International Directory of
COMPANY
HISTORIES

International Directory of
COMPANY
HISTORIES

VOLUME 103

Editor

Jay P. Pederson

ST. JAMES PRESS
A part of Gale, Cengage Learning

Detroit • New York • San Francisco • New Haven, Conn • Waterville, Maine • London

GALE
CENGAGE Learning™

International Directory of Company Histories, Volume 103

Jay P. Pederson, Editor

Project Editor: Miranda H. Ferrara

Editorial: Virgil Burton, Donna Craft, Louise Gagné, Peggy Geeseman, Julie Gough, Linda Hall, Sonya Hill, Keith Jones, Jodi Nazione, Lynn Pearce, Holly Selden, Justine Ventimiglia

Production Technology Specialist: Mike Weaver

Imaging and Multimedia: John Watkins

Composition and Electronic Prepress: Gary Leach, Evi Seoud

Manufacturing: Rhonda Dover

Product Manager: Jenai Drouillard

For product information and technology assistance, contact us at
Gale Customer Support, 1-800-877-4253.
For permission to use material from this text or product,
submit all requests online at **www.cengage.com/permissions.**
Further permissions questions can be emailed to
permissionrequest@cengage.com

Gale
27500 Drake Rd.
Farmington Hills, MI, 48331-3535

LIBRARY OF CONGRESS CATALOG NUMBER 89-190943
ISBN-13: 978-1-55862-637-9
ISBN-10: 1-55862-637-9

This title is also available as an e-book
ISBN-13: 978-1-55862-766-6   ISBN-10: 1-55862-766-9
Contact your Gale, a part of Cengage Learning sales representative for ordering information.

BRITISH LIBRARY CATALOGUING IN PUBLICATION DATA
International directory of company histories, Vol. 103
Jay P. Pederson
33.87409

Printed in the United States of America
1 2 3 4 5 6 7 13 12 11 10 09

Contents

Preface

The St. James Press series *The International Directory of Company Histories* (*IDCH*) is intended for reference use by students, business people, librarians, historians, economists, investors, job candidates, and others who seek to learn more about the historical development of the world's most important companies. To date, *IDCH* has covered more than 10,225 companies in 103 volumes.

INCLUSION CRITERIA

Most companies chosen for inclusion in *IDCH* have achieved a minimum of US$25 million in annual sales and are leading influences in their industries or geographical locations. Companies may be publicly held, private, or nonprofit. State-owned companies that are important in their industries and that may operate much like public or private companies also are included. Wholly owned subsidiaries and divisions are profiled if they meet the requirements for inclusion. Entries on companies that have had major changes since they were last profiled may be selected for updating.

The *IDCH* series highlights 25% private and nonprofit companies, and features updated entries on approximately 35 companies per volume.

ENTRY FORMAT

Each entry begins with the company's legal name; the address of its headquarters; its telephone, toll-free, and fax numbers; and its web site. A statement of public, private, state, or parent ownership follows. A company with a legal name in both English and the language of its headquarters country is listed by the English name, with the native-language name in parentheses.

The company's founding or earliest incorporation date, the number of employees, and the most recent available sales figures follow. Sales figures are given in local currencies with equivalents in U.S. dollars. For some private companies, sales figures are estimates and indicated by the abbreviation *est*. The entry lists the exchanges on which the company's stock is traded and its ticker symbol, as well as the company's NAICS codes.

Entries generally contain a *Company Perspectives* box which provides a short summary of the company's mission, goals, and ideals; a *Key Dates* box highlighting milestones in the company's history; lists of *Principal Subsidiaries*, *Principal Divisions*, *Principal Operating Units*, *Principal Competitors*; and articles for *Further Reading*.

American spelling is used throughout *IDCH*, and the word "billion" is used in its U.S. sense of one thousand million.

SOURCES

Entries have been compiled from publicly accessible sources both in print and on the Internet such as general and academic periodicals, books, and annual reports, as well as material supplied by the companies themselves.

CUMULATIVE INDEXES

IDCH contains three indexes: the **Cumulative Index to Companies**, which provides an alphabetical index to companies profiled in the *IDCH* series, the **Index to Industries**, which allows researchers to locate companies by their principal industry, and the **Geographic Index**, which lists companies alphabetically by the country of their headquarters. The indexes are cumulative and specific instructions for using them are found immediately preceding each index.

SPECIAL TO THIS VOLUME

This volume of *IDCH* contains an entry on Vulcabras S.A., the largest manufacturer of footwear in Latin America.

SUGGESTIONS WELCOME

Comments and suggestions from users of *IDCH* on any aspect of the product as well as suggestions for companies to be included or updated are cordially invited. Please write:

The Editor
International Directory of Company Histories
St. James Press
Gale, Cengage Learning
27500 Drake Rd.
Farmington Hills, Michigan 48331-3535

St. James Press does not endorse any of the companies or products mentioned in this series. Companies appearing in the *International Directory of Company Histories* were selected without reference to their wishes and have in no way endorsed their entries.

Notes on Contributors

M. L. Cohen
Novelist, business writer, and researcher living in Paris.

Jeffrey L. Covell
Seattle-based writer.

Ed Dinger
Writer and editor based in Bronx, New York.

Paul R. Greenland
Illinois-based writer and researcher; author of two books and former senior editor of a national business magazine; contributor to *The Encyclopedia of Chicago History, The Encyclopedia of Religion,* and the *Encyclopedia of American Industries.*

Robert Halasz
Former editor in chief of *World Progress* and *Funk & Wagnalls New Encyclopedia Yearbook*; author, *The U.S. Marines* (Millbrook Press, 1993).

Kathleen Peippo
Minnesota-based writer.

Nelson Rhodes
Editor, writer, and consultant in the Chicago area.

Carrie Rothburd
Writer and editor specializing in corporate profiles, academic texts, and academic journal articles.

David E. Salamie
Part-owner of InfoWorks Development Group, a reference

publication development and editorial services company.

Ted Sylvester
Photographer, writer, and editor of the environmental journal *From the Ground Up.*

Mary Tradii
Colorado-based writer.

Frank Uhle
Ann Arbor-based writer; movie projectionist, disc jockey, and staff member of *Psychotronic Video* magazine.

A. Woodward
Wisconsin-based writer.

List of Abbreviations

¥ Japanese yen
£ United Kingdom pound
$ United States dollar

A

AB Aktiebolag (Finland, Sweden)
AB Oy Aktiebolag Osakeyhtiot (Finland)
A.E. Anonimos Eteria (Greece)
AED Emirati dirham
AG Aktiengesellschaft (Austria, Germany, Switzerland, Liechtenstein)
aG auf Gegenseitigkeit (Austria, Germany)
A.m.b.a. Andelsselskab med begraenset ansvar (Denmark)
A.O. Anonim Ortaklari/Ortakligi (Turkey)
ApS Amparteselskab (Denmark)
ARS Argentine peso
A.S. Anonim Sirketi (Turkey)
A/S Aksjeselskap (Norway)
A/S Aktieselskab (Denmark, Sweden)
Ay Avoinyhtio (Finland)
ATS Austrian shilling
AUD Australian dollar
ApS Amparteselskab (Denmark)
Ay Avoinyhtio (Finland)

B

B.A. Buttengewone Aansprakeiijkheid (Netherlands)
BEF Belgian franc

BHD Bahraini dinar
Bhd. Berhad (Malaysia, Brunei)
BND Brunei dollar
BRL Brazilian real
B.V. Besloten Vennootschap (Belgium, Netherlands)

C

C.A. Compania Anonima (Ecuador, Venezuela)
CAD Canadian dollar
C. de R.L. Compania de Responsabilidad Limitada (Spain)
CEO Chief Executive Officer
CFO Chief Financial Officer
CHF Swiss franc
Cia. Companhia (Brazil, Portugal)
Cia. Compania (Latin America [except Brazil], Spain)
Cia. Compagnia (Italy)
Cie. Compagnie (Belgium, France, Luxembourg, Netherlands)
CIO Chief Information Officer
CLP Chilean peso
CNY Chinese yuan
Co. Company
COO Chief Operating Officer
Coop. Cooperative
COP Colombian peso
Corp. Corporation
C. por A. Compania por Acciones (Dominican Republic)
CPT Cuideachta Phoibi Theoranta

(Republic of Ireland)
CRL Companhia a Responsabilidao Limitida (Portugal, Spain)
C.V. Commanditaire Vennootschap (Netherlands, Belgium)
CZK Czech koruna

D

D&B Dunn & Bradstreet
DEM German deutsche mark
Div. Division (United States)
DKK Danish krone
DZD Algerian dinar

E

EC Exempt Company (Arab countries)
Edms. Bpk. Eiendoms Beperk (South Africa)
EEK Estonian Kroon
eG eingetragene Genossenschaft (Germany)
EGMBH Eingetragene Genossenschaft mit beschraenkter Haftung (Austria, Germany)
EGP Egyptian pound
Ek For Ekonomisk Forening (Sweden)
EP Empresa Portuguesa (Portugal)
E.P.E. Etema Pemorismenis Evthynis (Greece)
ESOP Employee Stock Options and Ownership
ESP Spanish peseta

Et(s). Etablissement(s) (Belgium, France, Luxembourg)
eV eingetragener Verein (Germany)
EUR euro

F
FIM Finnish markka
FRF French franc

G
G.I.E. Groupement d'Interet Economique (France)
gGmbH gemeinnutzige Gesellschaft mit beschraenkter Haftung (Austria, Germany, Switzerland)
G.I.E. Groupement d'Interet Economique (France)
GmbH Gesellschaft mit beschraenkter Haftung (Austria, Germany, Switzerland)
GRD Greek drachma
GWA Gewerbte Amt (Austria, Germany)

H
HB Handelsbolag (Sweden)
HF Hlutafelag (Iceland)
HKD Hong Kong dollar
HUF Hungarian forint

I
IDR Indonesian rupiah
IEP Irish pound
ILS new Israeli shekel
Inc. Incorporated (United States, Canada)
INR Indian rupee
IPO Initial Public Offering
I/S Interesentselskap (Norway)
I/S Interessentselskab (Denmark)
ISK Icelandic krona
ITL Italian lira

J
JMD Jamaican dollar
JOD Jordanian dinar

K
KB Kommanditbolag (Sweden)
KES Kenyan schilling
Kft Korlatolt Felelossegu Tarsasag (Hungary)
KG Kommanditgesellschaft (Austria, Germany, Switzerland)

KGaA Kommanditgesellschaft auf Aktien (Austria, Germany, Switzerland)
KK Kabushiki Kaisha (Japan)
KPW North Korean won
KRW South Korean won
K/S Kommanditselskab (Denmark)
K/S Kommandittselskap (Norway)
KWD Kuwaiti dinar
Ky Kommandiitiyhtio (Finland)

L
LBO Leveraged Buyout
Lda. Limitada (Spain)
L.L.C. Limited Liability Company (Arab countries, Egypt, Greece, United States)
L.L.P. Limited Liability Partnership (United States)
L.P. Limited Partnership (Canada, South Africa, United Kingdom, United States)
Ltd. Limited
Ltda. Limitada (Brazil, Portugal)
Ltee. Limitee (Canada, France)
LUF Luxembourg franc

M
mbH mit beschraenkter Haftung (Austria, Germany)
Mij. Maatschappij (Netherlands)
MUR Mauritian rupee
MXN Mexican peso
MYR Malaysian ringgit

N
N.A. National Association (United States)
NGN Nigerian naira
NLG Netherlands guilder
NOK Norwegian krone
N.V. Naamloze Vennootschap (Belgium, Netherlands)
NZD New Zealand dollar

O
OAO Otkrytoe Aktsionernoe Obshchestve (Russia)
OHG Offene Handelsgesellschaft (Austria, Germany, Switzerland)
OMR Omani rial
OOO Obschestvo s Ogranichennoi Otvetstvennostiu (Russia)
OOUR Osnova Organizacija

Udruzenog Rada (Yugoslavia)
Oy Osakeyhtî (Finland)

P
P.C. Private Corp. (United States)
PEN Peruvian Nuevo Sol
PHP Philippine peso
PKR Pakistani rupee
P/L Part Lag (Norway)
PLC Public Limited Co. (United Kingdom, Ireland)
P.L.L.C. Professional Limited Liability Corporation (United States)
PLN Polish zloty
P.T. Perusahaan/Perseroan Terbatas (Indonesia)
PTE Portuguese escudo
Pte. Private (Singapore)
Pty. Proprietary (Australia, South Africa, United Kingdom)
Pvt. Private (India, Zimbabwe)
PVBA Personen Vennootschap met Beperkte Aansprakelijkheid (Belgium)
PYG Paraguay guarani

Q
QAR Qatar riyal

R
REIT Real Estate Investment Trust
RMB Chinese renminbi
Rt Reszvenytarsasag (Hungary)
RUB Russian ruble

S
S.A. Société Anonyme (Arab countries, Belgium, France, Jordan, Luxembourg, Switzerland)
S.A. Sociedad Anónima (Latin America [except Brazil], Spain, Mexico)
S.A. Sociedades Anônimas (Brazil, Portugal)
SAA Societe Anonyme Arabienne (Arab countries)
S.A.B. de C.V. Sociedad Anónima Bursátil de Capital Variable (Mexico)
S.A.C. Sociedad Anonima Comercial (Latin America [except Brazil])
S.A.C.I. Sociedad Anonima Comercial e Industrial (Latin America [except Brazil])

S.A.C.I.y.F. Sociedad Anonima Comercial e Industrial y Financiera (Latin America [except Brazil])

S.A. de C.V. Sociedad Anonima de Capital Variable (Mexico)

SAK Societe Anonyme Kuweitienne (Arab countries)

SAL Societe Anonyme Libanaise (Arab countries)

SAO Societe Anonyme Omanienne (Arab countries)

SAQ Societe Anonyme Qatarienne (Arab countries)

SAR Saudi riyal

S.A.R.L. Sociedade Anonima de Responsabilidade Limitada (Brazil, Portugal)

S.A.R.L. Société à Responsabilité Limitée (France, Belgium, Luxembourg)

S.A.S. Societá in Accomandita Semplice (Italy)

S.A.S. Societe Anonyme Syrienne (Arab countries)

S.C. Societe en Commandite (Belgium, France, Luxembourg)

S.C.A. Societe Cooperativa Agricole (France, Italy, Luxembourg)

S.C.I. Sociedad Cooperativa Ilimitada (Spain)

S.C.L. Sociedad Cooperativa Limitada (Spain)

S.C.R.L. Societe Cooperative a Responsabilite Limitee (Belgium)

Sdn. Bhd. Sendirian Berhad (Malaysia)

SEK Swedish krona

SGD Singapore dollar

S.L. Sociedad Limitada (Latin America [except Brazil], Portugal, Spain)

S/L Salgslag (Norway)

S.N.C. Société en Nom Collectif (France)

Soc. Sociedad (Latin America [except Brazil], Spain)

Soc. Sociedade (Brazil, Portugal)

Soc. Societa (Italy)

S.p.A. Società per Azioni (Italy)

Sp. z.o.o. Spólka z ograniczona odpowiedzialnoscia (Poland)

S.R.L. Sociedad de Responsabilidad Limitada (Spain, Mexico, Latin America [except Brazil])

S.R.L. Società a Responsabilità Limitata (Italy)

S.R.O. Spolecnost s Rucenim Omezenym (Czechoslovakia

S.S.K. Sherkate Sahami Khass (Iran)

Ste. Societe (France, Belgium, Luxembourg, Switzerland)

Ste. Cve. Societe Cooperative (Belgium)

S.V. Samemwerkende Vennootschap (Belgium)

S.Z.R.L. Societe Zairoise a Responsabilite Limitee (Zaire)

T

THB Thai baht

TND Tunisian dinar

TRL Turkish lira

TWD new Taiwan dollar

U

U.A. Uitgesloten Aansporakeiijkheid (Netherlands)

u.p.a. utan personligt ansvar (Sweden)

V

VAG Verein der Arbeitgeber (Austria, Germany)

VEB Venezuelan bolivar

VERTR Vertriebs (Austria, Germany)

VND Vietnamese dong

V.O.f. Vennootschap onder firma (Netherlands)

VVAG Versicherungsverein auf Gegenseitigkeit (Austria, Germany)

W–Z

WA Wettelika Aansprakalikhaed (Netherlands)

WLL With Limited Liability (Bahrain, Kuwait, Qatar, Saudi Arabia)

YK Yugen Kaisha (Japan)

ZAO Zakrytoe Aktsionernoe Obshchestve (Russia)

ZAR South African rand

ZMK Zambian kwacha

ZWD Zimbabwean dollar

Actavis Group hf.

Dalshrauni 1
Hafnarfirdi, 220
Iceland
Telephone: (+354) 535 2300
Fax: (+354) 535 2301
Web site: http://www.actavis.com

Private Company
Incorporated: 1956 as Pharmaco hf.
Employees: 11,000
Sales: EUR 1.7 billion ($2.4 billion) (2008 est.)
NAICS: 325412 Pharmaceutical Preparation Manu-
    facturing

■ ■ ■

Actavis Group hf. is one of the largest producers of
generic pharmaceuticals in the world. In addition to its
more than 600 products on the market, the company's
pipeline includes hundreds of additional generic drugs
under development and pending regulatory approval.
Headquartered in Iceland with operations in 40
countries around the world, Actavis maintains
manufacturing facilities across Europe and in the United
States, China, India, and Indonesia. The United States is
the company's largest single sales market. Actavis gained
its position of prominence largely via an acquisition
spree that began in 1999 and encompassed more than
two dozen deals totaling more than $1.8 billion.
Icelandic billionaire Thor Bjorgolfsson, the firm's chairman since 2000, took Actavis private in August 2007.
In the global economic crisis that soon erupted,

however, Iceland's economy collapsed, which wiped out
a large portion of Bjorgolfsson's fortune. As a result, Actavis was placed on the auction block for sale either as a
single entity or in piecemeal fashion.

ORIGINS OF PHARMACO AND DELTA

Actavis traces its origins back to the 1956 founding in
Iceland of Pharmaco hf., which was set up as a purchasing alliance by seven of the island nation's pharmacists.
Four years later, Pharmaco began producing its own
pharmaceuticals, solely for the domestic market. In
1972 under new Icelandic legislation, pharmaceutical
supplies began to be managed by exclusive agents. Pharmaco became the authorized agent for such internationally prominent drugmakers as Astra AB and Aventis.
Under later legislation, Icelandic drugmakers were
permitted to register their products as proprietary
medicines. This led to Pharmaco's 1981 establishment
of Delta hf., which was charged with registering and
manufacturing pharmaceutical products. Pharmaco held
a two-thirds interest in Delta until 1992, when the two
companies parted ways to eliminate the conflict of
interests between Delta's production of its own products
and Pharmaco's distribution of the products of other
drugmakers. Delta soon strengthened its position within
the domestic market and began large-scale exporting of
its pharmaceuticals with its entry into the German
market.

Pharmaco remained focused on Iceland until 1999,
a critical year in Actavis's development. It was that year
that Björgólfur Thor Björgólfsson, better known

COMPANY PERSPECTIVES

We will become the champions of first-class generics by: adopting a challenger mindset; bringing a broad product line to market faster; using an aggressive approach to battle costs; [and] utilising global power and local know-how.

internationally as Thor (pronounced "tore") Bjorgolfsson, entered the picture. Born in 1967, Bjorgolfsson was descended from an Icelandic family long prominent in that small nation's business community. His determination to succeed in the business world stemmed in large measure from his desire to redeem his family's reputation after his father and other executives of Hafskip, a major Icelandic shipping line, became embroiled in a mid-1980s scandal centering on embezzlement and fraud. After earning a degree in finance from New York University in 1991, Bjorgolfsson enjoyed his first major success in Russia, where he set up a brewery in St. Petersburg in the late 1990s that he was eventually, in 2002, able to sell to Heineken N.V. for $350 million. Bjorgolfsson's share of the proceeds was $100 million.

Before cashing out that investment, however, Bjorgolfsson jumped at another opportunity in Eastern Europe presented to him by Deutsche Bank AG: investing in Balkanpharma, a small Bulgarian pharmaceuticals manufacturer. At the time Balkanpharma was seeking capital to purchase a number of Bulgarian generics producers that were being privatized. In 1999 Bjorgolfsson partnered with his father, who had moved on from Hafskip to a position with Pharmaco, and with Pharmaco itself in the purchase of Balkanpharma. A year later the two companies were merged, and Bjorgolfsson was named chairman of Pharmaco.

In the meantime, Robert Wessman had been running Delta as its CEO since 1999. He had taken over that firm at age 29 after gaining a business degree at an Icelandic university and then working for an Icelandic shipping company, where he eventually ran the firm's German operations. Wessman refocused Delta on the production of generic drugs and aimed to turn the company into a major player in the global generics market. Along these lines, Delta in 2001 acquired the Maltese firm Pharmamed Ltd., which operated a pharmaceuticals plant in Malta. Delta early the following year merged with the Icelandic company Omega Farma hf. to create the largest pharmaceutical company in Iceland. Also in early 2002, Delta acquired the Dan-

ish firm United Nordic Pharma AS (UNP). Established in 1990, UNP specialized in purchasing products from various producers of generic pharmaceuticals and selling them under its own brand names to pharmacies in Denmark.

2002: PHARMACO AND DELTA REUNITED

During the first half of 2002, Pharmaco placed its domestic wholesaling and distribution operations into a new subsidiary, which it then sold. This unit emerged as the independent firm PharmaNor hf., which later changed its name to Visitor hf. This divestment paved the way for the reuniting of Pharmaco and Delta under the former's name, with the merger completed in September 2002. Bjorgolfsson, who held a stake in Pharmaco of about 29 percent, remained company chairman, while Wessman was named CEO. At this stage in its development, Pharmaco was operating manufacturing facilities in Iceland, Bulgaria, and Malta; the bulk of its workforce of 5,300 was in Bulgaria; and its four largest markets, collectively accounting for 74 percent of total revenues, were Germany, Bulgaria, Russia, and the Netherlands. The company reported net profits for 2002 of ISK 3.17 billion ($39 million) on revenues of ISK 18.57 billion ($229 million).

As it continued to seek international expansion opportunities, Pharmaco leveraged its Icelandic base in one key way. Icelandic legislation enabled the company to formulate generic versions of drugs before the patents on them expired. This enabled Pharmaco to quickly enter a market with a generic drug upon the expiration of the corresponding patent.

Pharmaco began 2003 by completing another deal in Eastern Europe, in this case purchasing majority control of Zdravlje AD, which operated a manufacturing facility in Leskovac, Serbia, and ranked as that nation's third largest pharmaceutical company. Pharmaco entered another market and gained another manufacturing plant via the takeover of the Turkish generics firm Fako İlaclari AS, which was announced in 2003 and completed in January 2004. Purchasing Fako provided Pharmaco with a platform for expansion throughout southern Europe. Pharmaco also beefed up its research and development side with the 2003 purchase of an 86 percent stake in Colotech AS, a Danish firm specializing in the development of pharmaceuticals for the prevention and treatment of human cancers, and it also opened up sales offices in both Sweden and the United States. Entering the latter market was critical to the company's international ambitions as the United States was by far the world's largest generic pharmaceutical market and one in which ten of

KEY DATES

1956: Seven Icelandic pharmacists create a purchasing alliance called Pharmaco hf.

1960: Pharmaco begins manufacturing pharmaceuticals for the domestic market.

1972: Pharmaco starts distributing the pharmaceutical products of foreign drugmakers.

1981: Pharmaco establishes Delta hf. as its pharmaceutical manufacturing arm.

1992: The ties between Delta and Pharmaco are severed.

1999: Thor Bjorgolfsson engineers the purchase of Bulgarian generics producer Balkanpharma in partnership with Pharmaco; after being named CEO of Delta, Robert Wessman centers the firm on generic drugs and aims to make it a global player.

2000: Balkanpharma is merged into Pharmaco.

2002: Pharmaco and Delta merge under the former's name.

2004: Pharmaco is renamed Actavis Group hf.

2005: Actavis secures a major presence in the lucrative U.S. market by acquiring Amide Pharmaceutical, Inc., and the human generics business of Alpharma Inc.

2007: Through his investment vehicle Novator, Bjorgolfsson acquires the shares of Actavis he does not already own and takes the firm private.

2009: Bjorgolfsson has reportedly placed Actavis up for sale.

ever growing international operations under a single identity. The name itself was derived from two Latin words: *acta,* meaning action, and *vis,* meaning strength. Indeed, Actavis took action to further strengthen itself in 2004 by acquiring the sales and marketing offices in Norway and Finland of the Croatian firm Pliva d.d. The company thus secured a presence in the entire Nordic region (Denmark, Finland, Norway, Sweden, and Iceland).

At this time, Actavis was pursuing a twofold sales and marketing strategy in Europe. In central and Eastern Europe and the Nordic countries, the company was selling products under its own label that it had developed itself or had licensed from other companies. In Western Europe, particularly in Germany, the United Kingdom, Austria, and the Netherlands, Actavis focused on pursuing relationships with other pharmaceutical companies to have these companies sell Actavis products under their own labels. During 2004, Actavis introduced nine generic products within the European Union market; in five of these cases, the company was the first to market, a key to maximizing profits in the generics arena because an exclusive generic product can be sold for a higher price than one for which competition exists. Profits for the year jumped nearly 55 percent to EUR 62.7 million ($85 million), while revenues surged to EUR 451.7 million ($611 million), an increase of 42.9 percent. At year-end 2004, Actavis's market value stood at EUR 1.4 billion ($1.9 billion), making it the second most-valuable company on the Iceland Stock Exchange.

Actavis began an extremely busy 2005 with the February purchase of the Polish sales and marketing company Biovena Pharma Sp. Two months later, two more deals were completed: the acquisitions of Indian clinical research company Lotus Laboratories Ltd. and Pharma Avalanche s.r.o., a Czech generic pharmaceutical sales and marketing company that was active in the Slovakian market as well. Later in the year, Actavis bulked up further in Eastern Europe via the purchases of Higia AD, the largest pharmaceutical distributor in Bulgaria, and Kéri Pharma Generics Kft., a Hungarian firm specializing in the development, sale, and marketing of generic pharmaceuticals not only in Hungary but also in Slovenia, Slovakia, the Czech Republic, and the Baltic States.

billions of dollars of pharmaceuticals were scheduled to come off-patent over the next few years. Also during 2003, Pharmaco launched five products and began production of the generic drug ramipril, mainly used in the treatment of hypertension. As soon as the patent on ramipril expired in early January 2004, Pharmaco had 300 million tablets and capsules ready for export from Iceland into other European markets, starting with Germany, Britain, and Denmark. This effort was the firm's most ambitious product launch to that time.

EMERGING AS ACTAVIS IN 2004

In May 2004 Pharmaco changed its name to Actavis Group hf. The name change was part of a corporate branding program that aimed to unite the company's

ENTERING THE U.S. MARKET

In the most significant development of 2005, however, Actavis secured a major presence in the lucrative U.S. market by acquiring Amide Pharmaceutical, Inc., for $600 million in July and the human generics business of Alpharma Inc. for $810 million in December. Amide, founded in 1983 and based in Little Falls, New Jersey, generated about $100 million in annual sales from its portfolio of 67 marketed generic drugs. At the time of its acquisition, it had about 30 additional generic products in its pipeline and had 12 drug applications pending approval from the Food and Drug Administration (FDA). Its manufacturing plant in Little Falls had the capacity to produce 1.5 billion tablets and capsules per year. The Alpharma business that Actavis acquired, which had its origins in Norway in 1903, was a developer, manufacturer, and marketer of a broad range of solid, liquid, and topical forms of generic pharmaceuticals in both the United States and Europe and had generated sales of nearly $455 million during the first six months of 2005. This business ranked as the eighth largest generics company in the United States and the fourth largest in the United Kingdom; boasted strong positions in Scandinavia, the Netherlands, and Portugal; and had established a presence in China and Indonesia. The acquisition of the Alpharma business made Actavis one of the five largest players in the global generics market.

Actavis remained on the prowl in 2006 and set its sights on the Croatian firm Pliva, which operated a $1.2 billion generics business concentrated in Eastern and central Europe, along with Italy, Germany, and Spain. In March, Actavis made a $1.6 billion bid for Pliva, which was immediately rebuffed. Trying to fend off Actavis's overtures, Pliva put itself up for sale, which attracted a competing bid from the U.S.-based Barr Pharmaceuticals, Inc. In the bidding war that then ensued and stretched into September, Actavis lost out to Barr despite sweetening its offer to $2.5 billion. The company consequently had to settle for several smaller deals it completed during 2006: Sindan AG, a Hungarian generics company specializing in the production and distribution of oncology products; majority control of the Russian pharmaceutical manufacturer ZiO Zdorovje; and Abrika Pharmaceuticals Inc., a Fort Lauderdale, Florida-based producer of specialty generic pharmaceuticals such as controlled-release products. Actavis in 2006 also acquired a plant in India for the low-cost manufacturing of generic drugs for export to the United States and markets in Europe.

The company's acquisition spree sent sales soaring to EUR 1.38 billion ($1.82 billion) in 2006, while net income increased 27 percent to EUR 103 million ($136 million). North America accounted for 31 percent of the revenue, with Bulgaria generating 11 percent; Germany, 8 percent; and Turkey, the United Kingdom, and the Nordic countries, 7 percent each. At the end of the year, Actavis had around 650 products on the market, more than 350 products under development,

and about 50 pending approval in the United States from the FDA.

TAKEN PRIVATE IN 2007

Actavis was one of several parties that participated in the due diligence phase of an auction of the German firm Merck KGaA's generics arm but dropped out of the running in May 2007 before making a formal offer. Actavis's leaders were apparently concerned about the type of sensitive information it would have been required to reveal as an Icelandic public company. Bjorgolfsson, by this time a billionaire and still the company chairman with a stake of approximately 38 percent, decided it would be best to take Actavis private and thus eliminate the disclosure obligations entailed with public ownership. In August 2007, through his investment vehicle Novator, Bjorgolfsson acquired the shares of Actavis he did not already own for EUR 3.62 billion ($4.9 billion).

Ironically, in the immediate period following this latest twist in the Actavis saga, the company completed deals only of the minor variety. In January 2008 a manufacturing plant in Italy was acquired from Pfizer Inc., and then three months later Actavis acquired a 90 percent stake in Zhejiang Chiral Medicine Chemicals Company, a firm based in Hangzhou, China, specializing in the research, development, and manufacture of active pharmaceutical ingredients. In August 2008 Wessman stepped down as CEO and was replaced by Sigurdur Oli Olafsson, the former deputy CEO who had joined Actavis in 2003 after previous stints at Pfizer and Omega Farma. Later in 2008, the U.S. federal government forced the closure of Actavis's plants in New Jersey after the FDA had cited the facilities for violating good manufacturing practice requirements. The closures followed an earlier recall of all the products manufactured at the plants. By early 2009, Actavis was working to reopen the plants under the terms of a consent decree it had entered into with the FDA.

In the meantime, Actavis fell victim in an indirect way to the financial crisis that was wreaking havoc around the world and in particular on the once explosively growing Icelandic economy. In October 2008 Bjorgolfsson lost a large portion of his fortune when one of the companies he was heavily invested in, Landsbanki Islands hf., collapsed and was taken over by the Icelandic government. While the implosion of the Icelandic economy did not directly affect Actavis because the firm did business with international banks rather than the troubled Icelandic ones and because it generated only about 1 percent of its revenues at home, Bjorgolfsson was forced to place the company up for sale. Analysts originally estimated that Actavis could fetch as much as EUR 6 billion ($7.5 billion), but the company's ill-timed manufacturing troubles in the United States appeared to dampen the enthusiasm of potential acquirers. Another open question was whether the company would be sold as a single entity or in piecemeal fashion.

David E. Salamie

PRINCIPAL SUBSIDIARIES

Actavis hf.; Medis ehf.; Actavis Gmbh (Austria); Actavis EAD (Bulgaria); Actavis Operations Ltd. (Bulgaria); Higia EAD (Bulgaria); Actavis CZ a.s. (Czech Republic); Actavis A/S (Denmark); Actavis Nordic A/S (Denmark); Actavis Oy (Finland); Actavis Deutschland GmbH & Co. KG (Germany); Medis Pharma GmbH (Germany; 60%); Actavis Hungary Kft.; Actavis Ireland Ltd.; Actavis Italy S.p.A.; Actavis Ltd. (Malta); Actavis B.V. (Netherlands); Actavis Norway A/S; Actavis Polska Sp. z o.o. (Poland); Biovena Pharma Sp. z o.o. (Poland); Actavis Portugal AS; Actavis Romania; Zdravlje AD (Serbia; 73%); Actavis Trading Ltd. (Serbia); Actavis s.r.o. (Slovakia); Actavis AB (Sweden); Actavis Switzerland AG; FAKO İlaclari AS (Turkey); Actavis UK Ltd.; Medis Ltd. (UK); Actavis Inc. (USA); Actavis Australia Pty. Ltd.; Actavis (Foshan) Pharmaceutical Co., Ltd. (China; 90%); Actavis (China) Holding Ltd.; Zhejiang Chiral Medicine Chemicals Co. Ltd. (China; 90%); Zhejiang Chiral Medicine Chemicals Co. Ltd. (China; 90%); Actavis Pharma Development Centre Pvt. Ltd. (India); Lotus Laboratories Pvt. Ltd. (India); PT Actavis Indonesia; Actavis International Ltd. (Singapore).

PRINCIPAL COMPETITORS

Teva Pharmaceutical Industries Limited; Sandoz International GmbH; Mylan Inc.; Ratiopharm GmbH; STADA Arzneimittel AG; Watson Pharmaceuticals, Inc.; Ranbaxy Laboratories Limited; Sanofi-Aventis; Richter Gedeon Rt.

FURTHER READING

Appel, Heather, "Actavis Facing Trouble from Feds: Drug Maker Halts Production Locally," *West Paterson (N.J.) Herald News,* November 21, 2008, p. A1.

———, "Plant Vows Quick Fix," *West Paterson (N.J.) Herald News,* December 21, 2008, p. A1.

Brown-Humes, Christopher, "Pharmaco Plans Big Acquisition and LSE Listing," *Financial Times,* May 12, 2003, p. 24.

"A Chill Wind," *Economist,* October 25, 2008, p. 77.

Cunningham, Jennifer H., "FDA Orders Actavis to Close: Drug Plant Didn't Meet Standards," *Bergen County (N.J.) Record,* January 11, 2009, p. L7.

Farrow, Boyd, "Drugs Baron: Robert Wessman Revs Up Actavis," *European Business,* November 2006, pp. 25+.

Haddix, Dar, "Actavis Expands in Europe with Purchase of Bulgarian Distributor," *Generic Line,* September 21, 2005.

———, "Actavis to Buy Romania's Sindan," *Generic Line,* April 5, 2006.

Isenberg, Daniel J., *Robert Wessman and Actavis' "Winning Formula,"* HBS Case Study No. 9-808-127, Boston: Harvard Business School Publishing, 2008, 24 p.

Jack, Andrew, "Actavis Appoints Listing Advisers," *Financial Times,* January 24, 2005, p. 20.

———, "Actavis Buys U.S. Business As Generics Link," *Financial Times,* October 18, 2005, p. 30.

———, "Actavis Chief in Buy-Out Bid," *Financial Times,* May 11, 2007, p. 17.

———, "Actavis Looks at Targets," *Financial Times,* October 23, 2006, p. 22.

———, "Actavis Targets U.S. Through Amide Deal," *Financial Times,* May 20, 2005, p. 30.

———, "EUR 8bn Target for Actavis Sale," *Financial Times* (FT.com), January 8, 2009.

Jones, Elizabeth, "Novator Reacts to Actavis Buyout Report," *Generic Line,* October 29, 2008.

Jones, Elizabeth, and Christopher Hollis, "Actavis Expects to Resume Production Under Consent Decree," *Drug GMP Report,* January 13, 2009.

Kroll, Luisa, "Thor's Saga," *Forbes,* March 28, 2005, p. 138.

Niven, Michael, "Actavis Buys Alpharma's Generics Business for $810 Million," *Generic Line,* November 2, 2005.

Ramesh, Deepti, "Actavis to Build Three Plants in India; Opens Laboratories," *Chemical Week,* November 3/10, 2008, p. 31.

Schwartzkopff, Frances, "Actavis May Have to Lift Pliva Bid," *Wall Street Journal Europe,* April 5, 2006, p. 6.

Urquhart, Lisa, "Actavis Loses Out," *Financial Times,* September 19, 2006, p. 25.

"Viking Boss, Viking Strategy," *Economist,* April 14, 2007, p. 80.

Whalen, Jeanne, "Actavis Proposes Deal to Acquire Pliva of Croatia," *Wall Street Journal,* March 18, 2006, p. A7.

———, "Generic-Drug Firm Actavis May Be Sold," *Wall Street Journal,* October 17, 2008, p. B5.

Akeena Solar, Inc.

16005 Los Gatos Boulevard
Los Gatos, California 95032
U.S.A.
Telephone: (408) 395-7774
Fax: (408) 295-7474
Web site: http://www.akeena.net

Public Company
Incorporated: 2001 as Akeena, Inc.
Employees: 207
Sales: $40.76 million (2008)
Stock Exchanges: NASDAQ
Ticker Symbol: AKNS
NAICS: 221119 Other Electric Power Generation

■ ■ ■

Headquartered in Los Gatos, in the heart of California's Silicon Valley, Akeena Solar, Inc., is one of the country's leading designers and installers of solar power systems. The company markets, sells, designs and installs systems for residential and small commercial customers primarily in the state of California, the world's third largest market for solar power systems. Akeena also has branch offices in Colorado, Hawaii, and Connecticut, from which it reaches markets in New York, New Jersey, and Pennsylvania. The company stands out from its competitors with its proprietary solar module and installation technology called Andalay, a lightweight non-invasive "plug-and-play" design that incorporates all rooftop racking, wiring, and grounding into the solar panel itself.

STARTING AT THE TOP

Many companies have been started around kitchen tables, in basements, and in garages. Barry Cinnamon started his company, Akeena Solar, Inc., on the top of his garage. He began by installing some solar panels on his garage roof to see if they could actually reduce his electricity bill. Neighbors became curious and wanted systems for their own homes; one thing led to another and Cinnamon found himself in a growing business. "I founded Akeena Solar in 2001," said Cinnamon, "and started my work at the top, at the roof top, as a contractor and installer of solar power systems."

Cinnamon began his career in solar energy in the 1970s as a researcher at the Massachusetts Institute of Technology, where he earned a B.S. degree in mechanical engineering. In the 1980s, he designed and installed active solar, passive solar, and ground-coupled heat pump systems. Cinnamon's work in solar power computer modeling led him into the software industry, where he served as CEO of Soft Software Publishing Corporation. He founded Allegro New Media, a multimedia software publisher, which he took public in 1995. Cinnamon also acquired an M.B.A. in marketing from Wharton.

From the beginning, Akeena targeted residential and small commercial customers in areas with a combination of favorable public policy, high electric rates, and consumer environmental concerns. Initially, that meant concentrating sales efforts in the San Francisco Bay Area. The company marketed its product as a complete turnkey solution, including the system design, engineering work, building permits, rebate ap-

COMPANY PERSPECTIVES

Akeena Solar is a proven leader in the design and integration of solar power systems for residential and commercial customers in California, New York, New Jersey and Connecticut. Our skilled team of trained engineers are also dedicated environmentalists who take pride in exceeding customer expectations and protecting the environment. They have been immersed in leading-edge solar technology since its inception—and our growing list of over 1,200 satisfied customers underscores the successful outcome of our commitment to personal care and attention.

proval, utility hookups, and any potential maintenance work.

LAYING THE GROUNDWORK

Akeena Solar officially traces its company roots and the beginning of operations to February 2001, when Cinnamon created a California corporation under the name Akeena, Inc. On March 30, 2001, Akeena, Inc., purchased certain infrastructure and technology from Andalay, Inc., a Delaware corporation, in exchange for one million shares of Akeena, Inc.'s common stock at one penny per share.

Akeena never manufactured its own solar panels or modules. The company started out purchasing solar modules from Kyoto, Japan-based Kyocera Corporation. In 2002, Akeena also established a supply relationship with Sharp Electronics Corporation. In December 2002, Cinnamon established corporate headquarters in Los Gatos, California. By mid-2003, Akeena had added an East Coast presence with an office and warehouse in Fairfield, New Jersey, near New York City, and had begun installing rooftop solar electric systems in New York, Connecticut, and Pennsylvania.

In November 2003, Akeena filed suit against its hometown of Los Gatos, alleging the Town Council had violated the California Solar Rights Act. Ironically, Akeena had been denied a final building permit for a 6-kilowatt solar system installed on the roof of their headquarters in December 2002 because three of the solar panels were partially visible from the street.

BOOSTED BY PUBLIC POLICY

In August 2004, the California Environmental Protection Agency announced its proposed Million Solar

Homes Initiative. The plan was prompted by Governor Schwarzenegger's campaign promise of increased use of solar energy made and was initially designed to help one million Californians install solar energy systems at zero net costs. On September 25, 2004, the California governor signed an updated Solar Rights Act, which minimized aesthetic solar restrictions and limited the review of solar installations to items related to specific health and safety requirements of local, state, and federal law. The revised law took effect January 1, 2005, and led to the settlement of Akeena's lawsuit against its hometown.

In August 2005, as oil prices were climbing to record levels, and as the California state legislature began debate on the state's $3 billion "million-solar-roofs" proposal, Akeena released an influential "White Paper" that touted $9 billion in infrastructure, economic and environmental savings that could flow to the state from the ten-year program. In December 2005, company CEO Cinnamon was elected president of the California Solar Energy Industries Association, the largest state solar organization in the country. During the course of the year, Akeena began buying solar panels from San Jose-based Sun Power Corporation.

Akeena's New Jersey operations gained a boost in April 2006 when the state's Board of Public Utilities approved regulations requiring electric utilities to increase their use of renewable energy to 20 percent by 2020. The program specifically called for solar photovoltaic power to provide 2 percent of the state's electricity needs by 2020, which would require the installation of 1,500 megawatts of solar electric power. At the time, according to *PV News,* California and New Jersey accounted for 90 percent of the U.S. residential solar market.

TRANSITIONING TO PUBLIC COMPANY

In June 2006, Akeena, Inc., was reincorporated as a Delaware corporation, at which time its name was changed to Akeena Solar, Inc. On August 15, 2006, Akeena announced that it had completed a reverse merger and public transaction with Fairview Energy Corporation, Inc. Under the terms of the merger, 3.87 million shares of Fairview Energy common stock were canceled, and the remaining 3.65 million shares were converted into Akeena common stock for resale into the market. In connection with the merger, Akeena also closed a $2.5 million private placement of 2.5 million shares of its common stock at $1 per share. CEO and President Barry Cinnamon retained approximately 52 percent of the outstanding common stock. On August 31, 2006, company shares began trading as an over-the-

KEY DATES

2001: Akeena, Inc., begins operations in Los Gatos, California, in the heart of Silicon Valley.

2003: Company opens branch office in New Jersey to serve New York, Pennsylvania, and Connecticut.

2006: Akeena, Inc., becomes Akeena Solar, Inc.; goes public as over-the-counter stock.

2007: Company rolls out Andalay, its proprietary installation technology; company stock begins trading on the NASDAQ under the symbol AKNS.

2008: Akeena expands presence in California with six new sales and installation offices; firm moves New Jersey office to Connecticut; opens new branches in Colorado and Hawaii.

counter bulletin board stock under the ticker symbol AKNS.OB.

Also in August 2006, the California legislature approved the Million Solar Roofs bill, SB1, the largest state-sponsored solar bill in the country at the time. Earlier in 2006, the California Public Utilities Commission approved over $3 billion in solar incentives.

In the first public release of company financial information, Akeena in September 2006 reported net sales of $5.3 million for the six months ended June 30, 2006. While revenue grew 106 percent compared to the first half of 2005, Akeena's net loss of $0.03 per share remained the same for both periods. Investors also learned from the company's first conference call that Akeena had 41 employees and had been profitable in each full year of operation.

EXPANDING CALIFORNIA FOOTPRINT

On September 29, 2006, Akeena purchased certain solar electric energy generation contracts and fixed assets of Solahart All Valley Energy Systems, a Fresno-based installer of solar energy systems, solar hot water systems and solar pool heaters. The deal assigned solar pool and solar hot water segments to Solahart, and the solar electricity segment to Akeena, which included Solahart's ten solar electric employees and estimated annual revenues of $2 million to $3 million. Solahart owner Jeff Brown was retained as regional director to oversee Akeena's Central Valley expansion. In October, Akeena

CEO Cinnamon received a Business Commendation from the Town of Los Gatos, which thanked the company for its outstanding contributions to the community.

Financial results for the third quarter of 2006, as reported by Akeena in November 2006, showed a 62 percent increase in net sales to $3.6 million compared to the third quarter of 2005. Akeena also reported that it had installed 960 kilowatts in the nine months ended September 30, 2006, compared to 630 kilowatts for the same period in 2005 (the electrical needs for a typical California residence required a three kilowatt system). In December 2006, Akeena reported two significant commercial installations, a 134-kilowatt solar power system for a prominent biotech company based in Burlingame, California, and a 126-kilowatt system for the Peju Winery in California's Napa Valley.

Citing Southern California Edison's escalating electricity rates, Akeena opened a new office in Laguna Hills, California, on January 7, 2007, and began seeking business in Southern California's Orange County. The facility employed 11 people. In early February 2007, the company secured a $2 million line of credit from Comerica Bank, and in March, raised $4.1 million of working capital in a private investment in public equity.

REVENUES UP, PROFITS DOWN

As reported by the company on March 29, 2007, fourth quarter 2006 revenue was up 25 percent from the third quarter to $4.5 million, and 2006 revenue rose 86 percent to $13.4 million. Despite installing approximately 1,700 kilowatts in 2006, almost double the total of 2005, the company suffered a net loss for of $1.8 million, or $0.16 per share, marking Akeena's first unprofitable full year of operation. On December 11, 2006, Akeena common stock closed at $2.50 per share.

In April 2007, Akeena expanded its presence in California's Central Valley when it opened offices in the cities of Bakersfield and Manteca. It also announced a contract for a $2.2 million, 300-kilowatt, 566 solar panel installation for the California Air National Guard's Fresno armory. In May, Akeena acquired Alternative Energy Inc. of Santa Rosa, California, marking its fifth new location in the state since October 2006, and expanding the company's reach into Sonoma and Napa counties.

In mid-June 2007, the company moved into new corporate headquarters in Los Gatos, a 20,000-square-foot facility, where it consolidated its administrative, marketing, and sales management staff, as well as research and development, warehousing, fleet, and education facilities. In August 2007, Akeena opened its seventh California office in Palm Springs, with each new office costing approximately $600,000 in start-up costs.

ROLLING OUT ANDALAY

Akeena opened another California office in San Diego in mid-September 2007, just before receiving approval to trade the company's common stock on the NASDAQ Capital Market under the symbol AKNS. The company marked the September 24 milestone with an announcement that Suntech Power Holdings Co., Ltd., a China-based maker of photovoltaic (PV) cells and modules, would manufacture up to 14 megawatts worth of Akeena's state-of-the-art patent-pending Andalay solar panels.

The Andalay design, four years in the offing, was made to look like a glass skylight on the roof. The company claimed it reduced labor costs by 50 percent because it required 70 percent fewer parts and 25 percent fewer rooftop attachment points. The Andalay product rollout and the Suntech manufacturing agreement boosted Akeena stock to over $8 per share.

As reported by the company in early November 2007, Akeena substantially strengthened its financial flexibility when it secured $26.1 million through a private placement of equity. At the same time, the company's third quarter 2007 loss widened to $0.16 per share despite record-breaking sales and installations. Just as 2007 came to an end, Comerica granted the company an increase in its credit line from $7.5 million to $25 million.

THE CALM BEFORE THE STORM

Akeena began 2008 with a bang when it inked a licensing deal for Suntech to distribute an estimated 10 megawatts worth of Andalay solar panels in Europe, Japan, and Australia in 2008. The January 2 news caused company stock to surge 42 percent to $11.31. In February 2008, Akeena opened an office in Thousand Oaks, California, its ninth sales and installation office in the state. In March 2008, Akeena signed a strategic partnership with Kyocera Solar, Inc., the U.S. subsidiary of Kyocera Corporation, a supplier since 2001, for the manufacture and delivery of 1.6 megawatts of Andalay solar panels in 2008.

Year-end results for 2007, reported by Akeena in March 2008, were mixed. While net sales increased 140 percent to $32.2 million from 2006, the company's net loss ballooned from $0.16 per share to $0.52 per share. Akeena said operating costs for 2007 rose substantially as it expanded its infrastructure and significantly increased its sales, marketing, and installation staff. In April 2008, the company announced one of its largest installations ever, a 418-kilowatt project, housing 1,890 Akeena solar panels on the roof of Star Quality Concrete in downtown San Jose.

By June 2008, Akeena opened a new sales and installation office in Denver, Colorado. Citing flat demand in New Jersey compared to New York and Connecticut, Akeena announced in August 2008 that it was relocating its Fairfield, New Jersey, office to Milford, Connecticut. The company had already completed 40 installations in the state.

SIGNS OF A DOWNTURN

The company's financial results for the second quarter of 2008, as reported in August, began to show signs of the economic recession and a general tightening of credit. With commercial installations down 79 percent, revenue fell to $7.1 million from $12.2 million in the first quarter. The company's net loss for the first six months of 2008 rose to $9.7 million, or $0.35 per share, compared to $2.9 million, or $0.16 per share for the first half of 2007. The news dropped company stock on August 6 by almost 10 percent to around $4 per share. Also in August 2008, four years after the initial application, Akeena received approval of certain key elements of its Andalay technology from the U.S. Patent and Trademark Office.

By the start of October 2008, Akeena had opened another branch office in Hawaii. On October 3, 2008, the U.S. Congress passed the Economic Stabilization Act of 2008, which included an eight-year extension of the Solar Investment Tax Credit, originally introduced in 2005. The news was hailed as significant to the future of the solar energy industry in the United States, where the cost of both residential and commercial solar power system installations could be offset by as much as 30 percent through a federal tax credit.

Net sales for the third quarter of 2008 rebounded 31 percent to $10.6 million, as reported by Akeena in early November. Net loss for the third quarter was $5.5 million, or $0.19 per share. Backlog as of September 30, 2008, the company said, was a record $16.7 million, and revenue through the first nine months of 2008 was $29.9 million, up 36 percent compared to the first nine months of 2007. As the year ended, Akeena further lowered its 2008 revenue growth rate guidance. In March, the company predicted a 100 percent growth rate, which it lowered to 40 to 50 percent in May, then to 30 to 40 percent in August, and finally to 25 to 30 percent in mid-December.

As of mid-February 2009, Akeena's best hope to recover its financial momentum appeared to hinge on whether the company, the solar industry, and the economy as a whole, would benefit from the $787 billion economic stimulus package signed into law by President Obama on February 17, 2009. The solar industry in particular, including Akeena, stood to potentially benefit from parts of the stimulus plan designed to double the amount of alternative energy produced in the United States over the next three years. Also, as a company that actually installed solar panels on the roof, Akeena was positioned to benefit from a continuing drop in solar panel prices due to the overstocked inventories of the world's major solar panel manufacturers.

Ted Sylvester

PRINCIPAL COMPETITORS

SolarCity; Entech Solar, Inc.; SCHOTT Solar, Inc.; Ascent Solar Technologies, Inc.; SolarCraft Services Incorporated; ReGrid Power, Inc.; Borrego Solar Systems, Inc.; Advanced Solar Products, Inc.; Suntechnics Energy Systems, Inc.; SunPower Systems.

FURTHER READING

"Akeena Completes Solar Installation at Napa Valley's Peju Winery," *EnergyResource,* December 2006.

"Akeena Solar Shares Surge; Co. Reaches Licensing Agreement with Suntech Power," *AFX Asia,* January 2, 2008.

Baker, David R., "Tangled in Solar Paperwork," *San Francisco Chronicle,* August 17, 2007, p. D1.

Bogoslaw, David, "Solar Stocks Get Their Day in the Sun," *BusinessWeek Online,* January 3, 2008.

Bruce Allison, "Solar Energy Company Opens Office in T.O.," *Ventura County Star,* March 11, 2008.

Burgarino, Paul, "Solar Company Opens in Manteca," *Oakland Tribune,* April 23, 2007.

"CA Study Touts $6 Billion in Benefits from 'Million Solar Roofs,'" *Power Market Today,* August 26, 2005.

"CEO Interview: Barry Cinnamon—Akeena Solar, Inc. (AKNS)," *Wall Street Transcript,* December 15, 2008.

"Clovis Solar Company Teams with Akeena Solar," *Fresno Bee,* October 4, 2006, p. C2.

Gage, Jack, "High Energy Stocks; Demand for Energy Has Made It the Hottest Industry on Wall Street," *Forbes,* June 16, 2008.

"Op-Ed: Silicon Valley Leaders Speak Out on State Budget Crisis," *San Francisco Chronicle,* January 2, 2009, p. B9.

"Q2 2006 Akeena Solar Earnings Conference Call," *Voxant FD WIRE,* September 7, 2006.

Spence, Bruce, "Solar-Power Firm Opens Manteca Office: Fast-Growing Company Cites Rising Demand," *McClatchy-Tribune Regional News,* May 2, 2007.

"They Capture Sun Power," *NJBIZ,* May 16, 2005, p. 19.

Algar S/A
Emprendimentos e
Participações

———■———

Av Comendador Alexandrino Garcia 2689
Uberlândia, Minas Gerais 38402-288
Brazil
Telephone: (55 34) 3218-3300
Fax: (55 34) 3218-3303
Web site: http://www.algar.com.br

Private Company
Founded: 1954
Employees: 37,422
Sales: $1.41 billion (2007)
NAICS: 111110 Soybean Farming; 111998 All Other
Miscellaneous Crop Farming; 112990 All Other
Animal Production; 311225 Fats and Oils Refining
and Blending; 418211 Nonscheduled Charter Pas-
senger Air Transportation; 418212 Nonscheduled
Chartered Freight Transportation; 517212 Cellular
and Other Wireless Telecommunications; 541990
All Other Professional, Scientific, and Technical
Services; 551112 Offices of Other Holding
Companies; 561612 Security Guards and Patrol
Services; 561621 Security Systems Services (Except
Locksmiths); 712190 Nature Parks and Other
Similar Institutions

■ ■ ■

Algar S/A Emprendimentos e Participações is the holding company for a Brazilian family group called Grupo
Algar whose companies are mostly engaged in telecommunications and agriculture. Telecommunications, the
largest sector, includes holdings in both fixed-line and
wireless telephony. The chief agricultural activity is
processing soybeans for their yield of meal and oils, but
the group's enterprises also raise crops and livestock.
Grupo Algar is also engaged in other businesses, such as
security systems and services, aviation chartering and
maintenance, and operating a resort community.

THE EARLY YEARS: 1954–1987

Alexandrino Garcia was born in Portugal in 1907 and
came to Brazil with his parents and siblings in 1919. He
received little schooling, working for family businesses
in jobs such as driving trucks and as a "cerealista" who
tried, but failed, to market a rice husking machine,
before renting a gas station in Uberlândia, Minas Gerais,
in 1941, which he expanded. He became a General Motors (GM) dealer in 1947 and opened his own auto
dealership soon after, selling Ford as well as GM autos.

In the early 1950s Garcia took part in the group
that assumed control of Empresa Telefônica Texeirinha,
which, in 1954, became Companhia de Telefones do
Brasil Central (CTBC). This small company resisted
incorporation into Telecomunicações Brasileiros S.A.
(Telebrás), the government monopoly on telecommunications, and would become the nation's only
remaining private company alongside 28 public ones
providing fixed-line telephony.

CTBC's area of operation was a triangular, thinly
populated tract along the borders of the states of Minas
Gerais, São Paulo, Goiás, and Mato Grosso do Sul. The
company expanded by acquiring other small telephone
companies and was the only one to avoid being

COMPANY PERSPECTIVES

Mission: To develop relationships and sustainable businesses that generate perceived value, delighting people and promoting human potential.

nationalized in the 1960s by the military regime then ruling Brazil.

Because Garcia was not certain that he could maintain CTBC's independence, he next entered farming and ranching in central Brazil, establishing 11 properties with 20,000 head of cattle and the cultivation of grains and fruits. These holdings included the world's largest pineapple plantation in terms of continuous area cultivated. He took the name of ABC Algar (for Alexandrino and Garcia) for his holdings. In time his surviving son, Luiz Alberto, assumed a larger role in the family business, although Alexandrino did not retire until 1987.

DOWNSIZING AND RESTRUCTURING: 1987–91

Luiz Alberto loved agriculture and the countryside, but he studied electrical engineering and did not neglect CTBC. He introduced magnetic strip cards for public telephones in 1983. Uberlândia was one of the first four Brazilian cities to have cellular telephones. The Algar empire grew to 64 businesses encompassing civil construction as well as telephony, electronics, information, and agribusiness.

This surge of expansion ended in 1988, when the conglomerate lost $13 million and saw its debt climb to $170 million on revenues of $400 million. Employment fell from 13,200 to 6,000, and even relatives and close friends in charge of some of the businesses were dismissed. Luiz Alberto realized that the family enterprise needed professional management and hired as executive vice-president an Italian, Mário Grossi. Garcia went into exile, spending two years at Georgetown University, where he was enrolled in a program named Global Business Leadership.

Although a tough onetime submarine commander, Grossi established participatory management as a model. Once invited to speak up, employees exposed a number of errors, not sparing Garcia himself. A profit-sharing plan was adopted to motivate them to meet the enterprise's goals. Employees let go in the downsizing were encouraged to become contractors for functions

such as maintenance and technical assistance. After three years of restructuring and a reduction of $30 million in debt, a slimmed down Grupo Algar posted a profit of $10.6 million.

The restructuring also meant that Garcia had to humble himself and abandon his my-way-or-the-highway method of dealing not only with employees but with partners. In 1987, for example, he had broken with Telettra, the Fiat group firm that designed and built integrated telecommunications systems with Algar's Teleinformática. On its own, this business lost $40 million and ended up sold to the state-run Agência Nacional de Telecomunicações (Alcatel) in 1991 for only $19 million.

RENEWED PROSPERITY: 1991–95

By this time called ABC Algar, the conglomerate was confining its investments to telecommunications and agroindustry. The objective was to find foreign partners who would help it to earn one-third of its revenues abroad. An information technology joint venture, Algar Bull Computer & Communications (ABC&C), was formed in 1995 with the French company Bull S.A. to develop a complete line of information and telecommunications products and services, including software, consulting, and automatic banking. It included an earlier joint venture, ABC Bull, to build computers in Belo Horizonte, the capital of Minas Gerais. ABC Algar also established a joint venture with International Business Machines Corporation to make small computers.

One objective was to gain technology in order to build communications satellites. Another was to find a market in the United States for ABC X-Tal, which was manufacturing fiber optic products in Campinas, São Paulo, and would become Brazil's largest in this field. ABC Dados Informática signed technology agreements with two Italian firms and the public archive Aminet to produce and export data communications equipment. CTBC was investing in cellular telephony and planning to enter the field of high speed data transmission by means of the Brasilsat communications satellite.

ABC Algar's agricultural holdings, in three states, were exporting soybeans and soybean meal and were also producing soybean oil for domestic use. Green beans, peas, and pineapples were also being exported to Europe, and a plant established with technology from the Swiss company F. Hoffmann-La Roche Ltd. began to vacuum pack food products. Other units were raising dairy cows and animals for the export of specialty meats.

Grupo Algar's consolidated balance sheet for 1995 showed net assets of $844.6 million and debt below $20 million. The share of the Garcia family—which included, besides Garcia, his wife and two children, a

KEY DATES

1954: Grupo Algar's first business, the telephone company CTBC, is acquired.

1988: The group consists by this time of 64 enterprises, many focused on technology and agriculture.

1991: A drastically downsized Algar emerges from three years of austerity.

1995: Leaner but more prosperous, the Algar empire has made its owner a billionaire.

1998: Algar acquires a mobile telephone concession, ATL.

2000: CTBC Telecom is offering service in 300 cities in four Brazilian states.

2007: Telecommunications and agroindustry account for 95 percent of Algar's revenues.

sister, descendants of his deceased brother, and other relatives—was 56 percent. Garcia's own fortune was estimated by *Forbes* at $1.2 billion. The rest of Grupo Algar belonged to Bull, Telebrás, and other investors in telephony and in some local businesses of the group. Grupo Algar consisted of 23 businesses with 4,623 employees. The group's profit came to $27.3 million that year.

EMPHASIS ON TELECOMMUNICATIONS: 1998–2005

Grupo Algar's presence was naturally most evident in Uberlândia, where it owned a newspaper and a cable television company. Yet it was seeking cable contracts in a radius extending some 300 miles from this city and was, with a Canadian and a Korean group, seeking a government concession to operate a cellular telephone network reaching as far, perhaps, as São Paulo. In 1998 it submitted the winning bid for the Rio de Janeiro and Espírito Santo state concessions and founded and controlled, although it did not operate, the resulting enterprise, Algar Telecom Leste (ATL). Soon after, it bought a stake in Tess, the mobile phone operator for the interior of the state of São Paulo. By late 2000 CTBC Telecom was offering both fixed-line and cellular service in 300 cities in four states.

Brazil, however, was falling into a recession, and Grupo Algar lost money every year between 1998 and 2001. Although its revenues rose to BRL 1.42 billion ($602 million) in the final year, its debt reached the

equivalent of $1.8 billion. José Mauro Leal Costa, who had become executive vice-president in 1999, announced in 2002 that the enterprise was scaling back its ambitions in the telecommunications field. It would henceforth rely on CTBC Telecom's fixed-line holdings, which connected 800,000 phones in the group's home state of Minas Gerais and adjacent areas of Goiás, Mato Grosso do Sul, and São Paulo. The shares in Tess were sold in 2001 for $200 million, and part of the ATL stake in 2002 for $265 million. The shares in Algar Bull were sold for about $30 million.

Six of Grupo Algar's telecommunications companies were placed under the CTBC name in 2002. They included Engeredes, a fiber optic network that covered most of Brazil's biggest urban areas, and Net Site, an Internet provider with 40,000 subscribers in which the group had taken a majority stake. CTBC Cellular had 340,000 customers and 80 percent of its market. The only telecommunications company that remained outside the CTBC umbrella was ACS, a call and outsourcing center. It was later given the data center and service department of CTBC and also came to offer information technology. Grupo Algar was very much interested in adding and improving services to its customers, such as access to the Internet via cellular phone, data communications, and a data center that would create portals and sites such as telemedicine and education.

By 2005 Grupo Algar's telecommunications empire had been restored to health. CTBC's 2004 revenues of BRL 1.21 billion ($417 million) accounted for 60 percent of the group's total and its net profit of BRL 58 million ($20 million) comprised 37 percent of the total. For further growth, the enterprise was looking to services for corporations. Another goal was to connect 49 of the 81 municipalities in its fixed-line service area to its fiber optic network during the next three years.

A DIVERSIFIED EMPIRE: 2005–09

ABC Inco, the group's soybean processor, was the next largest business, with revenues of BRL 590 million ($203 million) in 2004. Business was even better in the ensuing year. With the establishment of a crushing unit in Porto Franco, Maranhão, in 2007, that could handle 1,500 metric tons of soybeans per day, exports rose to $100 million in 2007 and were expected to reach $250 million in 2008. The company was planning to build a soybean oil refinery and a port terminal in Itaqui, on the Uruguay River. In 2009 ABC Inco and ABC A&P (the crop cultivation and livestock raising unit) were merged and renamed Algar Agro. In all, Grupo Algar was expecting revenues of BRL 1 billion ($543 million) from agribusiness in 2008.

The telecommunications sector continued to be Grupo Algar's largest, accounting for 59 percent of its revenues in 2007. CTBC was renamed Algar Telecom in 2009, and ACS became Algar Tecnologîa. The former Sabe, which provided telephone books and the newspaper *Correio de Uberlândia,* became ABC Mídia. Engeset (Enghenaria e Serviços Telecomunicações) remained the name of this sector's subsidiary for integrated solutions with regard to information technology and telecommunications.

Services and tourism were accounting for about 5 percent, combined, of Grupo Algar's revenues. Space, which offered security services, became Algar Segurança in 2009. ABC Táxi Aéreo became Algar Aviation. This subsidiary was transporting light cargo as well as passengers, distributing and selling the TBM 850 aircraft as its exclusive distributor in Brazil, and maintaining jets and turboprop planes. Comtec and Rio Quente Resorts continued under their former names. Comtec was the concessionaire of public transport in Uberlândia. Rio Quente Resorts was an aquatic park with hot springs in Goiás.

EMPLOYEES AND FAMILY: A QUEST FOR HARMONY

Grupo Algar was reputed to be one of the best places to work in Brazil. In 2002, for example, the business magazine *Exame* ranked the company eighth among the 100 best enterprises for employment. Its corporate university was considered a benchmark for other businesses. In addition to professional training, which could put an employee on a track to executive advancement, a personal health program was offered that included a doctor, nutritionist, and personal trainer. Those enrolled in professional training, who were called associates rather than employees, could receive a 30 percent supplement to their salaries.

Grupo Algar had only three levels in the corporate hierarchy. It functioned with a high degree of internal transparency, with employees having the right to know the salary of anyone who worked there. In 2005 Grupo Algar required all its employees to sell the products and services that the enterprise offered, initially promising a bonus of 20 percent for each sale made. Those who were already sales executives were challenged to make sales outside their specialties.

By this time Garcia's son, Luiz Alexandre, had become president, or chief executive, of Grupo Algar, while his daughter, Eliane Garcia Melgaço, was commercial director. Their father, chairman of the board, worked only in the fortnight prior to presiding over each of the four board meetings per year. The 31 family members classified as inheritors were enrolled in 2001 in a council whose functions included establishing and maintaining the standards under which one of their number could be employed by Grupo Algar. Activities also included an annual reunion, visits to the various group businesses, lectures on subjects such as marketing and accounting, and exchanges with other such families. Those fourth-generation members not interested in a career with the enterprise were offered vocational guidance and an opportunity to prepare themselves for their roles as shareholders.

Robert Halasz

PRINCIPAL SUBSIDIARIES

ABC Norte (77%); Algar Agro; Algar Aviation; Comtec (50%); CTBC Telecom (84%); RG Empar (50%); Space.

PRINCIPAL OPERATING UNITS

Agro; Services; Telecom.

PRINCIPAL COMPETITORS

SLC Alimentos S.A.; Telemig Celular S.A.

FURTHER READING

Andrade, Lorna, "Os novos sabores da ABC Inco," *Dinheiro Rural,* August 2008, pp. 46–47.

Balarin, Raquel, "Algar investe na preparação de herdeiros," *Jornal Valor Econômico,* September 21–23, 2007, p. B2.

Caixeta, Nely, "Atendimento em ingles," *Exame,* April 13, 2005, p. 62.

Furtado, José Maria, "O milionário caipira," *Exame,* June 3, 1996, pp. 32–35.

———, "Novos impulses," *Exame,* May 29, 2002, pp. 64–66.

———, "Um pé lá, outro cá," *Exame,* August 16, 1995, pp. 44–45.

———, "Procurá-se um Sócio," *Exame,* July 28, 1999, pp. 52–54.

Gomide, Lívia, "Grupo Algar apresenta sua nova marca," *Correio de Uberlândia,* January 2, 2009, p. A4.

Herzog, Ana Luiza, "Todo empregado é um vendedor," *Exame,* August 17, 2005, p. 85.

Mano, Cristiane, "A aposta do Algar," *Exame,* September 28, 2005, p. 74.

Rocha, Márcia, "Maratona da saúde," *Exame,* September 18, 2002, supplement, pp. 62–63.

"Uma virada á mineira," *Exame,* April 29, 1992, pp. 44–45.

Wheatley, Jonathan, "Algar Sharpens Up Its Image," *Financial Times,* February 17, 1998, p. 29.

American Medical Alert Corporation

3265 Lawson Boulevard
Oceanside, New York 11572-3723
U.S.A.
Telephone: (516) 536-5850
Toll Free: (800) 286-2622
Fax: (516) 536-5276
Web site: http://www.amacalert.com

Public Company
Incorporated: 1983
Employees: 580
Sales: $38.58 million (2008)
Stock Exchanges: NASDAQ
Ticker Symbol: AMAC
NAICS: 541990 All Other Professional, Scientific, and Technical Services

■ ■ ■

With headquarters in Oceanside, New York, American Medical Alert Corporation (AMAC) is a medical communications company that provides personal emergency response systems (PERS) as well as call center solutions, selling to both healthcare organizations and direct to consumers. The company's Health and Safety Monitoring Services division manufactures, markets, and services remote patient monitoring systems, including the Medical Alert System, a two-way voice console unit that connects an existing telephone line to a lightweight medallion that a user can operate with the push of a button to summon help from a 24-hour call center in the event of a medical emergency. The product is marketed as Voice-

Care, Response Call, and Walgreens Ready Response as part of a joint venture with the Walgreens drugstore chain. The division also offers the MedSmart and Med-Time medication dispensers that sound an alarm and dispense a patient's proper medication at prescribed times while also providing event notification to caregivers and others; ResidentLink, a monitoring system for use in senior living communities; Intel Health Guide, a web-based, personal remote monitoring system that allows healthcare providers to manage the care of their patients; Health Buddy, an in-home device that connects to a home telephone line allowing patients and healthcare professionals to share real-time health information to reinforce regimen and prevent problems.

AMAC's other division, Telephony Based Communication Solutions, offers a wide range of call center services, including simple after-hours answering systems for physicians and healthcare organizations. Among the services the unit has to offer are appointment scheduling and confirmation, event/class/seminar registration, patient registration, insurance confirmation, critical care and emergency hotline, managed care provider and member services, physician's and information referral, satisfaction surveys, and clinical trial recruitment. Division brands include J-LINK On-Call, Live Message America, North Shore Answering Service, ACT Teleservices, MD OnCall, Capital Medical Bureau, and PhoneScreen. Altogether, AMAC operates nine call centers around the country and five regional sales and service offices. The company's SafeCom, Inc., subsidiary offers monitoring services to drugstores, pharmacies, and other retailers through the Silent Partner brand.

COMPANY PERSPECTIVES

Mission: Provide innovative technologies and monitoring services to assist the growing senior population's ability to engage in better self care activities and remain independent at home; Deliver superior monitoring and communication services through timely response and accurate delivery of critical, time sensitive information; Support the growing and changing demands for secure, health-centric communication services; Elevate the patient communication experience to best reflect the service mission of health services providers.

BEGINNINGS IN 1981

American Medical Alert Corporation was founded by its chairman, Howard M. Siegel, in 1981. A year earlier Siegel, who was running a burglar alarm company in the Long Island community of Oceanside, was contacted by the director of the Hartman YMHA (Young Men's Hebrew Association) who wanted to monitor the organization's senior citizens in Far Rockaway, New York. The medical alert system concept had already been pioneered by another company, Lifeline Systems, Inc., founded by Dr. Andrew S. Dibner and his wife six years earlier. A psychologist, Dibner was painfully familiar with the dangers facing the elderly and frail. As a child he witnessed the sudden death of his grandmother from a heart attack, and later an elderly family friend suffered a stroke while staying alone in a summer cottage and was not discovered until four days had passed. Dibner's solution was a timer-and-alert device that was regularly reset by a person's normal household routines, such as turning off lights or opening a refrigerator. Should that routine be broken the device automatically tapped into the telephone line and sent an alert. An operator would then call the patient. Dibner found an engineer to design the product and then contracted a burglar alarm manufacturer to produce it.

To fill the YMHA's request for a monitoring system, Siegel considered the Lifeline alert system, but did not believe it fit the bill. His own father, suffering from edema, resided in Florida, and Siegel knew that if he were in trouble and on the floor he lacked the strength to reach the phone. By the time someone could be dispatched it might be too late to save him. Siegel's idea was a panic button that established a two-way speakerphone call using a microphone and speaker strong enough to carry a conversation from anywhere in

a home. He found a company to manufacture his alert system, sold it to the Hartman YMHA and established a 24-hour monitoring center. Participants in the program paid $6 a month for the service and rented the equipment. Siegel's company, American Medical Alert, then looked to expand sales, marketing the device and system, which would take the name "VoiceEmitter" and subsequently "Voice of Help."

NEW YORK CITY CONTRACT AWARDS: 1983

"When I started this company," Siegel told the *New York Times* in 1987, "I was told one of the toughest things to sell is preventive health care because it's an admission of need. Many children wanted to buy it for their parents, but the parents rejected it." No matter how well the system worked, it was the stigma attached to personal alert systems that caused a lack of acceptance of the product in the marketplace. Hence, Lifeline early on had decided to target hospitals and nursing homes rather than the patients directly. For its part, AMAC won a contract in 1983 to provide PERS services to the City of New York Human Resources Administration, Homecare Service Program (HCSP), providing a steady revenue stream. Also in 1983 AMAC went public, raising funds from an initial stock offering to expand the company.

Unfortunately, Medicare, Medicaid, and most private insurers did not yet consider PERS to be essential, opting to categorize it as a preventive measure that did not warrant reimbursement. Meanwhile, the falling cost of personal alert systems in the 1980s provided only marginal help with consumers. To make matters worse, a television commercial promoting a device offered by the LifeCall company made potential customers even more reluctant to embrace alarm products. The crudely produced commercial attempted to dramatize the plight of Mrs. Fletcher, an elderly homebound person who falls in her bathroom and uses an emergency pendant to communicate with a dispatch service, exclaiming "I've fallen and I can't get up!" Unfortunately, comedians latched onto the phrase, which became a national punch line, making it even more difficult to convince people to make use of personal alert systems.

Regardless of initial consumer resistance, PERS gained traction with home care agencies and other institutions that recognized the cost-saving benefits that came with the remote monitoring of patients. Eventually insurers concurred and encouraged the use of PERS, and government money became available as well. Moreover, the population was aging, creating an ever growing pool of potential users, many of whom were

```
┌─────────────────────────────────────────────┐
│                                               │
│              KEY DATES                        │
│                  ■                            │
│  ─────────────────────────────────────────    │
│  1981:  Howard M. Siegel starts company.      │
│  1983:  Company incorporates and goes public. │
│  1991:  Contract is signed with Marriott Corp.│
│  2000:  Company begins diversification effort.│
│  2003:  Telephone answering service LMA is    │
│         acquired.                             │
│  2006:  Jack Rhian succeeds Siegel as chief   │
│         executive.                            │
│  2007:  Partnership is forged with Walgreens  │
│         Co.                                   │
│                                               │
└─────────────────────────────────────────────┘
```

comfortable using telephone answering machines, burglar alarm systems, and other electronics, breaking down their resistance to PERS devices.

LATE-CENTURY PROBLEMS ARISE

AMAC appeared to have turned the corner in 1991 when new contracts with HCSP and Marriott Corp. helped to boost annual revenues to more than $4 million, resulting in net income of $437,927. A year later, sales dipped to $3.6 million. Business then improved at a modest pace, reaching $6.2 million in 1995, and net income grew to $741,000. Investors in the public company were not impressed, however, and the price of AMAC shares rarely ventured above $4. In the second half of the decade sales improved to $9.2 million in 1999 and net income totaled $875,000 after approaching $1 million in 1998. The company was overly dependent, however, on its HCSP contract, which accounted for nearly half of AMAC's revenues, and in October 1999 it was informed that the City of New York was preliminarily awarding their business to another company. AMAC continued to serve the city through retroactive extensions and eventually the change in vendors did not go through, but it was clear to Siegel that after nearly 20 years in business the company had reached a crossroads. The time had come to sell or diversify the business to become less dependent on the city contract.

AMAC decided to remain independent and brought in new executives, including Jack Rhian, hired as COO in January 2000. A graduate of New York University with a master's degree in public administration, Rhian had experience as a hospital administrator, having spent six years as the COO of Nationwide Ambulance Service, and prior to joining AMAC he held the same position with Transcare New York, Inc., a medical transportation company. Rhian spearheaded AMAC's diversification effort to create new profit centers.

ENTERING DISEASE MANAGEMENT MONITORING: 2001

In November 2000 AMAC acquired Harriet Campbell, Inc., a company that provided telephone answering and office support services to New York City–area hospitals, clinics, and doctors. AMAC rebranded the services as H-LINK OnCall. A year later the company secured the North American distribution rights to market the high-tech Med-Time pill dispensing system, a device developed by Sweden's Pharmacell company to remind patients to take their medications and make sure that only the proper dosage was administered. Also in 2001 AMAC introduced a new product called VoiceCare Personal Emergency Response System, a device worn by patients that included their medical histories and emergency phone numbers.

Later in 2001 AMAC became involved in the disease management monitoring field, so-called tele-health, by forging an alliance with Health Hero Network, a Mountain View, California-based company that manufactured a home-based disease management appliance called Health Buddy. Plugged into a phone jack, it asked patients several questions related to their condition. Healthcare providers could then use the information to screen patients, determining whether office visits were required or other care needed. As a result, care providers could oversee as many as 150 patients, rather than the typical 13 to 30. Under terms of the arrangement between the two companies, AMAC was permitted to wed the Health Buddy technology to its PERS system. AMAC also supplemented the device with biometrics, providing such key information as glucose levels, blood pressure, and weight.

As a result of adding new products, AMAC increased sales to $13.9 million in 2001. Moreover, it was becoming less dependent on HCSP, whose contribution fell to 26 percent of the company's revenues in 2001. Diversification continued in 2002 when AMAC's Safe Com division leveraged the company's monitoring technology to introduce the Silent Partner system, carrying emergency signals between pharmacies and other retail establishments to AMAC call centers, which could then dispatch law enforcement as necessary. A further source of new income was added in June 2003 with the acquisition of LMA, a telephone answering service. Not only did it contribute $730,000 in sales, helping AMAC to build revenues to $16.6 million, it laid the foundation for the acquisition of similar services throughout the northeastern United States. In 2004 AMAC purchased AlphaConnect Inc., a Voorhees, New Jersey-based telephone answering service that served New Jersey and

Philadelphia hospitals and physicians. A year later Long Island Message Center Inc., a West Babylon call center, was acquired as well. Also of note in 2005, AMAC extended its contract with HCSP, but the business represented just 13 percent of annual revenues, which grew to $22.45 million in 2005.

SIEGEL RETIRES AS CEO: 2006

By this time Rhian had been named Siegel's successor as CEO, and at the end of 2006, the founder of the company turned over the reins, although he stayed on as chairman of the board and served as a senior adviser in a newly created position. At the end of his tenure AMAC acquired the PhoneScreen product, used to recruit patients for clinical trials. He left Rhian with a company that generated $30.8 million in 2006 and net earnings of $1.3 million. The company's prospects would be given a further boost early in 2007 when the Walgreens drugstore chain introduced Walgreens Ready Response, a medical alert system developed by AMAC. Walgreens then marketed its branded alert system through its network of more than 5,700 drugstores in the United States and Puerto Rico. AMAC's share in the business helped to grow its annual revenues to more than $35 million and net income to over $1.5 million in 2007. Two years later, sales had improved to $38.6 million although net income had decreased slightly. Given the aging of the population and the growing need for the products AMAC had to offer, there seemed reason to believe these totals would grow in the years to come.

Ed Dinger

PRINCIPAL SUBSIDIARIES

HCI Acquisition Corp.; LMA Acquisition Corp.; Safe Com, Inc.

PRINCIPAL DIVISIONS

Health and Safety Monitoring Services; Telephony Based Communication Solutions.

PRINCIPAL COMPETITORS

ADT Worldwide; Napco Security Systems, Inc.; Philips Lifeline.

FURTHER READING

Galant, Richard, "Staying Alert in an Expanding Market," *Newsday,* October 29, 2007.

Hirsch, James, "Emergency Help—With the Push of a Button," *St. Petersburg (Fla.) Times,* December 6, 1987, p. 6F.

Karlin, Rick, "Medical Pager Boom Could Signal Distress for Home Health Workers," *Albany (N.Y.) Times Union,* August 3, 1995, p. A1.

Powderly, Henry E., "Founder of American Medical Alert Corporation to Resign," *Long Island Business News,* November 21, 2006.

Reich-Hale, David, "Oceanside-Based American Medical Alert Corp. Takes Acquisition Route," *Long Island Business News,* September 20, 2005.

Schachter, Ken, "AMAC Shoots to Change Rules by Diversifying," *Long Island Business News,* May 10, 2002, p. 13A.

Talley, Karen, "American Answers Voice Alert Call," *Long Island Business News,* November 25, 1991, p. 3.

"Walgreens Launches Medical Alert System," *Chain Drug Review,* March 5, 2007, p. 3.

American Technology Corporation

15378 Avenue of Science, Suite 100
San Diego, California 92128-3407
U.S.A.
Telephone: (858) 676-1112
Fax: (858) 676-1120
Web site: http://www.atcsd.com

Public Company
Incorporated: 1980 as Chasko, Inc.
Employees: 33
Sales: $11.2 million (2008)
Stock Exchanges: NASDAQ
Ticker Symbol: ATCO
NAICS: 334310 Audio and Video Equipment
    Manufacturing

■ ■ ■

American Technology Corporation (ATC) is a NASDAQ-listed public company based in San Diego, California, that develops, manufactures, and sells innovative acoustics systems to the commercial, government, and military markets. Products are based on the company's HyperSonic Sound (HSS) and NeoPlanar technologies. HSS products focus sound into a tight beam, making them ideal as a way to cut through ambient noise, such as a railway station providing commuter information in a targeted area. Museums also make use of HSS to provide self-guided tour information, so that users can hear the information, yet other patrons, who may be standing only a few feet way, hear nothing. Retailers have also found HSS to be an effective way to impart information at points of purchase without creating a din. The company's NeoPlanar technology produces a column of sound, ideal for mass communication systems. Commercial products using this technology are sold under the NeoPlanar and SoundSaber labels.

ATC also produces the Long Range Acoustic Device (LRAD) that uses NeoPlanar technology to create a nonlethal device that can issue warnings as well as produce earsplitting sounds for crowd control and to deter attack. Because it is directed, the sound does not pose a threat to people on the periphery. LRAD products are used by the military and law enforcement as well as commercial users such as petrochemical and nuclear power plants enforcing exclusion zones. Cruise ships have also used LRAD to ward off pirate attacks. ATC holds more than 300 patents and patent filings in the United States and other countries, many of them held by the company's founder and chairman, Elwood G. "Woody" Norris.

FOUNDER: DEPRESSION-ERA BORN

Woody Norris was born in the late 1930s in Barrelville, Maryland, the son of a coal miner whose education did not surpass third grade. Norris's mother left school after the eighth grade. Although Norris would benefit from more formal education than his parents, much of his knowledge of electronics was self-taught. Fascinated by radio as a child, Norris began repairing broken sets for a local repair shop, working out of a chicken coop. After graduation from high school he applied for a job at a radio store, but being impatient, when he did not hear back quickly enough, decided to join the U.S. Air Force in 1956. In the service he received electronics training that would provide him with an important foundation.

Stationed on a New Mexico base, Norris trained at the University of New Mexico to be a nuclear weapons specialist, but overall found Air Force life to be tedious. His duties for the day completed by noon, Norris began working as a cameraman at an Albuquerque television station. After four years in the Air Force, he accepted a job fixing electronic equipment at the University of Washington. More importantly, the job allowed him to take classes for free. In addition to electronics engineering, he studied psychology, religion, and Spanish. He did not, however, fulfill the requirements needed to attain a degree. In his spare time, Norris also worked on an invention: a phonograph tonearm that corrected linear tracking problems created by a turntable.

A company in Salt Lake City, Protek Communications, learned of his abilities and hired him to develop a product for them, preferably a medical device because one of the four partners was a doctor. Over the course of a weekend, Norris, drawing on his knowledge of FM radio and radar from the Air Force, developed a method of emitting sound into the skin that could be bounced back to discern distinct sounds within the body, such as the heartbeat of a fetus. The underlying principles of Norris's invention would be employed in the creation of the sonogram, which translated the rebounding waves into pictures. His penlight-size transcutaneous Doppler would find ready use as a blood-flow monitor.

NORRIS SETS UP INVENTION SHOP: 1970

Norris's weekend of work provided him with 50,000 shares in the Salt Lake company, which became far more valuable after the company went public. With the shares worth $8, Norris cashed in during a secondary stock offering. He quit his job at the University of Washington in 1970, rented a shop, and filled it with all manner of tools and equipment. Norris devoted himself to the pursuit of his phonograph arm, which he eventually sold, and the development of other inventions that caught his attention. In 1980 he formed Chasko, Inc.,

to develop and market them. Two years later Chasko was renamed American Technology Corporation.

One of Norris's inventions resulted from a harrowing experience at Disneyland searching for a missing son. Inspired by it, he developed a child locator, the Guardian I, a small transmitter worn by the child. It emitted a beeping signal that could be picked up by a book-size monitor as far away as 500 feet. The device would also sound an alarm if the wearer wandered beyond 300 feet or the transmitter was removed, and it issued a different sound if immersed in water, such as a child falling into a pool of water.

In its first four years ATC mostly devoted its attention to the development of a two-speed cassette tape deck that could record continuously for 12 hours. This work led to a method of recording an entire unabridged novel on a single tape. Although the PocketTalk product was practical from the point of view of the listener, who no longer had to contend with multiple tapes to listen to an entire audiobook, Norris found that publishers and bookstores were not interested in a book on a single tape. Rather, they wanted to sell more tapes.

In September 1984 the focus of ATC shifted to technology acquired from another Norris company, Norcom Electronics Corporation, founded a year earlier to work on an ear radio that could fit entirely in the ear canal and an ear microphone that relied on the vibrations of head bones. ATC pursued the development of these products until March 1988 when most of the technology was assigned to Norris Communications, another Norris company. At this point, ATC became a dormant company, lacking the funds to pursue other business.

ATC RECAPITALIZATION: 1992

Norris also formed Patriot Scientific Corp. in 1987 to develop a ground-penetrating radar concept and other ideas. What he fell short in was management skills. Aside from ingenuity and incessant optimism, Norris also took advantage of his sales ability, something he honed during his days as a high school thespian. In fact, he had hoped to become an actor, only to have his skills as an inventor supersede that endeavor. Because of his enthusiasm and salesmanship, Norris was able to attract money to fund his inventions despite his shortcomings as a businessman. In 1992 he recapitalized ATC to further develop ear radios. An FM version was unveiled in September 1992 and an AM version followed in July 1995.

In the meantime, Norris began developing HSS technology, something he had been thinking about for 20 years. In developing HSS, Norris drew on his

KEY DATES

1980: Elwood Norris founds Chasko, Inc., to develop his inventions.

1982: Chasko is renamed American Technology Corporation (ATC).

1988: Financially strapped, company ceases operation.

1992: ATC is recapitalized.

1996: Norris initiates development of HyperSonic Sound technology.

2000: NeoPlanar technology is acquired.

2005: Pirate attack publicizes company's Long Range Acoustic Device (LRAD) products.

knowledge of color television, which relied on the mixing of red, blue, and green to trick the eye into seeing a variety of colors as the three mixed in the air as the light from the screen traveled to the eyes of the viewer. Even more influential to Norris was his reading of the works of the German scientist Hermann von Helmholtz in the 19th century. Helmholtz explained a phenomenon first noticed a century earlier by the Italian composer Giuseppe Tartini, who was puzzled when two loud organ notes produced a third note. The frequency of this third note, the so-called Tartini tone, Helmholtz explained, was actually the difference between the frequencies of the other two notes.

Norris's idea was to use a similar method of sound production to create a new type of loudspeaker. Although sound reproduction had taken greater strides in recent decades, speaker design had changed little, making it hi-fi's major weak link. Traditional speakers used oscillating cones to produce sound by moving air. Because no speaker driver could produce the full audio range, loudspeakers required three separate drivers: woofer, midrange, and tweeter. Even then, they could not reproduce the bottom 20 hertz of the audio range, and distortions were created from the crossover of the signals and the construction of the speaker enclosures. Waves bouncing off the walls behind the speakers also created a time-delay effect to further blur the sound.

COMPANIES SIGN ON TO TEST HSS TECHNOLOGY: 1998

Norris's idea to improve loudspeaker design was to use a crystal to produce two ultrasonic sounds, so high-pitched that the human ear could not detect them, then mix them in the air. The listener would then hear the

difference in the frequency between the two waves. This pure sound could then be thrown across the room onto a wall or other flat surface. As a result it could be directed like a spotlight and not disperse widely like traditional loudspeaker sound. A pair of speakers could also be extremely small, about the size of two Oreo cookies. The technology was so promising that in April 1998, Philips Consumer Electronics signed an agreement to consider incorporating the technology in its products. Two months later, Sanyo Technosound Co. Ltd. of Japan signed a similar agreement. Musician Ray Charles was so impressed by the sound the speakers produced that he agreed to endorse the speakers, something he had never done before.

More work, and many more millions of dollars, would be needed to develop HSS. Time would also be needed to persuade the marketplace to accept the new technology. By 2003 ATC spent $44 million on its development. Along the way, investors began to grow impatient and the company looked to diversify through acquisition. The company's NeoPlanar technology was acquired in 2000. In that same year, the U.S.S. *Cole* was attacked by terrorists on motorboats laden with explosives. The ship's crew members were not sure if the warnings it issued were heard, hesitated, and the ship was struck by the attackers. In answer to the obvious need for a better method of issuing long-range audio messages, ATC began development of its LRAD with financial help from the U.S. Navy. ATC took advantage of the NeoPlanar and HSS technologies to develop LRAD, which could not only deliver targeted warnings in a multitude of languages, it could also emit focused and highly painful sound waves, "sonic bullets" that could deter attacks without fatalities and without affecting the operator of the device or bystanders.

CEO RESIGNS: 2003

Although ATC held great potential, it was still an unprofitable company. In fiscal 2002 it posted sales of $1 million while losing $8.2 million, prompting its auditor to raise "substantial doubt" that the company could continue. To better organize ATC as it pursued the development, licensing, and marketing of HSS and NeoPlanar products, Norris hired James M. Irish in early 2003 to serve as chief executive officer. Irish quickly moved to raise $4 million in a private placement of stock and cut costs while hiring a sales force and rushing an HSS speaker into production. A $10 million investment round followed in July 2003. By late September 2003, however, Irish was gone after just eight months, resigning suddenly "by mutual agreement" with the board of directors, according to ATC.

The departure of Irish and no major contracts to announce cast a pall over ATC. Some good news came in February 2004, however, when the U.S. Marines purchased LRAD units for use in Iraq. Fitted with MP3 players the devices were used to issue prerecorded warnings in Arabic over long distances. In 2005 ATC received some much needed free publicity for LRAD, a nonlethal weapon (although it can cause major hearing loss), when a cruise ship used it to help ward off a pirate attack off the coast of Somalia.

With ATC's prospects improving, Norris hired a new chief executive officer in 2006, Thomas R. Brown, former president of Sony Electronics. He implemented new cost controls and focused the company's sales efforts on large customers, primarily governments, including the New York Police Department, the organizers of the Beijing Olympics, and the governments of the Republic of Georgia, India, and the United Arab Emirates. With LRAD sales leading the way, ATC increased revenues to $11 million in 2008. Because the market for LRAD was far from saturated and the company's HSS products retained a good deal of untapped potential, there was every reason to believe that ATC was on the verge of becoming a profitable concern.

Ed Dinger

PRINCIPAL COMPETITORS

Boston Acoustics, Inc.; IML Corp. LLC; Wattre Corp.

FURTHER READING

Armstrong, Larry, "The Cookie-Size Concert Hall," *Business Week,* December 2, 1996, p. 108.

Babyak, Richard J., "For Your Ears Only," *Appliance Manufacturer,* August 2003, p. 24.

Bigelow, Bruce V., "Inventor Strives for the Sound of Success," *San Diego Union-Tribune,* May 6, 1998, p. C1.

———, "Sound Waves Are Turned into Weapon by S.D. Firm," *San Diego Union-Tribune,* November 9, 2005, p. C1.

Fenton, Brian C., "Hypersonic Sound: Sound from Thin Air," *Popular Mechanics,* June 1997.

Foege, Alec, "Killer Sounds," *Fortune Small Business,* March 2009, p. 31.

Free, Cathy, "When Youngsters Stray Off to Parts Unknown," *People,* September 15, 1986.

Helman, Christopher, "Now Hear This," *Forbes,* September 15, 2003.

Jewell, Mark, "'Laziest Inventor You Ever Met?' Doubtful," *Minneapolis Star Tribune,* April 17, 2005, p. 11A.

Karp, Jonathan, "Hey, You! How About Lunch?" *Wall Street Journal,* April 1, 2004, p. B1.

Kauffman, Bruce, "Poway, Calif., Company Producing Speakers with Uncommon Technology," *North County Times* (Escondido, Calif.), August 4, 1998.

Maney, Kevin, "Sound Technology Turns the Way You Hear on Its Ear," *USA Today,* May 19, 2003.

Pae, Peter, "Weapon Sends Message That's Loud and Clear," *Los Angeles Times,* June 23, 2002, p. C1.

Weintraub, Arlene, "Here You Hear It, There You Don't," *Business Week,* February 17, 2003, p. 64.

Artisan Confections
Company

---

100 Crystal A Drive
Hershey, Pennsylvania 17033
U.S.A.
Telephone: (717) 534-4200
Web site: http://www.artisanconfections.com

Wholly Owned Subsidiary of The Hershey Company
Incorporated: 2005
NAICS: 311320 Chocolate and Confectionery Manufacturing from Cacao Beans; 311330 Confectionery Manufacturing from Purchased Chocolate

■ ■ ■

Artisan Confections Company is a wholly owned subsidiary of The Hershey Company that owns and manages three premium chocolate brands: Scharffen Berger Chocolate Maker, Joseph Schmidt Master Chocolatier, and Dagoba Organic Chocolate. The companies sell their chocolates in high-end food markets, specialty stores and department stores, and increasingly, in mainstream grocery stores. Joseph Schmidt has a permanent retail store in San Francisco, California, and one in San Jose, California. Scharffen Berger runs a factory store and a retail store in San Francisco.

HERSHEY BEGINS SELLING
ARTISAN CHOCOLATES: 2005

In 2005, The Hershey Company formed a wholly owned subsidiary called Artisan Confections Company to take advantage of and compete in the growing realm

of high-end chocolatiers, then a $1.7 billion industry segment. The impetus behind the explosion in dark chocolate offerings was the proliferation of artisan food items bolstered by the news that chocolate consumed in moderation is good for one's health. (There are many antioxidants in the cacao bean from which chocolate is made.) As a result, more people were purchasing premium chocolate and savoring its flavors as they would a fine wine or a dark roast coffee. In fact, dark chocolate sales were on the rise, increasing 15 percent from 2003 to 2006 as the percentage of households purchasing dark chocolate increased from eight in 2004 to 25 percent by 2006.

Artisan's first move was the double acquisition of Scharffen Berger Chocolate Maker, Inc., based in San Francisco, California, in July 2005 and Joseph Schmidt Master Chocolatier also of San Francisco, in August. Each company kept its own identity and staff and continued to make and market its distinctive line of gourmet products, using its signature recipes, but now bearing the new stamp of Artisan Confections in addition to its own brand name. The combined purchase price for Scharffen Berger and Joseph Schmidt was $47.1 million. In October 2006, Artisan Confections Company also purchased the assets of Dagoba Organic Chocolates, LLC, based in Ashland, Oregon, for $17 million.

SCHARFFEN BERGER
CHOCOLATES: 1996–2005

At the time of its purchase, Scharffen Berger owned and operated three specialty stores in New York, New York,

COMPANY PERSPECTIVES

The foundation of our marketing strategy is our strong brand equities, product innovation, the consistently superior quality of our products, our manufacturing expertise and mass distribution capabilities. We also devote considerable resources to the identification, development, testing, manufacturing and marketing of new products.

and in Berkeley and San Francisco, California. It was known for its high-cacao content dark chocolate bars and baking products sold online and in a broad range of outlets, including specialty retailers, natural food stores, and gourmet centers across the United States.

Scharffen Berger began in 1996, when Robert Steinberg, a former family medicine doctor and actor, and John Scharffenberger, the former owner of Scharffenberger Cellars winery, went into business together. Steinberg, a lover of chocolate, had left his practice in 1990 after being diagnosed with lymphoma; he traveled to France where he learned about cacao bean selection, blending, roasting, and conching (a process that enhances the product's smoothness and quality) chocolate at the renowned Bernachon Chocolatier in Lyons. Back home in the United States, he contacted his friend and former patient, Scharffenberger, who had just sold his winery and was taking time off.

The two men began experimenting with varieties of beans and chocolate liqueurs in Steinberg's kitchen in 1996, using makeshift chocolate-making equipment, such as a hair dryer, coffee grinder, and mortar and pestle. After rave reviews about their concoctions from family and friends, and even Julia Child, the team moved into a factory in 1997 and began to produce its first core product, 70 percent cacao bittersweet chocolate that it dubbed "the finest American-made dark chocolate."

Demand soon outstripped Scharffen Berger's tiny factory capacity as the company's following began to grow. Ignoring industry culture, the men opened their factory to the public and printed the percentage of cacao in each bar on the wrapper. They also spent considerable time visiting cacao farms around the world in search of the best beans and experimented with roasting methods for the best flavor profiles. Scharffen Berger grew rapidly and, in 2000, the chocolate maker pulled in $2.3 million in revenue. The following year, the company moved into a 27,000-square-foot factory in

Berkeley, increasing production capacity fivefold and growing its staff to 40. After expanding its product line and standardizing its packaging, that figure leapt to $4.1 million in 2002.

The next hurdle for Scharffen Berger to tackle was distribution. "The hard thing is getting distributors to understand exactly what our products are," Steinberg explained in a 2003 *San Francisco Business Times* article. "We need to be in more stores to get a critical mass with the population," a population of savvy foodies that had proven that it was willing to pay extra for artisanal cheeses, grass-fed beef, hand-crafted beers and wines. The company had by that time developed a strong relationship with Whole Foods and Peet's Coffee & Tea, as well as regional grocers, but found that it took sharing its product one-on-one to gain a following. Its next step, thus, was to open a retail store in San Francisco in late 2003 and a café at its factory in 2004 where it also introduced four new products in 2004: sweetened natural cocoa powder, chocolate-covered ginger, chocolate-covered cacao nibs, and chocolate-covered coffee beans.

Still, in 2003, after seven years of production, the company remained unprofitable, despite the popularity of its product. Consequently, Scharffenberger handed over management of the company to Jim Harris in January 2004. Harris increased profits by raising prices and investing in new machines that increased production sevenfold. The newly profitable company caught the attention of The Hershey Company when it began looking for high-end acquisitions in 2005 and offered to buy Scharffen Berger for a price about twice that of its then annual revenues of $10 million.

JOSEPH SCHMIDT MASTER CHOCOLATIER: 1983–2005

About a decade before Scharffenberger and Steinberg began developing their signature dark chocolate products, Joseph Schmidt, a native of Israel, born to Viennese parents, had begun to earn a reputation for his artistic truffles, his colorful chocolate mosaics, chocolate sculptures, and chocolate bowls. In 1983, he opened a small shop in San Francisco's Castro district where he began selling his chocolate confections.

Schmidt had arrived in the United States as a tourist in the early 1960s, after serving in the Israeli Army and training with European chefs. When his money ran out, he went to work as a dishwasher at a bakery and then worked his way up and learned to make pastries. Six years later, he headed west to San Francisco, where, after a few stints at various pastry shops, and a short time running his own ice cream store in the Marina,

KEY DATES

1983: Joseph Schmidt opens a small chocolate shop in San Francisco.

1996: Robert Steinberg and John Scharffenberger found Scharffen Berger Chocolate Maker.

1997: Joseph Schmidt builds a 95,000-square-foot chocolate factory in the Mission district of San Francisco.

2003: Joseph Schmidt relinquishes general management of his company to Charles Huggins.

2004: Jim Harris takes over management of Scharffen Berger; Dagoba moves into a 14,000-square-foot building in Ashland, Oregon, four times larger than its original facility.

2005: The Hershey Company founds Artisan Confections Company as a wholly owned subsidiary; Artisan purchases Joseph Schmidt Master Chocolatier and Scharffen Berger Chocolate Maker.

2006: Artisan purchases Dagoba Organic Chocolate.

2008: Steinberg dies.

Schmidt ended up at Fantasia Bakery where he worked for 11 years.

When Schmidt left Fantasia, he and his girlfriend and business partner, Audrey Ryan, started a pastry business. They had to order their chocolate in packages of at least 500 pounds apiece; thus Schmidt taught himself to make truffles as a way of using up the surplus. His egg-shaped American Truffle, with its creamy, flavored center, became an almost immediate success.

Then Schmidt discovered his special talent for sculpting in chocolate. He used a device similar to a potter's wheel, placing a mold on top of the wheel and coating it with melted chocolate. "Chocolate is one of the best ingredients to create sculptures from," said Schmidt in a 1992 *San Francisco Chronicle* piece. "'If you make a mistake, you can always re-melt it and try again.'"

Within three months of the opening of Schmidt and Ryan's business, a buyer from Neiman Marcus asked for permission to mention the couple's truffles in the store's Christmas 1983 gourmet catalog. The orders began to pour in, from I. Magnin, Saks, and Harrod's of London, and production went from a few hundred boxes of truffles a week to 6,000. During its first year in business, Joseph Schmidt revenues hit $400,000. A year later, Schmidt and Ryan were no longer making pastries, and Moreau chocolates, distributors of several European and American lines of candy, asked to sell their truffles.

By the late 1980s, Macy's and Neiman Marcus were selling Joseph Schmidt truffles, and Schmidt's bowls were part of a touring exhibit of confection art organized by the American Craft Museum in New York. In 1991, the company rang up sales of $5.5 million, a 25 percent increase from the year before. That same year, it added 150 new retail accounts, including upscale cookware chain Williams-Sonoma and Filene's, the New England department store chain. Bergdorf Goodman, an exclusive New York department store, became a customer in 1992. Schmidt also increased its sales to important existing customers Macy's and Neiman Marcus by 200 percent each in the second half of 1991. In addition, Schmidt expanded into mail-order sales for the first time, winning listings in four catalogs. By then, the company was using nearly 25 tons of Belgian chocolate per week in its Potrero Hill factory.

Joseph Schmidt was dreaming and working even bigger, breaking rules and inventing new ways of working in chocolate. "You cannot be a fanatic and stick to Old World rules on how to make certain things," he explained of his desire for freedom to exercise creativity in a 1994 *Chicago Sun-Times* article. His holiday-inspired creations, such as his largest in 1992, a five- by 29-foot Christmas fantasy with a three-and-a-half-foot tree and a box overflowing with toys (displayed in the lobby of One Market Plaza in San Francisco) used in the vicinity of 10,000 pounds of chocolate. Schmidt also worked small. In 1993, Joseph Schmidt Truffle Bars, made of Belgian Callebaut milk chocolate and manufactured on equipment purchased from Cadbury, became available in five flavors: amaretto, orange, coffee, white/dark, and milk/dark.

With a production growth rate of about 15 percent a year, the company's 40,000-square-foot plant became too small. The company's sales rose to $10 million in 1997, up from $8.7 million in 1996 and $7.7 million in 1995 on about 7,000 national accounts; orders to department stores jumped 30 percent. Schmidt was using 1.25 million pounds of chocolate annually at his factory in San Francisco. In 1997, Schmidt built a 95,000-square-foot chocolate factory in the Mission district, eventually adding 105 jobs to the company's total of 157 and boosting production by 30 to 40 percent, with an anticipated doubling of production within three years.

In 2003, Schmidt decided to concentrate full time on his truffle designs and Charles "Chip" Huggins, a longtime executive at See's, became Joseph Schmidt's chief executive officer. Schmidt continued to oversee production in the chocolate factory, while Audrey Ryan ran the retail store. By 2005, when the company was purchased by Hershey, it was selling about 20 million truffles a year to major department stores and gourmet food shops across the country, as well as exporting its products to England and Japan.

DAGOBA ORGANIC CHOCOLATE: 2000–06

Dagoba Organic Chocolate of Oregon, which Artisan purchased in 2006, had its origin in 1998, when Frederick Schilling began experimenting in his home kitchen with an idea he had had years earlier while working as a cook in a café in Boulder, Colorado. Schilling, who loved flavors, "just wanted to add some twists to chocolate," he recalled in a 2004 *Oregonian* article, and "had this idea that chai chocolate would be so good."

Schilling did some market research on chocolate bars and discovered that, while specialty chocolate was rising in popularity, it consisted primarily of dark or milk chocolate with or without almonds or hazelnuts. "In terms of an accessible chocolate bar that had a little more diversity of flavors and whatnot—it didn't exist at the time," he recounted in a 2004 *Oregonian* piece. Going on the positive response he had received from friends and family for his hot milk chocolate laced with tea, ginger, cardamom, cloves, and black pepper, he enlisted his father, Jon Schilling, a former IBM employee and "sales and marketing guru," and contracted to buy organic beans from small growers, the Bribri Indians, in the rain forests of Costa Rica and Panama. He leased some industrial space in Boulder, Colorado, and by 2000, he was marketing his "organic, fair trade" chocolate bars.

In 2001, Schilling and his girlfriend showed up at the Fancy Food Show in New York with "launch products," seven chocolate bars. After winning an award that year for best organic bar from *Food & Wine* and taking on its first East Coast distributor, the company moved to Ashland, Oregon, and in the summer of 2002 made its first $1 million in sales. Schilling was still, however, making each bar by hand, putting family and friends to work wrapping the bars when they came to visit. By the company's second anniversary, Schilling added a machine that automated the process of pouring chocolate into molds.

In 2002, the company moved from Boulder to facilities in Central Point, Oregon, and Schilling's mother and sister both came on board. Soon the company, named Dagoba Organic Chocolate (*Dagoba* is

a Sanskrit word meaning "Buddhist temple"), was producing some staples: New Moon, a 74 percent cacao bittersweet chocolate, and Eclipse, a very dark bittersweet at 87 percent cacao. Others followed: Mon Cheri, a 72 percent chocolate with berries and vanilla; Roseberry, 59 percent with dried raspberries and rose hips; Lavender, 59 percent with blueberries and lavender infusion; and Xocolatl, with chiles and cocoa nibs, nutmeg, and vanilla.

By this time, Dagoba had several awards to its name, including Best Chocolate from the *San Francisco Chronicle*. In 2004, it moved into a 14,000-square-foot building in Ashland, Oregon, four times larger than its original facility. There, about 12 people worked six days a week in double shifts, but the company, which produced chocolate bars, hot chocolate, and chocolate-covered coffee beans, which sold in natural food and gourmet stores across the United States, was still back-ordered several times a week.

Awards continued to pour in: *Food and Wine*'s 2005 Tastemaker Award and Best Organic Bar, the *San Francisco Chronicle*'s Best Dark Chocolate in 2005, the U.S. Environmental Protection Agency's 2005 Green Power Leadership Award, and the Organic Trade Association & Organic Farming Research Foundation's 2005 Spirit of Organic Award. Meanwhile, the company remained committed to its social ideals: providing a positive working environment for its 50 employees and "using cacao as a tool for positive ecological and social transformation" in the countries where it does business, according to its web site. Schilling increasingly traveled to cacao-producing communities to set up direct partnerships and collaborate on cacao processing with farmers and to ensure equitable trade agreements for communities and environment sustainability.

Although many of his friends accused him of selling out when Dagoba, with sales of $9 million, agreed to be acquired by The Hershey Company in 2006 for $17 million, Schilling and his family felt they had made the best decision for Dagoba's growth and the continued expansion of the high-end chocolate market.

EVERYDAY LUXURY CONCEPT: 2007–08

All three companies continued to grow as domestic sales of premium chocolate rose from $670 million in 2004 to an anticipated $850 million in 2009. In 2007, Steinberg and Scharffenberger's *Essence of Chocolate*, a historical cookbook of chocolate containing many recipes from Scharffen Berger's own kitchens, appeared in bookstores. At about the same time, single origin bars (chocolate made from the beans of a single cacao-producing region) became increasingly popular among chocolate connoisseurs. Dagoba produced single source bars from Ecuador, Peru, and Madagascar. Scharffen Berger meanwhile continued to purchase all of its beans from up to nine different cacao-growing regions and included the origin of each bar's cacao on the wrapper.

In 2008, Starbucks teamed with Artisan to create a line of Starbucks chocolates that included bars and squares, truffles, and milk chocolate-covered coffee beans. As the world of artisan chocolate makers mourned the passing of Robert Steinberg, cofounder of Scharffen Berger, the consumption of gourmet chocolate was still on the rise, with consumers seeking a quick, healthy, and relatively affordable fix for their growing lifestyle aspirations, especially during hard economic times.

Carrie Rothburd

PRINCIPAL COMPETITORS

Ghirardelli Chocolate Company; Chocolats Valrhona.

FURTHER READING

Beckett, Jamie, "How Sweet It Is for Schmidt," *San Francisco Chronicle,* February 14, 1992, p. B1.

Buford, Bill, "Extreme Chocolate: The Quest for the Perfect Bean," *New Yorker,* October 29, 2007, p. 68.

Clark, Kim, "Sowing the Seeds," *Earth Action Network,* December 25, 2006.

Crompton, Laura, "For the Love of Chocolate: Once Again, Bay Area Artisans Are at the Forefront of a Confectionary Renaissance," *San Francisco Chronicle,* September 6, 2006, p. F1.

Frost, Jim, "Schmidt: A Sculptor in Chocolate," *Chicago Sun-Times,* October 27, 1994, p. 1.

Kaminsky, Peter, "Magic Beans," *Condé-Nast Traveler,* August 2008, p. 61.

Smith, Susan, "Fast 100: Scharffen Berger Chocolate Maker Inc., Chocolate Maker Counts Converts, Not Beans," *San Francisco Business Times,* October 3, 2003, p. S8.

Stiles, Greg, "Hershey Co. Buys Oregon-Based Chocolate Producer," *Medford (Ore.) Mail Tribune,* October 20, 2006.

The official chocolate of everyday life."

Asher's Chocolates, Inc.

80 Wambold Drive
Souderton, Pennsylvania 18964
U.S.A.
Telephone: (215) 721-3000
Toll Free: (800) 438-8882
Fax: (215) 721-3265
Web site: http://www.ashers.com

Private Company
Incorporated: 1892
Employees: 120
Sales: $30 million (2008 est.)
NAICS: 311330 Confectionary Manufacturing from
    Purchased Chocolate; 311340 Nonchocolate Con-
    fectionary Manufacturing

■ ■ ■

Asher's Chocolates, Inc., produces a full line of milk, dark, and white chocolate molded confections and assorted candies as well as seasonal and holiday chocolates. The company has two state-of-the-art, in-line manufacturing plants in Pennsylvania with machinery for enrobing, extruding, and depositing candies; these include nonpareils, caramel patties, peanut butter cups, filled chocolates, cordial cherries, fudge, nut barks, coconut bonbons, mints, nougats, and chocolate-covered pretzels and potato chips. Asher's also makes more than 500 different varieties of Kosher chocolate confections and has the largest low-carbohydrate, sugar-free line in the industry. Vendors in all 50 states and Canada sell the company's products.

FROM HANDMADE TREATS TO MECHANIZATION

Chester A. Asher, a farm boy from Ontario, Canada, founded his own candy-making company in Center City Philadelphia, Pennsylvania, in 1892. Asher had worked for a short while in a candy factory in Boston, Massachusetts, before embarking on his own. However, Asher had a talent for business, and his company was so successful that, in 1905, he moved it to larger quarters in Philadelphia's Germantown section. There, in addition to making candies and chocolates, he sold maple syrup, jams and jellies, baked items, and ice cream, as well as some European-style bonbons and rare candies. Asher wrote out his own recipes on the back of sugar bags for production, which his staff of six scrupulously followed. Some of the company's original favorites included crystallized bonbons and handmade coconut fruits.

As John Asher Sr., Chester Asher's son, moved into the business, the company passed through some hard times, although it still managed to grow. By the time Asher Sr. died in 1966, leaving his sons, John (Jack) and Bob, to manage the business, Asher's Chocolates had purchased a neighboring movie theater, small department store, and restaurant in Germantown and converted them into candy-making facilities. However, the company was near collapse and on the verge of closing. Jack and Bob, intent on recovering the company's solvency, introduced mechanization to Asher's Chocolates' candy-making processes.

In the 1980s, a fourth generation of Ashers, David and Jeff, joined the Germantown company, which was

COMPANY PERSPECTIVES

Asher's success is due to the family's reputation for making quality candy with the freshest and purest ingredients available. Attention to detail, close supervision and adherence to its century-old mission statement assure that quality is maintained through every process and with every product.

now tight on space despite adding a second factory in York, Pennsylvania. Explained David Asher looking back in an article in *Candy Industry* in 1998, "[B]ecause the business had grown 10 percent or so a year, I could see that we were going to outgrow those facilities [in Germantown]." After renting 24,000 square feet of warehouse and office space beginning in 1988 in Montgomeryville, a suburb of Philadelphia, Asher's purchased 31 acres of farmland in Souderton, Pennsylvania, in 1993.

NEW MANAGEMENT AND A NEW FACILITY

In 1997, one year after David Asher became president and chief executive and Jeff Asher became vice-president of the business, the company began construction on a new $10 million, 125,000-square-foot facility in Souderton (of which $1 million went to purchase new equipment). By then, Asher's candies were distributed in 50 states and seven other countries. Asher's candies also were sold under the Asher's name at department stores, such as Strawbridge's and Boscov's, which sold candy in bulk; however, 95 percent of Asher's boxed and bulk chocolates were sold under other names.

The company, which had annual sales of about $21 million and produced five million pounds of candy a year, moved into its new facilities on schedule in 1998. The new facilities provided "the space to serve our current customer base and with extended capacity look down the road at other opportunities," according to Jeff Asher in *Candy Industry* in 1998.

Although the new factory offered only slightly more square footage than the company's previous five-building spread, "the efficiencies [of being under one roof] have been terrific and beyond our wildest dreams," according to David Asher in a 1999 *Candy Industry* article. In addition, while in Germantown, "we could not run a second shift because of the neighborhood ... up here we don't have that problem. There's still third

shift possibilities so we can easily double or triple the size of our business without expanding that back wall."

However, "that back wall" of their new home was designed to allow for growth. The factory was set up on a straight-through design with raw materials entering on one end and packaging occurring at the opposite end. According to Jeff Asher in the 1999 *Candy Industry* article, the design included a "pad that's graded along the side so we can basically double the size of the facility. The wall ... is designed to be knocked through and expanded."

Asher's did what it could to alleviate the hardship to some of its long-term employees introduced with the move. It organized field trips to the Souderton area before the new facility was complete to acquaint them with housing and shopping options, and, once the company had moved, it chartered vans for those who opted to make the daily hour and a half roundtrip commute. "We have management that's been with us 25-plus years and prior to the move our average tenure of line person was 15–20 years. When we say we're a family business we include all of our employees," David Asher explained in *Candy Industry* in 1998.

GROWTH THROUGH ACQUISITIONS

During the 1990s, Asher's also purchased two candy companies. The first of these was Goss Candies of Lewistown, Pennsylvania, acquired in 1991. Goss specialized in molded chocolates. The company was quite small when Asher's acquired it, with only seven employees and sales of $250,000 on 50,000 pounds of confections annually; however, under "retired" Jack Asher's direction, Goss Candies achieved $1.8 million in revenues by 1997. When, in 1998, Asher's purchased John F. Davis Candy Co. of Redding, Pennsylvania, it also acquired specialty chocolate and confectionery products and machinery. These products, including rainbow and watermelon coconut strips, were consolidated into Asher's Lewiston and Souderton facilities and distributed on a national basis.

REBOUND IN BULK

Asher's had made its name in the bulk and non-branded categories, but beginning in the mid- to late 1990s, the bulk market began having a hard time. By 1997, that market was in crisis as the bulk candy store concept waned, and traditional avenues for bulk chocolate sales (retail confectioners, department stores, and bulk candy stores) were closing down.

Interestingly, however, people still liked buying their candy in bulk. According to Jeff Asher, in a 2001 *Profes-*

```
┌─────────────────────────────────────────────┐
│                                               │
│               KEY DATES                       │
│                  ▪                            │
│   ───────────────────────────────────         │
│                                               │
│  1892:  Chester Asher founds a candy company  │
│         in Center City Philadelphia.          │
│  1905:  Company moves to Philadelphia's       │
│         Germantown section.                   │
│  1966:  John Asher Sr. dies; Jack and Bob     │
│         Asher take over managing the          │
│         business.                             │
│  1988:  Company rents additional warehouse    │
│         and office space in Montgomeryville,  │
│         Pennsylvania.                         │
│  1991:  Company buys Goss Chocolates of       │
│         Lewistown, Pennsylvania.              │
│  1993:  Company purchases 31 acres of         │
│         farmland in Souderton, Pennsylvania.  │
│  1998:  Asher's moves to newly built          │
│         facilities in Souderton,              │
│         Pennsylvania; Asher's buys John F.     │
│         Davis Candy Co. of Redding,           │
│         Pennsylvania.                         │
│                                               │
└─────────────────────────────────────────────┘
```

sional Candy Buyer article, although bulk in general was suffering, there was no evidence of "any reduction in people's desire to buy themselves a quarter-pound of chocolate. ... We see it in our own retail stores where we're bagging the most popular items ahead of time." In response, Asher's moved toward packing its bulk items, including introducing quarter and half-pound bags, to enhance bulk merchandising.

Asher's also began working with a major catalog company that began to capitalize on the bulk rebound by giving it an old-fashioned flair, selling bulk items packaged in kraft paper bags. By the early 2000s, the trend toward buying candy in bulk was catching on again, although it varied by region of the country with the West Coast and Northwest and, to some degree, the Midwest leading the way. On the East Coast, Asher's longtime customer Boscov's Department Stores took advantage of the shift back toward bulk by expanding the bulk candy departments in its 35 stores.

NEW EMPHASIS ON BRANDING AND PACKAGING

Asher's also embarked on a new marketing strategy with its move to the Souderton campus. According to Jeff Asher in *Candy Industry* in 1998, the decision was to "swing the emphasis to the Asher name ... as a brand nationally. We're hoping, through chains and larger merchandisers, to get items that we're not selling with retail manufacturers." At the same time Asher's began to place more emphasis on the packaging of its items as part of its branding strategy.

The redesign of Asher's box line led to growth in sales of its boxed chocolate offerings. In fact, in 2000, Asher's Chocolates' sales were up 61 percent overall over the previous year, and the company increased wages more than it normally had. The growth led to Asher's winning the Eastern Montgomery County Chamber of Commerce's excellence award in 2001. That same year, Asher's continued to slowly broaden its distribution nationally and began plans to triple its square footage in order to increase production on its entire product line.

It also began to focus on new offerings. "We try to stay current without replacing traditional favorites," explained Jeff Asher in a 2008 *Candy Industry* article. In 2004, company relabeled its sugar-free items as "low carb" and saw their sales skyrocket. A few years later, as the trend toward high-end chocolates caught on, the company increased focus on dark chocolates with higher cacao content and introduced its premium Majestic line. Asher's also began to offer an organic dark assortment with raspberry, mango, and black cherry flavors and introduced a walnut caramel patty.

As the end of the decade drew near, production was up at Goss Candies, which continued to do specialty work include chocolate molding and hand-crafted candy clustering. The Lewiston-based facilities took up 109,000 square feet and employed more than 100 workers. Asher's overall revenues were in excess of $30 million, and production topped ten million pounds of candy per year. The tightly held family company looked to a future of continued growth in its bulk categories, and increasingly, in its name brand and specialty offerings.

Carrie Rothburd

PRINCIPAL SUBSIDIARIES

Goss Candies.

PRINCIPAL COMPETITORS

The Hershey Company; Russell Stover Candies Inc.; Cadbury plc; Chocoladefabriken Lindt & Sprüngli AG; Dynamic Confections, Inc.; Endangered Species Chocolate, LLC; Ferrero S.p.A.; Ghirardelli Chocolate Company; Godiva Chocolatier, Inc.; Guittard Chocolate Company; Laura Secord; Nestlé S.A.; Purdy's Chocolates; Rocky Mountain Chocolate Factory, Inc.; See's Candies, Inc.

FURTHER READING

"Bulk Rebound?" *Professional Candy Buyer,* September 2001, p. 48.

Hildebrandt, Stephanie, "Staying Current," *Candy Industry,* July 2008, p. 27.

Klaus, Mary, "Lewiston, Pa.-based Candy Company Continues to Grow," *Harrisburg (Pa.) Patriot-News,* March 21, 1999.

Orenstein, Beth W., "Candy Maker Leaving Philadelphia for Franconia," *Eastern Pennsylvania Business Journal,* December 9, 1996, p. 11.

Thomas, Jennifer, "Lewistown Chocolatier to Be Honored for Decades of Work," *Centre Daily Times,* March 26, 2006.

Tiffany, Susan, "New Factory Stretches Opportunities for Asher's Chocolates," *Candy Industry,* August 1998, p. 22.

———, "Trouble-Free Partnership Conceives and Builds Dream Factory for Asher's Chocolates," *Candy Industry,* April 1999, p. 52.

Assicurazioni Generali S.p.A.

Piazza Duca degli Abruzzi, 2
Trieste, 34132
Italy
Telephone: (+39 40) 671-111
Fax: (+39 40) 671-600
Web site: http://www.generali.com

Public Company
Incorporated: 1831 as Assicurazioni Generali Austro-Italiche
Employees: 80,555
Total Assets: EUR 383.94 billion ($534.4 billion) (2008)
Stock Exchanges: Borsa Italiana
Ticker Symbol: G
NAICS: 524113 Direct Life Insurance Carriers; 524114 Direct Health and Medical Insurance Carriers; 524126 Direct Property and Casualty Insurance Carriers; 524130 Reinsurance Carriers; 525110 Pension Funds; 525910 Open-End Investment Funds; 551112 Offices of Other Holding Companies

■ ■ ■

Founded in Trieste in 1831, Assicurazioni Generali S.p.A. is the largest insurance company in Italy and the third largest in Europe. Very active beyond its home market from the beginning, Generali derives more than 60 percent of its premium income from outside Italy. Generali subsidiaries and agencies are located in more than 40 countries worldwide, with widespread coverage of Western Europe and significant market shares in Germany, France, Spain, Austria, and Switzerland. The company is also active in Central and Eastern Europe, the Middle East (particularly Israel), North and South America, and the Asia-Pacific region, including China and India. In addition to continuing to maintain its comprehensive insurance offerings, which encompass life, health, accident, property, and reinsurance, Generali has diversified its interests into the wider realm of financial and real estate services and asset management. Its nickname, the "Lion of Trieste," derives both from the city where it was founded, and is still based, and from its insignia featuring the winged lion of St. Mark.

1831 FOUNDING IN TRIESTE

Trieste's position on the Adriatic and its role as chief port of the Austro-Hungarian Empire made it a center of shipping and commerce, when the first ventures in maritime insurance were established in the mid-1700s after the Hapsburg King Charles VI had declared it a free port. Following the upheavals of revolution and the Napoleonic Wars, Trieste experienced an economic boom. In 1825 some 20 insurance companies were active, chiefly in maritime insurance.

Generali was founded by Giuseppe Lazzaro Morpurgo, a businessman from a leading family in Gorizia, who brought together a group of Trieste financiers and merchants in November 1831 to found the Ausilio Generale di Sicurezza. Their intention was to establish a company with sufficient capitalization to expand beyond the geographical territory reached by other Trieste houses. Like its chief competitor at the time, the Adriatico Banco d'Assicurazione—later known as Riunione

COMPANY PERSPECTIVES

The Generali Group mission sets out the following objectives: to become the leading insurance group, in terms of profitability, in the major European countries in which the Group operates and to play an important role in high-potential markets; [and] to grow in the retail and SME sectors by implementing a distribution strategy based primarily on agent networks and focused on a multi-brand and multi-local approach.

Adriatica di Sicurtà or RAS—the Ausilio Generale founding members were drawn from Trieste's multiethnic business community, which included Austrians, Slavs, Italians, Germans, and Greeks.

At the first shareholders' assembly, conflicts among the partners over statutes led to the dissolution of Ausilio Generale. A month later the remaining partners formed the Assicurazioni Generali Austro-Italiche, with an initial capitalization of two million florins, divided into 2,000 shares of 1,000 florins each. Statutes were approved on December 26, 1831. Almost immediately, founding member Giuseppe Morpurgo left Trieste to establish the company's Venice headquarters, which was placed under the direction of Samuel della Vida from Ferrara.

Other Generali founders included Marco Parente, a businessman with ties to the Vienna Rothschild family, and Vidal Benjamin Cusin, grandfather of two future secretary-generals of Generali, Marco Besso and Giuseppe Besso. The company's other members included Giovanni Cristoforo Ritter de Zahony, a Frankfurt native with a Hungarian title; the shipbuilder Michele Vucetich; Alessio Paris, who in 1826 had been a founder of the competitor Adriatico Banco; and Giambattista Rosmini, an Italian lawyer who managed the new company in his role as legal adviser.

The adjective *Generali* was intended to convey the fact that the company's activities were not limited to maritime and flood insurance but, as Article 2 of the first charter indicated, "insurance of land [i.e., fire and shipping insurance] ... security of the life of man in all its ramifications, pensions and whatever other area of insurance permitted by law." The first agencies were opened rapidly, amounting to some 25 in the principal cities of the Hapsburg Empire in the first two years. Branches, agencies, and affiliates were established in France in 1832, and in 1835 to the east in Switzerland and Germany, in Transylvania, and Galizia. Administra-

tion of the company was divided between the Trieste and Venice headquarters, with Venice in charge of operations in Italy and west Europe while the central management in Trieste handled operations elsewhere in Austria-Hungary and east Europe. In 1837 the Venice office began to operate in the field of credit insurance, while limiting its transport insurance solely to goods being shipped from Venice.

In 1835 a struggle for power developed between the chairman, Zahony, and legal administrator Giambattista Rosmini, with Morpurgo supporting the chairman. The board of directors sided with Rosmini, who succeeded in forcing Zahony and Morpurgo out of the company. At this time, the charter was rewritten and the position of chairman was abolished, to be reinstated in 1909. The dispute had a deleterious effect on business; four other board members left with Zahony and Morpurgo, and the directors compelled Rosmini to share power with Masino Levi, former agent in the Padua office, who was named secretary general.

PRODIGIOUS GROWTH UNDER MASINO LEVI

The following 40 years under Levi's direction saw unprecedented growth for Generali. Expansion was effected according to the company's geographical division, with activity on the Italian peninsula overseen by the Venice office, while Trieste was responsible for other European operations. Generali was especially active in East and Central Europe, where offices opened in Saxony, Prussia, and Silesia in 1837, expanding further in 1838 to Corfu, Bavaria, Russian Poland, Serbia, and Valacchia. The company's Hamburg operations center was run for many years by the mathematical prodigy Wilhelm Lazarus, who compiled the first mortality tables for Germany.

While growth was surging on the continent, expansion on the Italian peninsula was slower. Prior to the unification of Italy, protectionist laws in effect in the separate Italian states greatly restricted activity by foreign insurance companies. For example, until 1850 Generali representatives in the Bourbon kingdom of Naples frequently had to appeal to the throne to avoid suspension of their activity. In the Papal States, business was possible only in the Romagna region. In the kingdom of Piedmont, the Società Reale Mutua held a legal monopoly in fire insurance, and heavy legal hindrances existed in other fields until 1853. At Parma and Piacenza, Generali was able to begin activity only in 1837, when the Milan agency succeeded in winning monopoly rights in the region from the Bourbon duchess Maria-Luigia.

KEY DATES

■

1831: Giuseppe Lazzaro Morpurgo leads a group of Trieste entrepreneurs to found Assicurazioni Generali Austro-Italiche.

1832: Among numerous early growth initiatives, Generali expands into France.

1848: Company's name is simplified to Assicurazioni Generali.

1857: Generali's stock begins trading on the Trieste Stock Exchange.

1882: Transition to a group structure begins with the establishment of a subsidiary in Vienna specializing in accident insurance.

1918: Generali officially becomes an Italian company when Trieste is united with the Italian republic.

1933: Acquisition of Alleanza & Unione Mediterranea forms basis for the majority-owned Alleanza Assicurazioni.

1945: At the end of World War II, Generali loses most of its assets in Central and Eastern Europe.

1948: A push into the Americas includes the acquisition of a majority stake in the Argentinian company Providencia.

1956: Mediobanca, Italy's largest investment bank, acquires a stake in Generali through which it will influence the insurer's strategy for decades to come.

1966: Generali enters into a partnership with the U.S. firm Aetna Life & Casualty Company.

1989: Generali returns to Eastern Europe via a Hungarian joint venture.

1996: Purchase of Italian mutual fund manager Prime S.p.A. marks the first step in the company's diversification into the wider realm of financial services.

1998: Generali gains majority control of Aachener und Münchener Beteiligungs-AG, the third largest insurer in Germany.

2000: Instituto Nazionale delle Assicurazioni S.p.A. is acquired.

2006: Company purchases Toro Assicurazioni S.p.A.

2009: Generali announces plans to acquire full control of Alleanza Assicurazioni and then merge it with Toro.

Expansion throughout Europe was carried out by means of a tiered system. Territories were grouped around a central general agency responsible for gradually increasing growth in new expansion zones. Where Generali was unable to establish an autonomous agency, an affiliate was authorized. From its lucrative Pest agency in Hungary, Generali extended operations to Bucharest in 1847 and to Belgrade in 1856. In the following decade, operations started in Bosnia and the remaining area of Turkish domination, enlarging Generali's territory to include the whole of the Middle East, especially in the branch of fire insurance. The first fire insurance policies in Alexandria were issued by Generali in 1851, limited to the city's European quarter.

In the meantime, the revolutions of 1848 that particularly undermined the authority of the Austro-Hungarian Empire affected Generali as well. The company's association with the empire and its use of the imperial two-headed eagle as its symbol led revolutionaries to attack a number of Generali buildings in Italy. The board of directors reacted by stripping the Austro-Italiche appellation from the company's name, simplifying it to Assicurazioni Generali. It was at this time that the company adopted as a symbol for its operations on Italian peninsula the Lion of St. Mark. In 1857 Generali's shares were listed on the Trieste Stock Exchange for the first time.

Later in the 19th century, Generali's attention turned to eastern and other non-European countries. Between 1879 and 1882 Generali opened agencies or representative offices in the main ports of the Near East and the Far East, along the sea routes of the Lloyd Austriaco line, which had its terminal in Trieste: Generali's territory was thus extended throughout Greece, to Beirut, Tunis, Bombay, Colombo, Shanghai, and Hong Kong. Across the Pacific Ocean, agencies were opened in San Francisco, California, and in Valparaiso, Chile. New kinds of insurance were initiated; in 1877 Generali began extending coverage to plate glass, in 1881 to injury, and by the end of the century to theft.

MODERNIZATION AND DIVERSIFICATION UNDER MARCO BESSO

In 1878 Marco Besso replaced Masino Levi as secretary general, inaugurating a period of modernization and diversification. Besso had come to Generali in 1863 as the company's representative to Rome, where he successfully negotiated the acquisition of the Vatican's failing Pontificia insurance house. Taking over the company at the age of 35, Besso established Generali's life insurance activities and initiated a policy of real estate investment. During his period of tenure the company acquired the

Procuratie Vecchie, one of the Renaissance palaces on Venice's Piazza San Marco, and built its imposing Rome headquarters in Piazza Venezia.

Also during this period Generali laid the groundwork for its future as a major European group with the constitution of its first wholly owned subsidiaries. It established Cassa Generale Ungherese di Risparmio (General Savings Bank of Hungary) in 1881, followed by Erste Allgemeine Unfall und Schadensversicherung in 1882. The latter, based in Austria, was Generali's first insurance subsidiary, and it initially specialized in accident insurance.

Marco Besso was replaced by his brother Giuseppe Besso in 1885, who served as secretary general until 1894. Marco Besso continued to guide Generali, however, acting as chairman from 1909, when the position was reinstated, until his death in 1920. During the years 1894 to 1909, he acted as consulting director while the post of secretary general was filled by Edmondo Richetti, who had joined the company ten years earlier as director of the Austrian Unfall branch.

During these years Besso formed what was to prove a fruitful long-term relationship with Italy's principal merchant bank, the Banca Commerciale Italiana (COMIT), a relationship that continued throughout the 20th century. Less than two years after COMIT was founded in 1894, Besso was installed on the board of directors where he remained for life. Except for a ten-year period coinciding with World War II, Generali and COMIT traditionally held reciprocal seats on each other's boards. (COMIT was acquired by, and merged into, Banca Intesa S.p.A. at the beginning of the early 21st century. Banca Intesa later merged with Sanpaolo IMI S.p.A. to form Intesa Sanpaolo S.p.A.) Also during this period, Franz Kafka was hired by the company's general agency in Prague as an office worker. The aspiring novelist left after nine months, however, suffering from nervous ailments.

THE PRESSURES OF A WORLD WAR

In 1914, on the eve of World War I, Generali was enjoying a position of tremendous strength. Its assets totaled 12.6 million crowns (ITL 13.32 million). While the war brought unprecedented destruction to the very areas of Europe in which Generali was most active, the company suffered more from political pressures than from financial loss. At the outbreak of hostilities, Generali's two most important offices found themselves in opposing camps of warring nations. The Venice headquarters made every effort to be regarded as Italian, whereas Generali's Trieste office reaffirmed its loyalty to

the Hapsburgs. The governments of France and England regarded Generali as a part of the Austro-Hungarian Empire, and the company's activities were curtailed in both countries until 1916.

Generali, however, was viewed with equal suspicion in Vienna. The Trieste headquarters was relocated to the Austro-Hungarian capital, where activities were supervised by a substitute managing director, Emanuel Ehrentheil. Generali, like much of Trieste, had always divided its loyalties between Italy and the Hapsburgs. Because much of Generali's personnel transferred to Italy at the outbreak of fighting, the authorities placed most of Generali's officers on a list of suspected Italian nationalists. Claiming suspicion of foreign espionage, the Military Command investigated the directors and searched their homes. In 1916 the company's assets temporarily were sequestered under a decree to prevent the flight of foreign capital. Despite this, on May 31, 1918, a Generali life policy was written for the last Hapsburg emperor, Charles I.

AN ITALIAN COMPANY FROM 1918

In 1918, with the armistice, Trieste was united with the Italian republic and Generali assumed as its insignia the Lion of St. Mark, symbol of Venetian power and justice. After the collapse of the Hapsburg monarchy in Central Europe, new nationalist states replaced the politically united territories that Generali had cultivated for nearly a century. In addition to the damage inflicted by the fighting, the new order resulted in complex monetary, legal, and economic problems in the insurance industry. Authorized to continue its activity in all the former Austro-Hungarian territories, Generali initially restricted itself to handling life insurance in Czechoslovakia and Yugoslavia.

Adjusting for the devaluation of the lire from its 1913 rates, the company estimated that its assets had fallen by 17 percent since the outbreak of war, but two years later Generali was on the road to an impressive recovery, and under the direction of Edgardo Morpurgo, from 1920, the company marked its 100th anniversary in extraordinarily good health.

Despite the economic crisis of 1929, Generali's capital rose from ITL 13 million to ITL 60 million in ten years, and gross premiums in life insurance rose from ITL 1 billion to ITL 6 billion. The company boasted 3,150 representatives in Italy and 5,765 in foreign countries. It had 30 subsidiaries and associated companies, 6 in Italy and 24 abroad. Real estate holdings were valued at ITL 292 million, which then included urban and agricultural property in 17 different countries. Faced with the effects of the Great Depression in the United States and the need to have strong liquid assets readily available, the company established a new department at its central headquarters, solely in charge of financing.

Notable events in the 1930s included the acquisition of Alleanza & Unione Mediterranea in 1933, which was merged with Securitas Esperia, already controlled by Generali, to form Alleanza-Securitas-Esperia (Allsecures), no longer a part of the Generali group. Life insurance activities absorbed from this group formed the basis for the Alleanza Assicurazioni company, which became the largest private life insurance company in Italy, second only to the state-run giant, INA. Significant growth occurred, meanwhile, in Generali's French holding La Concorde, and the Austrian Erste Allgemeine. Benito Mussolini's alliance with Nazi Germany ensured that Italian interests in Austria were not lost after Adolf Hitler's *anschluss* in 1934.

WORLD WAR II AND THE POSTWAR PERIOD

The extension of Germany's anti-Semitic laws to Italy, however, had a devastating effect on the Generali group. With the rise of fascism in Italy, Morpurgo, who was Jewish, had struggled to maintain control, enrolling in the Fascist Party and appointing a staunch supporter of Mussolini as managing director. Gino Baroncini, who came to Generali from the Milan-based subsidiary Anonima Grandine, an insurer formed by Generali in 1890 to cover crop damage by hailstorms, was to determine the company's structure and course for much of the next 30 years. In 1938, however, Morpurgo was forced to leave the company, eventually fleeing to Argentina. He was replaced by Count Giuseppe Volpi di Misurata, who served until the fall of the Fascist government in 1943.

The company also lost 66 Jewish employees, including 20 directors. With Trieste under a German high command, Generali's central headquarters were moved to Rome, and its status as an Italian company was formalized by an official decree. Antonio Cosulich, a Trieste shipbuilder and member of the board, was named chairman and served until 1948, with Baroncini continuing as managing director.

The end of the war renewed prospects for a return to normal operating conditions in Western Europe, but in Eastern Europe all rights, property, and interests pertaining to Italy or Italian citizens were seized. Generali's agencies and affiliates in Hungary, Czechoslovakia, Poland, and Romania suffered the worst losses, while those in Yugoslavia, Bulgaria, Albania, and East

Germany fared slightly better. In all, the Generali group lost 14 subsidiaries as well as substantial real estate holdings in Eastern Europe. Efforts by Baroncini to recover some of the losses in Eastern Europe were only partly successful: ITL 13 billion was eventually restored to the company in payments from various countries, about one-tenth of what was lost. There were further losses in the former Italian colonies, such as Libya and Ethiopia.

However in 1945 tensions did not immediately ease in Trieste, where a bloody campaign of terror was waged by Yugoslavia at the end of the war, when Yugoslavian nationalists tried to win control of the city. After the declaration of the Free Territory of Trieste, the city led a tense existence from 1947 to 1954, until a hard-won international compromise resulted in the city's being awarded to Italy.

Generali's solid asset base made the work of reconstruction possible, and by 1948 the company's Western European operations were on the way to recovery. Spurred by the loss of Eastern and Central European markets, attention turned to Latin America, where a majority ownership was acquired in the Argentinian company Providencia. At the beginning of the 1950s, operations resumed in Greece and the Middle East and in Brazil, Guatemala, Venezuela, Ecuador, and Colombia. In South Africa, Generali acquired a controlling interest in the new Standard General Insurance, then in a phase of considerable expansion.

From 1948 to 1953, Senator Mario Abbate succeeded Cosulich as chairman of the company. Formerly Abbate had been chairman of the Milan subsidiary Anonima Grandine. Already elderly and in ill health, Abbate's was largely a titular chairmanship. Chief executive responsibility was shared by Baroncini and Michele Sulfina, a Generali manager who had served with Edgardo Morpurgo in the 1920s and 1930s. In 1950, during Abbate's tenure, direct operations resumed in the United States after Generali had obtained the necessary authorization to offer shipping and fire insurance as well as reinsurance. At this time, and as Italy entered its postwar economic boom, the company dedicated itself to reorganizing and restructuring its Italian assets. Thus in 1955 the two old Milan firms constituted to handle injury and hailstorm insurance in the 19th century, Anonima Infortuni and Anonima Grandine, were merged to form the Milan head office.

Mario Tripcovich, who succeeded the aging Senator Abbate as chairman in 1953, came from the Trieste shipbuilding concern founded in 1895 by his father, Diodato Tripcovich, himself a member of Generali's executive council for 20 years. The younger Tripcovich had spearheaded efforts to improve Generali's position in the United States, insisting on buying the Buffalo Insurance Company in 1950.

ALLIANCES AND THE ENTRANCE OF POWERFUL SHAREHOLDERS

Tripcovich was succeeded in 1956 by Camillo Giussani, who acted for a period as simultaneous chairman of Generali and the Banca Commerciale Italiana. The strengthening of bonds between the two companies was to continue in the decades that followed. As the Italian economy surged ahead, so did Generali, achieving first place among foreign insurers operating in Austria and France, thanks to its considerable presence in both countries, through La Concorde in France and Erste Allgemeine in Austria. The company was active in 60 different countries and was diversifying into previously unheard-of areas. When television came to Italy, Generali initiated policies covering equipment and antennae, fire, theft, and destruction of cathode tubes.

The decade was also characterized by the entrance of powerful shareholders into the elite group of Trieste financiers and industrialists who had traditionally occupied seats on Generali's executive council. In 1956 Mediobanca, Italy's largest investment bank, acquired a 3.5 percent share. Guiding this move was Enrico Cuccia, president of the bank since 1949, who was to have a hand in Generali's course in decades to come.

Baroncini, the engineer of Generali's postwar recovery, was named chairman in 1960 and served until 1968 when he was succeeded by another former official of the COMIT bank, Cesare Merzagora. In 1966 an international cooperation agreement was reached with a leading U.S. insurer, Aetna Life & Casualty Company, under which each company provided reciprocal services to the other's clients while abroad.

In the 1970s Generali rationalized its foreign activities, aiming at greater local integration. Companies such as Generali France, Generali Belgium and, in West Germany, Generali Lebensversicherung were created as domestic companies governed by local laws, and often were strengthened by mergers with local companies. Reinsurance activity was increased. The Europ Assistance companies were also established, providing tourist assistance in the European market.

Enrico Randone became Generali's chairman in 1979, taking over from Merzagora, who remained as honorary chairman. By this time the company had assumed its present name. Two years later a robust Generali celebrated its 150th anniversary. Total premiums amounted to ITL 1.39 trillion, real property was valued at ITL 581 billion, and equity investments at ITL 1.09 trillion. This marked the beginning of a significant

decade for the company. The prospect of a unified European market in 1992 prompted an increase in mergers and acquisitions in the major European markets, as Europe's large insurers prepared for tough competition.

Generali had distinguished itself in the postwar decades as a slow-moving giant, too dignified for U.S.-style hostile takeover bids. In 1988, however, the Italian company tried to acquire Compagnie du Midi, one of the larger French insurance groups. This bid was ultimately unsuccessful, as the threat of takeover drove Midi to seek protection in a merger with its largest competitor in France, the AXA Group. The widely publicized adventure ended in a boardroom battle between the two French managers. Midi's President Bernard Pagezy was driven out by his younger partner Claude Bébéar, while Generali won no more than a joint partnership with AXA-Midi, in accordance with French regulations on foreign investment.

During this period, the large shareholders controlling nearly 23 percent of Generali stock proved to be influential in determining company strategy. Mediobanca headed this list, controlling 5.6 percent. Another 4.8 percent was held by the Euralux investment group whose members included Italy's powerful Agnelli family. The Banca d'Italia owned a similar portion of shares.

RETURN TO EASTERN EUROPE AND ADDITIONAL OVERSEAS ADVENTURES

Generali closed the decade with the formation of AB Generali Budapest, the first mixed-ownership insurance company in Eastern Europe, 40 percent of the joint venture being owned by Generali and 60 percent by Allami Biztosito, a Hungarian state-owned insurer. This venture also marked the company's return to Eastern Europe, from which it had been expelled at the conclusion of World War II. In 1990 Generali made its first real entrance into the U.S. business world, buying the Kansas City, Missouri-based Business Men's Assurance Company of America from its parent BMA Corporation for about $285 million, or less than ITL 360 billion. Another significant achievement was Generali's linkup with Taisho Marine and Fire Insurance Company (later Mitsui Marine and Fire Insurance Company), the third largest insurer in Japan, whereby Generali was able to open a liaison office and general agency through Taisho Marine and Fire in Tokyo, and Taisho was able to operate in Italy through the offices of Generali subsidiary la Navale.

In 1991 Randone, the 80-year-old chairman, retired, along with several other senior officers who had guided Generali's policy for the past few decades. Taking over the chairmanship was Eugenio Coppola di Canzano. Coppola continued to seek opportunities for Generali outside Italy. Asia was one area targeted for growth as Generali expanded its presence there by opening agencies in Hong Kong and Singapore. Another was North America where Generali and New York-based Continental Corporation signed an agreement in 1991, whereby Continental would service and underwrite the North American portion of multinational policies covering commercial and personal property and casualty risks.

In Europe, Generali was experiencing a difficult period in the early 1990s. Its operations in England were consistently unprofitable because of huge underwriting losses. The poor ratio of underwriting losses to premium income of 113 percent in 1991 increased to 117 percent in 1992. Generali officials blamed the U.K. losses on several natural disasters, including Hurricane Andrew. Generali's French operations posted an overall loss in 1992 primarily because of large losses for the nonlife (property/casualty) insurance companies there. The problems were partially cyclical ones because the nonlife underwriting markets in both countries were suffering a general downturn. Some analysts, however, pinned at least part of the blame on mismanagement. Overall, Generali was able to maintain a steady level of profits during this period because its home operations had benefited from a government crackdown on crime and from improved risk management by the company's underwriters.

Elsewhere in Europe, Generali's fairly small operation in Switzerland was significantly enhanced by the 1994 acquisition of 56 percent of the voting rights of Swiss insurer Fortuna Holding from TA Media AG. As a result, Generali's premium income in Switzerland increased 379.1 percent in 1994 over 1993 results and nearly 6 percent of Generali's total premium income in 1994 came from the Swiss market.

Despite its difficulties in Europe, Generali enjoyed steady growth in the early 1990s. Gross premiums written increased 15.5 percent in 1994 to $17.63 billion and profits increased from $374.4 million in 1993 to $393.2 million in 1994. Through these uncertain years the company had maintained its number five position in the European insurance market.

The chairmanship of the company once again changed hands in 1995 after Coppola resigned and Antoine Bernheim took over. By early 1996, Bernheim appeared to have resolved Generali's vexing relationship with the French insurer AXA, which stemmed from Generali's unsuccessful attempt to take over Midi in 1988. Since the attempted takeover, Generali had held an indirect 16.9 percent stake in AXA but was unable to

exercise any influence in the company's decision-making process. Generali wanted to work together with AXA in foreign markets, particularly in Asia, but had consistently been ignored. After Generali threatened to sell its stake unless AXA cooperated with it, in early 1996 AXA appeared to finally give Generali the greater voice it wanted by realigning the links between the two firms. Consequently, Generali gained a direct 11 percent stake in AXA, with voting rights equivalent to 15.6 percent. Later in 1996, however, Generali elected to sell its stake back to AXA for $1.2 billion and pocket a capital gain of $420.3 million.

WIDENING INTERESTS INTO FINANCIAL SERVICES

In other 1996 developments, Generali led a consortium bid to acquire Creditanstalt, Austria's largest bank, hoping to use the bank's network of bank branches to rebuild its operations in Central and Eastern Europe. This takeover attempt was thwarted, however, after Bank Austria AG entered the fray with a larger offer. Deal-hungry Generali did complete one significant acquisition in 1996, the takeover of Prime S.p.A., a major Italian manager of mutual funds, for ITL 325 billion ($212 million). This acquisition was the first step in Generali's drive to diversify its interests beyond insurance into the wider realm of financial services. Important follow-up moves included the 1998 acquisition of Banca della Svizzera Italiana (BSI), a Swiss private bank with more than EUR 20 billion in assets under management, and the establishment that same year of Banca Generali S.p.A., which eventually developed into a subsidiary offering personal financial services through multiple channels.

At the same time, Generali continued to seek expansion opportunities within insurance markets outside Italy. In 1997, for instance, the company gained majority control of Migdal, an insurer that commanded a 32 percent share of the life insurance market and 17 percent of the nonlife insurance market in Israel. This takeover prompted immediate calls in Israel for a boycott against Migdal because of allegations that the heirs of Holocaust victims had not received payouts from insurance policies written by Generali group companies in Eastern Europe in the years leading up to World War II. Generali, which had been founded by a group of Jewish businessmen, had enjoyed a significant share of the market in Eastern Europe during that period, particularly among Jews. The company, however, initially maintained that it had no legal obligations in this matter because its assets in Eastern Europe had been seized by the Communist governments that took power. After receiving a great deal of bad press about this matter, Generali in 2000 finally agreed to allocate more than $100 million for the payment of Holocaust-era life and property insurance claims.

Ironically, Generali was concurrently continuing to rebuild its position in Eastern Europe. It was also seeking opportunities in other emerging markets. After setting up a representative office in Beijing in 1996, Generali four years later gained a license to enter the Chinese life insurance market. In 1999 the company became the leading insurer in Argentina via the purchase of a controlling interest in Caja de Ahorro y Seguro S.A.

TAKEOVERS OF AMB AND INA

In the meantime, against the backdrop of a rapidly consolidating European insurance industry, Generali in late 1997 turned bolder, launching a $9.35 billion, hostile takeover bid of Assurances Générales de France (AGF), one of the largest insurance companies in France. The bid escalated into a takeover battle with the appearance of Germany's Allianz AG on the scene as a white knight. Eventually, the rivals resolved their battle amicably. Allianz proceeded to acquire AGF, but it also agreed to sell its and AGF's minority stakes in Aachener und Münchener Beteiligungs-AG (AMB) to Generali. This enabled Generali to emerge in 1998 with majority control of AMB, the third largest insurer in Germany. AMB, active in the life, nonlife, and health sectors of the insurance industry, was one of Europe's oldest insurers, having been established in the Prussian city of Aachen in 1825. Generali later, in 2001, merged its existing German subsidiary, Generali Lloyd AG, with AMB to form AMB Generali Holding AG. In addition to gaining control of AMB, Generali through its agreement with Allianz was also able to move into sixth position among French insurers by purchasing three insurance companies in that nation that AGF had only recently acquired: GPA-Vie, GPA-Iard, and Proxima.

Late in 1998 Generali entered into an alliance with Commerzbank AG, which at the time was Germany's fourth largest bank. The companies bought minority stakes in each other, and they agreed to begin selling each other's products and services at their respective branches in Germany. In May of the following year, Bernheim was ousted from the Generali chairmanship in a move that the financial press claimed Mediobanca had engineered. The successor was Alfonso Desiata, the chairman of Generali's majority-owned subsidiary Alleanza Assicurazioni. During their terms, both Bernheim and Desiata served as nonexecutive chairman; the company's day-to-day operations had been handled since 1992 by Gianfranco Gutty.

Generali also entered into another major takeover battle in 1999. When Italian banking giant Sanpaolo IMI S.p.A. entered into negotiations with Instituto Nazionale delle Assicurazioni S.p.A. (INA) to create the largest banking/insurance company in Italy, Generali stepped in to head off this amalgamation with a hostile offer to take over INA for EUR 12 billion ($12.7 billion). By February 2000 Generali was able to complete its takeover of INA after agreeing to cede INA's majority stake in Banco di Napoli S.p.A., the largest bank in southern Italy, to Sanpaolo. Generali thus gained control of Italy's number two insurer, which not only solidified its commanding position in its home market, increasing its market share to 26 percent, but also made it the largest life insurer in Europe and propelled it into the number three position in the overall European insurance industry. Generali subsequently restructured its insurance operations in Italy so that several units operated independently but shared common service centers.

According to a series of reports in the financial press, Mediobanca continued to meddle in Generali's affairs. It was able to do so based on a stake of just 15 percent apparently because this stake in effect grew to a controlling one thanks to the sparse attendance at the insurer's annual meetings. In any event, Desiata was ousted from the chairmanship in April 2001, with Gutty named the successor. Then, a year later, Gutty was stripped of his executive powers. Giovanni Perissinotto and Sergio Balbinot, both career Generali employees who were then in their 40s, assumed the leadership mantle as co–chief executives. The subsequent firing of Gutty in September 2002 enabled Bernheim to return to Generali at age 78 as nonexecutive chairman, focusing on the firm's overall strategy. The rationale behind the rapid turnover at the top was difficult to determine given the secrecy under which Generali had always operated, but the backdrop for the changes in 2002 was a poor one. The company posted a net loss for the year of EUR 754.4 million ($791 million), its first year in the red since the 1970s, after having to write down the value of its investment portfolio and the stakes it held in such firms as Commerzbank by EUR 4 billion ($4.2 billion).

A NEW ERA OF OPENNESS

In a clear break from the past, Bernheim and the co–chief executives embarked on a new spirit of openness, one that was initially most evident in January 2003, when the company for the first time in its history made a public presentation of its future plans. In addition to setting specific targets for profitability and for the ratios that were key measuring sticks for insurance companies, the three-year plan aimed to cut annual operating costs by EUR 617 million ($660 million) in part by trimming 2,800 jobs, or about 5 percent of the workforce. It also called for growth to occur mainly within Generali's core European markets, particularly Italy, Germany, and France, with a secondary focus on areas with potential for high-revenue growth and above-average profitability, such as Eastern Europe and China. Indeed, among the key developments of 2003 was the acquisition of Le Continent Group for EUR 290 million ($327 million), a move that strengthened Generali's position in France.

Generali was again much in the news during 2003 because of its relationship with Mediobanca. After the death in 2000 of Enrico Cuccia, the investment bank's founder, at age 92, Mediobanca's power waned somewhat, and eventually several Italian banks, led by UniCredito, entered into alliance to dilute it still further. Because Generali had been Mediobanca's main tool for asserting its influence, the allied banks turned table on Mediobanca and made Generali their own pawn in this power struggle. The banks amassed nearly 20 percent of Generali's shares and were able to force the ouster of Mediobanca's chairman and install their own candidate in his place. For Bernheim and Generali's chief executives, this power play had the chief benefit of stabilizing the governance situation. At the April 2004 annual shareholders meeting, UniCredito and allies backed a resolution to extend the contracts of the management troika from the traditional one-year term to that of three years, providing the leaders with greater freedom to execute their strategic plans.

Among other restructuring moves carried out during its first three-year plan, Generali turned itself into a more coherent international group by improving coordination among its national subsidiaries. The restructuring and cost-cutting enabled the group to post 2005 profits of EUR 916.8 million ($1.09 billion). Over the three-year plan period, total premiums increased 28 percent, while profits jumped 67 percent. The investment community, traditionally skeptical about Generali's prospects because of its past penchant for secrecy and the machinations that resulted from its ties to Mediobanca, showed greater affection for the company as its shares rose 69 percent between the beginning of 2003 and the end of 2005.

With its second three-year plan, announced in early 2006, Generali planned to leverage its strong capital position by making large outlays of cash to buy out minority shareholders of several of its foreign subsidiaries and to buy back a large portion of its own stock. Thus, during 2006, the company acquired full control of both Generali Holding Vienna AG in Austria and Generali (Schweiz) Holding AG in Switzerland and also increased its stake in AMB Generali Holding in Germany to more than 85 percent, which gave it full

control of that firm's shareholders meetings. Elsewhere, Generali gained regulatory authority to enter the nonlife market in China while continuing to develop its life insurance business there; entered into a joint venture with Future Group India, that nation's largest retailer, to operate in the life and nonlife sectors in India; and purchased controlling interests in insurance companies in several Eastern European countries, including Bulgaria, Croatia, Serbia, and Ukraine. Back home, in its biggest 2006 deal, Generali canceled its planned stock buyback in order to finance the EUR 3.85 billion ($5.1 billion) acquisition of Toro Assicurazioni S.p.A. The addition of Turin-based Toro particularly served to solidify Generali in an area of weakness, auto insurance, and it increased the company's share of the overall nonlife market in Italy from 15.6 percent to 22.2 percent.

Generali's results for 2007 were quite positive, including a 2.6 percent increase in total premiums to EUR 66.2 billion ($103.8 billion) and a 21.2 percent increase in net profits to EUR 2.92 billion ($4.58 billion). Still the subject of criticism for its corporate governance practices, Generali during the year overhauled its board of directors to include more outside directors with business management backgrounds (the board's composition had been heavily tilted toward lawyers from companies connected to Generali through cross-shareholdings). After more than 175 years in business, the company also appointed its first chief financial officer in a further reform initiative.

FURTHER DEAL MAKING

Also in 2007, Generali announced two significant deals, both of which closed in early 2008. Generali and PPF Group N.V., a Dutch financial holding company, combined their operations in Central and Eastern Europe into a joint venture called Generali PPF Holding B.V. that was 51 percent owned by Generali and 49 percent by PPF. Generali PPF immediately ranked as one of the largest insurers in the region with gross premiums of about EUR 2.6 billion ($3.6 billion) and more than nine million customers in 12 countries, with leading positions in the Czech Republic, Hungary, and Slovakia. In the second deal, Generali acquired the Swiss private bank Banca del Gottardo from Swiss Life Holding for $1.63 billion. Gottardo was subsequently merged into Generali's existing Swiss private bank, BSI, pushing its assets under management to more than CHF 90 billion ($80 billion).

Although Generali's traditionally conservative investment philosophy enabled it to fare better than many of its peers in the initial period of the global financial crisis, the worsening economic climate eventually undermined even its investment portfolio. Generali operated in the red during the fourth quarter of 2008, and its profits for the full year plunged 70 percent to EUR 861 million ($1.2 billion) as a result of EUR 5 billion ($7 billion) in "impairments" stemming from the economic crisis. Seeking to take advantage of the depressed prices of stocks, Generali in February 2009 announced plans to buy out the minority shareholders of the publicly traded Alleanza Assicurazioni for a price totaling about EUR 2 billion ($2.5 billion). It then planned to merge Alleanza, which specialized in life insurance, with nonlife specialist Toro to create a new Italian company operating in both sectors. The company expected synergies from this combination to generate EUR 200 million ($250 million) in annual cost savings by 2012.

Paul Conrad
Updated, David E. Salamie

PRINCIPAL SUBSIDIARIES

Alleanza Assicurazioni S.p.A. (50.3%); Banca Generali S.p.A. (60.3%); Fata Assicurazioni Danni S.p.A. (99. 96%); Fata Vita S.p.A. (99.96%); Genagricola-Generali Agricoltura S.p.A.; Generali Immobiliare Italia SGR; Generali Investments Italy S.p.A.; BG Società di Gestione del Risparmio S.p.A.; Genertel S.p.A.; Ina Assitalia S.p.A.; La Venezia Assicurazioni S.p.A.; Toro Assicurazioni S.p.A.; BAWAG P.S.K. Versicherung AG (Austria; 50.01%); Europäische Reiseversicherung-AG (Austria; 74.99%); Generali Bank AG (Austria); Generali Holding Vienna AG (Austria); Generali Immobilien AG (Austria; 99.99%); Generali Rückversicherung AG; Generali Versicherung AG (Austria); Europ Assistance Holding S.A. (France; 99.94%); Generali France Assurance S.A. (99.98%); Generali France S.A. (99.98%); Generali IARD S.A. (France; 99.98%); Generali Immobilier Gestion S.A. (France; 99.98%); Generali Vie S.A. (France; 99.97%); L'Equité IARD S.A. (France; 99.98%); AMB Generali Holding AG (Germany; 86.9%); AachenMünchener Lebensversicherung AG (Germany; 86.9%); AachenMünchener Versicherung AG (Germany; 86.9%); AdvoCard Rechtsschutzversicherung AG (Germany; 87.04%); Central Krankenversicherung AG (Germany; 86.9%); Cosmos Lebensversicherungs AG (Germany; 86.9%); Cosmos Versicherung AG (Germany; 86.9%; Deutsche Bausparkasse Badenia AG (Germany; 86.9%); Dialog Lebensversicherungs AG (Germany; 87.7%); Envivas Krankenversicherung AG (Germany; 86.9%); Generali Deutschland Holding AG (Germany); Generali Deutschland Immobilien GmbH (Germany; 86.9%); Generali Deutschland Pensionsfonds AG (Germany; 86.9%);

Generali Deutschland Pensionskasse AG (Germany; 86. 9%); Generali Versicherung AG (Germany; 87.1%); Migdal Insurance and Financial Holding Ltd. (Israel; 69.8%); Migdal Insurance Company Ltd. (Israel; 69. 8%); Migdal Investments Management 2001 Ltd. (Israel; 69.8%); Generali PPF Holding B.V. (Netherlands; 51%); Banco Vitalicio de España-Compañia Anonima de Seguros (Spain; 99.9%); Cajamar Vida S.A. de Seguros y Reaseguros (Spain; 50%); Generali España Holding de Entidades de Seguros, S.A. (Spain); La Estrella S.A. de Seguros y Reaseguros (Spain; 99.8%); BSI S.A. (Switzerland); Fortuna Investment AG (Switzerland); Fortuna Rechtsschutz-Versicherungs-Gesellschaft AG (Switzerland); Generali (Schweiz) Holding AG (Switzerland); Generali Allgemeine Versicherungen AG (Switzerland); Generali Personenversicherungen AG (Switzerland).

PRINCIPAL COMPETITORS

Allianz SE; AXA; ING Groep N.V.; Zurich Financial Services; Milano Assicurazioni S.p.A.

FURTHER READING

Arnold, Catherine, "Generali to Pay Holocaust Claims," *National Underwriter—Life and Health/Financial Services,* December 18–25, 2000, p. 28.

Le Assicurazioni Generali: Cenni Storici, Trieste, Italy: Assicurazioni Generali, 1966.

Ball, Deborah, and Thomas Kamm, "Coup at Italian Insurer Deepens a Struggle in Financial Sector," *Wall Street Journal,* May 3, 1999, p. A16.

Ball, Deborah, and Vanessa Fuhrmans, "Running Scared: Generali Launches Hostile Bid for INA Valued at 12 Billion Euros," *Wall Street Journal Europe,* September 15, 1999, p. 1.

Ball, Deborah, and Yaroslav Trofimov, "Generali Shakes Up Management, Ousts Chairman Desiata," *Wall Street Journal Europe,* April 30, 2001, p. 13.

Balletta, Francesco, *Mercato finanziario e Assicurazioni Generali, 1920–1961,* Naples: Edizioni scientifiche italiane, 1995, 194 p.

Betts, Paul, "Bernheim's Cool Hand Trumps the Generali Activists," *Financial Times,* April 29, 2008, p. 14.

———, "Generali Confirms Sector Leadership," *Financial Times,* November 5, 1999, p. 30.

———, "The Questionable Logic of an Italian Financial Colossus," *Financial Times,* January 7, 2009, p. 18.

———, "Trieste's Architect of Alliances Is Revealed," *Financial Times,* February 12, 2001.

Betts, Paul, and Andrew Jack, "Generali Makes Its Move with Hostile AGF Bid," *Financial Times,* October 14, 1997, p. 32.

Bianchi, Federica, "Generali Strips Chairman Gutty of Executive Power in Revamp," *Wall Street Journal Europe,* April 29, 2002, p. M2.

Bianchi, Federica, and Brian Lagrotteria, "Generali Warns of Loss, Plans to Cut 2,800 Jobs," *Wall Street Journal Europe,* January 23, 2003, p. M1.

Boland, Vincent, "Generali Buy-Out Values Alleanza at EUR 4bn," *Financial Times,* February 24, 2009, p. 18.

"Can the Empire Strike Back?" *Economist,* April 25, 1998, p. 76.

Cohen, Sabrina, "Generali Looks to Expand After Profit Jumps by 21%," *Wall Street Journal Europe,* March 18, 2008, p. 6.

———, "Italy's Generali Rejects Shareholder Criticism," *Wall Street Journal,* February 5, 2008, p. C2.

Cohen, Sabrina, and Gabriel Kahn, "Insurer Generali to Buy Rival Toro for $4.82 Billion," *Wall Street Journal,* June 27, 2006, p. C4.

Fairlamb, David, Gail Edmondson, and John Rossant, "Power Struggle, Italian-Style: A Machiavellian Battle over Who'll Run Insurance Giant Generali," *Business Week,* May 7, 2001, p. 48.

"Fiasco: Fighting over Generali," *Economist,* March 8, 2003, p. 83.

Fleming, Charles, "Axa, Generali Go Own Ways, but Amiably," *Wall Street Journal Europe,* September 9, 1996, p. 11.

———, "Sinking Feeling: Italy's Top Insurer Is Struggling to Put the Past Behind It," *Wall Street Journal Europe,* July 4, 1997, p. 1.

———, "Top Executives at RSA, Generali Step Down," *Wall Street Journal Europe,* September 13, 2002, p. M1.

———, "War of Attrition: Long, Bitter Battle over AGF Highlights Upheaval in Industry," *Wall Street Journal Europe,* December 22, 1997, p. 1.

Galloni, Alessandra, and Marcus Walker, "The Italian Job: Banker Shakes Up Secretive World of Finance in Milan," *Wall Street Journal,* July 22, 2003, p. A1.

Generali Group: The Insurer Without Frontiers, Trieste, Italy: Generali Group, 1995.

"Generali Steps Out: Italian Insurer Generali Turns Over a New Leaf," *Economist,* November 23, 2002, p. 95.

Kapner, Fred, "Veteran Takes Insurer into a New Age," *Financial Times,* January 23, 2003, p. 25.

Kielmas, Maria, "Generali Takes Direct Stake in AXA," *Business Insurance,* January 22, 1996, pp. 23+.

Lagrotteria, Brian, "Italian Banks Part Ways on Generali, End Uncertainty," *Wall Street Journal Europe,* December 5, 2003, p. M5.

Lanchner, David, "Free Generali!" *Institutional Investor,* October 2003, pp. 119–22.

Lindner, Claudio, and Giancarlo Mazzuca, *Il leone di Trieste: Il romanzo delle Assicurazioni Generali dalle origini austroungariche all'era Cuccia,* Milan: Sperling & Kupfer, 1990, 286 p.

McDonald, Ian, "Generali, PPF to Join in a Venture," *Wall Street Journal Europe,* April 27, 2007, p. 19.

Michaels, Adrian, "Generali Defends Unorthodox Governance Style Against Critics," *Financial Times,* February 13, 2007, p. 23.

———, "Generali Poised to Appoint First Finance Chief in Drive to Reform," *Financial Times,* September 26, 2007, p. 17.

———, "Generali Quickens the Pace of Turnaround," *Financial Times,* September 28, 2006, p. 28.

———, "Generali Sells Non-Life Business to Groupama of France for EUR 1.25 Billion," *Financial Times,* August 3, 2007, p. 23.

———, "Generali Shrugs Off Demands by Activists," *Financial Times,* February 6, 2008, p. 14.

Michaels, Adrian, and Haig Simonian, "Swiss Life Sells Unit to Generali," *Financial Times,* November 8, 2007, p. 19.

Mijuk, Goran, "Italy's Generali Plans Revamping to Boost Profits," *Wall Street Journal Europe,* March 7, 2006, p. 6.

Palladini, Giovanni, "Le Compagnie di assicurazioni di Trieste," *Trieste Economica,* December 1966.

Pitt, William, "Generali, Continental Venture Targets French Multinationals," *Business Insurance,* June 29, 1992, pp. 95+.

Reilly, David, and Alessandra Galloni, "Italy's Generali Becomes Arena for Power Play," *Wall Street Journal Europe,* March 10, 2003, p. M1.

Rossant, John, "Divorce, Italian-Style: A Banking Upheaval Destroys an Old Alliance," *Business Week,* May 17, 1999, p. 54.

Schondelmeyer, Brent, "Generali Goliath Embraces BMA," *Kansas City Business Journal,* November 15, 1991, p. 19.

Stefani, Giuseppe, *Il centenario delle Assicurazioni Generali, 1831–1931,* Trieste, Italy: Editrice La Compagnia, 1931, 307 p.

"Stumbling Abroad," *Economist,* July 17, 1993, pp. 71–72.

Sturani, Maria, "Generali to Buy Two Units from UBS for $1.26 Billion," *Wall Street Journal Europe,* July 2, 1998, p. 15.

Sullivan, Ruth, "Gallic Blood Injects New Life into Generali," *European,* November 2, 1995, p. 28.

"Waking Up the Lion of Trieste," *Economist,* March 4, 2006, p. 87.

The Years of the Lion, Trieste, Italy: Assicurazioni Generali, 2008, 112 p.

BASIN ELECTRIC
POWER COOPERATIVE
A Touchstone Energy® Cooperative

Basin Electric Power Cooperative

1717 East Interstate Avenue
Bismarck, North Dakota 58503-0564
U.S.A.
Telephone: (701) 223-0441
Fax: (701) 557-5336
Web site: http://www.basinelectric.com

Cooperative
Incorporated: 1961
Employees: 1,800
Sales: $628.7 million (2007)
NAICS: 221110 Electric Power Generation

∎∎∎

Basin Electric Power Cooperative is a nonprofit electric generation and transmission cooperative based in Bismarck, North Dakota, supplying power to about 125 rural electric systems in nine states (Colorado, Iowa, Minnesota, Montana, Nebraska, New Mexico, North Dakota, South Dakota, and Wyoming) through coal-, oil-, gas-, and wind-powered generation facilities located in North Dakota, South Dakota, Wyoming, and Iowa. All told, Basin Electric provides electricity to 2.6 million consumers who, in effect, are the company's owners.

In addition, Basin Electric provides power marketing and telecommunications services and owns eight for-profit subsidiaries. The largest are Dakota Coal Company and Dakota Gasification Company. Dakota Coal is a financial backer of Beulah, North Dakota's Freedom Mine, producing lime reagent in Wyoming, and manages another subsidiary, Montana Limestone

Company, a limestone quarry and plant located near Warren, Montana. Dakota Gas produces synthetic natural gas at the Great Plains Synfuels Plant in the Beulah, North Dakota, area. Another subsidiary, Souris Valley Pipeline Ltd., delivers carbon dioxide to a pair of Canadian oilfields for use in enhanced oil recovery as well as sequestration (preventing the gas from exacerbating the earth's greenhouse gas problem). Basin Telecommunications Inc. is a regional provider of telecommunications and Internet services to individuals, and small and large businesses. Subsidiary Basin Cooperative Services serves electric plant facilities by acquiring necessary fuel, materials, and services. Finally, Basin is developing a pair of wind generation operations, PrairieWinds ND 1, Inc., and PrairieWinds SD 1, Inc., the former slated to become operational in late 2009 or early 2010, while the latter is expected to be commissioned in late 2010 or early 2011. Basin Electric is governed by a ten-member board of directors, elected by system members.

DEPRESSION-ERA RURAL ELECTRIFICATION EFFORT TAKES SHAPE

While urban America was wired for electric power by the early 1890s, allowing residents to take advantage of modern lighting and appliances, rural America was forced to rely on kerosene lamps, hand pumps, cellars for refrigeration, and other outdated methods because electric utility companies found it unprofitable to string wires and provide power to farmers and other residents in sparsely populated parts of the country. By the time Franklin Roosevelt was elected president of the United

States in 1932, only one in ten rural residents had electricity, a far cry from the 70 percent of city residents and the rural residents of many other countries around the world. In Basin's territory the situation was even worse, with only 3.5 percent of the population electrified. What made the situation even more egregious was that a solution, electric cooperatives, had been suggested by the Country Life Commission, established by President Theodore Roosevelt in 1908 to determine how to improve rural living conditions. Nearly 20 years passed before another Roosevelt in the White House took the next step, as part of his promise to offer the American people a "New Deal." More than just raising the standard of living of farmers, delivering electricity to the farm brought refrigeration for milk and irrigation systems to help increase productivity. In 1935 Roosevelt established the Rural Electrification Administration (REA) and provided it with $100 million in funding to bring electricity to the countryside. Privately owned utilities were far from enthusiastic about the idea, playing down the need for rural electrification. Thus, in 1936 Roosevelt signed into law the Rural Electrification Act of 1936, giving loan preference to public entities and electric cooperatives. Before the end of the year almost 100 cooperatives had secured loan agreements to build transmission facilities and electrical lines.

FORMATION OF BASIN ELECTRIC: 1961

A large number of the rural electric cooperatives bought power from private power companies. Much of the power came from dams that combined flood control with hydroelectric power generation. As demand for power escalated during the post–World War II era, the U.S. government in the late 1950s informed electric cooperatives that they would have to generate their own power to supply their needs beyond what the dams could allocate to them. Rather than cooperatives building a large number of small generating plants to meet their individual requirements, former Roosevelt Federal Power Commission Chairman Leland Olds made a convincing case to the cooperatives that they should band together to form regional "super" generation and transmission cooperatives (G&Ts) that could supply all of them with the power they needed. Hence, in April 1961, 67 distribution cooperatives from eight states met in Minneapolis to establish Basin Electric Power Cooperative. A month later it was incorporated in Bismarck, North Dakota.

Basin Electric's first general manager was James L. Grahl, formerly with the American Public Power Association, a service organization that supported community-owned electric utilities. At the time, another regional G&T was taking shape in the Missouri River basin, Lignite Electric, which was also interested in building a power plant. After meetings between the two organizations, it was agreed that Basin Electric's plant would serve a larger area than the one proposed by Lignite, prompting Lignite to support Basin receiving preferential treatment in its request for an REA loan. The REA loan was approved in 1963, and as part of the grant Basin Electric agreed to provide other cooperatives a chance to join. Several current members took the opportunity to become a part of the regional G&T.

FIRST POWER PLANT OPERATIONAL: 1966

Grahl's next major task was to find a site to build the plant that offered sufficient water and existing federal power lines and had access to low-cost fuel. The Stanton, North Dakota, area fit the bill, possessing water, proximity to supplies of lignite coal, and was located just 12 miles from the federal power grid. Ground was broken on Basin Electric's first power plant, a 21-megawatt facility that came on line in 1966. It was named the Leland Old Station (LOS), paying homage to the man who had played an important role in the creation of super G&Ts. Not only did the plant provide power to member cooperatives, it served as a backup supplier to the Western Area Power Administration (WAPA), which generated power from dams constructed by the U.S. Army Corps of Engineers. Under the terms of a pooling arrangement, Basin Electric delivered power across the federal transmission system, receiving backup power from WAPA should its power station go off line. By the same token, Basin Electric served as WAPA's backup, selling power to WAPA as necessary.

A few years later construction of a second, larger Basin Electric plant at Stanton was begun. What became known as LOS Unit 2 came on line in 1975. The new plant boasted a 440 megawatt capacity, and it too would become a backup facility. This time, as part of an REA loan provision, Basin Electric was required to join Mid-Continent Area Power Pool and serve as a much needed backup to the regional power pool. In the meantime Basin Electric had added another power plant

KEY DATES

1961: Basin Electric Power Cooperative is formed.
1963: Loan application is approved by Rural Electrification Administration.
1966: Basin Electric's first power plant comes on line.
1975: Second power plant comes on line.
1980: First Laramie River Station unit becomes operational.
1985: First manager, James L. Grahl, retires.
1988: Great Plains Synfuels Plant is acquired.
1993: Wyoming Lime Producers is established.
1996: Basin Telecommunications, Inc., is formed.
2004: Construction begins on four plants using heat-recovery systems.
2008: Two wind energy subsidiaries are formed.

through acquisition, in 1973 buying Minot, North Dakota-based William J. Neal Station from member cooperative Central Power, which had pledged upon joining Basin Electric in 1964 that it would eventually sell its generating assets to the larger entity.

Although Basin Electric possessed three power plants by the mid-1970s, it was well aware that it would find it increasingly difficult to keep up with the area's rapidly escalating demand for more electricity. Plans were in the works for further power plants, which often took ten years to complete. Power plants were planned for Wheatland, Wyoming, which broke ground in 1977, and Beulah, North Dakota. While these larger projects were developed, a stop-gap operation opened in 1978, the fuel oil-fired Spirit Mound peaking station in Vermillion, South Dakota, which came on line in 1978. The plant tapped into a nearby pipeline and generated electricity when the rest of the Basin Electric system was at peak capacity.

DELAY OF ANTELOPE VALLEY LAUNCH UNTIL 1984

The three units of the Laramie River Station in Wheatland, Wyoming, came on line between 1980 and 1982. The other major project developed in the 1970s, Antelope Valley Station, near Beulah, was delayed because demand for power had not grown as expected. Estimating power needs a decade ahead of time was far from an exact science. As the result of a power surplus, the first unit of Antelope Valley station did not come on line until 1984. To make matters worse during the mid-

1980s, costs increased, forcing Basin Electric to find ways to become more efficient, cut costs, and provide diversified services.

In 1985 Grahl retired and was replaced by Robert L. McPhail, a man better suited to operations than Grahl, who had been an ideal choice for Basin Electric during the construction phase of the co-op's first 25 years. McPhail took over during a difficult time for the entire energy industry, especially oil and gas, which saw a collapse in prices that led to numerous bankruptcies. One project in the Beulah area was impacted, the Great Plains Synfuels Plant, a coal gasification complex, built by five interstate pipeline companies. The majority partner of the venture, American Natural Gas, went bankrupt in 1985 when it defaulted on $1.5 billion in government loans and the Department of Energy gained possession. The $2.1 billion plant used coal to produce gas for pipelines and was the largest plant of its kind in the world. Conceived at a time of energy shortages, the original partners expected to sell gas at $10 per thousand cubic feet. The actual price the gas fetched in 1985 was just $6 per thousand cubic foot, an amount that would continue to fall, yielding not nearly enough to pay back the government loans. Basin Electric supplied power to the facility through the Antelope Valley Station, and the loss of it as a customer would not only cut revenues but hurt Basin Electric's ability to share the costs of coal and water. Deciding it was in everyone's best interest, the members of Basin Electric decided the G&T should acquire Great Plains and made an offer for the property. In 1988 the cooperative outbid eight other suitors, including two other finalists, paying $85 million in cash for the plant. A $105 million cash reserve fund was turned over to the government, which also could receive future profit sharing, tax credit waivers, and about $367 million in federal taxes, or a possible $1.8 billion over the next 21 years.

NEW CEO: 2000

McPhail's tenure as Basin Electric's CEO and general manager lasted until 2000. During the 1990s he continued to diversify the cooperative's services and improve operations. Basin Cooperative Services was formed to acquire supplies, fuel, and other products for electric plant utilities. In 1993 Wyoming Lime Producers was created to produce lime for power plant use. Basin Telecommunications, Inc., was then established in 1996 to provide telecommunications and Internet services. Souris Valley Pipeline Limited was established and in 1997 filed an application with Canada's National Energy Board to build a pipeline to deliver carbon dioxide to oilfields in southern Saskatchewan for use in enhanced oil recovery as well as for sequestration. It became operational in 2000.

McPhail's successor as CEO and general manager was Ronald R. Harper. A graduate of Southwestern State University in Oklahoma, he brought to the job 20 years of utility industry experience. Under his direction Basin Electric resumed its drive to add more power capacity in order to meet the needs of its members, pursuing a variety of means, including wind energy. In 2002 the cooperative signed an agreement with FPL Energy to build and operate a pair of 40-megawatt wind farms in Edgelery, North Dakota, and Highmore, South Dakota. Basin Electric also looked to heat recovery systems. In 2004 it began construction on four new power plants that took advantage of the hot exhaust gases emitted from compressor stations operated along the Northern Border pipeline. The recovered heat vaporized a fluid in order to drive a turbine and generate electricity. Basin Electric also began construction on a new clean-coal burning power plant. Other power generation projects were also in development. Basin Electric began work on its first Montana power plant, the Culbertson Generation Station, a natural-gas fueled peaking facility using gas supplied by Dakota Gasification Company.

Another project in development was the Dry Fork Station in Gillette, Wyoming, a coal-based power plant slated to open in 2011. A 700-megawatt baseload power plant was also expected to be built in Selby, South Dakota, and come on line in 2014. Basin Electric in 2008 also formed a pair of subsidiaries, PrairieWinds ND 1 and PrairieWinds SD 1, to develop wind projects in the Dakotas. In addition, Basin Electric initiated projects to bolster its transmission system, including the Hughes Transmission Project in northeast Wyoming and a pair of transmission lines to be built in western North Dakota.

Ed Dinger

PRINCIPAL SUBSIDIARIES

Basin Cooperative Services; Basin Telecommunications, Inc.; Dakota Gasification Company; Dakota Coal Company; Montana Limestone Company; PrairieWinds ND 1, Inc.; PrairieWinds SD 1, Inc.; Souris Valley Pipeline Ltd.

PRINCIPAL COMPETITORS

MidAmerican Energy Holding Company; Nebraska Public Power District; Xcel Energy Inc.

FURTHER READING

Carvlin, Elizabeth, "Energy Production Is a Growing Concern," *Bond Buyer,* March 28, 2007, p. 46A.

Donovan, Lauren, "Basin Picks Company to Build World's Largest Carbon Capture," *Bismarck Tribune,* March 14, 2008.

Duke, Paul, Jr., "U.S. Finds Buyer for Big Synfuels Plant but Won't Recoup Its Initial Investment," *Wall Street Journal,* August 8, 1988, p. 1.

"FPL Building 2 Wind Farms," *Palm Beach (Fla.) Post,* September 17, 2002, p. 6B.

Hanson, Mark, "Cooperative to Begin Construction on Four Power Plants in Dakotas," *Bismarck Tribune,* January 8, 2004.

"North Dakota Utility to Buy U.S. Synthetic-Fuels Plant," *New York Times,* August 6, 1988.

bebe stores, inc.

——■——

400 Valley Drive
Brisbane, California 94005
U.S.A.
Telephone: (415) 715-3900
Toll Free: (877) 232-3777
Fax: (415) 715-3939
Web site: http://www.bebe.com

Public Company
Founded: 1976
Employees: 4,400
Sales: $687.6 million (2008)
Stock Exchanges: NASDAQ
Ticker Symbol: BEBE
NAICS: 448120 Women's Clothing Stores

■ ■ ■

Fashion as "affordable luxury" is what bebe stores, inc., offers the chic shopper of the 21st century. The company designs, manufactures, and sells upscale separates for professional women, as well as sportswear and casual clothing for 20- and 30-somethings, and logo-conscious teens. With an ever increasing array of accessories and footwear, bebe and BEBE SPORT have conquered the market for trend-conscious shoppers looking for high fashion without the hefty price tag of couture.

THE EARLY YEARS: 1970S AND '80S

The bebe concept was created by Manny Mashouf, a former entertainment executive who specialized in restaurant and arena management. In the mid-1970s Mashouf saw an opportunity to profit from the growing niche market of womenswear designed specifically for the younger, trend-conscious consumer, so he opened the first bebe store in San Francisco in 1976. Mashouf chose the name "bebe" because it encapsulated many of the images he wanted the clothing to project; the name was a play on Hamlet's famous phrase "to be or not to be" and was also Turkish for "woman" and French for "baby." The name (pronounced "bee-bee") was also unique for its pithy sound, representing the sharp and youthful originality the company wanted to portray.

The store was a success, focusing primarily on suits for younger, urban working women. For its first several years, bebe remained a single boutique, only branching out in the northern California area after several years in business. Mashouf, as director of the company, was at first conservative in his approach to expansion, choosing to focus on the financial health of a handful of stores before opening new locations. The strategy worked, and the company grew slowly but steadily in the Northwest throughout the 1980s.

Part of what made bebe profitable was the company's tight control over its design and production costs. By manufacturing its own products and using primarily domestic materials, overhead costs were kept low. By designing, manufacturing, and marketing its clothing in-house, bebe benefited not only from saving

COMPANY PERSPECTIVES

The bebe brand: Through an edgy, high-impact, visual advertising campaign using print, outdoor, in-store and direct mail communication, we attract customers who are intrigued by the playfully sensual and evocative imagery of the bebe lifestyle. We also offer a line of merchandise branded with the distinctive bebe logo to increase brand awareness.

The bebe woman: The bebe woman is not defined by how she looks—she is defined by her attitude: assertive, sexy and stylish. She's confident and cutting edge, demanding the same cachet from her clothing. For her, bebe's signature look of hip, sophisticated, body-conscious fashion is the ultimate expression of her own style.

on costs, but maintaining a firm grasp on its overall image as well. From initial sketch to presentation at the store, Mashouf and his team were able to give the bebe label consistency in both quality and style. As the company's popularity grew, so did its product line, and by decade's end bebe had expanded from daytime suits and other form-fitting career wear to overtly sexy cocktail dresses and separates.

NATIONAL GROWTH: THE EARLY NINETIES

By the beginning of the 1990s bebe was ready to begin competing with national chains. Its stores had developed a loyal customer base who could find trendy looks at a fraction of the cost of more expensive lines such as Donna Karan and Ralph Lauren, and, unlike other chains such as the Gap and Banana Republic, the company made no secret of its dedication to a single niche market: the young, stylish woman with a sizable chunk of disposable income.

As the country's overall economy began to pick up and large, exclusive malls developed at a faster pace nationwide, the company had its first opportunity to grow from a successful regional chain to a nationally recognized label. In 1994 bebe began an aggressive expansion campaign and within 18 months had opened 38 stores in strategically located malls across the nation. New stores catered directly to youthful, sexy women, with prices ranging from $30 for a simple, tight T-shirt to $150 for a flashy, short cocktail dress.

To augment its expansion plans, the company launched major advertising spreads such popular magazines as *Vogue, Cosmopolitan,* and *Bazaar* reflecting bebe's vampy, trendy image. Models wore sheer, silky gowns with feather boas draped in seductive poses. The unique, highly sexualized image worked, and bebe's profits and name recognition soared.

THE MARRIAGE OF FASHION AND FAME: 1995

An important development in the fashion industry, particularly high fashion, was the increasingly involved relationship between individual celebrities and clothing labels in the 1990s. In couture, a celebrity could make a certain name or label a household word almost overnight, particularly if he or she wore the label to a highly publicized event such as the annual Academy Awards or Grammys.

In the mid-1990s, after its initial national growth, bebe took the unusual step of actively seeking out name recognition through not only its print advertising campaigns, but through celebrity exposure as well. If the bebe label was seen on the stars its customer base admired, both brand identity and sales would increase exponentially. Such was the case in 1995 when a phenomenally successful television show called *Melrose Place* showcased several young, attractive television stars whose distinctive wardrobes were mimicked across the nation. When one of the show's top stars, Heather Locklear, wore a bebe outfit, she ushered in a new era of advertising and sales far more effective than bebe's traditional ads.

After bebe's appearance on *Melrose Place* the label began showing up on other celebrities, all of whom appealed to the same customer base. Among them were Drew Barrymore, Alicia Silverstone, and Brooke Shields (who wore bebe on her television show *Suddenly Susan*), models Cindy Crawford and Christy Turlington, as well as Jennifer Lopez, Madonna, and Julia Roberts. The trend of presenting labels on specific television shows continued for the next several years, with bebe's wares making regular appearances on such shows as *Party of Five, Beverly Hills 90210, The Practice,* and *Ally McBeal.*

Consequently, while bebe capitalized on this new form of exposure, the relationship between clothes and entertainment proved to be an increasingly vital element to a show's success as well. In one episode of *Ally McBeal,* the entire plot line revolved around the controversial length of the skirt worn by the show's star, Calista Flockhart. The skirt was made by bebe, and orders for the skirt and others in the line went up around the country immediately after the program was aired.

designs within a matter of weeks. By following up a design or trend so quickly, bebe allowed its fashion-conscious customers to keep up with the dizzying vicissitudes of the retail trade.

Through imitating high-fashion labels and offering its merchandise at usually less than half of what a customer would pay for more upscale names, bebe had carved out an important place for itself in the growing niche market of trendy womenswear in the late 1990s. The company had managed to make its products appealing to both the label-obsessed celebrity and the image-obsessed consumer without sacrificing quality.

Another important factor in the company's growth was its "test and reorder" method, which allowed bebe to move inventory at a much faster pace than its competitors. Using this method, the company shipped only a limited amount of certain products to its stores early in a season, then waited to see what its customers would buy. If the product sold exceptionally well, the company would alter its inventory by changing factory orders to accommodate customer demand. bebe could do this quickly, because unlike many of its competitors, the company produced its own merchandise and had total control over both the speed and the amount of product created.

Considering the pace at which the trendier end of the retail market moved, the company's "test and reorder" philosophy became a vitally important aspect of the company's fiscal health. This process also ensured that bebe's merchandise would be constantly changing, revolving around the capricious demands of the fashion-conscious consumer, and enabled the company to keep up with trends from season to season and, in some cases, from region to region. A distinctive part of bebe's image, paradoxically, became its chameleon-like ability to change quickly, although the company never strayed far from its core devotion to snugly fitting, sexy apparel.

By the late 1990s bebe had evolved dramatically from the single, career suit-oriented boutique of less than two decades earlier, with the company gaining enough fiscal strength to go public in June 1998. The company had an initial public offering (IPO) of $11 a share, with 2.5 million shares sold. After the company's appearance on the stock exchange, Mashouf maintained 88 percent ownership and continued to play an active role in the company's designs and expansion as its chief executive.

bebe had always marketed itself to younger women, primarily in their 20s, but after its tremendous expansion the company began to appeal to an even younger age group by offering less expensive, logo-emblazoned shirts, sweaters, and jackets. The introduction of such merchandise not only brought in an expanded customer

---

KEY DATES

1976: Manny Mashouf opens the first bebe boutique in San Francisco.

1994: More than three dozen new bebe stores open across the nation.

1995: Actresses on popular television shows including *Melrose Place* and *Ally McBeal* sport bebe clothing.

1996: Greg Scott begins running bebe's design and merchandise department.

1998: Company goes public on the NASDAQ and begins offering online shopping.

1999: Sales for bebe stores hit $200 million.

2000: Merchandising guru Greg Scott leaves bebe.

2003: BEBE SPORT is launched featuring sportswear separates.

2004: Greg Scott returns to run bebe as chief executive.

2005: A flagship store on Rodeo Drive in Beverly Hills opens.

2006: bebe celebrates 30 years as Manny Mashouf is named to *Forbes* magazine's list of billionaires.

2007: *Desperate Housewives* star Eva Longoria is signed as BEBE SPORT's poster girl.

2008: Skechers and indie designer Tara Subkoff sign deals with the company.

2009: Mashouf returns as CEO upon Greg Scott's departure.

Like any advertising campaign, the courting of a star by a clothing company had to be strategic and shrewdly planned, forcing bebe to know not only the sartorial preferences of its customers, but also the stars, films, and television shows they admired and wished to imitate. No longer was bebe confined to considerations specific only to the retail industry; the company had become an active part of the entertainment industry as well.

FURTHER EXPANSION: 1996 AND 1997

Unlike high fashion and bridge labels such as Donna Karan or Ralph Lauren, bebe was not an innovator when it came to designs and trends. Instead, the key to the company's success was found in its ability to quickly and accurately mimic and expand upon key styles from season to season. When Karan came out with sheer, wispy dresses for one season, bebe followed with similar

base, but made the company's name more visible. In addition, while still focusing on suits and dresses as its primary inventory, bebe had also added lingerie and more casual wear to its collections.

NEW DIRECTIONS: 1998 TO 2003

In late 1998 bebe signed licensing agreements with Genender International Inc. (to produce inexpensively priced but fashionable watches) and Titan Industries (to design a footwear collection), both slated to be sold in bebe stores and upscale department stores. The company also contracted with California Design Studio to produce an eyewear collection with prices ranging from $50 to $150 a pair. In addition, bebe took its wares online, offering select items to Internet shoppers.

By May 1999 bebe had opened 11 stores in as many weeks, reaching the milestone of successfully operating 100 stores. Two of these stores bore international addresses, with one in Kent, England, and the other in Vancouver, British Columbia. The popularity of the newest locations inspired the company to look into other international regions such as Europe, Asia, and Israel.

bebe's almost fairy tale–like success was not without risk, however, as it appealed to a highly limited customer base and was frequently criticized for its small sizing and creating clothes into which only a tiny percentage of the American female population could fit. Such criticism, however, did not affect the slew of imitators who began offering similarly styled clothes in the same price range. Abercrombie & Fitch catered to thin, leggy teenagers with jeans and tees, while Juicy Couture, Diesel, and Lucky Brand marketed designer-label chic to young women and teenagers, the same demographic as bebe.

Regardless of the competition, bebe continued to attract 20- and 30-somethings who wore its labels with pride. Sales hit $200 million for 1999 and within three years had climbed to $316.4 million for 160 stores worldwide, including a new concept, BEBE SPORT, featuring sports-related and more casual clothing. Although expansion plans had been tempered after the September 11, 2001, terrorist attacks on the United States, bebe's workforce had grown to 2,400 and the company's identity and sales remained strong.

By 2003 although sales were relatively stable, bebe experienced a downturn in both its stock pricing and quarterly same-store sales. Some analysts blamed the company's seeming abandonment of its original customers, young, impossibly-thin career women, instead steering merchandise toward casual and sport clothing for younger shoppers, including teenagers who were primarily interested in logo tees and jeans. Despite the criticism, bebe managed to finish the fiscal year in June 2003 with sales of just under $326 million for its 185 stores (173 bebe, 12 BEBE SPORT) in the United States and Canada.

ONWARD AND UPWARD: 2004 AND BEYOND

In 2004 bebe weathered an executive shakeup when its newly hired chief executive, Gregory Gemette of American Eagle Outfitters, was sued for breach of contract as he defected to rival bebe. The resulting lawsuit made founder and chairman Mashouf move away from Gemette, leaving bebe vulnerable for a time before new president and CEO Greg Scott, who had been with the company from 1996 to 2000 as senior vice-president of merchandising, came back to take the reins.

Scott's reappearance at bebe ushered in a new era of focused control on bebe's core customers and image. Jazzy separates for professional women were ramped up, while casuals and sportswear were scaled back. Accessories such as bags, sunglasses, and jewelry were still available, while bebe's popular footwear line was expanded. In addition, Scott restructured operations for tighter control, and the results were positive: 2004 sales climbed to $372.3 million and by the following year, 2005, sales had mushroomed to $509.5 million with double-digit gains in net profit, helped in part by the opening of a huge flagship store on Rodeo Drive in Beverly Hills.

By 2006, the year of bebe's 30th anniversary, the company waxed nostalgic. Not only did Heather Locklear's *Melrose Place* micro-miniskirt and jacket ensemble make a comeback, but bebe had returned to its marketing strategy of featuring popular television actresses. Mischa Barton of *The OC* fame represented the company's bebe line in 2006 and 2007, and was replaced by *Ugly Betty* and *X-Men* actress Rebecca Romijn in 2007. Another new "face" was signed in 2007 as well, for BEBE SPORT, and the impact was immediate and enormous. Actress Eva Longoria of *Desperate Housewives* became the perfect poster girl for BEBE SPORT's sexy sportswear. Longoria's looks, personality, and diminutive size quickly boosted BEBE SPORT's image and bottom line, helping propel overall sales to $579.1 million for 2006 and $670.9 million for 2007.

As the new century's first decade came to a close, bebe and its ever popular sibling, BEBE SPORT, continued to prosper by offering teens and young professional women contemporary separates and sportswear at "affordable luxury" prices. Always looking to stay ahead of its rivals, bebe initiated a deal with Tara Subkoff (founding designer of indie label Imitation of Christ) in 2008 for a new collection and signed with Manhattan Beach, California-based Skechers for a BEBE SPORT footwear line. The company also opened two new stores in Chicago and a new store in Honolulu. A number of older locations underwent renovations in 2008 and 2009 in California, New Jersey, and New York.

In 2009 bebe took a hit as chief executive Greg Scott left the company for the second time, in the midst of a rather catastrophic economic downturn. With close to 300 North American locations and stores in Asia, the Middle East, Puerto Rico, Russia, South Africa, and the Virgin Islands, bebe and BEBE SPORT continued to offer fashion-conscious, savvy female shoppers luxurious clothes at prices lower than traditional designer duds. With the future of many higher-end fashion stores in peril, bebe seemed to be in capable hands with founder Manny Mashouf back at the helm of his retail empire.

Rachel H. Martin
Updated, Nelson Rhodes

PRINCIPAL COMPETITORS

A/X Armani Exchange; BCBG Max Azria Group, Inc.; Diesel SpA; Donna Karan International, Inc.; Gilly Hicks LLC; Guess? Inc.; Juicy Couture, Inc.; Liz Claiborne, Inc.; Wet Seal, Inc.

FURTHER READING

"Bebe Coming to Singapore via SSS Holding," *Women's Wear Daily (WWD)*, August 23, 1999, p. 2.

"Bebe Stores, Inc. Enters the Eyewear Business," *Business Wire*, July 29, 1998.

Jones, Rose Apodaca, "Monah Li Leaves Bebe Stores," *WWD*, January 2, 2002, p. 2.

Kaplan, Julee, "Bebe Teams with Subkoff," *WWD*, January 31, 2008, p. 16.

Maxwell, Alison, "Retailers Dress TV Stars to Woo Teens," *WWD*, August 19, 1999, p. 10.

Moin, David, "Contract Dispute Leaves Bebe in Flux," *WWD*, November 14, 2003, p. 11.

Poggi, Jeanine, "Bebe Net Up, Forecast Lowered," *WWD*, October 26, 2006, p. 3.

Ramey, Joanna, "Bebe Grows Up: New Concept, Affordable Luxury," *WWD*, November 29, 2006, p. 9.

Ryan, Thomas J., "Bebe Files IPO for 2.5 Million Shares," *WWD*, April 23, 1998, p. 8.

———, "Bebe Shares Plummet 20.8% As Greg Scott Plans to Leave," *WWD*, January 5, 2000, p. 11.

Sammon, Lindsay E., "Skechers Inks License for Bebe Footwear," *Footwear News*, December 3, 2007, p. 8.

Solnik, Claude, "Bebe Launching New Footwear Business," *Footwear News*, February 1, 1999, p. 108.

"US: CEO Gregory Scott Leaves Bebe Stores," *just-style.com*, January 12, 2009.

Vesilind, Emili, "Bebe Sport Names Eva Longoria As Face," *WWD*, January 5, 2007, p. 12.

Wilson, Beth, "Bebe Expands Presence in Chicago," *WWD*, April 16, 2008, p. 12.

Young, Kristin, "Bebe CEO Details Chain's Expansion," *WWD*, December 18, 2000, p. 18.

Boral Limited

Level 39
AMP Centre
50 Bridge Street
Sydney, New South Wales 2000
Australia
Telephone: (+61 2) 9220 6300
Fax: (+61 2) 9233 6605
Web site: http://www.boral.com.au

Public Company
Incorporated: 1946 as Bitumen and Oil Refineries
(Australia) Limited
Employees: 15,928
Sales: AUD 5.2 billion ($4.71 billion) (2008)
Stock Exchanges: Australian
Ticker Symbol: BLD
NAICS: 212313 Crushed and Broken Granite Mining
and Quarrying; 212319 Other Crushed and Broken
Stone Mining and Quarrying; 212321 Construction
Sand and Gravel Mining; 238110 Poured Concrete
Foundation and Structure Contractors; 321113
Sawmills; 321211 Hardwood Veneer and Plywood
Manufacturing; 321212 Softwood Veneer and
Plywood Manufacturing; 321911 Wood Window
and Door Manufacturing; 324121 Asphalt Paving
Mixture and Block Manufacturing; 327121 Brick
and Structural Clay Tile Manufacturing; 327310
Cement Manufacturing; 327320 Ready-Mix
Concrete Manufacturing; 327331 Concrete Block
and Brick Manufacturing; 327390 Other Concrete
Product Manufacturing; 327420 Gypsum Product
Manufacturing; 332321 Metal Window and Door
Manufacturing

■ ■ ■

Founded as an oil-refining company shortly after the conclusion of World War II, Boral Limited later divorced itself from its initial interests and diversified into a wide range of resource and material fields. In 2000 the company spun off its remaining energy operations to concentrate on building and construction materials, a field in which it ranks as one of the largest in Australia. During the 1990s and into the early 21st century, Boral expanded operations in the United States and Asia, but domestic operations still account for about nearly 80 percent of overall revenues. The company, through a number of subsidiaries as well as several joint ventures, is involved in quarrying, timber operations, and masonry, as well as the production of bricks, roofing tiles, cement, concrete, asphalt, windows, and plasterboard.

EARLY YEARS: FOCUS ON OIL REFINING

Boral, originally known as Bitumen and Oil Refineries (Australia) Limited, was incorporated in 1946. The new company was assisted financially by California Texas Oil Company (Caltex), a joint venture of Standard Oil Company of California (later Chevron Corporation) and the Texas Company (later Texaco Inc.). Caltex's Australian subsidiary purchased 40 percent of Bitumen and Oil's initial stock. Caltex also agreed to provide the new company with a 25-year supply of crude oil and technical assistance for three years. In return, Bitumen

COMPANY PERSPECTIVES

We are focused on delivering shareholder value, value to our customers and value to other stakeholders in our company. Our corporate Values of Leadership, Respect, Focus, Persistence and Performance are referred to in our Strategic Intent to reinforce their ongoing importance in Boral.

Our market driven focus reflects the increased importance we place on addressing market needs through improved product development and innovation processes. We must be aware of future market trends and anticipate the changing needs of our customers. In order to do this effectively we strive to understand what is important to our customers and what they value.

and Oil guaranteed Caltex a supply of refinery byproducts.

An entrepreneurial promoter named David Craig became the company's first chairman, and Elton Griffin was named chief executive. Griffin was an accountant by trade and maintained board positions with several other Australian companies, including the City Mutual Life Assurance Society Limited and e-mail Limited.

T. G. Murray, another founding director, succeeded Craig as chairman in 1947. Murray also served as board chairman for the City Mutual Life Assurance Society, where Griffin was a director, and was a board member of other major Australian companies.

Bitumen and Oil stock, issued in early 1946, represented the 60 percent of the company that Caltex did not own. Initially the stock did well on the market as a result of widespread interest in the new corporation. The stock soon fell victim to nose-diving prices, before leveling off once production began in late 1948.

When production finally commenced, it was on Botany Bay, New South Wales, at a new plant on land in Matraville, leased from the Australian government. Despite difficulties in obtaining permission to construct the facility on the Botany Bay parcel, near Sydney, construction schedules stayed on course.

By 1949 Bitumen and Oil's prospects were good. Chairman Murray told stockholders that year that increased government-sanctioned roadwork should benefit the company, although the cost of interstate transport and the limited supply of steel for drums

could hinder profits. The company closed out its first full year of production with a net profit of AUD 40,747.

Bitumen and Oil steadily increased production through the mid-1950s. In 1954 the company embarked on its first major expansion, and Queensland Oil Refineries Pty Limited, later known as Boral Resources (Queensland), was founded. Activities of the new operation included processing semirefined oil received from Matraville into heavy fuel oil and bitumen.

The company entered the field of petroleum tars that same year, with the purchase of a minority interest in Petroleum and Chemical Corporation, which provided an outlet for refinery byproducts. The acquisition of a smaller company, W. B. Constructions, during this same time gave Bitumen and Oil a base for the manufacture and distribution of emulsion and tars in the states of New South Wales and Victoria.

DIVERSIFYING IN THE SIXTIES

Bitumen and Oil made a number of acquisitions during the early 1960s that set the way for expansion in some areas and capital gains in others through the sale of new assets. In 1961 a controlling interest was purchased in Petroleum and Chemical Corporation. That same year Bitumen and Oil targeted Huddart Parker Industries, a shipping group, for its first major takeover. Bitumen and Oil sold some of Huddart Parker's assets shortly after the successful acquisition, but picked up bargaining power within the oil industry, having secured markets to store heavy fuel and diesel oil.

During this time the company also expanded bituminous operations in Victoria, with the formation of Reid Brothers & Carr Proprietary, an asphalt-manufacturing company owned jointly by Reids Quarries and Bitumen and Oil. Fowler Road Construction Proprietary was also purchased and later became the spray division of Boral Resources (Victoria). Bituminous surfacing operations were then extended into South Australia through the purchase of an interest in Bitumax Proprietary, which later became a wholly owned subsidiary.

In 1963 Bitumen and Oil acquired Mt. Lyell Investments, primarily because of its large interest in the fertilizer industry. Mt. Lyell was soon sold, after plans to manufacture fertilizer from refinery byproducts fell through because of unforeseen high costs.

Early in 1964 the Gas Supply Company was acquired, which included gas plants in Victoria, New South Wales, and Queensland. The Victorian operations

KEY DATES

1946: Bitumen and Oil Refineries (Australia) Limited is incorporated as an oil-refining firm.

1963: Company is renamed Boral Limited.

1964: Diversification into construction materials begins.

1969: Boral merges its oil-refining operations into a joint venture with Total, then exits entirely from oil refining two years later.

1976: Cyclone Company, a maker of fencing, prefab buildings, window frames, and other products, is acquired.

1979: Company enters U.S. market through purchase of partial interest in California Tile.

1980: Merry Group, a U.S. clay brick maker, is acquired.

1982: BMI Limited, a major Australian construction materials group, is purchased.

1987: Blue Circle Southern Cement Limited, the largest cement maker in Australia, is acquired.

1993: A variety of manufacturing operations outside building products and energy is spun off as Azon Limited; Sagasco Holdings, a gas firm, is acquired.

1997: Natural gas distribution operations are spun off to shareholders as Envestra Limited.

2000: Through a demerger, the energy operations are separated from the building and construction materials operations, which form the core of the new Boral.

2004: Boral breaks into the U.S. concrete and quarries sector.

were later sold. The Norman J. Hurll Group was acquired later that year, and went on to form an integral part of the Bitumen and Oil subsidiary Gas Group. During this same time the company also purchased a majority interest in Mt. Lyell Mining and Railway, a tin manufacturing company. Company officials later decided to abandon the tin field, and the mining company was sold for capital gain.

A 1964 decision to diversify into construction resources was the highlight of the period. This diversification marked the beginning of a shift in corporate focus. Two large quarry groups were purchased in 1964, paving the way for restructuring and

ultimately representing two major building blocks in the formation of the Boral of the early 21st century.

The two groups purchased, Albion and Reid, were consolidated under the name Albion Reid Proprietary, which later became the subsidiary Boral Resources (Victoria) Proprietary. Activities of smaller quarrying companies, including Carr Fowler, Reid Brothers & Carr, and Dammann Asphalt, were then incorporated into the interests of Albion Reid.

On November 19, 1963, the company adopted the name Boral Limited, which was an acronym for Bitumen and Oil Refineries (Australia) Limited. The new name signified the company's move away from its original core business, oil refining. With the formation of the Albion Reid group, Boral had entered the premixed-concrete industry in South Australia. Operations were later expanded to include quarrying, and the subsidiary became known as Boral Resources (South Australia) Proprietary. In 1966 Boral acquired its third major quarry company, Bayview, rounding out the group that was then Boral's foundation. That year Boral earned net profits of AUD 3.7 million on total sales of AUD 75.9 million.

Boral's acquisitions were put on hold for the next three years while company operations were consolidated. In April 1967 John O'Neill was named a company director and later that year was appointed chairman, following the retirement of T. G. Murray. O'Neill, a director of the City Mutual Life Assurance Society, brought a background to Boral that included the law, banking, oil exploration, and insurance.

EXITING FROM OIL REFINING, EXPANDING IN BUILDING AND CONSTRUCTION

Boral merged its oil interests with the French-based Total in 1969. Boral's previous attempts to provide larger coverage of the retail petroleum market and acquire an assured crude oil supply had been less than successful. In a major reorganization spanning the next two years, Boral sold its remaining oil interests to Total and completely separated itself from its original field.

With oil refining behind it, Boral became increasingly committed to expansion in the building and construction industries. Early acquisitions spurred by this new direction included Warringah Brick and Pipe Works in New South Wales, Brittain Bricks and Pipes Limited in Queensland, and Steel Mills Limited (later Boral Steel Limited) operating in New South Wales and Queensland.

Boral continued expansion into the brick field in the early 1970s, with the purchase of Glen Iris Bricks, later known as Boral Bricks (Victoria). Meanwhile, the company acquired a trio of concrete-masonry-block companies, including Besser Vibrapac of Queensland, Jaywoth Industries in New South Wales, and Hollostone, operating in Victoria and South Australia. Boral also expanded into the field of gas and asphalt early in the decade with the acquisition of Brisbane Gas Company, which became Gas Corporation of Queensland, and asphalt operations from Esso.

In 1973 Elton Griffin retired as CEO and was succeeded by Eric J. Neal. Neal, a ten-year veteran of the company, had served in various managerial roles before replacing Griffin. The new CEO was quick to direct other diversification moves, and in 1976 Boral purchased Cyclone Company of Australia, which became Boral Cyclone. The acquisition brought Boral into the fields of fencing, materials-handling equipment, prefabricated buildings, aluminum window frames and shower screens, wire screen cloth, and hand tools.

Peter Finley was named Boral's fourth chairman in 1976. Finley, a chartered accountant, would in 1990 become vice-chairman of the National Australia Bank and chairman of e-mail Limited, a company of which Elton Griffin had once been a board member.

In 1978 Boral Cyclone purchased the Melwire Group, whose operations included woven-wire conveyor belts, wire screens for heavy industry, and other woven-wire products. Melwire later acquired Mounts Wire Industries, a New Zealand company with similar operations. That same year Boral took over its first mining interest and a major gypsum producer, Australian Gypsum Industries. The subsidiary Boral Bricks Proprietary also acquired Albury Brickworks and Pacific Brick Proprietary about the same time. Meanwhile, Boral was also establishing its presence in the United States, with the 1979 purchase of a partial interest in California Tile Inc., a concrete-tile-manufacturing company based near Los Angeles (the remaining interest was purchased in 1980).

FURTHER ACQUISITIONS AT HOME AND ABROAD

Boral entered the 1980s joining a growing number of major Australian industrial suppliers diversifying into energy. Under an agreement with Esso Exploration and Production Australia, Boral began oil and gas exploration in Queensland's Galilee Basin in 1980. A few years later Boral acquired a 37 percent stake in the Oil Company of Australia (OCA), a Queensland-based gas exploration company. A subsequent purchase of additional interest in the oil company made OCA an 85 percent-owned subsidiary.

In 1982 the takeover of BMI Limited of Australia was completed, giving Boral full control over a major construction materials group. BMI's interests were complementary to those of Boral, and included operations in concrete, asphalt, and bricks. The newly enlarged Boral boasted the top position in the Australian building and construction materials markets. Boral also entered a new business, timber, via Allen Taylor and Co. Limited, which BMI had taken over in 1970. In addition, Boral gained bases in the United Kingdom and Indonesia. Around the time of Boral's takeover of BMI, Caltex sold its remaining 11 percent interest in Boral.

Expansion and diversification led to increasing sales, and by 1983 Boral passed AUD 1 billion in sales for the first time. The 1980 acquisition of the Augusta, Georgia-based Merry Group, the third largest manufacturer of clay bricks in the United States, made Boral the fourth largest brick manufacturer in the world. Once under Boral's wing, the Merry Group went on to acquire brickworks in Maryland, Oklahoma, Texas, Virginia, and South Carolina.

In 1985 Boral purchased Johns Perry, an Australian company involved in heavy engineering, ropes and strappings, and lifts and escalators. The following year the Edenhall Group, a U.K. producer of concrete products, was acquired.

In order to safeguard its cement supply, Boral bought Blue Circle Southern Cement Limited, in 1987. The AUD 630 million acquisition was Boral's costliest takeover thus far. Blue Circle, Australia's largest cement manufacturer, also had interests in coal and limestone. The purchase of Blue Circle and certain U.S. interests helped push Boral's sales over AUD 2 billion in 1987; the company posted AUD 2.37 billion in sales, more than double the total for 1983.

Also in 1987, Eric Neal retired as CEO. Neal had played a key role in Boral's expansion in the Pacific, the United States, and the United Kingdom. Neal was succeeded by Bruce R. Kean. Kean, who had joined Boral in 1968, had served as general manager of the company's energy group and later headed a number of building products, manufacturing, and overseas operations. Kean picked up where Neal left off, continuing expansion drives in the United States and Australia. The new CEO also led Boral into continental Europe. Acquisitions there included two clay-brick and tile operations and a limestone and gravel processing plant in West Germany, as well as two Dutch brick manufacturers.

During the late 1980s a handful of Australian companies agreed to be bought out by Boral, which led to further expansion into the tool manufacturing field. These acquisitions included the Bell quarrying concrete, asphalt, and tire business, based in Western Australia; Patience & Nicholson, a cutting-tool company; Trojan, a shovel and hand tool maker; the concrete and masonry manufacturing company Calsil Limited; and a window manufacturing company, Dowell Australia Limited.

Acquisition activity also picked up in the United States in the late 1980s, where Boral acquired Fontana Asphalt, a major southern California asphalt supplier and quarry operator. Other U.S. acquisitions in the late 1980s included Blair Paving and Vernon Paving; another southern California asphalt manufacturer; and U.S. Tile Company, a producer of clay roofing tiles.

LATE-CENTURY STRUGGLES AND RESTRUCTURING

Boral entered the 1990s on a wave of rising revenues, having posted annual profit increases for 19 consecutive years. Despite the spate of overseas endeavors, better than 80 percent of Boral's activities remained in its home country, and late in 1990 the company expanded its presence in Western Australia by acquiring Midland Brick Company. The economic downturn of the early 1990s hit Boral hard, given the company's exposure to the cyclical housing market. For the fiscal year ending in June 1991, the company's annual profits failed to increase over the previous year, the first time that had happened in 20 years. Boral also cut its dividend for the first time in 43 years. Profits fell further still in 1992.

In December 1991 Mobil veteran Jim Leslie succeeded Finley as chairman of Boral. One of the first major moves under his chairmanship was the bolstering of timber operations through the purchase of Pacific Dunlop's forestry products division for AUD 158 million. This move made Boral the leading hardwood timber producer in Australia, with operations added in New South Wales and Tasmania. The Leslie era was also noted for an increased concentration on Boral's core building products and energy businesses. To that end a hodgepodge of manufacturing operations outside the two core areas were spun off as Azon Limited in 1993. Seeking to increase the company's energy operations as a counter to the cyclical building industry, Leslie and Kean launched a takeover bid of Sagasco Holdings Limited, which operated South Australia's suburban gas network and held various production assets. Following some resistance from Sagasco and its major shareholders, Boral succeeded by increasing its bid to AUD 816 million. Shortly after the completion of this deal in late 1993, Tony Berg took over as managing director from the retiring Kean. Berg, with a background in investment banking, was a former head of Australia's Macquarie Bank. In November 1994 Leslie was succeeded as

chairman by Peter Cottrell, who had been on the Boral board of directors since 1992.

Under Berg's leadership, Boral aimed to be one of the world's leaders in building and construction and to be a major player in the Australian energy sector, focusing particularly on production and distribution of natural gas. Most of the remaining operations outside of these areas were soon divested. For example, in 1995 Boral sold its elevator business to Otis Elevator Co. of the United States. Although there were no acquisitions completed on the scale of the Sagasco purchase, Boral did gain the leading position in the U.S. brick market through the 1995 purchases of Bickerstaff Clay Products Company and Isenhour Brick and Tile Company. In addition to bricks, Boral's U.S. operations also focused on tiles, fly ash, and plasterboard. The other major overseas push came in Asia, where the company concentrated on plasterboard and premixed concrete activities in Indonesia, Malaysia, and China. In 1994 Boral began work on the first plasterboard factory in Indonesia and purchased the only plasterboard producer in Malaysia, Wembley Gypsum Products Sdn Bhd. Boral entered the rapidly opening Chinese market for the first time in 1995 when it established a joint venture with a local firm to construct the first plasterboard factory in Shanghai.

Net income dropped nearly in half for the fiscal year ending in June 1996 as Boral was buffeted by another downturn in the housing and construction markets. Seeking to cut its debt load, Boral in July 1997 spun off its natural gas distribution operations to shareholders as a new company called Envestra Limited, a move that gained the company AUD 899 million. Boral's net debt to equity ratio was thereby reduced to only 25 percent. Other businesses deemed noncore were sold off as well, including the North American gypsum and German tile operations.

EARLY 21ST CENTURY: NEWLY FOCUSED VIA DEMERGER

With the company's financial performance lagging behind that of its main building and construction material rivals, its share price depressed, and the Asian financial crisis hurting the company's operations in that region, Berg and Boral were under continuous pressure in the late 1990s from shareholders and the investment community. Many analysts advocated a company breakup into separate building and energy firms. In October 1999 Boral announced just such plans, with a demerger completed in February 2000. For various reasons, it was actually the building and construction materials business that was demerged from Boral. The old Boral, consisting of the energy operations, was renamed Origin Energy Limited, and the demerged entity took on the Boral Limited name.

With the completion of the demerger, Berg left the company, and Rod Pearse took over as managing director. Pearse had been hired by Berg in 1994 to head the construction materials division. A number of non-core operations were divested in the first several months following the demerger in order to reduce a newly enlarged debt load. Among these were the European brick operations, Boral Tyres, a woodchip operation in Tasmania, and the windows extrusion business. Boral also restructured its troubled Asian activities, in particular through the June 2000 establishment of an Asia-wide plasterboard joint venture with Lafarge S.A., a French building materials firm. The venture, called Lafarge Boral Gypsum in Asia Ltd., was initially 26.7 percent owned by Boral, but the company increased that ownership to 50 percent over the next few years by financing new projects.

By 2001, with the Australian housing and construction markets beginning to recover and Boral's financial state improving as well, Pearse began looking for acquisitions to further strengthen the company's position. In mid-2001 Boral completed the AUD 70.8 million purchase of Concrite Pty Limited, a privately held concrete maker based in Sydney. During the following two years, a number of additional, modest deals were completed. These included takeovers of Allen's Asphalt Pty Ltd. in southeastern Queensland; Stud & Track, the largest plasterboard distributor in New South Wales; and Franklin Industries Inc., the biggest independent brick distributor in the United States. By fiscal 2002–03, near-record demand in the Australian housing market helped push the company's profits up 47 percent, to AUD 283.2 million, while revenues advanced 10 percent to AUD 3.83 billion.

Boral's acquisition ambitions soon proved far larger as the firm in December 2003 unveiled an AUD 840 million ($624 million) hostile bid for Adelaide Brighton Limited (AdBri). The deal promised to unite the second and third largest cement companies in Australia (behind Cement Australia), as well as strengthen Boral's position in Queensland; greatly advance its limited presences in the cement markets of Western Australia, South Australia, and the Northern Territory; and provide an entry into the lime market. In January 2004 AdBri accepted a slightly sweetened bid of AUD 867 million. The Australian Competition and Consumer Commission (ACCC), however, launched a lengthy investigation of the takeover and eventually, in May, ruled against its completion on competition grounds, specifically its potentially adverse effects on downstream markets, namely, premixed concrete and concrete masonry. Boral

initially pressed ahead with its bid, setting the stage for a showdown in federal court, but it then threw in the towel in September 2004 when it became clearer that victory was unlikely.

Even before this lengthy takeover bid at home had reached its negative conclusion, Boral was continuing to seek growth overseas. In July 2004 the company acquired Hanson PLC's concrete and quarry operations in Thailand for AUD 65.9 million. In a deal completed in September 2004, Boral extended its U.S. operations into the concrete and quarries sector, having attained the number one position in the United States in both bricks and clay roof tiles. Boral spent AUD 93.2 million for Ready Mixed Concrete Company and the assets of Owens Brothers Concrete, two firms based in Denver, Colorado, with operations in concrete, quarrying, and concrete masonry.

ORGANIC GROWTH INITIATIVES, BATTLING HOUSING DOWNTURNS

Also during the 2004–05 fiscal year, Boral earmarked a significant allotment of capital for organic growth initiatives, including $35 million to build a new clay brick plant in Union City, Oklahoma, to replace a facility that had been shuttered, and $80 million for the joint venture with Lafarge to double its plasterboard capacity in China and South Korea. Boral that year managed a 2 percent increase in profits despite downturns in both the Australian housing market and the plasterboard market in South Korea. Aiding the company were strong markets in the United States for housing and nonresidential construction.

Over the next two years, organic growth remained high on the agenda. Boral boosted its manufacturing capacity with several new plants, including a plasterboard manufacturing and distribution center in Brisbane, Queensland; a clay brick plant in Terre Haute, Indiana; concrete roof tile plants in Las Vegas, Nevada, and Lake Wales, Florida; a clay roof tile plant in Ione, California; and, via the Lafarge Boral Gypsum joint venture, a plasterboard plant in Vietnam. In August 2007 Boral paid roughly AUD 95 million for two Oklahoma City-based construction materials businesses: Schwarz Readymix, a ready-mixed concrete and sand business, and the Davis Arbuckle Materials quarry.

By fiscal 2006–07, Boral was struggling under the weight of the continued downturn in the New South Wales housing market and the beginning of a severe slump in the U.S. housing sector. Net profits that year fell 18 percent to AUD 298 million, before dropping a further 19 percent a year later to AUD 243 million, the firm's worst showing in six years. The result for the latter year stemmed largely from a further deterioration in the U.S. housing market; Boral's U.S. operations posted a net loss of AUD 27 million, after having generated AUD 95 million in profits a year earlier. By early 2009 the company had laid off about half of its U.S. workforce and either cut production at or shut down most of its U.S. plants. It also announced that its profits for the first half of fiscal 2008–09 had plunged 44 percent to just AUD 75 million and that it expected its full-year profits to total only about AUD 120 million. Boral was clearly among the companies hit hardest by the global economic downturn. It also had to fend off ongoing speculation that it needed to raise equity to shore up its balance sheet. Adding to the uncertainty surrounding the company was the April 2009 revelation that the board of directors had begun an executive search, making it quite possible that a new CEO would be installed at the end of 2009 when Pearse's contract expired.

Roger W. Rouland
Updated, David E. Salamie

PRINCIPAL SUBSIDIARIES

Blue Circle Southern Cement Ltd; Boral Building Materials Pty Ltd; Boral International Pty Ltd; PT Boral Indonesia; Boral Concrete (Thailand) Ltd; Boral Quarry Products (Thailand) Ltd; Boral International Holdings Inc. (USA); Boral Asia Pacific Pte Ltd (Singapore); Boral Building Services Pte Ltd (Singapore); Boral Construction Materials LLC (USA); Ready Mixed Concrete Company (USA); Boral Industries Inc. (USA); United States Tile Co. (USA); Boral Bricks Inc. (USA); Boral Composites Inc. (USA); Boral Material Technologies Inc. (USA); Boral (UK) Ltd; Boral Investments BV (Netherlands); Boral Industrie GmbH (Germany); Boral Industries Ltd (New Zealand); Boral Building Products (NZ) Ltd (New Zealand); Boral Australian Gypsum Ltd; Boral Investments Pty Ltd; Boral Construction Materials Ltd; Boral Resources (WA) Ltd; Boral Resources (Vic) Pty Ltd; Boral Resources (Qld) Pty Ltd; Boral Resources (NSW) Pty Ltd; Boral Recycling Pty Ltd; De Martin & Gasparini Pty Ltd; Girotto Precast Pty Ltd (80%); Boral Construction Materials Group Ltd; Boral Transport Ltd; Bayview Pty Ltd; Oberon Softwood Holdings Pty Ltd; Allen Taylor & Company Ltd; Boral Bricks Pty Ltd; Boral Masonry Ltd; Boral Montoro Pty Ltd; Boral Windows Systems Ltd; Sawmillers Exports Pty Ltd; Boral Building Products Ltd.

PRINCIPAL DIVISIONS

Australian Construction Materials; Cement; Clay & Concrete Products; Plasterboard; Timber; Boral USA.

PRINCIPAL COMPETITORS

CSR Limited; Fletcher Building Limited; Holcim Ltd.; CEMEX, S.A. de C.V.; CRH plc; Lafarge S.A.; Acme Brick Company.

FURTHER READING

Beeby, Melanie, "Double Your Money: Berg Still Haunted by His Vision," *Australian Financial Review,* September 3, 1998.

Blue, Tim, "Building Suppliers Still in Trough," *Australian,* September 6, 2008, p. 34.

"Boral Rounds Recession Mark and Heads for Renewed Growth," *Rydge's,* October 1983, pp. 34+.

"Bottom Heavy Management for a Better Bottom Line at Boral," *Rydge's,* March 1986, pp. 42+.

Boyd, Tony, "How Boral Cemented Its Asian Future," *Australian Financial Review,* August 28, 1995, p. 24.

Brief History of Boral Limited, Sydney: Boral Limited, 1989.

Chong, Florence, "U.S. Housing Crisis Buffets Boral, but Australia Holds Up," *Australian,* February 14, 2008, p. 23.

Craig, Duncan, "Boral Puts Its Foot on the Gas," *Australian Financial Review,* September 13, 1996, p. 48.

Ferguson, Adele, "What Went Wrong at Boral," *Business Review Weekly,* July 22, 1996, p. 20.

Greenblat, Eli, "Boral on the Hunt for New Chief Executive," *Sydney Morning Herald,* April 7, 2009, p. 19.

Howarth, Ian, "For $800M, Boral Takes Sagasco: Now Watch the Changes," *Australian Financial Review,* October 15, 1993.

Hoyle, Simon, "Restructuring Has Delivered the Goods, Declares Boral," *Australian Financial Review,* September 4, 1997, p. 21.

Hughes, Anthony, "Back to the ACCC: Boral Bids for Rival," *Sydney Morning Herald,* June 5, 2001, p. 25.

———, "Boral Down, Will Keep Promise to Grow in U.S.," *Sydney Morning Herald,* February 15, 2001, p. 26.

———, "Boral's Losing Energy," *Sydney Morning Herald,* December 20, 1999, p. 31.

———, "It's Official: A Split Decision," *Sydney Morning Herald,* October 21, 1999, p. 25.

Hutchinson, Diane, "The Transformation of Boral: From Dependent, Specialist Bitumen Refiner to Major Building Products Manufacturer," *Business History,* July 2000, pp. 109+.

King, Stephanie, *From the Ground Up: Boral's First 50 Years,* Sydney: State Library of New South Wales Press, 1996, 104 p.

Kitney, Damon, "Boral's Building Blocks Cut for Expansion," *Australian Financial Review,* September 4, 2000, p. 20.

———, "Building Blocks Start Falling into Place at Boral," *Australian Financial Review,* March 19, 2001, p. 5.

Light, Deborah, "How Neal Charts the Course at Boral," *Business Review Weekly,* March 14, 1986, p. 14.

Maley, Karen, "Up and Down: Tony Berg's Career Path," *Australian Financial Review,* October 23, 1999, p. 30.

Marsh, Don, "Boral Limited in Name Only," *Concrete Products,* October 2004, p. 4.

McLachlan, Colin, and Brook Turner, "Boral Dividend Cut: The First in 43 Years," *Australian Financial Review,* September 3, 1991.

Ooi, Teresa, "Boral Blocked in by Housing Slump," *Australian,* August 17, 2005, p. 25.

———, "Boral Boss's Credo Set in Cement," *Australian,* July 12, 2004, pp. 27–28.

———, "Boral Dumps Troubled Bid for AdBri," *Australian,* September 28, 2004, p. 24.

———, "Boral Slashes 1,800 Jobs, Shuts Plants As Construction Tumbles," *Australian,* February 12, 2009, p. 22.

Pearse, Rod, "Boral's New Top Gun Ready for Tough Role," *Australian Financial Review,* December 6, 1999, p. 22.

Rennie, Philip, "Sir Eric Shows 'em How," *Rydge's,* May 1984, pp. 42+.

Ries, Ivor, "A Tense Time for Tony Berg," *Australian Financial Review,* November 14, 1998, p. 27.

Rochfort, Scott, "Booming Boral on the Prowl in U.S.," *Sydney Morning Herald,* February 11, 2004, p. 21.

———, "Boral Buys Hanson Out of Thailand for $61m," *Sydney Morning Herald,* July 20, 2004, p. 18.

———, "Boral Makes Hostile $840m Bid for AdBri," *Sydney Morning Herald,* December 17, 2003, p. 21.

———, "Boral Sees End to Bonanza," *Sydney Morning Herald,* August 18, 2004, p. 44.

———, "Boral Struggles on Slippery Slope," *Sydney Morning Herald,* August 16, 2006, p. 21.

———, "Boral Told to Raise Capital or Face Cut in Rating," *Sydney Morning Herald,* February 5, 2009, p. 23.

Sevior, John, "A 'Gleaming New Direction' for Boral," *Sydney Morning Herald,* October 21, 1993, p. 25.

Speedy, Blair, "U.S. Housing Woes Hit Boral Profits," *Australian,* January 29, 2009, pp. 17, 20.

Stensholt, John, "Concrete Optimism," *Business Review Weekly,* November 17, 2005, pp. 44+.

Sykes, Trevor, "Hard Men at the Top Ran a Tough Ship," *Australian Financial Review,* October 21, 1999, p. 27.

Syvret, Paul, "Boral's New Chief Has Eye on Asia," *Australian Financial Review,* August 30, 1993, p. 18.

Tabakoff, Nick, "Boral Makes Maiden Investment in China," *Australian Financial Review,* August 21, 1995, p. 19.

Tait, Nikki, "Bosses at Boral Build a Dynamic Image," *Financial Times,* October 21, 1993, p. 32.

West, Michael, "Berg: Surgeon or Grim Reaper?" *Sydney Morning Herald,* July 15, 1996, p. 37.

BP p.l.c.

1 St. James's Square
London, SW1Y 4PD
United Kingdom
Telephone: (44 20) 7496-4000
Fax: (44 20) 7496-4570
Web site: http://www.bp.com

Public Company
Incorporated: 1998 as BP Amoco PLC
Employees: 92,000
Sales: $365.7 billion (2008)
Stock Exchanges: New York
Ticker Symbol: BP
NAICS: 211111 Crude Petroleum and Natural Gas Extraction; 324110 Petroleum Refineries; 325188 All Other Inorganic Chemical Manufacturing; 551112 Offices of Other Holding Companies

■ ■ ■

Formed by the 1998 merger of British Petroleum Company and Amoco Corporation, BP p.l.c. is a leading global energy company. On the strength of approximately 92,000 employees, the company has operations in more than 100 countries. Its well-known brands include BP, Castrol, Arco, and Aral. By the end of the opening decade of the 21st century, BP had proved reserves equivalent to 18.1 billion barrels of oil. In addition to operating 17 refineries, the company was engaged in exploration and production initiatives in 29 countries. BP also operated 22,600 service stations worldwide.

BRITISH PETROLEUM: EARLY 20TH-CENTURY ORIGINS

BP originated in the activities of William Knox D'Arcy, an adventurer who had made a fortune in Australian mining. In 1901 D'Arcy secured a concession from the grand vizier of Persia (Iran) to explore for petroleum throughout most of his empire. The search for oil proved extremely costly and difficult, since Persia was devoid of infrastructure and politically unstable. Within a few years D'Arcy was in need of capital. Eventually, after intercession by members of the British Admiralty, the Burmah Oil Company joined D'Arcy in a Concessionary Oil Syndicate in 1905 and supplied further funds in return for operational control. In May 1908 oil was discovered in the southwest of Persia at Masjid-i-Suleiman, the first oil discovery in the Middle East. The following April the Anglo-Persian Oil Company was formed, with the Burmah Oil Company holding most of the shares.

The dominant figure in the early years of the Anglo-Persian Oil Company was Charles Greenway. Greenway began his career in the firm of managing agents who handled the marketing of Burmah Oil's products in India. Invited by Burmah Oil to help in the formation of Anglo-Persian Oil, he became a founding director, was appointed managing director in 1910, and took the position of chairman in 1914. The first few years of the company's existence were extremely difficult, and it survived as an independent entity in large part through Greenway's skill. Although Anglo-Persian Oil had located a prolific oilfield, it encountered major

COMPANY PERSPECTIVES

BP started life as a pioneering company, at the frontier of what was possible.

We continue to push back the boundaries, from the giant finds in the Middle East, to the frozen tundra of Alaska, and by securing access to new resources and markets around the world. The pioneering spirit that founded the company still drives us forward, confidently into our next 100 years.

problems in refining the crude oil. The company also lacked a tanker fleet and a distribution network to sell its products.

For a time Anglo-Persian Oil risked being absorbed by one of the larger oil companies, such as the Royal Dutch/Shell Group, with whom it signed a ten-year marketing agreement in 1912. However, in 1914 Greenway preserved the independence of Anglo-Persian Oil by a unique agreement with the British government. Under the terms of this agreement, negotiated with Winston Churchill, then first lord of the Admiralty, Greenway signed a long-term contract with the British Admiralty for the supply of fuel oil, which the Royal Navy wished to use as a replacement for coal.

At the same time, in an unusual departure from the United Kingdom's laissez-faire traditions, the British government invested £2 million in Anglo-Persian Oil, receiving in return a majority shareholding that it would retain for many years. The transaction provided the company with funds for further investment in refining equipment and an initial investment in transport and marketing in fulfillment of Greenway's ambition to create an independent, integrated oil business. In return for its investment, the British government was allowed to appoint two directors to the company's board with powers of veto, which could not, however, be exercised over commercial affairs. In fact, the government directors never used their veto throughout the period of state shareholding in the company. On paper Anglo-Persian Oil was state controlled until the 1980s; in practice it functioned as a purely commercial company.

GROWTH TO GLOBAL PROMINENCE DURING WORLD WAR I

World War I created considerable opportunities for the fledgling enterprise. Although within Persia the author-

ity of the shah had almost disintegrated, and in 1915 Anglo-Persian Oil's pipeline to the coast was cut by dissident tribesmen and German troops, demand for oil products was soaring. Between 1912 and 1918 there was a tenfold increase in oil production in Iran. The war also created opportunities for Greenway to further his ambition of establishing an integrated oil business. In 1915 Greenway founded a wholly owned oil tanker subsidiary, and within five years Anglo-Persian Oil had more than 30 oil tankers. In 1917, in his biggest coup, Greenway acquired British Petroleum Company, the British marketing subsidiary of the European Petroleum Union. The European Petroleum Union, a Continental alliance with significant Deutsche Bank participation, had been expropriated by the British government as an enemy property. In 1917 Greenway also decided to establish a refinery at Swansea, Wales, with improved refining technology that could produce petroleum products for British and European markets.

World War I, coupled with Greenway's skill, led to Anglo Persian Oil's emergence by the late 1920s as one of the world's largest oil companies, matching Royal Dutch/Shell and Standard Oil of New Jersey in stature. During the 1920s the company made a major expansion in marketing, establishing subsidiaries in many European countries and, after the expiration of the agreement with Shell in 1922, in Africa and Asia. New refineries were established in Scotland and France, and a research laboratory erected in Sunbury, Great Britain, in 1917 greatly expanded the company's activities. In the early 1920s there were some criticisms of the management of Anglo-Persian Oil within the British government and some suggestions that the state shareholding be privatized, but in November 1924 a decision was made to retain the government's equity stake.

Greenway's successor was John Cadman, a former mining engineer who had been a professor of mining at Birmingham University before World War I and who had become a major figure in official British oil policy during the war. In 1923 he became a managing director of Anglo-Persian Oil, and in 1927, chairman. He introduced major administrative reforms and, in the words of business historian Alfred Chandler, as quoted in *Scale and Scope: The Dynamics of Industrial Capitalism,* "was one of the few effective British organizational builders." Cadman was successful in overcoming the excessive departmentalism and lack of coordination that had formerly characterized the company. In 1928, he also joined forces with other leading oil companies in a clandestine price-fixing agreement among the world's largest oil companies.

KEY DATES

■

1889: Rockefeller's Standard Oil Trust establishes Standard Oil Company (Indiana).

1892: Standard Oil Trust is liquidated; Standard Oil (Indiana) becomes a subsidiary of Standard Oil Company (New Jersey).

1901: William Knox D'Arcy obtains a concession from Persia to explore for petroleum there.

1908: D'Arcy's company becomes the first to strike oil in the Middle East.

1909: D'Arcy and Burmah Oil form the Anglo-Persian Oil Company.

1911: The government orders Standard Oil Company (New Jersey) to relinquish control of its subsidiaries; Standard Oil (Indiana) becomes an independent company.

1914: The British government acquires a controlling interest in the Anglo-Persian Oil Company.

1915: Anglo-Persian forms an oil tanker subsidiary.

1917: Anglo-Persian acquires British Petroleum Company.

1923: Standard (Indiana) acquires 50 percent of the American Oil Company, which marketed an antiknock gasoline under the brand name "Amoco."

1925: Standard (Indiana) buys an interest in the Pan American Petroleum & Transport Company in the largest oil industry consolidation to date, giving Standard entry into oilfields in Mexico, Venezuela, and Iraq.

1929: Standard (Indiana) and five other Standard companies organize the Atlas Supply Company to sell automobile tires and other accessories.

1932: Standard (Indiana) sells Pan American's foreign interests.

1933: Persia signs a new 60-year concession with Anglo-Persian Oil.

1935: Anglo-Persian is renamed Anglo-Iranian Oil when Persia becomes Iran.

1945: Amoco Chemicals is formed.

1948: Standard (Indiana) forms a foreign exploration department to spearhead exploration efforts in Canada and other countries.

1951: The Iranian oil industry is nationalized, ousting Anglo-Iranian Oil.

1952: Standard Oil (Indiana) is the nation's largest domestic oil company.

1954: Anglo-Iranian Oil is renamed British Petroleum Company, returns to Iran.

1957: Standard (Indiana) reorganizes, consolidating nine subsidiaries into four larger companies.

1961: Standard (Indiana) begins to use the brand name Amoco heavily in its advertising and subsidiary names.

1967: British Petroleum (BP) becomes the second largest chemicals company in the United Kingdom.

1969: BP makes a major oil find at Prudhoe Bay in Alaska, partners with Standard Oil Company of Ohio (SOHIO) to develop the property.

1970: BP discovers the Forties field, the first major commercial oil find in British waters.

1978: Standard Oil (Indiana)'s tanker *Amoco Cadiz* runs aground, dumping thousands of tons of oil off the French coast.

1985: Standard Oil (Indiana) changes its name to Amoco Corporation.

1987: BP acquires SOHIO, forms BP America; the British government sells its shares of BP.

1988: Amoco buys Dome Petroleum, Ltd., of Canada.

1992: Amoco becomes the first foreign oil company to explore the Chinese mainland.

1994: Amoco restructures, replacing its three major subsidiaries with a network of 17 business groups.

1996: BP merges its European refining and marketing operations with Mobil Corporation.

1997: Amoco begins a divestiture program designed to shed noncore properties.

1998: British Petroleum acquires Amoco Corporation, forming BP Amoco PLC.

2000: BP Amoco acquires Atlantic Richfield Co. and Burmah Castrol, and changes its name to BP p.l.c.

2001: Madison Oil agrees to acquire BP's ARCO Turkey Inc. business for $3.4 billion.

2002: BP sells its Gelsenberg subsidiary for $2.3 billion.

KEY DATES CONT.

2003: In order to streamline operations, BP sells numerous refineries, plants, and retail operations throughout the United States, Canada, Singapore, Central Europe, and Germany, as well as ownership stakes in various projects.

2005: An explosion at the company's Texas City refinery in the United States results in 15 deaths and 170 injuries; company sells its Innovene chemicals business to the United Kingdom's Ineos Group for approximately $9 billion.

2006: BP contends with two oil spills in Prudhoe Bay, Alaska, resulting from corroded pipelines.

2007: Tony Hayward succeeds John Browne as CEO amid controversies surrounding the latter's personal life; BP agrees to pay $373 million in restitution and fines to settle illegal propane trading allegations, as well as alleged environmental violations surrounding the Alaskan pipeline leaks and Texas refinery explosion.

2008: Falling profits lead BP to announce 5,000 job cuts.

2009: BP celebrates its 100th anniversary.

DEPRESSION AND THE THREAT OF IRANIAN NATIONALISM IN THE THIRTIES

In the 1930s one of Cadman's greatest challenges came from the growth of Persian nationalism. Previously, in 1921, the old dynasty of shahs had been overthrown by an army colonel, Reza Khan, who made himself shah in 1925. Reza Khan was determined to reverse the foreign political and economic domination of his country. Anglo-Persian Oil had a symbolic role as a bastion of British imperialism, and, following growing resentment of declining royalty payments from the company due to its falling profits during the Great Depression, the government of Persia canceled its concession in November 1932. The dispute eventually went to the League of Nations, and in 1933 Persia signed a new 60-year concession agreement with Anglo-Persian Oil that reduced the area of the concession to about a quarter of the original and introduced a new tonnage basis of assessment for royalty payments. Anglo-Persian Oil had the formidable backing of the British government, and Persia gained little out of the dispute.

The oil company, which was renamed Anglo-Iranian Oil in 1935 (the year Persia became Iran), became a renewed target of nationalist discontent after World War II. The Iranians complained that their dividends were too small, and the signing of 50-50 profit-sharing agreements between governments and oil companies elsewhere (in Venezuela in 1948 and Saudi Arabia in 1950) fueled criticism of Anglo-Iranian Oil within Iran. Extensive negotiations ensued between the company and the Iranian government. Anglo-Iranian Oil eventually offered substantial concessions, but they came too late and were repudiated by the nationalist government of Muhammad Mussadegh.

On May 1, 1951, the Iranian oil industry was formally nationalized. Several years of complex negotiations followed. Eventually, a 1953 coup, in which the British government and the U.S. Central Intelligence Agency (CIA) were implicated, resulted in the overthrow of Mussadegh. After his removal from power, an agreement was reached that allowed the return to Iran of Anglo-Iranian Oil, renamed British Petroleum Company in 1954, but not on such favorable terms as the company had secured after the early 1930s dispute. Under the accord, which was reached in August 1954, British Petroleum held a 40 percent interest in a newly created consortium of Western oil companies, formed to undertake oil exploration, production, and refining in Iran.

DIVERSIFICATION: FIFTIES AND SIXTIES

The events from 1951 to 1954 had encouraged BP to diversify away from its overdependence on a single source of crude oil. The Iranian nationalization deprived the company of two-thirds of its production. The company responded by increasing output in Iraq and Kuwait and by building new refineries in Europe, Australia, and Aden (now part of Yemen). Oil exploration activities were launched in the Arabian Gulf, Canada, Europe, north Africa, east Africa, and Australia.

Meanwhile, BP, which had moved first into petrochemicals in the late 1940s, became the second largest chemicals company in the United Kingdom in 1967.

The company's future was secured at the end of the 1960s by major oil discoveries in Alaska and the North Sea. In 1965 BP found gas in British waters of the North Sea. In October 1970 it discovered the Forties field, the first major commercial oil find in British waters. Throughout the 1960s BP also had been looking for oil in Alaska, and in 1969 this effort was rewarded by a major discovery at Prudhoe Bay on the North Slope. In the previous year BP had acquired the U.S. East Coast refining and marketing operations from Atlantic Richfield Company, and the stage was set for a surge of expansion in the United States. Through its large share in Prudhoe Bay, BP owned more than 50 percent of the biggest oilfield in the United States, and it needed outlets for this oil.

The solution was a 1969 agreement with Standard Oil Company of Ohio (SOHIO), the market leader in Ohio and several neighboring states. Under the agreement, SOHIO took over BP's Prudhoe Bay leases as well as the downstream facilities acquired from Atlantic Richfield. In return, BP acquired 25 percent of SOHIO's equity. In 1970 BP and SOHIO engaged in a seven-year struggle to develop the Prudhoe Bay oilfield and construct the 800-mile Trans-Alaska Pipeline system, which was finally completed in 1977. By the following year BP had taken a majority holding in SOHIO. Later, in 1987, BP would acquire SOHIO outright and merge it with BP's other interests in the United States to form a new company: BP America.

OIL CRISIS DURING THE SEVENTIES

The oil price shocks and the transformation of the balance of power between oil companies and host governments that occurred in the 1970s caused many problems for BP, as for other Western oil companies. BP lost most of its direct access to crude oil supplies produced in countries that belonged to the Organization of Petroleum Exporting Countries (OPEC). The company's oil assets were nationalized in Libya in 1971 and Nigeria in 1979. BP and Shell clashed with the British government in 1973 over the allocation of scarce oil supplies. BP's chairman, Sir Eric Drake, refused to give priority to supplying the United Kingdom, despite forceful reminders from Prime Minister Edward Heath that the government owned half of the company.

Problems in the oil industry prompted BP to diversify away from its traditional role as an integrated oil company heavily dependent on Middle Eastern oil production. Beginning in the mid-1970s, BP built up a large coal business, especially in the United States, Australia, and South Africa. BP's chemical interests also expanded during this period, especially after 1978, when it acquired major European assets from Union Carbide and Monsanto. Also in the mid-1970s, BP became active in mineral mining, acquiring Selection Trust, a mining finance house based in Great Britain, in what was then the London stock market's largest ever takeover bid.

CEO Sir Peter Walters, who took BP's helm in 1981, guided a five-year acquisitions binge costing approximately £10 billion. It included the purchase of the Purina Mills animal feed company in 1986 as well as the purchase of the remaining shares in SOHIO. In 1981 SOHIO acquired Keiecott, the largest U.S. copper producer.

Seen retrospectively, this diversification strategy was not always a wise one. A major world recession after 1979 led to considerable overcapacity, forcing BP to close down or sell off parts of its chemicals business in the early 1980s. Late in the decade, the energy conglomerate sold its coal and minerals interests in the United States, Canada, Indonesia, Australia, and South Africa, netting £428 million in the process. BP started to consolidate its upstream business through divestment in the late 1980s. Another sale of selected worldwide oil and gas interests and assets brought in $1.3 billion. In 1990 and 1991 sales of exploration interests and assets in New Zealand, France, the Netherlands, and from the BP Exploration division in particular totaled £830 million.

One notably successful acquisition was Britoil, a company established by the British government in the 1970s to participate in North Sea oil exploration. Britoil had become one of the largest independent oil exploration and production companies, and in acquiring it, BP almost doubled its exploration acreage in the North Sea.

The late 1980s saw considerable changes at BP. In October 1987 the government under Prime Minister Margaret Thatcher sold its remaining shares in the company as part of a privatization program. The timing of the share issue was particularly unfortunate, as the world's stock markets collapsed between the opening and closing of the offer. One result of the sale was that by March 1988 the Kuwait Investment Office had built up a 21.6 percent stake in the company; government regulatory authorities subsequently reported that this share was reduced to less than 10 percent.

In the early 1990s British Petroleum sought to consolidate its activities to focus on its traditional areas of strength in "upstream" areas (oil and gas exploration, field development, production, pipeline transportation, and gas marketing) and "downstream" areas (oil supply trading, refining, and marketing) as well as in chemicals manufacturing. As a result of its corporate shuffling, BP focused on its three core businesses: oil exploration and production, oil refining and marketing, and chemicals.

PROJECT 1990 UNDER CEO HORTON

In 1990 BP announced Project 1990, a fundamental change of its corporate structure. The primary aims were to reduce organizational complexity, reshape the central organization and reduce its cost, and reposition BP for the 1990s. Project 1990 was the brainchild of BP's chairman, Robert Horton. Horton earned a reputation for saving money and rose to prominence at BP by cutting costs first at the company's tanker division, then progressing to BP's chemicals subsidiary. Eventually becoming chairman and chief executive officer of BP Oil in 1990, he set out to cut $750 million from BP's annual bottom line by revamping the corporate culture.

At the heart of the scheme was a conviction that BP had become overly bureaucratic and that strategic flexibility was handicapped as a result. In 1990, Horton said, "What I'm trying to do is simply, refocus, and make it clear we don't need to have hierarchies. We don't need to have baronial head office departments. This is a fundamentally different way of looking at the way you run the center of the corporation." Under Project 1990, nearly 90 percent of corporate center committees were abolished, with individuals taking responsibility instead. Hierarchically structured departments were to be replaced by small flexible teams with more open and less formal lines of communication.

Unfortunately, Project 1990 quickly came to represent wholesale job cuts and low morale. Between 1990 and 1992, more than 19,000 positions representing at least 16 percent of the total workforce were cut. The intended result of the job cuts was to shorten the lines of command and promote individual responsibility, but workloads were not redistributed in the process. Project 1990 earned a poor reputation among employees, because some of the most basic measures to promote good communication and efficiency were eschewed for job elimination. Horton also insisted on maintaining BP's dividend, despite cuts in other vital areas.

As a result of Project 1990's shortcomings, many employees lost faith in it, according to a 1991 internal survey. Horton's personal abrasiveness and tendency to dictate, rather than cultivate, change earned him an unflattering nickname: "The Hatchet." He was forced to resign on June 25, 1992, after BP sustained its first quarterly losses. Sales had slid from $66.4 billion in 1990 to $51.9 billion in 1992, and profits declined from $3.2 billion to an annual loss of £458 million ($811 million).

RESTRUCTURING UNDER NEW MANAGEMENT TEAM IN THE MID-NINETIES

Horton's role was split between Lord Ashburton, the nonexecutive director who had led the mutiny, and Sir David Simon, who advanced from chief operating officer to chief executive officer. Ironically, however, Simon and Ashburton soon found that they needed to accelerate, not reverse, Horton's plan. First, they organized the company's interests into three primary divisions: BP Exploration, BP Oil, and BP Chemicals. The new organizational scheme allowed the parent to better analyze and pinpoint underperforming and noncore assets with a view to improvement or elimination. Of the $4 billion in assets targeted for divestment were BP Nutrition and the company's controlling stake in BP Canada. The company also planned to reduce debt by $1 billion annually and invest $5 billion per year on capital projects.

From 1993 to 1995, BP cut another 9,000 people from the payroll, reducing employment to less than 54,000 by the end of 1996. Reorganization efforts also focused on the troubled American subsidiary, BP Oil, which contributed more than $20 million of the parent company's 1992 loss. Cost-cutting measures at the subsidiary ran the gamut, from selling 300 California and Florida gas stations, to employee buyouts eliminating 600 to 700 jobs, to the close scrutinization of travel vouchers.

The ongoing cuts (which were expected to bring employment down to 50,000) brought home a stern reality; as an unnamed source told *Oil & Gas Journal* in 1996, "There is no doubt among staff that BP is a lean and mean machine these days, and not the Rolls-Royce among oil companies it once thought itself." Ashburton and Simon also halved BP's "fat-cat" dividend, a measure Horton had been reluctant to take. In 1995, Sir John Browne, former chief of Exploration, took over as BP's chief executive. The change in leadership was to bring about even greater shifts in the company's focus, direction, and size.

Under Browne's guidance, BP accelerated its use of strategic partnerships to cut the cost of doing business around the world. In 1996, for example, the company merged its European fuel and lubricants business, including pipelines, terminals, road tanker fleets, refineries, depots, and retail sites, with Mobil Corporation. The joint venture operated in 43 countries and held a 12 percent share for fuels and an 18 percent share for lubricants in the European market. A joint venture with China's Shanghai Petrochemical Company expanded BP's chemical interests in Asia while limiting the company's liabilities. The company hoped to target Southeast Asia and Eastern Europe for new downstream operations. In 1997, BP announced that it would build its first service stations in Japan. Also in 1997, BP acquired a 10 percent equity stake in AO Sidanco, a major Russian oil and gas company, as well as 45 percent of Sidanco's majority interest in a separate Russian company with major oil and gas properties in east Siberia.

The partnerships and acquisitions of the mid-1990s were mere foreshadowings of much bigger deals to come. In 1998, BP made history by acquiring Amoco Corporation, the fifth largest oil company in the United States and the largest producer of natural gas in North America. The $50 billion deal was both the first megamerger in the oil industry and largest industrial merger ever made. It was a highly significant move for BP; not only did it add substantially to the company's oil operations, but more important, it gave the company a leadership position in natural gas. With demand for gas expected to grow much faster than demand for oil in the coming years, it was critical for BP to move in that direction.

EARLY DAYS AT AMOCO: THE LATE 19TH CENTURY

Amoco had been in business since 1889, although it had been known as Standard Oil Company (Indiana) until its name was changed in 1985. The company was formed outside Whiting, Indiana, a location chosen by John Rockefeller's Standard Oil Trust as a refinery site close enough to sites in the growing midwestern market to keep freight costs low, yet far enough away to avoid disturbing residents.

From the beginning, the Whiting facility was organized as a self-supporting entity, planning for long-term expansion. Although refining was its main activity, it also constructed oil barrels for transportation and manufactured an oil-based product line consisting of axle grease, harness oil, paraffin wax for candles, and kerosene produced from the crude oil. The oil itself flowed to Chicago and other midwestern cities via two pipes originating in Lima, Ohio. Land transportation began on the refinery's grounds, at a railroad terminal belonging to the Chicago & Calumet Terminal Railroad, a company over which a Standard Oil interest had gained control. This terminal's placement gave the company exclusive use of the tracks, access to the West and the Southwest, and a direct route that eliminated the expense of switching tolls.

Standard (Indiana) had no direct marketing organization of its own. After Standard Oil Trust was liquidated in 1892 by order of the Ohio Supreme Court, the 20 companies under its jurisdiction reverted to their former status and became subsidiaries of Standard Oil Company (New Jersey). The functions of Standard Oil (Indiana) were then expanded to include marketing.

The company's capitalization was increased from $500,000 to $1 million, which was divided into $100 shares. Standard Oil still owned about 54 percent of Standard (Indiana). Standard (Indiana) used the extra cash to buy Standard Oil Company (Minnesota) and Standard Oil Company (Illinois), formerly P.C. Hanford Oil Company, an oil marketing organization in Chicago. The extra capital expanded Standard's sales territory, which was broadened even further when the property of Chester Oil Company of Minnesota was bought. Other acquisitions followed, and by 1901 the company was marketing through its own organization in 11 states.

At first, Standard (Indiana) had few competitors in the petroleum-product market. It enjoyed about 88 percent of the business in kerosene and heavy fuel oil. After competition began to grow, Standard (Indiana) fought back with strategically placed bulk storage stations and subsidiary companies in competitive areas that cut prices and drove competitors out. Earnings rose from $605,781 in 1896 to a high of almost $4.2 million in 1899, but the company's competitive practices and its growing market share made it the target of government agencies.

INDEPENDENCE AND GROWTH THROUGH ACQUISITION: THE EARLY 20TH CENTURY

In 1911, after a court battle lasting almost three years, Standard Oil Company (New Jersey), the parent company to Standard (Indiana) and other Standard companies, was ordered to relinquish supervision of its subsidiaries. Gasoline sales had risen from 31.6 million gallons to 1.57 billion between 1897 and 1911. Once independent, Standard (Indiana) began to cater to the burgeoning automobile market, opening a Minneapolis, Minnesota, service station in 1912. Chicago's first service station opened in 1913, and by 1918, there were 451 altogether. Along with growing sales of road oil, asphalt, and other supporting products, the automotive industry provided one-third of all Standard (Indiana) business.

To get as much gasoline out of each barrel of crude as possible, Standard formulated the cracking process, which doubled the yield by separating the oil's molecules, by means of heat and pressure, into a dense liquid plus a lighter product that would boil in gasoline's range. The possibility of less expensive gasoline and a new line of petroleum-based products made the method attractive to other refiners, who licensed it, accounting for 34 percent of the company's total profits between 1913 and 1922.

With the end of World War I, company Chairman Colonel Robert Stewart's top priority was to find a secure source of crude oil, to meet the rapidly expanding demand for gasoline and kerosene. Before the war, Standard had depended on the Prairie Oil and Gas Company for its supply, but military needs diverted Prairie's crude to the refineries along the Atlantic seaboard. To obtain a reliable source of crude oil, Stewart acquired 33 percent of Midwest Refining Company of Wyoming, in 1920. A half interest in the Sinclair Pipe Company was purchased in 1921, for $16.4 million in cash, improving transportation capacity. Sinclair's 2,900 miles of pipeline ran from north Texas to Chicago, encompassed almost 6,000 wells, and ran through oil-rich Wyoming.

Standard bought an interest in the Pan American Petroleum & Transport Company in 1925. The interest, costing $37.6 million, was the largest oil consolidation in the history of the industry, giving Standard (Indiana) access to one of the world's largest tanker fleets and entry into oilfields in Mexico, Venezuela, and Iraq. In 1929 Standard (Indiana) acquired another chunk of Pan American stock through a stock swap, bringing its total ownership of Pan American to 81 percent.

Pan American also introduced Standard to the American Oil Company, of Baltimore, Maryland. Started by the Blaustein family, American Oil marketed most of Pan American's oil in the eastern United States and was 50 percent owned by Pan American and 50 percent owned by the Blausteins. The Blausteins were initiators of the first measuring gasoline pump and inventors of the high-octane Amoco-Gas that reduced engine knocking.

Although expensive, these investments proved to be sound; by 1929, the Depression notwithstanding, Standard Oil (Indiana) was second only to Standard Oil (New Jersey) as a buyer of crude oil. Equally profitable as a supplier, the company's net earnings for 1929 were $78.5 million after taxes.

In 1929 Stewart was followed as CEO by Edward G. Seubert, who continued to strengthen Standard's crude oil supply. With an eye to future supply security, Seubert shifted the emphasis to buying and developing crude oil-producing properties like McMan Oil and Gas Company, a 1930 purchase that provided 10,000 barrels daily. Also in 1930, Standard acquired both the remaining 50 percent interest in the Sinclair Pipe Line Company and the Sinclair Crude Oil Purchasing Company for $72.5 million, giving it control over one of the country's largest pipeline systems and crude oil buying agencies. These subsidiaries now became the Stanolind Pipe Line Company and the Stanolind Crude Oil Purchasing Company; they were joined in 1931 by the Stanolind Oil & Gas Company, a newly organized subsidiary absorbing several smaller ones.

In 1929 a retail venture called the Atlas Supply Company, which was co-organized with five other Standard firms, had been organized to sell automobile tires and other accessories nationwide. The Great Depression, however, made competition fierce by the end of 1930. Even worse conditions threatened after the largest oilfield in history was found in east Texas in late 1930. The new field caused production to rise quickly to a daily average of 300,000 barrels in 1931, glutting the market. Ruthless price-cutting followed. Standard (Indiana) did not engage in this practice, preferring instead to curtail exploration and drilling activities. As a result, only 49.9 billion barrels were produced in 1931, as against 55.1 billion the year before, and the company's 13 domestic facilities operated well below capacity. The 45,073 employees worked on construction projects, and accepted wage cuts and part-time employment to minimize layoffs. The flow of inexpensive crude oil continued, often in excess of limits set by state regulatory bodies; gas sales were accompanied by premiums including candy, ash trays, and cigarette lighters. Track-side stations, where gasoline was pumped from the tank car into the customer's automobile, posed another price-cutting threat. Also prevalent were cooperatives organized by farmers, who would buy tank cars of gasoline for distribution among members to save money. These conditions caused 1932 earnings to reach only $16.5 million, down from $17.5 million in 1931.

In 1932 Standard decided to sell Pan American's foreign interests to Standard Oil (New Jersey). These properties cost Standard Oil (New Jersey) slightly less than $48 million cash plus about 1.8 million shares of Standard Oil (New Jersey) stock.

By 1934 the worst of the Depression was over. Activities in Texas led the Stanolind Oil & Gas Company to the Hastings field, which held 43 producing wells by the end of 1935. Also in 1935, more oil-producing acreage in east Texas came with Stanolind Oil & Gas Company's $42 million purchase of the properties of Beaumont-based Yount-Lee Oil Company, an acquisition that helped Stanolind Oil & Gas to increase its daily average production to 68,965 barrels.

During the 1930s overproduction began to threaten, and federal and state governments tried to curb oil production with heavy taxes. Standard felt the bite in Iowa's 1935 chain-store tax, which could not be justified by its service stations' profit margin. Therefore, the company turned back leased stations to their owners, and leased company-owned stations to independent operators, to be operated as separate outlets. By the following July, all 11,685 Standard (Indiana) service stations were independently operated and the company was once more primarily a producer distributing oil at wholesale prices. This move spurred the newly independent entrepreneurs, whose increased sales helped to achieve a net profit for Standard of $30.2 million for 1935.

FOREIGN EXPLORATION, DOMESTIC REORGANIZATION AT MID-CENTURY

When Standard reached its 50th year in 1939, during World War II, its research chemists were working to improve the high-octane fuels needed for military and transport planes. Standard's engineers cooperated with other companies to build the pipelines necessary for oil transportation. By 1942, the "Big Inch" pipeline carried a daily load of 300,000 barrels of crude from Texas to the East Coast, where most of it was used to support the war effort. Loss of manpower and government steel restrictions curbed operations, yet the company produced 47 million barrels of crude and purchased about 102 million barrels from outside sources. Other wartime products from Standard plants included paraffin wax coatings for military food rations, toluene (the main ingredient for TNT), butane, and butylene for aviation gasoline and synthetic rubber.

On January 1, 1945, Seubert retired as president and chief executive officer of the company. He left behind him 33,244 employees, sales of crude oil topping the 1944 figure by 37.1 percent, and a gross income of $618.9 million. Seubert was succeeded as chairman and CEO by Robert E. Wilson, formerly president of Pan American Petroleum & Transport Company, and Alonzo W. Peake became president. Peake had been vice-president of production.

The management style instituted by Wilson and Peake differed from the centralized, solo authority Seubert preferred. The two men split the supervisory authority, with no overlap of direct authority. Wilson was responsible for finance, research and development, law, and industrial relations, while Peake's commitments

included refining, production, supply and transportation, and sales and long-range planning. Responsibility for operating subsidiaries was split between the two. The result was a decentralized organization, making for swifter, more cooperative decision making at all levels.

In 1948 Stanolind Oil & Gas formed a foreign exploration department to head exploration attempts in Canada and other countries. The new team spent more than $98 million by 1950, with Canada and the Gulf of Mexico its prime targets.

By 1952 Standard Oil (Indiana) was acknowledged as the nation's largest domestic oil company. It possessed 12 refineries able to market products in 41 states, plus almost 5,000 miles of crude oil gathering lines, 10,000 miles of trunk lines, and 1,700 miles of refined product pipelines. By 1951, gross income had reached $1.54 billion.

In 1955 Peake retired as president, to be succeeded by former Executive Vice-President Frank Prior, who inherited the problem of a decrease in allowable production days in the state of Texas, as a result of additions to oil reserves in the state. The rising amount of imported oil was another problem that surfaced during Peake's tenure. The total had swelled from 490,000 barrels per day in 1951 to 660,000 barrels in 1954.

Nevertheless, less expensive international exploration costs spurred Standard (Indiana) to again become active in the growing foreign oil arena that it had all but left in 1932 when it sold Pan American's foreign interests. To handle international land leasing and joint ventures, the company organized Pan American International Oil Corporation in New York, as a subsidiary of Pan American Petroleum. Foreign operations included exploration rights for 13 million acres in Cuba, obtained in 1955; a subsidiary company formed in Venezuela in 1958, for joint exploration of 180,000 acres with other companies; and 23 million acres obtained for exploration in Libya.

The traditional oil industry profit arrangement for international activities had been an even split between the company and the host government, although several firms had quietly bent the guidelines. Standard (Indiana) broke openly with this custom in a 1958 deal with the National Iranian Oil Company (NIOC), in which Standard (Indiana) split the profits evenly, then gave NIOC half of its own share, to which it added a $25 million bonus.

The late 1950s also saw domestic reorganization. In 1957 the company consolidated nine subsidiaries into four larger companies. Stanolind Oil & Gas Company became Pan American Petroleum Corporation, consolidating all Standard Oil (Indiana) crude oil and natural gas exploration and production. American Oil Pipe Line Company, a former subsidiary of American Oil, was merged into Service Pipe Line Company (which had been known as Stanolind Pipe Line Company until 1950), focused on oil transport. Crude oil and natural gas purchasing operations were combined to form the Indiana Oil Purchasing Company; and Amoco Chemicals Corporation consolidated all chemical activities into a single organization. Total income for 1957 was about $2 billion.

CHANGES UNDER CEO SWEARINGEN: SIXTIES AND SEVENTIES

In 1960 company President John Swearingen succeeded Prior as chief executive officer, the chairmanship being left vacant. Swearingen turned both domestic and foreign operations over to subsidiaries, making Standard Oil (Indiana) entirely a holding company. Operating assets were transferred to the American Oil Company, into which the Utah Oil Refining Company also was merged. American Oil's responsibilities now included the manufacture, transport, and sale of all company petroleum products in 45 states, although limited marketing operations in three other states also were maintained. This consolidation allowed the company to develop a national image and provided more efficiency in staff use and storage and transport flexibility. Coverage being national, the company was able to advertise nationally and demand better rates from ground and air transporters.

Standard (Indiana) also became concerned with product trade names. The 1911 breakup had left several former Standard (New Jersey) subsidiaries in different areas of the country with the Standard Oil name and rights to the associated trademarks. American Oil thus had the right to use the Standard name only in the 15 midwestern states that had been the company's original territory. Thus, in 1957, the word *American,* together with the Standard Oil (Indiana) logo, was used in all other states. Since a five-letter name was easier for motorists to note, in 1961 the company began to replace the brand name American with Amoco, the name first coined by American Oil's original owners for the high-octane, antiknock gasoline that had powered the Charles Lindbergh transatlantic flight. Familiar within the company since the 1945 organization of Amoco Chemicals Corporation, "Amoco" was used increasingly on products and by subsidiaries, until, by 1971, major subsidiaries everywhere had "Amoco" in their names.

In 1961 Standard's total income reached almost $2.1 billion, yielding net earnings of $153.9 million. Continuing with methodical reorganization, Swearingen oversaw the expansion and modernization of the company's domestic refining capacity as well as 11 of its 14 catalytic cracking units. An aggressive marketing program featured large, strategically placed retail outlets, plus the addition of Avis car rental privileges to the credit card services that had been in operation since the early 1930s. By the end of 1966 there were 5.5 million cardholders, encouraging American Oil to go national with its motor club.

Because only 8 percent of its assets was located overseas, Standard (Indiana) still lacked a large foreign market for crude oil. Swearingen moved swiftly to close the gap. By 1964 foreign explorations were taking place in Mozambique, Indonesia, Venezuela, Argentina, Colombia, and Iran. Refining and marketing also were flourishing, through the acquisition of a 25,000-barrel-per-day refinery near Cremona, Italy, and about 700 Italian service stations. About 250 service stations also were opened in Australia in 1961, along with a 25,000-barrel-per-day refinery. Other foreign refineries were to be found in West Germany, England, Pakistan, and the West Indies. In 1967 Standard began production in the Persian Gulf Cyrus field, by which time the huge El Morgan field in the Gulf of Suez was producing 45,000 barrels daily.

The market for Standard's chemical products also increased during the mid-1960s. To keep pace with demand for the raw materials used in polyester fiber and film, the company built a new facility at Decatur, Alabama, in 1965, adding another in Texas City, Texas, a year later. There were also 641 retail chemical fertilizer outlets in the Midwest and the South. The popularity of polystyrene for packaging also grew. All of these advances ensured profitability; overall chemical sales rose to $158 million by the end of 1967, on total revenues of almost $3.6 billion.

Fuel shortages and the wave of OPEC price rises, nationalizations, and takeovers of the early 1970s underlined the importance of oil exploration. Swearingen's strategy was to accumulate as much domestic exploration acreage as possible before other companies acted, while organizing production in developing foreign markets that were not too competitive.

To capitalize on concern about air pollution, the company introduced a 91-octane lead-free gasoline in 1970 at a cost in excess of $100 million. Although motorists were initially reluctant to accept the 2 cent-per-gallon price rise, the 1973 appearance of catalytic converters on new cars assured the success of the fuel.

Environmental matters came to the fore again in 1978, when an Amoco International Oil Company tanker, the *Amoco Cadiz,* suffered steering failure during a storm and ran aground off the French coast, leaking about 730,000 gallons of oil into the sea. The huge oil spill cost $75 million to clean up and left its mark on the area's tourist trade as well as its ecosystem. The French government brought a $300 million lawsuit against Amoco that eventually led to a $128 million judgment against Amoco. Amoco appealed the ruling, but the U.S. Circuit Court of Appeals in Chicago not only upheld the judgment but increased it to $281 million. Amoco chose not to appeal this ruling and paid the French government $243 million and the affected Brittany communities $38 million.

In late December 1978 the shah of Iran was overthrown, and Standard (Indiana) hurriedly closed its Iranian facility and evacuated American staff members after all American employees of Amoco Iran Oil Company received death threats. The year 1978 had seen record-breaking production in Iran, and its loss resulted in a 35 percent production decrease in the company's overseas operations. Despite these turbulent events, net income was $1.5 billion in 1971, on total revenues of $20.19 billion.

By the end of the 1970s, chemical production accounted for about 7 percent of company earnings. To gain more visibility with consumers, Standard (Indiana) began to stress end-product manufacture as well as the production of ingredients used in manufacturing processes. The trend had begun in 1968, when polypropylene manufacturer Avisun Corporation was purchased by Amoco Chemicals Corporation from Sun Oil Company. The $80 million price tag included Patchoque-Plymouth Company, maker of polypropylene carpet backing. By 1986 a 100-color line plus improved stain resistance made Amoco Fabrics & Fibers Company's petrochemical-based Genesis carpeting a serious competitor of the stain-resistant carpeting offered by du Pont. Other strategies focused on market stimulation for basic industrial products. Since this required specialized marketing skills, the company divided its chemical operations among four subsidiaries.

NAME CHANGE AND REORGANIZATION: EIGHTIES AND NINETIES

In 1983 John Swearingen retired as chairman of the board. In his stead came Richard W. Morrow, who had been president of Amoco Chemicals Corporation from 1974 until 1978, before assuming the Standard (Indiana) presidency in 1978. In 1985 Standard Oil Company (Indiana) changed its name to Amoco

Corporation. Morrow also presided over the 1988 acquisition of Dome Petroleum, Ltd., of Canada, which was later merged into Amoco Canada. Dome, owning 28.7 million acres of undeveloped, arctic region land, improved Amoco's oil and gas reserves. The Dome purchase was hard-won, costing Amoco $4.2 billion. Other chances to expand oil and gas exploration in 1988 came with the acquisition of Tenneco Oil Company's Rocky Mountain properties, for approximately $900 million.

Amoco Corporation began the 1990s with record revenues of $31.58 billion and net income of $1.91 billion. By 1990, the need for raw materials had expanded internationally, moving strongly toward Europe and the Far East. Joint ventures in Brazil, Mexico, South Korea, and Taiwan met the growing demand for polyester fibers, helping to generate about 35 percent of business overseas.

H. Laurence Fuller took over as chairman in 1991 amid a downturn in Amoco profits owing to weakening demand for petroleum products and reduced prices caused by the recession. Revenues fell to $28.3 billion in 1991 and to $26.22 billion in 1992, while net income declined to $1.17 billion and $850 million, respectively. Fuller aimed not only to turn around the company's fortunes but also to overtake Exxon, the top U.S. oil company, in profitability. Fuller began this effort with a 1992 restructuring intended to reduce costs and improve efficiency. Approximately 8,500 employees were axed, contributing to $600 million in savings. Exploration operations were cut back from a wildcatting strategy spread out over more than 100 countries to a targeted search for oil and gas in 20 countries with proven reserves. China became a prime target area; after establishing an offshore drilling operation in 1987, Amoco signed a deal in 1992 to become the first foreign company to explore the Chinese mainland, thought to hold more than 20 billion barrels of oil.

This restructuring served as prelude to an even larger reorganization effort initiated in 1994. A total of 4,500 more jobs would be cut over the next two years, with projected savings of $1.2 billion each year. Amoco's organizational structure was completely overhauled. The three major subsidiaries (Amoco Production Company, Amoco Oil Company, and Amoco Chemical Company) that had been responsible for the three major areas of operation were replaced by a decentralized structure with 17 business groups divided into three sectors: exploration and production, petroleum products, and chemicals. A Shared Services organization was created to share the resources of Amoco's support operations.

Amoco's chemical operations were overhauled during these restructurings by shedding such weak areas as oil well chemicals and by increasing expenditures in fast-growing areas such as polyester. One result was that profits from Amoco's chemical sector increased from $68 million in 1991 to $574 million in 1994 thanks in large part to its 40 percent share of the world market in paraxylene and purified terephthalic acid, both used to make polyester, the demand for which grew dramatically, especially in Asia.

New product expenditures also were bolstered during this period. With demand for alternative and cleaner-burning fuels on the rise, Amoco introduced Crystal Clear Ultimate, a cleaner-burning premium gasoline, and test-marketed compressed natural gas for use by fleet operators. Also tested were shared service stations that offered Amoco gas and fast food (from McDonald's and Burger King), or such services as dry cleaning (DryClean U.S.A.). These tests were so successful that Amoco planned to roll out 100 such units in 1995 at a cost of $100 million.

In 1994, Amoco made one of its largest natural gas finds off Trinidad and Tobago. The company embarked on a drive to become a leader in natural gas-powered electricity generation, creating Amoco Power Resources Corporation to pursue this venture and purchasing a 10 percent interest in electricity facilities in Trinidad and Tobago.

With the cost of oil and gas exploration soaring and lean operations not able to withstand the failure of a risky venture, more oil companies turned to joint ventures in the early and mid-1990s to spread the risk. Amoco was a member of a ten-company consortium that signed an agreement in 1994 with the Republic of Azerbaijan to develop oilfields in the Caspian Sea. Also in 1994 Amoco joined with rivals Shell Oil and Exxon to finance a $1 billion offshore oil platform in the Gulf of Mexico, to be the world's deepest. In 1995, Shell and Amoco created a limited partnership to develop oilfields in the Permian Basin area of west Texas and southeast New Mexico. In 1997, Amoco partnered with the Argentina oil company Bridas Corp. to form Pan American Energy, an exploration and production company that planned to conduct operations in Argentina, Brazil, Paraguay, and Uruguay.

The middle and late 1990s also were marked by continued divestitures. In 1995, the company sold its motor club business to a subsidiary of Montgomery Ward and its credit card operations to Associates First Capital Corporation, a Ford subsidiary. Two years later, it announced a major divestiture program, designed to shed nonfundamental properties and allow a tighter focus on core assets. The company sold Amoco Gas Co.,

a gas pipeline and processing unit in Texas, to Tejas Gas Corp. The same year, the company sold a large portion of its domestic exploration and production assets, including oil and gas properties in Oklahoma; upstream oil and gas operations in Colorado; production properties in Wyoming, Montana, Colorado, and North Dakota; and coal-bed methane reserves in Alabama's Black Warrior Basin.

BP AMOCO: AN ENERGY POWERHOUSE IN THE LATE 20TH CENTURY

The British Petroleum–Amoco merger was finalized at the end of 1998. The new company, named BP Amoco p.l.c., was 60 percent owned by BP shareholders and was headed by BP's CEO Sir John Browne. Amoco's former CEO, Laurance Fuller, was co-chairman of the board, an office he shared with BP Chairman Peter Sutherland. BP shareholders owned 60 percent of the company. The merger served a dual purpose for both BP and Amoco. In the short term, it reduced costs by eliminating areas of overlap between the two organizations, most notably, in the reduction of approximately 10,000 jobs. In the long term, the pooling of BP's and Amoco's assets and revenues allowed the company to finance more development and take on larger projects.

The oil giant's frenetic growth did not stop with the merger. Just a few months after closing the Amoco deal, the company announced another major acquisition: Atlantic Richfield Co. (Arco). Arco, which was based in Los Angeles, had been in the oil business since 1866, longer than either British Petroleum or Amoco. The company operated refineries and a 1,700-unit chain of gas stations in the western United States. It also held major oil and gas reserves, most of which were in Alaska. Together, in fact, BP Amoco and Arco would have controlled almost 70 percent of the oil production in Alaska, a degree of control that made the Federal Trade Commission (FTC) uncomfortable. The FTC refused to approve the merger until the company agreed to sell off Arco's Alaskan holdings, and the deal was delayed for months before finally closing in the spring of 2000.

Meanwhile, BP Amoco was pursuing still another acquisition. In March 2000, the company agreed to purchase Burmah Castrol, a U.K. lubricants group. Burmah Castrol was the maker of Castrol brand motor oil, one of the world's best-selling car motor oils. The company also manufactured chemicals used in the foundry, steel, and construction industries. The acquisition, which was finalized in mid-2000, gave BP Amoco the second largest market share in lubricants in Europe.

In addition, like Amoco and Arco, it allowed the company to reduce costs by eliminating redundant jobs.

The year 2000 also marked a major change in corporate identity. Known in the two years since the merger as BP Amoco, a marriage of two strong trade names, the company shed "Amoco" from its name, becoming simply "BP p.l.c." The well-known Amoco name and logo were replaced with a new BP logo and color scheme: a green and yellow sunburst. Industry analysts speculated that the changes were intended to help the company move away from its longstanding identity as an "oil company" and reposition itself as an "energy company," one with operations in oil, natural gas, and solar power.

Browne's aggressive acquisition strategy proved to be both well timed and well executed. The last years of the 20th century were marked by rapidly increasing prices in both crude oil and natural gas, hikes that paid off handsomely for BP. At the same time, the company began to realize the large cost reductions promised by its acquisitions. In 2000, the company made $12 billion in pretax profits, a record for a U.K. company.

STREAMLINING OPERATIONS: 2001–04

During the first half of the decade, BP sharpened its focus by shedding operations. In early 2001 the company revealed plans to sell its plastic fabrications arm, as well as its BP Amoco Fabrics & Fibres business unit, which collectively generated about $1 billion per year. Around the same time, Madison Oil agreed to acquire BP's ARCO Turkey Inc. business for $3.4 billion. Following the acquisition of Burmah Castrol in early 2000, BP moved forward with plans to divest that company's specialty chemicals operations, beginning with the sale of Foseco Inc. to Cinven in September 2001.

More significant developments unfolded in 2002. That year, E.ON and BP struck a $1.6 billion deal with Petro-Canada for Veba Oil's natural gas and oil exploration and production operations. BP then proceeded to acquire full ownership of Veba. The company secured a 51 percent stake in February for $1.6 billion, and acquired the remainder from E.ON in June for $2.4 billion. The following month, BP sold its Gelsenberg subsidiary for $2.3 billion.

Divestitures unfolded at a rapid pace in 2003. That year, BP sold numerous refineries, plants, and retail operations throughout the United States, Canada, Singapore, Central Europe, and Germany, as well as ownership stakes in various projects. Among the more notable transactions were the $275 million sale of the company's

interest in Indonesia's Tangguh liquefied natural gas project, and the $250 million sale of its stake in Kaltim Prima Coal.

BP also scaled back its operations in the United Kingdom during 2003. That year, the company shuttered its Coryton refinery's lubricants operation, as well as two acid manufacturing plants in Hull. In addition, BP's 96.14 percent stake in the North Sea's Forties oilfield was sold, along with gas fields in the Southern North Sea.

BP kicked off 2004 by generating $1.65 billion from the sale of its 2 percent stake in PetroChina Company Ltd. Another $700 million came from the sale of BP's stake in Sinopec. In August, the company merged the automotive lubricant operations of Petrolub International Co. Ltd. and BP Japan, forming a new enterprise named BP Castrol KK that held an estimated 7 percent of the Japanese automotive lubricant market.

DIFFICULT TIMES: 2005–07

A number of significant developments unfolded at BP in 2005. In March, an explosion at the company's Texas City refinery in the United States, considered to be one of the nation's worst refinery disasters, resulted in 15 deaths and 170 injuries. BP ended the year by acquiring a 20 percent interest in China Aviation Oil for $44 million and selling its Innovene chemicals business to the United Kingdom's Ineos Group Holdings p.l.c. for approximately $9 billion.

On the heels of the disaster at its Texas refinery, BP continued to face difficulties in 2006. That year, the company contended with two oil spills in Prudhoe Bay, Alaska, that resulted from corroded pipelines. In the United States, Robert A. Malone was named as head of BP America midway through the year. In July, BP CEO Lord John Browne announced plans to retire at the end of 2008. Significant deals in 2006 included the $1.3 billion sale of producing properties on the Gulf of Mexico's Outer Continental Shelf to Apache Corp.

In January 2007, BP announced that John Browne would step down as CEO sooner than planned. Exploration and production head Tony Hayward, who had joined the company as a geologist at age 25, was chosen to succeed Browne in July. However, the succession occurred earlier than planned when Browne resigned in May. His departure occurred amid controversies surrounding a sexual relationship with a younger man, which Browne admitted to being untruthful about in court.

Moving forward, Hayward, whose management style was considered to be more team-focused than Browne's, made plans to simplify the company's organizational structure. In addition, he had numerous challenges to contend with in his new role. By this time BP had settled approximately 1,350 lawsuits surrounding the refinery disaster in Texas City. However, hundreds of civil suits still remained. In addition, allegations that the company's BP Products North America business had engaged in illegal propane trading had resulted in a criminal investigation by the Commodity Futures Trading Commission. Finally, BP also was being investigated by the Department of Justice over alleged gasoline trading irregularities, as well as the aforementioned Alaskan oil spills.

In order to settle the illegal propane trading allegations, as well as alleged environmental violations surrounding the Alaskan pipeline leaks and Texas refinery explosion, BP agreed to pay $373 million in restitution and fines to the Department of Justice in October 2007. Two months later, BP revealed plans to sell 71 company-owned gas stations, as well as five franchised locations, in south Florida, for anticipated proceeds of $200 million to $300 million.

CHALLENGES CONTINUE: 2008–09

BP's annual profits had fallen 22 percent in 2007, reaching $17.3 billion. This prompted Hayward to announce 5,000 job cuts in early 2008. The eliminations, some 60 percent of which were corporate positions, were expected to take place by mid-2009.

During 2008, BP struggled with its operations in Russia. Specifically, the company found itself at odds with its Russian partners in the joint venture TNK-BP over management and operational issues. BP subsequently found itself contending with everything from police raids to problems with workers' visas.

On April 14, 2009, BP celebrated its 100th anniversary. The company had achieved remarkable growth throughout a century filled with its share of challenges. Moving forward, BP faced a number of difficulties as it began its second century. In addition to dire economic conditions, in early 2009 the State of Alaska, the Justice Department, the U.S. Environmental Protection Agency, and the U.S. Department of Transportation filed civil lawsuits against the company's BP Exploration business in connection with the oil spills in Prudhoe Bay.

Geoffrey Jones and Gillian Wolf
Updated, April Dougal Gasbarre; Shawna Brynildssen;
Paul R. Greenland

PRINCIPAL SUBSIDIARIES

Abu Dhabi Marine Areas (37%); Abu Dhabi Petroleum Co. (24%); Amoco Caspian Sea Petroleum (British Virgin Islands); Atlantic 4 Holdings (U.S.A.; 38%); Atlantic LNG Company of Trinidad and Tobago (Trinidad and Tobago; 34%); Atlantic Richfield Co. (USA); BP America (USA); BP America Production Company (USA); BP Amoco Chemical Company (USA); BP Amoco Exploration (Amenas); BP Australia Capital Markets; BP Berau (Indonesia); BP Canada Energy; BP Canada Finance; BP Capital (Netherlands); BP Capital Markets America (USA); BP Capital Markets; BP Company North America (USA); BP Corporation North America (USA); BP Developments Australia; BP Egypt Co. (USA); BP Egypt Gas Co. (USA); BP Espana (Spain); BP Exploration (Alaska) Inc. (USA); BP Exploration (Angola); BP Exploration (Caspian Sea); BP Exploration (El Djazair) (Bahamas); BP Exploration Op. Co.; BP Finance Australia; BP Global Investments; BP Holdings North America (USA); BP International; BP Nederland; BP Norge (Norway); BP Oil Australia; BP Oil International; BP Oil New Zealand; BP Oil UK; BP Products North America (USA); BP Shipping; Burmah Castrol; BP Southern Africa (South Africa; 75%); BP Trinidad (LNG) (Netherlands); BP Trinidad and Tobago (U.S.A.; 70%); BP West Coast Products (USA); BP West Java (Indonesia); Britoil; Calvary Neftegaz Holdings BV (Netherlands; 49%); Deutsche BP (Germany); Jupiter Insurance; Lukarco (Netherlands; 46%); Pan American Energy (U.S.A.; 60%); Ruhr Oel (Germany; 50%); Shanghai Secco Petrochemical Co. (China; 50%); South Caucasus Pipeline Co. (Cayman Islands; 26%); Standard Oil Co. (USA); The Baku-Tbilisi-Ceylan Pipeline Co. (Cayman Islands; 30%); TNK-BP (British Virgin Islands; 50%).

PRINCIPAL COMPETITORS

Chevron Corp.; Exxon Mobil Corp.; Royal Dutch Shell p.l.c.

FURTHER READING

Bahree, Bhushan, Christopher Cooper, and Steve Liesman, "Bigger Oil: BP to Acquire Amoco in Huge Deal Spurred by Low Energy Prices," *Wall Street Journal,* August 12, 1998, p. A1.

Beck, Robert J., "State Companies Lead OGJ 100 World Reserves, Production List," *Oil and Gas Journal,* September 28, 1992.

"Big Problems: British Petroleum," *Economist,* February 8, 1992.

"BP After Horton," *Economist,* July 4, 1992.

"BP Snaps Up Chinese Bargain," *Weekly Petroleum Argus,* December 12, 2005.

Bush, Jason, "BP: Roughed Up in Russia; The Oil Giant's Problems with Local Authorities Are Mounting," *Business Week,* June 16, 2008.

Chelminski, Rudolph, *Superwreck: Amoco, the Shipwreck That Had to Happen,* New York: Morrow, 1987.

Cook, James, "First-Rate Company," *Forbes,* May 1, 1989, pp. 84–85.

Cowell, Alan, "BP's Chief Quits over Revelations About Personal Life," *New York Times,* May 2, 2007.

Dedmon, Emmett, *Challenge and Response: A Modern History of Standard Oil Company (Indiana),* Chicago: Mobium Press, 1984.

Fairhall, David, *The Wreck of the Amoco Cadiz,* New York: Stein and Day, 1980.

Ferrier, R.W., *The History of the British Petroleum Company* (Vol. 1), Cambridge: Cambridge University Press, 1982.

Giddens, Paul Henry, *Standard Oil Company (Indiana): Oil Pioneer of the Middle West,* New York: Arno Press, 1976.

Guyon, Janet, "When John Browne Talks, Big Oil Listens," *Fortune,* July 5, 1999, p. 116.

Jones, Geoffrey, *The State and the Emergence of the British Oil Industry,* London: Macmillan, 1981.

Kemp, Peter, and James Batty, "Howard Takes on Browne's Mixed Legacy As BP's New Boss," *Oil Daily,* May 3, 2007.

Knott, David, "BP Sharpening Focus on Improved Shareholder Value, Efficiency," *Oil and Gas Journal,* July 8, 1996, pp. 22–26.

———, "British Petroleum Maps Strategy for Continued Gains," *Oil and Gas Journal,* March 22, 1993, pp. 25–29.

Mack, Toni, "Catching Up to Exxon," *Forbes,* March 13, 1995, pp. 64, 66.

Manor, Robert, "British Petroleum Sells U.S. Subsidiary for $9 Billion," *Chicago Tribune,* October 7, 2005.

Melcher, Richard A., Peter Burrows, and Tim Smart, "Remaking Big Oil: The Desperate Rush to Slash Costs," *Business Week,* August 8, 1994, pp. 20–21.

O'Connor, Brian, "Dealmaker Browne May Dazzle with Another Lightning Strike," *Daily Mail,* November 22, 2001, p. 77.

"An Oil Major Redefines Its Role," *Petroleum Economist,* February 1, 2001, p. 3.

Palmeri, Christopher, "A Good Match in the Oil Patch," *Forbes,* September 21, 1998, p. 88.

Strauss, Gary, and Thor Valdmanis, "BP, Amoco Nozzle Up: Oil Companies Pump Out $50 Billion Merger Deal," *USA Today,* August 12, 1998, p. 1B.

Therrien, Lois, "Amoco: Running Smoother on Less Gas," *Business Week,* February 15, 1993, pp. 110–12.

Werdigier, Julia, and Stephen Labaton, "BP, Under New Chief, to Pay a Big Settlement," *New York Times,* October 26, 2007.

White, Gary, "US Sues BP over Prudhoe Bay Oil Spill," *Telegraph,* April 1, 2009.

"Whittle-Down Economics," *Oil and Gas Investor,* November 1992, pp. 43–46.

Yerak, Rebecca, "Plugging the Drain at BP Oil," *Cleveland Plain Dealer,* January 26, 1993.

BRIO AB

Box 305, Nordenskioeldsgatan 6
Malmö, S-201 23
Sweden
Telephone: (+46 0479) 190 00
Fax: (+46 0479) 193 33
Web site: http://www.brio.net

Public Company (Majority Owned by Proventus Industrier AB)
Incorporated: 1884
Employees: 396
Sales: SEK 892.5 million ($104 million) (2008)
Stock Exchanges: Stockholm
Ticker Symbol: BRIO B
NAICS: 339932 Game, Toy, and Children's Vehicle Manufacturing

■ ■ ■

BRIO AB is the company behind one of the world's best-known children's toy brands. The Swedish company continues to produce its BRIO wooden train sets, as well as other toys targeting preschoolers. BRIO remains one of the world's leading producers of wooden toys. Through its BRIO Business Area, the company also produces lines of baby products and toys under the Carena and Simo brands, in addition to the core BRIO brand. This unit also markets the company's products to the Nordic, German, French, Belgium, U.K., and Japanese markets. In the United States, the company's distribution is conducted through a partnership with K'Nex Industries. The company's Scanditoy Business Area distributes branded and licensed toys to the Nordic market. BRIO's Partner Business Area oversees a network of BRIO-branded independent franchise shops, largely in Norway. BRIO has struggled to maintain a presence in the global toy market as traditional toys have faced enormous pressure from new generation toys and games, including electronic gaming devices. Despite successive restructuring and new product development efforts, BRIO continued to face mounting problems in the early 2000s. In 2008, for example, the company posted a net loss of SEK 75.5 million (approximately $10 million) on sales of SEK 892.5 million ($104 million). At the beginning of 2009, the company hired a new CEO, Andreas Sbrodiglia. BRIO is listed on the Stockholm Stock Exchange, but is majority controlled by private-equity group Proventus Industrier AB.

COMPANY ORIGINS

The roots of the BRIO organization can be traced to 1878 when 17-year-old Ivar Bengtsson invested his savings of 77 riksdaler (the Swedish currency of the time) in the purchase of woven slatted baskets to sell in neighboring Denmark. The youthful venture was a success, and by 1884 Bengtsson and his wife, Sissa, were operating a small basket factory out of their cottage in Boalt, just outside Osby, Sweden. By 1902 the basket company required larger facilities, and the company was moved to Osby, an expanding community in the province of Skåne. Osby's position on the main railway line in the country made it an excellent location for the growing wholesaling concern because it allowed Bengtsson to distribute his products across the region.

COMPANY PERSPECTIVES

Our Vision: To be the world's best-loved family brand. Our Mission: To create products for active, modern parents who want the best for their children.

Declaration of Independence: There are those who say that you can't eat out once you have children. That you'll never have time to read. That you can't travel. That you'll never dance on the tables again. There are those who say that you'll never wear white. That you'll put on a track suit every morning and never buy another pair of stilettos. There are those who say that the future looks bleak. We beg to disagree. We know that it isn't always easy to juggle family life with work, friends, ball games, shopping and everything else you want to do. But at BRIO, our goal is to make that life easier, fun-filled and joyful.

With its new location and facilities, the Ivar Bengtsson Basket Company was able to greatly expand its product line. The 1907 catalog lists more than 170 articles available for order. Among these items was the Göinge Horse, a traditional wooden pull toy. This small, painted horse on wheels marked BRIO's first entry into the wooden toy business that would become the company's hallmark product line.

In 1908, at the age of 47, Bengtsson decided to turn his business over to his sons, Viktor, Anton, and Emil Ivarsson. Although the three boys were still young, Bengtsson hoped that by giving them the management of the company they would be dissuaded from joining the waves of Swedish youths who were then immigrating to the United States. His ploy worked. The boys stayed in Sweden, and the company name was changed to BRIO for Bröderna Ivarsson of Osby (Ivarsson Brothers of Osby). The company continued to expand its range of product offerings so that by 1914 the BRIO catalog offered 6,000 items for sale by mail order and traveling salesmen. Product types included toys, ceramics, glass, and porcelain among other diverse merchandise. BRIO also opened a small retail shop, called the "15-öre Bazaar," to sell the company's products directly to Osby consumers.

BRIO BRANDS AND BARBIE: 1930–70

BRIO opened a new phase in its history in 1930 when the bold BRIO trademark was painted onto the side of two wooden cars distributed by the company. The development of the BRIO brand would become key to the growth of the company over the next 70 years. Some five years later the company lent its name to a line of baby carriages manufactured by another Osby firm but distributed by BRIO. By the mid-1930s, when BRIO was officially incorporated as a limited liability corporation, the company was employing 150 people and had achieved annual sales of SEK 4.3 million. BRIO's product line had begun to focus on the wooden toys and baby carriages that would become the core of the company's business.

Although BRIO had been placing its brand name on products distributed by the company since the 1930s, it was only after World War II that BRIO began its own manufacturing concern with the opening of a baby carriage factory in 1947. By the late 1950s the postwar baby boom had come into full swing and BRIO baby carriages became one of the best-selling brands in the country. This success was cemented in 1959 with the introduction of the Sylvana model, the first baby carriage in the world to be equipped with a fully welded collapsible frame.

BRIO toys received worldwide recognition with the introduction of the BRIO Labyrinth in 1946. The wooden maze toy, with its distinctive tilting box, was distributed throughout the world during the 1950s and 1960s and was largely responsible for the original dissemination of the BRIO brand name. Following the success of Labyrint, BRIO began to expand its line of wooden toys for the domestic and international markets. The 1950s saw the introduction of Bygg-BRIO, a wooden construction toy that was the predecessor to BRIO MEC, and, most significantly, the BRIO Wooden Railway, which was to become the best-selling wooden railway in the world and BRIO's most popular toy ever.

The 1960s were marked by growth in BRIO's importing and wholesaling business, which increased dramatically in 1963 when BRIO obtained the Scandinavian distribution rights to a new American fashion doll, Barbie. The attraction of this small plastic doll to little girls was apparently universal as total sales for BRIO jumped by over 30 percent in a single year thanks to the Barbie phenomenon. In 1964 the company set up new subsidiaries in Denmark and Finland, followed six years later by a Norwegian subsidiary, largely in order to distribute the fashion doll. Although sales for Barbie tapered off in following years, the doll remained a substantial part of the BRIO import unit through the 1970s and a factor in the company's sales in Norway through the 1990s.

KEY DATES

1884: Ivar Bengtsson establishes a factory making baskets in Osby, Sweden.

1908: Bengtsson turns over control of the company to his sons in order to prevent them from immigrating to the United States; the company changes its name to BRIO (Brothers Ivarsson of Osby).

1946: BRIO launches the BRIO Labyrinth and begins to focus on producing wooden toys and strollers, and toy distribution.

1963: BRIO acquires distribution rights to the Barbie brand in Scandinavia.

1977: BRIO founds a subsidiary in the United States.

1985: BRIO goes public on the Stockholm Stock Exchange.

2004: Amid falling sales and losses, the Ivarsson family sells 42 percent of the company to Proventus.

2009: BRIO brings in new CEO and announces an "acute liquidity shortage."

BRIO WOODEN TOYS FOR THE EXPORT MARKET: 1970–90

While in the domestic and Nordic markets the center of BRIO's business was toy wholesaling and baby carriages. Beginning in the 1970s, the export of BRIO brand wooden trains, construction toys, and preschool toys to the rest of Europe and North America became a substantial contributor to total revenues. Previously, BRIO toys had been exported via distribution agreements with toy wholesalers but in 1974 small subsidiaries were opened in the United Kingdom and Germany mainly in order to market the company's wooden toys.

It was the opening of the U.S. subsidiary BRIO Corp. in 1977, however, that changed the nature of BRIO's toy business. BRIO Corp. was largely the product of its president, Peter Reynolds, and his determination to create a market for the company's high-quality toys. Reynolds began his career as a salesman for a variety of British food distributors but had moved to Milwaukee when he was hired by a British jigsaw puzzle company that was one of the five agents for BRIO products in the United States. When that company went bankrupt in 1975, Reynolds persuaded BRIO to let him use the Milwaukee warehouse to establish a U.S. subsidiary.

From the start, Reynolds had his own approach to the marketing of BRIO's wooden toys, believing that they would sell only because they were truly good toys and that his job consisted of convincing parents that good toys were important to their children's development. Key to Reynolds's marketing philosophy was his insistence that the small retail stores that had traditionally sold the wooden toys were the best venue for promoting good play value. Even after sales of BRIO toys started to take off in the United States, Reynolds refused to market his product to such large superstores as Toys "R" Us that were taking over the U.S. toy retail industry. This strategy allowed BRIO Corp. to maintain a close relationship with the owners of small toy boutiques who did not have to worry about price undercutting by the big chains.

The relationship with small toy stores was crucial to the marketing of BRIO toys because it permitted Reynolds to run educational campaigns instructing salespeople about the benefits of the products. "We need people who'll tell the story, not just show the product," Reynolds told the *Seattle Times*. The story that Reynolds wanted told was that BRIO toys promote good play by catering to the "whole" child, which includes the child's physical, social, and intellectual development. Reynolds's campaigns also stressed the value of the high-priced BRIO toys. "BRIO-trained retailers are able to educate customers about the concepts of open-ended toys and playthings as an investment. For example, a $50 set of wooden blocks is both open-ended and an investment because it captures the child's attention and imagination in different ways over the years. Such a toy, if played with for five years, costs only $10 a year—a wise, long-term purchase," Reynolds wrote in a column in *Playthings*.

Reynolds had to convince not only store owners and parents about the importance of good play but his bosses in Sweden as well. "They didn't really understand the importance of play. Consequently, they didn't understand the value of their toys," he explained to the *Milwaukee Journal*. If Reynolds's philosophy had not sold the parent company on the merits of his approach, his results would have. When Reynolds started the U.S. subsidiary, sales of BRIO toys in the United States were under $4 million and accounted for only a small percentage of BRIO's total sales. By 1991, U.S. sales had mounted to $14.6 million and represented over 50 percent of BRIO wooden toys sold worldwide. Reynolds's approach to marketing was adopted wholeheartedly by BRIO AB, which began to actively promote the "good play" value of the company's wooden toys.

In 1985 a Canadian subsidiary, BRIO Scanditoy, was opened to further grow North American sales.

Under the direction of Kate Baldwin, BRIO Scanditoy adopted the same approach to marketing that had spelled such a success for BRIO Corp., emphasizing the company's relationship to the toy boutiques that sold BRIO products. Canadian sales reached about 5 percent of BRIO's wooden toy sales by the 1990s.

DOMESTIC GROWTH IN THE EIGHTIES AND NINETIES

In addition to growth in the export of BRIO's wooden toys, in the Nordic region the company's toy and baby carriage business continued to expand. In the early 1980s BRIO AB won the distribution rights to the American board game Monopoly from Sweden's leading game company, Alga, and then proceeded to buy the Alga subsidiary from the Bonniers Company outright. In the mid-1980s BRIO obtained the rights to a number of very successful promotional toys, including Trivial Pursuit and My Little Pony, as well as reaching a distribution agreement with General Mills toys. The combined sales of these products caused the company's total income to rise to a record SEK 68.3 million on sales of SEK 1 billion in 1987.

The management and ownership of BRIO AB had remained in the Ivarsson family throughout the century. In 1985 the balance of ownership changed somewhat when the company issued an initial public offering of shares on the over-the-counter market of the Stockholm Stock Exchange. This offering came in conjunction with a share offering to employees that saw 60 percent of BRIO employees buying a stake in the company.

In the 1990s a number of BRIO brand product introductions, including plush toys, bath toys, and child-sized gardening tools, along with a 1992 distribution agreement with Hasbro, created record income of SEK 85 million on sales of SEK 1.52 billion in 1994.

After the impressive results of the early 1990s, the company suffered a decline in sales toward the mid-1990s. A sharp drop in the Swedish birthrate coupled with the loss of the Hasbro license damaged the company's baby carriage and wholesale business in the Nordic region, and in 1997 BRIO suffered a net loss of SEK 28 million, the largest loss in the company's history. Restructuring costs involved with the purchase of Plasto Bambola, a maker of high-quality plastic toys, also added to the company's financial difficulties. By 1998 it appeared likely that the general restructuring of the worldwide toy industry, which was undergoing dramatic consolidation, would force BRIO to make changes in the company's toy wholesaling business.

STRUGGLING FOR SURVIVAL

BRIO's troubles continued to build leading into the new century. The company's wholesale operations continued to decline as it lost more licenses, including the rights to distribute Mattel toys. Other areas of BRIO's business, particularly its nursery division that produced baby carriages and other baby products, slipped into losses during the 1990s. In order to restore that operation's growth, the company agreed to merge its BRIO Baby arm into a joint venture with Simo, a Norwegian stroller and baby products manufacturer, creating European Nursery Group.

The surge in interest in wooden toys in general, and the BRIO train line in particular provided some hope for the company. Yet BRIO missed out on the licensing rights to the highly popular *Thomas the Tank Engine* television series, and now faced its first serious rival producing a similar toy train line. Other companies jumped onto the wooden train bandwagon. Ikea, for one, launched its own wooden train set at a far lower price, yet at a similar quality level, to BRIO's own. In the United Kingdom, the Tesco supermarket did the same.

Whereas the company had been able to face down this sort of product challenge because of the inferior quality of its imitators, this new generation featured quality levels largely similar to BRIO's own line. Yet BRIO, which was slow in shifting its manufacturing to low-wage markets in Asia and elsewhere, found itself unable to meet the lower prices of its rivals.

With the global economy in a slump, BRIO found itself further exposed to the changing trends in the world's toy industry. The rising strength of discount department stores such as Wal-Mart and Target, as well as the growth of a number of specialist toy chains including Toys "R" Us, had captured the major share of the toy sector. By 2000 the independent toy retailer sector, BRIO's core distribution channel, was disappearing rapidly.

Meanwhile, the toy industry itself was changing, as the appeal of traditional toys waned in the surge of interest in new generation toys, particularly those linked to television series and films, especially the growth of the electronic gaming industry. BRIO had been slow to adapt to the changes in the market, and its new product development had been lukewarm at best.

NEW OWNERS AND OLD TROUBLES

BRIO's losses mounted. The group sold its stake in its U.K.-based BRIO Wonderland retail group in 2002. By

2003 the group, saddled with debt and facing mounting pressure from its banks, launched a further restructuring of its operations, including shedding some 20 percent of its payroll in favor of a shift to sourcing products from China. In 2004 the company sold off its Finnish toy operations as well.

That same year, the Ivarsson family agreed to sell 30 percent of the company, and 42 percent of voting rights, to private-equity group Proventus. The deal reduced the family's own stake to just 29 percent, for 39 percent of voting rights. Proventus brought in a new management team, led by Thomas Brautigam.

The company launched a new restructuring effort, including taking full control of European Nursery Group in 2004. In 2005 the group eliminated another 100 jobs, including shutting down its factory in Kille-berg, Sweden. In the United States, BRIO turned over its distribution to K'Nex Industries Inc. in 2006, while also selling its Polish operations that year.

A licensing deal with Disney buoyed the group's spirits in 2007. Yet the company's losses continued to mount, nearing SEK 53 million ($7.5 million) on turnover of SEK 930 million that year. The increasingly disastrous economic climate, however, placed the company under still greater pressure through 2008. By the end of that year, the company had phased out most of its franchised retail network in Sweden, retaining only its franchise base in Norway.

Proventus, which increased its stake in the company to 55 percent, brought in a new CEO, Andreas Sbrodiglia, at the beginning of 2009. Yet the company remained in dire condition, announcing a net loss of SEK 75.5 million ($10 million) on sales of SEK 892.5 million ($104 million) in 2008. By March 2009, the group was forced to announce that it faced an "acute liquidity shortage." Despite a rich heritage as one of Sweden's and the world's most popular toy brands, BRIO appeared in need of a new locomotive in order to ensure its survival as an independent toy company in the 21st century.

Hilary Gopnik
Updated, M. L. Cohen

PRINCIPAL SUBSIDIARIES

BRIO Leksaker; BRIO Toy; Alga; BRIO Barnvagnar; BRIO Lek & Lär; BRIO A/S (Denmark); BRIO OY (Finland); BRIO AS (Norway); BRIO Ltd. (UK); BRIO Corp. (USA); BRIO Scanditoy Inc. (Canada); BRIO SA (France); European Nursery Group AB.

PRINCIPAL OPERATING UNITS

BRIO Business Area; BRIO Partner Business Area; Scanditoy Business Area.

PRINCIPAL COMPETITORS

Nintendo Company Ltd.; Perfekta Enterprises Ltd.; Mattel Inc.; Namco Bandai Holdings Inc.; Sega Sammy Holdings Inc.; Hasbro Inc.; Konami Corp.; Sammy Corp.; Tomy Company Ltd.; Egmont Group; LEGO Group A/S.

FURTHER READING

"Brio AB Divests Polish Operations," *Nordic Business Report,* December 19, 2006.

"Brio Acquires Remaining 50% of European Nursery Group AS," *Nordic Business Report,* December 22, 2004.

"BRIO Beefs Up Three Major Toy Lines," *Playthings,* February 1993, p. 117.

Foster, Janine, and Otte Rosenkrantz, "Child's Play," *London Business Monthly Magazine,* June 1997, pp. 18–22.

George, Nicholas, "Brio Cuts 20% of Jobs and Looks to Asia," *Financial Times,* September 3, 2003, p. 29.

———, "Brio Ousts Chief Executive," *Financial Times,* December 15, 2004, p. 29.

———, "Brio's Toy Trains Hit the Buffers," *Financial Times,* August 29, 2003, p. 10.

———, "Proventus in Push for Brio," *Financial Times,* July 7, 2004, p. 22.

Israelson, David, "Little Engines of Wood Scale Heights in Toy Trade," *Toronto Star,* February 6, 1996, p. D1.

Newhouse, David, "Beanie Babies Cross Toyland's Great Divide," *Seattle Times,* December 21, 1997, p. E1.

Peerson, Brian, "A 'Royal' Concern," *Playthings,* September 1, 2008, p. 13.

Reynolds, Peter, "'Children First' Focus Helps Specialty Retails," *Playthings,* February 1989, p. 278.

Schmelz, Abigail, "Swedish Toy Maker Says Business Not Child's Play," *Journal of Commerce,* December 23, 1996, p. A5.

Sharma-Jensen, Geeta, "The Mantra of Mr. Brio," *Milwaukee Journal,* December 19, 1993, pp. D1–D2.

"Swedish Toy Maker Brio AB Signs Licence Agreement with Disney," *Nordic Business Report,* October 30, 2007.

"Swedish Toymaker Brio AB Streamlines Operations, Cuts 30 Jobs," *Nordic Business Report,* November 26, 2008.

"Swedish Toys Maker Brio AB Posts Operating Loss of SEK 44.8m, Close to 'Acute Liquidity Shortage,'" *Nordic Business Report,* February 17, 2009.

Weiskott, Maria, "Weaving Success," *Playthings,* May 2002, p. 12.

Bucyrus International, Inc.

———■———

1100 Milwaukee Avenue
South Milwaukee, Wisconsin 53172-2013
U.S.A.
Telephone: (414) 768-4400
Fax: (414) 768-4474
Web site: http://www.bucyrus.com

Public Company
Founded: 1880 as Bucyrus Foundry and Manufacturing
    Company
Incorporated: 1927 as Bucyrus-Erie Company
Employees: 7,200
Sales: $2.51 billion (2008)
Stock Exchanges: NASDAQ
Ticker Symbol: BUCY
NAICS: 333131 Mining Machinery and Equipment
    Manufacturing; 811310 Commercial and Industrial
    Machinery and Equipment (Except Automotive and
    Electronic) Repair and Maintenance

■ ■ ■

Bucyrus International, Inc., is one of the world's largest manufacturers of surface and underground mining equipment for the extraction of coal, oil sands, copper, iron ore, and other minerals. The company spent the first 126 years of its existence concentrating on surface mining equipment, where its principal products in the early 21st century are electric mining shovels, used mainly for loading mined materials into trucks; draglines, used primarily in surface coal mining to remove overburden (the rock and dirt above a coal seam); and

rotary blasthole drills, used to bore large holes in mineral deposits or rock for the placement of the explosives to loosen minerals at mining sites. Then in 2007 Bucyrus expanded into the production of a wide range of underground mining equipment through the acquisition of DBT GmbH. In addition to manufacturing original equipment at plants in Australia, China, Germany, Poland, and the United States, the company provides aftermarket replacement parts and service for this equipment, all of which carries the Bucyrus brand. A little less than half of the company's sales are derived in the United States, with Germany accounting for about 21 percent; Australia, 11 percent; Chile, 6 percent; and Africa and Canada, 4 percent each.

DIGGING IN: 1880–1921

The birth of the excavating machine industry in the United States was directly tied to the construction of the infrastructure spurred by the nation's rapidly expanding geographical boundaries during the 19th century. Dredging rivers, harbors, and canals and laying railroad lines required reliable and efficient digging equipment, and during the 1880s a fledgling U.S. excavating machinery industry rose to meet the need. In 1880 a prosperous Ohio business magnate named Daniel P. Eells saw the opportunity to create a profitable new business sideline for the many railroads to which he had business associations. By purchasing the idle Bucyrus Machine Company of Bucyrus, Ohio, Eells and his associates founded the Bucyrus Foundry and Manufacturing Company, which quickly began producing handcars, locomotive drive wheels, car wheels and axles, and related components for the expanding railroad industry.

COMPANY PERSPECTIVES

We will strive to be the preferred supplier in the mining industry by achieving continuous improvement in all facets of our business performance; consistently delivering reliable and competitive products/services which meet and exceed the expectations of our customers.

Eells's business took a decisive turn when both the Northern Pacific and Ohio Central Railroads placed orders for steam shovels for their railroad construction operations in 1882. By deploying a sales force and advertising in trade journals, by 1889 Bucyrus's annual output had risen to 24 shovels, and its No. 10 shovel was being hailed by an industry newspaper as "the largest and most powerful steam shovel ever built in this country." Within a year, steam shovels accounted for 80 percent of Bucyrus's business. Because the demand for its standard shovels and dredges was unpredictable, however, Bucyrus increasingly began developing a reputation as a designer/manufacturer of specialized excavating equipment for mining and public works projects.

In 1893, seeking to attract businesses to southeastern Wisconsin, the county of South Milwaukee offered Bucyrus something it could not refuse: a 15-acre plant site and $50,000 toward construction of a new factory. Bucyrus signed on, and Eells and associates decided to transfer the company's assets to a new entity, Bucyrus Steam Shovel and Dredge Company of Wisconsin. Despite the new expanded facilities, by 1895 a national depression and Bucyrus's own troubles with its new Milwaukee labor force had pushed it to the brink of bankruptcy. Eells's son Howard was named the receiver in a court-arranged reorganization that offered Bucyrus's creditors a viable, ongoing business in the form of a new corporation, named The Bucyrus Company, that assumed the assets of the failing company. Realizing that expanded production was the only way to make Bucyrus solvent, Bucyrus increased the output of its new plant threefold between 1897 and 1901.

Production innovations such as a new steel foundry, the use of special-alloy steels, and the adoption of new heat-treating techniques began to enhance Bucyrus's reputation as a manufacturer of high-quality steel excavating equipment. Significant technological advances enabled Bucyrus to introduce such innovations as the

first 180-degree revolving steam shovel; the first back-acting shovel, which could dig below its own level and toward the cab; and, in 1910–11, the first Bucyrus dragline machines, the first Bucyrus tank-tread-style "crawler" shovels and draglines, and the first Bucyrus machines powered by an internal combustion gasoline engine. The entry into the dragline market was accomplished by purchasing the manufacturing rights to Heyworth-Newman dragline excavator in 1910. By the early years of the new decade heavy-duty railroad shovels were accounting for 62 percent of Bucyrus's output, dredges 29 percent, and railroad wrecking cranes and pile drivers 9 percent.

In 1904 a federal agency called the Isthmus Canal Commission ordered a 70-ton and two 95-ton Bucyrus shovels for the punishing excavation work that would eventually produce the historic Panama Canal. More orders followed, and between 1904 and 1907 the Bucyrus shovels delivered to the massive undertaking were accounting for a third of all large shovels sold by the firm. Almost all the earth and rock moved during the peak phase of the canal project was performed by Bucyrus machines. The Panama Canal project not only gave the company priceless public relations opportunities, including a famous photo with President Theodore Roosevelt perched on a Bucyrus machine, it also gave the company invaluable experience in mass-production manufacturing, enabling it to vie with Marion Steam Shovel Company for dominance in the manufacture of heavy shovels. For the period 1905–07 alone, Bucyrus's corporate profits totaled half a million dollars, and by 1911 its net worth had leaped to $2.3 million.

Bucyrus management quickly capitalized on its Panama Canal success. In 1910 it entered the small revolving steam shovel market by purchasing Vulcan Steam Shovel Company (and thus forming Bucyrus-Vulcan Company), acquired a new manufacturing site in Evansville, Indiana, and agreed to purchase the Atlantic Equipment Company. In 1911 the fusion of Bucyrus, Vulcan, and Atlantic produced a new public corporation, Bucyrus Company, thus ending the company's existence as a family corporation. In the same year W. W. Coleman replaced Howard Eells as company president and led Bucyrus through its brief incarnation as a munitions manufacturer in World War I. In 1915, in a joint venture with three other companies named the Mississippi Valley Products Co., Bucyrus began work on its first order for high-explosive shell blanks for the British government. The war also precipitated a boom in U.S. nonmilitary construction and mining work, which enhanced sales of Bucyrus's commercial products. Bucyrus created the Wisconsin Gun Company with three other Milwaukee firms to produce artillery barrel and breech mechanisms to meet this demand without

KEY DATES

1880: Daniel P. Eells and associates form the Bucyrus Foundry and Manufacturing Company in Bucyrus, Ohio.

1882: Company produces its first steam shovels.

1893: Company moves to South Milwaukee, Wisconsin, and reorganizes as Bucyrus Steam Shovel and Dredge Company of Wisconsin.

1895: Following another reorganization, company emerges as The Bucyrus Company.

1910: Bucyrus enters the dragline market and merges with Vulcan Steam Shovel Company to form Bucyrus-Vulcan Company.

1911: A further merger with the Atlantic Equipment Company results in a new public corporation, Bucyrus Company.

1927: Company is renamed Bucyrus-Erie Company following purchase of the Erie Steam Shovel Company.

1930: Bucyrus-Erie expands overseas with purchase of the British firm Ruston & Hornsby, Ltd.

1933: Company enters the drill market by purchasing Armstrong Drill Company.

1952: Bucyrus-Erie produces its first rotary blasthole drills.

1981: Western Gear Corporation, a California aerospace firm, is acquired.

1985: A holding company called Becor Western Inc. is formed to ward off a hostile takeover.

1988: Western Gear is sold off, and Becor is taken private through an LBO as B-E Holdings, Inc.

1994: Bucyrus-Erie Company emerges as a public company from the prepackaged bankruptcy of B-E Holdings.

1996: Company changes its name to Bucyrus International, Inc.

1997: Bucyrus acquires Marion Power Shovel Company; American Industrial Partners takes Bucyrus private.

2004: Bucyrus is taken public.

2007: Through the acquisition of DBT GmbH, Bucyrus diversifies into underground mining equipment.

interrupting its burgeoning nonmilitary production. By the war's end, Bucyrus's annual sales had reached $6.6 million, and by 1925 Bucyrus had definitively surpassed Marion to become the dominant supplier of large mining stripping equipment and medium-sized quarry and mine excavating machines.

DOMINANCE BY DIVERSITY

Despite buoyant sales and a growing domestic and overseas market, sales of Bucyrus's small revolving shovels lagged throughout the 1920s. Yet just as Bucyrus's purchase of Vulcan had enabled it to enter this lucrative new market in 1910, its decision in 1927 to acquire the Erie Steam Shovel Company, then the largest U.S. producer of small excavating machines, catapulted it to the top of the small shovel industry.

While the management of the new Bucyrus-Erie Company was reconciling the two firms' corporate structures and streamlining their overlapping product lines, it expanded again, adding a British manufacturing affiliate in 1930 with the purchase of Ruston & Hornsby, Ltd., the leading British excavating machinery maker, and in 1931 purchasing a controlling interest in Monighan Manufacturing of Chicago, a producer of walking dragline machines. To survive the Great Depression, management cut back on its workforce, closed the Evansville plant, loosened credit arrangements with customers, and minimized product development and plant improvements. Despite the devastation of the Depression, Bucyrus's tight-ship financial system, the assets accumulated through three decades of success, and holdover back orders from pre-Depression days enabled it to survive the early hardships of the 1930s. In 1932 Coleman announced that Bucyrus was determined to "go after all possible business with courage and the conviction that better times are ahead." Because of its austerity measures, Bucyrus was able to complete the acquisition of the Armstrong Drill Company of Iowa, a manufacturer of churn-type drills, in 1933—its entrée into the drill market—and healthy exports combined with a 1935 contract to supply industrial tractor producer International Harvester with tractor parts enabled Bucyrus to post 1937 profits of $2.1 million.

Bucyrus intentionally limited its involvement in munitions production during World War II. As in World War I, the conflict stimulated domestic and military-related sales of its commercial products, and Bucyrus excavators were purchased in dramatically increased numbers for mining domestic coal and minerals, export to U.S. war allies, and use by U.S. armed forces. Between 1940 and 1944, shipments of Bucyrus excavators totaled more than $44 million, and by 1945 3,000 shovels, draglines, and cranes had been sold directly to the military or U.S. allies. Still, nongovernment production stayed above 40 percent, and Bucyrus's only armaments work was for gun carriages and mounts.

Despite Coleman's conviction that the postwar economic boom would play out in two years, by 1947 he admitted that "the demand for Bucyrus-Erie products [was] beyond its capacity to produce." With the outbreak of the Korean War, any fears Bucyrus management had about declining demand were abandoned, and it concentrated on two problems that had bedeviled it in the prewar years: the rising strength of unions and the need to adjust its product lines and plant capacity to meet changing demand. Bucyrus initially took a hard-line stand with national unions, but damaging strikes in the late 1940s softened management's posture, and by the early 1950s the company was more willing to tolerate national union representatives in new labor contract negotiations.

Between 1945 and 1950, demand for smaller excavating machines had grown to $450 million, but Bucyrus represented only 12 percent of the excavating machinery industry's manufacturing capacity in this segment. Bucyrus therefore undertook a plant expansion program that by 1951 had increased its capacity by 25 percent and then followed it with the purchase of the National Erie Corporation, a steel foundry and machine shop less than a mile from Bucyrus's Erie plant. By combining and expanding the two Erie facilities Bucyrus increased its capacity by 50 percent. Bucyrus also expanded its product lines, changing some of the basic designs that had remained the same since the 1930s, and introduced ever bigger, more sophisticated versions of standard models capable of handling larger and larger loads. In 1952 it first began producing rotary blasthole drills, a brand-new technology that remained an integral part of its product line into the 21st century. By 1955, Bucyrus had grown into an industry behemoth employing 5,000 people and generating shipments of $72 million a year.

The construction of the St. Lawrence Seaway and the passage of the Federal Highway Act in the 1950s meant intensified demand for Bucyrus shovels and excavators. Bucyrus unveiled a new plant in Richmond, Indiana, in 1955, and the number of foreign markets placing orders had grown to 48. W. W. Coleman's retirement in 1956 fell just before a national recession produced layoffs at Bucyrus plants and the company's first net loss in more than a quarter century. Bucyrus promptly closed the new Richmond plant, slashed inventories, and consolidated and streamlined operations in South Milwaukee, Erie, and Evansville. In 1957 dwindling demand prompted the company to discontinue production of dredging equipment; the firm had produced 336 dredges over a 74-year span.

By 1963, Bucyrus had bounced back, and for the next decade and a half it would experience breakneck growth and record profits. Bucyrus soon claimed subsidiaries in Brazil, Japan, and Mexico; manufacturing operations on six continents; new plants in Idaho, Pennsylvania, and Racine, Wisconsin; and a backlog so congested it had to reject an offer by NASA to bid on the huge crawler transports for the Apollo moon mission.

The growth in offshore oil drilling offered Bucyrus a valuable new market in marine crane manufacture, and in 1969 Bucyrus unveiled its crowning engineering achievement, the 4250-W coal shovel. Said to be the largest mobile land vehicle ever built, the "Big Muskie" was powered by ten 1,250 horsepower motors and its bucket loaded 325 tons of material in a single pass. By 1971 Bucyrus had soared past the $185 million mark in shipments, and the onset of the energy crisis in 1973 seemed to augur even larger equipment sales to the coal mining industry. In 1973 Bucyrus arranged the third major U.S. equipment sale to the People's Republic of China with a $19 million deal for mining shovels and blasthole drills.

Demand was rapidly outstripping Bucyrus's ability to meet deadlines, and in 1974 management decided to expand its manufacturing facilities 200 percent, by relying on subcontracting and foreign manufacture. With Bucyrus factories virtually on a wartime footing, its workforce was expanded by 80 percent between 1974 and 1975, and in the same two-year period shipments climbed 35 percent to $353 million. The pace continued until by 1979 Bucyrus had broken past the $550 million mark in annual shipments. Bucyrus's production capacity had doubled, sales had grown sevenfold, and profits had skyrocketed 2,500 percent since 1962. The boom years of the 1970s seemed to put Bucyrus on solid financial ground as it prepared to celebrate its first centennial.

DISASTER: 1980–94

The celebrations surrounding the anniversary, however, masked a marked drop-off in sales. Confronted with a mature market, Bucyrus began diversifying, buying Western Gear Corporation, a California aerospace firm, in 1981, and closing its plants in Idaho and Pennsylvania. With profits still sinking, Bucyrus formed a holding company named Becor Western Inc. in 1985 to ward off a hostile takeover. By 1987, however, Becor's consultants reported that "profitability was not likely to improve until 1990, if then" and that Western Gear was an insupportable drain on the corporate purse. Becor's management then made a fateful decision: They decided to sell Western and, in concert with their investment bankers, Goldman, Sachs and Co., execute a leveraged buyout (LBO) of Bucyrus, a move that made the corporation a private company and therefore promised management greater flexibility in steering the company to financial safety. The LBO also promised high cash distributions to shareholders and tax advantages stemming from the service of the debt on the LBO's bonds. It was in the assumption of massive debt, needed to give management the wherewithal to buy Bucyrus out, however, that the inherent risk of the LBO lay.

Shareholders approved the plan, which was completed in February 1988, with Becor broken up into Bucyrus-Erie and a new holding company named B-E Holdings, Inc. Damaged by Goldman, Sach's hefty fees, the LBO debt almost immediately began to bury Bucyrus. By the end of 1988, corporate debt had risen to $100 million and equity had plummeted to $16 million. Within a year, B-E Holdings was paying out $21 million annually just to service the interest on its debt. Promising new orders only made matters worse. The LBO's financial projections were based on the assumption that Bucyrus would *lose* money in 1990 and 1991. Unanticipated profits meant only that Bucyrus would have to pay even higher levels of debt interest. Bucyrus returned to the financial market to raise more funds in order to avoid paying higher levels of debt interest. Rather than plow the money into much needed working capital, however, the new influx of cash was applied to debt payment, and Bucyrus was caught in a vicious cycle of acquiring new debt to pay off old.

Following heated negotiations with its creditors, in 1993 Bucyrus proposed a restructuring plan in which it would file for a Chapter 11 bankruptcy but arrange with its creditors beforehand to trade them a combined 87 percent share of Bucyrus stock in return for forgiving $135 million in debt. All Bucyrus's creditors agreed to this so-called prepackaged bankruptcy except Jackson National Bank, which claimed in a lawsuit that false statements about Bucyrus's true financial health had fraudulently seduced it into lending Bucyrus $60 million. Jackson's suit threatened to torpedo Bucyrus's only hope of emerging from bankruptcy intact, and as it headed toward federal court its losses continued to mount. In February 1994 Bucyrus officially filed for bankruptcy, with a ten-month window to secure the judgment before new tax laws went into effect forcing it into further, probably fatal levels of debt. After ten months of deliberation the federal court announced that Bucyrus had been awarded the debt-for-equity bankruptcy it sought and could retain control of its own fate. The worst crisis in its history was over, and in December 1994 Bucyrus-Erie Company emerged from bankruptcy as a public company having absorbed B-E Holdings, its former parent.

Ironically, Bucyrus remained not only a viable but also a significant player in the world excavation machinery business before its slide toward bankruptcy began to seem inevitable. The opening of the South African mining machinery market promised greater sources of new sales, and, more importantly, a 1988 contract to provide mining machines to China had been followed by an even larger Chinese order in 1993. China held the potential of becoming the largest customer for the mining machine industry in the world. If the U.S. market for new mining machinery was exhausted, a large untapped international market seemed capable of offsetting the loss, and between 1994 and 1995 Bucyrus's net sales actually increased almost 20 percent to $231.9 million.

FROM PUBLIC TO PRIVATE TO PUBLIC AGAIN: 1995–2004

In July 1995, three senior Bucyrus executives quietly resigned, and a management consulting group shepherded the company during a search for a new CEO. In March 1996 Willard R. Hildebrand became president and CEO. He announced the goal of making Bucyrus a customer-driven, employee-empowered enterprise with a modernized accounting system and a new computerized data system. With exports accounting for almost 70 percent of all shipments and new foreign markets offering Bucyrus a chance to grow itself back to health, shareholders in May 1996 officially approved the rebirth of Bucyrus-Erie as Bucyrus International, Inc. That year, Bucyrus eked out its first profit in several years, earning $2.9 million on sales of $263.8 million.

Bucyrus changed course again in 1997 through two transactions completed in August. The company bought its longtime competitor, Marion Power Shovel Company, for $36.7 million, reducing the makers of heavy-duty electric shovels and draglines to two, Bucyrus and crosstown rival Harnischfeger Industries, Inc. Founded in 1884 and based in Marion, Ohio, Marion Power Shovel had reported 1996 sales of $111.4 million. For Bucyrus, this deal was most significant as a way of strengthening its position overseas in such Marion strongholds as Canada, Australia, and South Africa. The same month of the Marion purchase, Bucyrus's latest stint as a public company ended after a little more than two and a half years when the San Francisco private-equity firm American Industrial Partners took the company private in a deal valued at about $189 million.

Late in 1998 Hildebrand stepped aside from his position as CEO and was named vice-chairman. He was succeeded by Stephen R. Light, who had served as vice-president and general manager of Harnischfeger's surface mining unit. Light came onboard at a difficult time as the Asian financial crisis helped spark a severe downturn in the world mining market, which led mining companies to cut back on purchases of mining shovels, drills, and draglines. Bucyrus was hurt further in 1999 when it lost three South American mining shovel orders to Harnischfeger, and the owners of the company expressed their unhappiness with the firm's direction by replacing Light with Theodore C. Rogers in December 1999. Rogers was one of the founders of American Industrial Partners. One other noteworthy development from 1999 was the April purchase of Bennett & Emmott Ltd., a Canadian firm providing field repair and servicing of surface mining equipment. This acquisition was particularly significant for the boost it gave to Bucyrus's position in the burgeoning field of oil sands mining in western Canada. For the year, Bucyrus suffered a net loss of $22.6 million on sales of $318.6 million.

Bucyrus's struggles continued into the new century, and during this period it carried out certain restructuring initiatives including the June 2000 closure of a manufacturing plant in Boonville, Indiana. The company survived mainly on the revenue generated from its provision of aftermarket parts and service to its $10 billion base of installed equipment. With sales of new equipment depressed, aftermarket revenues accounted for about 80 percent of overall sales during the downturn. The results for 2002 were even worse: sales of new machines generated just $47.6 million of the $289.6 million revenue total, or a little more than 16 percent. Bucyrus operated in the red throughout this period, although by 2003 it had shaved its net loss to just $3.6 million. Sales also improved in 2003, surging more than 16 percent to $337.7 million, with a nearly 38 percent improvement in sales of new machines leading the way.

Bucyrus's prospects improved even more in 2004, when a global commodities boom began and along with it a new upturn in the cyclical mining industry, which in turn quickly pushed demand higher for equipment to mine coal, iron ore, copper, and oil sands. One major factor behind the boom was rapidly growing China, which was displaying an unquenchable appetite for coal and iron ore. American Industrial Partners took advantage of this reversal and the potentially strong investor interest in Bucyrus to cash out. In July 2004 American Industrial sold the majority of its shares in Bucyrus, more than six million shares in total, in an initial public offering priced at $18 per share. For the third time in its long history, Bucyrus moved from private to public ownership with its stock trading on the NASDAQ. American Industrial disposed of its remaining Bucyrus shares in a secondary offering completed in

November 2004. Leading the company into this new era was Timothy W. Sullivan, who had been named president and CEO in March 2004 after serving as president and COO since August 2000. Rogers shifted over to the chairmanship.

GOING UNDERGROUND IN BOOM TIMES

The boom times in commodities, particularly in coal mining and oil sands extraction, led Bucyrus to ramp up its manufacturing capacity and sent the company's revenues and profits soaring. By 2006 the company was able to earn $70.3 million on sales of $738.1 million, more than double the total for 2003. Bucyrus's total order backlog stood at $895 million at the end of 2006, compared to the figure of just $234 million at year-end 2003.

Bucyrus leveraged its strengthened position into the largest acquisition in its history, the May 2007 purchase of DBT GmbH for $730.8 million. Buying DBT, which was based in Lünen, Germany, and generated annual sales of around $1 billion, propelled Bucyrus into the underground mining equipment sector. DBT particularly specialized in the production of equipment for mining coal underground, including roof support systems, armored face conveyers, plows, shearers, and continuous miners. Its eight facilities around the world were located in Germany, the United States, Poland, China, and Australia, and its strongest markets were in Europe and Asia. Coal mining in Europe in particular was typically done underground, in contrast to the surface mining more commonly used in North America. By acquiring DBT, Bucyrus placed itself into even more direct competition with Joy Global Inc., the name under which Harnischfeger Industries had emerged from bankruptcy in 2001, because Joy was already involved in both the surface and underground sides of the global mining equipment industry. The combination of Bucyrus and DBT created a company with an installed base of mining machinery valued at more than $25 billion, which the company claimed was the largest such base in the world, exceeding that of Joy Global.

The commodities boom lasted until the latter months of 2008, when the global economic crisis sent prices of coal, iron ore, copper, and other commodities lower. In addition, lower crude oil prices undermined the economic justification for some of the major oil sands projects in Canada. Mining companies thus began curtailing their expansion plans and equipment purchases, leaving Bucyrus staring at a potentially devastating drop-off in sales. The results for 2008, however, were unaffected by the economic turmoil as Bucyrus was still working through a huge order backlog.

Profits totaled a record $233.3 million on best-ever sales of $2.51 billion. With its massive installed base driving revenue for aftermarket parts and services and a backlog of equipment orders worth $2.5 billion at the end of 2008, Bucyrus International seemed poised for a solid 2009, but its prospects beyond that appeared quite uncertain.

Paul S. Bodine
Updated, David E. Salamie

PRINCIPAL SUBSIDIARIES

Boonville Mining Services, Inc.; Bucyrus (Africa) Surface (Proprietary) Limited (South Africa); Bucyrus America, Inc.; Bucyrus (Brasil) Ltda. (Brazil); Bucyrus Canada Limited; Bucyrus Field Services, Inc.; Bucyrus Holdings GmbH (Germany); Bucyrus Europe Holdings, Ltd. (UK); Bucyrus Europe Limited (UK); Bucyrus Germany Holdings GmbH; Bucyrus DBT Europe GmbH (Germany); Bucyrus Africa Underground (Proprietary) Limited (South Africa); Bucyrus Czech Republic, a.s.; Bucyrus Germany Service GmbH; Bucyrus Polska Sp. z o.o. (Poland); OOO Bucyrus Service (Russia); Bucyrus UK Limited; DPM Gesellschaft fur deutsch-polnischen Maschesenhandel und Leasing GmbH (Germany); DBT (Langfang) Mine Technik Co. Ltd. (China); Tangshan DBT Machinery Co., Ltd. (China); Bucyrus India Private Limited; Bucyrus Industries, Inc.; Bucyrus International (Chile) Limitada; Bucyrus International Hong Kong Limited; Bucyrus International (Peru) S.A.; Bucyrus (Mauritius) Limited; Western Gear Machinery Co.; Wisconsin Holdings Pty. Ltd. (Australia); Bucyrus (Australia) Surface Pty. Ltd.; Bucyrus Australia Underground Holdings Pty. Ltd.; Bucyrus Australia Underground Pty. Ltd.; Bucyrus Australia Underground LAD Pty. Ltd.

PRINCIPAL COMPETITORS

Joy Global Inc.; Atlas Copco AB; Sandvik Aktiebolag.

FURTHER READING

Aeppel, Timothy, "Investors Love the Big Machines," *Wall Street Journal*, January 25, 2005, p. C1.

Anderson, George B., *One Hundred Booming Years: A History of Bucyrus-Erie Company, 1880–1980*, South Milwaukee, Wis.: Bucyrus-Erie Company, 1980, 303 p.

Barnes, Brooks, "Bucyrus to Acquire One of Two Competitors," *Milwaukee Journal Sentinel*, April 9, 1997, Business sec., p. 1.

Barrett, Rick, "Bucyrus Gears Up to Meet Demand," *Milwaukee Journal Sentinel*, February 16, 2008, p. D1.

———, "Bucyrus to Buy German Firm," *Milwaukee Journal Sentinel*, December 18, 2006, p. A1.

———, "Dragline Domain: Milwaukee Manufacturers Command World Market for Huge Mining Machines," *Milwaukee Journal Sentinel*, April 15, 2007, p. D1.

———, "Mining Equipment Makers Hit Pay Dirt," *Milwaukee Journal Sentinel*, January 4, 2006, p. D1.

———, "Mining Equipment Makers Ponder Future," *Milwaukee Journal Sentinel*, February 15, 1999, p. D1.

———, "Mining-Equipment Makers Survive Crisis," *Milwaukee Journal Sentinel*, October 10, 2008, p. D1.

Content, Thomas, "Bucyrus International Shares Rise 26% on First Trading Day," *Milwaukee Journal Sentinel*, July 24, 2004, p. 1D.

Gallagher, Kathleen, "Investment Firm Buying Bucyrus," *Milwaukee Journal Sentinel*, August 1, 1997, Business sec., p. 1.

Gallun, Alby, "Bucyrus Rehires Top Executives," *Business Journal-Milwaukee*, January 21, 2000, p. 1.

———, "Bucyrus Stands to Gain from Harnischfeger's Pain," *Business Journal-Milwaukee*, June 11, 1999, p. 6.

Giesen, Lauri, "Bucyrus-Erie Plans to Leave Construction Equipment Field," *American Metal Market*, December 12, 1983, pp. 1+.

Gilbert, Nick, "Bleached Carcass," *Financial World*, September 1, 1994, p. 34.

Haddock, Keith, *Bucyrus: Making the Earth Move for 125 Years*, St. Paul, Minn.: MBI, 2005, 160 p.

Joshi, Pradnya, "A Surprise at Bucyrus-Erie: Three Execs Resign," *Milwaukee Journal Sentinel*, July 27, 1995, p. 1D.

Kirchen, Rich, "Bucyrus-Erie Sweep Wasn't a Surprise," *Business Journal-Milwaukee*, July 29, 1995, pp. 1+.

Lank, Avrum D., "The Battle over Bucyrus," *Milwaukee Sentinel*, July 25, 1994, p. 1D.

———, "Judge Approves Reorganization of Bucyrus-Erie," *Milwaukee Sentinel*, December 2, 1994, p. 1D.

Orlemann, Erik C., *Power Shovels: The World's Mightiest Mining and Construction Excavators*, St. Paul, Minn.: MBI, 2003, 160 p.

Osenga, Mike, "Bucyrus Looking to Its Future," *Diesel Progress Engines and Drives*, September 1996, pp. 10, 12, 16.

Savage, Mark, "Bucyrus CEO Is Replaced in Surprise Shake-Up," *Milwaukee Journal Sentinel*, December 18, 1999, p. 1D.

———, "Bucyrus-Erie Wins Big Chinese Contract," *Milwaukee Journal Sentinel*, August 22, 1995, p. 1D.

———, "Bucyrus Names New President, CEO," *Milwaukee Journal Sentinel*, December 10, 1998, p. 3D.

———, "Bucyrus's Losses Continue, but New Orders Fuel Hope," *Milwaukee Journal Sentinel*, March 7, 1996, Business sec., p. 1.

———, "Name Change Reflects Business: Bucyrus Taking on International Outlook," *Milwaukee Journal Sentinel*, May 24, 1996, Business sec., p. 3.

———, "A Private Stop on the Carousel," *Milwaukee Journal Sentinel*, September 28, 1997, Business sec., p. 1.

———, "Strategy in Place for Bucyrus Team," *Milwaukee Journal Sentinel,* April 29, 1996, Business sec., p. 3.

———, "Turnaround Artist Gives Focus to Bucyrus-Erie," *Milwaukee Journal Sentinel,* October 16, 1995, Business sec., p. 10.

Williamson, Harold Francis, and Kenneth Holston Myers, *Designed for Digging: The First 75 Years of Bucyrus-Erie Company,* Evanston, Ill.: Northwestern University Press, 1955, 384 p.

Cameron Hughes Wine

444 De Haro Street, Suite 101
San Francisco, California 94107-2349
U.S.A.
Telephone: (415) 495-1350
Toll Free: (800) 805-1971
Web site: http://www.chwine.com

Private Company
Incorporated: 2001
Employees: 17
Sales: $16 million (2008 est.)
NAICS: 424820 Wine and Distilled Alcoholic Beverage
    Merchant Wholesalers

■ ■ ■

Cameron Hughes Wine is a San Francisco, California-based "virtual winery" that offers premium-label wine. The company owns no traditional infrastructure of a typical wine company, such as vineyards and bottling facilities. Rather, it acts as a negotiant, acquiring high-quality juice on the spot market, excess product that mainstream wineries are unable to use, and blending it to create wines that are bottled under the Cameron Hughes label on a contract basis. The wines retail for less than $20, a price well below the inherent quality of the juices. The limited-edition wines are assigned a "Lot" number and sold through major retailers, primarily Costco, but also Sam's Clubs and Cost Plus. In addition Cameron Hughes sells an Evergreen Series wine through supermarket chains, including Safeway, Vons, and Lucky Stores. Unlike the Lot wines,

Evergreen wines are bottled once a year in large quantities and are thus available year-round. The company also offers large-bottle wines (1.5 liters) under the Rock Ridge Cellars label; a higher price-point wine under the Hughes Wellman label, a partnership between the father of Cameron Hughes and a friend; and the Flying Winemaker label, wines developed with winery partners and available on an ongoing basis to smaller groceries and retailers.

Cameron Hughes Wine is owned by Cameron Hughes and his wife, Jessica Kogan, who is responsible for marketing. A key to the success of the company is the palette of Cameron Hughes and his ability to quickly make decisions on what available juices to purchase. One wine broker told *Forbes* that suppliers appreciated his decisiveness: "Cameron tastes the wine, Cameron likes the wine, Cameron buys the wine." What requires minutes for him to decide takes days for others, and as a result Cameron Hughes has scored numerous coups that have established his label as a provider of premium wine at an excellent value.

CAMERON HUGHES: CHILDHOOD INTEREST IN WINE

Growing up in Modesto, California, about 100 miles from Napa Valley, Cameron Hughes became familiar with the wine business at an early age. His father, Steve Hughes, was a sales executive at The Wine Group. After earning a philosophy degree from the University of Colorado he was recruited by his father and went to work in direct marketing at The Wine Group in the mid-1990s. After four years he grew tired of working at a large company and in 1999 tried his hand at selling wine via the Internet, joining start-up Exceptionalwines.com. The idea was to buy French wine in bulk and sell it over the Internet at a discount. It was not, however, a business model that could survive the bursting of the tech bubble in 2001. "These guys had a luxury pricing model," Cameron explained to *Forbes* in 2009, "but the wine didn't have any branding beyond the label."

The idea to start his own virtual wine company occurred to Hughes in 2001 while creating wine mixes for fun with friends at dinner. From his experience in the wine industry he knew that surplus wine from upscale vineyards could be bought at reasonable prices. In fact, boxed-wine companies did just that but mixed the premium wine with mediocre juices to create large quantities. His idea was to hire winemakers to mix quality wines he bought to create a premium blend that could fetch a higher margin than boxed-wine. It would also occupy a much higher price point than the increasingly popular bottled blends offered by Bronco Winery through the Trader Joe's supermarket chain under the Charles Shaw label, known to most as "Two Buck Chuck." Moreover, Hughes believed the time was ripe for such an idea because of an oversupply of wine in the marketplace.

ORIGINATING IN A SAN FRANCISCO APARTMENT: 2001

To cofound the business, Hughes turned to his girlfriend at the time, Jessica Kogan, an experienced marketer having worked in fashion as well as dot-coms. Together they drew up a business plan, and to raise seed capital, Hughes sold his 40-case wine collection, which fetched $25,000, borrowed money from his father, and tapped their credit cards. Thus in October 2001 they launched Cameron Hughes Wine in their San Francisco apartment. In the spring of 2002 they brought their first wine to market. Sold under the Cinergi Napa Valley Red label, it was 50 percent Cabernet Sauvignon, 30 percent Merlot, 15 percent Zinfandel, and 5 percent Sangiovese. To market the product, which retailed for $15 to $17, Hughes hit the road visiting retailers, essentially selling the wine out of the back of a Volvo sta-

tion wagon. Kogan marketed the product from home through a web site she created, tapping into her collection of media contacts and sending out wine for tasting. The couple was able to place the Cinergi in a variety of retailers in Northern California, including Tresetti's Wine World, Tresetti's World Café, the Wine Shoppe in Modesta, and Restaurant 15-0-Five. Later in 2002 Cameron Hughes introduced a second Cinergi product. Retailing at $10 to $12 it was a blended white wine based on Sauvignon Blanc, relying on grapes from Monterey and Napa counties.

Cameron Hughes's introduction to the market was successful enough that the company was able to attract an investment group, put together by Centerra Capital, raising about $200,000. The young company also found a local distributor in Riverbank, California-based Dry Creek Beverage Inc., and nationally it lined up a network of brokers willing to represent the brand across the country. In the months following the terrorist attacks in the United States of September 11, 2001, the times were not particularly good for dinner parties and the wine that often went with it, so that Cameron Hughes had to endure some lean times before gaining any kind of security in the market. Both Hughes and Kogan had to take consulting jobs to help make ends meet, while at the same time they married and began raising a family in the same apartment where they ran the company. At one point they were saddled with $50,000 in credit card debt, yet they managed to keep their marriage intact and stay in business while waiting for a break. It came in 2004.

TURNING POINT: 2004 COSTCO DEAL

Late in 2003 Hughes was able to inexpensively acquire 1,800 cases of $40 Syrah from the Spencer Roloson Winery in St. Helena, California, provided he was circumspect about the deal. Hughes then began courting retailers to carry the wine at about $10 a bottle, including Trader Joe's and Safeway. For two or three months he tried in vain to reach the Costco buyer, Steve Coburn, by telephone. When he was finally able to make his pitch, Hughes promised that if Coburn did not like the sample he sent, he would never bother him again. Coburn agreed but made it clear that he was about to leave for France. Hughes immediately drove over a half-bottle of the Syrah. The next morning Coburn called to say he would take every case Hughes had available, but with one stipulation: Costco approved the labels. Hughes then paid $5,000 to an artist to create six designs of a Cameron Hughes label for Costco to choose from. He then had the wine hauled in 6,000-gallon tanks to bottling plants where his own bottles

KEY DATES

2001: Company is founded.
2002: First wine is offered.
2004: Costco begins carrying Cameron Hughes wine.
2007: Evergreen label is introduced.
2008: Bacchus Capital Management provides mezzanine financing.
2009: Flying Winemaker label is introduced.

were filled and corked and the Costco-approved label applied. Hughes promoted the wine, named Lot 1, at Costco stores. Although he was unable to offer samples to customers, he greeted potential customers and successfully pitched the wine to them.

Cameron Hughes offered more limited-edition wines to Costco in randomly numbered lots, which were shipped to select Costco stores. Soon customers came to expect a quality product under the Cameron Hughes name and because they realized that the wine was available in limited quantities, the stocks sold quickly, the pace quickening as the fear of losing out on a deal took hold. Adding to the mix was the knowledge that customers never knew when a new Cameron Hughes Wine would appear at their local Costco.

OFFICE OPENS: 2006

After selling just 500 cases of wine, mostly to small stores, in 2003, Cameron Hughes began to increase sales at a rapid pace, so that in 2005 revenues reached $771,676. A year later that amount increased to $2.3 million, as the wine became available to Costco stores outside of Northern California, spreading to Southern California as well as other states. In 2006 Hughes and Kogan were able to move the business out of their condominium, opening an office and hiring five employees. Cameron Hughes also took steps in 2006 to become less dependent on Costco, as other retailers impressed with the company's successful business model inquired about carrying the Cameron Hughes brand.

In 2007 the Evergreen label was introduced at the Safeway and Von's supermarket chains. Because supermarkets, unlike price clubs such as Costco, preferred a product they could count on year-round, the Evergreen label differed from the opportunistic approach taken in the Lot series. Instead, the wines were bottled

in large enough quantities to be available throughout the year. Cost Plus, the upscale retailer of mostly imported goods, also became a buyer in 2007. As a result, sales grew to $8.6 million for the year. Moreover, Costco's share of those sales fell to 80 percent after accounting for 90 percent the previous year.

EQUITY PARTNERS TAKEN: 2008

Dependence on Costco continued to decline in 2008 when Sam's Club became a buyer. Steps were also taken to place Cameron Hughes wine in independent stores in New Jersey and Massachusetts, and on the horizon were plans to enter such states as Colorado, Florida, and Texas. To keep pace with the growing business the company hired more people and tripled its office space to 3,000 square feet. In order to have the capital needed to accelerate that growth, Cameron Hughes arranged mezzanine financing (the next stage after venture-capital financing) from Bacchus Capital Management in October 2008, a new investment fund focused on the wine industry that concentrated on mezzanine and private-equity investments. The San Francisco–New York venture was founded a year earlier by managing partners Sam Bronfman, Peter Kaufman, and Henry Owsley. Bronfman, former chairman of Diageo Global Wines, possessed 25 years of experience in the wine business, while Kaufman and Owsley were well seasoned investment bankers, boasting 40 years of experience between them. They chose Cameron Hughes as their first investment. More than just money, Bacchus, primarily through Bronfman, brought an extensive network of useful connections to distributors as well as financial expertise.

Cameron Hughes posted sales of about $16 million in 2008. Despite a downturn in the economy, the company was positioned to do well during difficult conditions. While consumers were not yet ready to give up wine, they were becoming increasingly interested in finding the right balance between quality and price, a nexus that favored Cameron Hughes. While its Lot series continued to do well, the company looked to establish more permanency in its product offerings as a way to spur further growth. In keeping with that strategy, Cameron Hughes introduced the Flying Winemaker label to offer a wide variety of wines for sale at smaller groceries and retailers. Because of the change in consumer demand it was also likely that high-end winemakers would look to compete in the lower price points where Cameron Hughes prospered. Given Cameron Hughes's track record for making quick, intelligent decisions, there was every reason to believe that the company's nimbleness would continue to serve it well in the years to come.

Ed Dinger

PRINCIPAL COMPETITORS

Bronco Wine Company; Kendall-Jackson Wine Estates, Ltd.; The Wine Group, Inc.

FURTHER READING

Bishop, Amanda, "Cameron Hughes Uncorks Wine Sales Strategy," *San Francisco Business Times,* October 27, 2008.

Calvert, Robert, "Virtual Wines," *Austinwoman,* August 2008.

Farrell, Maureen, "Wine Workout," *Forbes,* March 30, 2009.

Hise, Phaedra, and Joanne Chen, "Unlimited Partnership," *Fortune Small Business,* February 2008, p. 68.

Holland, John, "From the Vine," *Modesto Bee,* January 6, 2007.

Moran, Tim, "Wine Notes," *Modesto Bee,* May 17, 2002.

———, "Wine Notes," *Modesto Bee,* November 1, 2002.

A NUON BIWATER COMPANY

Cascal N.V.

Biwater House
Station Approach
Dorking, Surrey RH4 1TZ
United Kingdom
Telephone: (44 1306) 746 080
Web site: http://www.cascal.co.uk

Public Company
Incorporated: 2000
Employees: 1,447
Sales: $160.64 million (2008)
Stock Exchanges: New York
Ticker Symbol: HOO
NAICS: 221310 Water Supply and Irrigation Systems

■ ■ ■

Surrey, United Kingdom-based Cascal N.V. is a leading global provider of water and wastewater services. The company is involved in building, refurbishing, owning, leasing, and operating facilities on four continents that collectively serve about 3.5 million people.

In addition to its headquarters and operations in the United Kingdom, Cascal maintains offices in Amsterdam, China, Hong Kong, and Singapore. The company's operations include sites in Panama, Chile, the United Kingdom, South Africa, China, the Philippines, and Indonesia.

FORMATIVE YEARS: 1999–2000

Although it was officially established in 1999, Cascal traces its roots back to 1989 when, as part of the Biwa-

ter plc, the company was involved in the privatization of the United Kingdom's water industry. Operations subsequently expanded beyond the United Kingdom, leading to the development of an international organization that played a role in water industry privatization efforts in other countries.

One example of Biwater's early international efforts was the formation of a headquarters facility in Bangalore, India, in early 1999. The company had secured a contract from the Bangalore Water Supply and Sewerage Board to work on the second phase of a project that, when completed, would add approximately 500 million liters of water per day to the reservoirs serving Bangalore.

During the company's early years, approximately three billion people throughout the world did not have access to clean, reliable sources of water. In addition, five billion people did not have access to adequate sanitation. Governments in developing countries began relying on private water and wastewater companies, which often had access to better technology, more efficient management methods, and additional capital.

On March 23, 1999, Biwater Capital BV was formally established as a private limited liability company in the Netherlands. Seven months later, on October 19, Biwater plc transferred its water sector operations to Cascal, along with a related management team. On March 31, 2000, Biwater sold a 50 percent equity stake in Cascal to a Netherlands-based energy company named nv Nuon for $125 million, creating a new joint venture named Cascal BV.

The company kicked off the new millennium on solid footing. Nuon brought additional financial capital to the organization, as well as experience in the area of utilities. This enhanced the established base of water-related assets and international management infrastructure that had been developed by Biwater. The company moved forward with a workforce of approximately 620 employees at operations located in Chile, Indonesia, Kazakhstan, the United Kingdom, South Africa, Mexico, and the Philippines. In 2000, David O. Lloyd served as Cascal's chairman and CEO.

EARLY DEVELOPMENTS: 2001–02

During its first full year of operations, Cascal developed a three-year business plan and invested $39.9 million in both existing operations, as well as the acquisition of new operations.

When the government of Belize sought to privatize its water and wastewater services midway through 2000, Cascal was among nearly 20 companies that entered the bidding. Its efforts were successful, and on March 31, 2001, the company acquired Belize Water Services Ltd.

Cascal's new enterprise in Belize joined an extensive base of international operations that included United Kingdom-based Bournemouth & West Hampshire Water plc; Puerta Vallarta, Mexico-based CTAPV; Philippines-based Subicwater; Batam, Indonesia-based Adhya Tirta Batam; and Telang Kelapa, Indonesia-based Adhya Tirta Sriwijaya.

Cascal also had significant operations in Chile. In Santiago, these included the operating companies SAPBSA and Aguas Chacabuco, as well as an investment company named Inversiones Libardon S.A. In Antofagasta, Cascal was involved in sewage treatment and collection via its BAYESA business, which also was engaged in the sale of treated effluent for water reuse. Additionally, the company operated a water and wastewater contracting operation named Servicios Y Construcciones B.S.A. (SYC), as well as a company named Aguas de Quetana S.A. that was involved in operating a sewage treatment business in Calama.

In 2001 Cascal reflected upon the first full year of operations in Nelspruit, South Africa. The company's Greater Nelspruit Utility Co. (GNUC) business began providing water and sanitation services to approximately 260,000 people across a 500-square-kilometer area in November 1999. Operations began following a period of negotiations with the Nelspruit Transitional Local Council and a subsequent concession agreement.

GNUC's first months were difficult ones. In addition to contending with noteworthy opposition to the concession, the company was impacted by record cyclone-related flooding after only four months of operations. The situation quickly escalated into a natural disaster, and many people were left without water as pump stations flooded, pipelines were washed away, and sewerage fermentation ponds eroded. GNUC did an effective job of providing emergency services and restoring regular water service quickly.

Cascal concluded 2001 by commencing construction of a pipeline and pumping stations to supply treated wastewater from its plant in Antofagasta, Chile, to an area 35 kilometers away. The delivery area, recognized as the driest spot on earth, was home to industrial companies that needed a consistent supply of water for operations such as copper production. Before the project, which was completed in April 2002, wastewater had been routed to the sea, resulting in coastal pollution. The initiative was so significant that it was designated as a 200th Anniversary of Chilean Independence-related project.

CONTINUING PROGRESS: 2003–05

By 2003, Cascal was led by CEO Stephane Richer, COO Paul Gledhill; Investment Director Simon Humphrey, Chief Commercial Officer David Sayers, Projects Director Andrew Young, and CFO Cees Zonneveld. That year, the company invested $21.8 million in its Bournemouth & West Hampshire Water operations in the United Kingdom. A variety of improvements were made in areas such as the environment and customer service. The company's efforts were recognized when it received an Investor in People award, as well as the government's Chartermark for excellence in public services.

Beyond the United Kingdom, Cascal also continued to make significant investments in its operations in Belize, where the company experienced a 21 percent increase in sales. In tandem with the government, Belize Water Services Ltd. began a four-month joint investment initiative to expand the country's water distribution network. Other examples of improvements in Belize included staff training initiatives and a new customer billing system for workers at the company's nine customer service centers.

KEY DATES

1999: Biwater Capital BV is formally established as a private limited liability company in the Netherlands; water sector operations of Biwater plc are transferred to Cascal, along with a related management team.

2000: Biwater sells a 50 percent equity stake in Cascal to the Netherlands-based energy company nv Nuon for $125 million, creating a new joint venture named Cascal BV.

2006: Full ownership of Cascal is acquired by Biwater when it buys out nv Nuon.

2009: Cascal completes a reorganization of its subsidiaries in the United Kingdom.

Improvements to Cascal's operations in Nelspruit, South Africa, included the refurbishment of a wastewater treatment plant, as well as the construction of a new one. In addition, the company also worked to expand the water distribution network in Nelspruit to additional rural areas.

Progress also was made in other areas of the world. In northern Chile, a new wastewater treatment plant was constructed in Calama. In Indonesia, Cascal's Adhya Tirta Batam operation experienced a 10 percent rise in water demand, along with an 18 percent rise in customer connections, which reached 69,000. The company also added a new customer service office in Batam Centre.

In all, Cascal's workforce totaled 792 in 2003. The company's employees benefited from various training initiatives, as well as an employee magazine.

Significant developments continued into the middle of the first decade of the 2000s. When Indonesia was impacted by a tsunami in 2004 that resulted in massive casualties and billions of dollars in damages, several of Cascal's companies provided assistance. These included PT Adhya Tirta Batam in Indonesia, as well as Bournemouth & West Hampshire Water in the United Kingdom. Together, these companies provided packaged water treatment plants, as well as skilled manpower.

In 2005 the government of Belize moved forward with plans to re-nationalize its water services. In August of that year, the government forged an agreement to buy back Cascal's stake in Belize Water Services in a deal worth $24.8 million.

BIWATER BUYOUT: 2006–08

A significant milestone was reached in mid-2006. In late June, Biwater bought out nv Nuon and acquired full ownership of Cascal, which became its flagship water and wastewater firm. The buyout occurred because Nuon changed its strategy and decided to focus solely on energy initiatives, as opposed to water-related projects. This had resulted in a lack of investment by Nuon in Cascal.

Following the ownership change, Cascal began evaluating opportunities to invest in new water projects. Around the same time of the Nuon buyout, Cascal shelled out $14.3 million to acquire Biwater's stake in the Panama City-based potable water supplier Aguas de Panama. Later in the year, Cascal parted with $25.1 million to secure an 87 percent stake in The China Water Company Ltd. from Thames Water, Sime Darby, and several other investors. Cascal planned to use China Water as a springboard for further investments in the Chinese water services market, where it had functioned as a contractor since the mid-1990s.

Growth continued in 2007, by which time Cascal employed a global workforce of approximately 1,200 people. Early in the year, Cascal's Bournemouth & West Hampshire Water business spent $8.9 million to acquire the gas installation and maintenance services company Pre-Heat Ltd. At the time, Bournemouth & West Hampshire Water was seeking to expand beyond the regulated water sector. Pre-Heat was combined with the company's existing Aqua Care arm, which provided customers in South England with plumbing, gas, drainage, and water hygiene services.

Another important development in 2007 occurred in May, when Cascal acquired a 73.4 percent stake in South Africa's Siza Water for roughly $2.9 million. The deal bolstered Cascal's presence in that country, as it gained a water and wastewater company that served some 50,000 people in South Africa's Dolphin Coast region.

CHINA EXPANSION: 2008–09

On March 31, Cascal capped off its 2008 fiscal year with revenues of $160.6 million, an increase of 32 percent over the previous year. Growth continued during the early part of the year when The China Water Company Ltd., in which Cascal held a majority stake, secured a 30-year concession contract with the government of Yancheng in Jiangsu Province for the provision of water services to approximately 600,000 people in Yancheng City. Specifically, China Water acquired a 49 percent interest in an equity joint venture named Yancheng China Water Co. in late April. After commencing operations on May 1, the new company was expected to employ a workforce of 600 within five years.

Prior to the Yancheng City project, Cascal had Chinese operations in areas such as Xinmin, Qitaihe, Fuzhou, and Yanjiao. Following the deal, the company served some 1 million people throughout China. This number swelled past the 1.5 million mark in June, at which time China Water secured a majority interest in Zhumadian China Water Co., a joint venture established with the Zhumadian Bangye Water Group, in China's Zhumadian City, Henan Province.

It also was in mid-2008 that Cascal expanded its footprint in Chile by acquiring the water and wastewater companies Servicomunal and Servilampa. Combined with its existing operations in Chile, Cascal saw its customer base there grow to more than 500,000 people.

In early 2009, Cascal completed a reorganization of its subsidiaries in the United Kingdom. By this time, the company served more than four million customers throughout the world. Since its beginnings during the 1980s, the company had established itself as a leader by designing and building more than 1,000 water or wastewater systems. Moving forward, Cascal seemed prepared for continued success.

Paul R. Greenland

PRINCIPAL SUBSIDIARIES

Agua Mexicana y Operaciones S.A. de C.V. (Mexico); Aguas Chacabuco S.A. (Chile); Aguas de la Portada S.A. (Chile); Aguas de Panama S.A.; Aguas de Quetena S.A. (Chile); Aguas Santiago S.A. (Chile); Aquacare (BWHW) Ltd.; Bayesa S.A. (Chile); Belize Water Services Ltd. (83%); Biwater Ingeniera y Proyectos S.A. de C.V. (Mexico); Bournemouth & West Hampshire Enterprise Ltd.; Bournemouth & West Hampshire Holdings Ltd.; Bournemouth & West Hampshire Water Group Ltd.; Bournemouth & West Hampshire Water Plc; Bournemouth Water Ltd.; Bournemouth Water Plc; BV Cascal Investment Ltd.; BWH Holdings (South Africa); BWH Investments BV; BWS Finance Ltd.; Cascal (Chile) S.A.; Cascal BV (Chile) Limitada; Cascal Operations (Pty) Ltd. (South Africa); Cascal Plc; Cascal Services Ltd.; China Water Company (Fuzhou) Limited (Hong Kong; 87%); China Water Company (Yancheng) Ltd. (Hong Kong; 87%); China Water Company (Yanjiao) Ltd. (Hong Kong; 87%); China Water Company (Zhumadian) Ltd. (Hong Kong; 87%); CWC Water Management Company Ltd. (British Virgin Islands; 87%); Fuzhou CWC Water Company Ltd. (China; 62.64%); Inversiones Aguas del Sur Limitada (Chile); Inversiones Cascal S.A. (Chile); Inversiones Libardon S.A. (Chile); Mill Stream Insurance Ltd.; P.T. Adhya Tirta Batam (Indonesia; 50%); P.T. Adhya Tirta Sriwijaya (Indonesia; 40%); Pre-Heat Ltd.; Qitaihe CWC Water Company Ltd. (China; 79.09%); Sanhe Yanjiao CWC Water Company Ltd. (China; 82.08%); Servicios y Construcciones Biwater S.A. (Chile); Siza Water Company (Proprietary) Ltd. (South Africa; 73.42%); Subic Water & Sewerage Company Inc. (Philippines; 30%); The China Water Company (Fuzhou) Ltd. (British Virgin Islands; 87%); The China Water Company (Mauritius) Ltd. (87%); The China Water Company (Qitaihe) Limited (British Virgin Islands; 87%); The China Water Company (Xinmin) Ltd. (British Virgin Islands; 87%); The China Water Company (Yanjiao) Ltd. (British Virgin Islands; 87%); The China Water Company Ltd. (British Virgin Islands; 87%); The Greater Nelspruit Utility Company (Pty) Ltd. (South Africa; 90%); West Hampshire Water Ltd.; West Hampshire Water Plc; Xinmin CWC Water Company Ltd. (China; 79.09%); Yancheng China Water Company Ltd. (42.63%).

PRINCIPAL COMPETITORS

Bechtel Group Inc.; GDF SUEZ; Veolia Environnement SA.

FURTHER READING

"Biwater Acquires 100% Control of Cascal, Looks for Investment Opportunities," *Business News Americas–English,* June 29, 2006.

"Cascal N.V. Announces Acquisition of Majority Stake in Zhumadian China Water Company; Acquisition Will Expand Cascal's Presence in China to More Than 1.5 Million Residents," *PR Newswire,* June 16, 2008.

"Cascal N.V. Completes Reorganization of United Kingdom Subsidiaries," *PR Newswire Europe,* February 26, 2009.

"Cascal N.V. Completes Two New Acquisitions in Chile; Acquisitions Increase Cascal's Presence in Chile to Nearly 500,000 Residents," *PR Newswire,* June 30, 2008.

"Wastewater Reuse Plant Supplies Industrial Water in Antofagasta, Chile: Cascal's Latest Chilean Project Treats Wastewater That Once Polluted Coastal Waters and Transports It to the North for Industrial Use; Industrial Water Supply," *Water and Waste Water International,* December 1, 2002.

"WATERThames Water Sells China Water Holding," *Utility Week,* November 24, 2006.

Charter Financial
Corporation

■

1233 O.G. Skinner Drive
West Point, Georgia 31833-1789
U.S.A.
Telephone: (706) 645-1391
Toll Free: (800) 763-4444
Fax: (706) 645-3070
Web site: http://www.charterbank.net

Public Mutual Company
Incorporated: 2001
Employees: 189
Total Assets: $794.6 million (2008)
Stock Exchanges: Over the Counter (OTC)
Ticker Symbol: CHFN
NAICS: 522120 Savings Institutions; 551111 Offices of
    Bank Holding Companies

■ ■ ■

Charter Financial Corporation is the parent company of
bank and federal savings institution CharterBank. Ten
bank branches serve communities along the I-85 corridor between Atlanta, Georgia, and Montgomery,
Alabama. In addition to the community banks, Charter-
Bank operates Georgia-based loan production offices.
Established in the 1950s, the financial institution
switched to a part-public, part-mutual ownership
structure in 2001. Holding company First Charter,
MHC owns more than 80 percent of the company's
stock, with the remaining shares of Charter Financial
Corporation sold over-the-counter. Long-held Freddie

Mac stock elevated dividends, until the U.S. housing
market collapse of late 2007 into 2008.

COMMITTED TO COMMUNITY:
1954–2001

Charter Financial Corporation took root in the mid-
20th century, a boom era in home ownership. "Charter-
Bank originated in 1954 with the intent of helping its
neighbors secure loans to buy the American dream ...
their first home," the company's web site history
recalled. John W. "Bubber" Johnson Jr., founder and
president, established a presence in communities of west
central Georgia and east central Alabama.

During the 1980s, Johnson led the company in the
acquisition of Freddie Mac stock. The U.S. Congress
created the charter for the Federal Home Loan
Mortgage Corp. (Freddie Mac) in 1970 to address
disparities in availability and in interest rates for home
mortgages. Freddie Mac bought mortgages from lenders,
bundled them into securities, and sold those financial
instruments to investors. Freed of home mortgages and
their inherent risks, the intent was for lenders to make
loans to Americans being excluded from home
ownership.

Johnson also encouraged engagement in civic and
charitable activities. In line with that commitment to
community, the bank (formerly Charter Federal Savings
and Loan Association) established the Charter Foundation, in 1994, to support social, cultural, artistic, and
economic efforts in its service region.

Upon the founding of Charter Financial Corporation in 2001, Johnson took the post of chairman. The

COMPANY PERSPECTIVES

As this institution continues its years of service in the Chattahoochee valley region, we affirm our commitment to you, and the communities we serve through the following statement: "In an age where promises are not kept and commitments are easily broken, people are drawn to deeper, more significant and long lasting relationships. CharterBank is a committed partner to our customers, neighbors, and community, with our roots in the best of banking tradition. It is a privilege to live and work here and we are honored to earn your trust."

new entity and CharterBank reorganized into a mutual holding company structure and issued a public stock offering.

STRIVING TO GROW: 2002–03

Seeking to expand the five-branch community bank, Charter Financial moved to take over FLAG Financial Corp. and its 16 Georgia branches. CEO and President Robert L. Johnson initiated an $86 million cash bid, as FLAG prepared to go private through a reverse stock split, according to *Mergers and Acquisitions Report.* FLAG management rejected the offer on February 15, 2002, and canceled plans to go private. Charter Financial stepped away from the buyout, which it planned to finance by selling some of its investments. (Johnson had succeed the founder as president in 1996.)

In September 2002, Charter Financial announced an $8 million cash deal for EBA Bancshares, Inc. Located in Opelika, Georgia, EBA Bancshares was parent company of Eagle Bank and its three Alabama-based branches.

Charter Financial recorded $2.9 million in net income for the fiscal year ending September 30, 2002, versus $4.8 million the prior fiscal year. "During our first year as a public company, we have been pleased with investor reaction to our stock as the price increased to $29 per share from the initial public offering price of $10 per share," Johnson said in a November 2002 *PR Newswire* release. "However, the stock-price appreciation also increased the cost of our stock-based benefits, which contributed significantly to lower earnings this year compared to last year."

Declining interest rates also created a bad news-good news scenario. On one hand the bank's interest

margins shrank, on the other, mortgage loan refinancing expanded.

The bump up in mortgage loans and service fees partially offset a $1.5 million loss related to the sale of a WorldCom, Inc., corporate bond. The communication company filed for bankruptcy in 2002. An additional loss in excess of $500,000 stemmed from a loan servicing partnership, according to the fiscal year-end news release.

The acquisition of EBA Bancshares was completed in early 2003. "The merger extends our presence in the Auburn-Opelika area and reflects a key part of our strategy of effectively deploying capital to benefit our shareholders, such as through acquisitions that build our retail banking franchise," Johnson announced on February 21. The *PR Newswire* release indicated Eagle Bank had merged into CharterBank. Headquartered roughly 20 miles to the northeast in West Point, CharterBank had operated in the Auburn-Opelika area since 1978. Eagle Bank, situated in a growing region northeast of Montgomery, helped drive an increase in core deposits and deposit fee income for Charter Financial during fiscal 2003.

Managing its 4.64 million shares of Freddie Mac stock represented another aspect of the company's corporate strategy. During the year, the company "initiated a pilot program of writing covered call options" on a half-million shares. Charter Financial earned income from writing the stock sale agreements and made gains on the sale of the stock.

OUTSIDE INFLUENCES: 2004–07

Charter Financial joined the NASDAQ Financial-100 index in February 2004. The Georgia-based operation had a market capitalization of $791 million.

Two factors contributed to a roughly 39 percent climb in net income during fiscal 2005. Loan portfolio growth improved the retail banking operation's net interest income, and increased gain on the sale of Freddie Mac stock drove up non-interest income.

Marketing efforts and a growing local economy aided Charter Financial's retail banking business during fiscal 2006. Continuing branch upgrades improved customer service and were expected to drive additional growth. The bank had already added a ninth branch location. A KIA Motors plant, under construction in West Point, Georgia, and set to employ approximately 2,800 people, sparked ancillary business activity.

On the national front, rising oil prices and falling consumer confidence helped stall the heady assent of the Dow Jones industrial average, the *Atlanta Journal-*

```
┌─────────────────────────────────────────┐
│                                         │
│             KEY DATES                   │
│                ■                        │
│  ─────────────────────────────────────  │
│  1954:  Home loan company is founded.   │
│  1980s: Company president leads drive to │
│         accumulate Freddie Mac stock.   │
│  1994:  The Charter Foundation is        │
│         established.                     │
│  2001:  Public offering accompanies      │
│         reorganization.                  │
│  2004:  Charter Financial Corporation    │
│         joins NAS-DAQ Financial-100      │
│         Index.                           │
│  2007:  Net income skyrockets with       │
│         partial sale of Freddie Mac      │
│         stock.                           │
│  2008:  Remaining Freddie Mac stock is   │
│         liquidated.                      │
│                                         │
└─────────────────────────────────────────┘
```

Constitution reported on November 10, 2006. Speculation regarding the power shift in Congress, from Republican to Democratic control, furthered feelings of uncertainty. The Dow had been trading in record territory, above 12,000. Charter Financial and several other Georgia-based firms, nevertheless, continued to trade at 52-week highs.

A case of mistaken identity, during 2007, put Charter Financial on the offensive. A similarly named Washington-based company was mistakenly linked with Charter Financial's trading symbol. The Georgia-based bank repeatedly countered reports of its acquisition, concerned about investors' reaction to the erroneous news.

Partial sale of Freddie Mac stock propelled net income 262 percent in fiscal year 2007, to $50.9 million. Charter Financial sold 1.035 million shares for a pretax gain of $69.5 million. CharterBank, meanwhile, opened a "grocery store branch" increasing its locations to ten, according to a year-end *PR Newswire* release.

In the realm of capital management, Charter Financial repurchased more than a half million of its own shares, distributed a special cash dividend of $2.50 per share to shareholders, and raised the regular quarterly dividend once again. Dividends totaling $13.35 per share had been declared since 2001.

AN ERA ENDS

John Johnson retired as chairman of Charter Financial in late 2007, at the age of 87. "His decision to invest in Freddie Mac long before it became the major force it is today is just one example of the vision he has shown for more than a half century," said his successor Robert Johnson, in a November 29 *PR Newswire* release. The founder's tenure had ended on an up note. Charter Financial's sale of 23 percent of its Freddie Mac stock had yielded an after-tax gain in excess of $41 million.

Nonetheless, trouble was on the horizon. The U.S. housing market downturn had hurt credit quality, an issue reflected in an uptick in non-performing assets, and sparked worries about increased charge-offs down the road. The government-sponsored enterprise (GSE), Freddie Mac, a huge player in the U.S. subprime mortgage market, saw its stock plummet in value. Furthermore, Charter Financial's region of operation contended with ongoing contraction of the textile industry.

In September 2008, the U.S. Treasury placed Freddie Mac under conservatorship of the Federal Housing Finance Agency. A further decrease in the value of Freddie Mac common stock, plus an uncertain future value, prompted Charter Financial to liquidate its holdings.

The loss of Freddie Mac stock reduced Charter Financial's total assets by $200.8 million, according to the company's year-end *PR Newswire* release. Net income dropped to $10.5 million, for fiscal 2008, largely due to lower gains from the earlier Freddie Mac stock sale. A weakening economy, and concerns regarding some of the loans on its books, prompted Charter Financial to make a provision for loan losses late in the fiscal year, thus increasing its reserves.

Freddie Mac holdings, over the years, had allowed Charter Financial to pay out substantially higher dividends than the retail banking operations alone could support. Nonetheless, Johnson remained optimistic in his January 14, 2009, letter to shareholders: "Our bank operations continue to be profitable and the opportunities in our markets are numerous. We are tightly focused on our own internal business without the distraction of a major outside investment."

Reflecting this confidence, Charter Financial's board of directors passed on participating in the Troubled Asset Relief Program (TARP). "After careful consideration, the Board determined that the Company's capital levels were sufficient to support its growth and that the Company does not need a taxpayer bail-out or government ownership or participation in our business," Johnson explained.

At the beginning of 2009, Charter Financial continued to hold hope for an expansion in its regional economy linked to the KIA Motors plant, scheduled to open in December. The plant and tier-one automotive suppliers had projected the creation of more than 10,000 jobs, when the plant reached full capacity. Global automobile sales, meanwhile, had plunged and the nation's big three manufacturers and their suppliers struggled to stay afloat. The housing market had yet to recover.

Kathleen Peippo

PRINCIPAL SUBSIDIARIES

CharterBank.

PRINCIPAL COMPETITORS

Bancorp South, Inc.; The Colonial BancGroup, Inc.; Synovus Financial Corp.

FURTHER READING

Cecil, Mark, "FLAG Elicits Flaky (Perhaps) Takeout Bid," *Mergers & Acquisitions Report,* February 25, 2002.

"Charter Financial Corporation Announces Earnings for Year," *PR Newswire,* November 14, 2002.

"Charter Financial Corporation Completes $8.4 Million Acquisition of Eagle Bank of Alabama in Auburn-Opelika Area," *PR Newswire,* February 21, 2003.

"Charter Financial Declares Quarterly Cash Dividend," *PR Newswire,* February 24, 2009.

"Charter Financial Reports 1st Quarter Fiscal 2009 Net Income of $957,000," *PR Newswire,* January 29, 2009.

"Charter Financial Reports Fiscal Year 2008 Net Income of $10.5 Million," *PR Newswire,* November 7, 2008.

"Charter Financial Reports Full-Year Earnings Up to $0.16 from $0.15, Q4 EPS Increases to $0.10 from $0.06," *PR Newswire,* November 4, 2003.

"Charter Financial Reports FY05 Net Income Increases 39%," *PR Newswire,* November 9, 2005.

"Charter Financial Reports FY06 Net Income Increases 17%," *PR Newswire,* November 7, 2006.

"Charter Financial Reports FY07 Net Income Increases Sharply," *PR Newswire,* November 20, 2007.

"Charter Financial, West Point, Ga., Reiterates It Has Not Been Acquired," *PR Newswire,* July 16, 2007.

"Charter Financial's Founder and Chairman to Retire," *PR Newswire,* November 29, 2007.

Forbes, Steve, "How Capitalism Will Save Us," *Forbes,* November 10, 2008, pp. 18–22.

"NASDAQ: Charter Financial Corporation to Join NASDAQ Financial-100 Index Beginning February 18, 2004," *M2 Presswire,* February 18, 2004.

Thompson, Laura K., "In Brief: Charter of Ga. Buying Ala. Bank," *American Banker,* September 16, 2002, p. 20.

———, "In Brief: Charter of Ga. Posts 58% Profit Increase," *American Banker,* November 5, 2003, p. 5.

Walker, Tom, "Dow Stalls over Consumer Doubts," *Atlanta Journal-Constitution,* November 10, 2006, p. F4.

Charter Manufacturing
Company, Inc.

1212 West Glen Oaks Lane
Mequon, Wisconsin 53092
U.S.A.
Telephone: (262) 243-4728
Fax: (262) 243-4767
Web site: http://www.chartermfg.com

Private Company
Incorporated: 1936 as Charter Wire Inc.
Employees: 1,050
Sales: $719.6 million (2007)
NAICS: 331111 Iron and Steel Mills; 332618 Other
    Fabricated Wire Product Manufacturing

■ ■ ■

Charter Manufacturing Company, Inc., is a privately
held manufacturing company based in Mequon,
Wisconsin, that produces steel and steel components
through four subsidiaries. The first, Charter Steel, is a
fully integrated maker of carbon and alloy steel bar, rod,
and wire products with operations in Saukville,
Wisconsin; Cleveland and Fostoria, Ohio; and Detroit,
Michigan. The Charter Specialty Steel division produces
stainless steel rod at its plant in Fond du Lac,
Wisconsin, serving the heading, spring steel, and bar
markets. Another subsidiary, Charter Wire, produces
cold-rolled flat wire, cold finish bar in standard squares
and rectangles and custom sizes, as well as special shapes
to fill customer needs. From its Milwaukee plant
Charter Wire serves agricultural, automotive, construction, defense, energy, general machinery, lawn and

garden, and recreation industries. Finally, Charter
Automotive supplies engineered components and as-
semblies to the automotive industry for engine,
transmission, and driveline applications. The unit
maintains manufacturing facilities in Milwaukee, the
United Kingdom, and China. Charter Manufacturing is
headed by the third generation of the Mellowes family.

BIRTH AND EARLY YEARS OF FOUNDER

Charter Manufacturing was founded by Alfred W. Mellowes, born in Dayton, Ohio, in 1880, the son of British immigrants. He would become better known as the
inventor of the first mechanical refrigerator. Mellowes
earned an engineering degree from Cornell University at
the age of 16 in 1906 and returned to his hometown to
work for Johns-Manville Company. He also began
development of his idea for an iceless refrigerator, and in
1915 quit his job to finish his invention in a backyard
wash house in Fort Wayne, Indiana. By attaching an
electric refrigeration unit to a wooden cabinet, he
invented the first true refrigerator. A year later he and a
group of investors formed the Guardian Frigerator
Company, which subsequently relocated to Detroit.
Manufacturing was slow, taking a week to turn out a
hand-assembled unit, and after two years Guardian was
on the verge of bankruptcy. The head of General Motors, William Durant, then stepped in to buy the
company, recognizing the potential of Mellowes's
design. He applied the mass production techniques used
by the auto industry to the production of refrigerators.
Durant also gave the product and company a new
name: Frigidaire. After Durant sold the business to

COMPANY PERSPECTIVES

For more than 70 years, Charter Manufacturing has adhered to a simple, successful formula: *"Do something different and do it right to achieve the highest-quality product."* This philosophy has allowed Charter to quietly develop leadership positions in several specialty steel markets.

General Motors, it came into its own and in many parts of the world Frigidaire became synonymous with refrigerator.

FORMATION OF CHARTER WIRE: 1936

After selling Guardian, Mellowes relocated to Milwaukee, going to work for Briggs & Stratton Corporation, a maker of automobile engines and parts, to establish a refrigerator division. In 1922 Mellowes started another business, Milwaukee Lock Washer Company, based on another one of his innovations, a new way to produce lock washers. Five years later he sold the company to National Lock Washer, becoming a vice-president and director while managing the Milwaukee plant. In 1936 he started a company to supply National Lock Washer with wire, calling it Charter Wire Inc., thus laying the foundation for Charter Manufacturing. Appointed to run the venture in Mequon, Wisconsin, was his son Charles N. Mellowes, who had also graduated from Cornell, earning his engineering degree in 1933.

A second division of Charter Manufacturing, now known as Charter Automotive, was added in 1948 at the request of Chrysler Corporation, which needed dipsticks. The result was Milwaukee Wire Products, which in short order became the leading U.S. manufacturer of fluid-level indicators for the combustion engine and powertrain industries. The company also began producing car trunk latches, intravenous bottle holders, and other metal items. It was also during the post–World War II era that the Mellowes family returned to the manufacture of lock washers. In 1951 National Lock Washer announced that it would no longer rely on Charter Wire, opting instead to roll its own wire. The Mellowes family responded by using its wire to produce lock washers, providing its former customer with stiff competition. Soon the Mellowes Company, as the venture was named, emerged as the

market leader. In 1968 the family acquired National Lock Washer.

THIRD GENERATION JOINS COMPANY: 1965

A third generation of the Mellowes family, John A. Mellowes, joined the company in 1965. Like his father and grandfather, he received an engineering degree from Cornell, class of 1960. When he arrived at Charter Manufacturing the company was generating about $5 million in annual sales. Having acquired a New Jersey company, Positive Lock Washer, the younger Mellowes was dispatched to run it as manager. Five years later John Mellowes returned to Milwaukee to take charge of Charter Wire and soon made his mark by removing the time clocks. The Mellowes family had always valued the contributions of its employees, as demonstrated in 1958 when it established a profit-sharing program. Without time clocks, Charter workers became salaried employees.

In 1973 John Mellowes succeeded his father as president of Charter Manufacturing. The operations soon developed a problem in securing supplies of adequate wire rod needed by the plants. The family decided to meet the challenge by starting its own melt shop and rolling mill, thus becoming vertically integrated. The first step was taken in 1975 when Charter acquired a mill from National Steel Corp.'s Great Lakes Steel division. The operation was combined with a Morgan No-Twist finishing line to outfit a mill that opened in Saukville, Wisconsin, in 1978 as Charter Rolling. It bought billets, which were rolled into rod, and supplied to its sister companies. The mill also became the first plant in the world to produce 4-millimeter wire rod.

Charter added melting capabilities in 1981 through the acquisition of a Chicago melt shop from bankrupt California Steel Co. (named for the Chicago street on which it was located, not the state). The quality of what Charter Electric Melting produced was barely adequate, but with some improvements to the operation, including the installation of a new electric-arc furnace, it was eventually capable of producing simple cold-heading grades of steel billets for the Charter Rolling mill. By this stage, Charter Manufacturing had increased sales to the $50 million level.

A number of other changes took place within the other Charter Manufacturing units in the 1980s. Milwaukee Wire Products opened a Detroit sales office in 1984 to better support its automotive customers, including purchasing, engineering, and assembly operations. A year later the Charter Processing unit began serving the specialty steel markets with the opening of a new processing plant that could clean, coat, anneal, and draw wire as needed. To develop new products as well as new manufacturing processes, Charter Manufacturing opened its Advanced Development Center in 1987. One of those new products, produced by Milwaukee Wire Products, was valve spring retainers, introduced in 1989.

CHARTER STEEL PLANT OPENS: 1991

Charter Manufacturing finished the 1980s with annual sales approaching $125 million, but soon faced a significant challenge. With the Chicago plant having reached its production capacity, Charter arranged for $25 million in financing in 1989 to build a minimill at the Saukville site in anticipation of further growth in demand for billets, which in addition to sister units Charter Rolling supplied to outside customers. The company went forward with the plans for the new mill despite rumblings from the auto industry about possible production reductions. By the time the project was complete in 1991, resulting in Wisconsin's first minimill, and Charter Rolling changing its name to Charter Steel, Charter Manufacturing was so short of cash that it had to implement a four-month wage freeze and ask vendors to grant it 70 days to pay its invoices instead of the usual 30. To make matters worse, the economy was still mired in recession with no immediate prospect of improvement and the auto industry, Charter's primary customer, was in a slump. The company received a much needed turn of good fortune in the spring of 1991 when Glenview, Illinois-based Illinois Tool Works Inc. made a bid for The Mellowes Co. The

manufacturer of lock washers and cotter pins contributed about 12 percent of Charter's sales, but it was no longer a core operation and was sold, thus easing the company's cash problem.

Having taken the risk of opening a new mill, Charter began to reap the benefits of becoming the only manufacturer in the country that could melt and produce bar, rod, and processed wire at one site. The company was able to move into a number of high-end and niche markets, all the while continuing to expand all of its operations. The early 1990s also brought a generational change. In 1991 John Mellowes's son, Charles A. Mellowes, joined the company, becoming the fourth generation involved in the family business. Two years later 82-year-old Charles N. Mellowes died, and John Mellowes assumed the chairmanship.

With the expansion of the Saukville site, the Charter Electric Melting operation in Chicago was closed and in 1994 the business was sold to J. Pitterick of Pittsburgh. In the second half of the 1990s further expansion took place as sales topped the $200 million level and continued to climb. The 81st Street facility in Milwaukee was completed in 1995 and two years later capacity was increased at the Saukville site to 400,000 tons annually as the result of a major expansion of the rolling mill and melt shop. In 1999 the Saukville processing facility was expanded as well, and Milwaukee Wire replaced its operation with a new manufacturing plant in Milwaukee. In addition, Charter Manufacturing built on a reputation for quality workmanship and responsible management. In 1997 Charter Steel and Milwaukee Wire received QS 9000 certification, a motor industry standard indicative of a company with a quality management system in place. In 2000 Charter Steel became the first U.S. steel company to receive environmental ISO 14001 certification, a voluntary standard concerning environmental management governed by the International Organization for Standardization.

OPENING OF CHARTER SPECIALTY STEEL: 2001

Expansion projects continued in the new century as Charter Manufacturing enjoyed a growth spurt. To better serve East Coast customers with just-in-time deliveries, Charter Steel opened a $16 million, full-service carbon and alloy steel bar, rod, and wire processing and distribution facility in Fostoria, Ohio, about 45 miles southeast of Toledo, in 2000. A year later a $60 million steel production plant was opened in Fond du Lac, Wisconsin, establishing Charter Specialty Steel and providing entry into the stainless steel market. The division quickly became a leading provider of coiled stainless steel rod in the United States. In addition, Charter Manufacturing grew by acquisition. In 2002 it bought the idle American Steel & Wire Corp. specialty steel bar mill located near Cleveland, Ohio, from Birmingham Steel Corp. Renamed Charter Steel – Cleveland, it resumed operations later in the year, bringing additional coil-making capacity and a wider range of products. Also in 2002 the Saukville plant completed another expansion, as Charter Manufacturing grew annual sales to $338 million. Just two years later sales increased to $623.1 million.

To maintain the company's growth, more expansion projects were undertaken, including the addition of a $90 million melting plant in Ohio to support Charter Steel – Cleveland. The Fostoria operation also completed a $12 million furnace expansion project in 2005. In that same year, Charter Manufacturing closed on a pair of acquisitions. A Canadian start-up company, ProTube Design Limited, was added to Milwaukee Wire to add further automotive tube products. Moreover, the Emerald Steel coil processing plant in Center Line, Michigan, was purchased and folded into the Charter Steel operations.

After posting sales of about $720 million in 2006, Charter Manufacturing took a major step to grow the business internationally. In 2007 Milwaukee Wire acquired Valve Train Components Ltd. of Lichfield, England, a supplier of components to the automotive industry, a move that brought new products, new customers, and new markets. As a supplier to a large number of the world's leading automobile manufacturers, Milwaukee Wire changed its name in 2007 to Charter Automotive.

In 2008 Charter Wire made plans to leave Milwaukee for a 7.8-acre site outside the city, one large enough to accommodate a wire plant. Limited by space the old plant had been forced to improvise: Production lines doubled back instead of running the length of the building. In addition, the property located in the Menomonee Valley Industrial Center could support further expansion. As the U.S. economy began to sag in 2008, however, expansion was no longer in the immediate plans of Charter Manufacturing. Fortunately, the company was prudent in the way it managed inventories

and melted steel only as orders warranted it. Some measures were taken to keep the company healthy in anticipation of difficult times to come, as demand for steel of all types weakened and the automobile industry faced especially difficult times. Plans were made to shutter Charter Specialty Steel in Fond du Lac and Detroit's Charter Steel plant. Moreover, Charter Automotive's dipstick and tube business was put up for sale. Charter Manufacturing appeared to be well positioned to weather the storm, however, and the Mellowes family anticipated that eventually another generation would take the reins and continue the tradition established by Alfred Mellowes.

Ed Dinger

PRINCIPAL SUBSIDIARIES

Charter Automotive; Charter Specialty Steel; Charter Steel; Charter Wire.

PRINCIPAL COMPETITORS

Nucor Corporation; Republic Engineered Products, Inc.; United States Steel Corporation.

FURTHER READING

Daykin, Tom, "Charter Wire Sees Potential in Valley," *Milwaukee Journal Sentinel,* April 3, 2008, p. D1.

Lanke, LuAnn, "In the Face of Cash Crunch, Charter Pounds Out Steel-Based Course," *Business-Journal Milwaukee,* May 23, 1992, p. S20.

Petry, Corinna, "Charter to Shut Two Plants," *American Metal Market,* November 14, 2008, p. 1.

Sacco, John E., "In Shift, Charter Targets Specialty Market," *American Metal Market,* May 24, 2000, p. 16.

Savage, Mark, "Charter Navigates Worker-Friendly Course," *Milwaukee Journal Sentinel,* September 9, 1996.

Schmid, John, "Charter Spans Out Globally," *Milwaukee Journal Sentinel,* February 16, 2007, p. D1.

Torinus, John, "Family-Owned Charter Looks Long-Term," *Milwaukee Journal Sentinel,* December 15, 2002, p. D3.

Woker, Craig, "From 150,000 to 500,000 Tons at Charter Steel," *New Steel,* July 1, 1998, p. 88.

Chevron Corporation

6001 Bollinger Canyon Road
San Ramon, California 94583-2324
U.S.A.
Telephone: (925) 842-1000
Fax: (925) 842-3530
Web site: http://www.chevron.com

Public Company
Founded: 1879 as Pacific Coast Oil Company
Incorporated: 1926 as Standard Oil Company of
California
Employees: 67,000
Sales: $273.01 billion (2008)
Stock Exchanges: New York
Ticker Symbol: CVX
NAICS: 211111 Crude Petroleum and Natural Gas
Extraction; 211112 Natural Gas Liquid Extraction;
324110 Petroleum Refineries; 324191 Petroleum
Lubricating Oil and Grease Manufacturing; 325110
Petrochemical Manufacturing; 447110 Gasoline
Stations with Convenience Stores; 447190 Other
Gasoline Stations; 486110 Pipeline Transportation
of Crude Oil; 486210 Pipeline Transportation of
Natural Gas; 486910 Pipeline Transportation of
Refined Petroleum Products

■ ■ ■

Chevron Corporation is the number two U.S.-based
integrated oil company (behind Exxon Mobil Corporation) and number four in the world, behind Exxon Mobil, Royal Dutch Shell plc, and BP p.l.c. The company

has some 11.2 billion barrels of oil and gas reserves and
daily production of around 2.5 million barrels. Major
producing areas include the Gulf of Mexico, California,
Texas, Canada, Argentina, Colombia, Trinidad and
Tobago, the North Sea, the Middle East, Angola, Chad,
Nigeria, Australia, Azerbaijan, Bangladesh, China,
Indonesia, and Kazakhstan.

On the downstream side, Chevron operates 18
refineries around the world with the combined capacity
to refine 2.1 million barrels of crude oil per day. The
company considers seven of these to be core refineries;
five of the core plants—located in Singapore, Thailand,
South Korea, and Richmond and El Segundo,
California—provide coverage of the Pacific Basin, with
the other two, located in Pascagoula, Mississippi, and
Pembroke, United Kingdom, supplying the Atlantic
Basin. Chevron's refined products are marketed through
approximately 25,000 retail outlets, which are mainly
located on the West Coast of North America, the U.S.
Gulf Coast, and in the Caribbean, Latin America, the
United Kingdom, Asia, and southern Africa. The
company uses three main brands for its products:
Chevron, Texaco, and Caltex.

In support of these operations, Chevron maintains
nearly 13,000 miles of pipeline in the United States and
abroad for the transport of crude oil, refined products,
natural gas, liquefied petroleum gas, and liquefied
natural gas. Among the firm's other operations and
interests are a 50 percent interest in Chevron Phillips
Chemical Company LLC, a major petrochemical
manufacturer (the other 50 percent is held by Conoco-
Phillips); equity interests in 13 power generation

COMPANY PERSPECTIVES

At the heart of The Chevron Way is our vision ... to be the global energy company most admired for its people, partnership and performance.

Our vision means we: provide energy products vital to sustainable economic progress and human development throughout the world; are people and an organization with superior capabilities and commitment; are the partner of choice; deliver world-class performance; earn the admiration of all our stakeholders—investors, customers, host governments, local communities and our employees—not only for the goals we achieve but how we achieve them.

projects worldwide; and a U.S.-based mining unit that produces and markets coal and molybdenum.

Chevron developed from modest California origins in the late 19th century to become a major power in the international oil market, aided by its association with the Standard Oil Trust (until its 1911 breakup). Dramatic discoveries in Saudi Arabia gave Chevron a strong position in the world's largest oil region and helped fuel 20 years of record earnings in the postwar era. The rise of the Organization of Petroleum Exporting Countries (OPEC) in the early 1970s deprived Chevron of its comfortable Middle East position, causing considerable anxiety and a determined search for new domestic oil resources at a company long dependent on foreign supplies. The firm's 1984 purchase of Gulf Corporation, at $13.2 billion, the largest industrial transaction to that date, more than doubled Chevron's oil and gas reserves but failed to bring its profit record back to pre-1973 levels of performance. By the mid- to late 1990s, however, Chevron was posting strong earnings, a result of higher gasoline prices and the company's restructuring and cost-cutting efforts. Two major acquisitions in the early 21st century helped keep the company among the world's oil giants. In October 2001 Chevron merged with Texaco Inc., a company whose history traces back to the early boom years of the Texas oil industry. The two firms' histories previously began to intertwine in the 1930s with the formation of the Caltex and Aramco ventures in the Middle East. The enlarged firm operated as ChevronTexaco Corporation until May 2005 when it reverted to the Chevron Corporation name. Later in 2005, Chevron acquired Unocal Corporation, which

had been one of the world's leading independent oil and gas exploration and production companies.

COMPANY ORIGINS: FROM PACIFIC COAST TO SOCAL

Chevron's oldest direct ancestor is the Pacific Coast Oil Company, founded in 1879 by Frederick Taylor and a group of investors. Several years before, Taylor, like many other Californians, had begun prospecting for oil in the rugged canyons north of Los Angeles; unlike most prospectors, Taylor found what he was looking for, and his Pico Well #4 was soon the state's most productive. Following its incorporation, Pacific Coast developed a method for refining the heavy California oil into an acceptable grade of kerosene, then the most popular lighting source, and the company's fortunes prospered. By 1900 Pacific had assembled a team of producing wells in the area of Newhall, California, and built a refinery at Alameda Point across the San Francisco Bay from San Francisco. It also owned both railroad tank cars and the *George Loomis,* an oceangoing tanker, to transport its crude from the field to the refinery.

One of Pacific Coast's best customers was Standard Oil Company of Iowa, a marketing subsidiary of the New Jersey–headquartered Standard Oil Trust. Iowa Standard had been active in northern California since 1885, selling both Standard's own eastern oil and also large quantities of kerosene purchased from Pacific Coast and the other local oil companies. The West Coast was important to Standard Oil Company of New Jersey not only as a market in itself but also as a source of crude for sale to its Asian subsidiaries. Jersey Standard thus became increasingly attracted to the area and in the late 1890s tried to buy Union Oil Company (later Unocal), the state leader. The attempt failed, but in 1900 Pacific Coast agreed to sell its stock to Jersey Standard for $761,000 with the understanding that Pacific Coast would produce, refine, and distribute oil for marketing and sale by Iowa Standard representatives. W. H. Tilford and H. M. Tilford, two brothers who were longtime employees of Standard Oil, assumed the leadership of Iowa Standard and Pacific Coast, respectively.

Drawing on Jersey Standard's strength, Pacific Coast immediately built the state's largest refinery at Point Richmond on San Francisco Bay and a set of pipelines to bring oil from its San Joaquin Valley wells to the refinery. Its crude production rose steeply over the next decade, yielding 2.6 million barrels a year by 1911, or 20 times the total for 1900. The bulk of Pacific Coast's holdings were in the Coalinga and Midway fields in the southern half of California, with wells rich enough to supply Iowa Standard with an increasing

KEY DATES

1879: Pacific Coast Oil Company is founded in California.

1900: Pacific Coast is purchased by the Standard Oil Trust.

1906: Pacific Coast is merged with Standard Oil of Iowa to form Standard Oil Company (California), known as Socal.

1911: The Standard Oil Trust is ordered dissolved by the U.S. Supreme Court; Socal emerges as an independent firm officially called Standard Oil (California).

1926: Socal merges with Pacific Oil Company, a division of Southern Pacific Railroad Company; company name is changed to Standard Oil Company of California.

1930: Socal strikes oil in Bahrain, beginning the firm's involvement in the Middle East.

1933: Company gains drilling rights in Saudi Arabia.

1936: Socal sells 50 percent of its drilling rights in Saudi Arabia and Bahrain to the Texas Company (later Texaco Inc.), forming a joint venture called the California-Texas Oil Company (Caltex); the Saudi arm of the Caltex venture is later called Arabian American Oil Company (Aramco).

1948: 30 percent of Aramco is sold to Standard Oil Company (New Jersey) and 10 percent to Socony-Vacuum Oil Company.

1961: Socal purchases Standard Oil Company of Kentucky to market gasoline in the southeastern United States.

1970s: Company is rocked by the OPEC oil embargo and the nationalization of a number of Caltex holdings.

1980: The government of Saudi Arabia nationalizes Aramco.

1984: Socal changes its name to Chevron Corporation; company purchases Gulf Corporation for $13.2 billion.

1993: Chevron forms joint venture with the Republic of Kazakhstan to develop the huge Tengiz oilfield.

1996: Company sells its natural gas gathering, processing, and marketing operations to NGC Corporation, gaining a 27 percent stake in a firm later called Dynegy Inc.

2000: Chevron combines its worldwide chemical operations with those of Phillips Petroleum Company (later ConocoPhillips), forming a 50-50 joint venture called Chevron Phillips Chemical Company.

2001: Chevron acquires Texaco in a $45 billion deal, forming ChevronTexaco Corporation.

2005: Company changes its name back to Chevron Corporation and acquires Unocal Corporation for $17.29 billion.

volume of crude but never enough to satisfy its many marketing outlets. Indeed, even in 1911 Pacific Coast was producing a mere 2.3 percent of the state's crude, forcing partner Iowa Standard to buy most of its crude from outside suppliers such as Union Oil and Puente Oil.

By that date, however, Pacific Coast and Iowa Standard were no longer operating as separate companies. In 1906 Jersey Standard had brought together its two West Coast subsidiaries into a single entity called Standard Oil Company (California), generally known thereafter as Socal. Jersey Standard recognized the future importance of the West and quickly increased the new company's capital from $1 million to $25 million. Socal added a second refinery at El Segundo, near Los Angeles, and vigorously pursued the growing markets for kerosene and gasoline in both the western United States and Asia. Able to realize considerable transportation savings by using West Coast oil for the Pacific markets of its parent company, Socal was soon selling as much as 80 percent of its kerosene overseas. Socal's head chemist, Eric A. Starke, was chiefly responsible for several breakthroughs in the refining of California's heavy crude into usable kerosene, and by 1911, Socal was the state leader in kerosene production.

The early strengths of Socal lay in refining and marketing. Its large, efficient refineries used approximately 20 percent of California's entire crude production, much more than Socal's own wells could supply. To keep the refineries and pipelines full, Socal bought crude from Union Oil and in return handled a portion of the marketing and sale of Union kerosene and naphtha. In the sale of kerosene and gasoline, Socal maintained a near-total control of the market in 1906, supplying 95 percent of the kerosene and 85 percent of the gasoline and naphtha purchased in its marketing area of California, Arizona, Nevada, Oregon, Washington, Hawaii, and Alaska, although its share dipped somewhat in the next five years. When necessary, Socal used its dominant position to inhibit competition by deep price cutting. By the time of the dissolution of the Standard Oil Trust in 1911, Socal, like many of the Standard subsidiaries, had become the overwhelming leader in the refining and marketing of oil in its region while lagging somewhat in the production of crude.

FROM 1911 TO WORLD WAR II: GROWTH AS AN INDEPENDENT COMPANY

In 11 short years the strength of Standard Oil and a vigorous Western economy combined to increase Socal's net book value from a few million dollars in 1900 to $39 million. It was in 1911, however, that Jersey Standard, the holding company for Socal and the entire Standard Oil family, was ordered dissolved by the U.S. Supreme Court in order to break its monopolistic hold on the oil industry. As one of 34 independent units carved out of the former parent company, Socal, sporting a new official name of Standard Oil (California), would have to do without Standard's financial backing, but the new competitor hardly faced the world unarmed. Socal kept its dominant marketing and refining position, its extensive network of critical pipelines, a modest but growing fleet of oil tankers, its many oil wells, and, most helpfully, some $14 million in retained earnings. The latter proved useful in Socal's subsequent rapid expansion, as did California's growing popularity among U.S. citizens looking for a fresh start in life. The state population shot up quickly, and most of the new residents found that they depended on the automobile, and hence on gasoline, to navigate the state's many highway miles.

The years leading up to World War I saw a marked increase in Socal's production of crude. From a base of about 3 percent of the state's production in the early part of the century, Socal rode a series of successful oil strikes to a remarkable 26 percent of nationwide crude production in 1919. The company expanded further in 1926 with the acquisition of the Pacific Oil Company, a division of Southern Pacific Railroad Company, a merger that led to the adoption of the name Standard Oil Company of California. As the national production leader, Socal found itself in a predicament that would be repeated throughout its history: an excess of crude and a shortage of outlets for it. For most of the other leading international oil companies, the situation was reversed,

crude generally being in short supply in a world increasingly dependent on oil. Particularly in the aftermath of World War I, of which the British diplomat George Curzon said "the Allies floated to victory on a wave of oil," there was much anxiety in the United States about a possible shortage of domestic crude supplies. A number of the major oil companies began exploring more vigorously around the world. Socal took its part in these efforts but with a notable lack of success, namely 37 straight dry holes in six different countries. More internationally oriented firms, such as Jersey Standard and Socony-Vacuum Oil Company, soon secured footholds in what was to become the future center of world oil production, the Middle East, whereas Socal, with many directors skeptical about overseas drilling, remained content with its California supplies and burgeoning retail business.

In the late 1920s Socal's posture changed. At that time Gulf Corporation was unable to interest its fellow partners in Iraq Petroleum Company in the oil rights to Bahrain, a small group of islands off the coast of Saudi Arabia. Iraq Petroleum was then the chief cartel of oil companies operating in the Middle East, and its members were restricted by the Red Line Agreement of 1928 from engaging in oil development independently of the entire group. Gulf was therefore unable to proceed with its Bahrain concession and sold its rights for $50,000 to Socal, which was prodded by Maurice Lombardi and William Berg, two members of its board of directors. This venture proved successful. In 1930 Socal geologists struck oil in Bahrain, and within a few years, the California company had joined the ranks of international marketers of oil.

Bahrain's real importance, however, lay in its proximity to the vast fields of neighboring Saudi Arabia. The richest of all oil reserves lay beneath an inhospitable desert and until the early 1930s was left alone by the oil prospectors. Yet at that time, encouraged by the initial successes at Bahrain, Saudi Arabia's King Ibn Saud hired a U.S. geologist to study his country's potential oil reserves. The geologist, Karl Twitchell, liked what he saw and tried on behalf of the king to sell the concession to a number of U.S. oil companies. None was interested except the now adventurous Socal, which in 1933 won a modest bidding war and obtained drilling rights for a £5,000 annual fee and a loan of £50,000. After initial exploration revealed the fantastic extent of Arabian oil, Socal executives realized that the company would need access to markets far larger than its own meager foreign holdings, and in 1936 Socal sold 50 percent of its drilling rights in Saudi Arabia and Bahrain to the Texas Company, later Texaco, the only other major oil company not bound by the Red Line Agreement. Thus the California-Texas Oil Company (Caltex) was created.

Once the oil started flowing in 1939, King Saud was so pleased with his partners and the profits they generated for his impoverished country that he increased the size of their concession to 440,000 square miles, an area the size of Texas, Louisiana, Oklahoma, and New Mexico combined.

POSTWAR EXPANSION

Socal and the Texas Company agreed to market their products under the brand name Caltex and developed excellent representation in both Europe and the Far East, especially in Japan. The new partners realized soon after the end of World War II, however, that the Saudi oilfields were too big even for the both of them, and in 1948, to raise further capital, they sold 40 percent of the recently formed Arabian American Oil Company (Aramco) for $450 million, 30 percent going to Jersey Standard (later Exxon Corporation), and 10 percent to Socony-Vacuum (later Mobil Corporation), leaving the two original partners with 30 percent each. With its crude supply secure for the foreseeable future, Socal was able to market oil around the world, as well as in North America's fastest-growing demographic region, California and the Pacific Coast. As a later company chairman, R. Gwin Follis, put it, Saudi Arabia was a "jackpot beyond belief," supplying Caltex markets overseas with unlimited amounts of low-priced, high-grade oil. By the mid-1950s Socal was getting one-third of its crude production out of Aramco and, more significantly, calculated that Saudi Arabia accounted for two-thirds of its reserve supply. Other important fields had been discovered in Sumatra and Venezuela, but Socal was particularly dependent on its Aramco concession for crude.

On the domestic scene, Socal by 1949 had grown into one of the few U.S. companies with $1 billion in assets. No longer the number one domestic crude producer, Socal was still among the leaders and had made plentiful strikes in Louisiana and Texas, as well as in its native California. In addition to its original refineries at Point Richmond and El Segundo, Socal had added new facilities in Bakersfield, California, and in Salt Lake City, Utah. Socal's marketing territory included at least some representation in 15 western states and a limited foray into the northeastern United States, mainly as an outlet for some of its inexpensive Middle Eastern oil. The heart of Socal territory was still west of the Rocky Mountains, where the company continued to control about 28 percent of the retail market during the postwar years, easily a dominant share in the nation's leading automotive region.

In the two decades following the war the U.S. economy became completely dependent on oil. As both

a cause and an effect of this trend, the world was awash in oil. The Middle East, Latin America, and Southeast Asia all contributed mightily to a prolonged glut, which steadily lowered the price of oil in real dollars. The enormous growth in world consumption assured Socal of a progressive rise in sales and a concomitant increase in profits at an annual rate of about 5.5 percent. By 1957, for example, Socal was selling $1.7 billion worth of oil products annually and ranked as the world's seventh largest oil concern. Its California base offered Socal a number of advantages in the prevailing buyer's market. By drawing on its own local wells for the bulk of its U.S. sales, Socal was able to keep its transportation costs lower than most of its competitors, and California's zooming population and automobile-oriented economy afforded an ideal marketplace. As a result, Socal consistently had one of the best profit margins among all oil companies during the 1950s and 1960s.

California crude production had begun to slow, however, and along with the rest of the world Socal grew ever more dependent on Middle Eastern oil for its overall health. The rich Bay Marchand strike off the Louisiana coast helped stem the tide temporarily. By 1961 Socal was drawing 27.9 million barrels per year from Marchand and had bought Standard Oil Company of Kentucky to market its gasoline in the southeastern United States. Yet the added domestic production only masked Socal's increasing reliance on Saudi Arabian oil, which by 1971 provided more than three-quarters of Socal's proven reserves. As long as the Middle Eastern countries remained cooperative, such an imbalance was not of great concern, and by vigorously selling its inexpensive Middle Eastern oil in Europe and Asia, Socal was able to rack up a record number of profit increases every year in the 1960s. By 1970, 20 percent of Socal's $4 billion in sales was generated in the Far East, with Japan again providing the lion's share of that figure. The firm's European gas stations, owned jointly with Texaco until 1967, numbered 8,000.

THE OPEC CHALLENGE

The world oil picture had changed fundamentally by 1970, however. The 20-year oil surplus had given way in the face of rampant consumption to a general and increasing shortage, a shift soon taken advantage of by OPEC members. In 1973 and 1974 OPEC effectively took control of oil at its source and engineered a fourfold increase in the base price of oil. Socal was able to rely on its Saudi partner for only a tiny price advantage over the general rate, and it was no longer in legal control of sufficient crude to supply its worldwide or domestic demand. The sudden shift in oil politics revealed a number of Socal shortcomings. Although it had 17,000 gas stations in 39 U.S. states, Socal was not a skilled marketer either in the United States or in Europe, where its former partner, Texaco, had supplied local marketing savvy. In its home state of California, for example, Socal's market share was 16 percent and continuing to drop, and Socal had missed out on both the North Sea and Alaskan oil discoveries of the late 1960s. Furthermore, the OPEC-spawned upheaval included the nationalization of a number of Caltex holdings in the Middle East, and in 1978 Caltex Oil Refining (India) Ltd. was nationalized by the government of India. A further blow to Socal's overseas operations came in 1980 when the government of Saudi Arabia nationalized Aramco.

Socal responded to these problems by merging all of its domestic marketing into a single unit, Chevron USA, and began cutting employment, at first gradually and later more deeply. Also, Socal stepped up its domestic exploration efforts while moving into alternative sources of energy, such as shale, coal, and uranium. In 1981 the company made a $4 billion bid for AMAX Inc., a leader in coal and metal mining but had to settle for a 20 percent stake. In 1984 Standard Oil Company of California changed its name to Chevron Corporation, tying the company more directly with its main marketing brand. Also in 1984, after a decade of sporadic attempts to lessen its dependence on the volatile Middle East, Chevron Corporation met its short-term oil needs in a more direct fashion by buying Gulf Corporation.

The $13.2 billion purchase, at that time the largest in the history of U.S. business, more than doubled Chevron's proven reserves and created a new giant in the U.S. oil industry, with Chevron the leading domestic retailer of gasoline and, briefly, the second largest oil company by assets. Certain factors made the move appear ill-timed, however. Oil prices had peaked around 1980 and begun a long slide that continued until the Gulf War of 1990, which meant that Chevron had saddled itself with a $12 billion debt at a time of shrinking sales. As a result, it was not easy for Chevron to sell off assets as quickly as desired, both to reduce debt and to eliminate the many areas of overlap created by the merger. Chevron eventually rid itself of Gulf's Canadian operations and all of Gulf's gas stations in the northeastern and southeastern United States, paring 16,000 jobs in the meantime, but oil analysts pointed to such key figures as profit per employee and return of capital as evidence of Chevron's continued poor performance.

DEVELOPMENTS IN THE NINETIES

In the early 1990s Chevron began publicizing its environmental programs, a response in part to public pressure on all oil companies for more responsible environmental policies. From 1989 to 1993 Chevron Shipping Company had the best overall safety record among major oil companies. In 1993, while transporting nearly 625 million barrels of crude oil, Chevron Shipping spilled an amount equaling less than four barrels. During this same period, Chevron Utilities Supervisor Pete Duda recognized an opportunity to convert an abandoned wastewater treatment pond into a 90-acre wetland. Fresh water and new vegetation were added to the site, and by 1994 the area was attracting a variety of birds and other wildlife, as well as the attention of the National Audubon Society, *National Geographic,* and the California Department of Fish and Game. The conversion saved Chevron millions, as conventional closure of the site would have cost about $20 million.

Financially the company began the 1990s with less than glowing returns. Chevron's 1989 results were poor, and in that year's annual report, Chairman Kenneth Derr announced a program to upgrade the company's efficiency and outlined as well a five-year goal: "a return on stockholders' investment that exceeds the performance of our strongest competitors." The company also took important new initiatives. In 1993 Chevron entered into a partnership with the Republic of Kazakhstan to develop the Tengiz oilfield, one of the largest ever discovered in the area.

In 1994, five years after Derr's announcement, Chevron had met its goal for stockholders, largely through restructuring and efforts to cut costs and improve efficiency. From 1989 to 1993 Chevron cut operating costs by more than $1 per barrel and the company's stock rose to an 18.9 percent return, compared with an average of 13.2 percent for its competitors. The company celebrated this achievement by giving 42,000 of its employees a one-time bonus of 5 percent of their base pay.

After meeting its five-year goal, Chevron continued its cost-cutting and efficiency efforts. In December 1995 the company announced a restructuring of its U.S. gasoline marketing unit. It combined regional offices, consolidated support functions, and refocused the marketing unit toward service and sales growth. One example of the company's new efforts toward marketing was a joint initiative with fast-food giant McDonald's Corporation. In April 1997, as a response to "one-stop shopping" marketing trends, Chevron and McDonald's together opened a new gas station and food facility in

Lakewood, California. The two companies shared the space, and customers could order food and pump gas at the same time. They could pay for the order with a Chevron card. More Chevron/McDonald's facilities were planned for California and elsewhere in the United States.

Chevron also cut its refining capacity, where margins were especially low in the early 1990s. Capacity dropped 407,000 barrels per day from 1992 to 1995. The company helped reduce its refining capacity by selling its Port Arthur, Texas, refinery in February 1995 to Clark Refining & Marketing Inc. Chevron controlled 10.2 percent of U.S. refining capacity in 1992 but just 7.5 percent by 1995. These measures seemed to improve the company's fortunes, as its earnings jumped in 1996 to more than $2.6 billion, an all-time high. Stockholder return for the year was 28.5 percent. High gasoline prices also contributed to Chevron's huge profits. The company was able to take advantage of high crude prices by increasing production at its Kazakhstan and West African facilities. Also during 1996, Chevron sold its natural gas gathering, processing, and marketing operations to Houston-based NGC Corporation, gaining a 27 percent stake in the Houston-based energy marketer and trader, which changed its name to Dynegy Inc. in 1998; Chevron retained ownership of its gas fields and its gas production operations. Late in 1997 Chevron sold the marketing side of Gulf Oil (Great Britain) Limited to a unit of Royal Dutch/Shell Group in a deal that included 450 service stations in the United Kingdom and three fuel terminals.

Cracks in the OPEC cartel and more efficient energy exploration technologies led to an oil glut and plunging oil prices in 1998 and 1999. With prices falling to as low as $10 per barrel, several major oil companies responded with a wave of megamergers that transformed the industry. Chevron, however, completed only two smaller acquisitions in 1999, picking up Rutherford-Moran Oil Corporation, a small U.S. independent with proven oil and gas reserves in the Gulf of Thailand, and Petrolera Argentina San Jorge S.A., the number three oil company in Argentina. The company made unsuccessful bids for both Atlantic Richfield Corporation and Amoco Corporation (both of which eventually were subsumed within BP p.l.c., the successor of British Petroleum Company PLC) and entered into advanced merger talks with Texaco in mid-1999. The latter discussions failed at least in part because the two sides could not agree on who should head the combined firm. Meanwhile, Chevron exited from offshore California production in early 1999 when it sold its share of the Point Arguello project, located offshore near the city of Santa Barbara, and the rest of its California offshore properties to Venoco Inc. At the end of 1999 Derr retired from Chevron after 11 years as chairman and CEO, with Vice-Chairman Dave O'Reilly taking over those positions.

FORMATION OF CHEVRONTEXACO IN 2001

In addition to the spate of megamergers, the period around the end of the millennium was also noteworthy for the number of major joint ventures that were formed between various petroleum companies. For its part, Chevron combined its worldwide chemical operations with those of Phillips Petroleum Company (later ConocoPhillips), forming a 50-50 joint venture called Chevron Phillips Chemical Company LLC. Created in July 2000, the new venture began with about $6.1 billion in total assets and $5.7 billion in annual revenues. The two companies anticipated annual cost savings of about $150 million from the combination, partly from the elimination of about 600 positions, or 10 percent of the combined workforce.

A few months after the consummation of this merger, Chevron belatedly joined the megamerger bandwagon with the announcement of the merger of Chevron and Texaco, the longtime Caltex partners. The deal was struck despite the spike in oil prices, which had reached about $30 a barrel by the time of the merger announcement in October 2000, and the paramount rationale for the combination was the potential for substantial cost savings. Initial estimates were for $1.2 billion in annual savings. Structured as a Chevron takeover of Texaco, the merger was completed on October 9, 2001, with Texaco shareholders receiving 0.77 shares of common stock in ChevronTexaco Corporation, the new name adopted by Chevron Corporation. The final value of the deal was $45 billion, including $38.3 billion in Texaco stock and $6.7 billion in Texaco debt. Texaco Inc. became a subsidiary of ChevronTexaco. Also becoming a wholly owned subsidiary of the newly enlarged firm was Caltex Corporation, which had moved its headquarters from Texas to Singapore in 1999 to be closer to its core markets. ChevronTexaco began with a market capitalization of $97 billion, enabling it to join the ranks of the so-called supermajor oil firms, which included Exxon Mobil Corporation, BP, and Royal Dutch/Shell. Headquarters for the company initially remained in San Francisco, but the head office was moved to a nearby San Ramon business park during 2002. The management team of ChevronTexaco were O'Reilly as chairman and CEO along with two vice-chairmen, Richard Matzke, who had been Chevron vice-chairman, and Glenn Tilton, who had become chairman and CEO of Texaco in February 2001.

In approving the merger, the Federal Trade Commission ordered the divestment of stakes in two refining and marketing joint ventures inherited from Texaco: Equilon Enterprises LLC and Motiva Enterprises LLC. These interests were transferred to a trust prior to completion of the merger. Then in February 2002 Shell Oil Company and Saudi Refining, Inc., purchased the interests for $2.26 billion in cash and the assumption of $1.6 billion in debt. Meanwhile, in October 2001, the development of the Tengiz field in Kazakhstan received a boost when a new pipeline came online. Previously much of the crude oil from the field had been shipped by rail through Russia to the seaport of Ventspils, Latvia. The new 900-mile, $2.6 billion pipeline, built by the Caspian Pipeline Consortium, 15 percent owned by ChevronTexaco, ran from the Tengiz field westward through Russia to the Black Sea port of Novorossiysk. This represented a much less costly form of transportation for exporting the crude oil.

Another development in late 2001 came through ChevronTexaco's equity stake in Dynegy. Energy trading giant Enron Corporation was on the verge of bankruptcy, with its stock price plunging, amid allegations of accounting and other improprieties. In November Dynegy announced an agreement to buy Enron for about $9 billion, and ChevronTexaco committed to inject an additional $2.5 billion into Dynegy in support of the merger. With the continuing collapse in Enron's stock price, however, Dynegy canceled the deal later in November. This led to Enron declaring bankruptcy and also suing Dynegy for withdrawing from the takeover, with a countersuit soon following. Dynegy turned financially troubled itself in 2002 and pulled out of the energy trading market. ChevronTexaco was forced to write off about $2.2 billion of its investment in Dynegy that year. The company sold its Dynegy stake in 2007, resulting in a gain of $680 million.

The initial postmerger integration efforts led ChevronTexaco to suffer a net loss of $2.52 billion for the fourth quarter of 2001. This included $1.17 billion in charges related to the merger, including severance payments for some of the 4,500 employees who lost their jobs as a result of the merger, facility-closure costs, and other expenses. The company took an additional $1.85 billion in write-downs of energy, mineral, and chemical assets as it looked closely at the combined operations and pared back on investments. ChevronTexaco eventually increased its estimate of the annual cost savings derived from the merger to around $2.2 billion. In its full-year results for 2001, ChevronTexaco reported net income of $3.29 billion on revenues of $104.41 billion.

In a plan launched in 2003 to boost profits, the company divested a substantial portion of its North American oil and gas fields. Most of these were mature fields with steadily declining production. ChevronTexaco elected to concentrate more of its resources on higher growth and potentially more lucrative projects overseas, including fields in West Africa, Venezuela, Australia, and Kazakhstan. Also in 2003, the company reached a settlement with the U.S. Justice Department and the Environmental Protection Agency to spend around $275 million to clean up emissions from five of its U.S. oil refineries, located in California, Mississippi, Utah, and Hawaii.

Soaring oil and natural gas prices propelled ChevronTexaco's profits up 84 percent in 2004, to $13.33 billion. The revenue total of $155.3 billion represented a 28 percent increase. Despite these prodigious numbers, ChevronTexaco faced significant challenges, particularly on the upstream side, as both its production and reserves were trending downward. The takeover of Texaco had produced its share of disappointments, including the discovery that some of Texaco's oilfields contained less oil than expected and the cropping up of political hurdles overseas that delayed the development of certain Texaco-originated projects, including a highly touted field off the coast of Nigeria. The desire to bulk up its production and reserves led ChevronTexaco to pursue another major acquisition.

2005 TAKEOVER OF UNOCAL

In early April 2005 ChevronTexaco entered into an agreement to buy its California neighbor, El Segundo-based Unocal Corporation, for $16.8 billion in cash and stock. A month later the company switched its name back to Chevron Corporation, ending some confusion that had arisen from the use of the hybrid name; Texaco nevertheless remained one of the firm's three main marketing brands, along with Chevron and Caltex. Soon thereafter, Chevron's takeover of Unocal was placed in doubt when CNOOC Limited, a major petroleum company controlled by the government of China, stepped in with its own offer for Unocal, an all-cash bid of $18.5 billion. A politically tinged takeover battle ensued, which Chevron managed to win after whipping up anti-China sentiment within what had been a solidly free-trade-backing U.S. Congress and by sweetening its original bid. When Chevron closed the deal in August 2005, the deal was valued at $17.29 billion. Unocal had accepted the lower bid after lawmakers in Washington inserted into an energy bill a provision requiring that a study be conducted into the economic and national security implications of a CNOOC takeover of Unocal. The required study would have left Unocal in a state of limbo for several months.

At the time of its takeover, Unocal was one of the world's largest independent oil and gas exploration and production companies. Acquiring Unocal boosted Chevron's oil and gas reserves by about 1.7 billion barrels, or roughly 15 percent, and added 400,000 barrels to its daily production output. Chevron gained a number of major long-term projects that were on the verge of paying off. The majority of these were in Asia, where half of Unocal's proven reserves had resided, and included Attaka, the largest oil and gas field in Indonesia; significant natural gas production in Thailand, which powered 30 percent of Thai electricity production; the Pattani oilfield in Thailand, where production doubled to 15,000 barrels per day in 2005; and the firm's 10 percent interest in a consortium controlling four billion barrels of oil in the Caspian Sea. In addition to the Southeast Asian properties, which served both local markets and oil-hungry China and India, and the Caspian Sea project, which was situated to supply the European and Russian markets, Unocal also had valuable properties in the Gulf of Mexico to supply the U.S. market.

By 2007 Chevron had leveraged soaring oil prices into record profits of $18.69 billion on record revenues of $220.9 billion. Profits would have been still higher, but the high cost of oil hurt the company's downstream operations, which were further affected by downtime at its U.S. refineries. During the year, Chevron's main regions for oil exploration included the offshore area of West Africa, the Gulf of Mexico, offshore northwest Australia, and the Gulf of Thailand. The company was also selected by PetroChina Company Limited to help develop a major natural gas field in Sichuan Province. Chevron's involvement in certain risky projects also came to the fore in 2007, when authorities in Kazakhstan slapped a $609 million fine for environmental violations on the Chevron-led consortium developing the Tengiz oilfield. Oil from this field contained deadly hydrogen-sulfide gas, and the authorities contended that the consortium was improperly storing the sulfur that it was stripping from the oil after its extraction. Also in 2007, Chevron sold its fuels marketing businesses in Belgium, the Netherlands, and Luxembourg to the Delek Group Ltd. of Israel for about $516 million.

Early in 2008, Chevron gained further prestige on Wall Street when its stock joined that of its main U.S. rival, Exxon Mobil, as one of the 30 components of the Dow Jones Industrial Average. For much of the year, Chevron enjoyed a continuation of a months-long gusher of profits stemming from record crude oil prices that peaked during the third quarter at a historic high of $145.29 per barrel. The global economic crisis that arose suddenly that same quarter, however, quickly undermined demand for petroleum products and pulled oil prices into a swift decline, down to around $45 per barrel by year-end. Although Chevron's downstream side benefited from this sudden reversal, the company eked out only the barest of profit increases for the fourth quarter. The full-year totals were nevertheless new records of $23.93 billion in profits on sales of $273.01 billion.

During this volatile year, Chevron pushed ahead with major projects around the world. In March, Chevron and its partners announced their intention to begin construction of a new $3.1 billion natural gas project in the Gulf of Thailand, with production expected to commence in early 2011. A Chevron-led consortium in August reached an agreement with the Canadian province of Newfoundland and Labrador to develop the Hebron offshore oilfield, which was estimated to contain 700 million barrels of heavy oil. The project, the cost of which was estimated at $6.6 billion, was expected to come onstream as early as 2016. Among the projects in which first production was achieved in 2008 was the deepwater Blind Faith project in the Gulf of Mexico, which was estimated to contain more than 100 million barrels of oil equivalent in the form of both crude oil and natural gas.

In the early months of 2009, Chevron unloaded a number of marketing operations overseas as part of an effort to refocus its downstream business on the Pacific Rim. In addition to divesting several fuels marketing businesses in Africa, the company also sold its fuel distribution assets in Brazil to the Brazilian firm Ultrapar Participações S.A. for around $720 million. Also under consideration was a rationalization of the company's refinery assets. Around this same time, John S. Watson was named Chevron's vice-chairman, which appeared to position him to succeed the 62-year-old O'Reilly as chairman and CEO. After leading the integration of Chevron and Texaco, Watson had served as CFO, headed an international production unit, and then served as executive vice-president of strategy and development. Chevron in March 2009 announced it had decided to curtail its spending on some oil- and gas-producing projects. Because the costs of certain goods and services had not fallen in concert with the decline in oil prices, the company concluded it made economic sense to delay certain investments until these costs came down. The result would be a short-term decline in production. While grappling with the consequences of the economic downturn, Chevron, along with its industry rivals, was gearing up to fight several initiatives from the nascent administration of Barack Obama, including proposals for a new excise tax on production in the Gulf of Mexico and the elimination of various tax breaks worth billions of dollars to the oil and gas industry. A centerpiece of President Obama's agenda was an effort to transition the country to clean-energy sources both to reduce dependence on foreign oil and combat global climate change.

Jonathan Martin
Updated, Terry Bain; David E. Salamie

PRINCIPAL SUBSIDIARIES

Cabinda Gulf Oil Company Limited (Bermuda); Chevron Africa and Latin America Exploration and Production Company; Chevron Argentina S.R.L.; Chevron Asia Pacific Exploration and Production Company; Chevron Canada Funding Corporation; Chevron Canada Limited; Chevron Europe, Eurasia and Middle East Exploration & Production Limited; Chevron Funding Corporation; Chevron Geothermal Indonesia, Ltd. (Bermuda); Chevron Global Energy Inc.; Chevron Global Power Company; Chevron Mining Inc.; Chevron Nigeria Limited; Chevron North America Exploration and Production Company; Chevron Oronite Company LLC; Chevron Pipe Line Company; Chevron Products Company; Chevron Thailand Exploration and Production, Ltd. (Bermuda); Chevron Transport Corporation Ltd. (Bermuda); Chevron U.S.A. Inc.; PT Chevron Pacific Indonesia; Saudi Arabian Chevron Inc.; Texaco Capital Inc.; Texaco Inc.; Unocal Corporation.

PRINCIPAL COMPETITORS

Exxon Mobil Corporation; Royal Dutch Shell plc; BP p.l.c.; TOTAL S.A.; ConocoPhillips.

FURTHER READING

Barrionuevo, Alexei, "Chevron and Phillips Petroleum to Form Venture with $5.7 Billion in Revenue," *Wall Street Journal,* February 8, 2000, p. A4.

Barrionuevo, Alexei, and Thaddeus Herrick, "Texaco to Sell Stakes in Two Joint Ventures," *Wall Street Journal,* October 10, 2001, p. A4.

Berman, Dennis K., and Russell Gold, "Chevron Raises Its Bid for Unocal," *Wall Street Journal,* July 20, 2005, p. A3.

Blackwood, Francy, "Chevron Environment Effort: Think Locally, Act Globally," *San Francisco Business Times,* November 4, 1994, p. 2A.

Brady, Rose, and Peter Galuszka, "The Scramble for Oil's Last Frontier," *Business Week,* January 11, 1993, pp. 42+.

Calvey, Mark, "Executive of the Year 2001: ChevronTexaco CEO David O'Reilly Runs Well-Oiled Machine," *San Francisco Business Times,* December 31, 2001.

"Chevron, Phillips to Form Giant Chemical JV," *Oil and Gas Journal,* February 14, 2000, pp. 24–25.

"Chevron Scaling Back Point Arguello amid Exit," *Oil and Gas Journal,* November 30, 1998, pp. 26–28.

"Chevron, Texaco Agree to Merge in All-Stock Deal," *Oil and Gas Journal,* October 23, 2000, pp. 28–30.

Cook, James, "Hungry Again," *Forbes,* March 7, 1988, pp. 68+.

Culbertson, Katherine, "Share of U.S. Refining Capacity Controlled by Top 4 Majors Dwindles, API Study Says," *Oil Daily,* July 31, 1996, p. 1.

Dorman, Shirleen, "Chevron's Net Income Soars," *Wall Street Journal,* November 1, 2008, p. B5.

Fan, Aliza, "Analysts Praise Chevron Restructuring As Bold Move to Boost Downstream," *Oil Daily,* December 19, 1995, p. 3.

Folmer, L. W., *Reaching for a Star: Experiences in the International Oil Business,* Austin, Tex.: L.W. Folmer, 1993, 243 p.

Gold, Russell, "ChevronTexaco to Acquire Unocal," *Wall Street Journal,* April 5, 2005, p. A3.

———, "Reserve Judgment: In Deal for Unocal, Chevron Gambles on High Oil Prices," *Wall Street Journal,* August 10, 2005, p. A1.

Gold, Russell, and Ben Casselman, "Chevron Warns of Hefty Drop in Earnings," *Wall Street Journal,* January 9, 2009, p. B1.

Hartley, Fred L., *"The Spirit of 76": The Story of the Union Oil Company of California,* New York: Newcomen Society in North America, 1977, 20 p.

Haynes, H. J., *Standard Oil Company of California: 100 Years Helping to Create the Future,* New York: Newcomen Society in North America, 1980, 22 p.

Herrick, Thaddeus, "ChevronTexaco Vows Not to Cut Output," *Wall Street Journal,* October 17, 2000, p. A3.

Hidy, Ralph W., and Muriel E. Hidy, *History of Standard Oil Company (New Jersey),* Vol. 1: *Pioneering in Big Business, 1882–1911,* New York: Harper & Brothers, 1955, 839 p.

Howe, Kenneth, "Chevron's Turn to Play?: Oil Giant Could Be Jumping on the Merger Bandwagon," *San Francisco Chronicle,* August 21, 1998, p. B1.

"Hunting the Big One," *Economist,* October 21, 2000, p. 71.

James, Marquis, *The Texaco Story: The First Fifty Years, 1902–1952,* New York: The Texas Company, 1953, 118 p.

Klaw, Spencer, "Standard of California," *Fortune,* November 1958.

Kolbenschlag, Michael, "The Luxury of Time," *Forbes,* September 14, 1981, pp. 42+.

Lazarus, David, "Vice Chairman Chosen to Lead Chevron," *San Francisco Chronicle,* September 30, 1999, p. B1.

Liesman, Steve, "Chevron and Texaco Argue That Size Isn't Everything: Companies Dissent, for Now, from Oil Industry's Megamerger Mindset," *Wall Street Journal,* December 30, 1998, p. B4.

Linsenmeyer, Adrienne, "Chevron's Oil Crisis," *Financial World,* October 30, 1990, pp. 26+.

Louis, Arthur M., "Deal's Done on Chevron-Texaco Merger," *San Francisco Chronicle,* October 17, 2000, p. A1.

Mack, Toni, "Can Ken Derr Turn Chevron Around?" *Forbes,* November 27, 1989, pp. 49+.

Mellow, Craig, "Big Oil's Pipe Dream," *Fortune,* March 2, 1998, pp. 158–60+.

Miller, William H., "Chevron Bridges the Gulf," *Industry Week,* May 12, 1986, pp. 65+.

Palmer, Jay, "Here Comes Chevron!: The Once-Lagging Oil Giant Steps Up the Pace," *Barron's,* May 6, 1991, pp. 16+.

Palmeri, Christopher, and Stephanie Anderson Forest, "An Oil Giant Springs a Leak," *Business Week,* August 5, 2002, pp. 78, 80.

Pederson, Barbara L., *A Century of Spirit: Unocal, 1890–1990,* Los Angeles: Unocal Corporation, 1990, 326 p.

Petzinger, Thomas, *Oil and Honor: The Texaco-Pennzoil Wars,* New York: Putnam, 1987, 495 p.

Quirt, John, "Socal Is Looking Homeward," *Fortune,* March 10, 1980, p. 66.

Racanelli, Vito J., "Bigger Really Is Better: Benefits of Chevron's Acquisition of Texaco Seem Underappreciated," *Barron's,* May 28, 2001, pp. 19–20.

Sampson, Anthony, *The Seven Sisters: The Great Oil Companies and the World They Made,* New York: Viking Press, 1975, 334 p.

Schwartz, Nelson D., "Chevron's Dave O'Reilly: Pumped Up," *Fortune,* September 5, 2005, pp. 119–20, 123–24, 126.

Shannon, James, *Texaco and the $10 Billion Jury,* Englewood Cliffs, N.J.: Prentice Hall, 1988, 545 p.

Shao, Maria, "Ken Derr's Got the Money—but What Will He Do with It?" *Business Week,* September 5, 1988, p. 27.

Texaco Today: The Spirit of the Star, 1902–1992, White Plains, N.Y.: Texaco Inc., 1992, 40 p.

Vitiello, Greg, *A Century of Energy,* Harrison, N.Y.: Texaco Inc., 2001, 82 p.

Welty, Earl M., and Frank J. Taylor, *The 76 Bonanza: The Fabulous Life and Times of the Union Oil Company of California,* Menlo Park, Calif.: Lane Magazine and Book Company, 1966, 351 p.

White, Gerald Taylor, *Formative Years in the Far West: A History of Standard Oil Company of California and Predecessors Through 1919,* New York: Appleton-Century-Crofts, 1962, 694 p.

Wilson, James W., et al., "The Chevron-Gulf Merger: Does It Still Make Sense?" *Business Week,* January 21, 1985, pp. 102+.

Winning, David, "Chevron Taps into China's Energy Output with Pact to Develop PetroChina Gas Field," *Wall Street Journal,* August 7, 2007, p. A3.

CHRISTIE®

Christie Digital Systems, Inc.

—•—

10550 Camden Drive
Cypress, California 90630
U.S.A.
Telephone: (714) 236-8610
Toll Free: (866) 880-4462
Fax: (714) 503-3375
Web site: http://www.christiedigital.com

Wholly Owned Subsidiary of Ushio, Inc.
Incorporated: 1929 as McColpin-Christie Corp., Ltd.
Employees: 751
Sales: $400 million (2008 est.)
NAICS: 334310 Audio and Video Equipment Manufacturing

■ ■ ■

Christie Digital Systems, Inc., is a leading manufacturer of video and film projection equipment. Its customers include such top names in the motion picture industry as Regal Cinemedia, Pixar, and Industrial Light & Magic; such major corporations as Boeing and AT&T; numerous government agencies; and producers of large-scale entertainment events. Christie has production facilities in California and Ontario, Canada, and maintains 13 sales offices around the world.

BEGINNINGS

Christie Digital Systems traces its roots to 1929, when Norwegian immigrant S. L. Christie helped found a company in Los Angeles to produce battery chargers and electrical power supplies. The latter were used by movie theaters and others to power carbon-arc lamps, and over time McColpin-Christie Corp. began providing other equipment to the film industry including projectors.

In the 1960s the firm partnered with bulb-maker Ushio, Inc., of Japan to develop a replacement for carbon-arcs, which had been the only light source bright enough to produce a good-quality image on a large screen. They required frequent attention, however, and did not burn for the full length of a feature film, which meant that projectionists had to change reels during a presentation so they could tend the carbons on the opposite machine. Starting with an ultra-bright bulb developed in Germany during World War II to direct antiaircraft fire at planes, they created the first practical pressurized xenon gas lamphouse for film projection, which could be used for a thousand hours or more with minimal attention.

The new, long-lasting lamps paved the way for single-machine, automated projection of films, which in turn helped facilitate the rise of multiplexes. During the 1970s Christie added related products including a platter system, in which a full-feature film could be spliced together on its side on a large metal disc, as well as film handling equipment sold under the name Autowind. The company became a leading provider of such products, and also added innovative new ones including a self-contained xenon lamphouse and power supply. Christie's accomplishments were recognized by the Academy of Motion Picture Arts and Sciences in 1983 with a Technical Achievement Award for the Ultramittent, a gearless version of a critical projector component that yielded a more stable image.

CHRISTIE SOLD TO USHIO IN 1992

In 1992 company head Tom Christie sold the firm to longtime partner Ushio, and in 1995 it set up an office in Singapore to sell products in Asia. A year later the company moved from Los Angeles to Cypress, California, the U.S. headquarters of Ushio, and in March 1998 Christie won a second technical Oscar for its Endless Loop film transport system.

Change was looming on the horizon, however, as technologies for digital image manipulation and display began to improve in quality and brightness. With Hollywood soothsayers foreseeing the demise of the cumbersome, fragile, and expensive medium of 35mm film for both production and distribution, in 1999 Christie acquired Kitchener, Ontario-based video projector maker Electrohome Projection Systems for CAD 38 million.

Electrohome's roots dated to 1907, when Arthur Pollock and engineer Alex Welker founded Pollock Manufacturing Co., Ltd., to produce a "hornless" phonograph called the Pollock Talking Machine. In 1933 the firm changed its name to Dominion Electrohome Industries to reflect a broadened product lineup that included electric fans and mixers. Revenues topped $1 million by 1938, and during World War II produc-

tion expanded to include airplane wings, tails, and related items. By the late 1940s the company employed 1,400.

During the 1950s the firm began manufacturing television sets and a wider range of appliances, and also launched radio and television stations in partnership with other investors. Over time its operations came to include a Canadian service network and a plant that made motors for the auto industry, and by the end of the 1960s Electrohome (as it was officially known) had taken its place as one of the nation's top consumer brand names, known for high-quality televisions, stereo systems, air conditioners, and other electronic products and furniture. In 1971 Harvard M.B.A.-degreed John Pollock took over as company president from his father Carl, who had held the position since his own father Arthur's death in 1951.

BEGINNING OF ELECTROHOME PROJECTION SYSTEMS: 1979

Electrohome employed 4,400 at five plants, but sales of the firm's electronics and furniture soon began to plummet due to competition from less expensive imports. Nearly bankrupt by the mid-1970s, the company began slashing costs and jobs while seeking new, more profitable ventures away from consumer markets. In 1979 Electrohome Projection Systems was formed to build on the firm's expertise in television manufacturing by developing specialized monitors and video projectors for use in boardrooms, educational institutions, and other applications including arcade games. After starting with the world's first large-screen data projection system, a three-lens unit, in 1983 the company brought out the first single-lens projector. The 75-pound ECP 1000 could project a four- by six-foot image from video or computer sources.

Over the next decade Electrohome continued to refine its business model, focusing on commercial electronics and television broadcasting while shedding other businesses. The projection unit continued to grow, gaining visibility in such venues as the O. J. Simpson trial, which used its projectors to display evidence. New products of this period included the Showstar, which could produce a bright image up to 25 feet wide.

In 1995 the company formed a partnership with Texas Instruments, Inc., to develop projection systems. The Vista Pro model, introduced the following year, used Texas Instruments' Digital Light Processing (DLP) three-chip system to produce an extremely sharp and bright image. Customers ranged from automakers BMW and Mercedes Benz to San Francisco's Bay Area Rapid Transit System, which used 15 ceiling-mounted units to track the status of its trains.

KEY DATES

1929: S. L. Christie founds company in Los Angeles to build electronic products.

1030s: Firm boosts offerings to motion picture industry.

1960s: Christie partners with Ushio of Japan to develop xenon projector bulbs.

1979: Electrohome Projection Systems is founded as unit of Electrohome, Ltd., in Canada.

1983: Christie wins technical Academy Award for Ultramittent projector gear.

1992: Ushio buys Christie, Inc., from heirs of S. L. Christie.

1998: Company receives second technical Oscar for Endless Loop film transport system.

1999: Christie purchases Electrohome Projection Systems for $38 million.

2000: Firm introduces first cinema projector with Texas Instruments DLP technology.

2005: Partnership with AccessIT creates Christie/AIX to fund digital cinema rollout.

2007: Vista Control Systems Corp. is acquired.

2008: Brilliant 3D is introduced; Christie projectors are used at Olympics opening ceremony.

During the mid-1990s Electrohome exited the radio business, sold its television stations to Baton Broadcasting for a combination of cash and stock, bought a stake in design partner Robotel Electronique of Quebec, and acquired computer monitor maker Display Technologies of Illinois, although it was sold just two years later at a loss. In April 1998 the firm was split into two halves, one to hold its stake in Baton Broadcasting and the other consisting of projector manufacturing and the new Advanced Visualization Group, which would hold stakes in Robotel and display software developers Fakespace and Immersion Studios.

Despite the positive response to products such as the new 6,000-lumen Roadie video projector for large-scale venues, Electrohome Projection Systems was struggling against global competitors including Sony and NEC, and in late August 1999 the division was sold to Christie, which had earlier approached it to develop digital movie projectors. The sale would not include the Advanced Visualization Group, the separate broadcast holding company, or Electrohome's 300,000-square-foot plant in Kitchener, the manufacturing portion of which Christie would lease and soon begin to upgrade.

FIRST DLP CINEMA OEM PROJECTOR DEBUTS IN 2000

After the sale was finalized, Electrohome Projection Systems was renamed Christie Digital Systems, which in 2000 also became the corporate name of Christie, Inc. During the year the firm was recognized as the first original equipment manufacturer (OEM) of DLP cinema projectors with Texas Instruments technology.

While the company continued to develop and sell digital projectors for a wide range of users including businesses, educational organizations, and government agencies, Christie had its roots in theatrical film exhibition and was working to get a toehold in this new market, which was expected to explode when the technology was mature. By 2001 there were still less than three dozen digital cinemas worldwide, however, and few films had been converted to a high-definition format. Exhibitors were resisting investing in the new projectors, which cost about triple the price of a conventional film unit, while standards for digital cinema had not yet been established. The industry's goal was an image that would look better than 35mm film in resolution, color fidelity, and dynamic range, and would be sharp and bright when projected onto a screen that might be 80 feet wide by four stories tall.

In 2001 Christie partnered with StereoGraphics Corp. of California to develop 3D projection equipment, and also sold its Marquee cathode-ray-tube video projector line to Video Display Corp. of Florida. The following year saw the first completely digital-originated feature film, *Star Wars Episode II: Attack of the Clones,* released. Producer Lucasfilm had used Christie equipment throughout production. Sales for fiscal 2002 were approximately $150 million.

In late 2002 the company announced it would supply digital projectors for pre-show ads and other programming to the world's top theater chain, Regal CineMedia, which would use the new ChristieNET network for distribution. The latter would also allow the firm to control and troubleshoot equipment from its Cypress headquarters. In early 2003 the company also created the Cinema Systems Group to offer turnkey digital cinema packages and signed a deal with Carlton Screen Advertising of the United Kingdom to install 1,000 digital projectors in its theaters.

Christie acquired video equipment rental wholesaler Nationwide in June 2003, and in the fall bought the Kitchener manufacturing facility it had been renting from Electrohome for $5.5 million, which also housed other tenants. The firm employed nearly 350 and had global sales of approximately $200 million. There were some 170 digital cinemas worldwide, 60 percent of which used Christie equipment.

In 2004 the company added a Tokyo sales arm and introduced the CP2000 cinema projector, which offered its highest resolution to date, 2.2 million megapixels at 2048 by 1080 pixel resolution. The firm also continued to sell projectors to corporate, institutional, and other clients.

FORMATION OF CHRISTIE/AIX: 2005

In June 2005 the company signed an agreement with digital film distributor Access Integrated Technologies, Inc., (AccessIT) to create a funding structure to help exhibitors install digital cinema equipment in several thousand U.S. theaters. A new AccessIT subsidiary, Christie/AIX, was formed to administer the plan, which was quickly followed by similar offerings from other pairings including Kodak and Belgian projector maker Barco.

Through Christie/AIX, theater owners would pay only a small portion of the cost of the expensive digital projection system (also agreeing to a long-term maintenance contract), while film studios would make up the difference by paying a "virtual print fee" of $1,000 per screen for each release (about half what a 35mm film print cost). Christie would sell the equipment to Christie/AIX, which would collect the fees.

In addition to the studios' savings on film printing and shipping (estimated at $1 billion per year), and the elimination of image deterioration through wear and tear, there were numerous advantages to exhibitors including the ability to screen live concerts and sports events, add more local or specially targeted advertising, and reduce labor costs for film handling. The studios had long voiced concerns about digital copies being pirated, which were finally addressed in July when the industry's official standards were published by the Digital Cinema Initiative group.

In September Disney's Buena Vista Pictures unit signed an agreement with Christie/AIX to pay the virtual print fee, and other top studios soon followed including Twentieth Century Fox, Universal, and Sony. They would also pledge to make 75 percent of feature releases available in digital format during the first year, and 90 percent in the second. Anticipating a surge in orders, the firm increased its workforce in Kitchener by a third, to nearly 300, and hired 50 more in the United States for distribution and installation. Production was slated to increase from 25 CP2000s per month to 100 as exhibitors began to convert their theaters.

In December the firm signed a deal to outfit the third largest multiplex chain in the United States, Carmike Cinemas, with digital projection systems. Some 2,300 of Carmike's 2,500 screens would be converted over the next two years. The contract, worth up to $300 million, would be administered by Christie/AIX, which had secured $217 million in credit from GE Commercial Finance.

DLP PROJECTOR INSTALLATIONS TOP 1,000 IN 2006

By the summer of 2006 the firm had installed 1,000 DLP cinema projectors and was continuing to hire workers in Kitchener to keep up with demand. Attractive benefits and perks like an in-house fitness facility and chef-run cafeteria kept the turnover rate low. During the year Christie also introduced the HD series of three-chip DLP projectors with native 1920 by 1080 resolution, which were intended for the rental, postproduction, broadcast, and religious markets.

In the summer of 2007 the firm acquired Vista Control Systems Corp., a maker of video processing systems that would be integrated into Christie products. The company had 3,000 digital cinema projectors installed (2,600 of them in the United States), and was completing 400 per month. The payroll in Kitchener stood at 385, nearly a third of whom performed research.

Sales remained strong in 2008, with highlights including the installation of 96 units at the NASDAQ to display trading information; a $4 million sale to Lockheed Martin for military flight trainers; Christie projectors used at the Democratic National Convention in Denver; and triumphing in a fierce competition with rival Barco for the opening ceremony of the 2008 Beijing Olympics. More than a billion people watched the stunning merger of 15,000 live performers and nearly 150 video projectors aimed at both the floor and the circular upper portion of the "bird's nest" stadium to create seamlessly blended images. After the Olympics, the machines were sold to Chinese movie theaters, allowing the Olympic committee to recoup much of their cost.

During 2008 Christie also built a 50,000-square-foot control center at its Cypress, California, headquarters that would allow it to remotely manage and maintain equipment in U.S. theaters. In October the firm unveiled Brilliant 3D, a single-lens theatrical projection system that offered lower cost and increased brightness. Studios were throwing their weight behind digital 3D, with Disney's Pixar unit announcing that all future releases would be produced in the format. In the fall Christie and AccessIT extended their relationship with a new commitment to install 10,000 more digital projectors in North America.

Despite the global economic meltdown, by early 2009 Christie was continuing to hire new employees. More than 5,000 of the firm's digital projectors were installed in theaters.

Eight decades after S. L. Christie first began selling equipment to the motion picture industry, Christie Digital Systems, Inc., had evolved into a leading provider of digital projection systems for theaters. The firm's product line also included projectors for boardrooms, control centers, concert venues, and other specialized applications, as well as traditional 35mm film equipment and support services such as remote monitoring and maintenance. With the movie industry's conversion to digital cinema still in its infancy, Christie looked toward strong sales growth for the foreseeable future.

Frank Uhle

PRINCIPAL SUBSIDIARIES

Christie Digital Systems, USA, Inc.; Christie Digital Systems Canada, Inc.

PRINCIPAL COMPETITORS

Barco NV; NEC Viewtechnology, Ltd.; Sony Corp.; Panasonic Corp.; Digital Projection International.

FURTHER READING

"Boxoffice Beacon Award: Christie Digital," *Boxoffice,* January 2009, p. 23.

Chilton, Susan, "Projecting a New Image," *Kitchener-Waterloo Record,* October 27, 2001, p. F7.

"Christie Acquires Vista Control Systems," *Broadcast Engineering,* July 23, 2007.

"Christie to Build Regal's Theater Network," *Digital Cinema,* February 1, 2003, p. 8.

Cruz, Sherri, "Firm Gains Foothold in Digital Cinema Through Theater Ads," *Los Angeles Business Journal,* September 22, 2003, p. 24.

Deagon, Brian, "Two Digital Cinema Companies Looking to Jump-Start Industry," *Investor's Business Daily,* June 22, 2005, p. A4.

Fritz, Ben, "Duo Project Digital Cinema Effort," *Daily Variety,* June 21, 2005.

Hammond, Mark, "Christie Digital Riding Out Economic Storm," *Waterloo Region Record,* January 9, 2009, p. D8.

Howitt, Chuck, "Christie Signs 'Historic' Deal with Disney," *Kitchener-Waterloo Record,* September 17, 2005, p. F1.

Koven, Peter, "Christie Digital Sharpens Image," *Financial Post,* October 18, 2006.

Lahey, Liam, "Projecting the Future of Film in the Digital Age," *Computer Dealer News,* September 28, 2001, p. 6.

Lukasiewicz, Mark, "Electrohome Puts Its Television Know-How to a Profitable Use in the Video Market," *Globe and Mail,* September 2, 1980, p. B1.

Luna, Nancy, "OC Digital Projector Maker Inks $300 Million Deal with Carmike," *Orange County Register,* December 20, 2005.

Robinson, Marcus, "Kitchener's Christie Leads D-Cinema Revolution," *Playback,* April 17, 2006, p. 20.

Simone, Rose, "Christie Goes Hollywood," *Kitchener-Waterloo Record,* December 30, 2003, p. C1.

Stanton, Raymond, "Electrohome Winds Down, Leaving Behind a Rich Legacy," *Kitchener-Waterloo Record,* June 2, 2008.

Strathdee, Mike, "Most of Electrohome Sold," *Kitchener-Waterloo Record,* August 23, 1999, p. A1.

Tolkoff, Sarah, "Christie Digital Sees $10M Sale for Olympic Projectors," *Orange County Business Journal,* September 1, 2008, p. 50.

Zaccaria, Joy, "Christie Digital 75 Years Later," *Systems Contractor News,* August 2004, p. 8.

Compton Petroleum
Corporation

———————————————■———————————————

3300 Fifth Avenue Place
East Tower, 425-1st Street Southwest
Calgary, Alberta T2P 3L8
Canada
Telephone: (403) 237-9400
Fax: (403) 237-9410
Web site: http://www.comptonpetroleum.com

Public Company
Incorporated: 1992 as 544201 Alberta Ltd.
Employees: 253
Sales: CAD 610.29 million (2008)
Stock Exchanges: Toronto New York
Ticker Symbol: CMT
NAICS: 211111 Crude Petroleum and Natural Gas
    Extraction; 213112 Support Activities for Oil and
    Gas Field Exploration

■ ■ ■

Compton Petroleum Corporation is an independent energy resources company involved in the exploration, development, and production of natural gas, natural gas liquids, and crude oil in the Western Canada Sedimentary Basin in Alberta, Canada. Compton Petroleum, almost entirely reliant on natural gas production, produces an average of 28,658 barrels of oil equivalent (boe) per day, primarily from its operations in southern Alberta. The company has 215,488 Mboe (thousand barrels of oil equivalent) in proved and probable reserves.

ORIGINS

During its first two decades of existence, Compton Petroleum never strayed far from its headquarters in Calgary. The company focused its exploration and production activities in Alberta, especially the southern portion of the province, concentrating primarily on tapping into deposits of natural gas. The company was incorporated in October 1992 under the name 544201 Alberta Ltd., a nondescript corporate title it kept until changing its name to Compton Petroleum Corporation in April 1993, three months before the company officially started operating as an oil and gas exploration concern.

At its inception, Compton Petroleum represented the leanest of operations. The company occupied a modest office in Calgary and employed a small technical team led by President and CEO Ernest G. Sapieha, an executive with more than a decade of experience in the oil and gas industry. The company possessed only CAD 1 million in capital, a meager sum in the oil and gas exploration business, but hoped to build up its coffers by using the most valuable asset aside from its technical team. Compton Petroleum possessed a large seismic database covering 12,000 kilometers in southern, central, and the Peace River Arch area in northwestern Alberta, the detailed information it would use to make its mark in the oil and gas industry.

In their Calgary office, Compton Petroleum officials sifted through the two-dimensional seismic data, using the information to develop an exploration strategy for the company. Their research, a lengthy process, convinced them to concentrate their efforts in southern

COMPANY PERSPECTIVES

Our goal is to be a premier Canadian intermediate exploration and production company that is recognized as an industry leader. Through implementation of a focused strategy that emphasizes natural gas and the development of committed and innovative people, we are dedicated to maximizing and creating sustainable and superior value for our shareholders.

Alberta, where they planned to implement an unconventional drilling strategy. Typically, drilling activity in the area was conducted according to the dictates of two strategies, or two types of resource "plays." Small companies tended to pursue shallow gas plays, drilling in shallow gas reservoirs at depths of less than 1,000 meters. At shallow depths, the drilling costs were low, but the pools and reserves per well were small, which required shallow gas players to replace their reserves on a continual basis. Large companies favored deep Paleozoic carbonate reservoirs, able to drill at deeper depths because they possessed greater financial resources than did small companies. Drilling at deeper depths incurred higher costs, but a deep gas play generally realized a long reserve life.

A STRATEGY IS DEVELOPED

Although its small stature cast it as a shallow gas player, Compton Petroleum bucked convention and chose to pursue a strategy that gave the company its distinguishing quality in Alberta's oil and gas industry. Sapieha and his team decided to make their living in medium depths and focused their exploratory efforts in the deep Lower Cretaceous sandstones in southern Alberta. Historically, oil and gas concerns had avoided the formations targeted by Compton Petroleum because they contained "tight" gas, or gas trapped in difficult-to-penetrate rock, limestone, or sandstone. Because of the difficulties involved in obtaining it, tight gas was referred to as an unconventional gas, but drilling technologies had improved, making it easier to tap into unconventional gas deposits such as tight sand, deep natural gas, and Devonian shale gas. Further, research into land ownership in southern Alberta revealed that large tracts of land were controlled by only a few companies, which encouraged Compton Petroleum to stake its future on locating tight gas formations in southern Alberta.

Years were spent developing the company's strategy, building the necessary infrastructure, and acquiring the land it intended to explore. Financially, the company's first years in operation were a struggle, as Sapieha and his team built up Compton Petroleum from scratch. Revenues only amounted to CAD 4.1 million by 1996, the year it converted to public ownership, but from there the company's annual volume began to increase exponentially.

Business activity was focused in the Western Canada Sedimentary Basin, a swath of land arcing southward from northwest Alberta to the U.S. border. In this region, the company completed several deals during the second half of the 1990s that helped it record financial growth. In 1997, Compton Petroleum raised CAD 25 million to purchase Canadian Occidental Petroleum's 62 percent interest in the Mazeppa gas plant and working interests in lands and wells in the Okotoks-Mazeppa area, which was located 30 miles from Calgary. The purchase increased Compton Petroleum's stake in the Mazeppa gas plant to 90 percent, which it sold the following year, along with a smaller gas plant, to Dynegy Canada Inc. for CAD 60 million. With the proceeds from the transaction, Compton Petroleum purchased J.M. Huber Canada Ltd. at the end of 1998. The purchase gave Compton Petroleum 12,000 Mboe and marked its entry into central Alberta.

After the series of acquisitions and divestitures, Compton Petroleum invested its resources in the area of its greatest success. In 2000, the company acquired 70 sections of contiguous land in the Basal Quartz section of the Hooker deep gas play, located immediately south of Calgary. The purchase nearly doubled the company's holdings in the Hooker area, making it the dominant landowner in the region. It also greatly brightened its prospects, giving the company the opportunity to double its existing reserves within the next two to three years.

A DOMINANT LAND POSITION SECURED BY 2001

On the heels of increasing its investment in the Hooker area, Compton Petroleum completed a larger deal, capping a five-year period of aggressive expansion. In May 2001, the company reached an agreement to acquire Hornet Energy Ltd., a Calgary-based oil and gas exploration and production company that was publicly traded on the Toronto Stock Exchange. With the addition of Hornet Energy, Compton Petroleum had purchased more than 560,000 acres of land between 1996 and 2001, giving the company the assets to produce robust financial growth. From the CAD 4.1 million recorded in 1996, annual revenues climbed

KEY DATES

1992: Compton Petroleum is incorporated.
1993: Company commences operations in July.
1996: Compton Petroleum completes its initial public offering of stock.
1998: Company enters central Alberta with the purchase of J.M. Huber Canada Ltd.
2001: Compton Petroleum acquires Hornet Energy Ltd.
2007: Compton Petroleum acquires Stylus Energy Inc.
2008: Under pressure from its largest shareholder, Compton Petroleum puts itself up for sale.
2009: Tim Granger is appointed president and chief executive officer.

energetically, reaching CAD 17.5 million in 1997, CAD 30.5 million in 1998, and CAD 97 million in 1999. In 2000, the company more than doubled its revenue, posting CAD 213.3 million. Net earnings for the year leaped upward as well, jumping from CAD 17 million to CAD 40 million. The significant increase in Compton Petroleum's financial totals reflected the progress it had made evolving from a purely exploration concern into a producing company, as its average daily production of boe swelled from 1,025 in 1996 to 23,404 in 2001.

Steady financial growth continued as Compton Petroleum increased its drilling activity during its second decade of business. The company, which had drilled 96 wells in 2000, drilled 342 wells in 2006, focusing its efforts on its four resources plays in the 1.4 million acres of contiguous land it owned. Compton Petroleum was involved in three deep gas resource plays: in the Basal Quartz sands at Hooker, the Foothills Upper Cretaceous Belly River area at Callum in southern Alberta, and the Gething/Rock Creek Sands at Niton in central Alberta. The company also had committed to a shallow gas resource play in the Plains Belly River and Edmonton Horseshoe Canyon zones in southern Alberta. As a way to generate cash flow to fund its shallow and deep gas plays, Compton Petroleum also was involved in a conventional oil play, drilling in the Peace River Arch area in northern Alberta, where it had developed properties that produced 7,000 boe per day. Combined, the company's drilling activities generated CAD 533 million in revenue in 2006, the company's tenth year of operating as a publicly traded concern.

Sapieha, who had presided over the company's development since the initial study of seismic data in Compton Petroleum's Calgary office, could look back on an enviable record of achievement. "Over the last 10 years, Compton has delivered a compound annual growth rate of 35 percent on our reserves ...," he said in the March 12, 2007 issue of *CNW Group.* "During this period, we've grown from a high risk, pure exploration company to a strong intermediate producer with low risk, high quality development assets ready for a large scale, accelerated drilling program."

ANNOUNCEMENT OF ACCELERATED EXPANSION: 2007

Sapieha was ready to ratchet up the company's pace of drilling, but before assuming a more aggressive posture, he brokered another deal to add to Compton Petroleum's reserves. In June 2007, he announced an agreement to acquire Stylus Energy Inc., a Calgary-based oil and gas company with operations in Alberta. Compton Petroleum agreed to pay CAD 91 million to acquire the company, which was expected to add 2,677 Mboe in proved reserves. "This transaction fits with our strategy of continued growth in our core areas and our focus on natural gas resource plays," Sapieha said in the June 25, 2007 issue of *CNW Group.* "The acquisition of Stylus creates significant operation synergies at Vulcan, Alberta, and adds an attractive portfolio of additional drilling prospects which will enhance our ability to execute our business plan."

Within weeks of announcing the Stylus Energy acquisition, Sapieha declared Compton Petroleum had reached a significant juncture in its development. In a July 11, 2007 interview with *CNW Group,* Sapieha said, "2007 is the year during which all the elements necessary for the company's next phase of growth will be put in place. We view 2007 as a transition year for Compton," he continued, "a year in which the stage is set for the large well counts that are necessary for production growth and the realization of the value inherent in our natural gas resource plays." Part of Sapieha's plan involved shedding the company's oil-related assets to make Compton Petroleum exclusively reliant on natural gas exploration and production. Toward that end, the company reached an agreement in September 2007 to sell its light oil assets at Worsley in the Peace River Arch area. Birchcliff Energy Ltd. agreed to pay Compton Petroleum CAD 270 million for the producing properties. Another, more important part of Sapieha's plan called for a significant increase in the company's drilling activity. Compton Petroleum planned to drill 435 wells in 2007, 600 wells in 2008, 800 wells in 2009, and up to 1,000 wells in 2010.

SHAREHOLDER ACTIVISM
PROMPTS SALE

As the company pressed forward with its growth plans, the specter of a contentious battle loomed. In December 2007, its largest shareholder, a hedge fund named Centennial Energy Partners LLC, sent a letter to Compton Petroleum's main offices. In the letter, Centennial Energy, which held a nearly 20 percent stake in Compton Petroleum, expressed concerns that Sapieha and his executive team did not have "a specific plan to eliminate the valuation discount [that had] developed between the underlying value of the company's asset base and the share price," as quoted in the December 18, 2007 edition of *Globe & Mail*. At the heart of the issue was Compton Petroleum's declining stock value, which had dropped more than 20 percent between May 2007 and November 2007, driven downward, according to Compton Petroleum, by the depressed state of Canada's natural gas industry and the high Canadian dollar.

Centennial Energy pressed Compton Petroleum for a review of the company's strategic options, including the potential sale of the company. Under pressure from its largest shareholder, Compton Petroleum agreed to conduct a strategic review of its operations in early 2008. "We want to follow the strategic plan, but we have a shareholder that has a different position than us," a Compton Petroleum spokesperson said in the February 29, 2008 edition of *Globe & Mail*. "The board is going to investigate the best direction to go in for all shareholders."

The strategic review, conducted by a committee that enlisted the help of Tristone Capital Inc. and USB Securities Canada Inc., was concluded in June 2008. Based on the recommendation of the committee, Compton Petroleum's board of directors announced the company would begin seeking a buyer for all the outstanding common shares of Compton Petroleum. The announcement lent an air of uncertainty to the company's future, but one matter was clear: Sapieha would not be present to lead the company into the future. Tim Granger, the vice-president and chief operating officer of Paramount Energy Trust, was appointed president and chief executive officer of Compton Petroleum in January 2009. Under his command, the company stood on the auction block, ready to be acquired by a new owner and ready to begin a new chapter in its history.

Jeffrey L. Covell

PRINCIPAL SUBSIDIARIES

Compton Petroleum Holdings Corporation; Compton Petroleum Finance Corporation; Hornet Energy Ltd.

PRINCIPAL COMPETITORS

Canadian Natural Resources Limited; EnCana Corporation; Husky Energy Inc.

FURTHER READING

"Compton Announces Major Extension of Hooker Deep Gas Play," *Canadian Corporate News,* October 6, 2000.

"Compton Announces Sale of Worsley for $270 Million," *CNW Group,* September 4, 2007.

"Compton Buys Canadian Firm," *Oil Daily,* December 8, 1998.

"Compton Petroleum Corporation Announces Sale Process," *CNW Group,* June 11, 2008.

"Compton Petroleum Corporation to Make Offer to Acquire Stylus Energy Inc.," *CNW Group,* June 25, 2007.

"Compton Petroleum Updates Status of Strategic Review," *CNW Group,* May 26, 2008.

"Hornet Energy Ltd.: Compton Petroleum Corporation," *Market News Publishing,* May 17, 2001.

Scott, Norval, "Compton Bows to Shareholder," *Globe & Mail,* February 29, 2008, p. B4.

———, "Compton 'Puzzled' by Shareholder's Call for Review," *Globe & Mail,* December 18, 2007, p. B7.

Sitaramiah, Gita, "Compton Petroleum Corporation—President and Chief Executive Officer," *America's Intelligence Wire,* January 9, 2009.

everyday products. extraordinary design.

CPP International, LLC

11707 Steele Creek Road
Charlotte, North Carolina 28273
U.S.A.
Telephone: (704) 588-3190
Fax: (704) 588-1123
Web site: http://www.carolinapad.com

Private Company
Incorporated: 1945 as Carolina Pad & Paper Company
Employees: 65
Sales: $50.9 million (2007)
NAICS: 322233 Stationery, Tablet, and Related Product Manufacturing

■ ■ ■

CPP International, LLC, is a privately held maker of school, office, and arts and crafts supplies based in Charlotte, North Carolina, doing business as Carolina Pad. Long a domestic manufacturer of commodity items such as standard legal pads and spiral notebooks, the company, once on the verge of bankruptcy, has transformed itself since 2000 into a producer of high-margin stylish products primarily targeting girls 8 to 12 years of age, the "tween" market. Designers are known to visit shopping malls to keep tabs on what fashion trends interest this key demographic. Spearheading the style change is chief designer Jacqueline Savage McFee whose "Jackie" brand includes a wide variety of colorful notebooks, folders, files, binders, student planners, journals, calendars, poster boards, sticky notes and flags, pens, and totes.

Other Carolina Pad brands include Notebound, offering notebooks and journals; U:create drawing pads, sketch diaries, and construction paper; the Sasquatch line of notebooks, binders, folders, and other products produced from plants and recyclable pulp; and Ghostline poster and display boards that offer faint grid lines to help guide users. Another major decision made to save Carolina Pad was to take manufacturing offshore to plants in China. As a result, the company maintains offices in Hong Kong and Shanghai. Products are sold through a wide range of retailers, including Wal-Mart, Target, Walgreens, Staples, and supermarket chains.

FOCUSING ON THE EDUCATION MARKET

Carolina Pad & Paper Company was founded in Charlotte in 1945 by former teacher, coach, and principal Joseph K. Hall II to sell quality notebooks and folders in a limited number of colors at a fair price. Initially selling out of the trunk of his car, Hall targeted regional school districts and colleges. The educational market remained the focus of the company for many years, and even after his son, Joseph K. Hall III, who went to work for the company in the 1950s, took the reins, novelty was hardly a catchword at Carolina Pad. The key to the company's success was its ability to spiral-bind loose-leaf notebook paper with a converting machine at its Charlotte facility. The solid-color cardboard covers were far from durable and issued no fashion statement, yet served the company well for many years.

Carolina Pad remained content to pursue a commodity business into the 1990s, although during that

COMPANY PERSPECTIVES

We will excite our customers by bringing extraordinary fashion and innovation to everyday products.

decade the company did add the innovative Ghostline product line, invented by sisters Mary Russell Sarao and Barbara Russell Pitts. Long frustrated with working with her daughter on art projects involving poster boards, Sarao woke up after dreaming about a solution to her problem: posterboard that used faint grid impressions that were nearly invisible from a few feet away. She and her sister developed the idea, receiving a patent on Ghostline in 1996. They sold the product on their own but soon found it the subject of a bidding war among manufacturers. Carolina Pad eventually beat out Mead Corporation and Pacon Company to acquire the exclusive rights to Ghostline.

LATE-CENTURY CHANGES CHALLENGE CAROLINA PAD

The pad business began to change radically in the 1990s. Increasingly, Carolina Pad relied on paper imported from Indonesia, but as a financial crisis enveloped Asia in the late 1990s, regional demand for paper fell, prompting the Indonesians to convert their excess paper into yellow legal pads and other commodity items that Carolina Pad specialized in and sell them in the United States. Other low-cost importers from Brazil and China followed suit. Carolina Pad also faced stiff competition at home from Mead, the industry leader, at the same time that mass retailers seized control of the school supply market. With their clout, Wal-Mart and other big-box superstores could demand lower-priced notebooks. As a result, Carolina Pad's margins were shaved razor thin and it became difficult to make money, and because so much of its capital was tied up in manufacturing operations, the company lacked the funds needed to develop new higher-margin products. Moreover, the company suffered from sagging employee morale. "We were a bunch of old paper guys," Hall told *Inc.* in 2009. "We knew we had to change but didn't know how."

To help resurrect the company, Hall stepped down as chief executive officer, although he stayed on as chairman, and brought in Clay Presley to take day-to-day control of the business. A former executive at the Christian publishing house Thomas Nelson, Presley had

been in charge of that company's gift division, C.R. Gibson of Nashville. "There," according to *Inc.*, "Presley had learned that products like photo albums and scrapbooks sell better when they are gussied up."

Shortly after taking the helm at Carolina Pad, Presley in November 2000 called in his senior managers for a two-day brainstorming meeting. Faced with dwindling sales, the company, on its way to losing $1 million on revenues of $26 million for the year, estimated that it would face bankruptcy in about three years if nothing were done. To avoid that fate, Presley declared, "We're going to be the best at something." He then asked, "What are we going to be the best at?" A number of ideas were rejected during the several hours of debate that followed, including transforming Carolina Pad into a private-label company, which would trade one low-margin business for another, and trying its hand with school locker products, but shelves, magnetic pen holders, and the like offered a very limited opportunity. What was not an option, everyone agreed, was staying the course.

Finally a senior vice-president of product development, Paul Wagner, showed the group a notebook he had designed that had a cardboard cover that looked like a piece of khaki fabric, inspired by what he saw retailer Old Navy offering to teens with great success. The notebook's clear plastic cover was also more durable than Carolina Pad's usual cardboard cover. What made the idea especially appealing was that its $2 price point was uniquely situated between the generic notebooks that could be bought for as little as 10 cents each and the $3 which a higher-quality notebook could fetch.

YOUNG DESIGNER HIRED

Carolina Pad's senior leaders knew that Wagner's prototype notebook was the answer they were looking for, but they were all middle-aged men and did not really know what products and designs would appeal to the market they wanted to tap into, young girls. Presley, however, knew someone from his days with a stationery company who fit the bill: Jacqueline Savage McFee. She graduated from Syracuse University with a dual degree in illustration and surface pattern design and then went to work for C.R. Gibson when Presley was in charge, followed by a stint with Amscan Inc. designing birthday party paper products. When Presley contacted her, McFee was contemplating doing design work for larger companies, but he persuaded the young designer to give up her Manhattan lifestyle for North Carolina to try her hand at an entirely new challenge, designing notebooks for young girls. Still in her 20s, McFee was close enough in age to the target market to know what might appeal

KEY DATES

1945: Joseph K. Hall II founds company.
2000: Clay Presley is named chief executive, leads turnaround.
2001: Company returns to profitability.
2008: Kendall Kollection, with a portion of the profits going to charity, is introduced.
2009: Presley survives US Airways Flight 1549 emergency landing in the Hudson River.

to them, and she agreed to become Carolina Pad's chief designer.

McFee designed a notebook that featured a checkered plaid design beneath a clear plastic cover, a product that would become a perennial favorite. She also assembled a design team and charged them with finding inspiration from a variety of sources as part of a new investment in market research. They visited the European trade shows to glimpse what colors and designs would soon be in fashion, frequented New York and Los Angeles hot spots to note what trendsetters were wearing, and they also visited shopping malls to see what colors and designs appealed to the girls who were the likely trendsetters in their schools. The children were divided into four groups: hip, edgy, conformist, and passive. Knowing that the edgy kids were too hard to predict, that the conformists emulated whatever fashion everyone else embraced, and that the passive kids accepted whatever was on the store shelves, the designers focused on the hip kids, determining what appealed to them and would drive the market.

A key to launching the new fashion notebook line was convincing the Wal-Mart buyers to take a chance and stock the item. Fortunately, the notebooks were an immediate success. McFee also played an important role in persuading major retailers to carry the products. According to *Inc.*, "Sales calls, once as plain vanilla as Carolina's notebooks, became performances in which McFee would use trend boards to demonstrate that products as diverse as Christmas trees and telephones were coming out in rich chocolate colors or in patterns echoing Victorian wallpaper. She would effuse over polka dots and show buyers with socks that matched the colors and patterns she was pitching." McFee also hired other women designers who were dispatched on sales calls, including Liz Diller, whose credits included collections for Target, Kmart, and Office Depot.

Another key to the successful turnaround of Carolina Pad was the outsourcing of manufacturing that accompanied the design changes. Rather than invest in the necessary four-color printing presses and equipment needed to produce acetate covers, the company focused its resources on design and marketing and turned to Asian contractors to handle manufacturing. Carolina's old equipment was sold to suppliers, and about three dozen factory jobs were terminated, although many of the employees found other positions in the company. There was also a turnover in the sales ranks as many representatives trained in commodity sales opted to leave.

After just one year Carolina Pad returned to profitability. By 2003 sales increased to $45 million. With success came competition as industry rivals soon introduced their own fashion notebook collections. Carolina Pad answered by turning over its product lines every year to 18 months, a far cry from earlier times when the same plain colors were offered year after year. The company also tried designing notebooks geared toward boys, employing sports themes, but the core customer remained tween girls. In addition, the company acquired brands and applied its newfound flair to a variety of new products, such as planners, pens, mousepads, and totes. Carolina Pad would even offer a brightly colored calculator.

LAUNCHING NEW PRODUCT LINES: 2008

Sales topped $50 million in 2007. To keep pace, a year later Carolina Pad introduced two new personal office product lines: Eye Candy and Simply Chic. The former offered large polka dots and stripes set against a bright white background, while the latter employed pinstripes, modern scrolls, and classic houndstooth patterns to create products with more of a sophisticated air. The company also unveiled the Kendall Kollection of school and office products, inspired by the daughter of one of McFee's cousins, a four-year-old who had been diagnosed with leukemia. Struck by the girl's courage, McFee persuaded Carolina Pad to develop the line. A portion of the profits was earmarked for The Leukemia & Lymphoma Society and its blood cancer research, patient education, and support services.

To help Carolina Pad maintain its competitive edge, a new designer was brought on board in the spring of 2008, Cathy Law, a 15-year veteran with Hallmark Cards, where she became a senior designer. For the past four years she had done design and illustration work on a freelance basis for Hallmark, Hasbro Inc., Target,

Nickelodeon, and others. Later in 2008 Carolina Pad created a new position, director of brand management, hiring April B. Whitlock to fill the post. Her focus was to shape the brand identities for all products.

CEO SURVIVES AIRLINER CRASH: 2009

As 2009 began, an online store was added to further drive sales. The company also escaped tragedy in the early weeks of that year. Presley and Vice-President Bill Nix were both returning from a trip to New York City when their US Airways plane, Flight 1549, was forced to make an emergency landing in the Hudson River. Both men survived, as did all the passengers, and a day later they returned to the office to continue their mission of growing Carolina Pad.

Ed Dinger

PRINCIPAL SUBSIDIARIES

Carolina Pad & Paper Company.

PRINCIPAL COMPETITORS

Avery Dennison Corporation; MeadWestvaco Corporation, MEGA Brands Inc.

FURTHER READING

Chitelle, Louis, "All That Glitters Isn't Gold," *New York Times,* November 10, 1998.

Choe, Stan, "Carolina Pad & Paper Finds New Market with Colorful, Trendy Products," *Charlotte Observer,* June 21, 2004.

———, "Charlotte, N.C.-based Paper-Product Maker Tries to Make What Tweens Want," *Charlotte Observer,* June 20, 2004.

Noone, Kelleyanne, "Poster-Board Invention Starting to Draw Interest," *Dallas Morning News,* August 17, 1996, p. 1H.

"The Ultimate Business Makeover," *Inc.,* March 2009, p. 58.

CRANE & CO.

Crane & Co., Inc.

—————————■—————————

30 South Street
Dalton, Massachusetts 01226-1751
U.S.A.
Telephone: (413) 684-2600
Toll Free: (800) 268-2281
Fax: (412) 684-4278
Web site: http://www.crane.com

Private Company
Founded: 1801
Incorporated: 1922
Employees: 1,200
Sales: $200 million (2008 est.)
NAICS: 322121 Paper (Except Newsprint) Mills;
322232 Envelope Manufacturing; 322233
Stationery, Tablet, and Related Product Manufacturing; 424120 Stationery and Office Supplies
Merchant Wholesalers; 511191 Greeting Card
Publishers

■ ■ ■

Crane & Co., Inc., is a family-owned papermaker
known for its high-quality stationery and for making
money, U.S. currency, that is. Since 1879 the company
has been the sole manufacturer of currency paper for the
U.S. Treasury. It also makes currency paper, and in some
cases prints the currency as well, for a number of
countries around the world, including Sweden, Egypt,
Saudi Arabia, India, and Paraguay. This international
business is conducted from its paper mill and printing
plant in Sweden, while Crane maintains domestic mills

in Massachusetts and New Hampshire. Instead of relying on wood pulp, Crane makes its currency paper from
a linen and cotton blend and its personal and business
stationery from cotton. Crane distributes its stationery
products through more than 2,000 independent retailers
across the United States. The company's nonwovens
division produces paperlike materials for a wide range of
industrial applications, including filtration and reverse
osmosis. More than two centuries after its founding,
Crane & Co. is managed by sixth- and seventh-
generation descendants of the founder, Zenas Crane.
Members of the Crane family continue to own about 80
percent of the company, while Lindsay Goldberg LLC, a
private-equity firm based in New York City, holds the
remaining 20 percent.

ZENAS CRANE FOUNDS A COMPANY: 1801–45

In 1799 Zenas Crane chose the small, agricultural town
of Dalton in western Massachusetts in which to build
his paper mill on the banks of the Housatonic River.
Zenas was following in a family tradition. His father,
Stephen, a papermaker, had sold a special security-type
paper to Paul Revere. Revere used that paper to print
the first banknotes in the colonies, in December 1775,
two years before Zenas was born.

Zenas learned the art and science of papermaking as
a teenager, how to clean old rags, then beat them into
pulp from which the paper was made. Wanting his own
mill, he looked west and found 14 acres near wood and
water and a population that could supply both the rags
and employees. It took him two years to raise the

money for the land and a mill. In 1801, Zenas and his two partners, Henry Wiswell and John Willard, were in business.

Local housewives provided the new mill with the rags needed to make paper. The company's first advertisement, reproduced in Wadsworth R. Pierce's history, *The First 175 Years of Crane Papermaking,* urged "that every woman, who has the good of her country, and the interest of her own family at heart, will patronize them, by saving her rags, and sending them to their Manufactory, or to the nearest Storekeeper—for which the Subscribers will give a generous price." Most of the rags the housewives offered were of a tough, homemade linen that was difficult to reduce to pulp, but made a very high grade of paper. This happenstance, combined with Zenas Crane's own perfectionism, established the firm's tradition of uncompromising quality in its products. Early customers included publishers, storekeepers, banks (many of which printed their own money), and the government of Massachusetts.

In 1822 Zenas bought out his partners and became the sole owner. At the same time, machines were playing a more important role in the industry: A cylinder machine replaced hand molding, and then steam-heated drying cylinders were introduced. Zenas developed a machine to automatically remove the paper from the papermaking machines. Around the mid-1930s the company began making what eventually became one of its best-known stationery lines: colored writing papers.

In 1842 Zenas turned management of the company over to two of his sons, Zenas Marshall Crane and James Brewer Crane. Two years later, Zenas Marshall developed a paper that significantly deterred the altering of banknotes. He was able to embed silk threads vertically into the paper to indicate the note's denomination: one silk thread for a $1 bill, two for a $2 bill, and so

on. The new paper meant that $1 bills could no longer become $10 bills with the addition of a "0." Banks quickly placed orders. In 1845 Zenas Crane died at the age of 68.

SECOND GENERATION OF CRANES: 1845–64

One of the company's biggest problems, transportation, was significantly reduced during the mid-1880s when the Boston and Albany Railroad came to Dalton. Now the Cranes could send their paper by rail instead of transporting it over land to the Hudson River and then downstream. The railroad also opened new markets, particularly in the West, and the Crane brothers built a second mill. Production was increased with the introduction of the Fourdrinier machine, which automated the papermaking process.

In 1851 the Cranes became the owners of a woolen mill that had gone bankrupt (Zenas had held the mortgage). They turned it over to brother Seymour, who converted it into a papermaking mill, which operated under the name Crane & Wilson and produced nothing but fine writing paper. Seymour's operation went out of business before the end of the decade, however, as the country moved toward civil war.

Although the two Crane mills in Dalton continued to operate once the Civil War began, they lost all their Southern customers and much of the money owed to them. The Confederacy refused to pay creditors in the North. According to Pierce, however, several of the businesses paid their debt to Crane in full after the war.

NEW USES FOR PAPER

During the economic depression following the assassination of President Abraham Lincoln, many Northern paper mills went bankrupt. In what could be considered an early marketing coup, Crane took a chance on a fashion fad and developed a new paper for men's collars. Men changed their collar every day, so the demand was great, and one of the company's two mills was kept busy making them. The new paper for the collars had to be stiff, fairly thick, and able to withstand damage from dirt and perspiration.

Although the rage for paper collars did not last long, its legacy within the Crane family was important. James Brewer Crane was granted patents in 1867 and 1868 for paper belts to drive machinery. He invented the belts in the process of developing the paper for the collars. The durability of these belts gradually won over the skeptics, as did the characteristic that they would not stretch or slip as did leather or rubber belts. James

KEY DATES

1801: Zenas Crane establishes a paper mill in Dalton, Massachusetts.

1842: The founder turns over management of the company to his sons Zenas Marshall Crane and James Brewer Crane.

1879: Company wins contract to make currency paper for the U.S. Treasury.

1922: Company is incorporated as Crane & Co., Inc.

1923: Winthrop Murray Crane Jr., great-grandson of the founder, is named president.

1932: The firm's stationery division is established.

1975: Benjamin J. Sullivan becomes the first nonmember of the Crane family to hold the company presidency; Crane & Co. opens its new Wahconah Mill for the manufacture of currency paper.

1985: Revenues top $100 million for the first time.

1995: Lansing Crane, a sixth-generation descendant of the company founder, is named CEO.

2002: Crane acquires AB Tumba Bruk, renamed Crane AB, a Swedish operator of a currency paper mill and a currency printing plant.

2008: Lindsay Goldberg LLC, a private-equity firm based in New York City, purchases a 20 percent stake in Crane & Co.

2009: Crane acquires Visual Physics, LLC, developer of anticounterfeiting technologies for currency.

Brewer's sons continued to make the belts into the 1880s at their mill in Westfield, which they operated as Crane Brothers.

Crane Brothers also manufactured baskets and cans, washtubs, toboggans, and even coffins out of a plastic-like paper product called Linenoid. Yet they did not stop there. They used their paper to make light, graceful boats. The company's web site once included a description of a boat the brothers had at their mill in 1876: "It was about 15 feet long and three feet wide, yet so light that a couple of men could carry it with ease. The frame of the boat was made of wood and then covered with paper, about one-eighth to one-quarter-inch thick."

One of their customers used Crane Brothers paper to make domes, including one containing 1,000 pounds of paper for the observatory at Rensselaer Polytechnic Institute. The dome built in 1881 for the U.S. Military Academy, with 36 sections and using about 2,500 pounds of paper, survived until 1959 when the building was torn down.

QUALITY STATIONERY AND SHELL WRAPPINGS: 1865–75

In 1865 Zenas Crane Jr., son of Zenas Marshall and grandson of the company founder, was put in charge of the old Crane & Wilson facility, which was renamed the Bay State Mill. There, he restarted the manufacturing of writing papers. Three years later, he had paid off the $54,000 mortgage on the building.

When the mill was destroyed by fire, a common occurrence in the industry and for the Crane family, Zenas Jr. went to Europe to study how papermakers there produced the tinted and colored stationery that was becoming tremendously popular in the United States. The social papers he made when he returned were so fine, the mill could not keep up with orders from customers including Tiffany in New York; Baily, Banks & Biddle in Philadelphia; Shreve, Crump & Low in Boston; and Marshall Field in Chicago. In 1886 Crane stationery was used for the invitations to the dedication of the Statue of Liberty.

Zenas's brother W. Murray Crane and cousin Frederick G. Crane joined him to form a partnership, Z. & W. M. Crane, to run the rebuilt Bay State mill. Murray was responsible for several Crane successes. In 1873 he helped develop a paper for the Winchester Arms Co. to be used as wrapping for the repeater shells of that company's new rifle. The specifications, according to Pierce, called for "a highly-combustible, strong-but-thin" paper that left "little or no ash."

MAKING CURRENCY PAPERS: 1876–1900

Murray's biggest contribution to the company occurred in 1879, when he won for Crane the contract to make currency paper for the U.S. Treasury. With a bid of 38.9 cents a pound of paper, he beat out J. M. Wilcox & Co. of Philadelphia, which had been supplying the paper, as well as other big paper companies. Murray developed a new paper based on his father's parallel silk thread security paper to meet Treasury specifications, and the company bought another mill, renamed Government Mill, that made nothing but the currency paper. By the end of the century, Crane had tripled the life expectancy of one dollar bills and more than tripled the tonnage shipped to Washington, D.C.

However, the United States was not the only country for which the Crane's Dalton company made currency paper. The American Bank Note Company was one of its biggest customers, supplying banknotes for 48 countries, as well as stock certificates, bonds, and checks. Pierce noted that "The Story of American Bank Note Company" (quoted in *The First 175 Years of Crane Papermaking*) described how one of that company's early partnerships introduced a new term to the industry. The partnership used Crane paper to print bonds, and sent the company an order for "more of that bond paper," to use for its letterhead.

Crane's researchers and developers were busy during the last half of the 19th century, introducing a thick paper to replace the parchment or sheepskin used for diplomas and certificates and a special thin paper for Bibles. However, even as Crane was finding new uses and customers for its fine rag paper, the paper industry discovered how to make paper with wood pulp, a much less expensive process than that needed for cotton and linen fiber. Although many papermakers switched, the Crane operations did not, continuing to develop and manufacture fine rag papers. However, the company now bought its cotton and linen directly from European and U.S. mills; housewives no longer supplied the rags.

THE THIRD 50 YEARS: 1901–51

The company celebrated its 100th anniversary in 1901, with four paper mills and nearly 1,000 employees. Murray Crane was governor of Massachusetts and would go on to serve as senator from 1904 to 1913.

The company was shipping its paper all over the country, and in 1903 Crane sent a salesman over the Rockies for the first time. He soon found a new customer with a new challenge: drafting paper that was strong and transparent. The tracing paper the company developed became one of its largest, although lesser-known, product lines and the foundation for its specialty papers.

By 1922, there were five Crane mills, and the several partnerships that operated them incorporated as Crane & Co., Inc. Frederick G. Crane, the son of James Brewer and grandson of the founder, was named the new company's first president. When he died a year later, Murray's son, Winthrop Murray Crane Jr., took over the position, holding it for 28 years, through the Great Depression, World War II, and the postwar period.

Crane & Co. did well during these years and shared its success within the community of Dalton, establishing a scholarship fund for local high school graduates. One of the early changes under Winthrop had to do with the currency paper. In 1928, to foil counterfeiters, the company began scattering the red and blue silk threads throughout the bills rather than embedding two lines of thread in each bill.

To keep going during the Great Depression, the company developed and produced cigarette paper, and in the process came up with a better carbon paper, which remained a major product line until computers reduced the need for carbon copies. In 1932 the company established its stationery division and opened a retail operation in Dalton. Employees of the new division cut the stock produced at the Bay State mill, cut and produced the envelopes and boxes, and hand-painted the colored borders on note cards and writing paper. A row of inspectors checked each piece of paper, discarding any sheet with the slightest flaw. Two years later, Crane & Co. bought Z. & W. M. Crane, which controlled the Bay State and Old Berkshire Mills, adding the stationery division to its operations.

During World War II, Crane operated 24 hours a day producing paper for currency, War Bonds, and finally, invasion money. The shortage of linen resulted in a new formula, reducing the amount of linen from 75 percent to 50 percent, and increasing the cotton content from 25 percent to 50 percent. The war also cut off Crane's access to European linen mills. To fill the need, the company used a linen byproduct from linseed oil mills in Minnesota.

EXPANSION AND MODERNIZATION: 1951–89

In 1951 Bruce Crane (another member of the fourth Crane generation) assumed the presidency of Crane & Co. when Winthrop became chairman of the board, a new position. In the mid-1950s, the company began a major project to clean up the Housatonic River. Over the next 20 years, the company spent more than $1.5 million installing improvements, including a pollution control system that sent most of the discharges from the mills to a central processing plant. "They were leaders in environmental pollution controls, very active very early on and very cooperative with the environmental program at the college," the chair of the local community college's Life Sciences Department told the *Los Angeles Times* in 1986.

Those expenditures were only a small portion of the $35 million the company spent modernizing and expanding during Bruce Crane's presidency. In 1956 Crane bought Dalton's other paper manufacturer, the Byron Weston Company, the original supplier of paper for social security cards. In addition to ledgers, which it had been producing since 1863, Byron Weston products included diploma parchment, bond, and index papers, as well as archival record paper used by local governments. That same year, the formula for the currency stock changed again, increasing cotton to 75 percent in response to a new printing process that printed the money on dry paper.

In 1968 the company invested heavily in its research efforts to develop new products, building the $300,000 Crane-Weston Development Center. The following year, Crane & Co. expanded into printing and engraving with the purchase of the Excelsior Printing Company and Excelsior Process and Engraving, Inc., in Massachusetts, and, in 1970, of Standard Process & Engraving, Inc., in California.

The company introduced Craneglas in 1970, after ten years of research. This new paper product used glass and other manmade fibers instead of cotton, and could be used for insulation, filters, and food packaging. The company continued to develop what it called "nonwoven" products, and within 20 years Crane nonwoven papers were being used in applications ranging from pipewrap to airplane firewalls to circuit boards to cafeteria trays to vertical window blinds.

Benjamin J. Sullivan was elected president in 1975, the first person to hold that office who was not a member of the Crane family. His grandfather, however, had worked for the company for some 50 years as a paper machine tender at the Bay State Mill. That same year also saw the opening of the new $8.5 million Wahconah Mill to manufacture paper for U.S. currency. Wahconah was the first complete Crane paper mill built in the 20th century.

Ten years later, in 1985, Sullivan was named chairman and CEO, and Thomas White became president. The company's sales topped $100 million for the first time, with sales to the Treasury accounting for a quarter of that amount.

During the 1980s, Crane expanded its sales of currency paper directly to other governments so that by 1990 it had about a dozen foreign customers. Over the years, those clients included Mexico, Bolivia, and Taiwan. "They're typically the underdeveloped countries, because as one could logically assume, the more developed a country becomes, the more likely it would be to have its own manufacturing facilities as well as printing facilities," a Crane official stated in a 1990 article in *Boston Business Journal.*

CONTINUING TO INNOVATE AND DEFENDING ITS TURF: 1990–2001

The early part of the decade saw several innovations. Crane received a new patent for a method to deter

counterfeiting by embedding in the paper clear polyester threads that failed to show up when the paper was photocopied. The company also returned to its tradition of using clothing rags to make paper. It introduced Crest R, a paper composed of 30 percent recycled cotton, such as old tablecloths, and 70 percent recovered cotton fiber. Then, in 1993, it developed a 100 percent denim paper made for Levi Strauss & Co. from recycled scraps of Levi blue jeans. The Levi company used the paper for letterhead, corporate checks, and envelopes. In addition to producing a distinctive and sturdy paper, the recycling process kept a large portion of Levi Strauss's over two million pounds of denim scraps out of landfills.

Continuing its creative reuse of materials, the following year Crane introduced its "Old Money" line of stationery, made from recycled U.S. dollar bills. Instead of trying to get the dark ink out of the bills, which would have caused a solid waste problem itself, Crane left the ink in, giving the paper the color of money. Each ream of Old Money contained nearly $15,000 worth of shredded bills.

In 1995 Lansing Crane, a sixth-generation descendant of the company founder, was named CEO. A year later, the U.S. Congress increased its efforts to have the Treasury Department seek more competition for its currency contract. The first move was a reinterpretation of a 1988 law to mean that a bidder had to be 50 percent U.S.-owned, thus opening the door to foreign companies. The Treasury also posted a draft solicitation for the currency contract on the Internet, offering subsidies for start-up costs and equipment.

Crane and its congressional representatives fought the effort over the next several years, and the subsidies were never approved. In 1998 the Government Accounting Office released a report concluding that Crane should face competition because the Treasury could not determine whether its prices were fair or not. "This has been a continuing and ongoing assault by international joint ventures to try and break through on this," Senator Edward M. Kennedy (D-Mass.) told the *Associated Press* in October 1998. The government took bids from several companies in addition to Crane for the contract to supply currency paper through 2002, but in early 1999 Crane won the contract, which was valued at about $262 million.

Soon after this threat was turned back, Crane & Co. faced a new challenge to its currency paper business, which accounted for about one-third of the firm's revenues. In 2000 the U.S. Mint began minting the Sacagawea dollar coin and within a year had released hundreds of thousands of the gold-colored coins into circulation. The possibility of a dollar coin serving as even a partial replacement for the $1 bill threatened Crane's core business as the paper dollar comprised nearly half of the company's currency paper business. The Sacagawea dollar, however, fared little better as a circulating coin than the Susan B. Anthony dollar had two decades earlier. Perhaps most crucial to this failure was that retailers did not begin stocking the coin to give out as change. Experts also noted that other countries that succeeded in introducing high-denomination coins had eliminated the corresponding paper bill. The U.S. Congress had yet to authorize such a step, and Crane continued to lobby diligently against it.

2002 FORWARD: INTERNATIONAL EXPANSION, SECURITY INNOVATIONS

At the beginning of 2002 Crane gained its first overseas operation when it acquired AB Tumba Bruk from Riksbanken, the Swedish national bank, for $15 million. Tumba Bruk, which had been producing Sweden's currency since its founding in 1755, operated both a paper mill for making currency paper and a currency printing plant, thus marking Crane's debut in printing money. In addition to being the sole supplier of Swedish currency, Tumba Bruk exported currency paper to and printed currency for other nations. It was one of the producers of the newly introduced euro notes. In addition to gaining a new base for international expansion and expanding into currency printing, Crane's takeover of Tumba Bruk was important on the security front. Both the Swedish krona and the euro note featured a distinctive holograph strip to thwart counterfeiting, and holographic technology was something Crane had not yet developed. Tumba Bruk was based in Tumba, near Stockholm.

Under Crane, Tumba Bruk was renamed Crane AB, and Crane's existing business in producing currency paper for nations other than the United States was shifted to its Swedish subsidiary. Following the takeover, Crane completely refurbished the currency papermaking plant and also overhauled the printing facility to transform it into a state-of-the-art currency design and printing center. Back home, Crane & Co. in late 2002 was awarded another four-year contract to supply U.S. currency paper, a contract valued at around $340 million. In October 2005 family member David Crane purchased Excelsior Printing Company from the Crane family, although Crane & Co. retained Excelsior's personalized stationery unit. The following year, Crane secured another four-year U.S. currency paper contract. Also in 2006, the company shut down or sold the two dozen or so retail stationery stores it had operated over the previous decade or more. Crane continued to sell

directly to consumers and businesspeople over the Internet while also distributing its stationery lines via more than 2,000 independent retailers across the United States. Crane's stationery division also pursued the development of cobranded stationery lines and eventually reached deals to create collections bearing the Kate Spade, Disney, and Martha Stewart names.

Around this same time, Crane began working on a new currency security feature with Visual Physics, LLC, an Atlanta-based subsidiary of Nanoventions Holdings, LLC. Crane licensed from Visual Physics a technology based on micro-optics called the Motion security thread, which it then first used on a Swedish 1,000-kroner note. The key feature of the Motion thread was an optical effect in which the images on the thread appear to move when the bill is twisted and turned in the light. In 2007 the International Association of Currency Affairs awarded the Motion technology its Best New Currency Feature. As part of its ongoing redesign of the U.S. currency to stay ahead of increasingly sophisticated counterfeiters, the Bureau of Engraving and Printing planned to incorporate the Motion security thread into the new $100 bill scheduled for release in 2010.

In 2007 Lansing Crane retired and was succeeded as chairman and CEO by Charles Kittredge, another sixth-generation descendant of Zenas Crane. By this time there were around 100 members of the Crane family holding shares in Crane & Co., and many of them were not involved in the business. Some of them wanted to turn at least some of their holdings into cash. To fund a stock buyback program to accommodate these wishes and as a way to fund further growth, Crane in July 2008 sold a 20 percent stake in the firm to Lindsay Goldberg LLC, a private-equity firm based in New York City. Thus, for the first time in the firm's 238-year history, the Crane family gave up its sole ownership position. Hard on the heels of this historic shift, Crane & Co. acquired Visual Physics from Nanoventions in a deal that closed in early 2009. Crane thus gained exclusive control not only of the Motion security thread but also of Visual Physics' entire line of Unison anticounterfeiting technologies. Securing ownership of these technologies was likely to help Crane both gain additional currency business overseas and fend off competitors at home hoping to unseat it from its coveted position as sole supplier of currency paper to the U.S. Treasury.

Ellen D. Wernick
Updated, David E. Salamie

PRINCIPAL SUBSIDIARIES

Crane's Personal Design Services; Visual Physics, LLC; Crane AB (Sweden).

PRINCIPAL COMPETITORS

De La Rue plc; Giesecke & Devrient GmbH; Gould Paper Corporation; International Paper Company; Sappi Limited.

FURTHER READING

Barry, Ellen, "Town Rebuffs New $1 Coin: Plan Holds No Currency in Paper-Money Center," *Boston Globe,* November 21, 1999, p. B1.

Bluestein, Adam, and Charles Kittredge, "Crane & Co.: 200 Years of Happy Customers, from Paul Revere to the Saudi Government," *Inc.,* October 2008, pp. 120+.

Boye, Roger, "New Roadblocks Due for Counterfeiters," *Chicago Tribune,* March 17, 1991, p. C11.

Donn, Jeff, "New England Firm Thrives on Paper," *Associated Press,* November 18, 1998.

Esper, George, "Crane Name Synonymous with Berkshire Hills Town Since 1801; Paper Mill's Good Neighbor Policy Pays Dividends of Respect, Affection," *Los Angeles Times,* October 12, 1986, p. 5.

Fischetti, Mark, "The Restoration at Crane & Co.," *Family Business Magazine,* Autumn 1996.

Gaines, Judith, "Levis; Leftovers Get a New Lease on Life," *Boston Globe,* February 21, 1993, p. 34.

Gavin, Robert, "Nothing Counterfeit About Success," *Boston Globe,* August 1, 2005, p. E4.

Gevirtz, Leslie, "Treasury Mulls Subsidies for Currency Contract," *Reuters Financial Service,* December 27, 1996.

Hopkins, Peter, "Making Money—Literally!" *Paper Age,* November/December 2004, pp. 40–43.

Hower, Wendy, "Dalton Mills Making Money Making Money," *Boston Business Journal,* March 5, 1990, p. 6.

Killian, Linda, "Crane's Progress," *Forbes,* August 19, 1991, p. 44.

Kingsbury, Kathleen, "Money's Paper Chase," *Time,* June 5, 2006, p. A31.

Knapp, Caroline, "The Buck Starts Here," *Boston Business,* September 1987, p. 18.

Nelson, Andrew, "Paper Maker Is Trying to Spare That Tree," *Quincy (Mass.) Patriot Ledger,* November 3, 1999, p. 20.

Olsen, Patricia R., "Changing Times for a Maker of Very Important Paper," *New York Times,* February 7, 2009, p. B2.

Palmer, Kimberly, "Money Maker," *Government Executive,* January 1, 2007.

Parker, Paul Edward, "Dough's Their Bread-and-Butter," *Providence (R.I.) Journal,* June 20, 2001, p. C1.

Pierce, Wadsworth R., *The First 175 Years of Crane Papermaking,* North Adams, Mass.: Excelsior Printing Company, 1977, 76 p.

Puner, Janice, "Moving Stationery," *Greetings Magazine,* November 1994, p. 4.

"A Real Tiger in the Paper Trade," *Fortune,* March 28, 1988, p. 52.

Robinson, Melissa B., "Crane Gets Reprieve in Congressional Spending Bill," *Associated Press,* October 9, 1998.

Siwolop, Sana, "Fed Has Money to Burn. Company Has Other Ideas," *New York Times,* May 28, 1995, p. F8.

Toland, Bill, "Firm Wants to Make Cash," *Pittsburgh Post-Gazette,* October 16, 2005, p. B1.

Tynan, Trudy, "Family Firm Finds Niche in Currency Paper, Fine Stationery," *Associated Press,* February 11, 2002.

Zitner, Aaron, "Crane Wins Currency Paper Pact," *Boston Globe,* February 12, 1999, p. A6.

Dare Foods Limited

—∎—

2481 Kingsway Drive
Kitchener, Ontario N2C 1A6
Canada
Telephone: (519) 893-5500
Toll Free: (800) 668-3273
Fax: (519) 893-8369
Web site: http://www.darefoods.com

Private Company
Incorporated: 1919 as C.H. Doerr Company
Employees: 1,300
Sales: $300 million (2008 est.)
NAICS: 311812 Commercial Bakeries; 311330 Confectionery Manufacturing from Purchased Chocolate; 311821 Cookie and Cracker Manufacturing; 424450 Confectionery Merchant Wholesalers; 424490 Other Grocery and Related Product Merchant Wholesalers

∎ ∎ ∎

Dare Foods Limited makes cookies, candies, crackers, fruit snacks, and fine breads, selling its products in more than 25 countries. The company operates seven manufacturing facilities in Canada and the United States to produce a variety of products marketed under more than a dozen brand names. Dare sells cookies under the brand names "Bear Paws," "Simple Pleasures," "Wagon Wheels," "Whippet," "Ultimate," "Normandie Meteo," "Traditions," and "Dare." Its crackers are sold under the brand names "Breton," "grainsfirst," "Vinta," "Bremner Wafers," "Vivant," "Cabaret," and "Crispy Baguettes."

The company's candy and fruit snacks products are sold under the "RealFruit" and "Dare" labels. The fine breads line, a category comprised of melba toast, bread sticks, croutons, flatbreads, and crisp breads, are sold under the "Grissol" label.

19TH-CENTURY ORIGINS

The more than century-long legacy of the Dare family's involvement in the cookie and candy industry began on the corner of Breithaupt Street and Gzowski Street in Berlin, Ontario. In 1889, Charles H. Doerr opened a grocery store at the location, but he found his true calling when he began making biscuits to sell in his store. Doerr began making biscuits in 1892, offering his homespun creation on the shelves of his general merchandise store. Before long, Berlin residents were frequenting Doerr's store solely to buy his biscuits, prompting the grocery store owner to remove his shelves and turn his business into a bakery.

During World War I, the residents of Berlin sought to distance themselves from any association with their overseas adversary and renamed their city Kitchener. Doerr, whose family would change its name at the conclusion of the next global conflict, enjoyed a bustling business by the time Berlin became Kitchener. The popularity of his biscuits had spread beyond the city, becoming a favorite throughout southwestern Ontario. To meet growing demand, Doerr built a larger bakery to replace his original facility in 1919, the same year he incorporated his business as C.H. Doerr Company and added a line of candy.

FOUNDER'S GRANDSON TAKES CHARGE IN 1941

C.H. Doerr survived its first great crucible, managing to remain solvent during the turmoil of the Great Depression. Doerr's grandson, Carl Doerr, joined the biscuit-and-candy company during the harsh economic climate, beginning a remarkably long 70-year tenure at the company in 1933. For the next eight years, Carl Doerr learned the nuances of the business from his grandfather, becoming the company's president in 1941, when Charles Doerr passed away.

Carl Doerr guided the family business through enormous changes during his six decades as president, taking the helm of a regional business and building it into a multinational competitor. His era of leadership began on a foreboding note when the bakery was destroyed by fire the year after he took control, but once a new bakery was built on an old airfield on the outskirts of Kitchener in 1943, his lengthy reign began an uninterrupted period of growth.

POST–WORLD WAR II EXPANSION

The Doerr family changed its name to Dare in 1945, which prompted a change in the name of the family business. C.H. Doerr Company became The Dare Company, Limited, a business that would shed its status as a regional concern and embark on steady geographic expansion during the post–World War II period. Dare began distributing its products throughout Canada during the 1950s and entered the U.S. market midway through the decade. The company's Canadian operations matured during the 1960s, as the expansion of distribution efforts during the previous decade was followed by the establishment of a physical presence to improve service to the country's provinces. In 1960, the company established its marketing and distribution organization in Quebec, Les Aliments Dare Limitée. In 1962, Dare opened a bakery and sales office in British

Columbia, enabling it to respond more quickly to customers in British Columbia, Manitoba, Saskatchewan, and Alberta.

Dare expanded through internal as well as external means. One of the first acquisitions completed by Carl Dare was the purchase of The Howe Candy Company, a Hamilton, Ontario-based company. Other acquisitions followed, including Saratoga Products, St. Jacobs Canning Company, Mother Dell's Bakeries, and Dairy Maid Chocolates, with each purchase adding to the array of products sold by the company.

INTRODUCTION OF BRETON CRACKERS: 1982

One of Dare's most successful products was introduced as the company neared its centennial, an instance of new product development that showed the ability to innovate had not been lost by the venerable cookie and cracker company in Ontario. In 1982, the company introduced Breton crackers and began distributing the crackers throughout Canada and the United States. Breton, along with its companion brands, Cabaret and Vivant, enjoyed an enthusiastic reception among consumers, enabling Dare to remain competitive in a market dominated by much larger concerns such as Nabisco Co. Another signature product was introduced on the 100th anniversary of the opening of Charles Doerr's grocery store, a product introduction made possible by the addition of a new manufacturing facility. In 1989, the company built a fully automated, soft-candy plant in Milton, Ontario. Once the facility was completed, a new product line of RealFruit Gummie candies was released.

Dare celebrated its 100th year in the cookie and candy business in 1992, observing the founding date recognized by the Dare family. The decade witnessed an increased interest in penetrating the U.S. market, beginning with the establishment of its first production plant across the border. In 1994, Dare built a new cracker bakery on a 33-acre site in Spartanburg, South Carolina. The other significant move to increase business in the United States occurred five years later, when Dare acquired a 134-year-old cracker company, a union that combined two of the oldest cracker makers in North America. The 1999 acquisition of Bremner Biscuit Company added the Bremner Wafer line of crackers to Dare's product portfolio and gave it a production plant in Denver, Colorado.

A year after Dare purchased Bremner, the dynamics of the cookie segment of the food industry were changed considerably by massive mergers. Consolidation became the dominant theme as Kraft Foods acquired

1889: Charles H. Doerr opens a grocery store in Berlin, Ontario.

1892: Doerr begins making biscuits to sell in his store.

1919: Doerr incorporates his business as C.H. Doerr Company and begins producing candy.

1941: Carl Doerr, Charles Doerr's grandson, is named president of the company.

1945: The Doerr family changes its name to Dare.

1956: Dare enters the U.S. market for the first time.

1982: Dare introduces Breton crackers.

1989: A soft-candy plant is constructed in Milton, Ontario.

1994: A cracker bakery, Dare's first production plant in the United States, is built in Spartanburg, South Carolina.

1999: Dare acquires Denver, Colorado-based Bremner Biscuit Company.

2001: Dare acquires Culinar from Saputo Inc., a purchase that doubles the size of its cookie business.

2002: Fred Jaques is named president, the first non-member of the Dare family to hold the position.

2004: Dare introduces a new line of Breton crackers under the label "Breton Gourmet."

2006: Dare unveils a new line of whole grain crackers marketed under the name "grainsfirst."

Nabisco, Kellogg acquired Keebler Foods, and Parmalat Finanziaria acquired Archway Cookies. The industry leaders joined forces, becoming behemoths, seeking to improve their competitive chances through economies of scale. Although Dare was far smaller than the upper tier giants (the Nabisco-Kraft Foods marriage created a $10-billion-in-sales powerhouse), it also looked at consolidation as a way to strengthen its position. The decision to search for a major acquisition target led to what was arguably the most significant event in the company's more than 100-year history.

ACQUISITION OF CULINAR IN 2001

In 2001, Dare offered its riposte to the actions of the previous year, concluding a partnership agreement with Saputo Inc. Saputo, the largest dairy processor in Canada and one of the largest cheese producers in North America, agreed to sell its cookie, fine breads, and soup operations to Dare. The operations, controlled by a subsidiary named Culinar, had been acquired by Saputo in 1999, giving it ownership of a business that traced its roots to 1867, to a small bakery in Montreal started by Charles-Theodore Viau. The acquisition represented a substantial addition to Dare's assets, making the company the second largest cookie producer in Canada and doubling the size of its cookie business. "It's an excellent fit," said Graham Dare, Carl Dare's son, who served as executive vice-president. "Culinar's strong presence in Quebec and popular chocolate-coated cookie brands perfectly complements Dare's Canada-wide reputation for plain and sandwich cookies and our worldwide success as the maker of Breton crackers."

The acquisition was completed in July 2001, a transaction that gave Saputo a 21 percent stake in Dare. The Culinar business added $83 million in annual sales to Dare's revenue total, giving it three manufacturing plants in Quebec and brand names such as Whippet, Wagon Wheels, Viva Puffs, Viau-McCormicks, and Grissol. Dare subsequently sold Culinar's line of Loney's soups, deeming the brand to be outside its strategic scope, but the rest of the assets made Dare a far more comprehensive competitor. The acquisition also led to another significant event in Dare's history, an unprecedented moment that marked the beginning of a decidedly different era.

Carl Dare, who had become president of Dare in 1941, ended his incredibly long run at the helm in early 2002, making way for only the third president in the company's 110-year history. He was succeeded by his son, Graham Dare, but the appointment lasted only a matter of months. The Dares, in the process of absorbing the Culinar operations, decided their company needed the help of an executive with experience in managing multinational, packaged-goods companies. For the first time in the history of their business, they looked outside the family for a leader. "This is another step in the company's growth," Carl Dare said in the December 5, 2002 issue of the *America's Intelligence Wire*. "It is becoming a bigger business. It is more complicated and we have to ensure that we have experienced, professional managers."

FRED JAQUES TAKES CHARGE IN 2002

To guide the company to the next level, the Dares turned to Fred Jaques, hiring him as president in late 2002. Jaques had headed Labatt Breweries' North American division and Kellogg's Canadian operations, learning the nuances of brand development, product innovation, and marketing that he would use to lead

Dare. "As fourth-generation members of a family-run business," Jaques said in the April 2004 issue of *Candy Industry,* "they were looking for help. The company needed a strategic plan, one that would transform Dare Foods from a manufacturing/sales push organization to a consumer-led group. It needed to become a branded products company."

Jaques implemented sweeping changes once he settled into Dare's Kitchener offices. He discarded brands that showed any signs of weakness, consolidated operations, and focused the company's efforts on marketing, bringing in executives to concentrate on brand innovation and renovation. During 2003, he spearheaded efforts to launch or to redesign 144 products in the company's branded and seasonal segments, instituting changes that delivered immediate financial results. Sales in the company's confectionery division, which represented nearly one-fifth of its business, grew 12 percent during the year, becoming Dare's fastest-growing segment. "How does a little, private food business like ours win against our big competitors in the game of new products and innovation?" Jaques asked in the January 2005 issue of *Snack Food & Wholesale Bakery.* "How do we bring better, smarter brands with significantly lower resources, because we're never going to outspend our major competitors?"

2004–06: PRODUCT LINE EXTENSIONS

Jaques's answer was to focus on product innovation and step up investments on marketing and manufacturing. In 2004, the company extended the Breton product line by introducing Breton Gourmet, a variety of cracker available in four flavors: Original, Asiago & Rosemary, Garlic & Fine Herb, and Pesto & Parmesan. Concurrent with the extension of the Breton line, the company added to its line of Ultimate cookies, introducing two new flavors, Vanilla Crème and Strawberry Crème, giving the company a total of 11 flavors in the Ultimate range. Later in the year, Dare added new flavors to its Bear Paws line as well, introducing Banana Bread, Homestyle Oatmeal, and Baked Apple.

Jaques fleshed out Dare's existing product lines and he also added new brands, a way of increasing sales and market share that he presumably would pursue in the future. In late 2006, Dare introduced "grainsfirst," a line of crackers baked with 11 whole grains and seeds. The product was released in two flavors, Autumn Harvest and Spring Harvest. In the years ahead, the focus on brand innovation and renovation were the ingredients for Dare's success, as one of the oldest cookie and candy companies in North America worked on becoming a branded products company.

Jeffrey L. Covell

PRINCIPAL SUBSIDIARIES

Dare Foods Inc.

PRINCIPAL COMPETITORS

Pepperidge Farm, Inc.; Voortman Cookies Limited; George Weston Limited.

FURTHER READING

"Dare Foods Expands Plant in Quebec," *Snack Food & Wholesale Bakery,* June 2003, p. 20.

"Dare Foods to Acquire Quebec's Culinar Businesses," *Resource News International,* June 18, 2001.

"Dare Foods/Bremner Biscuit," *Gourmet Retailer,* December 2000, p. 114.

Goldeen, Joe, "Dares Hand over Reins to Outsider," *America's Intelligence Wire,* December 5, 2002.

Hanacek, Andy, "Daring New Direction," *Snack Food & Wholesale Bakery,* January 2005, p. 18.

"Kitchener, Ont.-based Dare Foods Became the Second-Largest Player in the Canadian Cookie Market," *Snack Food & Wholesale Bakery,* June 2001, p. 11.

Malovany, Dan, "Under the Radar," *Snack Food & Wholesale Bakery,* July 2001, p. 18.

"Octocookie," *Snack Food & Wholesale Bakery,* June 2002, p. SI-23.

Pacyniak, Bernard, "Sweet Pickin's," *Candy Industry,* April 2004.

"Saputo Inc.," *Market News Publishing,* June 18, 2001.

"Snack Lovers Rejoice," *CNW Group,* April 23, 2007.

"Tasty, Safer Snacks for the Backpack: Dare Peanut-Free Products a Must Have for Back to School This Year," *CNW Group,* July 17, 2006.

De Agostini Editore S.p.A.

Via G da Verrazzano 15
Novara, I-28100
Italy
Telephone: (+39 0321) 4241
Fax: (+39 0321) 47128
Web site: http://www.deagostini.it

Subsidiary of De Agostini S.p.A.
Incorporated: 1901 as Istituto Geografico De Agostini
Employees: 2,270
Sales: EUR 1.62 billion ($2.07 billion) (2007)
NAICS: 511130 Book Publishers

∎ ∎ ∎

De Agostini Editore S.p.A. is one of the world's top ten publishing groups. The Novara, Italy-based company is active across a wide range of publishing areas, and is particularly well known for its range of partwork and installment publications. De Agostini Editore operates through seven business units. Partworks Editorial, the group's largest division, generates more than 58 percent of its annual revenues of EUR 1.6 billion ($2 billion) each year. This division focuses on the publishing and distribution of magazines, installment editions, and collector's series, primarily through the newsstand and kiosk business channel. Major subsidiaries in the Partworks division include Editions Atlas, in France, and a 50 percent stake in the Planeta De Agostini joint venture. Direct Marketing, which contributes 28.5 percent of revenues, is a mail-order distributor of books, DVDs, CDs, cards, and other products. Other divisions

include Direct Marketing, which sells encyclopedias, dictionaries, classic works, and related materials on a door-to-door basis; Education, which publishes school grade textbooks; Books and Cartography; Magazines; and Digital De Agostini, which operates digital television services and Internet-based content delivery. De Agostini Editore is present in more than 30 countries worldwide, with a focus on the European and Central and South American markets. The company has also launched operations in China.

Agostini Editore remains the heart of growing conglomerate De Agostini S.p.A., as the company launched a diversification effort in the late 1990s. De Agostini has added media and communications holdings, including the Antena 3 television network in Spain; lottery equipment and operations, including Lottomatica in Italy and Gtech in the United States; and insurance, through its stake in Toro, among other investments. De Agostini Editore continues to represent more than 44 percent of De Agostini S.p.A.'s total annual turnover. Paolo Boroli is Agostini Editore's president, while Pietro Boroli serves as chairman. The interrelated Boroli and Drago families maintain control of the entire De Agostini group.

ITALIAN ATLAS PIONEER IN 1901

Giovanni De Agostini was the brother of noted Italian explorer Alberto Maria, known for his travels to Patagonia at the start of the 20th century. De Agostini too shared an interest in geography, but his career took another direction altogether. In 1901, De Agostini founded a publishing house, called Istituto Geografico

COMPANY PERSPECTIVES

Our Mission: Innovation and Internationalization. The constant evolution of the markets—both in terms of the type of content and how it is created, and in the ways different forms of content are delivered to the consumer—presents an ongoing challenge. This can be met only by the flexibility and dynamism that allows the development of new business strategies, based on internationalization and innovation.

Technological developments, especially in the communications sector, have led to the creation of new media. De Agostini Editore is meeting the challenge such media present by drawing on its traditional strengths to channel its creative dynamism.

This combination of the company's heritage and its dynamism is at the core of the company's mission: a deep-rooted commitment to disseminating knowledge in all its potential forms. Our strength is based on our ability to know how to interpret consumer needs and interests, translating them into fresh and original products that are appreciated by millions of buyers in every continent.

Ideas, research and close observation of target markets make our company the absolute leader in consumer publishing, with confirmed levels of excellence both in terms of the quality of what we offer and the quality of our customer care.

De Agostini, with an office facing Rome's Trevi Fountain. From there, De Agostini published his first work, the *Atlante Scolastico Moderno* (*Modern School Atlas*).

While atlases were generally large and bulky works, De Agostini had the idea to publish a new atlas in a smaller, pocket-sized format. This led to the release in 1904 of the *Calendario Atlante De Agostini*, which became popularly known as the *Atlantino* (or *Mini Atlas*). The new atlas also combined features of the traditional almanac, while providing geographic facts and figures in addition to maps of the world.

The *Atlantino* was a major success for De Agostini and established the company's name among the leading Italian atlas producers. The company further solidified its reputation when it became the first to produce a complete map of Italy, which had only recently become

a unified country, in 1906. The work, which featured a scale of 1:250,000, had been developed for the Italian Touring Club, and became a popular consumer success.

The heart of the European cartography world, however, lay farther north, particularly in Germany, which had emerged as a leading center of precision cartography tools. De Agostini had also begun to build relationships with Italy's growing industrial sector, also largely situated in Italy's northern regions. As a result, De Agostini moved his own business north, setting up new headquarters in Novaro.

De Agostini continued to expand into the World War I years. Following the war, the company was taken over by new owners, Marco Boroli and Cesare Rossi. The partners then incorporated the company, with each taking an equal share. The new team continued to focus on the cartography market, expanding its scientific department, which was placed under Luigi Visintin. Into the 1920s, the company conceived of a new large-scale atlas capable of rivaling the most respected atlases from other countries. This resulted in the launch of the *Grande Atlante Geografico* (the *Complete Geographical Atlas*) in 1922.

DEVELOPING PRODUCT LINES IN THE FIFTIES

De Agostini had modernized its printing capacity in late 1927, investing in costly rotogravure printing presses. The new technology allowed the company to increase its production levels. The printing process also allowed the company to raise the quality of its illustrations amid a highly competitive cartography market.

The Boroli family bought out its partners and took full control of the company in 1946. At that time, Achille Boroli took the company's lead. Soon joined by his brother, Adolfo, Boroli sought to establish De Agostini as a leading player in Italy's publishing sector. After completing a capital increase in 1947, the company began developing new product lines, branching out from its initial focus on atlases and cartography.

The search for new products, and for new distribution models, led to the launch of *Il Milione,* one of the world's largest geographic encyclopedias. Over the course of time, the work spanned 15 volumes for a total of 10,000 pages and 16,000 illustrations. Another distinguishing feature of the encyclopedia was the company's decision to sell it in installments of 312, 32-page magazines. The low-price threshold, with a cost of just 200 liras for the first issue, made the encyclopedia extremely popular. The partwork model became a company mainstay.

The success of the partwork formula encouraged Istituto Geografico De Agostini to develop other distribu-

KEY DATES

1901: Giovanni De Agostini establishes a publishing company in Rome and launches his first atlas.

1908: De Agostini moves its headquarters to Rome.

1946: The Boroli family become sole owners of the company.

1959: De Agostini launches its first installment encyclopedia, *Il Milione.*

1971: The company spins off its printing operations to focus on developing international publishing operations.

1985: De Agostini forms a joint venture with Grupo Planeta and enters the Spanish, Portuguese, and Latin American markets.

1994: De Agostini founds an English-speaking subsidiary in London, then enters the United States and Canada.

1997: Marco Drago becomes chairman and leads the group on a diversification drive, creating De Agostini S.p.A. as a holding company.

2002: De Agostini acquires the Utet publishing company in Turin.

2004: De Agostini S.p.A. creates a dedicated publishing subsidiary, De Agostini Editore.

2008: De Agostini Editore launches a new division, Digital De Agostini.

---

tion models as well. Through the 1950s, the door-to-door sales channel had grown strongly in Italy and elsewhere. Door-to-door sales of encyclopedias, which were easily sold in installments, had long since become a fixture in the publishing world. De Agostini recognized the opportunity to extend its own publishing operations into this direction as well, and in 1962, the company launched its first installment sales products.

INTERNATIONAL GROWTH FROM THE SEVENTIES

Through the 1960s and 1970s, De Agostini expanded rapidly, and by the beginning of the 1980s had grown into one of Italy's leading publishing houses. A major step toward this achievement came with the decision to spin off the company's printing business into a separate company, called Officine Grafiche De Agostini, in 1971. Now dedicated to its publishing operations, Istituto Geografico De Agostini focused especially on building its partwork business. The company quickly launched a

wide range of products, enjoying particular success with the launch of a number of collector's series.

Having established a solid presence in Italy, De Agostini also targeted international expansion. Over the next decades, the company succeeded in becoming not only a leading player in the European publishing sector, but by the dawn of the next century had grown into one of the top ten publishing groups worldwide. Among the company's notable international successes was its control of Editions Atlas, in France, which launched its own partwork encyclopedia in that country in 1967. Atlas grew into one of De Agostini's largest subsidiaries, building its own international network. In addition to becoming one of the largest publishing groups in France, Editions Atlas also established itself as a major player in the partworks publishing sector in the German-speaking markets.

In 1987, Atlas expanded into a new area when it merged with the Guilde Internationale du Disque, becoming a major distributor of music CDs. This addition led De Agostini to develop a dedicated Direct Marketing division in 1989. The group's mail-order business combined the company's longstanding series sales model with a strong catalog of single titles. Through 2000, the company's direct marketing expanded its range to include cards and DVDs, in addition to books and music.

De Agostini moved into the Spanish publishing market in the mid-1980s, when it teamed up with Grupo Planeta to form Editorial Planeta De Agostini in 1985. The 50-50 partnership, based in Barcelona, not only gave De Agostini access to the Spanish and Portuguese markets, it also brought the company across the Atlantic, with operations throughout Latin America.

Into the 1990s, De Agostini targeted the English-speaking markets as well. For this the company set up its first subsidiary in London in 1994. By the following year, De Agostini had set up a U.S. subsidiary, launching its first list of titles for that market in 1995. For this, the company initially targeted the children's book market; by 1996, however, De Agostini had launched its first English-language adult titles in the United States as well.

DIVERSIFIED CONGLOMERATE

De Agostini entered a new era in the second half of the 1990s, following the death of Adolfo Boroli and his brother Achille's retirement. Taking the lead of the company was their nephew, Marco Drago, who had served as the group's managing director since the early 1980s. As chairman, Drago set his sights on re-creating De Agostini as a diversified media conglomerate. One of

Drago's first moves was to join the privatization of the SEAT industrial group, becoming a partner in the buy-out of SEAT Pagine Gialle, the Italian yellow pages and Internet operator. Drago quickly turned around De Agostini's minority stake in that business, selling it for a net gain of EUR 1.8 billion.

De Agostini targeted further media expansion at the beginning of the decade. Toward this goal, the group carried out a restructuring, creating a new holding company, De Agostini S.p.A. The company was then given a new divisional structure, including Publishing, Media and Communications, and Finance divisions. Over the next several years, De Agostini completed a flurry of new acquisitions. These included Italian lottery operator Lottomatica in 2002; majority control over Spanish radio and television broadcaster Antena 3; the Toro Assicurazioni insurance group in 2003, and U.S.-based lottery equipment giant Gtech in 2006.

De Agostini's publishing arm also grew strongly during this period. In 2002, the company acquired Utet (Union Tipografico Editirice Torinese), one of Italy's oldest and most prestigious publishers, with a catalog of more than 1,000 titles. Founded by bookstore owners in 1791, Utet had entered the encyclopedia market in 1841, publishing the *Nuova Enciclopedia Poolare*. In modern times, Utet launched the *Enciclopedia Europea* in 1976.

The growth of De Agostini's diversified holdings led the company to create a new dedicated subsidiary for its publishing operations, called De Agostini Editore, in 2004. The new subsidiary regrouped several business areas, including Partworks, Direct Marketing, Books and Cartography, School, General Reference, and Professional Publications. Taking the lead of the new subsidiary was Pietro Boroli, who had joined the company in the late 1970s.

De Agostini Editore continued its expansion, buying majority control of educational books publisher Sedes S.p.A. in 2006, followed by that of the educational publishing operations of Cedam S.p.A., part of the Wolters Kluwer group. In 2007, the group's educational sector expanded again, with the purchase of foreign-language publisher Cideb Editrice. By then, the company had also targeted new international expansion, developing its first two products, a children's collectible series and an encyclopedia of minerals, for the Chinese market.

De Agostini continued to augment its range of media interests through the end of the decade. Publishing subsidiary De Agostini Editore, which by the end of 2008 represented just 44 percent of total group turnover, also sought new publishing horizons. In that year, for example, the company established a new division. Digital De Agostini, in order to expand its presence in digital media platforms such as the Internet, mobile telecommunications, and digital television. De Agostini continued to chart new destinations as one of the world's leading publishing and media groups of the new millennium.

M. L. Cohen

PRINCIPAL SUBSIDIARIES

De Agostini Atlas Editions B.V.; De Agostini Deutschland GmbH; De Agostini Diffusione del libro S.p.A.; De Agostini Edizioni Scolastiche S.p.A.; De Agostini Hellas E.P.E.; De Agostini Japan K.K.; De Agostini LLC (Russia); De Agostini Netherland B.V.; De Agostini Partworks Holding B.V.; De Agostini Polska S.p.z.o.o. (Poland); De Agostini Scuola S.p.A.; De Agostini U.K. Holding Ltd.; Di. Ya. Ge. Int.l Books & Magazines Distribution Co. Ltd. (China); Editions Atlas (France) S.A.S.; Editions Atlas (Suisse) S.A. (Switzerland); Edito Service S.A.; Gruppo Planeta De Agostini S.L. (50%); Istituto Geografico De Agostini S.p.A.; Mach2 (36%); Main Equity Investments; m-dis Distribuzione Media S.p.A. (45%); Sedes S.p.A. (75%); U.T.E.T. (99.53%).

PRINCIPAL DIVISIONS

Partworks; Direct Marketing; General Reference; Education; Books and Cartography; Magazines.

PRINCIPAL COMPETITORS

Vivendi S.A.; Bertelsmann AG; Dr August Oetker KG; Reed Elsevier N.V.; Wolters Kluwer N.V.; Grupo PRISA; Pearson PLC; RCS MediaGroup S.p.A.; Bonnier AB; Verlagsgruppe Georg von Holtzbrinck GmbH; Arnoldo Mondadori Editore S.p.A.

FURTHER READING

"Acquisition of Cattleya Authorised," *European Report,* March 5, 2009.

"Another Italian Family Conglomerate in the Making," *Daily Deal,* April 7, 2003.

Clark, Simon, "To De Agostini Chief, Lottery Firm Is Safe Bet," *International Herald Tribune,* August 25, 2006, p. 13.

"De Agostini Offloads 30% of Toro in Bullish Eu613m IPO," *Euroweek,* June 3, 2005, p. 29.

"De Agostini Revenue Goes up to 2.2bn Euros," *Europe Intelligence Wire,* June 20, 2003.

"De Agostini Targets Double Growth of TV Arm," *Screen Digest,* December 2008, p. 376.

"Italy's De Agostini Ramps Up," *Hollywood Reporter,* September 17, 2002, p. 8.

McMahon, Kate, and Will Hurrell, "De Agostini Looks to UK to Kickstart Global Ambition," *Broadcast,* November 28, 2008, p. 3.

Reid, Calvin, "De Agostini Offers US Adult List," *Publishers Weekly,* November 4, 1996, p. 14.

Timmons, Heather, "A Conglomerate with Ambition Buys into the US," *New York Times,* January 23, 2006, p. C2.

Vivarelli, Nick, "A Fresh Chapter: Italo Publisher Collects TV Production Houses," *Variety,* September 15, 2008, p. 15.

———, "Italo Publisher Buys into Reality Producer," *Daily Variety,* January 11, 2007, p. 22.

Zecchinelli, Cecilia, "Publisher to Acquire Art Pic Distrib," *Variety,* July 29, 2002, p. 10.

Del Monte Foods Company

One Market @ The Landmark
San Francisco, California 94105-1390
U.S.A.
Telephone: (415) 247-3000
Fax: (415) 247-3565
Web site: http://www.delmonte.com

Public Company
Incorporated: 1916 as California Packing Corporation
Employees: 8,600
Sales: $3.74 billion (2008)
Stock Exchanges: New York
Ticker Symbol: DLM
NAICS: 311421 Fruit and Vegetable Canning; 311422 Specialty Canning; 311111 Dog and Cat Food Manufacturing

■ ■ ■

Del Monte Foods Company is among the largest producers and marketers of branded canned fruits and vegetables in the United States. Its main brands for packaged vegetables, fruits, and tomato products are Del Monte, S&W, and Contadina, and it also produces College Inn broths. In addition to its food products, which generate more than 60 percent of company revenues, Del Monte is also a major producer and marketer of branded pet food and snacks, with such nationally known labels as Meow Mix, Kibbles 'n Bits, 9Lives, Milk-Bone, Pup-Peroni, and Pounce. The company's facilities encompass 17 production sites and nine distribution centers in the United States, plus overseas production sites in Mexico and Venezuela. The vast majority, roughly 94 percent, of Del Monte Foods' revenues are generated in the United States, with the remainder originating in South America.

The tangled history of Del Monte Foods has led to an equally tangled array of companies that have a stake in the Del Monte brand. Del Monte Foods itself is involved in marketing only packaged food products under the Del Monte brand and only in the United States and South America; it has licensed the Del Monte brand to a number of other unaffiliated companies. For example, Kikkoman Corporation holds the rights to the brand in most of Asia and the South Pacific for packaged food products. Fresh Del Monte Produce Inc. markets fresh fruits, vegetables, and produce under the Del Monte brand throughout the world (including the United States), while its Del Monte International unit markets Del Monte–branded packaged food products in Europe, Africa, and the Middle East. Several other companies hold the rights to produce Del Monte packaged foods in Canada, Mexico, Central America and the Caribbean, the Philippines, and the Indian subcontinent.

EARLY HISTORY

Del Monte traces its origins to the pioneering 19th-century figures in West Coast canning, Daniel Provost and Francis Cutting. Along with the influx of settlers from the California gold rush came a need for new regional food manufacturers, and these men led the way. While Provost holds the distinction of forming the first foodpacking operation there, Cutting became the first of

COMPANY PERSPECTIVES

Our Vision & Mission: Del Monte is committed to enriching the lives of today's family—everyone in the family, including pets—by providing nourishing, great tasting and easy-to-use products that meet the needs of everyone in the home. We are driven by the consumer and deliver results through a partnership with our customers built upon superior brands and products, continuous innovation, excellent service and a commitment to quality in all we do. Our people are passionate about winning and take pride in Del Monte as they lead the company to achieve world-class performance and superior shareholder value.

a long line of entrepreneurs to manufacture metal and glass containers (rather than having them shipped from the East) and the first to export California-processed fruit back to the East Coast as well as Europe. As the California orchard industry grew, so did the canning industry; a virtual boom in agriculture came to the region during the 1800s, following construction of the first railroad networks, and dozens of canneries were established.

One such business, the Oakland Preserving Company, was launched in 1891. At this time, uniformity in labeling and product quality, under the auspices of the recently established California Canned Goods Association, was becoming a foremost marketing concern. The intent of this service organization was to ensure that the label "California grown" stood for an uncommonly high standard; its efforts ultimately led to effective legislation governing the canning industry. Oakland's own efforts in this area generated the Del Monte brand, a name that soon became synonymous with exceptional value.

During this time the need arose for sustaining high consumer demand within an industry that seemed to be rapidly outgrowing its economic limits. Talks of consolidation among canners eventually produced the California Fruit Canners Association (CFCA) in 1899. CFCA represented a historical merger of 18 separate canneries, including the Oakland Preserving Company. Upon consolidation, CFCA was so vast that it accounted for approximately half of the entire California canning industry and ranked, in effect, as the largest canner of fruits and vegetables in the world. There were several key promoters of the CFCA consolidation, including Frederick Tillman Jr. of Oakland Preserving;

Sydney Smith of Cutting Fruit Packing Company; Robert and Charles Bentley of Sacramento Packing; and Mark Fontana and William Fries of Fontana & Co. By popular assent, Fries became the company's president.

Given CFCA's wide area of operations and the strong wills of its various principals, true integration of the canneries never materialized. Furthermore, the retention of a large number of name brands prevented CFCA from developing a strong, cohesive marketing presence during its early years. Nonetheless, the multidimensional cannery prospered, spreading beyond the borders of California with the acquisitions of the Oregon Packing Company and the Hawaii Preserving Company. Like the other canneries already within the fold, these continued to operate fairly autonomously. However, as William Braznell pointed out in his *California's Finest: The History of the Del Monte Corporation,* "One notable concession made to corporate solidarity was the adoption of the *Del Monte* label as the association's premier brand." The brand name, courtesy of Tillman and the Oakland Preserving Company, was derived from a coffee blend prepared by Tillman and a partner for the Hotel Del Monte in Monterey as early as 1886. (*Del Monte* is a Spanish phrase meaning "of the mountain.") The Del Monte brand soon graced over 50 products, including squash, sweet potatoes, peppers, berries, jams, jellies, cranberry sauce, and olives. The famous Del Monte shield made its first appearance on a food can label in 1909.

FORMATION OF DEL MONTE PRECURSOR: 1916

CFCA's reliance upon commission agents to sell most of its produce led to a curious chain of events and, ultimately, the formation of the California Packing Corporation (Calpak), the immediate ancestor of the Del Monte Corporation. For some time, CFCA employed San Francisco-based J. K. Armsby Co., the West Coast's largest wholesaler, as its exclusive agent. After CFCA terminated the arrangement, Armsby sought out the region's second largest manufacturer, Central California Canneries (CCC). This new arrangement soured when the Armsby brothers, J. K. and George, began rapidly accumulating stock in CCC. George, the more aggressive and visionary-minded of the two, had begun to conceive of a single, dominant food concern that would, at the very least, include the Armsby Co., CCC, and CFCA. Although CCC president William Hotchkiss managed to repel the takeover attempt, he eventually proved amenable to the idea of such a merger.

On November 19, 1916, after numerous meetings, disagreements, and compromises, George Armsby's

KEY DATES

1909: The Del Monte shield makes its first appearance on a food can label of the California Fruit Canners Association (CFCA).

1916: CFCA merges with other major canners to form the California Packing Corporation (Calpak).

1967: Calpak changes its name to Del Monte Corporation.

1979: R. J. Reynolds Industries, Inc., (later RJR Nabisco, Inc.) acquires Del Monte.

1989: Following Kohlberg Kravis Roberts & Co.'s takeover of RJR Nabisco, substantial parts of Del Monte are sold, including its fresh fruits operations.

1990: What remains of Del Monte is acquired by an investor group led by Merrill Lynch & Co.; the European canned food operations are later sold, leaving Del Monte focused mainly on canned foods for the U.S. market.

1997: Texas Pacific Group acquires Del Monte Foods Company; firm acquires the Contadina brand of canned tomato products.

1998: The Del Monte business in Venezuela and the rights to the Del Monte brand in South America are reacquired.

1999: Del Monte Foods is taken public with a listing on the New York Stock Exchange.

2001: The S&W brand of canned fruit, vegetables, and bean products is acquired.

2002: Del Monte acquires several operations from H. J. Heinz Company, including its North American pet foods business (with the 9-Lives and Kibbles 'n Bits brands) and StarKist tuna.

2006: Company gains added scale in pet products by purchasing the Meow Mix and Milk-Bone brands.

2008: Del Monte's seafood business, including StarKist, is sold.

dream was realized and the monolithic Calpak was formed. Joining the three major companies in the merger were Alaska Packers Association and Griffin & Skelley. Save for Alaska Packers, all of the consolidated companies were headquartered in San Francisco within a short distance of each other. By 1917, a new head-quarters had been established and a committee system of management adopted. J. K. Armsby and Fries were elected to serve as president and chairperson, respectively. Like the CFCA merger, the Calpak merger presented a host of organizational problems for the new management, not the least of which was establishing production consistency within the 71 plants in California, Washington, Oregon, and Idaho, as well as the territories of Alaska and Hawaii. According to Braznell, what held everything together was the understanding by the owners that "California Packing Corporation would present a solid front in the market place. There would be only one premium Calpak label—Del Monte. It would stand for products of uniformly high quality, and it would be promoted for all it was worth."

A year after the merger, Calpak made promotional history by placing its first Del Monte advertisement in the *Saturday Evening Post*. Mass advertising was a new medium, and Calpak's intent was to use it to create a national market for its Del Monte label. What the company hoped to overcome was the prevailing image among consumers that canned goods were "rainy day" items, adequate though not preferable replacements for fresh produce. The concept of brand loyalty was another potential stumbling block for the company, because most grocers at the time were "full service," filling customers orders themselves and paying little attention to manufacturers or labels. Piggly Wiggly was among the first grocery chains to alter this practice. By the 1920s the evolution toward self-service supermarkets in the grocery industry was well underway, and the success of the Del Monte marketing plan was ensured.

Calpak nevertheless entered the 1920s in a precarious situation. Although earnings were about $7 million on revenues of $85 million following record-high commodity prices, an agricultural depression loomed, made worse by the plight of many farmers who had heavily mortgaged their land to sink new capital into their operations. The company weathered the crisis better than many of its growers, strengthening itself through the establishment of a national sales network and the initiation of mass production, quality assurance, and other internal systems that both improved efficiency and enhanced the Del Monte brand. A major development came in 1925, when Calpak acquired Rochelle Canneries of Rochelle, Illinois. The purchase of this Midwest company signified Calpak's expansion into corn and pea packing, then the two most lucrative segments of the vegetable canning industry. Related acquisitions included plants in Wisconsin and Minnesota. Several overseas ventures in such countries as the Philippines and Haiti also highlighted the decade.

LOSSES DURING THE GREAT DEPRESSION

With the onset of the Great Depression, Calpak's earnings crumbled. From 1930 to 1931 they fell from $6.16 per share to just 9 cents per share. In 1932 the company posted the worst losses in its history. Nonetheless, within two years, earnings began to rebound and, after one more unfavorable year, the company was firmly back in the black. In addition to the poor economy and fierce competition from other major canners, Calpak also faced pressure at the time from a flurry of new canneries. Enormous changes within the industry also came about as a result of the agricultural labor movement. The International Longshoremen and Warehousemen's Union, after demonstrating its clout through well-planned strikes, eventually won the right to represent cannery workers in wage, plant safety, and benefit negotiations.

Having aided the Allied effort during World War II, while sustaining profit losses and the temporary closing of operations in the Philippines, Calpak emerged a much stronger company during the late 1940s because of the postwar expansion and rising per capita consumption of canned products. In 1948 the company acquired East Coast producer Edgar H. Hurff Co. Two years later Calpak moved into new headquarters, and in 1951 the company named its seventh president, Roy Lucks. Braznell characterized him as: "coolly logical, an avid student of management sciences ... a leader who recognized no jurisdictional boundaries and no allegiances other than those owed to the corporation and its shareholders." Under Lucks, wrote Braznell, "Calpak/Del Monte moved into the modern era."

By 1951, Calpak had an estimated worth of $158 million and annual revenues of $223 million. Yet it remained an unwieldy business whose potential for growth had barely been tapped. Until the end of his presidency in 1963, Lucks drove the company forward not so much by acquisition as by a devotion to marketing research, field sales, new promotions, new product introductions (including fruit drinks), and a consolidation of its operating units. Of course one merger did prove singularly beneficial to Calpak. This was the purchase of a two-thirds interest in Canadian Canners Limited in 1956. The $14 million dollar deal attracted considerable attention from industry analysts, because it not only gave Calpak a controlling voice in the operations of the world's second largest fruit and vegetable canner, but it also ensured a dominant position for the company in the prized British trade bloc.

When Jack Countryman succeeded Lucks, he fortified Del Monte's competitive advantages by establishing a highly efficient warehouse distribution system. In 1967, in an attempt to heighten the company's profile and attract new management talent, he gave Calpak the name it had come to prize above all others, Del Monte. After streamlining its famous shield logo, the Del Monte Corporation launched boldly into the new territory of soft drinks (which was abandoned after four years) as well as an entire line of canned fruit drinks (which survived until 1974). Other forays included potato chips, frozen french fries, fruit turnovers, frozen prepared entrees, and real estate. Only the last two held any real promise for the company. Strong earnings growth typified the period not because of these attempts at diversification but because of Countryman's parallel commitment to international expansion. The president also proved astute in thwarting a potential takeover from United Fruit (later Chiquita Brands) by acquiring a Miami-based banana importer which, under a U.S. District Court antitrust ruling, nullified any such attempt. United later sold its Guatemalan operations to Del Monte for $20 million, thus conferring status on the canner as a potentially major player in the fresh fruit market. Alfred W. Eames Jr. assumed the reins from Countryman in 1968, just prior to a "canner's recession." Accordingly, profits during 1969 and 1970 dropped substantially. In 1971 Del Monte became the first major U.S. food processor to voluntarily place nutritional labeling on all its food products.

ACQUISITION BY RJR NABISCO IN 1979

Profit Improvement Project, or PIP, teams dominated Del Monte corporate culture during the 1970s. U.S. Grocery Products, U.S. Subsidiaries, International Grocery Products, and Seafood were named as the company's major divisions and decentralization became the guiding management philosophy. By 1978, Del Monte had weathered several economic crises (the devaluation of the dollar, rising manufacturing costs, and price freezes) to emerge with record sales of $1.56 billion. Through conservative management of its assets, it was positioning itself for a pivotal acquisition of large proportions that might render it less vulnerable to downswings in its core industry. The company's balance sheets were beginning to look so attractive, however, that its privately issued stock, which was once closely held but freely traded among a widening circle of private investors, began unexpectedly ratcheting upward. In August 1978 J. Paul Sticht and Joseph Abely Jr. of R. J. Reynolds Industries, Inc., (later RJR Nabisco, Inc.) arranged a meeting with the new Del Monte president, Dick Landis. In a little over a month an agreement to merge, worth $618 million, was reached and then officially ratified in early 1979, with Del Monte becoming the acquired rather than the acquirer.

For the next ten years, Del Monte benefited from the addition of RJR Foods labels (such as Hawaiian Punch, Chun King, and Patio) but also suffered from RJR managerial impulses. The company underwent at least four reorganizations, as well as a succession of managers, and saw its longtime San Francisco headquarters moved to Miami. All of this came to an abrupt end in 1989, when Kohlberg Kravis Roberts & Co. effected the biggest leveraged buyout in U.S. history, purchasing RJR Nabisco for more than $24 billion. In order to reduce debt incurred by the transaction, substantial portions of Del Monte were auctioned off to overseas buyers, including its fresh fruits operations (purchased by British-based Polly Peck International) and its processed foods and Japanese rights (purchased by Kikkoman Corporation).

A new Del Monte management team, led by Ewan Macdonald, who had served as marketing vice-president since 1985, salvaged the remainder of the business via another leveraged buyout in January 1990. The cost of this acquisition by an investor group led by Merrill Lynch & Co. was $1.48 billion, 80 percent of which was financed with outside capital. According to Fara Warner in *Adweek's Marketing Week:* "Del Monte is one of the success stories to come out of the RJR leveraged buyout, despite the heavy debt load the current owners incurred in buying Del Monte from RJR; sales have grown annually by 9 percent during Macdonald's tenure." Most attributed the success to Macdonald's strategy of advertising only in magazines. However, a $50 million campaign to introduce the failed Del Monte Vegetable Classics, a considerable portion of which was earmarked for television ads, belied this strategy. In addition, the debt load was reduced via the divestment of the Hawaiian Punch and the European canned food divisions.

STRUGGLING UNDER DEBT LOAD

Throughout all the turmoil, Del Monte maintained its good reputation. In 1992 it still ranked number one in brand preference in several categories and controlled 16 percent of the $3.5 billion canned vegetable market. A heavy debt load, however, gave the company little flexibility. Necessary computer upgrades had to be done on the cheap, and advertising expenditures remained relatively low. To lighten the debt burden, the company sold off further divisions in the mid-1990s; its dried fruit division went to Yorkshire Food Group in 1993 and its pudding division went to Kraft in 1995.

Moreover, demand for canned foods had been declining throughout the 1980s and 1990s, as Americans sought to increase their consumption of fresh fruits and vegetables. To combat this trend, Del Monte initiated an advertising campaign aimed at 18- to 34-year-olds. Using new print advertising, new packaging, and new products, the company appealed to young adult consumers, such as single parents and unmarried couples, who might not have time for preparing fresh fruits and vegetables.

Also during this time, the Federal Trade Commission ruled that a supply agreement Del Monte had with Pacific Coast Producers substantially reduced competition in the processed fruit market. The decision led Del Monte to pay out $4 million to settle an antitrust suit brought against them by Pacific Coast.

To offset this large debt, Del Monte's owners sought a purchaser for the company, coming close to closing a deal in the mid-1990s. Del Monte had agreed to a $1 billion takeover by Grupo Cabal, a group of investors led by Carlos Cabal, in 1994. The deal would have reunited some of the Del Monte brands because Cabal had already purchased Fresh Del Monte Produce from the liquidators of Polly Peck International in 1992. The deal fell through at the last minute, however, when Cabal disappeared after being charged with illegally transferring money from a trade finance firm to his personal accounts.

1997 ACQUISITION BY TEXAS PACIFIC

As the canned foods market continued to decline and as debts continued to burden the company, Del Monte sought another buyer. In the meantime, it announced in 1996 that it would reduce its workforce by 20 percent. The following year, another suitor appeared. The private-equity firm Texas Pacific Group had begun a food business shopping spree in 1995 and became known for buying up companies that most analysts regarded as trouble. Beginning with the purchase of Kraft Foods' marshmallow and confections operations, Texas Pacific was soon the fourth largest U.S. candy and confections company. In April 1997 Texas Pacific acquired Del Monte in a deal valued at about $840 million. As part of the transition, Richard Wolford, previously the president of packaged foods for rival Dole Foods, was named CEO of Del Monte.

Wolford led a concerted effort to revitalize what had become a stagnant business during its two decades under a succession of indifferent owners. New products and packaging were introduced, including the Orchard Select line of premium fruit in glass jars; the consumer promotions budget was nearly quadrupled to $46 million; and the first Del Monte advertising campaign in eight years was launched in the spring of 1999 centering around the tagline "Add imagination and serve."

Another strategy involved broadening the company's channels of distribution, and in particular pushing the Del Monte brand into high-growth retail sectors such as supercenters and warehouse club stores. Cost-cutting was also on the agenda as Del Monte in early 1998 announced the closure of two of its six plants in California and the elimination of about 1,000 jobs.

Del Monte also bulked up during this period through two important acquisitions. In December 1997 the company purchased the Contadina brand of canned tomato products from the U.S. unit of Nestlé S.A. for $195 million (with Nestlé retaining the Contadina line of refrigerated pasta and sauces). Like Del Monte, Contadina was another venerable California brand with a history dating back to 1916. Adding Contadina provided Del Monte with a more extensive line of tomato products, including tomato puree, tomato paste, crushed tomatoes, and pizza sauce. Adding value-added products such as these was a key goal for the company as it attempted to de-emphasize the more moribund and commoditized area of simple canned vegetables, where branding had grown ever less important. In August 1998 Del Monte regained a portion of its former international business from Nabisco, Inc., when it reacquired the rights to the Del Monte brand in South America and bought Nabisco's canned vegetable and tomato business in Venezuela, which included a food processing plant. The purchase price was $32 million.

1999 RETURN TO PUBLIC OWNERSHIP

For the 1997–98 fiscal year, Del Monte Foods Company eked out a net profit of $5 million on sales of $1.31 billion. In the summer of 1998 the company canceled a planned return to public ownership when the market for initial public offerings (IPOs) turned unfavorable. The following February, however, a second attempt at an IPO went through, and Del Monte began a new era as a public company. The firm sold 20 million shares of common stock on the New York Stock Exchange at $15 per share, yielding net proceeds of $230 million, which were used to shave a still-heavy debt load.

Del Monte began the 21st century with two more acquisitions of related brands. In September 2000 the company bought the SunFresh brand from UniMark Group, Inc., for $12.7 million. The SunFresh line included premium tropical and citrus fruit in glass jars and cans and thus fit in well alongside the Orchard Select line. Del Monte in March 2001 purchased the S&W brand from Tri Valley Growers, a grower-owned cooperative that had filed for Chapter 11 bankruptcy protection the previous July. Gaining the S&W brand in

this $35.4 million deal not only expanded Del Monte's presence in canned fruits and vegetables but also extended its line of products into canned baked beans as well as various flavored and unflavored beans, including kidney, black, garbanzo, and chili beans. Del Monte and S&W shared similar roots as the latter was founded in 1896 by three San Francisco grocery wholesalers.

EXPANSION INTO THE PET FOOD SECTOR

During the 2001–02 fiscal year, when the company netted $38.5 million on revenues of $1.32 billion, Del Monte completed the integration of S&W into its existing operations and also pared its debt by around $124 million, to $590.5 million. The reduction in debt helped lay the foundation for Del Monte's largest transaction to that time. In December 2002 H. J. Heinz Company spun off to a separate company several sluggishly growing businesses that had collectively generated annual sales of $1.8 billion: its North American pet foods business, including the 9-Lives, Kibbles 'n Bits, and Pup-Peroni brands, StarKist tuna, Nature's Goodness baby food, College Inn broths, and the firm's U.S. private-label soup and gravy products. This spinoff was then merged into Del Monte Foods Company, which subsequently commanded a much enlarged presence in the center aisles of grocery stores and gained clout in its dealings with retailers. Although Heinz considered the brands it offloaded underperforming, Del Monte officials were attracted by the higher margins that the pet food and tuna products in particular offered in comparison to its canned fruits and vegetables. Del Monte did, however, have to assume about $1.1 billion in debt from the businesses it swallowed, pushing its total long-term debt to $1.64 billion by the end of fiscal 2002–03.

Del Monte worked quickly to improve the fortunes of the long-neglected brands it had taken off Heinz's hands. More resources were devoted in particular to the pet food brands, with new products being developed and existing ones improved in quality. The early results were quite positive as the pet food brands during fiscal 2003–04 saw both their sales and earnings increase for the first time in seven years. That year, which featured the first full year of results following the Heinz transaction, net income surged 23.3 percent to $164.6 million, while revenues jumped 49.6 percent to $3.13 billion.

The next year profits fell as a result of both competitive pressures and increases in basic costs, such as steel, energy, and transportation. The company subsequently conducted a review of its product lines and elected to jettison its private-label soup and gravy businesses and its infant-feeding unit (but to retain the College Inn broth brand). These former Heinz operations were sold to TreeHouse Foods, Inc., in April 2006 for approximately $275 million. Just a month later, Del Monte gained added scale in the pet food sector by acquiring Meow Mix Holdings, Inc., from the private-equity firm Cypress Group for roughly $705 million, thereby securing the Meow Mix and Alley Cat brands of cat food. Del Monte further enlarged its position in pet products in July 2006 when it acquired the Milk-Bone line of dog treats from Kraft Foods Inc. for $580 million. These deals propelled Del Monte into second place in the North American pet food market, trailing only Nestlé, owner of the Purina brand. For fiscal 2006–07, Del Monte's pet products operations accounted for around 37 percent of overall sales, compared to the 28 percent figure of three years earlier. Even more importantly, the pet products brands generated more profits than Del Monte's core canned fruit and vegetables lines as 2006–07 operating income for the former totaled $234 million compared to $170.4 million for the latter.

In 2008 Del Monte elected to narrow its focus to two main areas: its founding fruit and vegetable business and its nascent pet food operations. Thus in October it sold its seafood business, including the StarKist tuna brand, to the South Korean company Dongwon Enterprise Co., Ltd., for around $360 million. The seafood unit had generated sales of $560 million in fiscal 2007–08. Overall revenues that year totaled $3.74 billion, an increase of 9.4 percent over the previous year, while net income amounted to $133.1 million, an increase of 18.2 percent. Future prospects for Del Monte Foods were uncertain given the potential impact of the global economic downturn on its operations. Cash-strapped consumers were increasingly trading down to less expensive brands and private-label products, possibly hurting the company's venerable brands, including Del Monte and Contadina, and the firm's pet food side faced a downturn of its own given that some consumers might be forced to abandon their pets to shelters while others elect not to get a pet. Nevertheless, Del Monte Foods possessed a strong stable of brands that could be found in eight out of ten households in the United States, and many of these brands had managed to survive through previous economic calamities.

Jay P. Pederson
Updated, Susan Windisch Brown; David E. Salamie

PRINCIPAL SUBSIDIARIES

Del Monte Argentina; Hi Continental Corporation; College Inn Foods; DLM Foods Canada Corp.; Del Monte Colombiana, S.A. (Colombia); Contadina Foods, Inc.; Marine Trading Pacific, Inc.; The Meow Mix Company, LLC; Meow Mix Decatur Production I LLC; S&W Fine Foods, Inc.; Del Monte Peru, S.A.C.; Del Monte Andina, C.A. (Venezuela); Industrias Citrícolas de Montemorelos, S.A. de C.V. (Mexico).

PRINCIPAL COMPETITORS

General Mills, Inc.; Con Agra Foods, Inc.; H. J. Heinz Company; Seneca Foods Corporation; Pacific Coast Producers; Dole Food Company, Inc.; Unilever; Campbell Soup Company; Nestlé S.A.; Mars, Incorporated; The Procter & Gamble Company; Colgate-Palmolive Company; Menu Foods Limited.

FURTHER READING

Anders, George, "Italian Financier Begins Talks Aimed at Buying Del Monte for $300 Million," *Wall Street Journal*, May 28, 1992.

Angwin, Julia, and Kenneth Howe, "Texas Group to Acquire Del Monte," *San Francisco Chronicle*, March 1, 1997, p. B1.

Barron, Kelly, "Breathing New Life into a Tired Old Brand," *Forbes*, November 30, 1998, pp. 190–91.

Berman, Dennis K., "Del Monte Nears $700 Million Deal for Meow Mix," *Wall Street Journal*, March 2, 2006, p. A11.

Braznell, William, *California's Finest: The History of the Del Monte Corporation and the Del Monte Brand*, San Francisco: Del Monte Corporation, 1982, 168 p.

Carlsen, Clifford, "Del Monte Charts a New Strategy After Canning Its IPO," *San Francisco Business Times*, September 25, 1998, pp. 3+.

"Del Monte: A New Marketing Formula Moves It Beyond Canned Foods," *Business Week*, July 5, 1982, pp. 92+.

DeNitto, Emily, "Del Monte Sets Its Sights Younger," *Advertising Age*, October 4, 1993, p. 8.

Dorman, Shirleen, "Del Monte Net Nearly Doubles amid Sale of Unit," *Wall Street Journal*, December 4, 2008, p. B3.

Eames, Alfred W., and Richard G. Landis, *"The Business of Feeding People": The Story of Del Monte Corporation*, New York: Newcomen Society in North America, 1974, 22 p.

Eig, Jonathan, and Robert Frank, "Heinz Spins Off Sluggish Units: Digestion of Brands Like 9-Lives, StarKist to Enlarge Del Monte," *Wall Street Journal*, June 14, 2002, p. B4.

Elliott, Dorinda, "Dole and Del Monte Are Staying Put—No Matter What," *Business Week*, November 18, 1985, pp. 58+.

Emert, Carol, "Del Monte Will Cut 1,000 Jobs," *San Francisco Chronicle*, January 31, 1998, p. D1.

Estrada, Richard T., "S&W Sale Is Final Today," *Modesto (Calif.) Bee*, March 14, 2001, p. A1.

Fass, Allison, "Animal House," *Forbes*, February 12, 2007, p. 72.

Fuquay, Jim, "Del Monte Plans to Go Public, Sell 20 Million Shares," *Fort Worth Star-Telegram,* January 20, 1999.

———, "Fort Worth Group to Buy Del Monte," *Fort Worth Star-Telegram,* March 1, 1997.

Johnson, Bradley, "Vexed over Vegetables: Churlish Children Hawk Del Monte's New Line," *Advertising Age,* January 14, 1991, p. 4.

Kindel, Sharen, "Bringing Mother Nature On Line," *Financial World,* December 8, 1992, pp. 78–79.

Lindeman, Teresa F., "Fresh Start—Again," *Pittsburgh Post-Gazette,* November 10, 2002, p. D1.

———, "A Shift in Focus for Del Monte: Food Giant Looks to Promote Brands, Simplify Its Business," *Pittsburgh Post-Gazette,* September 29, 2005, p. E1.

Loeffelholz, Suzanne, "Thrice Shy: Del Monte and Sansui Are the Jewels in Polly Peck's Crown," *Financial World,* May 29, 1990, pp. 46+.

Maremont, Mark, and Judith H. Dobrzynski, "Meet Asil Nadir, the Billion-Dollar Fruit King," *Business Week,* September 18, 1989, p. 32.

Paris, Ellen, "Swimming Through Syrup," *Forbes,* November 21, 1983, p. 328.

"A Peach or a Raspberry from Mexico?" *Economist,* July 2, 1994, p. 63.

Pimentel, Benjamin, "Brand New Mix: Del Monte Absorbs Products from Rival Heinz," *San Francisco Chronicle,* June 14, 2002, p. B1.

"Refinancing of Debt Related to Buy-Out Is Completed," *Wall Street Journal,* September 13, 1991.

Reyes, Sonia, "Breeding a New Cast of Characters," *Brandweek,* November 24, 2003, pp. 20–22, 24.

Sarkar, Pia, "Del Monte Goes for Bigger Bite of the Pet Food Market," *San Francisco Chronicle,* March 17, 2006, p. D1.

Sinton, Peter, "Del Monte Buys Contadina Line of Tomato Products," *San Francisco Chronicle,* November 15, 1997, p. D1.

Strasburg, Jenny, "Del Monte Reclaims Cannery," *San Francisco Chronicle,* October 3, 2004, p. J1.

Waldman, Peter, "RJR Completes Del Monte Sale for $1.48 Billion," *Wall Street Journal,* January 11, 1990.

Walsh, James, "Alone at Last," *California Business,* July/August 1991, pp. 18+.

Warner, Fara, "Del Monte Has a Rendezvous with an Italian Suitor," *Adweek's Marketing Week,* June 1, 1992, p. 4.

———, "What's Happening at Del Monte Foods?" *Adweek's Marketing Week,* November 18, 1991, p. 4.

Watson, Lloyd, "Slimmed-Down Del Monte Is Still 'Growing,'" *San Francisco Chronicle,* September 19, 1986, p. 41.

DELHAIZE ✱ GROUP

Delhaize Group

———— ● ————

Square Marie Curie 40
Brussels, 1070
Belgium
Telephone: (+32 32) 24122111
Fax: (+32 32) 24122222
Web site: http://www.delhaizegroup.com

Public Company
Incorporated: 1867
Employees: 141,000
Sales: EUR 19 billion ($27.8 billion) (2008)
Stock Exchanges: Euronext Brussels New York
Ticker Symbols: DELB; DEG
NAICS: 445110 Supermarkets and Other Grocery
    (Except Convenience) Stores; 452990 All Other
    General Merchandise Stores

■ ■ ■

Delhaize Group is an internationally operating retail food group with nearly 3,000 stores in seven countries. Brussels-based Delhaize is Belgium's second largest supermarket group, with more than 360 supermarkets (including Luxembourg and Germany), and more than 275 convenience stores. The group is also the leading pet store operator through its 136-strong Tom & Co chain. Delhaize's Belgian operations represented just 23 percent of the group's revenues in 2008, and just 18 percent of its profits. This is because Delhaize has been one of the few European retail groups to penetrate the U.S. market successfully. Delhaize's U.S. division includes nearly 1,600 stores operating under the Food

Lion, Bloom, Bottom Dollar, Harveys, Hannaford, and Sweetbays banners. Delhaize's U.S. operations focus on the East Coast markets, where it ranks number three; the company's U.S. division produces nearly 70 percent of group revenues, and nearly 80 percent of its operating profit. Delhaize is also a strong player in Greece, where it operates the 135-strong Alfa-Beta chain, as well as 54 convenience stores and ten cash-and-carry stores. Greece generates 7 percent of Delhaize's total turnover. Since the early 2000s, Delhaize has also been focusing on building a presence in a number of developing markets, including Romania and Indonesia, where the company operates 40 Mega Image stores and 63 Super Indo stores, respectively. The Rest of World division generates just 1 percent of group sales. The group's total turnover topped EUR 19 billion ($27.8 billion) in 2008. Delhaize is listed on both the Euronext Brussels and New York stock exchanges. The company is led by CEO and President Pierre-Olivier Beckers.

PUTTING RETAIL THEORY INTO PRACTICE IN THE MID-19TH CENTURY

Commercial sciences professor Jules Delhaize had developed his own theories about food retailing at the middle of the 19th century, and in 1867 he convinced his brother Edouard and their brother-in-law Jules Vieujant, who were also teachers, to join him in putting his theories into practice. Delhaize was convinced that he could revolutionize Belgium's grocery trade by creating a network of branch stores supplied by a central warehouse, which would enable the company to

COMPANY PERSPECTIVES

Strategy: Delhaize Group has leading positions in food retailing in key markets. The Group's position was established through strong local companies going to market with a variety of food store formats. The local companies benefit from and contribute to the Group's strength, expertise and successful practices. Delhaize Group is committed to offering a locally differentiated shopping experience to its customers, delivering high value and maintaining high social, environmental and ethical standards.

This strategy consists of the following building blocks: pursuing concept leadership; pursuing executional excellence; operating as a learning company; providing a more attractive workplace; and acting as a responsible corporate citizen.

eliminate the many middlemen involved in the grocery trade and cut down on costs. The company was then able to pass its savings onto its customers. Prices on store items, moreover, were to be clearly marked.

The Frères Delhaize company was formed in Charleroi in 1867, adopting Belgium's lion crest as its own symbol. The company's name later incorporated its symbol, becoming Delhaize "Le Lion." The symbol was later to become one of Belgium's most well-known brands. The Delhaize name also contributed to the success of another of the Delhaize brothers, Adolphe, who founded his own network of stores around the same time. In 1883, the company, which had moved to Brussels soon after its founding, moved headquarters for facilities closer to the city's Gare de l'Ouest train station. Featuring then state-of-the-art warehousing facilities, as well as a school and fire brigade, the new site also gave the company a rail link, increasing its distribution capacity. At this time too, the company branched out into manufacturing, producing a range of goods under the Delhaize brand name, including chocolates and biscuits, and coffee and spirits.

By the outbreak of World War I, Delhaize had expanded to a network of about 500 stores throughout Belgium. Following the war, the company sent representatives to the United States, where grocers were steadily introducing new innovations in areas such as store designs, displays, and service. The company's participation in international trade fairs enabled it to import new products for its stores. However, apart from

expanding its network to include the Belgian Congo, the company continued to focus exclusively on its domestic market. The economic crisis surrounding the Depression Era encouraged the company to add a new store banner, Derby, featuring deep-discount products. Despite the troubled economic climate, Delhaize continued to prosper, expanding its branch network to nearly 750 stores at the outbreak of World War II. In addition, the company's strong distribution network and its various production facilities enabled it to build a second network of affiliated, yet independent stores.

INTRODUCING SELF-SERVICE

Following World War II, the company shut down most of its manufacturing operations to focus its efforts on its retail and distribution activity. The company updated its wine and spirits warehouses, adopting innovations then being made in France. Delhaize grew externally in 1950, when the grocery chain founded by Adolphe Delhaize was merged into that founded by his brothers. That decade was to mark a revolution in the grocery industry, and the Delhaize company was to become one of the leaders in that revolution in Belgium.

The postwar reconstruction years had rapidly given way to a period of extended economic growth, particularly in Belgium. The low unemployment levels, rising wages, growing leisure time, as well as technological innovations, both in the stores and in the home combined to encourage the growth of a new grocery format, the supermarket. More consumers were adding refrigerators and freezers at home, making it possible to preserve fresh foods for longer periods. The same was true for the stores themselves, which rapidly added fresh fruits and vegetables, meats and fish, and other perishable items. Delhaize had continued to study innovations being made in the United States, which had pioneered the supermarket concept, and in 1957 the company opened Europe's first fully self-service supermarket. That supermarket incorporated a number of other features of the American supermarket, such as checkout counters, brightly colored stores, and fluorescent light fixtures.

Delhaize set about converting its network to the new supermarket format, a process that required a new distribution infrastructure, including cold-storage facilities. In order to finance the company's transformation, it took a listing on the Brussels stock exchange, changing its name to SA Delhaize Frères et Cie "Le Lion" in 1962. In 1963, the company added chilled warehouse facilities for stocking and handling fresh fruits and vegetables and dairy products. In 1967, the

KEY DATES

1867: Jules Delhaize sets up grocery branch network with brother Edouard and brother-in-law Jules Vieujant.

1871: Company moves to Brussels.

1883: Delhaize opens new state-of-the-art warehouse and headquarters facility.

1930: Company introduces Derby discount retail format.

1950: Company merges with grocery chain founded by Adolphe Delhaize.

1957: Company launches Europe's first fully self-service supermarket patterned after American supermarket concept.

1962: Company lists on Brussels stock exchange as SA Delhaize Frères et Cie.

1974: Company acquires 32 percent stake in Food Town Inc., with 22 stores in North and South Carolina.

1976: Company acquires majority control of Food Town Inc., begins rapid expansion in eastern United States, and launches DI health and beauty aid shops in Belgium.

1981: In Belgium, the company launches AD Delhaize affiliated store chain.

1983: Food Town renames itself Food Lion Inc., and boasts 225 supermarkets.

1985: Delhaize opens first Cub Foods store in Atlanta.

1989: Delhaize launches Caddy-Home, a home-delivery service, and Tom & Co, a pet foods and supplies chain in Belgium.

1992: Company acquires Alpha-Beta Vassilopoulos and enters Athens market with 15 supermarkets.

1994: Company acquires majority share in France's PG chain, with 38 Shopi and 14 March Plus stores.

1996: Company acquires Florida's Kash n' Karry chain.

2000: Delhaize completes takeover of Hannaford; acquires full control of Food Lion Thailand; and acquires 51 percent of Mega Image (Romania).

2001: Delhaize America becomes first Belgian company to take a listing on New York Stock Exchange.

2004: Delhaize acquires full control of Mega Image in Romania; Delhaize US begins converting Kash n' Karry to Sweetbays.

2007: Delhaize completes its exit from the Thai, Indonesia, Slovakian, and Czech markets.

2009: Delhaize becomes leading supermarket group in Bucharest region with purchase of four Prodas stores.

company added its own butchering facilities to supply its new in-store butcher shops.

During the mid-to-late 1960s, the company continued converting its branch network, shutting down a number of its former grocery shops and opening supermarkets, while converting a number of its existing stores to small-format self-service stores. By the middle of the 1970s, the company's supermarket network had grown to 80 stores. Yet the company faced the first of a series of so-called padlock laws that placed severe limits on the number of hypermarkets and supermarkets allowed to open in Belgium. Similar laws had begun to appear elsewhere in Europe, designed to protect small shopkeepers from being crushed by the small number of rapidly growing supermarket giants. Delhaize began developing other retail formats to circumvent the growth laws, launching its own chain of pharmacies and body care stores under the DI banner.

AMERICAN EXPANSION IN THE SEVENTIES

For its supermarket growth, Delhaize turned to a market where such restrictions were unlikely ever to appear: the United States. In 1974, the company made its first entry into that country, buying a one-third share of North and South Carolina-based Food Town Inc., which owned 22 supermarkets but had run out of cash for further expansion. Two years later, Delhaize acquired a majority share in that company. Food Town was to provide a springboard for the company's expansion in the United States. By 1983, the company had grown to more than 225 stores. In that year, Food Town changed its name to Food Lion, bringing it closer under Delhaize's wing.

In 1985, the company, which continued to target expansion in the markets on the eastern coast of the United States, opened its first Cub Foods store in

Atlanta. The company later boosted its share of that market with the acquisition of the Food Giant chain. Meanwhile, back home, the company launched a new chain, called AD Delhaize. Rather than being company-owned, the stores affiliated with the new banner remained independent, with Delhaize providing wholesale supply services and management advice.

Delhaize continued to branch out through the end of the 1980s, particularly by launching two new retail formats. The first was Caddy Home, which offered home-delivery services. The second was Tom & Co, which took the company beyond supermarkets into a retail pet foods and supplies format. These stores helped expand the company's holdings in Belgium to more than 400 stores, of which nearly 110 were supermarkets. Meanwhile, the company's United States' presence remained its driving force, with over 1,000 supermarkets under Food Lion's control by the beginning of the 1990s.

The 1990s saw Delhaize turn to an even wider international arena for its growth. The collapse of the Soviet Union and the subsequent opening up of the former Eastern Bloc countries presented Delhaize with an opportunity to expand into Central Europe. In 1991, the company launched a new subsidiary in the Czech Republic, Delvita, opening its first supermarket that year. The company's expansion in that country and neighboring Slovakia was rapid; by 1992 the company had opened seven Delvita supermarkets.

Delhaize continued to explore new foreign markets, despite the economic downturn of the period. In 1991, the company acquired a majority share in Greece's Alpha-Beta Vassilopoulos, which operated 15 supermarkets in Athens and surrounding areas. Delhaize next looked to neighboring France, buying a controlling stake in the PG group, which operated supermarkets under the Stoc banner and a network of grocery affiliates under the March Plus name. Despite growing PG to 38 supermarkets and 14 affiliates by the end of the decade, Delhaize was forced to withdraw from the bruising competitive climate of the French market, selling out its stake in PG to Carrefour in 2000.

U.S. PUBLIC OFFERING IN 2000

The United States, however, continued to provide good fortune for Delhaize. In 1996, the company expanded again, into the Florida market, with the acquisition of the Kash n' Karry chain. The following year, Delhaize targeted the other side of the world, setting up shop in Thailand and Indonesia. The company imported the Food Lion brand into Thailand, taking a stake in the new Food Lion Thailand and opening 15 stores, includ-ing the acquisition of six Sunny's stores, by the end of 1999. The following year, the company acquired full control of Food Lion Thailand. In Indonesia the company stores operated under the Super Indo banner, growing to 14 supermarkets by the end of the decade. At the same time, Delhaize moved into a new Asian market, Singapore, with the acquisition of 49 percent of that country's third largest supermarket group Shop N Save.

In Central Europe, Delvita established itself as a major retailer in the Czech and Slovakia markets with the acquisition of Interkontakt and its 50 supermarkets. The 2000 acquisition of 51 percent of Romania's Mega Image allowed the company to expand its presence in the region. In the United States, meanwhile, the company acquired the 28-store chain of Farmer Jack stores before announcing a far larger acquisition at the end of 1999.

That deal, which was closed in July 2000, called for Delhaize to acquire Hannaford Bros., a $3.3 billion company with 152 stores under the Hannaford and Shop 'n Save banners operating primarily in the northeastern United States but extending as far south as the Carolinas. At the same time, Delhaize announced it was setting up a new U.S. subsidiary company, Delhaize America, to group its growing U.S. holdings, including its 56 percent stake in Food Lion Inc. Hannaford was to remain a separately operating company under Delhaize America, signaling Delhaize's willingness to pursue further growth beyond the Food Lion banner, which, despite growing to nearly 1,200 stores, had been unable to extend its brand beyond its own core southeastern region. The Hannaford deal, which boosted the company's sales to EUR 18 billion by the end of 2000, made it the sixth largest supermarket group in the U.S. market.

At the end of 2000, the company announced its intention to buy full control of Food Lion Inc., a process completed in 2001. At that time, Delhaize America was listed on the New York Stock Exchange (NYSE), the first Belgian company to achieve a listing on the NYSE main board. Despite the United States' overwhelming position in Delhaize's balance sheet, accounting for 70 percent of sales and some 85 percent of its cash flow, the company continued to assert itself as a retail leader in its home base. By the end of 2001, the company revealed plans to boost its Belgian presence to more than 650 stores by 2006. Supermarket growth, which continued to be tightly controlled by the Belgian government, was to represent only a minor part of that expansion, with just three new supermarkets planned. Instead, the company was banking on the successful rollout of three new small-store formats, the center-city

Delhaize City stores; Shop n' Go, typically located next to filling stations and expected to grow to 50 outlets by 2003; and Proxy Delhaize, formerly known as Superettes Delhaize.

SEVEN-NATION ARMY

Delhaize continued to build its presence in the United States through the first decade of the new century. In 2003, it acquired the 43-supermarket Harveys chain, focused on south Georgia and part of Florida. The company also acquired Victory Super Market, a chain of 19 supermarkets in New England, which was then merged into the Hannaford chain. The company then began pruning underperforming stores from its U.S. portfolio, shedding 41 Food Lion and 34 Kash N' Karry stores in 2005. Delhaize then began rolling out a new format for its Florida operations, converting the Kash N' Karry chain to the Sweetbays name, a process completed by 2008.

By then, Delhaize's U.S. operations represented nearly 70 percent of the company's total revenues (down from 90 percent at mid-decade), and nearly 80 percent of operating profits. Delhaize had also been readjusting its international presence. The company became the second largest supermarket group in Greece after its acquisition of Trofo in 2001. Delhaize Greece reinforced its position in 2008 with the purchase of 34 supermarkets from Plus Hellas. At the same time, Delhaize announced its intention to launch convenience store operations in Greece, opening 54 stores under the City, Shop n' Go, and AB Food Market names.

In the meantime, Delhaize had narrowed the focus of its other international businesses. The company exited the Czech Republic in 2007, selling its operations there to Rewe, of Germany. The company also sold its holdings in Singapore, Thailand, and Slovakia in 2003, 2004, and 2005, respectively. Instead, the company focused on building its presence in Romania, where it acquired full control of Mega Image in 2004. This chain was expanded with the purchase of 14 La Fourmi stores in 2008, and then with four Prodas supermarkets in March 2009. These purchases made Mega Image the largest supermarket group in the Bucharest region.

Delhaize also continued building its domestic business. The group strengthened its presence in northeastern Belgium with the acquisition of the 43 Cash Fresh supermarkets. Delhaize's Belgium division also began its own international expansion, opening its first stores in Luxembourg, as well as establishing a small number of stores in Germany. In early 2009, amid rumors that France's Carrefour might be looking to unload its Belgian operations, Delhaize began jockeying,

announcing its interest in acquiring some or all of Carrefour's Belgian stores. With revenues of EUR 19 billion ($27.8 billion) and nearly 3,000 stores under its control, the Delhaize lion continued its growth into the new century.

M. L. Cohen

PRINCIPAL SUBSIDIARIES

Alfa-Beta Vassilopoulos S.A. (Greece); Atlas A.S. (Czech Republic); Bevermart NV; Delhaize America, Inc.; Delhaize Deutschland GmbH; Delhaize Luxembourg S.A.; Delhaize The Lion America, Inc.; Delhaize "The Lion" Nederland B.V.; Food Lion (Thailand), Ltd.; Hannaford Bros. Co. (USA).

PRINCIPAL COMPETITORS

Carrefour SA; Metro AG; Albertsons Inc; Koninklijke Ahold Nv; Aldi AG; Pathmark Stores, Inc; RALLYE S.A.; Safeway Inc.; Auchan Group; Arden Group Inc; Eagle Food Centers, Inc.; Fresh Brands Inc; Foodarama Supermarkets Inc; Gristedes Sloans Inc; The Kroger Company; Winn-Dixie Stores Inc.; Wal-Mart Corporation.

FURTHER READING

"American Operations Make Delhaize," *MMR,* May 9, 2005, p. 53.

Bickerton, Ian, "Ahold Drops Merger Plan with Delhaize," *Financial Times,* November 8, 2006, p. 30.

Carreyrou, John, "Belgium's Delhaize Raises Its Bid to Buy Rest of American Unit It Doesn't Own," *Wall Street Journal,* November 17, 2000, p. B6.

"Delhaize Builds on Strengths," *MMR,* May 13, 2002, p. 92.

"Delhaize Buys Romanian Supermarkets," *just-food.com,* March 19, 2009.

"Delhaize Completes La Fourmi Acquisition," *just-food.com,* September 2, 2008.

"Delhaize Eyeing Carrefour Supermarkets," *just-food.com,* March 27, 2009.

"Delhaize 'Le Lion' Buys US Supermarket Chain Hannaford," *Eurofood,* August 26, 1999.

"Delhaize Set to Open Discount Stores," *just-food.com,* July 31, 2008.

"Delhaize wil tegen 2006 650 voodingsverkooppunten," *De Financieel Economische Tijd,* June 27, 2001.

Domby, Daniel, "Belgian Retailer Reports Lower 2000 Profits," *Financial Times,* March 16, 2001.

Downey, John, and Lori Johnston, "Smaller Role for Food Lion in Expansion," *Business Journal,* August 20, 1999.

Frederick, James, "Food Lion Plans Pharmacy Test in Midst of Big Expansion Program," *Drug Store News,* March 20, 2000.

Garbato, Debby, "Lion's Pride," *Retail Merchandiser,* September 2006, p. 8.

Mitchell, Sue, "Food Lion's Local Links Uprooted by Foreign Buyer," *Business Journal,* December 1, 2000.

"Net Profit Soars 21% at Delhaize," *MMR,* March 23, 2009, p. 24.

Steen, Michael, "Ahold Brushes Aside Talk of Belgian Merger," *Financial Times,* March 7, 2008, p. 23.

"Unilever, Delhaize Settle Pricing Row," *just-food.com,* March 8, 2009.

Oberoi Hotels & Resorts

EIH Ltd.

————————— ■ —————————

4 Mangoe Ln.
Kolkata, 700 001
India
Telephone: (+91 033) 2248 6751
Fax: (+91 033) 2248 6785
Web site: http://www.oberoihotels.com

Public Company
Incorporated: 1949
Employees: 6,000
Sales: INR 11.51 billion ($227.9 million) (2008)
Stock Exchanges: Bombay
Ticker Symbol: 500840
NAICS: 721110 Hotels (Except Casino Hotels) and
    Motels; 722110 Full-Service Restaurants

■ ■ ■

EIH Ltd. is the publicly listed holding company for Oberoi Hotel & Resorts, the second largest operator of high-end hotels in India (behind ITC Limited). Oberoi operates 27 hotels in India, Egypt, Saudi Arabia, Indonesia, Australia, Bali, and Mauritius. The company's hotels operate under two primary brands, Oberoi, which focuses on the luxury leisure sector; and Trident, which provides five-star accommodations with a focus on the business traveler. Many of Oberoi's hotels are landmark buildings. The Oberoi Cecil, for example, located in Shimla, the former British protectorate's summer capital, was built in the 19th century. The company also owns the historic Grand Hotel in Kolkata (Calcutta), the Windsor in Melbourne, Australia, and the

Mena in Cairo, Egypt. Most of the company's hotels and resorts have nonetheless been purpose-built for the company. In addition to hotel operations, EIH is active in the luxury cruise segment on the Nile and in Kerala, India, with two small cruise vessels; charter flights, with two private jets; spa operations; and in-flight catering services, with its own network of flight kitchens. EIH planned to add ten new hotels, with the first two opening in 2009. The founding Oberoi family controls EIH through Oberoi Group's 46 percent stake in the company; Oberoi has announced its intention to raise its stake to more than 50 percent in 2009. The company is led by Prithvi Raj Singh (Biki) Oberoi, and his son, Vikram Oberoi, who serves as the company's CEO. In 2008, EIH posted revenues of INR 11.51 billion ($227.9 million).

INDIAN RAGS TO RICHES STORY IN THE 20TH CENTURY

Mohan Singh Oberoi was born in Bhaun, a village in Punjab (later part of Pakistan) in 1898. Oberoi's father died when he was only six months old, and Oberoi's family struggled through poverty. Nonetheless, Oberoi managed to complete his education, receiving a bachelor's degree at a university in Lahore. An outbreak of plague in 1922 prompted Oberoi to move to Shimla, the Himalayans-based summer capital of the British protectorate government.

Oberoi applied for a job at the prestigious Cecil Hotel. He so impressed the hotel's manager, Ernest Clarke, that Clarke gave Oberoi a position as a front desk clerk. Oberoi soon gained experience in other areas

COMPANY PERSPECTIVES

Mission: Our Guests. We are committed to meeting and exceeding the expectations of our guests through our unremitting dedication to every aspect of service. Our People. We are committed to the growth, development and welfare of our people upon whom we rely to make this happen. Our Distinctiveness. Together, we shall continue the Oberoi tradition of pioneering in the hospitality industry, striving for unsurpassed excellence in high-potential locations all the way from the Middle East to Asia-Pacific. Our Shareholders. As a result, we will create extraordinary value for our stakeholders.

of the hotel's operation. When Clarke acquired his own hotel, called the Clarkes Hotel, several years later, he offered Oberoi the job of manager. Oberoi managed that hotel for several years. Then, in 1934, Clarke offered to sell the hotel to Oberoi, who liquidated all of his assets, including his wife's jewelry, in order to meet the purchase price.

The Clarkes Hotel proved the starting point for what was to become one of India's greatest hotel success stories. Oberoi's next opportunity came in 1937, when he bought the famed Grand Hotel in Calcutta. Once a landmark hotel in that city, the Grand Hotel had fallen on hard times after an outbreak of cholera in the hotel forced its closure in the early 1930s. However, Oberoi recognized the potential for reviving the hotel, which had been shuttered for five years before Oberoi acquired it. Oberoi borrowed money for the purchase, placing his Shimla hotel up as collateral.

Oberoi completed an extensive renovation of the hotel, yet struggled to recruit clientele, who feared that the hotel's water supply was still tainted with cholera. Oberoi at last managed to convince his first customer to stay at the hotel by promising to serve meals that had been prepared outside of the hospital, as well as bottled water to drink. Oberoi's perseverance paid off, and the Grand Hotel soon became profitable.

Ownership of the Grand had its risks, however. With the start of World War II, the British army had begun requisitioning hotels for its troops. The Grand Hotel would have been taken over as well. Yet Oberoi managed to avoid losing his hotel by offering instead to reserve the premises for British army officers, at reduced room and meal rates. Instead, Oberoi made a handsome

profit selling alcohol to the hotel's guests. Oberoi's service to the British army earned him the title of Rai Bahadur.

BECOMING A MAJOR HOTEL PLAYER IN THE FORTIES

Oberoi set his sights on expanding his business. Using the profits generated at the Grand, Oberoi quietly began buying shares in the country's largest hotel group at the time, Associated Hotels of India Ltd. (AHI). By 1943, Oberoi had succeeded in gaining majority control of that company, and announced this by walking into that company's annual meeting with a suitcase filled with his shares in AHI.

Oberoi thus became the first Indian to gain ownership of that hotel company. Control of AHI gave Oberoi control of the Cecil in Shimla, as well as the Corstophans, also in Shimla, two hotels in Delhi, and four hotels situated in the future Pakistan, in Lahore, Murree, Rawalpindi, and Peshawar.

In 1949, Oberoi incorporated his own company, which later took on the name of EIH Ltd., as a holding company for his growing hotel empire. Following India's independence, Oberoi took steps to introduce modern hotel amenities and features to the country. Oberoi began planning his first modern hotel, the Oberoi New Delhi. In order to finance the project, Oberoi took his company public, listing its shares on the London Stock Exchange in 1956.

NEW BUSINESS AREAS IN THE FIFTIES

The opening of the Oberoi New Delhi proved a milestone in the Indian hotel industry, in more ways than one. Prior to independence, the country's hotels typically featured an army of staff, all male, with as many as five or six assigned to clean a single room. In 1957, however, Oberoi became the first in the country to employ chambermaids, working with vacuum cleaners, and scandalized public opinion.

Oberoi's business interests had also turned to ancillary markets. The company developed its own travel agency operation, Mercury, which grew into one of the largest in India. Oberoi also added a number of businesses in order to ensure the quality and supply of items used by the hotel, such as soaps, towels, and stationery. In 1974, for example, the company opened its own printing press at one of its hotels and began printing its own stationery, menus, and other items needed by the group's growing hotel chain.

Oberoi had also seen an opportunity to expand beyond the hotel industry proper. In 1959, the company

KEY DATES

1922: Mohan Singh Oberoi, a native of Punjab, moves to Shimla and begins working as a clerk at the Cecil Hotel.

1934: Oberoi buys his first hotel, Clarkes, in Shimla, then acquires the Grand Hotel in Calcutta in 1937.

1944: Oberoi gains control of Associated Hotels of India, the leading hotel group in India at the time.

1956: Oberoi lists the future EIH Ltd. on the London Stock Exchange.

1965: Oberoi opens the first fully air-conditioned hotel in India in Delhi.

1978: Company opens its first foreign hotel resort in Bali, and later enters Egypt and Saudi Arabia.

1986: Son Biki Oberoi oversees construction of the group's flagship, the Oberoi Mumbai.

1998: Oberoi establishes new luxury hotel standard with the Rajvilas in Jaipur.

2004: Company forms a marketing agreement with Hilton Hotels for its Trident business hotel brand.

2008: Oberoi announces plans to open ten new hotels; the Oberoi Mumbai is destroyed by a terrorist attack.

launched Oberoi Flight Services, becoming the first in India to position itself as a supplier of in-flight meals to the Indian airline industry. That operation grew strongly, establishing kitchens in New Delhi, Mumbai, Cochin, and Chennai (Madras).

Hotels, however, remained the center of Oberoi's enterprise. Joined by sons Tilak Raj (known as Tikki) and Prithvi Raj Singh (Biki), Oberoi began repositioning the company to focus on the luxury and high-end business markets. One of the company's first projects in this direction was a new hotel in New Delhi, which was to become the first fully air-conditioned hotel in India.

LUXURY IN THE SEVENTIES

Launched in the early 1960s, the project had run into an obstacle, when the Indian government's tight foreign exchange regulations made it difficult for the group to raise the capital in order to complete the hotel's construction. Oberoi persisted, however, and finally found a way around the regulations, developing a partnership with InterContinental, one of the world's largest hotel operators at the time. Oberoi then negotiated a loan from U.S.-based Ex-Im Bank, completing the hotel in 1965. The Oberoi InterContinental became the first modern luxury hotel in India. It also marked the first time that an Indian hotel group had joined forces with an international hotel group.

The Oberois also took steps to address another issue confronting the growth of the group's operations: the need to recruit qualified personnel. This led the company to found its own training academy, the Oberoi School of Hotel Management. The school soon achieved international recognition, notably from the Paris-based International Hotel Association, becoming the most important school of its type in India. As it broadened its curriculum, the school later changed its name to the Oberoi Centre of Learning and Development.

Oberoi's growing staff needs corresponded with the continued expansion of its operations. The company developed partnerships with a number of international hotel chains in an effort to encourage travel to India. With Western interest in the country running high in the late 1960s and into the 1970s, Oberoi helped develop the country as a high-end tourist destination as well. In order to attract an increasingly affluent clientele, Oberoi teamed up with the Sheraton hotel group to construct a new hotel in Mumbai (Bombay). Built on reclaimed land on the Bay of Bombay, the 35-story Oberoi Sheraton became a rival to the city's landmark hotel, the Taj. The new hotel proved particularly attractive to foreign travelers, who soon comprised as much as 85 percent of total clientele.

BUSINESS HOTELS IN THE EIGHTIES

By the late 1970s, Oberoi itself had begun to look beyond India as it set out to establish its name among the world's most prestigious hotel brands. The company recognized a new trend in travel, as affluent tourists began to seek more exotic destinations. Oberoi became one of the first to cater to this demand, agreeing to take over and manage an existing property on Bali's Legian Beach. The group redeveloped that site into its first luxury resort hotel. Instead of building a more standard hotel, the group introduced a villa concept in an attempt to capture the cultural spirit of Bali itself. The site also proved innovative in its feature offerings as well. Successive expansions and renovations of the site were to add a number of distinctive elements, such as private gardens, complete with private full-length lap pools, for each villa.

Oberoi's international expansion continued through the 1980s and into the 1990s. Egypt became one of the group's major foreign markets, as it built up a network of six hotels in that country. Oberoi also began operating cruises there, adopting an ultra-luxury vessel for its Nile cruises. The company also added hotels in Saudi Arabia and then entered Australia, where it acquired the landmark Windsor in Melbourne.

Tikki, who had been described as a "flamboyant playboy," had originally been tapped as M. S. Oberoi's successor. When Tikki died in 1984, that role fell to younger brother Biki, who had studied law in the United Kingdom before completing his studies at the École Hôtelière de Lausanne. Biki Oberoi oversaw the design and construction of the company's next landmark hotel, the Oberoi Mumbai, which opened in 1986. The new hotel featured a more modern, understated design than that traditionally found in India's high-end hotel sector. In this way, Oberoi helped to bring about a redefinition of the five-star business-class hotel in India.

DUAL BRANDS IN THE NEW CENTURY

Through the 1990s, Oberoi continued developing its hotel brands. The company targeted especially the highest ends of the market. As part of that process, the company reshuffled its portfolio of hotels, eliminating a number of its largest hotels in favor of smaller properties, with fewer beds and a staff to guest ratio of two to one. Oberoi also extended its cruise operations to Kerala, India, and acquired two private jets in order to provide charter flight services.

Oberoi's operations had come to focus on two primary brands: Trident, for its five-star business hotels, and Vilas, for its luxury hotels. The latter group included the Lombok, opened in 1997, and the Rajvilas, which opened in Jaipur in 1998, and was said to have established a new standard in the luxury hotel market. Over the next several years, Oberoi embarked on an ambitious expansion of its hotel chains, opening several hotels through 2002. Founder M. S. Oberoi died that year, at the age of 103. Biki Oberoi became the group's chairman, while his son, Vikram, became the group's CEO.

Oberoi's expansion made the group highly vulnerable to the global travel and tourism slump following the September 11, 2001, terrorist attacks on the United States. With occupancy rates dropping precipitously low, Oberoi sought a major international partner in order to enhance its own global marketing effort. This led the company to form a marketing agreement with the Hilton hotel group; as part of that agreement, Oberoi rebranded its Trident business hotels under the Trident Hilton brand. Oberoi continued to manage the hotels, while Hilton took charge of international marketing.

The marketing partnership ended in 2008, at which point the company rebranded its business hotel operations as Trident. By then, the company had also rebranded its luxury hotel segment, adding the Oberoi brand to the various Vilas properties. Despite the increasingly cloudy economic climate, Oberoi remained upbeat, announcing plans to open as many as ten new hotels from 2008. The first two were slated to open in 2009.

By then the company had begun to recover from a new setback, when the terrorist attack in Mumbai in late 2008 targeted two of the company's hotels. Oberoi, which had provided emergency and anti-terrorist training for its staff, was credited with saving many lives during the attack. Nonetheless, the group's flagship hotel, the Oberoi Mumbai, suffered from heavy damage. The company promised to rebuild the hotel, regardless of the cost. The Oberoi name had taken its place among the elite names in the global hotel industry in the new century.

M. L. Cohen

PRINCIPAL SUBSIDIARIES

EIH International; Mercury Travels; Mumtaz Hotels; Oberoi Kerala Hotels and Resorts; Rajgarh Palace Hotel and Resorts.

PRINCIPAL DIVISIONS

Luxury Hotels; Business Hotels; Luxury Cruises; Spas.

PRINCIPAL COMPETITORS

Hutchison Whampoa Ltd.; Loews Corp.; Orascom Group; Bertin S.A.; Jardine Strategic Holdings Ltd.; Compass Group PLC; Marriott International Inc.; AC-COR S.A.; Hilton Hotels Corp.; Bukhatir Group Ltd.; Three Cities Group; Tamimi Group; Pyramisa Hotels.

FURTHER READING

Bozec, Louise, "Oberoi Hotel Group Founder Dies at 103," *Caterer & Hotelkeeper*, May 16, 2002, p. 58.

"Enduring Elegance," *Euromoney*, June 2000, p. 58.

Karmali, Naazneen, "Meet India's Raja of Rooms," *Forbes*, January 12, 2009, p. 92.

Lewis, Paul, "Mohan Singh Oberoi, 103, a Pioneer in Luxury Hotels," *New York Times,* May 4, 2002, p. A13.

"Oberoi Enters Dubai Market," *Business Traveller Middle East,* September–October 2006, p. 6.

"Oberoi Group Has Been Picked by the Bangalore International Airport Limited to Operate India's First Airport Hotel," *Business Traveller Asian Pacific,* March 2007, p. 12.

"Oberoi Hotel Opens Two Restaurants," *Design Week,* April 7, 2005, p. 9.

"Oberoi in UK Sales Expansion," *Travel Weekly,* March 15, 2004, p. 32.

Ruggia, James, "The Uncommon Touch," *Travel Agent,* February 12, 2001, p. 42.

Salkin, Allen, "Jewels in the Crown," *TravelAge West,* February 21, 2005, p. 46.

Strauss, Karyn, "Hilton International, EIH Rebrand in India," *Hotels,* May 2004, p. 14.

FIFTH THIRD BANK

Fifth Third Bancorp

---

38 Fountain Square Plaza
Fifth Third Center
Cincinnati, Ohio 45263
U.S.A.
Telephone: (513) 579-5300
Toll Free: (800) 972-3030
Fax: (513) 534-0629
Web site: http://www.53.com

Public Company
Incorporated: 1908 as The Fifth Third National Bank of
    Cincinnati
Employees: 22,423
Total Assets: $119.8 billion (2008)
Stock Exchanges: NASDAQ Global Select Market
Ticker Symbol: FITB
NAICS: 522110 Commercial Banking; 522210 Credit
    Card Issuing; 522190 Other Depository Credit
    Intermediation; 551111 Offices of Bank Holding
    Companies; 522310 Mortgage and Nonmortgage
    Loan Brokers; 523930 Investment Advice

■ ■ ■

Fifth Third Bancorp ranks among the 20 largest bank holding companies in the United States. The $120 billion-asset operation serves its customers through 16 banking affiliates and their 1,308 full-service Banking Centers, 94 of which are grocery store locations open seven days a week. The bank also has 2,350 ATMs, spread throughout its midwest and southeastern U.S. markets. In addition to its home base of Ohio, the company operates in Kentucky, Indiana, Michigan, Illinois, Florida, Tennessee, West Virginia, Pennsylvania, Missouri, Georgia, and North Carolina. Fifth Third Bancorp's five main business segments are Branch Banking, Consumer Lending, Investment Advisors, Commercial Banking, and Fifth Third Processing Solutions. A 51 percent majority of the latter was sold in 2009 to raise needed capital.

PIONEER OF THE NATIONAL BANKING SYSTEM

Fifth Third Bancorp traces its history to the mid-19th-century formulation of the national banking system in the United States. Although national banks had existed since the late 18th century, a lack of consensus on the advantages of a national currency prevented the federal government from establishing a unified currency structure. Rampant inflation during the Civil War, however, prompted the 1863 ratification of the Federal Banking Act, thereby creating a uniform, government-backed national currency to replace the diverse currencies issued by state banks and other firms. That same year, a group of influential Cincinnati businessmen led by A. L. Mowry applied for and received one of the first national bank charters. Their institution, Cincinnati's Third National Bank, opened in a Masonic Temple later that year under a 20-year charter.

The firm that would become Fifth Third Bancorp evolved and grew through dozens of mergers over the ensuing decades. When the Third National Bank acquired the Bank of the Ohio Valley in 1871, the *Cincinnati Enquirer* hailed the union as "one of the best

COMPANY PERSPECTIVES
■

The Bancorp believes that banking is first and foremost a relationship business where the strength of the competition and challenges for growth can vary in every market. Its affiliate-operating model provides a competitive advantage by keeping the decisions close to the customer and by emphasizing individual relationships. Through its affiliate-operating model, individual managers from the banking center to the executive level are given the opportunity to tailor financial solutions for their customers.

managed banks in Ohio." The superlative descriptions continued when Third National was recapitalized in 1882 at $1.6 million, the highest-asset bank in the state.

The Panic of 1907 brought a run on banks and the first substantial banking and currency reform since the Civil War. Fearful of widespread bank failures, the federal government ordered the consolidation of several big-city banks to shore up weaker institutions. As a result, Third National merged with Fifth National to form The Fifth Third National Bank of Cincinnati, with a capitalization of $2.5 million and $12.1 million in deposits, in 1908. Fifth Third's 1910 acquisition of two other local banks, American National Bank and S. Kuhn & Sons, increased its capital to $3 million.

The Federal Reserve Act of 1913 organized a regional system of 12 Federal Reserve banks that were capitalized with contributions from national banks in each region. The legislation required each national bank to deposit 3 percent of its capital and surplus into its regional Federal Reserve bank. These moves helped inspire confidence in the national banks, thus preventing panics and runs on banks. The Federal Reserve Act also gave the federal government more control over the U.S. money supply, made commercial credit available, and discouraged venturesome banking practices. Although bankers initially resisted its creation, the Federal Reserve laid the groundwork for the country's modern banking system.

DEPRESSION AND WAR YEARS

Another bank industry consolidation followed World War I. The 1919 affiliation with Union Savings Bank and Trust Company, a state-chartered bank, brought several changes to Fifth Third's operations. Affiliation with a state bank permitted Fifth Third to circumvent

the stricture against national banks' establishment of branches. Before the end of the year, Fifth Third assumed control of the assets of several local banks, including Market National Bank, Security Savings Bank and Safe Deposit Company, Mohawk State Bank, and Walnut Hills Savings Bank. It operated these institutions as branch offices.

Although the 1920s were marked by increased governmental supervision and general economic prosperity, many U.S. banks remained weak. The situation gave Fifth Third the opportunity to continue to grow through the acquisition of four local banks. Fifth Third consolidated with the Union Trust Company to form the Fifth Third Union Trust Company in 1927. The advent of the Great Depression in 1929 intensified this activity somewhat, because Fifth Third was one of the stronger banks in the Cincinnati area. Fifth Third assumed control of three banks from 1930 to 1933.

The Great Depression also brought increased regulation of the banking industry, including expansion of the Federal Reserve Board's powers and the establishment of the Federal Deposit Insurance Corporation (FDIC). The economic crisis also spawned a plethora of federal and state legislation restricting interstate retail banking. Strong popular and governmental reaction to the Great Depression helped make banking one of the most regulated segments of U.S. industry (and inspired the *Economist* to call the American system "one of the world's wackiest banking systems" in 1988). These barriers effectively restricted Fifth Third's growth through acquisition until after World War II.

DIVERSIFICATION INTO PERSONAL AND COMMERCIAL BANKING: 1955–76

Distanced from the Great Depression by the trauma of global war, U.S. banks began to cautiously expand their operations to include a broader range of financial services, especially in the field of retail or personal banking, in the postwar era. Under the direction of G. Carlton Hill from 1955 to 1963, Fifth Third began to formulate its focus on retail or consumer banking. For example, the company established a travel department to issue traveler's checks and plan tours. These activities intensified during the presidency of Bill Rowe, who was the son of 1930s-era Fifth Third leader John J. Rowe. Over the course of the 1960s, the bank instituted a program of internal expansion with an emphasis on convenience and personal service. Advertising featuring the company's 5/3 shield logo promoted Fifth Third's many suburban locations and extended hours. During the 1970s, the bank shifted its lending emphasis from commercial or business loans to consumer credit. In

some of the most rigorous state banking regulations. This new corporate entity was not technically a bank and thus was exempt from laws that prohibited cross-county branching. By 1976 Fifth Third included 37 banking offices.

KEY DATES

1863:	The Third National Bank forms in Cincinnati, Ohio.
1908:	The Third National Bank merges with The Fifth National Bank to form The Fifth Third National Bank of Cincinnati.
1927:	Company merges with The Union Trust Company and establishes The Fifth Third Union Trust Company.
1969:	Fifth Third Union Trust Company is renamed Fifth Third Bank.
1975:	Fifth Third Bancorp incorporates.
1998:	Company completes two largest acquisitions to date, CitFed Bancorp, Inc., and State Savings Company; celebrates its 25th consecutive year of increased earnings.
2001:	Old Kent Financial Corp. acquisition increases Fifth Third's size by nearly 50 percent.
2004:	The 1,000th branch opens.
2007:	Real estate market crisis creates new problems for the bank.
2008:	Fifth Third taps into the federal government's Capital Purchase Program.
2009:	Majority of profitable payment-processing unit is sold.

1973, Fifth Third hired Johnny Bench, famed catcher for the Cincinnati Reds baseball team, as spokesman. It adopted the long-running slogan "The only bank you'll ever need" the same year.

"Back office" changes supported the bank's growth and profitability. Fifth Third, which had booted up its first computer in 1960, initiated home banking services and JEANIE automated teller machines (ATMs) in the 1970s. The institution's home banking system, which could be accessed via the average touchtone phone, was uniquely user-friendly. These electronic services formed the basis of what would become Fifth Third's Midwest Payment Services department. Later in the decade, the bank offered its automated services to other banks and corporate clients. By the early 1990s, Midwest Payment Services maintained ATMs and electronic cash registers for more than 1,000 clients. This lucrative business niche contributed one-third of the bank's annual income in the early 1990s.

The 1975 creation of a bank holding company, Fifth Third Bancorp, enabled the institution to sidestep

AGGRESSIVE GROWTH AND INCREASED ACQUISITIONS: 1980–89

The further liberalization of Ohio banking laws in the early 1980s expanded both the types of products banks were permitted to offer and the geographic reach they were allowed to attain. Strictures against growth outside the home bank's county were first to fall. Barriers to interstate branching continued to deteriorate in the early 1980s. In September 1985, federal and state banking regulations changed dramatically, freeing Ohio's banks to enter into agreements with banking organizations outside the state. Fifth Third became Ohio's first holding company to take advantage of the new legislation when it acquired American National Bank in Newport, Kentucky, just across the Ohio River, later that year. Fifth Third's roster of branches increased 125 percent over the course of the 1980s, and it expanded its reach from a single Ohio county to an interstate bank.

Much of this vigorous growth was inspired by a new corporate leader, Clement L. Buenger, who took the helm of Fifth Third in 1981. Buenger, who was called "one of the best acts in the business" in a 1991 *Fortune* article, brought his background in life insurance sales to the bank. The new president transformed the bank's corporate culture through innovative incentive programs and personal example. Whereas some Fifth Third offices were only open from 10:00 A.M. to 2:00 P.M., Buenger worked 10 to 12-hour days and expected many of his managers to do the same. The president (who later became CEO and chairman) even made cold calls on prospective clients. One incentive program, the "Shoe Leather Award," evolved from his passion for earning new business. A new pair of designer shoes was awarded to each month's best cold caller. In fact, all employees could earn sales incentives: *Fortune* noted in 1991 that the bank "already had several secretaries worth $500,000."

Fifth Third's focus on consumer banking and safe lending helped the bank avoid the real estate loans, Third World debt, and leveraged buyout problems that troubled many financial institutions during the 1980s. The "banking bust" that followed led *Fortune* to call the early 1990s "the hardest times for bankers since the Great Depression" in November 1991.

George Schaefer Jr. took Fifth Third's reins in 1989 at the age of 44. Schaefer was trained in engineering, but when a hoped for job designing a nuclear power plant fell through in 1969, he entered the bank's management trainee program. Some industry observers predicted that the new leader would be stymied, both by the shadow of his predecessor and by the difficult banking environment. Yet while literally hundreds of banks failed each year in the late 1980s and early 1990s, Fifth Third continued its outstanding performance and was even able to benefit from the misfortune of others by inexpensively acquiring dozens of new outlets. This allowed the bank to slowly expand its sphere of influence, yet maintain shareholder value.

CONTINUED GROWTH: 1992–94

In 1992 Fifth Third proposed a merger with Star Banc Corp. that would have unified the two largest Cincinnati-based financial institutions. Star had not grown as fast as Fifth Third, but its record of continued growth made it an enticing acquisition target. The alliance was viewed by many analysts and investors as a good deal for both banks. Fifth Third made a generous offer of $42 per share, which amounted to more than twice Star's book value. However, when CEO Schaefer prematurely publicized the heretofore private proposition, Star's longtime president, Oliver Waddell, balked, and the target's board unanimously rejected the offer.

Shunned by Star, Schaefer returned to Fifth Third's previous course of growth through relatively small acquisitions. Then, in 1994, the bank made two significant purchases: the 45-office Cumberland Federal Bancorporation in Kentucky, which had $1.1 billion in assets; and Falls Financial Inc. in northeastern Ohio, a company with $581 million in assets. The Cumberland acquisition became Fifth Third Bank of Kentucky, Louisville, and the Falls purchase was merged with Fifth Third Bank, Northeastern Ohio. According to the company's 1994 annual report, these two acquisitions contributed to the largest one-year increase in assets, 22 percent, in the institution's history. The purchases also made Fifth Third the preeminent operator of supermarket bank locations in the United States, with 81 full-service locations.

RAPID EXPANSION THROUGH ACQUISITIONS: 1995–99

Fifth Third moved aggressively through the second half of the decade, building upon its 20 consecutive years of increased earnings. To remain competitive and to ensure continued growth and strong earnings, the company stepped up its acquisition efforts and began to pursue new businesses, including mortgage brokering and investment services, and new territories. In mid-1995,

for instance, Fifth Third acquired Bank of Naples, Florida, and increased its assets in the Florida region, which Fifth Third first entered in 1989. Other acquisitions Fifth Third made in 1995 included Mutual Federal Savings Bank in Dayton, Ohio; Bank One Lebanon; PNC Bank's Dayton division; and seven offices of Bank One, Cincinnati. The PNC purchase, which included 12 offices, increased Fifth Third's banking centers in the Dayton area to 30, making it the fourth largest financial establishment in the region.

In the following years the firm continued to follow its strategy to increase market share in the Midwest by acquiring small businesses. Fifth Third made three acquisitions in 1996: the Ohio branch of 1st Nationwide Bank, the Ohio operations of First Chicago NBD Bank, and Kentucky Enterprise Bancorp, Inc., located in northern Kentucky. Four acquisitions were made the following year, all in Fifth Third's familiar midwest region. In June, Fifth Third purchased Gateway Leasing Corporation for $2.2 million, and a month later it bought Suburban Bancorporation, Inc., a savings and loan holding company. Fifth Third also acquired Heartland Capital Management Inc., a money managing company in Indiana, and Great Lakes National Bank Ohio, with eight branches in Ohio, in 1997.

Fifth Third found substantial support from industry analysts, who regarded the company's stock as reliable and profitable. From 1993 to 1998, according to the *Wall Street Journal,* Fifth Third's annual revenue increased 15.9 percent, about three points better than the industry average. To continue its streak of increased earnings, Fifth Third in 1998 branched into new business arenas and made some major acquisitions. To start out 1998, Fifth Third announced it would acquire CitFed Bancorp Inc. of Dayton and its subsidiary Citizens Federal Bank FSB for $661 million in stock. CitFed had 35 offices in Ohio. The acquisition, completed in June, created the largest bank in Dayton and boosted its market share there to 28 percent. Fifth Third's market share in its hometown of Cincinnati was 22.7 percent.

Also at the beginning of 1998 Fifth Third announced plans to buy State Savings Co. of Columbus, which would create the fourth largest bank in Columbus, and The Ohio Company, a brokerage and investment management firm with 49 offices in Ohio and four additional states. Fifth Third expanded into another business field when it acquired W. Lyman Case & Company, a commercial mortgage banking company with headquarters in Columbus. Also that year Fifth Third bought State Savings Company and its subsidiaries, State Savings Bank, Century Bank, and State Savings Bank, FSB, which provided Fifth Third access to a new territory: Arizona. Four offices of Bank

One were acquired as well, boosting Fifth Third's presence in southern Ohio. Fifth Third celebrated its 25th consecutive year of increased revenues at the end of 1998 and had increased the number of its branches from 35 to 468.

The year 1999 showed no signs of slowdown for Fifth Third. CEO Schaefer revealed in the *Cincinnati Business Courier* that he planned to continue expanding through acquisitions. "I see more opportunity for us now than at any point in the last 25 years," said Schaefer. "We continue to pick up market share in every market." The company completed the acquisition of Enterprise Federal Bancorp Inc., one of the biggest thrifts in the Cincinnati area. The purchase, estimated at $96.4 million, provided Fifth Third with 11 additional branches in greater Cincinnati. Fifth Third also acquired Ashland Bankshares, Inc., and subsidiary Bank of Ashland, both based in Kentucky. The $80 million purchase gave Fifth Third four more branches, as well as $160 million in assets. Fifth Third also began to implement plans to expand further into Florida and acquired South Florida Bank Holding Corp. in June, adding another four branches to its Florida roster. Additional expansion into the Cleveland, Ohio, area came with the acquisition of Emerald Financial Corp. for $204 million. Fifth Third also acquired Cleveland-based Emerald Financial Corp. and its subsidiary, Strongsville Savings Bank.

Fifth Third further strengthened its commercial banking services by acquiring Vanguard Financial Corporation, a commercial mortgage banking firm, in July 1999. Fifth Third merged Vanguard with previously acquired W. Lyman Case and created Fifth Third Real Estate Capital Markets Company. Prior to the purchases, Fifth Third offered three-year commercial real estate financing, which meant loans had to be renegotiated every three years. With the acquisitions, however, Fifth Third was able to provide long-term financing, thus better serving the business client.

In mid-1999 Fifth Third made its largest acquisition to date when it announced it would purchase CNB Bancshares Inc., the biggest independent bank holding company in Indiana. The $2.4 billion purchase propelled Fifth Third deeper into Indiana and made Fifth Third the third largest bank in Indiana, as well as the 28th biggest bank in the nation. CNB was the parent company of Civitas Bank and had 145 banking offices and $7.2 billion in assets. The CNB purchase also provided Fifth Third with an entry into insurance sales. Fifth Third quickly followed up the CNB purchase with another significant acquisition. Increasing its presence in the Indianapolis area, Fifth Third bought Peoples Bank & Trust Co. for $228 million. The buy moved Fifth Third from sixth place to fourth in the Indianapolis

market, with a market share of about 7 percent. Peoples had nine Indianapolis offices.

CEO Schaefer told the *Cincinnati Business Courier* that Fifth Third was ready to undertake additional billion-dollar deals and move away from smaller, million-dollar acquisitions. After accomplishing 12 deals, amounting to nearly $5 billion in a mere 16 months, Fifth Third was certainly on a fast track. In 1999 Fifth Third received the top ranking from Salomon Smith Barney in its Top 50 Bank Annual for the eighth consecutive year. Banks were rated according to profitability, operating efficiency, asset quality, capital strength, and operating growth. Its Midwest Payment Systems data processing subsidiary saw net income increase 34 percent in 1998 over 1997, and in mid-1999 the subsidiary's profits were up 37 percent from the previous year. Fifth Third's net income for the first half of 1999 was up 21 percent compared to the same period a year earlier. Reporter Geert De Lombaerde declared in the *Cincinnati Business Courier,* "Fifth Third is in the midst of a metamorphosis. It is no longer primarily a commercial bank—40 percent of revenues comes from fees—or just a strong performer in the middle-of-the-road Midwest. It is on the cusp of becoming a sizable national player."

NEW COMPLEXITIES: 2000–03

At the beginning of the new century, Fifth Third bolstered its payments business through mergers, two in 2000 and a third in 2001. Midwest Payment Systems was renamed Fifth Third Processing Solutions in January 2003.

Meanwhile, on the banking front, longtime CEO George Schaefer broke with a tried and true strategy. "His tightly focused, hands-on style worked smoothly over a decade of prosperity. He built up the company one safe little step at a time, largely through small acquisitions close to home," Jack Milligan observed in a March 2001 *American Banker* article. The deal to acquire Old Kent Financial Corp. of Grand Rapids, Michigan, struck in November 2000, was two times the size of any previous acquisition. The addition of Old Kent moved Fifth Third from 24th to 16th place among the largest U.S. banking companies, with $70 million in assets.

At the outset the new road seemed rocky, the economy was in a downturn, 15 percent of its new Old Kent workforce faced layoffs, and its stock price lagged behind its Midwest peers. Yet Fifth Third's integration strategy, by and large, had proved successful in the past. One exception was a 1998 regional brokerage acquisition. Brokers and client assets drained off, as staff took umbrage with the new management style.

"Of course, Mr. Schaefer isn't the only banker to stub his toe entering the securities industry, and he hasn't tried again since. But Fifth Third could join the noteworthy group of companies, among them Bank One, First Union, and Bank America, that have had trouble with very large acquisitions," Milligan surmised.

To bring this unprecedented acquisition into Fifth Third's culture, Old Kent would be divided into three affiliate banks, two under Fifth Third executives and one under an Old Kent executive. Moreover, Fifth Third quickly "exposed Old Kent to its aggressive sales style," according to Milligan. A sales push during 2000, produced earnings growth of nearly 18 percent for Fifth Third.

The $4.92 billion Old Kent acquisition, completed on April 2, 2001, taxed back-office operations; Fifth Third had not only increased in sheer size but also in complexity. To further complicate matters, a rash of wrongdoing by U.S. corporations and an attack on U.S. soil resulted in more stringent regulation of financial institutions in certain areas.

In September 2002, Fifth Third revealed a $54 million charge tied to an error "in the booking of certain securities transactions," Matthias Rieker reported in *American Banker*. In response, Ohio regulators and the Federal Reserve Bank of Cleveland imposed a moratorium on Fifth Third's acquisitions, halting one in its tracks.

In a March 2003 agreement among Fifth Third, the Cleveland Fed, and the Ohio Division of Financial Institutions, Fifth Third was cited for being out of compliance with holding company requirements of the Gramm-Leach-Bliley Act, in addition to other issues. "To the surprise of virtually all observers, the regulators required the banking company to comply with a long list of improvements of its controls and to submit to an independent review of its board, board committees, directors, management structure, and senior officers," Rieker explained.

RESHUFFLING: 2004–06

When the acquisition moratorium lifted, Fifth Third moved to complete the deal for Franklin Financial Corporation of Nashville, accomplished in June 2004. Fifth Third followed up with a bid for 16-branch First National Bankshares of Florida, Inc., the largest remaining independent bank in the state. Some analysts and investors questioned the premium price linked to the Florida expansion, *American Banker* reported. As for internal growth engines, Schaefer looked to fee generation, cross-selling, and new locations. The thousandth branch opened in August 2004.

The company's compensation committee pared back executive bonuses during 2005. CEO Schaefer and three other of the highest paid executives had failed to meet performance goals. Schaefer's base salary of $990,018, frozen for three years running, was slightly above the median base of peer comparison companies, *American Banker* reported.

The $106 billion-asset company's operational, financial, and regulatory problems translated into a downturn in its price per share. In early 2002, the stock traded at nearly $70 per share. In late August 2006, it traded at just below $40 per share.

Fifth Third shook things up, attempting to return to its previous glory days. A new management team comprised of experienced banking executives was put in place, led by Schaefer as chairman and Kevin Kabat, formerly head of Old Kent, as president and CEO. Improvements in retail banking service, product cross selling, technology, and communication with analysts and investors were on the to-do list. The balance sheet received a makeover.

American Banker explained in August 2006, "The company's sizable securities portfolio was ill-positioned for rising short-term interest rates and a flattening yield curve, causing much pain to earnings over the last two years. It was one of the last big banking companies to reshuffle its balance sheet when the yield curve started to flatten."

To further its reemergence, Fifth Third planned renewed merger and acquisition activity and continued organic growth. It had entered St. Louis and Pittsburgh and looked toward Baltimore, Charlotte, and Atlanta as target markets.

ECONOMIC UPHEAVAL: 2007–09

Unfortunately, massive upheaval in the mortgage market sent the U.S. economy into a tailspin in 2007. Real estate values fell and bank valuations tumbled. Michigan, Ohio, and Florida were hit hard by foreclosures, and less so, Indiana and Illinois.

While reporting that "Fifth Third does not originate or hold subprime loans, nor do we hold collateralized debt obligations (CDOs) or asset-backed securities backed by subprime loans," the bank was not immune to the economic downslide. Fifth Third posted charges linked to loan losses and soured investments. To mitigate further harm, the company began to intervene earlier in problem credit situations and exited riskier lines of business. The electronic payments processing segment, meanwhile, continued to be a pocket of strength.

In November 2007, Fifth Third acquired R-C Crown Bank and its 30 Florida and three Augusta, Georgia, locations. Fifth Third added nine Atlanta-area branches, in May 2008, and entered North Carolina in June, both through acquisitions. In a sign of the times, Fifth Third assumed about $250 million in deposits of an insolvent bank, in November, through FDIC action.

Despite the acquisition activity and declaration of capital strength, Fifth Third's future was less certain, as the economy continued to spiral down. The company posted a net loss of $2.2 billion in 2008, versus a net income of $1.1 billion a year earlier.

Fifth Third had tapped into the Troubled Asset Relief Program (TARP) to a tune of $3.45 billion, at the end of 2008. Just nine U.S. banks had received a greater infusion of federal money, the *Wall Street Journal* reported on March 28, 2009. Subsequent plans to renovate executive offices raised the hackles of those at odds with the massive bailout of the country's financial institutions.

In a move to further strengthen its capital base, Fifth Third agreed to sell 51 percent of its profitable payment-processing unit to private-equity firm Advent International Corp. for $561 million in cash. Fifth Third would retain 49 percent of the stand-alone company, Fifth Third Processing Solutions, LLC, and chipped in $1.25 billion in bank loans for the new company, evidence of the dearth of deal financing available in the skittish private market. The sale was expected to close in the second quarter of 2009. Meanwhile the federal government continued stress testing the nation's largest banks, hoping to forestall future failures.

April D. Gasbarre
Updated, Mariko Fujinaka; Kathleen Peippo

PRINCIPAL DIVISIONS

Fifth Third Bank (Greater Cincinnati); Fifth Third Bank (Central Ohio); Fifth Third Bank (Northwestern Ohio); Fifth Third Bank (Northeastern Ohio); Fifth Third Bank (Western Michigan); Fifth Third Bank (Eastern Michigan); Fifth Third Bank (Central Kentucky); Fifth Third Bank (Louisville); Fifth Third Bank (Tennessee); Fifth Third Bank (Central Indiana); Fifth Third Bank (Southern Indiana); Fifth Third Bank (Chicago); Fifth Third Bank (South Florida); Fifth Third Bank (Central Florida); Fifth Third Bank (Tampa Bay); Fifth Third Bank (Charlotte).

PRINCIPAL OPERATING UNITS

Branch Banking; Consumer Lending; Investment Advisors; Commercial Banking; Fifth Third Processing Solutions.

PRINCIPAL COMPETITORS

PNC Financial Services Group, Inc.; Bank of America Corporation; U.S. Bancorp.

FURTHER READING

Barnes, Jon, "Fifth Third Bancorp Expanding in Ohio, Data-Processing Field," *Investor's Business Daily,* November 18, 1998, p. B20.

Bennett, Robert A., "How to Earn 1.6% on Assets," *United States Banker,* January 1992, pp. 20–27.

Buenger, Clement L., *Fifth Third Bank: The Only Bank You'll Ever Need,* New York: Newcomen Society of the United States, 1991.

Davis, Paul, and Matthew Monks, "Fifth Third's Latest Deal: Too Little, Too Late?" *American Banker,* March 31, 2009, p. 1.

De Lombaerde, Geert, "Acquisitions Continue to Fuel Fifth Third's Growth," *Cincinnati Business Courier,* April 9, 1999, p. 30.

———, "Fast Times at Fifth Third," *Cincinnati Business Courier,* August 6, 1999, p. 1.

"Fifth Third Bank Provides More Information to Customers," *Investment Weekly News,* April 11, 2009, p. 177.

"Fifth Third Drops Offer to Buy Star Banc Corp.," *American Banker,* July 1, 1992, p. 1.

"Fifth Third, the 'Charlie Hustle' of Banking," *United States Banker,* April 1995, p. 24.

Fitzpatrick, Dan, "Corporate News: TARP Recipient Fifth Third Plans an Office Makeover," *Wall Street Journal,* March 28, 2009, p. B5.

Fraust, Bart, "Fifth Third to Enter Kentucky: Becomes 1st Ohio Holding Company to Acquire Out-of-State Bank," *American Banker,* July 31, 1985, p. 3.

Klinkermann, Steve, et al., "Fifth Third's Schaefer: Hard Work, Expense Control and the Secrets to Success," *American Banker,* December 19, 1994, p. 16.

Larkin, Patrick, "Fifth Third Expanding Its Reach," *Cincinnati Post,* June 9, 1999, p. C5.

Lattman, Peter, and Dan Fitzpatrick, "Fifth Third to Sell 51% Stake in Its Payment Unit to Advent," *Wall Street Journal,* March 30, 2009, p. C1.

Milligan, Jack, "Second Act for Fifth Third's Chief Exec," *American Banker,* March 23, 2001, p. 1.

Murray, Matt, "Fifth Third Bancorp Is First on Experts' List of Bank Stocks Due to High Revenue Growth," *Wall Street Journal,* January 13, 1998, p. C4.

Pare, Terence P., "Bankers Who Beat the Bust," *Fortune,* November 4, 1991, p. 159.

Peale, Cliff, "Merger Proposal Came Too Quickly for Star," *Cincinnati Business Courier,* May 4, 1992, p. 3.

Piggott, Charles, "The World's Best Banks: The Americans Bounce Back," *Euromoney,* August 1994, pp. 68–72.

Pramik, Mike, "Fifth Third Looms Larger," *Columbus Dispatch,* July 17, 1999, p. C1.

Rieker, Matthias, "Fifth Third CEO on Hard First Year," *American Banker,* April 15, 2008, p. 1.

———, "Fifth Third Says CEO's Pay Shrank in '05," *American Banker,* February 16, 2006, p. 19.

———, "New Team, New Plans: Fifth Third Sets Course," *American Banker,* August 24, 2006, p. 1.

"The Safest and Soundest of the Big Banks," *United States Banker,* July 1992, pp. 19–25.

Slater, Robert Bruce, "Banking's Cincinnati Kid," *Bankers Monthly,* January 1993, p. 14.

Slater, Sherry, "Fifth Third '08 Losses Reach $2.2 billion," *Fort Wayne (Ind.) Journal Gazette,* January 23, 2009, p. B13.

———, "Stumbles Haven't Altered Fifth Third Identity, Mission," *American Banker,* September 21, 2004, p. 1.

Smith, Brian, and Greg Feder, "Management Responsibility After Sarbanes-Oxley," *American Banker,* June 11, 2003, p. 10A.

Fujitsu Limited

Shiodome City Center
1-5-2 Higashi-Shimbashi
Minato-ku
Tokyo, 105-7123
Japan
Telephone: (+81-3) 6252-2220
Fax: (+81-3) 6252-2783
Web site: http://www.fujitsu.com

Public Company
Incorporated: 1935 as Fuji Tsushinki Manufacturing Corporation
Employees: 167,374
Sales: ¥5.33 trillion ($53.31 billion) (2008)
Stock Exchanges: Tokyo Osaka Nagoya Frankfurt London Swiss
Ticker Symbol: 6702
NAICS: 334111 Electronic Computer Manufacturing; 334112 Computer Storage Device Manufacturing; 334119 Other Computer Peripheral Equipment Manufacturing; 334210 Telephone Apparatus Manufacturing; 334220 Radio and Television Broadcasting and Wireless Communications Equipment Manufacturing; 334290 Other Communications Equipment Manufacturing; 334413 Semiconductor and Related Device Manufacturing; 334414 Electronic Capacitor Manufacturing; 334511 Search, Detection, Navigation, Guidance, Aeronautical, and Nautical System and Instrument Manufacturing; 511210 Software Publishers; 517110 Wired Telecommunications Carriers; 541511 Custom Computer Programming Services; 541512 Computer Systems Design Services; 541513 Computer Facilities Management Services; 541519 Other Computer Related Services

■ ■ ■

Fujitsu Limited is one of the world's leading makers of computers, semiconductors, and telecommunications equipment and is considered one of Japan's Big Five industrial-electronics companies, a group that also includes Hitachi, Ltd.; Mitsubishi Electric Corporation; NEC Corporation; and Toshiba Corporation. Historically, Fujitsu was best known as the world's number two maker of mainframe computers, behind IBM, but Fujitsu exited from that market at the beginning of the 21st century to focus its hardware efforts on servers, personal computers (vying with NEC for the top spot in Japan), and peripherals.

Of Fujitsu's three main business areas, its Technology Solutions division is its largest, generating more than 56 percent of overall revenues. This division is able to offer complete information technology solutions, encompassing both system platforms and services, including Japan's leading Internet service provider, or ISP, Nifty. Among the product offerings of the Ubiquitous Product Solutions division, responsible for more than 20 percent of revenues, are desktop and notebook PCs, mobile phones, and hard disk drives. Roughly 14 percent of sales stem from the Device Solutions division, producer of semiconductors and related electronic components. Fujitsu generates about 36 percent of its sales overseas, including 16 percent from Europe, the Middle East, and Africa; and roughly 10

COMPANY PERSPECTIVES

Through our constant pursuit of innovation, the Fujitsu Group aims to contribute to the creation of a networked society that is rewarding and secure, bringing about a prosperous future that fulfills the dreams of people throughout the world.

percent each from the Americas and the Asia-Pacific region (excluding Japan).

EARLY HISTORY

Fuji Tsushinki Manufacturing Corporation was created on June 20, 1935, as the manufacturing subsidiary of Fuji Electric Limited and charged with continuing the parent company's production of telephones and automatic exchange equipment. Fuji Electric, itself a joint venture of Japan's Furukawa Electric and the German industrial conglomerate Siemens, was part of Japan's attempt to overcome its late start in modern telecommunications. Spurred by Japan's expanding military economy, Fuji Tsushinki quickly branched off into the production of carrier transmission equipment in 1937 and radio communication two years later. Yet the country's telephone system remained archaic and incomplete, with German and British systems in use that were not fully compatible. World War II ruined a large part of this primitive system, destroying some 500,000 connections out of a total of 1.1 million, and leaving the country in a state of what might be called communication chaos. At the insistence of the occupying U.S. forces, Japan's Ministry of Communications was reorganized and nearly became a privately owned corporation that would have simply adopted existing U.S. technology to rebuild the country's telephone grid. A coalition led by Eisaku Sato, however, persuaded the government to instead form a new public utility, Nippon Telephone and Telegraph (NTT). Created in 1952, NTT soon became a leading sponsor and purchaser of advanced electronic research, and it continued to be one of Fuji Tsushinki's key customers.

The link with NTT may well have been Fuji Tsushinki's greatest asset, but Fuji Tsushinki was only one of a series of increasingly determined government partners for the country's young computer industry. Fuji Tsushinki first became interested in computers in the early 1950s, when Western governments and large corporations began making extensive use of them for time-consuming calculations. After a number of years of experimentation Fuji Tsushinki succeeded in marketing Japan's first commercial computer, the FACOM 100, in 1954.

This was a start, but the Japanese computer business was still in its infancy when IBM brought out the first transistorized computer in 1959. So great was the shock of this quantum leap in design that the Japanese government realized it would have to play a far more vigorous role if the country was not to fall permanently behind the United States. The government formulated a comprehensive plan that included restrictions on the number and kind of foreign computers imported, low-cost loans and other subsidies to native manufacturers, and the overall management of national production to avoid needless competition while encouraging technological innovation. Of equal importance, in 1961 the Japanese government negotiated with IBM for the right to license critical patents, in exchange allowing the U.S. giant to form IBM Japan and begin local production.

COMPUTER DEVELOPMENTS IN THE SIXTIES

Patents in hand, seven Japanese companies entered the computer race. All of them except Fuji Tsushinki quickly formed alliances with U.S. companies to further their research; Fuji Tsushinki, refused by IBM in a similar offer, remained the only "pure," or *junketsu,* Japanese computer firm, committed to the development of its own technological expertise. The other Japanese companies were all much larger than Fuji Tsushinki and devoted only a fraction of their energy to computers, whereas Fuji Tsushinki soon devoted itself to communications and computers.

Able to build on its substantial electronics experience Fuji Tsushinki was directed by the government to concentrate on the development of mainframes and integrated circuitry, and in late 1962 it was given the specific goal of developing a competitor to IBM's new 1401 transistorized computer. The government stalled IBM's plans for local production and enlisted Hitachi, NEC, and Fuji Tsushinki in what it called project FONTAC, the first in what would become a series of government-industry drives. From the perspective of the marketplace, FONTAC was a complete failure. Before it got off the ground IBM had launched its revolutionary 360 series, pushing the Japanese further behind than when they started. Yet as a first try at a coordinated national computer program, FONTAC proved to be extremely important. Fuji Tsushinki and the other Japanese manufacturers could afford poor initial performance, knowing that funds were available for further research and development. In particular, the

KEY DATES

1935: Fuji Tsushinki Manufacturing Corporation is created as a telecommunications manufacturing subsidiary of Fuji Electric.

1954: Fuji Tsushinki successfully markets Japan's first commercial computer, the FACOM 100.

1965: Company introduces the FACOM 230.

1967: Fuji Tsushinki officially changes its name to Fujitsu Limited.

1972: Fujitsu invests in Amdahl Corporation, a new venture formed to build IBM-compatible mainframes.

1970s: The M series of high-speed computers is introduced through a joint effort of Fujitsu and Hitachi.

1982: Fujitsu introduces the first Japanese supercomputer.

1990: Company purchases an 80 percent stake in International Computers Ltd. (ICL), the United Kingdom's leading mainframe maker.

1997: Fujitsu spends $878 million to take full control of Amdahl.

1998: Naoyuki Akikusa becomes company president and places increasing emphasis on software and services.

2000: Amdahl announces that it will exit from the mainframe market to focus on software, services, and consulting.

2002: Major restructuring involving job cuts totaling 16,400 jobs leads to a net loss of ¥193 billion ($1.45 billion).

2009: Fujitsu agrees to sell its hard-disk-drive business to Toshiba Corporation.

Japanese government had by this time formed the Japanese Electronic Computer Company (JECC), a quasi-private corporation owned by the seven computer makers but given unlimited low-interest government loans with which to buy and then rent out newly produced computers. In effect, this allowed Fuji Tsushinki and the others to receive full payment for their wares immediately, thus greatly increasing corporate cash flow and making possible the huge outlays for research and development.

The result of JECC's largesse was immediate: In the space of a single year, 1961 to 1962, Japanese computer sales increased 203 percent. In 1965 Fuji Tsushinki,

relying largely on technology developed as part of the FONTAC project, brought out the most advanced domestic computer yet built, the FACOM 230. The company had quickly become JECC's leading manufacturer, supplying approximately 25 percent of all computers purchased by the firm during the 1960s. In addition, Fuji Tsushinki had continued its substantial work for NTT, with over half of its telecommunications products going to the phone company by the end of the decade. NTT remained a critically important governmental agency for Fuji Tsushinki and the computer industry, routinely shouldering research-and-development costs and paying high prices to ensure that its suppliers remained profitable. NTT also sponsored a super-high-performance computer project in 1968, similar in design and scope to one begun the previous year by the Ministry for Trade and Industry (MITI), to develop a new computer for its complex telecommunications needs. Both of these ambitious programs were paid for by rival government ministries. In the meantime, in June 1967 Fuji Tsushinki officially changed its name to Fujitsu Limited.

DEVELOPMENT OF THE M SERIES

Despite this concerted effort, however, by 1970 the Japanese were suffering from IBM's introduction of its 370 line. Worse yet, under international pressure the Japanese government had agreed to liberalize its import policy by 1975, giving the local computer industry a scant five years in which to become truly competitive. MITI responded by making computer prowess a national goal, greatly increasing subsidies, and reorganizing the six remaining companies into three groups of cooperative pairs. Fujitsu, as the leading mainframe maker, was paired with its archrival Hitachi and given the task of matching IBM's 370 line with a quartet of its own heavy-duty computers, to be called the M series.

The need to build IBM-compatible machines led Fujitsu to an important decision. In 1972 the company invested a small but vital sum of money in a new venture started by Gene Amdahl, a former IBM engineer who had been largely responsible for the design of its 360 series computers. Amdahl Corporation had been formed with the express intent of building a less expensive, more efficient version of IBM's 370 line, which made a joint venture with Fujitsu highly advantageous for both partners. With its strong government support, Fujitsu had access to the capital Amdahl badly needed, while the U.S. engineer was a valuable source of information about IBM operating systems. Fujitsu and Amdahl persevered in what became a most profitable sharing of technology and capital.

A key factor in the Fujitsu-Amdahl deal was the Japanese company's confidence that it could rely on NTT to pay top dollar for whatever computer evolved from the new venture. In this, as in many other situations, NTT served as a kind of guaranteed market for Fujitsu, which in turn was well on its way to becoming a world leader in telecommunications technology and hence a more valuable supplier to NTT. The Fujitsu-Hitachi M series of high-speed computers emerged in the late 1970s. With the M series, the Japanese had achieved a rough parity with the IBM systems. Fujitsu had become one of IBM's very few real competitors in the area of general-purpose mainframe computers; in 1979 Fujitsu took a narrow lead over IBM in Japanese computer sales that held through the mid-1990s.

NEW INITIATIVES IN COMPUTERS, TELECOMMUNICATIONS, AND ELECTRONIC DEVICES

After the watershed events of the 1970s, Fujitsu in the 1980s pushed ahead with an impressive array of projects in each of its three main marketing areas. In computers, which generated 60 to 70 percent of overall corporate revenue, Fujitsu continued the success of its M series while branching out into minicomputers, workstations, and personal computers. The company spent much of the 1980s in a legal dispute with IBM over the latter's charge that Fujitsu had improperly copied IBM's software. An arbitrator decided in 1988 that, after $833 million in payments to IBM, Fujitsu could continue to buy access to IBM software for ten years at a cost of at least $25 million a year. The agreement was meant as a spur to further mainframe competition. After introducing the first Japanese supercomputer in 1982, Fujitsu became a leading manufacturer of supercomputers, with some 80 such units installed by the end of the 1980s. Although easily the leading mainframe maker in Japan, Fujitsu had little success exporting its products; with only 22 percent of corporate sales made overseas, Fujitsu remained overly dependent on its Japanese business. In particular, the company was unable to break into the U.S. market, where, in addition to the obvious presence of IBM, its mainframe bias was seen as somewhat outdated. The trend in large computer systems at the time was toward greater distribution of processing power, aided by individually tailored software applications, two areas in which Fujitsu was notably weak.

Fujitsu remained strong in telecommunications, however, continuing its close relationship with NTT as well as with the newly emerging New Common Carriers. In light of its origin in the telecommunications field, it was not surprising that Fujitsu became a world leader in the development of Integrated Services Digital Network (ISDN), a convergence of data processing and telecommunications aiming to carry voice, image, data, and text all on one system. Fujitsu was also active in other improvements in telecommunications such as COINS (corporate information network systems), PBXs (private branch exchanges), and digital switching systems. The company also provided important terminal and branching equipment for the Trans-Pacific Cable #3, the Pacific Ocean's first optical submarine cable.

Fujitsu maintained a strong presence in its third product area as well, electronic devices. In 1987 the firm was prevented by the U.S. government from acquiring Fairchild Camera, a leading U.S. manufacturer of memory chips, but it still managed to sell about $2.5 billion worth of chips annually. The very fact that Fujitsu was barred from purchasing Fairchild was a testament to the company's strength in semiconductors as well as computers. In conjunction with the Japanese government and other Japanese computer firms, Fujitsu continued to refine its chip technology in anticipation of the arrival of the fifth generation of computers, proposed machines that would be able to write their own software and in some meaningful sense "think."

PARTNERING AND RESTRUCTURING

In the end, however, Fujitsu's 1980s activities proved unable to carry a healthy firm into the 1990s. Observers noted (in hindsight) that the company had played a mainly follow-the-leader (IBM) strategy that emphasized mainframe computers. This began to catch up with Fujitsu in the early 1990s as the shift to networked systems and client-server systems accelerated, cutting the market for mainframes dramatically. Other initiatives undertaken in the 1980s to great fanfare proved less important long-term than little noticed projects; in telecommunications, for example, ISDN was still being touted as the system of the future as late as 1996, while Fujitsu's Nifty Serve online service, which debuted in 1986, was seen as the centerpiece of the company's telecommunications operation in the mid-1990s because of the emergence of the Internet (Nifty-Serve had about 1.6 million subscribers in Japan in 1996).

The year 1990, then, became a year of transition for Fujitsu upon the appointment of Tadashi Sekizawa, a telecommunications engineer, as president. Sekizawa wanted Fujitsu to be more aggressive in its pursuit of foreign markets (80 percent of revenue in 1989 came from Japan), to become more market-driven in general, and to lessen the stifling bureaucracy that impeded product development.

To bolster the firm internationally, Sekizawa continued to seek non-Japanese partners for growth, wishing to utilize local experts knowledgeable about local markets. Already having a partner in the United States through its 43 percent stake in Amdahl, Fujitsu gained a major European partner in July 1990 when it spent £700 million ($1.3 billion) for an 80 percent stake in International Computers Ltd. (ICL), Britain's largest and most important mainframe maker. Fujitsu and ICL, which had become a subsidiary of STC in 1984, had collaborated on several projects, beginning in 1981. Fujitsu's European operations were further bolstered in 1991 when ICL acquired Nokia's data systems group, which was the largest computer company in Scandinavia. The U.S. market was further targeted as well with a $40 million investment in HaL Computer Systems, Inc., a start-up firm aiming to develop UNIX systems, UNIX being an increasingly popular operating system.

Unfortunately for Fujitsu, the Japanese economic bubble burst in 1991 just as the company was beginning to implement Sekizawa's program. As a result, profits fell 85.2 percent from ¥82.67 billion in fiscal 1990 to ¥12.21 billion in fiscal 1991; the following two years, Fujitsu posted losses: ¥32.6 billion in fiscal 1992 and ¥37.67 billion in fiscal 1993. Looming over these figures was the downside of the company's huge investments of the 1980s, a $12.4 billion debt by 1992.

The recession precluded Fujitsu from making further international moves in 1991, and capital spending was slashed one-third that year. Strategically, however, research and development spending was not cut. Because the Japanese culture prevented companies in Fujitsu's position from making large workforce reductions to cut costs, Sekizawa dramatically cut the number of new hires. Meanwhile, to lessen its dependence on mainframe sales and strengthen its PC area, Sekizawa in 1992 established a cross-functional Personal Systems Business Group with the aim of speeding up product development. Also intended to improve product development speed was a restructuring that created a flatter organizational structure and lessened corporate bureaucracy.

Fujitsu's huge debt ruled out any major investments to create new products, so the company turned to partnerships to an even greater degree as the decade continued. The deals included: developing a next generation of less expensive mainframes with Siemens; establishing a joint venture with Advanced Micro Devices, Inc., called Fujitsu AMD Semiconductor Limited to produce flash memory; creating multimedia technology with Sharp Corp.; developing microprocessors for Sun workstations with Sun Microsystems; and

relying on Computer Associates to market Jasmine software in the United States.

SHIFTING EMPHASIS TO SOFTWARE AND SERVICES

Clearly, Fujitsu in the mid-1990s was juggling a number of initiatives as well as dealing with weakening mainframe sales and a difficult, highly competitive semiconductor market. Encouragingly, revenues rose sharply in fiscal 1994 (¥3.26 trillion) and 1995 (¥3.76 trillion), while the company also returned to profitability, posting net income of ¥45.02 billion in 1994 and ¥63.11 billion in 1995. Part of the sales increase in 1995 was attributable to a huge increase in sales of Fujitsu personal computers. During the year, by offering its models at extremely low prices, possibly at a loss, the company more than doubled its share of the Japanese PC market to 18.4 percent, placing it second to NEC; overall sales of PCs in Japan increased an astounding 70 percent that year as Japanese companies began making the transition from mainframes to networked PCs. Fujitsu also made a strong push to expand its share of the overseas PC market, aiming to become the number five computer maker by 2000. According to Sekizawa, the renewed PC drive had an ancillary benefit of providing Fujitsu with opportunities to develop a much stronger position in software and services connected with computer networks and with the broader and emerging Internet.

The heightened activity in the area of software and services became increasingly important in the late 1990s and into the 21st century as all of the Japanese electronics firms saw their profit margins on computers, semiconductors, and telecommunications gear decline steadily. Nowhere was the shift from hardware to software and services more apparent than in Fujitsu's floundering mainframe affiliate Amdahl. By mid-1997, Amdahl had posted six consecutive quarters in the red and appeared on the verge of bankruptcy. In September of that year, Fujitsu stepped in and purchased the 57 percent of Amdahl it did not already own for $878 million. The cash infusion saved Amdahl from bankruptcy, and the company began to place increasing emphasis on its software, services, and consulting operations. Similarly, ICL had also been transformed into a leading U.K. information technology services company by the time Fujitsu took full control of it in 1998. Under Fujitsu's new president, Naoyuki Akikusa, who took over during 1998, the transformation of Amdahl reached its logical conclusion when the firm announced in late 2000 that it would exit from the mainframe business altogether, reducing its hardware business to servers and storage systems.

Under Akikusa, Fujitsu adopted the slogan "Everything on the Internet," and these words were put into action in 1999 when the company gained full control of Nifty Serve, merged it with another online service, and thereby created the leading ISP in Japan. Akikusa also took decisive action within the company's semiconductor operations, which were losing money because of falling computer chip prices. He shut down Fujitsu's chip operations in England, taking a $480 million write-off (which contributed to a net loss for the 1999 fiscal year), closed older chip operations at home, and began buying more of the chips it needed for its own products from Taiwanese firms. Of its remaining chip operations, Fujitsu planned to scale back production of dynamic random-access memory chips (DRAMs), which were used in personal computers, in favor of an increased focus on advanced semiconductors used in such products as cellular phones. Alliances played a role in this shift as Fujitsu in May 2000 entered into an agreement with Advanced Micro Devices Inc. (AMD) of the United States to manufacture flash memory used in cellular phones, computer-network devices, digital cameras, car navigation systems, and other increasingly popular high-tech gear. Fujitsu was also involved in other semiconductor collaborations, including tie-ups with Sony to develop system large-scale integrated circuits (LSIs), which combined memory and processing in a single chip that could be used in digital audio-video devices and in mobile communications products; and with Toshiba to develop a next-generation, one-gigabit memory chip.

Another key alliance was launched in June 1999 with Siemens AG. A jointly owned company called Fujitsu Siemens Computers was created to combine the European computer operations of the two firms. After a troubled beginning marked by squabbling by the two partners over the direction of the joint venture, which initially focused on desktop PCs, Fujitsu Siemens shifted ground in late 2000, announcing plans to focus on selling servers and mobile computers to businesses and to enter the handheld computer segment. Back on the Internet front, Fujitsu and Sakura Bank Ltd. announced in July 1999 that they had formed a joint venture to establish the first Internet/online bank in Japan.

LOSSES FROM TECH DOWNTURN AND RESTRUCTURING EFFORTS

Fujitsu's shift of emphasis to the Internet, software, and services failed to buffet the firm from the effects of the severe downturn in the tech sector that began in the later months of 2000. The company faced a simultaneous slowdown in the U.S. telecommunications industry, weakening demand in the mobile phone market worldwide, a deep falloff in demand for computers from consumers and small businesses, and corporate belt-tightening that hit the tech sector particularly hard. Consequently, Fujitsu barely eked out a profit for the 2001 fiscal year. The company then launched a major restructuring in July 2001. The plan involved the merger of business units, the divestment of noncore operations, and the combination of several plants into one. One month later, Akikusa announced plans to cut 16,400 jobs, or about 9 percent of the company workforce as part of the restructuring. About 5,000 of the cuts came in Japan but did not involve any layoffs of full-time employees but rather were derived through attrition and the elimination of temporary positions.

This restructuring, one of the most dramatic undertaken by a major Japanese electronics firm, also involved a greater emphasis on the Fujitsu name outside Japan. Thus, the Amdahl name was largely relegated to history as that firm was renamed Fujitsu IT Holdings, Inc. (which itself was later subsumed within the U.S.-based Fujitsu Computer Systems Corporation). Likewise, U.K. subsidiary ICL was renamed Fujitsu Services Holdings PLC. Restructuring charges for fiscal 2002 totaled ¥417 billion ($3.14 billion), leading to a net loss for the year of ¥193 billion ($1.45 billion). Revenues fell nearly 9 percent to ¥5.01 trillion ($37.65 billion).

Sales fell nearly 8 percent more a year later as the economic climate remained challenging, but Fujitsu's restructuring efforts began to pay off with the firm achieving an operating profit of ¥100.4 billion ($837 million) compared to the previous year's operating loss of ¥74.4 billion ($559 million). Charges taken for additional restructuring initiatives resulted in another, though smaller, net loss of ¥61.3 billion ($511 million).

FURTHER ALLIANCES AND DIVESTMENTS

As Fujitsu returned to profitability in fiscal 2004 under the leadership of newly installed President Hiroaki Kurokawa, alliances remained an important component of the company's turnaround efforts. In July 2003, for example, Fujitsu's collaboration with AMD deepened when the two firms integrated their flash memory operations into a joint venture originally called FASL LLC but later renamed Spansion Inc. AMD initially held 60 percent of the venture and Fujitsu 40 percent, but Spansion became an independent public company via a December 2005 IPO. In semiconductors, Fujitsu needed new factory equipment to keep pace with other makers of small, low-power-consuming microchips, but its huge debt load of ¥1.4 trillion ($13.1 billion) provided an impetus for pursuing outside financing. Thus in the spring of 2004 U.S. chip-designer Lattice Semiconductor Corporation agreed to invest as much as $200 million toward Fujitsu's construction of an advanced semiconductor plant in Japan where Lattice-designed chips would be fabricated. Also in 2004, Fujitsu entered into alliances with Sun Microsystems, Inc., to jointly develop UNIX servers, and with Cisco Systems, Inc., to jointly develop basic software and to market cobranded products in the area of high-end routers and switches. In 2005 Fujitsu elected to exit from the increasingly cutthroat flat-panel display sector, selling its LCD operations to Sharp Corporation. This divestiture freed up funds that were needed for increased investment in the firm's semiconductor business.

In 2008 Kuniaki Nozoe was named president of Fujitsu. The new leader placed particular emphasis on continuing his predecessors' efforts to make the company more of a customer-centric organization. As he aimed to shift Fujitsu out of its emphasis on restructuring and toward more of a growth orientation, Nozoe saw three main platforms for future growth: moving beyond a concentration on customers' information technology needs toward improving a customer's entire business, a renewed effort at global expansion, and conducting business in a sustainable manner for the sake of the global environment.

With this new philosophical framework in place, a series of additional strategic moves once again altered Fujitsu's array of operations. In March 2008 the company placed its LSI chips business into the newly created subsidiary Fujitsu Microelectronics Limited in a move that analysts viewed as a prelude to a possible sale of the unit or its placement into a joint venture. Later in the year, Fujitsu agreed to buy Siemens out of their nine-year-old European joint venture, Fujitsu Siemens Computers (FSC), for about EUR 450 million ($569 million). Nozoe believed taking full control of this venture fit in well with his global growth strategy, although FSC was not profitable and was the likely subject of future realignment efforts. Early in 2009 Fujitsu decided to offload another loss-making operation, its hard-disk-drive business. It agreed to sell the unit to Toshiba and in doing so planned to absorb a special loss on the divestment of roughly ¥30 billion. As a result, Fujitsu expected to post a net loss of around ¥50 billion ($542 million) for the fiscal year ending in March 2009. The company had anticipated a year of red ink thanks in part to weakened demand for information technology products and services because of the global economic downturn, coupled with the impact of a stronger domestic currency, which was reducing

the value of overseas revenue after its conversion into yen.

Jonathan Martin
Updated, David E. Salamie

PRINCIPAL SUBSIDIARIES

Shinko Electric Industries Co., Ltd. (50%); NIFTY Corporation (66.59%); Fujitsu Component Limited (50.31%); Fujitsu Broad Solution & Consulting Inc. (56.44%); Fujitsu Business Systems Ltd. (52.64%); Fujitsu Frontech Limited (53.2%); Shimane Fujitsu Limited; PFU Limited; Fujitsu Isotec Limited; Fujitsu IT Products Ltd.; Fujitsu Access Limited; Fujitsu FIP Corporation; Fujitsu FSAS Inc.; Fujitsu Electronics Inc.; Fujitsu Laboratories Ltd.; Fujitsu TEN Limited; Fujitsu Personal System Limited; Fujitsu Microelectronics Limited; Fujitsu Mobile-phone Products Limited; Fujitsu Computer Products of America, Inc. (USA); Fujitsu Computer Systems Corporation (USA); Fujitsu Consulting Holdings, Inc. (USA); Fujitsu Network Communications, Inc. (USA); Fujitsu Europe Limited (UK); Fujitsu Services Holdings PLC (UK); Fujitsu Siemens Computers (Holding) B.V. (Germany); Fujitsu Taiwan Limited; Fujitsu Asia Pte. Ltd. (Singapore); Fujitsu Australia Limited; Fujitsu Computer Products Corporation of the Philippines; Fujitsu Microelectronics Asia Pte. Ltd. (Singapore); Fujitsu (Thailand) Co., Ltd.

PRINCIPAL DIVISIONS

Technology Solutions; Ubiquitous Product Solutions; Device Solutions.

PRINCIPAL COMPETITORS

NEC Corporation; Toshiba Corporation; Hitachi, Ltd.; Mitsubishi Electric Corporation; Sony Corporation; Hewlett-Packard Company; International Business Machines Corporation; Panasonic Corporation; Samsung Group; Intel Corporation; Dell Inc.; Sun Microsystems, Inc.; Sharp Corporation; SANYO Electric Co., Ltd.; Electronic Data Systems Corporation; Unisys Corporation.

FURTHER READING

Alabaster, Jay, "Fujitsu Moves to Split Off Chip Business," *Wall Street Journal,* January 22, 2008, p. B3.

Anchordoguy, Marie, *Computers Inc.: Japan's Challenge to IBM,* Cambridge: Harvard University Press, 1989, 273 p.

Brull, Steven V., and Gary McWilliams, "'Fujitsu *Shokku*' Is Jolting American PC Makers," *Business Week,* February 19, 1996, p. 50.

Brull, Steven V., Robert D. Hof, Julia Flynn, and Neil Gross, "Fujitsu Gets Wired: The Company Is Staking Its Future on the Still Elusive Frontiers of Cyberspace," *Business Week,* March 18, 1996, pp. 110–12.

Caulkin, Simon, "Fujitsu Sights Its Future," *Management Today,* December 1985, pp. 62+.

Clark, Don, "Fujitsu's Amdahl Plans to Stop Making IBM Compatibles, Seeing Little to Gain," *Wall Street Journal,* October 19, 2000.

Creative Partners in Technology, Santa Clara, Calif.: Amdahl Corporation, 1989.

Dvorak, Phred, "Fujitsu Thinks Out of the Box, but Its Finances Are Still Heavy," *Asian Wall Street Journal,* March 24, 2004, p. M1.

———, "Japan's Electronics Makers See Benefits from Restructuring," *Wall Street Journal,* April 28, 2003, p. B3.

Eisenstodt, Gale, "Race Against Time," *Forbes,* December 21, 1992, pp. 292–96.

"Fujitsu's Sekizawa: Dealing with Changing User Requirements," *Datamation,* September 1, 1992, pp. 87–89.

Gomes, Lee, "Amdahl's Autonomy Fades As Fujitsu Offers $850 Million for Remaining Stake," *Wall Street Journal,* July 31, 1997, p. A3.

Gross, Neil, and Robert D. Hof, "Fujitsu Gets a Helping Hand from an American Buddy," *Business Week,* June 28, 1993, p. 46.

Gross, Neil, and John W. Verity, "Can Fujitsu Break Big Blue's Grip?" *Business Week,* December 19, 1988, pp. 100+.

Guth, Robert A., "Eroding Empires: Electronics Giants of Japan Undergo Wrenching Change," *Wall Street Journal,* June 20, 2002, p. A1.

Hamilton, David P., "Harder Drive: Decade After Failing, Japan Firms Try Anew to Sell PCs in U.S.," *Wall Street Journal,* June 5, 1996, pp. A1+.

Hills, Jill, *Deregulating Telecoms,* Westport, Conn.: Quorum Books, 1986, 220 p.

Ishibashi, Kanji, "Fujitsu Is Aiming to Double Profits by Cutting Costs," *Asian Wall Street Journal,* May 27, 2004, p. M3.

"Japanese Semiconductors: Flat As a Pancake," *Economist,* May 4, 1996, p. 66.

"Japan's Less-Than-Invincible Computer Makers," *Economist,* January 11, 1992, pp. 59–60.

"Japan's Lou Gerstner," *Economist,* November 23, 1996, p. 80.

Johnston, Marsha W., "ICL Builds a Software House," *Datamation,* May 1, 1991, pp. 80–87.

Keenan, Faith, and Peter Landers, "Staggering Giants," *Far Eastern Economic Review,* April 1, 1999, pp. 10–13.

Kirkpatrick, David, "Your Next PC May Be Japanese," *Fortune,* October 28, 1996, pp. 141+.

Kunii, Irene M., Heidi Dawley, Robert D. Hof, and Neil Gross, "Fujitsu: Beyond Big Iron," *Business Week,* March 29, 1999, pp. 76, 78.

Landers, Peter, "Fujitsu Plans to Cut 9 Percent of Work Force, Citing Effects of Tech Slowdown in U.S.," *Wall Street Journal,* August 21, 2001, p. A16.

———, "Fujitsu Plans $2.43 Billion Charge Due to Slump," *Wall Street Journal,* July 30, 2001, p. A16.

———, "Japan's Fujitsu Looks to America Online As Model in Attempt to Become a Leader in E-Commerce," *Wall Street Journal,* August 10, 1999, p. A18.

McWilliams, Gary, Emily Thornton, and Paul M. Eng, "If at First You Falter, Reboot," *Business Week,* June 30, 1997, pp. 81–82.

Meyer, Richard, "Japan's Brave New World: The Industry Fears the Commodity Computer. Fujitsu Prepares for It," *Financial World,* January 21, 1992, pp. 48–49.

Meyer, Richard, and Sana Siwolop, "The Samurai Have Landed: How the Japanese Computer Makers Slipped into Europe Almost Unnoticed," *Financial World,* September 18, 1990, pp. 46–50.

Mood, Jeff, "Next Stop, World Markets," *Datamation,* August 1, 1989, p. 28.

Morris, Kathleen, "What IBM Could Have Done: IBM Almost Halved Its Staff, and It Still Has Problems. Fujitsu Thinks It Can Grow Its Way Out of Mainframe Dependence," *Financial World,* March 15, 1994, pp. 32–34.

Nusbaum, Alexandra, "Japan Inc.'s Internet Crusader: The President of Fujitsu Has Launched a Bold Mission to Put His Company at the Forefront of the Online Revolution," *Financial Times,* March 23, 2000, p. 24.

Preuschat, Archibald, and Yuzo Yamaguchi, "Fujitsu Buys Siemens's Share of Venture," *Wall Street Journal,* November 5, 2008, p. B5.

Schlender, Brenton R., "How Fujitsu Will Tackle the Giants," *Fortune,* July 1, 1991, pp. 78–82.

Sender, Henny, "Fujitsu Seeks to Become a Global Software Maker," *Asian Wall Street Journal,* September 26, 2000, p. 17.

Shimamura, Kazuhiro, "Fujitsu Net Drops 40% amid Restructuring," *Wall Street Journal Asia,* May 13, 2008, p. 8.

Tanzer, Andrew, "Fujitsu Fumble," *Forbes,* October 6, 1986, p. 96.

Yamada, Michele, "Toshiba, Fujitsu Reports Show Strong Results for Fiscal Year," *Wall Street Journal,* April 28, 2004, p. B4.

Yamaguchi, Yuzo, "Toshiba Buys Drive Unit from Fujitsu," *Wall Street Journal,* February 18, 2009, p. B7.

Galiform

Galiform PLC

—•—

1st Floor, 66 Chiltern Street
London, W1U 4JT
United Kingdom
Telephone: (+44 0207) 535 1110
Fax: (+44 020) 8913 5181
Web site: http://www.galiform.com

Public Company
Incorporated: 1964 as Mullard Furniture Industries
Employees: 6,101
Sales: £782.9 million ($1.02 billion) (2008)
Stock Exchanges: London
Ticker Symbol: GFRM
NAICS: 337110 Wood Kitchen Cabinet and Counter Top Manufacturing; 337122 Nonupholstered Wood Household Furniture Manufacturing

∎ ∎ ∎

Galiform PLC is the holding company for Howden Joinery Limited, one of the United Kingdom's leading suppliers of fitted kitchens and other joinery products, such as kitchen cabinets and doors, to the professional market. Howden operates a network of nearly 450 depots throughout the United Kingdom, serving exclusively the trade professional sector: primarily small, local builders. The company has three production and logistics facilities, in Cheshire, Northamptonshire, and Yorkshire, and annually supplies more than 400,000 fitted kitchens, four million kitchen cabinets, and two million doors to more than 230,000 builders. These operations generated revenues of £783 million ($1.02 billion)

in 2008. Until 2006, Galiform was more well-known as MFI Plc, which had been a leading retail distributor of flat-pack (build it yourself) kitchens and other furniture in the United Kingdom. Galiform was created after the company spun off MFI's struggling retail arm to focus entirely on the professional building sector. MFI subsequently declared bankruptcy and shut down all of its stores at the end of 2008. Galiform is listed on the London Stock Exchange and is led by Chairman Will Samuel and CEO Matthew Ingle.

FLAT-PACK SUCCESS IN THE SIXTIES

Galiform was founded during the United Kingdom's economic boom in the 1960s, a time during which the country's housing market underwent a major expansion. The period also marked the appearance of a new type of retail furniture model. Known as "flat-pack" furniture and made most famous by Sweden's Ikea, this type of furniture was not delivered fully assembled as in the case of traditional furniture. Instead, furniture was sold as kits and packed flat in boxes, which customers brought home to set up themselves. Furniture became less expensive to produce, and less costly to transport and stock in store warehouses, while also eliminating the need to deliver to the customer's home.

While the flat-pack market began to take hold in other markets, furniture retailing in the United Kingdom remained focused on the traditional sales model into the early 1960s. The gap in the market attracted the attention of Noel Lister and Donald Searle, who recognized the potential for developing a flat-pack based retail model in the United Kingdom. Lister and Searle had gotten to know each other through the war surplus sector, often meeting up at the many auctions for the surplus goods held in the United Kingdom in the postwar period. The surplus market had begun to slow by the late 1950s, however, as the economic boom produced a higher level of disposable income.

Lister and Searle decided to go into business together and founded Mullard Furniture Industries, based in Wembley, in 1964. The name for the company was taken from Searle's wife's maiden name. MFI, as the company soon became more popularly known, initially operated as a mail-order company, building a catalog of both self-assembled furniture and camping equipment. As furniture sales took off, however, the company began focusing on this sector, phasing out its camping supplies. Sales at the company quickly reached £500,000.

MFI quickly expanded beyond mail order, opening its first warehouse-showroom in 1966. At the time, most of the retail furniture centered on the country's "high streets," that is, the city center shopping districts. Few furniture retailers offered home delivery, or only at a significant price; yet customers seeking to pick up their furniture were confronted with the congested streets and difficult parking of the city center. For its move into retail, MFI deliberately avoided the congested high streets, the city center shopping districts in most British cities. The company's focus on flat-pack furniture made it much easier for its customers to transport their furniture to their own homes.

PUBLIC OFFERING IN 1971

Through the end of the decade, the company opened a series of "MFI Superstores," in Manor Park, Catford, Chiswick, and Balham. By 1970, the company had also opened a second warehouse showroom in Birmingham. The group's growing purchasing clout supported another important part of the company's business model, positioning itself as a furniture wholesaler selling directly to the public. Rising sales enabled the company to source its products directly from furniture manufacturers.

By the end of the 1960s, most of the group's catalog were items designed and developed specifically for MFI. At the same time, the company adapted its product range to focus especially on items that were most amenable to the flat-pack model. These included items such as desks, bookshelves, kitchen cabinets, and full-scale fitted kitchens.

With sales of £6 million, MFI went public in 1971, listing its shares under the name MFI Warehouses on the London Stock Exchange. The public offering raised nearly £16.5 million for the company, fueling further growth in the group's store network. Soon after the public offering, cofounder Donald Searle died. The company brought in a new chairman, Arthur Southon, then expanded its management, adding Derek Hunt, a former police officer, and, in 1974, Jack Seabright, as joint-managing directors.

MFI weathered a difficult patch in the early 1970s, when it was hurt by the British recession of the period. The company's mail-order business, then experiencing heavy competition, including from MFI's own retail shops, had become the most vulnerable part of the group's operations. In 1974, MFI decided to exit the mail-order business altogether, and refocus itself entirely around its growing number of retail furniture superstores. The company stepped up new store openings, while improving their profitability. By the mid-1970s, most of the company's new stores became profitable after just eight months. By 1976, the company's retail network had reached 50 stores, and by 1978, turnover had climbed to £50 million.

ACQUIRING SCALE IN 1980

MFI's growth remained strong, despite the deep recession in the United Kingdom at the end of the 1970s. By then, the company had grown into one of the country's leading furniture retailers. MFI's product line had also expanded strongly, adding living room and dining room furniture, including upholstered furniture. MFI's ambitions reached higher, however, as the company moved to establish itself on a truly national level.

This led the company to launch a bid to acquire Status Discount, in a deal worth more than £31 million. Status offered a profile similar to MFI's, with a focus on flat-pack kitchens and bedroom furniture, with annual sales of £41 million. While MFI's strength lay in the south of England, as well as in Scotland, Status's operations were especially strong in the north. Both companies also shared Humber Kitchens, a Jersey-registered furniture producer, as a major supplier of kitchens.

MFI's revenues soared, topping £177 million in 1982, despite the difficult economic climate. Nonethe-

KEY DATES

1964: Donald Searle and Noel Lister found Mullard Furniture Industries (MFI) in order to sell flat-pack furniture by mail order.

1966: MFI opens its first retail store.

1971: MFI goes public with a listing on the London Stock Exchange.

1974: MFI exits mail order and focuses entirely on retail.

1980: MFI acquires Status Discount, extending its operations into the north of England.

1985: MFI agrees to merge with Asda, becoming Asda-MFI.

1987: MFI is spun off in a management buyout and acquires the Hygena retail kitchen in the United Kingdom.

1992: MFI relists on the London Stock Exchange.

1995: MFI creates trade-only Howden Joinery kitchen and joinery products group.

2006: MFI sells its retail furniture arm and changes its name to Galiform PLC.

2008: The MFI furniture chain declares bankruptcy.

less, the group was forced to shut a number of unprofitable stores. At the same time, the company had been revising its supplier list and began turning to lower-priced markets in Asia and elsewhere. By 1982, non-U.K. suppliers accounted for 30 percent of the group's total.

As the U.K. economy recovered, MFI regained its own momentum. The company launched an ambitious expansion program toward the middle of the decade, reaching 120 stores by 1984. The company then set out to open as many as 20 new stores in 1985, and more than 30 stores before the end of the decade. MFI also continued to expand its range of products, adding electrical appliances to its kitchen line.

MERGER AND DEMERGER IN THE EIGHTIES

MFI's strong growth, and its interest in entering other, non-furniture categories, caught the attention of other growth-minded retail groups. In 1985, Associated Dairies, which operated the Asda supermarket chain, approached MFI with a buyout offer. The deal quickly made progress after cofounder Noel Lister sold his stake in the company for £43.5 million.

By April 1985, the companies announced that MFI had agreed to merge with Asda in a deal worth £1.8 billion. The combined group then became one of the largest retail groups in the United Kingdom, placing fourth behind Marks & Spencer, Sainsbury, and Great Universal Stores. Following the merger, the larger company took on the name of Asda-MFI. Derek Hunt remained on as the chief executive of the group's furniture and home furnishings operations.

The merger with MFI had been part of Asda's larger ambition to extend its operations beyond its core dairies and supermarkets to encompass a broader spectrum of retail businesses. In the end, the marriage with MFI proved an uncomfortable one. By 1987, Asda had decided to refocus itself around its core supermarket business, and began selling off its dairy and other operations.

MFI CEO Hunt sought to lead a management buyout (MBO), but met with resistance from the banks, which felt that MFI had grown too large and had too few assets for an MBO to be successful. However, Hunt finally found backing from merchant banker Charterhouse, which agreed to bankroll not only the buyout, but the £200 million purchase of the U.K. operations of the Hygena retail kitchens chain. The deal was completed just two weeks ahead of the stock market collapse of October 1987.

The addition of Hygena gave the company a new well-known fitted kitchens brand name and retail chain. The deal also brought MFI its own manufacturing base for the first time. Nonetheless, the stock market crash and subsequent collapse of the U.K. building sector, followed by the beginning of a new recession, soured the MBO and Hygena acquisition.

FADING FORTUNES INTO THE NEW CENTURY

MFI appeared to regain some of its momentum into the early 1990s, however. The company began to open new stores again, starting from 1990. By 1992, the company had returned to the stock exchange. Yet despite its efforts, the company's growth slowed again through that decade, in part because of the enormously successful entry of the Ikea chain into the United Kingdom. Into the late 1990s, MFI's new store opening rate slowed to a crawl.

While the group's retail business had begun to fade, MFI enjoyed strong growth elsewhere. In 1995, the company decided to create a new operation targeting the market for small and local building companies. The company named its new operation Howden Joinery, ostensibly built upon a small business established by brothers Jan and Eric Howden in the early 1930s. According to the company's web site, the Howdens started out by building chicken sheds. Following the war, they contributed to the reconstruction effort in the United Kingdom, transitioning into the production of kitchens.

Future Galiform CEO Matthew Ingle was placed in charge of establishing and building the Howden Joinery business. By the end of its first year, Howden boasted 25 depots, which were also open to retail customers, who could then place their order with craftsmen. Many of the Howden sites were located nearby MFI stores, and Howden itself became a major supplier of kitchens to the MFI chain.

Howden's growth was rapid. The company operated just 14 depots in 1995. By 1998, Howden oversaw a national network of nearly 120 shops. The company more than doubled this figure by 2002. By 2009, there were 450 Howden depots across the United Kingdom.

In the meantime, MFI's own problems continued. Part of the retail operations problems stemmed from the poor reputation of the MFI brand, customers began to complain about the quality of its goods. MFI's expanded product range, including an extension into house wares and textiles in the 1990s, also served to highlight lack of focus at the company. In order to revive its fortunes, MFI brought in a new chief executive, John Hancock, former chairman of WH Smith in the United States, in December 1998. The group attempted to revive its flagging sales with a move into the country's high streets, starting in 2001.

NEW NAME AND NEW FOCUS IN 2006

A disastrous switchover to a new £60 million supply chain platform in 2004 brought the group new problems. The breakdown in its supply chain led to long delivery delays, and ultimately to large numbers of canceled orders. Mounting losses were compounded by the write-off of a large part of the supply system's value. At the same time, the company's reputation suffered, and by 2005 the company exhibited a sharp decline in sales.

As MFI slipped into the red in 2006, the company appointed Ingle to take over as the company's CEO. Ingle at first attempted to rescue the retail operation, closing two of its factories and shutting 11 stores. MFI was then restructured into three divisions, retail, supply, and Howden Joinery.

These efforts proved too little too late, and in September 2006 the company agreed to sell the MFI retail division to Merchant Equity Partners for the symbolic sum of £1. MFI labored on over the next two years, but by November 2008, amid the new global economic collapse, the company was finally forced to declare bankruptcy.

Following the sale of the MFI retail wing, the company adopted a new name, Galiform PLC, which became a holding company wholly focused on its core Howden Joinery business. Howden's own operations had been growing steadily throughout the first decade of the 2000s, building its network of depots to 450, and its sales to £783 million by 2008. The company was not entirely unaffected by the collapse of MFI. In January 2009, Galiform announced that it had been hit by exceptional charges of £109 million.

Howden also remained exposed to the economic downturn, as the housing market slumped and consumer spending dipped. During the first months of the year, the company's sales had dropped nearly 11 percent. Having abandoned the flat-pack market, and switching its focus to the local builder, Galiform hoped to have found the right formula for the next phase in its 45-year history.

M. L. Cohen

PRINCIPAL SUBSIDIARIES

Galiform Holdings Limited; Houdan Menuiseries SA (France); Howden Joinery Limited; Howden Kitchens (Asia) Limited (Hong Kong).

PRINCIPAL DIVISIONS

Howden Joinery Supply; Health and Safety.

PRINCIPAL OPERATING UNITS

Howden Joinery.

PRINCIPAL COMPETITORS

Steinhoff International Holdings Ltd.; Homebase Ltd.; Tedco Ltd.; Ikea International AB; DFS Trading Ltd.; The Peacock Group PLC; Dunelm Group PLC.

FURTHER READING

Bowditch, Gillian, "When the Sums Don't Always Work," *Times,* February 5, 1990.

"Furniture Chain MFI Closes Down," *BBC News,* December 19, 2008.

"Galiform Builds on Howden Progress," *Investors Chronicle,* September 7, 2007.

"Galiform Leaves MFI Past Behind at Howdens," *Birmingham Post,* March 7, 2008, p. 24.

"Galiform Says Howden Fine," *Birmingham Post,* May 19, 2007, p. 21.

"Galiform to Trim Supply Arm and Jobs," *Cabinet Maker,* July 6, 2007, p. 5.

"Good Start for Galiform After Restructuring," *Birmingham Post,* September 7, 2007, p. 21.

Hall, James, "MFI Aims to Furnish a Better Future," *Sunday Telegraph,* July 24, 2005, p. 3.

"Howdens Rises from MFI Ashes," *Sunday Times,* October 22, 2006, p. 16.

Hume, Neil, and Robert Orr, "Speculation About Potential Buyers Pushes Galiform to Best Close Yet," *Financial Times,* November 7, 2006, p. 46.

Ramnarayan, Abhinav, "MFI: The Flatpack Giant That Fell on Its Back," *Guardian,* November 26, 2008.

Risen, Dennis, "Galiform Suffers from MFI Impact," *Investors Chronicle,* March 6, 2009.

Smith, Allison, "MFI Plans to Bolt Together a New Image," *Financial Times,* March 20, 2001, p. 26.

"Why MFI Needs a Little Distance," *Cabinet Maker,* October 14, 2005, p. 9.

Genesys Telecommunications Laboratories Inc.

1155 Market Street, 11th Floor
San Francisco, California 94103
U.S.A.
Telephone: (415) 437-1100
Fax: (415) 437-1287
Web site: http://www.genesyslab.com

Subsidiary of Alcatel-Lucent
Incorporated: 1990 as Enhanced Voice Processing Inc.
Employees: 1,100
Sales: $116.5 million (2008 est.)
NAICS: 511210 Software Publishers

■ ■ ■

A subsidiary of Paris-based Alcatel-Lucent, Genesys Telecommunications Laboratories Inc. is a leading developer of software used by contact centers (call centers). In addition to its California headquarters, the company has approximately 45 offices located throughout the world, where some 1,500 employees serve a base of more than 4,000 customers.

The company's Genesys Product Suite gives medium and large call centers the ability to handle customer contacts via a variety of channels including phone, e-mail, instant messages, and video. Specifically, its software is capable of routing some 40,000 e-mails and approximately one million calls per hour. In developing solutions for its customers, Genesys relies on approximately 300 different partners, including IBM, SAP, Accenture, Alcatel, and Oracle.

FORMATIVE YEARS: 1990–96

Genesys traces its roots back to October 11, 1990, when the company was established in California as Enhanced Voice Processing Inc. Cofounders Gregory Shenkman and Alec Miloslavsky, both Russian immigrants, had met in 1980 while playing cards in San Francisco.

Before establishing Enhanced Voice Processing, Shenkman became a successful salesman in the telecommunications industry. After attending the University of California at Berkeley, Miloslavsky earned a civil engineering degree and landed a job at Pixar. Ultimately, the friends decided it was time to start their own business. Start-up capital consisted of about $150,000 ($75,000 from each of their families).

Recognizing the importance of corporate call centers as the frontline interface between organizations and their various constituents, Shenkman and Miloslavsky set out to develop software that linked telephone and computer systems in order to improve the call center experience. In time, the company established itself as a pioneer in what became known as the computer telephony integration (CTI) industry.

Starting on a shoestring, Shenkman and Miloslavsky looked to their native Russia for employees who were willing to take a chance on the new venture. Among the company's first employees was one of Miloslavsky's childhood friends, who in turn helped them to find other Russian computer scientists that were willing to relocate to the United States.

The company's strategy of hiring talented workers from overseas gave it an edge in the highly competitive technology industry. However, it also caught the atten-

COMPANY PERSPECTIVES

Genesys enables companies to deliver a superior customer service experience in real-time.

tion of the Federal Bureau of Investigation, who called the firm in 1994 to learn more about its operations. "They thought we were a front for the Russian mafia," Shenkman explained in a July 6, 1998, *Forbes* article.

Measured progress continued into the mid-1990s. By 1995 the company's headquarters were located in San Bruno, California, and Shenkman was serving as CEO. New products included a computer-mediated communications technology called Netvectoring, which combined the company's telephony software with real-time, two-way video conferencing. Genesys showcased its new offering to the banking industry during an address by Microsoft founder Bill Gates at the Retail Delivery Show.

In 1996 the company furthered its expansion by partnering with New Brunswick, Canada-based Bruncor Inc. to establish a joint venture named Genesys Laboratories Canada Inc. The new enterprise joined existing operations in the United States, the United Kingdom, Japan, and Russia. Another key development occurred in August 1996, when Genesys relocated its headquarters to San Francisco. The company ended the year with revenues of $11.8 million, up from $8.3 million in 1995.

EARLY GROWTH: 1997–98

By 1997 Genesys employed about 500 people. Some 70 percent of the company's workforce, namely programmers and engineers, hailed from such foreign locations as the former Soviet Union and Eastern Europe. In order to ensure a steady flow of new talent, the company established recruitment relationships with Russian institutions such as Phystech and Moscow University.

Early in the year, the company acquired full ownership in Genesys Laboratories Canada Inc. and formed new subsidiaries in Japan, France, and Australia. In addition, Genesys forged a global distribution agreement with Unisys Corp. that allowed both companies to provide more sophisticated solutions to customers in the financial sector. Genesys's customer base had grown to include Sprint/United Management, MCI, Kaiser Permanente, Citibank, Ameritech, Canadian Tire, Charles Schwab NationsBanc, and British Telecom.

Progress continued midway through the year. In June Genesys went public, offering 2.5 million shares of stock for $18 per share and ultimately netting $39 million in cash. The following month, the company announced that revenues for its 1997 fiscal year had reached $34.9 million, an increase of 274 percent from 1996. In October Genesys announced a major leadership change when CFO Michael McCloskey was promoted to chief operating officer.

Genesys started off 1998 by acquiring Forte Advanced Management Software Inc., which marketed telecommunications and e-mail-related products under the brand name Adante. Around the same time, the company established its first office in South Africa. The new operation joined other wholly owned subsidiaries formed that year in locations such as Germany and South Korea. In addition, *Forbes* named Genesys to its *Forbes ASAP* Top 100 Dynamic Companies listing.

Midway through the year, Genesys unveiled a new product named Genesys E-Mail, which allowed call center agents to interact with customers via e-mail in an optimal manner. For example, the product distributed incoming messages and routed them to the appropriate agent.

For its fiscal year ending June 30, 1998, Genesys reported revenues of $68.97 million, an increase of 126 percent from 1997. In July, COO Michael McCloskey was promoted to president. He succeeded Gregory Shenkman, who relinquished his position as president and CEO, but remained on the company's board.

Developments continued during the latter part of the year. In October Genesys established a regional headquarters facility in Singapore to manage its business throughout Asia, with the exception of Korea and Japan, where offices already were in place.

Genesys concluded the year with several developments. In December, the company opened a new office near Stockholm, Sweden, which was its first Scandinavian facility. In addition, Ori Sasson was named as the company's new CEO, and Gregory Shenkman was appointed chairman. One final development that month was the acquisition of an early-stage technology company named Plato Software Corp.

ACQUIRED BY ALCATEL: 1999–2001

Progress continued in 1999. During the fourth quarter of its fiscal year, Genesys added 40 new customers. In June the company acquired California-based Next Age Technologies Inc. in a deal that gave it a new workforce management product. Sales continued to climb, reach-

KEY DATES

1990: Company is established in California as Enhanced Voice Processing Inc.
1997: Genesys goes public.
2000: French telecommunications equipment manufacturer Alcatel acquires Genesys for $1.5 billion.
2002: Company announces plans to relocate its headquarters from San Francisco to Daly City, California.
2009: Genesys serves 4,000 customers.

ing $139.1 million for the fiscal year. This marked an increase of 64 percent over 1998.

One of the most significant developments in Genesys's history occurred in September 1999, when the French telecommunications equipment manufacturer Alcatel revealed plans to acquire the company in a $1.5 billion deal. The deal was completed on January 21, 2000, at which time Genesys became a wholly owned Alcatel subsidiary.

Genesys received a great deal of recognition for its products during the early 2000s. In 2000 the company's Genesys Suite 6 received Product of the Year honors from *Computer Telephony*. Similar honors were received from *Communications Solutions* for its Genesys Workforce Management product. In addition, Genesys was honored with the 2000 Frost & Sullivan Market Engineering Award for Market Leadership and Excellence, as well as the 2000 Call Center CRM Solutions CRM Excellence Award.

The early 2000s also were a time of physical expansion for Genesys. In December 2000, the company revealed that it had leased 27,000 square feet of space in Long Creek, California. The new facility would house 175 employees who had previously worked at its main San Francisco location. Additionally, more space was needed in San Francisco to accommodate the hiring of additional employees there.

Frost & Sullivan bestowed a number of honors upon Genesys in 2001. That year, the firm ranked Genesys as the North American market leader in the computer telephony integration market. Additionally, Frost & Sullivan presented the company with its Market Engineering Award for Product Line Strategy, as well as its Market Engineering Award for Outstanding Market Performance for being the Asia Pacific region's leading CTI vendor.

By mid-2001 Genesys was at work on a project for Reuters, which was implementing the company's Enterprise Routing product at its customer relationship management centers in Sydney, Geneva, Chicago, New York, and London. Together, these facilities handled approximately 70,000 customer interactions per month. More geographic expansion occurred late in the year, when Genesys signed a seven-year, $5 million lease for a 33,000-square-foot facility in Cary, North Carolina.

CHANGING TIMES: 2002–05

In early 2002 Genesys announced plans to relocate its headquarters from San Francisco to Daly City, California, in a move that affected approximately 400 workers. That year, Frost & Sullivan once again bestowed the title of North American market share leader upon Genesys. The company's products continued to garner recognition from industry publications. For example, *Communications Solutions* named Genesys's Expert Contact as product of the year. In addition, *Customer Interaction Solutions* granted similar honors to the company's Genesys Voice Portal product.

In 2003 Genesys was honored with the *Customer Interaction Solutions* CRM Excellence Award. In addition, the company's Genesys Voice Callback solution received Product of the Year honors from *Customer Interaction Solutions,* and Genesys Express was similarly ranked by *Communications Solutions*. In particular, Genesys Express, an out-of-the-box product that could be used by single-location call centers, was driving the company's growth in the Middle East, Africa, and Europe, where Genesys had approximately 100 midmarket clients.

Several major leadership changes unfolded in early 2004. In late February, President and CEO Ad Nederlof was named chairman. At the same time, COO Laurent Philonenko was named president and CEO. By this point in time, the company's products routed approximately 100 million customer interactions daily for organizations in 80 different countries.

Honors in 2004 included Market Leadership and Market Engineering awards from Frost & Sullivan, as well as another *Customer Interaction Solutions* CRM Excellence Award. In December of that year, the company forged a global reseller agreement with the enterprise applications software leader PeopleSoft Inc.

Developments continued during the midpoint of the first decade of the 2000s. In February 2005, Genesys established a strategic relationship with speech software company TuVox, bolstering its abilities in the area of speech self-service. It also was in 2005 that the company teamed with Microsoft to offer customers a combined instant messaging/telephony solution.

Another major development in 2005 was a technology and reseller agreement with IBM for a product called WebSphere Voice Server, which offered voice recognition capabilities. Genesys continued to receive awards, including the 2005 Frost & Sullivan Market Leadership Award.

INDUSTRY LEADER: 2006–09

Progress continued in 2006 when Genesys secured Travelocity, then the fifth largest U.S. travel agency, as a customer. In addition, the company's contact center solutions for the banking industry were recognized with the IBM PartnerWorld Beacon Award, Global Solutions. Additional recognition came when *Customer Interaction Solutions* awarded Product of the Year honors to the company's Genesys 7.2 contact center software suite.

New customer growth continued in 2007. Earlier that year, Genesys announced that Pearson Digital Learning had selected the company's Genesys 7.2 Real-Time Interaction Suite and Customer Interaction Management platform to provide contact center support to teachers via voice, instant messaging, chat, and e-mail.

Several months later Genesys announced the availability of a new product, developed with the Finnish company Lekane, that enabled remote employees to become part of the call center through the use of mobile devices. Genesys concluded 2007 with the acquisition of the Atlanta, Georgia-based analytic software company Informiam LLC.

Midway through 2008, Genesys forged a partnership agreement with Consilium Software that enabled both parties to further their expansion into the regions of Southeast Asia and India. In August, more developments unfolded in India when the company announced the development of an educational facility named Genesys University. Developed in partnership with iSmart, the center focused on educating customers on both best practices and contact center technology.

The formation of new partnerships continued during the latter part of 2008. In September Genesys announced a collaboration with the audio search and speech analytics solutions developer Nexidia. In December, a partnership agreement was formed with the Agoura Hills, California-based web chat provider Conversive.

Genesys began in 2009 with a customer base that included some 4,000 different organizations. Leading

companies, government agencies, and others had grown to rely on the company's technology for the functioning of their contact centers. From its position of industry leadership, the company seemed well-suited for continued growth and development during the 21st century's second decade.

Paul R. Greenland

PRINCIPAL SUBSIDIARIES

Forte Advanced Management Software, Inc.; GCTI Telecommunications Laboratories GmbH (Germany); Genesys Australasia Pty Ltd. (Australia); Genesys Japan; Genesys Laboratories Canada Inc.; Genesys Telecommunications Laboratories (PTY) Ltd. (South Africa); Genesys Telecommunications Laboratories AB (Sweden); Genesys Telecommunications Laboratories Asia Pte Ltd. (Singapore); Genesys Telecommunications Laboratories B.V. (Netherlands); Genesys Telecommunications Laboratories S.L. (Spain); Genesys Telecommunications Laboratories S.r.l. (Italy); Genesys Telecommunications Laboratories-Europe Ltd. (UK); GTF Sarl (France); Next Age Technologies Inc.; Plato Software Ltd. (Israel).

PRINCIPAL COMPETITORS

Avaya Inc.; Cisco Systems Inc.; Nortel Networks Corp.

FURTHER READING

"Ad Nederlof Is Named Chairman of Genesys and Laurent Philonenko Appointed Chief Executive Officer of Genesys," *M2 Presswire,* February 24, 2004.

"Alcatel Completes Its Acquisition of Genesys," *M2 Presswire,* January 24, 2000.

"Genesys Acquires Informiam," *Wireless News,* December 16, 2007.

"Genesys and iSmart Join Hands (Open the First Genesys University in India)," *India Business Insight,* August 31, 2008.

"Genesys Labs Opens San Francisco Headquarters," *Business Wire,* August 13, 1996.

"Genesys Telecommunications Laboratories Inc. Announces Initial Public Offering of 2,500,000 Shares of Common Stock from Company and Certain Shareholders," *Business Wire,* June 17, 1997.

"Genesys Telecommunications Labs Recognized for Leadership Role in the Contact Center Market," *Business Wire,* October 12, 2004.

Ginsberg, Steve, "S.F. Loses Firm Headquarters, 400 Jobs: Genesys Willing to Pay Millions to Make Daly City Move," *San Francisco Business Times,* February 22, 2002.

McCormack, Scott, "The Russia House," *Forbes,* July 6, 1998.

Robson, Douglas, "To Be Transferred Out of Voice-mail Hell, Press Three," *San Francisco Business Times,* June 5, 1998.

Globex Utilidades S.A.

Av Tenente Rebelo, 675
Irajá, Rio de Janeiro 21230-900
Brazil
Telephone: (55 21) 2472-8245
Fax: (55 21) 3361-1956
Web site: http://www.globex.com.br

Public Company
Incorporated: 1981
Employees: 10,532
Sales: BRL 4.51 billion ($2.45 billion) (2008)
Stock Exchanges: Bolsa de Valores de São Paulo; Over the Counter (OTC)
Ticker Symbols: GLOB; GBXPY
NAICS: 442110 Furniture Stores; 443111 Household Appliance Stores; 443112 Radio, Television, and Other Electronics Stores; 443120 Computer and Software Stores; 522210 Credit Card Issuing; 522220 Sales Financing; 522291 Consumer Lending

■ ■ ■

Globex Utilidades S.A., by means of its Ponto Frio retail chain, is the second largest Brazilian retailer focusing on selling furniture and electric and electronic appliances. Other merchandise consists of jewelry, cameras, electronics, toys, and office products, including computers, cellular phones, and fax machines. It also sells products over the telephone, on the Internet, directly to companies, and as a wholesaler, principally to smaller retail chains. In addition, Globex offers customers credit, personal loans, and insurance, and is engaged in factoring and investment activities.

THE FIRST FORTY YEARS: 1946–86

Globex was founded in 1946, just after the end of World War II, by Alfredo João Monteverde, a young Romanian immigrant. Located in Rio de Janeiro, the company imported and sold home appliances such as sewing machines and refrigerators. As business grew, Monteverde opened a store in 1950 to sell these products. Since the U.S. Coldpoint refrigerator was very popular, the enterprise came to be known by its equivalent name in Portuguese, Ponto Frio, and it chose a penguin for its logo.

At the beginning of the 1960s Ponto Frio was initiating its entry into the new federal capital, Brasília, and the states of Goiás and Minas Gerais. In time, "Freddy" Monteverde, as he was known in society, acquired a wife, Lily. Freddy, who was her second husband, killed himself as his business fell into disarray. His widow inherited it and turned for help to Edmond Safra, a prominent banker from a close knit family of Syrian Jewish origin. The two were married in 1976.

Born in Lebanon, Safra entered the banking business first in Italy and later in Brazil, where he and his brothers Joseph and Moise established Banco Safra. Edmond Safra chose Simon Alouan, another Lebanese-born Jew who was serving as financial director of the bank, to administer Globex. Under his leadership Ponto Frio expanded further, opening stores in big cities such as São Paulo and Belo Horizonte as well as Rio de Janeiro, where it still had its strongest presence.

In order to sell its big ticket items to a large customer base, Globex established Banco Investcred as the financing arm of the corporation. This allowed Ponto Frio to finance its sales at lower interest rates than most other retail chains in its sector. Other factors in Ponto Frio's growth were low prices, good store locations, and a judicious choice of products.

TARGETING POPULOUS SÃO PAULO: 1987–97

In 1987 Alouan moved from Rio de Janeiro to São Paulo as part of an effort to augment Ponto Frio's presence in southern and southeastern Brazil, the more prosperous part of the country. Nevertheless, Ponto Frio had only 22 stores in the São Paulo metropolitan area, the most populous in South America, in 1992, when it purchased a competitor, Casas Buri, for an estimated $20 million to $30 million. The acquisition gave Ponto Frio 114 more stores, including 35 in greater São Paulo and 31 in the interior of the state. It promised to double Ponto Frio's share in these lucrative markets.

Globex's purchase of family-owned Casas Buri did not come easily. It took place after three years of sporadic negotiations and required a position for the founder's son. Another condition was that none of the 1,500 employees be dismissed. A Globex executive later described the unification of the two "cultures" as "complicated," and some 20 of the acquired stores were closed. Nevertheless, the acquisition served as the springboard for Ponto Frio's entry into three southern states.

By this time, Ponto Frio had 212 stores. In 1994 sales came to $983 million, of which the state of Rio de Janeiro accounted for about half and the state of São Paulo for 30 percent. Electric home appliances and audio and video components comprised 76 percent of the total. Of the 5,000 Globex employees, 2,200 were engaged in sales and more than half received some type of training, usually by the department of human resources. This enabled the company to achieve one of the highest ratios of sales per employee in Brazilian retailing.

Publicly traded since 1981, Globex was nevertheless principally in the hands of three persons: Lily Safra, with 32 percent of the shares; Carlos Monteverde, her adopted son, with 38 percent; and Simon Alouan, still the principal executive, with 16 percent. An investment firm held 7 percent, and the remaining 7 percent were owned by public shareholders. The company sold $58.5 million in American Depositary Receipts (ADRs) in 1996 and introduced an Internet site for Ponto Frio in that year. In 1997 Globex purchased J.H. Santos, a retail chain in southern Brazil.

Globex was diversifying Ponto Frio's mix of products, adding computers and cellphones, for example, and amplifying its wholesale operation. In this form the company was lessening its dependence on white goods, that is, large home appliances. The strategy was seen as allowing Globex to better its profit margins.

ALOUAN'S LAST YEARS: 1999–2003

Further expansion was also definitely part of Globex's program. In 1999 it acquired 22 stores in Minas Gerais from Kit Eletro. The following year it purchased the 81 points of sale of the Disapel chain in a public auction, thereby reinforcing its presence in three states of southern Brazil and taking the lead in Brazil in the number of stores for its particular market sector. That year, Ponto Frio introduced its first megastore, in São Paulo. In 2001 Globex sold half of Banco Investcred, its financial services arm, to Unibanco – União de Bancos Brasileiros S.A. for BRL 100 million ($42 million), and it became Banco Investcred Unibanco.

Brazil was still fighting to emerge from its latest economic downturn, but Ponto Frio had reached the height of its success. There were 369 stores in late 2000 and estimated revenues of BRL 2.3 billion ($1.3 billion) that year. A share of Globex stock had rocketed eightfold in value in only a year. Even so, Ponto Frio had lost leadership in the home appliance retail sector to Casas Bahia S.A., which was growing even faster. Also, as a human enterprise, Globex had fallen into trouble. Edmond Safra's faith in Alouan had proven fully justified, but, according to journalists' accounts, Lily Safra blamed him for the 1989 death of Cláudio Cohen, one of her two sons by her first marriage and Ponto Frio's marketing director. After a heated discussion with Alouan at Ponto Frio's headquarters in Rio de Janeiro, Cohen drove off to his weekend beachfront house but was killed, with his son, in a traffic collision. Lily was said to have expelled Alouan from the funeral.

When Edmond Safra died in a 1999 fire in his Monaco apartment, Alouan lost his protector. Finding a successor, however, was not easy, for Carlos Monteverde,

KEY DATES

1946: Founding of Globex in Rio de Janeiro.
1992: Purchase of Casas Buri raises the number of Ponto Frio stores to 212.
2000: Globex's stock value increases eightfold in a year.
2003: Simon Alouan, Globex's chief executive for more than a quarter century, resigns.
2006: Globex's next chief executive is fired after only three years.
2007: The company opens smaller stores under a new format, Ponto Frio Digital.
2008: The number of Ponto Frio stores reaches 447 at year's end.

based in London and Monaco, was more interested in racing cars than running the enterprise. Lily's other two children also lived abroad and did not seem inclined to seek its reins. When Alouan finally stepped down in 2003, the third year of falling revenues, he did so without choosing a successor. The new chief executive, appointed four months later, was Roberto Britto, formerly president of a supermarket chain.

YEARS OF TRANSITION: 2004–06

Britto inherited a difficult situation. Ponto Frio had sales of only $885 million in 2003, 40 percent lower than that registered in 2000, while Casas Bahia's sales grew 20 percent in the same period. The profit of only $1 million was its smallest ever. Another home appliance chain, Magazine Luiza, was gaining rapidly.

Britto's first priority was to cut costs. Almost immediately he closed 21 of the 354 stores. Next, he sought to motivate the executives, some of whom had moved on to other chains. The wholesale division, responsible for 10 percent of sales, had been completely paralyzed by the exodus of 29 functionaries. Also, the company tried to improve its relations with suppliers by offering them better terms. In addition, Ponto Frio's Unicard credit card was introduced in 2006.

By the close of 2005 Ponto Frio's sales had almost doubled and its profit margin was again comfortable. In spite of these numbers, Britto was fired in late 2006 by Michel Elia, another Lebanese-born financial executive closely tied to the Safra family and the son-in-law of Lily Safra. Although nominally only a counselor, Elia had been looking over Britto's shoulder for at least two

years, delving into every aspect of the chain, including selecting the location of new stores and weighing in on advertising campaigns. In the same style as Alouan, he kept an exceedingly low profile and was preoccupied with his security, traveling in armored cars and visiting the stores incognito. (In 2004 he survived an armed attack in a suburb of Rio de Janeiro; the attack was perhaps not aimed at him but rather the result of gang warfare.)

OPENING NEW STORES IN 2007

Six months passed before Globex appointed a new chief executive, Manoel Amorim. He immediately embarked on a tour of many of the stores and a round of meetings with the 29 principal executives and 17 major Ponto Frio suppliers. With the help of the U.S. business consulting firm McKinsey & Company, Amorim formed a 12-member group to monitor every aspect of the enterprise. About 250 administrators were dismissed. The number of items stocked by Ponto Frio was reduced from 10,000 to 7,000, and the average amount of time stocked in the stores dropped from 62 to 50 days.

At the same time Ponto Frio was growing rapidly in the number of points of sale, with a major push to the northeast. In partnership with local entrepreneurs, it was opening 50 units under a new format called Ponto Frio Digital: small stores that specialized in cellular phones and cameras. In all, some 59 stores opened in 2007. The company was also taking part in a project, named Casas Brasileiras, with two other firms, including Volkswagen do Brasil Ltda., to market products made abroad. Amorim was said to have more autonomy in running Globex than Britto had enjoyed.

GLOBEX AND PONTO FRIO IN 2008

There were 445 Ponto Frio outlets in September 2008, located in 11 states and the federal district. Fifty-five were Ponto Frio Digital units. The retail chain was in all southern states except remote Mato Grosso do Sul but in none north of Bahia. There were 111 stores in São Paulo and 84 in Rio de Janeiro. Two more stores opened in the remainder of 2008, to bring the increase during the year to 31, and 11 in early 2009, raising the total to 458.

Ponto Frio's stores were in four formats. Street stores depended on heavy pedestrian traffic and carried all the chain's product categories. Shopping center stores were smaller but also stocked all the chain's product categories. Megastores were far larger, more than

100,000 square meters in size, and not only stocked all products but also used part of the space to establish partnerships with suppliers that enabled them to demonstrate their product lines. By contrast, Ponto Frio Digital outlets had as little as 70 square meters of selling space, with the focus on technological products such as camcorders, audio and video equipment, cellular apparatus, and information technology.

By means of Banco Investcred Unibanco, Globex claimed to be the first retail chain owner in Brazil to widely offer financial products and services. These included personal loans and easy payment plans. In early 2008, 62 percent of Ponto Frio's sales were by credit, of which 29 percent were by credit card and 71 percent by Banco Investcred Unibanco.

Globex's revenues rose almost 7 percent in 2008, but this was because of the increase in Ponto Frio's units. Sales per square meter of space fell slightly, and net profit dropped 64 percent. Lily Safra and Carlos Monteverde were reported to be talking to another retail chain in 2009 about selling their shares. Their 70 percent stake was valued at about BRL 600 million (about $245 million).

Robert Halasz

PRINCIPAL SUBSIDIARIES

Banco Investcred Unibanco S.A. (50%); Globex Administração de Consórcios Ltda.; Globex Administração e Serviços Ltda.; Globex Factoring Comercial S.A.; Ponto Frio Administração e Importação de Bems Ltda.; Pontocredit Negocios de Varejo Ltda.; S.A.B.A.R.A. S.A.

PRINCIPAL COMPETITORS

Casa & Video; Casas Bahia S.A.; Fast Shop; Magazine Luiza S.A.

FURTHER READING

"O bonzão ficou muito maior," *Exame*, May 13, 1992, p. 50.

Carvalho, Denise, "A eminência parda do Ponto Frio," *Exame*, November 22, 2006, pp. 60–61.

Correa, Cristiane, "Uma corrida para tirar o atraso," *Exame*, August 1, 2007, pp. 88–89.

Ferraz, Eduardo, "Lily sai de cena," *Exame*, November 1, 2000, pp. 56–58.

"Globex: Continuing Market Leadership," *Institutional Investor*, October 1996, pp. IB12+.

Paduan, Roberta, "A agenda do Ponto Frio," *Exame*, October 13, 2004, pp. 48–50.

"Pingüim gosta mesmo é de muito calor," *Exame Melhores e Maiores*, August 1995, pp. 148, 150, 152.

Vassalo, Cláudia, "Apesar de Você," *Exame*, November 4, 1998, pp. 68–70.

Weiss, Gary, "The Mystery Man of Finance," *Business Week*, March 7, 1994, pp. 98–105.

GN ReSound

GN ReSound A/S

Postboks 99, Lautrupbjerg 7
Ballerup, DK-2750
Denmark
Telephone: (+45) 45 75 22 22
Fax: (+45) 45 75 22 29
Web site: http://www.gnresound.dk

Subsidiary of GN Store Nord A/S
Incorporated: 1943 as Danavox
Employees: 3,775
Sales: DKK 3.18 billion (2008)
NAICS: 339113 Surgical Appliance and Supplies
Manufacturing; 334510 Electromedical and Electro-
therapeutic Apparatus Manufacturing; 334515
Instrument Manufacturing for Measuring and Test-
ing Electricity and Electrical Signals

■ ■ ■

GN ReSound A/S is a world-leading developer of hearing aids, and is also the world's leading developer and
producer of audiology equipment. Based in Bellerup,
Denmark, GN ReSound is one of the two operating
divisions (alongside headset producer GN Netcom) of
parent company GN Store Nord A/S. ReSound develops
and distributes hearing aids under three primary brands:
ReSound, which provides cutting-edge hearing aid
technologies; Beltone, the North American retail brand
leader; and Interton, the company's wholesale hearing
aid brand. Hearing aid sales accounted for 87 percent of
GN ReSound's total turnover of DKK 3.2 billion in
2008. The remainder was produced by the group's GN

Otometrics division, which develops and distributes
measurement and diagnostic equipment for the audiology sector, hearing aid fitting and verification equipment, as well as testing and diagnostic equipment for
balance-related disorders. GN Otometrics operates
through three main brands, Madsen, Aurical, and ICS.
GN ReSound maintains a global presence, with
subsidiaries across the world and distribution to more
than 70 countries. Europe accounts for 45 percent of
the company's turnover, with North America adding 36
percent and Asia and the rest of the world contributing
19 percent to sales. GN ReSound's share of parent
company GN Store Nord's total turnover reached 57
percent in 2008. GN ReSound is led by CEO Mike van
der Wallen.

ORIGINS IN THE FORTIES

While GN ReSound itself was formed only in 1999, its
roots stretch back to the 1940s especially to the development of modern audio technology in the post–World
War II period. The invention of the telephone had
provided the basis for the first electrical hearing aid
devices in the 1870s. The earliest electrical hearing aids
were bulky, required a lot of power to operate, and
provided only limited audio quality. The introduction of
vacuum tubes in the 1920s represented a major step
toward overcoming these problems. By the 1940s, hearing aid manufacturers had introduced the first wearable
hearing aids.

The hearing aid industry remained closely linked to
developments in audio and radio technology, including
sound capture and sound reproduction. As a result, a

number of hearing aid companies had their origins in the audio sector. Such was the case with Danavox, a company founded by Gerd Rosenstand in Denmark in 1943 in order to produce loudspeakers. Danavox introduced its first hearing aid in 1947, laying the foundation for the future GN ReSound group.

The year 1947 marked a new milestone not only for the hearing aid industry, but also for the electronics industry as a whole. The introduction of the transistor that year paved the way toward the dramatic miniaturization of electronic circuits, giving birth to the modern technological era. The earliest transistors were not efficient enough for commercial use. This changed, however, in 1952 with the introduction of new germanium-based transistors. Hearing aids were the first commercially available products to incorporate transistors that year.

Denmark by then had begun its development into one of the major world centers for hearing aid technology. This came about in large part because of the Danish government's decision in 1950 to provide free hearing examinations and hearing aids. The guarantee of a market provided fertile ground for the industry's growth, as researchers and the audio industry collaborated on developing new technologies. A major figure in this effort was Poul Madsen, an electronic engineer who had begun his career with the famed Bang & Olufsen company.

Madsen founded his own company, Amplex, in 1955, and began working with Dr. Ole Bentzen, a leading audiology researcher, to develop the first instruments capable of measuring hearing loss. Madsen sold Amplex, based in Odense, in 1960 in order to move to Copenhagen to work on a new project to develop an instrument capable of taking impedance measurements of the middle ear. To this end, Madsen set up a new company, Madsen Electronics.

GROWTH IN THE FIFTIES

Danavox in the meantime claimed a position among the Danish leaders, as it joined in the race to develop smaller, less obtrusive, less visible hearing aid devices. In 1955, for example, Danavox adopted an idea developed in the United States and produced its first hearing aid incorporated into an eyeglass frame. The company called the model "Lunettes" (French for eyeglasses). Further improvements on the design led to the launch of the "Royal" in 1960. The company also continued to develop its other audio operations, including expanding into the production of headsets (headphones). Headsets, in particular for the telecommunications sector, later became the group's audio product focus.

Danavox's growth remained strong into the middle of the 1960s. The company developed an international distribution network early on, adding sales operations in Germany, the Netherlands, and the United Kingdom, before entering other markets. Yet Rosenstand proved a better engineer than business manager. Through the 1960s and into the 1970s, Danavox's corporate structure, including a number of subsidiaries and sales operations, had become increasingly complex and inefficient.

Rosenstand was said to have retained "exorbitant" amounts of Danavox's capital for himself, before retiring to Switzerland, leaving fewer resources for the company's research and development efforts. Rosenstand's son-in-law remained with the company as its technical director, and Rosenstand continued to hold the chairman's seat. The transition to new management, however, went less than smoothly, as management and the founding family came into conflict. These factors resulted in Danavox losing its technological footing. Major competitors, including Widex and Oticon, took the lead in the country's hearing aid market. Into the early 1970s, the company's revenues languished at DKK 35 million.

ACQUIRED BY GN IN THE SEVENTIES

Danavox's board of directors turned to outside help to restore the company's growth. In 1975, the company asked Erik Rasmussen, then chairman of the Great Northern Telegraph Company (later known as GN Store Nord), to take a seat on the board. With Rasmussen's assistance, Danavox regained some of its momentum. By the end of 1976, the company's sales had grown to DKK 48 million. Danavox continued to extend its operations as well. In the mid-1970s, for example, the company set up a new production facility in New Washington, near Birmingham in England.

GN was then in the process of redefining its own operations. Founded in 1869, GN had been responsible for setting up Denmark's telegraph network. By 1872,

KEY DATES

1940: Beltone is founded in Chicago by Sam Posen.

1943: Gerd Rosenstand founds Danavox in Denmark to produce loudspeakers.

1947: Danavox produces its first hearing aid.

1958: Poul Madsen founds Madsen Electronics and begins developing audiology equipment.

1977: GN acquires Danavox, which becomes GN Danavox.

1990: GN Danavox acquires Madsen Electronics.

1999: GN merges with ReSound Corporation, becoming GN ReSound; acquires Danplex and Rastronics.

2000: GN ReSound acquires Beltone.

2001: GN ReSound merges all audiology operations into GN Otometrics, which becomes a world leader.

2005: GN ReSound forms wholesale division through purchase of Interton.

2006: GN agrees to sell GN ReSound to Sonova of Switzerland, but deal falls through.

2009: GN ReSound launches first "invisible" hearing aid.

the company had linked the country to the developing international telegraph grid. In that year, GN became the first to provide a telegraph connection between Europe and the Far East.

Telegraph's obsolescence into the middle of the 20th century forced GN to seek new business areas. The company targeted the electronics sector for growth in the 1950s, acquiring a number of businesses through the 1970s. In 1976, Rasmussen proposed to GN's board that the company acquire Danavox as well. By 1977, GN succeeded in negotiating the purchase, for DKK 24.5 million. Rasmussen then replaced Rosenstand as the company's chairman.

Under GN, Danavox underwent a new surge in sales, which topped DKK 100 million by the end of the decade. The company restructured its network of international subsidiaries, putting into place a new sales and distribution organization. At that time, the company's operations spanned Brazil, Canada, France, Germany, the Netherlands, the United Kingdom, and the United States. From this base, the group's distribution reached more than 70 countries.

HEARING AID SPECIALIST IN 1986

While GN Danavox, as the company became known, invested strongly in its marketing effort into the 1980s, other areas of the group's operations were being overlooked. The company's manufacturing network had become highly inefficient; in the mid-1980s, the group's production reached just 65 percent of its total production. The company also was dogged by a number of quality issues, damaging its reputation among major customers. By the middle of the decade, GN Danavox had begun to hemorrhage badly. In 1985, its losses reached DKK 6 million. The following year, the company's losses swelled to DKK 49 million.

GN brought in new management for the company, and carried out a reorganization of its operations. This involved the spinoff of the group's headset business into a new company, GN Netcom. That company quickly became profitable.

The situation at GN Danavox was more delicate, however. Now focused entirely on the hearing aid market, GN Danavox continued to struggle through the end of the decade. The company brought in a new managing director, Anders Grandt, who set out to rebuild the company. Grandt's early efforts were unsuccessful, however. By 1988, the company was forced to turn to GN for a capital injection of DKK 58 million.

GN debated whether to divest GN Danavox and exit the hearing aid industry altogether. Yet Grandt convinced the board of the future opportunities represented by the hearing aid industry. At the time, the industry remained highly fragmented. The largest hearing aid company had a market share of just 15 percent. GN Danavox's own share remained strong, at nearly 5 percent. The fragmentation of the industry offered the possibility of growth through acquisition. At the same time, the huge baby boomer population, the first of whom would turn 50 in the middle of the decade, promised a strong future market for hearing aids. The baby boomer generation also held the distinction of having grown up during an era of significant improvements in audio amplification. Exposure to loud music for long periods had left many with hearing impairments, and at an earlier age than previous generations.

GAINING SCALE

GN decided to keep GN Danavox and instead invest in building the company into a world leader. Acquisitions and mergers were to play a prominent role in the company's success through the 1990s. Yet GN Danavox also revitalized its research and development effort, enabling it to claim a place among the cutting-edge leaders.

GN Danavox's acquisition of Madsen Electronics in 1990 allowed the company to extend its operations into the related field of audiology measurement and diagnostic instruments. The purchase also helped expand GN Danavox's own technology base. Most importantly, Madsen had been one of the pioneers in the implementation of computer and software technologies for use in auditory measurement. This expertise provided GN Danavox with a new milestone. In 1992, GN Danavox became the first in the world to begin marketing a hearing aid incorporating digital sound processing technology.

In 1996, GN Danavox formed a partnership with U.S.-based ReSound Corporation, founded in California in 1984. The companies began collaborating on developing the world's first software-based hearing aids. The partnership's success quickly led the companies to agree to a merger. In May 1999, parent company GN paid $167 million to acquire ReSound. GN Danavox and ReSound were then merged together, becoming GN ReSound.

The creation of GN ReSound came amid a general consolidation of the hearing aid industry. A driving factor behind the industry consolidation was the rapidly increasing costs of research and development. New products often cost up to $30 million to develop. Nonetheless, in part because of the rapid gains in technology, the average life cycle of a product was less than three years.

HEARING AID LEADER

GN ReSound carried out a number of acquisitions in 2000. The most important of these was its purchase of U.S.-based Beltone, one of that country's most well-known hearing aid brands. Beltone had been founded in Chicago in 1940. The company had completed its own series of acquisitions, including J.W. Childs in 1997, and Philips Hearing Technologies in 1999, before becoming part of GN ReSound. Beltone then took its place as one of GN ReSound's flagship brands.

GN ReSound also moved to position its audiology equipment operations as a world leader. Toward this end, the company acquired several rival companies, including Danplex (which had evolved from Amplex) and its subsidiary Rastronics, in 1999, and then of ICS Medical and Hortmann in 2000. In 2001, GN ReSound merged all of its audiology instrumentation businesses into a single company, GN Otometrics. That company then became the world's largest producer of audiology equipment.

In the hearing aid division, meanwhile, the company continued to establish industry milestones. In 2003, for example, the company debuted its Air technology, which provided sound reinforcement without blocking the ear canal, thereby preventing the occlusion that often reduced sound quality and made hearing aids uncomfortable to wear. Other technological breakthroughs posted by the company included the Pulse, the first rechargeable hearing aid, and the "dot," which the company claimed was the world's smallest hearing aid, in 2008. Then, in 2009, the company extended its miniaturization with the launch of "be," which the company claimed to be the first "invisible" hearing aid.

GN ReSound completed a new acquisition, Interton, in 2005. That company allowed GN ReSound to move into the wholesale market, supplying hearing aids to third parties. The following year, parent company GN Store Nord announced that it had agreed to sell GN ReSound to rival Sonova, part of the Swiss Phonak Group for $2.8 billion. The sale soon fell through, however, after the German monopoly commission struck down the deal, claiming that it would create an "oligopoly" in the German market. The decision led GN Store Nord to abandon the idea of selling its hearing aid division, at least for the time being. Meanwhile, GN ReSound had claimed a spot among the global hearing industry's leaders.

M. L. Cohen

PRINCIPAL SUBSIDIARIES

American Hearing Systems Inc. (USA); Beltone Europe Holdings A/S; GN GROC Ltd. (China); GN Group Solutions GmbH (Germany); GN Hearing Care Corporation (USA); GN Hearing Care S.A. (Spain); GN Otometrics A/S; Interton Electronic Hörgeräte GmbH (Germany); Interton Ltd. (UK)

PRINCIPAL DIVISIONS

Hearing Instruments; Hearing and Balance Instrumentation and Software.

PRINCIPAL COMPETITORS

Sonova AG; Amplifon GmbH; Siemens Healthcare GmbH.

FURTHER READING

Caldwell, Douglas E., "Having a Ball," *Silicon Valley/San Jose Business Journal,* August 30, 2002.

Christ, Bjørn, "ReSound Rebounds from Blocked Merger with Backlog of Innovation," *Hearing Review,* April 2008, p. 54.

"First Invisible Hearing Aid Set to Revolutionise Hearing Instruments," *Tone Magazine,* March 22, 2009.

"GN Explores Options for Hearing Care Divisions," *Hearing Review,* August 2006, p. 8.

"GN ReSound Purchases Danplex," *Hearing Journal,* October 1999.

Hanson, Monte, "Hearing-Aid Maker Discusses Its Future in Industry," *Finance and Commerce Daily Newspaper,* May 24, 2001.

Iversen, Martin J., *GN Store Nord: A Company in Transition, 1939–1988,* Copenhagen: Copenhagen Business School Press, 2005.

Jones, Claire, "Sound Swiss Organization on Phonak Deal," *International Tax Review,* November 2006.

Moore, Janet, "Hearing-Aid Maker GN ReSound Growing Quietly," *4Hearingloss.com,* April 18, 2005.

"New Leadership at ReSound and Otometrics," *Hearing Review,* March 2008, p. 12.

Greater Washington Educational Telecommunication Association

2775 South Quincy Street
Arlington, Virginia 22206
U.S.A.
Telephone: (703) 998-2600
Fax: (703) 998-3401
Web site: http://www.weta.org

■ ■ ■

Nonprofit Corporation
Incorporated: 1953 as Greater Washington Educational Television Association
Employees: 236
Operating Revenues: $87.34 million (2007)
NAICS: 515100 Radio and Television Broadcasting

■ ■ ■

Greater Washington Educational Telecommunication Association (GWETA), based in Arlington, Virginia, is a nonprofit company that operates Public Broadcasting Service WETA-TV channel 26 and National Public Radio station WETA-FM 90.9, serving the greater Washington, D.C., community. The organization also maintains web sites for both broadcasters as well as four television digital subchannels: WETA HD, airing WETA programming in high definition; WETA Create, focusing on travel, cooking, and how-to programming; WETA Kids Channel, offering a 24-hour schedule of family fare; and The WETA Channel, focusing on public affairs programming, news, and documentaries. In addition, WETA is a major producer of PBS programming, including *The NewsHour with Jim Lehrer,* *Washington Week with Gwen Ifill & National Journal,*

The Kennedy Center Presents, and coproducer with Ken Burns of his documentary series. WETA also serves an educational mission through children's learning and development programs, including WETA's Reading Rockets program, funded by the U.S. Department of Education to improve reading proficiency across the country; WETA's Ready to Learn program, which trains adults to make use of WETA-TV programming to improve school readiness of Greater Washington children; and WETA's LD Online web site, providing online information and support related to children with learning disabilities.

PUBLIC TELEVISION TAKES SHAPE IN POST–WORLD WAR II AMERICA

The emergence of television in the United States was interrupted by World War II, but soon after the war ended in 1945 and the U.S. economy enjoyed a boom following a brief postwar recession, commercial enterprises began a stampede for television broadcasting licenses. The crush was so great that many stations sharing the same channel interfered with one another's signals, and in 1948 the Federal Communications Commission (FCC) implemented a four-year freeze on new licenses in order to determine how to increase the number of available channels, which at the time was limited to a dozen, two through 13 (channel 1 had been assigned for land-mobile use). Groups that wanted to make use of television for public and educational purposes took advantage of that respite to lobby the FCC, which in 1952 agreed to reserve 242 television stations for educational purposes, albeit many of them were on the new bank of ultrahigh frequency (UHF) channels, 14 to 83, that most televisions could not yet receive, and even when converters became available the picture was poor. In Washington, D.C., channel 26 was allocated for educational television.

To develop programming for channel 26, Greater Washington Educational Television Association was formed in 1953 by a group of educators and cultural leaders. The driving force behind the organization was Elizabeth Pfohl Campbell. Born in 1902 and raised in the Moravian faith, Campbell was a longtime educator. After earning an undergraduate degree from Salem College and a master's from Columbia University and further study at the University of Pennsylvania and the University of Michigan, she was named dean at the Moravian College for Women in Bethlehem, Pennsylvania, when she was just 25 years of age, and was later named dean of Mary Baldwin College in Staunton, Virginia. After marrying attorney Ed Campbell she moved to Arlington, Virginia, began raising a family, twin boys, and soon became concerned about her children's education. She cofounded the Rock Spring Cooperative Nursery School in Arlington, and then, dissatisfied with the public school, she enrolled her sons in the private National Cathedral School, paying for it by teaching two classes of Latin. Rather than simply ignore Arlington's public schools, she ran and was elected to the school board in 1947, becoming the only woman in the state to serve on a school board.

CAMPBELL RECOGNIZES TELEVISION'S POWER TO TEACH

Campbell had been aware of the power of television since 1941 when her boys watched *Howdy Doody* with the son of a neighbor that owned one of the early television sets. "I found out from my experience that they wanted to buy everything that had been advertised around *Howdy Doody* and that they could recount for me the story,' Campbell recalled in a 1993 interview with *Current.* "The two things that are important in education are: first, information and second, motivation. Both of these they were getting from television." As a

member of the Arlington school board she saw television as a possible tool to address some of the inadequacies in the school, in particular music and fine arts. It was with this in mind that she helped organize GWETA and spearheaded its development. In 1957 she was elected GWETA's president.

When Campbell took charge of GWETA its purpose was to produce television programs for the schools, which determined what subjects they wanted covered and provided the teachers. Campbell canvassed 11 schools who told her that they needed a science enrichment program, and with a grant from the Meyer Foundation, GWETA developed a show called *Time for Science,* which featured a classroom teacher, T. Darrell Drummond, offering science lessons and conducting experiments with schoolchildren. Because channel 26 was not operational and even if it were, few television sets in the area could receive the signal, the program would have to be broadcast on one of the three commercial television stations in the area. Washington's WTTG channel 5 finally agreed, but only if GWETA agreed to pay the costs of production. In addition, the organization had to allow a commercial to lead into the program. The station manager planned on an ad promoting the Living Bra, but finally settled on a milk commercial at the suggestion of Campbell. All told, it cost $30,000 to produce the 30-minute *Time for Science* in a makeshift studio in the Raleigh Hotel. It ran from 1958 to 1961.

ACTIVATION OF WETA: 1961

After Campbell submitted the necessary paperwork, GWETA received a license from the FCC to activate channel 26 in October 1961. With a $75,000 equipment grant, a $175,000 pledge from the schools, and a staff of eight, the new station established a studio in a converted shop room at Yorktown High School in Arlington, Virginia. Broadcasting under the call letters WETA, it went on the air for the first time on October 2, 1961, relying on a former WTTG transmitter. By early 1963 GWETA was serving 18 area school systems five days a week, offering a selection of science, mathematics, art, music, geography, and language programs from 9 A.M. to 3 P.M. on weekdays during the school year. The station would then go dark until the early evening when programming for children was shown, followed by adult fare later at night.

WETA was very much a shoestring operation, with business functions carried out in Campbell's home. GWETA's days as a school program feeder soon came to an end. Virginia and Maryland began receiving programming from their state public broadcast stations. The District of Columbia schools had never participated

KEY DATES

1953: Greater Washington Educational Television Association is formed.
1961: WETA-TV begins broadcasting.
1967: *Washington Week in Review* debuts.
1970: WETA-FM radio station is launched; company is renamed Greater Washington Educational Telecommunication Association.
1972: Broadcast facilities open in Arlington, Virginia.
1981: Annual Capital Fourth program begins.
1990: *The Civil War* documentary debuts.
1992: WETA pioneers high definition television.
2001: Reading Rockets program begins.
2004: Founder Elizabeth P. Campbell dies at age 101.

with GWETA, and as a result, much of the organization's financial support dried up. In addition to foundations, WETA began seeking support from the public in 1963. The creation of the Corporation for Public Broadcasting in 1967 added federal funds to the coffers. As for programming, WETA carried shows produced by National Educational Television in New York, sent by plane on tape for broadcast. To fill the daytime hours that had once offered school programming, WETA focused on a preschool audience and began airing *Sesame Street* and *Mister Rogers*.

WETA was forced to move out of the classroom it occupied at Yorktown High, which needed the space to accommodate the community's rising population. The station moved to a small studio offered by American University, and then found more permanent accommodations in 1964 when Howard University made an abandoned gymnasium available. Not only did the station receive much needed studio space, it was able to pay the rent by providing Howard students with television training. In that same year a WETA production won the station's first Emmy award: *English—Fact and Fancy*, a humorous take on ordinary speech hosted by linguist James Bostain. With its new facility, WETA was also able in 1966 to add weekends to its schedule. A year later the station began producing *Washington Week in Review*, a journalist roundtable to discuss news of national importance. It would be picked up by PBS, becoming the first station-produced program to be selected for national distribution, and in 1969 WETA received $750,000 in funding from the Ford Foundation to attract journalists.

ADDITION OF RADIO STATION: 1970

In 1970 GWETA expanded beyond television when it launched a radio station that combined news and a variety of music, including classical, jazz, and folk. The addition of the radio station necessitated a change in the name of the parent organization, which was rechristened Greater Washington Educational Telecommunication Association. When Howard University decided to build its own television station, steps were taken to move out of the Howard gymnasium into a new office and production headquarters located in the Shirlington section of Arlington that opened in 1972. Just prior to the move, in 1971, Campbell stepped down as president, but she stayed on as vice-president for community affairs, serving as the liaison between the station and its viewers while never accepting a salary. Mrs. C., as she was known, continued to keep close tabs on the station. Her office located near the restrooms insured she interacted with staff members on a regular basis. She remained the head of community affairs until January 2004 when she died at the age of 101.

With its new facilities WETA was able to expand its production efforts. In 1973 WETA received accolades for its live gavel-to-gavel coverage of the Senate Committee Watergate hearings provided to PBS stations across the country, followed by the impeachment hearings of President Richard Nixon. In 1976 the station joined forces with New York's WNET to coproduce the *MacNeil-Lehrer Report*, now known as *The NewsHour with Jim Lehrer*. The 1970s also saw WETA begin raising funds from the public through pledge week activities.

More production credits were to follow in the years to come. In 1981 WETA broadcast *A Capitol Fourth*, a concert from the West Lawn of the U.S. Capitol building, which featured celebrity performers and a fireworks display on the National Mall. The show became a popular annual event for PBS stations. The 1980s also saw a relationship forged with Ken Burns, as WETA coproduced the filmmaker's epic documentary *The Civil War*. The 11-hour series was shown on five consecutive nights in September 1990, drawing 40 million viewers to make it the most watched program in PBS history. It would remain popular for many years to come. Other coproductions between WETA and Burns would follow as well.

WETA PIONEERS HDTV: 1992

WETA was also an innovator on the technology front, becoming a pioneer in high-definition television (HDTV). In 1992 the station broadcast the first over-the-air HDTV signal in the United States, showing a 12-minute 1,050-line video that was transmitted from WETA's suburban Maryland transmitter to an antenna mounted on the U.S. Capitol building some ten miles away. Later in the decade WETA built an HDTV broadcast facility and a year later began testing a full-power HDTV transmitter. HDTV broadcasts were then showcased to the public in 1999. Simultaneous broadcasts of standard-definition analog and HDTV digital were made available to allow television retailers to provide side-by-side demonstrations. In the meantime WETA also pursued digital television, setting up an experimental DTV transmitter and receiving FCC permission in 1996 to air DTV signals on channel 34. In 1996 WETA-TV and KCTS-TV in Seattle formed the Public Television Digital Alliance to accelerate the introduction of digital television to public broadcasting.

WETA was also quick to embrace the Internet, in 1995 becoming one of the first PBS stations to launch a web site. In that same year, GWETA acquired the CapAccess interactive computer network, which was used to help connect public schools, public libraries, as well as local government agencies to the Internet. GWETA also leveraged the Internet for national education projects. LD Online was established in 1996 to provide information and advice regarding learning disabilities and ADHD.

WETA-TV produced a wide variety of television programming in the 1990s, including *National Geographic, In Performance, The Kennedy Center Presents,* and *Nova* specials, as well as interviews with major newsmakers. in the *Talking with David Frost* series. The station also took advantage of its location to cover important congressional proceedings, including the Whitewater Hearings, the Waco Hearings, terrorism hearings, and a number of confirmation hearings. New Ken Burns documentaries were also coproduced, including series on the history of baseball, Thomas Jefferson, Lewis and Clark, Frank Lloyd Wright, and the story of Elizabeth Cady Stanton and Susan B. Anthony.

GWETA and its units remained in the forefront of media development as the new century dawned. The Reading Rockets program was launched in 2001, providing a multimedia approach to helping young children learn to read. Two years later Colorin Colorado was spun off, offering a free web-based service to help Spanish-speaking families of English-language learners. WETA-TV became one of the first television stations in the United States to offer digital subchannels. Three years earlier WETA had attempted to launch a new public affairs channel but had to shelve the idea because it was unable to receive enough carriage commitments

from Comcast Corp., the largest cable operator in the area. The new digital subchannels included WETA Prime, WETA Plus, and WETA Kids. After PBS closed PBS You and PBS Kids, the subchannel lineup was revamped in 2006 to include WETA Create, WETA Family, and WETA Kids.

WETA-TV also remained a major producing station for PBS. The *America at a Crossroads* series was introduced and *American Masters, Kennedy Center,* and *In Performance* programs continued, as did Ken Burns, who contributed *Jazz* in 2001, a documentary on Mark Twain in 2001, *The Rise and Fall of Jack Johnson* in 2004, and in 2007 *The War,* a documentary that focused on the home front during World War II. More programming was also in development. Burns was slated to present *Baseball: The Tenth Inning,* an update and follow-up to his previous work on baseball. Burns also had a series in development on the people behind the U.S. National Parks. Other WETA-produced shows underway included *Circus,* a reality show following the Big Apple Circus, and the documentary *Faith and America's Founders,* exploring the religious background of the country's founders and how their beliefs impacted the development of the United States.

Ed Dinger

PRINCIPAL SUBSIDIARIES

WETA-TV; WETA-FM.

PRINCIPAL COMPETITORS

WJLA-TV; WRC; WUSA; WUPN; WNVC.

FURTHER READING

Bernstein, Adam, "WETA Founder Elizabeth Campbell Dies at 101," *Washington Post,* January 10, 2004, p. B1.

Brennan, Patricia, "Elizabeth Pfohl Campbell; A TV Pioneer: WETA's Founder, Grande Dame," *Washington Post,* October 22, 1989, p. Y07.

Gould, Jack, "Education TV to Undergo Major Restructuring," *New York Times,* October 10, 1969, p. 95.

Halonen, Doug, "D.C. Public Affairs Channel Plan Dead," *Electronic Media,* November 15, 1999, p. 41.

"'I Didn't Have Time to Have Doubts,'" *Current,* February 15, 1993.

Lambert, Peter, "By HDTV's Early Light," *Broadcasting,* March 30, 1992, p. 10.

Przybyla, Heidi, "Restructured WETA Wants More Money," *Washington Business Journal,* May 15, 1998, p. 3.

The Grocers Supply Co., Inc.

───────■───────

3131 East Holcombe Boulevard
Houston, Texas 77021-2199
U.S.A.
Telephone: (713) 747-5000
Fax: (713) 746-5611
Web site: http://www.grocerssupply.com

Private Company
Incorporated: 1923
Employees: 8,900
Sales: $2.72 billion (2007)
NAICS: 424410 General Line Grocery Merchant
　　Wholesalers

■ ■ ■

The Grocers Supply Co., Inc., is a privately held grocery wholesaler based in Houston, Texas, operating in a 350-mile radius of the city, including parts of five states. The company serves 650 grocery stores, including a pair of ethnic supermarket chains it owns: Fiesta Mart, with about 50 stores, mostly in Houston; and the 37 units of Minyard Food Stores Inc., which includes about two dozen Carnival Super Market stores, as well as several stores flying the Minyard banner and about ten Sack 'n Save warehouse operations. Grocers Supply provides retail customers with a number of private brands in partnership with the Federated Group, including the Good Sense, Better Valu, Parade, VIP, and 3 Ring brands. A subsidiary, Grocers Supply Produce Company, supplies fresh produce and related items to supermarkets, while sister companies, Quality Banana

and C&M Potato Prepack, focus on the distribution of bananas and potatoes, respectively.

Grocers Supply also owns a subsidiary to serve non-supermarket customers. The Grocers Supply Institutional and Convenience unit (GSIC) serves about 1,200 convenience stores and drugstores in Texas and Louisiana, supplying them with grocery items as well as cigarettes, candy, beverages, and other merchandise. GSIC also serves about 200 schools, providing them with menu items for breakfast and lunch programs. Another subsidiary, GSC International, supplies oil company operations, U.S. embassies, and other international customers. In addition, Grocers Supply maintains a real estate division and a printing service unit to print advertising circulars for its retail customers. The company maintains a distribution center about 750,000 square feet in size, plus a cooler-freezer facility and four satellite warehouses in Houston, as well as a delivery fleet of more than 200 tractors and more than 700 trailers. The company is owned and managed by the family of its founder.

FOUNDER: RUSSIAN BORN, LATE 19TH CENTURY

Grocers Supply's founder, Joe Levit, was born in Russia in the late 1800s and immigrated to the United States at the age of 16 in 1914. According to family lore he had just $7 in his pockets when he arrived. In typical rags-to-riches fashion, Levit worked hard, attending school while taking on a part-time job at the Magnolia Paper Company, where in time he became a stenographer. In 1917 he entered the grocery business, purchasing a grocery store located at the corner of Winter and Colorado streets in Houston. He would eventually sell this store and buy another one in town before deciding to turn his attention to the wholesale business.

Houston did not lack grocery suppliers. About a dozen companies vied for the business of area retailers, but Levit knew from direct experience as a grocer that independent stores were poorly served by these suppliers. In 1923 he turned over the management of his store to his wife, Dora, and set up a wholesale operation, Grocers Supply Co., in a 7,500-square-foot building he leased, conveniently located on Houston's Produce Row, a two-block portion of Commerce Avenue near Market Square. In the early decades of the 1900s a number of produce houses had set up shop in this area to import fruits and vegetables for distribution to Houston grocers.

Levit's instincts proved correct, and he developed enough customers that after five years he was employing more than 40 people and operating a fleet of ten trucks to make deliveries throughout Houston. Having outgrown his warehouse, Levit moved to a larger Commerce Avenue facility. Located close to the bayou, the warehouse was damaged by the flood of 1936, prompting another change of address. This time the company relocated to a new three-story building at the corner of Commerce and Jackson Street, several blocks from the original Produce Row. Grocers Supply continued to grow, despite the Great Depression, and eventually moved across the street to an even larger, more modern facility.

COMPANY MOVES: 1956

Levit was joined by his sons Milton, Max, and George in the post–World War II economic boom years. The business thrived and in 1956 the operation was moved to Holcombe Boulevard, which remained its location into the 21st century. With ample room for growth, the facility would be expanded a number of times, eventually to almost 750,000 square feet in size. In 1983

Grocers Supply added a 105,000-square-foot cooler-freezer facility across the street. It too would be expanded, eventually exceeding 210,000 square feet in size. Smaller satellite warehouses were also added in Houston, including one distribution center the company picked up from the Eagle Supermarket chain when that retailer exited the fiercely competitive Houston market in 1985.

The Levit family kept its business dealings closely guarded, but according to *Forbes* magazine, Grocers Supply employed 1,100 people and was doing about $1 billion in annual business in 1990, putting it in the top 400 largest private companies in the United States. For decades Grocers Supply, like hundreds of wholesalers across the country, followed a business model that focused on pure logistics, receiving supplies and distributing them efficiently to supermarket clients. In the 1990s that approach began to become obsolete as competition in the grocery business intensified. A harbinger of what was to come took place in Houston in 1991 when the parent company for the southwestern-based Stop N Go convenience store chain filed for Chapter 11 bankruptcy protection. Beset with stiff competition and a recession, the chain was unable to stay profitable, leaving Grocers Supply holding $7.3 million in debt.

LATE-CENTURY SUPERMARKET CONSOLIDATION AFFECTS WHOLESALERS

Consolidation in the supermarket field in the 1990s greatly thinned the ranks of independent grocers and created larger regional and national chains, who increasingly began to establish their own buying and distribution networks. The reduced need for wholesalers to serve this market began to shrink their numbers also, as they either fell by the wayside or combined with other firms to create larger, more efficient operations. Unlike the systems and distribution centers created by the supermarket chains, however, the wholesalers could not take full advantage of new business practices and technologies because the stores they served lacked common ownership and therefore lacked common systems to exploit. To make matters worse, Wal-Mart, which had always been self-distributing, expanded into the food business. Supermarket chains and independents alike had to contend with a retailing behemoth, leading to further consolidation as chains sought to grow ever larger, and independents and smaller chains, unable to make it alone, sold out.

As Grocers Supply entered the new century, there continued to be a need for wholesalers, but in order to remain successful, they had to offer more than the mere

KEY DATES

1917: Joe Levit opens grocery store in Houston.
1923: Levit establishes Grocers Supply.
1956: New headquarters opens.
1983: Cooler-freezer facility opens across the street from main distribution facility.
2000: Handy Andy stores are acquired.
2004: Fiesta Mart chain is acquired.
2008: Company buys assets from Minyard Food Stores.

consolidation of shipments. To serve the new marketplace they had to help customers with value-added services such as marketing by gathering and analyzing product information data so that retailers could increase sales and margins. In some cases, wholesalers also had to acquire struggling customers in order to keep their business.

In 2000 Grocers Supply began returning to its retailing roots when a San Antonio-based customer, the Handy Andy grocery store chain, lapsed into bankruptcy. Handy Andy actually began in Miami, Florida, in the 1920s, but in the wake of a hurricane it moved to San Antonio. The chain thrived until the 1970s, when it underwent a bankruptcy, but rebounded and in the 1980s emerged as one of the United States' largest Hispanic-owned companies. The business declined steadily through the remainder of the century, however. Handy Andy found it increasingly difficult to compete against larger chains, which could leverage their scale to offer lower prices. Moreover, high interest and lease rates crippled Handy Andy, the ownership of which changed hands twice in the 1990s. The chain tried to expand in 2000 by acquiring a pair of stores, but not only was it a matter of too little, too late, it was more than the parent company, H.A. Assets Inc., could afford. Later that year it defaulted on a $12 million loan to Grocers Supply, the chain's wholesaler, which took control of the chain in November 2000. A subsidiary, Bexar County Markets, was formed to manage Handy Andy. Improvements were made to some stores, but many units were simply closed. In another foray into retailing, in 2002 Grocers Supply bought four Albertsons stores, which were then leased back to Food Town.

ACQUISITION OF FLEMING COMPANIES' ASSETS: 2003

Simply taking over struggling customers was far from a foolproof formula of success for wholesalers, witness the

plight of Dallas-based distributor Fleming Companies. In the 1990s it had to contend with the loss of a major customer, the Albertsons supermarket chain, which opted to become self-distributing. Fleming responded by acquiring discount supermarket chains and landing a major distribution deal with Kmart to supply Super Kmart Centers with groceries in Fleming's area of operation. In 2002 the company added a convenience store distribution business. Fleming clearly had size. Doing $20 billion in business, it was one of the largest wholesalers in the country, but after cutting ties with Kmart and saddled with underperforming supermarkets, the company was forced into Chapter 11 bankruptcy protection in 2003. Without a line of credit in hand, however, Fleming fell into a death spiral rather than being able to use Chapter 11 protection to reorganize. Unable to pay its bills, the company inflated deductions to their invoices, resulting in suppliers cutting back on deliveries, making it impossible for Fleming to adequately conduct business. As a result, management had no choice but to put its assets up for sale. Grocers Supply was one of the buyers, acquiring a distribution center in Garland, Texas. Grocers Supply sold the Garland facility, more interested in the 100 accounts it inherited from Fleming.

Grocers Supply's next step in adding a retail element to its business came in 2004 when it acquired one of its customers, the 50-unit Fiesta Mart chain, with 34 of the units located in Houston. Primarily, the move was a defensive action. A major self-distributing supermarket chain was looking to buy Fiesta, which had been put up for sale, and Grocers Supply did not want to lose the business. Nevertheless, Fiesta was a good fit for the wholesaler. The chain had been established by Donald Bonham and O. C. Mendenhall in Houston in 1972 to serve the city's Hispanic population. Although neither man was Hispanic, Bonham was well familiar with the customer base, having supervised the development of a supermarket chain in Chile. Supposedly, the two men were unable to decide on the name of their first store and simply chose "Fiesta" because they spotted a sign bearing that word on a vacant building. They bought the sign and Fiesta Mart was born. What made the acquisition of the chain more than palatable to Grocers Supply was that it served a niche, ethnic market and was less threatened by the larger supermarket chains. Moreover, Grocers Supply had the capital necessary to invest in Fiesta, grow the chain, and thereby create business for its wholesale operation.

ACQUISITION OF MINYARD FOOD STORES' ASSETS: 2008

Although the Fiesta acquisition grew out of necessity, the next acquisition of a retail operation was by choice.

In 2008 Grocers Supply solidified its presence in the Hispanic food market by acquiring stores from Minyard Food Stores Inc. The 37 stores in the Minyard deal included 23 Carnival Super Market stores, one Sack 'n Save warehouse-format store, and five Minyard stores. The chain had experienced some financial difficulty but was well established in its markets, in particular Dallas and its growing Hispanic population. Adjusting to the new realities of its business by embracing niche opportunities, Grocers Supply appeared to be well positioned to remain a viable wholesaler for years to come.

Ed Dinger

PRINCIPAL SUBSIDIARIES

C&M Potato Prepack; Grocers Supply Institutional and Convenience; Grocers Supply Produce Company; Quality Banana; GSC International.

PRINCIPAL COMPETITORS

GSC Enterprises, Inc.; McLane Company, Inc.; Nash-Finch Company.

FURTHER READING

"Houston-Based Supply Firm Takes Over San Antonio, Texas-based Grocery Chains," *San Antonio Express-News,* December 6, 2000.

Howell, Debbie, "Candy Update," *DSN Retailing Today,* September 20, 2004, p. 16.

Huddleston, Scott, "Then & Now: Casualty of 'Food Wars,'" *San Antonio Express-News,* December 4, 2005, p. 2B.

Kaplan, David, "Grocers Supply Bags Fiesta," *Houston Chronicle,* August 26, 2004, p. A1.

———, "Newly Bought Texas Grocery Chain Fiesta Likely to Stick with Its Philosophy," *Houston Chronicle,* August 27, 2004.

Karolefski, John, "The Domino Effect," *Food Logistics,* September 15, 2003, p. 31.

———, "Ready for Retail," *Food Logistics,* September 15, 2004, p. 36.

Shlachter, Barry, "Ethnic-Oriented Houston Grocery Chain Is Bought by Supplier in Defensive Move," *Fort Worth Star-Telegram,* August 27, 2004.

Wollam, Allison, "Grocers Supply Digs Deeper into Dallas Market with Minyard Buy," *Houston Business Journal,* August 4, 2008.

Zuñiga, Jo Ann, "Levit, 80, a Grocery Wholesaler," *Houston Chronicle,* June 27, 2004, p. 31.

Gruma, S.A.B. de C.V.

Calzada del Valle 407 Oriente
Colonia del Valle
San Pedro Garza García, Nuevo León 66220
Mexico
Telephone: (+52-81) 8399-3300
Fax: (+52-81) 8335-9900
Web site: http://www.gruma.com

Public Company
Founded: 1949
Incorporated: 1971
Employees: 12,384
Sales: MXN 44.79 billion ($3.24 billion) (2008)
Stock Exchanges: Bolsa Mexicana de Valores New York
Ticker Symbol: GRUMAB (Bolsa Mexicana); GMK (New York)
NAICS: 311211 Flour Milling; 311830 Tortilla Manufacturing; 311919 Other Snack Food Manufacturing; 551112 Offices of Other Holding Companies

■ ■ ■

Gruma, S.A.B. de C.V. is a holding company based in Mexico whose operating subsidiaries collectively rank as the world's leading producer of corn flour and corn tortillas. The publicly traded Grupo Industrial Maseca S.A.B. de C.V. (Gimsa), which is 83 percent owned by Gruma, is the largest corn miller in Mexico and is well known for its flagship Maseca corn tortillas. About 24 percent of Gruma's revenues are attributable to Gimsa. Gruma generates nearly half of its sales from Gruma Corporation, its wholly owned U.S. subsidiary, which produces corn flour, Mission and Guerrero brand corn and wheat tortillas and tortilla chips, and Maseca brand tortillas and tortilla chips. Mission is positioned as the firm's national U.S. brand for the general consumer market, while Guerrero is targeted at the U.S. Hispanic market. Gruma Corporation also holds an 80 percent stake in Azteca Milling, L.P., a U.S.-based corn miller 20 percent owned by food processing and distribution giant Archer Daniels Midland Company (ADM). Gruma and ADM are also involved in a Mexican wheat-milling joint venture. Additionally, Gruma Corporation has begun to penetrate the European market with the opening of a tortilla plant in Coventry, England, and the purchases of a corn flour plant in Italy, a tortilla plant in the Netherlands, and a Newscastle, England-based manufacturer of tortillas and other flat breads. Other Gruma, S.A.B. de C.V. subsidiaries produce corn flour, tortillas, and tortilla chips in Central America, Venezuela, China, Malaysia, and Australia. Gruma's founder, Roberto González Barrera, and other family members own about 56 percent of Gruma's stock, while ADM maintains a stake in Gruma of around 23 percent.

A DRY PROCESS FOR MAKING TORTILLAS

The humble tortilla, essentially a corn pancake that also doubles as a sandwich-like wrapper for a variety of fillings, is a staple of the Mexican diet. For at least 1,000 years the making of tortillas involved husking ears of corn, boiling the kernels in water to which lime has been added, and then forming a patty of the wet dough and placing it in a flat earthenware pan for frying. Unfortunately, the traditional tortilla becomes stale a mere four or five hours after frying.

In 1949 Roberto M. González and his son, Roberto González Barrera, established a plant producing 15 tons of corn flour a month in Cerralvo, a community in the state of Nuevo León. Only 18 at the time, González Barrera had dropped out of school at 11 and was a traveling salesman for Mexico's largest industrial enterprise, Petróleos Mexicanos (Pemex), before going into business for himself. After years in the corn flour business, during which they researched and tested new technologies, González Barrera and his associate Manuel Jesús Rubio took out a patent, in 1965, on an improved tortilla apparatus and production method. At the beginning of 1971 González's enterprise consisted of seven plants. Although widely known as Maseca ("dry dough") for the brand name of its product, the company's name was Gruma (an acronym for Grupo Maseca).

The Maseca process of preparing the raw material for a tortilla consisted of boiling corn for 30 minutes, drying the kernels instantly by injections of hot air, and milling them into flour prior to humidifying the product into a mass suitable for making tortillas. This had certain advantages over the traditional wet dough prepared by thousands of small shops as well as millions of homemakers. Not only was the Maseca product more sanitary and uniform in quality, it had a longer shelf life. Moreover, Gruma's machines were better than the ones already in existence, which made only 30 to 40 tortillas per minute. Gruma's machines were not only faster, they used less water and fuel per tortilla and made 20 percent more tortillas per kilogram of corn.

Gruma collaborated with research groups in the design of plant and equipment processes and products. Elektra Good Machinery Co. began making the machines in 1976 and also was responsible for roasting, frying, packing, mixing, and cutting. Enrichment of Maseca corn flour with vitamins and proteins began in

the 1970s at the San José, Costa Rica, tortilla plant Gruma had established in 1972. The largest such facility in the world, the plant also converted soy meal to protein.

According to the Mexican weekly *Proceso,* González Barrera enjoyed political support from General Bonifacio Salinas Leal, a governor of Nuevo León, and Raúl Salinas Lozano, minister of trade and industry from 1958 to 1964, who extended loans and special permits during this period. However, González later told Jorge Monjaras of the Mexican business magazine *Expansión* that he was handicapped by heavy government regulation of the tortilla industry. "One couldn't just open a mill," he complained, adding, "One had to obtain permission, and production was limited by a quota. Similarly, one couldn't just open a tortilla shop anywhere. A certain number of inhabitants were required for each store." Selling the product directly to homes was forbidden. Existing artisanal tortilla producers stifled potential competition through these means, with the help of allies in the nation's ruling Institutional Revolutionary party.

In spite of these restraints, Gruma was 46th in size among reporting Mexican companies in 1979, with sales of MXN 4.16 billion ($183.9 million), compared to MXN 1.65 billion ($72.2 million) in 1977. By this time its annual production was 750,000 tons of flour. Gruma also opened its first U.S. plant in 1977 in Canoga Park, California, and began marketing tortillas, tortilla chips, and taco shells under the Mission Foods name. Automatic International Corp. was Gruma's research and development company in the United States, while Asesoria de Empresas S.A. was the Mexican subsidiary established in 1979 to provide the others with technical, financial, commercial, and administrative assistance. There were 16 affiliated companies in 1978 and a total of 8,500 employees. The 12 plants in Mexico included one that produced air conditioners. In 1982 Gruma established its first corn flour mill in the United States, located in Edinburg, Texas.

GIANT STRIDES FORWARD

The main Mexican subsidiary, Grupo Industrial Maseca, S.A. (Gimsa), tripled in sales in real terms between 1987 and 1989 and became a public subsidiary in 1990, selling 15 percent of its shares and using the proceeds to add three more plants. Another 7 percent of the company was quickly sold in two secondary offerings. The three new plants raised Gimsa's production from 1.2 million to 1.65 million tons of flour. By the end of the year Gimsa held 61 percent of the Mexican market for industrialized corn flour. Nevertheless, 73 percent of

KEY DATES

1949: Roberto González Barrera and his father open a corn flour plant in the Mexican state of Nuevo León.

1972: Gruma establishes the world's largest tortilla factory, in San José, Costa Rica.

1977: The company's first plant in the United States is opened, in Canoga Park, California.

1990: Gruma takes its main Mexican subsidiary, Grupo Industrial Maseca S.A. (Gimsa), public.

1992: Gruma goes public.

1996: Archer-Daniels-Midland Company (ADM) buys a 22 percent stake in Gruma; the two firms also form two joint ventures.

2000: Company begins penetrating the European market with the opening of a tortilla factory in Coventry, England.

2006: Gruma opens its first plant in China, located in Shanghai.

the nation's tortillas still were being made by the traditional wet dough method.

Gruma was at this time a privately owned conglomerate of 80 companies engaged in a host of activities, including the fabrication of machinery for the food sector, the development of technology for the corn industry, and the Mexican operation of fast-food restaurant chains such as Burger Boy and Pizza Hut. It had also opened a tortilla plant in Honduras in 1987.

Gruma became a public company in 1992, and its shares began trading on the Mexican stock exchange in 1994. González Barrera became director in 1992 of the Banco Mercantil del Norte (Banorte), which was privatized after a decade in government hands. Gruma acquired 10 percent of the bank's shares. The company discontinued its operations in the fast-food restaurant business in 1994. It had in the meantime, in 1993, expanded its core corn flour/tortilla business into El Salvador, Guatemala, and Venezuela.

Of Gruma's 1990 sales of about $800 million, $220 million were in the United States. In 1991 Gruma Corporation, the U.S. subsidiary, was operating 12 plants in five states. By 1994 Gruma Corp. accounted for almost 40 percent of the parent company's revenue. Sales consisted of corn flour, tortillas, snack foods, and bakery products sold under the brand names Mission and Guerrero. Mission, a more upscale brand, made

packaged tortillas and served institutional customers such as Taco Bell, which was buying one-third of its taco shells. (Guerrero Foods, a Los Angeles-based company, had been purchased by Gruma in 1988.)

Still, González Barrera was not satisfied with the results his firm had achieved in the United States. "In that country there's lots of discrimination," he told an *Expansión* reporter in 1994. "We struggle to win the confidence of supermarkets, to prove that we're as good as other suppliers," he added.

In Mexico, Gruma benefited greatly from support by Carlos Salinas de Gortari, who was president from 1988 to 1994. In 1990 the Mexican government committed itself to promoting the substitution of corn flour for dough in the production of tortillas. Conasupo, the government agency that distributed basic foods, resolved that the following year, in any part of Mexico where new corn flour plants were built, it would phase out its program of supplying millers of corn for traditionally made tortillas with cheap corn. If the millers paid the higher market price, the ministry of commerce said it would not let them pass on the higher price to consumers. Furthermore, according to a 1996 *New York Times* article, millers who still refused to convert corn to flour received strictly limited amounts of Conasupo's worst corn. Seven thousand Mexican tortilla-making shops closed between 1993 and 1995.

At the same time, government subsidies to Gruma grew. According to *Proceso,* between 1989 and 1992 producers of corn received subsidies of more than $7 billion. Because Gimsa and other millers were the ones who had to pay the growers the government-guaranteed price of corn, higher than the international market price, and were required to sell to tortilla producers at a fixed price, they went to the government for the difference as a rebate, which in 1992 represented about 35 percent of Gimsa's MXN 1.93 billion ($492.6 million) in revenue. This subsidy grew to 43 percent of Gimsa's revenue in 1994. Practically the only flour making alternative to Gimsa was Miconsa, a poorly run public enterprise that was later privatized. By this time Gonzalez was a billionaire; his net worth was estimated at $1.7 billion in 1997.

To *Proceso* and other critics of the Mexican government and ruling party, the tortilla policy was a prime examples of *amiguismo,* the Mexican version of crony capitalism. González Barrera had come to the aid of Raúl Salinas Lozano, father of the president, when he fell into disgrace in the 1970s. Moreover, he was related by marriage to Carlos Hank González, secretary of agriculture in the Salinas administration. In 1996, after the end of Salinas's term in office, the Mexican government imposed quotas on sales of subsidized corn in order to combat fraud and waste. Corn subsidies and tortilla price controls were phased out during 1998 and eliminated at the end of the year.

ALLIANCE WITH ARCHER-DANIELS-MIDLAND

U.S.-based Archer-Daniels-Midland Company (ADM) purchased a 22 percent stake in Gruma for $258 million in 1996. The transaction also established two joint ventures. Azteca Milling, L.P., 80 percent owned by Gruma, the largest corn flour producer in the United States, combined the U.S. corn flour operations of both companies, representing about 25 percent of the U.S. market. Gruma Corp. was running the biggest tortilla factory in the world in the Los Angeles area, with the capability of making 800,000 tortillas per hour.

The other joint venture, Molinera de México, S.A. de C.V., involved two new wheat flour mills that ADM had opened in Mexico. The share split for this venture was 60 percent to Gruma and 40 to ADM. The alliance with ADM gave Gruma the technology and financial backing to break into Mexico's $1.5 billion per year wheat flour and bread market, dominated by Grupo Bimbo, S.A. de C.V., which held about 95 percent of the nation's packaged bread market. By the fall of 1997, Molinera de México had acquired three more mills and two wheat flour brands and was scheduled to provide the flour for a bread plant to open in Monterrey.

Gruma Corp. had sales of MXN 6.62 billion ($670 million) in 1998, with 12 tortilla plants and five corn flour plants in the United States. The company held 83 percent of the U.S. corn flour market under the Maseca label and 24 percent of the tortilla market under the Mission and Guerrero labels. At the beginning of 1999 it acquired four more tortilla producing plants. Gimsa, in the meantime, had 18 corn flour plants in Mexico in 1998. The parent company's sales from this 71 percent owned subsidiary came to MXN 5.07 billion ($512.7 million). The corn flour industry had a 47 percent market share in the production of tortillas in Mexico (excluding self-production), of which Gimsa's share came to 69 percent.

Gruma Centro America had five corn flour plants and five other plants in 1998, including a bread factory and two bakeries opened in San José, Costa Rica, in 1995. Products included packaged bread and tortillas, tortilla chips, and pastries as well as corn flour. Sales in 1998 came to slightly more than MXN 1 billion ($101 million). In August 1999 Gruma purchased the Venezuelan operations of International Multifoods Corporation, Molinos Nacionales, C.A., which included facilities producing wheat and corn flour, for $94 million.

Molinera de México, the parent company's 60 percent owned joint venture, had seven wheat flour mills, 9 percent of the Mexican wheat flour market, and 1998 sales of MXN 791 million (about $80 million). Productos y Distribuidora Azteca, manufacturer and marketer of packaged corn and wheat tortillas under the Mission label, introduced in 1994, and bread under the Breddy brand, had three tortilla plants and one bread plant. By 1999 Gruma claimed to have captured a 12 percent share of the bread market in northern Mexico with the Breddy brand. The Gruma empire also included tortilla machines and related equipment sold to supermarkets.

VENTURING INTO EUROPE

Gruma began laying the foundation for an expansion into the European market in 1997, with the opening of a sales office in London, England. Three years later, the company opened its first European tortilla factory in Coventry, England. Mexican food was more or less a novelty cuisine in Europe at this time, so to a degree Gruma had to create demand for its tortillas, in part by educating foodservice and institutional customers on how to incorporate tortillas into their food offerings.

In July 2004 the company strengthened its position in Europe by completing two acquisitions. Gruma paid about $12.8 million for Ovis Boske, a Dutch firm producing tortillas, wraps, pita bread, Swedish flatbread, and other grain-based foods and distributing them throughout the continent. In the second deal, Gruma purchased a 51 percent stake in Nuova De Franceschi & Figli, S.p.A., an Italian corn flour maker serving the corn chip, cereal, and beer industries in a number of countries, including Germany, Poland, Croatia, Israel, and Saudi Arabia. As part of Gruma, this company began supplying corn flour for corn chips produced at the Coventry plant. In 2006 Gruma bought the 49 percent of Nuova De Franceschi & Figli it did not already own. That October, Gruma spent $33 million for Newcastle, England-based Pride Valley Foods, a manufacturer of tortillas and other flat breads, including pita bread, naan, and chapati (the latter two being staples of the cuisines of the Indian subcontinent). Annual sales at Pride Valley had been about $40 million prior to the acquisition. Even before these latest moves, Gruma had been generating 3 percent of its overall sales in Europe.

In North America, Gruma faced some significant challenges during this period. In October 2000 Gruma Corp.'s Mission Foods division was forced to recall all of its yellow corn tortillas, tortilla chips, taco shells, and other products, and Azteca Milling recalled all of its yellow corn flour, after concerns were raised that StarLink, a genetically modified yellow corn (used in animal feed) that had not been approved for human consumption, had entered into the companies' chain of production. Over the next year, Mission Foods and Azteca produced their products using only white corn. After implementing stricter testing methods to identify the presence of genetically modified organisms in the corn they purchased, as well as requiring their suppliers to certify their products and facilities, the companies began once again producing yellow corn products.

In 2001 Gruma was sued by several U.S. tortilla makers claiming the company violating U.S. antitrust laws because of the payments it paid to supermarkets to carry its products. These so-called slotting fees were not illegal in and of themselves but could be deemed so if used to drive out competition or dominate a market. In early 2004 a federal judge dismissed the case, ruling that the plaintiffs had lost space on grocers' shelves because of competition and their refusal to pay slotting fees, not from any unfair business practices. In the meantime, Gruma in 2001 decided to refocus on its core corn-based business and therefore unload its unprofitable bread business. Its bread operations in Costa Rica and the United States were sold off, and its Mexican bread business was wound down.

EXPANDING IN NORTH AMERICA AND ASIA

In its two main markets, the United States and Mexico, Gruma pushed ahead with expansion of its core business. Seeking to double its U.S. sales by 2009, the company purchased a tortilla plant in Las Vegas, Nevada, in 2004 and completed an expansion of its corn flour plant in Evansville, Indiana, a year later. In May 2005 Gruma purchased the tortilla assets of Cenex Harvest States Cooperatives, which included plants in New Brighton, Minnesota; Railhead, Texas; and Phoenix, Arizona. That year, in a separate transaction, the company also acquired a small tortilla plant located near San Francisco, and it opened its 25th U.S. plant, a $33.9 million, 110,000-square-foot tortilla plant located in Pennsylvania's Luzerne County. In Mexico, Gimsa in August 2005 acquired Agroinsa, a group of Monterrey-based companies engaged primarily in the production of corn flour. Gruma in 2006 entered into an agreement to sell a 40 percent stake in the Venezuelan firm Molinos Nacionales to its Venezuelan partners in the corn flour venture Derivados de Maíz Seleccionado, C.A.

By 2005, Gruma's profits had increased to MXN 1.19 billion ($111.6 million) on sales of MXN 26.68 billion ($2.51 billion). Seeking another avenue for future growth, the company stepped up its efforts to penetrate markets in Asia, which it had been serving via

exports from its U.S. and U.K. facilities. In 2006 Gruma purchased two small tortilla plants in Australia and also opened its first plant in China, located in Shanghai. The Shanghai facility, which began producing wheat tortillas, corn tortillas, and tortilla chips, was set up to serve not only the Chinese market but also other markets in eastern Asia. Gruma's initial investment of $100 million in the 96,000-square-foot plant was justified by the rapidly growing demand for tortillas in China; exports of tortillas into China had reached $420 million by 2003. Gruma initially served foodservice clients in China, particularly YUM! Brands, Inc.'s KFC fast-food chain, which used Gruma tortillas for the chicken wrap sandwiches featured on the menu of its 1,800 restaurants in China.

In 2007 Gruma's Asia expansion continued as it purchased a tortilla plant in Malaysia and began building a new tortilla plant in Melbourne, Australia. The capacity of the latter facility, built to replace the two small plants purchased a year earlier, was similar to that of the plant in Shanghai. Gruma was also investigating the construction of another Asian plant, potentially located in either South Korea or Japan.

Such expansion plans were soon scaled back after Gruma ran into major financial problems stemming from currency hedges it had taken prior to the plummeting of the peso from the six-year high against the dollar it had reached in early August 2008. By the end of 2008, the company was reporting that losses from these hedges totaled MXN 11.54 billion ($834 million). The resulting net loss for the year amounted to MXN 11.76 billion ($850 million). In March 2009 Gruma announced deals with several banks to exchange its loss-making currency positions for debt. Once these transactions were completed, Gruma's debt was expected to rise two-thirds to about MXN 24.12 billion ($1.68 billion). Although the increased debt load was sure to at least delay the firm's expansion, Gruma was on track for a record-breaking year in 2009 despite its currency hedging travails and the global economic crisis.

Robert Halasz
Updated, David E. Salamie

PRINCIPAL SUBSIDIARIES

Grupo Industrial Maseca, S.A.B. de C.V. (83%); Molinera de México, S.A. de C.V. (60%); Productos y Distribuidora Azteca, S.A. de C.V.; Investigación de Tecnología Avanzada, S.A. de C.V.; Gruma Corporation (USA); Azteca Milling, L.P. (U.S.A.; 80%); Gruma Centroamérica, LLC (USA); Molinos Nacionales, C.A. (Venezuela; 57%); Derivados de Maíz Seleccionado,

C.A. (Venezuela; 57%); Mission Foods (Shanghai) Co. Ltd. (China); Gruma Oceania Pty. Ltd. (Australia); Mission Foods (Malaysia) Sdn. Bhd.

PRINCIPAL COMPETITORS

Grupo Bimbo, S.A.B. de C.V.; Grupo Minsa, S.A. de C.V.; Tyson Foods, Inc.; Cargill, Incorporated; Hormel Foods Corporation; Flowers Foods, Inc.; General Mills, Inc.; Santa Maria AB.

FURTHER READING

Black, Thomas, "Tortilla Plan Rolled Up for Now," *Houston Chronicle,* January 2, 1998, pp. 1C, 6C.

DePalma, Anthony, "How a Tortilla Empire Was Built on Favoritism," *New York Times,* February 15, 1996, pp. A1, A12.

Duffy, Tim, "Mexico Tortilla Deregulation Doesn't Boost Sales," *Wall Street Journal,* January 8, 1999.

Duggan, Patrice, "Tortilla Technology," *Forbes,* April 29, 1992, p. 48.

Emmond, Kenneth, "Gruma: Mexican Staple Makes Waves Around the World," *Business Mexico,* April 2005, p. 25.

Fowler, Tom, and Ruth Rendon, "Bakers Sue over Space on Shelves," *Houston Chronicle,* August 30, 2001, Business sec., p. 1.

"Gruma to Compete with Bimbo in Mexico's Bread Market," *Milling and Baking News,* September 30, 1997, p. 14.

"Grupo Maseca: En el principio sola era maíz," *Expansión,* December 12, 1979, pp. 65–68.

Guadarrama H., José de Jesús, "Maseca, un 'taco de alta technologia,'" *El financiero,* November 4, 1997, p. 30.

Hanacek, Andy, "Mission Accomplished," *Snack Food and Wholesale Bakery,* September 2004, pp. 26+.

Jacquez, Antonio, "La riqueza de Roberto González Barrera," *Proceso,* February 19, 1996, pp. 14–18, 20–21.

Kilman, Scott, and Joel Millman, "ADM, Showing New Interest in Mexico, Agrees to Buy 22% Stake in Gruma SA," *Wall Street Journal,* August 23, 1966, p. C15.

"Mexican Manufacturer Sites in Luzerne County," *Northeast Pennsylvania Business Journal,* March 1, 2005, p. 14.

Millman, Joel, "Corn Products Are Recalled by U.S. Units of Mexico Firm," *Wall Street Journal,* October 16, 2000, p. A25.

———, "Mexican Baker Turns Up the Heat on Rivals," *Wall Street Journal,* August 27, 1999, p. A7.

———, "Mexican Tortilla Firms Stage U.S. Bake-Off," *Wall Street Journal,* May 10, 1996, p. A6.

Moffett, Matt, "Mexico's Campaign to Modernize Sparks Battle over Tortillas," *Wall Street Journal,* September 9, 1993, pp. A1, A14.

Monjaras Moreno, Jorge, "La modernización de la tortilla," *Expansión,* February 20, 1991, pp. 46–48, 51.

———, "Roberto González Barrera: El hombre de *Expansión,*" *Expansión,* January 12, 1994, pp. 32–33, 35, 37, 40.

Moreno, Jenalia, "It's a Wrap for Tortilla Suit: Judge Throws Out Case Against Gruma," *Houston Chronicle,* January 7, 2004, Business sec., p. 2.

———, "Ruling Could Favor Tortilla Giant," *Houston Chronicle,* November 27, 2003, Business sec., p. 1.

Rueda, Marisol, "Tortilla King," *Latin Trade,* July 2006, p. 60.

Smith, Geri, and Michael Arndt, "Wrapping the Globe in Tortillas," *Business Week,* February 26, 2007, p. 54.

Hannaford Bros. Co.

145 Pleasant Hill Road
Scarborough, Maine 04074-9309
U.S.A.
Telephone: (207) 883-2911
Toll Free: (800) 442-6049
Fax: (207) 885-2859
Web site: http://www.hannaford.com

Wholly Owned Subsidiary of Delhaize Group
Founded: 1883
Incorporated: 1902
Employees: 27,000
Sales: $2.2 billion (2008 est.)
NAICS: 445110 Supermarkets and Other Grocery
(Except Convenience) Stores; 424410 General Line
Grocery Merchant Wholesalers

■ ■ ■

Hannaford Bros. Co. is one of the leading food retailers
in northern New England. Based in Maine, the
company operates upscale supermarkets in that state, as
well as in New Hampshire, Massachusetts, Vermont,
and upstate New York. Major markets include Portland
and Bangor, Maine; Manchester, New Hampshire; Burlington, Vermont; and Albany, New York. The 167
Hannaford stores are an average of 48,400 square feet in
size, and they vary in format; while some are
conventional supermarkets, others are conventional
supermarkets with pharmacies, so-called combination
stores selling both food items and general merchandise,
or combination stores with pharmacies. Hannaford

stores place a particular emphasis on fresh products and
perishables, and they attempt to maintain a competitive
edge through an everyday low price policy. The
company supplies its stores from three distribution
centers located in South Portland and Winthrop, Maine,
and Schodack, New York. These facilities and the firm's
trucking subsidiary also supply food items, general
merchandise, and pharmaceuticals on a wholesale basis
to 29 independent supermarkets. Since July 2000
Hannaford Bros. has been a subsidiary of Delhaize
America, Inc., the U.S. division of Brussels-based Delhaize Group. Delhaize America owns several other major
supermarket chains in the eastern United States, including Food Lion in the Southeast and Mid-Atlantic and
Sweetbay Supermarket in Florida.

WHOLESALE BEGINNINGS

In 1883 Arthur Hannaford left the Hannaford family
farm in Cape Elizabeth, Maine, to open a small shop on
the Portland, Maine, waterfront as an outlet for the
variety of fruits and vegetables grown on the farm. By
1894, Howard and Edward Hannaford had joined their
brother in the fledgling enterprise, which over time
became a major produce wholesaler, operating out of a
Portland warehouse. Within a few more years, the
company expanded beyond wholesaling produce from
the family farm, adding poultry, butter, and eggs to
their offerings. Arthur Hannaford eventually left to
pursue other interests, but Howard and Edward carried
on and incorporated the company as Hannaford Bros.
Co. in 1902. Howard held the company presidency
until 1906 when Edward began a 33-year stint at the
helm.

COMPANY PERSPECTIVES

Hannaford is a full-service supermarket committed to listening to consumers and meeting their needs. We will deliver an outstanding shopping experience so customers will recognize Hannaford as the best choice for quality products, exceptional service and great value. We will be a responsible, respectful employer and corporate citizen, actively serving the interests of our associates and the local community.

Hannaford Bros. enjoyed steady growth during the first few decades of the new century. It remained focused primarily on southern Maine although it eventually began shipping products to northern Maine by steamboat and down to Boston via railcar. The company expanded into the wholesale grocery business in 1939 when it acquired H. S. Melcher Co., a grocery wholesaler and franchiser of the Red & White stores in Maine. That same year, Edward Hannaford sold the firm to Stewart Taylor, a company vice-president. Taylor brought in Walter F. Whittier as a minority partner. Whittier was a banker who had helped finance the deal.

GRADUAL SHIFT TO RETAIL

Whittier played a key role in Hannaford Bros.'s gradual shift from being primarily a wholesaler to primarily a retailer. This move began in 1944 when the company opened its first grocery store in partnership with William T. Cottle but accelerated in the early 1960s after Whittier's ascension to the presidency in 1960. Under Whittier, the company began to purchase equity interests in supermarket chains. The strategy was based on the knowledge that these equity partnerships yielded a much higher profit margin than did straight wholesale relationships. The linking of wholesale distributors with retailers in the grocery business was revolutionary at the time, and Hannaford Bros. was at the forefront of this movement. In the meantime, the company laid the groundwork for an expansion of its retail operations into northern Maine with the 1955 purchase of wholesaler T. R. Savage Co. Also aiding growth was the opening in 1960 of a modern, 200,000-square-foot warehouse in South Portland, Maine.

By the middle of the 1960s, Hannaford Bros. was distributing to about 100 stores, mostly located in Maine. Although that number remained fairly constant over the next several years, the size of the stores grew, as smaller units shut their doors and new, bigger locations were built. In 1966 the company bought the 31-unit Sampson's supermarket chain for $4.5 million. These stores, all located in Maine, had been Hannaford wholesale customers before the acquisition. Thirty percent of the Sampson stock was then immediately sold off to a group of investors involved in the stores' operation. This was typical of the equity partnership arrangement with Hannaford Bros.'s other stores, most of which operated under the Shop 'n Save name. In 1967 Hannaford opened a store in Burlington, Vermont, its first outside Maine. By 1970 the company owned majority interests, usually between 51 percent and 70 percent, in 58 of the 103 stores it supplied. The rest were served strictly as wholesale customers, although Hannaford was also landlord to several of them. For 1970 the company returned a profit of $844,000 on sales of $124 million.

In 1971 James L. Moody, a 12-year company veteran, became Hannaford's president, with Whittier continuing in his role as chairman and chief executive. Moody took over the CEO spot two years later. The year 1971 was a landmark one for the company in several other ways. Hannaford common stock was sold publicly for the first time that year, although a large portion of its stock remained in the hands of insiders. It also marked the first time that the company generated net earnings in excess of $1 million. The trend toward retailing continued into the mid-1970s. By 1974 Hannaford was the regional leader in both the wholesale and retail sale of groceries. Company officials attributed this success largely to the equity partnership system, which remained fairly unusual in the supermarket industry. By this time, the company had 58 equity partnership stores, which bought about 65 percent of their merchandise from Hannaford's distribution center; 16 wholly owned outlets; and 38 independent retail customers. Between those three types of stores, Hannaford was supplying about a quarter of all the food sold in Maine's supermarkets. Annual sales had reached $200 million by this time.

Around the same time, Hannaford began its push into the retail drugstore business. The company opened three Wellby Super Drug Stores in Maine in 1973, and several more Wellby openings followed during the next few years. Unlike its grocery outlets, all of these initial entrants into the pharmacy business were owned outright by Hannaford.

During the rest of the 1970s, Hannaford Bros. retreated somewhat from its equity partnership concept, choosing instead to purchase full interest in its retail operations. By 1981 the company had 73 stores in its stable, 52 of them wholly owned. The remaining 21 stores operated according to the company's well-

KEY DATES

1883: Arthur Hannaford opens a small produce outlet in Portland, Maine; he is later joined by his brothers Howard and Edward.

1902: After Arthur's departure from the firm, Howard and Edward Hannaford incorporate it as Hannaford Bros. Co.

1939: Hannaford family involvement ends with Edward Hannaford's sale of the firm.

1944: Hannaford Bros. opens its first grocery store via a partnership arrangement.

1966: The 31-unit Sampson's supermarket chain in Maine is acquired.

1967: Opening of store in Burlington, Vermont, marks first retail foray outside Maine.

1971: Hannaford goes public.

1973: Company launches the Wellby drugstore chain.

1984: Company opens its first combination food-and-drugstore.

1987: Hannaford expands into Massachusetts and upstate New York; sales hit $1 billion.

1990: The 11-unit Alexander's chain in northeastern Massachusetts and southern New Hampshire is acquired.

1992: Company sells its freestanding drugstores.

1994: In first venture outside the Northeast, Hannaford acquires Wilson's Supermarkets, operator of 20 supermarkets in North and South Carolina.

1995: For the first time, stores are opened under the Hannaford banner; the name is first used for new stores in the Southeast.

2000: Belgium's Delhaize Group acquires Hannaford Bros. for $3.6 billion; to secure antitrust approval, Hannaford is forced to divest all its southeastern stores.

2003: Company completes the rollout of the "Festival for the Senses" format; all stores sport the Hannaford banner.

2004: Hannaford acquires Victory Super Markets, operator of 19 stores in Massachusetts and New Hampshire.

Hannaford also bought the outstanding equity in Progressive Distributors, a supplier of health and beauty aids and other general merchandise, during 1981. Progressive had been an equity partnership since 1967. As the growth in New England's population outpaced the national average, new Shop 'n Save and Sampson stores were opened throughout the region, and sales approached $500 million.

AGGRESSIVE EXPANSION PROGRAM

Hannaford continued to grow impressively in the 1980s. In keeping with its aggressive expansion program, the company sought innovative ways to stay ahead of the supermarket pack. Technology was one area in which Hannaford's progressive philosophy was apparent. The company had scanning capability in 18 stores by 1982, and its internally developed computer programs for inventory and other financial procedures was advanced enough to be coveted by other supermarket firms. Hannaford Trucking Company, a wholly owned subsidiary, was founded in 1982, giving the company more flexibility and control over its distribution system. In 1984 Hannaford opened its first superstore. Called Super Shop 'n Save, the outlet was the largest of its kind in the northern New England region. In addition to the usual supermarket products, the 42,000-square-foot unit included a pharmacy, hardware, automotive items, a plant department, and a bulk food area. The Super Store concept, the result of several years' planning and fine-tuning, was part of a national trend toward larger format supermarkets. Also in 1984, Hugh G. Farrington, who had joined the company as a management trainee in 1968, was named president of Hannaford. Moody stayed on as chairman and CEO.

The expansion program continued during the second half of the 1980s. In 1986 Hannaford Bros. stock began trading on the New York Stock Exchange. Sales for that year totaled $910 million. By 1987 the company was operating 66 supermarkets under the names Shop 'n Save, Martin's, and Sun Foods. In addition, 36 Wellby Super drugstores were in business by that time. Sales at Hannaford broke the $1 billion barrier for the first time in fiscal 1987. That year, the company made its move into the upstate New York and Massachusetts markets. Plans for expansion into these areas included a Sun Foods super warehouse store in Lowell, Massachusetts, and New York stores to be located in Glens Falls, Plattsburg, Amsterdam, and Albany. Most of these new stores were either combination or superstores, selling general merchandise as well as groceries, as the trend toward larger facilities continued to gain momentum. At the same time, the

established equity partnership pattern. The 1981 purchase of the outstanding equity in the Sampson chain accounted for a good part of that shift in balance.

company's home turf of Maine, New Hampshire, and Vermont remained an important part of the mix. In many of those states' markets, larger stores were built to take the place of small, outmoded locations.

THRIVING THROUGH RECESSION AND IN FACE OF INCREASED COMPETITION

As the 1980s drew to a close, Hannaford continued to thrive, despite a recession that dragged down much of New England's economy. For the entire decade, the company's profits had increased an average of 18 percent annually, compared to 13 percent for the seven companies tracked by Standard and Poor's Food Chains index. The company's expansion into upstate New York continued, assisted by computerized marketing surveys that focused on areas where supermarket chains were sparse. By 1989 Hannaford's sales had grown to $1.52 billion, with a healthy $39 million in net earnings. Part of the company's success had to do with its adoption of a "socio-technical system" of management, based on Japanese factory management ideas. Under this system, decision making was decentralized. Small groups including both managers and employees were given a great deal of autonomy in areas such as hiring, pay scales, and general rules.

In December 1990 Hannaford added 11 supermarkets to its collection at once by acquiring the Alexander's chain in northeastern Massachusetts and southern New Hampshire for $73 million. The deal also brought two freestanding drugstores and three freestanding bakery shops into the Hannaford fold. That same year, Hannaford bought out its last equity partner, so that all of its retail outlets were wholly owned, and it also opened a state-of-the-art distribution center in Schodack, New York. The early 1990s saw the rise of a new and potent type of competitor: the membership club. With the spread of wholesale clubs such as Sam's and BJ's into Hannaford's home-base states, the company faced more of a threat to its market share than ever before. To remain competitive, Hannaford introduced a number of institutional-size items and other club-style merchandise under the name Budget Values. In spite of the increased competition, Hannaford managed to boost its sales even further, reaching $2 billion for fiscal 1991 and keeping pace with the company timetable.

The Hannaford empire consisted of 129 stores by 1992. That year Farrington added CEO to his existing titles of president and chief operating officer, while Moody retained his chairmanship. As competition from the clubs and from Wal-Mart Stores, Inc., continued to heat up, Hannaford's management made the strategic

decision to get out of the drugstore business, where deep discounting was making it increasingly difficult to turn a profit. In May 1992 Hannaford sold 34 of its 41 freestanding drugstores to the Rite Aid Corporation. The sale of those Wellby outlets, which had generated less than 5 percent of Hannaford's total sales, enabled the company to concentrate its efforts more fully on its core supermarket business.

The ongoing recession and the elimination of revenue from the drugstores led to Hannaford's first decrease in annual sales in 1993, although the drop was small. Meanwhile the company managed to increase its earnings by 15 percent to $56.7 million. By the end of 1993, Hannaford was operating a total of 93 food stores, more than half of them in Maine. Fifty-seven of the company's stores were large combination stores offering a broad range of nonfood merchandise, four were super-warehouse units, and the rest were conventional supermarkets. Among the company's new openings in 1993 were two combination food/drugstores in New York State; one in Concord, New Hampshire; and one in Farmington, Maine, that replaced a smaller unit. The Gloversville, New York, store was the first Hannaford store to go head-to-head with a Wal-Mart in the same shopping complex.

One way in which Hannaford retained a competitive edge was by continuing its history of technological innovation. In 1994, for instance, the company began installing a strategic information system for groceries and perishables that was based on actual sales to customers rather than on inventory shipments to stores. The system enabled Hannaford to improve its inventory control and fine-tune its merchandising and marketing efforts, all leading to higher profits.

SOUTHERN FORAY

In 1994 Hannaford made its first foray out of the Northeast by acquiring Wilson's Supermarkets, based in Wilmington, North Carolina, for $120 million. Wilson's, a privately owned 20-store chain with units in both North and South Carolina, had expected sales of over $200 million in 1994. The deal also included five additional store sites (three already under construction) and several shopping centers. By September 1994, Hannaford had opened the 21st Wilson's, located in Fayetteville, North Carolina. Day-to-day management of the Wilson's chain remained in the hands of the Wilson family, which had run the stores since the company's inception in 1919.

Further expansion in its new southern area of operations soon followed. In 1995 Hannaford expanded into Virginia with the purchase of six Farm Fresh stores.

The company also opened a number of new stores in the region, concentrating particularly on larger markets, including Charlotte, Raleigh, and Wilmington, North Carolina, and Richmond, Virginia. These new food-and-drug superstores, modeled on the company's latest prototype in the Northeast, opened under the Hannaford banner, the first such use of the corporate name. Because of trademark issues, the company had been precluded from using the Shop 'n Save name in its new region. Also in 1995, four Sun Foods stores in New York and New Hampshire and five Martin's stores in Vermont were converted to the Hannaford banner.

Throughout its stores in the Northeast and Southeast, Hannaford in 1996 launched an expanded line of private-label products under the Hannaford name. To buttress its southeastern stores, the company opened a new, 465,000-square-foot warehouse in Butner, North Carolina. Late in 1996, Hannaford announced plans to close two Wilson's stores and convert five others to the Hannaford banner. The five converted stores were enlarged into superstores. A further retrenchment occurred during the fourth quarter of 2007 when Hannaford closed seven stores located in smaller markets in North Carolina and Virginia in order to focus on its remaining 40 stores in larger southeastern markets. In conjunction with these closures, the company wrote down the value of its $120 million Wilson's acquisition by $40 million. Sales for 1997 passed the $3 billion mark for the first time, while profits fell 20 percent, to $59.6 million, because of the write-off.

2000 ACQUISITION BY DELHAIZE GROUP

By 1999 Hannaford Bros. was operating more than 150 stores under the Shop 'n Save and Hannaford banners, the Wilson's name having been retired. The company's future as an independent operator was placed in doubt that spring when the Sobey family, which controlled one of the largest supermarket chains in Canada, decided not to renew a standstill agreement governing its 25 percent stake in Hannaford. The Sobeys had long held a significant stake in Hannaford but had agreed to neither increase nor decrease their holding. The ending of this agreement opened the door for Belgium's Delhaize Group to step forward in August 1999 and work out a deal to acquire Hannaford for $3.6 billion in cash and stock. Delhaize already owned Food Lion, Inc., operator of more than 1,100 stores in the Southeast and Mid-Atlantic region.

Delhaize's takeover of Hannaford did not close until July 2000 because of a lengthy antitrust review. To secure federal approval for the deal, Hannaford agreed to divest all of its southeastern stores, which eliminated

overlap with the Food Lion chain. The 40 stores were subsequently sold or closed, thereby ending Hannaford's foray into the Southeast. Under Delhaize, Hannaford remained an autonomous entity as it became a subsidiary of the newly formed Delhaize America, Inc., which served as a holding company for Delhaize's U.S. operations. Hannaford's headquarters remained in Scarborough, Maine.

Farrington remained CEO of Hannaford following the takeover, but company veteran Ronald C. Hodge was named president and COO. Hodge was named CEO a year later, while Farrington became a Delhaize Group executive vice-president and board member. In the fall of 2001, Hannaford introduced its "Festival for the Senses" strategy for its 11 stores in southern Maine. In addition to a name change from Shop 'n Save to Hannaford, these stores were overhauled to sport a new format featuring 40 percent more space devoted to fresh produce and meat, stepped-up customer service, and an environment meant to engage customers' full range of five senses. The emphasis on fresh foods was designed to provide the stores with a competitive advantage at a time when packaged goods had become more or less commoditized because of their wide availability at convenience stores, discount stores, and other outlets. The initial results for the format were quite positive as the number of customers, number of departments visited by the average customer, average order size, and overall sales all increased. The new format was rolled out over the next two years to encompass the entire 122-store chain. Thus by the fall of 2003 all the stores carried the Hannaford banner.

Hannaford in November 2004 filled in some gaps in its geographic footprint, particularly in Massachusetts, when it acquired the privately held Victory Super Markets for $175 million. Victory, which had been owned by the DiGeronimo family since the first store opened in 1923, ran 17 stores in central and southeastern Massachusetts and two stores in southern New Hampshire. At the time of the purchase, Hannaford operated just six stores in Massachusetts and had two more under construction. All of the Victory stores were rebranded under the Hannaford banner during 2005.

MAINTAINING A HISTORY OF INNOVATION

During this period, Hannaford also incorporated into some of its stores a special section called Nature's Place that featured organic and natural food items. By 2006, pharmacies had been added to most Hannaford stores, and the company that year accelerated its pace of growth, opening 14 new stores, the most the firm had ever opened in a single year. The year 2006 also marked Hannaford's introduction of its Guiding Stars nutritional information system. Hannaford analyzed the content of more than 30,000 name-brand and private-label products and assigned them a rating of one to three stars, with three stars given to the most nutritious items. The ratings were placed on food shelf tags throughout all of Hannaford's stores and were designed to make it easier for consumers to select more nutritious foods. Analysis from a year's worth of data showed the program was succeeding in this goal as, within certain categories, sales of higher rated items increased while sales of lower rated items decreased. A survey found that more than 40 percent of Hannaford's customers were regularly using the Guiding Stars ratings. The program was later introduced into Hannaford's sister chains within Delhaize America, including Sweetbay Supermarket in Florida and Food Lion. In 2008 Hannaford began exploring the possibility of expanding the system to other retailers as well as to food manufacturers and foodservice operations in schools and other institutions through licensing deals.

Continuing its history of innovation, Hannaford in late 2007 announced plans to build a new store in Augusta, Maine, that it claimed would be the first platinum-certified Leadership in Energy and Environmental Design (LEED) supermarket. To obtain the platinum designation, which was the highest certification awarded by the nonprofit U.S. Green Building Council, Hannaford sought to create a store over 40 percent more energy efficient than a typical supermarket. Green elements included geothermal heating and cooling, solar photovoltaic panels, high-efficiency refrigeration, energy-efficient lighting, and a plant-filled roof providing insulation and helping to control stormwater runoff. The store was slated to open in the summer of 2009.

At the end of 2007, Hannaford began experimenting with a smaller, 35,000-square-foot format at a new store in Dover, New Hampshire. The concept aimed to provide the breadth of the chain's typical product offerings in a smaller footprint, using different merchandise arrangements, a smaller backroom area, and higher shelving. Seven store openings in 2007 brought the chain total to 165.

Hannaford's reputation took a hit when as many as 4.2 million credit and debit card numbers were compromised as a result of a breach of the computer system handling credit- and debit-card transactions at the company's stores that occurred between December 2007 and March 2008. Fraudulent activity was subsequently reported on at least 1,800 cards, and the numerous lawsuits that were soon filed against

Hannaford were consolidated into a class-action suit. To prevent future theft of card numbers, the company by April 2008 had upgraded the security of its data networks, in part by investing in new equipment and software that kept card numbers encrypted during the entire time of their transmittal through the system.

At this same time, competition in the food retailing sector remained fierce, and Hannaford in particular faced increased pressure as Wal-Mart made a renewed push into Maine with plans for several more supercenters. Hannaford lowered prices on more than 1,500 items throughout its stores in mid-2008, and in early 2009 it launched an initiative to cut operating costs by tens of millions of dollars by trimming about 50 head-office positions and slashing its advertising and marketing budgets. The company nevertheless remained in growth mode, with plans for four more stores in Maine alone.

Robert R. Jacobson
Updated, David E. Salamie

PRINCIPAL SUBSIDIARIES

Athenian Real Estate Development, Inc.; Boney Wilson & Sons, Inc.; Guiding Stars Licensing Company; Hannbro Company; Hannaford Licensing Corp.; Hannaford Procurement Corp.; Hannaford Trucking Company, Inc.; Martin's Food of South Burlington, Inc.; Plain Street Properties, Inc.; Progressive Distributors, Inc.; Shop 'n Save - Mass., Inc.; Victory Distributors, Inc.

PRINCIPAL COMPETITORS

The Stop & Shop Supermarket Company; Shaw's Supermarkets, Inc.; Wal-Mart Stores, Inc.; The Golub Corporation; Demoulas Super Markets Inc.

FURTHER READING

Autry, Ret, "Hannaford Brothers," *Fortune,* November 19, 1990, p. 174.

Berner, Robert, and Steven Lipin, "Food Lion Agrees to Acquire Hannaford," *Wall Street Journal,* August 19, 1999, p. A3.

Bivins, Jacquelyn, "James Moody: A Master of Understatement," *Chain Store Age Executive,* October 1985, pp. 11+.

Blom, Eric, "Hannaford a Model for Sister Stores," *Portland (Maine) Press Herald,* March 19, 2004, p. 1C.

Brumback, Nancy, "Hannaford Cites Recession, Competition for Tough Year," *Supermarket News,* May 25, 1992, p. 9.

Calkins, Jan, "Hannaford Gears for Expansion," *Supermarket News,* April 20, 1987, p. 2.

Campanella, Frank, "Warehouse Expansion, New Stores Enhance Hannaford Bros. Profits," *Barron's,* December 13, 1971, p. 34.

Garry, Michael, "Hannaford to Roll Out Automated Store Ordering," *Supermarket News,* May 8, 2006, p. 137.

"Geography Lesson," *Forbes,* August 1, 1994, p. 120.

Hamstra, Mark, "Bright Ideas," *Supermarket News,* July 28, 2008, p. 14.

———, "Nutritious Items 'Star' at Hannaford," *Supermarket News,* September 11, 2006, p. 6.

"Hannaford Expects $1 Billion Annual Sales in '80s," *Supermarket News,* May 10, 1982, p. 20.

"Hannaford's Home-Grown Savvy," *Dun's Review,* June 1974, p. 106.

Hench, David, "Full Story of Hannaford Breach Has Been Slow to Reach the Public," *Portland (Maine) Press Herald,* April 6, 2008, p. A1.

Martin, Andrew, "Store Chain's Test Concludes That Nutrition Sells," *New York Times,* September 6, 2007, p. C3.

Mehlman, William, "Hannaford Continues Mastery of Yankee Grocery Retailing," *Insiders' Chronicle,* April 21, 1986, pp. 1+.

Murphy, Edward D., "Food Lion's Owner Buys Hannaford," *Portland (Maine) Press Herald,* August 19, 1999, p. 1A.

———, "Hannaford Buying Victory Chain," *Portland (Maine) Press Herald,* September 25, 2004, p. D9.

———, "Hannaford Selling Stores in Southeast," *Portland (Maine) Press Herald,* June 1, 2000, p. 8B.

———, "Life in the Slow Aisle: Hannaford Bros., Retreating from a Foray into Unfamiliar Territory, Returns Home to Confront the Problems of Flat Sales and Slow Growth," *Portland (Maine) Press Herald,* April 7, 1998, p. 1C.

———, "Regulators OK Hannaford Deal," *Portland (Maine) Press Herald,* July 26, 2000, p. 6C.

Netzer, Baie, "How About a Grocer in the Northeast!?" *Money,* February 1992, p. 50.

Orgel, David, "Food Lion on the Prowl with Deal for Hannaford," *Supermarket News,* August 23, 1999, p. 1.

———, "Hannaford Moves South with Deal to Buy Wilson's," *Supermarket News,* June 27, 1994, p. 1.

Outwin, Charles Patrick Maxwell, "A History of the Hannaford Bros. Co. of Maine," Ph.D. diss., University of Maine, 1995, 77 p.

Redman, Russell, "Hannaford Brand Is Replacing Shop 'n Save Throughout Chain," *Supermarket News,* January 29, 1996, pp. 29+.

Rosebaum, Clarence, "Hannaford Bros. Co. in the Vanguard of the Food Distribution Revolution," *Journal of Commerce,* December 7, 1971, p. 7.

"Shop 'n Save Getting New Name," *Portland (Maine) Press Herald,* July 27, 2001, p. 1A.

Springer, Jon, "Hannaford to Exit South to Get OK of Delhaize Deal," *Supermarket News,* June 5, 2000, p. 1.

Turcsik, Richard, "Hannaford Battling Club Assault," *Supermarket News,* November 4, 1991, p. 1.

Turkel, Tux, "Company Response to Breach Criticized," *Portland (Maine) Press Herald,* March 21, 2008, p. A1.

Weinstein, Steve, "Hannaford's Southern Exposure," *Progressive Grocer,* May 1995, pp. 58–60.

Wickenheiser, Matt, "Hannaford Steps Up Security," *Portland (Maine) Press Herald,* April 23, 2008, p. A1.

Zwiebach, Elliot, "Hannaford Bros. Gets Victory in Southern New England Market," *Supermarket News,* October 4, 2004, p. 4.

———, "Hannaford Name to Go Southeast," *Supermarket News,* May 29, 1995, pp. 3+.

———, "Hannaford's Winding Road to Retailing," *Supermarket News,* July 28, 2008, p. 18.

HFF, Inc.

1 Oxford Center
301 Grant Street, Suite 600
Pittsburgh, Pennsylvania 15219-1503
U.S.A.
Telephone: (412) 281-8714
Fax: (412) 281-2792
Web site: http://www.hfflp.com

Public Company
Incorporated: 2006
Employees: 400
Sales: $131.7 million (2008)
Stock Exchanges: New York
Ticker Symbol: HF
NAICS: 522320 Financial Transactions Processing, Reserve, and Clearing House Activities

∎ ∎ ∎

HFF, Inc., is a New York Stock Exchange–listed commercial real estate capital intermediary company offering a full range of real estate transaction services through six lines of business: debt placement, investment sales, private equity and corporate finance, structured finance, note sales and note sale advisory, and loan servicing. Among HFF's debt placement offerings are construction loans, fixed-rate loans, bridge-acquisition loans, credit-tenant lease transactions, forward loans, and tax-exempt loans. The investment sales group relies on the company's CapTrack proprietary database of debt and equity market information in the United States to sell all major types of commercial properties and portfolios.

Through HFF Securities L.P., the company is involved in the private equity and corporate finance arena, helping clients to raise capital from a variety of public and private sources, including banks, insurance companies, pension funds, and endowments. HFF also offers structured finance services, including mezzanine debt, convertible mortgages, entity investments and ventures, preferred equity, participating mortgages, single-asset and portfolio joint ventures, single-asset and portfolio recapitalizations, and restructuring. The firm's note sales and note sale advisory unit serves institutional investors, helping them restructure mortgage portfolios through the sale of structured and non-structured notes.

Finally, HFF offers commercial loan services, including asset management, accounting, payment processing, tax administration, insurance monitoring, financial statement analysis, and property inspections. While HFF lists Pittsburgh, Pennsylvania, as its headquarters, the company takes a decentralized approach, maintaining home offices in 18 other U.S. cities to do business across the country as well as in Puerto Rico, Canada, and Mexico.

FORMATION OF HOLLIDAY FENOGLIO: 1982

HFF, Inc., was created in 1998 when the company of partners Harold E. Holliday Jr. and John Fenoglio was combined with that of John P. Fowler. Both native Texans, Holliday and Fenoglio were colleagues, fellow vice-presidents at First Mortgage Company of Texas Inc. in the 1970s. Upon learning that the company was being sold to a savings and loan, they decided to quit and

COMPANY PERSPECTIVES

As one of the largest and most successful commercial real estate capital intermediaries in the country, HFF incorporates capital markets knowledge with local real estate expertise to successfully complete any type of real estate transaction, regardless of size or complexity. HFF consistently maintains the capital markets relationships critical to accomplishing your specific needs in today's highly complex and rapidly shifting capital markets environment.

start their mortgage banking firm. "We knew S&Ls were going to make a pretty big mess on the real estate scene," Holliday recalled in a 1997 interview with *Houston Business Journal.* "We knew we didn't want to go the S&L route." In November 1982 they formed Holliday Fenoglio & Co. and set up shop in Houston.

Holliday Fenoglio enjoyed a successful start, but around the same time oil prices began to decline, the beginning of a severe slump in the energy sector that would have a devastating effect on the Houston real estate market, which collapsed in the middle of the decade. The two partners had to take stock of their situation. Rather than dissolve, move to another market, or turn their attention to some other sector, they elected to stay the course and pursue the mortgage business in Houston. Because Holliday Fenoglio was a new company it held a distinct advantage over more established firms, free of a large portfolio of old loans that had to be serviced. Another saving grace of the difficult economic climate was a sudden lack of competition. Transactions, however few in number, continued to crop up and it seemed that whenever Holliday Fenoglio had the chance to make a quote it won the business.

ADDITION OF RESEARCH DEPARTMENT: 1987

To drum up new business, in 1987 Holliday Fenoglio created a research department, the first commercial mortgage banking firm in the country to take such a step. Through research the firm was able to find new opportunities, such as supermarket-anchored shopping centers, which enjoyed higher, more stable occupancy rates than other types of properties. Moreover, these were deals they could recommend to investors that could still be accomplished despite tough economic conditions. The firm was also nimble enough to find

borrowers who still had a need to maximize loan proceeds and remained interested in real estate investments.

Holliday Fenoglio added a branch office in Dallas and then in 1989 expanded to New York State, opening an office in the fall of 1989 in Albany. Several months later, in May 1990, the firm opened a second New York office in Buffalo. In addition to Buffalo, this branch served the Rochester and Syracuse markets. By this point in the firm's history it was servicing about $700 million in commercial mortgages for lenders and since its inception had closed $2.2 billion in commercial mortgages. A fifth office also opened in the early 1990s in Boca Raton, Florida.

FIRM MERGES WITH AMRESCO

Holliday and Fenoglio decided in 1994 to join forces with Dallas-based financial services company Amresco Inc., selling the business for about $33 million in cash, stock, and other payments. The company now operated under the name Holliday Fenoglio Inc. Publicly traded Amresco was the former Financial Resource Management, Inc., (FRMI) subsidiary of NationsBank Corp., which acquired the failed banks of Dallas-based First Republic Bank Corporation in 1988 and two years later formed FRMI to manage the troubled assets. Early in 1992 NationsBank reorganized FRMI and provided it with a new name, Amresco, in an effort to gain a fresh start. Amresco then initiated an acquisition spree in order to achieve some diversity and grow its residential- and commercial-mortgage divisions, leading to the purchase of Holliday Fenoglio.

Under Amresco's ownership, Holliday Fenoglio enjoyed strong growth. Seven more offices were added over the next three years, the 12th in Boston at the end of 1997. In order to become the Northeast's largest commercial mortgage banking firm, Amresco then engineered in early 1998 the acquisition of Boston-based Fowler, Goedecke, Ellis & Connor for $16 million in cash and stock. The firm was created in 1981 when John P. Fowler and Peter Goedecke merged their company with Leggat McCall & Werner Financial Corp. It grew into a six-office concern, with branches in Rochester and Albany, New York; Saddlebrook, New Jersey; and Hartford and Westport, Connecticut. Amresco combined the Holliday Fenoglio and Fowler operations to create Holliday Fenoglio Fowler, L.P. (HFF). The firm was soon supplemented with the acquisition of Pittsburgh, Pennsylvania-based PNS Realty Partners. With offices in Louisville and Lexington, Kentucky; and Indianapolis and Merrillville, Indiana, PNY Realty allowed HFF to expand its reach into the Midwest.

```
┌─────────────────────────────────────────────┐
│                                               │
│              KEY DATES                        │
│                 ■                             │
│  1982:  Holliday Fenoglio & Co. is founded in │
│         Houston.                              │
│  1987:  Research department is established.    │
│  1990:  Office opens in Buffalo, New York.     │
│  1994:  Amresco Inc. acquires firm.            │
│  1998:  Firm is combined with Fowler, Goedecke,│
│         Ellis & Connor to create Holliday     │
│         Fenoglio Fowler, L.P.                 │
│  2000:  Lend Lease Corp acquires HFF.          │
│  2003:  HFF principals acquire firm.           │
│  2007:  HFF, Inc., completes initial public    │
│         offering of stock.                     │
│                                               │
└─────────────────────────────────────────────┘
```

Before the end of 1998, both Holliday and Fenoglio left HFF. In July 1998 Fenoglio announced that he was taking a one-year leave of absence to spend more time with his family and the Texas Families for a Healthy Environment nonprofit organization. He did not return, however. In January 2000, he and fellow HFF executive David Aaronson cofounded Live Oak Capital Ltd., a full-service commercial real estate investment firm. Other colleagues from HFF would join them as well, including Harold Holliday in October 2000.

SALE OF HFF: 2000

After Fenoglio's departure in 1998, HFF experienced a tough patch, due to global economic problems, leading to some cost-cutting measures in 1999. Carrying a heavy debt load, about $1.7 billion, the parent company fared far worse. In 1999 it began negotiations with Atlanta-based Lend Lease Real Estate Investments, the U.S. subsidiary of Australia's Lend Lease Corp., a major international real estate and financial services group. For a time, all of Amresco was on the block, but not all of the units were worth buying and the deal almost collapsed. In the end, Lend Lease acquired five business lines, including HFF, in a deal that closed in March 2000, leading to Harold Holliday's departure.

Under Lend Lease's ownership, HFF and its 18 offices (Chicago was added in 2002) serviced an $11.3 billion commercial real estate loan portfolio and completed 790 transactions worth more than $13.25 billion in 2002. A year later, a group of HFF principals arranged to purchase the firm from Lend Lease in a deal valued around $10 million. The transaction closed in June 2003. During the year, transaction volume increased 20 percent to $16.2 billion.

In April 2004 HFF formed HFF Securities LP, relying on former executives of the Los Angeles-based investment banking firm Chadwick & Saylor to create a real estate banking affiliate to provide financial advice and help raise funds for real estate companies. In this way HFF could better serve providers as well as users of capital in the commercial real estate market, making the firm something of a one-stop shop. The firm recorded total revenues of $143.7 million, resulting in net income of $29.4 million in 2004. A year later revenues increased to $205.85 million and net income grew to more than $48 million.

HFF GOES PUBLIC: 2006

HFF took steps to go public in 2006. A new Delaware corporation was formed under the named HFF, Inc., which would become the new parent company of Holliday Fenoglio Fowler L.P. and HFF Securities L.P. After generating revenues of $229.7 million and earnings of $51.55 million in 2006, HFF held its initial public offering of stock in February 2007, grossing $296 million and netting $271.6 million. Shares were then listed on the New York Stock Exchange. The proceeds were used to purchase the HFF entities and $56.3 million was earmarked to pay down debt.

Due to increased production, revenues increased 11.3 percent over the previous year to $255.67 million in 2007. Operating expenses were much higher as well, leading to a decrease in net income to $14.42 million. Compared to what transpired the following year, however, such a result was more than satisfactory. Not only did the U.S. and global economies slow dramatically in 2008, the capital and credit markets dried up, bringing production to a standstill by the end of the year. As a result, HFF's total revenues dropped 48.5 percent to $131.69 million in 2008. The firm remained profitable, but barely, netting just $229,000.

With poor economic conditions continuing into 2009 and likely to cloud the foreseeable future, HFF took steps to reduce operating costs in order to weather the storm. By the end of 2008 the firm had completed a thorough review of its business lines and support functions, and isolated places where it could trim expenses, including the workforce. As a result, HFF cut employment 12 percent, eliminating 57 positions across the country. Further expense reductions followed in April 2009. Another 44 positions, or 10.2 percent of the workforce, were eliminated. Matching 401(k) payments were also suspended and some support staff employees received salary reductions. Senior executives also took salary cuts. CEO John H. Pelusi Jr., for example, reduced his own base salary by 33 percent, or $150,000. Other executives received 25 percent salary cuts. HFF also consolidated its Westport, Connecticut, office with the New York City office.

The lack of available funds in the capital market adversely impacted HFF's clients as well. To find capital market solutions for them was clearly a challenge but obviously a necessary focus of HFF, at least in the short-term. The few areas where management sensed an opening to generate revenues was multifamily debt and investment sales, distressed debt and REO business (foreclosed or forfeited property in the possession of a lender), the note sales and note sale advisory business, the investment banking advisory business, and the servicing line of business. The economic situation was not expected to improve quickly, but there was every reason to expect that HFF would successfully navigate the turbulent waters.

Ed Dinger

PRINCIPAL SUBSIDIARIES

Holliday Fenoglio Fowler L.P.; HFF Securities L.P.

PRINCIPAL COMPETITORS

CB Richard Ellis Group, Inc.; Cushman & Wakefield, Inc.; Jones Lang LaSalle Incorporated.

FURTHER READING

"Amresco Sale Hits Snag," *National Mortgage News,* September 20, 1999, p. 1.

Bell, John, "Holliday Fenoglio Fowler's Success," *Mortgage Banking,* November 2004, p. 76.

Bergsman, Steve, "After the Fall," *Mortgage Banking,* November 1998, p. 52.

Brown, Steve, "Principals to Buy Houston-Based Commercial Real Estate Investment Firm," *Dallas Morning News,* June 19, 2003.

Cook, Lynn J., "Holliday Fenoglio Fowler Sold to U.S. Lend Lease Subsidiary," *Houston Business Journal,* December 24, 1999, p. 5.

"Houston Mortgage Firm Opens Buffalo Office," *Business First of Buffalo,* May 14, 1990, p. 5.

Kindleberger, Richard, "Mortgage Banking Firm Found Itself a Deal," *Boston Globe,* February 28, 1998, p. G1.

Stromberg, Laura A., "Magnates of Mortgage Banking," *Houston Business Journal,* December 19, 1997, p. 14.

IDEX Corp.

630 Dundee Road, Suite 400
Northbrook, Illinois 60062
U.S.A.
Telephone: (847) 498-7070
Fax: (847) 498-3940
Web site: http://www.idexcorp.com

Public Company
Incorporated: 1987
Employees: 5,813
Sales: $1.49 billion (2008)
Stock Exchanges: New York Chicago
Ticker Symbol: IEX
NAICS: 333911 Pump and Pumping Equipment
    Manufacturing

■ ■ ■

Headquartered in Northbrook, Illinois, IDEX Corp. is a diversified engineered products company. It focuses mainly on four industry sectors: dispensing equipment, including paint dispensing stations used at leading home improvement stores; fire and safety products that include the well-known Jaws of Life brand; fluid and metering technologies; and health and science technologies. The products manufactured by IDEX are sold to both consumers and original equipment manufacturers.

FORMATIVE YEARS: 1987–95

Although IDEX was established on September 24, 1987, the company's operations are rooted in a company named Houdaille, which the investment firm Kohlberg Kravis Roberts & Co. took private in 1979.

IDEX's formation happened in an interesting way. In 1986, London-based TI Group PLC offered to acquire Houdaille's John Crane business, a manufacturer of mechanical seals. At the time, Houdaille decided not to pursue the deal. However, in August 1987 TI agreed to acquire all of Houdaille for $500 million. Because it was really only interested in John Crane, TI put the six other operating units that comprised Houdaille up for sale.

Houdaille's former executive team established IDEX for the purpose of acquiring the six units that TI was selling. The $220 million deal was concluded in January 1988. IDEX moved forward under the leadership of former Houdaille CEO Donald N. Boyce, who had joined the company's Akron, New York-based Strippit business in 1969. Under his leadership, IDEX embarked upon a strategy of growing via acquisitions.

Among IDEX's early acquisitions were Madison, Wisconsin-based KLS in August 1989, and Oklahoma City, Oklahoma-based Corken International Corp. in May 1991. That same year, IDEX sold Creative Concepts, an in-house advertising agency that was part of its Strippit Division, to Strippit Communications-Marketing Manager Susan Augustine.

IDEX continued to grow via acquisitions during the early 1990s. International expansion occurred in early 1992, at which time a CAD 9.5 million deal was made to acquire the Pump Group of Devjo Industries. The transaction involved three Canadian companies:

Calgary, Alberta-based Western Pump & Machinery; Viking Pump of Windsor, Ontario; and Toronto, Ontario-based Atlas Engineering & Machine. Another international acquisition took place later in the year when IDEX obtained the United Kingdom's Johnson Pump. Domestic growth also occurred in 1992, when IDEX snapped up Rochester, New York-based Pulsafeeder Inc.

IDEX rounded out the first half of the 1990s with more acquisitions. These included Signfix Holdings Ltd. in Bristol, United Kingdom, as well as a $90 million deal for Hale Products Inc. in 1994. Midway through 1995 IDEX parted with $32 million to obtain Micropump Corp., followed by a $35 million deal for LUKAS Hydraulik GmbH.

EARLY GROWTH: 1996–97

Growth continued in 1996. IDEX acquired Fluid Management for $135 million in July. By late 1996 IDEX had a market capitalization of $777 million. The company had acquired ten other firms since its formation during the late 1980s, and it had plans to continue doing more of the same. In the December 16, 1996, issue of *Mergers & Acquisitions Report,* Chairman and CEO Donald Boyce provided insight into the company's strategy, commenting: "We are very selective. Our ideal acquisition candidate is a producer of proprietary industrial products that have an engineering content, serving diverse markets, with a leadership position in a niche market. Our acquisition strategy is focused—we don't want to be a conglomerate."

IDEX was recognized by the Association for Corporate Growth's Chicago Chapter in September 1996, at which time it received the 1997 Emerging Company Award. Specifically, IDEX was honored for having the strongest three-year growth rate among companies with annual revenues less than $500 million. The company ended the year by leaving that category, as

its annual sales rose from $487.3 million in 1995 to $562.6 million in 1996.

International growth continued in 1997. In April of that year IDEX purchased U.K.-based Terry Harrison Holdings Ltd., which manufactured air-operated diaphragm pumps.

Midway through the year, IDEX announced several leadership changes. In May, the company named Steven E. Semmler as president of its Corken Inc. business, which was located in Oklahoma City, Oklahoma. At the same time, Jeffrey L. Hohman was appointed president of IDEX's Vancouver, Washington-based Micropump Inc. business.

Another leadership change followed in December, when IDEX named Frank J. Hansen as president and chief operating officer. Donald Boyce remained with the company as chairman and CEO. Around the same time, IDEX also acquired Costa Mesa, California-based Knight Equipment International in a cash deal worth $38 million. The new enterprise joined IDEX's Pulsafeeder operation.

IDEX ended 1997 on a high note, breaking records in both sales and net income. Specifically, sales increased 13 percent, totaling $636.1 million. In addition, the company's net income climbed 17 percent, reaching $58.6 million.

ACQUISITIONS CONTINUE: 1998–2000

Acquisition activity continued during the late 1990s. In January 1998, IDEX shelled out $118 million to acquire Benton Harbor, Michigan-based Gast Manufacturing Corp., a maker of air motors, regenerative blowers, fractional horsepower compressors, and vacuum pumps that had annual sales of approximately $100 million. In addition to operations in Michigan, Gast also operated manufacturing sites in both England and Wales.

In April 1998, IDEX took a brief pause from its acquisition strategy and announced plans to divest its Vibratech and Strippit divisions, which had generated a collective $90 million in sales during 1997, but were no longer considered to be core operations. The company indicated it would use proceeds from the divestitures to reduce its $384 million debt load.

The $23 million sale of Vibratech was concluded in mid-1998, via a management buyout involving Ridge Capital Corp. The divestiture of Strippit followed in August, when Gullegem, Belgium-based LVD Company NV agreed to acquire the company in a cash deal valued at $19.5 million.

KEY DATES

1987: IDEX is established.
1996: IDEX receives the 1997 Emerging Company Award from the Association for Corporate Growth's Chicago Chapter.
1997: Frank J. Hansen is named president and chief operating officer.
1999: Donald Boyce retires as CEO but remains chairman; Frank Hansen is named CEO.
2000: Chairman Donald Boyce retires; General Electric Co. executive Dennis K. Williams is named chairman, president, and CEO.
2003: A sales and manufacturing operation is established in China.
2004: Lawrence D. Kingsley is named chief operating officer.
2005: Kingsley succeeds Dennis Williams as president and CEO.
2008: In the fourth quarter, IDEX buys back 2.3 million shares of its stock for $50 million.

In December 1998, Chairman and CEO Donald Boyce announced his intention to step down as CEO on March 31, 1999. However, he intended to remain with the organization as its chairman. Frank Hansen was named as Boyce's successor, effective April 1, 1999.

Midway through 1999, IDEX acquired the Cinisello, Balsamo, Italy-based refinishing and color-formulation equipment manufacturer FAST S.p.A. for $62 million. That November, another leadership change unfolded when President and CEO Frank Hansen revealed plans to retire, capping off a 24-year career with the company. Hansen agreed to remain with IDEX until a suitable replacement could be found.

IDEX ushered in the new millennium with more changes in the executive suite. Chairman Donald Boyce retired from the organization on March 31, 2000. About two weeks later, General Electric Co. executive Dennis K. Williams was named as the company's new chairman, president, and CEO.

In the midst of these leadership changes, IDEX continued along the acquisition path. Glattbrugg, Switzerland-based Ismatec SA, which manufactured metering pumps, process controllers, and sample preparation systems, was acquired in mid-April. In late May, the company parted with $35 million to acquire Trebor International Inc.

SUCCESS IN DIFFICULT TIMES: 2001–04

Progress continued in 2001. In early January, IDEX acquired Class 1 Inc. Around the same time the company acquired a business named Liquid Controls LLC, which generated annual revenues of approximately $50 million from the manufacture of flow meters and process control systems. In June, Liquid Controls was merged with IDEX's Corken operation. That same month, the company also acquired Versa-Matic Tool Inc., along with affiliated businesses named Pumper Parts LLC and Dominator Pump AB.

When the September 11, 2001, terrorist attacks against the United States resulted in the collapse of the World Trade Center in New York, IDEX did its part to help by sending 55 skids of Hurst Jaws of Life rescue tools, as well as two related training vehicles, to the disaster site.

Following difficult economic conditions in 2001, activity continued at IDEX during 2002. That year, the company made a number of acquisitions, beginning with Bridgeport, Connecticut-based Halox Technologies Inc. in April.

That same month, Kohlberg Kravis Roberts & Co. revealed plans to sell a sizable share of its holding in IDEX. Some 14 years after an initial $7.3 million investment in IDEX, the firm stood to generate roughly $131 million through a secondary stock sale of 2.9 million shares by its general partner, Idex Associates, and another 560,801 shares by partner KKR Associates LP.

Midway through the year, Rheodyne L.P. became part of IDEX's corporate family, bolstering its offerings in the areas of injectors, valves, fittings, and accessories. Finally, the company purchased Waukesha, Wisconsin-based Wrightech Corp. in October.

IDEX started off 2003 with news that KKR Associates LP planned to sell 1.35 million additional shares of the company's common stock via a secondary public offering. Acquisitions that year included the Westminster, South Carolina-based precision turbine flow meter manufacturer Sponsler Co. Inc., which joined IDEX in July. In addition, Classic Engineering Inc. was acquired in September.

Other highlights from 2003 included the formation of a sales and manufacturing operation in China. IDEX capped off the year with sales of $797.9 million, up 8 percent in 2002.

In January 2004 IDEX bought Manfred Vetter GmbH, which joined the company's Hale Products arm. In April, IDEX announced a three-for-two stock split. That same month, Systec LLC was acquired, followed by the life sciences company Scivex LLC in May. Scivex operated Santa Clara, California-based J.L. White; Oak Harbor, Washington-based Upchurch Scientific; and Pocasset, Massachusetts-based Sapphire Engineering.

Two important developments occurred in mid-2004, including the acquisition of Tianjin Dinglee Machine and Motor Co. Ltd., and the appointment of Lawrence D. Kingsley as chief operating officer. IDEX ended the year on a high note. Orders totaled $942.4 million, an 18 percent increase from 2003. This supported a 16 percent increase in sales, which reached a record $928.3 million. Net income totaled $86.4 million, up 39 percent from 2003.

CONTINUING GROWTH: 2005–09

In February 2005, IDEX announced that Lawrence Kingsley had been chosen to succeed Dennis Williams as president and CEO on March 22. Williams agreed to remain with the company as chairman until March 31, 2006. For the year, orders increased 12 percent, reaching $1.06 billion. Sales totaled $1.04 billion, a 12 percent increase, and net income jumped 27 percent, totaling $109.8 million.

IDEX kicked off 2006 by expanding its Hale Products operation. In January, the company acquired the assets of Direct Equipment West Ltd.'s British Columbia, Canada-based Airshore International business, which manufactured fire and rescue-related items such as stabilization struts for collapsed vehicles and buildings.

Midway through the year, IDEX acquired Bristol, Connecticut-based Eastern Plastics Inc. Around the same time, the company sold its Warrensville Heights, Ohio-based Lubriquip Inc. business to Graco Inc. Activity continued during the latter part of the year, when IDEX purchased the assets of Crawfordsville, Indiana-based Banjo Corp. for $183 million. That deal was followed by the acquisition of Longwood, Florida-based Toptech Systems Inc. in December, strengthening the company's offerings in the oil, gas, and refined fuels sectors.

More growth in IDEX's oil, gas, and refined fuels business occurred during the later years of the first decade of the 2000s. On the international front, IDEX purchased the La Ferte Bernard, France-based metering technologies business Faure Herman SA in February 2007. In October, a $101 million deal was made for the Germany-based specialized pumps, valves, and control equipment manufacturer Richter Chemie-Technik GmbH. IDEX rounded out the year by acquiring Isolation Technologies of Hopedale, Massachusetts, which became part of its Sapphire Engineering operation.

More growth took place in January 2008, at which time IDEX parted with $160 million in order to obtain ADS LLC. Three additional deals unfolded in October of that year. In addition to acquiring Ipek Spezial-TV of Hirshegg, Austria, and IETG of the United Kingdom, the Rochester, New York-based optical filter company Semrock became part of IDEX toward the end of the month.

IDEX was faced with a very challenging economic climate during the later years of the first decade of the 2000s. In 2008 the company reduced the size of its workforce and shuttered two facilities as part of a restructuring initiative that stood to save $20 million in 2009. In the fourth quarter of 2008, IDEX spent $50 million to buy back 2.3 million shares of its stock.

Despite the difficult economy, in early 2009 IDEX reported that orders had increased 9 percent in 2008, and sales had increased 10 percent. Combined with the company's efforts to reduce costs, IDEX seemed to be on solid footing as it approached the 21st century's second decade.

Paul R. Greenland

PRINCIPAL SUBSIDIARIES

Band-It Clamps (Asia) Pte. Ltd. (Singapore); Band-It Company Ltd. (UK); Band-It IDEX Inc.; Banjo Corp.; Blagdon Pump Holdings Ltd. (UK); Class 1 Inc.; Corken Inc.; Dominator Pump AB (Sweden); E.P.I. Realty LLC; Eastern Plastics Inc.; FAST & Fluid Management Australia Pty. Ltd.; FAST & Fluid Management East Europe Sp. z.o.o. (Poland); FAST & Fluid Management France SARL; FAST & Fluid Management Iberica S.A. (Spain); FAST & Fluid Management S.r.l. (Italy); FAST & Fluid Management U.K. Ltd.; Faure Herman Meter Inc.; Faure Herman SAS (France); Fluid Management Canada Inc.; Fluid Management Espana SLU (Spain); Fluid Management Europe B.V. (Netherlands); Fluid Management GmbH (Germany); Fluid Management Operations LLC; Fluid Management Servicos e Vendas Ltda. (Brazil); Fluid Management Inc.; FM Delaware Inc.; FM Investment, Inc.; Gast Asia Inc.; Gast Manufacturing Company Ltd. (UK); Gast Manufacturing Inc.; Godiva Limited (UK); Godiva Products Limited (UK); Hale Products Europe GmbH (Germany); Hale Products Europe Limited (UK); Hale Products Inc.; IDEX Asia Pacific Pte. Ltd. (Singapore); IDEX Dinglee Technology (Tianjin) Co. Ltd. (China); IDEX Europe GmbH (Germany); IDEX Holdings, Inc.; IDEX a Private Ltd. (India); IDEX Leasing GmbH (Germany); IDEX Middle East FZE (United Arab Emirates); IDEX Precision Products (Suzhou) Co.

Ltd. (China); IDEX Receivables Corp.; IDEX Service Corporation; IDEX Technology (Suzhou) Co. Ltd. (China); IDEX Trading (Shanghai) Co. Ltd. (China); Ismatec Laboratoriumstechnik GmbH (Germany); Ismatec S.A. (Switzerland); Johnson Pump (UK) Ltd.; JUN-AIR (UK) Ltd.; JUN-AIR AB (Sweden), JUN-AIR Benelux B.V. (Netherlands); JUN-AIR France S.A.S.; JUN-AIR Inc. USA; JUN-AIR International A/S (Denmark); JUN-AIR Norge A/S (Norway); Knight (Canada) Limited; Knight Equipment Australia Pty. Ltd.; Knight Europe B.V. (Netherlands); Knight LLC; Knight U.K. Limited; Knight Inc.; Liquid Controls (India) Pvt. Ltd.; Liquid Controls Europe SpA (Italy); Liquid Controls LLC; Liquid Controls Sponsler Inc.; LUKAS Hydraulik GmbH (Germany); M. BOS Srl (Italy); Micropump Limited (UK); Micropump Inc.; Pulsafeeder Europe B.V. (Netherlands); Pulsafeeder Inc.; Quadro (US) Inc.; Quadro Engineering Corp. (Canada); Rheodyne Europe GmbH (Germany); Rheodyne LLC; S.A.M.P.I. SpA (Italy); Sapphire Engineering Inc.; SAS Paros (France); Scivex, Inc.; Signfix Holdings Limited (UK); Signfix Limited; Systec LLC; Tespa GmbH (Germany); Tianjin Dinglee Machine and Motor Co. Ltd. (China); Toptech Europe N.V. (Belgium); Toptech Systems Inc.; Trebor International Inc.; Upchurch Scientific Inc.; Versa-Matic Pump Inc.; Vetter GmbH (Germany); Viking Pump (Europe) Ltd. (Ireland); Viking Pump Latin America S.A. de C.V. (Mexico); Viking Pump of Canada Inc.; Viking Pump Inc.; Warren Rupp Europe Ltd. (UK); Warren Rupp Inc.; Wright Flow Technologies Inc.; Wright Flow Technologies Limited (UK).

PRINCIPAL COMPETITORS

Dover Corp.; Roper Industries Inc.; Thomas Products.

FURTHER READING

Giesen, Lauri, "IDEX Acquires Six Operating Units from TI: Company Reacquires Division Sold in 1987," *Metalworking News,* February 1, 1988.

"Idex Continues Build-On Acquisition Plan," *Mergers & Acquisitions Report,* December 16, 1996.

"IDEX Corporation Announces Retirement of Donald N. Boyce As Chairman," *PR Newswire,* April 3, 2000.

"IDEX Corporation Announces That KKR Associates, L.P. Will Sell 1.35 Million Shares of IDEX Common Stock," *PR Newswire,* January 14, 2003.

"IDEX Corporation Names Dennis K. Williams As New Chairman, President and Chief Executive Officer; Frank J. Hansen to Retire," *PR Newswire,* April 14, 2000.

"IDEX Corporation Reports 2008 Results; 9% Orders Growth, 10% Sales Growth, Adjusted EPS up 4%," *Investment Weekly News,* February 21, 2009.

"Lawrence D. Kingsley Named President and Chief Executive Officer of IDEX Corporation; Dennis K. Williams Retains Role As Chairman of the Board," *Business Wire,* February 28, 2005.

Murphy, H. Lee, "Idex Strategy Focuses on Divesting, Investing," *Crain's Chicago Business,* April 6, 1998.

Jimmy John's Enterprises, Inc.

2212 Fox Drive
Champaign, Illinois 61820-7553
U.S.A.
Telephone: (217) 356-9900
Toll Free: (800) 546-6904
Fax: (217) 359-2956
Web site: http://www.jimmyjohns.com

Private Company
Incorporated: 1983
Employees: 350
Sales: $600 million (2008 est.)
NAICS: 722211 Limited-Service Restaurants

∎∎∎

Jimmy John's Enterprises, Inc., is the holding company for the Jimmy John's Gourmet Sandwich Shops chain of fast-food restaurants. The privately held, Champaign, Illinois-based company operates and franchises more than 700 stores in 35 states, as well as a handful of stores in Central America. The key to the chain's success has been a focus on a limited menu, fresh ingredients, delivery, and college town locations. The stores offer eight-inch and 16-inch sub sandwiches, a variety of club sandwiches, and lettuce-wrap versions of both the sub and club sandwiches. Side items are limited to soda, one brand of potato chips, kosher dill pickles, and giant chocolate chip or oatmeal raisin cookies. Boxed lunches and party platters are also available. Bread is baked fresh in the stores each day and served warm from the oven. All meats and cheeses are fresh and cut daily. The

company is majority owned by its founder, chairman, and chief executive officer, James (Jimmy) John Liautaud. The San Francisco private-equity firm of Weston Presidio has owned about one-third of the company since 2007 and plays an important role in driving the growth of the chain.

FOUNDER GRADUATES NEAR BOTTOM OF 1982 HIGH SCHOOL CLASS

Jimmy John Liautaud was born in Arlington Heights, Illinois, in 1964. His father, Jim Liautaud, was a mechanical engineer who in 1968 started his own company, Capsonic, which merged metals and plastics. It was a high-flying company for several years but because of Liautaud's neglect, it was on the verge of bankruptcy before he turned it around. Jim Liautaud's financial difficulties had an adverse impact on his son as Jimmy attempted to fit in at a private prep school, Elgin Academy. The heavyset youngster was rebellious, often tardy, and became involved in fights. After his junior year the school's faculty urged that he be expelled, but coming to his defense was the dean of discipline, James Lyons, who believed the young man was simply insecure and acting out because of problems at home. Lyons mentored Liautaud and provided advice as graduation neared in 1982. Money was still tight at home and Liautaud's grades were poor—he would finish second from the bottom of his graduating class—essentially eliminating college as a choice. Lyons urged him to pursue his passion: food. Jim Liautaud, who had successfully turned around his company, then offered to provide $25,000 to start a business. Should he fail, the younger Liautaud agreed to join the U.S. Army.

Liautaud initially wanted to start a Chicago-style hot dog stand modeled after the famous Portillo's chain. He spent three weeks studying the business and realized that even if he purchased used equipment, at the very least he needed $43,000 in start-up funds. His father was unwilling to increase the loan, forcing Liautaud to look for a new idea. It was while visiting a friend at Marquette University in Milwaukee, Wisconsin, that he found an alternative. They went to a local sandwich shop to eat and Liautaud realized that the only equipment there was a meat slicer and a beer cooler. Deciding to open a sandwich shop, he devoted the next few months to driving around the country visiting local sandwich shops, collecting menus. Back at home he began to make his own sandwiches. Disappointed with the available bread, he decided to bake his own loaves. After some study at the library, he and his mother spent three days experimenting until they found a bread recipe he liked. Liautaud then created six sandwiches, using friends and family to test them. Everyone agreed that four of the sandwiches should make the menu. His personal favorite, made with liver, sausage, onion, and mayonnaise, did not.

FIRST SHOP OPENS 1983

Before Liautaud started his sandwich shop, his father provided him with a checkbook and two pieces of advice: Put your money in the bank every day and always pay cash on delivery. Liautaud decided to open his sandwich shop in Charleston, Illinois, where his brother and cousins were attending Eastern Illinois University. He rented and converted a 600-square-foot former garage. Although located close to campus, it was hardly an ideal location and had already failed as a pizza shop, and the house it was attached to had previously failed as a Dixie Cream Donut Shop. Nevertheless, he signed a five-year lease and installed a new oven, a secondhand meat slicer, a used Sears chest freezer, and half-a-dozen old bread pans. His mother donated some old Tupperware and an oven mitt. Altogether he spent $23,871. On January 13, 1983, the day after his 19th

birthday, Liautaud opened the doors of Jimmy John's Gourmet Sandwiches to the public, which greeted the new establishment by purchasing all of two $1.25 sandwiches.

Convinced that people would make their way to the former garage once they tasted his four-item menu, Liautaud began to give out sample-size sandwiches, visiting office buildings by day and bars at night. Sampling worked, and soon he had a steady stream of customers. To drum up further business Jimmy John's began to deliver to dormitories, something that other restaurants in the area would not do. Thus, one major aspect of the Jimmy John's business model was purely the result of necessity.

Liautaud's on-the-job business training was far from over, however. As the owner, he elected to give himself weekends off and assigned the hardest shifts to two friends who had joined him in the enterprise. With nothing at stake, they did not last long. The first left after a month, the second two months after that. Liautaud had to assume all of their shifts and found himself working open to close seven days a week, something he would do for 120 straight days. It was an exhausting stretch, but it served the young businessman well in the long run. He came to know his customers and he came to discern the most efficient way to do things. He began writing down all of his procedures, which he would then refine. In time, this information would lay the groundwork for the opening of additional stores and eventually franchising. Liautaud also learned the importance of accounting. During a college break when he had some free time, he balanced his checkbook. It was then that he realized he had yet to send the state the sales tax he had been collecting. His father hired an accountant who determined that the store owed $12,000. Liautaud contacted the state about the problem and a sympathetic supervisor was sent to visit the store. Liautaud escaped penalty, but learned the importance of keeping close tabs on the books.

REPAYS FATHER: 1985

With his business under control, Liautaud was once again ready to hire an employee. This time, however, he kept the tough work for himself and delegated the easy tasks. When the first year came to a close, Jimmy John's posted sales of $155,000. For his efforts, Liautaud calculated that he had made about 92 cents per hour. The second year the shop took in $188,000. By this time his father had made $45,000 on the venture, prompting Liautaud to declare that the two were even. His father disagreed, reminding him that he still owed $25,000 plus 10 percent interest. In 1985 Liautaud paid off his debt in cash.

KEY DATES

1983: Jimmy John Liautaud opens first Jimmy John's Gourmet Sandwich shop.
1986: Second shop opens.
1993: Franchising begins; corporate headquarters are established in Elgin, Illinois.
2003: Chain opens 200th unit.
2005: Headquarters are relocated to Champaign, Illinois.
2007: Weston Presidio acquires 33 percent stake.

Now a businessman completely on his own, Liautaud was ready to expand. It was at this juncture that he found a new mentor, Jamie Coulter, a Pizza Hut franchisee who was a friend of his father. Coulter would later found and serve as chief executive of the Lone Star Steakhouse & Saloon, Sullivan's, and Del Frisco's chains. For Jimmy John's, Coulter played a key role in teaching Liautaud how to run multiple units, and he emphasized the value of keeping a limited menu. In 1986 Liautaud opened a second store in another college town, Macomb, Illinois, and worked there for a year to get it established. A friend who was to help run it died, and once again Liautaud found himself working double shifts. A third store was added in 1987, and once again Liautaud devoted a year of his time to the new venture.

HEADQUARTERS IN ELGIN

By 1993 Liautaud had opened another eight stores; established a corporate headquarters in Elgin, Illinois; and began making plans to franchise Jimmy John's, something he had initially resisted, fearful of losing quality control. Franchised shops then opened in Illinois, Indiana, Iowa, and Wisconsin. In 1996 Jimmy John's ventured into Central America through franchisees Lucia and Edwin Escobar. As M.B.A. students at Northwestern University in 1995, they became regular customers of Jimmy John's and contacted Liautaud about taking the concept to Latin America, where in Guatemala Lucia's family were major retailers. Five sandwich shops then opened in Guatemala City, and in 1996 the Escobars signed an area-development agreement to expand into El Salvador.

Jimmy John's enjoyed steady growth in the second half of the 1990s, as Liautaud remained faithful to a simple format. Although the menu had expanded to include 23 sandwiches, the main ingredients were limited to five meats, one cheese, and two bread doughs.

Two kinds of chips and one type of cookie, baked by the same baker, were shipped frozen to the stores for thawing (the stores did not offer breakfast or specialty items). The stores also adhered to three different formats: units about 1,160 square feet offering 70 seats, delivery and takeout-only shops of about 300 square feet, and units of 150 square feet that sold sandwiches prepared from a commissary. Average unit sales reached $568,000 in 1997, about half of which came from delivery, the company's not-so-secret key to success and a feature that separated it from other sandwich shops. By the end of the decade the chain consisted of 61 units, of which nine were company owned.

The pace of Jimmy John's expansion picked up, primarily through franchising. In 2000, 26 new stores opened, followed by 31 in 2001. Moreover, same-store sales continued to grow, increasing from $677,183 in 2000 to $838,946. Systemwide sales improved from $55 million in 2000 to $85 million in 2001. The menu changed slightly, as one more meat and canned tuna were added to the mix, as was seven-grain bread to allow for the addition of club sandwiches. Much of the sales growth in the company-owned stores was attributed to the renovation of older units and the 20 percent increase of meats and cheeses to the sandwiches without an increase in price. In addition, Liautaud paid store managers a bonus for growing sales, a policy that he urged franchisees to follow as well.

Systemwide sales in 2002 increased to about $135 million from 15 company-owned stores and 152 franchised units. To help spur further growth, Liautaud in 2003 hired John Matthews to serve as president and spearhead nationwide expansion. Matthews was the former national marketing director of Little Caesars and prior to joining Jimmy John's was vice-president of Clark Retail Enterprises, a convenience store company with 1,250 units under the Clark and White Hen Pantry banners. In July 2003 Jimmy John's opened its 200th restaurant. Although college towns and locations near campus remained an important element of Jimmy John's success, the chain looked for more traditional business locations. Yet the company found it increasingly difficult to secure desirable locations. The chain came to have more potential franchisees than locations.

Other challenges cropped up as well early in the first decade of the 2000s, when after a decade of double-digit gains Jimmy John's units experienced a decrease in same-store sales. In answer, portion sizes were increased while delivery areas were drawn in. In this way, delivery times were shortened, and customers responded by giving more business to Jimmy John's. In 2004 Matthews left the company.

SELLING A STAKE IN THE COMPANY: 2007

In 2005 Jimmy John's developed a television marketing campaign as a prelude to an expansion beyond the Midwest to such areas of the country as New York, Maryland, and Seattle. To keep pace with the chain's growth, the corporate headquarters were moved from Elgin to larger accommodations in Champaign, Illinois, in 2005. By the start of 2007 Jimmy John's totaled 475 stores. Real estate remained an impediment to further growth, however. To help in this regard as well as spur expansion in other areas, Liautaud searched for a strategic partner. After narrowing the field to five private-equity firms, he settled on San Francisco-based Weston Presidio (a company that also held stakes in Jet-Blue Airways and Wild Oats Markets), selling to them a 33 percent interest in Jimmy John's. The relationship paid immediate dividends. In the first year with Weston Presidio, the chain was able to close on more than 100 real estate deals.

With over 700 stores in 35 states and systemwide sales of $600 million by the start of 2009, Jimmy John's was poised for even greater success. Its founder was a notable success, his autograph sought after. Yet he had not forgotten his old prep school and James Lyons, the man who kept him from being expelled. He donated $1 million to Elgin Academy to help fund a new academic center, asking that the building bear Lyons's name. In the end he agreed to share the billing with Lyons because it was felt that his story would inspire other students. Lyons also felt uncomfortable with his name above the door, but liked the idea of a student and educator joined together. Thus the Liautaud-Lyons Upper School opened in late 2008, in many ways a testament to someone who followed his passion: food.

Ed Dinger

PRINCIPAL SUBSIDIARIES

Jimmy John's Franchise, LLC; Jimmy John's Inc.

PRINCIPAL COMPETITORS

Doctor's Associates Inc.; Kahala Corp.; The Quiznos Master LLC.

FURTHER READING

Casey, Erin, "Hard-Earned Success: Jimmy John Liautaud Combined a Small Loan and Strong Work Ethic to Build a Nationwide Chain," *Success,* April 2009, p. 28.

Johnson, Dirk, "Troublesome Student Makes Good, and Honors Disciplinarian," *New York Times,* December 31, 2008, p. A14.

Koprowski, Gene, "No Honor Roll, No College Degree, No Problem," *Chicago Tribune,* August 17, 1997, p. 1.

Medill, David Dolan, "Jimmy John's Tasty Sandwiches Creating Legions of New Fans," *Arlington Heights (Ill.) Daily Herald,* May 26, 2004, p. 1.

Meyer, Ann, "Checklist Frees Franchisees," *Chicago Tribune,* May 16, 2005, p. 3.

Nachtrab, Julianne, "Entrepreneur Jim Liautaud: Hard Work and Examination Pulled Him Up," *Investor's Business Daily,* April 30, 2001, p. A04.

Rohland, Pamela, "Just Jimmy John," *QSR Magazine,* March 2003.

Van Houten, Ben, "Papa Jimmy?" *Restaurant Business,* July 1, 2000, p. 16.

Walkup, Carolyn, "Jimmy John's 'Delivers' on Growth," *Nation's Restaurant News,* January 14, 2002, p. 1.

———, "Jimmy John's Founder Liautaud Plots Growth, Keeps Focus," *Nation's Restaurant News,* September 7, 1998, p. 24.

———, "Jimmy John's Sandwich Chain to Jump-Start Growth," *Nation's Restaurant News,* August 18, 2003, p. 28.

Walkup, Carolyn, and Susan Cavanaugh, "Jimmy John's Puts Bite on College Market Share," *Nation's Restaurant News,* June 27, 1994, p. 12.

Weingartner, Nancy, "Reflections of a Big Man on Campus," *Franchise Times,* May 2008.

JTH Tax Inc.

———■———

1716 Corporate Landing Parkway
Virginia Beach, Virginia 23454
U.S.A.
Telephone: (757) 493-8855
Toll Free: (800) 790-3863
Fax: (800) 880-6432
Web site: http://www.libertytax.com

Private Company
Incorporated: 1997
Employees: 125
Sales: $75.14 million (2007)
NAICS: 541213 Tax Preparation Services

■ ■ ■

JTH Tax Inc. is the entity that owns Liberty Tax Service, a franchiser of tax preparation offices in North America. Liberty has agreements with more than 1,600 franchisees who operate 3,000 offices that prepare tax returns for individuals. The company is led by John Hewitt, a former H&R Block regional director who founded Jackson Hewitt Tax Service.

FOUNDER'S BACKGROUND

In the tax preparation industry, it is difficult to find a more influential figure than John Hewitt, an entrepreneur who left an indelible mark on the profession he embraced early in life. After earning his high school diploma in 1967, Hewitt attended the University of Buffalo, where he signed up for a non-curricular course during his sophomore year that galvanized his professional aspirations. The course was offered by H&R Block, Inc., the Kansas City, Missouri-based leader in the tax preparation industry. After Hewitt completed the tax preparation course, he dropped out of the University of Buffalo and sought employment from the company that had offered what he described as the most interesting course he had ever taken.

Hewitt joined H&R Block as a tax preparer and began a meteoric rise through the company's hierarchy. After his first year at H&R Block, Hewitt was promoted to the position of assistant manager for the company's Buffalo district. Next, he was appointed district manager in Elmira, New York, a post he held from 1975 to 1980. Hewitt made company history with his next advancement within H&R Block's management ranks, becoming the youngest individual ever to hold the position of regional director. Hewitt oversaw 250 branch offices as an H&R Block regional director, managing more than 2,000 tax preparers in one of the company's largest districts.

INNOVATION LEADS TO INDEPENDENCE

Hewitt, the H&R Block wunderkind, immersed himself in the tax preparation business. When his father purchased an Apple personal computer in the early 1980s, Hewitt looked at the device and envisioned its capabilities as a tool to prepare tax forms. He and his father developed software that offered responses to individual tax questions, creating a decision-tree tax interview application that was one of the first of its

COMPANY PERSPECTIVES

At Liberty Tax Service, being a principles-led company is more than a list of ideals—it is part of our mission. Since 1997, a mission statement that seeks to balance strong growth, best business practices, social responsibility, and a fulfilling life experience for our franchisees and employees has guided us. Our Mission Statement of "Set the Standard, Improve Each Day, Have Some Fun," calls us to use our business model to improve the quality of life of our community, country and the world.

kind. He took the program to his superiors at H&R Block, hoping to sell the software to the company, but his offer was rebuffed. His response to the apathy of his employers was to strike out on his own, believing the software he had developed, dubbed "Hewtax," could form the basis of a new tax preparation venture.

Hewitt left H&R Block ready to make his mark in the tax preparation industry. He suffered from no lack of ambition, setting goals for himself that required phenomenal success with his first entrepreneurial attempt. "The biggest thing I fear is that I won't be No. 1," he said years later in the October 13, 2003 edition of the *Buffalo News*. "Do I really want a gravestone that says, 'No. 2 in the tax business?'" he asked. To launch his assault on H&R Block, Hewitt purchased a small tax preparation company in Hampton Roads, Virginia, named Mel Jackson Tax Service. The transaction, completed in 1982, gave him control of six offices operating in the Hampton Roads area.

Hewitt expanded his company at a feverish pace. He changed its name to Jackson Hewitt Tax Service and began selling franchises throughout the country, using the company's proprietary software to create a new powerhouse in the industry. By 1992, a decade after Hewitt started the venture, Jackson Hewitt Tax Service had eclipsed all rivals except for H&R Block, ranking as one of the fastest-growing companies in the country, as determined by *Inc.* magazine. In 1994, Hewitt took his company public, selling shares in his franchised operation on the New York Stock Exchange.

LESSONS LEARNED FROM JACKSON HEWITT TAX SERVICE

Jackson Hewitt Tax Service's stature by the mid-1990s was impressive, but the sprawling operation created by Hewitt suffered from financial and organizational problems. Not long after Hewitt invited shareholders to take ownership stakes in the company, the company's situation became dire, resulting in a turn of events that pocked the record of the former H&R Block wunderkind. The company, which had been suffering from cash flow problems, defaulted on its bank loans in 1995, requiring it to agree to a costly restructuring of its loans with its primary lender, NationsBank. Unhappy with the financial results recorded by the company, Jackson Hewitt Tax Service's board of directors took action in 1996, engineering Hewitt's ouster. Keith E. Alessi, the former leader of the Farm Fresh Inc. grocery store chain, was hired as Jackson Hewitt Tax Service's new chief executive officer, which prompted Hewitt to resign shortly thereafter, ending his relationship with a company that he had built into a 1,345-store chain.

Hewitt conceded he had made mistakes while orchestrating the fast-paced expansion of Jackson Hewitt Tax Service. His allocation of company resources for software development and marketing was one regrettable move. "We spent millions of dollars and tons of time on the software, but we did a bad job getting people in the door," he said in the November 3, 1998 edition of the *Virginian-Pilot*. His biggest blunder occurred in 1988, when he negotiated a deal that allowed Jackson Hewitt Tax Service to open offices within Montgomery Ward department stores. The agreement called for Hewitt's company to open tax preparation offices in 180 Montgomery Ward stores in 20 states, but the expansion proved disastrous, spreading the company's presence too thinly. Halfway through the 1989 tax-return season, Hewitt was forced to shutter one-third of its Montgomery Ward offices.

Mistakes had been made with Jackson Hewitt Tax Service and Hewitt was forced to make an ignoble retreat, but he had no intention of forsaking his dream of building the largest tax preparation company in the United States. "I'm a shameless self-promoter," he said in the October 13, 2003 edition of the *Buffalo News*. "Probably one of the biggest you'll ever see. Sometimes I go a little too far, but if you're not out there pushing yourself, pushing your company, you shouldn't even be in this business." The irrepressible Hewitt was ready for more, still wishing to reign supreme in his profession, but his goal of dominating the tax preparation industry had been made more difficult by his own actions. He had to beat H&R Block, a company with more than 8,700 offices in 1997, and he had to contend with the industry's second largest competitor, the company he had built and the company that still bore his name. "It's a little weird," he said of his battle with Jackson Hewitt Tax Service in the November 3, 1998 edition of the *Virginian-Pilot*, "but it's even weirder for them."

KEY DATES

1997: John Hewitt acquires U&R Tax Depot, a Canadian company he will use to build a North American tax preparation chain.

1998: Hewitt enters the U.S. market and changes the name of U&R Tax Depot to Liberty Tax Service.

1999: Hewitt's non-compete agreement with Jackson Hewitt Tax Service expires, freeing him to ramp up his expansion efforts in the United States.

2001: With 551 offices in the United States and Canada, Liberty's revenues reach $10.7 million.

2003: Expansion increases the number of Liberty offices to 919 and lifts revenues to $28.5 million.

2007: Hewitt acquires eSmartTax from C&S Technologies, enabling him to offer online tax preparation services.

JTH TAX INC. FORMED IN 1997

Hewitt was eager to launch his second tax preparation business, but contractual restrictions with Jackson Hewitt Tax Service barred a full-fledged assault on the U.S. market. He had signed a non-compete agreement with the company he had formerly led that prohibited him from operating throughout much of the country; the agreement expired on April 30, 1999. Instead of waiting, Hewitt headed north, escaping the purview of his non-compete agreement. He formed JTH Tax Inc. to facilitate his reentry into the tax preparation business and acquired a Canadian tax franchiser named U&R Tax Depot on September 1, 1997.

Having learned from his mistakes at Jackson Hewitt Tax Service, Hewitt was determined not to repeat them. He intended to expand at a rapid rate, particularly once he was free to operate without restrictions in the United States, but he vowed to concentrate store locations in every market he entered, thereby avoiding the Montgomery Ward debacle that hobbled his ability to build brand recognition. He also established performance requirements that franchisees had to fulfill. If a franchisee failed to prepare at least 1,000 tax returns by his or her third year in business, the franchisee would be terminated.

Hewitt, who had an insatiable appetite for expansion, expanded on two fronts with his new venture, opening offices in Canada and in the United States. In 1998, the year he changed U&R Tax Depot's name to Liberty Tax Service, he opened his first offices in the United States, selecting a market excluded from his non-compete agreement. He opened a cluster of five offices in Columbus, Ohio, the first of 1,500 offices he planned to open in the country by 2003. At the time, Liberty operated 207 offices through franchise agreements in Canada, a number he planned to increase to more than 700 by 2003. In early 1999, during the last months of his non-compete agreement, Hewitt increased Liberty's presence in the United States, entering four new markets (Providence, Rhode Island; Williamsport, Pennsylvania; Chattanooga, Tennessee; and Seattle, Washington) giving him a total of 35 offices in the country. Franchisees, in a letter excerpted in the March 30, 1999 edition of the *Virginian-Pilot,* were promised far more office openings once Hewitt's efforts were unfettered by his contractual obligations to Jackson Hewitt Tax Service. "We will acquire existing competitor locations, buy land and build locations, and employ aggressive local store marketing," Hewitt wrote. "We will buy competitors and/or hire their best people."

RAPID EXPANSION

In terms of expansion, Hewitt accomplished more in a shorter period with Liberty than he had with Jackson Hewitt Tax Service. During his first three years at the helm of Liberty, Hewitt opened as many offices as he had during his first decade in charge of Jackson Hewitt Tax Service. By 2001, the network of Liberty stores comprised 551 offices operated by 248 franchisees, which enabled JTH Tax to record $10.7 million in revenue for the year. During the next two years, the chain recorded robust physical growth, expanding to 919 offices. Revenues nearly tripled in response, jumping to $28.5 million by 2003. Hewitt's growth projections by this point were as ambitious as ever, calling for the chain to double in size during the ensuing two years and to double in size again by 2008, when Hewitt hoped to have 3,600 Liberty offices in operation in the United States and Canada.

As Liberty neared the end of its first decade in business, it was closing fast on Jackson Hewitt Tax Service, touting itself as the fast-growing tax preparation company in North America. Between 2003 and 2007, the number of Liberty offices increased from 919 to 2,363, while the number of franchisees swelled from 551 to 1,607. Liberty's tenth anniversary in 2007 was a milestone Hewitt could celebrate with a good measure of pride, particularly because Liberty recorded a greater increase in the number of raw tax returns during the year than H&R Block and Jackson Hewitt Tax Service recorded combined. "Moreover," Hewitt wrote in the company's 2007 annual report, "we accomplished that with just 2,000 offices compared to 19,000 offices for the competition. We have made history in the income tax industry." Further cause for celebration during the year was the company's financial performance. Revenues increased nearly 14 percent to $75 million and net income nearly doubled, increasing 90 percent to $15.7 million.

ACQUISITION OF ESMARTTAX IN 2007

Liberty's tenth anniversary also included an expansion of the services offered by the company. For nearly four years, Hewitt had negotiated with Intuit Inc., seeking to form a joint venture with the developer of TurboTax, a tax preparation application. The discussions failed to produce any meaningful results, which prompted Hewitt to approach San Jose, California-based C&S Technologies. Hewitt acquired eSmartTax from C&S Technologies in 2007, a purchase that was expected to generate additional revenue for Liberty franchisees because less than one third of the individuals who started to file their returns online completed the process. Individuals who failed to complete the eSmartTax process online were referred to their local Liberty office. For each individual that completed the eSmartTax process, Liberty agreed to pay a 14 percent royalty to the franchisee in whose territory the customer resided.

Looking ahead, there was every expectation Hewitt would continue to increase the number of Liberty offices. He wanted nothing less than to preside over the largest tax preparation company in North America, a goal that would require him to expand aggressively in the years ahead. By 2009, H&R Block operated more than 13,000 offices. Jackson Hewitt Tax Service controlled a chain of nearly 7,000 offices. Hewitt, with more than 3,000 offices in operation in 2009, had come a long way in a short time. Nonetheless, to realize his dream of supremacy, much needed to be accomplished as he plotted his future course.

Jeffrey L. Covell

PRINCIPAL SUBSIDIARIES

Liberty Tax Service; Liberty Tax Service Canada.

PRINCIPAL COMPETITORS

H&R Block, Inc.; Jackson Hewitt Tax Service Inc.; Intuit Inc.

FURTHER READING

Dennis, Staci, "For Company, Lady Liberty Represents Different Tradition," *Virginian-Pilot,* November 4, 1999, p. 4.

"Liberty Tax Service Scores Again by Obtaining College Credits for Its Training Courses," *Mental Health Weekly Digest,* November 24, 2008, p. 174.

Phillips, Noelle, "Need It Now: Bad Economy Creating Early Filers," *Columbia (S.C.) State,* January 18, 2009.

Purdy, Kevin, "Entrepreneur with Hamburg, N.Y., Ties Tries to Build Largest Tax Franchise," *Buffalo News,* October 13, 2003.

Shean, Tom, "A Celebrated Return," *Virginian-Pilot,* March 30, 1999, p. D1.

———, "Federal Court Gives Tax Preparation Chain Time to Look for Violations," *Virginian-Pilot,* March 1, 2001.

———, "Hewitt's New Tax Service," *Virginian-Pilot,* November 3, 1998, p. D1.

———, "Liberty Buys eSmartTax to Tap into Online Business," *Virginian-Pilot,* January 9, 2007.

Kemps LLC

—■—

1270 Energy Lane
St. Paul, Minnesota 55108
U.S.A.
Telephone: (651) 379-6500
Toll Free: (800) 322-9566
Fax: (651) 379-6803
Web site: http://www.kemps.com

Division of HP Hood LLC
Incorporated: 1914 as Kemps Ice Cream Company
Employees: 1,450
Sales: $650 million (2008 est.)
NAICS: 311511 Fluid Milk Manufacturing; 311520 Ice
    Cream and Frozen Dessert Manufacturing; 424430
    Dairy Product (Except Dried or Canned) Merchant
    Wholesalers

■ ■ ■

Kemps LLC is a leading U.S. dairy products manufacturer, with a strong presence in markets in the upper Midwest, the Northeast, the mid-Atlantic, and the Gulf States regions. Kemps is well known for its Kemps brand milk and ice cream. The brand is also a market leader in frozen yogurt and in Yo-J, a yogurt-juice drink the company pioneered. Kemps also sells dairy products under the brand names Hood, Hagan, Green's, and Arrowhead. Its plants include five fluid milk and ice cream facilities in Minnesota, a foodservice distributorship in Chicago, an ice cream plant in Connecticut, and a fluid milk processing plant in Cedarburg, Wisconsin. Kemps traces its lineage back to a small ice cream

manufacturer in Minnesota. However, it grew through many mergers, and for much of its history was known as Marigold Foods, Inc. Since 2004, Kemps has been a division of the Lynnfield, Massachusetts, dairy company HP Hood LLC.

SMALL BEGINNINGS

The history of Kemps LLC reflects the development of the U.S. dairy industry as a whole. Beginning as a tiny family-owned company, it later merged with other local players and became better known throughout its region. An accelerated pace of industry mergers and acquisitions ultimately left Kemps one of the largest companies in the market, with distribution throughout significant portions of the nation. Despite many twists and turns and changes in ownership, the Kemps brand name held on.

Kemps Ice Cream Company was a small, family-owned creamery in southern Minnesota. It was founded in 1914. Kemps remained a local phenomenon all the way through the Great Depression and World War II. In the postwar years, Kemps combined with other regional players. In 1961, Kemps Ice Cream, then based in Minneapolis, merged with a neighboring dairy in St. Paul, Minnesota, called Crescent Creamery. At the same time, the two Minnesota companies merged with a dairy based in Wisconsin, Dolly Madison Dairies. The three together took the new name Marigold Foods, Inc.

As a larger player, spanning two states in the upper Midwest, Marigold hoped to build up its market share. The new company was indeed more profitable than its small components had been, and within six years,

Marigold had doubled in size. By 1967, Marigold had sales of about $33 million. Yet it still did not have the capital it needed to grow further. Another merger took place in 1968 when Marigold was acquired by Ward Foods, Inc. Under Ward's umbrella, Marigold continued to grow rapidly. At the end of a decade, the company had seen sales increase from $33 million to as much as $86 million. At that point, Marigold found a new owner in the Dutch company Wessanen.

GROWTH UNDER WESSANEN

Royal Wessanen NV was a Dutch company with a lineage going back more than 200 years. It made a range of food products at facilities in the Netherlands and elsewhere in Europe. In 1978, it made its first venture into North American markets with its purchase of Marigold. Marigold was run by the company's U.S. holding company, Wessanen USA, which had headquarters in Ridgewood, New Jersey. With the Dutch company's deep pockets, Marigold began a quick upward course of expansion through acquisition, product development, and innovative marketing.

In the first two years of its new ownership, Marigold acquired several regional dairies. It bought the Clover Leaf Creamery in 1979. Clover Leaf was based in Minneapolis, where it processed fluid milk. The next year, Marigold bought the Eastern dairy division of Fairmont Foods. This purchase brought it two Wisconsin plants, one in Green Bay and one in the small town of Kewaskum. Also in 1980, Marigold entered a joint venture with a large regional milk producer, Associated Milk Producers, Inc., known as AMPI. The two partnered in operating a milk facility in Duluth, Minnesota. By the end of the 1980s, Marigold had increased its penetration through the Midwest, and distributed its products beyond Minnesota and Wisconsin into Illinois,

Indiana, Iowa, Michigan, Ohio, and North and South Dakota. As a subsidiary of Royal Wessanen, Marigold did not release its own sales figures for the 1980s. Marigold, though, was estimated to have grown 3 to 4 percent per year during the decade.

Marigold's growth was not only due to acquisitions. Beginning in 1986, the company began to invest significantly in marketing. Marketing was something of a foreign concept to Marigold at the time, but with people and capital devoted to promoting new products and hyping its brands, the company was soon a model for other regional dairies. Savvy marketing helped Marigold determine new yogurt flavors, for example. It differentiated between lower-priced yogurt mothers might buy for their children and more upscale flavors women might buy for their own consumption. Marigold was also successful with some health-oriented products, such as milk enhanced with acidophilus. In addition, Marigold attached the Kemps brand name to a simple slogan, "It's the cows." This led to humorous spots on both television and radio, and Kemps logo items such as pencils and T-shirts.

Marigold also spent significantly in the 1980s under Royal Wessanen to upgrade its plants. The company plunged $30 million into capital investments at the end of the decade. It built a new ice cream plant in Rochester, Minnesota, and installed the latest technology for handling and packaging at several other facilities.

SISTER COMPANY CROWLEY

Royal Wessanen bought another regional dairy firm in 1983, Binghampton, New York-based Crowley Foods, Inc. Wessanen was eager to grow in the U.S. market, and it spearheaded its acquisitions through both Marigold and Crowley. These two companies operated separately, in different parts of the country. However, they overlapped in distribution of some products, and were in a sense siblings, both reporting to the same Dutch parent.

Crowley also grew rapidly through acquisition after it was bought by Wessanen. By the end of the 1980s, Crowley operated five subsidiaries in the Northeast. These were Axelrod Foods, of Paterson, New Jersey; Heluva Good Cheese, Inc., of Sodus, New York; Green's All-Star Dairy of York, Pennsylvania; and a dairy in Massachusetts and another in New Hampshire. In total, Crowley operated ten facilities. While all its plants were in the Northeast, its marketing territory stretched all the way along the East Coast from Maine to Florida, with some products making it as far west as Michigan.

By the late 1980s, both Crowley and Marigold were doing some $300 million in sales annually. Royal Wes-

KEY DATES

1914: Kemps Ice Cream Company is founded.
1961: Kemps and two other dairies merge, forming Marigold Foods.
1968: Marigold is acquired by Ward Foods.
1978: Dutch company Wessanen buys Marigold from Ward.
1983: Wessanen acquires Crowley Foods.
2001: National Dairy Holdings buys Marigold and Crowley from Wessanen.
2004: Crowley and Marigold are acquired by HP Hood, united as Kemps LLC.

sanen's U.S. operations accounted for more than 50 percent of its total sales volume. The two divisions, Crowley and Marigold, worked well together. For example, Marigold's Kemps brand of frozen yogurt was among its most profitable products. The brand had strong recognition in the Midwest. Yet Marigold was able to get Kemps frozen yogurt into markets Crowley handled. It was unusual for a regional brand to have such wide penetration. Marigold hoped to push at least the frozen yogurt products into the South and West, confident that it had the know-how and corporate backing to stretch itself a little. Both Crowley and Marigold thrived in the 1980s and through the 1990s under the umbrella of their Dutch corporate parent.

MORE ACQUISITIONS

Marigold had made several acquisitions in the first two years it was owned by Royal Wessanen. After that, it spent significantly on capital improvements. Yet it was not until 1993 that Marigold began acquiring again. In that year it made two purchases, Cedarburg Dairy, Inc., of Cedarburg, Wisconsin, and Brown's Velvet Ice Cream, located well south, in New Orleans, Louisiana. Marigold expanded its options when it acquired Becker's Dairy, in Chicago, in 1998. While the other dairies it had purchased were producers of milk and ice cream, Becker's was actually a distributor, moving milk throughout the densely populated Chicago area.

Marigold's territory expanded westward with its purchase in 1999 of Gillette Dairies, of Rapid City, South Dakota, and Nebraska Dairies, of Norfolk, Nebraska. These two western dairies had been owned by Marigold's Minneapolis neighbor Nash Finch. Nash Finch was a food supplier to supermarkets and military bases, and it sold the dairies in order to concentrate on its core business. The Gillette and Nebraska dairies had combined sales of roughly $45 million, and they did business in areas west of Marigold's usual territory, reaching through Nebraska, Kansas, the Dakotas, and all the way to Wyoming. The next year, Marigold made one more purchase, taking on another Minneapolis area dairy, Oak Grove Dairy.

These acquisitions swelled Marigold at a time when other industry players too were growing and consolidating. Marigold had also wisely invested in up-to-date packaging, distribution, and product development. Its marketing efforts were admired, and a December 2002 profile of the company in the industry journal *Dairy Foods* said Marigold looked "like a company with a 10-year head-start on the competition."

Although Marigold and its sister company Crowley had grown significantly under the tutelage of Wessanen, the dairy industry was seeing even more radical consolidation leading to much bigger major players. Dean Foods was a regional dairy that had at first been centered in northern Illinois. A family-run company founded in 1925, by 1981 it was a public company listed on the New York Stock Exchange and one of the nation's leading milk companies. The Texas-based Suiza, by contrast, was only founded in 1993. Yet by 1997, Suiza too was listed on the New York Stock Exchange, and by 2000 it had made over 40 acquisitions. These two giants prepared to merge in 2001. The combined firm, which carried on the name Dean Foods, became a $3 billion company, the market leader not only in the United States but in the United Kingdom as well. While the Dean-Suiza merger was underway, it was clear to other dairy veterans that the milk market would soon be very different. Some players pulled out, while other mergers seemed suddenly urgent. It was in this climate that Wessanen put Marigold and Crowley up for sale in 2000. They were offered both separately and together. Ultimately, they were sold as a pair in 2001 to a new company, National Dairy Holdings.

INDUSTRY SHIFTS

National Dairy Holdings (NDH) was formed in 2001 by a trio of Texas dairy industry veterans and the 25,000-member dairy farmer cooperative Dairy Farmers of America. The first move of the brand new company was to buy Marigold and Crowley for $400 million. NDH then consolidated the two former Wessanen offspring under the Marigold name. As of September 2001, Crowley and Marigold operated as Marigold Foods, LLC.

The huge Dean-Suiza merger led to some other buying opportunities. Federal regulations forced the new

Dean Foods to sell off some of its subsidiaries. National Dairy Holdings snapped up 11 more milk and dairy facilities from Dean. NDH stood as the second largest U.S. dairy, controlling some 10 percent of the U.S. fluid milk market. However, it was still dwarfed by the number one company, Dean, which had a U.S. market share of around 30 percent.

As early as 2002, NDH began negotiating with a large East Coast dairy, HP Hood, about a possible merger. HP Hood sold New England's best-known brand of milk, and had sales of about $1 billion annually. Hood and NDH moved forward with their merger plans, but soon ran into regulatory difficulties. At the same time, two other major food industry entities, Nestlé and Dreyer's, were encountering roadblocks with their own attempted merger. Hood and NDH decided, based on the Nestlé-Dreyer precedent, to restructure their merger. The two became jointly managed, with Hood CEO John Kaneb CEO of both firms. Similarly, NDH's president and chief operating officer also became president and COO at Hood. As part of the new arrangement, in 2004 Crowley and Marigold became subsidiaries of HP Hood. Marigold and Crowley took the name Kemps LLC.

The company had grown greatly, and Marigold headquarters in Minneapolis had already stretched between two different buildings. In 2005, the new Kemps moved into a bigger headquarters across the river in St. Paul, Minnesota. Kemps relished its Minnesota roots, as many of its ice cream brands had fanciful names with a regional lilt, such as Hockey Puck and Sub Zero. Nevertheless, the Hood leadership also broadened Kemps' vision and reach. One new development was the 2005 partnership with General Mills, one of the nation's leading food companies, to co-brand some products. General Mills owned the Pillsbury brand, and in a new venture, Kemps brought out some new ice cream flavors featuring the iconic Pillsbury Doughboy. The Pillsbury Doughboy had market recognition across the country, meaning the regional Kemps could stretch into markets far from its principally midwestern territory.

Milk remained a very competitive market through the first decade of the 2000s. While consumption of organic milk grew in double-digits, conventional milk producers had to try hard to come up with ways to position themselves with consumers. Kemps was one of only a few brands profiled by *Dairy Foods* in an overview of the U.S. milk market published in February 2008. Kemps did well by promoting its brand as

healthful. It brought out Kemps Plus Healthy Lifestyle Milk and Kemps Plus Healthy Kids Milk, which both contained extra calcium and the fish oil extract omega-3 EPA/DHA. The Kids Milk also contained vitamin C. These new lines were in accord with current consumer thinking, paraphrased by a milk industry watcher in *Dairy Foods* as "What can I put into my diet to be healthier?" That is, rather than consumers looking to cut down on certain foods to lose weight, people were more likely to respond to products with added healthy ingredients. Kemps under Hood seemed to be continuing its strength as a market innovator and leader.

A. Woodward

PRINCIPAL COMPETITORS

Dean Foods Co.; Dreyer's Grand Ice Cream Holdings, Inc.; Wells' Dairy, Inc.

FURTHER READING

"Acquisitions Give DFA 10% of Milk Market," *Feedstuffs,* October 8, 2001, p. 7.

"Hood Acquires Marigold and Crowley from NDH," *Ice Cream Reporter,* April 20, 2004, pp. 1, 4.

Ingrassia, Robert, "Minneapolis-Based Ice Cream Maker to Move Headquarters to St. Paul," *Saint Paul Pioneer Press,* March 16, 2005.

"Kemps Tickles the Doughboy," *Dairy Foods,* March 2005, p. 30.

Kimbrell, Wendy, "Marigold Foods, Minneapolis," *Dairy Foods,* February 1990, p. 63.

———, "Wessanen: Poised for U.S. Growth," *Dairy Foods,* November 1989, p. 86.

———, "Wessanen USA," *Dairy Foods,* April 1990, p. 66.

"Marigold Adds Oak Grove Dairy," *Ice Cream Reporter,* March 20, 2000, pp. 3–4.

"Marigold Buys Nash Finch Dairies," *Ice Cream Reporter,* July 20, 1999, p. 2.

"Marigold Foods Comes of Age," *Dairy Foods,* December 2002, pp. 24–31.

Phillips, David, "Hood's Dairy Nation," *Dairy Foods,* December 2004, pp. 16–22.

———, "Whatever Floats the Boat," *Dairy Foods,* February 2008, pp. 40–48.

Smith, Rod, "Hood Acquires Crowley Foods, Marigold Dairies," *Feedstuffs,* April 26, 2004, p. 8.

"Wessanen Puts Marigold, Crowley Up for Sale," *Dairy Foods,* November 2000, p. 11.

Kruger Inc.

3285 chemin Bedford
Montreal, Quebec H3S 1G5
Canada
Telephone: (514) 737-1131
Fax: (514) 343-3124
Web site: http://www.kruger.com

Private Company
Founded: 1904
Incorporated: 1921 as Kruger Paper Company Limited
Employees: 9,000
Sales: CAD 2.5 billion ($2.04 billion) (2008 est.)
NAICS: 321113 Sawmills; 321211 Hardwood Veneer and Plywood Manufacturing; 322110 Pulp Mills; 322121 Paper (Except Newsprint) Mills; 322122 Newsprint Mills; 322130 Paperboard Mills; 322212 Folding Paperboard Box Manufacturing; 322222 Coated and Laminated Paper Manufacturing; 322291 Sanitary Paper Product Manufacturing

■ ■ ■

The privately owned Kruger Inc. is a major Montreal-based forest products company. Its core operations are in publication papers, including newsprint and coated, magazine, and directory paper; tissue products, including bathroom and facial tissue, paper towels, and hand towels, marketed under such brands as Cashmere, Scotties, SpongeTowels, and White Swan; packaging products, including linerboard, corrugated boxes, and point-of-purchase displays; and wood products, including lumber, panels, and subflooring. The plants and mills of these units are located in Quebec, Alberta, British Columbia, Newfoundland and Labrador, Ontario, Tennessee, and the United Kingdom. Kruger is also a major recycler of paper and paperboard at wholly or partly owned facilities in Quebec, Ontario, and New York, and is involved in a handful of hydroelectric and wind energy projects. The company ventured further afield in 2006 when it acquired a controlling interest in Maison des Futailles, a leading Quebec-based winemaker and distributor of wines and spirits.

EARLY 20TH-CENTURY ORIGINS

The first stirrings of what eventually became one of the largest, privately owned forest products companies in Canada began in New York at the turn of the 20th century. It was there and then that the patriarch of the Kruger family, Joseph Kruger, worked as a paper merchant, plying his trade in a business that would make the Kruger name synonymous with the production of paper products for the next century. Along with the inseparable link connecting the Kruger family name with paper production came enormous wealth and widespread prominence for Joseph Kruger's descendants, but the family did not begin its rise until Joseph Kruger decided to settle elsewhere. New York proved to be only a way station along the family's path to greatness. It was in Montreal that the Krugers rose to distinction in the paper products industry, establishing a business legacy there that was renowned for its privacy and astute management, and one that began in 1904 when Joseph Kruger moved from New York and settled in Montreal, where he established a wholesale fine papers business.

COMPANY PERSPECTIVES

The mission of Kruger Inc. is to provide our customers with products and services that continually fulfill their expectations.

This is achieved by all employees optimizing the quality of each action that takes place in the business of buying, producing, selling and servicing our products—all within a safe work environment that encourages personal development and satisfaction.

Kruger Inc.'s objective is to be the quality leader and low-cost producer within our industry, while taking a leadership role in respecting the environment and the principle of sustainable forest development.

In 1921 Kruger incorporated his business as Kruger Paper Company Limited, predecessor to Kruger Inc. Although Joseph Kruger had founded the family business, the credit for developing the business into one of Canada's largest companies fell to his two sons, Gene and Bernard. The duties of stewarding the fortunes of the family business were passed to these two second-generation representatives of the Kruger family at an early age, for six years after he officially established Kruger Paper Joseph Kruger died, never knowing that the small business he had created would develop into one of Canada's preeminent enterprises.

At the time of Joseph Kruger's death, Kruger Paper employed a total of five employees. Four workers were assigned to the company's warehouse to distribute the fine paper sold to wholesale customers, and the remaining member of the company's payroll wore two hats, serving as Kruger Paper's secretary and bookkeeper. At the age of 25, Gene Kruger took control of the enterprise. He had spent the previous five years working at Kruger Paper with his father; his brother Bernard, 15 years old at the time of his father's death, remained in school. A year later, in 1928, Bernard joined his brother at Kruger Paper, marking the beginning of a fraternal partnership that would span a half century.

The transformation of Kruger Paper from the small, wholesale fine papers business left by Joseph Kruger into one of the largest newsprint producers in North America began quickly under the guidance of the two Kruger brothers, albeit in a direction far removed from newsprint production. In 1929 the Krugers diversified into the aluminum business, founding Aluminum Rolling Mills and Dominion Foils Ltd. Both were based in

Quebec, with Dominion Foils registering the greatest success of the two. A manufacturer of foil for the packaging industry, Dominion Foils was one of the first companies to master the production process involved in combining foil and soft paper for holding cigarettes in their packaging, spurring the two Kruger brothers forward in their involvement in the aluminum business. In the decade leading up to World War II and after the war, the Krugers continued to invest in aluminum production properties by acquiring or building plants throughout Canada and in Holland.

Within a few short years of their father's death, Gene and Bernard Kruger had distanced themselves from the business that Joseph Kruger had created. Joseph Kruger had established a business that never pretended to be more than a small-scale, entrepreneurial venture capable of supporting a family. The Kruger brothers, on the other hand, quickly embarked on a course that, in retrospect, pointed to the development of a business empire. Although the two Kruger brothers kept both their personal and business dealings close to the chest, preferring to remain out of the public spotlight, later publicity about the power dynamics between the two brothers cast the elder brother, Gene, as the orchestrator of all that followed the death of Joseph Kruger.

For nearly all of their years spent together directing their family-owned business, Gene and Bernard maintained a low social profile and avoided political involvement. During the decades that spanned the development of their family fortune, however, a few employees and friends shed light on what was occurring within the Kruger inner circle. To a reporter from *Maclean's,* a former employee noted that Gene Kruger was always on the phone "yelling and screaming." The same employee described Bernard as the epitome of affability, remarking that, in contrast, Bernard was a gentle and gracious person who mixed easily with his employees. The divergent personalities of the brothers defined their dealings with each other: Gene was in charge and Bernard generally responded dutifully to his brother's bidding. Bernard admitted as much, confiding to a *Maclean's* reporter that "if there was a disagreement, we would do things Gene's way." Consequently, Gene Kruger received much of the credit for the success recorded by Kruger Paper and later by Kruger Inc., earning a reputation within the Canadian forest products industry that perhaps was justly deserved. One industry consultant later remarked, "Gene Kruger was always one of the brightest and most innovative men in the business." Despite the uneven power relationship between the two brothers and the accolades heaped upon Gene Kruger, there was no power struggle between the two brothers. In one of his few comments

KEY DATES

1904: Joseph Kruger establishes a wholesale fine paper business in Montreal.

1921: Company is incorporated as Kruger Paper Company Limited, forerunner of Kruger Inc.

1927: Upon the founder's death, leadership passes to his two sons, Gene and Bernard.

1950: Kruger Paper acquires its first newsprint mill, located in Bromptonville (later Sherbrooke), Quebec.

1952: Company buys its first corrugated packaging plant.

1973: Through the acquisition of Three Rivers Pulp and Paper Company, Kruger gains a second major paper mill located in Trois-Rivières, Quebec.

1988: When Gene Kruger dies, his son Joseph Kruger II takes over as chairman and CEO.

1991: With its purchase of a sawmill in Parent, Quebec, Kruger Inc. completes its first outright acquisition in the wood products sector.

1997: Company makes a major push into the Canadian tissue products market by acquiring Scott Paper Limited.

2006: Kruger acquires control of Maison des Futailles, a Quebec-based winemaker and distributor of wines and spirits.

to the press, Bernard Kruger described his feelings for his brother to a *Canadian Business* reporter, explaining, "It was the greatest relationship in the world; we trusted each other implicitly."

POST–WORLD WAR II EXPANSION

The Kruger brothers worked well together, and the growing magnitude of their business interests reflected as much. While the pair built up their holdings in the aluminum business before and after the war, they did not neglect the development of the paper business. Increasingly, the brothers became involved in paper production and related ventures, executing their boldest moves following the conclusion of World War II. In 1950 they completed their first major acquisition when they purchased the Richmond Pulp and Paper Company in Bromptonville, Quebec. The acquisition gave the Kruger business a newsprint mill that would serve as the

company's flagship paper facility for the remainder of the century, touching off decades of energetic physical growth, as the two brothers narrowed their sights on the paper business. It was during this period that Gene Kruger's strategy for growth was most discernible. As the company grew exponentially from the 1950s forward, it did so by purchasing old pulp and paper mills and then revamping them into modern production facilities. This approach predicated the company's expansion strategy for the decades ahead, remaining a key tenet of Kruger Inc.'s development even after the departure of Gene and Bernard Kruger.

During the early 1950s, the Kruger brothers launched an acquisition spree, adding to the breadth of their paper business over the course of several years. Among the companies acquired during the decade were Sherbrooke Paper Products Ltd. in Sherbrooke, Quebec, which produced corrugated boxes and was purchased in 1952 (and was later relocated to LaSalle, Quebec), and Montreal-based Turcot Paperboard Mills Ltd., a producer of recycled linerboard bought in 1960. By 1961, the Krugers owned ten pulp and paper companies and ranked as a leading paper producer in their home province of Quebec; their nonpaper business interests, meanwhile, were gone. As the brothers increased their stake in paper production, they concurrently began shedding businesses that did not add to their stature as a paper producer. By the beginning of the 1960s, all of the nonpaper operations had been divested (the last business was sold in 1961), leaving the Krugers entirely dependent on, yet strongly supported by, the growing roster of pulp and paper facilities composing their growing empire.

Expansion continued under the aggressive and ambitious tutelage of Gene Kruger throughout the 1960s and 1970s, both within Canada and abroad. In 1955 the Krugers acquired 50 percent interest in, and then later purchased the balance of, Papeles Venezolanos C.A., a Venezuela paper mill company. Although this property was organized as a company separate from Kruger Inc., the move to foreign shores established a precedent. Gene Kruger also helped a group of local industrialists found another affiliated South American company, Papeles Nacionales, S.A., which was organized in Colombia in 1960. Production began from this firm's tissue machine and manual converting equipment two years later. On the domestic front, a second box production plant was erected in Rexdale, Ontario, in 1964, and a second paper mill was added in 1973 through the purchase of Three Rivers Pulp and Paper Company. The paper mill, located in Trois-Rivières, Quebec, represented a significant addition to the company's operations, ranking as important as the purchase of the Bromptonville plant 23 years earlier.

By the time the Trois-Rivières plant was acquired, Kruger Inc. had completed a sweeping modernization program. Many of the company's facilities were thoroughly revamped to meet the mounting need for paper products, particularly for newsprint, which ranked as Kruger Inc.'s single most important product. The investment in the Bromptonville plant represented a telling example of the company's commitment to establishing itself as a large-scale paper producer. It also provided a glimpse into Gene Kruger's strategy to purchase old plants and enhance their technological capabilities and capacities. When the Krugers purchased the Bromptonville newspaper mill in 1950, the plant contained one machine that could produce roughly 9,000 metric tons of newsprint per year. By 1973, after years of investment, the plant housed three machines capable of producing 168,000 metric tons of newsprint per year.

After the modernization program was completed, Kruger Inc., to a certain extent, was beginning anew; a gradual change in the company's leadership added to the sense that a new chapter in the company's history was beginning. In 1968 Gene Kruger's son Joseph Kruger II was appointed to Kruger Inc.'s board of directors. By the mid-1970s, Gene was giving his son more responsibilities and, according to Bernard, Joseph began to wield this newfound power freely, occasionally stepping on his uncle's toes as he did so. Before long, Bernard began to feel uneasy about the situation at Kruger Inc. In his mind, his position was being eroded by his nephew. Bernard Kruger no longer knew where he stood and saw no resolution to the new power dynamics reshaping Kruger Inc.'s executive ranks without creating considerable friction among family members. In 1979 Bernard Kruger left the company of which he had been an integral part for 51 years, opting to retire rather than engaging in a power struggle at the company's headquarters.

FAMILY FEUD ERUPTS IN THE EIGHTIES

Bernard's departure did not ease the troubles that began brewing in the late 1970s. The uneasiness remained, particularly in Bernard's mind, as he began to wonder exactly how much he owned of the family's various ventures and what his own children could expect as an inheritance. Inquiries into these matters caused Gene to take umbrage, and quickly the dispute turned into a battle waged in the courts and in Kruger Inc.'s boardroom. In 1982 a legal fight over the central issue of Bernard's family's rights as minority shareholders was brought to the courts. Bernard charged that his brother and representatives had attempted to bilk his family out of its fair share of Kruger Inc. and other offshore ventures. Further, Bernard contended that Gene's family, who owned 61 percent of Kruger Inc.'s shares, was not paying out sufficient dividends, that he had stopped receiving his CAD 40,000-per-year pension, that his secretary had been fired, and that his company credit cards had been canceled. As the owner of 32.5 percent of Kruger Inc.'s 11 million shares, Bernard's family asked the courts for compensation for years of low dividend payments, a demand that Gene and his son found specious. Although Gene's side of the family kept their comments to the press to a minimum, flatly stating that Kruger Inc.'s dividend policy was "moderately reasonable," the family feud was the stuff of headlines. The bitter battle brought the lives of a family that had shunned the scrutiny of the public eye for decades into the open.

Amid the turmoil, however, Kruger Inc. continued to perform admirably. Despite board meetings that Bernard's son David, a Kruger Inc. board member, compared with "the way Lee Iacocca described Ford meetings under Henry Ford," the company reigned as a dominant force in the Canadian forest products industry. The dispute between Gene and Bernard was eventually settled during the late 1980s in a secret, out-of-court deal in which Joseph agreed to buy Bernard's 32 percent share in the company for CAD 99 million. When Gene died in 1988, Joseph Kruger II took over as chairman and CEO.

In spite of this family feud, Kruger Inc. never missed a step throughout the decade. While tempers were at their hottest during the early and mid-1980s, the company had secured a major contract with Gannett Supply to provide newsprint for the publisher's new newspaper, *USA Today*. The deal was significant not only for the volume of business it represented but also because *USA Today* required the most demanding quality specifications in the newsprint business, which meant that Kruger Inc. could count itself among the most sophisticated newsprint producers on the continent. The newspaper's four-color pages were the first in the industry, and Kruger Inc. was one of the first newsprint suppliers to qualify as a supplier. By the late 1980s, when newspaper publishers were rapidly moving toward color printing, there was a dearth of qualified newsprint mills capable of meeting the expected demand. There were, in fact, only eight newsprint mills in North America that qualified as suppliers for *USA Today*, and Kruger Inc. operated two of them.

One of these was the firm's newsprint mill in Corner Brook, Newfoundland. This mill, which dated back to 1925, was acquired by Kruger in 1984 and then thoroughly modernized over the course of a number of years. Also acquired along with the mill was a hydroelectric power plant at nearby Deer Lake, which generated much of the energy the mill needed to operate.

Kruger Inc.'s strong technological lead over many of its North American competitors during the late 1980s served the company well as it entered the 1990s. Newsprint production would continue to be the company's mainstay business in the decade ahead, but, with Joseph Kruger at the helm as chairman and CEO, Kruger Inc. also made an aggressive effort to strengthen its position in the recycling business, specifically in its capacity to produce recycled newsprint. Toward this end, the company purchased Manistique Papers, Inc., in February 1991 for roughly $68 million. Located in Michigan, the Manistique mill accelerated Kruger's foray into recycled newsprint production and strengthened the company's presence south of the border, where the bulk of its newsprint shipments were delivered. Next, the company acknowledged its need to develop further its operations in the United States by forming a U.S. subsidiary in 1992. The subsidiary operation, located in Albany, New York, was established to generate baled wastepaper for use by the company's linerboard and newsprint mills in Quebec. Concurrent with this move, the company also opened a $55 million deinking facility at its mill in Bromptonville. Deinking equipment is used to remove printing ink from wastepaper to create deinked pulp, which can then be turned into recycled paper.

By the mid-1990s, Kruger's strength was considerable. The company's largest market share continued to be in newsprint production, which was generated by ten machines capable of producing approximately 980,000 tons of newsprint per year. All totaled, the company's facilities were capable of producing 1.8 million metric tons of paper products per year, making Kruger Inc. the largest, privately owned paper products company in Canada.

EXPANDING INTO WOOD PRODUCTS AND TISSUE PRODUCTS

In the meantime, the company had also ventured into wood products. Kruger's first foray into this sector occurred in 1987 when it acquired a minority interest in Gérard Crête & Fils Inc., an operator of softwood sawmills based in the Mauricie region of Quebec. Kruger upped its stake in Crête to 50 percent in 1992. A year earlier, the company had completed its first outright acquisition in this sector by acquiring Scierie

Parent, operator of a sawmill in Parent, Quebec. It later acquired additional Quebec sawmills in Forestville and Longue-Rive. In April 1996 Kruger purchased Longlac Wood Industries, a producer of wood panels based in Longlac, Ontario. Eventually, in 1998, the company consolidated all of its Quebec sawmills and woodlands under a newly created Forest and Wood Products division.

Kruger by this time had been involved in the production of tissue products for decades through its Colombian and Venezuelan affiliates, and also owned three tissue plants in the United Kingdom, but in June 1997 the company made a great leap into this sector at home. That month, the company completed its takeover of the previously publicly traded Scott Paper Limited, which had been majority owned by Kimberly-Clark Corporation. The deal cost Kruger about CAD 350 million in cash, and it also had to assume around CAD 100 million in debt. Scott Paper operated mills in Crabtree, Lennoxville, and Gatineau, Quebec, and in New Westminster, British Columbia. It sold several branded products to consumers, including Cottonelle, Purex, and White Swan bathroom tissue, ScotTowels and Viva paper towels, and Scotties facial tissue, and also provided tissue, soaps, and dispensing systems to industrial and commercial customers.

Of these brand names, Kruger gained ownership of Purex, White Swan, and Scotties outright, but for Cottonelle, Viva, and ScotTowels, Kimberly-Clark would grant Kruger the rights to use the names in Canada for only ten years. Eventually, Kruger changed the name of Cottonelle to Cashmere, ScotTowels was transformed into SpongeTowels, and the White Swan brand grew to encompass not only bathroom tissue but also facial tissue, paper towels, and napkins, and in the process subsumed the Viva line. Ultimately as well, Scott Paper evolved into the Kruger Products division. This division ventured south of the border in 2002 by acquiring a large, idle tissue mill in Memphis, Tennessee, investing $35 million to modernize the plant, and restarting operations in 2003.

By the end of the 1990s, Kruger Inc. was generating more than CAD 2 billion in annual revenues. The company continued to invest heavily in its existing facilities to increase capacity, improve product quality, develop new products, and cut costs. Acquisitions stayed on the agenda as well. In early 2000 the company gained its first pulp holding when it entered into a joint venture with Tembec Inc. to acquire a pulp mill in Marathon, Ontario, with an annual capacity of 180,000 metric tons.

FURTHER EXPANSIONS AND NEW VENTURES

Around this time, the Quebec government provided financing assistance for several of Kruger's expansions as it intervened in the marketplace to forestall facilities closures and thereby save jobs and stimulate the economy. In 2001, for instance, Kruger Wayagamack Inc. was formed to acquire a newsprint mill in Trois-Rivières that had been mothballed by Abitibi-Consolidated Inc.; the joint venture was 51 percent owned by Kruger Inc. and 49 percent by Société générale de financement du Québec, a provincial lending agency. CAD 500 million was then invested in the plant in part to construct a new coated paper machine capable of producing 200,000 metric tons of ultralightweight coated paper used for magazines, catalogs, and advertising supplements. Late in 2002 Kruger announced a CAD 116.4 million plan to upgrade its tissue mills in Crabtree and Lennoxville that was partly financed by the provincial government.

In August 2002 Kruger's Longlac Wood Industries unit opened a new plant in Mississauga, Ontario, for the manufacture of a new type of subflooring called DRIcore that was designed to provide a warm, dry surface over concrete basement floors. That same year, the company organized its operations into five business units focusing on publication papers, containerboard, tissue, forest and wood products, and recycling.

At Kruger's Corner Brook newsprint mill in Newfoundland, a 15-megawatt cogeneration system began operating in 2003. This system converted mill waste into steam and electricity, both of which were put to use in the plant. A year later, the company set up Kruger Energy as a sixth business unit to manage its various energy projects. Additional Kruger Energy projects soon followed, including a 23-megawatt biomass cogeneration system installed at the Bromptonville mill that commenced operation in 2007. Meanwhile, late in 2005, the Ontario Ministry of Energy selected Kruger Energy to build a 101.2-megawatt wind farm at Port Alma, on the shore of Lake Erie. The project and its 44 wind turbines were started up in November 2008, generating enough electricity to power about 30,000 Ontario homes. In early 2009 Kruger Energy was selected to build a second wind farm of a similar size located adjacent to the first farm.

CONFLICT WITH INNU, INDUSTRY DOWNTURN

During 2005 Kruger Inc. was temporarily barred from logging on Île René-Levasseur, a huge island in northeastern Quebec where it had been granted logging rights from the provincial government in 1997. The native Innu had sued to stop the logging on the island, which was situated in the heart of the territory claimed by the Innu and was considered sacred to them. In April 2006, however, an appeals court decision overturned an earlier court injunction, and Kruger was able to resume logging and supplying wood to its three sawmills in the area. Also in 2006, Kruger acquired the 50 percent of Gérard Crête & Fils it did not already own, gaining full control of the wood products company, which was running two sawmills in the Mauricie region of Quebec. Kruger in September 2006, having already diversified into wood products, tissue products, and wind power, ventured much farther afield by purchasing a 75 percent controlling stake in Maison des Futailles, a leading Quebec winemaker, bottler, and marketer of wines and spirits. Kruger also sold Manistique Papers, which since its purchase by Kruger 15 years earlier had evolved into a producer of recycled uncoated specialty papers, in 2006.

In 2007 Kruger's lumber operations, which exported about 90 percent of their products to the United States, were battered by the combination of a high Canadian dollar and a steep drop-off in demand stemming from the slumping U.S. market for new home construction. Consequently, in March the company idled four of its Quebec sawmills and laid off more than 1,000 workers. This prolonged downturn also prompted Kruger in December 2008 to enter into an agreement with Norbord Inc. to combine their respective hardwood plywood operations into a joint venture that would rely exclusively on Norbord's facility in Cochrane, Ontario. Kruger subsequently shut down its Longlac plywood plant. In early 2009 Kruger also announced the sale of its Forestville softwood sawmill to Boisaco Inc.

Kruger's publication papers unit was also suffering from the high Canadian dollar and a drop in demand, and a series of temporary and permanent closures of plants and machines were announced throughout 2007 and 2008. The market for newsprint was particularly troubled at this time as the U.S. newspaper industry fell into an accelerating state of decline highlighted by the loss of both readers and advertising to the Internet. Circulation fell; newspapers shrank the physical size of their pages, reduced their page count, or both; and a number of newspapers began cutting their number of publication days or shifting to an online-only format. Some newspapers simply went bankrupt. Newsprint producers were therefore dealing with chronic overcapacity in North America, and Kruger responded by planning a 25,000-metric-ton cut in its newsprint production during the first half of 2009, which amounted to a reduction in its annual output of about 2.5 percent.

Jeffrey L. Covell
Updated, David E. Salamie

PRINCIPAL SUBSIDIARIES

Corner Brook Pulp and Paper Limited; Deer Lake Power Company; Gérard Crête & Fils Inc.; Hydro Bromptonville Inc.; Kruger Energy Inc.; Kruger Wayagamack Inc. (51%); Longlac Wood Industries Inc.; Maison des Futailles (75%); Papeles Nacionales S.A. (Colombia); Kruger Tissue (Manufacturing) Limited (UK); Kruger Tissue (Industrial) Limited (UK); Kruger Recycling, Inc. (USA); Kruger Pulp and Paper Sales, Inc. (USA); K.T.G. (USA) LP; Papeles Venezolanos C.A. (Venezuela).

PRINCIPAL OPERATING UNITS

Publication Papers; Kruger Products; Forest and Wood Products; Krupack Packaging; Energy; Recycling; Wines and Spirits.

PRINCIPAL COMPETITORS

AbitibiBowater Inc.; White Birch Paper Co.; International Paper Company; Catalyst Paper Corporation; Boise Inc.; Georgia-Pacific LLC; Smurfit-Stone Container Corporation; The Procter & Gamble Company; Cascades Inc.; Kimberly-Clark Corporation; Weyerhaeuser Company; West Fraser Timber Co. Ltd.; Canfor Corporation; Irving Tissue, Inc.; Atlantic Packaging Products Limited.

FURTHER READING

Barton, Christopher, "Kruger Buys Paper Mill Equipment," *Memphis (Tenn.) Commercial Appeal,* August 27, 2002, p. B7.

Beirne, Anne, "Kruger vs. Kruger; Gene and Bernard Kruger Spent More Than 50 Years Building Kruger Inc. into a Giant Paper Company," *Canadian Business,* January 1986, pp. 61+.

Cody, Harold M., "Kruger Upgrades Newsprint and Coated Paper Lines to Keep a Competitive Edge," *Pulp and Paper,* February 2002, pp. 45–49.

Gibbens, Robert, "Kruger Shutting Down Two Quebec Paper Mills," *Montreal Gazette,* October 3, 2007, p. B2.

Glowacki, Jeremy J., "Kruger Inc.: Newsprint Market Dominance, Leadership Continues," *Pulp and Paper,* February 1996, pp. 34–35.

Hill, Bert, "Kruger to Change Scott Name As Kimberly-Clark Deal Ends," *Ottawa (Ont.) Citizen,* October 11, 2006, p. D2.

Ingman, Lars C., "Kruger Inc. … One of the Quality Leaders," *Pulp and Paper,* August 1989, p. 135.

"Kruger Buys U.S. Tissue Mill," *Pulp and Paper,* April 1999, p. 25.

"Kruger Feud Erupts with C$40-Million Lawsuit," *Pulp and Paper,* June 1993, p. 29.

Kruger, 1904–2004: 100 Years of Commitment to Innovation, Montreal: Kruger Inc., 2005, 44 p.

"Kruger Plans to Idle All SC Capacity," *Pulp and Paper,* December 2007, pp. 11–12.

Lush, Patricia, "Kruger Alters Bid for Scott Paper," *Globe and Mail,* May 21, 1997, p. B10.

———, "Kruger Launches Bid for Scott," *Globe and Mail,* March 5, 1997, p. B1.

Marotte, Bertrand, "Kruger Shuts Four Sawmills, Cuts Jobs in Quebec," *Globe and Mail,* March 31, 2007, p. B5.

Marowits, Ross, "Slumbering Market Pushes Kruger to Close Mills," *Montreal Gazette,* March 31, 2007, p. C3.

McGowan, Kathy, "Marathon Mill Sale Boosts Confidence," *Northern Ontario Business,* March 1, 2000, p. 20.

Moore, Lynn, and Hubert Bauch, "Kruger to Build De-inking Plant with Lots of Help from Quebec," *Montreal Gazette,* February 24, 2007, p. C2.

Moore, Lynn, and Kevin Dougherty, "Kruger Wins Access to Island," *Montreal Gazette,* July 7, 2005, p. B1.

Patrick, Ken L. "Kruger Boosts Newsprint Production with New Machines at Trois-Rivières," *Pulp and Paper,* August 1991, p. 100.

Silcoff, Sean, "Kruger Taps Quebec Again for Financing," *National Post,* November 19, 2002, p. FP10.

Wallace, Bruce, "A Family Dynasty on Trial," *Maclean's,* June 2, 1986, p. 42.

LinkedIn Corporation

2029 Stierlin Court
Mountain View, California 94043
U.S.A.
Telephone: (650) 687-3600
Fax: (650) 687-0505
Web site: http://www.linkedin.com

Private Company
Incorporated: 2002
Employees: 345
Sales: $17 million (2008 est.)
NAICS: 518210 Data Processing Services

■ ■ ■

LinkedIn Corporation operates a social networking web site for businesspeople, providing a way for professionals to communicate with colleagues and to meet new colleagues. The web site LinkedIn.com has over 40 million members in 200 countries, growing by one new member approximately every second. Membership is free, but the company also offers premium services and accounts for monthly and yearly fees. Several venture capital firms have financed the company's development, notably Sequoia Capital, Greylock Partners, and Bessemer Venture Partners. LinkedIn maintains a customer service office in Omaha, Nebraska, and operates satellite offices in San Francisco, California, and New York City, New York. The company's European headquarters are located in London, England.

THE FOUNDERS

By 2008, five years after the LinkedIn.com web site was launched, there were 33 million users composing the network, a virtual community equivalent in size to the population of Canada. The legions of LinkedIn members were linked, by various degrees of separation, to the five founders of the business-oriented social network: Allen Blue, Jean-Luc Vaillant, Eric Ly, Konstantin Guericke, and Reid Hoffman. Of the five founders, four became actively involved in managing the company, none more prominently than Reid Hoffman.

Raised in Berkeley, California, Hoffman earned his undergraduate degree at Stanford University, where he studied symbolic systems. He distinguished himself at Stanford, earning a Marshall Scholarship, a prestigious award given to only 40 U.S. undergraduates each year. As a Marshall Scholar, Hoffman received full funding to study in the United Kingdom, which led to his enrollment at Oxford University, where he earned a graduate degree in philosophy in 1993.

When Hoffman returned to the United States at the age of 26, he began his remarkable rise in the technology sector. He spent four years working for Apple Computer and Fujitsu Software Corp. before launching his career as an entrepreneur. In 1997, Hoffman and a fellow Stanford graduate, Konstantin Guericke, started SocialNet.com, a social networking web site that visitors used to meet people and to share interests in recreational and professional activities. Not long after starting SocialNet.com, Hoffman became an executive vice-president at PayPal, a company that facilitated electronic payments for online purchases. Hoffman, in

COMPANY PERSPECTIVES

Your professional network of trusted contacts gives you an advantage in your career, and is one of your most valuable assets. LinkedIn exists to help you make better use of your professional network and help the people you trust in return.

Our mission is to connect the world's professionals to accelerate their success. We believe that in a global connected economy, your success as a professional and your competitiveness as a company depends upon faster access to insight and resources you can trust.

charge of PayPal's corporate development, forged vital business ties with Visa, MasterCard, and Wells Fargo and played an instrumental role in the company's $1.5 billion sale to eBay in 2002. The transaction gave Hoffman the financial freedom to pursue his interests, financing his activities as an investor. Over the course of the next several years, he helped finance more than 60 companies, including more than 25 from initial conception. He also provided the seed money for an altered version of SocialNet.com, a start-up formed in 2002 under the banner LinkedIn Corporation.

Hoffman initially invested $700,000 to start LinkedIn, forming the company in late 2002, when company headquarters were established in his living room. The homespun start-up, created to facilitate business-oriented networking, began with its own, small network, drawing upon the connections of its founders. Reid and Guericke, both Stanford graduates, enlisted the help of Allen Blue, a Stanford alum who had worked as a subcontractor for PayPal and served as the director of product design for SocialNet.com. Blue became LinkedIn's vice-president of product strategy. Jean-Luc Vaillant, LinkedIn's chief technology officer, held engineering management positions at Fujitsu Software, where Reid had worked after studying at Oxford University, and he served as vice-president of development at MatchNet, the company that acquired SocialNet.com. in 2001.

LAUNCHING THE WEB SITE: MAY 2003

On May 5, 2003, a day company employees later referred to as "Cinco de LinkedIn," the LinkedIn.com web site was launched, creating a new, virtual meeting place for business professionals to communicate with existing colleagues and to make new contacts. By posting a personal profile on the LinkedIn.com web site, a LinkedIn user could expand his or her network of contacts by using existing relationships to cultivate new relationships. The founders launched the web site by inviting 300 of their professional contacts to join LinkedIn, the base from which the most popular business-oriented social network began. By the end of the first month, online introductions among the first 300 users increased LinkedIn's membership to 4,500.

Hoffman, serving as the company's chief executive officer, pinned the success of LinkedIn on the ability of the company's web site to attract new members. The company, which offered its service for free, could not expect to implement a revenue-generating business model until it reached a critical mass in membership. The larger the membership base, the greater potential usefulness of the network, and the greater the usefulness of the network, the greater its ability to attract new members. Although Hoffman later expressed disappointment at the pace of LinkedIn's growth during its first years of existence, investors were impressed with the potential of the network, enabling Hoffman to attract the first sizable investment in his company. In November 2003, Sequoia Capital, a venture-capital firm that had backed Google, Yahoo!, and PayPal, invested $4.7 million in LinkedIn. In the years ahead, Hoffman would rely on financial support from venture capital firms to finance the growth of his network.

When Sequoia Capital made its financial commitment to LinkedIn, the network was facilitating more than 1,000 referrals per month, doubling in size every six weeks. The company ended the year with 81,000 members, and reached its first major membership milestone in April 2004, when the network comprised 500,000 users. The rapid growth attracted additional financing in October 2004, when Greylock Partners, an early stage venture capital firm, invested $10 million in LinkedIn. By the end of the year, there were 1.6 million members, roughly half of whom resided outside the United States, convincing Hoffman that he had reached the point where he could begin to make LinkedIn a revenue-generating enterprise.

LINKEDIN CHASES PROFITS

Although LinkedIn continued to offer its service for free, from 2005 forward it began to experiment with charging members for particular services. The transition began in March 2005, when LinkedIn Jobs, the company's first premium service, was launched. The service, which functioned as a job board on the Internet, was free to job seekers, but a fee was charged each time

KEY DATES

2002: LinkedIn is formed in the living room of cofounder Reid Hoffman.

2003: LinkedIn.com web site is launched on May 5.

2004: In April, LinkedIn reaches 500,000 members.

2005: Company's first premium service is introduced, LinkedIn Jobs.

2006: LinkedIn turns its first profit in March, when membership reaches five million users.

2007: Dan Nye is hired as LinkedIn's chief executive officer.

2008: LinkedIn secures $75 million in funding.

2009: Number of LinkedIn members reaches 40 million.

a human resources manager or recruiter posted a job offering. "We focused on that area because classified employment is the biggest money maker and the one that has moved most significantly online," Guericke explained in the March 16, 2005 issue of *Business Week Online*. In August 2005, the company began offering LinkedIn Business Accounts, a premium service that gave recruiters the ability to search the entire LinkedIn network, as opposed to having to go through intermediaries. For between $15 and $50 per month, recruiters and human resource professionals could gain access to the professional experience posted by LinkedIn's 3.3 million members, enabling users to "search a space 10 times larger, [making them] 10 times more likely to find the right person," according to an August 8, 2005 LinkedIn press release.

FIRST PROFIT AND NEW CEO: 2006-07

As LinkedIn entered its fourth year of existence, the business-oriented social network was growing at a robust rate. There were four million members by the end of 2005, a figure that swelled to five million by March 2006, the month Hoffman announced LinkedIn had turned its first profit. It was difficult to determine how successful the foray into fee-based products had been because the company refused to release any financial figures and it refused to reveal how many of its users were paying for premium services, but March 2006 represented a breakthrough moment in LinkedIn's development, nevertheless. In the years ahead, Hoffman and his management team would continue to add subscription services in an effort to turn the ever-expanding LinkedIn network into a profit-producing enterprise.

LinkedIn gained the financial support of another venture-capital firm in 2007, a year that saw the company move to new corporate headquarters and hire new leadership. In January 2007, Bessemer Venture Partners and European Founders Fund gave LinkedIn $12.8 million in funding, money Hoffman intended to use to fund the company's expansion and to develop new products and services. The following month Hoffman relinquished some of his duties to Dan Nye, who was appointed LinkedIn's chief executive officer. A Harvard Business School graduate, Nye spent six years working for software developer Intuit, where he rose to the post of vice-president before joining another software developer, Advent Software, in 2002. Nye's appointment as LinkedIn's chief executive officer left Hoffman with the responsibilities of chairman and president. In May 2007, the two senior executives moved into new offices when LinkedIn transferred its headquarters from Palo Alto to Mountain View, California.

INTERNATIONAL GROWTH

From their new offices, Hoffman and Nye presided over a rapidly growing virtual empire. LinkedIn, with ten million members in April 2007, reached 15 million members in September 2007, the month users were given the opportunity to post portrait photographs on their profile page. The two senior executives also watched over an expanding international network. From its first year in existence, the company's web site had attracted a strong international following, drawing members from Canada, Asia, and Europe. The company's membership in the United Kingdom surpassed the one-million mark in October 2007, prompting the establishment of a European headquarters in London, England, in January 2008 that became its first international office. The continued expansion of the overseas network led to the launch of a Spanish version of LinkedIn in July 2008, a French version in November 2008, and a German version in January 2009.

LinkedIn's international expansion, as well as continued growth on the domestic front, benefited from additional infusions of capital from outside investors. In June 2008, the company received the largest financial package in its history. Bain Capital Ventures, leading a group that also included Sequoia Capital, Greylock Partners, and Bessemer Venture Partners, invested $53 million in LinkedIn. In October 2008, when membership reached 30 million LinkedIn users, the company raised additional capital. Goldman Sachs, The McGraw-

Hill Companies, and SAP Ventures (along with a reinvestment by Bessemer Venture Partners) contributed $22.7 million to LinkedIn's cause. "We secured this investment with innovators in enterprise software, investment banking, and business information who see the potential to create value and transform industries through the LinkedIn platform," Nye said in an October 23, 2008 LinkedIn press release. "These leading companies understand that LinkedIn is building a network with broad and enduring value."

As LinkedIn prepared for the future, the company boasted the world's largest professional network, one that was expanding by one new member every second in mid-2009. The years ahead promised to see continued efforts to make LinkedIn an indispensable tool for businesses and professionals alike. The company was well funded, experiencing no difficulty in attracting the capital required to support and to expand its operations. During its first six years in operation, the web site's network had increased in size from the initial 300 contacts to over 40 million, providing a valuable database whose worth was set to increase in the years ahead.

Jeffrey L. Covell

PRINCIPAL COMPETITORS

Facebook, Inc.; Jigsaw Data Corporation; Spoke Software, Inc.

FURTHER READING

Copeland, Michael V., "The Missing Link," *Business 2.0,* December 2006, p. 118.

"How LinkedIn Broke Through," *Business Week Online,* April 10, 2006.

Johnson, Kimberly S., "California-Based Website LinkedIn.com Offers Forum for Business Networking," *Denver Post,* April 7, 2006.

Lacy, Sarah, "LinkedIn Expands Its Connections," *Business Week Online,* March 16, 2005.

"LinkedIn Premium Services Finding Rapid Adoption," *Internet Wire,* March 7, 2006.

"LinkedIn Raises $12.8 MLN from Bessemer Partners, European Fund," *AsiaPulse News,* January 30, 2007.

Moore, Cathleen, "LinkedIn Expands into Paid Services," *Infoworld.com,* July 19, 2005.

Pont, Jonathan, "Recruiters Now Have to Chip In to Use LinkedIn," *Workforce Management,* September 1, 2005, p. 33.

Ricadela, Aaron, "Smile, You're on LinkedIn," *Business Week Online,* September 27, 2007.

Lodge Manufacturing Company

204 East 5th Street
South Pittsburg, Tennessee 37380
U.S.A.
Telephone: (423) 837-7181
Fax: (423) 837-8279
Web site: http://www.lodgemfg.com

Private Company
Incorporated: 1896
Employees: 200
NAICS: 331511 Iron Foundries; 421620 Electrical Appliance, Television, and Radio Set Wholesalers

■ ■ ■

Lodge Manufacturing Company, the oldest family-owned and -operated cookware business in the United States, produces a wide selection of cast-iron goods for cooking using its privately held metal formula. It also manufactures other cast-iron products, such as doors to cast-iron stoves, cooking stove parts, and other pieces-to-order at its foundry. Lodge's products can be found worldwide at Wal-Mart, Target, Bass Pro, Williams-Sonoma, and Sur La Table, in hardware stores, online at Amazon.com, on its web site, and in mail-order catalogs.

LODGE MANUFACTURING COMPANY INCORPORATES: 1896–1910

In 1896, in the town of South Pittsburg, Tennessee, during the first presidential term of William McKinley,

Joseph Lodge founded Blacklock Foundry. Lodge, who had relocated to Tennessee from Pennsylvania in 1876, originally worked for the Southern State Coal and Land Company, which was known as the "The Old English Company" in honor of its English investors. By 1882, Lodge had become the superintendent for The Old English Company's blast furnaces and coal mines.

When The Old English Company went belly up in the 1890s, it was sold to the Tennessee Coal, Iron, and Railroad Company. About the same time, in 1892, Joseph Lodge and his brother, William James Lodge, started the Shuster Foundry, which manufactured soil pipe. Four years later, Lodge, then 48, began his first cast-iron foundry where he manufactured "stove and country hollowware, ... grates, fenders, kitchen sinks" as well as cast-iron skillets, Dutch ovens, and griddles, according to Lodge historical material. He named the company in honor of Rector Joseph Blacklock of Christ Church Episcopal in South Pittsburg and leased facilities at Cedar Avenue and 1st Street from the TCI&RR Co.

Seven years later, in 1899, a New York company named the Central Foundry Company bought the Shuster Foundry and engaged Lodge to start the Central Coal and Iron Company near Tuscaloosa, Alabama. Henry Blacklock, son of Joseph Blacklock, became the manager of the Blacklock Foundry in South Pittsburg after Lodge left for Alabama in 1901.

Lodge remained in Alabama for seven years. He resigned the presidency of The Central Coal and Iron Company in Tuscaloosa in 1906 and went to work for Woodward Iron Company of Woodward, Alabama. In

COMPANY PERSPECTIVES

Our success lies in our people. We have the latest technology, the latest equipment, but without people, you have nothing.

1908, he returned to South Pittsburg to manage the Blacklock Foundry.

Two years later, in May 1910, a portion of Lodge's foundry burned to the ground. Two months later, Lodge rebuilt his company at a site he had purchased for $6,000, the home of the current Lodge facility. Lodge chose the South Pittsburg area because of its supply of iron ore and access to river transportation. The company reorganized as Lodge Manufacturing Company with Joseph Lodge as president and incorporated on August 10, 1910. The molders poured the first castings at the new foundry on August 26, 1910. The company manufactured kettles, frying pans, skillets, ovens, irons, grates, and mantels.

A BRIEF HISTORY OF CAST IRON

Cast iron is humankind's oldest form of cookware, valued for its even heating properties, its non-stick finish, the flavor and trace amounts of iron that a well-seasoned pot adds to any meal, and the fact that pieces can go from stovetop to oven and improve with age. During Edward III's reign in the 14th century, the monarch's iron cookware was considered part of the crown jewels. In the 15th century, Christopher Columbus brought cast-iron cookware to the New World. The first family of the United States used cast iron in the White House, and families carried iron pots and pans as they moved west in covered wagons.

The sandblasting process for making iron cookware has remained virtually the same from its origins to the present. Iron scrap and pig iron is heated to 2,800 degrees Fahrenheit, and the molten metal is poured into a sand mold made at high pressure of sand, clay, and water. Once cooled, the cooking item is pelted with abrasive steel shot or BB pellets to achieve a smooth finished surface, then washed and coated in food-grade wax to prevent rusting. At Lodge, beginning in the 1980s, the manufacturing process included eight minutes in a vibratory drum with TRG (Tennessee River gravel) to achieve a smooth grain finish, but otherwise the production process remained unchanged until the start of the next century.

Early competition for the company was limited primarily to two other domestic manufacturers of cast iron. The Wagner Manufacturing Company was founded in Sidney, Ohio, in the 1890s and grew to become one of the largest makers of cast-iron cookware domestically. Selden & Griswold of Erie, Pennsylvania, was founded in 1865 by two families, who entered the cast-iron market as door hinge makers and branched out into cast-iron cookware.

"Back then what people wanted was wash pots and rendering pots, tea kettles and irons," according to Robert Kellermann, the company's fourth chief executive officer, in a 2003 *Washington Post* article. However, as technologies developed, all three cast-iron manufacturers faced increased competition as other companies introduced the first lines of stainless steel, copper, and other cooking sets in the 1940s. Eventually Wagner acquired Griswold in 1957, although it continued the Griswold name and trademark until 1959 when it transferred Griswold trademark rights to Textron Inc. (Randall Company of Sidney, Ohio). In August 1969, General Housewares Corp. acquired all rights to both the Griswold and Wagner trademarks.

After Joseph Lodge died in 1931, the company passed to Richard Lodge, his son, who remained president until 1949. Charles (Dick) Kellermann, a third-generation Lodge family member, became the third company president and held his position until 1973; his two brothers, Leslie and Francis, also took part in company management. Leslie Kellermann served as president from 1973 to 1984. Robert F. Kellermann, Francis Kellermann's son, began to work for the family business in 1969 after completing college at the University of Tennessee and serving in the U.S. Navy Reserve; he took over marketing for the company after his father suffered a stroke in 1969. In 1984, he became company president. In 2001, Kellermann became chief executive of Lodge and Henry Lodge, another of Joseph Lodge's great grandsons, became president.

DECLINE IN POPULARITY, INCREASE IN COMPETITION: SEVENTIES AND EIGHTIES

By the 1970s, cast iron no longer enjoyed its former widespread popularity. Southern cooks, the Amish, Mormons, and outdoor cooks remained steadfast proponents, but cast iron had sunk to the single digits as a percentage of the total range-top cookware sold in the United States. In fact, the 1973 version of the *Joy of Cooking* disparaged cast-iron cookware because it had "low conductivity, rusts easily and discolors acid foods." Despite such misinformed press, the company continued to turn out its products. During the 1970s, it

KEY DATES

1896: Joseph Lodge and his brother open the Black-lock Foundry.

1901: Lodge heads to Alabama to start the Central Coal and Iron Company.

1908: Lodge returns to South Pittsburg to manage the Blacklock Foundry.

1910: The company reorganizes as Lodge Manufacturing Company and incorporates.

1931: Joseph Lodge dies and son Richard Lodge becomes company president.

1949: Charles (Dick) Kellermann becomes the third company president.

1973: Leslie Kellermann becomes the fourth company president.

1984: Robert Kellermann becomes the fifth company president.

1991: Company replaces its cupola melting system with the more environmentally friendly induction melt system.

1996: Company doubles production with the addition of two new automatic molding machines.

2001: Robert Kellermann becomes chief executive of Lodge, and Henry Lodge becomes president.

2002: Company introduces the Lodge Logic line of pre-seasoned cookware.

2004: Company introduces Lodge Enamel.

2006: Company introduces Lodge Color.

2007: Lodge introduces its Signature Series of cast-iron items with stainless steel handles.

replaced its wooden plant with a steel building, and began to stamp its skillet and egg logo on the underside of its pots.

RENEWED INTEREST IN CAST IRON: EIGHTIES AND NINETIES

Then the mid-1980s saw renewed interest in cast iron as the Cajun cooking craze took hold and the American Dietetic Association confirmed that cast-iron cooking adds iron to foods. Sales for cast iron increased 35 percent in 1985 and another 60 percent in 1986. Lodge Manufacturing, with about 30 percent of the cast-iron market, returned to full production in 1986 after two years of reduced output, rebranding some of its products as the Original Cajun Cast Iron by Lodge and selling them in five-piece sets.

In 1991, the company replaced the old coke-fired cupola it used for melting iron with two electric burners. About this time, Lodge implemented a global marketing strategy after taking part in a housewares show in Europe and began to compete globally. "As a result of that, we redesigned our skillets from being slightly concave with a ridge around them to round-bottomed," Robert Kellermann later explained in a 1998 *Chattanooga Times* article.

Retail demand drove investment as, during the late 1990s, the market for kitchenware also grew, increasing a little more than 7 percent to $6.1 billion in 1999. High-end cookware was one of the fastest-growing segments. In 1996, the company doubled production with the addition of two new automatic molding machines capable of producing more than 400 molds per hour and an auto-pour system for pouring molten iron into molds. By 1998, the company was processing more than 85 tons of iron per day and producing more than 50 percent of the nation's cast-iron cookware.

However, Lodge faced competition from other technologies, including the enameled cast iron of Le Creuset and Staub, and inexpensive Chinese cast-iron imports. It also had to compete with itself. "One problem is that our stuff doesn't wear out," Kellermann explained in a 2003 *Washington Post* article. To add to sales, Lodge began to introduce new specialty items for campers and foodservice companies, and in 2000, it manufactured a trio of commemorative items for sale at the Winter Olympics: a Dutch oven (which got its name because the Dutch would go door-to-door selling cookware, according to Lodge literature), skillets, and spoon rests.

"It's an interesting story as to how we got involved with the Olympics," Kellermann explained in a 2001 *Chattanooga Times Free Press* article. "[W]e had to tie the Dutch oven into the history of the state." Lodge did so in part with a cookbook it produced in cooperation with the Utah-based International Dutch Oven Society. The items were a success, and Kellermann was invited to run a segment of the Olympic Torch Relay.

As the century drew to a close, Lodge became the sole remaining domestic manufacturer of cast-iron cookware as World Kitchen acquired the Wagner name through the purchase of General Housewares Corp. in October 1999 and ceased production of cast iron shortly thereafter. In 2002, Lodge, whose 180 employees were producing 10,000 pieces of cast iron per day, rolled out a new line of pre-seasoned cast-iron cookware. Lodge Logic's 28 items were coated with a vegetable spray that was then baked onto the cookware. The items sold at Bed, Bath & Beyond, Linens 'N Things, Williams-Sonoma, and Wal-Mart.

In 2003, Lodge Logic received *Good Housekeeping's* "Good Buy" award, and along with the Historic Preservation Society of South Pittsburg, Lodge compiled *A Skillet Full of Traditional Southern Lodge Cast Iron Recipes and Memories.* By 2004, the pre-seasoned line had expanded to 80 items, and sales of American-made cast iron had doubled as a result. The company, straining to keep up with demand and despite lower profit margin attributable to the rising cost of pig iron and steel scrap, added a new production line for seasoning Lodge Logic items.

It also continued to add new items: Lodge Enamel in 2004, a new line of high-priced, enamel-coated cookware, and Lodge Color in 2006, a moderately priced line of enameled cast iron. Both enameled lines were manufactured in China. In 2007, Lodge introduced its Signature Series of cast-iron items with stainless steel handles for ease of handling. The Signature Series 12-inch cast-iron skillet won "Best of the Best Gold" at the Fifth Annual Housewares Association assuring continued growth for Lodge's long-lasting products for years to come. Even as the U.S. and world economy declined in 2008, sales of Lodge's moderately priced items remained solid.

Carrie Rothburd

PRINCIPAL COMPETITORS

Le Creuset; Staub; All-Clad Metalcrafters.

FURTHER READING

Combs, Candice, "Kellermann to Bear Olympic Torch," *Chattanooga Free Times,* November 28, 2001, p. B2.

Demski, Joanne Kempinger, "Black Magic," *Milwaukee Journal Sentinel,* November 1, 2001, p. 1G.

Hyatt, Beenea A., "Business Cast in Iron; Lodge Has Served Up Quality Cookware Since 1896," *Chattanooga Times,* June 3, 1998.

Nicholls, Walter, "From Its Home in Tennessee, the Lodge Family Has Been Creating Cast-Iron Cookware for 106 Years," *Washington Post,* April 2, 2003, p. F1.

Porter, Thyra, "Meeting Demand," *HFN,* June 5, 2000, p. 53.

Mattress Giant Corporation

———————— ■ ————————

14665 Midway Road, Suite 100
Addison, Texas 75001
U.S.A.
Telephone: (972) 392-2202
Toll Free: (800) 544-4244
Fax: (972) 392-7308
Web site: http://www.mattressgiant.com

Private Company
Incorporated: 1992
Employees: 900
Sales: $220 million (2008 est.)
NAICS: 442110 Furniture Stores; 442299 All Other
Home Furnishings Stores

■ ■ ■

The fifth largest mattress retailer in the United States, Mattress Giant Corporation has more than 360 bedding stores in and around big cities in Delaware, Florida, Georgia, Illinois, Maine, Maryland, Massachusetts, Minnesota, Missouri, New Hampshire, New Jersey, Pennsylvania, Rhode Island, and Texas. The company sells brand-name mattresses as well as futons, daybeds, headboards and footboards, pillows, comforters, and other sleep-related products. Its non-mattress business accounts for less than 10 percent of sales. Mattress Giant has experienced enormous growth in the early years

of the 21st century due in part to its intense focus and commitment to sales training and customer service.

ABE LANG MANAGES FIRST GROWTH SPURT: 1992–96

Mattress Giant was founded in 1983 by Sam Capps. Nine years later, in 1992, when Phil Lang and his brother, Abraham Isaac (Abe) Lang, took over management of the business it was an eight-store chain in Fort Lauderdale, Florida. Abe Lang had been in business for himself since, as a teenager, he had opened a sandwich shop at the University of Maryland. Later he went on to operate restaurants in Maryland and Texas.

Abe Lang served as president of Mattress Giant from 1992 to 1996, and his vision for the company led to its expansive growth. Lang was intent on establishing long-term brand recognition for the company. One of his strategies in the fight for market dominance was the chain's "Ooh-ahh" jingle, an upbeat tune with a hint of country and jazz. Mattress Giant also employed special promotions, advertised on billboards and in newspaper ads, and offered great prices on known brands to drive its sales. Under Abe Lang's leadership, same store sales increased every quarter.

Lang remained integral to Mattress Giant even after he resigned as president in 1996; he joined Sam Capps, then chairman of the board, on the company's board of directors. Upon his brother Abe's resignation, Phil Lang took over the company's day-to-day operations. Phil Lang had first entered the bedding business in the late 1980s when he earned a reputation as a hard worker at the Mattress Discounters chain.

COMPANY PERSPECTIVES

Shop Smart Sleep Better embodies our philosophy to provide great value, customer service and our commitment to help customers sleep better.

PHIL LANG CONTINUES AGGRESSIVE EXPANSION: 1997–98

Shortly after he became president of Mattress Giant, Lang moved its headquarters to Dallas, Texas, and acquired a controlling interest in the company from his brother and two other partners. By that time, Mattress Giant had grown to more than 60 stores in Fort Lauderdale, Florida, Houston, Texas, and St. Louis, Missouri, each ranging from 3,200 to 8,000 square feet. According to Phil Lang in a 1997 *HFN* article, "Our growth has been a direct result of Abe's work as past president and Mr. Capps' direction and knowledge of the business. Mr. Capps brought to the table a philosophy of being good to people and being honest with our vendors. Abe ... continued that philosophy and added a push, a futuristic mentality, a vision of what Mattress Giant could be. I rely on both of them for advice and direction."

By 1997, the company had sales of $81 million. According to Lang in a 1997 *HFN* article, while the Mattress Giant brand brought customers into its stores, it was selection, price, and customer service that achieved sales. "We are a discount superstore. We give consumers a wide variety of choice and can save consumers from $50 to $200 over department and furniture store prices." In addition, Mattress Giant sold higher-end products than most discounters or sleep shops.

Lang continued the aggressive expansion program begun by his brother. In 1998, as the first step in the company's five-year plan to become one of the 25 largest stores in the domestic bedding market, a management-led group bought the assets of the chain. "We felt that most of the previous partners were not working in the company on a daily basis and we felt this was the right timing to go ahead and purchase the company," explained Lang in *HFN* in 1998.

The company also instituted a high-end bedroom look—big windows, metal beds, and lots of lighting—designed to make the customer feel comfortable buying from a discount superstore and to avoid the image of a warehouse. Mattress sets were arranged in rows, by price and feel, instead of by brand, to allow consumers to focus on comfort and price. "People are beginning to understand sleep more," attested Lang in a 1998 *HFN* article. "Luxury bedding not only feels good and gives consumers proper support, but it also gives them more of a quality night's sleep, and I think that's where the interest comes from."

ACQUIRING THE COMPETITION: 1999

Mattress Giant had sales of $110 million in 1998, and by 1999, it owned 110 stores in Texas, Florida, Minnesota, Illinois, Massachusetts, Missouri, and New Hampshire, each averaging about 6,000 square feet. Its competition came mainly from department stores and furniture stores. Then in 1999, with the bedding industry consolidating, the company purchased the ten-store American Bed chain as a springboard for expansion in central Florida.

It also acquired Nationwide Discount Sleep Centers of Philadelphia, Pennsylvania, which operated 48 stores throughout Philadelphia, New Jersey, and Delaware under several trade names. With a total of 175 retail locations, Mattress Giant became the largest privately held bedding retailer in the United States, operating in 11 markets, mostly in the Midwest and the East, and with annual sales of approximately $170 million in 1999.

Changes were afoot in the bedding industry, however. The retail mattress business, once controlled by local furniture shops and department stores, was rapidly being taken over by fast-growing specialty and discount chains. The competition had turned so intense that many of these undercapitalized mattress retailers were struggling to stay afloat. With the bedding industry consolidating, furniture stores and chains accounted for 44 percent of the $47 billion mattress industry, specialty stores 27 percent, department stores and national chains 18 percent, mass merchants 10 percent, and clubs the remaining 1 percent. Mattress Giant itself was almost purchased by Fenway Partners, a New York-based private investment firm, but the sale was forestalled in 1999 due to the economy. That same year, Abe Lang returned to Mattress Giant as a vice-president; unfortunately, he died of a heart attack shortly thereafter.

FOCUSING ON CUSTOMER SERVICE: 2002–08

Phil Lang left his position as chief executive officer of Mattress Giant, by then a top 100 company of *Furniture Today,* in 2002. Barrie Brown from Sleep Country USA

KEY DATES

1983: Sam Capps founds Mattress Giant in Florida.

1992: Abe and Phil Lang become the company's managers.

1996: Abe Lang resigns as president and joins the board of directors; Phil Lang takes over day-to-day operations of the business; company headquarters move to Texas.

1998: A management-led group buys the assets of the chain.

1999: Mattress Giant purchases American Mattress (doing business as American Bed) of Orlando, Florida, and Nationwide Discount Sleep Centers of Philadelphia, Pennsylvania.

2002: Barrie Brown becomes chief executive officer and president of Mattress Giant, succeeding Phil Lang; the company moves its headquarters to Addison, Texas.

2005: Back to Bed, Inc., purchases all 29 Mattress Giant stores in the Chicago area.

2006: Freeman Spogli & Co. investment firm purchases Mattress Giant.

2008: Company closes its distribution centers in Orlando and Largo, Florida, and opens a new distribution center in Davenport; company purchases Mattress Expo of Georgia and Clearwater Mattress of Florida.

succeeded him. Lang had seen the company grow from fewer than 100 stores to nearly 230 locations in several markets from 1996 to 2002.

Brown's first year was "a down year in a challenging environment," as he described it in *HFN* in 2003. The following year, Brown focused on training his salespeople to explain the importance of quality sleep and to focus on customer service. The 240-outlet chain also embarked on a new advertising campaign in all of its 14 states. This was a significant undertaking for a company long identified by its jingle. Launched during May, the industry's annual sleep month, Mattress Giant's "Z's" were the center of its print, television, radio, and outdoor ads. Accompanying the sleepwalking letters was the new tagline, "Shop smart. Sleep better."

Mattress Giant moved up one slot to number six among *Furniture Today*'s top 25 domestic bedding retailers with a 2.2 percent sales increase to $188 million in 2003 as bedding retailers as a group boosted their sales.

Collectively bedding sales grew from $3.02 billion in 2002 to $3.37 billion in 2003. This increase in sales was most probably due to the increased presence of baby boomers. Although the average customer only bought a mattress once every seven years, the older and less fit boomers were beginning to place a higher priority on getting a good night's sleep and buying new beds.

The following year, when a hurricane ripped through Florida on Labor Day weekend, the storm caused considerable damage to 69 of Mattress Giant's Florida stores and two of its distribution centers. In all, the company counted $4 million in lost sales. Still, by 2005 the company ranked number six on *Furniture Today*'s list of the top 25 bedding retailers. Most of the $11 billion-a-year retail industry was dominated by private equity-owned companies, but Mattress Giant remained independent. In order to simplify operations, it sold all 29 of its Chicago area stores to Back to Bed, Inc., of Itasca, Illinois, and decreased its number of brands sold.

The following year, it agreed to be sold to a private equity firm, Los Angeles-based Freeman Spogli & Co. The sale had no impact on day-to-day operations and allowed for further growth, which Mattress Giant undertook with zeal in 2007. With stores approaching the 250 mark and employees numbering 750, the chain had sales of about $208 million in 2006, up 4.5 percent from 2005. In 2006, *Furniture Today* named the company a "retail giant of bedding" and placed it at number seven on its list of the top 25 domestic bedding retailers. Although bedding specialists' 2007 performance as a whole was not as strong as in 2006, the company added 100 stores and saw its sales jump by almost 16 percent.

Continuing its growth, Mattress Giant acquired two growing sleep shop chains in the southeast in 2008, entering Georgia with the purchase of Mattress Expo, which had 24 stores in the metro Atlanta area, and the Tampa Bay market, with the acquisition of Clearwater Mattress's 21 stores. The two acquisitions brought Mattress Giant's total number of retail outlets to 340 in 14 states.

As both chains remodeled to match Mattress Giant's in-store formats and focused on sales training and customer service to develop what the company called "engaged employees," Mattress Giant focused its attention on Florida. Closing its distribution centers in Orlando and Largo, as part of efforts to consolidate operations, it added a $5.4 million, 83,000-square-foot distribution center in Davenport, Florida.

The 25-year-old company, ranked the fifth largest bedding retailer in 2008 by *Furniture Today*, commemorated its anniversary with kind words for its native state of Florida. "Starting here in Miami has allowed us to grow and attain dependable tenure in a highly competitive industry. The loyalty of our Miami area customers has been a springboard to our growth across the U.S.," said Barrie Brown in a company press release. "We've grown at a fast clip for the past several years but have never forgotten where we came from." Mattress Giant, with 360 locations, was still intent on growing.

Carrie Rothburd

PRINCIPAL COMPETITORS

Select Comfort Corporation; Sleepy's, Inc.; Slumberland, Inc.; 1800mattress.com; J. C. Penney Corporation, Inc.; Mattress Holding Corp.; Sam's Club; Sears Holdings Corporation; Tempur-Pedic International Inc.; Macy's, Inc.; Mattress Discounters Corporation.

FURTHER READING

Farrell, Nina, "Texas-Sized Growth Plan," *HFN,* July 6, 1998, p. 32.

Garau, Rebecca, "Mattress Giant's Got 'Em Singing," *HFN,* August 25, 1997, p. 15.

Godinez, Victor, "Mattress Giant Changes Hands: Equity Firm Purchase Won't Affect Operations, Official Says," *Knight-Ridder/Tribune Business News,* August 5, 2006, p. 1.

Kunkel, Karl, "No Time to Rest: Mattress Specialty Retailers Are Working Hard to Prepare for the New Year After a Tough 2002," *HFN,* January 20, 2003, p. 19.

"Mattress Merchants Multitask," *Home Textiles Today,* April 9, 2007, p. 1.

Perry, David, "Let's Shorten Warranties, Sell Profitable Extensions," *Furniture Today,* May 22, 2006, p. 30.

———, "Mattress Giant Buys Two Chains," *Furniture Today,* January 7, 2008, p. 1.

———, "Three Specialists Lead Bedding Growth Parade," *Furniture Today,* June 9, 2008, p. 24.

———, "Top 25 Bedding Retailers Boost Sales 11.7 Percent," *Furniture Today,* November 29, 2004, p. 6.

Pohl, Kimberly, "Back to Bed Puts Mattress Giant to Sleep," *Daily Herald,* December 24, 2005, p. 1.

Switzer, Liz, "Mattress Giant Sold," *HFN,* February 23, 1998, p. 10.

Williams, Steve, "His Side of the Mattress," *CIO,* September 15, 2002, p. 1.

Maverik, Inc.

———————■———————

1014 South Washington Street
Afton, Wyoming 83110
U.S.A.
Telephone: (307) 885-3861
Toll Free: (877) 936-5557
Fax: (307) 885-3832
Web site: http://www.maverik.com

Private Company
Incorporated: 1928
Employees: 2,500
Sales: $370 million (2008 est.)
NAICS: 447110 Gasoline Stations with Convenience
Stores

■ ■ ■

Maverik, Inc., operates a chain of service stations and convenience stores under the name "Maverik Country Stores," ranking as the largest independent marketer of gasoline, diesel, and convenience products in the Intermountain West. The family-owned and -managed company operates in a seven-state region, boasting 170 locations in Wyoming, Idaho, Utah, Montana, Colorado, Nevada, and Arizona, and billing itself as "Adventure's First Stop." Each store employs between ten and 20 workers, stocking food items such as doughnuts, pizza, burritos, and hamburgers and featuring an in-store bakery. To promote itself, the company produces a television program called *Kick Start* that features river rafting, sky diving, and other outdoor

recreational activities. The company is led by Mike Call, who represents the third generation of family leadership.

ORIGINS

In the small, rural community of Afton, Wyoming, Reuel T. Call played the role of a serial entrepreneur, pursuing varied business interests in the town his family had helped establish. Afton, a Mormon community located in western Wyoming near the Idaho border, was incorporated in 1902, with Anson Vasco Call II (Reuel Call's uncle) as its first mayor. In Afton, Call launched several business ventures, but his most enduring entrepreneurial creation was a business that became known as Maverik Country Stores, a retail chain that would employ generations of his descendants and ensure that the bond between Afton and the Call family would remain intact into the 21st century.

Never lacking ambition, Call "thought big, he planned big, and he accomplished big," as the *Intermountain Retailer* remembered the Afton native in the publication's 2004 Industry Directory. Among his business creations was the Callair Airplane Factory, a company he founded that manufactured STOL (short take-off and landing) aircraft. Callair airplanes, built in both passenger and spray-plane configurations, were designed for short, high-altitude runways and outfitted with wheels for summer flying and with skis for winter flying. Call, who was issued a patent in 1950 for his design of an "Aircraft Ski," also launched another transportation business venture. He used an aircraft engine and a propeller to make what he dubbed a

COMPANY PERSPECTIVES

◾

Maverik is a values based company. That means that decision making by all Maverik employees are values centered. Our values are unconditional, it is not situations that determine our actions but our values. Therefore, it is imperative that Maverik employees' personal values align with Maverik's values and operating principles. This assures employees that personal integrity will never be compromised in the name of business and assures Maverik customers that this organization expects them to be served courteously with respect, honesty, and impeccable principles—which includes a healthy helping of fun!

"Snowcar," a machine designed for cross-country travel in the mountains of Wyoming that represented an early version of a snowmobile.

When Call decided to enter the petroleum business, the foundation for Maverik Country Stores was set. The foray also provided a springboard for his entry into several related business areas. He made his move in 1928 by forming a small company that hauled gasoline in wooden barrels, a distribution venture that relied on horse-drawn wagons to deliver its supply of fuel.

ONE OF THE FIRST SELF-SERVICE OPERATORS

Call soon turned his gasoline distribution company into an operator of gasoline service stations. He opened his first station in Afton, starting what became a chain of service stations that also sold snacks and a limited range of groceries. The remarkable attribute of Call's business was its format, a format that made the self-described maverick's service stations stand out from nearly all of the competition. Instead of staffing his gas stations with service attendants, Call left the chore of pumping gas to his customers, which enabled him to offer discounted prices for his fuel. Full-service stations were the norm throughout the country, but Call's Maverik Country Stores were self-service stations, giving his chain its distinguishing quality.

DIVERSIFICATION INTO PETROLEUM REFINING

Expansion into new markets occurred at a measured pace during Call's first decades in business. Maverik

Country Stores did not impress by size, but it did in other ways, as Call built a vertically integrated operation that gave him a level of control over his business that few of his competitors enjoyed. A major impediment to growth was the availability of gasoline, which was in scarce supply. Hamstrung by an unreliable supply of gasoline, Call took proactive action, responding to the situation by again donning the hat of an entrepreneur. Between 1960 and 1975, he constructed two refineries, one in Woods Cross, Utah, and the other near Farmington, New Mexico, to fulfill his own needs and to supply other independent operators in need of a dependable supply of gasoline. As he was beginning his foray into the refining and distribution sector of the petroleum industry, he developed his own brand of gasoline, Maverik, and converted his stores to the brand in 1964.

Maverik Country Stores' presence expanded along highway corridors in a handful of states neighboring Wyoming. New locations, a combination of service stations and convenience stores, were established in Nevada, Arizona, Colorado, and Montana, but most of the new units were opened in Utah and Idaho, particularly along Interstate 84 and Interstate 15. The expansion occurred as management of the company passed from one generation to the next, a transfer of power that saw Reuel Call's son take control of the company before the reins of command were passed to the third generation of family management. The third generation's ascension to power marked a period of significant change that etched a new identity for the business founded by Reuel Call.

Maverik Country Stores' took a turn in its development at the end of the 1990s, its seventh decade of operation. The decade marked the passing of Reuel Call, in 1994, and the appointment of his grandson, Mike Call, as president and chief executive officer, duties he assumed when his father announced his retirement late in the decade. Mike Call was joined by cousin Brad Call, who became Maverik Country Stores' general counsel and vice-president after serving as a lobbyist for Fluor Corp. between 1995 and 1998. Brad Call's role as vice-president, which put him in charge of marketing, human resources, and public relations, was influential in shaping the new direction taken by the company. Maverik Country Stores suffered from the same marketing and branding problem plaguing nearly all of its rivals: how to distinguish itself from the competition. "Part of the problem with the convenience store industry is that it's very generic," Brad Call explained in the Summer 2004 issue of *GW Law School.*

CREATION OF ADVENTURE THEME

Brad Call spearheaded the development of a new corporate image and marketing strategy for Maverik Country Stores. For years, the company had used a Western theme to promote itself, but Call believed the family business needed to revitalize its image. A new corporate slogan was created, "Adventure's First Stop," along with signage, new print and television advertisements, and artwork that tapped into the popularity of outdoor recreational activities. "We implemented a fun adventure theme to distinguish ourselves from the crowd," Brad Call explained to *GW Law School.* "We run adventure TV ads, have adventure murals in all our stores, and our tanker trucks sport jeeps and wave runners," he said.

Shortly before the company's new brand identity was created, one of the few major acquisitions in its history was completed. The company was looking to add to its nearly $300 million in annual revenue and to increase its presence in its stronghold, the Utah market. To secure discounts from wholesalers and refineries (Maverik Country Stores had exited the refinery business years earlier), convenience-store chains needed to cluster their stores in markets. Maverik Country Stores, with 62 of its 140 stores located in Utah by the end of the 1990s, greatly increased its presence in Utah by acquiring 38 Circle K stores from Circle K's parent company, Tosco Marketing Co., in 1999. The purchase gave the company 100 units in Utah, including more than 30 stores in the Salt Lake City market.

As Maverik Country Stores entered the 21st century, it represented a formidable force among independent operators. The 50 largest convenience store chains in the country controlled 43 percent of the

market, leaving more than half the market to the second tier of competitors. Within the group of second tier operators, Maverik Country Stores figured as a prominent player, ranking as the seventh largest operator in terms of store count.

ENVISIONING A 300-STORE CHAIN

For the decade ahead, the Call family had ambitious plans for growth, although the implementation of any major expansion campaign would be slow to occur. To prepare for the expected expansion, the Calls made improvements to the infrastructure of their operations. Midway through the decade, Mike Call invested in a new call center, aware that his current system, four phone lines and four computers, could not adequately support a larger chain. Call hired a specialist from Continental Airlines, John Patterson, to serve as Maverik Country Stores' new call center manager. Patterson, attempting to prepare the chain for an expansion to 300 stores by the end of the decade, installed a state-of-the-art call center that used voice over Internet protocol (VoIP) technology.

To promote its stores, Maverik Country Stores devoted a considerable amount of its resources toward developing marketing and promotional campaigns. The company introduced an "Adventure Club Card" program that enabled customers to earn "Trail Points." By using the company's Adventure Club Card at the pump or in the store, customers earned points—one point for every gallon of fuel and one point for every dollar spent—that were tallied every fiscal quarter. Customers were mailed gift cards in various denominations depending on the number of points they accumulated. Maverik Country Stores also produced its own television show to promote itself, creating *Kick Start* in 2008 with the help of a Salt Lake City production studio, 8fish. The program aired once a week, featuring risk-averse individuals participating in outdoor activities such as sky diving, rock climbing, and river rafting.

By the time Maverik Country Stores' 80th anniversary arrived, the company had yet to make any significant strides toward its goal of operating 300 stores. In 2008, the company operated roughly 170 stores, leaving much work to be done before the family realized its expansion plans. The Calls intended to reach their objective, however, announcing plans in 2008 to open 15 new stores annually in the coming years.

Further expansion in its core operating area of Utah, Idaho, and Wyoming was likely, but perhaps the greatest opportunities for expansion existed in areas where Maverik Country Stores maintained only a limited presence. The company operated at only one location in Montana, a store in Bridger, south of Billings. Maverik Country Stores operated only one store in Colorado as well, a unit in Cortez near the Utah border. Arizona, home to seven stores, and Nevada, where half a dozen stores were in operation, also figured as areas for further expansion.

Whether or not Maverik Country Stores realized its growth projections, the company stood as one of the largest independent operators of convenience stores and service stations in the country. During its first 80 years of existence, the company had demonstrated an ability to adapt to changing market conditions and to withstand the competitive pressures inflicted by its much larger rivals. In the years ahead, the company's entrenched position in Utah, Wyoming, and Idaho, promised to serve it well, ensuring that Reuel Call's

entrepreneurial effort would continue to employ generations of his descendants.

Jeffrey L. Covell

PRINCIPAL COMPETITORS

7-Eleven, Inc.; Exxon Mobil Corporation; Flying J Inc.

FURTHER READING

Boulton, Guy, "Country-Store Chain Buys Utah Circle K Stores," *Knight-Ridder/Tribune Business News,* March 10, 1999.

"Discounter Maverik Abandons Old Image in Five-Year Revamp Plan," *Oil Express,* June 4, 2001, p. 7.

Enis, Matthew, "Growing Steady," *Convenience Store News,* September 25, 2000, p. 21.

"Maverik Country Stores Utilizes Site Selection Software," *Convenience Store News,* October 16, 2008.

Rapp, Meik, "Maverik Country Stores Celebrates 75 Years," *Intermountain Retailer,* 2004 Industry Directory, p. 8.

"A True Maverik," *GW Law School,* Summer 2004.

Melco Crown
Entertainment Limited

36th Floor, The Centrium
60 Wyndham Street
Central District
Hong Kong
Telephone: (+852) 2598-3600
Fax: (+852) 2537-3618
Web site: http://www.melco-crown.com

Public Company
Incorporated: 2004 as Melco PBL Entertainment
    (Macau) Limited
Employees: 4,803
Sales: $1.41 billion (2008)
Stock Exchanges: NASDAQ
Ticker Symbol: MPEL
NAICS: 721120 Casino Hotels

∎∎∎

Melco Crown Entertainment Limited is a developer and operator of casinos in the Macau Special Administrative Region, part of the People's Republic of China. Melco Crown operates the Altira Macau, a resort with a 216-room hotel and a multilevel casino with 240 gaming tables and 240 gaming machines. Altira Macau, a $512 million project, is located on Macau's Taipa Island. A much larger resort, the $2.1 billion City of Dreams project, is scheduled to open in 2009 on Macau's Coloane Island. Featuring a 420,000-square-foot casino with 550 gaming tables and 1,500 gaming machines, the City of Dreams resort includes restaurants, nightclubs, a performance hall, and 2,200 guest rooms

in three hotels and an apartment complex. Melco Crown also intends to develop a third property on the Macau peninsula. Aside from its casino operations, the company operates six Mocha Club locations in Macau that offer more than 1,000 electronic gaming machines. Melco Crown is led by Co-Chairmen Lawrence Ho and James Packer.

MONOPOLY IN MACAU

In the early 21st century, Las Vegas lost its supremacy in the global gaming industry, falling behind Macau as the greatest producer of gambling revenue in the world. Macau held the distinction of being the first and the last European colony in China, an area administered by the Portuguese from 1557 until 1999, when sovereignty was transferred to the People's Republic of China. The transfer of control gave China its first casinos, an industry in Macau thoroughly dominated by Macau's wealthiest person, a multibillionaire named Stanley Ho.

Ho secured a stranglehold on Macau's gaming industry when the area was a Portuguese colony. In 1962, Ho, promising to promote tourism and to develop infrastructure in Macau, won the public tender for gaming in Macau, giving him absolute control over the industry. Through his company, Sociedade de Turismo e Diversoes de Macau, SARL, Ho built the Lisboa Casino, which became the foundation upon which the "King of Gambling," as Ho was referred to, created his gaming empire.

Ho reigned supreme in Macau for four decades. When his grip over gaming activities began to loosen, the door was opened to other investors and casino

Through the implementation of innovative products and services and by working hand-in-hand with globally renowned brands, Melco Crown Entertainment fully intends to offer the best entertainment experience to the broadest spectrum of customers and thereby become the leader of Macau's gaming industry. In this endeavor, we have a number of projects currently underway or planned in the region.

operators, providing a business opportunity that was highly attractive. Macau, comprising a peninsula and two islands, was located roughly 40 miles southwest of Hong Kong, whose seven million inhabitants could reach Macau within an hour via a 24-hour ferry service. Spreading farther out to include capital cities within a 2,500-mile radius, Macau could court a potential customer base of two billion people, drawing clientele from Taiwan, Japan, Korea, Thailand, Malaysia, Singapore, Indonesia, and the Philippines. The area also could expect legions of visitors from mainland China because of the government's liberalization of policies related to travel visas and currency conversion.

MARKET OPENS UP

Macau, as a gaming market, had all the attributes to attract billions of dollars of investment, but not while Ho enjoyed absolute control over all casino activities. Everything changed in 2002, when the Macau government ended the monopoly system and sold two casino licenses, which subsequently were divided into subconcessions. For the first time in 40 years, the market was open to other casino operators, and the biggest names in the business wasted little time before drawing up multibillion-dollar development projects.

The Las Vegas Sands Corporation, led by Chairman Sheldon Adelson, was the first major player to stake a physical presence in Macau. When the company opened the Sands Macao, a variant of Macau, in 2004, the 229,000-square-foot property became the first foreign-owned casino in Macau. The Wynn Macau, built by Las Vegas-based Wynn Resorts, Limited, became the second foreign-owned casino to open in Macau, a 600-room, 250,000-square-foot resort whose grand opening in September 2006 occurred in the same fiscal quarter that saw Macau overtake Las Vegas as the greatest producer of gaming revenue. Both Las Vegas Sands and Wynn Resorts were planning additional, far more ambitious

development projects, as were other concerns, including a company led by the King of Gambling, Stanley Ho.

THE ARCHITECTS OF MELCO CROWN

Ho, the Macau tycoon, controlled numerous companies, including Melco International Development Limited, which he managed along with his son, Lawrence Ho. Melco International was involved in various business activities, overseeing, through subsidiaries, interests in information technology services, investment banking and financial services, and restaurants in Hong Kong and Macau. The company would be used by the Hos to develop new casinos in Macau, an effort that largely would be led by Lawrence Ho, a University of Toronto graduate who was the eldest of Stanley Ho's 17 children.

Melco's foray into the casino development business was made with a partner, Australia's Publishing and Broadcasting Limited (PBL). PBL ranked as the largest media and entertainment company in Australia, owner of, among numerous businesses, the Crown Casino Melbourne in Melbourne, Australia, and the Burswood Casino in Perth, Australia. The company was led by James Packer, the son of Australia's wealthiest citizen, Kerry Packer. In 2004, PBL and Melco formed a joint-venture company, Melco PBL Entertainment (Macau) Limited, the predecessor to Melco Crown Entertainment Limited.

Melco PBL, formed just before Sands Macao opened its doors, was created to launch an ambitious assault on the Macau casino market. Ho, 28 years old, and Packer, 37 years old, served as co-chairmen of the venture, intending to develop projects on a massive scale, but before they revealed their first project, an acquisition was completed to give their start-up enterprise a source of revenue. In June 2004, Melco PBL acquired Mocha Slot Group Limited. Mocha Slot, conducting business under the Mocha Club banner, operated at six locations scattered throughout Macau, drawing revenue from more than 1,000 electronic gaming machines. The company controlled more than 20 percent of Macau's electronic gaming market, giving Melco PBL a steady supply of cash while the company plotted its first major move in the casino market.

FIRST DEVELOPMENT PROJECT, THE CROWN MACAU: 2004

In September 2004, Ho and Packer announced Melco PBL's first casino development project, a property designed to become Macau's first six-star casino hotel.

```
┌─────────────────────────────────────────────┐
│                                             │
│              KEY DATES                      │
│                   ■                         │
│  ─────────────────────────────────────────  │
│                                             │
│  2004:  Melco PBL, the direct predecessor   │
│         to Melco Crown, is formed as a      │
│         joint-venture company by Melco      │
│         International Development Limited    │
│         and Publishing and Broadcasting     │
│         Limited.                            │
│  2006:  Construction of City of Dreams,     │
│         the company's second development    │
│         project, begins.                    │
│  2007:  Crown Macau, later rebranded as     │
│         Altira Macau, opens.                │
│  2008:  Melco PBL changes its name to       │
│         Melco Crown Entertainment Limited.  │
│                                             │
└─────────────────────────────────────────────┘
```

Dubbed the Crown Macau, the $512 million project included 240 gaming tables and 240 gaming machines, restaurants, bars, a spa, and the 216-room, 38-story Crown Towers. Construction at the Crown Macau site, located on Macau's Taipa Island, began in December 2004, with completion of the project scheduled for the first half of 2007.

Melco PBL's second development project was exponentially larger than Crown Macau, reflecting the ambitious intentions of Ho and Packer. In Cotai, on Macau's southernmost island of Coloane, they planned to build the City of Dreams, a $2.1 billion development project described by the company as "an integrated urban entertainment resort." The project included a 420,000-square-foot, underwater-themed casino with 550 gaming tables and 1,500 gaming machines, the focal point of a complex that provided 2,200 guest rooms at two deluxe hotels and one apartment complex. A shopping mall, a 2,000-seat performance hall, and a host of restaurants and bars added to the depth and breadth of the project. Construction at the site began in April 2006, with the completion date set for 2009.

GOING PUBLIC AND OPENING THE CROWN MACAU: 2006-07

By mid-2006, Ho and Packer had committed more than $2.5 billion to build two casino resorts, but the pair had yet to acquire a gaming concession or subconcession. Melco PBL had been operating its Mocha Slot chain under the terms of a service agreement with Sociedade de Jogos de Macau, S.A., another one of Stanley Ho's companies, but it did not possess a gaming license. In September 2006, Melco PBL acquired a Macau subconcession from U.S. gambling magnate Stephen Wynn, paying $900 million to become one of only six opera-

tors licensed to operate casinos in Macau. The hefty price tag, nearly twice the cost of the Crown Macau resort, prompted the next move by Melco PBL's co-chairmen: filing for an initial public offering (IPO) of stock in the United States. The company registered with the U.S. Securities and Exchange Commission (SEC) in December 2006, hoping to raise nearly $1 billion to defray the cost of the casino license and its two resorts.

When Ho and Packer filed for an IPO with the SEC, the investment community was well aware of the rapid growth of the gaming industry in Macau, which had just eclipsed Las Vegas as the world's greatest generator of gambling revenue. Ho and Packer had intended to sell 53 million shares for between $16 per share and $18 per share when they filed with the SEC, but the excitement generated by the filing in the weeks to follow encouraged the two executives to increase the number of shares for sale and to increase the share price of the offering. When Melco PBL became a public company in late December 2006, the company raised $1.15 billion by selling 60.3 million shares for $19 per share.

After completing an IPO that exceeded expectations, Ho and Packer next celebrated the grand opening of their first casino resort. In May 2007, Crown Macau opened for business, giving Melco PBL its first major stream of revenue. In 2006, when the company relied entirely on its chain of Mocha Club units for income, Melco PBL collected $36.1 million in revenue. In 2007, the company leaped to a higher plateau, generating $358.4 million in revenue. The following year, the first full year of operation for Crown Macau, Melco PBL collected $1.41 billion in revenue.

FUTURE EXPANSION PLANS

To keep pace with their rivals, Ho and Packer mapped out expansion plans while construction at the City of Dreams site pressed ahead. The exclusive group of casino operators in Macau was spending billions of dollars on development projects, such as the $1.8 billion Venetian Macao. When Las Vegas Sands opened the Venetian Macao in September 2007, it became the largest casino in the world, part of the company's plans to spend as much as $11 billion to build a complex of hotels in the former Portuguese colony. Ho and Packer intended to follow suit, revealing expansion plans that promised to fuel continued financial growth. They were searching for a site on the Macau peninsula near the ferry terminal, where they planned to spend an estimated $700 million on a casino and apartment complex. They also hoped to build a casino at Macau

Studio City, a retail and entertainment complex scheduled to open in 2009.

As Melco PBL neared its fifth anniversary and the expected June 2009 opening of City of Dreams, Ho and Packer made several changes to the company, preparing for the next phase of expansion. In May 2008, they appointed Greg Hawkins as CEO of City of Dreams and Keith Heise as chief executive officer of Crown Macau. Hawkins joined Melco PBL in January 2006, when he was hired as the chief executive officer of Crown Macau, recruited by Ho and Packer after serving as the general manager for gaming at SKYCITY Entertainment Group, a gaming and entertainment company with properties in Australia and New Zealand. Heise joined Melco PBL after serving as vice-president at Venetian Macao. The same month Hawkins and Heise assumed their new responsibilities, Melco PBL changed its name to Melco Crown Entertainment Limited.

Melco Crown was establishing a substantial presence in the world's largest and fastest growing market for gaming. In 2006, gaming revenues in Macau reached $6.87 billion, a 23 percent increase from the previous year's total. In 2007, revenues increased a staggering 46.6 percent, leaping to $10.4 billion. In this fertile environment, Melco Crown was set to unveil its flagship property and begin reaping the rewards of its $2.1 billion investment. As the ground opening of City of Dreams approached, the company rebranded its only operating casino, changing the name of Crown Macau to Altira Macau in April 2009, and pressed ahead with its two development projects, occupying an enviable position in the world's largest gaming market.

Jeffrey L. Covell

PRINCIPAL SUBSIDIARIES

MPEL Holdings Limited (Cayman Islands); MPEL International Limited (Cayman Islands); MPEL Nominee One Limited (Cayman Islands); MPEL Investments Limited (Cayman Islands); MPEL Nominee Three Limited (Cayman Islands); MPEL Nominee Two Limited (Cayman Islands); Melco Crown Gaming (Macau) Limited; Melco Crown (COD) Hotels Limited (Macau); Melco Crown (CM) Hotel Limited (Macau); Melco Crown (CM) Developments Limited (Macau); Melco Crown (Macau Peninsula) Hotel Limited; Melco Crown (Macau Peninsula) Developments Limited; MPEL (Macau Peninsula) Limited.

PRINCIPAL COMPETITORS

Wynn Resorts, Limited; Las Vegas Sands Corp.; MGM Mirage; Sociedade de Turismo e Diversoes de Macau, SARL.

FURTHER READING

Cheung, Clare, "Melco PBL Seeking $1.1 Billion IPO in U.S.," *International Herald Tribune,* December 4, 2006, p. 14.

Jordan, Lara Jakes, "Melco PBL Entertainment Prices Nasdaq Initial Public Offering at US$19 per Share," *America's Intelligence Wire,* December 19, 2006.

"Make Way for the 'Las Vegas of the East,'" *Institutional Investor International Edition,* September 2006, p. S3.

"Melco PBL Entertainment," *Euroweek,* February 17, 2006, p. S11.

"Melco PBL Entertainment Names Greg Hawkins Chief Executive Officer of City of Dreams and Keith Heise Chief Executive Officer of Crown Macau," *PrimeZone Media Network,* May 14, 2008.

Wong, Kelvin, "A Macao Feather for PBL's Crown," *International Herald Tribune,* May 9, 2007, p. 14.

———, "Melco PBL Share Sale Brings in $1.14 Billion," *International Herald Tribune,* December 20, 2006, p. 16.

National CineMedia, Inc.

9110 East Nichols Avenue, Suite 200
Centennial, Colorado 80112-3405
U.S.A.
Telephone: (303) 792-3600
Toll Free: (800) 828-2828
Fax: (303) 792-8800
Web site: http://www.ncm.com

Public Company
Incorporated: 2006
Employees: 598
Sales: $369.5 million (2009)
Stock Exchanges: NASDAQ
Ticker Symbol: NCMI
NAICS: 541870 Advertising Material Distribution
Services

■ ■ ■

National CineMedia, Inc., operates the largest digital
network providing pre-movie marketing content to
movie theaters nationwide. With more than 17,300
screens at 1,380 theaters showing National CineMedia
material, the company reaches nearly half of the movie-
going audience in the United States, about 643 million
patrons annually. National CineMedia's network
includes the three largest theater chains in the United
States, as well as several affiliates in smaller chains. The
company's primary product is FirstLook, a 20- to 30-
minute package of continuous-play advertising and
original entertainment. It is a pre-show segment that
ends immediately before the movie trailers. FirstLook

Play provides pre-show content appropriate to children
viewing G-rated, animated films.

Lobby Entertainment Network (LEN) provides
marketing and advertising content, displayed on 2,600
plasma televisions located in the lobbies, restrooms, and
other common spaces of 1,150 theaters. Digital
Broadcast Network (DBN), known as Fathom, features
live events, such as musical performances and sporting
events. Digital Content Network (DCN) offers
prerecorded events for theater showing. Standard or
high-definition digital media events are available live in
500 theaters nationwide, while prerecorded events are
available at any network theater equipped with a digital
screen. CineMeetings and Events provides complete
meeting planning services, including theater rental and
single-site or multisite broadcast of corporate meetings
and religious worship services. The company web site
hosts online social marketing and provides opportunities
for social interaction among movie fans.

JOINT VENTURE TAPS POTENTIAL OF IN-THEATER MARKETING

There are two strands to the formation of National CineMedia, Inc., from the founding of the National
Cinema Network (NCN) by AMC Entertainment, Inc.,
in 1985 and of Regal CineMedia by the Regal
Entertainment Group in 2002. Both organizations took
advantage of the captive audience of the cinema as they
developed pre-movie original entertainment and offered
pre-movie advertising to national and local companies,
as well as for theater concessions. NCN and Regal Cin-

COMPANY PERSPECTIVES

The definitive resource for cinema advertising and unique in-theatre events.

eMedia provided the material to their parent company theaters, to be shown prior to the previews of upcoming movies.

The advent of digital technology facilitated the development of new in-theater marketing and event strategies. In 2002 NCN began to offer live and prerecorded digital broadcasts of entertainment at AMC theaters, including concerts of nationally known performers and popular sporting events, such as the Rose Bowl. Regal CineMedia developed "The 2wenty" pre-show, which upgraded the format from a repeating slideshow to a continuous, 20-minute digital presentation. Regal CineMedia installed digital equipment in all of its 562 theaters and sold all of the advertising time available. Regal CineMedia signed contracts to obtain pre-show content with NBC, followed by Universal Pictures and Turner Broadcasting. Sony Pictures Entertainment became a content partner in 2003. When Georgia Theater Company became an affiliate in 2004, the digital format allowed Regal CineMedia to tailor pre-show content for that company's 257 screens in Georgia, Virginia, and South Carolina.

National CineMedia LLC (NCM) was formed in March 2005 as a joint venture of NCN and Regal CineMedia. The combined organization encompassed 11,200 screens which accounted for 36 percent of national box-office proceeds. NCM integrated the two digital networks, as it developed a proprietary digital distribution technology to cover its 8,200 digital screens. The company combined and streamlined their advertising sales formats as well. Such integration was expected to reduce costs while maximizing the potential of the growing marketing medium.

NCM retained the Regal CineMedia headquarters in Denver, and satellite offices in New York, Chicago, Detroit, and Los Angeles. NCN's main office in Kansas City closed, and sales representatives were given the option to take positions at another office. Kurt Hall, president and CEO of Regal CineMedia, became CEO of the new company.

Cinemark joined NCM as a founding member in July 2005 by purchasing a 21 percent interest in the company. NCM determined joint ownership proportionate to audience size and number of screens,

so AMC's stake was reduced to 29 percent. The entry of Cinemark added 180 theaters in Texas, including 2,300 screens. The venture combined the three largest movie theater chains in the United States.

NCM expanded further when AMC purchased Loews Cineplex Entertainment in January 2006 and added the AMC Loews theaters to the NCM network in June 2006. A $21 million investment supported the upgrading of Loews facilities to digital equipment. However, an existing contract prevented the Star Theaters, with 148 screens at nine theaters, from joining the network until the spring of 2009.

NEW COMPANY DEVELOPS DIGITAL INFRASTRUCTURE

NCM initiated a business plan to develop a digital cinema network, available to all exhibitors, not only its own theaters. NCM negotiated with digital equipment manufacturers to obtain a volume purchase price that would be passed along to its theaters, affiliates, and other exhibitors that purchased NCM's pre-show content. Satellite equipment installed on movie theater complexes allowed the pre-show material to be distributed from a central location. The technology allowed NCM to change advertising content easily, especially compared to the previous method of including footage on the 35 millimeter film that contained the feature movie presentation. In addition to providing flexibility for national and local business advertising from one location, the digital format reduced production and distribution costs.

In conjunction with the launch of pre-show content at Cinemark theaters on January 1, 2006, NCM introduced a new pre-show brand, FirstLook. With new, original content, the pre-show material was designed to amuse moviegoers before the movie trailers. NCM signed content partnership agreements with A&E Television Networks, Walt Disney Studios Home Entertainment, Universal Studios, Sony Picture Entertainment, and Warner Bros. By offering a marketing outlet for prominent entertainment companies, FirstLook provided them with a target audience of movie-lovers. The challenge of content partners involved enhancing the moviegoer's experience without intruding with overt advertising. NCM kept content fresh by circulating a different mix on a bimonthly basis. NCM issued new versions every month, with content adapted to age and audience interest, based on the movie being presented.

NCM offered theaters an extension of FirstLook for theater common areas. The Lobby Entertainment Network (LEN) provided similar entertainment advertising over plasma screens placed in high-traffic areas of movie theater lobbies, such as near concession stands

KEY DATES

1985: AMC Entertainment forms National Cinema Network to create cinema pre-show advertising and entertainment.
2002: Regal Entertainment Group begins production of advertising and original pre-show content; AMC and Regal form a joint venture, National CineMedia; Cinemark joins company.
2006: Initial public offering of stock funds transition to digital format.
2008: NCM becomes market leader over Screenvision.

and restrooms. Available at theaters with digital equipment, LEN displayed five segments of entertainment content, with advertising aired between the 30-minute repetitions.

In order to facilitate the growth of its digital market, NCM sought to develop a fully integrated digital product that suited the needs of exhibitors who would purchase the digital equipment, while it enabled them to use NCM's pre-show content. Toward that end, in August 2006 NCM signed an agreement with Kodak to develop software that could manage ticket sales, pre-show advertising, trailers, and movie presentation from a single computer application. Hence, pre-show advertising and digital cinema projectors, operated separately, were combined to handle all aspects of the moviegoer experience within one user interface. One of the challenges of the transition involved convincing movie producers to distribute first-run movies in digital format, rather than on film. NCM retained Travis Reid, who oversaw the integration of Loews Cineplex with AMC, to lead the transition.

In October 2006, NCM began consulting with JP-Morgan Chase to develop financial support for its transition from film to digital film presentation. National CineMedia incorporated in 2006 in preparation for a public offering of stock, which took place in February 2007. NCM offered 38 million shares at $21 per share, reaping gross proceeds of $798 million.

DIGITAL BROADCAST NETWORK EXPANDS SERVICE CAPABILITY AND CONTENT

NCM expanded the variety of digital content through partnerships with cultural and corporate organizations.

Under the Fathom brand, NCM offered live and prerecorded events. In November 2006 the Metropolitan Opera began to broadcast live from New York City to participating movie theaters nationwide. NCM provided digital transmission of the operas to AMC, Cinemark, and Regal Entertainment theaters in 25 markets. Prerecorded broadcasts were available at theaters in another 25 markets.

An offshoot of Fathom involved a business development project called CineMeetings, which used live and prerecorded broadcasts for business meetings and corporate events. In addition to providing single-site meeting services, CineMeetings used the Fathom network to broadcast corporate meetings live to outlying locations. Held during periods of slow theater traffic, Monday through Thursday daytime hours, such events included product launches, training seminars, and sales and marketing events. CineMeetings offered complete event planning and management services, including theater rental. The group offered meeting and entertainment packages, such as Meeting and a Movie or Meeting and a Fathom Event.

NCM continued to expand its pre-show and theater content in 2007. In January the company signed a multiyear contract with Discovery Communications to obtain pre-show content for FirstLook from cable channels TLC, Animal Planet, and Travel Channel. The following April NCM signed an exclusive contract with DMI Music & Media Solutions for all music programming. DMI's Private Label Radio provided music and video content for theater lobbies, restrooms, and other common areas, as well as for pre-show entertainment. The agreement with DMI streamlined NCM's music programming.

An exclusive content agreement with A&E Television Network involved pre-show content for 13,500 screens, such as advertising derived from A&E's television series, mini-series, and specials, and material from the History Channel. A&E agreed to provide content for theater lobbies, including LEN's video and high-definition plasma screens, available in 780 movie theaters. The April 2008 content agreement with Disney included advertising for home-entertainment movie titles as well as "behind-the-scenes" documentaries about movie production.

To prepare for widespread use of the digital media format, NCM formed Digital Cinema Implementation Partners (DCIP), a separate entity owned by AMC, Cinemark, and Regal. In early 2008 DCIP began distribution of digital cinema projectors and servers to theaters. Along with Warner Bros. and Universal Studios, DCIP began to develop technology that would transfer digital movie files to theaters via broadband or satellite, rather than on hard drive. Warner Bros. and Universal intended to use the technology to reduce the cost of distribution for the industry, not as a product to drive profits.

GAINING NEW AFFILIATES AND MARKET SHARE

The cinema pre-show advertising medium and digital entertainment continued to develop in quality and breadth. NCM signed affiliate agreements with Goodrich Quality Theatres, Marcus Theaters, and Kerasotes ShowPlace Theatres. The agreement with Kerasotes included pre-show content, in-theater events, such as NCM Fathom live and prerecorded entertainment, as well as meeting and event services. The agreement covered 96 theaters encompassing 853 screens in several major markets, including Denver, Minneapolis, Chicago, and Indianapolis.

Taking effect after a contract with Screenvision expired in 2008, the agreement with Kerasotes gave NCM a market lead over Screenvision, its closest competitor, However, NCM counted 12,600 digital screens, of 14,000 screens in its network, while Screenvision had 7,000 digital screens. Also, NCM had the advantage of 30-year contracts with affiliates, while Screenvision carried contracts for a much shorter term.

NCM's network expanded further in March 2008, when Hollywood Theaters became an affiliate. Covering locations in 15 states, the contract for services included FirstLook, CineMeetings, and NCM Fathom live and prerecorded entertainment. In April 2008, Regal Entertainment acquired Consolidated Theaters. After meeting existing contractual obligations, the 28 theaters, with 399 screens, would become part of DCN in January 2011. In January 2009, Cobb Theaters joined NCM's Fathom network, beginning with nine locations in Florida and Alabama.

Live broadcasts on the Digital Broadcast Network (DBN) resulted in a 110 percent increase in revenues for Fathom in 2008. NCM installed digital equipment at 150 locations, for a total of 500 locations equipped to provide Fathom/CineMeetings live events. Fathom became an integral component to transforming movie theaters into multipurpose community centers. In addition to the live music and sporting events, Fathom presented live radio programs and town hall meetings.

The ease of distributing pre-show content in the digital format made the new marketing medium an attractive alternative to analog formats on the decline, such as print, network television, and radio. Moreover, the cinema context of FirstLook stimulated creative approaches to advertising as it increased the sophistication

of long-form commercials that met the requirements of both entertainment and advertising. These commercials lasted from 60 to 90 seconds, sometimes up to two minutes long. A typical television spot lasted 30 seconds. With creative and media support from NCM, clients produced quality advertisements recognized with CAC Creative Advertising Awards and Telly Awards. NCM encouraged its customers to use the theater as a first-release medium, in that advertisements appeared in theaters before they appeared on television, as occurs with feature films. NCM extended FirstLook content to the Internet, adding another medium to the advertising package for its customers.

As in-theater marketing became a more attractive alternative to analog media, NCM experienced increased interest from a wider array of businesses. New national advertisers included Wendy's, J. C. Penney, LG Electronics, and Army National Guard. Toy makers, retail stores, packaged goods producers, and quick-service restaurants were a natural fit for in-theater advertising, as movie theaters tended to be located at shopping malls where these goods and services could be found. As NCM captured advertising market share, the company expanded its advertising sales team to 175 representatives who covered 1,100 theaters nationwide.

Mary Tradii

PRINCIPAL DIVISIONS

FirstLook; Fathom; CineMeetings and Events.

PRINCIPAL COMPETITORS

Cinedigm Digital Cinema Corporation; Screenvision Cinema Network, LLC; Technicolor Digital Cinema.

FURTHER READING

Bond, Paul, "Big Picture Better for CineMedia: Analysts See Opportunity for Sagging Stock with Loews Ad Deal," *Hollywood Reporter,* January 24, 2008, p. 9.

———, "Business Is Good for National CineMedia," *Hollywood Reporter,* March 20, 2007, p. 69.

Fuchs, Andreas, "Big Rollout: Digital Technology Lures New Screen Advertisers," *Film Journal International,* October 2007, p. 26.

———, "Digital Development: National CineMedia Eyes Major Transition," *Film Journal International,* October 2006, p. 20.

Paoletta, Michael, "Music Before Movies: National CineMedia Taps DMI for Audio," *Billboard,* April 7, 2007, p. 10.

Sperling, Nicole, "CineMedia Ups Ad Space Visibility: Cinemark Chain Acquires 21% Stake, Adds Its Theaters," *Hol-*

lywood Reporter, July 18, 2005, p. 5.

———, "Cineplex Part of NCM Digital Plan," *Hollywood Reporter,* September 1, 2006, p. 4.

———, "Regal AMC Join Forces: New Ad Firm Makes 36% of B.O.," *Hollywood Reporter,* March 30, 2005, p. 1.

———, "Regal Extending Deals with NBC, Universal,

Turner," *Hollywood Reporter,* October 26, 2004, p. 6.

———, "Top Exhibitors Team up to Take D-Cinema Wide," *Hollywood Reporter,* December 15, 2005, p. 1.

Vuong, Andy, "CineMedia Reels in Ads—Shown in Theaters," *Denver Post,* December 2, 2007, p. C2.

National Penn Bancshares, Inc.

Philadelphia and Reading Avenues
Boyertown, Pennsylvania 19512
U.S.A.
Toll Free: (800) 822-3321
Fax: (610) 369-6118
Web site: http://www.nationalpennbancshares.com

Public Company
Incorporated: 1982
Employees: 1,780
Total Assets: $9.4 billion (2008)
Stock Exchanges: NASDAQ
Ticker Symbol: NPBC
NAICS: 522110 Commercial Banking

■ ■ ■

National Penn Bancshares, Inc., grew to the fifth largest bank holding company headquartered in Pennsylvania through a series of acquisitions beginning in the early 2000s. The majority of the acquired banks operate as divisions of National Penn Bank, including FirstService Bank, HomeTowne Heritage Bank, KNBT, and Nittany Bank. Delaware-based Christiana Bank & Trust Company is a wholly owned subsidiary of the holding company. Affiliations allow National Penn to offer a full range of financial services. The bank takes pride in consistently producing increased earnings and dividends for its shareholders, but a contracting economy creates a spate of challenges going forward into 2009.

BANKING ON TRADITION:
1982–93

National Penn Bancshares formed in 1982 as parent company of National Bank of Boyertown. The small town bank, established in 1874, had built a regional presence in southeastern Pennsylvania and banked on further growth.

Retaining headquarters in Boyertown, the bank worked to keep its hometown feel. The long-held tradition of serving a family-style dinner at the annual meeting, for example, continued into the early 1990s. Viewed by some as a perk of ownership, protests arose when cost-cutting measures included the elimination of after-dinner dessert.

"The complaint may sound trivial to some, but National Penn's 2,700 shareholders have little else to be concerned about; for the past five years, their community bank's earnings have hit record levels while many regional banks struggled to stay in the black. The key, the bank executives and shareholders say, is the company's commitment to its customers and stockholders," Constance Walker wrote in Allentown's *Morning Call* in 1993.

The Boyertown-based bank, centrally located southwest of Allentown, northwest of Philadelphia and east of Reading, had grown to assets of about $861 million and 25 full-service banks, in Berks, Bucks, Chester, Lehigh, and Montgomery counties.

Wayne R. Weidner headed the bank, rising in his 31 years with the company from teller to president. In the early 1960s, the bank held $15 million in assets and two branches.

COMPANY PERSPECTIVES

Our people are the secret behind our history of increased earnings and dividends. After all, it's our employees, not our products and services, who listen to customer needs and wishes, and then going beyond the expected to craft solutions that help our customers achieve their dreams.

Our attention is focused on helping clients realize financial success. Our goal is to be their trusted financial advisor.

Lawrence T. Jilk, a 17-year veteran and president and CEO of National Penn Bancshares, planned continued expansion, filling in gaps in the company's service region. "We will build or buy new offices within or adjacent to existing markets," he told Walker in July 1993.

MEASURING SUCCESS: 1994

Despite increased earnings, National Penn Bancshares' stock price fluctuated during 1994. A period of takeover speculation had driven up Pennsylvania bank valuations. When it cooled, it took some of the heat out of the market. Specific to National Penn, some analysts labeled the bank overvalued, putting additional downward pressure on the stock, according to an August *American Banker* article.

The bank's strength kept its price from falling too far. The super community bank traded at 2.5 times book value (the difference between assets and liabilities) in November 1994. For three consecutive years, National Penn had traded at three times book value, a feat *American Banker* called "astounding."

Weidner, wrote Jeffrey Zack, attributed the success to "net interest margins that have been at or above 6.00% for three years, the sales culture it has built over the last decade, lean staffing, a series of aggressive but prudent acquisitions, and the stability of the markets where it does business."

The company's growth prompted a new identity. National Bank of Boyertown and all but three other holding company affiliates changed their names to National Penn Bank, in May 1994. Philadelphia's Chestnut Hill National Bank branches, acquired about a year earlier, were the only holdovers. The bank's home base of Boyertown along with its surrounding area,

roughly 18,000 people, produced about 10 percent of business, Weidner explained.

The bank had established itself in new locations through opening "easy-to-start" limited production offices: full-service banking but in rented space. "After we have a year or 18 months under our belt and like what we see, then [we can] go into a permanent site," Weidner told *American Banker.*

Along with growth came challenges. Acquisitions initially took a toll on efficiency. National Penn responded by quickly eliminating duplicate systems. The bank holding company also invested in technology upgrades to handle increased business volume and aid sales.

The genesis of National Penn's sales culture began with a cross-selling push, during the 1980s. Then in the beginning of the 1990s, a commission program was established for branch managers. Compensation increases were tied to sales. In 1994, about 9 percent of the company's 600 employees were dedicated to sales. Weidner wanted to double the number of sales-only staff within the next year and a half, Zack reported for *American Banker.*

The management structure, furthermore, was tailored to keep costs down. Each of the eight branch managers oversaw five additional locations. Branches, averaging $30 million in deposits, operated with one full-time manager, two full-time tellers, and one customer service representative. Sixty percent of staffing was from part-time employees, according to Weider.

The recession of the early 1990s had steered the bank back to an emphasis on community banking. (Upon Jilk's arrival, in the 1970s, the bank had tipped toward commercial lending.) Facing a trend toward declining interest spreads, National Penn looked toward other sources of revenue.

MAKING CHANGE: 1995–2001

National Penn's predecessor company had received its trust powers in 1930. Operating as a division of the bank, the small trust business had untapped potential. Three experienced trust bankers were brought aboard in February 1994, and in June, the trust business spun off as Investors Trust Company. The new subsidiary would sell trust services to smaller banks.

National Penn added retail brokerage services the following year, and in 1998 created Penn Securities. The moves brought the $1.6 billion in assets community bank a step closer to becoming a full-service financial institution.

Also in 1998, National Penn moved on its first acquisition since early in the decade, striking a $102

1982: Holding company is formed for National Bank of Boyertown.

1994: Bank changes name to National Penn.

1999: Competition prompts move into niche banking.

2003: Series of purchases is begun.

2007: National Penn embarks on largest acquisition in its history.

2008: U.S. Treasury bank bailout program puts $150 million in coffers.

BUYING SPREE: 2003–08

The $3 billion-asset, financial services company maintained its commitment to the manufacturing niche, in 2003, despite 32 consecutive months of job loss in the sector. An industry downturn intensified in the wake of the September 11, 2001, terrorist attacks and subsequent economic decline. While some banks in the country pulled away from lending to manufacturers, National Penn had added three more manufacturing-dedicated lenders, according to an April *American Banker* article.

National Penn also continued to serve its governmental and international niches and had added Small Business Administration lending. The Panasia Bank, though, was sold to a subsidiary of Korean-based Woori Financial Group for $34.5 million in September 2003.

The bank embarked on a series of acquisitions on the heels of the sale. HomeTowne Heritage Bank was purchased in December 2003 and People's First, Inc., in June 2004.

Desiring to "expand fee income and exploit cross-selling opportunities," Penn National then acquired three insurance agencies in about a six-month period. The company continued to expand its southeastern Pennsylvania insurance business during the year.

Through the purchase of Nittany Financial Corp., in January 2006, National Penn entered the community banking market in central Pennsylvania and bolstered its wealth management business.

In June 2007, National Penn Bancshares agreed to purchase wealth-management specialist Christiana Bank & Trust Company, for $56.5 million, gaining a foothold in neighboring northern Delaware.

Three months later, the company announced its largest acquisition to date: an all stock $464.6 million deal for KNBT Bancorp Inc. The Bethlehem-based KNBT would become a division of National Penn, but retain its name and the name of its subsidiary, Tony Lucia reported for the *Reading Eagle*.

The deal for KNBT prompted reorganization under four regions reporting to Scott V. Fainor, the president and CEO of KNBT. Fainor, as senior executive vice-president and COO of the holding company and president and CEO of National Penn Bank, would report to Moyer. Five KNBT directors were to join ten National Penn directors on the board.

National Penn Bancshares completed the acquisitions of KNBT and Christiana Bank & Trust Company of Greenville, Delaware, in early 2008. The transactions bumped National Penn's assets to $8.9 billion and assets

million stock deal for Elverson National Bank. The premium price bought National Penn seven branches in Chester County, an area long targeted for expansion. Glenn E. Moyer, Elverson president, would stay on to head the new division. National Penn's other targeted market divisions included 1st Main Line Bank, Chestnut Hill National Bank, and National Asia Bank, according to a July *American Banker* article.

A competitive market, dominated by First Union and Summit Bank, led National Penn to seek new niches, according to *Small Business Banker*. Following a canvassing of manufacturing firms, the bank launched a Manufacturing Group, in 1999, focusing on the needs of manufacturing customers. Generally serving operations with less than $10 million in sales, the bank also developed alliances to link manufacturers with non-financial services, such as equipment leasing.

National Penn expanded its niche program to government entities during 2001. The bank tailored money management products in line with funding patterns of local school districts, municipalities and townships, offering special rates of return and deposit and withdrawal flexibility. In addition to the governmental and manufacturing niches, National Penn was readying an international banking group, targeting companies set to enter the global marketplace.

Meanwhile, the bank attended to opportunities and challenges inherent to its Asian market niche. National Penn had acquired New Jersey-based Panasia Bank in July 2000 and about a year later folded in its Asian division. Panasia Bank clients often engaged in international trade, which served as a catalyst for the international banking division. Problems stemming from cultural differences, though, arose as the Asian and American banks merged their businesses.

under management to $8.2 billion, increasing the first by more than half and the second by nearly three times. National Penn also climbed to fifth spot in terms of assets among Pennsylvania-headquartered banks. Moreover, the company gained "well-established brands in wealthy markets in the Lehigh Valley and neighboring Delaware," Bonnie McGeer wrote in *American Banker*.

National Penn planned to convert its existing branches in Northampton and Lehigh counties to the KNBT brand to capitalize on its market strength. Wachovia Corporation topped the ranks in terms of deposits in Lehigh Valley, ahead of KNBT. Christiana, meanwhile, afforded wealthy customers legal and tax advantages unavailable in Pennsylvania and generated more fee income and cross-selling opportunities for National Penn.

The acquisitions were necessary to continue the streak of 30 consecutive years of higher earnings per share and dividends, according to the McGeer article. Since 2002, National Penn had grown from 58 offices and just under $3 billion in overall assets, to about 130 offices and more than $9 billion in assets, according to *Morning Call*.

UNCERTAIN FUTURE

National Penn Bancshares decided to participate in the U.S. Treasury Department's Capital Purchase Program to "thaw frozen credit markets and prop up financial institutions," *Morning Call* reported in December 2008.

Moyer said that although National Penn continued to be "well-capitalized by all regulatory standards and has a long history of financial strength," the taxpayer money would help them "stimulate economic recovery" in their region. The additional resources would go toward consumer and business loans and, possibly, acquisitions.

The $700 billion bank bailout package came with stipulations, including prior approval for dividend payments and changes related to executive pay. In return for the capital infusion, the Treasury Department would receive senior preferred stock, warrants for common stock and 5 percent interest for the first five years.

Across the country increasing mortgage default rates had crippled banks and driven down credit availability for consumers and businesses. Banks themselves stopped lending to one another, fearful of their stability. In the first quarter of 2007, National Penn had "ceased participating in wholesale mortgage originations."

National Penn Bancshares received $150 million through its sale of stock to the U.S. government, in December. Warrants for 1.47 million shares of common stock at $15.30 per share were also issued.

National Penn posted net income of $32.27 million or $0.42 per diluted share for 2008, versus $65.23 million and $1.31 per share the prior year. Increased reserves for loan losses, failed investment securities, and a fraud loss factored into the decline.

Kathleen Peippo

PRINCIPAL SUBSIDIARIES

National Penn Bank; Christiana Bank & Trust Company.

PRINCIPAL COMPETITORS

Fulton Financial Corporation; Harleysville Corporation; Wachovia Corporation.

FURTHER READING

Agosta, Veronica, "National Penn's Niching Goes Government," *American Banker*, May 23, 2001, p. 7.

"Bank Swat Team Snags Clients," *Small Business Banker*, December 2000, p. 31.

Fontana, Dominick, "National Penn Makes CEO Jilk Chairman, Taps New President," *American Banker*, May 7, 1998, p. 12.

Gottlieb, Jenna, "National Penn's Agency Deals Eye Fees, Cross Selling," *American Banker*, January 6, 2005, p. 7.

Lucia, Tony, "Bank Suit Claims Millions Missing: National Penn Bancshares Inc. Alleges a Fired Vice President and Relatives Took the Money," *Reading (Pa.) Eagle*, December 6, 2008.

———, "National Buys KNBT Bancorp: The Largest Acquisition in the Boyertown-Based Bank's History Gives It a Foothold in Lehigh Valley," *Reading (Pa.) Eagle*, September 8, 2007.

McGeer, Bonnie, "National Penn Celebrates Two Transformative Deals," *American Banker*, March 10, 2008, p. 6.

"National Penn Announces Reorganization," *Reading (Pa.) Eagle*, December 20, 2007.

"National Penn Bancshares Completes Sale of $150 Million in Senior Preferred Shares to U.S. Treasury," *U.S. Newswire*, December 12, 2008.

"National Penn Settles Lawsuit Against Party in Fraud Case," *Reading (Pa.) Eagle*, December 30, 2005.

Reosti, John, "Building a Niche Many Lenders Shun," *American Banker*, April 10, 2003, p. 1.

———, "For National Penn, $3.4M Tab for Fraud," *American Banker*, February 24, 2005, p. 1.

———, "National Penn Eyes Expansion for Asian Unit," *American Banker*, November 12, 2001, p. 5.

Ring, Niamh, "Small Pennsylvania Bank to Seek Broker-Dealer License," *American Banker,* June 3, 1998, p. 15.

Soper, Spencer, "National Penn in Line for Bailout Money," *Allentown (Pa.) Morning Call,* December 2, 2008, p. A1.

Tomasula, Dean, "National Penn Stuck at 52-Week Low After a Big Selloff," *American Banker,* August 31, 1994, p. 20.

Walker, Constance, "Commitment Given to Customers Equally Enjoyed by Shareholders," *Allentown (Pa.) Morning Call,* July 26, 1993.

Whiteman, Louis, "Pa. Bank Pays Big Premium in Deal for Small Neighbor," *American Banker,* July 23, 1998, p. 6.

Zack, Jeffrey, "National Penn: Writing a Continuing Success Story," *American Banker,* November 7, 1994, pp. 1A+.

National Wildlife Federation

11100 Wildlife Center Drive
Reston, Virginia 20190-5362
U.S.A.
Telephone: (703) 438-6000
Toll Free: (800) 822-9919
Fax: (703) 438-6468
Web site: http://www.nwf.org

Nonprofit Company
Founded: 1936 as General Wildlife Federation
Employees: 400
Operating Revenues: $88.54 million (2007)
NAICS: 813312 Environment, Conservation, and
Wildlife Organizations

■ ■ ■

National Wildlife Federation (NWF) is a nonprofit member-supported conservation group comprised of state and territorial affiliates, associate members, and individual contributors. All told, the Reston, Virginia-based organization boasts more than five million members and supporters, making it the largest private conservation education and advocacy organization in the United States. The primary mission of NWF is to preserve wildlife and other natural resources as well as the earth's environment in a sustainable manner. NWF also promotes the appreciation of wildlife and wild places. To support its goals, NWF publishes magazines, such as *Wild Animal Baby* for toddlers, *Your Big Backyard* for preschoolers, *Ranger Rick* for children aged seven to 12, *Ranger Rick Just for Fun* activity books, and

National Wildlife and *International Wildlife* for adults.

NWF also publishes an annual Conservation Directory and operates National Wildlife Productions, Inc., to produce television programs and films. Other NWF programs include Backyard Wildlife Habitat, showing people how to provide friendly conditions for wildlife in their yards and communities; and Campus Ecology, building support among college and university students through education events and the provision of resources and technical support. NWF also maintains nine regional field offices to support specific, local environmental needs as well as the National Advocacy Center in Washington, D.C., to lobby the federal government and promote its position to the media.

POLITICAL CARTOONIST DRIVING FORCE BEHIND NWF'S ORIGINS

The man who inspired the creation of the National Wildlife Federation was Pulitzer Prize–winning political cartoonist Jay Norwood "Ding" Darling. Born in 1876 in Norwood, Michigan, Darling grew up in Elkhart, Indiana, and attended high school in Sioux City, Iowa, close to where the Iowa, Nebraska, and South Dakota borders converged. The area was far from developed, allowing Norwood to enjoy the pleasures of an unsullied prairie and develop an enduring love of the outdoors and wildlife. He also developed a gift for sketching that turned into a facility for caricaturing individuals. After graduating from Beloit College he had intended to study medicine and to make money to pay for it he took a job as a reporter for the *Sioux City Journal.*

Unable to take a photograph of a lawyer to accompany an article he wrote, Darling supplied a sketch. It was so well received that he began drawing pictures of prominent Sioux City residents in a series called "Local Snapshots." For the next several years he continued to combine reporting and drawing until the *Des Moines Register and Leader* hired him as a cartoonist. Aside from a brief stint working for the *New York Globe,* Darling spent his half-century career in Des Moines. In 1923 he gained national prominence by winning the Pulitzer Prize for best cartoon. He would win a second Pulitzer in 1943.

In addition to his newspaper work, Darling became active in promoting his passion for the outdoors, helping to organize the Des Moines chapter of the Izaak Walter League, which advocated the preservation of natural resources, and serving on the Iowa Fish and Game Commission. He also helped to landscape the local parks and establish a wildlife research unit at Iowa State College that served as a model for similar endeavors across the country. Darling opposed the election of Franklin Roosevelt to the presidency in 1932, and lampooned Roosevelt's New Deal slate of progressive programs, yet in 1934 President Roosevelt appointed him to a committee to develop a migratory waterfowl plan and he was subsequently offered the post as chief of the U.S. Bureau of Biological Survey, a job that paid $8,000 a year. Darling, whose income was $100,000 a year, accepted.

While he may have lacked administrative experience, Darling's energy was never in short supply. In the 20 months that he headed the Biological Survey, the predecessor to the U.S. Fish and Wildlife Service, he secured $20 million for wildlife conservation and 4.5 million acres were set aside as refuge land. He also created the Federal Duck Stamp Program, which raised money from waterfowl hunters through the required purchase of stamps for the acquisition of wetlands for wildlife habitat protection.

CONFERENCE OF 1936 LEADS TO NWF

In 1936 Darling persuaded Roosevelt to convene a conference in the capital to bring together agencies, organizations, and individuals interested in the conservation and restoration of wildlife habitats. Held in February of that year, just after Darling resigned as the chief of the Biological Survey, it was called the North American Wildlife Conference. Out of the meeting emerged the General Wildlife Federation, an organization that would be dominated by sportsmen but one that at the behest of Darling included unaffiliated individuals and non-sporting groups. Darling was elected as the first president, and the first annual meeting was held in March of the following year in St. Louis with delegates from 42 states and the District of Columbia. It was here that Darling made it clear to the delegates that the group would have to become politically active in order to achieve their goals, one of which he urged should be clean water. It would become a major NWF issue for the next half century. Delegates to the first conference also endorsed a plan to create an annual National Wildlife Restoration Week, the first celebration of which was held in 1938. In time, Restoration Week would be spearheaded by a celebrity chairperson, starting with Bing Crosby in 1950, and focus on a theme, such as "Save the Key Deer" and "Waterfowl for the Future." In brief, the four objectives of the Federation were the organization of conservation groups, development of a comprehensive conservation program, the education of the public, and cooperation with other conservation organizations.

NEW PRESIDENT BRINGS CHANGES: 1950

General Wildlife Federation, which initially operated out of the American Wildlife Institute offices in Washington, quickly sought to influence legislation by advocating for the Federal Aid in Wildlife Restoration Act, passed in 1937. Known as Pittman-Robertson, it created a federal excise tax on firearms. The money it raised was used to match funds provided by states for wildlife management, including the acquisition, restoration, and maintenance of habitats. The organization took the name National Wildlife Federation in 1938. A year later Darling turned over the presidency to David Archer Aylward, who would hold the post until 1950, running the organization from an office in Boston. Darling remained involved, however, and during the early years when NWF struggled financially he paid some of the day-to-day expenses of the organization, which was always teetering on the edge of bankruptcy. Not only was Conservation Week a money-losing proposition, the wildlife stamps the NWF produced to raise money did not cover the cost of their printing, the Federation shouldered the expenses of maintaining dual offices in Boston and Washington, and an education program also drained the coffers. The program produced

KEY DATES

1936: North American Wildlife Conference creates General Wildlife Federation.
1938: General Wildlife Federation changes name to National Wildlife Federation.
1956: Annual revenues top $1 million mark.
1962: *National Wildlife* begins publishing.
1981: Jay D. Hair is named president.
1994: National Wildlife Productions, Inc., is formed.
2001: Headquarters is moved to Reston, Virginia.
2004: Larry J. Schweiger is named president.

pamphlets that were to be sold for $1 each, with 35 cents of the proceeds earmarked for local and state conservation councils and 65 cents for NWF. Of the 150,000 pamphlets produced by 1942, only 30,000 were sold.

Because of poor record keeping no one really knew how much had been spent. Estimates ranged from $110,000 to $197,000, but there was no doubt that expenses far exceeded the $13,000 taken in. The Federation was forced to beg creditors not to press their claims for a year to provide some breathing room. NWF scraped by and under the leadership of Treasurer Louis Wendt it was financially stable enough by the end of the 1940s to hire its first full-time executive director.

In the late 1940s NWF lobbied for the passage of two major pieces of legislation. In 1947 President Harry Truman signed into law the Federal Insecticide, Fungicide, and Rodenticide Act, the first time the federal government addressed the problem of toxic chemicals in the environment. A year later The Transfer of Certain Real Property for Wildlife Conservation Purposes Act allowed unneeded federal agency land that could be of value to migratory birds to be transferred to the secretary of the interior or a state agency for wildlife conservation.

In 1950, with the resignation of Aylward, the Boston office closed, saving money as the Washington office carried on the legislative work as well as serving as the Federation's headquarters. A new change in administration also led to improved fund-raising ventures. A Christmas card and gift promotion worked well for a while in the early 1950s and a Christmas stamp promotion in 1956 helped NWF top the $1 million mark in annual income for the first time. This suc-

cess was followed by a sheet of stamps aimed at the school market, another profitable venture.

On the legislative front in the 1950s, NWF lent its weight to the passage of several important bills. The Federal Aid in Fish Restoration Act, taxing sportfishing equipment to fund sport fisheries, was passed in 1950. The landmark Water Pollution Control Act followed in 1956, making federal funds available for the construction of water treatment plants. In that same year the Fish and Wildlife Reorganization Act was signed into law, separating commercial fisheries and sports fisheries into distinct bureaus of the Fish and Wildlife Service, and in 1958 the Pesticide Research Act directed the Fish and Wildlife Service to study the impact of pesticides on wildlife.

CAPITAL OFFICE OPENS: 1961

The profits of stamp ventures as well as a large bequest allowed NWF to build a Washington, D.C., headquarters, which opened in 1961. In that same year a change in the bylaws shifted the emphasis of the organization away from sportsmen affiliates by creating a new class of associate memberships and the addition in focus from just "wildlife resources" to "other natural resources." With the expansion of the organization's membership and purview, momentum increased for the publication of a magazine, something that had been discussed for years. A joint venture was established with Milwaukee's W. A. Kreuger Company, which would design, print, and distribute the magazine while the Federation was responsible for the editorial content and selling it to its members. In November 1962 the first issue (December–January 1962–63) of *National Wildlife* was published.

The shift in editorial direction of the magazine over the next 20 years mirrored the evolution of NWF, as its focus moved from conservationism to environmentalism. A key turning point came in 1969 when *National Wildlife* began offering its annual Environmental Quality Index, essentially a report card on the state of the earth's environment. By 1971 a turning point had been reached and environmentalism became the hallmark of both the magazine and NWF. Around this time a second magazine, *International Wildlife*, was launched. Earlier, in 1966, NWF began publishing a children's magazine, *Ranger Rick*, which grew out of a Federation book published in 1959, *The Adventures of Rick Raccoon*. In 1980 *Our Big Backyard* was introduced for children too young to read.

The type of legislation for which NWF advocated was also indicative of the increasing emphasis on the environment. The Clean Air Act of 1963 was a key bill, as was the National Environmental Policy Act of 1969, which required all federal agencies to provide the public with environmental impact statements on any proposed legislation that might have a serious impact on the environment. Other major legislation lobbied by NWF in the 1960s included the Sikes Act, 1960, requiring the military to provide conservation programs for its reservations; the 1961 Wetlands Loan Act, providing funding for wetlands appropriations; the Wilderness Act of 1964, creating the National Wilderness System; also in 1964, the Land and Water Conservation Fund Act; the Endangered Species Preservation Act of 1966; the Wild and Scenic Rivers Act and National Trails System Act, both in 1968; and a year later, the Endangered Species Conservation Act and Water Bank Act, providing further protection for the wetlands.

In the 1970s NWF continued to advocate for a variety of legislation. In 1972 five major pieces of legislation were enacted: The Coastal Zone Management Act; amendments to the Clean Water Act through the Federal Water Pollution Control Act Amendments; Marine Protection Research and Sanctuaries Act, also known as the Oceans Dumping Act; Federal Environmental Pesticide Control Act; and the Marine Mammals Protection Acts. Other laws supported by NWF in the 1970s included the Endangered Species Act in 1973, followed a year later by the Forest and Rangelands Renewable Resources Planning Act; the Federal Land Policy and Management Act, Toxic Substance Control Act, and National Forest Management Act, all in 1976; the Surface Mining Control and Reclamation Act in 1977; and the National Parks and Recreational Act of 1978, which greatly added to the National Park System as well as the Wild and Scenic River System, and the National Scenic Trails System.

JAY HAIR BECOMES PRESIDENT: 1981

Another watershed moment for NWF came in 1981 when Jay D. Hair was named Federation president. He completed the organization's transformation from a loose federation of sportsmen interested in preserving hunting lands and fishing waters to a grassroots environmental group with a diverse agenda. Hair took over just as the Reagan administration had assumed office and he quickly became a feisty adversary, one who vehemently objected to the administration's budget cuts and reorganization that he viewed as an attempt to roll back hard-won environmental protections. Serving as the spur to action for Hair and other environmentalists was head of the Department of Interior, James Watt, who advocated increased development of public lands, including drilling for oil in wildlife preserves. Watt was

soon forced from his post, but served as a catalyst for Hair in his efforts to grow NWF into a grassroots movement. Membership increased from 4.2 million in 1981 to six million in 1994.

Hair also made NWF into a more media-savvy organization. In 1989, for example, following the *Exxon Valdez* oil spill in Alaska, Hair was quick to arrive at the scene, the first major environmentalist to do so. To make his point about the dangers of drilling and transporting oil in environmentally sensitive areas, he sent government officials oil-soaked rocks in plastic bags. Under his leadership in the 1980s, NWF was in the forefront of support for the Endangered Species Act Amendments of 1982, the Food Security Act (Farm Bill) of 1985, and the 1986 Superfunds Amendments and Reauthorization Act that put teeth, and money, into the 1980 Superfund legislation dealing with toxic contamination.

With greater membership came increased revenues from dues. NWF also proved to be a good merchandiser. By 1990 the Federation made $30 million each year on the sale of calendars, T-shirts, Christmas cards, and other items, while the magazines fetched another $35 million. With extra funds at his disposal, Hair built up the organization's staff of lawyers, lobbyists, and scientists. He was not without his share of critics, however. A firm believer in the free enterprise system, he tried to work with corporations, sitting on a number of boards, a conciliatory approach dubbed "cooperative conservation" not shared by other environmental groups. Hair was also criticized for his high salary and for maintaining the large, expensive headquarters the organization moved into in 1989. In the early 1990s a further split between NWF and other environmental groups resulted from the North American Free Trade Agreement (NAFTA). Taking what they called a practical approach to the legislation, NWF along with the National Audubon Society and others endorsed NAFTA while the Sierra Club, Greenpeace, and a large number of community groups opposed it.

NWF added a new way to spread its environmental message in the 1990s, establishing a film production unit in 1994. The proliferation of cable television channels created an increased need for content, providing NWF with an opening in the marketplace. Federation productions were carried by TBS, Discovery, Disney, the Travel Channel, Home and Garden Television, and the Outdoor Life Network. Moreover, the unit also produced IMAX films. The first IMAX production, *Whales,* was narrated by actor Patrick Stewart. In addition, NWF offered an educational guide, companion book, CD-ROM, and exhibit kiosk. IMAX films on wolves and bears followed later in the 1990s.

Hair left NWF in 1995, replaced as president by Mark Van Putten a year later. Under his watch, NWF sold its headquarters, deemed too large by the organization, to a church in 1999 and in 2001 moved into a new home in Reston, Virginia. Although designed to be as environmentally benign as possible (parking lot rainwater, for example, was purified by cattails before running into a nearby pond and the front desk was made from wood harvested from ecologically managed forests), the new headquarters had its share of critics, who charged NWF with contributing to urban sprawl.

Van Putten was succeeded as president by Larry J. Schweiger in 2004. He was well familiar with NWF, having served as the publisher of the group's magazines from 1981 to 1995. He then went to head the Western Pennsylvania Conservancy before returning to NWF. Schweiger's primary goal, and that of NWF, was to address the challenge of global warming and need for a comprehensive climate and energy policy. With the election of Barack Obama as president in 2008, NWF hoped that after years of fruitless advocacy on behalf of climate legislation, it would enjoy greater success in helping to shape a response to what it regarded as a global crisis.

Ed Dinger

PRINCIPAL SUBSIDIARIES

National Wildlife Productions, Inc.; National Wildlife Foundation, Inc.

PRINCIPAL COMPETITORS

Greenpeace International; National Audubon Society; The Sierra Club.

FURTHER READING

Allen, Thomas B., *Guardian of the Wild,* Bloomington and Indianapolis: Indiana University Press, 1987, 212 p.

Brennan, Patricia, "So Many Channels, So Few Films," *Washington Post,* November 3, 1996, p. Y07.

"Ding Darling, Cartoonist, Dies," *New York Times,* February 13, 1962.

Gutfeld, Rose, and Allanna Sullivan, "Exxon, Alyeska Pipeline Are Sued by Wildlife Group over Oil Spill," *Wall Street Journal,* August 18, 1989, p. 1.

"Offering Business a Peace Pipe," *Business Week,* February 21, 1983, p. 98H.

Schneider, Keith, "Environment Groups Are Split on Support for Free-Trade Pact," *New York Times,* September 16, 1993, p. A1.

Whoriskey, Peter, "Eco-Friendly Is in Eye of Beholder," *Washington Post,* March 21, 2001, p. B01.

"Wildlife Experts Gather at Capital," *New York Times,* February 2, 1936.

Netto International

Mimersvej 1
Køge, 4600
Denmark
Telephone: (+45 43) 56 88 22
Fax: (+45 43) 56 88 12
Web site: http://www.netto.co.uk

Private Subsidiary of Dansk Supermarked
Incorporated: 1980
Employees: 15,000
NAICS: 445110 Supermarkets and Other Grocery
(Except Convenience) Stores

■ ■ ■

Netto International is a leading European operator of
discount supermarkets. Based in Køge, Denmark, Netto
is part of Dansk Supermarked, the country's leading
retail group, which itself is jointly owned by A.P. Møller
- Mærsk A/S and F. Salling A/S. Netto operates more
than 1,100 stores, focusing on the Danish, Swedish,
U.K., Polish, and German markets. The company's
Denmark operations include 400 stores under the Netto
name; the company has also rolled out a smaller
convenience store format, DøgnNetto. In Germany, the
company is represented by 285 Netto stores (but is
unaffiliated with rival Netto Marken-Discount, owned
by the Edeko retail group). Netto's U.K. operations are
directed by Netto Foodstores Limited, and includes 195
stores. The company has indicated its interest in
expanding its U.K. operations to as many as 1,000 in
the 21st century. In Poland, Netto operates 157 stores,

while the group's youngest market, in Sweden, launched
in 2002 as part of a joint venture with that country's
ICA, numbers 102 stores. Netto seeks to differentiate
itself from its hard discount competitors, such as Aldi
and Lidl, by developing higher-quality lines of private-
label goods, which offer branded goods at discounts up
to 30 percent of mainstream supermarket pricing. The
company's private-label lines vary according to their local markets, and typically feature domestically produced
foods and local specialties. Netto International employs
more than 15,000 people. The company does not
provide sales data.

ROOTS IN EARLY 20TH CENTURY

Netto International's origins lay in the growth of the
Dansk Supermarked group. That company had its start
in the early 20th century, when Ferdinand Salling set up
a department store in the town of Aarhus in 1906. His
son Herman Salling took over the business in 1953 and
launched a major expansion drive, opening a number of
new department stores throughout Denmark.

Toward the 1960s, Salling decided to travel abroad,
where he was introduced to the new retailing trends being pioneered in the United States and elsewhere.
Returning to Denmark, Salling decided to introduce the
supermarket concept to the country. In 1960, Salling
renamed his company as Jysk Supermarked. In that year,
the company opened its first supermarket, called Fotex,
featuring a mix of grocery items, as well as hardware,
clothing, and other textiles.

From the start, Salling sought to develop the chain
store model that had led to the growth of major retail

COMPANY PERSPECTIVES

Netto is common sense. Netto's business concept is based on common sense. The store design is simple, and Netto customers are offered quality products and weekly special offers at low prices. Netto's range covers almost 90 percent of the average consumer's convenience goods needs, and it is constantly being expanded to meet customer requirements.

groups in the United States and elsewhere. To this end, Salling teamed up with Danish industrial and shipping conglomerate A.P. Møller - Mærsk A/S, which acquired a 50 percent stake in Jysk Supermarked in 1964. Soon after, the company changed its name to Dansk Supermarked.

Through the 1970s, Dansk Supermarked expanded its retail network, opening its first hypermarket, Bilka, in 1970, and later adding other department stores, as well as clothing and retail stores. At the beginning of the 1980s, however, Dansk Supermarked found its grocery operations under threat from a new challenger.

HEADING OFF THE COMPETITION IN 1980

While the self-service supermarket format had been transforming the retail sector across all of Europe, the economic crisis of the 1970s had inspired the development of new grocery retailers focused on the discount market. Among the pioneers of the so-called hard discount format was the German Aldi group, which had launched its international expansion by the beginning of the 1980s. The first Aldi in Denmark opened in 1980, and set itself apart from the mainstream supermarket sector with its stripped-down, no-frills stores, its limited selection, and, especially, its extremely low pricing.

Dansk Supermarked recognized that it needed to strike back in order to head off Aldi's growth into the Danish market. In 1981, therefore, Dansk Supermarked launched its own deep-discount subsidiary, called Netto. As with the other retail businesses in the Dansk Supermarked group, Netto operated as an independent company. At the same time, Netto was able to tap into the strong financial position of its parent companies in order to drive its expansion throughout Denmark.

By the early 1990s, Netto topped 150 stores in Denmark. Through the end of the century, Netto became a mainstay of the Danish supermarket sector,

building up a network of more than 400 stores. Netto also became one of the country's most well-known brands, enjoying brand recognition rates on a par with Danish iconic brand Lego. Netto's growth was all the more remarkable given the relatively small size of the Danish population of just five million.

INTERNATIONAL AMBITIONS IN THE NINETIES

Dansk Supermarked was not the only retail group in Europe to develop the Netto format. In Germany, the Edeka supermarket group launched its own version of the Netto concept, which grew into the 1,000-store Netto Marken Discount chain. Similarly, in France, the Intermarche supermarket chain, working in partnership with the Spar supermarket group, developed its own chain of Netto stores operating both in France and Spain.

Dansk Supermarked decided to extend the reach of its own Netto operations at the beginning of the 1990s. The company at first targeted Germany, and specifically the newly reunited northeastern region. In 1990, Netto created a new subsidiary, OHG Netto Supermarkt, which opened its first store in Anklam, in the Mecklenburg-Vorpommern region, in September of that year.

Netto's strategy in Germany focused on steadily building a major regional presence, rather than pursuing a rapid national expansion. The group's German presence received a boost in 1992 when it formed its own joint-venture partnership with Spar Handels AG to develop the Netto chain. Over the next decade, Netto built a solid presence in the German northeast.

After claiming the leadership in the discount market in that region, Netto then began to expand into other German markets, notably Schleswig-Holstein and Hamburg. By the later years of the first decade of the 2000s, Netto's German network numbered 285 stores. By then Dansk Supermarked had also regained a controlling interest in the joint venture, holding 75 percent, with the remaining held by Edeka.

BUILDING A U.K. PRESENCE

Germany was not the only target for Netto's expansion in the early 1990s. Shortly after entering Germany, Netto also launched a subsidiary in the United Kingdom, called Netto Foodstores Limited. That company then set up its first store in Leeds in December 1990. Netto's entry into the United Kingdom came on the heels of a more high-profile drive by rival Aldi to move into the U.K. market.

KEY DATES

1981: Dansk Supermarked establishes a discount grocery chain, Netto.

1991: Netto establishes subsidiaries in Germany and the United Kingdom, opening its first stores there.

1995: Netto expands into Poland.

2002: Netto adds operations in Sweden in a joint venture with ICA.

2009: Netto enters Ukraine with plans to open as many as 30 stores in its first year.

While Aldi's entry proved highly controversial in the United Kingdom, where the discount grocery format had failed to gain significant market share, Netto quietly built up its own U.K. presence. Part of Netto's success in the United Kingdom lay in its policy of stocking its store shelves with a product selection geared to local preferences. Netto stores, like their hard discount rivals, featured only a limited selection of products. In general, each product category offered a brand leader, as well as a corresponding private-label product. Unlike Aldi, which sourced much of its product offering from outside the United Kingdom, and therefore stocked its shelves with brands unrecognized by British consumers, Netto's own supply network was largely based in the United Kingdom.

This policy allowed Netto to avoid the negative publicity generated by Aldi. Because of the furor surrounding Aldi (the company was accused of selling at a loss, for example) the German discounter found it difficult to acquire existing properties. Instead, the company was forced to build new stores from scratch. In contrast, Netto's lower profile helped the company in its search to acquire and convert existing properties to the Netto format. The lower costs associated with conversion, as opposed to building from scratch, enabled Netto to pass these savings along to its customers in the form of lower prices.

By May 1991, Netto had opened five stores. As with the group's German expansion, Netto Foodstores maintained a similar strategy of focusing its initial strategy on a single region. Yet Netto Foodstores, led by Henrik Gundelach, quickly developed its own personality. In a departure from the group's Danish operations, for example, the company began developing its own private-label product range for the U.K. market. For this, Netto emphasized the high-quality segment, seeking to emulate the brand leaders, rather than the generally lower-quality generic product segment.

STRUGGLING IN THE UNITED KINGDOM IN THE LATE NINETIES

The Netto U.K. operation grew quickly in its early years. By 1993, the company also boasted 60 stores in the United Kingdom covering most of northern England and into Scotland. Netto maintained its growth into the middle of the decade, topping 100 stores by 1995. Part of this growth came from the acquisition of 13 Ed discount stores, which Netto Foodstores took over from France's Carrefour in 1995. Gundelach left the company that year.

Netto Foodstores prepared to move into the southeast region, particularly the London area, in the second half of the decade. In support of this effort, the company added a new warehouse and distribution facility in Reading in 1996. Yet Netto failed to achieve its growth ambitions, in large part because of the United Kingdom's resistance to the discount grocery formula.

While the company struggled to overcome consumer resistance, Netto was also faced with the problem of finding new locations. The U.K. competition authority had come out in favor of the country's major multiple supermarkets, claiming that the discounters, because of the limited selection of products they offered, hampered competition. This meant that Netto, like its discount rivals, was severely limited in the types and numbers of properties it was allowed to acquire. The company's new store openings slowed to a crawl, averaging just five or six per year in the second half of the decade.

In the meantime, the major supermarket chains had begun to fight back, introducing their own low-priced labels to undercut the hard discount sector's consumer appeal. These moves helped limit the discount sector's ability to take market share. Into the late 1990s, total hard discount sales represented only 9 percent of the retail grocery market. Netto's own share of the U.K. market struggled to reach just 1 percent.

While Netto Foodstores' sales neared £300 million ($500 million), the company struggled to achieve profitability, and even slipped into losses in 1996. As a result, Netto carried out a management change, bringing Henrik Gundelach back to revive the group's U.K. fortunes. Over the next two years, Gundelach managed to restore the company's profitability, as well as its growth. The company once again began expanding its store network. By 1999, Netto Foodstores operated 188 stores.

SEEKING NEW MARKETS

With its U.K., Danish, and German operations all growing strongly, Netto cast its sights on entering new markets. The transition of the former Eastern Bloc countries to free market economies in the 1990s provided one direction for Netto's expansion. In 1995, the company entered Poland, establishing subsidiary Netto, Artykuly Zywnosciowe.

The new subsidiary once again adopted Netto's regional focus strategy, building up an initial presence in the northwest region of Poland. Following its successful entry into that market, the company shifted its attention to expansion into the southern and southeastern regions. By 2009, Netto had developed a strong national network of nearly 160 stores.

Netto looked closer to home for its next international extension in the early 2000s. In 2002, the company reached an agreement with Sweden's ICA supermarket group to form a new joint venture. Called Netto Marknad, the new company targeted an extension of the Netto brand and discount format into the Swedish market. For this, the company's focus fell on the more populated southern regions around the main urban centers of Göteborg and Malmö.

Into the second half of the first decade of the 2000s, Netto bustled with optimism as its total network topped 1,000 stores. By the end of 2008, the company's network contained more than 1,100 stores, a figure the company hoped to double in the years to come. In Sweden, for example, the company announced its plans to open as many as 150 stores through 2010, and ultimately expand its network there to as many as 400 stores. In the United Kingdom, meanwhile, the group suggested that its total presence might one day climb to as high as 1,000 stores. At the same time, Netto Foodstores had begun a drive to reposition itself away from its origins as a discount grocer and more toward that of a mainstream supermarket group.

The economic crisis near the end of the first decade of the 2000s provided a new lift for Netto's operations, as harried consumers turned increasingly to the hard discount sector for their shopping needs. Netto responded by expanding its own range of goods, adding low-fat, organic, and other items in an effort to position its stores as one-stop shopping destinations. At the same time, Netto launched preparations to enter a new market, Ukraine. The company expected to be operational in that market in 2009, with as many as 30 stores to be opened by the end of that year, and an ultimate goal of as many as 1,000 stores for the Ukraine market in the future. Netto had positioned itself as a leading European low-priced retailer in the new century.

M. L. Cohen

PRINCIPAL SUBSIDIARIES

Netto Foodstores Limited (UK); Netto Marknad AB (Sweden); Netto, Artykuly Zywnosciowe Sp.Z.o.o. (Poland); OHG NETTO Supermarkt GmbH & Co. (Germany).

PRINCIPAL COMPETITORS

Aldi Group; EDEKA ZENTRALE AG and Company KG; Kwik-Save Ltd.; Lidl Stiftung and Company KG; Metro AG; REWE-Zentral AG.

FURTHER READING

Cripps, Peter, "Netto's Top Dog," *Grocer*, September 13, 2008, p. 48.

———, "New Netto Chief Aims to Accelerate Sales Growth," *Grocer*, February 7, 2009, p. 58.

Davis, Glynn, "The House of Lancaster," *Grocer*, January 12, 2008, p. 34.

Harrison, Liz, "Ways to Help the UK Choose Netto," *Grocer*, August 7, 2004, p. 30.

Jones, David, "Cost-Cutting the Danish Way," *Daily Post*, April 26, 2006, p. 19.

Kuipers, Pascal, "Netto's Growth Imperative," *Elsevier Food International*, February 2006.

Lewis, Helen, "Hard Discounter Strategies and Major Players in the UK," *just-food.com*, June 15, 2008.

"Netto 'Eyeing Online Launch,'" *just-food.com*, August 8, 2008.

"Netto Fastest-Growing Chain in 'Year of the Value Retailer,'" *Grocer*, March 22, 2008, p. 5.

"Netto Hits 1,000 and Plans 2,000," *Grocer*, October 13, 2007, p. 11.

"Netto Plans 20 Stores a Year and Sharpens Up Pricing Act," *Grocer*, July 26, 2008, p. 4.

"Netto Reveals Ambitious Plans," *Farmers Guardian*, October 17, 2008, p. 12.

"Netto to Step Up Expansion of Stores from Denmark to Sweden," *Quick Frozen Foods International*, July 1, 2005.

Smith, Chloe, "Netto Takes on Mults with Premium Range," *Grocer*, February 23, 2008, p. 59.

The New School

66 West 12th Street
New York, New York 10011
U.S.A.
Telephone: (212) 229-5620
Fax: (212) 229-5648
Web site: http://www.newschool.edu

Nonprofit Company
Incorporated: 1919
Employees: 855
Operating Revenues: $261.4 million (2008)
NAICS: 611310 Colleges, Universities, and Professional
Schools

■ ■ ■

The New School is a New York-based educational institution that offers degree and non-degree instruction through eight colleges that include Parsons, Milano, Mannes, and Eugene Lang. Students can receive undergraduate and graduate certificates in the liberal arts, social sciences, business, music, drama, and design, or enroll in short-duration continuing education classes on topics that range from art, cooking, and computer skills to literature and foreign affairs. The school serves nearly 10,000 students in its 70 degree-granting programs and more than 13,000 for continuing education.

BEGINNINGS

The New School was founded in 1919 in New York City. Its creation was sparked by the resignation of

noted historian Charles A. Beard from Columbia University, in protest over the dismissal of two colleagues for their strong antiwar views. His departure was followed by that of James Harvey Robinson, and they and others subsequently began meeting at the offices of the left-leaning *New Republic* magazine to formulate a plan to offer ungraded lectures for adults on subjects in the social sciences.

The school's founders included noted academics Beard, Robinson, James Dewey, Felix Frankfurter, and Thorstein Veblen, associate *New Republic* editor and economist Alvin Johnson, and philanthropic women Mrs. Thomas W. Lamont and Mrs. Learned Hand. In 1919 operations began in rented quarters in Manhattan's Chelsea district with a variety of courses in the social sciences and economics. Some two-thirds of early students were female, a much higher percentage than at other educational institutions of the day.

In 1922 the organization was restructured and Alvin Johnson was named president of what would be called The New School for Social Research. The mix of classes was also shifted to encompass a broader palette, with psychology, philosophy, literature, art, and music added and the social sciences reduced in prominence. Several founders, including Robinson and Beard, quit over the changes, having wanted to turn the school into a research-focused institution, but the move was supported by many students and board members and enrollment grew.

As the institution's initial ten-year lease neared expiration, Johnson began seeking a permanent home, and secured pledges of funding from his board of

COMPANY PERSPECTIVES

The New School is a legendary, progressive university comprising eight schools bound by a common, unusual intent: to prepare and inspire its 9,400 undergraduate and graduate students to bring actual, positive change to the world. From its Greenwich Village campus, The New School launches economists and actors, fashion designers and urban planners, dancers and anthropologists, orchestra conductors, filmmakers, political scientists, organizational experts, jazz musicians, scholars, psychologists, historians, journalists, and above all, world citizens—individuals whose ideas and innovations forge new paths of progress in the arts, design, humanities, public policy, and the social sciences. In addition to its 70 graduate and undergraduate degree-granting programs, the university offers certificate programs and more than 1,000 continuing education courses to 13,000 adult learners every year.

trustees. He commissioned architect Joseph Urban to create a new building on West 12th Street in Greenwich Village that would include a 600-seat auditorium and studios for dance, theater, music, and art. Murals were also commissioned from Mexican social-realist painter José Clemente Orozco and American Thomas Hart Benton. The new building was opened in January, 1931. Although it had enjoyed relative prosperity in the late 1920s, the Great Depression took a toll and at one point the school's mortgage payment was made by heiress Doris Duke.

"UNIVERSITY IN EXILE": 1933

During the 1920s Johnson established ties to a number of scholars in Europe while serving as associate editor of the *Encyclopedia of the Social Sciences,* and from them learned of the danger posed by Germany's emerging National Socialist Party. After Adolf Hitler took power in 1933 many Jewish or anti-fascist professors were expelled from their teaching posts, and Johnson quickly approached the Rockefeller Foundation for funds to bring some to the United States. With support from that institution and other donors such as Hiram Halle, The New School was able to underwrite transportation costs and help them secure visas.

Informally known as the University in Exile, The New School's foreign scholars would officially become part of its new Graduate Faculty of Political and Social Science, which began in 1935 to grant its first degrees. Over the next two decades the school would bring 183 scholars and their families to the United States from countries including Italy, Spain, France, Poland, Czechoslovakia, and Russia, despite some resistance from the U.S. government. While many moved on to posts at other institutions, a core group of nearly two dozen stayed in New York. Notable names included Max Wertheimer, who brought Gestalt psychology to the United States; art psychology theorist Rudolf Arnheim; and theater director Erwin Piscator, who would exert a major influence on such students as Marlon Brando and Tennessee Williams.

In 1943 The New School was reorganized into two units, the School of Politics and the School of Philosophy and Liberal Arts. Anticipating the needs of returning servicemen, the institution also began granting a bachelor's degree in the social sciences. In 1945 Alvin Johnson was named president emeritus and Bryn Hovde took the top post until his resignation in 1949, after which German émigré Hans Simons became the school's president.

In 1956 The New School broke ground on a $2.5 million expansion that would add an eight-story annex to its West 12th Street building and a four-story library nearby. It was completed in 1959, at which time the school's original building was renamed in honor of Alvin Johnson. With the additional space, by 1964 adult education enrollment had doubled.

During this period the school's curriculum evolved into a less demanding one that emphasized shorter-duration courses on more popular topics. Celebrity lecturers were also engaged to draw students, and some criticized the courses as being intellectually undemanding.

In 1964 Jack Everett took over as president and began another round of expansion, with the J.M. Kaplan Center for New York City Affairs established that same year to study the metropolitan area. The New School's annual budget was $2 million.

In 1966 a master of arts in liberal studies program was created through a Ford Foundation grant, and in 1968 The New School announced an ambitious new ten-year, $37 million building campaign.

MERGER WITH PARSONS IN 1970

In 1970 The New School, which served some 16,000 students annually, merged with Parsons School of Design, a highly regarded art school that had been founded in 1896. Parsons, which had enrollment of 650, was moved two years later from midtown to Greenwich Village.

KEY DATES

1919: Group of scholars begins offering ungraded classes in New York.

1922: Institution takes name The New School for Social Research.

1931: New building is completed on 12th Street in Greenwich Village.

1933: School begins helping German and other European scholars immigrate to the United States.

1944: Undergraduate degree program is created for returning servicemen.

1959: A $2.5 million expansion adds library, eight new stories of classroom space.

1964: J.M. Kaplan Center for New York City Affairs is established.

1970: New School merges with Parsons School of Design.

1985: Eugene Lang College is created to expand offerings for undergraduates.

1989: Mannes College of Music becomes part of New School.

1994: Drama program is launched in partnership with Actors Studio.

1997: Name is changed to New School University.

2001: Bob Kerrey becomes president, begins boosting fund-raising and full-time faculty.

2003: Nine-year expansion project is completed; online classes debut.

2005: Institution is rebranded as The New School, college names are revised.

In 1975 the J.M. Kaplan Center was expanded and renamed the Graduate School of Management and Urban Policy, and in 1978 Parsons merged with the Otis Art Institute of Los Angeles, which dated to 1918.

The New School's full-time teaching ranks were thinning due to death or retirement, and in 1978 it came close to being ordered by the State of New York to close its graduate programs in philosophy, political science, and sociology. In response to this crisis the school began recruiting new professors and created the Seminar College, which awarded four-year degrees in the liberal arts.

In 1982 Jonathan Fanton took the job of president, and the former University of Chicago vice-president for planning further boosted its rebuilding efforts by raising funds for teaching chairs and the endowment. The school also sold its famous Thomas Hart Benton murals for a reported $2 million, ostensibly over concerns that it could not afford to care for them, while working to restore the Orozco murals, which could not safely be removed.

CREATION OF EUGENE LANG COLLEGE: 1985

In 1985 the Seminar College was renamed the Eugene Lang College after New School trustee Lang, who had given the largest gift in the school's history, $5 million, to expand it. A year later the Rose and Erwin Wolfson Center for National Affairs was created, and a new jazz and contemporary music program was launched.

By this time the school had 5,000 degree students and upward of 30,000 non-degree ones, with about 200 full-time professors and administrative staff and 2,500 adjunct professors, who might teach as little as one course per year. A 1986 marketing survey found that the school's typical continuing education student was an employed female college graduate in her early 30s. Non-degree course offerings, which had evolved over the years in reflection of current trends, covered topics ranging from "Summer Salads and Soups" (in the recently created department of Culinary Arts) to "The New Narcissism." The school continuously added and dropped courses, depending on popularity, and spent $700,000 per year of its $40 million budget on newspaper and radio advertisements, as well as relying on a printed catalog that typically had a cover drawn by a well-known artist. Celebrity teachers ranged from José Ferrer, Vincent Price, Mia Farrow, Howard Cosell, and folksinger Mary Travers, to high-powered academics including Irving Howe and Robert Heilbronner.

In 1989 The New School merged with Mannes College of Music, a small, 73-year-old New York conservatory that had been losing money in recent years. While continuing to offer classes on 85th Street, it would begin holding others in Greenwich Village.

In 1994 The New School began a partnership with the Actors Studio Drama School, the legendary institution that had been founded in 1947 by a group that included director Elia Kazan, and had educated such noted performers as Marlon Brando, Paul Newman, and Marilyn Monroe.

In 1995, The New School named its graduate school of management and urban policy for Robert J. Milano, a longtime trustee and donor, and two years later the institution became known as the New School University. It had also completed $5 million in improvements to the Lang College that included a new outdoor courtyard. In 1998 the school formed a partnership with the Joffrey Ballet to offer a degree program in dance.

BOB KERREY TAKES TOP POST IN 2001

In January 2001 Jonathan Fanton stepped down as president of The New School, and his job was taken by former U.S. Senator Bob Kerrey, who like Alvin Johnson hailed from the state of Nebraska. Kerrey had a reputation as an intellectual and a vigorous fund-raiser, and was also reputedly motivated to take the job by his relationship with *Saturday Night Live* writer Sarah Paley, whom he married shortly after taking office. The school had some 7,000 degree-seeking students and 30,000 adult education participants.

In 2003 The New School began collaborating with the Open University of the United Kingdom to offer online education, starting with a five-course certificate program in management. During the year it also completed a decade-long, $40 million renovation of a nine-story building on West 13th Street, which would provide space for computer labs, a jazz performance venue, and more. It also featured a painting donated by artist Sol Le Witt.

In 2005 the New School University was rebranded as simply The New School, with a new graffiti-style logo and individual school names lengthened to include The New School name. During the year the organization also created the India-China Institute to research connections between India, China, and the United States; created its own drama school after breaking ties with the Actors Studio; and recognized the labor union formed by its adjunct professors after a protracted fight.

Although sometimes controversial with the liberal New School student body for his participation in raids that killed civilians in the Vietnam War, his vocal support of the decision to invade Iraq, and his selection of friend John McCain as the New School commencement speaker in 2006, during his tenure Kerrey engineered a dramatic improvement in the school's fortunes. By the fall of 2007 enrollment had increased almost 30 percent versus 2000, while the school's endowment had grown from $93.8 million to $232.2 million and nearly $200 million had been raised to fund scholarships, hire faculty, add to facilities, and support research and conferences. More than 50 new full-time professors had been hired at the Eugene Lang College alone, with enrollment at the undergraduate school increasing by 125 percent to 1,323, though tuition for undergrads had also increased by 50 percent to $30,660.

Continuing to move the school toward a more weighty curriculum, by 2009 the number of noncredit enrollments had fallen by 56 percent to 13,000 while the undergraduate and graduate population reached 9,400 and full-time faculty more than doubled to 350, with tenured positions offered for the first time. Parsons had grown to become the most popular unit, as well as the most profitable, and plans were announced to better integrate the school's eight divisions so that students could take some courses between them.

In early 2009 New School President Kerrey received a vote of no confidence from a majority of the school's full-time faculty while facing protests from students who were upset about the treatment of adjunct professors. In May, Kerrey announced he would step down in 2011 after completing his second five-year term in office.

Nearing the end of its first century, The New School had grown to serve nearly 10,000 undergraduate and graduate students, as well as 13,000 continuing education enrollees each year. It was in the process of evolving from a group of separate schools into a unified institution of higher learning.

Frank Uhle

PRINCIPAL DIVISIONS

The New School for General Studies; The New School for Social Research; Milano The New School for Management and Urban Policy; Parsons The New School for Design; Eugene Lang College The New School for Liberal Arts; Mannes College The New School for Music; The New School for Drama; The New School for Jazz and Contemporary Music.

PRINCIPAL COMPETITORS

City University of New York; New York University; Columbia University; The Cooper Union; School of Visual Arts; Learning Annex Holdings LLC; 92nd Street Young Men's and Young Women's Hebrew Association.

FURTHER READING

Carmody, Dierdre, "New School Graduate Unit Rebounds," *New York Times*, July 15, 1987, p. B3.

Chan, Sewell, "Kerrey Will Leave New School in 2011," *New York Times*, May 7, 2009.

Currivan, Gene, "Parsons School of Design Joins in Affiliation with New School," *New York Times*, February 22, 1970, p. 72.

Fiske, Edward B., "New School Facing Need to Rebuild with Approaching Change in Leaders," *New York Times*, May 13, 1982, p. B1.

Fung, Amanda, "New School's Growing Pains," *Crain's New York Business*, January 26, 2009, p. 15.

Gravois, John, "New School Adjuncts Get Union Contract," *Chronicle of Higher Education,* November 11, 2005.

Hevesi, Dennis, "Mannes College Joins the New School," *New York Times,* February 9, 1989, p. B4.

Hurley, Joseph, "A Degree of Excellence," *Newsday,* July 18, 1986, p. 2.

Karni, Annie, "How Kerrey Gave New School Growth and Its Own Eclat," *New York Sun,* September 12, 2007.

Kennedy, Dana, "Bob Kerrey, New New Yorker," *New York Times,* May 5, 2002, p. CY1.

McKinley, Jesse, "New School, in Split with Actors Studio, to Create Own Program," *New York Times,* May 26, 2005.

Messina, Judith, "Bob Kerry's Curriculum," *Crain's New York Business,* August 6, 2001, p. 15.

"'New School' Marks 25th Anniversary," *New York Times,* May 23, 1944, p. 25.

Rutkoff, Peter M., and William B. Scott, *New School: A History of The New School for Social Research,* New York: Free Press, 1986.

Salmans, Sandra, "Adult Education Goes to Market," *New York Times,* August 3, 1986, p. EDUC43.

Schumach, Murray, "$37-Million Expansion Planned by the New School," *New York Times,* December 12, 1968, p. 59.

Teltsch, Kathleen, "Financier Nurtures Youths' Dreams," *New York Times,* February 17, 1985, p. 58.

"Two Buildings Planned for the New School," *New York Times,* May 9, 1955, p. 1.

Weber, Bruce, "The New School Is Creating a School for Performing Arts," *New York Times,* May 11, 1995, p. B3.

New York Yacht Club, Inc.

37 West 44th Street
New York, New York 10036-6613
U.S.A.
Telephone: (212) 382-1000
Fax: (212) 391-6368
Web site: http://www.nyyc.org

Private Company
Incorporated: 1865
Employees: 100
Operating Revenues: $3.1 million (2008)
NAICS: 813410 Civic and Social Organizations

■ ■ ■

New York Yacht Club, Inc., is home to one of the world's most important private yacht clubs, best known for originating the America's Cup racing competition. The club is comprised of 3,200 invitation-only members, little more than half of whom own yachts of some sort. The organization maintains dual headquarters: a Beaux Arts clubhouse in New York City's theater district, a National Historic Landmark that houses a massive model room filled with replicas of historically important yachts, including *America,* for which the America's Cup is named; and the Harbour Court clubhouse in Rhode Island, the organization's waterfront facility and former mansion of John Nicholas Brown, a onetime commodore of the New York Yacht Club. Both clubhouses provide dining to members, the Grill Room in New York and Bolero Grill in Rhode Island, as well as bars. Overlooking Benton's Cove, Har-

bour Court has played host to numerous yachting events. Each year the club holds a celebrated regatta, with well over 100 yachts competing. Every two years it holds Race Week, offering one-design, handicap, and distance races. New York Yacht Club is also involved in team racing, dinghy racing, youth sailing, and also participates in international regattas and sponsors occasional transatlantic races. A separate organization, the New York Yacht Club Foundation, raises money to maintain and restore its historic New York and Rhode Island buildings.

MID-19TH-CENTURY ORIGINS

The New York Yacht Club was established in 1844 at the suggestion of John Cox Stevens, a member of one of the United States' most prominent families. His grandfather was a member of the Continental Congress, while his father served as a colonel in the Revolutionary War and along with his sons made a fortune in steamboats. The younger Stevens was a successful railroad and steamship line promoter and, from childhood, an avid sailor. It was aboard his yacht, *Gimcrack,* that eight other New York yachtsmen met on the afternoon of July 30, 1844, to form the third U.S. yacht club (following Boston and Detroit). They were Hamilton Wilkes, William Edgar, John C. Jay, George L. Schuyler, Louis A. Depew, George B. Rollins, James M. Waterbury, and James Rogers. After they elected Stevens to serve as the club's first commodore, they selected the New York Yacht Club name and appointed a committee to establish the club's rules and regulations. The club's first activity was a cruise, which became an annual event, as did the regatta, the first of these races held on

COMPANY PERSPECTIVES

Today's members come primarily from the New York metropolitan area and New England as well as across America and around the world. They are cruising sailors, powerboaters, Corinthian racers, professional sailors, team-racers, match-racers, Olympic medalists, America's Cup skippers and crews, and sailmakers, yacht designers and boatbuilders. They are distinguished by one thing: an abiding passion for yachting.

July 16, 1845. In fact, the main purpose of the club in the early days was the racing for prize money and wagering, although the club also successfully lobbied the government in 1847 to free private yachts from the annoyance of being inspected each time they entered a U.S. port by Treasury inspectors looking to collect tariffs. Because the yachts were not engaged in commerce, and inspecting them was an unnecessary expense for the government, the boats were licensed and given an ensign to fly to allow them to enter American harbors unimpeded.

The first clubhouse, a modest gingerbread-style structure, was built in 1846 at Elysian Field, Hoboken. Hudson River traffic eventually created too many problems for the yachtsmen, who also outgrew the house. The club reached a turning point in 1865 when it was incorporated, and a newer generation of members began hiring professional captains. In 1866 a ship captained by a professional won a famous transatlantic race. Growing ever larger, the club relocated to a house on Staten Island in 1868. Four years later a town house was acquired in Manhattan at the corner of 26th Street and Madison Avenue. The club moved again to 67 Madison Avenue in 1884.

AMERICA'S CUP RACING DATES TO 1851

The history of the America's Cup, all but synonymous with the history of the New York Yacht Club, dates to 1851 when as part of the Great Exposition of 1851 in England the British decided to hold a regatta at the Isle of Wight, the country's center for yacht racing, and were looking for a fast New York pilot schooner to join the fray. Stevens, a keen competitor and a betting man, was quick to accept the challenge. He put together a syndicate of six men, who spent $30,000 for a racing schooner designed by George Steers and built by New

York shipwright William Brown. It was christened *America.* The ship sailed to France where it was painted a pirate black and outfitted with racing sails. At the regatta held in August 1851 it took on 17 British yachts in a 58-mile course around the Isle of Wight, easily winning in a time of ten hours and 37 minutes, 18 minutes faster than its nearest competitor. Stevens took home the trophy, the "One Hundred Guinea Cup," an ornate silver urn, but left *America,* which he sold for $25,000. The trophy was then given to the New York Yacht Club in 1857 to serve as the America's Cup (regarded as the oldest trophy in the sports world), named for the yacht that won it, for which any foreign yacht club could issue a race challenge.

Eleven years passed before anyone offered a challenge, the honor going to Englishman James Ashbury. When he arrived in New York in 1870 he would find that to win the cup he would have to defeat a fleet of 17 schooners, the same odds *America* faced when it took the original cup. Ashbury made a game attempt, finishing eighth, and returned a year later for another try. This time the New Yorkers agreed to just a single defender, and a best-of-seven race format, albeit they permitted themselves a new boat each day. The third challenge for the cup came from Canada in 1876, and this time the rules called for a single defender, establishing the single challenger, single defender format for the America's Cup that would be in place ever after. In 1876 New York defended the cup in a best-of-three format, which would change to best-of-five from 1893 through 1903 and best-of-seven through most of the 20th century. All told in the 1800s, the New York Yacht Club successfully defended the Cup ten times. Until 1893 the races were held in New York Harbor and afterward were moved to the New York–New Jersey coast. Nevertheless, the defenders retained a significant advantage because of their intimate knowledge of the local waters.

MANHATTAN CLUBHOUSE OPENS: 1901

One of the most famous commodores of the New York Yacht Club was banker J. Pierpont Morgan, who held the post from 1898 to 1899. It was Morgan who was responsible for the 44th Street clubhouse. In 1898 he donated three lots on 44th Street in the heart of what was the clubhouse district, years before the Broadway theater district took shape. More than a dozen architects were invited to compete for the commission, which called for special emphasis on a model room that could be used on public occasions, capable of holding 300 people, a library that could accommodate some 15,000 books, and a chart room where captains could plan

┌───┐

KEY DATES

∎

1844: New York Yacht Club is established.
1851: *America* wins English regatta, taking home the "100 Guinea Cup."
1857: Cup is offered to the New York Yacht Club and intended as the prize for future race challenges, creating the America's Cup competition.
1901: New clubhouse opens on 44th Street in Manhattan.
1930: Sir Thomas Lipton fails in fifth attempt to win the America's Cup.
1983: *Australia II* becomes first challenger to win the America's Cup.
1987: Newport, Rhode Island, clubhouse is acquired.
1999: Original clubhouse is moved to Newport.
2001: America's Cup Jubilee celebrates 150th anniversary of *America*'s winning the "100 Guinea Cup."

└───┘

cruises. Architects were given just one month to make their submissions, resulting in seven sets of plans from which a winner emerged. The new building would be designed in the Beaux Arts style by Whitney Warren and Charles D. Wetmore. The *New York Times* referred to the architecture as "the modern Renaissance of the French school." The model room, which Warren maintained was in essence the club, was the crown jewel of the building, which opened in 1901. The original clubhouse was not forgotten, however. After serving as the home to the New Jersey Yacht Club it was set to be demolished in 1904 when New York Yacht Club Commodore Frederick G. Bourne arranged to have it moved to Glen Cove, Long Island. In 1949 it would be moved again to Mystic Seaport in Connecticut.

The most tenacious challenger for the America's Cup was the Irish tea merchant Sir Thomas Lipton. His first attempt with a schooner dubbed *Shamrock* was defeated in 1899. A second *Shamrock* suffered the same fate in 1901, and a third lost in 1903. Following World War I, Lipton brought *Shamrock IV* to challenge the New York Yacht Club in 1920. By that time, even Lipton was growing distraught over the prospect of defeating the New Yorkers in their home waters, and the club announced that Newport, Rhode Island, would be the site for the next race. Lipton tried a fifth and final time to wrest the America's Cup from the grasp of the New

York Yacht Club in 1930, but at the age of 80 he and *Shamrock V* were defeated in four straight races. According to lore, Lipton was heard to say following his final bid to win the cup, "I canna win, I canna win." His only consolation was a silver loving cup presented to him by New York Mayor Jimmy Walker on behalf of the American people.

POSTWAR CHANGES TO AMERICA'S CUP RACING

The New York Yacht Club defended the Cup twice more in the 1930s before World War II intervened and the world was preoccupied with more weighty affairs than a 100 Guinea Cup. After the war it appeared that America's Cup racing might never resume, due in large measure to the expense involved in building the large J-class yachts that had been adopted for use in the competition. To address that concern, the New York Yacht Club switched to the smaller and less-expensive 12-meter class. The first competition in this new era came in 1958, but once again the American boat easily dispatched its British challenger.

The switch to 12-meter yachts had the desired effect of stimulating competition. Support for the Cup defense also shifted to the West Coast, in particular the San Diego Yacht Club, which would play a prominent role in keeping the Cup in U.S. hands. The Cup was challenged three times each in the 1960s and 1970s, albeit not without incident. In 1967 a controversial ruling that went against the Australian challenger resulted in an American race win by default, almost leading to Australia withdrawing its ambassador from the United States in protest. The Australians ultimately lost the challenge series but became devoted to the mission of taking the America's Cup from the New York Yacht Club, especially the wealthy Alan Bond who bankrolled the effort after 1970.

Aiding in Bond's quest was another change in the rules that had favored the American defenders. The New York Yacht Club had always insisted that competing yachts be built and equipped in their home countries, meaning that they could not make use of American-made electronics, Kevlar sails, and other equipment. In the early 1980s that rule was waived, greatly leveling the playing field. Bond was not alone in challenging for the cup in 1983. His yacht, *Australia II,* would have to defeat two other Australian entries as well as yachts from Britain, France, Italy, and Canada before taking on Dennis Conner of the San Diego Yacht Club and his ship *Liberty.* Bond's boat, although smaller than the other boats, featured a keel that was literally shrouded in mystery. When the boat was lifted from the water its keel was covered to keep prying eyes from seeing its secret: fins that improved speed and increased maneuverability. Although he lacked the technical advantage, Conner won three of the first four races. Under skipper John Bertrand, however, *Australia II* then won three in a row to win the America's Cup.

While losing the Cup was a bitter pill for the New York Yacht Club, it was to the benefit of America's Cup racing. Public interest increased, corporate sponsorship followed, as did television ratings. Four years after losing the Cup and being vilified in some circles, Conner and his boat *Stars & Stripes* defeated the Australian challenger and won back the Cup, but instead of returning to a display case in the New York Yacht Club, it made its home in the clubhouse of the San Diego Yacht Club. America's Cup competition had taken on a life of its own, forcing the New York Yacht Club to reinvent itself.

PURCHASE OF NEWPORT CLUBHOUSE: 1987

In 1987 the New York Yacht Club acquired the former Newport summer home of Commodore John Nicholas Brown, adding a second clubhouse, which opened a year later. The new Harbour Court waterfront facility provided a much needed charge of energy to the club, which in the 1990s began hosting a variety of events, including the club's Sesquicentennial Celebration in 1994. Four years later, with sponsorship by Rolex, it hosted Race Week at Newport, which included the Disabled World Sailing Championship as well as the ILC Maxi World Championship. Newport also became the new home for the original New York Yacht Club clubhouse, which was moved there in December 1999. The Manhattan site also remained involved, hosting the Atlantic Challenge Cup in 1997, a transatlantic race that followed the same course as the 1905 race won by *Atlantic*.

The New York Yacht Club and Harbour Court continued to host a variety of sailing competitions in the new century. The U.S. Junior Championships for Sears, Bemis, and Smythe Trophies was held in 2000. Two years later the Intercollegiate Sailing Association Sloop National Championship was hosted by the club with Brown University. Also in 2002 an international match-racing championship, the UBS Challenge, was held by the club, and in 2006 it hosted the Blind Sailing World Championships. The Intercollegiate Sailing Association National Championships were hosted in 2008. In addition, the New York Yacht Club worked in concert with other major yacht clubs. In 2001 it worked with the Royal Yacht Squadron for the America's Cup Jubilee, a weeklong regatta to celebrate the 150th anniversary of the regatta that begat the America's Cup. In 2003 the club supported the DaimlerChrysler North Atlantic Challenge, a new transatlantic race organized by Norddeutscher Regatta Verein. Two years later, New York Yacht Club again joined with the Royal Yacht Squadron to host the Atlantic Challenge Cup, rechristened the Rolex Transatlantic Challenge. Anticipating its 175th anniversary, the New York Yacht Club remained a sailing institution, one that was sure to maintain a place of prominence for many years to come.

Ed Dinger

PRINCIPAL SUBSIDIARIES

New York Yacht Club Foundation.

PRINCIPAL COMPETITORS

San Diego Yacht Club; Royal Perth Yacht Club; Royal Yacht Squadron.

FURTHER READING

"The Brave, the Bold, and the Brash," *New Straits Times* (Malaysia), December 30, 2002.

Callahan, M. Catherine, "Auld Mug's First Appearance in Newport Was Its Farewell," *Newport Daily News,* September 26, 2003.

Cole, Timothy H., "Corporations Put New Wind in Yachting's Sails," *New York Times,* July 17, 1983.

"Fifty Years of Yachting," *New York Times,* July 29, 1894.

McQuade, Walter, "High Tech Chases the America's Cup," *Fortune,* May 2, 1983, p. 172.

"The New York Yacht Club," *New York Times,* April 30, 1899.

"N.Y. Yacht Club Is Just 70 Years Old," *New York Times,* June 22, 1914.

Wallace, William N., "A Corporate Tinge to Financing the America's Cup," *New York Times,* August 17, 1980.

News Communications,
Inc.

2 Park Avenue, Suite 1405
New York, New York 10016-5701
U.S.A.
Telephone: (212) 689-2500
Fax: (212) 689-1998
Web site: http://www.thehill.com

Public Company
Incorporated: 1986
Employees: 96
Sales: $12.2 million (2004)
Stock Exchanges: Pink Sheets
Ticker Symbol: NWCM
NAICS: 511110 Newspaper Publishers

■ ■ ■

News Communications, Inc., (NCI) is the former publisher of a chain of community newspapers, sold off in the early 2000s. The New York City-based company has reconfigured its holdings to include *The Hill* and Marquis Who's Who LLC. Published by subsidiary Capitol Hill Publishing Corp., *The Hill* is a free Washington, D.C., newspaper that focuses on the work of Congress, covering both policy and political topics. The newspaper has a print circulation of more than 21,000 and also makes its editorial content available online. NCI's other main enterprise, *Marquis Who's Who*, has been profiling distinguished people in print, and now online, since 1899. Reference titles bearing the Who's Who label include *Who's Who in America, Who's Who in the World; Who's Who in American Law, Who's*

Who of American Women, Who's Who in American Education, Who's Who in Finance and Business, Who's Who in American Politics, Who's Who in Medicine and Healthcare, and *Who's Who in Science and Engineering.* A subsidiary of Who's Who is National Register Publishing, a reference publishing company whose titles include *The Official Catholic Directory, The Official Museum Directory, The Corporate Finance Sourcebook,* and *Direct Marketing Market Place.* NCI is still considered a public company, but its shares are now relegated to Pink Sheet status and not traded, making it essentially a private company. Primary shareholders include Chairman Jerry Finkelstein; his son James Finkelstein, the company's CEO; and investors Wilbur L. Ross, Gary Weiss, and Morton Davis.

FIRST PUBLICATION: 1985

News Communications got its start in 1985 when Jerry Finkelstein launched a free weekly newspaper in New York City called the *West Side Spirit,* which focused on news of special interest to Manhattan's Upper West Side residents and later under the *Manhattan Spirit* name it expanded to include coverage of lower Manhattan. In his late 60s, Finkelstein had already enjoyed a long career that mixed industry, publishing, and politics. The son of a small businessman, Finkelstein was born around 1916. He graduated from New York Law School in 1938 but never practiced law. Instead he became a reporter for the *Mirror* and then in 1939 joined forces with the publisher's son to launch the *Civil Service Leader.* He also became involved in Democratic Party politics, managing Mayor William O'Dwyer's successful reelection campaign in 1949. The grateful mayor appointed him chairman of the City Planning Commission. Finkelstein then began accumulating a fortune, using Wall Street contacts to buy into the Fifth Avenue Coach Company with $85,000 in borrowed money. He later sold his stake for about $1 million and became an industrialist. In 1963 he gained control of the *New York Law Journal*, a publication covering legal news in New York City since the late 1880s. To what had long been a collection of calendars, legal opinions, and notices, he added news stories related to the legal profession and opinion columns written by practicing lawyers. As publisher of the *Law Journal*, Finkelstein wielded a great deal of power because he decided what city and state opinions warranted publishing and perhaps one day would be cited as precedents. This fact was not lost on the judges writing these opinions.

With wealth and the power of the press behind him, Finkelstein became a political power broker, holding forth from his usual table at "21." In the 1960s he fund-raised for the presidential campaigns of John F. Kennedy and Lyndon B. Johnson, Robert Kennedy's New York senate campaign, and in the early 1970s Finkelstein became chairman of the New York City Democratic Committee. Finkelstein used some of his political clout to promote the political aspirations of his eldest son, Andrew Stein, who shortened his last name, he said, as a way to declare independence from his powerful father. Nevertheless, it was likely that the $300,000 his father spent was the key factor in Stein's election to the State Assembly in 1968 when he was 27 years old.

In 1985 Finkelstein sold The New York Law Journal Publishing Company to Price Communications Corporation for $21 million. He stayed on as publisher

until 1988, when another son, 39-year-old James A. Finkelstein, succeeded him. By the time the elder Finkelstein started the *West Side Spirit*, Andrew Stein was New York's City Council president and a likely candidate for mayor. According to press speculation, Finkelstein created the new weekly newspaper as a way to promote his son's candidacy, a charge that would be echoed by political opponents but one that he consistently denied.

COMPANY TAKEN PUBLIC: 1987

Whatever his original motivation, Finkelstein began building a chain of similar community newspapers. His company was incorporated in Nevada in 1986 and then taken public a year later in a reverse merger with a shell corporation, Applied Resources Inc., which then took the name News Communications, Inc. The company, run by its president, former television newsman Steve Bauman, began expanding in 1988 with the acquisition of Dan's Papers, a group of five idiosyncratic newspapers serving the Hamptons area of Long Island. They were founded by Dan Rattiner in 1960 when he was a 19-year-old college student and started the *Montauk Pioneer*. He wrote most of the articles, employing an irreverent, satirical, self-referential style that made him into a Hamptons institution. Rattiner retained a 20 percent stake in Dan's Papers and remained editor and publisher under a long-term employment contract. At the same time Dan's Papers was purchased, NCI began a joint venture to develop business-oriented publications and professional directories. Out of this effort grew *Office Life*, a monthly magazine that served as a business-to-business directory for the midtown Manhattan office market. A few years later *Office Life* would be incorporated into *Manhattan Spirit* as a section.

NCI's next acquisition came in May 1989 when the company paid $2.82 million for Tribco Incorporated, the publisher of *Queens Tribune*, a chain of six weekly newspapers covering communities in the New York City borough of Queens that had been in business since 1970. Later in 1989 NCI launched another start-up newspaper, *Neighborhood Life*, a monthly shopping service magazine distributed to Manhattan's Upper East Side. New York City community newspapers appeared to offer a great deal of potential. They appealed to specific audiences that advertisers deemed attractive, and residents not only found the free cost appealing, the newspapers covered issues of local importance that were overlooked by New York's daily newspapers. Moreover, the city was rife with writing and editing talent that could be secured at reasonable rates.

KEY DATES

1985: The *West Side Spirit* is launched.
1987: News Communications, Inc., is taken public.
1988: Dan's Papers is acquired.
1991: *Our Town* is acquired.
1994: *The Hill* is launched.
2000: Company begins divesting community weeklies.
2006: Marquis Who's Who LLC is added.
2007: Dan's Papers is sold.

ACQUISITION OF *OUR TOWN:* 1991

NCI's expansion continued in the 1990s. Queens Tribune added the *Western Queens Tribune* in May 1991, its three editions serving the western part of the borough. In that same month NCI paid $1 million for *Our Town,* a weekly newspaper covering Manhattan's Upper Eastside with 119,000 readers. Also in 1991 NCI created a new division, Media Venture Group, Inc., an investment company targeting media entities, providing loans as well as buying equity positions. Near the end of 1991 Bauman resigned as president to "pursue other interests," and was replaced by Michael Schenkler, the president of Tribco Inc.

In March 1992 NCI signed a letter of intent to acquire five more community newspapers, including three in Manhattan, *Downtown Express, Chelsea Clinton News,* and the *Westsider,* as well as a pair of New Jersey weeklies, *Ocean County Review* and *Sun 'N' Fun.* In 1992 Andrew Stein made a bid to run for mayor of New York, and political rival Rudolph Giuliani was quick to accuse Jerry Finkelstein, NCI's largest shareholder, of buying metropolitan newspapers as a way to aid his son's political ambitions. Again, Finkelstein vehemently denied such a plan was the motivation behind NCI's growth. In fact, after Stein eventually dropped out of the mayoral race, NCI continued to add to its portfolio of print properties. After Giuliani's election as mayor, the company acquired Parkchester Publishing Co. Inc., the publisher of the *Bronx Press Review,* begun in the late 1940s. In 1993 another Bronx weekly was launched as well, the *Riverdale Review,* which covered the affluent Riverdale section of the borough. At the end of the year NCI also acquired eight Nassau County newspapers. In addition, NCI began publishing a glossy monthly magazine, *Manhattan File,* in 1993. For the first time in its history, NCI turned a profit in fiscal 1993. Revenues that had totaled just $1.5 million

three years earlier, approached $9 million, resulting in net earnings of $233,000.

DEBUT OF *THE HILL:* 1994

The future appeared bright for the 16-publication chain. Finkelstein, who had become NCI's chairman, became even more ambitious. In 1994 NCI entered the Washington, D.C., market, starting *The Hill,* a free weekly to compete against the twice-weekly *Roll Call,* owned by the Economist Newspaper Group, Inc., a publishing venture of the *Economist* magazine. The first issue of *The Hill,* covering Congress, was distributed September 21, 1994. Although many thought it would have a difficult time establishing itself in the market, *The Hill* soon found its niche and became a profitable enterprise.

Revenues increased to $18.1 million in fiscal 1995, but because of start-up costs for *The Hill,* as well as the escalating price of newsprint, the company posted a net loss of $1.7 million, leading to some cost-cutting measures. Investment banker Wilbur L. Ross Jr., husband of then Lieutenant Governor Betsy McCaughey Ross, bought a controlling interest in NCI in October 1996. He took over as CEO, although Finkelstein stayed on as chairman. Like Finkelstein, Ross was accused of buying into the newspaper chain for political reasons, to help advance his wife's political ambitions. He also insisted that his interest in the community newspapers was strictly a business decision. He also recruited others to participate in his $2 million investment in NCI, including journalist Carl Bernstein, Broadway producer Robert Nederlander, and retailer Sy Syms.

Revenues improved only modestly for NCI in fiscal 1996 to $18.3 million, while the net loss increased to $3.8 million. In the words of *Crain's New York Business,* NCI was "battling mounting competition and a somewhat dowdy image." Moreover, "costly technological improvements [were] putting further pressure on the bottom line." Early in fiscal 1997 the financial outlook improved, as some of the changes Ross brought to NCI began to pay dividends. While some departments experienced cuts, additional salespeople were hired, and the publications were redesigned. Not only were the papers more colorful and sophisticated in style, they adopted a standard size to improve efficiencies.

To further improve its fortunes, NCI looked to new niche opportunities in 1997. It joined forces with *Washington Blade,* a gay newspaper, to launch *New York Blade News* and compete against *LGNY,* a New York gay and lesbian publication. In November NCI added to its Nassau County publications, acquiring *South Shore*

Record to provide what Ross called "a great cross-trading opportunity" with the company's 11 other weeklies in the county.

The changes implemented by Ross did not produce the desired effects, however. Revenues dipped to $17.8 million in 1998 and only improved marginally to $81.3 million in 1999, when NCI posted a net loss of $3.83 million, compared to a net loss of $2.71 million the prior year. In August 1999 Ross resigned as CEO, although he remained a director and a major investor. Taking over the reins was Steven Farbman, the COO of American Lawyer Media, Inc.

RESTRUCTURING

As the new century dawned, NCI began to restructure its operations. In 2000 it sold its interest in *New York Blade News.* Later in the year the *Bronx Press Review* and *Riverdale Review* were sold. The company lost another $1.6 million in 2000, on revenues of $18.7 million, a performance that hardly inspired investors. Because of the low trading price of its stock, about 33 cents, NCI was delisted from the NASDAQ SmallCap Market in May 2001. At the heart of the company's problems, according to some critics, was its excessively large distribution area and exorbitant salaries paid to some of the senior officers. Moreover, former board member Carl Bernstein observed, as reported by *Columbia Journalism Review,* "Seems to me that this is an enterprise that's become a play toy for people, none of whom have demonstrated a legitimate interest in journalism."

Notorious penny stock investor J. Morton Davis acquired a major stake in NCI and then in June 2001 James A. Finkelstein acquired majority control of the company and took over as CEO, replacing his father who filled in after Farbman's unexplained departure some months earlier. The younger Finkelstein then made plans to sell the community weeklies to concentrate on *The Hill* and *Dan's Papers.* In August 2001, four Manhattan weeklies were divested, fetching about $1 million: *Our Town, West Side Spirit, Chelsea Clinton News,* and the *West Sider.* The remaining community weeklies would experience the same fate. In an effort to build on its core properties, NCI launched *Hamptons Style* in 2003, appealing to wealthy Hamptons seaside communities. In 2005 *The Hill* extended its brand, launching *The Hill Health Watch,* an online subscription service covering health legislation issues.

In the meantime, Wilbur Ross in 2003 acquired Marquis Who's Who LLC and National Register Publishing from London-based Reed Elsevier and James Finkelstein was installed as president. In 2006 Who's Who and its National Register subsidiary were folded into NCI, and Finkelstein looked to aggressively build on the Who's Who brand. *Who's Who in Asia* was launched at the end of 2006, and *Who's Who in American Art* became available online. A gallery of artwork of prominent artists was added to the 2008 print edition and subsequently made available online as well, as were other Who's Who titles.

In 2007 NCI elected to divest Dan's Papers, selling the unit to Brown Publishing Company, an Ohio-based family-owned newspaper publishing company, for about $20 million. As a result, NCI was reduced to *The Hill, Who's Who,* and the National Register publications. With no market for its stock, and unwilling to incur the costs associated with filing the necessary paperwork with the Securities and Exchange Commission, NCI began taking steps to go private. While the future of the company was uncertain, there was no doubt that the brands it held offered some promise. Whether they would form the platform for growing NCI into a larger media concern or eventually be sold off piecemeal remained uncertain.

Ed Dinger

PRINCIPAL SUBSIDIARIES

Capitol Hill Publishing Corp.; Marquis Who's Who LLC.

PRINCIPAL COMPETITORS

LexisNexis People; National Journal Group Inc.; Roll Call Inc.

FURTHER READING

Appel, Adrianne, and Madeline Gaughran, "Over the Hill," *Columbia Journalism Review,* May 2001, p. 11.

Arnold, Martin, "Jerry Finkelstein: A Study in Personality and Politics," *New York Times,* July 5, 1972.

Bagli, Charles V., "McCaughey Ross's Husband Is Expected to Buy Weekly Newspapers," *New York Times,* October 2, 1996.

Barron, James, "Quirky Hamptons Paper, Reading for Rich, Is Sold," *New York Times,* July 24, 2007.

Childs, Kelvin, "The Hill Has Arrived," *Editor & Publisher,* September 6, 1997, p. 10.

Denitto, Emily, "The Mini-Murdoch of Metro New York," *Crain's New York Business,* April 28, 1997, p. 4.

Glaberson, William, "New Paper to Vie for Readers on Capitol Hill," *New York Times,* May 25, 1994, p. A22.

Herzlich, Jamie, "Media Baron Acquires Stake in Dan's Papers," *Newsday,* June 28, 2002, p. A54.

Levy, Clifford, "Weeklies See Profits Without a Charge," *New York Times,* February 10, 1992, p. D8.

Linden, Dana Wechsler, and Vicki Contavespi, "Media Wars," *Forbes,* August 19, 1991, p. 38.

Mitchell, Alison, "Father's Papers and a Son's Politics," *New York Times,* April 3, 1992, p. B1.

Morgan, Richard, "News Communications Gets Father-Son Duo," *Daily Deal,* June 5, 2001.

Ruffini, Gene, "Free Weekly Group Turns It Around in New York City," *Editor & Publisher,* April 30, 1994, p. 27.

Sanger, Elizabeth, "Publisher Plans to Sell Queens Tribune," *Newsday,* June 6, 2001, p. A42.

Newsday Media Group

—■—

235 Pinelawn Road
Melville, New York 11747-4250
U.S.A.
Telephone: (631) 843-2175
Fax: (631) 843-2986
Web site: http://www.newsday.com

Subsidiary of Cablevision Systems Corporation
Incorporated: 1940 as Newsday, Inc.
Employees: 2,900
Sales: $59.8 million (2007 est.)
NAICS: 511110 Newspaper Publishing

■ ■ ■

Newsday Media Group, based in Melville, New York, is the corporate parent of Long Island's largest daily newspaper, *Newsday,* and is in turn owned by Cablevision Systems Corporation, a major cable television provider. *Newsday* boasts a daily circulation of nearly 380,000 and Sunday circulation of about 450,000, numbers that have both been in decline, mirroring the general fate of newspapers in the Internet age. While a tabloid in size, *Newsday,* which also serves a portion of New York City, distinguishes itself from other area tabloids, the *New York Post* and *Daily News,* by shying away from sensational front page headlines and strident prose. Over the years, *Newsday* has garnered about 20 Pulitzer Prizes as well as numerous other major media awards.

Newsday Media also publishes a free New York City newspaper, *amNewYork,* claiming a daily circulation of

335,000. Subsidiary Star Community Publishing is a major weekly shopper publishing operation, serving the northeastern United States with about 180 editions, resulting in a total circulation of more than 2.5 million. Products include *This Week* and *This Week's Pennysaver,* delivered as a *Newsday Sunday* insert as well as a separate Saturday publication for non-subscribers; 82 editions of *Shopper's Guide, Yankee Trader,* and *Huntington Pennysaver,* mailed twice weekly to Long Island residents and businesses; *Newsday Marketeer,* with 35 editions covering Brooklyn, Queens, and Staten Island; and *What's Happening,* a glossy magazine provided to *Newsday* Friday home subscribers ten times a year and on a quarterly basis to New York City boroughs. Another publishing venture, Island Publications, offers 17 lifestyle, visitor reference, and economic development magazines related to Long Island, including *This Month on Long Island, Long Island Travel Guide, Long Island Lodging Guide, Hamptons Travel Guide, Wine Country, Parents & Children,* and *Career Island.* In addition, Newsday Media includes Newsday Interactive, reaching more than three million unique monthly visitors to such web sites as Newsday.com, amny.com, ExploreLI.com, and Newsday.com/NZon, a high school sports destination.

FOUNDER'S FAMILY: 19TH-CENTURY NEWSPAPER LINEAGE

Launched in 1940, *Newsday* is a relatively young newspaper, but one with deep connections. It was founded in Hempstead, Long Island, by Alicia Patterson, whose family was steeped in the newspaper

COMPANY PERSPECTIVES

The Vision: Connect Long Islanders to one another, their communities and their passions.

industry. Her great-great grandfather, James Patrick, came from Ireland in the early 1800s to become a county judge and start a weekly newspaper in New Philadelphia, Ohio. He took under his wing a young lawyer named Joseph Medill, who had become more interested in journalism than practicing law, learning the rudiments of the newspaper business from Patrick while romancing his daughter. The couple wanted to marry, but Patrick insisted that Medill must first secure his finances. Thus, in 1852 Medill started a Cleveland newspaper and two years later was offered the job as managing editor of the *Chicago Tribune*. He turned it down but soon found a partner to acquire the newspaper and take over as editor and publisher, a position of power that he would use to promote the presidential aspiration of an Illinois lawyer-politician, Abraham Lincoln. His son-in-law, Robert Wilson Patterson, the paternal grandfather of Alicia Patterson, succeeded Medill as editor and publisher of the *Tribune*. Her father, Joseph Medill Patterson, became the founder and publisher of the *New York Daily News*, and in addition a cousin, Robert R. McCormick, became editor and publisher of the *Tribune*, and an aunt, Eleanor Medill Patterson, became owner of the *Washington Times-Herald*.

ALICIA PATTERSON BORN: 1906

Alicia Patterson was born in 1906, the second child of Joseph Patterson who already had a daughter and was so bitterly disappointed that Alicia was not a boy, he greeted her birth by slamming the door and not returning home for days. Another daughter would follow, forcing Patterson to find one of the girls to serve as a suitable substitute for a son, although he eventually adopted a boy to bear his name. Patterson was an iconoclast in many ways. Born to wealth and educated in private schools, he became a Socialist, and later became disillusioned with that as well, having come to the conclusion that people will work only if there is a profit in it. Like the rest of his family, however, he was interested in newspapers. During a stint in the military in World War I he became familiar with a British tabloid, the *Daily Mirror*, and decided the concept could work in the United States as well. In 1919 he began publishing the *Illustrated Daily News* in New York, soon

changing the name to the *Daily News*. The small size proved to be ideal reading matter for subway riders, and the focus on sex and crime helped to grow circulation. The paper added more national and international news in the 1930s as it attempted to gain more respectability, and by the end of the 1930s emerged as the newspaper with the country's largest daily circulation.

Alicia Patterson was 12 years old when the *Daily News* was launched, and like her father was a bit of a rebel, entering and leaving a succession of private schools. Her nickname was "Violet Roughneck." She tried her hand as a reporter, but made an egregious error by mixing up the names in a divorce story, leading to a libel suit. Her father fired her from the paper, not so much because of the suit but because he thought a dismissal would be good training for a journalist, who often had to hunt for a new job. Instead, she threw a tantrum and returned to Chicago to lead the life of a playgirl, although she would also become a staff writer for one of her father's magazines and serve as book review editor for the *Daily News*. She was married and divorced twice before her 1939 wedding to Harry F. Guggenheim, a millionaire businessman and diplomat. While on their honeymoon, they learned that Long Island's *Nassau County Journal*, a failed newspaper, was up for sale. With $70,000 of her husband's money she purchased the equipment of the *Journal* in early 1940 and assumed the lease on the Hempstead, Long Island, plant and former automobile showroom.

PUBLICATION OF FIRST ISSUE: 1946

Patterson assembled a staff of former *Daily News* employees as well as newcomers to the trade, and on September 3, 1940, they published the first issue of a new Long Island tabloid, which she dubbed *Newsday*. The early days were a struggle as the new venture gained its feet, an effort soon complicated by the institution of a military draft and the subsequent entry of the United States into World War II. The resulting shortage of employees hindered *Newsday's* ability to develop a professional staff. On a positive note, the conditions allowed employees to be experimental. The newspaper was also fortunate in its rivals. Its chief competitor, the *Nassau Daily Review-Star*, had long since grown complacent. By the end of the war, *Newsday* had surpassed the *Review-Star* in daily circulation and continued to grow while the latter experienced no gains. In the midst of the war, *Newsday* expanded beyond Nassau County to add a Suffolk County edition. This move paid dividends during the postwar years as suburbs were established throughout Long Island to provide housing for the baby boom generation, allowing *Newsday* to outmaneuver the

KEY DATES

1940: Alicia Patterson founds *Newsday.*
1949: Operations move to Garden City, New York.
1954: *Newsday* wins first Pulitzer Prize.
1963: Patterson dies.
1970: Tribune Company acquires *Newsday.*
1985: *New York Newsday* is launched.
1995: *New York Newsday* is closed.
2003: *amNewYork* begins publishing.
2008: Cablevision acquires Newsday Media Group.

New York City dailies as well as the *Brooklyn Eagle,* all of which had failed to establish strongholds on Long Island when they had the opportunity. By the time they made the effort, *Newsday* had solidified its hold on the rapidly growing Long Island counties.

After her father died in 1946, Patterson began receiving an income from the trusts he had established to distribute his wealth. With some money at her disposal Patterson tried to acquire a controlling interest in *Newsday,* but her husband would relinquish only a minority share. Although she would hold a 49 percent interest and presumed she would gain the rest of the business following his death, that 2 percent difference became a major bone of contention between the couple, as did the money the paper lost in the early years. With the arrival of Levittown and other large Long Island residential communities, however, the financial picture began to improve. Not only were there an increasing number of potential subscribers on Long Island, there was no shortage of merchants looking to reach them through advertisements in *Newsday.* To keep pace with increasing print runs, *Newsday* gave up the old automobile showroom for a new plant in Garden City in 1949.

NEWSDAY WINS FIRST PULITZER PRIZE: 1954

Newsday relied on three columns rather than the usual five employed by other tabloids, resulting in innovative page layouts as well as industry awards for topography, makeup, and printing. The newspaper also improved editorially. It won its first Pulitzer Prize in 1954 for "meritorious public service," the result of uncovering payments building contractors at Roosevelt Raceways were forced to pay union leader William De Koning, who was eventually convicted of extortion. Aside from the credibility that came with the prize, around this

time the *Review-Star* folded, leaving *Newsday* as Long Island's undisputed number one newspaper. It solidified its reputation by opening a Washington bureau and carrying more national and international news.

Patterson would have likely divorced Guggenheim, their relationship having long since grown cold and distant, but she knew quite well that leaving him meant giving up the newspaper. Although she was a dozen years younger than Guggenheim, he survived her. Alicia Patterson died at the age of 56 in July 1963. She left behind a newspaper with a circulation of 370,000. The 72-year-old Guggenheim took over as publisher. Despite a lack of journalism experience, he enjoyed success during the time he ran the newspaper, but by 1967 he was ready to turn over the reins to someone new. His choice as *Newsday*'s new publisher was the 32-year-old press secretary for President Lyndon Johnson, Bill Moyers, a man who would later make his mark in television news.

Moyers made it clear that he and Guggenheim were not likely to agree on politics, and indeed they eventually had a falling out, a situation exacerbated by Guggenheim's failing health. Rather than allow Moyers to gain control of *Newsday,* Guggenheim secretly reached a deal to sell the paper to the Times Mirror Company. Once he learned of Guggenheim's intentions, Moyers offered to resign as publisher, but Guggenheim was determined to sell. Moyers had the financial backing to pay more than the Times Mirror offer, and still Guggenheim, whom Moyers later described as "adamant and irrational," refused to change his mind.

TIMES MIRROR ACQUIRES *NEWSDAY*

Times Mirror and its head Otis Chandler took control of *Newsday* in 1970. The newspaper's corporate parent proved to be patient and supportive as *Newsday* began turning its attention westward, gaining a toehold along the edges of New York City in Queens and Brooklyn. In the early 1980s *Newsday* saw an opening in the metropolitan New York City market where both tabloids, the *Post* and the *Daily News,* were struggling. Assuming that one of them would fold, *Newsday* in 1985 launched a competing urban daily, *New York Newsday,* bringing its more benign tabloid personality to the city in hopes of peeling away the upper demographic end of the *Daily News* readership that advertisers found especially attractive.

A decade-long tabloid war embroiled New York City, as all three tabloids fought for subscribers and in the process lost significant amounts of money. In the meantime, *Newsday* expanded in a different direction in 1990 when it acquired Alternate Distribution Systems and its slate of free "shoppers." In essence, the deal was a way to leverage *Newsday's* distribution system to create an additional revenue stream. Any funds that could be brought in were obviously welcome in light of the ongoing fight to establish *New York Newsday.* Cost-cutting was also in order. In the early 1990s Newsday allowed its workforce to decrease from 3,300 to 3,000 through attrition and early retirement. Unpaid voluntary summer furloughs were also used to trim expenses without resorting to layoffs, but in 1992 the company decided more drastic measures were needed and the decision was made to reduce the workforce by another 10 percent, eliminating about 300 jobs.

Although well respected in the industry, a winner of three Pulitzer Prizes, *New York Newsday* continued to drain the coffers of its parent company, losing from $8 million to $14 million each year according to press reports. A shakeup in management ranks was in order, and in November 1994 *Newsday's* publisher, Robert M. Johnson, who had held the post since 1986, resigned due to what was described as "differences in business philosophy." No change at the helm, however, could correct the problems with *New York Newsday,* which began to experience a serious erosion in circulation. Rather than outlasting the other tabloids and inheriting a cache of readers and subscribers, *New York Newsday* was the one forced from the field. In July 1995 the newspaper published its last issue, a mere six weeks after a new CEO took charge of Times Mirror. Over the course of a decade the venture lost approximately $100 million.

Newsday focused on its home territory where it remained strong and retained a minor presence in New York City, the Long Island paper still distributed by independents in portions of the outer boroughs. There was even talk in the early 2000s about reviving *New York Newsday,* but with the rise of the Internet and the availability of free news content, all newspapers began to suffer and *Newsday* was more concerned with holding onto the readers it had than making another attempt to invade New York City, although in 2003 Times Mirror helped launch *amNewYork,* a free daily that found a niche in the market, and later acquired complete control of the venture. Changes were also taking place with the newspaper's owner. In 2000 Times Mirror merged with the Tribune Company, which owned the *Chicago Tribune* as well as other newspapers, WGN-TV and radio, and the Chicago Cubs baseball team.

CABLEVISION ACQUIRES NEWSDAY MEDIA GROUP: 2008

At the end of 2007 Chicago real estate mogul Sam Zell took Tribune Co. private and Newsday Media Group was put on the block. Suitors for the property included the owners of the *Daily News,* Mortimer Zuckerman, and the *New York Post,* Rupert Murdoch and News Corp., but in the end Long Island-based Cablevision Systems Corp. bought Newsday Media Group for a reported $650 million in May 2008, money greatly needed by Tribune Co., which was saddled with nearly $13 billion in debt. The Newsday Media Group assets Cablevision acquired included *Newsday, amNewYork,* Newsday Interactive, Star Community Publishing, and Island Publications. In an effort to achieve some synergy with other Cablevision properties, Newsday.com became the host site for several other sites: Optimum Autos, Careerbuilder.com, Homefinder.com, and Apartments.com.

Despite the change in ownership, the fundamentals of the newspaper business continued to deteriorate, furthering the need for cost containment. In December 2008 *Newsday* cut its workforce another 5 percent, or 100 jobs. The following year there was talk of eliminating the Saturday edition to save money and perhaps charging for its online content, something the newspaper had tried a decade earlier without success. Clearly the business model that had once well served the newspaper business was no longer viable, making the future for *Newsday* and virtually all other newspapers far from certain.

Ed Dinger

PRINCIPAL SUBSIDIARIES

Island Publications; Newsday, Inc.; Newsday Interactive; Star Community Publishing.

PRINCIPAL COMPETITORS

Daily News, L.P.; News Corp.; The New York Times Company.

FURTHER READING

Cohen, Roger, "New Aggressiveness at Times Mirror," *New York Times,* December 3, 1990, p. D1.

"Early Reactions to Cablevision/'Newsday' Deal," *Editor & Publisher,* May 12, 2008.

Fabrikant, Geraldine, "Newsday Buys a Business That Distributes 'Shoppers,'" *New York Times,* September 13, 1990, p. D19.

Glaberson, William, "Decade-Old New York Newsday to Cease Publishing Tomorrow," *New York Times,* July 15, 1995, p. A1.

———, "Future of Newsday Edition in New York Is Weighed," *New York Times,* June 20, 1995, p. B3.

————, "Newsday Publisher Departs," *New York Times,* November 2, 1994, p. D1.

Jochum, Glenn, "NY Newsday Laid to Rest," *Long Island Business News,* July 24, 1995, p. 1.

Jones, Alex S., "In New York's Newspaper War, Tabloids Race to the Final Battle," *New York Times,* December 2, 1987, p. B1.

————, "Newsday Seeks to Cut Work Force," *New York Times,* May 6, 1992, p. D19.

Keeler, Robert F., *A Candid History of the Respectable Tabloid,* New York: William Morrow, 1990, 790 p.

Reich-Hale, David, "Experts: New York-based Newsday's Pay-for-Play Model Will Fail," *Long Island Business News,* February 27, 2009.

nobia

Nobia AB

———— ■ ————

World Trade Center
Klarabergsviadukten 70 A5
P.O. Box 70376
Stockholm, S-107 24
Sweden
Telephone: (+46 08) 440 16 00
Fax: (+46 08) 503 826 49
Web site: http://www.nobia.se

Public Company
Incorporated: 1996
Employees: 8,871
Sales: SEK 15.99 billion ($1.8 billion) (2008)
Stock Exchanges: Stockholm
Ticker Symbol: NOBI
NAICS: 337110 Wood Kitchen Cabinet and Counter-
top Manufacturing

■ ■ ■

Nobia AB is a leading European specialist in the manufacturing and retailing of fitted kitchens. The Stockholm, Sweden-based company is also leading the consolidation of the European fitted kitchens sector, having acquired more than a dozen companies since its creation in 1996. Nobia's operations are organized into three geographic divisions. The Nordic region contributed 37 percent of the group's revenues for 2008, and includes such brands as Marbodal and Myresjökök in Sweden; HTH, Invita, and Uno Form in Denmark; Petra, A la Carte, and Parma in Finland; and Sigdal and Norema in Norway. The U.K. region ac-

counted for 31 percent of 2008 revenues, generated through the Magnet, Magnet Trade, and Gower brands. In continental Europe, Nobia has built up operations in Germany, Austria, and France, with brands including Poggenpohl, Optifit, and Pronorm in Germany; Hygena in France; and Ewe and FM in Austria. Nobia is also a partner in the Netherlands-based Culinoma joint venture with De Mandemakers Groep, which operates primarily in Germany through the Plana, Marquardt, and Asmo brands.

Nobia maintains dedicated manufacturing facilities for nearly all of its brands; in addition, the company operates a number of brand-specific retail networks. In 2009 the company operated a total of 694 retail stores, of which 219 were franchise businesses. The Culinoma joint venture operates 88 stores. Nobia is listed on the Stockholm Stock Exchange and is led by CEO Preben Bager.

STORA SPINOFF IN 1996

Nobia was founded in 1996 as part of the streamlining of Stora AB, ahead of its merger with Finland's Enso, which created the forestry-products giant Stora Enso in 1998. Stora had become involved in the building products and kitchen and interior fittings markets in the late 1980s, after its acquisition of Swedish Match. That company, founded in 1917, had diversified into building materials in the 1950s. Through the 1980s Swedish Match had developed a range of diversified operations, including the manufacturing of fitted kitchens, as well as other products, such as flooring and doors.

Stora acquired Swedish Match in 1988, then split its operations into two parts, selling its lighter, matches, and tobacco businesses (which kept the Swedish Match name) in 1990. In 1993 Stora regrouped its various building materials and related operations into a single subsidiary, Stora Byggprodukter AB. That company's three main divisions were then fitted kitchens, the production of doors and windows, and a wholesale building materials business.

The subsidiary, however, proved a loss maker, as Sweden, like most of Europe, suffered the effects of the long recession of the early 1990s. Stora Byggprodukter's losses continued to mount into the middle of the decade, leading to Stora's decision to sell these operations. In 1996 the Swedish investment group Industri Kapital led a buyout of Stora Byggprodukter, which was acquired through a newly established company, Nobia AB.

Nobia inherited operations producing nearly SEK 3.5 billion ($375 million) in revenues each year. Exports, primarily to the Nordic region, accounted for approximately half of those revenues, but also for a great deal of the company's losses. Nobia's management set out to devise a new strategy for the company, restructuring its operations, notably by ending its money-losing export operations, and restoring its profitability.

KITCHEN SPECIALIST

Nobia nonetheless maintained an international profile, through its portfolio of kitchen brands. These included HTH in Denmark, Marbodal in Sweden, and Norway's Sigdal. Nobia launched a new marketing effort, in order to raise the profile of its kitchen brands in their respective markets. The company also developed a new decentralized management structure, placing each subsidiary's management in charge of ensuring profitability.

Nobia's restructuring continued into 1997, as the company streamlined its manufacturing operations. No-bia also worked on developing more-efficient production and distribution systems. The company also continued its branding activities, helping its brands grow into market leaders. By the end of that year, Nobia had become a profitable business overall, with all of its divisions in the black by the end of the decade.

During this period Nobia sought to increase its fitted kitchens operations. The company also began selling off a number of noncore operations. At the same time, Nobia began seeking out acquisitions to expand its geographic reach and to establish itself as a European leader in the kitchen segment. Nobia completed its first acquisition in 1998, buying Finland's fitted kitchen leader, Novart Oy. The addition of that company, established in 1964, gave Nobia three new brands: A la Carte, Petra, and Parma.

CONSOLIDATOR IN THE 21ST CENTURY

By 1999 Nobia had committed to a new strategy based on reinventing itself as a specialist producer and distributor of fitted kitchens. As a result, the company launched the sell-off of its remaining operations, a process that was largely completed early in the first decade of the 2000s.

In the meantime, Nobia sought to expand its operations beyond the Nordic market, and establish itself as a leading player in the highly fragmented European kitchens market. Acquisitions were to form a major part of the group's new expansion strategy, as it positioned itself as an industry consolidator into the new century.

Nobia's acquisition drive got off to a strong start in 2000. In July of that year, the group agreed to acquire Poggenpohl, based in Germany but owned by Sweden's Skanska construction group. Poggenpohl, founded in 1892, had grown into one of the best known and most respected kitchen brands, and added more than SEK 2 billion ($230 million) to Nobia's turnover. Other operations in Germany added that year included Pronorm Einbauküchen and Optifit Jaka Möbel. Optifit produced flat-pack kitchens, that is, kitchens delivered in kit form, which purchasers put together themselves.

Nobia next acquired Norway's Norema, another leading name in fitted kitchens. Norema brought Nobia a number of showrooms, as well as a strong business supplying the construction sector. Also in 2000, Nobia bought Invita, founded in 1974 and based in Bording, Denmark. By the end of the year, Nobia's operations had topped the SEK 6 billion ($700 million) mark.

KEY DATES

1996: Industri Kapital leads a buyout of Stora Bygg-produkter AB from Stora AB, including the HTH (Denmark), Marbodal (Sweden), and Sigdal (Norway) kitchen brands, and renames business as Nobia AB.

1998: Nobia acquires Novart in Finland.

2000: Company refocuses as kitchen specialists and launches international acquisition drive.

2002: Nobia goes public on the Stockholm exchange.

2005: EWE-FM in Austria is acquired.

2006: Nobia acquires Hygena in France.

2007: With De Mandemakers Groep, company forms 50-50 joint venture Culinoma in Germany.

ENTERING THE UNITED KINGDOM IN 2001

Nobia's expanding interests led it to the United Kingdom in 2001. In that year, the company acquired one of the United Kingdom's leading kitchen specialists, Magnet, from Enodis, a company that otherwise manufactured catering equipment. Nobia paid £134 million for Magnet, which included its C.P. Hart bathrooms brand (later sold). The addition of Magnet helped boost Nobia's total turnover closer to the SEK 10 billion mark. By then, too, Nobia had completed its acquisition of Swedish kitchens group Myresjökök, a company founded in 1946.

Nobia completed its divestment program in 2002. In that year, the company prepared for its future expansion by going public, with a listing on the Stockholm Stock Exchange. The offering provided Industri Kapital with the opportunity to begin paring its holding in Nobia; by 2004 Industri Kapital had sold all of its shares in Nobia. The sale allowed Industri Kapital to multiply its initial investment in Nobia by more than eight times. By then, too, Nobia had long since been profitable, posting profits of more than SEK 400 million on net sales of SEK 9.6 billion that year.

Acquisitions remained an important part of Nobia's strategy through the first half of the first decade of the 2000s. The company returned to the United Kingdom in 2003, buying Gower Furniture Ltd. That company was one of the leading suppliers of flat-pack kitchens to the U.K. retail market.

Nobia also continued in its efforts to improve the efficiency of its operations, as part of its four-pronged strategy at the dawn of the 21st century. Nobia had already put into place the first two parts of this strategy, notably the decentralized management of its subsidiaries and the development of a multibrand and multichannel business. The third prong fell into place as the group developed its own supply chain management system, which included coordinating purchasing operations throughout its subsidiaries, as well as emphasizing the use of standardized components across its various kitchen brands.

CONTINUING GROWTH

The fourth prong of Nobia's strategy called for "profitable growth." Toward this end, the company continued to seek new acquisitions. In 2005, for example, the company entered the Austrian market, taking over that country's EWE-FM, the leading manufacturer of fitted kitchens for that market. EWE had begun producing kitchens in 1967, developing a strong distribution network throughout Austria, before launching sales in Germany and Switzerland as well.

Next, Nobia entered France, buying that country's Hygena chain in 2006. Hygena had been created by the United Kingdom's MFI in 1983, and had grown into a leading player in the French kitchens market. Nobia paid MFI £92 million for Hygena, including its 138-store network throughout France. Nobia celebrated its ten-year anniversary that year with revenues of more than SEK 15.5 billion.

Acquisitions, however, were only one part of Nobia's profitable growth strategy. Through the middle of the first decade of the 2000s, Nobia pursued a major expansion of its retail operations. In the United Kingdom, where the company operated a total of 200 stores, Nobia announced plans to open as many as 100 new Magnet stores starting in 2007. At the same time, the group announced its intention to boost the number of Hygena stores to as many as 215 throughout France. Hygena also became the company's spearhead into the Spanish market, with the opening of four stores around Barcelona that year.

Meanwhile, the group's Poggenpohl brand, which operated 27 stores, began rolling out its own retail expansion, with as many as 60 stores expected to open before the end of the decade. This expansion program also included plans to open a number of Poggenpohl stores in the United States.

Nobia's effort to expand its retail network then turned to Germany. In 2007 the company joined with the Netherlands' De Mandemakers Groep to form a

50-50 joint venture, Culinoma GmbH. Nobia had long been a major supplier to De Mandemakers's operations in the Netherlands. Through Culinoma, both companies targeted expansion into the German fitted kitchen retail sector. The partnership got off to a strong start, acquiring the Asmo, Plana, and Marquardt brands. By the end of 2008 Culinoma claimed the lead in the German market, with a total of 88 stores. In the meantime, the addition of Culinoma had helped raise the company's total revenues to nearly SEK 16.7 billion at the end of 2007.

Fueled by acquisitions and its own organic growth, Nobia had maintained steady growth through most of the first decade of the 2000s. In 2008, however, as the impact of the global economic collapse began to be felt, Nobia's sales began to slip. The group's U.K. operations were particularly hard-hit. By the end of the year, the company's total revenues had slipped back by 1 percent to SEK 15.99 billion. Nonetheless, Nobia had established itself as a leading player in the European kitchen market for the new century.

M. L. Cohen

PRINCIPAL SUBSIDIARIES

Culinoma BV (Netherlands; 50%); EWE Küchen GmbH & FM Küchen GmbH (Austria); Gower Furniture Ltd (UK); HTH Køkkener A/S (Denmark); Hygena Cuisines SAS (France); Invita Køkkener A/S (Denmark); Magnet Ltd. (UK); Marbodal AB (Sweden); Myresjökök AB (Sweden); Norema AS (Norway); Novart Oy (Finland); Optifit Jaka Möbel GmbH (Germany); Poggenpohl Möbelwerke GmbH (Germany); Pronorm Einbauküchen GmbH (Germany); Sigdal Kjøkken AS (Norway).

PRINCIPAL DIVISIONS

Kitchen Stores; Furniture Stores; Builders' Merchants and DIY Chains; Prefab Housing and Construction Companies.

PRINCIPAL OPERATING UNITS

UK Region; Nordic Region; Continental Europe Region.

PRINCIPAL COMPETITORS

Vorwerk & Co. KG; Galiform PLC; AFG Arbonia-Forster-Holding AG; Nobilia-Werke J. Stickling GmbH and Company KG; Corona Corp.; ALNO AG; Glunz AG; Ballingslöv International AB; Häcker-Küchen GmbH + Company KG; Sabag Holding AG.

FURTHER READING

"Contract Kitchens Boost Nobia Sales," *Cabinet Maker,* November 3, 2006, p. 6.

"Extra Stores Boost Magnet," *Cabinet Maker,* February 15, 2008, p. 6.

"Kitchen Focus Pays at Nobia," *Cabinet Maker,* May 4, 2007, p. 6.

"Kitchens Dip," *Cabinet Maker,* May 2, 2008, p. 7.

MacCarthy, Clare, "Nobia in Deal to Buy Poggenpohl," *Financial Times,* July 8, 2000, p. 18.

"Nobia AB and De Mandemakers Groep Holding Acquire German Kitchen Retail Chain," *Nordic Business Report,* October 12, 2007.

"Nobia AB Completes Acquisition of EWE-FM in Austria," *Nordic Business Report,* December 29, 2004.

"Nobia AB to Establish New Store Chain in Finland," *Nordic Business Report,* June 16, 2005.

"Nobia Puts Store in Kitchen Growth," *Cabinet Maker,* April 9, 2004, p. 5.

"Swedish Kitchen Company Nobia AB Divests UK Bathroom Stores Chain CP Hart," *Nordic Business Report,* December 14, 2007.

"Swedish Kitchen Company Nobia AB Reorganises Production in Denmark," *Nordic Business Report,* February 11, 2009.

"Swedish Kitchen Company Nobia AB to Expand European Store Networks," *Nordic Business Report,* July 19, 2007.

Star brite®

Ocean Bio-Chem, Inc.

4041 Southwest 47th Avenue
Fort Lauderdale, Florida 33314-4023
U.S.A.
Telephone: (954) 587-6280
Toll Free: (800) 327-8583
Fax: (954) 587-2813
Web site: http://www.oceanbiochem.com

Public Company
Incorporated: 1973 as Star brite Corporation
Employees: 108
Sales: $21.3 million (2007)
Stock Exchanges: NASDAQ
Ticker Symbol: OBCI
NAICS: 325612 Polish and Other Sanitation Good
   Manufacturing

■ ■ ■

Based in Fort Lauderdale, Florida, Ocean Bio-Chem, Inc., (OBC) manufactures and distributes maintenance and care products for boats, cars, motorcycles, recreational vehicles (RVs), and aircraft, mostly under the Star brite name but also as private labels. Marine products include different formulations of polishes, cleaners, protectants, and waxes. OBC also offers motor oils, lubricants, antifouling additives, antifreeze coolants, gaskets, and sealants. In addition to polishes and cleaners, automotive products include hydraulic gear and motor oils, Star Tron fuel treatments, brake and transmission fluids, antifreeze, and windshield wash. RV products also include a wide variety of polishes, cleaners,

and protectants, as well as sealants, waterproofers, gasket materials, degreasers, and toilet treatment fluids. The marine, automotive, and RV care products are also marketed for use with motorcycles and aircraft. The Star brite name is also applied to mops, brushes, and handles; tie-downs and straps; sail lashes and bungee cords; and miscellaneous hardware, including sockets, eyelets, studs, and snaps. In addition, OBC serves the home market with patio/deck furniture and umbrella maintenance products; barbeque cleaning kits; rust removers; epoxies; mildew treatments and dehumidifiers; and liquid electric tape.

OBC products are sold through mall outlets and such major retailers as Wal-Mart, Home Depot, Kmart, West Marine, Boater's World, and Boat America. Manufacturing is done mostly at a plant in Montgomery, Alabama, supplemented by contract work conducted strategically at plants across the country. OBC manufactures its own polyvinyl chloride (PVC) and high-density polyethylene (HDPE) molded bottles, which are also sold to outside customers. Although a public company listed on the NASDAQ, OBC is mostly owned, about 63 percent, by cofounder, Chairman, and CEO Peter G. Dornau.

PETER DORNAU, CO-OWNER OF TROUBLED COMPANY

Peter Dornau grew up the son of a gas-range manufacturer, and learned the rudiments of business, especially marketing, from his father. "By osmosis, you pick that up across the dinner table," he recalled in a 1995 interview with the *Miami Herald*. A graduate of

COMPANY PERSPECTIVES

Ocean Bio-Chem, Inc., is a manufacturer and distributor of maintenance and care products for boats, recreational vehicles, automobiles, motorcycles and aircraft.

Brooklyn Polytechnic Institute in New York City in the 1960s, where he earned a degree in mechanical engineering and received a background in chemistry, Peter Dornau put some of that knowledge to work while still in his 20s by starting a company with his older brother, Fred R. Dornau. Called Ra-Dor Industries, it manufactured materials used in defense contracts. In 1967 the business was relocated from the Bronx to Sarasota, Florida, where it struggled and went bankrupt by the spring of 1969. The brothers then had to contend with fraud charges, brought by the U.S. Department of Defense, which paid $137,000 for missile containers it never received, and investors who claimed the Dornaus made misrepresentations about the business.

In October 1969 Peter Dornau, the company's vice-president, was indicted in the U.S. District Court for the Southern District of New York on 15 counts of mail and wire fraud as part of an alleged effort to defraud investors, including a forged contract purporting that the government owed Ra-Dor more than $240,000. The charges were later dropped, however, when a judge dismissed the indictment because it was determined that the prosecutor had relied heavily on testimony Peter Dornau had given during a May 1969 meeting with creditors as part of bankruptcy proceedings. According to the Bankruptcy Act, Dornau's testimony was covered by a grant of immunity. The judge determined that the evidence in the prosecution's case was not sufficiently derived from legitimate independent sources.

FORMING STAR BRITE CORPORATION: 1973

While his legal entanglements were being worked out, Peter Dornau worked as a consultant. In 1971 he was hired to write a marketing plan for a manufacturer who had acquired car and boat polish formulas from a German chemist. When the client was unable to act on the plan because of a lack of funds, Dornau stepped in to find investors; in 1973 he and his partners raised about $500,000, bought out the client, and established Star brite Corporation, named after the Miami company's single product, Star brite Auto Polish. Dornau's ex-client

manufactured the product, which became a major success in the 1970s, due in large part to innovative marketing. In television commercials Star brite was used in automobile makeovers, "Junkyard Tests," turning unsightly vehicles into sparkling wonders in a matter of minutes. Building on the product's early success, other automotive products followed.

By the early 1980s car sales were down because of a recession and many of the companies that depended on those sales failed, including some that owed money to Star brite. To make matters worse for the company, Dornau took it public in 1981 but because the underwriter did not issue as many shares as planned, Star brite raised less money than it needed from its initial public offering (IPO) of stock. Clearly an adjustment was in order. While car sales languished, boat sales were thriving, a fact well known to Dornau, a boating enthusiast who had bought his first boat at the age of 13. In 1981 Dornau decided to shift the focus of Star brite Corporation from cars to boats, and he restructured its operations to emphasize marine products, supported by an abundance of ads in marine publications. The shift in focus worked, and the company returned to profitability in 1983.

ADOPTION OF OCEAN BIO-CHEM NAME: 1984

A year later the company changed its name in keeping with the change in focus, becoming Ocean Bio-Chem, Inc. In the final five years of the decade, OBC took advantage of a marine market that grew at an annual rate of 15 to 20 percent. Net sales increased to $3.7 million in 1987 and $4.5 million a year later. OBC was also doing extremely well in the RV market. The company estimated it held a 70 percent market share in boat and RV polishes. OBC also did well with products it introduced to the marine market, one of them a paint additive called Compound X, which kept barnacles from adhering to hulls and slowing boats. It was developed by a doctor who realized while studying the way antibiotics attacked calcium in the body that barnacles, which contain calcium, would be similarly affected by the drugs. Also of note during this period, the company relocated to facilities in Fort Lauderdale in 1988.

In the first half of the 1990s, OBC increased revenues from $6.2 million in 1991 to $9.7 million in 1995, while net income improved from $380,000 to more than $540,000. Much of the company's growth was due to the introduction of new products, some of which were developed internally. Others were external additions, such as the Mil-Du Gas product line added in 1994 when OBC struck a distribution deal with M-D-G Corp. The nontoxic mildew and moisture

KEY DATES

1973: Company is founded in Miami as Star brite Corporation.
1981: Company is taken public.
1984: Name is changed to Ocean Bio-Chem, Inc.
1988: Headquarters are moved to Fort Lauderdale, Florida.
1996: Facilities in Montgomery, Alabama, are acquired.
1998: License is granted on Teflon.
2003: Alabama facilities are expanded.
2008: Company receives delisting notice from the NASDAQ.

inhibitors were then sold under the Star brite label, taking advantage of the brand name and OBC's established distribution network. The company was so well entrenched and respected in its markets that later in the decade E.I. du Pont de Nemours & Co. awarded OBC the exclusive license to its venerable Teflon brand for the marine and RV markets in the United States and Canada. Other companies in the field would have to go through OBC first in order to use the Teflon name. Moreover, OBC gained access to the du Pont laboratories to improve existing formulations and develop new marine and RV products with Teflon. OBC also looked to diversify into other product categories. In 1995 it began producing straps, tie-downs, and bungee cords for sale under the Star brite label.

ACQUISITION OF KINPAK FACILITY: 1996

OBC added its Montgomery, Alabama, facility in February 1996 when it purchased assets from Kinpak, Inc., including a lease for about 20 acres of property in Montgomery, a 50,000-square-foot plastic bottle manufacturing plant, a chemical mixing facility, massive storage tanks with a total capacity of 1.2 million liquid gallons, and a docking facility on the Alabama River that had access to the Gulf of Mexico along with a rail operation that could handle as many as 30 freight cars for loading or unloading onto barges and trucks. OBC also acquired machinery, equipment, and inventory. The addition of the Kinpak operations provided a substantial savings in the cost of bottles as well as warehousing, both of which had been contracted out previously. As a result, OBC gained a competitive edge in its efforts to maintain a dominant market position.

The addition of straps and brushes, new marine products, and Teflon-related products introduced into the marine market at the end of 1998 helped to drive sales increases at the end of the 1990s into the new century. Revenues grew from $12.85 million in 1997 to nearly $16 million in 1999. After posting a net loss of about $170,000 in 1997, OBC returned to profitability in 1998 and netted $430,000 in 1999. Although the company increased sales to more than $18 million in 2000, higher interest rates and raw material costs led to a net loss of about $245,000. To improve the cost side of the business and prepare for the addition of a new automotive line, OBC invested in upgrades of the Kinpak facility. Completed in March 2001, the project included improvements to the tank farm, and the addition of new high-speed filling lines to help in PVC production. A year later OBC successfully arranged a $3.5 million industrial development bond through the city of Montgomery to fund a 70,000-square-foot addition to the manufacturing plant, along with the necessary new machinery and equipment. The work was completed by the end of 2003.

WAL-MART ADDS STAR TRON LINE: 2007

New automotive lines and a private-label marine oil supply contract helped to increase sales from $19.9 million in 2001 to $22.7 million, and net income from $106,384 to $134,518. A year later revenues dipped slightly, yet because of lower overhead, OBC was able to grow net income to more than $345,000. Sales improved to $24.4 million in 2004, but as the price of oil and other raw materials escalated, the company was unable to remain profitable. Net income fell to $134,554 in 2004. A year later sales fell to $19.7 million and OBC reported a net loss of $1.8 million. OBC rebounded in 2006, returning to profitability and netting $392,000 on sales of $20.4 million, due in large measure to improved national distribution of automotive and marine products and efficiencies at the Kinpak plant. A year later revenues increased to $21.3 million. A major factor was the introduction of OBC's line of Star Tron fuel additives for gas and diesel engines at Wal-Mart. Moreover, net income surged to $725,000 in 2007.

Wal-Mart's move to stock up on Star Tron products led in early 2007 to a sudden spike in the price of OBC stock, which in a matter of just two days tripled in value from $1.94 to more than $6. It was not a level that could be sustained, however, and the price plummeted despite the company's performance in 2007. The company launched the Sea Safe line of environmentally friendly boat cleaners, leading to even better results in

2008. Nonetheless, the price of OBC stock languished below the $1 mark, prompting the NASDAQ to issue a notice of noncompliance in October 2008. The company had until July 2009 to increase the bid price of its stock to $1 for a minimum of ten business days. By the end of March 2009, the price was less than 50 cents, making it highly uncertain whether OBC would retain its NASDAQ listing. Nevertheless, the company remained a leader in its field.

PRINCIPAL SUBSIDIARIES

Star brite Distributing, Inc.; Star brite Distributing Canada, Inc.; D & S Advertising Services, Inc.; Star brite Staput, Inc.; Star brite Service Centers, Inc.; Star brite Automotive, Inc.; Kinpak Inc.

PRINCIPAL COMPETITORS

Ashland Inc.; Meguiar's Inc.; Turtle Wax, Inc.

FURTHER READING

Croghan, Lore, "Boat Cosmetics Firm Churns Up a Market," *Miami Herald,* September 11, 1989, p. 13BM.

DuPont, Dale K., "Marketing Keeps Firm's Star Shining Bright," *Miami Herald,* May 22, 1995, p. 9BM.

Katz, Ian, "Stocking Up on Cleaning Products: Wal-Mart Deal a Big Win for Ocean Bio-Chem," *South Florida Sun-Sentinel,* February 19, 2007.

"2 Accused of Fraud in $137,000 Claims for Missile Service," *New York Times,* October 11, 1969.

Orange 21 Inc.

■

2070 Las Palmas Drive
Carlsbad, California 92009
U.S.A.
Telephone: (760) 804-8420
Fax: (760) 804-8421
Web site: http://www.orangetwentyone.com; http://www.spyoptic.com

Public Company
Incorporated: 1992 as Sports Colors, Inc.
Employees: 94
Sales: $46.5 million (2008)
Stock Exchanges: NASDAQ
Ticker Symbol: ORNG
NAICS: 339115 Ophthalmic Goods Manufacturing; 423460 Ophthalmic Goods Merchant Wholesalers; 315212 Women's, Girls', and Infants' Cut and Sew Apparel Contractors; 315223 Men's and Boys' Cut and Sew Shirt (Except Work Shirt) Manufacturing; 315224 Men's and Boys' Cut and Sew Trouser, Slack, and Jean Manufacturing; 315232 Women's and Girls' Cut and Sew Blouse and Shirt Manufacturing; 315991 Hat, Cap, and Millinery Manufacturing; 315999 Other Apparel Accessories and Other Apparel Manufacturing

■ ■ ■

Orange 21 Inc. is a holding company for two brands of eyewear, Spy Optic and E Eyewear. The company manufactures premium fashion sunglasses, women-specific sunglasses, performance sport sunglasses, motocross and snow goggles, and apparel and accessories for the action sports (surfing, skateboarding, and snowboarding) and youth lifestyle markets. Orange 21 sells its products in close to 40 countries at 8,300 retailer locations.

STAKING OUT A NICHE IN THE SPORTS AND YOUTH LIFESTYLE MARKETS: 1994–2004

In 1984, Jeff "Beaver" Theodosakis and brothers Mark and Brian Simo were living in Florida, racing dirt bikes and running a wood-chopping business, when they founded Life's a Beach and pioneered the trend in knee-length shorts. "People thought we were idiots," at first, explained Theodosakis, until then-motocross superstar Ricky Johnson began to wear their pants, sending the new company scrambling for sewing machines and fabric.

The company grew, but the friends had a falling out, and in 1987, the Simo brothers left Life's a Beach. They founded No Fear on their own in 1992. Theodosakis rejoined the Simo brothers in 1994, and the three incorporated Sports Colors as a subsidiary of Spy Optic, Inc. They gathered together a roster of high-profile athletes to endorse their new products, found an Italian manufacturer to make them, and, in 1995, Spy shipped its first sunglasses. The trio thought, as Theodosakis recalled in 2003 in the *San Diego Union-Tribune*, "[Y]ou put them on a shelf and there's no sizes. It should be a simple business." They soon discovered

COMPANY PERSPECTIVES

The Spy brand was created by the passion of a group of over-achieving athletes and enthusiasts seeking a new visual perspective on technical eyewear products. Our values are not bound by tradition, but based on the core ideals of young-at-heart pioneers, those whose needs to express freedom and innovation are stronger than the rules and conventions of the day. Our Spy Brand DNA melds an action sports heritage with an affection for fashion-forward styling. Constantly evolving the relationship between material, function and design, our DNA generates an obsession with progress. Spy finds itself at the intersection of retro-futuristic design and optical innovation, while at the same time expressing its identity through the iconic minds, bodies and vision of the world's greatest athletes and artists.

that while they knew how "to create a brand," they "just didn't know anything about the eyewear business."

Early on, Spy Optic had to deal with heavy competition for the Southern California action sports crowd, especially from publicly traded Oakley, whose sales were in the hundreds of millions. From 1999 to 2002, the company's own revenues increased from $11 million to $27.4 million in 2004. By 2003, the company had added products for the sports and youth lifestyle markets and prescription glasses to its lines. By 2004, Spy had offices both domestically and internationally and about 100 employees; it sold about one million pairs of sunglasses through 4,500 retail outlets in the United States, Canada, Western Europe, Japan, and Australia.

2004: ORANGE 21 REINCORPORATES UNDER NEW MANAGEMENT

By this time, the action sports market, which centered around the surf, skate, and board sports lifestyle of California, was becoming increasingly popular. In fact, half of Spy's business came from Gen-Yers in California alone. Yet increasing opportunities translated to increasing competition and necessitated changes within the company. In late 2004, Barry Buchholtz replaced Mark Simo as chief executive officer. Buchholtz had joined the company in 1997 and had a background in the computer industry; he had served as president of Orange 21 since January 2000.

Shortly thereafter, in December 2004, the company reincorporated as a holding company called Orange 21 Inc. in Delaware with Spy Optic, Inc., as its wholly owned subsidiary. No Fear, which then operated about 30 retail stores under CEO Simo, had a 23 percent interest in Spy, which went public with an initial public offering (IPO) of common stock on the NASDAQ. The IPO was a huge success, raising $30 million, and, by the next day, Orange 21's stock price had increased 14 percent. For 2004, Orange 21 had revenues of $33.56 million, a 22.5 percent increase over 2003.

2005: CHANGES IN MARKETING AND PRODUCTS

Immediately, Spy instituted changes in the way it marketed its goggles, sunglasses, and accessories. It converted its business model from relying upon distributors to becoming a direct dealer with regional sales representatives in France and Italy. It also began advertising on the East Coast of the United States with a new sales management team.

Additionally, the company introduced the E Eyewear brand of sunglasses in 2005, named after Dale Earnhardt Jr., aiming to appeal to a slightly older demographic than Spy Optic with broader distribution at lower price points. It also expanded its apparel and accessories business, which then accounted for 10 percent of its overall business, striving to further connect with young customers through items such as T-shirts that afforded increased brand exposure.

The company also expanded its lines in 2005, introducing new handcrafted designs reminiscent of the 1960s and 1970s and a line of exotic leather eyewear. It engineered and marketed lenses that adjusted to varying light conditions, its Delta Photochromic line, and ventilated motocross racing goggles with a "face foam system," its Magneto line. More innovations followed in 2006 with the introduction of Spy's Gemini line of goggles intended for high performance at high altitudes where bubbling or warping of a non-depressurized lens sometimes occurred.

Lastly, in a move to minimize production costs, Orange 21 purchased its Italian manufacturer, LEM S.r. l., in December 2005. LEM, which was founded in 1984 and manufactured 79 percent of Orange 21's products at the time of the purchase, became a wholly owned subsidiary of Orange 21 Inc.

KEY DATES

1992: Company is incorporated as Sports Colors, Inc.
1994: Company changes its name to Spy Optic, Inc., and begins operations.
1995: Spy ships its first sunglasses.
2004: Company reincorporates and changes its name to Orange 21 Inc.; Barry Buchholtz replaces Mark Simo as chief executive officer.
2005: Spy Optic launches E Eyewear; Orange 21 purchases Spy's Italian manufacturer, LEM S.r.l.
2008: A. Stone Douglass replaces Simo as chief executive.
2009: Orange 21 launches a rights offering for its stock owners; company applies to transfer from the NASDAQ Global Market to the NASDAQ Capital Market.

INCREASES IN SALES CANNOT PREVENT LOSSES: 2005–08

Spy's innovations proved successful, and, despite the ongoing competition, by mid-decade Spy had become an increasingly strong brand with five consecutive years of substantial increases in sales. For 2005, Orange 21's revenues were $38.6 million, a 14.9 percent increase over 2004. However, the company reported a net loss for the year of $1.7 million.

Unfortunately, losses continued into 2006, when the company reported a shortfall of $7 million on revenues of $42 million. The company was not able to capitalize on its growth in orders because of productivity problems at LEM. It struggled to improve its material planning process and internal operations.

Further, while domestic sales increased only incrementally, international sales declined dramatically mid-decade, leading Spy Optic to change international distributors. In an effort to recover international growth, Spy signed a distribution agreement with Marmalade Group PTY LTD in 2006 to distribute Spy Optic products in Australia, and a second agreement with Surf Sales to distribute its products in the United Kingdom and Ireland. Buchholtz left his position as chief executive of Orange 21 to become president of European operations and sales that same year. Mark Simo, who had been chairman of the board, once again assumed the role of chief executive officer, stepping down as the CEO of No Fear.

Later in 2006, Orange 21 signed two separate distribution agreements in Australia, replacing Marmalade as its distribution agent. The first of these was with Quattro Action Sport Distribution, the leading distributor of U.S. youth and board sports brands, the second with GAS MX Distribution, a leading distributor for the motocross and motorcycle markets.

Increased sales and marketing efforts, including an augmented sales force and an improvement in product mix, boosted Orange 21's revenues to $46.5 million for 2006 with a net loss of $8 million. However, Spy Optic also faced challenges of a different sort in 2006. That fall, a raid of two warehouses and two retail stores in downtown Los Angeles produced 20,000 units of counterfeit Spy Optic sunglasses, the estimated value of which was $1.7 million.

In 2007, Orange 21 considered buying Carlsbad-based No Fear's retail stores subsidiary, and then backed down. No Fear had annual sales of around $9 million and 300 employees in about 40 stores and was among the largest sellers of Spy Optic eyewear. No Fear, which then owned about 15 percent of Orange 21's stock, urged Orange 21 to reconsider the merger, but Orange refused. No sooner had it done so than New York-based Costa Brava Partnership III, a hedge fund that owned 10 percent of Orange 21's shares, placed its offer to buy Orange 21 on the table.

2008–09: DOUGLASS ATTEMPTS TO TURN ORANGE 21 AROUND

Simo's tenure as chief executive ended in October 2008. A. Stone Douglass, who specialized in turning around troubled companies, replaced Simo at the helm. Douglass's first move was to initiate a comprehensive strategic review of Orange 21 with the aim of streamlining operations and reworking the company's executive compensation scheme to increase shareholder returns; his announced goal was to achieve $3 million in cost savings during his first year.

Douglass would have a tough road ahead as sales for 2008 were $47.3 million, only a 2 percent increase over 2007, while losses almost doubled to $15.2 million for the year. In January 2009, Orange 21 launched a rights offering entitling stock owners to buy additional shares of its stock, to raise money for research and development, capital expenditures, working capital, and general expenses. In April, it applied to transfer from the NASDAQ Global Market to the NASDAQ Capital Market because it no longer met the continued listing standards for stockholder returns for the NASDAQ Global Market. The company intended to focus on expanding distribution outside the action sports market in the eastern United States and reorganizing its global distribution.

Carrie Rothburd

PRINCIPAL SUBSIDIARIES

Spy Optic, Inc.; LEM S.r.l.

PRINCIPAL COMPETITORS

Oakley, Inc.; Gianni Versace S.p.A.; Luxottica Group S.p.A.; Mountain Shades Distributing Company, Inc.; Von Zipper, Ltd.; Electric Visual Evolution LLC.

FURTHER READING

"CEO Interview: Barry Buchholtz—Orange 21 Inc.," *Wall Street Transcript,* September 26, 2005.

Davies, Jennifer, "Carlsbad, Calif.-based Sunglasses Maker Sees Stock Climb 14 Percent After IPO," *San Diego Union-Tribune,* December 15, 2004.

Dougherty, Conor, "Made with the Shades: Action Sunglass-Maker Spy Optic Has Prescription for Success," *San Diego Union-Tribune,* November 9, 2003, p. N4.

Freeman, Mike, "Two Sports Companies Divided over Merger Idea; No Fear Turns Up Heat on Orange 21," *San Diego Union-Tribune,* November 19, 2008, p. C1.

"Orange 21 Inc. Announces New CEO and Strategic Review," *Science Letter,* October 14, 2008, p. 3845.

The Orchard Enterprises, Inc.

23 East 4th Street, 3rd Floor
New York, New York 10003
U.S.A.
Telephone: (212) 201-9280
Fax: (212) 201-9203
Web site: http://www.theorchard.com

Public Company
Incorporated: 1998
Employees: 101
Sales: $57.36 million (2008)
Stock Exchanges: NASDAQ
Ticker Symbol: ORCD
NAICS: 533110 Owners and Lessors of Other Non-Financial Assets

■ ■ ■

The Orchard Enterprises, Inc., serves as a middleman between independent record labels and digital music sales outlets including Apple's iTunes, eMusic, and Verizon Wireless. The firm's library encompasses more than 1.3 million recordings from 91 countries, as well as over 4,000 videos, and includes American roots music from Vee Jay and Smithsonian Folkways; hard rock from Amphetamine Reptile, SST, and Lookout!; and vast amounts of international music from Rotana, EMI Pakistan, Saregama, Discos Musart, and others. The Orchard also helps license tracks to film and TV producers, videogame makers, advertisers, and for cellphone ringtones; offers distribution of compact discs or vinyl records; and provides promotion and marketing services. The publicly traded firm's majority shareholder, Dimensional Associates, owns music download service eMusic.

BEGINNINGS

The Orchard was founded in 1998 by music industry veterans Richard Gottehrer and Scott Cohen to promote and distribute music by independent recording artists. An industry force since the early 1960s, CEO Gottehrer had been a hit songwriter ("I Want Candy," "My Boyfriend's Back"), producer (Blondie; the Go-Gos), and artist (as one-third of faux Australian beat group The Strangeloves), and had cofounded pioneering U.S. punk/new wave label Sire (Talking Heads, Ramones). Named after the street in New York where its offices were located, the new company commenced operations in November 1998.

Targeting musicians that had issued their own compact discs (CDs) but had no means for national promotion or distribution, The Orchard provided them a web page that could include photos, artwork, and text, with sound samples and tour information available for an additional fee. Links for consumers to purchase discs via e-commerce sites including CDNow or Amazon.com were available, as was a conduit for wholesale orders through Valley Media. The artist would pay a one-time fee of $40 per release plus 30 percent of sales, with albums sold on a consignment basis and the proceeds paid quarterly. Sales of a typical release were in the range of 500 to 1,000 copies, far less than major record labels would bother with but enough to turn a profit for the firm and possibly break even for the artist.

COMPANY PERSPECTIVES

The Orchard licenses and globally distributes more than 1.3 million songs and over 5,000 video titles through hundreds of digital stores (e.g. iTunes, eMusic, Google, Netflix, V CAST) and mobile carriers (e.g. Verizon Wireless, Vodafone, Bell Canada, 3). With operations in 29 regions around the world, The Orchard drives sales for its label, retailer, brand, and agency clients through innovative marketing and promotional campaigns; brand entertainment programs; and film, advertising, gaming and television licensing. Through its recently acquired TVT Distribution division, The Orchard also offers physical distribution solutions of music in CD and vinyl format for select record label partners. A pioneer in digital music and media services, The Orchard fosters creativity and independence.

With no promotional efforts, by the following spring The Orchard had begun distributing more than 1,000 releases. In its first year the company also formed an alliance with Philadelphia-based duplication firm Disc Makers, waiving its $40 fee for performers who used it, as well as with EZCD, which offered custom compilation CDs of music by Orchard acts. In the fall of 1999 the company launched an imprint called Orchard Records whose initial release was a benefit compilation album for victims of the war in Kosovo.

The firm continued to add clients over the next several years, and in 2002 found sales success with Danish rock band The Raveonettes. The Orchard was reportedly operating in the red, however, and gained a reputation for being late with payments to performers.

SALE TO DIMENSIONAL ASSOCIATES IN 2003

In April 2003 control of The Orchard was purchased by Dimensional Associates, a unit of New York equity firm JDS Capital which also owned Dimensional Music Publishing and music download service eMusic. After the deal was finalized former McKinsey & Company media consultant Greg Scholl was brought in to serve as president and CEO, with Gottehrer remaining on tap as chairman and Cohen moving to the position of president of international operations, which were rapidly growing.

Scholl quickly took steps to repair the firm's damaged reputation by paying off past-due accounts and implementing more transparent accounting procedures and web-based information access. Capitalizing on the popularity of Internet-based music file-sharing, and the spring of 2003 debut of Apple's iTunes store, he also began to focus the firm's efforts on developing revenue streams from music downloads, and soon licensed tracks to iTunes, Napster, MSN Music, Yahoo, and other services in the United States and abroad. The Orchard was charging labels $99 to begin distribution as well as taking a 30 percent cut, offering contracts that ranged from three to ten years.

The firm's music library soon began to expand as it signed such labels as Lookout!, home to alternative/hard rock bands Green Day, The Donnas, and Rancid; Amphetamine Reptile; Amulet; Document; Universal Egg; Invisible; Shanachie; and Saregama, India's largest and oldest music company, which controlled over 300,000 songs. By the spring of 2004 The Orchard boasted one million paid downloads and streams. By then it had a workforce of 60, and had opened a second office in London.

In mid-2005 the company introduced a turnkey digital retail option for labels that they could operate from their own web sites, with the company providing fulfillment. In the fall The Orchard also began marketing its extensive catalog of Chinese music via iTunes, including the song "Mouse Loves Rice," which had already been downloaded 100 million times. The firm assisted the launch with a marketing campaign.

In May 2006 The Orchard signed a deal with the Harry Fox Agency to ensure proper licensing of digital downloads, and in June reached an agreement for Integrated Copyright Group of Nashville to perform administration for its music publishers worldwide.

ORCHARD MUSIC SERVICE: 2006

Seeking new uses for its library by movie/TV production companies, videogame makers, and providers of cellphone ringtones, in 2006 the firm created a unit called Orchard Music Services to pursue opportunities in the so-called synchronization business. As with digital downloads, the company would take a percentage for each track licensed, and it soon began to work with such ad agencies as BBDO Worldwide and Peterson Milla Hooks.

By mid-2006 The Orchard's music library had grown to include one million music tracks. It had content from 73 countries, with newly added material coming from Spain, Portugal, Russia, Argentina, Israel, Kenya, Australia, and Uzbekistan. It also continued to

KEY DATES

1998: The Orchard is founded in New York to distribute independent CD releases.

2003: Dimension Associates buys control of firm; Greg Scholl is named CEO; under new owners, firm adds labels and shifts emphasis to downloads.

2006: Orchard Music Service is launched to license music for TV, movies, and other outlets.

2007: Merger with Digital Music Group Inc. places firm on the NASDAQ.

2008: Acquisition of TVT brings company record label, physical distribution.

find new download customers, with signings including U.S. wireless operator Amp'd Mobile, advertiser-supported peer-to-peer music sharing network QTRAX, and leading Chinese download site top100.cn. Revenue for the year was $15 million, although the firm continued to lose money.

In early 2007 The Orchard signed a marketing and licensing agreement with background music provider Muzak that would put its recordings in some of that firm's 400,000 locations. The company also unveiled a proprietary content delivery platform called V.E.C.T. O.R. to speed downloads, and added a music search program to help licensing clients locate material.

MERGER WITH DMGI IN 2007

In July 2007 The Orchard merged with smaller rival Digital Music Group, Inc., (DMGI) of Sacramento, California, in a deal valued at $61 million. Founded in 2005, Digital Music Group had begun trading on the NASDAQ in February 2006, and the deal was structured as a reverse merger of The Orchard into DMGI. The expanded company would take ticker symbol ORCD and officially became known as The Orchard Enterprises, Inc. The two firms were the largest of their kind and had combined revenues of about $25 million, but neither had turned a profit. After the merger, Orchard President and CEO Greg Scholl would remain in the top posts, and DMGI's West Coast offices were closed.

The Orchard's library would include video content, having gained over 1,000 hours of material from DMGI including vintage television programs *Gumby*, *My Favorite Martian*, and *I Spy*. The firm had also recently

signed deals to represent a slew of additional labels including SST, Surfdog, Delicious Vinyl, Norton, Sanctuary, Snapper, Smithsonian Folkways, Discos Musart, Mu-Yap, EMI Pakistan, and Rotana, the latter of which was the largest label in the Middle East. In December it added Vee-Jay, a key U.S. record company of the 1950s and 1960s with a deep catalog of blues, jazz, R&B, and gospel music.

At year's end The Orchard also created a new brand entertainment division to seek further song placements with advertisers. It continued to boost wireless sales, as well, having by that time established relationships with more than 100 carriers worldwide. For 2007 the company reported sales of $28.5 million and a loss of $7.6 million.

ACQUISITION OF TVT IN 2008

In June 2008 The Orchard won an auction for the assets of bankrupt independent label TVT Records, which brought it new artists including rappers Lil' Jon and Pitbull, a sizable back catalog of releases, and a distribution network for CDs and vinyl albums. The deal was reportedly worth upward of $5 million. Several months later The Orchard announced it would begin offering physical distribution of discs for its member labels, in response to changes in the industry in which some record companies had begun shifting digital downloads to their distributors.

During 2008 The Orchard also resolved a dispute with social networking site MySpace to become one of the first independent music providers to license its catalog to users; began distributing music through the new Nokia "Comes with Music" cellphone/MP3 player plan; and signed a deal with Sony/ATV Music Publishing to license its recordings outside North America.

In September CEO Scholl publicly took issue with SoundExchange, a nonprofit, quasi-governmental agency that had been launched in 2001 to collect and distribute broadcast royalties for recording artists. About half of the 1.2 million songs in The Orchard's library were eligible for payments, but Scholl complained that the money was slow in coming and "incongruous" with the songs it had registered. SoundExchange countered that it was in fact more efficient than similar organizations and returned the vast majority of funds collected to artists.

Although it had been losing money for a decade, The Orchard was nearing profitability and for 2008 reported revenues of $57.4 million and a net loss of $2.3 million. Music sales accounted for 89 percent, with Apple's iTunes making up 55 percent of the overall total. Licensing of tracks to films, TV shows, videogames, advertisers, and ringtone providers, as well as physical sales and other miscellaneous income, comprised the remainder. The firm delivered 54.8 million music tracks during the year, with three-fifths of its library being downloaded at least once. Just over two-thirds of total revenues were paid out to labels and other content owners in royalties. In January 2009 the company moved into the former offices of TVT in New York.

In just over a decade, The Orchard Enterprises, Inc., had become one of the top digital music aggregators, serving thousands of independent record labels by licensing and distributing their content to hundreds of providers worldwide. With the shift away from physical media gaining traction, the firm looked to be strongly positioned for profitability and continued growth.

Frank Uhle

PRINCIPAL SUBSIDIARIES

Digital Rights Agency, Inc.; eMusicLive, Inc.; Orchard Enterprises NY, Inc.; Orchard Management, Inc.; The Orchard EU Ltd. (UK); The Orchard Enterprises, Ltd. (Hong Kong).

PRINCIPAL COMPETITORS

Independent Online Distribution Alliance; ONEDigital/INgrooves; IRIS; PAIS; Believe; edelNet; Koch Entertainment; Sony/RED; Universal Music Group/Fontana; EMI/Caroline; Warner Music Group/ADA.

FURTHER READING

Atwood, Brett, "Online Dist. Orchard Gives New Acts Access," *Billboard*, March 6, 1999.

Christman, Ed, "The Orchard: Let's Get Physical," *Billboard*, August 23, 2008.

Garrity, Brian, "Bankrupt TVT Records Finds New Life in The Orchard," *New York Post*, June 19, 2008.

Harding, Cortney, "Whose 'My' Space?" *Billboard*, April 26, 2008.

Jain, Anita, "Breaking Online Records: The Orchard's Head Is Seeding the Web with the Music of Independent Artists," *Crain's New York Business*, December 1, 2003, p. 4.

Levine, Robert, "Buying Music from Anywhere and Selling It for Play on the Internet," *New York Times*, January 9, 2006, p. 1C.

Paoletta, Michael, "That Synching Feeling," *Billboard*, September 9, 2006.

Scholl, Greg, "Editorial: A Sound Exchange?" *Billboard*, September 6, 2008.

Simson, John, "Editorial: The Promise of SoundExchange," *Billboard*, October 4, 2008.

Swett, Chris, "Online Music Has a New Duet," *Sacramento Bee*, July 12, 2007, p. D1.

Pearson plc

80 Strand
London, WC2R 0RL
United Kingdom
Telephone: (44 20) 7010-2000
Fax: (44 20) 7010-6060
Web site: http://www.pearson.com

Public Company
Incorporated: 1897 as S Pearson & Son Ltd.
Employees: 34,000
Sales: £4.81 billion (2008)
Stock Exchanges: London New York
Ticker Symbol: PSON (London); PSO (New York)
NAICS: 511110 Newspaper Publishers; 511120 Periodical Publishers; 511130 Book Publishers

■ ■ ■

Since the mid-1990s, Pearson plc has transformed itself from an industrial holding company with a large and sometimes confusing group of interests into the world's largest publisher of educational materials with three major business groups. Pearson Education is a leading education company, serving 100 million people throughout the world with textbooks, testing programs, and multimedia learning tools. The Financial Times Group is a leading business information company. Finally, The Penguin Group serves the consumer market with everything from classics and novels to cookbooks and children's titles.

EARLY GROWTH AS A BUILDING AND CONTRACTING FIRM

In its early years, the business was dominated by Weetman Dickinson Pearson, and later First Viscount Cowdray, who transformed it into an international contracting concern, which he subsequently converted to an investment trust-type operation. Pearson's roots can be traced to Weetman's grandfather, Samuel Pearson, who in 1844 became an associate partner in a Huddersfield-based building and contracting firm. In 1856, his eldest son, George, entered the business, which became known as S Pearson & Son, "sanitary tube and brickmakers and contractors for local public works in and around Bradford."

Contracts undertaken at this time were locally based and were for railway companies and, more frequently, for the provision of water supply, drainage, and sewerage facilities to expanding industrial cities. The business developed rapidly, moving its head office in 1857 to nearby Bradford, Yorkshire, and expanding its associated brick-making, glazed tile, and sanitary pipe activities. In 1873, Weetman Pearson entered the business and received a share in its ownership on the retirement of Samuel in 1879.

Pearson, increasingly under the direction of Weetman, began to make a quick metamorphosis into an internationally based concern. In the late 1870s, contracts outside the north of England were undertaken for the first time, and the head office was moved to London in 1884. Five years later projects were in progress as far afield as Egypt, the United States,

Canada, and Mexico with port works, railway construction and tunneling, and water supply and drainage predominating. Between 1884 and 1914 some 67 projects, with a total value of almost £43 million, were undertaken. Of these, 36 (valued at £16.5 million or 38 percent of the total) were located outside Great Britain and Ireland; with 10 percent in the United States and Canada; 45.5 percent in Central and South America; and 7 percent in Egypt, Spain, China, Malta, and Bermuda.

The British government was a major client, as were municipalities, railway and harbor companies, and water utilities. Contracts of particular note included the Admiralty Harbour at Dover; the Blackwall Tunnel under the River Thames in London; the East River Railway Tunnels, New York, for which a U.S. subsidiary, S Pearson & Son Inc., was formed to carry out the work; Malta Dry Docks and Breakwaters; and Halifax Dry Dock in Canada.

However, Mexico was the country where Pearson made its greatest mark, to the extent that Weetman Pearson, who had become a member of Parliament, was dubbed in the House of Commons and elsewhere as the "Member for Mexico." The first contract for the Mexican government, which ran from 1890 to 1896, was for the construction of the Mexican Grand Canal to drain Mexico City and its surrounding area. A succession of other government-owned or sponsored projects followed: the £3 million conversion of Vera Cruz harbor into a modern seaport; the £2.5 million reconstruction of the Tehuantepec Railway and its associated terminal ports, linking the Atlantic and Pacific Oceans; and the Salina Cruz harbor and docks, at £3.3 million.

EXPANSION INTO OIL AND ELECTRIC POWER

A growing confidence between Mexican dictator Porfirio Díaz and Weetman Pearson consolidated Pearson's Mexican interests. Under the Tehuantepec Railway contract, Pearson built the facilities at cost, provided part of the capital, and then managed the railway and ports, taking part of the profits as remuneration. This entry into the mainstream of Mexican business soon led to other interests, most importantly oil. In 1901, Pearson began to acquire oil-bearing land and by 1906 owned 600,000 acres and had royalty leases over about another 250,000. Oil refining began, and in 1908 Pearson entered the Mexican oil retail trade in direct competition with Walter Pierce Oil Company, mostly owned by Standard Oil Company, resulting in severe price competition.

However, it was not until 1910 that the business was transformed into an international oil concern with the discovery of the Potrero de Llano oilfield. The Aguila (Mexican Eagle) Oil Company Ltd. was formed to take over most of Pearson's oil interests and make a public issue of securities. In 1912, as a means of extending this business, the Eagle Oil Transport Company Ltd. and the Anglo Mexican Petroleum Company Ltd. were formed to focus on international distribution and sales. Some £12 million of Pearson capital had been committed to Mexican oil. During World War I, an immense trade was done in supplying the British government. In 1919, the Royal Dutch group acquired a large shareholding in the Aguila and took over management control, although for many years Pearson continued to own a large part of the company. In 1919, Whitehall Petroleum Corporation Ltd. was formed to take over Pearson's oil interests and prospect, mostly unsuccessfully, for oil worldwide. Its most notable action was the establishment of the Amerada Corporation, a major U.S. oil company, in 1919.

Another feature of Pearson's diversification after 1900 was the generation, supply, and application of electric power in Latin America. This began when Díaz invited Weetman Pearson to electrify and then manage the tramway system, later extended to electricity supply generally, in Vera Cruz, a service that was carried into effect by the Vera Cruz Electric Light, Power, and Traction Company Ltd. Soon Pearson developed similar schemes elsewhere in Mexico. After World War I, these developments were extended outside Mexico, when undertakings in Chile were acquired. The Chilean interests were subsequently modernized and managed by Pearson's Cia. Chilena de Electricidad. All these electri-

KEY DATES

1844: Samuel Pearson becomes an associate partner in a building and contracting firm.

1910: The Aguila Oil Company Ltd. is created to oversee most of Pearson's oil interests.

1919: Whitehall Petroleum Corporation Ltd. is formed to take over Pearson's oil interests; Whitehall Trust is created as a finance and issuing house.

1957: Pearson acquires an interest in Financial News Ltd.

1969: The company goes public.

1979: A controlling interest in Camco Inc. is purchased.

1984: The company's name is changed to Pearson plc.

1985: Subsidiary Penguin Publishing Co. Ltd. acquires Viking of the United States and the Michael Joseph and Hamish publishing houses.

1987: U.S.-based publisher Addison Wesley is purchased.

1988: The firm buys Les Echos Group.

1989: Pearson begins divesting its oil businesses.

1993: The company begins to focus on its media

businesses related to information, education, and entertainment.

1994: Software Toolworks is purchased and renamed Mindscape.

1996: HarperCollins Educational, Twenty-First Century Business Publications, and Putnam Berkeley are acquired; Westminster Press is sold.

1998: Pearson acquires Simon & Schuster's education, reference, and business and professional publishing division.

2002: Pearson sells its 22 percent stake in RTL Group to Bertelsmann AG.

2007: In a $950 million deal with Reed Elsevier, the company agrees to acquire both Harcourt Assessment and Harcourt Education International; the online educational services business eCollege is acquired for $477 million.

2009: The *Financial Times* introduces *China Confidential,* a fortnightly, subscription-based digital newsletter devoted to Chinese investment intelligence.

cal interests were consolidated into Whitehall Electric Investments Ltd. in 1922.

In 1897, Pearson, which was then reckoned to be the world's leading contractor, was converted into a limited company with an issued share capital of £1 million, all of which was owned by the Pearson family or by non-family directors. In 1907, Whitehall Securities Ltd. was formed to take over all of Pearson's non-contracting activities, while in 1919, S Pearson & Son (Contracting Department) Ltd. took over the firm's contracting interests. S Pearson & Son Ltd. became the group's holding company.

POSTWAR EXPANSION

During World War I, the contracting company was preoccupied with military contracts, of which the huge munitions plant at Gretna Green in Scotland, worth £9.2 million, was the largest. However, in the late 1920s the construction business was closed down, not sold, as

a going concern apparently as a result of family whim. By that time, however, Pearson had diversified well beyond the supplying of oil and electricity. In 1908, Weetman Pearson was a member of a large syndicate that acquired the London evening newspaper the *Westminster Gazette*. After the war, he acquired total control of the newspaper, converted it into a morning daily, and began to build around it a group of provincial newspapers. In 1919, the company established Whitehall Trust Ltd. as a finance and issuing house, and at about the same time its principal asset, a substantial interest in Lazard Brothers & Company, the London merchant bank, was acquired. A partnership was formed with Dorman Long & Company Ltd. to develop a coal mining and iron and steel industry in Kent, although this project was not to figure prominently in Pearson's affairs.

When Lord Cowdray died in 1927, he had completely reshaped his family's business. He was succeeded as chairman by his second son, Clive, while his eldest son, Harold, played a significant part in the development of Westminster Press Ltd. The management philosophy was to develop and extend the core businesses through local management. In 1929, the electricity businesses in Mexico and Chile were sold, but similar electricity undertakings were developed in southwest England. The company played a substantial role in establishing British Airways Ltd. (not the state-owned business that came to be known as British Airways PLC) in 1935.

The most significant result of World War II was the purchase of strategic Pearson assets by the British government. These included the airline interests but, much more significantly, the interest in the Amerada Petroleum Corporation, which was compulsorily acquired in 1941. The year 1948 saw the nationalization of the electricity undertakings in the west of England.

In the 1950s, the general strategy of Pearson, which from 1954 was under the chairmanship of the Third Lord Cowdray, was to concentrate on well-defined sectors and within them build up specialist niche businesses producing quality products, with much decision making devolved to local management. This was to be a successful and enduring philosophy. The five legs on which the business now stood were financial services, publishing, oil, manufacturing, and investment trusts.

ACQUISITIONS AND DIVESTITURES: 1950s TO 1980s

In 1945, the surviving oil interests were largely confined to oil and gas properties owned by Rycade Corporation of the United States. In the 1950s, the activities of this company were extended, while particularly successful expansion also occurred in western Canada through Whitehall Canadian Oils Ltd. In addition, a small interest in Amerada was reacquired. Publishing was strengthened in 1957 when a substantial interest was taken in Financial News Ltd., which in turn owned a large interest in the *Financial Times* and a small range of quality periodicals. In 1960, the last of the overseas electricity utilities was disposed of when the business of Athens Piraeus Electricity Company, which had operated under a concession granted in 1925, was sold to the Greek state, although a smaller trolley bus operation in Athens was retained until about 1970. In the manufacturing industry, a substantial interest in Acton Bolt Ltd., makers of nuts and bolts, was sold to GKN Ltd. in 1959, and another in Saunders-Roe Ltd., builder of helicopters, was sold to Westland Aircraft Company Ltd. in 1959.

In 1969, for tax and fiscal reasons, the business was converted into a quoted company and 20 percent of the equity was sold to the public. The company was then valued at £20 million, and profits before tax, attributable to shareholders, totaled almost £7 million. About 25 percent of profits came from financial services which largely consisted of Lazard Brothers & Co. Ltd., which was now almost fully owned by Pearson and Whitehall Securities Corporation, which provided services to the group. An additional 30 percent of profits were generated from a 51 percent holding in the publicly quoted S Pearson Publishers Ltd., owner of the *Financial Times;* Westminster Press Ltd., controller of about 60 local and provincial newspapers; and the Longman Group Ltd., a general publishing house. Oil interests in North America, which were reorganized at the end of the 1960s, provided about 20 percent of profits. Manufacturing, where the chief asset was a 59 percent interest in Standard Industrial Group Ltd., another publicly quoted company, included interests in pottery, glass, engineering, and warehousing. This contributed about 7 percent of profits. Finally, 15 percent of profits were contributed by investment trusts.

In the 1970s, the North American interests of Pearson were mostly represented by the holding in Ashland Oil, held by Midhurst Corporation. This holding was slowly reduced and the proceeds used to acquire other North American interests, especially in oil exploration and production services, as part of an effort to extend Pearson's interests outside the United Kingdom and into North America. The most significant move was the acquisition of Camco Inc., supplier of services and equipment to the oil industry on a worldwide basis, in which a controlling interest had been purchased by 1979. This business was subsequently built up by acquisition. Lignum Oil Co. and Hillin Oil, involved in the acquisition and development of oil producing properties, were also acquired, but were sold in 1989 as part of a divestment of oil exploration activities which also included the sale of Whitehall Petroleum.

Financial services remained grouped around the merchant bank of Lazard Brothers in which Pearson, in 1990, had a 50 percent interest, reduced from 79 percent. This decrease followed an ownership reorganization in 1984 when, as an early response to increasing internationalization of the securities industry, Lazard of London and two other Lazard houses, in Paris and New York, became more closely linked. An exchange of ownership interests resulted in Pearson having a 10 percent profit interest in both these houses. Notwithstanding the acquisition in 1976 of the unowned part of Embankment Trust Ltd., investment trust and other portfolio-type investments were decreased in order to fund acquisitions.

At the time, Pearson's interests in manufacturing were concentrated in the Doulton fine china business, which emerged as a world leader with a strong overseas distribution network. The engineering interests were strengthened in 1980 by the acquisition of the high technology businesses of Fairey Industries Ltd., and their merging with Pearson's other engineering interests in 1982. However, these relatively minor activities were disposed of in 1986 as part of group policy to focus more on core activities. Similarly, involvement in the manufacture of specialist glass, which had expanded rapidly in the 1970s, was terminated in 1982 with the sale of Doulton Glass Industries Ltd.

The minority interest in Pearson Longman Ltd. was acquired in 1982. Publishing, the division of Pearson with the highest proportion of profits, embraced financial publications that included not just the *Financial Times,* the world's leading financial newspaper, but also a host of important financial periodicals, including the *Economist,* in which Pearson had a 50 percent interest, and the *Investor's Chronicle,* as well as online electronic publications. Longman by acquisition and organic expansion, emerged as a major publisher of professional, educational, medical, and general reference publications. Penguin also held a strong international position in publishing both paper- and hard-back fiction and expanded its operations through the acquisition, among others, of Viking of the United States and the Michael Joseph and Hamish Hamilton publishing houses in 1985. Westminster Press expanded into newspapers distributed free of charge and disposed of several newspapers paid for by readers, as it concentrated resources in areas where it was a clear market leader. In 1987, the acquisition of Addison Wesley of the United States, with a strong schools and college list, confirmed Pearson as a major international publishing group. The global holdings increased in 1988 by a share swap with Elsevier, a leading Dutch publishing company, and through the acquisition of the French Les Echos Group. The swap with Elsevier was undone in 1991, when the two companies were unable to devise merger terms acceptable to all parties.

One new interest, since the mid-1980s linked to the publishing division, was the expansion into daytime family entertainment. Although Pearson had owned Chessington Zoo for many years, this area was fully established through the acquisition of Madame Tussauds in 1978. Since then a number of acquisitions were made and developed, virtually all U.K.-based. Further developments in this general sector included the acquisition of a 25 percent holding in Yorkshire Television Ltd. in 1981, and a less than successful involvement, which was terminated, in filmmaking. It also gained a 16 percent share in BSkyB, the first satellite television service in the United Kingdom, in 1990.

While Pearson's shares became much more widely held, the Pearson family continued to hold a large, but not controlling, share of the equity in the late 1980s. The Third Lord Cowdray retired from the chairmanship in 1977 and was succeeded by Lord Gibson and then by Lord Blakenham in 1983, both of whom were family members. The company's name was changed to Pearson plc in 1984, and by the early 1990s, the company could claim to be one of the most successful British-based companies.

FOCUS ON MEDIA-RELATED BUSINESSES: 1990–99

Indeed, Pearson had become quite large with considerable holdings spread across many industries. In an attempt to increase profits, the company began its migration towards focusing solely on its media businesses related to information, education, and entertainment. For the remaining years of the 1990s, Pearson accelerated its acquisition and divestiture activity to mold itself into a publishing industry giant.

Pearson's purchases included Extel Financial Ltd. for £74 million in 1993, Thames Television, and Software Toolworks, renamed Mindscape, for £312 million in 1994. The company also acquired the Register Group Ltd. and Future Publishing Ltd. that year, along with Interactive Data Corporation in 1995. The firm beefed up its entertainment holdings by purchasing stakes in several television concerns along with Grundy Worldwide Ltd. and ACI. At the same time, the company sold its interest in Camco International Inc., Yorkshire Tyne-Tees TV, its 9.75 percent direct holding in BSkyB for £560 million, and Westminster Press.

Pearson added to its publishing arsenal in 1996 by acquiring HarperCollins Educational, Twenty-First Century Business Publications, and Putnam Berkeley, which was renamed Penguin Putnam Inc. The most dramatic changes, however, came in 1997 with the appointment of Marjorie Scardino as CEO. The first woman to lead a major British concern, Scardino immediately set plans in motion to increase revenue growth and bolster the firm's reputation in the media industry. She was joined by Lord Dennis Stevenson, the company's first non-family chairman, who had replaced Blakenham earlier in the year.

In an attempt to boost U.S. sales of its *Financial Times* newspaper, Pearson began heavily investing in advertising and printing, hoping to capitalize on the paper's global business coverage, coverage that its competitors lacked. The duo also stepped up the pace of the firm's restructuring program, and divested its Troll,

TVB, and Churchill Livingstone holdings in 1997. The following year it sold the famed Tussauds Group, Capitol Publishing, Future Publishing, Mindscape, and its Law and Tax publishing concerns. The company also made several key purchases, including All American Communications Inc., Resource Data International, and several newspaper concerns. The most significant acquisition, however, was that of Simon & Schuster's education, reference, and business publishing arm for $4.6 billion. The deal secured Pearson's position as the world's largest educational publisher.

In 1999, the company continued to trim its portfolio with the sale of its Lazard holdings for £410 million. It also sold its Macmillan Library and General Reference businesses, Jossey-Bass, and various other non-core holdings. It also purchased E Source Inc. and Thomson Financial Securities Management.

A NEW MILLENNIUM: 2000–03

Pearson entered the new millennium looking much different than it had just five years earlier. Scardino's strategy of streamlining company operations appeared to be paying off as revenues had doubled since 1996 and were climbing to the £4 billion mark. Operating profit had also tripled during that time period to £686 million. The company continued to make strategic purchases to complement its media holdings. In 2000, National Computer Systems Inc. was acquired for $2.5 billion and merged into its Pearson Education unit. Dorling Kindersley plc was also purchased and its operations were folded into The Penguin Group. Pearson then combined its asset valuation business with Data Broadcasting Inc. In July 2000, the company merged its television holdings with CLT-Ufa to form the RTL Group S.A. It made its final exit from television, however, when it sold its 22 percent stake in RTL to Bertelsmann AG in 2002. By that time, the company stood as a global media company with its businesses concentrated on education, business information, and consumer publishing.

While Pearson had made great strides in becoming a leading media concern, the company faced economic challenges. During 2001, the firm was forced to cut its Internet spending related to the *Financial Times* web site. The Penguin Group was also hit by an industry-wide drop-off in backlist sales. The Latin American market weakened and advertising sales in the company's publications fell dramatically. As such, profits in the Financial Times Group fell nearly 40 percent in 2001. As economic hard times continued, Pearson cut costs and revised its business strategies in order to combat the financial downturn.

Following a difficult year, Pearson continued to grow throughout the remainder of the early 2000s. In 2002 the company sold its 22 percent interest in RTL Group to Bertelsmann AG in a EUR 1.5 billion deal and added the travel and music writing publisher Rough Guides to its Penguin business. Two additional acquisitions were made in April of that year. In a deal with Netfolio Inc., the company acquired *Hulbert Financial Digest*. In addition, Pearson Education acquired Lebanon, Indiana-based DDC Publishing, which served the high school and postsecondary education markets, as well as the corporate, home, and government sectors, with computer training software.

More growth occurred in 2003. That year, Edexcel, the largest examination awarding body in the United Kingdom, was acquired. Additionally, several developments occurred within the company's Financial Times Group, which established its first Chinese-language business web site, Chinese.FT.com, and also introduced an Asian edition of the *Financial Times*. Finally, in November Pearson acquired Scholar Inc.

FOCUSED GROWTH: 2004–07

Pearson started off 2004 by striking a $101 million deal with Dow Jones & Co. for the sale of its 22 percent stake in MarketWatch. That year, the Financial Times Group continued to pursue a strategy of international growth. In addition to establishing printing operations in Sydney, Australia, a 13.85 percent ownership interest in the Indian financial newspaper *Business Standard* was secured. One final development in 2004 took place in December, when Pearson arranged for the sale of its 79 percent stake in the Spanish media enterprise Recoletos to the investment firm Retos Cartera in a EUR 743 million deal.

Despite growth within the overall Financial Times Group, the publication of the same name had struggled during the early 2000s, recording a $17 million loss in 2003, followed by a $62 million loss in 2004. On November 3, 2005, Editor Andrew Gowers resigned over strategic differences with the company, and the paper moved forward with Lionel Barber, who had served as editor in the United States, as its new head.

A number of significant developments occurred in 2005. In January the company sold its Capella Education Co. business for $62.5 million. Pearson also bolstered its special education testing and publishing business by forging a $270 million deal with WRC Media for the acquisition of AGS Publishing.

Pearson kicked off 2006 by strengthening its Pearson VUE professional testing business. This was accomplished via a $42 million cash deal with Houghton

Mifflin for Bala Cynwyd, Pennsylvania-based Promissor Inc., which provided state and federal regulatory bodies with licensing exams. In September, Pearson acquired the New York– and London-based financial information company Mergermarket Ltd.

Pearson continued to make key acquisitions as the company headed into the later years of the first decade of the 2000s. In a $950 million deal with Reed Elsevier, the company agreed to acquire both Harcourt Assessment and Harcourt Education International in 2007. In addition, Pearson Education acquired the online educational services business eCollege for $477 million.

In addition to acquisitions, 2007 also included several key divestitures. Early in the year, the company sold its Pearson Government Solutions business to Veritas Capital. In December, Pearson agreed to sell its Les Echos SA business to the luxury goods company LVMH for 240 million. The sale included leading French economic newspaper *les Echos,* as well as the economic magazine *Enjeux.*

INTERNATIONAL DEVELOPMENTS: 2008–09

Pearson proceeded to divest more of its operations in 2008. In January, the company agreed to sell a 50 percent interest in Financial Times Deutschland to Gruner + Jahr AG. The following month, Pearson agreed to sell several tests, including the Harcourt Behavior Assessment System and the Pearson Oral and Written Language Scale, in order to meet U.S. Department of Justice requirements surrounding the acquisition of Harcourt Assessment. It also was in February that M & F Worldwide Corp. acquired Pearson's Data Management operation in a deal worth $225 million.

On the growth side, 2008 included the acquisition of Money-Media in January. In addition, Pearson revealed plans to introduce a daily business newspaper in India. The new publication was planned through an alliance with Network 18 Media and Investments Ltd.

In March 2009, the *Financial Times* introduced *China Confidential,* a fortnightly, subscription-based digital newsletter devoted to Chinese investment intelligence. The publication, which included a related web site, focused on consumer trends, as well as political and economic issues in China.

Pearson approached the 21st century's second decade on solid footing. The company had successfully transformed itself into a leading media enterprise. After defining its focus in the areas of education, business

information, and consumer publishing, the company had experienced significant growth in each.

John Orbell
Updated, Christina M. Stansell; Paul R. Greenland

PRINCIPAL SUBSIDIARIES

Dorling Kindersley Holdings Ltd.; Edexcel Ltd.; Interactive Data Corporation (U.S.A.; 62%); Mergermarket Ltd.; NCS Pearson Inc. (USA); Pearson Education Inc. (USA); Pearson Education Ltd.; Penguin Group (USA) Inc.; The Economist Newspaper Ltd. (50%); The Financial Times Ltd.; The Penguin Publishing Co. Ltd.

PRINCIPAL SUBSIDIARIES

Operating Units: Pearson Education; The Penguin Group; The Financial Times Group.

PRINCIPAL COMPETITORS

Editis; News Corp.; Random House Inc.

FURTHER READING

Colby, Laura, "Yankee Expansionist Builds British Empire," *Fortune,* March 16, 1998, p. 102.

Jeffrey, Don, "All American Acquired by Pearson," *Billboard,* October 11, 1997, p. 96.

Milliot, Jim, "Acquisitions Boost Pearson Book Sales to $1.5 Billion," *Publishers Weekly,* April 28, 1997, p. 11.

Morais, Richard C., "The U.S. Is a Very Noisy Place," *Forbes,* June 16, 1997, p. 54.

Patrick, Margot, "Pearson to Pay $477 Million for Education Site eCollege," *Wall Street Journal Europe,* May 15, 2007.

"Pearson Is Slashing Its Spending on the *Financial Times* Web Site," *Marketing,* March 15, 2001, p. 2.

"Pearson Plc Issues Trading Update," *Business Wire,* December 18, 2001.

Reed, Stanley, "The Red Ink at Pearson's Pink Paper; The *Financial Times* Has Been Losing Money, Circulation, and Prestige. Now It Has Lost Its Editor As Well," *Business Week Online,* November 4, 2005.

Spender, J. A., *Weetman Pearson. First Viscount Cowdray,* London: Cassell & Co. Ltd., 1930.

"Weetman Dickson Pearson. 1st Viscount Cowdray," *Dictionary of Business Biography: A Biographical Dictionary of Business Leaders Active in Britain in the Period, 1860–1980,* Vol. IV, edited by David Jeremy, London: Butterworth & Co. Ltd., 1985.

Young, Desmond, *Member for Mexico. A Biography of Weetman Pearson, First Viscount Cowdray,* London: Cassell & Co., Ltd., 1966.

PODS Enterprises Inc.

5585 Rio Vista Drive
Clearwater, Florida 33760
U.S.A.
Telephone: (727) 538-6300
Toll Free: (866) 220-4120
Web site: http://www.pods.com

Private Company
Incorporated: 1998
Employees: 1,200
Sales: $340 million (2007 est.)
NAICS: 493190 Other Warehousing and Storage

∎ ∎ ∎

PODS Enterprises Inc. has more than 130,000 steel-frame containers in service throughout a network of franchises located in the United States, Canada, and Australia. PODS uses its unique hydraulic lift system, PODZILLA, to minimize the shifting of containers' contents while transporting them to storage or to a client's new location. Atlanta-based Arcapita, an investment firm and affiliate of Bahrain's Arcapita Bank, purchased the company in 2008.

AN INNOVATOR IN STORAGE AND MOVING CONCEPTS: 1998–2004

Peter Warhurst, a former firefighter, started PODS (Portable On-Demand Storage) Enterprises in the Tampa Bay area of Florida in 1998. After selling his EAI Systems, a dispatch software provider, Warhurst decided to invest in mini-storage. He already owned one storage site when, while out looking for a second site, he got the idea for mobile storage containers from his colleague who pondered out loud the possibility of bringing storage units to people. "With that comment," recalled Warhurst in a 2007 *Business Review* article, "we stopped looking for a piece of property."

The team instead invested in portable on-demand storage containers, PODS, that were eight feet high and eight feet wide and came in two lengths, 16 feet and 12 feet. "We really thought we'd have 100 to 200 boxes as an adjunct to our fixed-base business," explained Warhurst, but instead the concept took off, revolutionizing the moving and storage industry, and growing Warhurst's new business 100 percent a year.

Before PODS, people could move themselves in rented moving trucks or hire a moving company. When it came to storing their possessions temporarily or long-term, they could rent a storage unit close to home. With PODS sturdy, wind- and weather-resistant containers, capable of withstanding gusts up to 110 miles per hour, they could park a storage unit outside a home or office, transport it to a secure PODS warehouse, or ship it from state to state.

The company's success lay in the versatility of the container itself, according to Warhurst. As the company grew, customers invented new ways to use the PODS that Warhurst had never imagined. For example, PODS worked with several military bases and government office buildings "to facilitate and expedite renovations," as described by Warhurst in a 2007 *Business Review* article. "Using PODS mitigate[d] the disruptions to military and government personnel, eliminating the need for them to rent a truck and move their items during renovations." Additionally, the company began to play a role in the government's disaster relief and emergency preparedness plans at the local, state, and federal levels.

MORE CONTAINERS IN MORE CITIES AND COUNTRIES: 2004–06

In 2004 and 2005, another use for PODS emerged. The PODS Rapid Response Team collaborated with municipalities in Florida after the state experienced a series of especially extreme hurricanes. During these storms, PODS shipped thousands of containers, mostly for storage and salvage, but some desperate survivors took up temporary residence in PODS containers.

The company continued to grow significantly throughout 2006, causing management to modify and add to PODS' existing infrastructure. In May, the company logged its 500,000th customer reservation and manufactured its 100,000th container. PODS also launched its new "urban model" container with a side door in Chicago, Illinois, in 2006 to accommodate customers in high-traffic markets with limited delivery space.

By midyear, PODS itself was on the move, expanding into Toronto, Canada, in August and into Sydney, Australia, in November (where the company established a manufacturing facility as well as a call center and satellite office). Its sales for the year reached $200 million. Before the end of the year, there were also locations in Adelaide, Brisbane/Gold Coast, and Newcastle. At the end of the year, the company had in the vicinity of 110,000 containers in 46 states and provinces, and was sending out 25,000 containers each month. It had played a role in more than 87,000 inter-franchise moves.

As the company continued to grow, management put its energy into further developing its infrastructure, investing money mid-decade into a global positioning system that allowed it to track its drivers. In addition, it engineered and then contracted for the manufacture of $150 million worth of fold-down containers in 2006. The new units, which folded down to 18 inches tall, were as strong and durable as the original containers and could be stacked 18 high on a single trailer, thereby increasing the company's efficiency. In January 2007, PODS opened a manufacturing facility in Tennessee for making the fold-down containers.

NEW DIRECTIONS, PORTABLE ON DEMAND SHELTER: 2007

By 2007, PODS' manufacturing facilities were capable of producing a container every three minutes. Midyear, the company added its Value Added Reseller Program, which targeted household movers and self-storage operations. Program participants, business owners themselves, had the option of offering PODS for domestic moves. PODS also began plans for offering shipment of large items, domestically and internationally, and opened its second Canadian office in Vancouver.

Also in 2007, PODS launched its Portable On Demand *Shelter* as a low-cost response to the need for temporary housing. This idea was developed by the PODS Rapid Response service team, whose members functioned as first responders. Eight- by eight- by 16-foot PODS containers were decked out with an efficiency kitchen with stovetop, microwave, and refrigerator; toilet and shower; table and beds for five; and seating areas with television to serve as temporary housing. The company marketed these units as "the perfect solution for individuals in need of temporary shelter and for those companies and agencies committed to meeting the needs of their customers and employees in need of emergency or temporary shelter" in a 2007 *Canada NewsWire.*

The units, which cost $10,000 to $13,000 to build, were outfitted by Warsaw, Indiana-based R-Vision, a motor home manufacturer; they could be delivered on the back of a truck. PODS began talking to the Federal Emergency Management Agency and Florida emergency management officials about ordering the temporary shelters that PODS stored in its warehouses and would deploy as needed. For Warhurst, as quoted in the 2007 *Tampa Tribune,* the shelters went "all the way back to my roots: I was a firefighter, a paramedic. I want us to be a community partner."

THE SEARCH FOR A BUYER: 2007–08

Not everyone was happy with PODS, however. Increasingly, homeowners and municipal officials protested the

KEY DATES

1998: Warhurst founds PODS Enterprises.
2006: PODS expands into Canada and Australia.
2007: The company introduces the Portable On Demand Shelter.
2008: Arcapita purchases PODS Enterprises; Tom Ryan replaces Warhurst as company president and chief executive officer; the company introduces a reduced-size container.

spread of the containers as unsightly and a parking impediment. Local businesses, especially storage businesses, objected to them because PODS was not paying taxes to the counties in which it did business, yet benefited from the billboards emblazoned on its containers' sides.

Another challenge the company faced increasingly as it grew was in keeping all franchisees focused on the same goals and vision and getting them to buy into a company identity. As interviewed in the 2007 *Tampa Tribune,* Warhurst acknowledged that, while he could require conformity, he would "rather sell them on the concept, get them to see how [companies such as] UPS and FedEx have a single image," and how it would benefit PODS to do the same.

Warhurst also confessed to having difficulty motivating his franchisees to grow. "They sometimes get to the point where their warehouse is full, and they need to get the next warehouse and 300 to 400 new PODS. If they don't and they want to grow revenue, they'll have to raise prices, and that opens the door for competition."

SLOWER GROWTH IN A DECLINING HOUSING MARKET: 2008

In fact, growth slowed overall due in large part to the decline in the housing market, and competition was on the upswing. PODS held its own among its rivals, upgrading its web site to expedite reservations and to prepare for its push into the e-commerce market in 2008. The idea was that, with PODS at their disposal, people would be encouraged to sell larger items online and then use PODS to ship them.

PODS faced the challenge of educating consumers about its containers' varied uses through targeted mailings and television ads. Several seasonal stores started

working with PODS as a means of storing their goods for sale cheaply during the nine months of the year when they remained closed. In addition, PODS began to deliver containers to restaurants, such as Wendy's and McDonald's, to hold furniture and restaurant equipment during remodels.

PODS had more than 100 franchises and about 128,000 pods in service in the United States, Canada, and Australia and revenues of $350 million in 2007. Warhurst stepped down in 2008, after selling PODS to Arcapita, the U.S. arm of Bahrain-based Arcapita Bank, a Middle East firm that invests in compliance with Islamic law. The decision to sell PODS was a well-planned one; in 2007, PODS had hired Morgan Stanley to seek buyers, having decided against going public in order to give its early investors the opportunity to recoup their investment.

As Tom Ryan took over as president and chief executive officer of PODS, Warhurst remained confident that his company would achieve its goal of becoming an international business. Ever expanding and still the industry leader, the company introduced a smaller, seven- by seven- by 12-foot container in 2008 and made plans to offer personal movers to assist homeowners in packing their goods and loading their container.

Carrie Rothburd

PRINCIPAL COMPETITORS

Door to Door Storage, Inc.; Smart Move, Inc.; Uni-Group, Inc.; 1-800-PACK-RATS; Box Cart; Mobile Mini Inc.

FURTHER READING

Baschuk, Bryce, "Invasion of the POD People: Fairfax Firms, Homeowners Try to Contain Storage Trend," *Washington Times,* February 22, 2007, p. C9.

Dorich, Alan, "Leading Alternative: After Achieving a Leadership Position in Its Industry, PODS Enterprises Inc. Is Looking Forward to Expanding Its Services into More Regions," *U.S. Business Review,* January 1, 2007, p. 56.

"Executives of the Year: Editor's Choice," *U.S. Business Review,* December 1, 2007, p. 5.

Mullins, Richard, "Buyout in Works, Not Done, PODS Says," *Tampa Tribune,* December 6, 2007, p. 1.

———, "PODS Looks to Expand Business," *Tampa Tribune,* September 27, 2007, p. 1.

"PODS Enterprises Inc. Introduces a New Concept in Temporary Housing," *Canada NewsWire,* July 11, 2007, p. 1.

Simanoff, Dave, "PODS," *Tampa Tribune,* July 26, 2007, p. 1.

Stacy, Mitch, "PODS People Planning on People PODS," *Connecticut Post,* July 25, 2007.

Praktiker Bau- und Heim-
werkermärkte AG

Am Tannenwald 2
Kirkel, D-66459
Germany
Telephone: (+49 06849) 95 00
Fax: (+49 06849) 95 22
Web site: http://www.praktiker.de

Public Company
Incorporated: 1978
Employees: 29,000
Sales: EUR 3.91 billion ($4.89 billion) (2008)
Stock Exchanges: Frankfurt
Ticker Symbol: PRA
NAICS: 444190 Other Building Material Dealers;
    444120 Paint and Wallpaper Stores; 444130
    Hardware Stores

∎ ∎ ∎

Praktiker Bau- und Heimwerkermärkte AG is
Germany's second largest do-it-yourself (DIY) retail
operator and one of the leading players in the East
European DIY market. Based in Kirkel, Praktiker operates more than 420 stores in Germany and elsewhere.
Germany remains the company's primary market,
covered by nearly 340 stores. Most of these trade under
the Praktiker signage; since 2007 the company's German operations have also included 76 stores under the
Max Bahr name. The German operations include an
expanded retail format, extra Bau + Hobby, present in
19 stores by the end of 2008. The group's international
operations include Luxembourg, where it trades under

the Bâtiself name, and Albania, Bulgaria, Greece,
Hungary, Poland, Romania, Turkey, and Ukraine. The
company ranks first or second in nearly all of these
markets, with the exception of Poland, where the group
claims the fourth place position. Praktiker is also ranked
fourth in the overall European DIY market. Altogether,
the company operated 100 international stores at the
beginning of 2009. International sales represented nearly
32 percent of the group's revenues of EUR 3.9 billion
($4.9 billion) in 2008. The group's international opera-
tions are also its strongest area of growth, posting
revenue gains of more than 14.5 percent, as opposed to
a 6.9 percent drop in the company's German revenues.
Formerly part of the giant Metro retail group, Praktiker
was spun off in a public offering on the Frankfurt Stock
Exchange in 2005. Wolfgang Werner is the company's
chairman and CEO.

SUPERMARKET EXTENSION IN
1978

Praktiker Bau- und Heimwerkermärkte was created in
the late 1970s as an offshoot of the German
supermarket group Asko Deutsche Kaufhaus AG, based
in Saarbrücken. The Praktiker format enabled Asko to
extend its own range of operations from a focus on
supermarket retail to include the relatively new and fast-
growing DIY sector. Although traditional hardware
stores had long been in operation throughout Germany,
the DIY format offered extended product ranges, often
with a focus on interior decoration. In this way the
larger DIY stores provided a one-stop shopping experience for the home improvement hobbyist.

Although Germany was to remain the primary market for Asko's Praktiker format, the company actually tested the DIY waters in Luxembourg. For that market, the company created the Bâtiself retail format, opening its first store there in 1978. This store was also Luxembourg's first specialized DIY store.

By 1979 Asko had refined its DIY concept for the German market as well, and rolled out its first four stores under the Praktiker signage. The company took advantage of its parent's strong retail presence and launched a rapid expansion strategy. For this, the company combined new store openings and the acquisition of existing stores. In 1979, for example, the company acquired the nine-store chain of BayWa home improvement centers.

Praktiker's sales built quickly and by 1980 the company passed the DEM 100 million mark. Yet into the early years of the decade, the company found itself confronted with a surge in competition in the DIY market. Nevertheless, the company recognized an opportunity to distinguish itself by narrowing its focus to the discount sales segment. This change of strategy was carried out in 1982.

MOVING TO EASTERN GERMANY IN THE NINETIES

Asko's own acquisitive growth strategy provided much of the fuel for Praktiker's expansion through the 1980s and into the 1990s. In 1985 the company added 12 former Wickes stores to its portfolio, boosting its payroll past 1,000 employees for the first time. Accompanied by the group's own new store openings, the acquisition allowed the company to expand its total sales surface area to 100,000 square meters by 1986. By 1987 Praktiker's sales had topped DEM 500 million.

Praktiker continued to add new stores through the end of the decade. By 1988 the company's total network had reached 50 stores. This expansion also led to a doubling of the company's workforce by the end of the decade. By the 1990s Praktiker claimed the leadership of the western German DIY sector. The company's strong growth also provided it with significant purchasing power, particularly as it sought to maintain its reputation as a DIY discounter.

Parent company Asko provided it with a new boost in 1990 when Praktiker took over the purchasing and procurement operations for all hardware and home improvement needs for the entire Asko retail group. This move also included the integration of the operations of another Asko-controlled DIY retail chain, real-kauf, in 1990. By the end of that year, Praktiker's revenues had topped DEM 1 billion for the first time.

The toppling of the Berlin Wall and the subsequent reunification of Germany at the beginning of the decade presented a new growth opportunity for Praktiker. By 1991 the company had launched its first stores in the former East Germany, where decades of Communist rule had left the country's retail sector largely undeveloped.

Nonetheless, the opening of the former East Germany market was not enough to ensure Praktiker's long-term growth. The newly reunified country was struggling through a deep recession, resulting in a drop in consumer spending. At the same time, Praktiker was confronted with the reality of an increasingly mature DIY retail market. Indeed, by the middle of the 1990s, the German DIY sector was showing signs of reaching saturation.

PUBLIC OFFERING IN 1995

Consolidation offered one growth outlet for the company, as the group reinforced its position among the leaders in the German DIY market. Parent company Asko once again provided a boost to the group's strategy. In 1992 Praktiker acquired the real-kauf DIY chain outright. At the same time, the company bought out another Asko home improvement format, Extra.

Asko's own acquisition drive provided further expansion for Praktiker, as the supermarket group turned over the DIY operations of its acquisitions to Praktiker. In 1993, for example, Praktiker acquired 29 new stores from Asko, including 11 Massa stores, as well as stores under the Huma, BLV, and MHB signages. The expansion of the group's retail network provided a new boost for its revenues, which neared DEM 3.75 billion by the end of 1994. This growth allowed Praktiker to claim, if only temporarily, the position of Europe's largest DIY retail group in terms of turnover.

Praktiker's expansion plans into the middle of the decade ran into a significant hurdle. The lingering recession and the uncertain retail market in Germany had caused German banks to become reluctant to finance the company's further expansion. As a result, Asko

```
┌─────────────────────────────────────────────┐
│                                               │
│              KEY DATES                        │
│                  ■                            │
│  ─────────────────────────────────────────   │
│                                               │
│  1978:  German supermarket group Asko Deutsche│
│         Kaufhaus opens its first do-it-yourself retail │
│         store in Luxembourg, then opens a chain of │
│         Praktiker stores in Germany.          │
│  1991:  Praktiker expands into former East Germany │
│         market, and opens its first store in Greece. │
│  1995:  Company is listed on the Frankfurt Stock │
│         Exchange.                             │
│  2002:  Metro AG acquires 100 percent control of │
│         Praktiker.                            │
│  2005:  Metro lists 60 percent of Praktiker's shares on │
│         the Frankfurt Stock Exchange.         │
│  2008:  In its latest international expansion, Praktiker │
│         opens its first store in Albania.     │
│                                               │
└─────────────────────────────────────────────┘
```

decided to raise capital through a partial public listing of Praktiker's shares. The company completed its initial public offering (IPO) on the Frankfurt exchange in 1995.

Soon after, Praktiker found itself with a new majority shareholder, Metro AG, which became Germany's leading supermarket following the merger of Asko and Metro Cash & Carry in 1995. Following the merger, Praktiker took over 27 Bauspar stores, which had previously been acquired by Asko from the Spar supermarket group. The Bauspar stores were integrated into Praktiker in 1996.

Praktiker's future growth in the German market nonetheless remained limited by the maturity of the market and by the presence of other major chains, including perennial rival OBI and smaller rival Rewe. In the early 1990s Praktiker had already taken the first step in the development of a new strategy to ensure its potential for further growth.

INTERNATIONAL GROWTH IN THE LATE NINETIES

Luxembourg had remained Praktiker's sole foreign market through the 1980s. Yet foreign expansion provided the greatest potential for future growth for the company. This potential had become all the more evident as the Central and Eastern European markets began to emerge from the shock of transitioning to free-market economies in the early 1990s. Nonetheless, for its first new move into the international market, Praktiker turned to another developing European market,

Greece. The company opened its first store in Greece in 1991. The following year, Praktiker expanded its presence there, buying three more stores, operating under the Esbella, Extra, and Continent names. The company raised its Greek network to six, with the opening of two more stores in 1995. By the dawn of the 21st century, Praktiker had become the dominant DIY player in Greece, ultimately expanding its network there to ten stores by 2009.

Praktiker's foreign expansion effort turned to new markets in the mid-1990s. Austria appeared a natural candidate for Praktiker's extension, as it shared a border with Germany. The company opened its first store in Austria in 1996 and by the end of 1997 operated four stores there. Yet Austria's DIY scene was already dominated by two large players, limiting Praktiker's own growth potential there.

Instead, the company looked eastward, setting up its first store in Poland in 1997. This market became the country's largest international market. By the later years of the first decade of the 2000s, the company's Polish network had grown to 20 stores. Success in Poland led the company into Hungary in 1998, which also became a significant foreign market for the company. In that same year Praktiker expanded into Turkey as well.

CHANGING STRATEGY

Back at home, meanwhile, Praktiker had begun to rethink its discount strategy. For much of its first two decades, the company had competed largely on price. Through much of the first half of the 1990s, the DIY sector had been somewhat protected from the lingering German recession, in part because reunification had created a building boom. When that slowed into the middle of the decade, Praktiker's competitors began competing on price as well. As a result, Praktiker lost its reputation as a low-cost DIY retailer, and by the end of the decade had lost its leadership in the sector to OBI, owned by the Tengelmann retail group.

With much of the DIY sector competing on price, Praktiker's new strategy therefore focused on providing added services. In order to reinforce this strategy, the company took over the 60-store DIY chain Wirichs in 1997. The takeover not only expanded Praktiker's network, as well as adding nearly DEM 1 billion to its turnover, it also brought Wirichs's own strong reputation for the quality of its sales service.

The Wirichs acquisition became part of a new consolidation wave in Germany's DIY market. Praktiker played its part in the trend, buying 25 franchised stores that had been operating under the Extra signage in 1998. In 2000 the company bought 27 Top-Bau stores.

By 2002 the group's total German network neared 300 stores, while its international operations reached more than 50 stores. The foreign operations included the company's first stores in Romania, added in 2002.

The service-oriented strategy fell short of Praktiker's goals, however, and led to a management and shareholder shakeup. Metro moved to buy out the company's minority shareholders, raising its own holding to 99 percent in 1999. By 2002 Metro had completed a "squeeze out" of the remaining shareholders, gaining 100 percent control. The company's new management team refocused the company around a low-price strategy.

When this effort proved unsatisfactory, however, Metro announced its interest in selling the Praktiker chain in 2003. Unable to find a buyer, Metro instead decided to spin off Praktiker as a public company. As such, Praktiker completed a new public offering, as Metro placed 60 percent of the company's shares on the Frankfurt exchange in 2005.

INTERNATIONAL OPPORTUNITIES FUEL GROWTH FOR THE FUTURE

Praktiker continued to seek growth opportunities for its German operations through the first decade of the 2000s. A new boost for the company came in 2006, when it acquired the 76-strong chain of Max Bahr home improvement centers. Founded in the late 1870s, Max Bahr also enabled Praktiker to extend its operations into the high-end DIY segment for the first time, while maintaining its focus on the low-price channel.

With future large-scale acquisition prospects limited in Germany, however, Praktiker's greatest long-term growth potential lay in its continued foreign expansion. The company added a new market, Bulgaria, in 2004. The company quickly expanded its network there, to four stores by the end of 2005. This was enough to give the group the number two position in the Bulgarian market. At the same time, the company had boosted its market position to the leading spot in Greece, Hungary, Luxembourg, and Turkey.

In 2007 Praktiker targeted a new foreign market, adding its first store in Ukraine that year, beating out rival OBI. Praktiker then announced plans to open three to five stores per year in that country, with plans to expand its Ukrainian network to as many as 25 stores into the next decade. In the meantime, the company's foreign expansion included another new market, as it opened its first store in Albania in 2008.

Praktiker's foreign expansion helped buffer its balance sheet amid the broad economic crisis at the end of

2008. Although the company's turnover in Germany shrank by nearly 7 percent, the group's foreign operations grew more than 14 percent. In this way, Praktiker limited the drop in its overall revenues to just 1 percent for the year. Like the rest of the European retail sector, Praktiker braced itself for the new economic crisis, hoping its 30-year history as a leading DIY retailer remained a strong foundation for future success.

M. L. Cohen

PRINCIPAL SUBSIDIARIES

Bâtiself S.A. (Luxembourg; 62%); BMH Baumarkt Holding GmbH; KIG GmbH; Küchen DIY Vertriebs-GmbH; Max Bahr Holzhandlung Baumarkt GmbH; Max Bahr Holzhandlung GmbH & Co. KG; Max der kleine Baumarkt GmbH; Praktiker Albanien Sh.p.k.; Praktiker Baumärkte GmbH; Praktiker EOOD (Bulgaria); Praktiker GmbH; Praktiker Group Buying HK Ltd. (China); Praktiker HELLAS A.E. (Greece); Praktiker International AG (Switzerland; 99.99%); Praktiker Polska Sp. z o.o. (Poland); Praktiker Romania S.R. L.; Praktiker Services GmbH; Praktiker Ukraine TOV; Praktiker Ungarn Kft. (Hungary); Praktiker Yapi Marketleri A.S. (Turkey).

PRINCIPAL DIVISIONS

Category Management; Distribution Germany; extra Bau + Hobby; International Business and Internationalisation; Location Management Germany; Marketing; Max Bahr; Personnel; Product Controlling.

PRINCIPAL COMPETITORS

The Home Depot, Inc.; The Lowe's Companies, Inc.; Wolseley plc; Kingfisher plc; Partidis S.A.S.; AGRAVIS Raiffeisen AG; B&Q PLC; Castorama France SASU; toom BauMarkt GmbH.

FURTHER READING

"DIY Retailer Praktiker Opens First Ukrainian Store," *Economist Intelligence Unit,* December 12, 2007.

"Germany DIY Chain Praktiker's Hungarian Unit Opens New Store in HUF 1.6 Bln Project," *Hungary Business News,* September 27, 2007.

"German DIY Retailer Makes Bid," *Home Channel News News-Fax,* May 21, 2007, p. 1.

"Germany's Praktiker Will Open at Least Two Hypermarkets in Ukraine by 2010," *Russia & CIS Business and Financial Newswire,* January 19, 2009.

"Metro Sells Out of Praktiker After Shares Gain 50% Since IPO," *Euroweek,* April 13, 2006, p. 24.

"Metro to Spin Off DIY Stores in Hot German Market," *Euro Property,* October 1, 2005.

"Praktiker IPO Plays on CEE Growth Story," *Euroweek,* November 11, 2005, p. 31.

Wiesmann, Gerrit, "Praktiker Store Chain Eyes M-Dax," *Financial Times,* November 23, 2005, p. 28.

Preferred Hotel Group

———— ■ ————

311 South Wacker Drive, Suite 1900
Chicago, Illinois 60606-6676
U.S.A.
Telephone: (312) 913-0400
Fax: (312) 913-0444
Web site: http://www.preferredhotelgroup.com

Private Company
Incorporated: 1998
Employees: 100
Sales: $7.4 million (2007 est.)
NAICS: 813910 Business Associations

■ ■ ■

Preferred Hotel Group ranks among industry leaders as a provider of technology, business solutions, and sales support for independent high-end hotels. More than 625 hotels and resorts across the globe are listed under Preferred Hotel Group's five brand names: Preferred Hotels & Resorts, Preferred Boutique, Summit Hotels & Resorts, Sterling Hotels, and Historic Hotels of America. The affiliation provides smaller operations with the clout to compete with larger chains while maintaining a distinctive identity. Preferred Hotel Group receives a percentage of room revenue and other fees for its back-of-room services. In 2007 the company expanded beyond its role as a hospitality industry service provider when it entered the luxury real estate market.

MAKING CONNECTIONS: 1968–92

Seeds for the Preferred Hotel Group were planted in 1968 when six independent hoteliers established a representation and referral organization. Their effort targeted hotels with "similar services and top-quality standards," the company's web site recounted. Preferred Hotels and Resorts Worldwide added reservations, sales, and marketing services during the 1980s.

Business as usual changed for the hotel industry in the 1990s, providing dangers as well as opportunities. The debt-financed building frenzy of the previous decade collapsed in on itself when the economy declined. U.S. hotels lost $5.7 billion in 1990, according to *Business Week Online*.

The recession drove industry consolidation and spurred the introduction of new technology and business practices. Large, deep-pocketed chains forced smaller independent operations to move beyond the traditional trade group concept of referrals, social networking, and limited group buying to remain competitive. Preferred offered an alternative to selling out, franchising, or, in the worse case, going under.

In 1992 approximately 65 percent of Preferred Hotels & Resorts' members were in the United States, 20 percent in Central Europe, and 10 percent in the Asia/Pacific region, according to *Travel Weekly*. Hoping to increase membership by 15 percent a year, the company looked toward the Mideast, Africa, northern Europe, and the Mediterranean. Domestically, Houston, Atlanta, and Chicago were on the short list.

COMPANY PERSPECTIVES

Preferred Hotel Group is a global leader in the hospitality industry. This creative, cutting-edge company is designed for a new era in travel—an era in which travelers embrace the individuality of distinctive hotels and resorts—yet desire a consistent commitment to excellence. The five renowned brands of Preferred Hotel Group represent a collection of the finest hotels and resorts in the world.

CASE MADE: 1994–2000

Peter Cass joined Preferred Hotels & Resorts in 1994, bringing airline, travel, and marketing experience. He established a return-on-investment program, showing member hotels how commissions and fees translated into revenue.

In 1998 the organization switched from an Illinois-based nonprofit to a Delaware-based C Corporation. Members of the association received stock. The ownership structure created a "stronger commitment to the enterprise," Cass said in *Business Week Online.* Preferred Hotels & Resorts also needed a way to "finance the future." He anticipated significant expenditures in major technology and expanded sales and marketing.

Preferred Hotels & Resorts created a holding company in 2000 to serve as an umbrella organization for multiple brands of independent hotels and resorts. Shareholders traded their stock for shares in IndeCorp Corporation. President and CEO Peter Cass said, in a 2000 *Business Wire* release, the new model served as a "protector of independent hotels—adding resources by sharing overhead, administrative and technology costs, while preserving and reinforcing the strengths, culture and qualities of the individual brands and their independent member hotels."

For the fiscal year ending June 30, 2000, Preferred Hotels & Resorts reported that it generated in excess of $100 million in revenue for more than 110 independent luxury properties across the world. The Chicago-based company had sales offices in New York, Los Angeles, San Francisco, London, Paris, Milan, and Frankfurt.

BRANDS BROADENED: 2001

IndeCorp bought Summit Hotels & Resorts and Sterling Hotels & Resorts from Pegasus Solutions for $12 million, *Hotel & Motel Management* reported in March 2001. Summit, found in more than 125 city centers and resort destinations, consisted of 167 upper-upscale independently owned hotels. Sterling, a reservations and representation operation, served 141 independent upper-upscale hotels in key business and resort destinations. Both operated worldwide and provided sales and marketing resources to the independent properties.

The purchase boosted the number of properties under IndeCorp to 418. The two new brands added geographic and market diversity. Sterling was strong in North America while Summit was strong in Europe and South America. Both had a presence in Asia. Moreover, Sterling targeted meeting planners and travel agents.

Although IndeCorp did not own or manage the properties, it did manage the brand. Hotels and resorts were expected to "adhere to a quality-assurance program that includes an annual, third-party, unannounced audit of 1,600 standards and practices," according to John P. Walsh, writing in *Hotel & Motel Management* in March 2001. Of approximately 100 groups of independent hotels in the industry, a quarter of them had brand potential of possible interest to IndeCorp.

IndeCorp moved toward the creation of a centralized web presence in May 2001, in anticipation of continuing strong growth of the online travel market. The investment company Bear Stearns had estimated 22 percent of U.S. hotel rooms were available for booking over the Internet, according to *Business Wire.*

Independents needed whatever edge they could get, holding 30 percent of the U.S. hotel industry, an 8 percent decline over the past decade. Cass claimed an 11-to-1 return on dues and fees for its independent members, an August 2001 *Business Week Online* article reported. Members paid about 1 to 1.5 percent of the hotel room revenue and received up to 35 percent of business through the independent hotel consolidator.

The 120-employee IndeCorp, though, had to contend with a drop-off in the number of business travelers. The economy had begun to slow early in the new century. Among the glitches was a technology sector meltdown.

The outlook, however, took a dramatic turn for the worse when hijacked planes slammed into the Twin Towers of the World Trade Center in New York City, the Pentagon in Washington, D.C., and a field in Pennsylvania. The terrorist attacks of September 11, 2001 (9/11), completely shut down air traffic for a time and dramatically altered future plans for many business and pleasure travelers.

KEY DATES

1968: Hoteliers join forces to establish independent operator organization.
1998: Group transforms into for-profit corporation.
2000: Holding company is created.
2001: Two hotel brands, Summit and Sterling, are acquired.
2004: John Ueberroth gains control of company.
2005: Boutique, small luxury hotel concept, is created.
2007: Historic Hotel Group becomes the fifth brand; plans are made for luxury real estate market program.

UNSETTLED TIMES: 2002–03

Hotel rates and occupancy experienced downward pressure into 2002. IndeCorp, nevertheless, prepared to launch a branded group of convention hotels. The Conference Collection would compete against big chains, which dominated the convention sector.

Moreover, convention bookings had been declining in early 2001. The 9/11 attacks worsened matters, as meetings were canceled or postponed, "leaving huge blocks of hotels' guest rooms and ballrooms empty," Christina Binkley of the *Wall Street Journal* explained in February 2002.

Primarily, independent hotels served more of the "transient travelers," who paid higher room rates but spent less on hotel food and drink, Binkley wrote. Single rooms also rang up higher administrative costs. Large chains had the advantage of worldwide sales forces and incentives to draw groups. IndeCorp planned to target meeting planners via trade magazines and the mail.

Cass departed in March 2003 after nine years with IndeCorp. The privately held, for-profit, shareholder-owned company had three brands of independent hotels on five continents, with sales offices on seven. Brand subsidiaries Preferred Hotels & Resorts Worldwide, Summit Hotels & Resorts Worldwide, and Sterling Hotels & Resorts operated more than 300 luxury independent hotels and resorts in 51 countries. In addition to sales and marketing, IndeCorp provided quality assurance, e-commerce, customer relationship management, and loyalty programs for member properties. Stepping into an interim position as head of the company was Onno Poortier, former president of the Hong Kong-based Peninsula Hotels.

IndeCorp established an Asia-Pacific headquarters in Hong Kong toward the end of 2003. The company had expanded sales efforts and was seeking new hotels. Health fears related to the SARS (severe acute respiratory syndrome) outbreak had subsided and Asian travel had begun to revive. Hotel construction underway also held the promise of new opportunities. In addition to Hong Kong, IndeCorp had branded properties in mainland China, Japan, Indonesia, Singapore, the Philippines, Thailand, and Australia.

IN EXPERIENCED HANDS: 2004

In 2004 John A. Ueberroth brought more than 30 years of travel industry experience to the helm of IndeCorp. Investing "less than $10 million," Ueberroth took control of the company, *Hotels* reported in May. "My short-term goal is to analyze everything—people, locations, offices, and everything we do," Ueberroth told Brice Adams of *Hotel & Motel Management* in May 2004. "In the long term, we want to be the best group producing in the business. We want to make sure that our brands be exactly what they stand for and be better known to consumers and trades. We will get some programs in place to make that happen."

Ueberroth, the new chairman, chief executive officer, and largest shareholder, planned to continue operating in the full-service niche, expanding the number of member hotels from 300 to 400 by the end of 2005. Board member Poortier, familiar with European as well as Asian markets, was tapped to help with brand growth.

According to *Hotel & Motel Management*, Ueberroth saw effective use of the Internet as the biggest challenge to the industry. The hospitality sector also had to contend with issues related to the economy, terrorism, and seasonal fluctuation.

Ueberroth had entered the travel industry in 1967 with Transportation Consultants International (TCI). Teaming with his brother Peter, the company was built into a large travel representation concern. When TCI acquired Ask Mr. Foster, John Ueberroth became president of the travel agency, beginning in 1971. Carlson Companies bought TCI in 1980 and Ueberroth was named president of Carlson Travel Group. A stint as chairman and CEO of Hawaiian Airlines followed, from 1990 to 1993. Ueberroth served as chairman of the Travel Industry Association of America and the U.S. Tour Operators Association, before turning his talents to IndeCorp. He resigned as cochair and board member of Ambassadors International, Inc., a travel services and performance improvement company, but continued as chairman of a spinoff company, Ambassadors Group, Inc.

ALL IN THE NAME: 2005–08

IndeCorp changed its name to Preferred Hotel Group in 2005, part of Ueberroth's drive to strengthen the brand name and further differentiate its various property groups. Ueberroth envisioned using the word *preferred* in new marketing campaigns along with an updated logo. After coming aboard, Ueberroth also implemented the restructuring of management and sales teams into North American, European, Middle Eastern, and Asia/Pacific regions and bolstered support in Central and South America. The sales force was also increased, with an emphasis put on group sales.

Around mid-year 2005 a fourth brand was unveiled. The brainchild of Lindsey Ueberroth, the daughter of John, the Boutique brand featured small luxury hotels. During 2006 the company instituted the I Prefer Global Guest Benefit program. The program offered membership benefits, such as early check-in/late checkout, and hotel specific services, such as spa deals.

Preferred Hotel Group partnered in 2007 with a nonprofit group working to save historic places in the United States. The move to license Historic Hotels of America from the National Trust for Historic Preservation created a fifth brand and added more than 200 new hotels to the portfolio. The year also marked Preferred Hotel Group's entry into the luxury real estate market. Preferred Residents was launched as a membership and exchange program for shared ownership resorts.

Interval International "expressed interest in Preferred setting luxury hotel standards for its offerings," Carlo Wolff reported in *Lodging Hospitality* in 2008. The target date for first phase completion of the resort, located 40 miles northwest of Puerto Vallarta, Mexico, was set for June 2009.

Wolff continued: "While Ueberroth acknowledges today's dicey economic situation, folding Interval into the Preferred mix should help. 'Say someone was going to sell a single ownership for $2 million,' he suggests. 'If you divide it 12 ways, at $200,000 each, it's $2.4 million, and you have to make 12 sales rather than one. But every cost is a lot less and brings it within reach. If you own a second home, whether you go there or not, you have to have upkeep. Lighten that 12 ways, it's a lot cheaper.'" Preferred Hotel Group went on to pursue other global venues for the Preferred Residents concept during 2008.

Kathleen Peippo

PRINCIPAL SUBSIDIARIES

Preferred Hotels & Resorts; Preferred Boutique; Summit Hotels & Resorts; Sterling Hotels; Historic Hotels of America.

PRINCIPAL COMPETITORS

Accor S.A.; Hilton Hotels Corporation; Marriott International, Inc.

FURTHER READING

Adams, Bruce, "New IndeCorp President Aims to Define, Grow Brands," *Hotel & Motel Management,* May 3, 2004, p. 4.

Binkley, Christina, "Managers & Managing: IndeCorp to Launch Brand of Hotels for Conventions," *Wall Street Journal* (Europe), February 25, 2002, p. A13.

Cain, Sandi, "Another Ueberroth Making Name in Hotel Business," *Orange County Business Journal,* September 18–24, 2006, pp. 4, 15.

———, "Latest Ueberroth Hotel Venture Draws in Second Generation," *Orange County Business Journal,* November 27, 2006, p. 12.

Eisen, David, "Hotelier: Ueberroth, CEO of Preferred Hotel Group," *TravelAgent,* December 4, 2006, pp. 29, 76.

"Historic Hotels of America Joins Preferred Hotel Group Brand," *Business Wire,* October 25, 2007.

"In with the Inn Crowd," *Business Week Online,* August 30, 2001.

"IndeCorp Becomes Preferred Hotel Group, Adds New Boutique 'Brand' to Stable," *Hotels,* June 2005, p. 18.

"IndeCorp Chooses K2 Digital to Build CRM and e-Commerce Services for Independent Hotel Brands," *Business Wire,* May 14, 2001.

"Preferred Aims to Expand 15% Year over Year," *Travel Weekly,* October 5, 1992, p. 23.

"Preferred Hotel Group Plans Major Expansion in India," *Asia Pulse,* September 10, 2008.

"Preferred Hotels & Resorts Worldwide Announces a Plan to Create a New Business Organization to Allow Independents to Compete Successfully Against Hotel Goliaths," *Business Wire,* August 14, 2000.

"Preferred Hotels Reverts to Original Name," *Lodging Hospitality,* June 2005, p. 15.

"Preferred Set to Axe Middle Man," *Travel Trade Gazette UK & Ireland,* November 25, 2005, p. 36.

Sternthal, Erin F., "The ABCs of Hotel Associations," *TravelAgent,* March 27, 2006, pp. 62–64.

Strauss, Karyn, "IndeCorp's New Chairman, CEO Invests in Company's Future," *Hotels,* May 2004, p. 14.

"Under Global Leadership of CEO Ueberroth, IndeCorp Moves Forward As Preferred Hotel Group with New Look, New Boutique Brand, New Direction and Increased Expansion," *Business Wire,* May 10, 2005.

"US Hotel Marketing Firm Picks HK for Asia-Pacific HQ," *Xinhau News Agency–CEIS,* October 3, 2003.

Walsh, John P., "IndeCorp Helps Independent Hotels Share Back-Office Costs," *Hotel & Motel Management,* March 5, 2001, p. 6.

Wolff, Carlo, "A Marriage of Convenience and Class," *Lodging Hospitality,* April 15, 2008, pp. 46, 48.

PT Gudang Garam Tbk

Jl. Semampir II/I
Kediri, 64121
Indonesia
Telephone: (+62 0354) 682 091
Fax: (+62 0354) 681 555
Web site: http://www.gudanggaramtbk.com

Public Company
Incorporated: 1958
Employees: 43,000
Sales: IDR 28.16 trillion ($2.55 billion) (2007)
Stock Exchanges: Jakarta
Ticker Symbol: GGRM
NAICS: 312221 Cigarette Manufacturing

■ ■ ■

PT Gudang Garam Tbk is one of Indonesia's top three producers of kretek cigarettes, a blend of tobacco, cloves, and other ingredients. One of the world's most populated countries, Indonesia also boasts one of the highest tobacco consumption rates, with as many as 65 percent of adult males counted as smokers. Gudang Garam's share of the market stood at 25 percent into 2009, down from a high of 49 percent a decade earlier. Gudang Garam manufactures traditional hand-rolled kretek cigarettes, including its earliest brand, Kretek Klobot Manis and flagship hand-rolled brand GG Merah King Size. The company workforce of more than 43,000 produces approximately eight billion "sticks" per year. Gudang Garam is also present in the machine-made cigarette category, which represents the bulk of the

company's revenues of IDR 28 trillion ($2.5 billion) per year. Brands in this category include GG Filter International Merah and GG Filter Surya. Since the early 2000s the company has also launched production of so-called light cigarettes as well as a low-priced line of cigarettes. Total manmade production nears 56 billion sticks per year. Indonesia remains Gudang Garam's main market, with exports reaching just 5 percent of the group's total revenues. The company also operates its own paper production subsidiaries, specialized in the production of cigarette paper and packaging papers, as well as a distribution subsidiary set up in 2005. Gudang Garam is listed on the Jakarta stock exchange. The founding family retains control of 67 percent of the company's shares.

ON HIS OWN IN THE FIFTIES

Gudang Garam was founded by Surya Wonowidjojo, who was born in the Fujian Province of China in 1923 as Tjoa Ing Hwie. Surya's family moved to Indonesia when he was four years old. While Surya's father opened a shop in Sampang, Madura, his uncle moved to Kediri, in East Java, where he became one of the early entrants into the kretek cigarette industry.

Kretek, which derived its name from the crackling sound the cigarettes made as they burned, was an invention of the late 19th century that combined tobacco with one of Indonesia's major crops, cloves. The cigarettes were initially meant as a health remedy for sore throats, asthma, and other lung conditions. This was because the burning of cloves released the chemical substance eugenol, which acted as a numbing agent.

Kretek cigarettes, traditionally wrapped in klobot, or dried corn husks, quickly became popular among Indonesian smokers. Kreteks were to retain their dominance into the 21st century, accounting for more than 92 percent of Indonesia's total cigarette market.

Surya's uncle's company, NV Jiou San (later NV Sembilan Tiga), produced the Cap 93 brand. Through the 1930s and into the 1940s, Cap 93 became one of the best-selling kretek brands in the East Java region. In the late 1940s, Surya was offered a job at the Cap 93 factory, where he received training in tobacco selection and, especially, the creation and production of "sauce," that is, the blend of cloves and other ingredients that imparted a brand's particular flavor to the tobacco.

Surya rose quickly in his uncle's business, becoming head of Tobacco and Sauce, and then being named a company director. Yet in the mid-1950s, Surya became determined to set up his own company. In 1956, he left his uncle's company and set up his own tobacco rolling workshop in a small, 1,000-square-meter facility in Kediri.

GOOD LUCK IN 1958

Surya's company initially employed 50 people, most of whom had left with Surya from his uncle's company. Surya created his first "sauce" that year, which he marketed under the Inghwie name. A hand-rolled, klobot kretek, Ingwhie brought Surya's company its first success. Before long, the Inghwie brand was even outselling the Cap 93 brand.

This success allowed Surya to expand his workforce, and in just two years the company boasted more than 500 workers. The increase in headcount enabled a surge in productivity, and by the end of 1958, the company was capable of producing more than 50 million "sticks," or individual cigarettes, per year.

By then, Surya had changed the company's name to Pabrik Rokok Tjap Gudang Garam. According to company legend, the change in name came about as a result of a dream, in which Surya had recognized an old salt warehouse that stood across the road from his uncle's factory. One of Surya's employees suggested that the name might bring the company good luck, and Surya agreed, renaming the company Gudang Garam, which literally meant "Salt Warehouse." Surya's employee then drew a picture of the warehouse, which served as a logo for the company and its fast-growing brand.

The success of Gudang Garam's kretek continued into the 1960s. In order to keep up with demand, the company expanded its production facilities. By the middle of the decade, the Gudang Garam factory was the largest kretek cigarette plant in all of Indonesia. Total production grew to nearly 500 million sticks by 1966, and then jumped again to nearly 865 million sticks by 1969.

ADDING MACHINERY IN 1979

Surya was joined in the business by his eldest son, Rachman Halim, born in 1947 under the Chinese name Tjoa To hin. Rachman's own career with the company began as a foreman overseeing the construction of the company's Unit II production plant. Following that project's completion, Rachman began his training in kretek production.

In 1969, Surya reincorporated the company as a partnership; in that year, the company also received financing from state-owned Bank Negara Indonesia. By 1991, Gudang Garam had reincorporated again, as a limited liability company, with Rachman joining his father on the board of directors.

Rachman's entry into the company proved the start of the group's growth into Indonesia's kretek powerhouse. A major factor in the company's later success was its decision, prompted by Rachman, to launch industrialized production in the late 1970s. Until then Gudang Garam, like the other players in the kretek industry, focused its production entirely on hand-rolled cigarettes.

In 1979, however, the company became the first in Indonesia to add machine-made kretek cigarettes, installing 30 rolling machines at its plant. The company then developed a blend specifically adapted to the new machine, launching the first machine-made kretek brand that year. The higher production rates allowed the company to price the new cigarettes at a discount to traditional hand-rolled cigarettes. As a result, the new cigarettes became another major success for the company, particularly among Indonesia's vast low-income population. By 1980, the company's total production neared seven billion cigarettes per year.

KEY DATES

1956: Surya Wonowidjojo founds a kretek (clove) cigarette factory in Kediri, East Java, Indonesia, which becomes Gudang Garam two years later.

1971: Gudang Garam reincorporates as a limited liability company.

1979: Company becomes the first to install cigarette rolling machinery for production of kretek cigarettes.

1990: Gudang Garam goes public, then diversifies into paper and packaging production.

1997: Company's market share peaks at 49 percent.

2002: Gudang Garam launches its own "light" cigarette brands.

2009: Gudang Garam's market share slips to 25 percent.

PUBLIC OFFERING IN 1990

While the Indonesian public responded to Gudang Garam's brands, part of the company's success lay in the founding family's relationship with Indonesia's ruling Suharto family. This relationship led Surya to found a joint venture to produce cigarette paper with Probosutedjo, one of Suharto's brothers, in 1984. Surya then turned over the chairmanship of Gudang Garam to his son that year. A year later, Surya himself passed away.

Throughout the company's history, Surya had remained focused on cigarette production. This set Gudang Garam apart from most of Indonesia's other business moguls, particularly the country's large group of highly successful Chinese-born entrepreneurs, who built highly diversified conglomerates in the years since Indonesia's independence. Rachman, however, adopted a more diversified view, leading the family's investments into the hotel, banking, and leisure industries. This diversification played a role in Rachman's emergence as Indonesia's wealthiest person in the 1990s. Cigarette production nonetheless remained the foundation of the family's fortune.

Into the 1990s, Gudang Garam had not only become Indonesia's largest kretek company, it had become one of the largest companies in the entire national economy. As a result the family-owned company came under pressure, reportedly from President Suharto himself, to open up its capital to outside investors. This was accomplished through a listing of approximately 12 percent of the company's shares on the Surubaya Stock Exchange. Soon after, the company listed an equivalent amount of its stock on the Jakarta Stock Exchange as well.

Gudang Garam continued to sell more shares to the public through the 1990s. The founding family nonetheless retained majority control of the company. At the same time, the public offering provided the basis for new expansion for the company. In 1991, Gudang Garam launched a vertical integration drive, establishing two paper production subsidiaries. The company then built two adjoining factories, the first for the production of cigarette rolling paper, the second for the production of heavier papers for the group's packaging needs. As these subsidiaries ramped up production through the decade, they also began supplying third parties.

STRUGGLING THROUGH THE ASIAN ECONOMIC CRISIS

The 1990s represented Gudang Garam's heyday as the company made impressive gains in market share. At the beginning of the decade, the company commanded a respectable 35 percent share of the kretek market. By 1997, however, the company became the true dominant player, expanding its share to nearly 50 percent.

Gudang Garam's growth was cut short, however, by the economic crisis that swept through most of the Asian region at the end of the decade. As the Indonesian economy collapsed, consumers were forced to reduce their non-essential spending, leading to a major reduction in tobacco consumption.

The slump in the market continued beyond 2000. With consumption dropping, Gudang Garam also found itself confronted with the growth of a discount cigarette market, which further eroded the company's market share. Yet the group's true troubles were caused by its own inability to recognize a growing trend in the country's kretek market.

While smoking rates remained extraordinarily high in the country (smokers represented as much as 65 percent of the male population), the health concerns surrounding tobacco use had begun to reach Indonesia. These concerns were all the more important for the country, as kretek cigarettes typically delivered nicotine and tar rates as high as double those of tobacco-only cigarettes. As a result, a new market appeared for so-called light cigarettes, which promised lower tar and nicotine levels.

MISSING THE LIGHT TREND

Gudang Garam ignored the new trend, instead remaining focused on its traditional brands. Major competitors such as Djarum and Sampoerna quickly established themselves as the leaders in the light cigarette segment, which rapidly gained market share at the expense of traditional blends. Gudang Garam was forced to play catch-up, and only launched its own light brands beginning in 2002. By then, however, the segment's leaders had established a strong degree of brand loyalty.

Gudang Garam's oversight resulted in a dramatic drop in market share. By the end of 2008, the company's share of the market had been nearly cut in half, dropping to as low as 25 percent. By then, the company faced new pressures. For one, rival Djarum had been acquired by global tobacco powerhouse Philip Morris International, providing that company with the financial and marketing clout to establish itself as the new leader in the Indonesian kretek industry. At the same time, the company reeled from the effects of two increases in excise taxes imposed on cigarette sales in a one-year period, raising the prices of cigarettes by more than 20 percent.

Gudang Garam also suffered another blow, when Rachman Halim died in July 2008. His death prompted rumors suggesting that Gudang Garam itself had become a takeover target, possibly by another global industry giant, British American Tobacco. For the time being, the founding family remained in control of the company, as a number of people in the third generation took up positions within the company. Nonetheless, the health issues surrounding tobacco use were expected inevitably to lead to a decline in Indonesian kretek consumption. Gudang Garam's future, like the tobacco industry in general, remained clouded into the new century.

M. L. Cohen

PRINCIPAL SUBSIDIARIES

PT Graha Surya Media; PT Surya Madistrindo; PT Surya Pamenang.

PRINCIPAL OPERATING UNITS

Graphics Department; Hand Rolled (SKT) Department; Processing Department; Production Department (Gempol unit).

PRINCIPAL COMPETITORS

Yunnan Yuxi Hongta Tobacco (Group) Company Ltd.; Philip Morris International Management S.A.; Japan Tobacco Inc.; Djarum, PT; Sumatra Tobacco Trading Company, N.V.; Hanjaya Mandala Sampoerna Tbk, PT; H M Sampoerna Tbk.

FURTHER READING

Aglionby, John, and Taufan Hidayat, "Jakarta Tax to Hit Cigarette Maker," *Financial Times,* December 5, 2006, p. 22.

"Clouds Darken Industry Horizon," *Asiamoney,* October 2006.

"An Empire Built from a Superstition," *Jakarta Post,* August 4, 2008.

"The Gudang Garam Group: Consistent in the Cigarette Business," *Indonesian Commercial Newsletter,* July 13, 1994, p. 34.

"Gudang Garam's Net Profit Declines to RP 2 Trillion," *Jakarta Post,* June 10, 2002.

Pappens, Rita, "Surya Cultivates Can-Do Will-Do Attitude," *Pulp & Paper International,* September 1993, p. 58.

Rendi Akhmad Witular, "Gudang Garam Splutters on Cheap Cigarettes," *Jakarta Post,* August 1, 2006.

"Two Indonesians Named in Billionaires Club," *Jakarta Post,* June 24, 2001.

"'234' Belongs to Gudang Garam," *Jakarta Post,* March 2, 2002.

PT Semen Gresik Tbk

Gedung Utama Semen Gresik, Jl. Veteran 10
Gresik, 61122
Indonesia
Telephone: (+62 031) 398 1732
Fax: (+62 031) 398 3209
Web site: http://www.semengresik.com

Public Company
Incorporated: 1953
Employees: 6,843
Sales: IDR 12.21 trillion ($1.11 billion)
Stock Exchanges: Jakarta
Ticker Symbol: SMGR
NAICS: 327310 Cement Manufacturing

■ ■ ■

PT Semen Gresik Tbk, or Gresik, is Indonesia's largest cement producer, commanding a 44 percent share of that country's cement market. Headquartered in Gresik, the company's total production reached 18.2 million tons in 2008, and is expected to top 20 million tons by 2011. The company produces the full range of ordinary and pozzolana portland cement varieties, based on a network of 12 factories. All of the company's cement plants use the more energy-efficient dry production process. Gresik serves as a holding company for three formerly state-owned enterprises: Semen Gresik, PT Semen Padang, and PT Semen Tonasa. Semen Gresik, the largest of the three, operates five cement plants that had a total output of 9.2 million tons in 2008. PT Semen Padang produced 5.4 million tons from four factories,

and South Sulawesi-based PT Semen Tonasa added 3.6 million tons from its three plants. Gresik also operates subsidiaries that make the paper sacks that get filled with cement, and that oversee the group's heavy equipment fleet. PT Semen Gresik remains under the auspices of the Indonesian government, which controls 51 percent of its shares. Blue Valley Holdings, Ltd., an Indonesian investment group, holds another 25 percent of the company. The rest is traded on the Jakarta Stock Exchange. Gresik is led by President Dwi Soetjipto. In 2008 the group's total revenues reached IDR 12.21 trillion ($1.11 billion).

CEMENTING INDEPENDENCE IN THE FIFTIES

The origins of PT Semen Gresik stem from the early years of Indonesian independence, as the young Indonesian government sought to develop the country's domestic resources. The need to construct the country's industrial and public infrastructure stimulated the rising demand for cement. Although a number of cement factories had been established under Dutch colonial rule, notably the company that became Semen Padang, founded in 1910, demand quickly outstripped supply. In 1953, therefore, the Indonesian government backed the founding of a new company, called NV Pabrik Semen Gresik.

The company then launched construction of its first cement plant, in Gresik, in east Java. Completed in 1957 and inaugurated under the auspices of Sukarno, the first Indonesian president, the Gresik plant was capable of producing as much as 250,000 tons of ce-

---

COMPANY PERSPECTIVES

Vision: To become a leading cement company with international reputation and capable of creating added value to stakeholders.

---

ment per year. The original Gresik plant was based on the earlier "wet" process of producing cement. Under this method, the basic materials of cement production underwent the grinding and mixing stages while already wet. This highly energy-intensive process was later phased out in favor of the latterly developed "dry" process, in which the grinding and mixing stages were performed on basic materials before being mixed with water.

Gresik and the country's other cement producers at first operated as private enterprises. The increasingly autocratic rule of the Sukarno government, however, led to the nationalization of large portions of the country's economy. The cement industry's turn came in the 1960s, with the passage of new legislation placing the industry under government control. In 1961, therefore, Semen Gresik was reincorporated as a state enterprise, or "Persero."

EXPANDING UNDER SUHARTO

Sukarno's economic policies brought Indonesia to the edge of collapse by the mid-1960s, setting the stage for the coup that placed Suharto in power as the country's strongman for the next 30 years. The oppressive and notoriously corrupt Suharto regime nonetheless put into place ambitious modernization and industrialization policies that led to massive investments in the country's infrastructure.

As a result, demand for cement grew strongly from the late 1960s through the next decades. Gresik, which reincorporated as PT Semen Gresik (Persero) in 1969, played a major role in the construction of Indonesia, growing into one of the dominant cement producers in the Java region.

Gresik's operations remained focused on its initial Gresik site. The company completed a series of expansions of the plant, including opening a second cement factory at Gresik. By the early 1990s it had reached a production capacity of 1.8 million tons per year. Yet the company faced competition from a growing number of cement producers, including companies founded in the 1970s after the Suharto regime began authorizing the development of private enterprises in the sector.

PRIVATIZATION IN THE NINETIES

The Suharto regime began implementing the privatization of parts of the Indonesian economy at the beginning of the 1990s. The government tested the waters, in fact, with Semen Gresik, which became the first state-owned company to list its shares on the Jakarta Stock Exchange, in 1991. Although the Indonesian government retained 73 percent of Semen Gresik, the offering allowed the cement manufacturer to launch a major expansion program.

Semen Gresik embraced the dry process technology, and began construction on a new cement plant at Tuban, located on the Java coast near Gresik. The new facility added 2.3 million tons per year to Semen Gresik's total production capacity, which topped four million tons per year. Tuban I, as the plant was called, went into production in 1994.

By then, the company had begun plans for an even more ambitious expansion program. In order to generate funding for this plan, which included the construction of two more cement production facilities at Tuban, the company proposed to carry out a new rights issue. The proposal called for the government to reduce its position in Gresik to that of a minority shareholder.

The government balked at relinquishing control over what was fast becoming Indonesia's largest cement producer. Instead, the Suharto government pushed through the merger of two of its other state-owned cement companies, Semen Padang and Semen Tonasa, into Semen Gresik, thereby once again raising its share in the company to 65 percent. The merger was hotly contested by some members of the government. In the end, the merger went through after a compromise was reached, under which Semen Padang and Semen Tonasa were granted the right to operate as autonomous businesses.

MERGING FOR LEADERSHIP IN 1995

Semen Padang was the older and larger of the two companies, tracing its origins back to 1910. In that year, a number of Dutch business partners founded what was to become Indonesia's first cement company, NV Nederlandsche Indische Portland Cement Maatschappij. Construction of the first plant, at Indarung on the large Sumatra island, began that year, and by 1913 the company had launched production. At the time, the new company's annual capacity remained below 23,000 tons per year. By 1939, however, the Padang site had raised its production levels to 170,000 tons per year. During World War II, the plant was taken over by the Japanese, then returned to Dutch control in the 1950s.

KEY DATES

1910: Dutch investors found NV Nederlandsche Indische Portland Cement Maatschappij (later Semen Padang) in Indarung, on Sumatra, and build Indonesia's first cement factory.

1957: Semen Gresik, incorporated in 1953, launches production at a cement factory in Gresik, on Java.

1961: Both Semen Gresik and Semen Padang become state-owned companies.

1968: Semen Tonasa, founded in 1960, launches production at its factory in Tonasa, South Sulawesi.

1991: Semen Gresik becomes the first state-owned company to be privatized and listed on the Jakarta Stock Exchange.

1995: Semen Gresik merges with Semen Padang and Semen Tonasa and becomes the leading cement producer in Indonesia.

1998: Cemex of Mexico acquires a stake in Semen Gresik.

2006: Cemex sells its shareholding in Semen Gresik to Blue Valley Holdings.

2009: Semen Gresik announces plans to spend $1.4 billion expanding production facilities by five million tons per year by 2012.

In 1958, however, Sukarno carried out a nationalization of all businesses owned by Dutch interests; like Semen Gresik, the Padang site, renamed as Semen Padang, became a state-owned company in 1961.

Over the next three decades, Semen Padang grew into one of the single largest cement facilities in Indonesia. After a series of plant expansions, production at the Indarung operation placed the company as the second largest in the country. By 1994 Semen Padang's total production had topped 3.2 million tons.

Semen Tonasa, in contrast, began life as a cooperation agreement formed between the Czechoslovakian and Indonesian governments in 1960. The agreement called for the joint development of a cement factory, based on the wet process, to be built in the village of Tonasa, in South Sulawesi, another of Indonesia's major islands. Construction of the factory stretched on through much of the decade. By 1968 Semen Tonasa had launched production, at an initial capacity of 110,000 tons per year.

The first Tonasa plant was phased out in 1984. Its place was taken by two new factories, both of which incorporated dry process production technologies. The first of the new plants, Tonasa Unit II, was built in cooperation with the Canadian government, and launched production with a capacity of 510,000 tons per year in 1980. The third plant, completed in 1984, was built in cooperation with the Indian and West Germany governments; it added another 590,000 tons per year, also through the dry process method.

NEW SHAREHOLDER IN 1998

The merger of Semen Padang and Semen Tonasa into Semen Gresik, which effectively became a holding company for all three companies, established Semen Gresik as the Indonesian leader, with a total production of more than eight million tons per year. In the meantime, the rights issue carried out by Semen Gresik in 1995 allowed the company to proceed with its two new expansion efforts. The first of the new Tuban plants was completed in 1997, with the second starting up operations in 1998. The company's annual total neared the 18 million tons per year mark.

Indonesia's economic collapse, amid the wider economic crisis that swept the Asian region in the late 1990s, forced the Indonesian government to carry out a number of reforms, including the further privatization of the cement industry. In 1998, therefore, the government announced its intention to accept bids to buy an initial 14 percent stake in Semen Gresik. In the end, Cemex S.A. de C.V. of Mexico was chosen to acquire the shares. Under the purchase agreement, Cemex also received the right to expand its shareholding in Semen Gresik, and even take majority control over the company. Accordingly, Cemex subsequently increased its shareholding to 25.5 percent in 1999.

The Indonesian government declared its intention to sell its remaining stake in Semen Gresik, 51 percent, to Cemex in 2001. Yet the announcement touched off a conflict between Semen Gresik and its Semen Padang subsidiary. The management of the latter, backed by opposition leaders in the Sumatra region, announced their refusal to allow Semen Padang to be taken over by a foreign company. The conflict reached its height when Semen Padang's management barricaded themselves in the factory, and refused to turn over control of the operation to a new management team sent by Semen Gresik. The conflict lasted until well into 2003, when Semen Gresik at last regained management control of Semen Padang.

Cemex maintained its stake in Semen Gresik through the middle of the decade. In 2006 the Mexican cement giant at last found a buyer for its stake, in the form of Blue Valley Holdings, an investment wing of the Indonesian conglomerate Rajawali Group. Blue Valley's stake stood at 24.9 percent, compared to the government's 50.01 percent and the 24.09 percent floated on the Jakarta exchange.

NEW EXPANSION TARGETS FOR 2012

With the conflicts surrounding its shareholder status largely resolved, Semen Gresik turned its attentions to further expansion as the decade's end approached. The company continued to raise its production levels, which reached 15.8 million tons in 2005, then climbed to 16.8 million tons at the end of 2007. By the beginning of 2009, Semen Gresik's total production topped 18 million tons.

Nevertheless, Semen Gresik set its sights on still higher production levels. At the beginning of 2009 the company's shareholders agreed to back a $1.4 billion investment program calling for the construction of two new cement factories, as well as a power plant. The first factory, to be built on Sulawesi near the Tonasa operations, was expected to add 2.5 million tons of capacity by 2011. The second factory, to be located in central Java, was slated for completion in 2012, adding another 2.5 million tons.

Most of this bump up in production was meant to meet the anticipated increase in demand in Indonesia over the next several years. Indeed, of the more than 18 million tons of cement produced by Semen Gresik in 2008, only one million tons or so had gone to the export market. Yet Semen Gresik's dominant position in the Indonesian market left it with limited future growth potential there. In 2009, therefore, the company announced its interest in establishing an international presence by acquiring cement companies in the Asian region. Having laid a solid foundation as Indonesia's cement leader, Semen Gresik hoped to concretize its dream of international expansion.

M. L. Cohen

PRINCIPAL SUBSIDIARIES

PT Industri Kemasan Semen Gresik; PT Kawasan Industri Gresik; PT Semen Gresik; PT Semen Padang; PT Semen Tonasa; PT United Tractors Semen Gresik.

PRINCIPAL DIVISIONS

Cement Production; Clinker Production; Engineering; Logistics and Inventory; Marketing Development; R&D Quality Assurance; Raw Material Production; Sales; Technical; Transportation & Distribution.

PRINCIPAL COMPETITORS

CRH plc; Tata Sons Ltd.; Holcim Ltd.; Lafarge S.A.; Grupo Ferrovial, S.A.; Cemex S.A. de C.V.; HeidelbergCement AG; The Siam Cement Public Company Limited; Liaoning Gongyuan Cement Company Ltd.

FURTHER READING

"Brisk Business Ahead for Semen Gresik Despite Challenges," *Jakarta Post,* August 25, 2008.

"Cemex to Become Majority Shareholder in Semen Gresik," *Jakarta Post,* March 6, 2000.

"Confronted by Elders, Gresik Claim to Protect Environment," *Jakarta Post,* September 12, 2008.

Donnan, Shawn, "Gresik Back in Control of Revel Division," *Financial Times,* September 10, 2003, p. 20.

"Economists Hail Government's New Plan on Semen Gresik," *Jakarta Post,* December 4, 2001.

"How Semen Gresik Got into This Mess," *Jakarta Post,* April 28, 2003.

"Indonesian Cement Co. Semen Padang to Build New Factory," *AsiaPulse News,* March 31, 2009.

"Indonesian Cement Industry to Be Dominated by Foreign Cartels," *Indonesian Commercial Newsletter,* May 8, 2001, p. 32.

Kasparman, Pilang, "Padang's Takeover a Success," *Jakarta Post,* September 9, 2003.

Klyne, Sharon, "Indonesia Announces New Semen Gresik Deal," *Privatisation International,* October 1998, p. 43.

"Semen Gresik Almost Doubles Net Profit on High Sales," *Jakarta Post,* October 28, 2005.

"Semen Gresik Cements Expansion Drive," *Jakarta Post,* January 31, 2009.

"Semen Gresik Expands Production Capacity," *Indonesian Commercial Newsletter,* July 9, 2002, p. 45.

"Semen Gresik Privatization Delayed," *Jakarta Post,* December 11, 2001.

"Semen Padang in Severe Financial Trouble Seeks Help," *Jakarta Post,* April 12, 2002.

@radical.media

435 Hudson Street
New York, New York 10014
U.S.A.
Telephone: (212) 462-1500
Fax: (212) 462-1600
Web site: http://www.radicalmedia.com

Private Company
Incorporated: 1993 as Sandbank, Kamen & Partners
Employees: 240
Sales: $175 million (2008 est.)
NAICS: 512110 Motion Picture and Video Production

∎∎∎

@radical.media produces television commercials, TV shows, films, music videos, web content, videogames, and photography for such clients as Pepsi, Nike, Ford, Sony, and American Express. Its efforts have included stylish commercials for Apple's iPod; reality-based shows *Battlegrounds* for MTV and *The Life* for ESPN; Burger King web site subservientchicken.com; video-on-demand automotive cable channel DriverTV; and the Oscar-winning documentary *The Fog of War* and Independent Spirit Award–winning *Metallica: Some Kind of Monster*. The firm's principals, Jon Kamen and Frank Scherma, are based in New York and Los Angeles, respectively, and the company also maintains offices in London, Paris, Berlin, Sydney, and Shanghai.

ORIGINS

@radical.media was formed in 1993 as an outgrowth of television commercial production company Sandbank and Partners. Founded in New York in 1975 as Sandbank Films by director Henry Sandbank and young producer Jon Kamen, it moved to larger quarters north of New York in 1984 and added a second office in Los Angeles in 1988, which was managed by former Chiat Day producer Frank Scherma.

Believing that cable television and the Internet would bring major changes to the way advertisers connected with their audience, Kamen, a high school dropout who had started in advertising as a 16-year-old photographer's assistant, began envisioning new projects such as brand-connected films and interactive media content that would bridge the gap between entertainment and marketing. In late 1992 he bought out Sandbank's stake in the firm, renaming it Sandbank, Kamen & Partners, and in January 1993 moved its headquarters back to New York City. A year and a half later it was again rebranded with the then cutting-edge name of @radical.media, with Kamen and West Coast-based Frank Scherma the two principals. The company's slogan, "never established," was a twist on the typical business practice of noting the founding date, and was intended to signal its willingness to break from the norm.

@radical, commonly known as Radical, would continue to rely on television commercial assignments from ad agencies, but increasingly sought other opportunities for projects that stretched the definition of a commercial production house. Jobs of this period

COMPANY PERSPECTIVES

We believe that the future belongs to those who can connect with an audience in lots of different ways. Which is why @radical.media has evolved into a multi-disciplinary integrated media company.

We make commercials for clients and agencies, television shows for networks and brands, feature films and documentaries, shorter length films for online, photography for advertising, music videos, design animation, motion graphics, games, and rich/interactive media.

We connect brands with content, channels with talent, and everyone with an audience that appreciates what we make.

included television spots for agency Wieden & Kennedy clients Nike and ESPN, a Nike-sponsored TV show for Japan called *The Hoop Hop Tour,* as well as work developing videogames for CD-ROM.

In 1995 Radical partnered with Spots Films of California, London, and Paris, pooling resources for production and marketing. During the year the firm was hired to help develop web sites for Hachette Filipacchi magazines including *Elle, George,* and *Car and Driver;* shot a half-hour special for the latter publication; and made ads for Jaguar, Porsche, DHL, Burger King, and Range Rover, among others.

Radical's talent pool included some of the industry's top commercial directors as well as feature-film artist Terry Gilliam, and during the mid-1990s it added more including documentary director Errol Morris and the single-named Tarsem, who left Spots just before that concern folded. Several also departed, some of whom formed a rival called Hungry Man. After the demise of Spots, the company retained its offices in London and Paris.

RADICAL WINS CANNES ADVERTISING PALME D'OR IN 1998

In June 1998 Radical was presented with the Cannes International Advertising Festival Palme d'Or for top commercial production firm, as well as awards for eight spots it produced for Miller Lite, Budweiser, and Jack in the Box restaurants. It had also been named top production house for several years running by the Association of Independent Commercial Producers. Other clients at this time included Boeing, Philips, Southwest Airlines, John Hancock, and IBM.

In the fall of 1998 Radical formed an alliance with web site company iXL to collaborate on projects, having completed software design assignments for Sotheby's and Bombardier. Early the next year an office was opened in Sydney, Australia, which offered solid technical facilities and lower production costs, as well as helped the company further embrace the global reach of its clients. During 1999 the firm also signed *What's Eating Gilbert Grape* director Lasse Hallström to its roster.

In June 2000 Radical formed a partnership with Copenhagen-based Zentropa Production, after which *Dancer in the Dark* director Lars von Trier's company would share work and talent with the firm. In October Radical acquired Outpost Digital, a year-old New York video postproduction house whose services it had been utilizing. In addition to performing work for its new owner, Outpost would continue to assist a client base of some 300 other firms, and soon expanded its staff from seven to ten. Radical's deal with iXL had ended, with interactive projects handled internally via its own Emerging Media Group unit.

In addition to shooting commercials, which continued to account for some 90 percent of revenues, Radical was also producing a 32-episode TV series for ESPN, *The Life,* which gave a behind-the-scenes look at professional athletes, and had developed a web site for Beatle George Harrison to promote the reissue of his classic *All Things Must Pass* album. With Wieden & Kennedy, the company formed Willing Partners to produce entertainment projects including Savion Glover's basketball-themed theater musical *Ball;* made a documentary for Court TV and another on cyclist Lance Armstrong; produced independent feature films for several of its directors including Tarsem's *The Cell;* and worked with The New York Times Co. to develop a multimedia project that would combine print, television, and web facets. The company employed 140 worldwide, as well as several hundred freelancers.

In June 2001 Radical partnered with FourHundred Films of London, which brought it the services of successful directors including Sharon Maguire of *Bridget Jones' Diary* fame. Another office had been added in Berlin. During the year Radical also won a second Palme d'Or at the Cannes Advertising Festival.

Building on its success with *The Life,* during the early 2000s the firm began taking on more television and film projects than ever before, including *Report from Ground Zero* for ABC (the firm's New York office was just a few blocks from the World Trade Center); girls' basketball series *Cyclone Season* for WB television; and

KEY DATES

1993: Sandbank, Kamen & Partners is formed as successor to Sandbank Films.

1994: New York/L.A.-based firm is rebranded as @radical.media.

1995: Partnership with Spots Films adds presence in London and Paris.

1998: Company wins its first Cannes Advertising Festival Palme d'Or.

2000: Outpost Digital is acquired.

2002: Company purchases Stiefel + Company, which becomes West Coast branch of Outpost.

2003: Radical-produced documentary *The Fog of War* wins Academy Award.

2004: Company launches print division.

2006: @radical.thinking is created to oversee branded entertainment efforts.

2007: FremantleMedia begins selling firm's branded entertainment abroad.

pilots for Showtime and VH1. Long-form programming soon grew to account for about a fifth of revenues.

ACQUISITION OF STIEFEL + COMPANY: 2002

In the fall of 2002 the firm bought L.A. production house Stiefel + Company, which would morph into the West Coast office of Outpost Digital, while head Frank Stiefel was named an executive vice-president at Radical. Commercial work included a series of Errol Morris spots for Apple and a set by Tarsem for T-Mobile, as well as others for Budweiser and FedEx. The company also designed an installation at Walt Disney's Epcot Center for IBM; created uniforms for four teams at the Winter Olympics; put together the opening film for the 2002 Academy Awards ceremony; and produced Errol Morris's documentary *The Fog of War*, which took home an Oscar the following year.

In 2003 Radical nearly doubled its office space in New York's Hudson Square area to 50,000 square feet, and also created a music video division; formed a joint venture with British producers Done & Dusted to produce a televised Victoria's Secret fashion show; and partnered with videogame designer American McGee to develop mini-games for use as online marketing tools.

In 2004 Radical added a print division headed by Michael Ash, whose Creative Management it would

absorb. Successes included American Express's The Adventures of Seinfeld and Superman campaign, a series of iconic Apple iPod television spots, the creation of subservientchicken.com for Burger King, and the Nike-sponsored MTV street basketball series *Battlegrounds*. The firm also received a prestigious National Design Award from New York's Cooper-Hewitt Museum, although at year's end it lost Errol Morris to rival Moxie Pictures.

In 2005 Radical won a Grammy for Best Long-Form Music Video for its George Harrison tribute *Concert for George*, and also took home an Independent Spirit Award for *Metallica: Some Kind of Monster*. The firm was preparing for the launch of video-on-demand cable channel DriverTV, which would offer car buyers short demonstration videos of new vehicles. Over the next year profiles were created for the vast majority of cars on the market.

BIRTH OF @RADICAL.THINKING: 2006

In 2006 a new unit called @radical.thinking was created to oversee the development and distribution of branded entertainment content including film, television, and digital media. It would be headed by Bob Friedman, a former executive at Viacom and New Line. Radical was also named Production Company of the Year by *Advertising Age*, with its work including *The Iconoclasts* series for the Sundance Channel; Emmy-winner *10 Days That Unexpectedly Changed America* for the History Channel; ads and a one-hour MTV special called *Gamekillers* for Axe deodorant; Internet video series *Bold Moves* for carmaker Ford; music videos for U2 and Green Day; and ads for Puma, Cadillac, Mercedes, ESPN, and Virgin Mobile.

In the spring of 2007 Radical reached an agreement with Bertelsmann unit FremantleMedia to distribute its branded entertainment programs overseas. Fremantle-Media, which represented such top properties as *American Idol*, would help with funding. Jon Kamen's original vision of moving the firm beyond commercial production had become a reality as advertisers increasingly sought new ways to stand out from the clutter of television advertising, and the company was recognized as a top creator of engaging brand-building content that featured subtle connections to products rather than an overt pitch.

In 2008 Radical opened an office in Shanghai, and early the next year it produced the opening segment for the 81st Academy Awards. Other projects included the pilot for American Movie Classics' popular series *Mad Men;* documentary *Britney: For the Record* for MTV; and

Ironic Iconic America for Bravo, produced in conjunction with designer Tommy Hilfiger.

Some 15 years after its founding, @radical.media had realized Jon Kamen's vision of creating brand-enhancing content across multiple formats that engaged consumers in fresh, memorable ways. The firm boasted a roster of top talent and a list of household-name clients, and had numerous industry awards to show for its efforts. As advertising continued to evolve in new directions, @radical.media appeared likely to remain a leader in its field.

Frank Uhle

PRINCIPAL SUBSIDIARIES

Outpost Digital; @radical.media print; @radical. thinking.

PRINCIPAL COMPETITORS

Anonymous Content; Believe Media; Biscuit Filmworks; Epoch Films; Gorgeous Enterprises; HSI Productions; Hungryman, Inc.; Moxie Pictures; Partizan; RSA; Stink Films.

FURTHER READING

Anderson, Mae, "@radical Print Unit Taps Ash," *Adweek,* August 9, 2004, p. 28.

Austin, Jane, "Blow to Spots As Tarsem Departs," *Campaign,* May 3, 1996, p. 3.

Berger, Warren, "The Creativity Interview: Jon Kamen," *Advertising Age's Creativity,* November 1, 2001, p. 26.

Caranicas, Peter, "@radical.media Seeks Lead in Breaking Spot Production Mold," *Shoot,* September 16, 1994, p. 1.

DeSalvo, Kathy, "@radical.media Forms Alliance with iXL," *Shoot,* September 11, 1998, p. 7.

————, "@radical.media Opens Office in Australia," *Shoot,* April 30, 1999.

Diaz, Ann-Christine, "Radical Revisited," *Advertising Age's Creativity,* September 1, 2005, p. 52.

Goldrich, Robert, "@radical.media Links with Zentropa," *Shoot,* June 16, 2000, p. 1.

————, "@radical Reaches Agreement to Acquire Stiefel + Company," *Shoot,* September 13, 2002, p. 1.

————, "Spots Films, @radical.media Enter into Alliance," *Shoot,* May 12, 1995, p. 1.

————, "U.S. Captures Advertising's World Cup, Dominates Lions," *Shoot,* July 3, 1998, p. 1.

Iezzi, Teressa, "Special Report: Top Production Companies - @radical.media," *Advertising Age's Creativity,* September 1, 2002, p. 36.

Kotkin, Joel, "Jon Kamen, @radical.media," *Inc.,* July 1, 2000, p. 112.

Oberlag, Reginald, "Errol Morris to Join @radical.media for Spots," *Shoot,* December 19, 1997, p. 7.

"Production Company of the Year: @radical.media," *Advertising Age's Creativity,* December 1, 2006, p. 36.

Pytlik, Mark, "Production Company of the Year: The Never Establishment," *Boards,* February 1, 2005, p. 24.

Schiller, Gail, "Friedman Tapped Chief of New Radical Thinking," *Hollywood Reporter,* August 2, 2006.

Schmuckler, Eric, "Totally Radical," *Shoot,* November 17, 1995, p. 58.

Vagnoni, Anthony, "Radical Departure," *Advertising Age,* June 25, 2001, p. 14.

Vranica, Suzanne, "Spreading 'Branded' Shows Overseas," *Wall Street Journal,* June 6, 2007, p. B3.

Woodward, Sarah, "@radical.media Buys Outpost Digital," *Shoot,* October 20, 2000, p. 1.

Reed's, Inc.

13000 South Spring Street
Los Angeles, California 90061
U.S.A.
Telephone: (310) 217-9400
Toll Free: (800) 997-3337
Fax: (310) 217-9411
Web site: http://www.reedsgingerbrew.com

Public Company
Incorporated: 1991 as Original Beverage Corporation
Employees: 60
Sales: $15.27 million (2008)
Stock Exchanges: NASDAQ
Ticker Symbol: REED
NAICS: 312111 Soft Drink Manufacturing

■ ■ ■

Reed's, Inc., is a leader in the natural soda market, marketing a range of flavored ginger ales, root beers, and colas. The company also makes ginger candies and ginger ice creams. Its flagship brand of ginger ales, which are brewed at a company-owned brewery in Los Angeles and through a co-pack agreement with a brewery in Pennsylvania, consists of six flavors: Reed's Original Ginger Brew, Reed's Extra Ginger Brew, Reed's Premium Ginger Brew, Reed's Raspberry Ginger Brew, Reed's Spiced Apple Brew, and Reed's Cherry Ginger Brew. In the root beer segment of the market, Reed's, Inc., sells Virgil's Root Beer, Virgil's Cream Soda, Virgil's Black Cherry Cream Soda, Virgil's Orange Cream Soda, and Virgil's Real Cola. A third brand, China

Cola, ranks as the top selling cola in the natural foods market. The company's candies and ice creams are marketed under the Reed's label. Reed's, Inc., sells its products in North America, Asia, Europe, and the Middle East, using a network of natural, gourmet, and independent distributors.

FOUNDER'S BACKGROUND

Christopher J. Reed was designing liquefied natural gas plants when he decided to make a dramatic change in his life. "I bought a guitar, moved to Hollywood, and decided I was going to live large and do my dreams," he said in a March 2008 interview with *Beverage Industry.* A musical career was not on the horizon, but Reed did want to give more attention to his passion for yoga, meditation, and most significantly, herbal medicine. A chemical engineer who received his undergraduate degree in 1980 from Rensselaer Polytechnic Institute in Troy, New York, Reed embarked on his new career path during the late 1980s, settling in Venice Beach, California, as a self-described hippie bearing all the trademarks of his subculture: a beard, shaggy hair, a tie-dyed T-shirt, a Volkswagen Bug, and a guitar.

Reed's fascination with herbal medicine centered on ginger, a plant considered by Indian and Chinese herbalists to relieve numerous medical problems such as arthritis, migraine headaches, and inflammation. He began researching old recipes for ginger ale in 1987, using his kitchen in Venice Beach as a laboratory. He found the recipes using the entire ginger root to be the most compelling, recipes that typically dated from the 19th century. "From an herbal standpoint, here was the

COMPANY PERSPECTIVES

Back in the early log cabin days, the pioneers couldn't go to the store and buy soft drinks, they made their own. They didn't make them the way modern commercial soft drinks are made, even the so called natural ones. They brewed them in their kitchens, directly from roots, spices and fruits. These early soft drinks, besides being delicious, were also used as herbal tonics. Reed's brews are delicious revivals of this lost brewing art. Each batch is hand crafted with pride, carefully brewed and aged like fine wine in small batches by our expert brewmasters. They choose only the finest fresh herbs, roots, spices and fruits. They won't let sugar, preservatives or artificial anything spoil Reed's natural taste.

whole wheat bread to the white bread," he said in his interview with *Beverage Industry*. His experimentations with various recipes continued for several years until he found an old Jamaican recipe that used ginger, citrus juices, honey, and exotic spices.

By 1989, Reed had fine-tuned the concoction he wanted to bring to market. He purchased 90 pounds of ginger root for his first batch of what would become known as "Original Ginger Brew" and drove his key ingredient to a local brewery, where he borrowed a vat and used a canoe paddle to mix the ginger with water, spices, and juices. He poured his ginger ale into bottles, used a glue stick to affix labels on the bottles, and began hawking his natural soda beverages to health food stores, delicatessens, and, in the first example of his desire to penetrate all markets, he sold an order to a Philly cheesesteak restaurant.

FIRST FORAY OUTSIDE LOS ANGELES IN 1990

Reed's homespun business enjoyed immediate success. A turning point in its development occurred not long after he began using his Volkswagen to ferry bottles of Original Ginger Brew around the Los Angeles area. He filled his backpack with bottles of his creation and walked into Natural Foods Expo West 1990, where he managed to sign agreements with several distributers. By the end of the year, his ginger ale was being brewed at the Boulder Brewing Company in Boulder, Colorado, where monthly production exceeded 2,000 cases. The brewing agreement with Boulder Brewing opened up

the distribution of his products to nearby Aspen and Denver, giving his business a three-market operating territory.

In 1991, Reed incorporated his business under the name "Original Beverage Corporation" and moved the company's production to Pennsylvania, where he signed a co-pack agreement with The Lion Brewery, Inc. The ensuing years were devoted to stoking interest in Original Ginger Brew, as Reed traveled the circuit of natural and specialty food trade shows and showcased his product. His decade-long efforts paid dividends, bringing his ginger ale, which began to appear in different varieties, into new markets. The period also saw Reed sign his first agreement with a mainstream supermarket distributor.

A NEW BREWERY AND NEW PRODUCTS

Entering the new century, Reed charged forward on all fronts. He expanded his product line, completed acquisitions, and diversified into new product categories. The cyclone of activity began in 1999, when he purchased the Virgil's Root Beer and Cream Soda brand from Crowley Beverage Company, using a $250,000 loan from his father, a U.S. Army colonel, to complete the deal. In 2000, he completed another acquisition, purchasing the China Cola brand, a brand he had been licensing since 1997. The year also witnessed the debut of three new products: Reed's Original Ginger Ice Cream, Reed's Cherry Ginger Brew, and Reed's Crystallized Ginger Candy. At the end of 2000, Reed took a bold step forward and purchased an 18,000-square-foot warehouse in Los Angeles that he converted into a brewery. He continued to rely on his co-pack agreement in Pennsylvania to reach eastern markets, but the brewery in Los Angeles, which produced its first products in 2003, became the hub of his business, serving as the headquarters for his company, which was reincorporated as "Reed's Inc." in 2001.

All the progress achieved between 1999 and 2001 cost money. To pay for the warehouse in Los Angeles and his other growth initiatives, Reed raised money through a special stock offering known as a Small Corporate Offering Registration, or SCOR, which allows companies to sell up to $1 million worth of stock without having to endure the lengthy and costly approval process required for a traditional initial public offering (IPO) of stock. Reed, aping the approach taken by ice cream maker Ben & Jerry's, solicited his SCOR by attaching neck tags on bottles of his natural soda, using what was referred to as "tombstones" to invite his customers to become shareholders for $2 per share. The reception to the offering was lackluster, nearly prompt-

KEY DATES

1987: Christopher J. Reed begins experimenting with recipes for ginger ale in his Venice Beach, California, kitchen.

1989: Reed begins selling bottles of "Original Ginger Brew."

1990: After gaining valuable exposure at Natural Foods Expos West 1990, Reed begins selling his ginger ale in Aspen, Colorado, and Denver, Colorado.

1991: Reed's business is incorporated as "Original Beverage Corporation."

1999: The Virgil's brand is acquired from Crowley Beverage Company.

2000: The China Cola brand is acquired.

2001: The name of the company is changed to "Reed's, Inc."

2003: An attempt at an initial public offering (IPO) of stock is terminated.

2004: A second attempt at an IPO is launched.

2006: Reed's, Inc., completes its IPO, raising $8 million.

2008: International sales increase 207 percent.

ing Reed to shut down the SCOR. During the first nine months of the offering, he raised only $50,000, but after a stockbroker friend, Peter Sharma, urged him to print thousands more tombstones, the offering raised $900,000 in its last three months. Reed raised the capital by incurring only $20,000 in costs.

REED BEGINS COURTING WALL STREET IN 2001

For Reed, the SCOR was deceptively easy and inexpensive to complete. His next attempt to raise money from investors would be exceedingly more difficult and exponentially more expensive. Within months of completing the SCOR, Reed was in desperate need of cash to fund his company's expansion, which prompted him to begin planning for Reed's, Inc.'s IPO. He took his first steps in 2001, beginning what became a protracted, five-year-long struggle to secure clearance from the U.S. Securities and Exchange Commission (SEC). He hoped to spend only $250,000 to complete the IPO, expecting to raise $18 million from his company's debut on Wall Street, but nothing about the IPO went according to plan. "You have to work hard to create that much trouble," Reed said in a February 2008

interview with *Inc.,* commenting on the debacle that preceded Reed's, Inc.'s conversion to public ownership.

Reed was determined to keep his IPO-related costs as low as possible, but nearly every effort to save money backfired. His troubles started when he began searching for a company to sell his stock. "The broker-dealers wanted $800,000 just to have their name on the cover [of the prospectus]," he explained in his interview with *Inc.,* "and we were like, 'To hell with that.'" Reed decided a more inexpensive alternative to paying a broker was to purchase a brokerage company, which led him to Blue Ray, a company based in Washington State. Blue Ray's owner did not want to sell his company, but he agreed to let Reed's stockbroker friend, Sharma, sell Reed's, Inc.'s stock under Blue Ray's auspices. It was not the standard approach to executing an IPO, and neither was Reed's idea to sell the stock over the Internet. The SEC, whose preference for convention clashed with Reed's iconoclastic inclinations, looked at the first draft of Reed's, Inc.'s prospectus and expressed its displeasure with the document. The exchanges between the SEC and Reed about the prospectus dragged on for more than a year, resulting in 13 amendments to the document before it was approved at the end of 2002.

CANCELLATION OF IPO: 2003

Once he was cleared for the offering, Reed expected to raise $18 million worth of stock within a matter of months. Shares in the company sold slowly, however, frustrating Reed. By the end of the first fiscal quarter of 2003, he had sold only $10,000 worth of stock, a woeful start to his company's IPO that he blamed on the looming invasion of Iraq by U.S. troops. Blue Ray's owner, Dale Garnett, put the blame for the tepid response from Wall Street squarely on Reed's shoulders. "Part of the arrangement was Peter was going to be in charge of all the selling," Garnett said in the February 2008 issue of *Inc.,* "and he didn't sell any." While Reed watched the IPO flounder, he learned he would need to have Reed's, Inc.'s 10-K (an annual financial statement required by the SEC) filed by the end of March 2003, which would add another $50,000 to the $300,000 he already had spent on the offering. The costs, Reed believed, were spiraling out of control, prompting him to abort the offering and to return the money the offering had raised to investors. "Management was me," he said in his February 2008 interview with *Inc.* "I was the CFO, CEO, COO. So management was pissed and upset and saddened and bent down and frustrated and everything else. It was not an easy decision."

SECOND ATTEMPT AT AN IPO: 2004

Reed decided to bide his time before attempting another IPO. He waited for conditions to improve, and by mid-2004 he was ready to turn to Wall Street again. Sales for the first half of the year reached $4.5 million, putting the company on pace to eclipse the $6.8 million it generated in 2003. To excite potential investors further, Reed had made impressive progress on the distribution front, signing an agreement that put his company's products in movie-studio commissaries, independent grocery stores, and industrial foodservice chains. He submitted his registration statement with the SEC in November 2004, seeking to sell two million shares at $4 per share.

Reed's second attempt at an IPO proved to be more troublesome than his first attempt at an offering. He stumbled immediately, experiencing a host of problems with his registration statement, ranging from failing to use the formatting mandated by the SEC to failing to coordinate the approval of federal and state regulators in an efficient manner. The SEC made 69 comments on Reed's registration statement, which delayed approval of the document until May 2005. Another three months passed before Reed met all the demands of state regulators, which meant he did not begin selling stock until August 2005. Once he received clearance from federal and state regulators, his company received the same lukewarm reception it had two years earlier. During the first two months of the $8 million offering, Reed's, Inc., sold only $90,000 worth of stock. The offering was teetering on the brink of failure when Reed received more unwelcome news in February 2006. The SEC informed him that all his financial information needed to be updated, presenting another costly delay in the IPO process. Reed was preparing to leave for India for several weeks when the SEC informed him of its demand. He instructed his lawyer to take care of the matter, but when he returned home the SEC informed him that the agency had not cleared the offering and, consequently, he was selling stock illegally.

The saga continued, stretching into its fifth year. Nearly every attempt by Reed to save money had failed miserably, which finally convinced him to alter his stance. He hired an expensive lawyer and launched a rescission, returning the money he raised to investors but not before clearing a new public offering document

to start selling stock again. He waited several months for the SEC to complete the process, paying $835,000 in rescission costs, and completed the IPO in October 2006 after spending five years and more than $3.1 million to complete the offering. The IPO sold out in two months, raising $8 million.

Reed wasted no time before putting the IPO proceeds to use. He focused his efforts on forging new distribution agreements to bring his products to as many markets as possible, and he made great strides. Within two-and-a-half years of Reed's, Inc.'s public debut, the company's products were available at 10,500 locations in the United States, appearing in supermarket chains, natural food stores, retail stores, and restaurants. Reed also pressed forward on the international front, signing distribution agreements that brought his products into Canada, Mexico, Europe, Asia, and the Middle East. Looking ahead, Reed saw abundant opportunities for expansion, confident his passion for ginger would one day be shared by consumers throughout the world.

Jeffrey L. Covell

PRINCIPAL COMPETITORS

Jones Soda Co.; Snapple Beverage Corporation; Buderim Ginger Company; Ben & Jerry's Homemade Inc.

FURTHER READING

"Breaking News: Reed's, Inc. Announced Launch of New Diet Versions of Soda for the Virgil's Brand," *Europe Intelligence Wire,* March 28, 2007.

"Bubbling to the Top: One Entrepreneur Is Making His IPO Really Pop by Advertising Directly to His Customers," *Entrepreneur,* March 2006, p. 55.

Clifford, Stephanie, "His Way," *Inc.,* February 2008, p. 90.

Green, Mike, "Nascent Food Signs Mexican Distribution Agreement for Reeds," *America's Intelligence Wire,* March 2, 2007.

Theodore, Sarah, "Reed's Inc.: Old-Fashioned Recipe Makes Modern-Day Success," *Beverage Industry,* March 2008, p. 32.

Wilson, Jane, "Aspenites Among the First to Taste Jamaican Ginger Brew," *Aspen Times,* March 15, 1990, p. 12B.

York, Bryson, "Healthy Alternative?" *Los Angeles Business Journal,* March 19, 2007, p. 6.

REWE-Zentral AG

Postfach 10 15 28
Cologne,
Germany
Telephone: (+49 221) 1490
Fax: (+49 221) 1499000
Web site: http://www.rewe.de

Cooperative Company
Incorporated: 1927
Employees: 290,000
Sales: EUR 45.1 billion ($57.0 billion) (2008)
NAICS: 445110 Supermarkets and Other Grocery (Except Convenience) Stores; 424410 General Line Grocery Merchant Wholesalers; 561510 Travel Agencies

■ ■ ■

REWE-Zentral AG, also known as REWE Group, is one of the world's top retail groups and a major player in the European travel and tourism sector as well. The cooperative company, based in Cologne, Germany, is that country's second largest food retailer, holds the number three position in the total European market, and ranks number seven worldwide. REWE operates nearly 10,000 stores throughout Germany, as well as nearly 3,500 stores across 15 countries. The company's retailing operations form the largest part of the group's annual revenues, which topped EUR 45 billion ($57 billion) in 2008.

REWE's retailing divisions include: National Full-Range Stores (24 percent of group sales), including the REWE, and Toom brands; International Full-Range Stores (16 percent), including Billa, Merkur, Standa, and Bipa; National and International Discount Stores (20 percent), largely through 5,000 Penny Market stores; Specialist Stores and Co-operations (5 percent), including the toom DIY store chain; Business-to-Business (13 percent), including the REWE wholesale operations Selgros and Prodega. The company's Travel & Tourism division operates under a number of brands, including ITS, Billa Reisen, ITS Coop Travel, and Dertour, and accounts for 9.5 percent of group turnover. International revenues represent approximately 30 percent of the group's total turnover. REWE is led by CEO Alain Capparos.

PURCHASING COOPERATIVE IN 1927

The cooperative movement played a significant role in a number of industries in Germany in the beginning decades of the 20th century. The first cooperatives had appeared in the previous century, particularly among the agricultural community, but had extended into other areas, such as banking and insurance, by 1900. Food retailing too became an important area for the cooperative movement, as consumers and retailers grouped together to form wholesale purchasing cooperatives.

The turbulent economic climate in Germany following the country's defeat in World War I encouraged the growth of the cooperative movement. For the most part, the early cooperatives remained small, largely locally focused businesses with a small number of members.

COMPANY PERSPECTIVES

We consistently unite the traditional ideas behind co-operatives with the latest demands of globalisation. After an intense phase of restructuring and integration, we are exceptionally well positioned to shape our socially responsible, sustainable trading and business practices even more comprehensively. We intend to bring the economic, ecological, social and cultural of what we do into greater harmony. This continues to serve as the guiding principle behind all of our entrepreneurial decisions.

The transition toward a smaller number of larger cooperatives grew apace in the 1920s. Larger groupings provided greater purchasing power, which in turn provided the cooperatives with a stronger platform from which to negotiate with food producers. In the Cologne region, a group of 17 purchasing cooperatives joined in on this trend, reaching an agreement to found a central purchasing body in 1926.

The new business was launched the following year, under the name Revisionsverband der Westkauf-Genossenschaften, or "Auditing Association of Western Purchasing Cooperatives." The group quickly adopted the initials REWE as the group's name. By 1932, the group had developed REWE into a full-fledged brand with its own logo. The cooperative then began extending the REWE brand into its retail operations. The first REWE-branded stores appeared by 1935.

NEW START IN THE POSTWAR PERIOD

REWE's growth was cut short by World War II. Bombing raids destroyed a significant part of the group's facilities, and by 1945 REWE had ceased operation. However, soon after the German capitulation, REWE had reestablished its headquarters and began rebuilding its business.

The German economic boom during the period following World War II provided the foundation for RE-WE's own strong growth. The cooperative supplemented its purchasing operations with the addition of an import subsidiary, called REWE-Zentralimport, in 1947. By the end of the 1950s, REWE had also added wholesale operations, and had launched an export business as well. As in the case of many cooperative businesses, REWE also developed its cooperative credit wing for its members.

REWE also responded to the introduction and subsequent rise to dominance of the self-service supermarket format in Germany. The appearance of a number of large-scale supermarket groups during the 1960s had begun to place the country's independent grocers under a great deal of pressure. This in turn provided REWE with the opportunity to extend its own reach, as it set itself up as a partner to the independent retail sector.

The growing competition in the food retailing sector also led the cooperative to restructure its organizational structure in the early 1970s. As part of this restructuring, the REWE-Zentralimport was reincorporated as REWE-Zentral AG, which became responsible for the cooperative group's trading operations. The group's credit and financial operations were placed under a new body, REWE-Zentralfinanz AG, which became both a subsidiary of and a major shareholder in REWE-Zentral. The cooperative organization model took on a three-pool structure, based on its head office, retail, and wholesale businesses.

FIRST ACQUISITIONS IN THE SEVENTIES

Following its restructuring, REWE-Zentral launched an effort to increase its penetration of the independent grocery sector. The company actively sought partnerships with retailers, developing more attractive purchasing terms. The company also established a new retail business model, called REWE Trading Companies, in which REWE became full partners with its retailers, acquiring up to 50 percent of each store.

REWE also sought to attract other cooperative bodies to its membership. In 1973, for example, the company added a new member, Für Sie-Discount AG, which operated as a retail cooperative group similar to REWE itself. At the same time, REWE sought partnerships beyond the cooperative movement. In 1974, for example, the company acquired a 50 percent share in Leibbrand Group. Based in Bad Homburg and founded in 1961, Leibbrand had been developing its own portfolio of retail brands. These included supermarket brands HL, Minimal, the discount operation Penny, the Idea drugstore chain, and toom, a do-it-yourself (DIY) hardware chain.

Through the 1970s, REWE remained a largely regional player in the German retail sector. The arrival of Hans Reichl as head of the cooperative toward the end of that decade represented the start of a new era. Under Reichl, REWE set out to establish itself as a nationally operating retail leader. At the same time, the group also entered the cash and carry market, establishing subsidiary REWE-Wibu in 1980.

KEY DATES

■

1927: Seventeen food purchasing cooperatives join together to form Revisionsverband der Westkauf-Genossenschaften (REWE) in Cologne, Germany.

1947: REWE launches an import subsidiary.

1959: REWE expands into the wholesale and export sectors.

1970: REWE-Zentral AG is created as part of the REWE cooperative group.

1974: Company acquires 50 percent of the Leibbrand Group, including its Penny discount supermarket brand.

1983: REWE acquires a stake in Kaiser + Kellermann, operator of the Globus hypermarket chain.

1988: REWE acquires stake in travel and tourism operator Atlas Reisen.

1993: Company makes first international acquisition, of 26 percent of Budgens in the United Kingdom.

1996: Company acquires BML in Austria, then expands into Eastern and Central Europe.

2005: REWE enters Russian market with stores in Moscow.

2008: REWE acquires 320-store Plus discount supermarket group in Germany.

2009: REWE enters Bulgaria and Ukraine.

The company took a new step in this direction in 1983, when it formed a partnership with the Kaiser + Kellermann group. Based in Kirchhunden, Kaiser + Kellermann had been developing its own network of Globus-branded hypermarkets. The following year, REWE consolidated its position as a leader in the Cologne market, buying a 51 percent stake in supermarket operator Cornelius Stüssgen AG.

BUILDING A NATIONAL NETWORK FROM THE EIGHTIES

The year 1988 marked a new milestone in REWE's growth. In that year, the company completed the acquisition of Deutscher Supermarkt Handels GmbH, based in Düsseldorf. The purchase added that company's own retail brands, which included Deutscher Supermarkt, Hill, Otto Mess, and Desuma.

REWE also moved to gain more control of its various retail partnerships. This led the company to acquire majority control of Kaiser + Kellermann in 1988, and then of Leibbrand Group and Cornelius Stüssgen in 1989. REWE's expansion effort also led the company to look beyond food retailing. In 1988, the company targeted the travel and tourism sector, buying a 50 percent stake in Atlas-Reisebüro. That Cologne-based company operated a national chain of some 300 travel agencies by the time REWE took full control in 1994.

In the meantime, REWE had restructured its operations, putting into place a new two-tier organization. The new structure eliminated the former wholesale wing, which was instead transferred to the head office. With control over the group's purchasing operations, this in effect established REWE-Zentral as the central force in the REWE operation. Most of the group's wholesale cooperatives agreed to move, transferring their activities to REWE-Zentral. Only REWE-Dortmund balked against giving up its independence, and remained a separate company, while nonetheless affiliated with the REWE group.

The reorganization came ahead of REWE's entry into the East German market in the 1990s. REWE had begun building a presence in East Germany even before the fall of the Berlin Wall and the subsequent German reunification, setting up its first stores in Weimar and Potsdam. REWE then took a major step toward establishing itself as a truly nationally operating retail group, buying Co-op AG and its nearly 400 supermarkets.

FIRST INTERNATIONAL EXPANSION IN 1993

By the early 1990s, REWE had established itself, if only temporarily, as one of Germany's and Europe's largest trade groups. Indeed, the company claimed the German leadership, and the number two spot in the full European market. Subsequent consolidation efforts among the group's rivals saw REWE's ranking slip later in the decade, however.

REWE's focus remained on the German market at the start of the decade. By 1990, the group's operations included more than 7,300 stores, as well as 17 wholesale operations, providing the company with a total sales surface of 3.95 million square meters. REWE also oversaw a growing family of more than ten brands, including the REWE and Globus names. Into the early 1990s, the company's market share in Germany reached 15 percent.

While REWE would continue to expand in Germany, the group began targeting international expansion in the 1990s. The creation of the European Union and the dropping of trade barriers among the member nations had introduced a new era of competition and opportunity in the retail sector. REWE became one of the first to join in the new cross-border race for market share, buying a 26 percent stake in U.K.-based Budgens in 1993. REWE also announced its intention to roll out a network of discount supermarkets in the United Kingdom.

Discount operations represented approximately 25 percent of REWE's total retail network, which topped 8,000 stores in 1993. Germany had pioneered the so-called hard discount supermarket format, which generally featured no-frills store interiors, with limited product ranges, and into the 1990s the discount sector had become a major retail sales channel. The rest of Europe had been slower to adopt the hard discount model, however, providing REWE with a number of growth opportunities.

Penny Market, the company's core discount brand, became REWE's international flagship as well. In 1994, for example, the company entered the Southern European market, setting up a Penny Market subsidiary in Italy. France became a new market for the company as well, following the purchase of 40 supermarkets from Vendex in 1995. These stores were then converted to the Penny Market name. The company also moved into Austria, buying the BML group in 1996. This purchase gave REWE a new range of store banners, including the Billa supermarket chain; Merkur groceries; a discount chain, Mondo; and others including the Bipa drugstore chain.

MANAGEMENT TROUBLES

From Austria, REWE moved into Central and Eastern Europe, setting up shop in Poland and Hungary. Other acquisitions made by REWE through the end of the decade included BLV Grossverbraucher Service, a cash and carry operation, which was merged with REWE-Wibu to form REWE Grossverbraucher Service in 1997.

REWE established itself as a leading player in the fast-growing DIY retail sector, buying 138 Stinnes stores and 52 Götzen stores in 1998. These were rebranded under the group's core DIY brand, toom, which then became one of the German leaders of that retail segment. The following year, the group claimed the leadership of the Austrian food retail market, buying the more than 160-store Meinl chain. Then, in 2001, the company stepped up its operations in Italy, buying that country's Standa supermarket group.

During the period, REWE had also been building its travel and tourism division. For this the company completed a number of acquisitions, notably of ITS, based in Kauthof, in 1995; DER Group in 2000; and the LTU tour group in 2001. Travel and tourism would come to represent nearly 10 percent of REWE's total turnover.

By the time Hans Reichl retired in 2004, REWE had grown from a small regional cooperative into one of Europe's and the world's most powerful retail groups. The departure of Reichl, who some said had ruled the company in the style of an "enlightened monarch," left REWE in some disarray. The company was forced to unravel the complex organizational system put in place by Reichl in order to consolidate his control over the group's operations. At the same time, REWE was hit by scandal when Ernst Dieter Berninghaus, appointed as CEO to replace Reichl, was indicted several months later on embezzlement charges.

REWE's management instability continued through the next year. Finally the appointment of Alain Caparros, who had led the Penny discount branch, as CEO appeared to bring new calm to the group's management structure in 2006. In that year, REWE, by then present in more than a dozen markets, with more than 10,000 stores and a growing number of store brands, carried out its "big bang" rebranding effort. The company adopted a new name, REWE Group, and streamlined its overall brand portfolio. In the process, REWE became the company's core mainstream supermarket brand, while Penny Market became the group's discount brand, while DIY operations were placed under the toom name.

EUROPEAN RETAIL LEADER

REWE once again turned its attention toward expansion. The company continued to seek new markets, such as Russia, where it established 18 Billa-branded supermarkets in the Moscow area in 2005. REWE added the Czech Republic the following year, buying the Delvita supermarket chain of 95 stores from Belgium's Delhaize Group in 2006. This purchased followed on REWE's acquisition of Delvita's Slovakian operations the previous year.

REWE continued to seek new international markets. The company entered Turkey in 2008. By 2009, the company had also launched plans to enter Bulgaria and Ukraine. REWE expected to open ten stores in each of these markets by the end of that year.

In Germany, REWE expanded its DIY business with the purchase of Marktkauf, a chain of 133 DIY stores, from the Edeka retail group. At the same time, REWE announced its intention to launch a major investment in the German market, targeting an increase in market share to as much as 20 percent by 2011. The group took a major step toward this end in November 2008, when it received approval to acquire 328 Plus-branded discount supermarkets. The deal was expected to boost REWE's total turnover, which topped EUR 45 billion ($57 billion) that year, by more than EUR 1 billion. The deal helped consolidate REWE's status as one of the top German food retailers, and its status as one of Europe's top three retail groups.

M. L. Cohen

PRINCIPAL SUBSIDIARIES

ATLAS REISEN GmbH; BILLA AKTIENGESELL-SCHAFT; DELUS GmbH & Co.; DELVITA a.s. (Czech Republic); DERTOUR America Inc.; GO!Reisen GmbH; ITS REISEN GmbH; Penny GmbH; REWE-Aktiengesellschaft; REWE-AUSTRIA AG; REWE Italia srl; REWE Polska Sp. z o.o.; REWE Romania SrL; REWE Schweiz AG; toom BauMarkt GmbH.

PRINCIPAL DIVISIONS

Food Trading; Travel and Tourism; Specialist Stores.

PRINCIPAL OPERATING UNITS

Business-to-Business; International Full-Range Stores; National and International Discount Stores; National Full-Range Stores; Specialist Stores and Co-operations; Travel and Tourism.

PRINCIPAL COMPETITORS

Carrefour SA; Metro AG; Casino Guichard-Perrachon SA; Royal Ahold N.V.; Lidl Stiftung and Company KG; Tengelmann KG; EDEKA ZENTRALE AG and Company KG.

FURTHER READING

Awbi, Anita, "Rewe's 'Big Bang' Rebrand," *FoodanddrinkEurope.com,* June 21, 2006.

Ehrenstein, Claudia, "Bio-Ware Beim Discounter," *Die Welt,* January 12, 2006.

"Europe's Shoppers Turn to Discount Food Stores," *International Supermarket News,* March 2, 2009.

Francis, Krishan, "Delhaize Sells Czech Activities to REWE-Zentral," *AP Worldstream,* November 13, 2006.

"The German Cartel Office Has Given Its Approval for REWE Group's Penny Chain to Acquire 328 Plus Outlets," *Grocer,* November 29, 2008, p. 9.

Kuipers, Pascal, "A Snake Pit Named REWE," *Elsevier Food International,* November 2006.

"Penny Market to Open in Bulgaria This Year," *International Supermarket News,* April 8, 2009.

Proissl, Wolfgang, "Neue Einkaufsallianz Fordert nur Niedrige Rabatte," *Financial Times Deutschland,* February 17, 2006.

Reich, Ingo, "Germany's REWE Will Acquire Italy's Standa Chain," *Wall Street Journal Europe,* December 28, 2000, p. 4.

"REWE Set for Launch in UK," *Super Marketing,* April 30, 1993, p. 7.

"REWE-Zentral Satiates Appetite for German Issuance," *Private Placement Letter,* October 18, 2004.

Ronke, Christiane, "REWE Kippt Bischerige Strategie," *Financial Times Deutschland,* January 25, 2007.

Rhythm & Hues Studios, Inc.

5404 Jandy Place
Los Angeles, California 90066
U.S.A.
Telephone: (310) 448-7500
Fax: (310) 448-7600
Web site: http://www.rhythm.com

Private Company
Incorporated: 1987
Employees: 1,000
Sales: $55.2 million (2008 est.)
NAICS: 512110 Motion Picture and Video Production;
512191 Teleproduction and Other Postproduction
Services

■ ■ ■

Rhythm & Hues Studios, Inc., is a leading producer of computer-generated animation for movies and television commercials. The firm's credits include work for *Night at the Museum, The Sum of All Fears, The Chronicles of Narnia: The Lion, the Witch and the Wardrobe,* Visual Effects Oscar-winners *Babe* and *The Golden Compass,* and Coke's polar bear and Geico's gecko lizard ads. Rhythm & Hues also performs design work for a variety of other projects including theme park motion rides, video games, and print media, and has announced plans to branch out into producing feature films of its own. The Los Angeles-based firm has operations in Mumbai and Hyderabad, India, and Kuala Lumpur, Malaysia.

EARLY YEARS

Rhythm & Hues was founded in April 1987 by a group of former Robert Abel and Associates animators. Abel's firm had begun operations in 1971 and produced stop-motion and early computer animation effects for award-winning commercials, television programs, and films including Disney's groundbreaking *Tron,* released in 1982 Abel sold the firm in 1986, but early the next year its new owners defaulted on investments and shut it down, leaving its talented staff at loose ends.

Suddenly unemployed, John Hughes, Keith Goldfarb, Pauline Ts'o, Frank Wuts, Chris Boule, and Charlie Gibson decided to band together as Rhythm & Hues. The Los Angeles-based firm would be led by former Abel production head Hughes, with key staffer Gibson having served as its senior technical director and software designer. The new firm would utilize a single Silicon Graphics workstation computer that ran its own proprietary animation software. Although it started out working on television commercials, the company's long-term goal was to complete a fully computer-animated feature film.

Rhythm's early assignments included commercials for the Pacific Bell yellow pages, the Korean Summer Olympics, and Sunbeam microwave ovens, and it soon began winning a string of ad industry Clio awards for its efforts. The company also sought work in television and feature films, and by the early 1990s commercials were accounting for only about half of revenues, with movie visual effects, music videos, and animation for theme park motion ride clients including Disney, MCA, and the World's Fair making up the remainder. Ad

COMPANY PERSPECTIVES

At Rhythm & Hues we believe that the highest quality work is created in an environment where people enjoy working and where people are treated fairly, honestly and with respect.

Recognizing the collaborative nature of our medium, our designers actively seek input and advice from others, but ultimately a single individual is responsible for the final design decisions.

Our building is designed to bring people together into natural gathering places where chance encounters can stimulate new ideas. Our space itself is a physical counterpoint to the aesthetic problems that our designers are solving. Sunlight and shadow play off intersecting planes and surfaces.

It is our hope that this sensitivity to the human needs of our people will result in the creation of products which will entertain people the world over.

clients of this period included Reebok, Kellogg's, and Coke, for which the company made spots featuring animated polar bears on assignment from Creative Artists Agency.

In 1992 Rhythm branched out to form a live-action commercial division, which soon developed a roster of about a half-dozen directors. The company quickly became reliant on renting studio space for these projects, as well as ones involving miniatures and motion-control cameras, and in 1994 it bought a 35,000-square-foot, three-soundstage facility in North Hollywood from Praxis Film Works that included art department, model-making, and lighting operations. Praxis head Robert Blalack, who specialized in blending live action and digital effects and had shared the 1978 Best Visual Effects Oscar for his work on *Star Wars,* would begin handling assignments for Rhythm. In addition to serving its own productions, the renamed Rhythm & Hues Studios would offer soundstage and equipment rental under the name Avalon Stages.

Rhythm was also working on a ride called Seafari for a Matsushita theme park in Japan, and in 1994 it formed an interactive division to produce video games and educational materials. By 1995 the company employed 200 and was using 100 Silicon Graphics computers.

RELEASE OF *BABE:* 1995

In 1995 Rhythm won widespread acclaim for its work on the popular Universal Pictures release *Babe,* about a pig that wants to be a sheepdog. The firm had spent 18 months completing more than 130 effects shots for the movie, which made real animals appear to have human qualities. After film was shot in Australia it was scanned to digital form and then modified in California with software the firm had developed. Animators used mirrors to view their own faces as models for the animals' expressions, inserting a computer-generated lower lip or other features to the filmed images. As each sequence was finished, it was transmitted by telephone link to Australia in Avid editing format for integration into the film.

In March 1996 the firm's work on *Babe* won an Academy Award for Best Visual Effects, and during the year Rhythm also partnered with New York postproduction/computer animation company Manhattan Transfer/Edit to share work and facilities, giving it a presence on the East Coast and additional resources to complete projects. Assignments at this time included commercials for Kraft and work on the action film *Speed 2: Cruise Control,* the latter in conjunction with George Lucas's Industrial Light & Magic. Although its plate was full and it had taken home a coveted Oscar, profit margins were thin and the company recorded a loss for the year.

Assignments for 1997 included features *Face/Off* and *Mouse Hunt,* and work on motion-simulator ride films for "Star Trek: The Experience" at the Las Vegas Hilton and "Race for Atlantis" for Caesars Palace Las Vegas, the latter in the IMAX 3-D format. The firm's financial picture was improving, and it finished the year with a record profit.

In January 1998 founding partner Charles Gibson left Rhythm for a career as a freelance visual effects supervisor and sold his stake in the firm. The company would continue to be headed by president and CEO John Hughes. Feature work during the year included *Babe: Pig in the City, Soldier,* and *The Parent Trap.*

In the spring of 1999 Rhythm bought 20th Century Fox special effects unit VIFX, keeping about two-thirds of the 108 it employed to boost its workforce to 320. The purchase price was an estimated $3 million, less than half what Fox had paid for it three years earlier, with the unit having consistently lost money in part because it was not kept busy by its owner. VIFX President Richard Hollander, whose credits included *The X-Files, Alien: Resurrection,* and *Star Trek: Insurrection,* would become the head of Rhythm's feature film and theme park divisions, and its operations were moved into the company's 70,000-square-foot campus in Los

KEY DATES

1987: Rhythm & Hues is founded by group of ex-
Robert Abel animators.

1994: Firm buys Praxis studio operation, becomes
Rhythm & Hues Studios.

1995: *Babe* is released; talking pig wins visual effects
Oscar the following year.

1999: Acquisition of 20th Century Fox effects unit
VIFX.

2001: Indian unit is added in Mumbai.

2007: Second Indian facility is added in Hyderabad.

2008: Company shares second visual effects Oscar
for *The Golden Compass*.

2009: Firm adds operation in Kuala Lumpur,
Malaysia.

Angeles. Work during the year included commercials for Dodge, Mazda, Huggies, Nesquik, Sony, and Geico, the latter featuring an animated gecko lizard; and feature films *Mystery Men, The Flintstones in Viva Rock Vegas, The Green Mile,* and *End of Days.*

As the millennium turned the industry suffered slowdowns caused by an actors' strike and the U.S. economic downturn. The computer animation field was also becoming crowded with new studios, and budgets were tightening as bidders tried to undercut each other for jobs. In response, the firm restructured some operations and cut its workforce to about 300, and in the fall of 2000 launched a new unit called ToolBox, which would market its animation and visual effects services to outside commercial producers. Work during this period included *Cats & Dogs, Dr. Dolittle 2, Lord of the Rings,* and *Planet of the Apes.* In some cases Rhythm was still completing all effects shots for a feature, but studios were increasingly farming out work to multiple animation houses for a complicated film.

LAUNCH OF INDIAN OPERATION: 2001

The firm had for some time been finding it hard to recruit qualified personnel locally, and when a contract for the Fox movie *Daredevil* brought a sudden influx of work it decided to open a new office in Mumbai, India. The speed and capacity of international data connections had grown, and animators in California and India would be able to work side by side on projects that both could see together in real time. Unlike some competitors, who sent work overseas primarily to save costs and

with lower quality expectations, Rhythm's Indian operation was considered of equal stature and its animators were extensively trained and overseen by the firm's American staff.

Work during 2002 included ads for Cingular and Burger King, and feature films *Gigli* for Columbia, *Scooby-Doo* for Warner Brothers, and *The Sum of All Fears* for Paramount. The latter, a nuclear war action thriller, was a coup for the firm, whose reputation as "the house of talking animals" was largely based on its success with the *Babe* series. Rhythm also began selling its computer-generated animation models online during the year to computer artists and others via web site TurboSquid.com.

In 2003 and 2004 Rhythm was kept busy with assignments that included *The Cat in the Hat, Elf, Lord of the Rings III, X-Men 2, Around the World in 80 Days, Garfield,* and *Scooby-Doo 2,* as well as ads for Skippy snack bars. The firm also created nearly 400 effects shots for Disney's *The Chronicles of Narnia: The Lion, the Witch and the Wardrobe,* which required several effects houses to complete. The company worked on crowd action scenes as well as creating several key characters including Aslan, lion-ruler of Narnia. Although computer technology had improved dramatically since the firm's early days, the process of animation rendering could still take up to six hours per frame of film (24 of which were required per second), given the greater detail that could be achieved. The film took two years to complete, and was nominated for an Oscar for best visual effects.

In 2005 Rhythm also created a digitized version of the late Marlon Brando for *Superman Returns* based on his performance in a 1978 film, and in 2006 it worked on *Night at the Museum, Charlotte's Web, Evan Almighty,* and *Happy Feet.* Continually upgrading its equipment, during the year the firm added a new digital archive storage system from Sun Microsystems. In December 2006, Division President Richard Hollander left for a position at Pixar Animation Studios, and was replaced several months later by Lee Berger.

ADDITION OF SECOND INDIAN FACILITY: 2007

During 2007 the growing Rhythm opened a new animation facility in Hyderabad, India, to perform modeling, animation, and compositing. The firm was also named lead visual effects studio for *The Incredible Hulk* and did the majority of effects shots for *The Golden Compass,* with nearly 500 working on the project including 150 in India. Other work during the year included *Alvin and the Chipmunks* and *The Kingdom.*

In February 2008 Rhythm won its third Scientific and Technical Achievement Academy Award for software that animated fluids, as well as sharing the Oscar for Best Visual Effects for *The Golden Compass.* In May the firm announced plans to open an additional facility in Kuala Lumpur, Malaysia, which would eventually employ as many as 200. While a facility was constructed, it began training workers in India.

In early 2009 Rhythm announced that it planned to begin producing feature films on its own, which would include both a blend of live-action and animation and fully animated projects. The firm employed 735 in California and 280 in India, with the new Malaysian facility expected to begin operations by midyear. Current projects included *Land of the Lost, Night at the Museum: Battle of the Smithsonian, They Came from Upstairs, Cirque du Freak,* and *State of Play.*

Nearing the quarter-century mark, Rhythm & Hues Studios, Inc., had become a leading name in the field of computer animation. The firm's credits included work on more than 100 films and hundreds of commercials, and it was preparing to expand into production of its own features. With the movie industry increasingly reliant on digital visual effects, the firm appeared poised for continued growth.

Frank Uhle

PRINCIPAL SUBSIDIARIES

Rhythm & Hues Commercial Studios.

PRINCIPAL COMPETITORS

Industrial Light & Magic; Pixar Animation Studios, Inc.; Dreamworks Animation SKG; Sony Pictures Imageworks, Inc.; Animal Logic; Digital Domain, Inc.; Digiscope LLC; Cinesite (Europe) Ltd.; The Mill; Gray Matter FX; Rainmaker Entertainment, Inc.

FURTHER READING

Chaudhuri, Arcopol, "Rhythm & Hues Charting Westside Story," *DNA,* January 17, 2008.

Clark, Michael, "Rhythm & Hues Stages Frozen Follies for Coke, CAA," *SHOOT,* August 4, 1995, p. 12.

Cohen, David S., "Rhythm & Hues Cues Feature Biz," *Daily Variety,* February 8, 2009.

Crabtree, Sheigh, "R&H's Hollander Drawn to Pixar," *Hollywood Reporter,* December 4, 2006.

———, "Rhythm & Hues Changing Spots for 'Sum' Work," *Hollywood Reporter,* May 30, 2002, p. 1.

Denslow, Phil, "Cartoony Computer Animation at Rhythm & Hues," *Animation Magazine,* Summer 1988.

Giardina, Caroline, "Rhythm and Hues, MT/E Form Co-Venture," *SHOOT,* February 16, 1996, p. 1.

———, "Rhythm & Hues Sets Up Malaysian Shop," *Hollywood Reporter,* May 22, 2008.

Goldrich, Robert, "Charles Gibson Resigns from Rhythm & Hues," *SHOOT,* January 9, 1998, p. 1.

———, "Rhythm & Hues Acquires Praxis Stage Facility," *SHOOT,* July 29, 1994, p. 1.

———, "Rhythm & Hues in Rhythm for Second Year with CGI, Graphics Clio Award," *Back Stage,* June 29, 1990, p. 7.

Guarin, Evangeline, "Rhythm & Hues Completes Effects for Babe," *SHOOT,* August 19, 1995, p. 17.

"Hollywood Effects in HiTec City," *New Indian Express,* July 21, 2007.

"No Blues for Rhythm & Hues," *UNIX Today!* April 17, 1989, p. 30.

"Rhythm & Hues Rounds Up VIFX," *Hollywood Reporter,* March 3, 1999, p. 4.

Robertson, Barbara, "Offshore 3D," *Computer Graphics World,* October 2003, p. 20.

Takaki, Millie, "Rhythm & Hues' Spot Division Opens Tool-Box," *SHOOT,* October 20, 2000, p. 7.

Turnbow, Gene, "Pushing Light," *Computer Graphics World,* April 2007, p. 8.

Turner, Brook, "Oscar Hopes Ride on the Sheep's Back," *Sydney Morning Herald,* February 22, 1996, p. 17.

Roberts Dairy Company

———— ■ ————

2901 Cuming Street
Omaha, Nebraska 68131-2134
U.S.A.
Telephone: (402) 344-4321
Toll Free: (800) 779-4321
Fax: (402) 346-0849
Web site: http://www.robertsdairy.com

Private Company
Incorporated: 1911 as Roberts Sanitary Dairy
Employees: 900
Sales: $259.5 million (2007)
NAICS: 311511 Fluid Milk Manufacturing

■ ■ ■

Roberts Dairy Company is a regional producer of fluid milk, half-and-half, cream, butter, cottage cheese, sour cream and dips, yogurt, ice cream, and frozen treats. The Omaha, Nebraska-based private company also of- fers orange, apple, and grape juice; as well as lemonade, iced tea, and fruit punch. Roberts owns and operates three fluid milk and juice plants in Omaha; Kansas City, Missouri; and Iowa City, Iowa; and manages a joint venture with Hiland Dairy, the Hiland-Roberts Ice Cream Company plant in Norfolk, Nebraska. Through ten distribution centers in Nebraska, Iowa, Kansas, and Missouri, Roberts serves retail food and foodservice customers in those states and parts of Illinois, Colorado, and South Dakota. Roberts is co-owned by a pair of

dairy cooperatives: Prairie Farms Dairy, the managing partner, and Dairy Farmers of America.

DELIVERING MILK IN LINCOLN, NEBRASKA: 1906

Roberts Dairy was established in Lincoln, Nebraska, in 1906 as Roberts Sanitary Dairy when farmer James R. Roberts began providing home delivery of milk produced by his 60-cow herd. The business did well and two years later Roberts was able to move operations from his milkhouse to a new plant in downtown Lincoln. As his delivery territory grew, Roberts began using horse-drawn delivery wagons around 1910. He then incorporated the company in 1911 and moved to an even larger, modern plant in Lincoln, the only dairy in the area capable of offering pasteurized milk and the benefits of extended shelf life.

Roberts expanded beyond Lincoln in 1918 by opening a branch in Sioux City, Iowa. Four years later the company entered the Omaha market, where it enjoyed rapid growth. (In the early 1930s the company would establish its headquarters in Omaha.) His own herds unable to meet demand, Roberts began buying raw milk from other dairy farmers, who used five-gallon cans to make deliveries to the dairy each day. The company, reincorporated as Roberts Dairy Company in 1928, continued to rely on horse-drawn wagons until the end of the 1920s. One of the horses, Old Tom, became a company legend. In the harness for nearly 20 years, he was estimated to have delivered about three million bottles of milk, traversing some 75,000 miles. He died at the age of 22 in 1930.

Roberts Dairy Mission Statement: To provide products of superior quality and value while maintaining an atmosphere of teamwork, trust and high business ethics. Strive to maintain growth and profitability for the Company and our customers. To listen and respond to our Associates' suggestions, provide opportunities for them to advance their careers and maintain an environment where they may perform to their highest potential.

JAMES G. ROBERTS JOINS COMPANY: 1932

James R. Roberts grew ill in 1932 and his son, James Gordon Roberts, stepped in to help out, becoming president in 1939. Still in his early 20s when he joined the dairy, the younger Roberts had never planned to make a career out of the milk business and as a result took an unusual, often eccentric, approach to the business. Without his father's knowledge, he helped employees to form a labor union, primarily to afford them protection from a despotic foreman. Something of a philosopher, he also had interests that extended well beyond the dairy industry. He became a regular columnist for the *Omaha World Herald* in the late 1940s, writing for the paper well into the 1960s. His essays were part Roberts Dairy advertisement, part reflection on important events of the day and Roberts's musings about capitalism, taxation, the pursuit of happiness, and other topics he found of interest. In 1952 he wrote and self-published a short book called *A Rational Route to Peace and Prosperity in Our Time*. His milkmen were then charged with selling the book on their routes, the proceeds intended to fund an employee health and welfare fund. During the height of the Cold War when many people were concerned about nuclear war and fall-out shelters became commonplace, Roberts in the early 1960s built the country's first fall-out shelter for cows, one that could accommodate 250 Guernsey cows and three handlers, along with milking machines to presumably resume dairy production once conditions permitted.

Roberts did not neglect the family dairy business, however. He, in fact, became quite passionate about the subject of milk, drinking about two quarts each day as he sought ways to improve, package, and market it. Under his leadership in the 1950s Roberts Dairy introduced 2 percent milk fortified with vitamins A and

D, an endeavor that put him at odds with local officials. For a time he was also blocked from making yogurt. Another innovative item the dairy offered in the 1950s was a patented "Ready Egg" product. He also sought a patent on an imitation butter spread. During the decade, Roberts Dairy was in the vanguard of dairies switching from glass bottles to paper carton containers.

EXPANSION THROUGH ACQUISITIONS: 1960–70

The 1960s brought a period of rapid expansion for Roberts Dairy, which grew into a much larger concern through a series of acquisitions. The Skyline Dairy in Lincoln and the Royal Dairy in Omaha were purchased. In addition, the company acquired three dairies in Denver, Colorado (Sterns Dairy, Robinson Dairy, and Arvada-Gibson Dairy) and Roberts Perfection Foods was added in Orlando, Florida.

In 1967 Roberts married a portrait artist and moved to Florida. Roberts Perfection Foods was divested in 1971, the same year that Fairacres Foods of Grand Island, Nebraska, was acquired. In 1972 he decided to sell Roberts Dairy to Omaha-based American Beef Packers, Inc. Although he regretted the loss of the family business, he remained interested in milk, which he believed contained untapped cancer-fighting abilities. In 1977 he published *Cancer: How and Why It May Be Wiped Out* through Roberts Cancer Research Publications. He lived until 1996, dying at the age of 87 in a Florida nursing home.

DAIRY COOPERATIVES BUY COMPANY: 1980

Roberts Dairy enjoyed some growth under American Beef's ownership. It acquired a controlling stake in Platte Valley Foods, known for its french-fried onion rings, in 1973. A year later Roberts added a wholly owned subsidiary, Plasti-Cyc, a company that recycled plastic gallon milk jugs and other containers into a reusable plastic material. Roberts Dairy's connection with American Beef was short lived, however. In 1975 the company declared Chapter 11 bankruptcy and the dairy was put on the block. The Denver operation was sold back to the Robinson family (who had previously sold the Robinson Dairy to Roberts Dairy), while Cal Fisher and Dick Westin bought Roberts Dairy. Fisher assumed the presidency but the dairy did not do well during his tenure. By the end of the decade the business was losing about $150,000 a month. In January 1980 Roberts was sold to a dairy cooperative, Springfield, Missouri-based Mid-America Dairymen. Fisher left to establish Fisher

KEY DATES

1906: James R. Roberts begins delivering milk in Lincoln, Nebraska.

1911: Company incorporates as Roberts Sanitary Dairy.

1928: Business reincorporates as Roberts Dairy Company.

1939: Founder's son, James G. Roberts, becomes president.

1972: Dairy is sold to American Beef Packers, Inc.

1975: After American Beef declares bankruptcy, Roberts is sold.

1980: Mid-America Dairymen and Prairie Farms Dairy acquire Roberts.

1994: Ice cream production moves to plant in Norfolk, Nebraska.

2005: Production ceases at Des Moines, Iowa, plant.

Foods in Nebraska to produce custom stocks and broths.

Mid-America had taken shape in the late 1960s. First, three Missouri and Illinois co-ops (Sanitary Milk Producers, the Producers Creamery Co., and Square Deal Milk Producers) merged in 1966, creating the St. Louis-Ozarks Marketing Agency (SLOMA). It operated under Associated Dairymen, a two-year-old federated cooperative that itself had been formed within the National Milk Producers Federation, part of an effort to address regional and local problems facing co-op members. In 1968 another Missouri co-op, Producers Creamery Company, and the newly formed Mid-America Dairymen of Kansas City were brought into the SLOMA fold, but rather than keeping the nondescriptive SLOMA name, the members chose to appropriate the Mid-America Dairymen name. The organization survived growing pains in the 1970s (at one point almost forced into bankruptcy), but a restructuring effort led by Gary Hanman, the former chief executive of Square Deal, allowed Mid-America to gain its footing. After thinning the ranks of top management, selling factories as well as company aircraft, and eliminating the use of company cars, Hanman returned the cooperative to profitability in just one year. He then reduced Mid-America's dependency on commodity sales, forming a marketing subsidiary to promote the Mid-America Farms brand and better compete with larger competitors including Land O'Lakes and Kraft.

MID-AMERICA AND PRAIRIE FARMS ESTABLISH JOINT VENTURE: 1979

Other keys to Mid-America's success were joint ventures Hanman engineered with other companies. He took on a partner for Roberts Dairy, Carlinville, Illinois-based cooperative Prairie Farms Dairy, which became the managing partner of the Nebraska dairy. Prairie Farms was established in the early 1930s as a way for small farmers to join forces to sell their excess cream at a better price for butter production. The Producers Creamery of Carlinville opened its own butter-churning plant in 1938. During World War II the plant turned its attention to the collection of whole milk to produce powdered milk and also began selling cream and some bulk milk. Sweetened condensed milk for sale to ice cream manufacturers followed in 1945, leading to a change in name to Prairie Farms Creamery of Carlinville. Starting in 1954 Prairie Farms enjoyed steady growth through a series of mergers and acquisitions. In 1978 the cooperative shifted gears to pursue a strategy of achieving growth through joint ventures. In 1979 it joined forces with Mid-America to acquire Hiland Dairy, with the former supplying the milk and the latter assuming management of the operation. A year later the two companies again teamed up with a similar arrangement involving Roberts Dairy.

Roberts's new owners quickly moved to turn around the business. The manager of the Prairie Farms dairy in Des Moines, Iowa, 60-year-old Randall E. Winters, was installed as president. Roberts's headquarters were shifted to Des Moines as Winters took charge of the rescue effort. The new owners invested about $6 million in new equipment. Cost-cutting measures were also initiated, productivity was increased, and the dairy placed a renewed emphasis on quality. The delivery fleet was also upgraded, as were the accounting system and office operations. As a result, when good fortune took place the company was ready to take advantage of it. In Omaha the Hy-Vee Foods Co. supermarket chain acquired ten shuttered Safeway stores and awarded the dairy business to Roberts, which could put to better use a plant designed to process 20 million pounds of milk per month, which until that point had contracts for only ten million pounds of milk per month. The more efficient Omaha plant also took over milk production from other cooperative-owned plants.

In addition to capital and management, Roberts's new co-owners supplied new facilities. In 1980 Home-Town Dairy of Iowa City was added, and soon Prairie Farms contributed a fluid milk dairy in Des Moines. In the meantime, Roberts closed its plants in Lincoln,

Grand Island, and Sioux City. By 1987 the three remaining plants were generating about $130 million, a significant improvement over the $80 million they combined to produce just six years earlier. At the start of 1988 Winters retired, and Roberts's headquarters returned to Omaha.

ICE CREAM PRODUCTION MOVES: 1994

Winters was succeeded as president by the general manager of the Omaha plant, Ronald Richardson. The company continued to grow under his leadership. In 1989 it acquired the Fairmont-Zarda milk and ice cream plants in Kansas City, Missouri. Two years later Roberts took on the management of the Norfolk, Nebraska, Gillette ice cream and fluid milk plant owned by Mid-America. In 1994 the production of ice cream was transferred from Kansas City to the Gillette plant. A few months earlier the dairy had consolidated its three ice cream brands, opting to discontinue the Roberts brand and combine the Fairmont and Gillette names to create the Fairmont/Gillette brand. The Roberts label continued to adorn milk and other products. In 1996 Mid-America sold the Gillette ice cream plant to a joint venture created between Roberts and Springfield, Missouri-based Hiland Dairy, resulting in Hiland-Roberts Ice Cream Company. A year later the Fairmont name was dropped from the label and ice cream was sold under the Gillette name alone. Also of note in the late 1990s, Mid-America merged with three other cooperatives to create Dairy Farmers of America, Inc., the United States' largest dairy co-op, which became Roberts's co-owner.

In 2000 Richardson stepped down as president after 14 years in office, turning over the helm to Jeff Powell, a dairy industry veteran with 24 years of experience in both sales and plant operations. He took over a successful company, but one that did not lack for new challenges, primarily due to supermarket consolidation that threatened to slow growth. To spur milk sales the dairy launched a campaign to encourage milk consumption among children. Other measures would also be necessary. In 2005 production was terminated at the Des Moines plant, leaving just the three production plants in Omaha, Kansas City, and Iowa City, as well as the Hiland-Roberts ice cream plant in Norfolk.

Ed Dinger

COMPANY CELEBRATES 100TH ANNIVERSARY

Roberts celebrated its 100th anniversary in 2006. It generated annual sales of more than $250 million but in the next few years had to contend with a spike in the price of fuel as well as ever increasing insurance premiums and other escalating operational costs. Nevertheless, it had the advantage of being owned by a pair of companies with deep pockets, providing some level of assurance that Roberts Dairy would continue to prosper well into the second century of its existence.

PRINCIPAL SUBSIDIARIES

Roberts Dairy Omaha; Roberts Dairy Kansas City; Roberts Dairy Iowa City.

PRINCIPAL COMPETITORS

Dean Foods Company; Kemps LLC; Land O'Lakes, Inc.

FURTHER READING

Beeder, David C., "Roberts Dairy Turns Profit Center," *Omaha World-Herald,* October 12, 1984.

Dudlicek, James, "100 Years and Growing," *Dairy Field,* September 2006, p. 20.

Gersten, Alan, "50 Years in the Business Retiring Dairy Head Recalls Challenges," *Omaha World-Herald,* December 6, 1987.

Norris, Melinda, "Gillette Dairy to Drop Fairmont Name," *Omaha World-Herald,* February 1, 1997, p. 26.

"Powell Takes Roberts Dairy into 21st Century," *Dairy Foods,* December 2000, p. 16.

"Roberts to Remove Name from Ice Cream," *Omaha World-Herald,* May 11, 1993, p. 14.

Rowell, Rainbow, "James Roberts, Dairyman with Innovative Ideas," *Omaha World-Herald,* November 10, 1996, p. 1B.

Ruff, Joe, "Roberts Celebrates a Century in Business," *Omaha World-Herald,* May 19, 2006.

Rockwell Automation

Rockwell Automation, Inc.

1201 South Second Street
Milwaukee, Wisconsin 53204-2410
U.S.A.
Telephone: (414) 382-2000
Fax: (414) 382-4444
Web site: http://www.rockwellautomation.com

Public Company
Incorporated: 1928 as North American Aviation
Employees: 21,000
Sales: $5.7 billion (2008)
Stock Exchanges: New York
Ticker Symbol: ROK
NAICS: 333612 Speed Changer, Industrial High-Speed Drive, and Gear Manufacturing; 334290 Other Communications Equipment Manufacturing; 334513 Instruments and Related Products Manufacturing for Measuring, Displaying, and Controlling Industrial Process Variables; 335311 Power, Distribution, and Specialty Transformer Manufacturing; 335314 Relay and Industrial Control Manufacturing; 335999 All Other Miscellaneous Electrical Equipment and Component Manufacturing; 511210 Software Publishers

∎ ∎ ∎

Rockwell Automation, Inc., specializes in industrial automation products, software, systems, and services. Among the company's offerings are controllers, variable-speed drives, input/output (I/O) systems, sensors, power supplies, network and communications devices, and signaling equipment, along with the computers and software that tie such devices together. Main brand names include Rockwell Automation, Allen-Bradley, A-B, ICS Triplex, Rockwell Software, and FactoryTalk. Rockwell Automation serves a wide range of industries in more than 80 countries using a combination of direct sales and sales through distributors. About half of the firm's sales are generated outside the United States, with Canada, the United Kingdom, Italy, China, Brazil, and Germany comprising the largest foreign markets. Rockwell Automation emerged in the early 21st century as the successor to Rockwell International Corporation, which was best known as a major defense and aerospace firm, after the latter made a series of strategic divestments starting in the mid-1990s.

EARLY HISTORY OF NORTH AMERICAN AVIATION

Charles Lindbergh's flight across the Atlantic in 1927 generated such interest in aviation that suddenly even small aviation companies were deluged with money from investors. So much capital was made available by investors (almost $1 billion by 1929) that holding companies created hundreds of airlines and airplane manufacturers. Three companies in particular emerged in the late 1920s as the largest aeronautic concerns: the Aviation Corporation of the Americas (Avco), run by Averell Harriman and the Lehman Brothers investment firm; the Boeing/Rentschler consortium known as United Aircraft and Transportation; and North American Aviation, the predecessor of Rockwell International, organized by a New York financier named Clement Keys.

Once the engine manufacturer Pratt & Whitney
had secured two airplane manufacturers and a major
airline, the United Aircraft consortium, as exclusive
customers, Clement Keys recognized that his company
needed a similar affiliation if it was to survive. He finalized an arrangement wherein the Wright Engine
Company became the exclusive supplier of engines for
North American Aviation.

North American's major airline, National Air
Transport, was one of 45 aviation companies operated
by Keys; the list also included the Curtiss Aeroplane &
Motor Company and Wright Engine. Curtiss was a successful manufacturer of such airplanes as the Condor,
and Wright manufactured some of the highest quality
aircraft engines of the day. North American also owned
Eastern Air Lines, the pioneer of air service along the
eastern coast of the United States, and Transcontinental
Air Transport. These subsidiaries made the parent
company's stock even more attractive. Money continued
to flow into North American from investor groups,
making the original stockholders (Keys among them)
extremely wealthy.

The bright future of the aviation companies came
to an abrupt end on October 24, 1929, when a financial
disaster hit Wall Street. Virtually all stocks were inflated
in value and backed only with borrowed funds. When
investors realized that the market could no longer support the inflated values of their stock, they flooded
brokerage houses with orders to sell. The large number
of claims led people, banks, and companies into
bankruptcy. The resulting stock market crash brought
about a ten-year world depression.

In 1930 North American lost its majority control of
National Air Transport to the United Aircraft company.
The buyout provided temporary relief to financially
troubled North American, which was purchased by
General Motors four years later. General Motors was

one of the few companies with capital available to
refinance a business that held such promise for the
future. General Motors acquired North American in an
attempt to diversify, because its own product was not
selling well during the Great Depression.

Keys retired from business in 1932 because of ill
health, and James Howard Kindelberger, who was with
Donald Douglas during development of the DC-1 and
DC-2, was made president of North American in 1935.
He was trained as an engineer but knew the automotive
business so well that his managerial acumen
overshadowed his engineering skills.

General Motors, which held a substantial amount
of stock in Trans World Airlines, sold its holdings in
that company in 1936. In the same year, North
American (still a subsidiary of General Motors) sold its
Eastern Air Lines unit to the airline's director, Eddie
Rickenbacker. The divestiture of airline companies from
airplane manufacturers was forced upon the three largest
aeronautic conglomerates by Senator Hugo Black, who
also advocated the breakup of numerous other
monopolies. North American Aviation was no longer an
airline company but merely a manufacturer of airplanes
and airplane parts.

During World War II, North American
manufactured thousands of P-51 Mustangs for the U.S.
Army Air Corps. The P-51, one of the last mass-
produced piston engine airplanes, saw action in every
theater during the war. The company also built the B-25
Mitchell bomber and T-6 Texan trainer. The company
built more airplanes for the U.S. military than any other
company during the war years. The rapid expansion of
the company was financed mostly by the government,
which was North American's largest customer.

DEFENSE AND AEROSPACE
CONTRACTING IN THE
POSTWAR ERA

When the war ended, North American's military
contracts also ended. Like Grumman Corporation,
North American opted to avoid entering the competitive
commercial airliner market. Instead, the company
focused its resources on the development of the next
generation of military aircraft, namely, jets. Working
from designs and prototypes of jet aircraft captured
from the Germans after the war, North American built
its first fighter jet, called the F-86 Sabre. Because the
Sabre's supersonic wings were developed from German
designs, the company saved millions of dollars in
research and development costs.

In the years after the war, North American attempted to enter the private airplane market, with a

KEY DATES

1903: Lynde Bradley and Dr. Stanton Allen create the Compression Rheostat Company.

1909: Compression Rheostat is renamed Allen-Bradley Company.

1919: Willard Rockwell founds Wisconsin Parts Company.

1928: North American Aviation is established and soon becomes one of the three largest aeronautic concerns in the country.

1930: Collins Radio Company is founded to build and sell radio transmitters.

1948: North American Aviation begins diversification into rockets, guidance systems, and atomic energy.

1953: Rockwell merges Wisconsin Parts and two other firms to form Rockwell Spring and Axle Company.

1958: Rockwell Spring is renamed Rockwell-Standard.

1967: Rockwell-Standard merges with North American Aviation to form North American Rockwell.

1973: North American Rockwell acquires Collins Radio; following merger with Rockwell Manufacturing, the company is renamed Rockwell International.

1985: Rockwell acquires Allen-Bradley Company of Milwaukee, thereby entering the industrial automation sector.

1995: Rockwell acquires Reliance Electric.

1996: Graphic systems and defense and aerospace businesses are sold off.

1997: Automotive business is spun off to shareholders as Meritor Automotive Inc.

1998: Company spins off its semiconductor operations to shareholders as Conexant Systems, Inc.

1999: Rockwell relocates to Milwaukee.

2001: Rockwell Collins is spun off to shareholders; Rockwell International changes its name to Rockwell Automation, Inc.

2007: Rockwell Automation divests the bulk of its power systems business, including the Reliance line of industrial electric motors.

small four-passenger plane called the Navion. Poor sales of the Navion, however, convinced company management of the futility of entering the private market. In 1947 the design and production rights to the Navion were sold to Ryan Aeronautical.

North American continued to develop new equipment for the military. The company built a number of fighters and trainers for the Navy's aircraft carriers, in addition to a new jet called the F-100 Super Sabre. North American also constructed the first experimental supersonic aircraft, the rocket-powered X-15 and X-70.

When General Motors sold its share of the company in 1948, North American diversified its product line, becoming involved in the development of rockets, guidance systems, and atomic energy. It created Rocketdyne, Autonetics, and Atomics International as new divisions to pursue research in those individual fields. Here again, Rocketdyne was assisted by the Germans; much of its rocket and missile technology was acquired from captured German data.

Kindelberger, who had been promoted to chairperson, and the company's new president, J. L. Atwood, planned the company's diversification before the war ended. They both knew that in order for the company to survive the postwar environment, they would have to prove the company's worth to the government by leading the development of the newest defense systems. The government could then justifiably be asked to fund much of the costly development of any new systems.

The company's greatest success was in its Rocketdyne division, which produced the Thor, Jupiter, Redstone, and Atlas rockets. The research and development of an atomic-powered missile was abandoned when the system was declared impractical and unworkable. Research from the ambitious but ill-fated project was converted for use in the development of nuclear reactors.

When the Soviet Union put Yuri Gagarin into space in 1961, the U.S. space program was jolted into action. North American's Redstone rocket was used to launch Alan Shepard and Virgil "Gus" Grissom into space during the Mercury space program in 1961. Later, John Glenn was launched into orbit aboard a Mercury spacecraft perched atop an Atlas rocket. North American Aviation enabled the United States to recover its technological edge in the space race with the Soviet Union.

In order to meet President John F. Kennedy's challenge to land a man on the moon before 1970, the National Aeronautics and Space Administration (NASA) contracted North American to build the three-passenger

Apollo 1 space capsule. On January 27, 1967, a flash fire swept through the manned capsule during a ground test. Killed in the accident were Grissom, Edward White II, and Roger Chaffee. The astronauts' widows each received $350,000 in a legal settlement, but North American was still harshly criticized. Despite the fact that most of its business involved government contracts, the company suffered severe financial reverses that threatened it with bankruptcy. Within two months of the accident, North American Aviation was a prime candidate for a takeover.

MERGER WITH ROCKWELL-STANDARD

Rockwell-Standard made a $922 million bid for North American Aviation in March 1967. Rockwell-Standard was established in Wisconsin in 1919 as a manufacturer of truck axles and was initially known as Wisconsin Parts Company. Willard Rockwell was the company founder. Rockwell later took over Timken Detroit Axle and Standard Steel Spring Company, the latter based in Coraopolis, Pennsylvania. In 1953 Rockwell merged these three companies to form Rockwell Spring and Axle Company, which was renamed Rockwell-Standard in 1958. By 1967 Rockwell-Standard was the world's leading producer of mechanical automotive parts, including parts for both light and heavy vehicles, in addition to being a manufacturer of industrial machinery.

Under the terms of the merger, J. L. Atwood, president and CEO of North American, would assume the same duties at the new company, while Colonel Willard Rockwell, of Rockwell-Standard, would serve as chairperson. The merger was delayed for a few months by the Justice Department, which argued that the merger would be anticompetitive. The problems were finally resolved and the smaller Rockwell, with sales of $636 million, took over North American, with sales of $2.37 billion.

Atwood said the merger was "in furtherance of North American's previously announced objective to diversify its activities into the commercial and industrial sector." What the company management really wanted was to improve its public image. Its association with the Apollo space capsule tragedy was never forgotten. The merger with the Rockwell company would recover the reputation of integrity that management thought North American deserved. It was clear that Colonel Rockwell would be firmly in charge of the new company, which was called North American Rockwell.

Rockwell's role in the U.S. space program continued, but the company maintained a low profile. It spent much of its first years after the merger

manufacturing car and truck parts, printing presses (following the 1969 acquisition of Miehle-Goss-Dexter), tools, industrial sewing machines, and electronic instruments for flight and navigation. The company devoted much of its resources to the development of space systems, including the enormous Saturn V rocket engines, which launched subsequent Apollo missions to the moon. Later, the company was chosen as the primary contractor for NASA's space shuttles. During this time, it also became NASA's largest contractor, a position it continued to hold into the 1990s.

EMERGENCE OF ROCKWELL INTERNATIONAL

In 1973 the company acquired Collins Radio Company, which had been founded in 1930 and began selling amateur radio transmitters in 1933. The company developed the first modem in 1955, which was as large as a refrigerator and weighed 700 pounds. Collins became the cornerstone of Rockwell's avionics and communications operations. North American Rockwell also merged in 1973 with the Rockwell Manufacturing Company, a separate company created by Willard Rockwell Jr. Following this merger, the company changed its name to Rockwell International.

Willard Rockwell Jr., who took over from his father in 1967, retired in 1979, and Robert Anderson assumed the position of chairperson. Anderson had joined Rockwell in 1968 after he left Chrysler Corporation. He was named president of Rockwell in 1970 and CEO in 1974. Anderson's background in the automotive business made him a conservative and cautious manager. Generally regarded as an engineer more than as a financial manager, he had a strategy for the company's growth and expansion that was markedly different from that of his predecessor. Anderson himself later remarked, "it's fair to say that we disagreed on the direction of the company altogether."

Under the junior Rockwell, the company made some risky acquisitions, stretching its balance sheet to an uncomfortable degree. At one point the company was reportedly losing a million dollars a day. Rockwell was trying to establish the firm's business in high-profile consumer markets, such as Admiral television, which Anderson sold in 1974.

Anderson, who was originally hired to smooth the transition of management and resources during the 1967 merger, had little tolerance for the waste usually associated with defense contracts. He introduced the General Motors policy, which required all company divisions to submit profit goals for various production periods. As a result of Anderson's strict management,

Rockwell's debt-equity ratio (the company's debt divided by its net worth) fell from 99 percent in 1974 to 50 percent in 1977 and to 9 percent in 1983.

DEVELOPMENTS IN MILITARY/AEROSPACE CONTRACTING

Rockwell had initially planned to build the B-1 bomber, but in 1977 the administration of President Jimmy Carter canceled the program, favoring instead the development of Northrop's stealth bomber. By 1983, however, the Reagan administration had reactivated the B-1 project as part of its ambitious military program. Production of the B-1 bomber was expected to generate a profit of approximately $2 billion a year for Rockwell, but subsequent orders for more of the bombers ceased. Once again, Rockwell and its B-1 were summarily excluded from consideration for the production of the next U.S. strategic bomber. The company still had other defense contracts, however: the MX "Peacekeeper" missile (designed to replace the nation's stock of aging minuteman missiles), five space shuttles, and a navigation satellite called Navstar.

Willard Rockwell Jr. resigned as a consultant to Rockwell in 1984 because of a conflict of interest between the company and a separate concern he founded in 1979 called Astrotech. Astrotech was negotiating to purchase one or more of NASA's space shuttles in the belief that only private enterprise could make shuttle flights profitable.

That venture was indefinitely postponed by the explosion of the space shuttle *Challenger* in January 1986. An investigation of the accident later revealed that one of the booster rockets malfunctioned and caused the rocket to collide with the huge external fuel tank. The resulting explosion decimated the orbiter and killed all seven of its astronauts. A few months later President Ronald Reagan announced the order for a new shuttle from Rockwell to replace the *Challenger.*

Shortly before the accident Rockwell was implicated in a government investigation into illegal overcharges on various government contracts. The company was banned from further contract awards until Anderson himself convinced Air Force Secretary Vernon Orr to reinstate the company in December 1985. Anderson promised to fire senior managers involved in any illegal activities.

ENTRY INTO INDUSTRIAL AUTOMATION VIA 1985 PURCHASE OF ALLEN-BRADLEY

In 1985 Anderson oversaw the first major acquisition of his career at Rockwell with the $1.65 billion purchase of the Allen-Bradley Company of Milwaukee. Rockwell was suffering from a decrease in business after the cancellation of the B-1 bomber and the completion of the space shuttles. Allen-Bradley provided Rockwell with steady profits from its operations and helped to reduce the company's dependence on government contracts. Allen-Bradley, a successful manufacturer of industrial automation systems, traced its origins back to 1903, when Lynde Bradley and Dr. Stanton Allen created the Compression Rheostat Company, which adopted the Allen-Bradley name in 1909. A key introduction came in 1920: the "Bradleystat," a rheostat (a resistor that regulates a current) designed for automotive dashboards and radios; sales of the Bradleystat exceeded $1.1 million by 1924. By 1985, Allen-Bradley was the number one maker of industrial automation equipment in North America, with revenues of more than $1 billion.

Robert Anderson retired in 1988, relinquishing control of the company to its president, Donald R. Beall, who had been priming himself for Rockwell's leadership position for a decade. Ten years earlier, in 1978, when Beall was president of Rockwell's electronic division in Dallas, he reportedly spent one evening composing some 14 pages of notes delineating what he would do if given control of Rockwell. He was finally given that opportunity and immediately set himself the task of redefining the company's future.

A principal component of Beall's strategy was to reduce Rockwell's dependence on federal defense contracts and increase its presence in the electronics market. Specifically, this meant an expansion of Rockwell's telecommunications operations and a more significant role for the company's Allen-Bradley subsidiary, which Beall had encouraged Anderson to acquire. To make the company more responsive to customers, Beall granted company managers nearly autonomous control of their operations and then sharply reduced the bureaucratic layers of management that had accumulated over the years. Seven management levels were compressed into three, the company's headquarters staff was cut by more than half, and Rockwell's various businesses were reorganized into four major categories: electronics products, automotive products, a graphics unit (which manufactured high-speed newspaper presses), and aerospace.

TRANSFORMING ROCKWELL IN THE LATE 20TH CENTURY

In the early 1990s, before Beall could complete his transformation of Rockwell, however, economic conditions soured, sending the national economy into a tailspin and shrouding Beall's efforts to create a more diversified, commercially oriented company. Despite the economic downturn, Beall funneled more than $250 million into Allen-Bradley to create a new generation of factory automation products, which, coupled with the company's commanding presence in the market for high-speed modems (a product of Rockwell's 1973 acquisition of Collins Radio), provided two stable, commercially oriented legs for the company to stand on once economic conditions improved.

When conditions did improve, the fruits of Beall's strategy were unveiled. Government-funded business, which in 1988 had accounted for 50 percent of Rockwell's revenues, contributed only 23 percent to the company's sales total in 1993, a span during which 40,000 government-funded jobs within the company had been eliminated. Conversely, Rockwell's commercial business had grown substantially, fueled by Beall's efforts to expand the company's telecommunications business and bolster Allen-Bradley's market position. By 1994, Rockwell's telecommunications unit was manufacturing 80 percent of all modems in computers and fax machines sold throughout the world, while the company's investment in Allen-Bradley began paying dividends, buoyed by a more favorable economic picture. In early 1994, Allen-Bradley was recording $8.1 million in sales per day, the greatest amount in the company's history and cause for much optimism for Rockwell's future as a more dynamic player in the commercial electronics market.

Rockwell solidified its move into industrial automation in January 1995 with the acquisition of Reliance Electric Company for $1.6 billion, outbidding General Signal Corporation in a several-months-long takeover battle. The addition of Reliance made industrial automation Rockwell's largest business, accounting for 28 percent of overall revenues in fiscal 1995. Reliance was a producer of electric motors and drives used in factories, making for a strategic fit with Allen-Bradley's factory automation systems. Reliance traced its roots back to the founding in 1904 in Cleveland, Ohio, of Lincoln Electric Manufacturing Company, whose first product was the Type AS DC motor. In 1967 Reliance acquired Dodge Mechanical Company, a firm specializing in gear reducers, mounted bearings, and power transmission components.

In mid-1995 Don H. Davis was named president, with Beall remaining chairman and CEO. Shortly thereafter, Rockwell began a series of moves that dramatically changed the nature of the company. Seeking to focus the company on the potentially higher growth areas of electronics and communications, Beall and Davis began divesting operations outside of these areas. In 1996 Rockwell sold its graphic systems business to Stonington Partners Inc. for $600 million. Then

late in 1996 the company sold its defense and aerospace businesses—its best-known operations—to Boeing for $3.2 billion, one part of an ongoing consolidation of the U.S. defense industry. Following the latter sale, business with the Defense Department and NASA accounted for only 6 percent of Rockwell revenues. A further concentration on core areas came in September 1997 when Rockwell spun off its automotive business to shareholders as Meritor Automotive, Inc.

The divestments left Rockwell with three core businesses: automation, avionics and communications (known as Rockwell Collins), and semiconductors. Rockwell Collins was beefed up in December 1997 through the purchase of the in-flight entertainment business of Hughes-Avicom International, Inc. In early 1998 Beall retired and Davis took over as chairman and CEO.

Davis quickly left his own mark on the company with another spinoff. Facing a sluggish and potentially volatile market for semiconductors, Rockwell in December 1998 spun off its semiconductor operations to shareholders as Conexant Systems, Inc. This move also precipitated a shifting of the company headquarters in 1999 from California to Milwaukee, where its industrial automation business was located. Meantime, the company launched a sweeping restructuring of its automation operations in mid-1998 that included the layoff of about 3,000 of the unit's 27,000 employees, the closure of factories and the exit from certain product lines, and special charges of nearly $600 million. Consequently, for the fiscal year ending in September 1998, Rockwell posted a net loss of $437 million on sales of $6.75 billion.

EARLY 21ST CENTURY: EMERGENCE OF ROCKWELL AUTOMATION

In the final chapter of the dramatic transformation of Rockwell International, the company spun off Rockwell Collins to shareholders in June 2001. Other than both being in the general field of electronics, the two remaining legs of Rockwell International had little in common, giving impetus to the breakup. Davis remained chairman and CEO of the automation firm, which began operating under the name Rockwell Automation, and later officially changed its corporate name to Rockwell Automation, Inc. Just prior to the completion of the spinoff, Rockwell announced plans to cut 1,000 jobs and close one factory in an effort to trim expenses by $100 million in the face of a stagnating U.S. economy. The newly incarnated Rockwell Automation thus began on rather shaky ground, but Davis was confident that his company's business would rebound when the general U.S. industrial sector entered a new period of growth.

As U.S. manufacturers cut back on their orders for automation equipment during the economic downturn, Rockwell responded by trimming its staff by a couple thousand and pushing its consulting services to counter the drop-off in manufacturing revenue. The firm also completed a series of strategic acquisitions to fill in particular product, technology, and geographic gaps in its operations. For instance, the January 2002 purchase of Tesch GmbH bolstered the company's safety product portfolio and its position in Europe, while the acquisition of Propack Data GmbH expanded Rockwell's presence in the provision of information systems for the pharmaceutical, food and beverage, and specialty chemicals markets. Growth returned to Rockwell in fiscal 2003, when net income nearly doubled to $286 million while sales edged up 5 percent to $4.1 billion.

In February 2004 Keith Nosbusch was named CEO. Davis remained chairman for an additional year, at which point Nosbusch assumed that post as well. The new leader was a company veteran who had risen through the engineering ranks at Allen-Bradley and Rockwell and had spent about six years heading Rockwell's control systems division. At this time, the market for automation equipment in the United States was limited more to upgrading existing systems than installing new ones in concert with capacity upgrades. Nosbusch thus placed increasing emphasis on overseas markets where new factories were still being built. By fiscal 2005, non-U.S. revenue had reached more than 38 percent of the total, with the Asia-Pacific and Latin American regions leading the way with sales increases of 16 percent and 27 percent, respectively. One of Rockwell's fastest growing markets was China, where sales reached $145 million by 2005. Other important growth markets included India, Mexico, Brazil, and Central and Eastern Europe.

In 2006 Rockwell Automation and its Rockwell Collins spinoff sold their jointly owned research and development unit, Rockwell Scientific Company LLC, to Teledyne Technologies, Inc. A much more significant divestment occurred in January 2007 when Rockwell Automation sold the bulk of its power systems business to Baldor Electric Company for $1.83 billion in cash and stock. Included in the divested assets, which had generated about $1 billion in annual sales, were the Reliance line of industrial electric motors and the Dodge line of power transmission products. Rockwell thus became even more focused on high-tech factory automation systems and services based on computers and advanced software.

Rockwell proceeded to complete a string of acquisitions, particularly of software companies, that filled in gaps in its core business. The largest during this period was the July 2007, $218 million purchase of Industrial Control Services Group Limited, which operated under the name ICS Triplex. This British firm specialized in the supply of control and safety solutions for the oil and gas, chemical, and power generation industries.

Rockwell remained solidly profitable through fiscal 2008, when net income totaled $577.6 million on sales of $5.7 billion. The overseas push reached milestone status that year when half of the company's sales were generated outside the United States. Rockwell aimed to increase its non-U.S. revenues to 60 percent of the total by 2013 by targeting faster-growing markets such as China. At the same time, Rockwell was developing the ability to offer manufacturers integrated control, power, communications, and information technology systems, and by doing so the company hoped to capture a greater share of its customers' business systems investments. The global economic downturn, however, posed new challenges for the firm over the course of 2008 and into 2009 as manufacturers severely reined in their capital spending. By February 2009 Rockwell had announced plans to reduce its costs for the 2009 fiscal year by $240 million to mitigate the effects of this particularly steep economic slump.

Jeffrey L. Covell
Updated, David E. Salamie

PRINCIPAL SUBSIDIARIES

Allen-Bradley Company; ICS Triplex Holdings Inc.; Industrial Control Services Group Limited (UK); PT Rockwell Automation Indonesia; Rockwell Automation (China) Co., Ltd.; Rockwell Automation (Malaysia) SDN. BHD.; Rockwell Automation (N.Z.) Ltd. (New Zealand); Rockwell Automation (Philippines), Inc.; Rockwell Automation (Proprietary) Ltd. (South Africa); Rockwell Automation (Xiamen) Ltd. (China); Rockwell Automation A.B. (Sweden); Rockwell Automation A.G. (Switzerland); Rockwell Automation A/S (Denmark); Rockwell Automation Argentina S.A.; Rockwell Automation Asia Pacific Business Center PTE. Ltd. (Singapore); Rockwell Automation Asia Pacific Limited (Hong Kong); Rockwell Automation Australia Ltd.; Rockwell Automation B.V. (Netherlands); Rockwell Automation Bolivia Srl; Rockwell Automation Canada Control Systems; Rockwell Automation Canada Inc.; Rockwell Automation Canada Nova Scotia Co.; Rockwell Automation Chile S. A.; Rockwell Automation Control Solutions (Shanghai) Co. Ltd. (China); Rockwell Automation de Mexico S.A. de C.V.; Rockwell

Automation de Peru S.A.; Rockwell Automation de Venezuela, C.A.; Rockwell Automation do Brasil Ltda. (Brazil); Rockwell Automation Ecuador Compania Limitada; Rockwell Automation Europe B.V. (Netherlands); Rockwell Automation European Headquarters S.A./N.V. (Belgium); Rockwell Automation Finland Oy; Rockwell Automation G.m.b.H. (Germany); Rockwell Automation Germany G.m.b.H. & Co. KG; Rockwell Automation GesmbH (Austria); Rockwell Automation Guatemala, Limitada; Rockwell Automation Holdings B.V. (Netherlands); Rockwell Automation Holdings G.m.b.H. (Germany); Rockwell Automation India Ltd.; Rockwell Automation International Holdings LLC; Rockwell Automation Japan Co., Ltd.; Rockwell Automation Korea Ltd.; Rockwell Automation Limitada (Portugal); Rockwell Automation Limited (Ireland); Rockwell Automation Limited (UK); Rockwell Automation Manufacturing (Shanghai) Limited (China); Rockwell Automation Monterrey Manufacturing, S. de RL de CV (Mexico); Rockwell Automation Monterrey Services, S. de RL de CV (Mexico); Rockwell Automation of Ohio, Inc.; Rockwell Automation Puerto Rico, Inc.; Rockwell Automation Research (Shanghai) Company Limited (China); Rockwell Automation S.A. (Spain); Rockwell Automation S.A./N.V. (Belgium); Rockwell Automation S.r.l. (Italy); Rockwell Automation s.r.o. (Czech Republic); Rockwell Automation Sales Company, LLC; Rockwell Automation SAS (France); Rockwell Automation Services s.r.o. (Czech Republic); Rockwell Automation Slovakia s.r.o.; Rockwell Automation Solutions G.m.b.H. (Germany); Rockwell Automation Southeast Asia Pte. Ltd. (Singapore); Rockwell Automation Sp.z.o.o. (Poland); Rockwell Automation Taiwan Co., Ltd.; Rockwell Automation Technologies, Inc.; Rockwell Automation Thai Co. Ltd. (Thailand); Rockwell Automation Trinidad and Tobago Unlimited; Rockwell Automation Uruguay, Srl; Rockwell Columbia S.A.; Rockwell Comercio e Servicos de Automacao Ltda. (Brazil); Rockwell European Holdings Ltd. (UK); Rockwell FSC Ltd. (Barbados); Rockwell International (UK); Rockwell International Overseas Corporation; Rockwell International Pension Trustees Limited (UK); Rockwell Otomasyon Ticaret A.S. (Turkey); Rockwell Services, Inc.; Rockwell Tecate S.A. de C.V. (Mexico).

PRINCIPAL OPERATING UNITS

Architecture & Software; Control Products & Solutions.

PRINCIPAL COMPETITORS

Siemens AG; Mitsubishi Corporation; ABB Ltd.; Honeywell International Inc.; Schneider Electric SA; Emerson Electric Co.

FURTHER READING

Anderson, Robert, *Through Turbulent Times,* New York: Newcomen Society, 1984, 24 p.

Barrett, Rick, "Bigger Not Better for Rockwell: Newly Named Chairman Nosbusch Says Specialization Keeps It Competitive," *Milwaukee Journal Sentinel,* February 7, 2005, p. D1.

———, "Rockwell Adds Staff to Reignite Growth in Asia," *Milwaukee Journal Sentinel,* January 25, 2007, p. D1.

———, "Rockwell to Divest Research Firm," *Milwaukee Journal Sentinel,* July 28, 2006, p. D3.

———, "Rockwell to Sell Power Systems Unit," *Milwaukee Journal Sentinel,* November 8, 2006, p. D1.

Berman, Dennis K., and J. Lynn Lunsford, "Rockwell Firms to Sell R&D Unit," *Wall Street Journal,* February 7, 2006, p. A18.

Bright, Charles D., *The Jet Makers: The Aerospace Industry from 1945–1972,* Lawrence: Regents Press of Kansas, 1978.

Brinton, James B., "Reborn Rockwell Rolls Toward 2000," *Electronic Business Today,* December 1996, pp. 45–47.

Brousell, David R., "For Rockwell, Breaking Up Is the Thing to Do," *Managing Automation,* January 2001.

Changing with the Times: A History of the Allen-Bradley Company, Milwaukee, Wis.: Allen-Bradley, 1987, 110 p.

Cook, Nick, "Who's Winning the U.S. Combat Airframe Battle?" *Interavia Business and Technology,* May 1994, p. 22.

Deady, Tim, "Rockwell's Earnings Socked by Recession," *Los Angeles Business Journal,* April 22, 1991, p. 8.

Donlon, J. P., "Rockwell Comes in from the Cold (War)," *Chief Executive,* December 1996, pp. 38–41.

Franson, Paul, "Rockwell Dangerfield: Born Again As an Electronics Company, Rockwell Isn't Getting the Respect It Deserves on Wall Street," *Electronic Business,* March 1998, pp. 36–40, 87.

Gertzen, Jason, "Rockwell Names New Chief: Nosbusch Plans to Focus on Overseas Sales, Expansion of Services, Consulting," *Milwaukee Journal Sentinel,* December 5, 2003, p. 1D.

———, "Rockwell Puts Its Focus on the Factory," *Milwaukee Journal Sentinel,* July 1, 2001, p. 1D.

———, "Rockwell Sees Future in Services," *Milwaukee Journal Sentinel,* January 1, 2002, p. 1D.

Gurda, John, *The Bradley Legacy: Lynde and Harry Bradley, Their Company, and Their Foundation,* Milwaukee, Wis.: Lynde and Harry Bradley Foundation, 1992, 170 p.

Hinton, Christopher, "Rockwell Automation Posts a 24% Fall in Net," *Wall Street Journal,* February 3, 2009, p. B6.

Lipin, Steven, and Jeff Cole, "Rockwell's Beall Takes Big Step Toward Strategy Goal: CEO's Deal with Boeing Advances Aim of Refashioning His Company," *Wall Street Journal,* August 2, 1996, p. B4.

Lubove, Seth, "New-Tech, Old-Tech," *Forbes,* July 17, 1995, p. 58.

MacKnight, Nigel, *Shuttle,* Osceola, Fla.: Motorbooks International, 1985.

Miller, William H., "Don Beall: Conglomerateer," *Industry Week,* January 22, 1996, pp. 13, 15–16.

Mrozek, Donald J., "The Truman Administration and the Enlistment of the Aviation Industry in Postwar Defense," *Business History Review,* Spring 1974, pp. 73–94.

Nelson, Brett, "Choreographer of the Assembly Line," *Forbes,* November 15, 2004, pp. 194, 196, 198.

Ordonez, Jennifer, and Andy Pasztor, "Rockwell Will Spin Off Avionics Division in 2001, Retaining the Automation Unit," *Wall Street Journal,* December 11, 2000, p. A6.

Perry, Nancy J., "Getting Out of Rocket Science," *Fortune,* April 4, 1994, pp. 101+.

"Rockwell International: Reaching for the Automotive Market Abroad," *Business Week,* May 5, 1980, p. 87.

Rose, Frederick, "Rockwell International, Shifting Focus, to Spin Off Automotive-Parts Business," *Wall Street Journal,* March 18, 1997, p. A3.

———, "Rockwell to Spin Off Chip Operations, Cut Work Force," *Wall Street Journal,* June 30, 1998, p. B4.

———, "Rockwell Wins Battle to Buy Reliance Electric," *Wall Street Journal,* November 22, 1994, p. A3.

Schmid, John, "A Milestone, and a Warning: Rockwell Gets More Than Half Its Sales Abroad, but Sees Tough Year Ahead," *Milwaukee Journal Sentinel,* November 12, 2008, p. D1.

———, "Rockwell Buys British Firm: ICS Triplex Purchase Stretches Global Reach," *Milwaukee Journal Sentinel,* May 25, 2007, p. D2.

———, "Rockwell Buys Software Firm," *Milwaukee Journal Sentinel,* April 23, 2008, p. D3.

———, "Rockwell Plans Sale of Hardware Division," *Milwaukee Journal Sentinel,* June 21, 2006, p. D1.

———, "Rockwell to Cut 600 Jobs," *Milwaukee Journal Sentinel,* October 1, 2008, p. B7.

———, "Rockwell to Tighten Belt Further As Earnings Erode," *Milwaukee Journal Sentinel,* February 3, 2009, p. D1.

Velocci, Anthony L., Jr., "Rockwell Collins Granted Autonomy," *Aviation Week and Space Technology,* December 18/25, 2000, pp. 15–18.

Wartzman, Rick, "Rockwell Touts Non-Aerospace Business: Only a Quarter of Its Work Comes from Pentagon," *Wall Street Journal,* December 27, 1989.

Weimer, De'Ann, "Will Rockwell Find Some Roots?" *Business Week,* May 10, 1999, pp. 77, 80.

Woolley, Scott, "This Pasture Looked Greener," *Forbes,* October 20, 1997, pp. 294–95.

Wrubel, Robert, "Cliff Function: Don Beall Is Proving Rockwell's Critics Wrong, There Is Life After the B-1B Bomber," *Financial World,* August 8, 1989, p. 30.

Sally Industries, Inc.

745 West Forsyth Street
Jacksonville, Florida 32204
U.S.A.
Telephone: (904) 355-7100
Fax: (904) 355-7170
Web site: http://www.sallycorp.com

Private Company
Incorporated: 1977
Employees: 40
Sales: $8 million (2008 est.)
NAICS: 333319 Other Commercial and Service
Industry Machinery Manufacturing

■ ■ ■

Sally Industries, Inc., operating as Sally Corporation, is the world's leading independent manufacturer of "dark rides" for amusement parks, and also creates animatronic characters for retailers, museums, trade shows, and other uses. The firm's productions range from licensed Scooby Doo rides for young children and families to the 17,200-square-foot, 54-character Challenge of Tutankhamon, built for Six Flags Belgium. Sally rides are noted for creativity and quality, as well as their interactive elements, which allow patrons to affect the outcome by shooting laser guns at digital targets.

EARLY YEARS

Sally Industries was founded in 1977 in Jacksonville, Florida, by three friends. The firm's beginnings can be traced to a robotic talking head made by John Rob Holland, a dental student with an engineering background. It had been built to read a report to a college class whose instructor had advised him to "be creative," but when John Fox saw it gathering dust in the garage the pair brainstormed a plan to build talking mannequins to sell as marketing tools. Enlisting John Wood to serve as sales manager, they named the new firm Sally Industries, after the classmate who had allowed Holland to make a mold of her face.

Starting out in the same garage, they built five prototypes and Wood took to the road with a mannequin in the passenger seat of his car to deliver the sales pitch. The firm's early orders included a schoolmarm character for the Oldest Schoolhouse attraction in St. Augustine, Florida, but sales of just ten mannequins during the first year fell far short of the partners' business plan to produce 150.

Sales gradually picked up during the late 1970s as Sally received commissions to create such characters as Santa Claus, the Keebler cookie elf, and Elvis Presley. One popular design was a talking tooth fairy produced for dental offices to teach children about proper brushing.

A growing fad for entertainment-themed family restaurants including Chuck E. Cheese's soon took Sally in a new direction, however. The firm began to create robotic, or "animatronic" shows, the first of which featured a re-creation of Mark Twain that told humorous stories while five dogs called Daniel and the Dixie Diggers "played" jazz. Having earlier moved out of Holland's garage, the firm found a larger production space to accommodate these more complex projects. Clients at this time included several U.S. restaurant chains, resorts, and amusement parks, among them Adventureland and Hersheypark.

The animatronic technology of this era was relatively primitive, with sound and control signals recorded onto eight-track tape cartridges and movement accomplished by means of compressed air, also known as pneumatics. Because the recording of information for multiple characters had to be done together for synchronization purposes, creating an ensemble might require many "takes" to get a perfect result. Over time Sally engineers would be able to greatly improve results through the use of computers, although movement remained pneumatic because the technology was highly reliable and yielded the most realistic motion.

To build a character Sally started with an artist's rendering, after which a steel skeleton of the proper size was built and fitted with tubes for the compressed-air movement system. This was then covered with a cast plastic or fiberglass body, molded silicone hands and face, hair, fur/feathers, teeth, and clothing. Multiple skilled artisans would work on a single figure, with others taking care of programming, character voicing/ music, script writing, and whatever else was needed.

With the entertainment-restaurant craze fading by the mid-1980s, Sally began seeking more overseas business and looked into such new product categories as industrial robots and medical education devices. The company also boosted its focus on amusement park projects, and found work building animatronic characters for an indoor Six Flags park in Baltimore as well as several children's shows based on the licensed Care Bears stories. One of the latter, which featured six animated bears in a castle, was priced at approximately $150,000, while a standard human-size standing character cost $20,000 and smaller projects like a talking parrot might go for $5,000.

SALLY TARGETS DARK RIDES IN 1986

Building on its entertainment experience, Sally management (led by new president, broadcasting industry veteran Howard Kelley) also began to pursue work developing amusement park "dark rides." Such entertainments dated back more than 100 years to so-called scenic railway and tunnel of love rides, in which patrons traveled through an enclosed, darkened space and encountered various lighted displays (which were sometimes scary, but not necessarily so). In modern times they had been refined with animatronic and other theatrical effects by The Walt Disney Company, in popular theme park rides including Pirates of the Caribbean, The Haunted Mansion, and Space Mountain.

Taking a bold step, Sally licensed the rights to the hit film *Ghostbusters* and built a mock-up for the 1986 amusement industry convention. Although it did not find a buyer, the firm won contracts to upgrade a number of existing rides, starting with Around the World in 80 Days for England's Alton Towers. Over the next few years Sally helped revamp others including The Haunted Mine at Canobie Lake in New Hampshire and Universal Studios Florida's E.T.'s Adventure.

In 1987 the company was split into two operating units, Sally Corporation, to work on rides, and Exhibit Resources, which focused on trade shows and museums as well as building background sets for Sally Corp. projects. By 1988 cofounders John Fox and John Rob Holland had returned to their careers as building contractor and dentist, respectively, and in 1989 John Wood was named chairman.

In 1990 Sally formed a joint venture with the Sofran Group to develop an entertainment complex for a Jacksonville oceanside tourist development, but the plan was later scrapped in the face of a U.S. economic downturn. The firm was working on projects for parks in the United States, Spain, France, Japan, and Taiwan, with nearly two-thirds of sales being made overseas. Other assignments of this period included animatronic Elsie cows for Borden, large stuffed animals for FAO Schwarz, and a musical ensemble for New England furniture store Cardi's.

In the summer of 1992 Sally unveiled its first completely original dark ride, Zombie Paradise, which was created in partnership with Togo International. Installed in Tokyo's Korakuen Park, it featured 54 animatronic characters with numerous visual and audio effects on multiple sets. Patrons rode in six-passenger electric, computer-controlled trackless carriages which could be dispatched every 25 seconds, for a total of up to 1,000 riders per hour. Another notable project of the early 1990s was a music-themed environmental show

KEY DATES

1977: Sally Industries is founded in Florida to make talking mannequins.

1980s: Sales grow with boom in entertainment-themed restaurants.

1986: Sally builds first dark ride mock-up, begins rejuvenating older rides.

1987: Company splits operations into Sally Corp. and Exhibit Resources units.

1992: First original dark ride, Zombie Paradise, is completed in Japan.

1995: Interactive family ride, The Great Pistolero Roundup, debuts to acclaim.

1997: Company moves to new facility in downtown Jacksonville.

2000: Exhibit Resources is sold to Manager Don Lyon; first licensed Scooby-Doo ride is built for Paramount Parks; Labyrinth of the Minotaur opens in Spain's Terra Mitica.

2003: Challenge of Tutankhamon is completed for Six Flags Belgium.

complete with exploding volcano and talking Tiki god for Taiwan's Woozland.

INTERACTIVE GREAT PISTOLERO ROUNDUP OPENS IN 1995

Seeing demand for a less-elaborate ride for families with small children, Sally created The Great Pistolero Roundup, which opened in the spring of 1995 at Doogom Land park in Korea and was later replicated for several other customers. In the new, interactive concept, riders in a small car shot at targets with laser pistols, activating pop-up cartoon characters and other props, with their score displayed inside the vehicle. The ride was subsequently named "Best New Product" at the amusement industry's annual awards, and served as the template for a number of interactive spinoffs including Den of Lost Thieves, North Pole Adventure, and Ghost Blasters (aka Ghost Hunt).

Other popular offerings of the era were dinosaur-themed rides, exemplified by the $1.5 million, 10,000-square-foot Escape from Dinosaur Beach built for a New Jersey amusement park, which featured a life-size Tyrannosaurus Rex. Work for corporate clients was continuing to grow as well, with such projects as the $120,000 "Maestro," an animatronic symphony conduc-

tor built for a Hong Kong retail/office complex that "conducted" a water fountain to the accompaniment of symphonic music.

For 1996, Sally had sales of approximately $4 million, of which dark rides accounted for about one-fifth. During the year John Wood added the title of CEO to his role of chairman.

In the summer of 1997 Sally moved into a 40,000-square-foot facility leased from the city of Jacksonville, which had been renovated at the cost of $1.75 million, two-thirds of which came from a city redevelopment fund intended to lure tenants (and jobs) to a blighted downtown area. The company later bought the property, and added a vacant lot next door for future expansion. Tours of Sally's manufacturing facility were popular with school groups who enjoyed seeing animatronic dinosaurs and other creatures that were being readied for shipment, as well as their manufacturing processes.

In the late 1990s Paramount Parks asked Sally to create a new interactive children's ride similar to Ghost Hunt. The firm soon developed one based on the popular Scooby-Doo cartoon characters, which it licensed from Hanna-Barbera. The first example opened in 2000, and its popularity led to assignments to build variations for several other Paramount locations and a Six Flags park.

LABYRINTH OF THE MINOTAUR OPENS IN 2000

In 2000 Sally partnered with Global Estudios of Spain to launch its largest dark ride to date, Labyrinth of the Minotaur. Built for the new Terra Mitica theme park, the 1,500-patron-per-hour capacity ride immediately became its most popular. The interactive Labyrinth featured 76 animatronic figures and cars with six crossbow-style laser guns. A low score resulted in ejection at either of two points, while a higher one enabled the riders to do battle with a 12-foot Minotaur. Like a video game, the experience was different each time depending on which targets were hit. The popularity of dark rides was growing in part because parks were pulling back from a recent competition to build ever-larger roller coasters, which cost as much as $25 million but could be trumped by a competitor the next year. An interactive dark ride was unique, less expensive, encouraged repeat business, and also appealed to all ages, while roller coasters skewed heavily toward teens and young adults.

During 2000 the firm also sold Exhibit Resources to division head Don Lyon, in part because it needed additional production space to fulfill growing dark ride orders. Exhibit Resources would continue to perform work for Sally Corp. under contract.

In 2001 sales hit $7 million, and during the following year the firm reached an agreement with MGM Consumer Products to license films including *Robocop* and *The Jungle Book* for rides. By that time, the company had installed its dark rides in nine different countries, and the category had grown to account for 80 percent of business. Sally was now billing itself as "The Great American Dark Ride Company."

CHALLENGE OF TUTANKHAMON DEBUTS IN 2003

In May 2003 a spectacular new interactive dark ride called the Challenge of Tutankhamon opened at Six Flags Belgium, which further cemented the firm's status as a world leader in its field. Riders spent 4½ minutes exploring King Tut's tomb, in which there were 16 different scenes, 54 animatronic characters, and 130 targets to shoot at. The 17,200-square-foot ride, which offered three different outcomes depending on score, could accommodate 900 riders per hour. Industry sources estimated its cost at $7 million.

The early 2000s also saw Sally rework a 1,200-foot water ride for Rye, New York's Playland with features that included animatronic gnomes and a dragon. The firm carefully retained the historic character of the 1920s-era attraction, which had been given National Landmark status. The company was completing an average of three major projects annually.

In the fall of 2004 Sally signed a two-year license agreement with comic publisher Marvel Enterprises to use its characters for rides. The firm also added more sales representatives abroad to a network that encompassed Europe, the Middle East, Asia, and India.

Sally was continuing to build more Scooby-Doo rides and also developed new concepts such as the Reese's Xtreme Cup Challenge, which opened in early 2006 at Hersheypark in Pennsylvania. Two teams (named chocolate and peanut butter) tried to best each other in ten competitions based on sports including sky diving and skateboarding. The firm also built characters and sets for a water-based ride called El Ultimo Minuto for Spain's Dinopolis park that featured 39 creatures including dinosaurs, wooly mammoths, and a saber-toothed tiger. For 2006, Sally's revenues were just under $10 million.

In December 2007 President Howard Kelley retired. The following October, the firm signed a licensing agreement with Scholastic, Inc., for the popular Goosebumps children's book characters. Rides had been built for clients in Sweden, China, and the United Kingdom.

With a spike in gasoline prices followed by the world economic crisis causing park operators to cut back on ride orders, in January 2009 Sally shut down operations for two weeks and laid off 16 of its 41 employees. Sales were expected to remain soft in the near term, but CEO Wood vowed to sit tight and wait out the lull until demand picked up again.

More than three decades after it began producing talking mannequins, Sally Industries, Inc., had evolved into the leading independent manufacturer of dark rides for amusement parks. Although orders had temporarily dropped off due to the ailing economy, the firm's reputation was strong and its experienced management appeared capable of pulling it through the hard times.

Frank Uhle

PRINCIPAL SUBSIDIARIES

Sally Corporation.

PRINCIPAL COMPETITORS

The Walt Disney Company; Merlin Entertainments Group, Ltd.; Kokoro Company Ltd.; Garner Holt Productions; LifeFormations; Advanced Animation; Farmer Attraction Development Ltd.; David Aldridge Animations Ltd.; Heimo; Klosterman Design GmbH Co. KG; Creative Works, Inc.; Eos Rides Srl; Etf Ride Systems; Gerstlauer Amusement Rides GmbH; Pan Amusements; Jora Vision BV; Mack Rides GmbH.

FURTHER READING

Barrier, Michael, "Creating Some Serious Fun," *Nation's Business,* December 1, 1997, p. 54.

"Florida Company Sending Care Bears to Indonesia," *St. Petersburg Times,* September 14, 1986, p. 18.

Jackson, Anna, "Sally Corp.: The Road to Becoming the Great American Ride Company," *Haunted Attraction,* Issue 35, 2003.

Koranteng, Julianna, "King Tut Ride to Scare Up Biz for SF Belgium," *Amusement Business,* February 10, 2003, p. 5.

"Lyon Buys Sally Division," *Jacksonville Business Journal,* May 18, 2000.

Muret, Dan, "Sally Corp. Foresees Big Increases in Dark Ride Business for Parks," *Amusement Business,* November 8, 1993, p. 54.

Nifong, Christina, "Action Figures That Really Act," *Christian Science Monitor,* July 14, 1998, p. 8.

O'Brien, Tim, "From Cartoon Characters to Giant Insects, Sally Animatronics Getting Rave Reviews," *Amusement Business,* November 16, 1992, p. 46.

———, "July Opening Set for Tokyo's Indoor Ride," *Amusement Business,* January 6, 1992, p. 18.

———, "New Attractions Open at Playland, Rye, N.Y.," *Amusement Business,* July 15, 2002, p. 5.

———, "$140 Mil Seacentre Project Scrapped," *Amusement Business,* September 2, 1991, p. 20.

———, "Sally Corp. Sheds New Light on Traditional Dark-rides," *Amusement Business,* December 23, 2002, p. 15.

Pipkin, Wanda R., "Sally Industries Exhibits Technology's Lighter Side," *Jacksonville Business Journal,* July 17, 1998.

Richards, Gregory, "Who's Afraid of the Dark?" *Florida Times-Union,* October 28, 2002, p. FB12.

Szakony, Mark, "Sally Corp. Scares Up Profits on Dark Rides," *Jacksonville Business Journal,* October 26, 2007.

Turner, Kevin, "Smiles Turn to Frowns As Fun-Park Orders Dwindle," *Florida Times-Union,* January 28, 2009.

Sociedad Química y
Minera de Chile S.A.

■

El Trovador 4285
Las Condes, Santiago
Chile
Telephone: (56 2) 425-2000
Fax: (56 2) 425-2493
Web site: http://www.sqm.com

Public Company
Incorporated: 1968
Employees: 3,746
Sales: $1.77 billion (2008)
Stock Exchanges: Bolsa de Comercio de Santiago New
    York
Ticker Symbol: SQM
NAICS: 212391 Potash, Soda, and Borate Mineral Min-
    ing; 212393 Other Chemical and Fertilizer Mineral
    Mining; 325181 Alkalines and Chlorine
    Manufacturing; 325311 Nitrogenous Fertilizer
    Manufacturing

■ ■ ■

Sociedad Química y Minera de Chile S.A. (Soquimich,
or SQM), Chile's leading chemicals producer, has been
a spectacular success as a privatized company. It is the
world's only commercial producer of natural sodium
nitrate and its derivatives, such as potassium nitrate
(saltpeter), a fertilizer, or plant nutrient, that is its major
product. SQM is the world's leading producer of potassium nitrate. Potassium chloride (from brine deposits)
and sodium nitrate (in Spanish, *salitre,* and often called
Chile saltpeter) from caliche ore are the raw materials in

the production of potassium nitrate. SQM is the world's
leading producer of iodine, which is also obtained from
the extraction processes that result in potassium nitrate.
The company is also the world's leading producer of
lithium and its derivatives. In addition, the company
produces potassium sulfate, sodium potassium nitrate,
and more than 200 blends of specialty fertilizers. It is
the leading distributor of fertilizers in Chile.

A TREASURE HOUSE OF
MINERALS

The Atacama Desert, a barren stretch of northern Chile
at an altitude of 10,000 feet, yields vast amounts of caliche, a mineral ore that contains high concentrates of
sodium nitrate and iodine in layers no more than ten
feet below the surface. It includes the Salar de Atacama,
a dried-up salt lake that, below the surface crust, holds a
brine with high concentrations of potassium, lithium,
and boron. Commercial exploitation of the deposits
began in the 1830s, when sodium nitrate was extracted
for explosives and fertilizer. The trade was so valuable
that Chile fought, and won, a war with Peru and Bolivia
(1879–83) for possession of the Atacama Desert. By the
end of the century nitrate production had become
Chile's leading industry.

Chile was supplying the world with 65 percent of
its fertilizer in 1910, when ammonia sulfate was
synthesized in Germany, leading to the eventual end of
dependence on natural nitrates for this purpose. Despite
the rapid commercial development of synthetic
nitrogen-based fertilizers in the 1920s, the Guggenheim
mining interests, paramount in mining Chile's copper,

acquired productive land in northern Chile to exploit the deposits. The Guggenheims bought the Lautaro Nitrate Company in 1929.

The first facility for this purpose, María Elena, opened in 1926, and the second, Pedro de Valdivia, in 1931. However, the global economic depression of the 1930s further damaged the natural nitrate industry in Chile, and it operated at reduced levels into the 1960s. According to an article in *Engineering & Mining Journal,* the industry survived only by exploiting the richest deposits under "deplorable" labor conditions. Only two companies were conducting major operations: Compañía Salitrera Anglo-Lautaro S.A. and Empresa Salitrera Victoria, S.A., which had come under Corporación de Fomento de la Producción (Corfo), the government's development agency. Anglo-Lautaro, by far the larger, was losing money and suffered a seven-week strike in 1967.

A MOSTLY PUBLIC ENTERPRISE: 1968–88

SQM was founded in 1968 by Anglo-Lautaro, which held five-eighths of the shares, and Corfo, which held the remainder. Following the accession in 1970 of Salvador Allende, a Marxist socialist, as president of Chile, however, Corfo purchased enough shares to take a majority stake. Anglo-Lautaro, still losing money and bedeviled by labor unrest, sold its remaining interests (stock, debentures, and debt owed) to Corfo for $6 million in 1971.

Although Allende was overthrown in a 1973 military coup led by General Augusto Pinochet, SQM remained under full state control for another decade. After earning a profit in 1974, the enterprise suffered six consecutive years of losses. Pedro de Valdivia and María Elena remained the most important of the four mines in operation. The miners were, in 1975, receiving free housing and medical care but only $1 per day in wages.

Julio Ponce Lerou, a forestry engineer and son-in-law of Pinochet who had been executive vice-president of Corfo, became president of SQM in 1981. He and his successors reorganized the company, contracted out many of its activities, and reduced the workforce. SQM became profitable again in 1983, the year the enterprise began its return to the private sector. The company succeeded in underselling its synthetic competitors and by the end of the 1980s was the world's only significant producer of sodium nitrate.

The privatization process was completed in 1988, when all SQM's shares were listed on the Bolsa de Comercio de Santiago. Chile's private pension funds took a 22 percent stake in the company. Sociedad de Inversiones Pampa Calichera, created in 1986 with profit-sharing funds allotted to the workers, acquired an 8.3 percent stake in 1987. Pampa Calichera had been organized by Ponce, who resumed the presidency of SQM in 1987.

FOCUSING ON POTASSIUM NITRATE: 1986–95

By this time SQM was diversifying its chemical output. The company in 1986 began producing potassium nitrate, a nutrient-rich, water-soluble specialty fertilizer that soon came to be regarded as ideal for crops grown in greenhouses. It became the world's leading producer of potassium nitrate, a specialty fertilizer providing two of the three essential plant nutrients. Yet about half of its revenues were coming from industrial rather than agricultural applications. The products for industrial use were, besides sodium nitrate, sodium sulfate and iodine. Sales of SQM products totaled $205 million in 1988.

Potassium nitrate was being produced from the chemical reaction of sodium nitrate with potassium chloride (potash), imported mostly from Canada. Iodine, rapidly growing in importance for SQM, was being produced partly by means of a new solar evaporation plant, expansion of existing facilities, and recovery of additional quantities from previously worked ores.

SQM was also modernizing its mining equipment and production, railroad, and port facilities, and it had established a research and development center in Antofagasta. In order to cut costs and raise productivity, the labor force was once more considerably reduced. A 1993 offering of American Depositary Shares in Europe and the United States raised funds for a $234 million capital program. A second offering followed in 1995.

SQM's aim was to free itself from reliance on imported potash to create potassium nitrate. Minsal, a joint venture in which Amax Inc. held the majority stake, was building a $200 million facility in the salt basin to produce 750,000 metric tons a year of the chemical. By late 1993 SQM had acquired Amax's shares in taking a 75 percent stake in Minsal.

KEY DATES

■

1968: Founding of SQM as a public-private partnership.

1986: Company begins producing potassium nitrate, a specialty fertilizer.

1988: After almost two decades of state control, SQM is fully privatized.

1989: Company is the only significant producer of sodium nitrate.

1995: SQM has begun to free itself from imported potash for making potassium nitrate.

1997: SQM begins commercial production of other chemicals from mineral-rich brine.

2001: Potash Corporation of Saskatchewan begins an effort to take control of SQM.

2008: SQM's revenues double, and its net income almost triples.

PRODUCING OTHER CHEMICALS:
1995–2004

The Minsal project, completed in 1995, involved using giant tractors to excavate mounds of mineral-rich brine from below the surface of the desert, dry them in solar-evaporation ponds, and then extract potash from the rest of the material. Recovery of other salts from the brine soon followed. In 1997 Minsal began commercial operations at a plant that removed, by evaporation, potassium and magnesium chlorides from the brine, yielding a solution that contained lithium chloride, which was then concentrated and mixed with soda ash in a chemical plant in Antofagasta in order to produce lithium carbonate. This substance was being used by the specialty glass and aluminum industries.

Potassium chloride output also began in 1997. Potassium sulfate and boric acid production were initiated the following year. In all, SQM spent $300 million for its brine-extraction and solar-evaporation system and in production plants for potassium chloride, potassium sulfate, lithium carbonate, and boric acid.

SQM built a new potassium nitrate plant in 2000 and one in Pasadena, Texas, for the production of butyl lithium, in 2002. In 2004 it acquired plants in Turkey and Thailand, and a urea phosphate factory in Dubai. The company also purchased a Netherlands-based producer of iodine and iodine derivatives. These were years of increasing prosperity, and the price of SQM's stock increased fivefold between 2000 and 2007.

STRUGGLE FOR CONTROL:
2001–08

Ponce's control, through Pampa Calichera, of SQM was threatened in 2001 when Potash Corporation of Saskatchewan (PCS) became a major stakeholder by purchasing 18 percent of the shares from pension funds for $129 million. PCS raised its equity stake in 2002 to the maximum allowed. Ponce controlled the same amount through SQ Holding, a joint venture established in 2001 with the Norwegian company Yara International ASA, the world's leading provider of mineral fertilizers and agronomic solutions. Yara received a 49 percent stake in this holding company.

Although his personal stake in SQM was estimated at only 4 to 6 percent, Ponce had been able to maintain control of the enterprise through a leveraged "cascade" of three intermediary companies. He was aided by company statutes, which he had established, that forbade any single shareholder from owning a majority of SQM's stock. Moreover, no shareholder was allowed to name more than three of the eight board directors. Apparently to enable Ponce to maintain control more easily, the stock was divided into two series in 1993. Series A shareholders were entitled to elect seven of the eight board members; Series B shareholders, only the remaining one.

PCS attempted to gain control of the board in late 2004 by purchasing the 8.3 percent stake held by Israel Chemicals Limited, which had one seat on the board, for $100.4 million. Since the acquisition placed PCS over the shareholding limit, SQ Holding objected, and the Canadian company had to auction 3.2 percent of its shares, which were mostly acquired by Pampa Calichera. PCS thereby was held to only three board seats. In 2008 Yara sold its stake in SQM to entities controlled by Ponce.

SQM IN 2008

SQM experienced a record-breaking year in 2008. Its revenues increased by half, reaching $1.77 billion, and its net income almost tripled, to $501 million. The *Wall Street Journal* rated the company's American Depositary Shares, or Receipts, as the best performer among large-cap stocks, with a 38 percent gain during the year.

Specialty plant nutrition led the way, accounting for 55 percent of revenues and 47 percent of the world market share. This sector included potassium nitrate, sodium nitrate, sodium potassium nitrate, and potassium sulfate. Additionally, SQM was offering more than 200 specialty blends for all types of applications.

Iodine and iodine derivatives accounted for 14 percent of company revenues and 33 percent of world market share. Demand for iodine salts, used in the production of polarizing films for LCD displays, was proving particularly notable. Lithium and lithium derivatives accounted for 10 percent of company revenues and 30 percent of world market share. With 27 percent of world lithium reserves, the Salar de Atacama was dubbed "The Saudi Arabia of Lithium" in a *Forbes* article. The lightest metal, lithium was necessary in rechargeable batteries for cellphones and laptop computers. Lithium-ion batteries were expected to be in use in hybrid automobiles.

Potassium chloride accounted for 8 percent of SQM's revenues in 2008, and industrial chemicals accounted for 7 percent. Export sales represented 81 percent of the company's total in 2007. North America led the way, with 24 percent, and Europe was next, with 20 percent. Seeking the way to increase its sales in China, SQM took a half-share in a joint venture with Migao Corp. in 2008 for the production and distribution of potassium nitrate. A production facility was expected to be completed in early 2009.

SQM was planning to spend $1 billion by 2010 on projects that would include expansion of its productive capacities. The most significant would boost its combined capacity to turn out potassium chloride and potassium sulfate. A new potassium nitrate plant was also planned for completion in 2010. The funds were to come primarily from internal cash flow.

Robert Halasz

PRINCIPAL SUBSIDIARIES

Ajay-SQM Chile S.A. (51%); Minera Nueva Victoria S.A.; Servicios Integrales de Tránsitos y Transferencias S.A.; Soquimich Comercial S.A.; SQM Industrial S.A.; SQM Nitratos S.A.; SQM Salar S.A.

PRINCIPAL OPERATING UNITS

Industrial Chemistry; Iodine; Lithium; Specialty Plant Nutrition.

PRINCIPAL COMPETITORS

Badische Anilin und Soda Fabrik AG (BASF); Chemetell GmbH; FMC Corporation; Great Salt Lake Minerals Corp.; Ise Chemicals Ltd.; K+S KALI Gmbh; S.C.M. Virginia; Tessenderlo Chemie.

FURTHER READING

"Chile Gears up Nitrate Mining in Response to Price Boom and Growing Demand," *Chemical Engineering and Mining Journal,* May 1975, p. 39.

"Chile's SQM Sets the Stage for '90's Growth," *Chemical Marketing Reporter,* August 14, 1989, pp. 7+.

Costa R., Paula, "Salitre y pólvora," *Capital,* May 18–31, 2007, pp. 50–52, 54–55.

Durruty, Ana Victoria, *Salitre, harina de la luna llena,* Antofagasta, Chile: 1993.

Fazio Rigazzi, Hugo, *Mapa de la extrema riqueza al año 2005,* Santiago: LOM Ediciones, 2005, pp. 328–30.

Koemer, Brendan I., "The Saudi Arabia of Lithium," *Forbes,* November 24, 2008, p. 34.

McCoy, Michael, "Chilean Inorganics Muscle into Market," *Chemical and Engineering News,* August 2, 1999, pp. 11–16.

Medel, Lorena, "SQM: Lucha de poderes," *Capital,* April 8–April 21, 2005, pp. 58–59.

Sim, Peck Hwee, "PCS Raises Its Stake in SQM," *Chemical Week,* May 29, 2002, p. 14.

"Soquimich," *LatinFinance,* March 1994, pp. 62, 64.

Sonic Corp.

———■———

300 Johnny Bench Drive
Oklahoma City, Oklahoma 73104
U.S.A.
Telephone: (405) 225-5000
Fax: (405) 280-7696
Web site: http://www.sonicdrivein.com

Public Company
Incorporated: 1959
Employees: 21,383
Sales: $804.7 million (2008)
Stock Exchanges: NASDAQ (GS)
Ticker Symbol: SONC
NAICS: 722211 Limited-Service Restaurants

■ ■ ■

Sonic Corp. franchises and operates the United States' largest chain of drive-in restaurants and ranks as one of the largest hamburger chains. As the end of the first decade of the 2000s approached, there were more than 3,500 Sonic restaurants in operation, averaging sales of approximately $1.11 million each. Under the slogan "America's Drive-In," a Sonic restaurant features fast service by roller-skating carhops and a limited menu of cooked-to-order items, including hamburgers, hot dogs, French fries, tater tots, and onion rings, and a wide variety of soft drinks and frozen desserts.

OKLAHOMA ORIGINS

The Sonic concept originated in Shawnee, Oklahoma, in the early 1950s. Troy Smith, a World War II veteran,

operated a small diner called the Cottage Café, which, with only four booths and 12 counter seats, could not support him and his family. Smith sold the diner and opened a larger restaurant, called Troy's Panful of Chicken. His attempts to expand into multiple locations were not successful, and by 1953 Smith's chicken restaurants had failed.

Smith next dreamed of running an upscale steak house. In 1953 he purchased land on the edge of Shawnee, a five-acre property that held a log cabin and included a root beer stand called the Top Hat. Smith's original intent was to operate his steak house in the log cabin and to tear down the root beer stand to make more room for parking. In the meantime, the root beer stand, which sold hot dogs and hamburgers, was averaging sales of $700 in cash per week. Customers would park, walk up to the stand to get food, and eat in their cars.

The postwar boom in automobile purchases created an increasingly mobile public, and businesses developed to serve this new population. Fast-food restaurants began to appear across the country; in California, many operated as "drive-ins," with covered parking spaces and a wait staff that roller-skated to customers' cars. The drive-in concept soon spread across the country, particularly in the warm-weather states. While traveling in Louisiana, Smith stopped at one of these new restaurants. It had an intercom system with homemade speakers that allowed customers to remain in their cars while they placed their order. Smith contacted the inventor of that system and ordered intercoms for his Top Hat root beer stand. Smith also constructed parking canopies, which allowed him to control parking in the root beer stand's lot, and hired carhops to serve his customers. Sales at the stand jumped to $1,750 in the first week after the intercom system was installed, and Smith quickly lost interest in his steak house.

The Shawnee restaurant remained the sole Top Hat until 1956. In that year, Smith met Charles Pappe, a manager of a Safeway supermarket in the Oklahoma town of Woodward who was interested in starting his own restaurant. Pappe, visiting Shawnee, met Smith, and, as the two discussed Pappe's restaurant plans, Smith convinced him to dub his drive-in a Top Hat as well. They began to operate their restaurants under the slogan "Service at the Speed of Sound" and developed paper goods with the Top Hat name. By 1958 two more Top Hats opened, in Enid and Stillwater, Oklahoma.

"SONIC" IN THE JET AGE

Smith and Pappe made plans to step up their franchise business. They soon discovered, however, that the name Top Hat had already been copyrighted. The pair consulted the dictionary, where they found the word *sonic*. The term fit neatly with their slogan. New signs and paper goods were developed, and in 1959 the Stillwater restaurant became the first to adopt the Sonic name.

The partners soon received requests from other entrepreneurs to open their own Sonic Drive-ins. Smith and Pappe assisted these new owner-operators with choosing locations and designing the restaurant layout and operations. Formal franchise agreements were drawn up for the new restaurants. The new owners paid a royalty fee of one penny per sandwich bag, purchased through a central supplier. These franchise agreements contained no provisions for advertising, territorial rights, or fixed menus. Instead, Smith and Pappe's business operated mostly on handshake deals. Sonic operators were still most likely to be local businessmen, owning in part or in full their restaurants, and restaurants were often family-run.

Sonic grew modestly through the 1960s. By 1967, the year of Charles Pappe's death, there were 41 Sonics in operation. Smith brought in two longtime Sonic restaurant franchisees, Matt Kinslow and Marvin Jirous, to run Sonic Supply, the company's supply and distribution division, while Smith continued to develop the company's franchise operations. Franchises appeared in Texas and Kansas, and, by 1972, there were 165 Sonic Drive-ins.

OVER-THE-COUNTER IN 1973

The company had grown too large for Smith, Kinslow, and Jirous to run alone. In 1973, Sonic restructured as a franchise company under the name Sonic Systems of America. Shortly thereafter it became Sonic Industries, Inc., which was a company composed of ten key franchise owners who served as officers and directors of the new company. Smith became chairman of the board and Jirous was named president. Sonic purchased the rights to the name, logo, trademark, and slogan from Smith, and the supply company from Kinslow and Jirous. Each owner also was offered 1,250 shares at $1 per share, and the volume of shares pushed the company to become an over-the-counter, publicly traded company. By year-end 1973, there were 200 Sonic Drive-ins. An additional 75 opened in 1974, and by 1975 Sonic was operating in 13 states.

The 1970s saw a dramatic growth in the number of Sonic restaurants. This growth was attributable to Sonic's second generation of owner-operators. Employees, many the sons and daughters of the original franchisees, were encouraged to become managers and supervisors and to open stores of their own. The company's franchise structure became increasingly complex. As former CEO and President C. Stephen Lynn related to *Restaurant Business,* "[Troy Smith] would perhaps sell a one-unit franchise to a small town man. That man might train his high school buddy. ... When he knew the business, another franchisee might recruit him to manage a second unit. All three might own a piece of the unit. ... Nearly all of our franchisees own pieces of each others' stores, which were often structured as general partnerships."

Between 1973 and 1978 more than 800 new restaurants opened; during one two-year period, more than one new Sonic Drive-in opened each day. The rapid expansion of the chain created a shortfall in the number of trained managers. Despite the establishment of a Sonic School manager training program in the mid-1970s, a number of restaurants began to fail. Rising inflation rates and higher gasoline prices as a result of the oil crisis of 1973 also placed pressure on the drive-in restaurant business. In addition, the company lacked a

KEY DATES

■

1953: Troy Smith acquires the Top Hat root beer stand.

1956: Charles Pappe starts his own Top Hat restaurant in cooperation with Smith.

1959: The "Sonic" name is introduced.

1973: Sonic becomes Sonic Systems of America and begins trading over the counter.

1977: The first Sonic TV commercial appears.

1983: New CEO Stephen Lynn sets out to unify the franchises.

1986: Lynn takes Sonic private.

1991: Sonic begins trading publicly again.

1998: A new "retro-future" look is introduced for the drive-ins.

2001: Plans are formed to open the first Mexican Sonic drive-in.

2003: Sonic celebrates its 50th anniversary.

2004: President Pattye Moore resigns, and Chairman and CEO Clifford Hudson assumes the additional role of president.

2008: Scott McLain is promoted to president and Mike Perry is named chief operating officer.

2009: The company has more than 3,500 locations nationwide.

systemwide advertising program through most of the 1970s.

To boost advertising, the company established the Sonic Advertising Trust, requesting drive-ins to contribute 1.5 percent of their gross. Participation, however, was voluntary, and the first Sonic television commercials did not appear until 1977. By 1979 profits began to fall nonetheless. A new advertising campaign, budgeted at only $5 million, could not reverse the decline, and by 1980 the company posted a net loss of almost $300,000. Overall revenues and per-store sales were down. In that year, 28 company-owned stores were closed, and by 1981, 300 stores had closed.

COOPERATING IN THE EIGHTIES

Jirous, Kinslow, and other original directors and officers left the company to focus on their own franchises. A new president was hired in 1981 but was replaced by Troy Smith in 1982. The following year, C. Stephen Lynn, formerly with Kentucky Fried Chicken and Century 21, took over the leadership of the company.

Lynn identified a number of problems facing Sonic. Its licensing agreements—there were as many as 20 different agreements throughout the chain—did not bring in the revenue the company needed to provide support services across a system that had spread through 19 states. Many of the drive-ins were two decades old and had become shabby, and many were losing money. Most important, the restaurants continued to operate more or less independently, with little cooperative purchasing and advertising.

Lynn worked to unify the company. By promising to cut food costs by 3 percent and to increase sales by 15 percent, he convinced 200 restaurants to consolidate their purchasing and to contribute 1 percent of sales to an advertising program. A new franchise agreement in 1984, adopted by nearly 90 percent of the franchisees, provided the company with ascending royalties, beginning at 1 percent of gross sales and rising to 3 percent, depending on store volume. By 1986, more than one-third of the stores in the chain were working cooperatively. Per-store sales grew to an average of $350,000 per year, with new stores averaging up to $550,000.

In 1986, Lynn, along with a group of investors, performed a leveraged buyout for approximately $10 million and took the company private. Calling franchisees "partners," Lynn was able to increase chain-wide cooperation, forming advertising groups focused on key markets. Sonic put together a low-cost remodeling package, initially priced at $20,000, to encourage older restaurants to revitalize their image. At the same time, the new structure price was set at around $140,000. Lynn also moved to fix the Sonic menu to a limited number of basic items and regional specialties. Soon, Sonic was once again growing. In 1987 it built its 1,000th restaurant.

PUBLIC AGAIN IN 1991

Sonic's growth continued into the 1990s. It went public again in 1991, raising $52 million in its initial public offering (IPO). Lynn had increased cooperative advertising participation to 93 percent of the restaurants, which by then contributed an average of 2.25 percent of gross sales. Between 1990 and 1994 Sonic added nearly 400 new restaurants, tagging on more than 120 in 1994 alone. Systemwide sales rose from $454.6 million to $776.3 million; same-store sales rose from $446,000 to $585,000; and company revenues grew from $45.8 million to $99.7 million. In 1993, Sonic's market value was estimated at $200 million. Sonic had grown to the fifth largest hamburger chain in the United States and the top drive-in chain.

Sonic's growth remained relatively flat after 1992. After reaching a high of $33, its stock price slipped to around $23 per share in 1995. Per-store sales seemed stagnated between $515,000 and $585,000. Sonic, which traditionally owned its rural and suburban southern markets, was facing increasing competition from drive-through chains such as Checkers and Rally's (these two would merge in 1999), while the giants of the industry, McDonald's and Burger King, with their ability to discount, began to invade its territory. Meanwhile, despite discussion of acquiring a Northern-based partner, Sonic clung to its traditional market, making few inroads outside of the warm-weather Southern areas. The company faced additional trouble in 1994 when it was forced to take a $3.9 million write-down charge for discontinuing its five company-owned properties, including two closed restaurants in south Florida that had suffered as a result of the hurricane that devastated the area in 1992.

In 1994, after more than a year of often bitter talks with franchisees, Sonic renegotiated its franchising contracts. The new contract, good for 20 years with a ten-year option to renew, raised graduated royalties to 4 percent and increased advertising contributions to a fixed 2.5 percent while granting Sonic control over a systemwide advertising program. It also fixed a sole soft-drink supplier. In addition, Sonic collected conversion fees from franchisees signing new contracts. In return, the company agreed to give up its first right of refusal for franchisees wishing to turn over restaurants to their heirs or partners, and agreed to fewer audits of franchisees' books. Franchisees also gained wider territorial protection guarantees, with a protected trade radius of 1.5 miles in larger cities, and up to three miles in rural areas. About two-thirds of Sonic franchisees accepted the new contract.

The terms gave Sonic increases of $5 million in royalties and conversions and allowed it to raise its advertising budget to $20 million. With the discontinuation of its Florida operations, Sonic saw its total revenues rise 24 percent, to $123.75 million in 1995. At the beginning of that year, Lynn, who owned approximately 12 percent of the company, named J. Clifford Hudson, former executive vice-president and COO, to take over as president of the company. When Lynn left Sonic to become chief executive officer and president of the beleaguered Shoney's restaurant chain, Hudson was appointed chief executive officer as well.

The typical Sonic restaurant of the mid-1990s remained true to the 1950s-style carhop concept: customers drove up to one of an average of 24 covered parking spaces, placed orders through an intercom, and were served at their car. Restaurants also offered drive-through service, with some restaurants operating as drive-throughs only. The absence of indoor dining allowed the company to maintain one of the highest-margin restaurant operations in the country, with a new construction package costing less than $515,000 per unit and first-year sales of more than $700,000. Average per-store sales were around $585,000 per year in 1995.

The company owned and operated, often through various franchise and partner agreements, 178 restaurants going into 1995. Company restaurants, together with franchise royalties and conversion fees, generated $123.75 million in revenues. Growth in the number of units was averaging 26 percent for franchised restaurants and 106 percent for company-owned restaurants over the five years from 1990 to 1994. Approximately two-thirds of franchisees were represented by the National Association of Sonic Drive-in Franchisees, which operated entirely separately from the company. Sonic entered the late 1990s with a new executive team, including former executives from Coca-Cola, Taco Bell, McDonald's, and Wendy's, and plans for 125 new franchised and company-owned restaurants in 1996.

In September 1995, Sonic Corp. restructured its holdings into two subsidiaries, Sonic Industries Inc., which handled franchising, and Sonic Restaurants, Inc., which handled company-owned restaurants. Sonic's equipment sales unit was sold to Columbus, Ohio-based N. Wasserstrom & Sons, Inc., in February 1996.

Sales boomed in the mid-1990s, with the company opening 100 to 150 new restaurants a year. Sonic's large variety of drinks and a new line of ice cream desserts won repeat business, and the chain added a grilled chicken sandwich for health-conscious diners.

A BRAND NEW LOOK IN 1998

Sonic updated its image as it entered the late 1990s. The novelty of a 1950s drive-in was not enough to keep people coming back. In fact, a 1995 survey indicated people identified the company most strongly not with its unique food items but with Frankie Avalon, the icon of 1960s beach films who pitched Sonic in television ads from 1987 to 1993.

The company began to develop the Sonic brand as never before. Its new advertising focused on the signature carhops and food offerings that differentiated Sonic from other national fast-food chains, items such as hot dogs, tater tots, and cherry limeades. Through its Sonic 2000 retrofit program, in 1998, the chain set out to redesign all of its 1,750 stores in neon-illuminated "retro-future" mode. Soon, Sonic was leading all other fast-food restaurants, including McDonald's, in customer frequency rates: between eight and nine visits a month.

In 1998, *Nation's Restaurant News* and *Inc.* magazine each profiled the D.L. Rogers Group, a Bedford, Texas-based Sonic franchisee that operated 54 drive-ins generating $42 million in annual sales. Its founder, Don Rogers, an Oklahoma oilman, had opened his first Sonic Drive-In in 1962. The group was credited with introducing the ice cream concept to the Sonic system after proving it at its own restaurants.

Jack Hartnett, president since 1983, led the Rogers Group to more than a dozen years of record profits and the highest unit volumes of any Sonic franchise. His style of "extreme managing" included a great deal of interpersonal contact and early morning phone calls. Eight terse, old-fashioned rules including "If I have to do your job, I want your money" and ending with "I will only tell you one time" contained the essence of his managing philosophy. In spite of Hartnett's authoritarian style, *Inc.* writer Marc Ballon credited his success with the stable, predictable environment he created for his managers, or "owner-operators," as Hartnett called them. They were in fact required to buy 25 percent shares in the drive-ins they managed. Hartnett, a demanding, "larger than life" figure, paid his managers as much as three times the industry average. Turnover at the Rogers Group was a fraction of that at other fast-food restaurants.

Feeling its stock undervalued, Sonic Corp. began to buy back shares in March 1998. The press agreed with its valuation. In April 1999, *Investor's Business Daily* included Sonic in its list of the country's 200 best stocks. In November, *Forbes* called Sonic one of the 200 best small companies in the United States. By August 2000, the company had bought back $53 million of its common stock and had authorized another $20 million for that purpose.

A NEW MILLENNIUM

The updates in menu and image were working. Sonic Corp.'s revenues rose 18 percent in 1999 to $257.6 million. Seasonal offerings such as the Chocolate Cream Pie Shake, complete with graham cracker crumbs, kept repeat business up. Still, a new restaurant expected to have the most business during its "honeymoon." Omaha's first Sonic Drive-In served 4,000 customers in its first two days.

An important milestone was reached in 2001, when the holding company Fidelity de Mexico, S. de R.L. de C.V. announced plans to open the first Mexican Sonic drive-in, with a location in Monterrey, Mexico. In April of that year, the company snapped up 35 franchise restaurants in the Tulsa, Oklahoma, area in a $21.9 million deal with Larco Enterprises Inc. Growth continued at Sonic in 2002. That year, the company announced plans to open 190 new drive-ins. In addition, 23 franchised restaurants in the Wichita, Kansas, area were acquired for $19.4 million.

Difficult economic conditions during the early 2000s resulted in price wars within the fast-food industry. However, instead of implementing deep discounts for signature items, Sonic focused on unveiling new products, such as jumbo popcorn chicken with dipping sauces, and emphasizing value items in its promotions.

Sonic reached a special milestone in 2003, when the company celebrated its 50th anniversary. That year, the company added a breakfast menu chainwide, after rolling out the offering at some 800 drive-ins in 2002. Sonic also continued to acquire existing units from its franchisees in 2003. In February alone, the company acquired 51 restaurants for $34 million. By this time Sonic operated approximately 450 company-owned locations, in addition to 2,150 franchised sites. Moving forward, Sonic had plans to open between 800 and 1,000 new drive-ins by 2008.

Sonic proceeded to put significant marketing muscle behind its brand promotion. Following media expenditures of $90 million during its 2002 fiscal year and $100 million in 2003, the company announced it would raise promotional spending to $110 million in 2004. Growth continued that year as Sonic revealed plans to acquire 22 drive-ins from a franchisee in Colorado. One final development in 2004 occurred in October, when President Pattye Moore resigned following a 12-year career with the company. At this time Chairman and CEO Clifford Hudson assumed the additional role of president, Mike Perry was named president of Sonic Restaurants Inc., and W. Scott McLain was named president of the company's Sonic Industries franchising business.

CONTINUING GROWTH AND CHANGE

Sonic acquired more drive-ins from franchisees in 2005, including a deal for 15 locations in Tennessee. In April of the following year, the company's market capitalization reached $2 billion. At that time its board of directors approved a three-for-two stock split, and increased an existing stock buyback authorization from $34.6 million to $110 million. In the fall of 2006, Sonic secured $775 million in credit, some $560 million of which was earmarked for buying back up to 25.5 million shares of the company's stock.

Following the addition of new locations in Washington, Oregon, and Pennsylvania, Sonic revealed plans to continue its expansion beyond the Sun Belt during the latter part of the decade. In 2007 plans were made to open a new location in Columbus, Ohio, which would be followed by approximately 25 new drive-ins around central Ohio. In addition, the company also revealed plans to expand into the Chicago area with four new drive-ins.

More leadership changes occurred in 2008. In April, Scott McLain was promoted to president of Sonic Corp., in addition to his role as president of the company's franchising business. At this time, Mike Perry was promoted to the newly created role of chief operating officer, while Eddie Saroch became president of Sonic Restaurants. On the operations front, a major change was implemented when the company decided to reclassify its carhops from hourly to tipped employees.

Along with the rest of the fast-food industry, Sonic faced dire economic conditions in late 2008. In an effort to maintain wallet share among consumers, plans were made to introduce a value meal that included select items priced around $1. Sonic headed into 2009 with 3,500 locations nationwide. Despite the difficult economic climate, the company had demonstrated an ability to expand beyond its traditional market and entice consumers with its unique menu and service approach.

Mickey L. Cohen
Updated, Frederick C. Ingram; Paul R. Greenland

PRINCIPAL SUBSIDIARIES

America's Drive-In Brand Properties LLC; America's Drive-In Restaurants LLC; Sonic Capital LLC; Sonic Community Development Inc.; Sonic Industries LLC; Sonic Industries Services Inc.; Sonic Partnership Interests Inc.; Sonic Property Development LLC; Sonic Restaurants Inc.; Sonic Technology Fund LLC; Sonic Value Card LLC; SPOTlight LLC; SRI Real Estate Holding LLC; SRI Real Estate Properties LLC.

PRINCIPAL COMPETITORS

Burger King Holdings Inc.; McDonald's Corp.; Whataburger Restaurants LP.

FURTHER READING

Alva, Marilyn, "Season of the Switch," *Restaurant Business,* February 10, 1995, pp. 56–64.

Ballon, Marc, "Extreme Managing," *Inc.,* July 1998, p. 60.

Berta, Dina, "49 Consider Addition by Subtraction: Sonic Corp. Implements Tip Credit in Effort to Improve Overall Service," *Nation's Restaurant News,* January 26, 2009.

Bunn, Dina, "It's a Sonic Boom: New Drive-Ins on Way," *Denver Rocky Mountain News,* June 24, 1999, p. 2B.

Fuller, Jennifer Mann, "Being Different Is Paying Off for Sonic Corp. Analyst Says," *Kansas City Star,* November 3, 1996, p. F6.

Gindin, Rona, "Everything Old Is New Again," *Restaurant Business,* February 10, 1987, pp. 150–59.

Hassell, Greg, "Fresh Ways to Get Folks to Drive In," *Houston Chronicle,* Business sec., May 13, 1998, p. 1.

Hogan, Gypsy, "Drive-Through Restaurant Chain Squeezes into Prime Space in Oklahoma City," *Daily Oklahoman,* June 24, 1999.

Hughlett, Mike, "Booming Sonic Plans to Enter Chicago Area," *Chicago Tribune,* June 19, 2008.

Keenan, John, "Carside Service: Sonic Drive-In Finds Diners Willing to Wait for a Stall," *Omaha World-Herald,* Business sec., August 10, 2000, p. 20.

King, Ronette, "Meals on Wheels—Sonic Makes a Comeback with a Dash of Nostalgia," *New Orleans Times-Picayune,* October 25, 1996, p. C1.

Lynn, C. Stephen, *Sonic: 40 Years of Success 1953–1993,* Oklahoma City: Newcomen Society, January 12, 1993.

"OKC-Based Sonic Corp. Approves Stock Split," *Oklahoma City Journal Record,* April 7, 2006.

Peters, James, "Sonic Discounts Price War, Aims for Sales Boom with Extra Value," *Nation's Restaurant News,* January 20, 2003.

Robertson, Nancy Love, "The Long and Winding Road: Sonic Turns 40," *What's Cookin': Sonic Industries News Magazine,* Spring 1994, pp. 9–16.

Ruggless, Ron, "D.L. Rogers Group: Sonic Drive-Ins Franchisee Succeeds by Putting Its People First," *Nation's Restaurant News,* NRN Fifty Special Issue, January 1998, p. 68.

"Sonic Corp., Parent of the 3400 Unit Drive-In Brand, Has Revamped Its Executive Lineup, Effective May 1, Including the Promotion of Scott McLain to Corporate President," *Nation's Restaurant News Daily NewsFax,* April 22, 2008.

"Sonic Escapes Frankie's Shadow," *Houston Chronicle,* Business sec., February 16, 2000, p. 1.

Wood, E. Thomas, "Shoney's New Chief Hungry for a Rebound," *Chicago Sun-Times,* Financial sec., April 30, 1995, p. 37.

Sovereign Bancorp, Inc.

75 State Street
Boston, Massachusetts 02109
U.S.A.
Telephone: (610) 378-6159
Toll Free: (877) SOV-BANK
Web site: http://www.sovereignbank.com

Wholly Owned Subsidiary of Banco Santander, S.A.
Incorporated: 1984 as Penn Savings Bank, F.S.B.
Employees: 11,643
Total Assets: $77.09 billion (2008)
NAICS: 522120 Savings Institution

■ ■ ■

Sovereign Bancorp, Inc., a wholly owned subsidiary of Banco Santander, S.A., primarily operates in the northeastern United States. Its financial services include retail, business, and corporate banking; cash management; capital markets; and wealth management. Subsidiary Sovereign Bank serves Mid-Atlantic and New England states through more than 750 community banking offices and 2,300 ATMs. Sovereign grew through a series of mergers and acquisitions, until its appetite for growth opened the door for its own sale. Santander acquired the remainder of Sovereign it did not already hold in January 2009.

A GROWING BANKING CONCERN: 1987–2004

Sovereign Bancorp, Inc., incorporated in 1987 as the holding company for Sovereign Bank. The latter formed in 1984, as Penn Savings Bank, F.S.B., through the merger of two financial institutions primarily operating in Berks and Lancaster counties, west of Philadelphia. The bank's roots, though, extend back to 1902 and a building and loan association serving textile workers eager to buy their own homes.

Penn Savings, renamed Sovereign Bank in December 1991, added branch offices, largely in the New Jersey area but also in Pennsylvania and Delaware, through a series of mergers and acquisitions through 1999. During the decade, Sovereign also acquired consumer/commercial loans, commercial bank deposits, and a New York-based specialty leasing company.

The $35 billion-asset company entered New England—Connecticut, Massachusetts, New Hampshire, and Rhode Island—in 2000, in a branch acquisition deal of unprecedented size, buying 285 branches and related deposits from FleetBoston Financial Corp. The three-stage purchase, stretching from March to July, garnered criticism of some analysts as the company racked up greater than expected special charges and had to raise additional capital, *American Banker* reported in November.

Sovereign implemented a restructuring following the creation of Sovereign Bank New England, cutting 6 percent of its workforce and eliminating management and back-office redundancies. The company's largest operations, located in Pennsylvania, Rhode Island, and Massachusetts, took the biggest hits. The streamlining was necessary to meet target return on equity of 15 to 16 percent by the end of 2002, Jay Sidhu, president and CEO, told *American Banker.*

COMPANY PERSPECTIVES

In joining Santander, Sovereign is poised to offer even better services and more innovative products than ever before—from the same people you already know and trust. You can also continue to count on the close, personal attention you've come to expect—and you'll understand why we say "Our Future is Bright."

Founded in Northern Spain in 1857, Santander has a successful history in retail and commercial banking, and has grown to become one of the five largest banks in the world by profit.

Executives, meanwhile, were realigned along product lines: consumer banking, commercial banking, and trust and private banking. The bank had established a Boston-based capital markets group, and opened a trust company, brokerage, insurance agency, and Internet-only bank during the year.

Sovereign, led by Sidhu, continued its acquisitive ways, adding branches in Pennsylvania, New Jersey, Massachusetts, New Hampshire, and Maryland from March 2002 to January 2005. Further growth via acquisition would require outside help.

HELPING HAND: 2005–06

Toward the end of 2005, Sovereign management struck a deal to sell 19.8 percent of the company to Banco Santander Central Hispano, S.A. The $2.4 billion deal also afforded the Spanish bank a first right of refusal to buy the rest of Sovereign after two years. Sovereign, in turn, would gain the needed capital to make another acquisition.

Pressed by investors to improve performance, Sovereign had set its sight on Independence Community Bank Corp. of Brooklyn. The 120-plus branch bank filled a significant gap in its northeastern U.S. footprint. Sovereign was ready to pay a premium price of $3.6 billion in cash to enter the New York metropolitan area.

Santander, for its part, wanted to reenter the market, the *New York Times* reported in October. The bank had sold a previous U.S. community banking investment in 1996 for a profit.

Small- to medium-sized operations provided a relatively affordable point of entry into U.S. retail banking for foreign banks. Santander, the world's ninth largest bank, had been forgoing riskier for more well-established markets, Heather Timmons explained in the *Times* article. Santander's existing U.S. presence included a private banking business in Miami and an investment-banking branch in New York.

Sovereign's deal for Independence, nevertheless, raised some concerns despite the benefits related to obtaining the New York franchise. Earnings across the industry were projected to decline, according to the *American Banker*. While one analyst called Independence "one of the premier franchises left to be acquired in the metro New York marketplace," others questioned Sovereign's ability to generate enough earnings growth to justify the deal.

The acquisition of the $19.8 billion bank was completed on June 1, 2006, following Santander's purchase of a stake in Sovereign. In addition to the Santander equity offering, Sovereign used proceeds from securities and cash on hand to fund the purchase.

As agreed upon in the acquisition deal, Santander purchased additional shares in Sovereign on the open market, increasing its holding to just under 25 percent, *American Banker* reported in September 2006. The $1 trillion asset bank retained the option to buy Sovereign in its entirety.

WAITING GAME: 2007–08

At year-end 2007, Sovereign Bank was an $85 billion financial institution, operating about 750 community banking offices and employing about 12,000 people. In addition to "attracting deposits" through the bank network, the company originated "small business and middle market commercial loans, multifamily loans, residential mortgage loans, home equity loans and lines of credit, and auto and other consumer loans." Sovereign had "acquired 28 financial institutions, branch networks and/or related businesses since 1990." Eighteen of those acquisitions were made since 1995, totaling about $52 billion in assets, according to the company's annual report.

Sovereign reported a net loss of $1.35 billion for the year; perhaps suggesting size does not always count. Deteriorating credit quality, a troubled residential mortgage market, and charges related to expense reduction contributed to the steep drop-off. Sovereign had produced a $137 million net profit in 2006.

In May 2008, Sovereign made a $1.9 billion equity offering to raise capital. The move reduced the ground floor offer required of Santander for the remainder of the company, from $40 to about $38 per share. Sovereign shares were trading at about $8.51, down 25.4 percent from the beginning of the year, on top of a

55.1 percent decline during 2007, according to a May 27 *American Banker* article.

Sovereign CEO Joseph P. Campanelli said neither a sale nor acquisition was on the immediate horizon. Although the company wanted to expand in New York, the company's performance needed to improve first.

As for Santander, the Spanish company said it had formed no definitive plans regarding Sovereign. Moreover, the minimum purchase price, set during the initial acquisition, would lapse by agreement down the road.

Campanelli, who succeeded the ousted Sidhu on an interim basis in October 2006 and was named CEO in January 2007, led the company through a year and a half of restructuring. Accomplishments included the reversal of retail banking account losses, the elimination of some underperforming assets, and improved risk control mechanisms, *American Banker* reported. From the viewpoint of some shareholders, though, much more needed to be done to root out poorly executed strategies, some of which were tied to Campanelli.

LOSS OF INDEPENDENCE

Festering problems bloomed into an all out financial crisis for the U.S. financial industry in the fall of 2008. As institutions teetered on the brink of disaster and the federal government debated a course of action, the stock market executed a nosedive, taking big bank stock for the ride.

Eric Dash wrote for the *New York Times* on September 30, "Regional banks were punished even more severely as investors scrambled to figure out which of them might fall next in the absence of a bailout plan. National City Corporation, Downey Financial Corpora-

tion and Sovereign Bancorp, lenders pressured by substantial exposure to soured mortgages, were especially hard-hit, falling 63 percent, 48 percent and 36 percent respectively on the heels of the government's seizure … of Washington Mutual, the largest savings and loan."

Santander, in October, struck a deal to acquire the 75.65 percent of Sovereign it did not already own. Valued at $1.9 billion or $3.91 per share, the acquisition enhanced Santander's geographic diversification and afforded a source of future earnings, according to a company press release. Sovereign, meanwhile, faced a possible uptick in deposit losses, as banking customers sought safe havens, according to the *Wall Street Journal.*

Bad news continued to surface on the broader financial front with the revelation of a massive fraud scheme perpetrated by Bernard Madoff. Santander was listed among those faced with potentially millions in investment losses, according to a December *McClatchy-Tribune Business News* story.

Close to year-end, Sovereign announced an 8 percent cut in the workforce, a cost reduction measure, according to the *Philadelphia Inquirer.* At the top, Campanelli had been replaced. Broadly speaking, U.S. banks had been cutting staff as losses accumulated with increased loan default and problem mortgage-backed securities. The country was in the grip of a deepening recession.

Significant charges, including $575 million on preferred shares of Fannie Mae and Freddie Mac coupled with other big losses, produced a net loss of $2.36 billion for the year. Sovereign also reported that it was no longer considered well capitalized.

Sovereign finally became a wholly owned subsidiary of Santander in January 2009. Two ratings agencies moved to upgrade Sovereign's debt rating in the wake of the sale.

"Sovereign is now part of one of the world's largest, most successful banks with $1.2 trillion in deposits and funds under management for over 80 million customers in 40 countries worldwide. We offer that strength, stability and security to our customers across the Sovereign footprint and the new ratings upgrades reflect that," newly named Sovereign Chairman and CEO Gabriel Jaramillo said in a February 3, 2009 press release.

Kathleen Peippo

PRINCIPAL SUBSIDIARIES

Sovereign Bank.

PRINCIPAL COMPETITORS

Bank of America Corporation; Citizens Financial Group, Inc.; The PNC Financial Services Group.

FURTHER READING

Dash, Eric, "The Banking Crisis Trickles Up," *New York Times,* September 30, 2008, p. C1.

————, "Sovereign Bank Settles Dispute with Shareholder," *New York Times,* March 23, 2006, p. C18.

Davenport, Todd, "Sovereign: Independence Is Worth the Price," *American Banker,* December 9, 2005, p. 24.

Fitzpatrick, Dan, Robin Sidel, and John Hilsenrath, "The Financial Crisis: Bailout Politics: Deposits Flow to Healthier Banks," *Wall Street Journal,* October 16, 2008, p. A6.

Leibowitz, Alissa, "Sovereign Realignment Includes 500 Job Cuts," *American Banker,* November 28, 2000, p. 1.

Mondics, Chris, "List of Those Hurt by Madoff Grows," *McClatchy-Tribune Business News* (Washington), December 16, 2008.

Rieker, Matthias, "Some Grilling for Sovereign's CEO," *American Banker,* September 21, 2006, p. 2.

————, "Sovereign CEO: We're 'Positioned' for a Sale," *American Banker,* September 15, 2006, p. 1.

————, "Sovereign, Smaller, Sees Progress on Many Fronts," *American Banker,* May 27, 2008, p. 1.

Schweizer, Paul, "Sovereign Bancorp to Cut 1,000 Jobs," *Philadelphia Inquirer,* December 20, 2008.

"Sovereign Revises Deal with Santander," *New York Times,* November 23, 2005, p. C4.

Timmons, Heather, "Santander Investing in Philadelphia Bank," *New York Times,* October 25, 2005, p. C4.

Spar Handelsgesellschaft mbH

———■———

Osterbrooksweg 35-45
Schenefeld, D-22867
Germany
Telephone: (+49 040) 83 94 0
Fax: (+49 040) 83 94 411 63
Web site: http://www.spar.de

Subsidiary of Edeka Zentrale AG
Incorporated: 1952 as Deutsche Spar
Employees: 273
Sales: EUR 469.7 million ($587 million) (2007)
NAICS: 424490 Other Grocery and Related Product
   Merchant Wholesalers; 445110 Supermarkets and
   Other Grocery (Except Convenience) Stores

■ ■ ■

Once one of Germany's leading supermarket groups, Spar Handelsgesellschaft mbH has refocused its operations around the Spar Express convenience store format. The Schenefeld company, which remains affiliated with Spar International, one of the world's leading retail associations, operates 470 stores throughout Germany, generating EUR 470 million ($587 million) in revenues. Spar Express stores are small, with an average size of less than 250 square meters, and focus primarily on fresh and convenience foods, including "food to go" items such as coffee, juices, ready-made meals, and snacks. In addition to its self-standing stores, Spar Handels operates a number of smaller, airport-based Spar Express shops in partnership with Lufthansa's Market Place Shops. Spar also operates service station-based convenience stores; including those of the Jet service station chain. Spar Handels has been part of German supermarket leader Edeka Zentrale, which absorbed Spar's supermarkets, wholesale operations, and discount supermarkets, since 2005.

SPAR'S ORIGINS IN THE EARLY 1950s

Spar's co-op origins were influenced by an existing model in the Netherlands. In 1932 Dutch grocery wholesaler A. J. M. van Well founded the first cooperative grocery chain in Europe. At that time cooperation between wholesale and retail businesses was uncommon. Van Well and his business partners, 16 of his retail customers, decided to work together in harmony in order to secure profits on a regular basis. In the reconstruction years after World War II, the concept became popular among German midsized grocery wholesalers and retailers. Many of them were concerned about their ability to compete with large conglomerates on the one hand and the widespread produce cooperatives at the other end of the market.

At an international wholesale trade meeting on February 16, 1952, the president of the German grocery trade organization VDN, Rolf Knigge, and two state chapter heads, Werner Hagen from North-Rhine Westphalia and Franz Weissbecker from Bavaria, founded the Deutsche Spar modeled after the Dutch organization. By the end of 1952, 20 wholesalers belonged to the group, loosely organized into northern and southern German groups, which met several times to exchange ideas and experiences. At one such meeting, on October

KEY DATES

1949: Handelshof GmbH, a German wholesale business, is founded.

1952: Deutsche Spar co-op is founded.

1953: Handelshof and Spar merge, forming Handelshof Spar GmbH, which is incorporated in Frankfurt.

1972: Spar delegates agree on updated Spar principles.

1982: First Kodi nonfood discount stores open in Düsseldorf.

1985: The largest Spar members merge to form Spar Handels-AG.

1988: Company goes public.

1990: First Spar supermarket opens in former East Germany.

1995: Spar logistics center in Mittenwalde near Berlin starts operations.

1997: French trade group ITM, operator of the Intermarché supermarket group becomes Spar's majority shareholder.

1999: Spar enters a partnership with Lufthansa to open airport-based Spar Express convenience stores.

2005: ITM agrees to sell Spar to Edeka Zentral.

2009: Refocused as a convenience store specialist, Spar operates 470 stores.

8, 1952, in Frankfurt, they decided to make their enterprise and the Spar trademark public.

The idea of about 50 cooperating wholesalers was not well-received by other parts of the industry. Many retailers were afraid they would have their choice of suppliers restricted. Many wholesalers did not sympathize with Spar, which they saw as a growing new competitor in its own right. The food industry even stopped delivery of goods to one Spar wholesaler, I.A. Schnell, in the German town of Hohenwestedt. However, other Spar wholesalers helped out with the goods that were not delivered to the Schnell business, and soon they started looking for ways to jointly purchase certain products for all Spar members.

To coordinate the group's activities, Centrale der Arbeitsgemeinschaft Spar was founded in the German city of Münster. At a meeting in January 1953 the foundation was laid for the group's further development. The gathered Spar members agreed on a set of core principles and the first Spar logo. They

decided to transform the Münster-based Handelshof GmbH, a private wholesale business founded in 1949, into Spar's central purchasing organization. At the same time, the principals of the Handelshof GmbH agreed to sell their capital to the Spar members and to move the company's headquarters to Frankfurt/Main. On August 19, 1953, the renamed Handelshof Spar GmbH was officially registered in Frankfurt.

The Handelshof Spar GmbH was the umbrella organization for all Spar wholesalers. It purchased products centrally from manufacturers, developed and managed central advertising campaigns, consulted its members on best business practices, and issued licenses to new Spar wholesalers. In 1953 four regional purchasing organizations were set up, serving the German North, South, West, and Southwest. The first Spar brand products were developed in the same year.

In July 1955 the Deutsche Handelsvereinigung Spar e.V. was founded to serve as the central committee for all Spar member businesses. Each regional Spar group was represented by a wholesaler and a retailer. Delegates had one vote, each representing 100 Spar retailers, and decisions were made at central delegates meetings. Thus Spar members were able to influence business politics of the group.

By 1958 the number of Spar member wholesalers peaked at 55. At the same time there were approximately 12,000 retail stores bearing the Spar banner. In 1959 the first Spar supermarket opened in Hersfeld, and the following year the first Spar mail-order catalog was introduced and the first nationwide advertising campaign, worth DEM 2.5 million, was launched.

By 1964 there were 26 Spar brand products, and that number would increase to 540 by the end of the decade. During this time, four subsidiaries were founded to run wholesale businesses and offer services such as electronic data processing, purchasing, and bookkeeping. Moreover, the Deutsche Spar Handels GmbH & Co. (DSH) was founded to purchase primarily nonfood products for the whole Spar group and to centralize invoicing and payment processes for Spar member firms and the industry suppliers.

The 1970s were characterized by a process of concentration and restructuring of the German retail landscape. The shrinking of Germany's retail food market segment had begun in 1968, and in the ensuing years the number of Spar wholesalers and delivery districts decreased by about one-third to 33, while the number of Spar independent retailers shrank by 40 percent to 6,200 stores. As the number of stores went down, the remaining stores started growing in size. To make up for losses in the grocery segment, the group also started to diversify into nonfood markets. As a result, Spar's wholesale revenues more than doubled during the 1970s and even sales of the traditional Spar retailers rose almost 50 percent.

The Spar principles, which were agreed to by all participating businesses, were the basis for the group's success. While they were regularly interpreted, updated, or modified according to changes in business environment, they remained the same in essence, and every member of the Spar organization had to adhere to them or be excluded from the group. A catalog agreed on by Spar delegates in November 1972 listed the main obligations and services for Spar members which remained unchanged up until the 1990s. They included guaranteed minimum sales for Spar wholesalers and retailers and a minimum sales area size for Spar retailers; the full product range to be offered; the obligation for retailers to order most products from Spar wholesalers; exclusive use of the uniform Spar logo in predefined sizes; participation in all Spar organs and services; openness of financial statistics; controls on competition between Spar members by means of assigned territories; and the right of first refusal by the group whenever a Spar store was put up for sale.

FORMATION OF SPAR HANDELS-AG

The 1980s were a decade of stabilization for the German Spar. The number of Spar wholesalers remained at about 30. While several wholesale businesses merged during that period, new wholesalers joined the group. The number of Spar retailers decreased, reaching about 5,400 by the mid-1980s. In 1982 Spar member company Koch & Sohn, based in Düsseldorf, established a new brand for the group, the Kodi nonfood discount stores. In 1985 the three leading German Spar wholesalers Pfeiffer & Schmidt (Schenefeld), Karl Koch & Sohn (Düsseldorf), and Kehrer & Weber (Munich) merged to form Spar Handels-AG. The following year Spar Handels-AG acquired shares in eight midsized German grocers. In 1988 the company's stock was first traded on the stock market.

The second half of the decade saw the number of Spar retailers rise once again, the result of takeovers and consolidation in the grocery industry. Spar's strong market position was reflected in increasing sales. Sales of Spar retailers rose one-third, from DEM 8.9 billion in 1980 to DEM 11.7 billion in 1990. The wholesale side of the business grew even faster. In 1980, 30 Spar wholesalers grossed DEM 5 billion; by 1990, although the group had shrunk to include nine Spar wholesale businesses, sales had jumped by 80 percent to DEM 9 billion.

EXPANSION: 1989-95

Immediately after the Berlin Wall came down in 1989, Spar developed a crash program to help about 3,000 East Germans set up their own Spar neighborhood stores. The first Spar supermarket on the territory of the former German Democratic Republic opened in March 1990. Designed in the style of markets in the West and stocked with products from the West, by the beginning of April 1991 there were more than 1,500 retail stores in the new East German states that purchased products from Spar and were interested in becoming independent Spar retailers.

A subsidiary, Spar Nordost, was founded to serve the new German states of Saxony, Saxony-Anhalt, Mecklenburg-Vorpommern, and Brandenburg. Thuringia, the fifth new state, was served from the Spar subsidiary in Friedewald near Bad Hersfeld in former West Germany. When the East German centrally administered grocery wholesale and retail industries were privatized, Spar Nordost took over 400 supermarkets in good locations and 1,600 other grocery stores from the former East German Handelsorganisation. Spar also acquired warehouses from ten former East German wholesale firms. Thus, with this East German expansion, the number of Spar wholesale customers suddenly increased significantly; the total number of Spar retail customers grew by 2,000 between 1990 and 1992, an increase of almost 30 percent.

The next step was the integration and modernization of the new facilities. Before new facilities were available, 86 warehouses taken over by Spar served the new Spar retailers. Four central warehouses in Rostock, Magdeburg, Potsdam, and Döbeln became key locations. At the beginning of 1992 Spar Nordost was merged with Spar Handels-AG. The new wholesale warehouses were transformed into modern logistics centers. Between 1992 and 1995 Spar invested more than DEM 1 billion into modernizing its logistics network in the new German states. In April 1995 a brand-new Spar logistics center started operations in Mittenwalde near Berlin. The whole Nordost territory was served by three central warehouses in Mittenwalde, Rostock, and Döbeln, as well as two regional and three discount warehouses.

In 1995 there were about 1,340 independent Spar retailers in the new German states, 11 Eurospar hypermarkets, 8 self-service department stores, 211 Netto food discount markets, and 18 Kodi nonfood-discounters. In addition Spar delivered to over 800 other retail customers including 20 food departments of the Karstadt and Hertie department stores.

Combined sales of Spar wholesale and retail businesses rose more than 43 percent between 1990 and

1995. In the new German states alone Spar grossed DEM 5.5 billion, a market share of between 13 and 14 percent. In 1993, 30 percent of Spar's net sales derived from the new German states. By the mid-1990s, 1,200 out of 1,600 Spar neighborhood stores in East Germany were managed by independent retailers.

RECESSION AND REORGANIZATION: 1995-2000

Spar's horizon was soon darkened, however, by fierce competition in the grocery retail industry, especially for market share in the new German states, along with a significant drop in fruit, vegetable, and meat prices and increasingly frugal shopping behavior. Spar, and the industry as a whole, entered a period of ruinous price competition. This was particularly hard on independent Spar retailers in East Germany, since they had not yet had the time to build a sustainable neighborhood customer base. Already, in the early stage of building their businesses, they were often in the red, their very existence threatened by other grocery chains. Moreover, they had to fight daily for the best purchasing modalities and began to feel that the Spar wholesale conditions did not meet their needs.

In August 1995 a group of disgruntled Spar retailers in Saxony-Anhalt, Mecklenburg-Vorpommern, and Thuringia founded an interest group called "Interessengemeinschaft der möglicherweise Spar Geschaedigten e.V.," the "Interest Group of those Possibly Harmed by Spar." They accused their regional Spar wholesalers of unrealistic sales projections, overpriced rents, and unfavorable prices and conditions. The group's story was featured in *Der Spiegel,* Germany's premier news magazine, and the Spar headquarters then accused those business owners of suboptimal management practices. In the following internal and external information campaign, Spar leaders admitted minor problems and promised help to struggling East German Spar retailers, except for those belonging to the Interest Group. The disputes were eventually more or less settled, at least in public. Membership of the Interest Group fluctuated between 60 and 100 during the late 1990s. One of the several pending lawsuits against Spar was settled in February 2000 in favor of Spar.

The increasingly competitive marketplace put Spar under pressure to find new markets and competent partners for strategic alliances. Beginning in 1995 Spar stocked the shelves of 50 Hertie grocery departments in addition to the 71 Karstadt grocery departments it had supplied since 1991. One year later it started deliveries to 600 VeGe/Vivo markets formerly owned by Contzen. Spar's endeavor to find new strategic partners bore fruit in 1997. After an alliance with the Tengelmann Group,

another leading German retail supermarket and distribution group, failed in 1995, the French trade group ITM, operator of the Intermarché supermarket group became majority shareholder of Spar through its Swiss subsidiary Intercontessa AG in the summer of 1997. The group, with retail sales of over DEM 40 billion, had a structure similar to Spar's, with 2,200 independent retailers in France, Portugal, Spain, Italy, Belgium, and Poland.

Beginning in 1996 Spar went on an unprecedented acquisition spree. Between 1996 and 1998 it took over 66 Bolle Markets in Berlin; 36 large Continent self-service department stores from the French Promodès trade group with annual sales of about DEM 2 billion; the wholesale business of Kathrainer AG; eight self-service department stores from Holzer Parkkauf GmbH; the Karlsruhe-based Pfannkuch Group with 212 markets in southwest Germany and net sales of DEM 1.1 billion; 152 PRO Hamburg markets in the Hamburg area and 34 markets around Kassel.

However, the weight of those new acquisitions was proving too heavy for Spar. In particular, venturing into the department store market segment seemed an unfavorable risk. The transformation of the Continent stores into Interspar self-service department stores was costly, and the ongoing price war in Germany diminished sales. Spar was deep in the red, by over DEM 300 million, in 1998. Moreover, since the engagement with Intermarché, Spar preferred shares lost 80 percent of their value. In 1998 a new strategy was developed, focusing on small and midsized grocery and convenience stores. Some 74 large Interspar self-service department stores were sold to U.S. giant Wal-Mart in a $658 million deal, while another 44 stores of the same format were integrated into the Eurospar distribution line. In November 1999 Spar wholesaler L. Stroetmann GmbH & Co. did not extend its contract with Spar and joined competitor Edeka Zentrale.

CONVENIENTLY FOCUSED

The marriage between Spar and Intermarché proved an unhappy one. Spar pushed through the conversion of its supermarkets to the Intermarché format. The costly conversion failed to excite German shoppers however, and into the new century Spar found itself burdened by debt and mounting losses. By 2002 the company's losses had reportedly risen to EUR 220 million, and the company was forced to turn to parent ITM for a bailout.

By the end of that year, the company announced plans to sell its supermarket operations in order to focus around a new core of its Netto discount chain and its wholesale business. As such Spar Handels sold off the Kodi chain, as well as its wholesale division and its home shopping business. The company struggled to find a buyer for its supermarkets, however.

ITM continued to pour money into the ailing Spar; the French company was estimated to have spent as much as EUR 1.3 billion keeping Spar afloat into the middle of the decade. By then, ITM was reportedly in talks with a number of Spar's rivals for a possible sale of the entire Spar business.

These reports soon revealed themselves to be true. In April 2005, ITM announced that it had agreed to sell its German operations to rival Edeka Zentrale AG, one of the country's leading retail groups. As part of the sale, ITM also entered into an international partnership with Edeka and Spain's Eroski Group, forming a EUR 75 billion ($97 billion) supermarket alliance.

Edeka's main target was the entry into the hard discount sector through its control over the Netto discount chain. Following the completion of the Spar takeover, Edeka dismantled the group, absorbing the supermarket operations into its own network, and splitting the Netto chain into a separate division.

Spar Handels was refocused as Edeka's convenience store division, with the launch of a new format, Spar Express. In addition to its network of small shops, which averaged 250 square meters in size, Spar Handels began developing partnerships with the service station sector, and particularly with the Jet service station chain. Spar Handels also oversaw a thriving airport-based business, opening shops in cooperation with Lufthansa's Market Place. By 2009, Spar Handels had been transformed from one of Germany's leading retail groups to a moderate-sized player in the convenience sector, with 470 stores and sales of EUR 470 million.

M. L. Cohen

PRINCIPAL SUBSIDIARIES

Spar Dienstleistungsgesellschaft mbH; Spar Einkaufsgesellschaft mbH; Spar Inkassokontor GmbH & Co. KG; Spar Projektentwicklung GmbH.

PRINCIPAL DIVISIONS

Spar Express.

PRINCIPAL COMPETITORS

The Schwarz Group; Lidl Stiftung and Company KG; Aldi Einkauf GmbH and Company OHG; REAL SB-Warenhaus GmbH; Plus Warenhandelsges Mbh; Metro AG; Plus Warenhandels GmbH; Anton Schlecker; Marktkauf Holding GmbH; Netto Marken-Discount GmbH and Company KG.

FURTHER READING

"Angeschlagene Handelskette Spar Steht vor dem Verkauf," *Handelsblatt,* February 16, 2004.

"Debts Plague Spar Handels Restructure," *Grocer,* June 8, 2002, p. 12.

"Die Spar Handels-AG spuert die Folgen der Rezession," *Frankfurter Allgemeine Zeitung,* June 3, 1994, p. 16.

"Edeka Announces Europe-wide Alliance and Takeovers of Spar, Netto," *just-food.com,* April 28, 2005.

"Edeka Deal OK," *Grocer,* September 3, 2005, p. 10.

"Neue Spar," *Frankfurter Allgemeine Zeitung,* May 21, 1996, p. 19.

"New Concept," *Grocer,* July 24, 2004, p. 13.

Roessing, Sabine, "Vom Debattierclub zum Machtfaktor," *Lebensmittel Zeitung,* February 16, 1996, p. 38.

Spar—gröte Freiwillige Handelskitte, Cologne, Germany: Euro-Handelsinstitut e. V., 1997, 52 p.

"Spar Handels Looks to Future," *Grocer,* July 13, 2002, p. 14.

"Spar Handels Revamp Begins," *Grocer,* December 8, 2001, p. 12.

"Spar Mus Schrumpfen," *Suddeutsche Zeitung,* May 16, 2003.

"Spar to Sell 350 Eurospar, Intermarché Stores," *Suddeutsche Zeitung,* October 29, 2002, p. 27.

"Spar Wird Edeka zur Last," *Handelsblatt,* February 10, 2006.

"Wal-Mart's Hyper Deal," *Grocer,* December 12, 1998, p. 5.

"Wir stehen bei der Spar vor einem Scherbenhaufen," *Lebensmittel Zeitung,* July 9, 1999, p. 6.

SPX Corporation

13515 Ballantyne Corporate Place
Charlotte, North Carolina 28277-2706
U.S.A.
Telephone: (704) 752-4400
Fax: (704) 752-4505
Web site: http://www.spx.com

Public Company
Incorporated: 1912 as The Piston Ring Company
Employees: 17,800
Sales: $5.86 billion (2008)
Stock Exchanges: New York
Ticker Symbol: SPW
NAICS: 332911 Industrial Valve Manufacturing; 332912 Fluid Power Valve and Hose Fitting Manufacturing; 332919 Other Metal Valve and Pipe Fitting Manufacturing; 333311 Automatic Vending Machine Manufacturing; 333415 Air-Conditioning and Warm Air Heating Equipment and Commercial and Industrial Refrigeration Equipment Manufacturing; 333911 Pump and Pumping Equipment Manufacturing; 333913 Measuring and Dispensing Pump Manufacturing; 333994 Industrial Process Furnace and Oven Manufacturing; 333995 Fluid Power Cylinder and Actuator Manufacturing; 333996 Fluid Power Pump and Motor Manufacturing; 333999 All Other Miscellaneous General Purpose Machinery Manufacturing; 334220 Radio and Television Broadcasting and Wireless Communications Equipment Manufacturing; 334512 Automatic Environmental Control Manufacturing for Residential, Commercial, and Appliance Use;

334513 Instruments and Related Products Manufacturing for Measuring, Displaying, and Controlling Industrial Process Variables; 334514 Totalizing Fluid Meter and Counting Device Manufacturing; 334515 Instrument Manufacturing for Measuring and Testing Electricity and Electrical Signals; 334516 Analytical Laboratory Instrument Manufacturing; 334519 Other Measuring and Controlling Device Manufacturing; 335311 Power, Distribution, and Specialty Transformer Manufacturing; 335999 All Other Miscellaneous Electrical Equipment and Component Manufacturing

■ ■ ■

With beginnings as an auto parts manufacturer, SPX Corporation has evolved over its 95-plus-year history into a wide-ranging maker of various industrial products and a provider of related services. The company's subsidiaries and units are divided into four segments: flow technology, test and measurement, thermal equipment and services, and industrial products and services. The flow technology segment includes fluid-handling products such as pumps and valves as well as air and gas filtration and dehydration products. The test and measurement segment includes automotive diagnostic service equipment, fare-collection systems, and cable and pipe locators. The thermal equipment and services segment includes various cooling, heating, and ventilation products for industrial, commercial, and residential markets as well as thermal components for power and steam-generation plants. The industrial products and

COMPANY PERSPECTIVES

From power generation to food processing, SPX solutions are helping to meet the needs of a growing, ever-changing world. We don't just talk about ideas. We make them happen—in our customers' manufacturing plants, on their construction sites, in their laboratories, underground and even in cyberspace.

Whether producing innovative process equipment and diagnostic tools or helping to develop global infrastructure, SPX is transforming ideas into powerful solutions.

services segment includes power transformers, industrial tools, and television and radio broadcast antennas. The company also holds a 44.5 percent stake in EGS Electrical Group, LLC, which is controlled and operated by Emerson Electric Co.; EGS is a manufacturer of electrical fittings, hazardous location lighting, and power conditioning products. SPX has operations in more than 40 countries and generates sales in more than 150 countries around the world. Approximately 48 percent of revenues originate outside the United States, with three countries leading the way: Germany (15 percent of overall sales), China (5 percent), and the United Kingdom (5 percent).

PISTON RING BEGINNINGS

SPX's foundations were laid on December 20, 1911, when two friends, Charles E. Johnson and Paul R. Beardsley, each deposited $1,000 in the National Lumberman's Bank of Muskegon, Michigan. The money served as the initial working capital of their new single product firm, The Piston Ring Company, which was officially founded in 1912. Johnson, a mechanic, and Beardsley, a salesman, foresaw the need for automotive parts for the burgeoning automotive industry in Michigan. The two partners personally delivered the first piston rings manufactured in their rented 30-by-60-foot factory to the firm's first customer, Continental Motors Corporation. In its first years, the aptly named Piston Ring Company devoted itself entirely to the production of piston rings for leading engine builders. The advent of World War I brought a huge increase in the demand for engine parts for the war effort, and The Piston Ring Company responded by undertaking a major plant expansion.

In the years between the two world wars, The Piston Ring Company began a series of acquisitions and

expansions, a pattern of growth for the company for the next 60 years. In 1923 the firm bought the No-Leak-O Piston Ring Company, which allowed it to further increase its production of the crucial engine component. By 1925, the company was able to begin exporting its product and to enter the increasingly lucrative replacement parts market. The acquisition in 1931 of the Accuralite Company, a maker of pistons and cylinder sleeves, marked a crucial step for the growing firm. This diversification of the product line would become a fundamental component of the company's strategy in later years. In order to reflect this new diversity, the company also changed its name from the simple "The Piston Ring Company" to the more evocative "Sealed Power Corporation."

The post–World War II years were a period of major expansion for Sealed Power. In 1946 the company opened its first plant outside Muskegon with the construction of a piston ring machining facility at St. John's, Michigan, closer to the huge Detroit automakers that were its primary customers. Two years later the company built a cylinder sleeve machining facility in Rochester, Indiana, and in 1957 it added a Replacement Distribution Center in LaGrange, Indiana. This distribution center, which serviced 33 smaller distribution outlets in key cities throughout the United States and Canada, was indicative of the growing role of replacement parts marketing in the company's business strategy. By 1959, replacement parts accounted for about 50 percent of Sealed Power sales and served as an important hedge against the highly cyclical original equipment market. The automotive aftermarket is not only relatively free from the sharp ups and downs of the original parts industry but actually tends to increase during downturns in the original automotive market. When people are not in a position to buy new cars they have their old ones repaired instead.

Sealed Power's relatively rapid expansion in the 1950s led to the company's first public offering of common stock in 1955. The company also increased exports, distributing their original and replacement parts in 78 countries by the end of the decade. Even more significantly for its global presence, by the dawn of the 1960s Sealed Power had opened plants in Stratford, Canada, and in Mexico City. This expansion in both production and market diversity was accompanied by a major product breakthrough in 1956 when Sealed Power introduced the first stainless steel piston ring. The ring quickly achieved 100 percent original and replacement market acceptance, according to company sources.

KEY DATES

1912: The Piston Ring Company is founded in Muskegon, Michigan, to manufacture piston rings for automakers.

1931: Acquisition of Accuralite Company, maker of pistons and cylinder sleeves, marks first diversification of product line; company changes its name to Sealed Power Corporation.

1955: Company goes public.

1982: Kent-Moore Corporation is acquired.

1988: Company changes its name to SPX Corporation.

1989: Major restructuring is launched involving the sale of a majority stake in all of SPX's original equipment operations.

1993: Automotive replacement parts division is sold to Federal-Mogul Corporation; SPX regains full control of its original equipment operations.

1997: The Sealed Power Division, the company's founding business, is sold to Dana Corporation.

1998: General Signal Corporation, maker of products for the process control, electrical control, and industrial technology industries, is acquired for $2.3 billion.

2001: United Dominion Industries Limited, a diversified manufacturer of engineered products, is acquired for about $1.9 billion.

2002: Company headquarters are moved to Charlotte, North Carolina.

2004: A series of controversies leads to the resignation of CEO John Blystone.

2005: Under new leadership, SPX divests several noncore businesses, including its Bomag, Edwards Systems Technology, and Kendro units.

2007: Process equipment specialist APV is acquired.

PERIOD OF STEADY GROWTH

At the beginning of the 1960s, in spite of product diversification over the previous 50 years, the sale of piston rings for both the original and replacement markets still accounted for over 65 percent of Sealed Power's sales. These sales made up about one-quarter of the total U.S. market for piston rings and made Sealed Power the second largest manufacturer of piston rings in the country. Cylinder sleeves and pistons made up the bulk of the company's remaining sales, although by this time it was also producing a variety of small engine parts, such as valves and tappets. By the end of the decade, Sealed Power, determined to decrease its reliance on a single product, implemented a planned program of product diversification. In 1968 the company acquired another cylinder sleeve plant in Mexico as well as the Consolidated Die Cast Corporation (later renamed Contech), a Michigan firm that produced precision die castings. During the next six years it acquired a manufacturer of valve tappets (later renamed the Hy-Lift Division), a manufacturer of transmission fluid filters (later renamed the Filtran Division), and a manufacturer of small alloyed castings. It had also opened a sealing ring plant in Franklin, Kentucky, a tappet facility in Zeeland, Michigan, and a new piston ring plant in Liege, Belgium, to serve the European market.

Sales rose steadily during the 1960s and 1970s as Sealed Power expanded. From annual sales of $25 million in 1960, the company's sales had grown to over $200 million by 1977. Although sales grew, earnings remained heavily dependent on fluctuations in the auto industry. In 1974, for instance, a year in which American car and truck production plummeted, earnings fell to $1.46 per share from the previous year's $2.19. Diversification had meant that piston rings made up a smaller percentage of sales than they had in the early 1960s; nonetheless, Sealed Power's original engine parts group, which included sealing rings, valve tappets, and transmission filters in addition to the company's long-standing engine products, still accounted for 42 percent of sales in 1975. With over three-quarters of these sales coming directly from the auto industry, Sealed Power's fortunes were inextricably tied to that of the major American automakers. In a 1980 press release, Edward I. Schalon, the company president, stated that "as a supplier of engine parts to the motor vehicle industry we are adversely affected by the proliferation of cars and trucks imported into the United States. This situation is compounded by the growing number of vehicles which bear domestic nameplates, but are powered by engines manufactured overseas."

CONTINUING ACQUISITIONS AND DIVERSIFICATION

Diversification continued to dominate Sealed Power's long-term business strategy in the 1980s. In early 1982 the company acquired Kent-Moore Corporation in a cash and stock transaction valued at $70 million. Kent-Moore, headquartered in Warren, Michigan, was a major manufacturer of specialized service tools, equipment, and diagnostic instrumentation for the transportation industry. An important step in Sealed Power's campaign to diversify its product line, the acquisition of Kent-Moore provided a new direction for Sealed Power's relationship with the auto industry. Although Kent-Moore dealt directly with the same automakers that Sealed Power had supplied since its beginnings in 1911, the specialty tools that it produced relied on the introduction of new automotive models rather than on the volume of production. Each new car model required a set of specialized tools with which dealers could service the vehicles, and the Kent-Moore division worked directly with manufacturers before new vehicles were introduced. Kent-Moore also had significant overseas operations, including a partnership in Japan, that allowed Sealed Power to expand its foreign presence. In 1982, the first year of the acquisition, Kent-Moore contributed some $86 million to Sealed Power's $366 million sales total.

Sales continued to grow during the 1980s, topping $400 million in 1983 and placing Sealed Power within the *Fortune* 500. Earnings, however, continued to fluctuate. In 1983 and 1984, when domestic automobile production soared, Sealed Power's earnings rose an impressive 27 and 17 percent, respectively, only to fall back again in 1985 and 1986 when both the original equipment and replacement markets flattened out. By 1985, as it became clear that the American auto industry would be unstable for at least the immediate future, stock analysts began to stress the advantages of the aftermarket over the original equipment market. After the Kent-Moore purchase the proportion of sales contributed by each of Sealed Power's product groups began to shift. In 1982, the year of the Kent-Moore acquisition, aftermarket sales made up 39 percent of total sales, original equipment contributed 35 percent, and specialty service tools took over 22 percent of total revenues.

In 1985 Sealed Power further expanded its specialty tool product segment through the acquisition of the Owatonna Tool Company and its subsidiaries, later the Power Team and Truth divisions of SPX. Owatonna, a producer of specialty tools and electronic repair equipment, allowed Sealed Power to expand its market in this area. Power Team and Truth further diversified Sealed Power's product line with the addition of high-pressure hydraulic pumps and other equipment for industrial applications as well as window and door hardware for the home construction industry. Also acquired in 1985 was the V.L. Churchill Group of Daventry, England, a major supplier of specialty tools and service products in Europe, further expanding Sealed Power's overseas presence. In order to respond to the growing threat of Japanese automobile imports, Sealed Power also set up a joint agreement with the Riken Corp., Japan's largest manufacturer of piston rings, to allow Sealed Power to distribute Riken's engine parts for repair and maintenance of Japanese cars in the United States. Sealed Power continued its program of diversification and expansion through acquisitions into the late 1980s. In addition to a number of smaller businesses, the company purchased the piston ring operations of TRW Inc. in 1987, resulting in a reorganization and consolidation of Sealed Power's piston manufacturing plants and the laying off of some 400 employees.

1988 EMERGENCE AS SPX

The late 1980s were a critical period for Sealed Power. By 1988 Sealed Power's products ranged from piston rings to door hardware and were sold to a wide range of markets. Original equipment motor parts sales had fallen to only 28 percent of total company revenues, whereas replacement parts constituted 36 percent of sales, service products and specialty service remained steady at 22 percent of corporate volume, and window and door hardware assumed 14 percent of total sales. In recognition of the changing nature of the company, the decision was reached to change the company name from Sealed Power Corporation to SPX Corporation. Robert D. Tuttle, then company chairman and CEO, stated in a press release that the name change was necessary because the Sealed Power name did not reflect the scope of the company's diversity in products and markets nor the range and depth of its vision of the company's future.

Acquisitions had greatly increased SPX's total sales, which rose from $250 million in 1980 to $632 million in 1989. Net income, however, failed to rise as consistently and the still considerable original equipment segment continued to be tied to the fluctuations in the automobile industry. The acquisition in 1988 of Bear Automotive Service Equipment Company increased SPX's presence in the specialty service equipment field. In 1989 the company reached a major crossroads; diversification had transformed it from an engine parts maker with some other interests, to a replacement parts and specialty service tool manufacturer that also made piston rings.

A rumor was reported in early 1989 that corporate raider Arthur Goldberg was making a move toward SPX and had actually purchased a 4 percent stake in the company. Whether or not these rumors were heeded by SPX management, they clearly thought that strong action was needed to maintain shareholder confidence in the diffuse company. That action came in April 1989 when it was announced that the company would undergo a major restructuring. The key component of this restructuring would be the sale of a majority stake in all of SPX's original equipment operations.

A new partnership, to be called Sealed Power Technologies Limited Partnership, would be formed from four Sealed Power divisions specializing in original equipment manufacture. The partnership would be controlled by a joint agreement between Sealed Power, who would retain a 49 percent stake in the companies, and Goldman, Sachs & Co., a New York securities firm that would assume control of 49 percent of the partnership. The remaining 2 percent stake would be owned by company management. This partnership would operate independently of SPX's other operations and would leave SPX free to concentrate more heavily on its replacement and specialty service tools segments. In addition, SPX would establish an employee stock ownership plan, in an apparently defensive move, to make unfriendly takeovers more difficult. "The restructuring will allow SPX to concentrate fully on a market segment that has higher margins and is more resistant to recessions than the original equipment business," CEO Robert Tuttle was quoted as saying in an article in the *Grand Rapids (Mich.) Business Journal.*

STRUGGLES IN THE EARLY 1990s

The resistance to recession that SPX believed it would gain from concentrating its resources on the automobile aftermarket and construction industries failed to materialize. Instead, 1990 proved a very poor year for all sectors of SPX, with the exception of such environmentally driven products as refrigerant recycling equipment from the Robinair division. Net income dropped from $23.6 million in 1989 to only $17.7 million in 1990 (not including income or losses from Sealed Power Technologies), mostly because of weak demand in the automotive replacement business and a major downturn in the housing industry. If 1990 was disappointing for the reorganized SPX, 1991 was disastrous. For the first time in over 50 years SPX recorded a net loss, totaling $19.4 million. Sales were down in all sectors, but continued losses in the Bear Automotive Service Equipment division were particularly worrisome.

Faced with increasing pressure to restabilize the company, Dale A. Johnson, SPX CEO since 1989, essentially reversed the restructuring that had taken place in the late 1980s. The first step in the repositioning of the company was the sale of the automotive replacement parts division to Federal-Mogul Corporation in September 1993. Then, in late 1993, the company decided to repurchase the outstanding 49 percent stake in the Sealed Power Technologies Partnership. With the

reacquisition of the four divisions that had made up the partnership, in addition to the sale of SPX's door and window hardware division, SPX was firmly back into the original automotive equipment market. The restructuring itself, however, had demanded a substantial outlay, and SPX faced another substantial loss by the end of 1993. Johnson, commenting on the $40.6 million loss in a press release, maintained that "operating performance for 1993 was sharply impacted by steps taken to complete the strategy for transforming the company into a global market leader in specialty service tools and original equipment components for the motor vehicle industry."

As the new SPX emerged in 1994, its operations were tightly focused in two distinct arenas. Specialty Service Tools made up 54 percent of sales and were produced and distributed by the Automotive Diagnostics (created by the merging of Bear Automotive with the newly acquired Allen Testproducts), Dealer Equipment and Services, Kent-Moore, OTC, Power Team, and Robinair divisions of SPX. The Original Equipment Components Group, formed by the Acutex, Contech, Hy-Lift, and Sealed Power divisions, contributed 46 percent of revenues. A substantial recovery in the motor vehicle industry occurred in 1994, making SPX's reentry into the original equipment market seem well timed. Sales surged past the $1 billion mark for the first time, registering at $1.09 billion, although net income was a fairly paltry $14.1 million.

TRANSFORMATION INTO A DIVERSIFIED INDUSTRIAL MANUFACTURER

Midway through 1995, with the company again struggling to make a profit and in fact on its way to a net loss for the year of $5.3 million, and with the company stock price on the decline, Johnson was forced to resign from his position as chairman and CEO. Charles E. Johnson II, grandson of the company cofounder, was named interim leader (Dale A. Johnson was not related to the founding Johnson family). In December 1995 John B. Blystone was named SPX's new chairman, president, and CEO. Blystone was a longtime executive with General Electric Company with nearly 20 years of experience managing various businesses, most recently Nuovo Pignone SpA, a $2 billion conglomerate based in Florence, Italy.

Blystone had experience turning companies around, and he moved quickly to change SPX's fortunes. The company began to divest unprofitable or noncore operations and strengthen and grow the remaining core units. Among the first divestments, in a clear signal of a new era, was the company's Sealed Power Division, its founding business, which was sold to Dana Corporation in early 1997 for $223 million. Other early moves in the Blystone era were the consolidation of divisions to save costs and the elimination of 1,100 jobs by mid-1997. SPX posted a net loss of $62.3 million in 1996, but this resulted largely from the recording of unusual expenses, including a $67.8 million write-off of goodwill and $20 million in restructuring charges. The improved financial condition of the firm was evident from the operating profit of $24.6 million reported in 1996, a substantial gain over the $7.7 million figure of the preceding year.

Acquisitions, fueled by the firm's rich stock price, began to be sought to bolster the core units. During 1997 SPX acquired A.R. Brasch Marketing, producer of automotive owner's manuals and technical service and training materials, a company that fit perfectly alongside the specialty service equipment operations. In early 1998 SPX made a surprising $3 billion hostile takeover bid for Echlin Inc., a much larger auto parts supplier. SPX withdrew its bid after Dana Corporation stepped in with a richer offer. Undismayed, SPX succeeded later in 1998 with a $2.3 billion stock-and-cash takeover of General Signal Corporation, a firm with 1997 revenues of $1.95 billion, more than double the revenues of the acquirer. The acquisition, completed in October 1998, enabled SPX to substantially diversify its product portfolio beyond the automotive industry. Based in Stamford, Connecticut, General Signal was a leading maker of products for the process control, electrical control, and industrial technology industries, such as ultra-low-temperature laboratory freezers and industry valves and radio-frequency transmission equipment. Late in 1998 SPX announced a restructuring program. As part of its integration of General Signal, SPX closed 18 manufacturing, sales, and administrative facilities and eliminated about 1,200 jobs. Substantial special charges related to the restructuring led to a net loss for the year of $41.7 million, but the company's revenues nearly doubled to $1.83 billion. Only about 14 percent of the sales were generated by the firm's founding sector, automotive parts.

SPX continued to restructure, divest selected units, and complete acquisitions in 1999. Four more facilities were closed during the year, leading to the elimination of more than 600 additional jobs and a special charge of $38.4 million. Divestments included Best Power, a maker of uninterruptible power supplies that had been acquired in 1995, which was sold to London-based Invensys plc for $240 million; and the Acutex division, which produced solenoid valves and transmission products and was sold to Hilite Industries, Inc., for $27 million. In September 1999 SPX paid $86 million in cash to Rockwell International Corporation for North American Transformer, Inc., manufacturer of large power transformers. Revenues surged to $2.71 billion in 1999, while net income was a strong $101.5 million.

INCREASING ACQUISITIVENESS

The story was similar in 2000 although there were no major divestitures and the company's acquisitiveness increased. Restructuring efforts led to the closure of ten manufacturing plants and sales offices, job cuts of more than 700, and $90.9 million in special charges. SPX spent about $225 million during 2000 to complete 21 acquisitions, most of which were small, strategic purchases. The largest of the group included Copes-Vulcan, a maker of control valves and turbine bypass systems purchased for $35 million; Pittsburgh-based Computerm Corporation, a producer of channel extension products, bought for $30 million; Fairfax, Virginia-based Varcom Corporation, a specialist in network management hardware, software, and services, acquired for $25 million; and Fenner Fluid Power, a division of Fenner plc of Yorkshire, England, specializing in medium-pressure hydraulic power system components, which was bought for $64 million. Also during 2000 SPX completed an initial public offering of 10.5 percent of class B stock in Inrange Technologies Corporation, a subsidiary specializing in the design, manufacture, marketing, and service of networking and switching products for storage, data, and telecommunications networks; it was actually Inrange that made two of the key 2000 acquisitions: Computerm and Varcom. SPX retained 100 percent of the class A stock and the remaining 89.5 percent of the class B, giving it voting power of about 98 percent. Proceeds of $128.2 million were raised through the offering. Revenues actually declined slightly for the year, to $2.68 billion—with the company feeling the impact of the midyear decline in the global economy—but net income increased 86.7 percent, totaling $189.5 million, although this figure was inflated by a $98 million gain on the issuance of Inrange stock.

In May 2001 SPX completed the acquisition of United Dominion Industries Limited in an all-stock transaction valued at about $1.9 billion, including the assumption of $876 million in debt. Based in Charlotte, North Carolina, United Dominion was a diversified manufacturer of flow technology, engineered machinery, test instruments, and other products. The firm had annual sales of about $2.4 billion. This acquisition marked a significant and further diversification of the SPX product mix. In April 2001 SPX announced that it planned to purchase VSI Holdings Inc., a Bloomfield Hills, Michigan-based provider of integrated marketing services mainly to the automotive industry, for $197 million. SPX soon pulled out of the deal, however, leading VSI to file a class-action lawsuit on its own behalf and on behalf of the company's shareholders alleging breach of contract and requesting that the court require SPX to complete the acquisition. The two sides eventually reached an out-of-court settlement that required SPX to make a $20 million payment of VSI. In the meantime, in July 2001, SPX completed its largest bolt-on acquisition to that time, beefing up its life-sciences business unit via the $320 million purchase of Kendro Laboratory Products, L.P., maker of a variety of laboratory equipment, including centrifuges, incubators, ovens, freezers, and clean-air equipment.

As the integration of United Dominion got underway, SPX announced in August 2001 that it would cut 2,000 jobs and close 49 manufacturing, sales, and administrative facilities by the end of 2002. That same month, the company announced that it would relocate its company headquarters from Muskegon to Charlotte, North Carolina. In a press release, Blystone explained the reasoning: "In choosing Charlotte, we considered total corporate costs, labor pool, access to metropolitan airports that offer better domestic and international flights, affordable housing, employment opportunities for dual income families and overall quality of life." The move was completed in early 2002.

The acquisition of United Dominion along with a number of other purchases helped send SPX revenues soaring past the $5 billion mark for 2002, nearly doubling the total for 2000. Operating income of $586.6 million more than doubled the $276.1 million figure for 2000, while net income before a change in accounting principles for 2002 was $276 million. At this time, Blystone was still receiving accolades for his stewardship of the company since late 1995, during which time he had engineered both a remarkable financial turnaround and a major transformation in the mix of SPX operations. He had also managed to maintain solid levels of profitability for SPX through the difficult economic times of the 21st century's initial years.

During 2003, in addition to spending an aggregate $244 million on a series of smaller acquisitions of 14 companies, SPX also divested Inrange Technologies, its publicly traded subsidiary specializing in networking and switching products. SPX sold its approximately 91 percent stake in Inrange to Computer Network Technology Corporation in May 2003 for roughly $190 million.

Blystone's reputation took a quick turn south early in 2004 when it was revealed that SPX had managed to meet its estimate for 2003 earnings only by including a one-time, $60 million settlement of a patent-infringement lawsuit. Further consternating shareholders

was that Blystone sold a large portion of his SPX stock holdings in the weeks leading up to the company's release of its 2003 earnings, although this sell-off was apparently part of an existing arrangement that did not violate restrictions on insider trading. He was also the subject of criticism for his outsized compensation package. Amid mounting criticism and a looming proxy fight led by shareholders seeking to add outside directors to the company board, Blystone resigned in December 2004. The debacle led to several class-action lawsuits against the company, which were eventually settled with SPX agreeing to pay about $13.6 million.

TURNAROUND UNDER NEW LEADERSHIP

Christopher J. Kearney, who had served as vice-president, secretary, and general counsel of SPX since 1997, was named the new president and CEO. Kearney's immediate first goal was to place the company on a firmer financial footing by slashing the hefty $2.4 billion load of debt his predecessor had amassed to finance his acquisition spree. SPX quickly identified a number of noncore businesses and placed them up for sale, in the process incurring $246.8 million in charges for goodwill impairment, which led to a net loss for 2004 of $17.1 million. A series of divestments ensued in 2005. Bomag, a German maker of soil, asphalt, and waste compactors, was sold in January to the French firm Groupe Fayat for $447.3 million. In March, SPX sold Edwards Systems Technology, which specialized in fire detection and building life-safety systems, to General Electric Company for $1.39 billion. In May, the Kendro laboratory and life-sciences unit was sold to Thermo Electron Corporation for $828.8 million.

Proceeds from the asset sales enabled SPX to reduce its debt by 70 percent, to about $721 million, which provided the company with a great deal more financial flexibility. In addition, Kearney placated investors by returning more than $700 million to them in the form of dividends and the repurchase of 14.7 million shares of common stock. He also revamped the firm's compensation system, while the board of directors was overhauled to include six independent directors out of the seven total. To improve earnings, Kearney introduced a more disciplined, centralized structure that brought more financial discipline to what had been a loosely run amalgamation of independent units. SPX's remaining operations were reorganized into four divisions: flow technology, test and measurement, thermal equipment and services, and industrial products and services.

SPX under Kearney also made a concerted effort to expand its presence in overseas markets. This effort was well timed as a global infrastructure building boom was underway, and the company included in its array of businesses a number that were active in the areas of electrical power, energy, and telecommunications. China was a particularly key market. SPX enjoyed a nearly 70 percent increase in its revenues from that nation in 2005 and by 2006 was operating a dozen manufacturing plants there. In 2007 the company opened a corporate office in Shanghai to facilitate future growth in China, which that year accounted for about 5 percent of overall sales.

Acquisitions played a key role in the overseas push, most notably the December 2007 purchase of APV from the British firm Invensys plc for $524.2 million. APV was a global manufacturer of process equipment and engineered products, including pumps, valves, heat exchangers, and homogenizers for the food, dairy, beverage, and pharmaceutical industries. This acquisition strengthened SPX's flow technology division and particularly its position in Europe and the Asia-Pacific region. This and other overseas acquisitions, coupled with organic growth initiatives, propelled the portion of revenues that SPX generated outside the United States from 30 percent in 2004 to nearly 50 percent by 2008.

By mid-2008, SPX's stock price had tripled over the three and a half years of the Kearney era in a clear signal of Wall Street's approval of the company overhaul. The stock fell sharply in the latter months of the year as the economic downturn accelerated, but SPX still managed to post healthy full-year profits of $247.9 million on sales of $5.86 billion. The 28 percent revenue increase that year was largely attributable to the purchase of APV. Of the three main areas SPX was focusing on at this time, the global infrastructure market saw its growth slowing in concert with the economic downturn, and the company's diagnostic tools operations faced an even bleaker outlook because of the travails gripping the automotive industry. In process technology, the company's third growth engine, prospects were brighter, particularly in the food and beverage equipment area that had been bolstered by bringing APV aboard. In early 2009 SPX announced a restructuring plan to shave costs and counter the effects of the economic decline, with the plan entailing the slashing of about 1,700 workers from the workforce, a downsizing of nearly 10 percent.

Hilary Gopnik
Updated, David E. Salamie

PRINCIPAL DIVISIONS

Flow Technology; Test and Measurement; Thermal Equipment and Services; Industrial Products and Services.

PRINCIPAL COMPETITORS

ABB Ltd.; Airmaster Fan Company; Alfa Laval AB; ALSTOM; Baltimore Aircoil Company Inc.; The Babcock & Wilcox Company; BBT Thermotechnik GmbH; Broan-NuTone LLC; Burnham Holdings, Inc.; Cadet Manufacturing Company; Chemineer, Inc.; EKATO Corporation; Evapco, Inc.; Fisher Controls International LLC; Fristam Pumpen F. Stamp KG (GmbH & Co.); GEA Group Aktiengesellschaft; General Electric Company; Glen Dimplex Group; Hayward Industries, Inc.; King Electrical Manufacturing Company; Kuhlman Electric Corporation; LEWA, Inc.; Ouellet Canada Inc.; Robert Bosch GmbH; Siemens AG; Snap-on Incorporated; Südmo North America Inc.; Systemair AB; TPI Corporation.

FURTHER READING

Alexander, Dave, "Firm's Poor Showing Forces SPX Head to Quit," *Grand Rapids (Mich.) Press*, June 29, 1995, p. B7.

————, "Muskegon's Largest Corporation Leaving for Charlotte, N.C.," *Grand Rapids (Mich.) Press*, September 1, 2001, p. D3.

————, "SPX Shakeup: Blystone Out, Johnson In," *Muskegon (Mich.) Chronicle*, December 9, 2004, p. A1.

Blake, Laura, "SPX Sees Profit with Acquisition," *Grand Rapids (Mich.) Business Journal*, July 5, 1993, p. B7.

————, "Technology Keys SPX into Future," *Grand Rapids (Mich.) Business Journal*, December 12, 1994.

Burton, Jonathan, "The House That John Built," *Chief Executive*, May 1997, p. 24.

Deogun, Nikhil, "SPX to Buy United Dominion for $954 Million in Stock Deal," *Wall Street Journal*, March 12, 2001, p. A6.

Dorfman, Dan, "Money Follows Goldberg's Moves," *USA Today*, March 3, 1989, p. 4B.

Downey, John, "Blystone Exits As Head of Struggling SPX," *Charlotte (N.C.) Business Journal*, December 10, 2004, p. 3.

————, "Chris Kearney Leading SPX Turnaround," *Charlotte (N.C.) Business Journal*, August 29, 2008, pp. 1+.

————, "SPX to Cut 400 U.S. Jobs As Part of Restructuring," *Charlotte (N.C.) Business Journal*, January 23, 2009.

"Greater Efficiency, New Items Spark Advance in Earnings of Sealed Power," *Barron's*, November 6, 1961, p. 21.

Hopkins, Stella M., "Game Plan: Hard Work Nets Success," *Charlotte (N.C.) Observer*, March 4, 2007, p. 1D.

————, "SPX to Settle Fraud Lawsuits," *Charlotte (N.C.) Observer*, January 9, 2007, p. 2D.

Laing, Jonathan R., "Numbers Game: The Clever Accounting at SPX, a Mini Conglomerate, Can't Work Forever," *Barron's*, September 13, 2004, pp. 20–21, 24.

Lipin, Steven, "SPX Is Buying General Signal for $2 Billion," *Wall Street Journal*, July 20, 1998, p. A3.

Lloyd, Mary Ellen, "SPX Chief Blystone Steps Down amid Criticism and Proxy Fight," *Wall Street Journal,* December 10, 2004, p. B2.

Lunan, Charles, "SPX to Shift from Buying to Selling," *Charlotte (N.C.) Observer,* August 3, 2004, p. 1D.

Maher, Tani, "SPX Cannot Unseal Its Past," *Financial World,* September 6, 1988, p. 16.

Novoselick, Paul, "After Merging with Giant General Signal, 1999 Promises to Be the Year of the New ... SPX," *Muskegon (Mich.) Chronicle,* September 13, 1998, p. F1.

————, "SPX Wins, Despite Losing Bid for Takeover," *Grand Rapids (Mich.) Press,* May 18, 1998, p. B4.

Novoselick, Paul, and Dave Alexander, "SPX Doubles in Size with Purchase," *Muskegon (Mich.) Chronicle,* March 12, 2001, p. A1.

Sabo, Mary Ann, "SPX Looks for Come-from-Behind Win over Losses," *Grand Rapids (Mich.) Press,* April 24, 1997, p. A15.

"Sealed Power Corp. Extends Solid Earnings, Recovery of Final Half of Last Year," *Barron's,* March 16, 1959, p. 28.

"Sealed Power: Engine Parts Maker Revved Up for Record Earnings," *Barron's,* May 10, 1976, pp. 32, 34.

Sechler, Bob, "SPX Finds Success Overseas," *Wall Street Journal,* February 27, 2008, p. B3C.

Sendler, Emily R., "SPX Agrees to Acquire General Signal in $2 Billion Deal for Stock and Cash," *Wall Street Journal,* July 21, 1998, p. A4.

————, "SPX Plans to Trim Sites, Jobs in Restructuring," *Wall Street Journal,* December 29, 1998, p. A4.

"SPX Corp. Selects Veteran of GE, Other Companies As Its New Leader," *Grand Rapids (Mich.) Press,* December 1, 1995, p. A17.

Turner, Mike, "The New Look of Muskegon's SPX," *Grand Rapids (Mich.) Business Journal,* April 17, 1989, p. B1.

Tuttle, Robert D., *A Tradition of Achievement: The Story of Sealed Power Corporation,* New York: Newcomen Society of the United States, 1986, 24 p.

Wieland, Barbara, "SPX Chief: 'The Rules Have Changed,'" *Grand Rapids (Mich.) Press,* November 14, 2000, p. A22.

SSI (U.S.), Inc.

---

401 North Michigan Avenue, Suite 3400
Chicago, Illinois 60611
U.S.A.
Telephone: (312) 822-0088
Fax: (312) 822-0116
Web site: http://www.spencerstuart.com

Private Company
Incorporated: 1956
Employees: 1,600
Sales: $375 million (2009 est.)
NAICS: 561312 Executive Search Services; 541612 Human Resources Consulting Services

∎ ∎ ∎

SSI (U.S.), Inc., otherwise known as Spencer Stuart Management Consultants, is a private, well-established, highly successful executive search and consulting firm. Based in Chicago, the company has 51 offices dotting the globe and is continually sought to fill C-level (high corporate-level) positions for many of the world's top-grossing companies. Spencer Stuart not only searches for top management talent but provides the corporate world with numerous studies and consulting services, including its annual Spencer Stuart Board Index, including in-depth coverage of the S&P 500's boards of directors.

ORIGINS: FIFTIES AND SIXTIES

On April 1, 1956, Spencer R. Stuart opened an executive search consulting firm on Michigan Avenue in Chicago, Illinois. Stuart had worked for many years at the well-known management consulting firm of Booz, Allen & Hamilton, located in Chicago. When he journeyed out on his own, Stuart was convinced a new kind of executive search firm was needed, one that was not just a recruiting agency, but an executive search firm as well. Executive search firms were a new breed during the late 1950s, and the changes many U.S. corporations were experiencing at the time demanded a comprehensive, systematic, and thoroughly disciplined approach to executive placement services.

Listening closely to his clients, Stuart developed a multifaceted approach to finding the right candidate: he profiled the company's organizational structure and corporate culture; prepared written descriptions of the required personnel; developed a highly sophisticated search tailored to the client's specific industry; analyzed and appraised candidates for the management position; and designed a plan to assimilate the new executive within the client company.

Stuart's first assignment was to find an executive to manage a pharmaceutical firm in Caracas, Venezuela. The firm needed an individual who was fluent in Spanish, familiar with the methods of doing business in South America, possessed knowledge and/or a background in the pharmaceutical industry, and whose family would be able to adapt to living in Venezuela. Stuart immediately hopped on a plane and found the right person for the job, someone already living in Caracas. By 1958 Stuart had filled numerous high-profile international placements and business was booming. He had taken more than three dozen flights to Europe and South America during the year, and

COMPANY PERSPECTIVES

As a global firm, we foster teamwork through our highly effective international practice structure, while retaining strong local capabilities in each of our 51 offices.

This distinctive culture continues to attract exceptional people to our firm and we are resolved to continue reaching for the highest standards of professionalism in our work. We take pride in our position as one of the world's leading professional service firms, but we do not allow ourselves to become complacent: we value our relationships with our clients and we are always striving to improve.

demand for his consulting services grew so rapidly Stuart established offices both in Mexico City and in Zurich, Switzerland, in 1959.

By the following year, the company had completed executive search assignments in over 25 countries including Brazil, Denmark, England, France, Germany, Italy, and other countries throughout Europe and South America. Clients included firms in the food, machinery, construction equipment, cosmetics, banking, and pharmaceutical industries. Stuart's firm had placed more than a dozen presidents or chief executives at companies around the globe. By 1961 new offices in London and New York were opened to meet the rapidly growing demand. As offices were planned for Brussels, Frankfurt, Paris, and Sydney, Australia, Stuart established a companywide policy that all international locations be managed and operated by nationals.

Throughout the remainder of the decade, Spencer Stuart pursued a long-range strategy of growth through expansion as numerous copycat firms popped up across the country and abroad. Spencer Stuart, however, continued to benefit through its association with larger corporations. Near the end of 1969, Stuart implemented an international management group to strengthen worldwide communications among satellite offices and, at the same time, to prepare for his own departure.

NEW LEADERSHIP: SEVENTIES

By 1973 Spencer Stuart had nine offices in the United States, Europe, and Australia, staffed with approximately 55 full-time executive search consultants. At this point, Stuart decided to retire from his duties as chief executive

officer and chose two partners to replace himself: an Englishman by the name of Peter Brooke, and a Frenchman named Jean-Michel Beigbeder, both graduates of Harvard University's Business School. Stuart also decided to sell the entire share of his ownership in the company to the new managing partners.

The transition from one-man leadership to a professional management team took place smoothly and Spencer Stuart & Associates began to grow both in size and revenue. Brooke and Beigbeder began to capitalize on new opportunities within the executive search industry, finding many firms preferred to bring in an outsider rather than promote from within. Instead, many clients sought senior level individuals who brought experience and a novel perspective to the issues confronting the company. In addition to the increasing demand for external executive searches came a growing acceptance of management recruiting firms. Presidents and comptrollers of companies were too busy to spend hours and hours reviewing and interviewing candidates for executive positions.

As the demand for executive search services grew, Spencer Stuart soon found itself as one of more than 900 U.S. executive search firms in the mid-1970s, although many concentrated on providing services for a particular industry, geographical location, or function. Although many of the search firms were small, with between one and three consultants, a handful of executive recruiting firms became major competitors for Spencer Stuart. To maintain its edge, the company once again looked outside the United States, to expand its international practice. More offices were opened throughout Europe, but much effort went into developing the company's services in Canada, South America, Australia, and Southeast Asia.

During the mid- and late 1970s locations in Europe and Asia more than doubled while the company explored markets in Africa, China, and the Middle East. Domestically, Spencer Stuart opened new offices in Atlanta, Cleveland, Dallas, Houston, Los Angeles, San Francisco, and Stamford, Connecticut. With over 100 consultants and 35 research associates, the company had become one of the largest executive search firms in the world and was focused on solidifying its stature within the industry.

As part of its growth strategy for the next decade, a new president and managing partner was named in 1979. Thomas J. Neff, a graduate of Lafayette College with an M.B.A. from Lehigh University, had begun working at the company in 1976 before working at Chicago's famed Booz, Allen & Hamilton, former stomping ground of Spencer Stuart's founder.

KEY DATES

1956: Spencer R. Stuart founds an eponymous placement firm in Chicago.

1959: Company opens international offices in Mexico City, Mexico, and Zurich, Switzerland.

1961: Spencer Stuart expands into New York City and London with new offices.

1973: Company founder Stuart decides to pass the reins to two managing partners.

1979: Company installs a new president and managing partner, Thomas Neff.

1992: Spencer Stuart and its top rival are hired to find a new chief executive for IBM.

1993: New office in Johannesburg marks the company's arrival in the African job market.

1995: Firm expands into the financial services sector.

1999: Company executives Thomas Neff and James Citrin publish *Lessons from the Top: The Search for America's Best Business Leaders.*

2002: New recruiting office is opened in Stockholm, Sweden.

2003: Spencer Stuart expands into the educational and nonprofit job sector.

2006: Company celebrates its 50th anniversary.

2007: Office is opened in Dubai, launching the firm's Middle East operations.

2008: Company further expands into Canada, opening an office in Calgary.

MAJOR GROWTH AND COMPETITION

By the early 1980s Neff was firmly ensconced as Spencer Stuart's leader and continued the company's expansion. Nine new U.S. offices opened along with locations in Amsterdam, Brussels, Düsseldorf, Frankfurt, Geneva, London, Madrid, Manchester, Milan, Paris, and Zurich. Offices were also opened in Australia, Brazil, Canada, and Hong Kong. Neff also supervised the addition of new managing partners and directors to create an international board comprised of representatives from six countries and the United States to run the increasingly renowned search firm.

The most important of Neff's contributions to the company during the 1980s, however, involved his development of executive search and management consulting ideas. As companies became more demanding in their expectations of what constituted a solution to a problem in management, Neff developed and refined the notion of management *consulting* in the executive search. Neff believed it was important to focus on what happened during the period previous to and following the recruitment process, and the company began focusing on succession planning, preparing boards for new executives, designing compensation packages, and the general problems involved with introducing new executives into an organization.

Near the end of the decade, two search or "headhunting" companies had emerged as the preeminent firms of the industry: Spencer Stuart & Associates and Heidrick & Struggles, both based in Chicago. Heidrick & Struggles, like Spencer Stuart, had successfully placed numerous high-profile candidates and served *Fortune* 500 companies. The two came head-to-head in 1992 when hired by IBM (International Business Machines) Corporation to find a successor for its chief executive, John Akers. The search caused a significant amount of controversy within the industry. Knowing placement firms were bound by certain limitations, including the general agreement prohibiting them from pursuing executives they had already placed, and a two-year restriction to not recruit from a client company where a placement had been made, IBM's management hired both companies so they could steal high-level executives from each other's previous clients.

The strategy, according to IBM, was to garner as much coverage of the market as possible, and it worked. Heidrick & Struggles eventually found IBM's new chief, Louis V. Gerstner Jr., but the ploy earned the executive search industry and its top players an enormous amount of publicity, both flattering and not, from such business magazines as *Business Week, Fortune, Forbes,* and the *Economist.*

A SHARPER FOCUS: 1995–99

In 1993 Spencer Stuart ventured to South Africa, opening its first office in the country in Johannesburg. The firm continued to scout new locations and had increased its international presence to six continents. The following year brought another innovation to shore up its business relationships, by offering a client satisfaction survey, the first of its kind in the executive recruitment industry.

By the mid-1990s as Spencer Stuart approached four decades in the executive recruiting business, the company remained at the top of its game and was well managed by Neff. Under his leadership, the company continued to distinguish itself from rivals, choosing to open new offices rather than gobble up smaller rivals in the manner of Heidrick & Struggles, New York-based Egon Zehnder International, and the Los Angeles-based behemoth, Korn/Ferry International. In 1995 Spencer Stuart took another gamble by segueing into a new search area, financial services, a pivotal and prescient move.

In 1998 the company unveiled a new program, Global Intelligence, to provide information and services related to mergers and acquisitions, executive assessments, and succession planning. The following year, 1999, Spencer Stuart's own executive suite gained recognition as Neff, now U.S. chairman, and James Citrin, one of the firm's managing directors, published *Lessons from the Top: The Search for America's Best Business Leaders.*

The book, published by Doubleday, became a widely read and respected business resource. Unfortunately for Neff and Citrin, a few of the chief executives profiled in the book, including Kenneth Lay of Enron, Dennis Kozlowski of Tyco, and Bernard Ebbers of WorldCom, later gained fame for the very public implosion of their companies. The fall of these corporate giants, however, did not affect Spencer Stuart's reputation or revenues and both Neff and Citrin continued their writing endeavors.

THE NEW MILLENNIUM

The early 2000s brought problems for C-level recruitment firms as the economy turned sour and clients were not as willing to pay five- and six-figure fees to find executives. Human resources or newly coined "human capital" departments took on broader responsibilities, including those previously held by firms such as Spencer Stuart. As the industry struggled, most of the top recruiters streamlined their organizations and Spencer Stuart was no exception. As the company reviewed underperforming offices and consolidated operations, it also turned to the Internet, a low-cost way to expand through both its web site (www.spencerstuart.com) and the launch of "Talent Network," a career services site for managers and executives considering a change.

The economy also took its toll on Spencer Stuart's major rivals, as Heidrick & Struggles and Korn/Ferry significantly reduced their workforces. All three executive search firms, however, began to bounce back by late 2003. For Spencer Stuart, it was partly from expansion into the industrial, education, nonprofit, and legal sectors; as well as continued publishing exposure: *Zoom: How 13 Exceptional Companies Are Navigating the Road to the Next Economy* (Neff and Citrin, Doubleday, 2002) and *The Five Patterns of Extraordinary Careers: The*

Guide for Achieving Success and Satisfaction (Citrin, Crown, 2003).

In 2004 Spencer Stuart was deemed the "most productive" of the United States' large executive recruiting firms in a study by market research firm Hunt-Scanlon Corporation. During this time Spencer Stuart also widened its scope again, moving into top-level marketing executives. Next came the opening of a new office in Mumbai, India, and another successful book by Neff and Citrin, *You're in Charge—Now What? The 8-Point Plan* (Crown, 2006). The company also passed another milestone in 2006: 50 years in the recruiting industry.

In 2007 Spencer Stuart's Global Intelligence program was renamed Spencer Stuart Executive Assessment Services, while Citrin's latest business book hit the shelves: *The Dynamic Path: Three Stages to Greatness in Business, Sports, and Life* (Rodale, 2007). Bigger news was the company's expansion into the Middle East with a new office in Dubai, followed the next year with increased coverage in Canada with a new office in Calgary, Alberta.

As Spencer Stuart looked to the next decade, its sixth in the recruiting industry, the firm remained one of the world's largest and most respected companies. Heidrick & Struggles and Korn/Ferry International, Spencer Stuart's top rivals, continued to best the firm in size but had turned over control to shareholders as public companies. Spencer Stuart's executives continued to resist the urge to go public, primarily to maintain control of the company and its highly prized integrity. When the economic downturn of late 2008 and 2009 threatened the livelihood of recruiters large and small, Spencer Stuart's reputation served it well as the company remained among the most sought-after search firms in the world.

Thomas Derdak
Updated, Nelson Rhodes

PRINCIPAL COMPETITORS

Challenger, Gray & Christmas, Inc.; Egon Zehnder International; Heidrick & Struggles International, Inc., Korn/Ferry International; Russell Reynolds Associates, Inc.

FURTHER READING

Bainbridge, Jane, "Could Recruiting Be Just the Job?" *Marketing*, September 18, 1997, p. 59.
Byrne, John A., "Can Tom and Gerry Find a Big Cheese for Big Blue?" *Business Week*, February 22, 1993, p. 39.

Citrin, James M., *The Dynamic Path: Three Stages to Greatness in Business, Sports, and Life,* New York: Rodale, 2007.

Citrin, James M., and Richard A. Smith, *The Five Patterns of Extraordinary Careers: The Guide for Achieving Success and Satisfaction,* New York: Crown Business, 2003.

Crawford, Kim, "The Rough Guide to Recruitment," *Marketing,* May 25, 1995, p. 28.

Curan, Catherine, "New Executive: Recruiter Pulls Rank; Moves Up to Run Spencer Stuart Firm," *Crain's New York Business,* July 21, 2003, p. 10.

Deutsch, Claudia H., "A Good Director Is Becoming Harder to Find," *New York Times,* April 28, 2002, p. BU4.

Fleming, Charles, "Hollywood Hunt Is on for Executive," *Variety,* March 23, 1992, pp. 125–26.

Hemple, Peter, "How to Find the Perfect Match," *In-Store Marketing,* September 2001, pp. 23+.

"IBM Hires Two Firms to Help Search for a Chief," *New York Times,* January 30, 1993, p. 37.

Jones, Del, "Revolving Door to Executive Suite Has Slowed," *USA Today,* July 19, 2007, p. 01B.

McClain, Dylan Loeb, "Headhunters Edge Toward Consulting," *New York Times,* May 5, 2002, p. BU18.

Morgenson, Gretchen, "Remember When Ken Lay Was a Genius?" *New York Times,* January 16, 2005, p. BU1.

Neff, Thomas J., and James M. Citrin, *Lessons from the Top: The Search for America's Best Business Leaders,* New York: Doubleday, 1999.

————, *You're in Charge—Now What? The 8-Point Plan,* New York: Crown Business, 2005.

Pasquarelli, Adrianne, "Recruiter Puts Women on Boards," *Crain's New York Business,* October 1, 2007, p. W13.

Sasseen, Jane, "Brief Encounters Management," *International Management,* September 1992, pp. 44–46.

Scism, Leslie, "Prudential May Seek Outsider to Succeed Chairman Winters When He Retires," *Wall Street Journal,* September 28, 1994, p. B10.

"Spencer Stuart Launches Money Management Group," *Pensions & Investments,* July 11, 1994, p. 28.

Stamler, Bernard, "Headhunters Seek 30–45 Age Group with New Campaign," *New York Times,* February 21, 2001, p. C10.

Stuart, Spencer R., and Thomas J. Neff, *Spencer Stuart & Associates,* New York: Newcomen Society, 1981.

"These Headhunters Seek Bigger Game," *Business Week,* March 20, 2000, p. 8.

Tsuruoka, Doug, "Ringing in Changes for CEO Selections: Honchos Need New Skills to Win Board Approval," *Investor's Business Daily,* July 30, 2007, p. A07.

Watson, Noshua, "Not Your Average Headhunter," *Fortune,* July 21, 2003, p. 40.

Wighton, David, "Headhunters Hit Out over Public Search for Successor of Morgan Stanley Resignation," *Financial Times,* June 15, 2005, p.29.

Williamson, Christine, "Headhunting: Recruiters' Golden Rule Violated in Search for CSAM," *Pensions & Investments,* July 21, 2003, p. 3.

Sunshine Village
Corporation

550 11th Avenue Southwest, Suite 400
Calgary, Alberta T2R 1M7
Canada
Telephone: (403) 277-7669
Toll Free: (877) 542-2633
Fax: (403) 705-4015
Web site: http://www.skibanff.com

Private Company
Incorporated: 1981
Employees: 800
Sales: CAD 59.43 million (2008)
NAICS: 713920 Skiing Facilities; 721110 Hotels
(Except Casino Hotels) and Motels

■ ■ ■

Sunshine Village Corporation, operating on land owned by the Canadian government, owns the Sunshine Village Ski and Snowboard Resort in Banff National Park, an hour's drive west of Calgary, Alberta. Sunshine Village enjoys the longest ski season in the region, averaging more than 30 feet of snow annually, which enables the resort to operate from mid-November to mid-May. The resort's lifts provide access to three mountains, Standish, Lookout, and Goat's Eye, including 3,358 acres of ski-able area serviced by 12 lifts: one eight-person gondola, seven quad chairlifts, one triple chairlift, one double chairlift, and two rope tows. The property includes the 84-room Sunshine Mountain Lodge, the only on-mountain accommodations in Banff National Park. The hotel features a heated, outdoor swimming pool, sauna,

exercise room, dining room, lounge, coffee shop, and pastry shop. Sunshine Village is owned and managed by the Scurfield family.

ORIGINS

Before Sunshine Village was measured in hectares, it was measured in feet. The ski resort began as a small log cabin built in 1928 by Canadian Pacific Railway (CPR), which had completed construction of a railway connecting eastern Canada and western Canada nearly a half-century earlier. After completing the trans-Canada route, CPR began building hotels to encourage tourists to travel across Canada. In the area surrounding Sunshine Village, CPR constructed the luxurious and massive Chateau Lake Louise and the Banff Springs Hotel, a landmark in downtown Banff. The site occupied by Sunshine Village received far less attention from CPR. The company spent CAD 300 to build a modest cabin for travelers on horseback, a stopping point conveniently located on the route to nearby Mt. Assiniboine.

While well-heeled tourists summered at Chateau Lake Louise, an entirely different sort of clientele frequented the log cabin located near Standish and Lookout mountains. Packhorses, mountains guides, surveyors, trappers, and hunters used the cabin, stopping generally no more than one night before continuing on their trek either to or from Mt. Assiniboine. The log cabin began to evolve from a secluded waypoint into a ski resort when Jim and Pat Brewster leased the cabin from CPR in 1934. The Brewsters expanded the cabin, envisioning a mountain retreat that could attract winter enthusiasts fond of Nordic skiing. Guests would spend an entire day making the five-mile trip from Banff to the cabin, a journey that required a Model-T, a horse, and a sled to complete. They charged guests CAD 30 for a week's stay, meals included.

The Brewsters turned the cabin into a vacation destination. In 1938, they hired Swiss ski guides to assist their guests. In 1941, they built a rope tow, giving the area the first modern amenity of a ski resort. Decades later, when Sunshine Village ranked as the second largest ski resort in Alberta, two ski trails at the resort paid homage to the fledgling years of the property: "Packer's Trail" was named after the guests who first stayed at the cabin and "Brewster Rock" passed by the lunchtime resting spot of ski touring parties led by Jim Brewster.

After World War II, control over the property was in flux. Numerous parties managed the ski area after the short yet pivotal Brewster era, but one enduring vestige of the postwar period was the first appearance of the Sunshine Village name. George Encil, who owned the Norquay ski resort on the outskirts of Banff, was credited with giving the area the name, and later became the owner of the resort he had christened.

THE WHITES PURCHASE SUNSHINE VILLAGE IN 1960

Steady management arrived when Cliff and Beverly White purchased Sunshine in 1960. When the couple acquired the property, which sat on land owned by the federal government and managed by Parks Canada, the Trans-Canada Highway was nearing completion. The Whites, like the Brewsters, were determined to develop the property, convinced the new highway had the potential to bring skiers to Sunshine Village in droves. The Whites eventually sold the property to other parties including Power Corporation and Warnock Hersey International, but the Whites served in managerial capacities after they sold Sunshine Village. During this period, the White era that spanned from 1960 to 1981,

the first major development projects at Sunshine Village were completed. Cliff White provided shuttle buses, built a T-bar lift to tow skiers up the mountain, and he completed his crowning achievement in 1980, a CAD 12 million gondola that ferried guests from the Bourgeau parking lot three miles up the mountain to the center of Sunshine Village.

SCURFIELD ERA BEGINS IN 1981

After the White era, development of the resort occurred under the direction of one of Canada's most successful executives, Ralph T. Scurfield. Scurfield was born in Broadview, Saskatchewan, in 1928, but his earliest recollections were of Ninga, Manitoba, where his father worked as a stationmaster for CPR. Scurfield worked as a carpenter to pay for his college tuition, earning his degree in 1948 from the University of Manitoba. After a two-year stint as an elementary school teacher, he returned to carpentry, moving in 1951 to Edmonton, Alberta, a city enjoying rapid economic growth driven by an expanding oil industry.

In Edmonton, Scurfield began working for a residential construction company, McConnell Homes, beginning his career in the industry as a crew foreman. Before long, his employer asked him to move to Calgary, Alberta, to take over the management of a struggling house builder named Nu-West Homes. Scurfield accepted the offer, but only after being allowed to purchase a one-third stake in the ailing company. He mortgaged his home to pay for his ownership stake, and in 1957, at the age of 29, became president of the company he would transform into a diversified, financial empire.

Scurfield worked wonders with Nu-West Homes. To restore the company's reputation, he fixed previously constructed homes free of charge, turning the ailing homebuilder into a reputable company. In 1969, he took Nu-West public and used the proceeds from the initial public offering of stock to purchase land in Edmonton. By building houses in Calgary and Edmonton, Scurfield turned Nu-West into the largest residential construction company in the province, giving him the operational might to begin expanding throughout Canada and into the United States. By the end of the 1970s, Scurfield's company ranked as the largest residential construction company in Canada, boasting a payroll of nearly 4,000 employees and CAD 1.9 billion in diversified holdings.

Scurfield used his wealth to make investments that reflected his love of ice hockey, football, skiing, fishing,

KEY DATES

1928: Canadian Pacific Railway builds a log cabin at the site later occupied by Sunshine Village.

1934: Jim and Pat Brewster lease the log cabin from Canadian Pacific Railway and begin charging guests for weeklong stays.

1960: Cliff and Beverly White acquire Sunshine Village and turn the property into a ski resort.

1980: A gondola is built to carry guests from the parking lot to Sunshine Village.

1981: Ralph T. Scurfield purchases Sunshine Village.

1988: The Angel Express is built, becoming the first high-speed, quad chairlift in Banff National Park.

1995: Goat's Eye Mountain becomes part of the ski resort, giving guests access to three mountains.

2001: A new gondola system is built, representing the largest investment in the history of the resort.

2003: Sunshine Mountain Lodge is renovated.

2008: Sunshine Village celebrates its 80th anniversary.

and golf. In 1981, he became an owner of the National Hockey League's Calgary Flames Hockey Club, one year after the franchise moved from Atlanta, Georgia. The year also saw Scurfield acquire Sunshine Village, giving the resort a deep-pocketed benefactor to finance its development.

The first decade of the Scurfield era brought new development to the resort and it also brought tragedy to the Scurfield family. In 1985, while on a heli-skiing trip in British Columbia, Scurfield was killed in an avalanche, an accident that left Sunshine Village Corp. without a leader. Ralph Scurfield's sons, Ralph Jr., John, and Sergei, stepped in to fill the void, led by Ralph Jr., who became the company's president.

NEW CHAIRLIFTS IN THE EIGHTIES

The Scurfields, like the Whites before them, focused their energies on developing the resort. In 1984, the family added a new chairlift, the Wheeler Chairlift, and they renovated Sunshine Inn, turning it into a lodge that, for the first time, allowed skiers to stay overnight.

In 1988, they built the Angel Express, the first high-speed, quad chairlift in Banff National Park. The CAD 3.5 million chairlift was capable of carrying up to 2,400 skiers per hour from the village to the top of Lookout Mountain, transporting twice as many skiers at twice the speed as the chairlift it replaced. Aside from Angel Express, Sunshine Village had one triple chairlift, five double chairlifts, three T-bar lifts, and the gondola system that carried skiers from the parking lot to the village.

PARKS CANADA AND THE SCURFIELDS

Sunshine Village's gondola system played a prominent role in a protracted battle between the Scurfield family and Parks Canada. Sunshine Village operated under the terms of a perpetually renewable lease with Parks Canada, which meant the resort needed approval from the federal government, Canada's Environment Department and Parks Canada, before beginning any substantial development project. At the end of the 1980s, the largest development project in the history of the resort was submitted for approval, a project four years in the planning that touched off a contentious battle between the Scurfields and Parks Canada.

The Scurfields' CAD 75 million expansion project, in part, sought to improve one of the fundamental weaknesses of Sunshine Village. The resort was not accessible by road in the winter, a problem Cliff White addressed with the construction of the gondola system. The gondola, a dramatic improvement when it first was put in service, was deemed inadequate by the Scurfields, however. The gondola was more expensive to operate than a quad chairlift and, more problematic, it could no longer accommodate the number of skiers arriving at the parking lot each morning. Long lines formed in the morning, and for the rest of the day the gondola rarely was used, with most Sunshine Village skiers skiing out to the summer road after their day on the mountain. The Scurfields wanted to build a new, 1,100-car parking lot higher up the mountain, from which they planned to provide access to the village with a high-speed, quad chairlift. Their project also included the construction of a six-story, 300-room hotel in the village to replace the 84-room Sunshine Inn. Parks Canada, as well as environmental groups such as the Alberta Wilderness Association, looked at the proposal and voiced concerns.

In 1989, the Scurfields' proposal was rejected, thwarting their ambitious expansion plan. During the next two years, the proposal was revised on several occasions, reducing the scope of the project to between CAD 35 million and CAD 45 million. The Scurfields spent nearly CAD 1 million attempting to gain federal approval, but their persistence failed to sway federal officials. Parks Canada, in a letter published in the March 29, 1991 edition of the *Globe & Mail,* explained the reasoning behind the agency's refusal to give the Scurfields its nod of approval. "The guiding principle is clear: wherever conflicts occur between resource protection and increased use and development, protection will take precedence." Frustrated, the Scurfields went as far as retaining RBC Dominion Securities Ltd. in 1991 to sell Sunshine Village Corp., but the family later took the property off the auction block.

EXPANSION AND A NEW GONDOLA

For the Scurfields, disappointment gave way to joy in the years that followed the rejected expansion plan. In 1995, a third mountain, Goat's Eye, became part of the resort, representing the largest amount of new terrain opened anywhere in the Canadian Rocky Mountains. The following year, the resort's Continental Divide double chairlift, which transported skiers and snowboarders back and forth across the Alberta-British Columbia border on its way up Lookout Mountain, was replaced with a high-speed, quad chairlift.

New development projects highlighted the resort's progress in the early 21st century. No project was bigger than the installation of a new, eight-person gondola to carry guests from the parking lot to the village. Billed as the world's fastest gondola when it opened in November 2001, the lift represented the largest investment in the history of the resort. Between 2002 and 2003, the WaWa quad chairlift was constructed and the TeePee Town chairlift was replaced. The period also saw the remodeling of the resort's hotel, which had been renamed Sunshine Mountain Lodge. The lobby was relocated, the property's lounge was expanded, and the size of the pub was increased as well. The renovation of the hotel was completed by the time the resort celebrated its 75th anniversary in 2003.

During the years leading up to the 80th anniversary of Sunshine Village, capital expenditures were devoted to improving the resort's amenities. Guest and restaurant facilities were renovated further in Sunshine Mountain Lodge. The base area received attention as well, improved by the expansion of the dining area in the Creekside Restaurant, a new locker room, and renovated guest services facilities. The Scurfields' record of consistent improvements to the resort promised to continue in the years beyond Sunshine Village's 80th anniversary in 2008, as each new decade moved the resort further away from its humble origins as a rest-stop cabin along the route to Mt. Assiniboine.

Jeffrey L. Covell

PRINCIPAL COMPETITORS

Intrawest ULC; The Lake Louise Ski Area Ltd.; Resorts of the Canadian Rockies Inc.

FURTHER READING

Gaines, Lisa, "Skiing Banff: A Tale of Three Resorts," *Travel Weekly,* December 5, 1991, p. 18.

Govier, Katherine, "My Favourite Place: A Flirtation with the Dangerous Beauty of Banff's Sunshine," *Globe & Mail,* August 4, 2001.

"Scurfields Selling Sunshine," *Globe & Mail,* March 19, 1991, p. B9.

Strachan, Al, "Ottawa's Park Policy Is Driving Alberta Ski Operators Downhill," *Globe & Mail,* March 29, 1991.

Volgenau, Gerry, "Canada's Banff Area Offers Majestic Mountains, Spectacular Skiing," *Detroit Free Press,* December 1, 2000.

Woeber, Patricia, "Skiing the Backbone of North America," *Globe & Mail,* December 9, 1989, p. F15.

Sweetbay Supermarket

3801 Sugar Palm Drive
Tampa, Florida 33619-8301
U.S.A.
Telephone: (813) 620-1139
Fax: (813) 626-9550
Web site: http://www.sweetbaysupermarket.com

Wholly Owned Subsidiary of Delhaize Group S.A.
Founded: 1947 as Big Barn
Employees: 10,000
Sales: $1 billion (2008 est.)
NAICS: 445110 Supermarkets and Other Grocery
   (Except Convenience) Stores

■ ■ ■

Sweetbay Supermarket is one of the largest supermarket operators along Florida's West Coast. Its more than 100 stores are sited as far south as Naples and as far north as Gainesville but the majority are located in the Tampa–St. Petersburg area. The supermarkets range in size from 38,000 to 49,700 square feet, and each store carries between 34,000 and 38,000 products. While its positioning is upscale, Sweetbay aims to offer its customers value, quality, and variety in stores tailored to local communities. Partnerships with Florida growers help to keep the stores stocked with abundant fresh produce, including exotic produce sought by Florida's large Hispanic community. Sweetbay Supermarket evolved out of Kash n' Karry Food Stores, Inc., founded in 1947. Sweetbay is a subsidiary of Delhaize America, Inc., the U.S. division of Brussels-based Delhaize Group

S.A. Delhaize America owns several other major supermarket chains in the eastern United States, including Hannaford Bros. Co. in the Northeast and Food Lion in the Southeast and Mid-Atlantic.

ORIGINS: FROM BIG BARN TO KASH N' KARRY

The history of the company dates back to 1947, when the Greco family founded its first Big Barn grocery store in Plant City, Florida. By 1962 the family-run business had expanded to nine stores and the Grecos opted for a new name, Kash n' Karry. Tampa Wholesale Co., whose principal shareholders were the Greco and Dominguez families, was operating Kash n' Karry in the 1970s. This firm had an estimated $32 million in annual sales and some 1,000 employees by 1968. The Kash n' Karry chain expanded in the 1970s partly through the acquisition at various times of about a dozen A&P stores. There were 46 Kash n' Karry supermarkets in a seven-county area on Florida's Gulf Coast in 1978. Kash n' Karry was believed to be in third place among supermarkets in the Tampa–St. Petersburg–Clearwater area, with about 9 percent of the market. In Hillsborough County, where it operated most of its stores and which includes Tampa, it held more than 50 percent of the market. The chain's annual sales were estimated at more than $150 million.

Most Kash n' Karry food stores were 20,000 to 23,000 square feet in size at this time. In 1974 the chain opened its first supermarket-drugstore combination in Tampa, in collaboration with Kare Drugs. Other

COMPANY PERSPECTIVES

Sweetbay Supermarkets blends passion, knowledge and excitement with outstanding quality, value and variety to offer a one-of-a-kind shopping experience to Floridians. Each store is a cornucopia of enticing sights, scents and textures. You'll always find an abundance of fresh-picked produce, top-quality meats, diverse ethnic offerings, oven-fresh baked goods, an expansive deli selection and well-stocked grocery aisles. In every department, our helpful associates share their expertise and passion for food.

As a "rewarding place to work," Sweetbay is a company where differences are not merely tolerated, but embraced to develop and leverage our associates and grow our business. As an inclusive company, we reach out to every level of the workforce, maximizing the potential of all associates while achieving our individual and organizational goals. This creates a competitive advantage, mirrors our communities and provides a culture where our associates bring their whole selves to work.

such combination stores soon followed. They were about 43,000 square feet in size, with an area between 7,000 and 10,000 square feet operated by Kare.

THE LUCKY STORE ERA

Kash n' Karry was sold to Lucky Stores, Inc., of Dublin, California, in 1979 for $26.8 million in cash and stock. The chain grew rapidly in the 1980s, both in size and market penetration. It competed aggressively for business, lowering prices on 3,000 items in 1985, when there were 84 stores, stretching from Fort Myers in the south to Gainesville in the north. "Kash n' Karry has managed to sell a total concept in the Tampa market," an observer told *Supermarket News,* "one that appeals to low-price-oriented shoppers and to more upscale shoppers alike."

Having established a reputation for low prices, Kash n' Karry launched a television advertising campaign in 1988 emphasizing the quality of its services. The first phase of the campaign consisted of conversations with employees about the services Kash n' Karry workers provided, including fast checkout and help in product selection. The second phase used employees only as extras, hiring actors to portray the delicatessen, bakery,

and produce people who described and discussed their work. In-store and newspaper advertising supported the TV campaign, featuring photos of as many as 100 of the chain's employees.

In July 1988 Kash n' Karry opened a 40,000-square-foot prototype store in Largo with aisles wider than in older stores and many amenities. This store carried vast supplies of bulk produce, a huge frozen food section, a wine and cheese island, and a "nutritional information center" offering brochures on healthful dining. The Largo store was among more than two dozen Kash n' Karry outlets with floral departments. The 94 Kash n' Karry stores operating at this time averaged 28,000 square feet in size. The chain had passed Winn-Dixie Stores, Inc., to take second place in its field in the Tampa–St. Petersburg area, with market share of 29 percent. Annual sales came to about $900 million.

RETURN TO INDEPENDENCE

Kash n' Karry regained its independence after Salt Lake City-based American Stores Company acquired Lucky Stores in 1988 and decided to unload the Florida chain. Kash n' Karry was acquired by its management for $305 million in October 1988, by means of a leveraged buyout in partnership with the New York City-based investment banking firm of Gibbons, Green, van Armerongen Ltd. Fulcrum III Limited Partnerships, managed by Gibbons, Green, van Armerongen, emerged with a majority of the stock until November 1991, when Los Angeles-based Leonard Green & Partners invested $27.7 million to become the controlling shareholder. Green & Partners was acting as general partner for Green Equity Investors L.P. In 1994 Green Equity Investors L.P. held 60.9 percent of Kash n' Karry Food Stores, Inc.'s common stock, and Fulcrum III Ltd., 33.8 percent.

Even before the leveraged buyout was completed, Kash n' Karry purchased 24 Florida Choice Food & Drug units and 24 adjacent liquor stores from Kroger Co. for $55 million. The acquisition enabled Kash n' Karry to pass Publix Super Markets, Inc., and take the number one position in the Tampa–St. Petersburg area, where half of the acquired Florida Choice units were located. These units ranged in size between 25,000 and 54,000 square feet, while about two-thirds of Kash n' Karry's stores were about 40,000 square feet. Kroger's president said the Florida Choice stores had been unprofitable for some time.

In 1990 Kash n' Karry established, at a cost of more than $3 million, a prototype store in Tampa. One of its most distinctive features was the exterior, with

KEY DATES

1947: The Greco family founds its first Big Barn grocery store in Plant City, Florida.

1962: Having expanded the business to nine stores, the Grecos opt for a new name, Kash n' Karry.

1979: Company is sold to Lucky Stores, Inc.

1988: Kash n' Karry Food Stores, Inc., regains its independence via a management-led leveraged buyout.

1994: Company restructures its debt under a prepackaged bankruptcy filing.

1995: Company goes public with a listing on the NASDAQ.

1996: Kash n' Karry is acquired by Food Lion, Inc., which is itself majority owned by Belgium's Delhaize.

2001: Kash n' Karry becomes a subsidiary of a newly formed Delhaize unit called Delhaize America, Inc., and also begins association with a sister Delhaize grocery company, Hannaford Bros. Co.

2004: Company unveils a new store format, under the name Sweetbay Supermarket, with an emphasis on food quality and variety.

2007: Final Kash n' Karry store is converted into a Sweetbay.

redesigned signage and more glass for an airy look. All future stores were to have this basic design. National brand sale items were promoted inside with highly visible front end and in-aisle signage. The company was converting its Lady Lee store brand to the Kash n' Karry private label. Most locations began staying open 24 hours a day in 1991. Kash n' Karry began offering shopping and delivery services in Hillsborough County in 1993.

Kash n' Karry in 1992 acquired from Wetterau Incorporated three super warehouse stores, one of which was subsequently closed, operating under the "Save n' Pack" name. Ranging in size between 76,000 and 88,000 square feet, these around-the-clock units featured some of the lowest prices on basic items carried by supermarkets and were designed to meet the needs of low-income households. In its Kash n' Karry outlets, too, the company continued to emphasize its everyday low prices.

BANKRUPTCY-AIDED RESTRUCTURING

By 1994 Kash n' Karry had annual sales of $1.2 billion. Same store sales fell to a five year low, however, during fiscal 1994 (the year ended July 31, 1994), and the company lost nearly $38 million in the face of intense competition from four major supermarket operators with greater financial resources. Kash n' Karry closed 17 stores but could not overcome the heavy debt load it had incurred, mainly in its leveraged buyout: $331 million in 1991, compared to only $12 million in 1988. The company filed for Chapter 11 bankruptcy in November 1994, listing assets of $389.9 million and liabilities of $446.3 million, of which $326.2 million was unsecured debt.

Shortly before the end of the year Kash n' Karry emerged from bankruptcy under a plan that was intended to reduce its debt burden by one-third and interest expenses by more than one-third, or $12 million a year. As part of the restructuring, Green Equity Investors traded its controlling interest in the company for a lesser stake of 15 percent. Shortly thereafter, however, Green Equity bought $12.9 million worth of Kash n' Karry's common stock, raising its stake to more than 22 percent. In 1995 the company's stock began trading on the NASDAQ.

Ronald E. Johnson was appointed in 1995 as Kash n' Karry's new chairman, president, and CEO. He began a 16-store remodeling program that featured more perishables and more seasonal nonfood merchandise. The new format included 3,500 square feet of space for a bakery, 3,000 square feet for the traditional deli, and 3,500 square feet for a food court and prepared foods area. The latter included pizza and coffee shops and carving, salad, and sandwich stations, plus a sushi bar.

PART OF FOOD LION: 1996

Kash n' Karry Food Stores, Inc., reported net income of nearly $2 million on sales of $1.02 billion for fiscal 1996. In December of that year, Kash n' Karry was purchased by Food Lion, Inc., for $341 million, including assumption of $221 million in long-term debt. Food Lion, based in Salisbury, North Carolina, had been majority owned by the Belgium firm Delhaize Frères & Cie, "Le Lion," since 1974, and thus Kash n' Karry fell within Delhaize's orbit. At this time, the 100-unit Kash n' Karry chain continued to center on the Tampa–St. Petersburg area but ranged from Gainesville, about 130 miles to the north, to Bonita Springs, about 150 miles to the south. Its market share of around 22 percent for the Tampa–St. Petersburg–Clearwater area placed it slightly ahead of Winn-Dixie Stores but behind market leader Publix Super Markets.

Johnson left Kash n' Karry upon the completion of the takeover, and Food Lion brought Ronald E. Dennis onboard as the new president. Dennis had been in charge of the Florida division of Albertsons Inc. Food Lion extended the store remodeling program that Johnson had begun, budgeting $150 million to complete a multiyear, full chain makeover. Although Kash n' Karry remained a chain distinct from the Food Lion stores, the Florida company's back office operations were integrated into those of Food Lion. In addition, Food Lion closed Kash n' Karry's 625,000-square-foot distribution center in Tampa, and Kash n' Karry began using Food Lion's 758,000-square-foot warehouse in Plant City.

An apparent culture clash led to Dennis's quick departure. Food Lion veteran Mike Byars was named COO in September 1997. Over the next year or so, nine unprofitable Kash n' Karry outlets were closed, and the chain introduced a card-based frequent shopper program in part to try to regain customers lost during the transition period that followed the Food Lion takeover. During 1999, most of Food Lion's 50 or so stores in central and southwestern Florida were converted into Kash n' Karry stores.

In 2000 Delhaize acquired Hannaford Bros. Co., a leading food retailer in northern New England. This takeover ultimately brought profound changes to Kash n' Karry. Most immediately, Delhaize in 2001 restructured its U.S. operations, creating a U.S. holding company called Delhaize America, Inc., which counted Kash n' Karry, Hannaford, and Food Lion among its subsidiaries. Also, responsibility for overseeing Kash n' Karry was shifted from Food Lion to Hannaford. Kash n' Karry and Hannaford stores were similar in size and typically larger than the average Food Lion outlet, and the former chains were also positioned more upscale than Food Lion.

METAMORPHOSIS INTO SWEETBAY

At this time, Kash n' Karry was struggling to find a successful niche for itself within an increasingly competitive marketplace. Publix, the clear leader in the Florida grocery sector, had entrenched itself on the upper end with its exceptional customer service, while Wal-Mart Stores, Inc., was rapidly expanding on the discount side. This left Kash n' Karry in the middle with Winn-Dixie and Albertsons. In June 2003 Delhaize sent Shelley Broader from Hannaford to Tampa to turn Kash n' Karry around. Broader, named president and COO,

and her associates conducted a great deal of customer research before implementing sweeping changes.

First, in early 2004, the company announced it would retrench back to the Tampa Bay area and Florida's West Coast and shut down most of the stores in central Florida and along the Atlantic Coast it had inherited from Food Lion. This left the firm with about 100 stores. Then, later in 2004, Broader began to reinvent Kash n' Karry from the ground up. A new store prototype was unveiled in Seminole, Florida, where the emphasis was on food, both food quality and variety, and on customer service as the decision to take the chain upscale became clear. The main store entrance opened into a large produce section that included 40 percent more variety than previously found at the chain, and the larger number of products overall, an increase from 41,000 to 58,000, included a wide variety of specialty products designed to appeal to food lovers. Other features included an open-air butcher shop, a new line of frozen food called the On the Go Bistro, and more international food, particularly Hispanic food given the state's demographics.

The most startling change, however, was the store banner, Sweetbay Supermarket rather than Kash n' Karry. Adopting a new name enabled the company to essentially restart the chain without any of the baggage carried by the old name, which had also grown passé in the age of credit and debit cards. The name was derived from a type of magnolia tree found across the Southeast, including Florida. One other change for Sweetbay was that it did not employ a loyalty card as Kash n' Karry had. By the end of 2006, all but 31 of the Kash n' Karry stores had been converted into Sweetbay outlets.

After seeing strong initial sales gains for the converted stores, Sweetbay Supermarket experienced disappointing sales by late 2006 in part because of perceptions among some shoppers that the stores were high priced. The company attempted to counter this image through advertising and in-store signage emphasizing everyday savings on particular items. Price reductions implemented in 2007 helped stabilize the overall sales results. In August of that year, the final Kash n' Karry store was converted into a Sweetbay, completing the transformation. Sweetbay Supermarket ended 2007 operating 106 stores.

Many elements of the Hannaford chain had been incorporated into Sweetbay, including the former's "everyday low price" positioning and its Hannaford line of private label products. In 2007 Sweetbay adopted the Guiding Stars nutritional information system that Hannaford had developed to make it easier for consumers to select more nutritious foods. Products were assigned nutritional ratings from one to three stars, which were placed on food shelf tags throughout the store. The sister companies also shared information systems, including the transaction processing system. Both chains were thus affected when hackers tapped into this system to steal credit and debit card numbers between December 2007 and March 2008. Fraudulent activity was subsequently reported on at least 1,800 cards, numerous lawsuits were soon filed against Hannaford and Sweetbay, and the companies quickly tightened the security of the transaction system.

In March 2008 Delhaize Group incurred an $18.6 million charge to write down the value of 25 underperforming Sweetbay stores. Sweetbay, although its sales were improving, had yet to turn a profit since its emergence from Kash n' Karry. When Broader left in June 2008 to become president and COO of Michaels Stores, Inc., Mike Vail was promoted from senior vice-president of retail operations to president and COO of Sweetbay. The new leader aimed to turn Sweetbay Supermarket into a profitable operation by 2010, at which point a growth phase was likely to be implemented. In the meantime, the drive for profitability led Sweetbay to announce the closure of seven of its 108 stores in early 2009. Delhaize took a pretax charge of $23.8 million for the closures and incurred an additional charge of $21.4 million to write down the value of 19 other underperforming Sweetbay locations.

Robert Halasz
Updated, David E. Salamie

PRINCIPAL COMPETITORS

Publix Super Markets, Inc.; Winn-Dixie Stores, Inc.; Wal-Mart Stores, Inc; Albertsons LLC.

FURTHER READING

Albright, Mark, "Food Lion to Change Florida Store Names," *St. Petersburg Times,* July 8, 1999, p. 1E.

———, "Grocer Beefs Up Hacker Security," *St. Petersburg Times,* April 23, 2008, p. 1D.

———, "Grocer Credit Data Is Swiped," *St. Petersburg Times,* March 18, 2008, p. 1D.

———, "It's All About the Food," *St. Petersburg Times,* November 6, 2004, p. 1D.

———, "Kash n' Karry Out, Sweetbay In," *St. Petersburg Times,* March 9, 2004, p. 1D.

———, "The Lion Lurks in State's Supermarket Wars," *St. Petersburg Times,* July 28, 1997.

———, "Speeding Toward Sweetbay," *St. Petersburg Times,* August 12, 2005, p. 1D.

———, "Taking Stock," *St. Petersburg Times,* August 3, 1998.

Beres, Glen A., "New Kash n' Karry Chief Lists Plans," *Supermarket News,* February 20, 1995, p. 4.

Buss, Dale, "Survival in the Fast Lane," *Florida Business–Tampa Bay,* August 1989, p. 30.

Clancy, Carole, "Buyout Firm Ups Its Stake in Kash n' Karry," *Tampa Bay Business Journal,* February 24, 1995, p. 1.

Dowdell, Stephen, "Passion Play," *Progressive Grocer,* March 1, 2005, pp. 28–30+.

Duff, Mike, "People Power Key to Kash n' Karry Campaign," *Supermarket Business,* November 1988, pp. 68–69.

Fisher, John, "Eberhard in Talks to Acquire Kash n' Karry, Florida Chain," *Supermarket News,* April 10, 1978, pp. 1, 10.

"A Full-Scale Approach," *Progressive Grocer,* July 1996, pp. 102–04.

Hamstra, Mark, "Delhaize to Close Seven Sweetbays," *Supermarket News,* January 26, 2009.

———, "A Fresh Start: Kash n' Karry Is Seeking to Tap a New Niche in Florida with Its Sweetbay Supermarket Banner," *Supermarket News,* November 15, 2004, p. 32.

———, "Kash n' Karry to Rebanner As Sweetbay Supermarkets," *Supermarket News,* March 15, 2004, p. 1.

Hau, Louis, "Kash n' Karry to Shed Stores, Jobs," *St. Petersburg Times,* January 16, 2004, p. 1A.

Hundley, Kris, "Grocery Settles over Pay Problems," *St. Petersburg Times,* August 20, 2003, p. 1E.

"Kash n' Karry Restructure Complete," *Supermarket News,* January 2, 1995, p. 4.

Keller, Amy, "Food, Glorious Food: Kash n' Karry Is Remaking Itself As Sweetbay," *Florida Trend,* November 2005, p. 66.

Lewis, Len, "Florida Facelift," *Progressive Grocer,* June 1997, pp. 37–38.

Linsen, Mary Ann, "Price Isn't Everything at Kash n' Karry," *Progressive Grocer,* September 1991, pp. 95, 98, 100–01.

Mayk, Lauren, "Internal Takeover," *Sarasota (Fla.) Herald-Tribune,* September 18, 2006.

Merrefield, David, "Tampa: A Market in Transition," *Supermarket News,* December 9, 1985, sec. 2, p. 28.

Ossorio, Sonio, "Chain Plans Debt Swap; Income Up," *Tampa Bay Business Journal,* May 1, 1992, p. 1.

Reinan, John, "Kash Flow Has Been a Winning Combination," *Tampa Tribune,* April 12, 1999.

Sasso, Michael, "Pricey Image Changing, Sweetbay Reports," *Tampa Tribune,* March 16, 2007.

———, "Sweetbay's Bright Outlook," *Tampa Tribune,* June 26, 2005.

———, "Sweetbay's New Chief Tackles Job," *Tampa Tribune,* January 25, 2009.

Shedden, Mary, "The Smell of Success: Shelley Broader Turns Heads in the Grocery Industry with Her Three-Year Plan to Cash Out Kash n' Karry and Reinvent the Decades-Old Chain," *Tampa Tribune,* July 22, 2007.

Springer, Jon, "Sweet Success," *Supermarket News,* September 10, 2007.

Zwiebach, Elliot, "American Stores Close to Kash n' Karry Sale," *Supermarket News,* August 8, 1988, p. 2.

————, "Kash Investments," *Supermarket News,* April 24, 1995, pp. 1, 132–33.

————, "Kash n' Karry to Buy Block of Florida Choice Stores," *Supermarket News,* August 29, 1988, pp. 1, 38.

————, "Remodels Set As Food Lion's First Step for Kash n' Karry," *Supermarket News,* November 11, 1996, p. 1.

TALISMAN
ENERGY

Talisman Energy Inc.

Suite 2000
888 - 3rd Street S.W.
Calgary, Alberta T2P 5C5
Canada
Telephone: (403) 237-1234
Fax: (403) 237-1902
Web site: http://www.talisman-energy.com

Public Company
Incorporated: 1925 as Supertest Petroleum Corporation
Employees: 2,966
Sales: CAD 9.81 billion ($9.2 billion) (2008)
Stock Exchanges: Toronto New York
Ticker Symbol: TLM
NAICS: 211111 Crude Petroleum and Natural Gas
    Extraction

■ ■ ■

Talisman Energy Inc. is one of Canada's largest
independent oil and gas exploration and production
companies. Proven reserves stood at 1.43 billion barrels
of oil equivalent at the end of 2008, and its daily
production totaled 432,000 barrels. Talisman centers its
exploration and production activities on North America,
the North Sea, and Southeast Asia. Its Canadian and
U.S. operations are focused on deep natural gas fields
and unconventional gas assets, the latter including gas
located in shale strata. Talisman operates more than 40
oilfields in the North Sea and also holds extensive
exploration acreage offshore of Norway. Its Southeast

Asian assets include substantial long-life natural gas
reserves in Indonesia, Malaysia, Vietnam, and Australia.
Other production fields are located in North Africa and
Trinidad and Tobago, while Talisman maintains additional exploration activities in Colombia, Peru, Qatar,
and the Kurdistan region of northern Iraq. Talisman
emerged in 1992 after its former parent, British
Petroleum Company plc, sold its 57 percent interest in
the Canadian concern, which had been known as BP
Canada. After becoming independent, Talisman Energy
grew rapidly through a series of acquisitions under the
leadership of James W. Buckee, who retired in 2007.

EARLY HISTORY OF SUPERTEST PETROLEUM AND BP CANADA

Talisman's roots can be found in the Supertest
Petroleum Corporation, established on December 17,
1925, with the opening of a corner gas station in
London, Ontario. The company immediately began
building a network of gas stations, and in 1926 it
bought the gas and oil interests of Ensign Oil Company,
based in Montreal. Growth for Supertest was slow during the economic depression of the 1930s, when
unemployment and persistent economic downturns affected the ability of Canadians to buy and drive cars.

The rival British Petroleum Company plc (BP)
made its first large foray into the Canadian market in
1953. BP, headquartered in London, England, had its
earliest roots in the Middle East, where extensive gas
and oil interests were found and exploited, in Iran and
Saudi Arabia in particular. As early as 1926, the

COMPANY PERSPECTIVES

We create value for investors through successful exploration and development of a diverse global asset base.

company considered expanding outside of the Middle East. Specifically, Arnold Wilson, who succeeded F. G. Watson as managing director of D'Arcy Exploration Company, a division of BP, told company directors that disappointment with drilling in Asia and Africa led him to consider drilling opportunities in Canada or South America. As it happened, BP did much to explore new opportunities before it entered the Canadian market in a substantial way. Between 1927 and 1930, company geologists showed considerable interests in possible fields in British Columbia, New Brunswick, and Alberta. The geologists, however, could not agree on whether potential gas and oil reserves in the Canadian hinterland warranted further investment toward drilling.

In 1953 BP bought a minority stake in Triad Oil Company, a small exploration company based in Calgary with large exploration holdings in western Canada. Four years later, BP entered the Quebec market. By 1960, when the company's first refinery opened for business in Montreal, BP had over 800 service stations in the French-speaking province. Now operating as rivals, both companies expanded during the 1950s and 1960s. Earlier, in 1959, Supertest merged into its own operations those of Reliance Petroleum Ltd., also based in Calgary. In 1964 BP bought the eastern Canadian interests of Cities Service, comprising 750 retail gas stations and a refinery at Oakville, Ontario. This acquisition brought to just under 1,800 the number of retail gas stations that BP had in Ontario and Quebec and added to its sales and service teams for home heating and the agricultural, commercial, marine, and aviation industries.

In 1969 BP's holding company in Canada was renamed BP Canada, and the principal marketing company was renamed BP Oil Ltd. Put another way, BP's Canadian operations had two arms, an upstream arm (oil and gas exploration and production) and a downstream arm (refining and marketing). A year later, all BP's marketing and refining interests in western Canada were put under the corporate umbrella of BP Oil and Gas Ltd., including the interests of the former Triad Oil Company.

1971: MERGER OF BP CANADA AND SUPERTEST

The discovery in August 1969 of giant oil reserves at Prudhoe Bay, Alaska, convinced BP headquarters in London that it had a significant future in northern Canada. In August 1971 BP Canadian Holdings Ltd., then BP Canadian Ltd., and a division of BP in Britain offered to buy a controlling interest in Supertest. The British parent exchanged for shares all of its petroleum marketing, refining, and exploration interests in Canada. These entailed all the outstanding stock of BP Oil Ltd., an associate company mainly engaged in marketing and refining in eastern Canada, and a 65.9 percent interest in BP Oil and Gas Ltd. The BP offer was accepted by Corlon Investments Ltd., which then held an 83.7 percent stake in Supertest. It sold its entire stake for CAD 10 a share. By November of that year, BP had bought 97.8 percent of Supertest, having paid CAD 16.50 per share for that holding.

Immediately upon buying Supertest, the new company, BP Canada Ltd., set about securing new oil and gas acreage holdings in the Arctic Islands region of Canada. The idea was to explore for possible oil and gas reserves in the regions adjoining the 1969 Alaskan oil and gas discoveries. Once located, substantial oil and gas reserves would be extracted from the earth via drilling rigs and then refined downstream before being sold to consumers through a network of gas stations. Other oil companies tended to be specific about identifying and taking aim at oil targets. BP Canada, on the other hand, had a "shotgun," as opposed to a "rifle," approach. It explored in many places in search of leads and eventual discoveries.

Total acreage in 1970 for BP Canada amounted to 26.7 million gross acres, up from 19.3 million gross acres held a year earlier. Of particular interest was a 1.2-million-acre tract of property purchased for exploration on Vanier, Emerak, and Prince Patrick Islands where actual drilling was to commence in 1971. BP Canada's net production of crude oil and natural gas in 1970 amounted to 18,582 barrels daily, up 17 percent on production a year earlier. Sales of natural gas had jumped 24 percent to an average of 62.4 million cubic feet per day, compared with production in 1969. In 1971 the company drilled its first Arctic well on Vanier Island, and labeled it "BP et al Panarctic Hotspur J-20." It then added two more, one on Prince Patrick Island ("BP et al Panarctic Satellite F-68") and the other on Graham Island ("BP et al Graham C-52"). BP Canada also purchased considerable acreage holdings in northern Alberta and British Columbia for possible exploration and drilling in those regions.

KEY DATES

1925: Supertest Petroleum Corporation is founded with the opening of a gas station in London, Ontario.

1953: British Petroleum Company (BP) enters the Canadian market through the purchase of a minority stake in Calgary-based Triad Oil Company.

1969: BP's Canadian holding company is renamed BP Canada.

1971: BP acquires 97.8 percent of Supertest, which it renames BP Canada Ltd. and merges with its other Canadian interests.

1992: BP sells its 57 percent stake in BP Canada to the public; BP Canada is renamed Talisman Energy Inc.

1993: James W. Buckee takes over the helm as president and CEO; Encor Inc. is acquired.

1994: Bow Valley Energy Inc. is acquired for CAD 1.82 billion, giving Talisman properties in the British North Sea and in Indonesia.

1996: Company completes three deals that substantially increase its North Sea production.

1997: Hostile bid for Wascana Energy Inc. is scuttled by a higher offer from Canadian Occidental Petroleum Ltd.; Talisman acquires Pembina Resources Limited from Loram Corporation for CAD 605 million.

1998: Company acquires Arakis Energy Corporation and its 25 percent stake in a major oil production project in Sudan for CAD 277.5 million.

1999: Rigel Energy Corporation is acquired for CAD 1.12 billion.

2001: Talisman acquires Petromet Resources Limited for CAD 823 million and Lundin Oil AB for CAD 504.8 million; the company announces major oil discoveries in Trinidad.

2003: The firm divests its Sudanese holdings.

2005: Talisman significantly boosts its North Sea assets through the CAD 2.56 billion takeover of Paladin Resources plc.

2008: Newly installed CEO John A. Manzoni unveils a shift in corporate strategy that in part seeks to secure long-term growth via the development of unconventional natural gas fields in North America.

A year later, the former offices of Supertest Investments and Petroleum in Calgary had been closed as management of the new company was moved to the Montreal-based headquarters of BP Oil and Gas Ltd. Production for the company jumped substantially in 1972. Sales of petroleum products averaged 94,400 barrels daily, whereas production of crude oil and natural gas was posted at an average 22,132 barrels daily. To accommodate this increased production, the company announced plans in 1972 to add a further 40,000 barrels per day of refining capacity at its Trafalgar Refinery facility in Oakville, Ontario. Products produced there would be marketed under the BP and Supertest brand names.

In April 1972, just months after the Supertest merger, company President Derek Mitchell, who had initially come to the position in 1966, outlined his business strategy to shareholders in the company's 1971 annual report: "Your company is now firmly established as a major marketer and refiner of petroleum products in Ontario and Quebec, is well placed as a producer of oil and gas in western Canada, and has an important stake in the exploration activity rapidly gaining momentum in Canada's frontier areas." BP Canada was establishing upstream exploration and production facilities in western Canada to serve key downstream markets in Ontario and Quebec, where oil and gas products could be sold directly to consumers.

SURVIVING THE OIL SHOCKS OF THE SEVENTIES

By late 1972, the company was beginning to feel the effects of higher world prices for a barrel of oil caused by the efforts of the Organization of Petroleum Exporting Countries (OPEC) cartel. Essentially, a higher price paid for imported crude oil forced BP Canada to pay more for the energy reserves it required to replace petroleum products sold earlier downstream in the marketplace.

This trend worried Mitchell, who said in the company's 1972 annual report: "The comparative stability of the 1960s is giving way to a decade likely to be characterized by rising prices for petroleum and growing government interest in the industry's affairs, both at the political and at the technical levels." Mitchell's words were to prove prophetic. Throughout 1973, OPEC instigated production cutbacks and embargoes among its customers, which played havoc with the global oil industry. The price of oil on the global market went up, and the world supply seemed to be shrinking.

Turmoil and confusion gripped the oil industry. Responding, BP Canada began moving crude oil from western Canada to Montreal through the St. Lawrence

Seaway, and later through the Panama Canal during the winter freeze-up. A thorn in the company's side was the growing involvement of the Canadian government in Ottawa in the domestic oil industry. Specifically, the government was calling on the industry to hold down anticipated price rises for Canadian oil products, which would grow costlier as they were affected by the rising world oil prices charged by OPEC member countries. Such restraint was meant to allow the government to develop a Canadian pricing policy to cushion the impact on consumers from rising world oil prices and provide an incentive for the domestic oil industry to develop new energy sources.

As a measure of the growing spread between domestic and world oil prices, a barrel of Canadian crude oil rose 85 cents to around CAD 4.50 in Toronto in the 12 months leading up to January 1, 1974. During that same period, the cost of imported crude oil rose by some CAD 8 to over CAD 11 a barrel in Montreal. BP Canada was making increased profits from selling petroleum products to consumers at higher prices, but it had to restore energy reserves it had sold by buying imported crude oil at around twice the December 1973 level. According to the company, it was under-recovering its cost of crude oil by about CAD 300,000 per day in the second half of 1973.

BP Canada might have been trading in crisis-ridden conditions in 1974, but it still managed to see profits rise 82 percent to CAD 39.5 million that year. Even so, the company still found grounds to complain in its 1975 annual report about growing royalties and income taxes owed to Canada's provincial and federal governments. What is more, by the end of 1974, world oil prices had risen to five times the mid-1973 level. The unprecedented price hikes had led to increased production, and ultimately a glut in the world oil market. The net result manifested itself in lower margins for BP Canada products in an ever more competitive market.

In 1975 the company began exploring for oil off Newfoundland, on Canada's easternmost seaboard. Also that year, the expansion of the Trafalgar Refinery was completed, but only after delays and cost overruns. A year later, BP Canada bought the remaining 65 percent stake in British Columbia Oil Sands Ltd. to take full control of the company. Paying CAD 20 per share in the transaction, the company gained ownership of oil and gas acreage in the Yoyo, Kotcho, Cabin, and Louise gas fields of northeastern British Columbia. Cost-cutting measures that year included reducing the number of retail outlets selling BP petroleum brand products in Ontario and Quebec from just over 3,000 to around 1,800. The company also introduced BP no-lead gasoline at its remaining retail outlets.

Early in 1977, BP Canada signed an agreement with the Alberta Oil Sands Technology and Research Authority that would see the government body contribute half the CAD 18 million cost of testing a sequential steam heating system to extract heavy crude oil (thick sludge used as highway asphalt) in the Wolf Lake area of Alberta. These tarlike deposits are filled with impurities but can be upgraded to light, valuable crude oil; the process is worthwhile if there is a CAD 3 to CAD 5 spread between the light and heavy crude oil variants. At the time, the price of oil on the world market was rising too quickly, compared with the price for domestically produced oil, to fully justify the development of heavy oil upgraders. The Wolf Lake project was noteworthy for its incentives to develop new sources of oil and gas in Canada. Companies such as BP Canada often had to extract heavier crude oil reserves at greater than average expense and longer than usual lead times before it could deliver a refined product to consumer markets in a light crude form.

BP Canada in the 1970s continued its thrust into the rugged terrain of the Monkman area in northeastern British Columbia. It held interests from 25 percent to 64 percent in 204,000 acres and 100 percent of 94,000 acres in the region, which was thought to hold vast natural gas reserves. The British Columbia Petroleum Corporation announced plans to build a pipeline and plant facilities to bring the Monkman-area natural gas to market in 1980.

In 1978 BP Canada saw its profits rise over the CAD 40 million mark for the first time. This record, however, was reached at a time when the industry as a whole was experiencing a market glut because of excess refining capacity and reduced consumer demand for petroleum products because of the unexpected success of conservation measures. The Iranian revolution in 1979 caused another jump in the price of oil on the world market. BP Canada saw its offshore supply drop substantially because of embargoes. To replace the shortfall, the company arranged to send Canadian crude oil from western Canada to northern-tier U.S. refiners, who in turn would divert their imported oil to the Montreal refinery.

At this time, BP Canada also faced a glut in the natural gas market, then a key earner for the company. Production in 1979 was 109.5 million cubic feet per day, down from 122.7 million cubic feet per day a year earlier. Purchasers had essentially been unable to take all the gas they had contracted to buy. Sales of natural gas continued slowly in 1980, but the company did manage to post profits of CAD 63.1 million for fiscal 1979, up 93 percent from the year before. A jump like that had

Mitchell (at that time chairman and CEO) defending the company's performance, given its persistent calls for less government control over the oil industry. Suspicions abounded in the 1970s that the oil industry as a whole was manipulating the OPEC crisis for its own profitable ends.

DEVELOPMENTS IN THE EIGHTIES

Speaking to shareholders, Mitchell repeated his company's call for regulatory restraint in the company's 1980 annual report: "There is no doubt that given appropriate policies—higher crude oil prices, a fair and stable tax and royalty system which will allow adequate netbacks to the industry, a commitment to allow companies to reap the fruits of their endeavors, and the encouragement of fuels substitution and energy conservation—Canada can again become self-sufficient in oil." If Mitchell sought government restraint, he ended up with greater intervention still. The Conservative government, entering the 1980 federal election, had proposed an 18-cents-a-gallon gasoline tax to subsidize more expensive oil imports. That proposed excise tax in part led to the Conservative government's downfall at the polls. The incoming Liberal government introduced the National Energy Program in October 1980. It painted foreign oil companies as profit-hungry conglomerates and gave support to Canadian-owned companies such as Petro-Canada.

Mitchell complained in March 1981 in the company's 1980 annual report: "The government is now hell-bent on putting on a circus for the benefit of the media and the public. ... The principal purpose will, doubtless, be to try to justify by propaganda and by 'trial' in the media the federal government's already well-demonstrated xenophobic prejudices against one of Canada's vital and most successful industries."

Although the Liberal government became a foul word in the BP Canada boardroom, the company's fortunes did not suffer. For the first time in 1980, gas from the Sukunka-Bullmoose area of northeastern British Columbia reached the market after many years of exploration. It was also announced that year that BP Canada's headquarters would move from Montreal to Toronto. The relocation served two purposes: It would remove the company from the separatist tensions then developing in Quebec and would place the headquarters in Ontario, the location of 70 percent of the company's assets.

Profits for 1980 were posted at CAD 104.3 million, 56 percent over the previous year. The rate of return on investment was 17.3 percent, a company record. Despite the government's aim to restrain foreign oil companies in Canada and support the domestic sector, the multinationals were doing better than ever.

Mitchell died suddenly on October 29, 1981, and was replaced by R. Hanbidge as president and CEO. A year later, BP Canada shelved plans to proceed with developing the Sukunka coal mine in northeastern British Columbia. Low coal prices on the world market accounted for the strategic move. The company in 1984 completed work on its Wolf Lake project, which came onstream five months ahead of schedule and with a price tag of CAD 110 million. Full production of 1,100 cubic meters of fuel per day was achieved in September 1985, and expanded production at Wolf Lake was forecast at 5,600 cubic meters per day by the end of the decade.

The falling price of oil on the world market hit BP Canada's earnings in 1985. Cash flow fell 17 percent, and net profits fell 55 percent to CAD 20 million, compared with results for the year earlier. Continuing success at energy conservation during the 1980s also cut into production at BP Canada. In 1985 sales of light and medium oil were down 10 percent on sales a year earlier, and 15 percent of production was lost during the first quarter of 1987. Also that year, production at the Wolf Lake project stood at 1,140 cubic meters per day, not far above production figures when the project came onstream in 1984.

For these reasons, the company attempted to curb its operating costs to maintain profitability. M. A. Kirkby, president of BP Canada, told shareholders in the 1987 annual report: "While we cannot control the worldwide prices of oil, gas and metals, we are constantly working to reduce our costs and to improve our netbacks within the market." Cost-cutting measures helped boost BP Canada's net profits to CAD 44.6 million in 1987, an all-time high. The very next year, however, net profits were down to CAD 10.3 million. The main reason was that world oil prices fell 27 percent in 1988.

In 1989 David Claydon replaced Kirkby as president of BP Canada. That year, he ordered environmental audits of all BP Canadian operations in response to growing concerns about possible environmental damage from oil exploration and refining. The company also announced plans to boost its natural gas exploration and reserves, recognizing that natural gas was a clean-burning fuel considered more environmentally sound by consumers than oil or coal.

1992 TRANSITION INTO THE INDEPENDENT TALISMAN ENERGY

In 1991 mounting debt and losses prompted a management shuffle and a worldwide review of operations by the head office of BP in London. By mid-1992, BP announced it would sell off its 57 percent stake in BP Canada through a secondary offering of shares. The *Financial Times of Canada* reported that Canadian employees responded with a burst of applause on hearing the news. To sell its stake in a highly profitable company with prospects that greatly encouraged Canadian and American investors, BP in London clearly had priorities elsewhere.

Upon being sold in June 1992, Talisman's share price stood at CAD 13.00. At the end of July 1993, the share price had climbed to CAD 26.50. The company had James W. "Jim" Buckee at its helm as president and CEO. The British-born businessman, Oxford-educated and with a Ph.D. in astrophysics, transformed Talisman in the 1990s into a smaller company focused on oil and gas exploration and production. For example, the company sold its Wolf Lake oil sands assets to Amoco Canada Petroleum Company in April 1992. Talisman then bought Encor Inc. the following year, gaining a company that held the oil and gas assets that once belonged to TransCanada PipeLines Limited. The purchase price comprised CAD 239 million worth of treasury shares.

No longer subservient to a British multinational parent, Talisman was free to seek international operations. The company had gained Encor's foreign activities in Algeria and Indonesia, but Buckee was seeking more substantial overseas holdings to balance Talisman's domestic operations. Bow Valley Energy Inc. was quickly identified as a prime target, and with a willing seller in the form of 53 percent owner British Gas PLC, a deal was soon struck. Talisman completed its acquisition of Bow Valley in August 1994, through a CAD 1.82 billion transaction consisting of CAD 627 million in cash, CAD 899 million in stock, and CAD 297 million in assumed debt. The purchase made Talisman the third largest gas producer in Canada but more importantly gave the company substantial properties in the British North Sea and in Indonesia, some of which were already in production and some of which were still at the prospecting stage. To reduce debt in the wake of the deal, Talisman sold some assets, including a group of oil and gas fields in southwestern Saskatchewan inherited from Bow Valley.

During 1996, Talisman substantially increased its North Sea holdings through three transactions. In January, Goal Petroleum plc was acquired for CAD 275 million. The deal doubled Talisman's oil production from the North Sea to nearly 39,000 barrels of crude oil per day, nearly equal to its production in western Canada. Later in the year, Talisman purchased a 52 percent stake in the North Sea's Ross field, which was expected to come onstream in the late 1990s with 20,000 barrels per day for Talisman. In the third deal, the company paid BP more than CAD 100 million for controlling stakes in three North Sea fields, adding another 16,000 barrels per day to Talisman's production.

Continuing its aggressive approach to expansion in 1997, a year in which the company was listed on the New York Stock Exchange, Talisman made a hostile CAD 1.56 billion bid for Wascana Energy Inc. The deal would have doubled Talisman's oil and gas properties in western Canada, but Canadian Occidental Petroleum Ltd. stepped in as a white knight with an offer that topped Talisman's, scuttling the bid. Talisman succeeded, however, with a CAD 605 million purchase of Pembina Resources Limited from Loram Corporation. Completed in October 1997, the transaction included Pembina's oil and natural gas operations in western Canada and Ontario with daily production of 10,000 barrels of oil and gas liquids and 92 million cubic feet of natural gas.

CONTROVERSIAL VENTURE IN SUDAN

One year later, Talisman acquired Calgary-based Arakis Energy Corporation for CAD 277.5 million in stock. Already operating in such politically risky areas as Indonesia and Algeria, Talisman gained Arakis's 25 percent stake in a major crude oil production and pipeline project in Sudan. Arakis had been attempting to develop the project for some time but had been unable to raise the funds necessary to move the project forward because of the turbulent situation in Sudan, which was in the 42nd year of a civil war pitting the Islamic government of the north against mainly Christian and animist groups in the south. In late 1996 Arakis had brought partners into the project: China National Petroleum Corporation, which took a 40 percent stake; Malaysia's Petronas Carigali Overseas Sdn. Bhd. (30 percent); and Sudapet Ltd., owned by the Sudanese government (5 percent). Ominously for Talisman, just three days after the company announced that it would purchase Arakis, the U.S. government launched cruise missiles at a purported nerve gas factory in the Sudanese capital of Khartoum. Talisman shares soon plunged nearly a third before recovering, and the deal was completed. In managing the crisis brought on by the missile strike, Buckee emphasized the long-range potential of the project and that the revenues from the oilfields could help to alleviate some of the strife plaguing Sudan.

Talisman completed a noncontroversial acquisition in September 1999, purchasing Calgary-based Rigel Energy Corporation for CAD 1.12 billion (CAD 735.8 million in stock, CAD 57 million in cash, and CAD 329.4 million in assumed debt). This deal significantly increased Talisman's natural gas production in western Canada and its oil production in the North Sea. It also helped to catapult the company into the top spot among Canadian oil and gas production companies in 2000.

The purchase of Rigel received little notice compared to the reams of negative publicity that Talisman was receiving over its Sudanese operations, publicity that increased in intensity in 1999 when oil began flowing through the completed pipeline and the government of Sudan began receiving hundreds of millions of dollars in oil revenues. Talisman was accused of helping to fund the government in its war against the rebels in the south, a government that was widely accused of committing human rights violations against its own citizens. Among the allegations, the government was accused of condoning slavery and forcing villagers to relocate to make way for the oil project. Human rights and religious groups called for the U.S. and Canadian governments to place sanctions on Talisman and put pressure on investment firms to withdraw their investments in Talisman. The U.S. government imposed sanctions on Talisman in February 2000, banning the refinement of Sudanese oil in the United States, but the Canadian government elected not to impose sanctions, despite a scathing report by a government-appointed special investigator, John Harker. In his report, Harker wrote that "Sudan is a place of extraordinary suffering and continuing human rights violations, and the oil operations in which a Canadian company is involved add more suffering." Talisman continued to maintain that its involvement in Sudan would lead to improvements in the human rights situation and help bring peace, and it also signed the International Code of Ethics for Canadian Business and in early 2001 released its first corporate social responsibility report on its Sudanese operations.

By the end of 2000, Talisman Energy's annual revenues were approaching CAD 4 billion, and its proven oil and gas reserves had reached 1.2 billion barrels of oil equivalent, up from 485 million barrels in 1995. In May 2001 Talisman acquired Calgary-based Petromet Resources Limited for CAD 765.9 million in cash and the assumption of CAD 57 million in debt in a deal that further expanded the company's natural gas

operations in Canada. Then in August of that same year, Lundin Oil AB was acquired for CAD 434.6 million in cash and CAD 70.2 million in assumed debt. Based in Sweden, Lundin had oil and gas interests in the North Sea, Malaysia, Vietnam, and Papua New Guinea that were conveyed to Talisman. Crucially, Lundin's operations in Sudan, Russia, and Libya were divested prior to the completion of the purchase.

Pressure on Talisman to exit from Sudan increased following the terrorist attacks on the United States of September 11, 2001, particularly because the Sudanese government was accused of harboring and aiding the Al Qaeda terrorist network. The U.S. Congress began serious consideration of a bill that would strip Talisman of its New York Stock Exchange listing, a potentially devastating blow to the company. Then in November 2001 human rights activists in New York filed a class-action lawsuit against Talisman on behalf of the southern Sudanese alleging that the company was complicit in human rights abuses in Sudan.

Around this same time, Talisman announced that it had made major oil discoveries in Trinidad potentially as large or larger than its Sudanese operations. The Trinidad discovery, combined with the international operations newly acquired via the Lundin purchase, provided the potential pretext for the company's exit from Sudan. It appeared likely that Talisman could divest itself of its Sudanese operations without suffering a drastic reduction in oil output or revenues. By the spring of 2002 the company had indeed placed its Sudanese holdings on the auction block, and in October of that year it had reached an agreement to sell the stake to a subsidiary of India's national oil company, Oil & Natural Gas Corporation Limited, for about CAD 1.2 billion. With the closing of the deal in March 2003, Talisman had finally rid itself of its Sudanese albatross and all the distractions and negative publicity that had come with it. It also netted a CAD 340 million after-tax gain on what amounted to a four-year investment. The final chapter to this saga was written in September 2003 when a U.S. district judge dismissed the civil lawsuit that had been filed against Talisman two years earlier.

GROWTH IN CORE AREAS OF NORTH AMERICA, THE NORTH SEA, AND SOUTHEAST ASIA

One of Talisman's main growth areas following its exit from Sudan was in the Appalachian area of upstate New York, where its focus was on deep natural gas wells. In a series of deals completed between October 2002 and June 2004, Talisman acquired about 978,000 acres of land for natural gas drilling. By 2005, the company was selling 105 million cubic feet per day of natural gas, making it the largest natural gas producer in New York State. Access to the energy-hungry northeastern U.S. market made this foray a particularly attractive one. During this same period, Talisman continued its active exploration for and production of natural gas within the Western Canadian Sedimentary Basin; made its first foray into the Middle East with a deal to explore for oil in Qatar; and entered the Norwegian North Sea by purchasing interests in a series of producing and prospective oilfields.

The firm's fastest-growing core area, however, was Southeast Asia, and in August 2004 Talisman announced it had signed a 17-year deal to sell natural gas to Indonesia's national gas distributor. The deal was expected to help Talisman sell 2.3 trillion cubic feet of natural gas from its Corridor project in Indonesia. The company was also working to develop oil and gas fields in Malaysia and Vietnam.

In November 2005 Talisman significantly augmented its North Sea assets via its largest acquisition to that time, a £1.22 billion (CAD 2.56 billion) takeover of the U.K. firm Paladin Resources plc. The interests it held in North Sea fields accounted for about 75 percent of Paladin's oil production and reserves; the remainder stemmed from fields in Australia, Indonesia, and Tunisia. At the time of its acquisition, Paladin was producing about 46,000 barrels of oil per day, but Talisman officials expected to boost this production to 70,000 barrels by 2009.

In the spring of 2006 Talisman launched a rationalization program centering on the sale of a number of North Sea and Canadian assets deemed noncore. By early 2007 the company had netted gross proceeds of nearly CAD 2 billion from the sale of such properties. A number of the assets sold entailed fields in which the company was only a passive partner. The divested properties also included the firm's very small stakes in two Canadian oil sands projects. Much of the proceeds from the unloaded properties was used to fund a stock buyback program.

NEW LEADERSHIP, SHIFT IN STRATEGY

Buckee, who had led Talisman since soon after its 1992 split from BP, retired in September 2007. While building the company into a leading independent petroleum explorer and producer with a far-flung array of assets, the outgoing leader during his long tenure had provoked controversy not only with his foray into Sudan but also

with his frequently voiced contention that global warming was not being driven by human activity. His successor as president and CEO was John A. Manzoni, a veteran BP executive who had most recently served as head of that firm's refining and marketing division.

After a lengthy review of the company's operations and assets, Manzoni in the spring of 2008 unveiled a major change in corporate strategy. Under the plan, Talisman stopped seeking growth from mature fields in the U.K. North Sea and Alberta and also planned a further round of divestments of noncore assets, including holdings in the Netherlands and Trinidad. In addition, while continuing to maintain a core set of international assets in the Norwegian North Sea, Southeast Asia, and South America, Talisman sought to attain sustainable long-term growth by developing unconventional natural gas fields in North America. With the latter effort, the company aimed to tap its vast 2.5 million acres of landholdings in North America, where substantial deposits of natural gas were trapped in shale, sand, and silt; the only way to unlock such deposits, which were typically shallow but wide, was through unconventional drilling techniques, such as horizontal drilling.

In June 2008, soon after launching this new strategy, Talisman added a new core international area of interest by taking stakes in two oil blocks in the Kurdistan region of northern Iraq. This move was risky given the instability in Iraq, but it provided Talisman with an early entry into oil-rich Kurdistan. In September 2008 the company entered into an agreement to sell its Dutch offshore assets to a unit of TOTAL S.A. for $480 million; the sale was completed in January 2009.

The record-high oil prices that prevailed for much of 2008 helped Talisman post record cash flow of CAD 6.16 billion ($5.78 billion) and record profits of CAD 3.52 billion ($3.3 billion) for the year. The revenue figure of CAD 9.81 billion ($9.2 billion) represented another all-time high. During the final months of the year, however, the global economic crisis quickly undermined demand for petroleum products and pulled oil prices into a swift decline, down to around $45 per barrel by year-end. The lower oil prices coupled with still-high costs for exploration and drilling prompted many petroleum producers to slash their 2009 spending. In concert with this trend, Talisman in early 2009 announced plans to spend just CAD 3.6 billion on exploration during the year, down from the CAD 5 billion spent the prior year. The company also continued to offload noncore assets. In March 2009 it announced an agreement to sell its oilfield assets in the Bakken region of southeastern Saskatchewan and northeastern Montana for CAD 720 million.

Etan Vlessing
Updated, David E. Salamie

PRINCIPAL SUBSIDIARIES

Talisman (Corridor) Ltd. (Barbados); Talisman Energy Canada; Talisman Energy Norge AS (Norway); Talisman Energy (UK) Limited; Talisman North Sea Limited (UK); Transworld Petroleum (UK) Limited.

PRINCIPAL COMPETITORS

Imperial Oil Limited; BP Canada Energy Company; EnCana Corporation; Canadian Natural Resources Limited; ConocoPhillips; Shell Canada Limited; Suncor Energy Inc.; Petro-Canada; Nexen Inc.; Husky Energy Inc.; Syncrude Canada Ltd.

FURTHER READING

Bott, Robert, "Fueled for Takeoff: Jim Buckee's Talisman Energy Leads the Way As One of the Most Dynamic Oil and Gas Players in a Reborn Calgary Oil Patch," *Globe and Mail*, Report on Business Magazine, November 25, 1994, p. 50.

"BP Canada Cut Loose As British Parent Sells Stake," *Globe and Mail*, May 13, 1992.

"BP Plans Further Cutbacks," *Globe and Mail*, May 6, 1992.

Brethour, Patrick, "Talisman Trims North Sea Assets," *Globe and Mail*, May 27, 2006, p. B5.

Brown, Mark, "Out of Africa," *Canadian Business*, December 9, 2002, pp. 21+.

Carlisle, Tamsin, "Talisman Agrees to Buy Rigel Energy in $563.2 Million Cash-and-Stock Deal," *Wall Street Journal*, August 24, 1999, p. B9.

———, "Talisman, Chasing Prized Natural Gas, to Buy Petromet in $469.7 Million Deal," *Wall Street Journal*, April 11, 2001, p. C14.

———, "Talisman Makes Purchase Offer for Bow Valley," *Wall Street Journal*, May 18, 1994, p. A3.

———, "Talisman Plans Unsolicited Bid for Wascana," *Wall Street Journal*, February 14, 1997, p. B23.

———, "Talisman to Buy British Oil Producer," *Wall Street Journal*, October 21, 2005, p. C6.

Chase, Steven, "Talisman Bids for Arakis Energy," *Globe and Mail*, August 18, 1998, p. B1.

———, "Talisman Cools on Quitting Sudan," *Globe and Mail*, May 3, 2000, p. B4.

———, "Talisman Stares Down Sudan Strike," *Globe and Mail*, October 9, 1998, p. B25.

———, "Talisman to Acquire Smaller Peer Rigel," *Globe and Mail*, August 24, 1999, p. B1.

Chase, Steven, and Jeff Sallot, "Heat Grows on Talisman over Sudan," *Globe and Mail*, May 4, 2000, p. A1.

Drohan, Madelaine, "Into Africa: Talisman Energy Wants Shareholders to Believe That Its Investment in Sudan Is Secure," *Globe and Mail*, Report on Business Magazine, September 24, 1999, p. 82.

———, "Sudan Play Bad Timing for Talisman," *Globe and Mail*, October 27, 1999, p. B2.

Ebner, Dave, "North Sea Sale Pares Talisman Portfolio," *Globe and Mail*, January 17, 2007, p. B3.

———, "Talisman CEO Touts Benefits of Going It Alone," *Globe and Mail*, March 2, 2006, p. B1.

———, "Talisman Makes $2.5-Billion Foray into North Sea," *Globe and Mail*, October 21, 2005, p. B1.

———, "Talisman Rejected Bid from 'Major,'" *Globe and Mail*, November 17, 2005, p. B1.

———, "Talisman Sells Second Batch of Oil, Gas Assets," *Globe and Mail*, June 15, 2006, p. B4.

———, "Thick-Skinned Iconoclast Packs It In," *Globe and Mail*, May 31, 2007, p. B1.

Fitz-James, Michael, "Talisman Turns the Tables: Responding to Social Protest Doesn't Necessarily Mean Backing Down," *Corporate Legal Times*, October 2001.

"Free of Stodgy Parents and Gushing Profits," *Financial Times of Canada*, July 31, 1993.

"Fueling a Fire," *Economist*, September 2, 2000, pp. 62–63.

Ingram, Mathew, "Talisman Deep in Sudan Quagmire," *Globe and Mail*, November 1, 1999, p. B2.

———, "Talisman Pumps Itself Up," *Globe and Mail*, October 14, 1996, p. B2.

Jang, Brent, "Talisman Bets on North Sea: Calgary Company Pays Over $100-Million for Controlling Stakes in Three Offshore Oil Fields," *Globe and Mail*, August 21, 1996, p. B1.

———, "Talisman Finds Huge Gas Pool in Alberta," *Globe and Mail*, August 15, 1997, p. B1.

———, "Talisman Looks Around for Bargains: Acquisitions Could Top $1-Billion," *Globe and Mail*, January 30, 1997, p. B1.

———, "Talisman Profit Cracks $1-Billion Mark for First Time," *Globe and Mail*, March 4, 2004, p. B4.

Leitch, Carolyn, "Talisman Kills Wascana Bid," *Globe and Mail*, April 10, 1997, p. B1.

Lem, Gail, "Talisman Makes Bid for Encor," *Globe and Mail*, March 11, 1993, p. B9.

McCarthy, Shawn, "From Bad Boy to Poster Boy: Talisman's Journey," *Globe and Mail*, April 30, 2008, p. B3.

McClearn, Matthew, "The End of the Affair," *Canadian Business*, September 25, 2006, pp. 11+.

Motherwell, Cathryn, "Talisman Bids $1.8-Billion for Bow Valley," *Globe and Mail*, May 18, 1994, p. B1.

Nguyen, Lily, "Suit Filed in U.S. Against Talisman: Sudan Class Action Disappoints Firm," *Globe and Mail*, November

9, 2001, p. B3.

————, "Talisman Heralds 'Major' Oil Discovery off Trinidad Coast," *Globe and Mail,* December 5, 2001, p. B1.

————, "Talisman Oil Find Could Add Major Area of Operation," *Globe and Mail,* November 7, 2001, p. B7.

————, "Talisman to Pull Out of Sudan," *Globe and Mail,* October 31, 2002, p. A1.

Nikiforuk, Andrew, "Company Loves Misery," *Canadian Business,* March 20, 2000, p. 16.

————, "Oil Patch Pariah," *Canadian Business,* December 10, 1999, pp. 69–70, 72.

Parkinson, David, "Turnaround Time for Talisman," *Globe and Mail,* March 31, 2008, p. B12.

Pitts, Gordon, "NGOs to Confront Talisman CEO," *Globe and Mail,* October 16, 2001, p. B8.

"Religious Groups Challenge Oil Giant," *Christian Century,* April 19–26, 2000, p. 450.

Scott, Norval, "New CEO Overlooked for Top Job at BP," *Globe and Mail,* May 31, 2007, p. B8.

————, "Roving Talisman Casts Its Eyes Homeward," *Globe and Mail,* May 1, 2008, p. B1.

————, "Talisman Strikes Deal for Iraq Fields," *Globe and Mail,* June 24, 2008, p. B1.

————, "This Is Not Jim Buckee's Talisman," *Globe and Mail,* December 13, 2008, p. B3.

Simon, Bernard, "A Canadian Oilman Gives In," *New York Times,* November 10, 2002, p. BU2.

————, "Oil Company Defends Role in Sudan," *New York Times,* October 17, 2001, p. W1.

"Talisman Grapples with Negative Publicity over Its Oil Project in War-Torn Sudan," *Oil and Gas Journal,* January 17, 2000.

"Talisman in a Flurry of Changes," *Globe and Mail,* April 14, 1993.

Wallace, Bruce, "A Sliding Moral Scale," *Maclean's,* February 28, 2000, p. 25.

Walton, Dawn, "Talisman Plans Huge Wind Farm," *Globe and Mail,* September 27, 2003, p. B2.

Willis, Andrew, "Streetwise Talisman Lost a Fair Fight," *Globe and Mail,* April 11, 1997, p. B11.

Yedlin, Deborah, "Wanted: Another Sudan; Well, Sort Of," *Globe and Mail,* Report on Business Magazine, May 30, 2003, p. 35.

TCF Financial
Corporation

200 Lake Street East
Wayzata, Minnesota 55391-1693
U.S.A.
Telephone: (612) 661-6500
Toll Free: (800) 228-8892
Web site: http://www.tcfbank.com

Public Company
Founded: 1923 as Twin City Building and Loan Association
Employees: 7,802
Total Assets: $16.74 billion (2008)
Stock Exchanges: New York
Ticker Symbol: TCB
NAICS: 522110 Commercial Banking; 551111 Offices of Bank Holding Companies; 522291 Consumer Lending; 522210 Credit Card Issuing

■ ■ ■

TCF Financial Corporation, a national financial holding company, markets aggressively to middle- and lower-income customers touting a range of free features, convenient hours, and locations. The $17 billion-asset company offers retail and commercial banking services through 448 offices located in Minnesota, Illinois, Wisconsin, Indiana, Michigan, Arizona, and Colorado. Other businesses include leasing and equipment finance in all 50 states, through TCF Equipment Finance, Inc., and Winthrop Resources Corporation, and commercial inventory finance in the United States and Canada, through TCF Inventory Finance, Inc., which was cre-

ated in 2008. TCF no longer sells investment and insurance products to retail banking customers.

EARLY LEADERSHIP: 1923–72

Twin City Building and Loan Association opened its doors on April 2, 1923, in downtown Minneapolis. "The firm was organized by a life insurance man who thought the savings business would feed his life business," Leonard Inskip reported in the *Minneapolis Tribune* in 1960. In the 1920s, real estate investors were also setting up savings and loans (S&Ls) as affiliated business ventures to drive up profits.

The operation, though, was not a sure bet. Public skepticism borne of the failure of other S&Ls initially made the hunt for investors a challenge. The membership fee was $2 per share, and investors in the savings and loan association would receive dividends at a rate of 7 percent.

However, persistence paid. By April of the next year, a second office had opened across the Mississippi River in neighboring St. Paul, Minnesota, and held nearly $50,000 in resources. During its second year of operation the Twin City Building and Loan Association grew nearly fivefold. The rapid growth prompted a move to larger facilities in both cities.

The economic hardships of the early 1930s cut into the association's earnings. In turn, interest rates were pared down, falling to a low of 2.5 percent. The mid-1930s introduction of a government insurance program for S&Ls proved to be a catalyst for growth in the industry and the Minnesota operation.

COMPANY PERSPECTIVES

TCF strives to place The Customer First. We believe providing great service helps to retain existing customers, attract new customers, create value for our stockholders, and build pride in our employees. We also respect customers' concern about privacy and know they place their trust in us. TCF is committed to protecting the private information of our customers and retaining that trust is our priority.

Twin City Building and Loan, upon receiving a federal charter in 1936, changed its name to Twin City Federal Savings and Loan Association. Its resources were $3.5 million at that time but grew to $10 million over the next three years.

Calendar years 1941 and 1942 proved to be stellar ones. Member accounts increased over $7 million, a growth rate near if not at the top of the industry for the time period. By 1943, the operation's 20th year of business, the association was the seventh largest savings and loan in the nation, holding over $20 million in resources. During its first two decades, Twin City Federal disbursed to its members approximately $2.9 million in dividends while also financing 14,126 homes.

Roy W. Larsen, who had been on board from day one, led the company as president although its growth spurt. Assets doubled every few years: $50 million in 1946; $100 million in 1951; $200 million in 1955. Another man on hand in 1923, Vice-President and Secretary Burch N. Bell, still served alongside Larsen as the 1960s approached.

In the fall of 1959, Twin City Federal had surpassed in terms of total size its biggest competitor in the Minneapolis/St. Paul savings market. With year-end assets of $357 million, the S&L was also closing in on some of St. Paul's largest banks.

Twin City Federal's rapid rate of growth had been propelled by a number of factors. S&Ls could offer larger interest rates on savings accounts than banks, which were capped by law at a rate of 3 percent. In addition, Twin City Federal had been spending some $700,000 annually on self-promotion. Moreover, the post–World War II housing boom helped the S&L grow: most of its funds were dedicated to long-term mortgages. Finally, there was Larsen's leadership and drive to beat out competitors. "Business is a game, and I have a competitive urge," he told Inskip. "If I didn't like

to win I would have quit years ago." He continued to man the helm even as others his age retired.

In 1960 Twin City Federal had about 26 percent of total assets held by the state's savings institutions. The bulk of the S&L's assets came from its savings account volume, primarily in the Twin Cities of Minneapolis and St. Paul. Yet about 20 to 25 percent came from customers outside the Twin Cities, from folks seeking more interest for their deposits than what local banks offered. "It's not just that we pay a higher rate for money than the country people," Larsen said in the *Minneapolis Tribune.* "A lot of people just don't want the rest of the people in their home town knowing how much money they've got salted away." Originating from rural northwestern Minnesota himself, Larsen led the urban operation for over four decades. Two other company veterans followed in the wake of his tenure. Under those early leaders, the company grew to $1 billion in assets, a milestone reached in 1972.

STORM ON THE HORIZON

The new leadership of the 1970s inherited an operation which was at the top of the local thrift market "thanks largely to an aggressive, personality-driven marketing strategy," wrote John R. Engen for *Corporate Report Minnesota.* A popular local radio host, an outspoken Twin's baseball manager, a gregarious Viking's football player, and droll comedian Jack Benny all promoted Twin City Federal. "That and a strong branch network, sports team sponsorships, a few catchy jingles ('Tuckabuckadayaway'), and the omnipresent premium giveaways add up to TCF's oldtime formula for success," observed Engen.

S&Ls had historically been tied to the strength of the economy and the home building industry: approximately 40 percent of all home loans were made by S&Ls at the beginning of the 1960s. By the late 1970s, though, many of the nation's thrifts, including Twin City Federal, were chasing commercial real estate ventures and other activities promising higher return on investment.

Skyrocketing inflation and interest rates eroded the value of traditional fixed-rate mortgage portfolios, according to Engen. Thrifts posted losses in the early 1980s. Margins shrank, as interest paid out on savings accounts rose, but interest coming in on loans remained the same. Moreover, federal legislation had changed the lending and investment landscape, leaving S&Ls looking for new ways to drive up profits.

By the mid-1980s, the cyclical nature of interest rates was the least of the S&L industry's problems: It was about to sink in a sea of red ink created from risky

KEY DATES

1923: Twin City Building and Loan Association is founded in Minneapolis, Minnesota.

1936: The business is granted a federal charter and changes its name to Twin City Federal Savings and Loan Association.

1943: Twin City Federal ranks as the seventh largest S&L in the nation, with $20 million in assets.

1972: Twin City Federal reaches $1 billion in assets.

1986: Company goes public under name TCF Banking and Savings, F.A.

1987: TCF Financial Corporation is formed as a holding company.

1988: TCF opens first supermarket branch location.

1989: TCF switches to a federal savings bank and begins trading on the NYSE.

1997: Company converts to a national bank charter.

1999: TCF opens its one-millionth retail checking account.

2002: TCF posts record earnings.

2005: Executives reap the reward of hitting incentive goal.

2009: TCF rethinks participation in government capital purchase program.

ventures and questionable business practices. The federal agencies regulating the S&Ls would be overwhelmed by the sheer number of thrifts that were insolvent or teetering on the brink.

The weight of ventures such as condominium conversions on the Upper East Side of Manhattan and interest rate swap contracts was about to kill off Twin City Federal. William Cooper, named CEO in the spring of 1985, was charged with keeping the operation alive.

Coming from a working-class background, Cooper served as a Detroit police officer while studying to become an accountant during the mid-1960s. A CPA job with Touche Ross would lead him to Michigan National Bank, where he was mentored in retail banking by the company vice-chairman. He held executive positions with Huntington Bancshares in Ohio and American Savings & Loan Association in Miami before arriving in Minnesota.

Cooper returned Twin City Federal to the basics, cutting expenses and revamping the culture. He stripped the corporate headquarters of its luxuries, including

expansive executive suites fragrant with orchids tended by flower ladies. Thirty-five upper level officers would retire or be fired during Cooper's first three years in command. Branch managers found their incomes tied tightly to performance.

Seeking capital, Twin City Federal went public in 1986, under the name TCF Banking and Savings, F.A. (TCF Bank). Meanwhile, Cooper continued to clean house. He shut down the company's New York real estate subsidiary, incurring a loss of more than $200 million; a $40 million racetrack construction loan was sold off; and a billion in interest rate contracts, used by his predecessor to lock in high rates, were canceled to the tune of $70 million.

While tearing down on one end of the spectrum, TCF built on the other. Totally Free Checking was introduced in 1986 to court low- and middle-income customers. Thrift patrons paid for their checks but incurred no other service fees on the noninterest-bearing accounts. Cooper believed that this strategy would drive up net interest margins. He intended to draw in a large number of small deposits, on which TCF paid little or no interest, and use that cheap source of money for higher-yielding consumer loans. By 1988 TCF's consumer loan portfolio including home-equity, credit card, and direct auto and recreational loans had climbed to $1 billion from about $200 million in 1986.

Cooper also began an expansion drive. During 1987, TCF acquired approximately $300 million of insured deposits from an S&L in Illinois. The holding company TCF Financial Corporation was also formed. The next year, TCF entered the supermarket sector, opening a branch in an Eagan, Minnesota, Cub Foods store. At decade end, TCF converted to a federal savings bank, operating under the name TCF Bank Savings fsb, and company stock began trading on the New York Stock Exchange.

Despite Cooper's moves, TCF's future was still in the balance in 1990. The firm remained in the red, and federal regulators watched it closely. During a period of three years, from 1989 to 1991, the government seized 633 thrifts, and the industry faced ever tighter controls. "In those dark times TCF's management bought heavily into the stock while the board, under Cooper's direction, turned to stock-driven incentives as a bigger part of the pay formula," wrote Engen.

TCF, unlike so many others, survived. Entering the last quarter of 1991, TCF had reduced its nonperforming assets to $87.3 million, down from $156 million at the end of 1986. The company's commercial real estate portfolio was split about evenly between multifamily loans, such as for apartment buildings, and higher risk loans for retail development and office space. A record

$1 billion in new mortgages was generated by TCF Mortgage Corporation, TCF Bank's mortgage lending subsidiary.

WARP SPEED: 1993–98

By 1993, TCF had boosted its share of Minnesota's consumer banking market to 18 percent, up from 8 percent in 1986, according to a May 1993 *American Banker* article by Brian Hellauer. Its figures surpassed larger commercial banks Norwest Corp. and First Bank Systems Inc.

In addition to growing market share by aggressively selling its banking services, TCF was beefing up profits with technology. According to Hellauer, a lean data-processing operation allowed the company to continue to service mortgages while other operations farmed the work out to third parties. Furthermore, TCF's widespread automated teller machine (ATM) network generated income with each transaction.

"We charge for just about everything, and we charge for things other people don't charge for," Cooper told Hellauer. "We're very aggressive pricers, but we give people a lot of service—longer hours, a broader base of products, more access to ATMs."

Through the mid-1990s, TCF relied heavily on acquisitions to build business in Illinois, Wisconsin, and Michigan. In 1993, TCF acquired $960 million-in-assets Republic Capital Group, Inc., of Milwaukee, Wisconsin. The company also spent about $14.5 million to buy $220 million of deposits and 15 branches of the failed thrift First Federal Savings and Loan Association of Pontiac, Michigan. TCF added 39 offices in Michigan when it acquired a struggling $2.4 billion Great Lakes Bancorp in 1995.

By 1996 TCF was clearly on solid ground, ranked among the best-performing thrifts in the nation, according to *Corporate Report Minnesota*. It was the 14th largest savings bank in the United States, holding just over $7 billion in assets. In 1997, Cooper led TCF's conversion from a thrift to a bank.

Also in 1997, TCF entered the leasing business through the acquisition of Winthrop Resources Corporation. The operation leased computers and other equipment to businesses nationwide. Additionally, banking operations were expanded to Colorado.

TCF directed a lot of attention to the Chicago area in 1997 and 1998, first purchasing the Bank of Chicago and then acquiring 76 bank branches in Jewel-Osco stores from BankAmerica Corp. The supermarket branches had failed to turn a profit under Bank of America: Its upscale product was not in line with the

profile of the typical Jewel customer. TCF turned the branches around by marketing products such as Totally Free Checking to modest-means customers.

"A small number times a large number equals a large number," Cooper told *Crain's Chicago Business* in 2000, citing the same strategy that had worked so well in the Twin Cities market. In terms of total number of branches in Chicago, TCF ranked second only to Bank One Corp.

MIXED RESULTS: 1999–2001

From 1990 to 1998 TCF's stock rose spectacularly, exceeding the pace of even strong industry performers. Yet as its earnings growth slowed in 1998, the stock nosedived. A February 1999 *American Banker* article reported profits were hurt by a $10 million price tag to open 105 supermarket branches; mortgage prepayments; and the discontinuation of its indirect automobile lending operation.

"Cooper's investor-relations problems coincided with voter dissatisfaction with his politics," wrote John Engen in a June 2001 *American Business* article. In 1990, Cooper served as finance chairman for a Republican gubernatorial candidate. Arne Carlson's unexpected victory in strongly Democratic Minnesota gave Cooper a solid foothold in the party, and in 1997, as party chairman, he helped bring in record contributions. Another unexpected victory took the shine off Cooper's political star. Ex-professional wrestler Jesse Ventura defeated both the Democratic and Republican candidates for governor in 1998. Cooper was not shy about exchanging barbs with the colorful new governor. Engen wrote, "Mr. Cooper displayed a bumper sticker that said, 'Your governor is smarter than my governor.'" In 1999, Cooper stepped down as party chairman, but he remained politically active, serving as finance chair.

Meanwhile, TCF opened its one-millionth retail checking account. In other business sectors, TCF both expanded and contracted in 1999. Leasing operations grew with the establishment of TCF Leasing, Inc. However, the company sold substantially all of its remaining automobile loan portfolio. Additionally, TCF sold its title insurance and appraisal operations and formed a strategic alliance with the buyer.

In 2000, TCF surpassed $1 billion in supermarket branch deposits. The Minnesota-based bank was the fourth largest operator of supermarket bank branches in the country with over 200. TCF also ranked as the 16th largest issuer of Visa debit cards in the United States with 1.1 million cards in circulation; TCF had introduced the card that worked like a check to its Minnesota customers in 1996. During 2000, TCF's debit card transactions produced $28.7 million in revenue, an increase of 47 percent over 1999.

TCF continued to apply technology as a means to draw customers: phone cards were introduced as part of a customer loyalty program and an Internet banking site was launched in 2000. As committed as ever to the concept of convenience, in 2001 TCF expanded Sunday hours to some of its traditional banking locations, a practice already in place in its supermarket sites. Its investment business was also expanded in 2001 with the introduction of a discount brokerage service. TCF had begun offering annuities in the 1980s and mutual funds in the 1990s.

REAPING REWARDS: 2002–07

TCF initiated some business activity outside its markets of Colorado, Illinois, Indiana, Michigan, Minnesota, and Wisconsin in the new millennium. Its venture capital unit planted seed money in new banks: the company's first two investments were made in Florida. TCF intended to invest between 5 and 25 percent of needed start-up capital. In addition to Florida, TCF was looking toward the Southwest for start-up bank locations, particularly in areas in which there had been a merger or buyout of a community bank, according to a February 2002 *American Banker* article.

During the year, TCF increased its core of deposits, providing additional low-cost funds for loans. Strong commercial real estate and commercial lending activity, in turn, helped TCF post record earnings of $233 million.

Cooper snagged *American Banker*'s Innovator of the Year award in 2004. "By challenging Visa, infiltrating the electronics payments association Nacha, enhancing debit cards, and grabbing the initiative in e-bill payment, Mr. Cooper, 61, is taking a stand. In the process, he is leading the way for smaller banks, though he says that is not his intent," W. A. Lee wrote in December. TCF had not only found ways to increase debit related profits but had positioned itself to influence the future of payment systems.

In January 2005, top TCF executives received 1.07 million shares of stock valued at about $33 million, an incentive tied to achieving a 75 percent increase in earnings per share over the base year of 1999. While attributing some of the bank's success to its strategy of gathering billions in low-cost savings and checking deposits, the *Minneapolis Star Tribune* also pointed to recent moves in balance sheet management.

"To avoid having too many fixed-rate loans on its books as interest rates rose, the bank forfeited millions

of dollars in interest income by letting $1.3 billion in mortgages and mortgage-backed securities roll off its balance sheet. It was the central reason that TCF's profits declined in 2003 and management had to forgo bonuses," Chris Serres explained. U.S. mortgage volumes were expected to drop off going forward.

In 2006 TCF and the University of Minnesota reached a naming rights agreement for the new football stadium, scheduled to open in September 2009. The $35 million deal included stipulations related to debit card marketing, logo placement, and campus branch location.

The midwest-based bank followed snowbirds to the Southwest in 2007, setting up a branch in Phoenix, Arizona. TCF had sold slower-growth branches in Michigan to fund the expansion, according to *American Banker*. "We concluded that a better use of shareholders' capital would be in faster-growing areas like Denver or Arizona," CEO Lynn A. Nagorske reported at a June investor conference. The TCF president had succeeded Cooper, who remained chairman, at the end of 2005.

TOUGH TIMES: 2008–09

TCF opened 11 branches during 2008, compared with 20 new branches opened in 2007. Just three were scheduled for 2009, according to the company's 10K report. Overall, TCF operated 236 supermarket, 197 traditional, and 15 campus branches.

The campus-based business had become an important retail niche. At year-end 2008, TCF ranked sixth in the country in terms of "campus card banking relationships" and held $218 million in campus deposits. TCF had alliances with ten colleges.

TCF Financial and TCF Bank, according to the 10K report, were "well-capitalized" as defined by the Federal Deposit Insurance Corporation Improvement Act of 1991 (FDICIA). In that light, the bank took part, at year-end, in the Treasury Department's capital infusion program, issuing $361 million in preferred stock and a warrant to purchase about 3.2 million shares in TCF common stock.

Attached to the agreement were restrictions related to dividends, stock buybacks, and executive compensation, according a November 2008 *Star Tribune* article. With the nation's flow of capital shut off by an onslaught of mortgage defaults, the federal government planned to funnel funds into the economy through solid financial institutions under the guise of the Emergency Economic Stabilization Act of 2008.

The nation's financial crisis, meanwhile, pulled Cooper out of retirement and back to the helm of TCF as CEO, following Nagorske's departure in July 2008. Looking back at the year, in his letter to stockholders, Cooper wrote: "TCF did not engage in the activities that have created so many problems in the financial industry." Nevertheless, the bank was "not immune to the effects of these devastating headlines, the reduction in home values and the general state of the economy, as evidenced by a 24 percent decline in our stock price."

During the year, the bank saw rising consumer home-equity delinquencies and net charge-offs. Similar problems with the commercial portfolio led to a shakeup of management in that area. Among other moves, TCF discontinued sales of investment and insurance products and created a commercial loan origination subsidiary. TCF Inventory Finance, Inc., would target electronics and appliance retail markets at the outset. Despite the myriad of challenges during the year, TCF remained profitable, a scenario only in the dreams of many U.S. bankers.

Early in 2009, the Minnesota-based bank got a taste of the criticism being directed at the nation's financial institutions, in particular ones that accepted money from the Troubled Asset Relief Program (TARP). Referring to a partially company-funded senior management trip to an Aspen area ski resort, Cooper said in *American Banker*, "We do take into consideration anything that would look bad, and we don't want to put the bank in a bad light, but this isn't one of them." He added, "It was a team-building event for people who have been under tremendous pressure, who didn't get bonuses." In the light of a 50 percent drop in full-year earnings, Cooper himself "chose to forgo both his salary and bonus," Katie Kuehner-Hebert reported.

TCF, meanwhile, sought regulatory approval to move TCF National Bank's legal headquarters to South Dakota, a state with beneficial tax laws and lending rules. The lack of interest rate caps, for example, had drawn Citibank's credit card business two decades earlier, according to a February 2009 *Star Tribune* article. Mortgage fee rules were also less restrictive than many other states: A South Dakota-based lender could impose a prepayment penalty. A 6 percent franchise tax was applied to profits earned in the state, but TCF had just one branch set to open in Sioux Falls.

In March TCF joined a growing list of companies seeking to return TARP money. While Cooper previously had been critical of some aspects of the program, he viewed continued participation as detrimental to the bank. Change in the program's rules had led to the perception that a TARP bank was a weak bank. Initially, TARP was "a way to encourage healthy banks to lend more but has morphed into a means to buoy weak banks," Kuehner-Hebert explained for *American Banker*.

Cooper told *American Banker* TCF would remain well-capitalized without the government money and that an internally run stress test indicated it had "adequate capital to survive anything." Nevertheless, unemployment continued to rise across TCF's market area and home prices had yet to stabilize, by no means good news for its sizable home-equity portfolio.

Kathleen Peippo

PRINCIPAL SUBSIDIARIES

TCF National Bank; TCF National Bank Arizona.

PRINCIPAL COMPETITORS

Associated Bank-Corp.; U.S. Bancorp; Wells Fargo & Company.

FURTHER READING

Alexander, Steve, "Two More Large Banks to Get Cash Injections," *Minneapolis Star Tribune*, November 4, 2008, p. 1D.

Anderson, Mark, "TCF Financial Positions Itself for Rising Interest Rates," *Finance and Commerce Daily*, April 17, 2003.

———, "TCF Financial Puts Stop to Executive Loans," *Finance and Commerce Daily*, May 21, 2002.

———, "TCF Financial Reports Yearly Income of $12B," *Finance and Commerce Daily*, January 16, 2003.

Arndorfer, James B., and Julie Johnsson, "Grocery Outlets a Real Jewel for TCF," *Crain's Chicago Business*, September 4, 2000, p. 1.

Bielski, Lauren, "Blue-Collar Bank: Led by CEO William Cooper, TCF Financial Profits Handsomely from Its Focus on Everyday Folks Who Don't Have a Lot of Time for Banking," *ABA Banking Journal*, December 2003, pp. 24+.

Chase, Brett, "High-Performing TCF Defies Banking Wisdom," *American Banker*, July 12, 1996, p. 4.

———, "TCF Bids for Respect with Conversion to Bank Charter," *American Banker*, April 7, 1997, p. 6.

———, "TCF Isn't Ready to Check Out of Supermarket Strategy," *American Banker*, February 25, 1999, p. 5.

———, "TCF's Check Mastermind to Retire on New Year's Day," *American Banker*, October 6, 1997, p. 8.

Conroy, Bill, "Minnesota's S&Ls: Asset or Liability?" *Minneapolis–St. Paul CityBusiness*, October 21, 1991, pp. 1+.

Engen, John R., "CEO Cooper—Wrestled Ventura, Sluggish Earnings—Won't Budge," *American Banker*, June 15, 2001, p. 1.

———, "A Master of Marketing—Supermarketing, That Is," *American Banker*, April 4, 1994, pp. 6+.

———, "Pin Money," *Corporate Report Minnesota,* October 1996, pp. 46+.

Hellauer, Bill, "TCF Financial Finds Fees, Profits Catering to Mass Market," *American Banker,* May 10, 1993, pp. 1A+.

Inskip, Leonard, "Twin City Builds Pennies into 373 Million Dollars," *Minneapolis Tribune,* April 24, 1960, pp. 9, 11.

Jackson, Ben, "Start-Up Investor TCF Says Control Is Not Its Goal," *American Banker,* February 4, 2002, p. 5.

———, "TCF Financial Introduces Sunday Hours," *American Banker,* October 26, 2001, p. 1.

Kaszuba, Mike, "TCF Perks Go Beyond Stadium's Name at U," *Minneapolis Star Tribune,* July 9, 2006, p. 1A.

Kennedy, Patrick, "CEO Pay Watch: TCF Financial Corp.," *Minneapolis Star Tribune,* February 28, 2009, p. 1D.

Kimelman, John, "Thrifts Slow to Abandon Traditional Ways," *American Banker,* November 1, 1999, p. 25.

Kuehner-Hebert, Katie, "Execs: Trip Criticism Inevitable but Off-Base," *American Banker,* February 10, 2009, p. 4.

———, "TCF: Another Bank Bailing Out of Bailout," *Minneapolis Star Tribune,* March 4, 2009, p. 1.

Lee, W. A., "In New Payments Era, Cooper Plays Hardball," *American Banker,* December 2, 2004, p. 12A.

Leuty, Ron, "TCF Fills Its Shopping Bag with Old BofA Branches," *San Francisco Business Times,* September 15, 2000, p. 15.

Mazzucca, Tim, "Why Midwest Bankers See an Opportunity in Arizona," *American Banker,* June 26, 2007, p. 1.

Rieker, Matthias, "TCF Financial of Minnesota Wins Praise from Merrill," *American Banker,* May 10, 2001, p. 20.

Schafer, Lee, "Alive and Well Among the Living Dead," *Corporate Report Minnesota,* December 1988, pp. 51–54.

Schwab, Paul, "TCF Launches Discount Brokerage," *Business Journal–Milwaukee,* June 29, 2001, p. 9.

Serres, Chris, "Taking the TC Out of TCF: Bank Moving to Sioux Falls," *Minneapolis Star Tribune,* February 13, 2009, p. 1D.

———, "TCF; They Cashed in Finally," *Minneapolis Star Tribune,* January 13, 2005, p. 1D.

Shenn, Jody, "TCF Cooling on Mortgages, Cites Volatility, Accounting," *American Banker,* September 10, 2004, p. 1.

Silvestri, Scott, "TCF Plans to Stock Up on Store Branches," *American Banker,* September 12, 2000, p. 1.

Twenty Million in Twenty Years, Minneapolis: Jones Press and Twin City Federal Saving and Loan Association, 1943.

Ter Beke NV

———■———

Beke 1
Waarschoot, B-9950
Belgium
Telephone: (+32 09) 370 12 11
Fax: (+32 09) 370 16 16
Web site: http://www.terbeke.com

Public Company
Incorporated: 1948
Employees: 1,838
Sales: EUR 393.2 million (2008)
Stock Exchanges: NYSE Euronext Brussels
Ticker Symbol: TERB
NAICS: 311612 Meat Processed from Carcasses; 311423
    Dried and Dehydrated Food Manufacturing

■ ■ ■

From tiny Waarschoot, Belgium, Ter Beke NV has grown into one of the leading producers of processed meats and fresh ready-meals in Europe. The Processed Meat division, grouped under subsidiary Ter Beke-Pluma NV produces a full range of deli meats, patés, and other processed meat products. The company's retail brands in this category include L'Ardennais, Daniel Coopman, and Pluma. In Belgium, the company operates a multi-channel approach, supplying fresh and packaged meat products to the retail sector, as well as supplying the wholesale butcher and professional catering sectors. The group's international operations, which include the Netherlands, Luxembourg, Switzerland, Germany, the United Kingdom, France, and Spain,

focus on the retail sector. Through its Ready Meals division, grouped under subsidiary Fresh Meals NV, Ter Beke has become a leading supplier to the fresh ready-to-eat category, through its Come a Casa and Pronto (retail) and Vamos (professional) brands. This segment focuses especially on the Italian and Mediterranean segments, producing a range of pasta and pizza dishes. Ter Beke is the leading supplier of ready-to-eat lasagna in Europe. Ter Beke's production is carried out through a network of factories in Belgium, with additional production facilities in the Netherlands and France. The company is listed on the NYSE Euronext Brussels exchange, while the founding Coopman family remain major shareholders. Luc De Bruyckere, who joined the company in the early 1970s, remains its chairman, while Marc Hofman serves as managing director. In 2008, the company's sales were EUR 393.2 million.

FROM BUTCHER SHOP TO DELI MEATS IN THE FORTIES

Ter Beke's roots reach back to the 1920s, when Frans Coopman began working as an itinerant butcher, buying and slaughtering poultry and rabbits. By the 1930s, Coopman had opened his own butcher shop, selling fresh meats as well as prepared meat products. In 1934, Coopman moved to a larger shop in Beke, a hamlet attached to the town of Waarschoot, in Belgium's Flanders region.

Coopman's business expanded over the next two decades, adding horsemeat and other fresh meat products. In 1948, Coopman founded a new company, Ter Beke, initially as a specialist in horsemeat products. Soon after, however, the company turned its focus toward the production of deli and other processed meats, particularly regional salami and sausages. Ter Beke grew steadily through the 1950s, supplying the region's butchers as well as a growing retail grocery market. By the end of the 1950s, Coopman's company had grown to 16 employees.

By then, Coopman had been joined in the business by his youngest son, Daniel. While a number of Coopman's other sons had gone on to found their own meat processing companies, including Copra, Plumaco, and Deva, Daniel was the only one to be formally trained, attending a butchers' training school. Daniel Coopman's involvement in his father's business began when Daniel was 14 years old. When Frans Coopman retired in 1959, the younger Coopman, then 21 years old, took over the company. As Coopman told *Nieuwsblad:* "I never thought about the decision. I'd been going along with my father since I was fourteen and when he retired, I couldn't think of anything better to do than to take over the company."

Over the next year, Coopman courted and then married Edith de Baets, who lived nearby. Coopman's choice of a bride proved an important element in the company's future success. Backed by Edith's degree in economics, the company expanded strongly through the 1960s. Edith Coopman handled the company's administrative side, while Daniel Coopman oversaw its production operations.

PROFESSIONAL MANAGER IN THE SEVENTIES

Ter Beke quickly broadened its range of products from sausage meats to a full line of fresh and processed meats. Before long, the company was able to provide a full selection of meats to the region's butchers. The Coopmans began to eye further growth, seeking to expand the company's reach from a regional to national level.

The Coopmans recognized that they did not possess the necessary skills to achieve this growth by themselves. At the beginning of the 1970s, the Coopmans decided to begin recruiting a professional management team from the country's business schools. This led Daniel

Coopman to offer a job to Luc De Bruyckere, a recent graduate with a degree in business psychology from the Vlerick business school.

While Coopman remained an active leader in the company, and retired only in 2007, De Bruyckere rapidly took over the direction of the group's operations and became the architect of its successful expansion into one of Belgium's, and Europe's, leading meat-processing groups. Among the company's first moves following De Bruyckere's hire was the decision to expand its operations into the Netherlands. This entry proved successful, and Ter Beke developed a strong reputation for its deli meats. Through the next decades, the company's Dutch operations focused largely on the over-the-counter and butcher shop sales channels. In support of its growing operations, the company acquired new deli meat production facilities in the late 1970s.

ACQUIRING SCALE INTO THE NINETIES

By 1986, Ter Beke's strong growth and plans for future expansion brought the company to the stock market, with a listing on the Brussels stock exchange. The public offering enabled the company to put into place a new acquisition-driven growth phase.

The company's first acquisition, however, came in large part as a response to the first of a number of health crises afflicting the Belgian meat industry. An outbreak of swine fever had been ravaging much of the Flanders region in the late 1980s. In order to ensure its supply of pork, Ter Beke took the decision to add new facilities in another part of the country altogether. The choice fell to the Ardennes region, in the French-speaking south, where the company acquired Salaisons Ardennaises Heinen, based in Malmedy, in 1987. That purchase also provided the company with the right to use the Ardennes label, which became protected in the next decade, on its products.

This first acquisition provided Ter Beke the appetite for more. In 1988, the company made a new purchase, of Ruiselede-based Reiners. Then in 1991 the company returned to the Walloon-region, buying Hollandia, a deli meats producer based in Vivegnis. Also that year, the company launched a new line of deli meats, targeting the professional catering sector, under the Daniel Coopman brand.

READY-MEALS TO THE RESCUE IN 1994

Despite its strong growth, Ter Beke was nonetheless confronted with a number of disturbing trends in the early 1990s. The different branches of the meat industry continued to be affected by recurrent health crises,

KEY DATES

1934: Frans Coopman opens his first butcher shop in Beke, Waarschoot, in Belgium.

1948: Coopman founds Ter Beke initially as a horsemeat processor, but then as a deli meats producer.

1959: Daniel Coopman takes over the business from his father and leads its expansion.

1971: Coopman turns over the direction of the company to Luc De Bruyckere, who expands the company to a national level.

1986: Ter Beke goes public on the Brussels exchange and launches an acquisition strategy.

1994: Ter Beke decides to enter the ready-meals segment, acquiring the Vamos and Come a Casa pasta brands.

1996: Ter Beke acquires Unilever's chilled foods division, as well as the Pronto (pizza), L'Ardennais (deli meats), and Les Nutons (pasta and paté) brands.

2003: Ter Beke completes first international acquisition, of Di Pasto, in France.

2006: Ter Beke merges with Pluma, becoming Belgium's leading meat processor.

2007: Daniel Coopman retires at the age of 70.

which only heightened at the end of the decade, with the outbreak of mad cow disease, public outcry over animal feed policies, and, particularly for Ter Beke, the dioxin crisis at the end of the 1990s.

At the same time, new nutritional guidelines had been calling for the reduction in consumption of red meats, especially of fattier, saltier deli meats. As a result, meat consumption had begun to decline by the beginning of the 1990s. By then, Ter Beke had also found it necessary to respond to another trend, as the supermarket sector had grown to dominate the retail markets in both Belgium and the Netherlands. While Belgium remained a strong market for over-the-counter meat sales, in the Netherlands, the self-service meat channel became the dominant model. By 2000, more than 90 percent of Dutch deli and other meat sales came from the self-service counter.

The rise of the self-service channel was in itself part of another fast-moving consumer trend. As more households switched to a two-earner model, people were able to spend less time in food preparation. Manufacturers rushed to supply this new market, developing new frozen, chilled, and fresh foods. Retailers too recognized the potential of focusing sales on the prepared foods sector, which offered far higher margins than basic foods. The ready-to-eat sector soon became the fastest-growing foods segment.

These factors led Ter Beke to make the important decision in the early 1990s to diversify into the ready-meals market. For this, the company sought a new acquisition that would at once provide Ter Beke with an entry into this channel, while also taking it away from its core meats focus. By 1994, the company had found its first target, with the purchase of Vamos, based in Wanze, Belgium. That company specialized in the production of ready-to-eat pasta dishes, including a leadership position in the chilled lasagna segment. Vamos brought Ter Beke that brand, which focused on the professional market, and the Come a Casa retail pasta brand. Ter Beke initially acquired a 74 percent stake in Vamos, but in 1996 acquired the remaining 26 percent.

The year 1996 proved a turning point for the company's efforts to establish itself as a dual-focus company. In that year, the company reached an agreement to take over the chilled foods division from Unilever, followed by the takeover of pizza brand Pronto. The company then rounded out its ready-meal expansion with the purchase of Les Nutons, based in Marche-en-Famenne, a producer of pastas as well as paté meats.

The gathering crises in the meats industry, culminating with the dioxin scandal in 1999, had led to further consumer confidence in the fresh meats sector. Ter Beke was also faced with corresponding rises in its raw materials costs, particularly with the wide-scale culling of European herds, and the banning of British beef from the continent, carried out in order to contain the growing range of diseases affecting the heavily industrialized meat market.

The company's move into ready-meals nonetheless provided the company with the balance it needed to survive this period. In the meantime, not all of the meats industry had been as hard hit by the crisis. The deli meats sector in particular proved more resistant, and continued to grow through the decade. Ter Beke responded to this trend by boosting its own deli meats operations, buying the well-known L'Ardennais brand of dried sausages, as well as Heku, a specialist deli meat slicer. The addition of sales and distribution company Europal that year also boosted the group's reach, particularly as it began to develop an international expansion strategy.

ACQUIRING THE LEAD

Ter Beke returned to Unilever in 1998, buying that company's Zwan Salami brand. Yet the gathering clouds over the meats industry had finally begun to catch up to the company. Faced with rising competition and raw material costs, growing pricing pressure from the large-scale supermarket groups, and the collapse of consumer confidence, Ter Beke was forced to restructure its operations. The company launched its "Aurora" plan in 1998, which involved a consolidation of its then 11 production facilities. By the end of the restructuring effort the following year, Ter Beke had closed down three of its plants and had shed a number of its least profitable food lines. The company also boosted its financial position, issuing a EUR 200 million Automatic Convertible Debenture in 1999.

Ter Beke's strategic focus turned to further expansion of its ready-meal operations. The company also sought to broaden its geographic spread, targeting increased sales to the French and German markets, and then to other European markets. In this, the company's Come a Casa brand became a corporate flagship, and rapidly grew into the leading European chilled lasagna brand. Into the new decade, the company's sales grew to include Spain, the United Kingdom, Portugal, the Scandinavian markets, Ireland, and the Czech Republic, in addition to its Benelux base.

By 2003, Ter Beke had renewed its acquisition strategy. The company reinforced its French sales entry with its first international acquisition, of the Di Pasto chilled pasta division of Agis. Other acquisitions soon followed, including the purchase of Netherlands-based Langeveld Sleegers, one of that country's leading processed meats groups, in 2005. In late 2007, the company acquired a second Dutch company, Berkhout Verssnijlijn, a leading meat slicing and prepacking company in the Netherlands.

By then, Ter Beke had grown into a European food processing leader. In 2006 the company reached an agreement to acquire its major Belgian competitor Pluma. The merger transformed Ter Beke into the clear leader in Belgium, placed it among the top three in the Benelux market, and positioned the company among the European leaders in the processed meats and ready-to-eat pasta segments. Following that acquisition, Ter Beke restructured its operations under two primary subsidiaries, Ter Beke-Pluma, for its processed meats, and Ready Meals, for its ready-to-eat foods. The company then acquired U.K.-based SDF Foods Ltd., which had been Pluma's sales agent in that market.

With sales approaching EUR 400 million in 2008, Ter Beke remained on the lookout for fresh growth opportunities. The company acquired France's Normandie Plats Cuisinés (NPC), a fresh pasta meals producer. Then, in 2008, the company launched talks to acquire Marcinelle-based Fresh Concept SA, a provider of meat slicing services.

Ter Beke itself had seen a changing of the guard, as Daniel Coopman retired to an honorary chairmanship in 2007. De Bruyckere became the company's chairman, while Marc Hofman, who had joined the company as its chief financial officer in 1997, became managing director. Ter Beke set its sights on consolidating its position among the European leaders in the processed meats and ready-meals markets.

M. L. Cohen

PRINCIPAL SUBSIDIARIES

Binet SA; Come a Casa SA; Fresh Meals Nederland BV; Fresh Meals NV; Fresh Meals UK Ltd.; Landeveld-Sleegers BV (Netherlands); Les Nutons SA; NS Vamos et Cie SA; NV Heku; NV Pluma; NV Ter Beke Immo; NV Ter Beke Vleeswarenproduktie; NV Ter Beke-Pluma; Pluma Fleischwarenvertrieb GmbH (Germany); Ter Beke (Deutschland) GmbH; Ter Beke France SA; Ter Beke Iberica SL (Spain); Ter Beke Pluma France SA; Ter Beke Pluma UK Ltd.; Ter Beke-Pluma Nederland BV.

PRINCIPAL DIVISIONS

Processed Meat; Ready Meals.

PRINCIPAL COMPETITORS

Unilever N.V.; VION Holding N.V.; DANISH CROWN AmbA; Nestlé France S.A.S.; Terrena S.C.A.; Myasomolprom Industrial Group; Sadia S.A.; Ebro Puleva S.A.; B and C Toennies Fleischwerk GmbH und Company KG; Fleury Michon SA.

FURTHER READING

El Amin, Ahmed, "Ter Beke Hit by Margin Fall Due to Higher Costs, Retailer Pressure," *Meatprocess.com,* September 15, 2006.

Fonteyn, Guido, "En Flandre, On Est 'Les Wallons,' Ici, 'Les Flamands,'" *La Libre,* July 9, 2005.

"Introducing Ter Beke," *Gondola,* December 1, 2006.

"Merger Creates Biggest Processed Meat Co.," *just-food.com,* March 17, 2006.

Scheir, Olivier, "Onze Carrièreplanning Was Álles Geven voor de Zaak," *Nieuwsblad,* March 7, 2007.

Suy, Pieter, "Familie Coopman Verstevigt Belang in Ter Beker," *De Tijd,* May 8, 2008.

"Ter Beke Expands into France," *Bakeryandsnacks.com,* July 3, 2003.

Van Thuyne, Dirk, "Welk Vlees Heeft Ter Beke in de Kuip?" *Trends,* March 23, 2006.

TITAN MACHINERY Your Solutions Dealer

Titan Machinery Inc.

——————■——————

4876 Rocking Horse Creek
Fargo, North Dakota 58104
U.S.A.
Telephone: (701) 356-0130
Fax: (701) 356-0139
Web site: http://www.titanmachinery.com

Public Company
Incorporated: 1980 as Titan Machinery, LLC
Employees: 716
Sales: $432.97 million (2008)
Stock Exchanges: NASDAQ
Ticker Symbol: TITN
NAICS: 423820 Farm and Garden Machinery and
Equipment Merchant Wholesalers; 423810
Construction and Mining (Except Oil Well)
Machinery and Equipment Merchant Wholesalers

■ ■ ■

Titan Machinery Inc. owns a chain of agricultural and construction dealerships in the upper Midwest. The company's stores, which range in size from 5,000 square feet to 40,000 square feet, serve farmers, construction contractors, public utilities, municipalities, and maintenance contractors in North Dakota, South Dakota, Minnesota, Iowa, and Nebraska. Titan Machinery's stores primarily sell and service equipment made by CNH Global N.V., a Dutch manufacturer based in Amsterdam that produces farm and construction equipment under the Case IH, Case Construction, New Holland, and New Holland Construction brand names. Titan Machinery ranks as the largest retail dealer of Case IH agricultural equipment in the world. Equipment stocked in the more than 60 stores operated by the company includes combines, tractors, sprayers, cranes, excavators, forklifts, and backhoes. Titan Machinery also operates internationally, selling equipment to customers in Eastern Europe.

ORIGINS

For roughly its first 20 years in business, Titan Machinery kept a relatively low profile, relative to the decidedly more aggressive and ambitious posture it assumed during the ensuing years. A dramatic change in a company's personality typically occurred alongside a change in management, but in Titan Machinery's case its two dissimilar eras of existence were governed by the same individual, David Meyer. Meyer founded the company in 1980 after spending the previous four years as a partner in an agricultural equipment dealership, managing precisely the type of company he would acquire as CEO of Titan Machinery.

IMPORTANCE OF THE CASE AND NEW HOLLAND BRAND NAMES

Meyer's North Dakota-based dealership sold agricultural equipment marketed under the brand names Case and New Holland. The tractors, combines, sprayers, and related equipment he sold in the towns of Lisbon and Wahpeton were manufactured by two U.S.-based companies, Case Corporation and Sperry New Holland. The two companies were of vital importance to Meyer, providing nearly all the equipment that would be sold at his dealerships for more than 30 years. Case, founded in the mid-19th century, manufactured a full range of agricultural and construction equipment, holding sway as a $2 billion powerhouse when Meyer operated his dealerships in Lisbon and Wahpeton. Sperry New Holland, founded in 1895, was a market leader as well, having revolutionized the harvesting equipment market with the introduction of the world's first twin-rotor combine in the mid-1970s. The company manufactured a family of products coveted by several corporate suitors. After being acquired by Sperry Corporation in 1947, the company was purchased by Ford Motor Co. in 1986, operating as Ford New Holland, Inc., until Italian conglomerate Fiat S.p.A. purchased the company in 1991, using it to form a Netherlands-based subsidiary named New Holland N.V.

After founding Titan Machinery in 1980 in Fargo, North Dakota, Meyer set out to acquire other dealerships, positioning himself as a consolidator of retail businesses operating in the upper Midwest. Although his dealerships stocked equipment made by companies such as Deere & Company and Caterpillar Inc., Meyer primarily focused on dealerships that had forged wholesale agreements with Case and New Holland.

Meyer's business grew slowly during the 1980s and 1990s, building a foundation in North Dakota and in neighboring Minnesota. By the end of the 1990s, Titan Machinery, after 20 years of growth, was a financially healthy, midsized business. As Titan Machinery entered the 21st century, however, its size began to increase at a pace unseen during its first two decades of business. Meyer, like a jockey on a racehorse, went to the whip, spurring Titan Machinery forward to a point where Wall Street investors took notice of his actions.

At the end of the 1990s, the principal brands stocked in Meyer's dealerships were joined under one corporate umbrella. In 1999, New Holland acquired Case, creating a new behemoth in the industry, CNH Global N.V. CNH Global, at the time of the merger, ranked as the second largest manufacturer of agricultural equipment, trailing Deere & Company, and the third largest producer of construction equipment, trailing Caterpillar and the Japanese giant Komatsu Ltd. Under the CNH Global umbrella, a handful of agricultural and construction brands were pertinent to Titan Machinery's dealerships: Case IH Agriculture, New Holland Agriculture, Case Construction, and New Holland Construction. Within a decade of the New Holland and Case union, Meyer would make Titan Machinery the world's largest retailer of Case IH Agricultural equipment and a major U.S. retailer of the New Holland Agriculture, Case Construction, and New Holland Construction brands.

PETER CHRISTIANSON JOINS TITAN MACHINERY IN 2002

Titan Machinery began to increase in size at a rapid rate not long after New Holland acquired Case. Beginning in 2001, Meyer acquired dealerships in earnest, completing 18 transactions during the ensuing five years. One of the most important acquisitions came early on in the acquisition spree, a purchase that gave Meyer another dealership and his aide-de-camp for the expansion campaign set to unfold. In 2002, Meyer acquired C.I. Farm Power, Inc., a two-store dealership owned by Peter Christianson. Christianson was appointed president of Titan Machinery in 2003, the same year his brother, Ted Christianson, was appointed chief financial officer.

THE TITAN OPERATING MODEL

With the infusion of new executives, Titan Machinery set out to secure control of the upper Midwest, seeking to billow in size by adding new dealerships to its ranks. As Meyer led his team forward, he applied what the company referred to as the "Titan Operating Model" to each acquisition he completed. The organizational approach encouraged entrepreneurship among Titan Machinery's dealers, promoting "front-line decision making," according to Peter Christianson in the November 14, 2006 issue of *Agweek*. Store managers enjoyed considerable control over their stores, earning a salary based upon their stores' revenue, profitability, and market share, and by meeting predetermined balance sheet objectives. Each store's parts manager, service manager, and field marketers reported directly to the store manager, who determined the mix of the store's inventory and the prices of the equipment stocked in the store. At company headquarters in Fargo, store managers received the support of Titan Machinery's

KEY DATES

1980: David Meyer establishes Titan Machinery in Fargo, North Dakota.

2002: Meyer acquires C.I. Farm Power, Inc., a dealership owned by Peter Christianson, who becomes Titan Machinery's president in 2003.

2004: Titan Machinery makes its first overseas sale, selling 16 used combines to a customer in Ukraine.

2007: Titan Machinery completes its initial public offering of stock.

2008: With the acquisition of Mid-Land Equipment Co., Titan Machinery gains its first location in Nebraska.

"Shared Resource Center," which performed numerous tasks that independent dealerships had to complete on their own. Matters related to accounting, human resources, information and technology services, advertising, administration, and training were handled on the corporate level in Fargo, leaving store managers free to concentrate on parts, sales, and services to their customers.

2003–05: EXPANDING THE DEALERSHIP NETWORK

With new management in place and the Titan Operating Model ready to be applied to an expanding network of dealerships, Meyer began acquiring Case and New Holland dealerships. In 2003, he purchased North Dakota-based Krider Equipment Co., Inc., an acquisition that added stores in Fargo and Bismarck. He also acquired Fargo Tractor & Equipment, Inc., which operated a store in West Fargo. By the end of the year, Titan Machinery generated $66.5 million in revenue. The company collected the bulk of its revenue, $43.5 million, from new equipment sales and generated the remainder of its volume from parts and service sales.

After shoring up his company's presence in North Dakota in 2003, Meyer turned his attention to expanding into neighboring states. In early 2004, he acquired Consolidated Ag Services, Inc., which operated three stores in the Minnesota communities of Graceville, Marshall, and Pipestone. Next, he advanced into Iowa, completing three separate acquisitions in 2005 that added a half-dozen new stores to Titan Machinery's fold. In March 2005, Smith International, Inc., was

acquired, giving the company a store in Waverly. In November 2005, two transactions were completed, the purchase of Walterman Implement, Inc., which operated a store in Dike, and the purchase of Vern Anderson, Inc., a dealership with stores in Anthon, Cherokee, Kingsley, and Le Mars. The year also included one acquisition outside Iowa, the purchase of H.C. Clark Implement Co., Inc., a New Holland dealership with a store in Aberdeen, South Dakota.

By the end of 2005, the Titan Operating Model had been applied to 18 farm and construction equipment stores. The shared resources group in Fargo provided support to dealerships in the four-state territory of North Dakota, South Dakota, Iowa, and Minnesota, and the store managers, in turn, produced laudable financial results. By the end of the year, Titan Machinery's revenues had reached $162 million, two-and-a-half times the total generated two years earlier. During the next two years, the company's revenues nearly doubled again, as Meyer and Christianson pressed ahead with their expansion campaign.

TITAN MACHINERY LOOKS ABROAD

The scope of Titan Machinery's expansion campaign broadened considerably after Christianson joined the company. International expansion had become a focus of the company's plans, drawing its impetus from Christianson. Christianson began forming business relationships in Ukraine in 1998 while he was managing his own dealership, C.I. Farm Power, Inc. He met a Ukrainian distributor of Case equipment who invited him to visit Ukraine. "He wanted me to assess their farm equipment deal distribution network, Christianson explained in the January 15, 2008 issue of *Agweek*. "They were farming with 1950s machinery," he added. The region, known as the breadbasket of Europe, represented an ideal export market for a company such as C.I. Farm Power, but while Christianson was in Ukraine, the Russian ruble plummeted in value, forcing Christianson to wait for economic conditions to improve before courting customers in the region.

By the time Christianson joined Titan Machinery in 2002, the economic climate in Ukraine had improved. The first steps toward forging ties in Ukraine were taken in 2003, when Titan Machinery hired Olga Vasilyeva, a native of Irkutsk, Siberia, who had earned a graduate degree in international marketing. "We made a commitment that after she got our domestic marketing developed that we would look at any possibilities in international marketing," Christianson said in the January 15, 2008 issue of *Agweek*. Within a year, the marketing department in Fargo was running smoothly enough to permit Titan Machinery's first look overseas. In April 2004, Vasilyeva organized a trip to visit U.S. Commerce Department trade offices in Ukraine and Russia, giving Titan Machinery executives, Christianson included, the opportunity to build a customer base. "We called on three businesses a day for 10 days—cold calls," Christianson told *Agweek*. Within two weeks, Christianson and his colleagues celebrated their first overseas sale, an order for 16 used combines placed by a customer in Ukraine.

CONVERSION TO PUBLIC OWNERSHIP IN 2007

Back on the domestic front, Titan Machinery's acquisition campaign charged ahead, increasing in intensity in the months leading up to the company's initial public offering (IPO) of stock. In 2006, two acquisitions were completed, Farm Power, Inc., of Minnesota and Piorier Equipment Company, Inc. The two purchases gave Titan Machinery three stores in Minnesota, two stores in South Dakota, and one unit in Iowa. At the end of the year, Christianson announced the company planned to acquire three or four dealerships a year as it pressed forward, but Titan Machinery exceeded projections in 2007. The company completed five acquisitions during the year, adding three stores in North Dakota, three stores in South Dakota, and two stores in Minnesota. Titan Machinery concluded the year by making its debut on Wall Street, completing an IPO in December that raised roughly $42 million.

ANTICIPATION OF FURTHER ACQUISITIONS

With the proceeds from the IPO, Meyer was armed to ratchet up his acquisitive efforts. "I've got a full pipeline of future acquisitions of dealerships who have called me," he said in the February 20, 2008 issue of *Investor's Business Daily*. "If you look at the demographics, you've got aging dealers in a fragmented industry. You've got a lack of capital and a lack of succession [options]." The years ahead promised to see Titan Machinery especially active on the acquisition front, as Meyer embraced the role of industry consolidator. "Nobody of any size or scale that we are aware of is trying to consolidate their industry," an analyst explained in the February 20, 2008 issue of *Investor's Business Daily*. There's always some level of competition from smaller mom-and-pops trying to expand their presence, but they tend not to have the access to capital to be really competitive in a bid against Titan."

In the years leading up to Meyer's 30th anniversary in charge of Titan Machinery, the company recorded robust financial growth. Revenues swelled from $66 million in 2003 to $432 million in 2008, driven upward by the nearly two dozen acquisitions completed during the five-year period. The purchase of Des Moines, Iowa-based Mid-Land Equipment Co. in mid-2008 signaled that the years ahead would see Meyer extend the boundaries of his operating territory. The acquisition added six stores and nearly $50 million in annual revenues, but, most important, the acquisition marked the company's entry into Nebraska, giving Titan Machinery a presence in five states. With more than 700 CNH Group dealers in the country representing potential acquisition targets, Meyer had a wealth of opportunities for expansion as he sought to secure a stranglehold on the Case and New Holland retail market.

Jeffrey L. Covell

PRINCIPAL SUBSIDIARIES

Transportation Solutions, LLC.

PRINCIPAL DIVISIONS

Agricultural; Construction; International.

PRINCIPAL COMPETITORS

Deere & Company; RDO Equipment Co.; Caterpillar Inc.

FURTHER READING

DeWitte, Dave, "Mid-Land Equipment Acquired by Titan Machinery," *Cedar Rapids (Iowa) Gazette,* May 13, 2008.

"HC Clark Implement Inc. Sold to Titan Machinery of Fargo, N.D.," *Aberdeen (S.Dak.) American News,* June 25, 2005.

Lee, Stephen J., "Titan's Rapid Rise," *Grand Forks (N.Dak.) Herald,* January 21, 2008.

"N.D. Machinery Company Helps Change Face of Farming in Ukraine," *Agweek,* January 15, 2008.

Pates, Mikkel, "Titan Machinery Cited by Trade Journal," *Agweek,* November 14, 2006.

Reeves, Amy, "Titan Machinery—Fargo, North Dakota Farm Equipment Distributor Grows by Acquiring Mom-and-Pop Shops," *Investor's Business Daily,* February 20, 2008, p. A6.

Tomra Systems ASA

P.O. Box 362
Asker, N-1372
Norway
Telephone: (+47 66) 79 91 00
Fax: (+47 66) 79 91 11
Web site: http://www.tomra.com

Public Company
Incorporated: 1972
Employees: 2,022
Sales: NOK 3.62 billion ($580 million) (2008)
Stock Exchanges: Oslo
Ticker Symbol: TOM
NAICS: 333999 All Other Miscellaneous General Purpose Machinery Manufacturing

∎ ∎ ∎

Tomra Systems ASA is the world's leading producer of reverse vending machines (RVMs) for the recovery and recycling of deposit bottles and other refillable containers. RVMs essentially reverse the retail process: customers return their refillable bottles and other containers and receive their deposit fee back. The Asker, Norway-based company, which pioneered this category, remains the dominant player, and at times has enjoyed a market share as high as 95 percent in Europe and 80 percent in North America. In 2009 Tomra Systems counted an installed base of more than 65,000 RVMs in 40 countries. Europe is the group's primary market; other major markets include the United States and Canada. In the United States, Tomra is also a major player in the materials handling sector, operating beverage container collection centers, as well as the pickup, transportation, sorting, and compaction of these containers. The Material Handling division is active especially in California.

Since early in the first decade of the 2000s, Tomra has launched an effort to reduce its reliance on the deposit-container segment, grouped under its Collection Technology Deposit Solutions division. The company has been developing two new business units, Collection Technology Non-deposit Solutions and Industrial Processing Technology. The former has been developing automated container collection technologies to serve as container recycling centers. The latter business unit focuses on developing recognition and sorting technologies, as well as compaction machinery, for waste materials handling and recycling centers.

Tomra's efforts to diversify its revenue stream have enabled the company to reduce its dependence on the Collection Technology Deposit Solutions division, which represented just 49 percent of the group's revenues at the end of 2008, down from 80 percent just the year before. Material Handling added 29 percent to revenues, while Industrial Processing Technology accounted for 19 percent. The Collection Technology Non-deposit Solutions division, while generating just 3 percent of revenues, has been buoyed by a contract for 100 recycling centers from the United Kingdom's Tesco retail group. Tomra is listed on the Oslo Stock Exchange and is led by CEO and President Amund Skarholt. In

```
┌─────────────────────────────────────────┐
│                                         │
│     COMPANY PERSPECTIVES                │
│                  ■                      │
│                                         │
│   Mission: Helping the world recycle. Vision: A leading │
│   global provider of advanced solutions enabling │
│   recovery and recycling of materials.  │
│                                         │
└─────────────────────────────────────────┘
```

2008 the company posted total sales of NOK 3.62 billion ($580 million).

PIONEERING RVMS IN THE SEVENTIES

Tomra Systems was founded by brothers Petter and Tore Planke in the town of Asker, Norway, in 1972. The idea behind the company came from Petter while he was working as a salesman selling labeling and pricing equipment to the Norwegian supermarket sector at the beginning of that decade.

In 1971 the head of a large supermarket chain approached Petter Planke to ask if his company had a solution for processing the large quantity of deposit bottles returned to the supermarket chain each day. Planke's company did not, however, produce this type of equipment. Instead, Planke proposed that the supermarket head discuss the matter with Tore Planke, a mechanical engineer then working for the Norwegian Institute of Technology's Foundation for Scientific and Industrial Research.

Tore Planke's focus at the foundation had been on developing the world's first fully automated navigational system for use by supertankers. Nonetheless, he agreed to take on the project, combining his mechanical engineering background with his experience working with cutting-edge microelectronics technology.

Working in his spare time, Tore Planke came up with his first design by the end of 1971. The supermarket owner agreed to fund the construction of a prototype, and by the beginning of January 1972, the Plankes had placed their first RVM in a store.

By April of that year, Petter Planke had secured orders for 15 more machines. The brothers then decided to found their own company, joined by their father, Sverre Planke, who became the company's first chairman. The company quickly began filling its order book, and by the end of 1972 had placed 29 machines in Norwegian shops. Word of the innovative machinery spread quickly, and by October of that year the young company had shipped its first RVM to the United States.

TECHNOLOGICAL SUCCESS IN 1977

Other markets quickly followed; by 1973 the company had begun to supply machinery across Europe. A new milestone for the company came in 1974, when Tomra received a contract for 100 specially designed machines for Sweden's Systembolaget, which controlled the country's state-owned retail alcohol monopoly. The contract provided Tomra with the financial basis for building a new 1,000-square-meter factory that year.

Through the middle of the 1970s, Tomra's RVMs relied on photocell technology for bottle recognition and handling. Yet the use of photocells was both costly and cumbersome, requiring that the RVM machine be manually adjusted for each bottle type. The rapid advances in electronic technology made during the decade provided Tomra with its next breakthrough product. In 1978 the company introduced its Tomra SP, for self-programmable, RVM, which used microprocessors to recognize and adjust automatically to different bottle types.

The launch of the SP allowed Tomra to stay ahead of the growing field of competitors. Indeed, one of the company's largest competitors at the time was Hugin Kassaregister AB, which had released its own RVM equipment. Following the release of the SP, however, Hugin decided to abandon its own RVM production. Instead, Hugin formed an agreement to market Tomra's machines, giving the smaller company access to Hugin's European-wide sales and distribution network. In exchange, Tomra agreed to sell Hugin a 33 percent share of the company.

The deal with Hugin enabled Tomra to do more than just expand sales of its RVM systems throughout Europe; the company quickly gained a dominant position in the European markets. Through the 1990s, Tomra's market share reached as high as 95 percent. By 1981 the deal with Hugin had provided Tomra with a solid foundation for its future international growth. In that year, therefore, Tomra and Hugin ended their agreement, and Tomra repurchased its shares from Hugin.

INTERNATIONAL UPS AND DOWNS IN THE EIGHTIES

Tomra began setting up its own sales and distribution network, opening its first subsidiary in the Netherlands in 1983. Soon after, the company added subsidiaries in Germany, Denmark, and the United States. At the same time, Tomra, fearful of the possibility that the European Community (EC) was preparing to establish new import regulations, decided to set up a manufacturing facility in the EC as well. Their choice of location was the

1972: Petter and Tore Planke debut their first reverse vending machine (RVM) for deposit bottle collection and found Tomra Systems.
1978: Introduction of self-programmable RVM.
1985: Tomra goes public on the Oslo Stock Exchange.
1992: Company adds a Material Handling division focused on the North American market.
2002: New division, Industrial Processing Technology, is launched to develop sorting and compacting systems for the recycling industry.
2008: Tomra establishes a new Collection Technology Non-deposit Solutions division and receives a major order from the Tesco supermarket group.

Netherlands, where the company acquired a factory in 1984.

Tomra's revenue growth remained in the double digits through the first half of the 1980s, posting an average annual growth rate of 36 percent. This set the stage for the company's decision to go public, with a listing on the Oslo Stock Exchange in 1985. The listing came ahead of the group's decision to expand on a large scale into the United States.

This effort nearly bankrupted the company. Although several states in the United States maintained deposit packaging laws, the majority did not. Tomra's attempt to expand its U.S. operations into the nondeposit states depended on high aluminum prices to build incentive for its RVMs. In 1986, however, the price of aluminum collapsed, following the Soviet Union's decision to dump millions of tons of aluminum into the world market. Faced with difficult market conditions in the deposit states as well, Tomra was forced to abandon its U.S. business, and posted a heavy loss for the year.

The company's European operations remained sound, however, and enabled a return to profitability by the following year. Also in 1987, Tomra debuted its newest generation of RVM technology, the Tomra 300, which became hugely successful. Within two years, the group's sales had grown by nearly two-thirds. The company also extended its sales and distribution operations to a number of new markets, including Italy and Finland. The success of the Tomra 300 also encouraged the company to try its luck in the United States again. This time, the company took a more prudent approach

to the market, establishing operations only in New York and Connecticut, both deposit states, before rolling out operations elsewhere.

MATERIALS HANDLING IN THE NINETIES

Tomra restructured its manufacturing base in the early 1990s, once it became apparent that the European Union (EU) was not going to impose import restrictions. The company shut down its Netherlands factory and consolidated all of its manufacturing operations at its Asker headquarters. This move led the company to invest in expanding its production capacity, and in 1994 Tomra unveiled a new 10,500-square-meter facility. Within a year, the company's output had grown more than one-third.

Much of Tomra's growth through the 1990s, however, came from its U.S. operations. In the early 1990s the company acquired one of its major distributors, Neroc Inc., which focused on the New York and Connecticut markets. This acquisition enabled the company to achieve significant growth rates in these markets. In 1993 sales jumped by 81 percent, followed by a new sales increase of 46 percent in 1994. By the middle of the decade, Tomra's U.S. sales accounted for some 38 percent of the group's total revenues.

Legislation helped the company's sales growth, both in the United States and in Germany. The latter market opened up for Tomra as the German government passed laws seeking to reach a 90 percent return rate on beverage containers by 1997. Similarly, in the United States, ten more states adopted bottle-return laws. As a result, Tomra's sales expanded to Michigan, Oregon, Maine, and Massachusetts.

Tomra had also begun to explore other operational areas. In 1992 the group decided to enter the materials handling market, that is, the collection, transporting, and sorting of recyclable containers and packaging. The new operations provided an important extension to the company's RVM business. At the same time, the company was able to penetrate new markets, particularly California, where the company rapidly became the leading player in the sector.

NEW MARKETS FOR THE NEW MILLENNIUM

Tomra also completed a number of acquisitions through the 1990s, in order to build its U.S. presence. In 1996 the company acquired the Deposit Legislation division of RRT Inc., part of Waste Management Inc., and active in the Syracuse and Rochester markets in New York

State. The following year, Tomra acquired Albany, New York-based Carco Inc. for $3 million. Then, in 1998 Tomra took a 50 percent stake in Wise Recycling LLC, which itself had acquired the national recycling operations of Reynolds Metals Co. By the end of the 1990s, Tomra's U.S. operations generated more than half of the group's total turnover. By then, the company's turnover had also passed the NOK 2 billion mark.

The company turned its attention to the Latin American markets at the start of the 21st century. The group gained a foothold on the South American continent in 2001 through a joint-venture agreement with beverage can manufacturer Latas de Alumínio. In 2005, however, Tomra abandoned Brazil, selling its holdings there to Aleris of the United States. In Europe, meanwhile, Tomra increased its dominance of the continent's RVM sector by taking over the RVM portfolio from Eleiko, of Sweden.

Tomra's near-monopoly status in Europe soon brought it difficulties from the EU competition authorities. In 2006 the company was accused of abusing its market dominance during the period between 1998 and 2002, and was hit by a fine of EUR 24 million.

DIVERSIFYING TOWARD 2010

As it moved into the new century, however, Tomra adopted a new strategy in order to reduce its dependence on the deposit-return sector. The company saw an opportunity to extend its expertise into the broader recycling industry. Toward this end, in 2002 the group inaugurated a new division, Industrial Processing Technology. This division then began targeting growth in recognition and sorting systems, as well as compacting equipment, for the recycling sector.

The new division became active starting from 2004, when Tomra acquired TiTech, a company that specialized in sorting technologies. By 2005 Tomra had also acquired the Orwak Group, adding that company's expertise in compacting systems. Tomra's Industrial Processing division grew again in 2006, as the company acquired Wedel, Germany-based CommoDaS, which developed recognition and sorting technologies.

Rising environmental concerns, particularly in Europe, encouraged Tomra to begin branching out from its core deposit-based packaging operations. The company added another business unit, Collection Technology Non-deposit Solutions, and began developing automated packaging collection centers. This effort received a boost in 2007 when the United Kingdom's Tesco supermarket group placed an order for 100 recycling centers. Tomra also formed joint ventures with

companies in Japan and Greece to develop its recycling operations in those markets as well. By the beginning of 2009, Tomra had succeeded in reducing its reliance on the deposit-bottle sector, which accounted for just 49 percent of sales. Tomra had prepared itself to remain a major player in the future recycling market.

M. L. Cohen

PRINCIPAL SUBSIDIARIES

B-burken AB (Sweden); Camco Recycling Inc. (Canada); Compactus AB (Sweden); Halton System GmbH (Germany); Halton System Inc. (USA); Orwak Group AB (Sweden); OY Tomra AB (Finland); Presona GmbH (Germany); QVision AS; Titech Visionsort AS; Titech Visionsort Co., Ltd. (Korea); Tomra AG (Switzerland; 50.5%); Tomra Baltic OÜ (Estonia; 40%); Tomra Butikksystemer AS; Tomra Canada Inc.; Tomra Europe AS; Tomra Japan Asia Pacific KK; Tomra Leergutsysteme GmbH (Austria); Tomra of North America Inc. (USA); Tomra Pacific Inc. (Canada); Tomra Production AS; Tomra s.r.o (Czech Republic; 40%); Tomra System AS (Denmark); Tomra Systems AB (Sweden); Tomra Systems BV (Netherlands); Tomra Systems GmbH (Germany); Tomra Systems Inc. (Canada); Tomra Systems Ltd. (UK); Tomra Systems NV (Belgium); Tomra Systems SA (France); UBCR (U.S.A.; 51%).

PRINCIPAL DIVISIONS

Collection Technology Deposit Solutions; Collection Technology Non-deposit Solutions; Material Handling; Industrial Processing Technology.

PRINCIPAL COMPETITORS

Wincor Nixdorf GmbH; Digi/Repant ASA; Envipco Inc.; Metal Management, Inc.; Biffa plc; CMA Corporation Pty Ltd.

FURTHER READING

Marley, Michael, "Aluminum Scrap Price Gains Lift Tomra Results," *American Metal Market,* February 15, 2007, p. 8.

"Record Fine for Tomra Group for Abuse of Dominant Position," *Europe Agri,* April 7, 2006.

Reinhardt, Andy, "Tomra Systems," *Business Week,* January 26, 2004, p. 60.

Schaffer, Paul, "Tomra Hoping Smaller Machine Lifts US Role," *American Metal Market,* December 19, 2008, p. 10.

———, "Tomra Tries to Break Reverse Vending Machine Reliance," *American Metal Market,* November 10, 2005, p. 7.

"Tomra Books German Vending Machine Order," *American Metal Market,* January 18, 2006, p. 8.

"Tomra, Sumitomo Ink Recycling Deal," *American Metal Market,* May 24, 2006, p. 8.

"Tomra Systems Signs Accord to Work with Brazil's Latasa," *American Metal Market,* November 27, 2000, p. 22.

"Tomra to Acquire Sorting Technology Developer," *American Metal Market,* June 13, 2006, p. 8.

Worden, Edward, "Norway's Tomra Plans to Devour More UBCs," *American Metal Market,* July 3, 1997, p. 6.

———, "Tomra Gets US Boost," *American Metal Market,* March 2, 1999, p. 9.

———, "Tomra Schedules Writedowns As Recycle Rates, Prices Slump," *American Metal Market,* January 16, 2002, p. 6.

Tri-State Generation and Transmission Association, Inc.

1100 West 116th Avenue
Westminster, Colorado 80234-2814
U.S.A.
Telephone: (303) 452-6111
Fax: (303) 254-6013
Web site: http://www.tristategt.org

Private Company
Incorporated: 1952
Employees: 1,137
Sales: $1.16 billion (2008)
NAICS: 221112 Fossil Fuel Electric Power Generation; 221119 Other Electric Power Generation; 221122 Electric Power Distribution

■ ■ ■

Tri-State Generation and Transmission Association, Inc., manages power generation, transmission, and distribution for its 44 rural electricity cooperatives in Wyoming, Colorado, Nebraska, and New Mexico. The organization dispatches energy from its headquarters in Westminster, Colorado, to local member utilities, who serve more than 13 million customers, including residential, farm, industrial, and commercial customers. In addition to acquiring 1,078 megawatt hours from western hydroelectric sources, Tri-State produces 2,458 megawatt-hours at 11 owned, partially owned, or leased generating stations. Coal powers approximately 72 percent of electricity produced by Tri-State, and Tri-State owns interests in coal mining operations that supply the organization's power plants. Natural gas, oil, and

alternative energy sources, such as wind and solar power, supply the balance of energy produced or purchased. With 5,206 miles of transmission lines, the organization dispatches 19 million megawatt-hours of electricity to members and five million megawatt-hours to nonmembers each year.

SUPPLY CRISIS DURING THE FIFTIES

The roots of Tri-State Generation and Transmission Association originated in the 1930s, when President Franklin D. Roosevelt's New Deal programs funded development of consumer-owned, electric cooperatives in rural areas too expensive for the large companies to serve. The Bureau of Reclamation handled the marketing and distribution of federal hydroelectric power to rural electric cooperatives, and "Bureau power" was the cooperatives' primary source of electricity. The formation of Tri-State stemmed from a projected shortage of electricity as demand increased during the early 1950s. The Bureau warned that supply would not meet demand after 1956.

In 1951 the representatives of 15 rural cooperatives met to discuss meeting projected electricity demand. The meeting prompted each organization to conduct surveys of future usage, and when the group reconvened two months later, the surveys confirmed that a shortage of electricity would occur in four to five years. The cooperatives decided to join together to create a more reliable and cost-effective system of power generation and transmission. An informal association was empowered to begin feasibility studies for a thermal generating plant. The articles of incorporation for Tri-State Generation and Transmission Association were signed May 19, 1952, with 26 rural cooperatives in Wyoming, Colorado, and Nebraska becoming owner-members of the association.

Initially, Tri-State intended to develop its own power sources. The organization applied to the Bureau of Reclamation to produce 75,000 kilowatts of firm power and 50,000 kilowatts of seasonal power, the latter to meet periods of high demand. In 1956 Tri-State received a $9.96 million loan from the Rural Electrification Administration (REA), intended to be applied toward construction of a 40 megawatt thermal plant. However, as the federal government developed new power generation and transmission projects, the need for private power plants diminished. Tri-State renegotiated the contract with its members to cover only the acquisition of power for resale. The association purchased electricity from the Missouri River Basin, as allocated by the Bureau of Reclamation, and began billing its members in October 1957 from its office in Loveland, Colorado. During the first year of operation, Tri-State delivered 37.45 million kilowatt hours through 100 points of delivery.

Demand for electricity continued to increase during the early 1960s, along with economic activity. Agriculture, especially irrigation pumping, oil and gas development, mining, residential growth, as well as military intercontinental ballistic missile systems in Colorado, drew from Tri-State's power resources. The situation required Tri-State to develop power transmission lines and new power supplies. In 1965 Tri-State obtained approval to apply funds from the REA loan to construct three transmission lines and substations. The infrastructure supported new power supply obtained from Basin Electric Power Cooperative, which provided electricity to Tri-State members in Nebraska beginning in 1966. After several years of actively supporting development of the Colorado River Storage Project (CRSP), a series of 11 hydroelectric plants along the Colorado River and its tributaries, Tri-State gained ac-

cess to electricity for its Colorado and Wyoming members in February 1969. By 1971 approximately 25 percent of Tri-State's electricity supply came from CRSP, and association members enjoyed many years of low rates.

A problem developed in serving Tri-State's Nebraska members, located primarily on the United States' eastern energy supply grid. The "DC Tie," completed in 1967, connected the power transmission lines of the eastern and western United States for the first time. The event was compared to the joining of the transcontinental railroad in the mid-19th century. The DC Tie allowed Tri-State to purchase and transmit 100 megawatts of power across the grid. The DC Tie resolved national transmission problems, also, as the Bureau of Reclamation required the facility to transmit power. Located at the Stegall, Nebraska, station, the tie became permanent in 1976.

DEVELOPING POWER SUPPLIES, MEETING NEW RESPONSIBILITIES: SEVENTIES

After many years of solving power access and transmission problems, Tri-State decided to undertake power generation development. A 1970 study revealed potential power shortages by 1975. To handle short-term increases, Tri-State built two small, oil-fired combustion turbine plants in Colorado. The Republican River Station in Wray began operation in June 1975, producing 210 megawatts at peak demand. Burlington Station opened in the town of the same name in 1977; it provided 100 megawatts of electricity.

Tri-State's first large scale power generation development, the Yampa Project, involved construction of three coal-fired generating units at Craig, Colorado. The Salt River Project of Arizona, the Colorado-Ute Electric Association, and the Platte River Power Authority partnered in the plant, called the Laramie River Station. Tri-State owned a 24 percent share in the Craig facility, which began operations in 1979. Tri-State obtained 205 megawatts from Units 1 and 2, the organization's first coal-fired operations.

The DC Tie made possible the Missouri Basin Power Project (MBPP), which involved six partners across the eastern and western grids: Tri-State, Basin Electric, Wyoming Municipal Power Association, Western Minnesota Municipal Power Agency, Heartland Consumers Public Power District, and Lincoln Electric. MBPP's Laramie River Station began operations in 1982. Tri-State's 24.13 percent share of the 1,650 megawatt coal-fired plant reaped 398 megawatts of electricity for member cooperatives.

The two power generating projects required Tri-State to invest in every aspect of power generation and transmission. To ensure adequate fuel for the plants, Tri-State co-charted the Western Fuels Association (WFA), a coal acquisition cooperative that reduced the resource costs for Tri-State and its partners. Also, the Yampa Project participants purchased the Trapper Mine, adjacent to the Craig facility. At the power plants themselves, new environmental laws required the installation of scrubbers to reduce pollution emissions. Tri-State installed several miles of transmission lines to carry electricity, at 115 kilovolts and 230 kilovolts. Even after rapid expansion during the early 1970s, Tri-State's transmission infrastructure doubled from 650 miles of line in 1976 to 1,308 miles of line in 1982. Furthermore, expansion and infrastructure projects required Tri-State to double its staff, and Tri-State began construction of a new headquarters in Thornton, Colorado, north of Denver, in 1975.

When the Western Area Power Administration (WAPA) began managing federal hydropower facilities in 1977, Tri-State was required to begin dispatching electricity to its customers, a responsibility previously handled by the Bureau of Reclamation. Tri-State started planning for a state-of-the-art Energy Management System, which involved installation of 35 microwave communication towers. Integration of that system with the Supervisory Control and Data Acquisition System allowed Tri-State to monitor generation and substation voltages and frequency and circuit breaker status. This information provided the foundation for efficiently predicting daily and seasonal power usage, then dispatching electricity to members reliably.

NEW SURGE IN DEMAND AND PLANT DEVELOPMENT

Extensive infrastructure development caused a significant increase in the cost of operations by the late 1970s, and loan repayment brought an end to low utility rates for Tri-State customers. While hydroelectric power had cost 6 mills per kilowatt hour, new power sources cost 12 to 14 mills during normal usage and 50 mills at peak usage. By 1979, Tri-State customers paid an average of 32.97 mills, for which Tri-State paid 28.37 mills. Tri-State raised rates to accommodate its operational needs, but the organization was well prepared for future growth.

After frantically building power generation and transmission infrastructure, demand for electricity began to slow during the early 1980s. Although the association experienced a decline in revenues, it used this time to refine its processes and become more efficient. Having overbuilt its power capacity, Tri-State found itself with a surplus of energy, which it sold to other utility companies, including Public Service Company of Colorado (later Xcel Energy). Some contracts extended to 2001. Revenues from surplus energy increased from $23 million in 1983 to $73 million in 1989. The availability of a surplus meant that member cooperatives overpaid for earlier projects, so Tri-State refunded $9 million to members in 1990.

As demand for electricity increased during the mid-1980s, Tri-State began building infrastructure and investing in the future. New projects included transmission lines and substations as well as the acquisition of the Dry Fork Mine, a low-sulfur coal mine in Gillette, Wyoming. In 1988 Tri-State began negotiations to acquire assets from Colorado-Ute Electric Association, then in bankruptcy reorganization. The sale of the Republican River Station, for $22 million, in 1989, offset the costs of new projects. In 1994, Tri-State acquired a small interest in the San Juan Generating Station, in northwestern New Mexico. The new power source compensated for the decline of electricity available from hydropower.

COLORADO GROWTH DOMINATES TRI-STATE ACTIVITIES

During the 1990s, Colorado experienced tremendous population and economic growth, which created a need for new sources of electricity in that state. No new plants had been built in Colorado since the 1980s, and the only increase in supply came from conversion of a nuclear plant to natural gas by the Public Service Company. In time to meet that demand, and after four years of extensive negotiations, Tri-State purchased two major assets from Colorado-Ute Electric, valued at $400 million. In 1992, Tri-State obtained ownership of the 100 megawatt Nucla Station in southwestern Colorado and the lease of Unit 3 of the Craig Station. The new systems added ten new member cooperatives to Tri-State, allowing the organization to disperse operating costs over a larger consumer base, thus reducing costs for all members. The Colorado-Ute deal included an ownership interest in the Trapper Mine, increasing Tri-State's ownership share to 33.67 percent of the coal mine.

Originally a stoker boiler facility, the Nucla Station had been a demonstration project for "clean coal," coal with low sulfur content. Implementation of a circulating fluidized-bed combustion technology, designed for burning low-sulfur coal, successfully lowered pollution emissions. Tri-State tested three kinds of Western coal, ranging in sulfur content from 0.4 percent to 1.5 percent, raising expectations that sulfur dioxide (SO_2) emissions would be reduced by 90 percent and nitrogen oxide (NO_x) by 82 percent. Once the acquisition of the Nucla facility was complete, the U.S. Department of Energy (DOE) provided a $19.9 million loan toward upgrading the facility. The $54 million project involved installation of ten-megawatt atmospheric circulating fluidized bed (ACFB) technology. In August 1995, Tri-State reported that implementation of the technology exceeded early testing, with emission reductions of SO_2 at 95.8 percent and NO_x at 95.4 percent. The efficiency of the plant positively affected operating revenues and enabled Tri-State to begin repayment of the loan, in biannual increments based on a percentage of net revenues.

Expected deregulation of the electrical utilities prompted Tri-State to implement a reorganization plan that would reduce costs. In 1996, Tri-State sold properties in Montrose, Colorado, which came with the Colorado-Ute deal, and consolidated field offices at a central location in Westminster, thus reducing travel expenditures. Tri-State began construction on a new headquarters adjacent to a power dispatching facility in Westminster, north of Denver. The $13.3 million

project enabled Tri-State to eliminate duplicate operations, locating information systems, scheduling, inventory control, engineering, finance, human resources, communications, and procurement at one site.

By 1998 load growth and record heat in the Rocky Mountain region prompted Tri-State to develop new sources of electricity. Tri-State reactivated Burlington Station and purchased an option for power at American Atlas 1 at Rifle, Colorado. After purchase, the latter property was renamed the Rifle Generating Station.

In June 1998 Tri-State announced plans to develop renewable energy resources, such as wind and solar generation, as well as existing hydroelectric power, for its Colorado cooperative members. The decision stemmed from a movement toward environmental sustainability in Colorado, where a majority of Tri-State's members resided. By 1999 Tri-State offered wind energy in 100 kilowatt blocks. The organization sold the electricity at a premium add-on of $2.50 per month, or 2.5 cents per kilowatt hour, to offset costs of acquiring the energy.

To deal with short-term increases in supply needs, Tri-State purchased existing generating plants. Tri-State completed two construction projects in Colorado in 2002. The Limon Generating Station, near Limon, in eastern Colorado, and the Knutson Generating Station at Brighton, northeast of Denver, were commissioned that spring. The gas-fired plants, with two units each, generated 70 megawatts per unit.

PURSUING OPPORTUNITIES IN NEW MEXICO AND KANSAS

In June 2000, Tri-State completed negotiations to merge with Plains Electric Generation and Transmission in Albuquerque, New Mexico. Tri-State outbid 18 other utility companies as it offered to assume $411 million in debt. The agreement yielded the Escalante 250-megawatt coal-fired plant and a 50 percent ownership in a 45 megawatt gas-fired plant. The addition of 272.5 megawatts brought Tri-State generation to 1,524.5 megawatts. Tri-State attained access to purchase a 160-megawatt block of hydroelectric power from the WAPA. To link system power sources, Tri-State planned to invest $30 million in a new electric line. The acquisition increased Tri-State's membership to 44 cooperatives and created access to Arizona and California energy markets.

A year later, Tri-State completed construction of the Pyramid Generating Station, near Lordsburg, New Mexico. Commissioned in April 2003, the station provided power for high-peak electricity usage and back-up to cooperative members in southern New Mexico.

In 2005, Tri-State approved a resource development project that would double the organization's capacity by building two new power plants. Tri-State planned a $2.5 billion, 600-megawatt plant for Holcomb, Kansas, expecting the project to begin in 2010. In southeast Colorado, Tri-State planned to begin construction on a $1.8 billion, 600-megawatt, coal-fired plant in 2016. It was the first such plant under consideration in more than a decade. Problems with acid rain from coal-fired plants made natural gas the fuel of choice; however, higher prices for natural gas renewed interest in coal as a power resource. Environmentalists began forming resistance, as the company began acquiring water rights. Concerns about emissions from a coal-fired plant stalled progress in 2008, however.

Tri-State expected that new power projects required $700 million in new transmission lines. With the Eastern Plains Transmission Project, Tri-State intended to install a 1,000 mile, high-voltage line that would transmit wind-generated power. The line could carry up to 1,000 megawatts purchased from outside sources. With an environmental impact statement in process, Tri-State hoped to bring the project online by 2012. A memorandum of understanding with Xcel Energy promised future cooperation in developing transmission infrastructure to meet growing energy needs.

NEW AND SUSTAINABLE POWER SOURCES

As the public became more aware of the need for energy independence and the potential of renewable sources of electrical power, Tri-State acted to secure alternative energy sources. Tri-State initiated a solar energy project, Cimarron 1, a 30-megawatt power plant, enough to supply 9,000 homes. Tri-State contracted with First Solar to supply the 500,000 solar panels to be located on 250 acres in northeastern New Mexico. Construction was scheduled to begin by April 2010. Intended to meet a new legal minimum requirement for renewable energy resources in New Mexico, the plant would be one of the largest solar power plants in the world.

In July 2003, Tri-State partnered with El Paso Electric, Xcel Energy, and PNM Resources, in the first large-scale development of a commercial solar generating plant in the United States. To be located in New Mexico, the plant would use parabolic trough technology, with thermal energy the preferred method of storage. The partners sought generation at a minimum of 211,000 megawatts, up to 375,000 megawatt-hours per year. That level of power would serve between 29,000 and 52,000 average homes in New Mexico. Pending regulatory approvals, the project would be in operation by the end of 2011.

To provide power to New Mexico residents over the short term, in 2006 Tri-State completed construction of a 418 megawatt coal-fired power unit in Springerville, Arizona, near the New Mexico border. Tri-State leased the Springerville Generation Station Unit 3 from the owner. After the 34-year lease ended, Tri-State would have the option of acquiring the unit.

Environmental initiatives included exploration of transforming power plants into hybrids by adding solar panels to coal-fired power plants, to reduce greenhouse emissions. In early 2009 Tri-State announced its participation in a test project for the Ion Transport Membrane (ITM) technology developed by Air Products. By separating oxygen from air, the ceramic membrane potentially reduced power consumption at an integrated gasification combined-cycle plant that burned low-sulfur coal. The ITM showed promise to make power generation more efficient.

Mary Tradii

PRINCIPAL COMPETITORS

Basic Electric Power Cooperative; Nebraska Public Power District; PacifiCorp.; PNM Resources, Inc.; Xcel Energy, Inc.

FURTHER READING

Aven, Paula, "Long-Term Contracts Snarl Deregulation Issue," *Denver Business Journal*, September 5, 1997, p. 12A.

———, "Tri-State Generation Consolidating Offices," *Denver Business Journal*, March 8, 1996, p. 5A.

Best, Allen, "Coal Under Fire: Colorado's No. 2 Electric Provider, Tri-State Generation and Transmission Association, Faces Pressure to Reassess Its Reliance on Coal—Now 70 Percent of Total Output," *ColoradoBiz*, March 2008, p. 24.

"DOE Gets Return on Clean Coal Investment," *Coal & Synfuels Technology*, December 5, 1994, p. 3.

Dowling, Mark, and J. Barry Winter, "Tri-State: Generations of Power," Westminster, Colo.: Tri-State Generation and Transmission Association, Inc., 2002.

"New Mexico Utilities Partner on Solar Project," *Space Daily*, July 3, 2008.

Raabe, Steve, "Tri-State Turns Its Gaze Toward Renewables: The Power Wholesaler Issues a Request for Proposals for Clean Sources of Energy," *Denver Post*, January 4, 2008, p. C1.

Smith, Jeff, "Power Co-op Girds for Summer," *Rocky Mountain News*, June 1, 2001, p. 4B.

Smith, Jerd, "More Power Shortages Possible This Winter; Electric Generator Warns That Demand Is Still Growing," *Rocky Mountain News*, August 26, 1998, p. 1B.

"Tri-State and First Solar Sign Major Development Agreement," *Space Daily*, March 26, 2009.

Trina Solar Limited

—————————■—————————

No. 2 Xin Yuan Yi Rd.
Electronics Park, New District
Changzhou, Jiangsu 213031
China
Telephone: (+86 519) 548-2008
Web site: http://www.trinasolar.com

Public Company
Incorporated: 1997 as Changzhou Trina Solar Energy
    Co., Ltd.
Employees: 5,000
Sales: $831.9 million (2008)
Stock Exchanges: New York
Ticker Symbol: TSL
NAICS: 334413 Semiconductor and Related Device
    Manufacturing .

■ ■ ■

Trina Solar Limited is one of the fastest-growing solar products companies in the world. From its manufacturing facilities in Changzhou, China, the company takes raw and recycled silicon, casts it into ingots, slices the ingots into very thin wafers, uses the wafers to make solar cells, then assembles the cells into modules. Trina markets these solar systems components and the assembled modules to other solar products manufacturers and systems integrators in Europe, Asia, and North America from offices in China, Germany, Spain, and the United States. The company's main focus is the production and commercialization of a wide variety of photovoltaic (PV) modules, both monocrystalline and multic-

rystalline, with power outputs ranging from 165 to 230 watts.

ROOTS IN ALUMINUM SIDING

When Jifan Gao founded the company that became Trina Solar Limited in Jiangsu Province in December 1997, the solar PV industry in the People's Republic of China was still in its infancy. Gao later explained that he was inspired to start the business by a June 26, 1997 speech to the United Nations by President Bill Clinton, in which he outlined an ambitious Million Solar Roofs Initiative for the United States. Spurred by the potential growth of the solar PV industry abroad and believing the Chinese market would soon develop, Gao's initial plan was to create a solar PV installation company focused on providing solar energy to different regions in China.

As cofounder and head of Guangdong Shunde Fuyou Detergent Factory from 1989 to 1992, and founder and head of Wujin Xiehe Fine Chemical Factory from 1992 through 1997, Gao already had an impressive business resume when he established Trina Solar's parent company, Changzhou Trina Solar Energy Co., Ltd., or Trina China, as it was called. As founder, Gao also served from the start as the company's chairman and chief executive officer.

When the company got rolling in 1998, however, its main focus was the aluminum siding business, which included the production, marketing and sale of aluminum exterior wall products used on buildings and houses. Aluminum siding operations were housed in a

7,600-square-meter facility in Changzhou, about 30 miles from the coastal city of Shanghai.

SOLAR BABY STEPS

Trina China's solar PV business began to take shape in 1999 when the company founded the Trina Solar Research Center. With a master's degree in physical chemistry from Jilin University in 1988, Gao, and a small group of scientists, began research and development efforts in solar products, and by October, Trina China had obtained its ISO 9002 Certificate.

As a foreign-invested enterprise engaged in a manufacturing business, Trina China benefited from a two-year exemption from China's enterprise income tax for the company's first two profitable years of operation, which were 1999 and 2000. The firm gained notoriety in August 2000 when it developed the first solar PV house in China as part of the Beijing Olympics Green Campaign. In September 2000, Trina China hosted the First International Solar Power Technology and Marketing Forum in Changzhou.

Gao's original vision for the business came a step closer to reality in 2002 when Trina China launched its solar power systems integration business, which focused on the design, testing, and installation of interconnected solar modules with system components such as batteries and inverters.

WORKING THE SYSTEM

In 2002, Trina China helped draft the National Technical Standards for Off-Grid PV Systems and was chosen by the Chinese government as the first privately held company to participate in its Western Brightness Program, an initiative aimed at bringing electricity to remote regions in China. Subsequently, in mid-2003, Trina Solar completed its first solar energy system project with an installation of 40 solar power generation stations in Tibet. The company netted $2.7 million from the job, which had a total power output of 715 kilowatts.

Trina China continued to take advantage of very favorable tax rates granted by the Chinese government to start-up businesses in certain sectors of the economy. When the firm relocated in 2002 to a high-tech zone in Changzhou, it qualified for a preferential enterprise income tax rate of 15 percent for 2002 and 2003. Combined with a 50 percent reduction of its income tax rate for the years 2001 to 2003, Trina China had a tax rate of 7.5 percent in each of 2002 and 2003.

In 2004, Trina China continued to garner recognition and influence in China's developing solar PV industry. It helped draft the country's first Renewable Energy Law, completed the "Solar Energy Power Generation Commercialization" project for the government, and founded (through Chairman Gao) the Changzhou Solar Association. During the fall of 2004, Trina China launched the company's third business segment, its solar module production business. The company made its first commercial shipment of solar modules in November 2004.

TRINA'S GREAT LEAP FORWARD

In 2005, Trina China's aluminum siding and systems integration business segments began to take a backseat to its growing solar module business, which prompted the company to move to the New District Industrial Park and expand its Changzhou-based manufacturing facilities. After opening a solar module production facility in early 2005, the company produced its first monocrystalline ingot in August, and its ingot production lines became fully operational in October. From the start, Trina tried to lower silicon costs by using recycled silicon scrap obtained from the tech sector. The company claimed that it could make high-quality ingots with up to 80 percent reclaimed silicon.

In its first full year of operations, Trina China's solar module business in 2005 skyrocketed the company's total revenues to $27.3 million from $413,632 in 2004, with net income going from a loss of $366,647 to a profit of $3.2 million. Solar module sales volume significantly increased from 0.12 megawatts in 2004 to 6.79 megawatts in 2005, while the average selling price rose from $3.45 per watt to $4.02 per watt.

KEY DATES

1997: Jifan Gao establishes Changzhou Trina Solar Energy Co., Ltd., in Jiangsu Province, China.
1998: Company begins operations in aluminum siding business.
2002: Solar power systems integration division is launched.
2004: Trina makes first commercial shipment of solar modules.
2005: Silicon ingot production begins.
2006: Firm starts manufacturing solar wafers; Trina Solar Limited is incorporated; company makes NYSE debut.
2007: First solar cell production lines become fully operational.
2008: Company stock loses over 80 percent of its value by end of year in global economic meltdown.

The company sold about 97 percent of its solar modules to systems integrators outside of China. Additionally, as Trina China ramped down its aluminum siding business in 2005, its net income from that fading business segment dropped to $91,010 from $354,237 in 2004.

In February 2006, Trina continued its expansion plan and began manufacturing solar wafers, which are the main component of solar cells. The move was part of Trina's overall strategy to eventually produce all of the components of solar modules from silicon ingots to wafers to cells to modules.

PREPARING TO LAUNCH

Anticipating an initial public offering (IPO) later in the year, on March 14, 2006, Trina Solar Limited, or Trina, was incorporated in the Cayman Islands and through a series of transactions acquired all of the equity interests of Changzhou Trina Solar Energy Co., Ltd., or Trina China.

In April 2006, Trina landed one of many contracts in Germany, at the time one of the fastest-growing solar energy markets in the world. Solar station developer and operator Phönix SonnenStrom of Sulzemoos, agreed to purchase two megawatts of solar modules from the company. On June 30, 2006, Trina ceased all aluminum siding operations and transferred the segment's employees to solar module operations. In mid-2006, the firm obtained one final round of private funding from

Milestones Capital, Good Energies, and Merrill Lynch before its public launch.

According to documents filed with the U.S. Securities and Exchange Commission, as of September 30, 2006, Trina had 910 full-time employees, including 805 in manufacturing, 25 in research and development, 12 in sales and marketing, and 68 in general and administrative. All of Trina's research, development, and manufacture of ingots, wafers, and solar modules were conducted at its 53,000-square-meter facility in Changzhou.

A SUNNY MARKET DEBUT

On December 19, 2006, opening under the symbol "TSL" on the New York Stock Exchange, Trina completed the trading day at $20.28 a share, up 10 percent from its initial public offering price of $18.50. The company raised $98 million from the sale of 5.3 million American Depositary Shares (ADS). Gao's stake in the company fell from 27.34 percent to 20.53 percent after the offering. Also in December, Trina sold the manufacturing equipment and buildings that were used for its former aluminum siding business.

In an attempt to secure a stable and affordable supply of polysilicon, an essential raw material in the production of solar wafers, Trina began 2007 by signing a six-year supply agreement with Germany-based Wacker Chemie AG that started in 2009. A similar agreement with Korea-based DC Chemical followed in February. The month also brought a strategic agreement with Q-Cells AG, another German company. The deal called for Trina to supply wafers for Q-Cells to process into solar cells, which were then used in Trina's module manufacturing lines.

Trina's 2006 expansion efforts showed up in its financial report for the year, released by the company in mid-February 2007. Revenues rose 319 percent to $114.5 million and net income was up 275 percent to $12.4 million. While prices for its panels fell, company sales were boosted by a higher demand for solar modules in Germany, Spain, and Italy, where government incentives encouraged the consumption of solar energy. By February 26, 2007, company stock soared above $50 a share.

ESTABLISHING IDENTITY

In May 2007, Trina's first 50-megawatt solar cell production line became fully operational, another significant step in the company's plan to vertically integrate its operations. In June, the company raised about $155 million in a second offering of 3.6 million shares, saying the funds were needed to expand ingot, wafer, solar cell, and module manufacturing production lines.

In July 2007, Trina announced new multiyear module supply contracts with three Italy-based companies: six megawatts with Enerpoint SRL; 22 to 33 megawatts with Tecnospot SRL; and 20 megawatts with Enereco SRL. It also landed a 40-megawatt deal with Germany-based IBC Solar AG.

In August, the company rolled out a new line of solar modules manufactured entirely from Trina-made ingots, wafers, and cells. The new product boasted power output that ranged from 180 watts to 220 watts. A long-term silicon supply agreement signed by Trina in October 2007 with the Nitol Group, a Moscow-based chemical company, secured a five-year flow of the feedstock starting in 2009. Also in August, based on revenue growth for the last three years, Trina was named the fastest-growing technology company in China in the "Deloitte Technology Fast 50 China 2007" program.

November 2007 brought a polysilicon supply agreement for mid-2008 through 2013 with Sichuan Yongxiang Polysilicon. Even though the company continued to source up to 80 percent of its feedstock requirements from reclaimed sources, it was constantly faced with rising prices associated with an industry-wide persistent short supply of silicon. In December 2007, Trina announced plans to build a multiphase polysilicon production facility. The proposed 10,000 metric ton capacity plant had a $1 billion price tag and was targeted for completion by 2012.

BUILDING CHARACTER

With sales from Germany, Spain, and Italy accounting for over 90 percent of the company's revenues in 2007, Trina began 2008 with an eye on expanding its module manufacturing capacity and increasing its presence in the developing solar markets of the Netherlands, Belgium, France, Greece, Korea, and the United States.

In February 2008, the firm moved into a new, more environmentally friendly, solar panel–powered office building. Net revenues for 2007, as reported in March 2008, grew 163 percent to $301.8 million while net income jumped a like amount to $34.9 million. Earnings per share amounted to $1.47. Trina's stock rose on the news by almost 10 percent to over $35 a share.

In April 2008, Trina signed an eight-year supply deal with China-based GCL Silicon Technology Holdings Ltd. for enough virgin polysilicon to produce approximately 2,600 megawatts of solar modules. At the same time, the company announced the cancellation of

its planned $1 billion polysilicon plant project. Trina ended the month by inking a smaller long-term polysilicon supply agreement with Italy-based SILFAB S.p.A., followed by a similar deal in May with Jupiter Corp. Ltd.

Trina continued to make inroads into the European market in June 2008 with two sales agreements; one with German photovoltaic wholesaler Solarmarkt AG, and a $158 million deal with Italy-based ErgyCapital SpA. In July 2008, faced with growing concerns over free cash flow generation due to rising capital investment requirements, raw material prepayments and a tougher equity-funding environment, solar stocks in general, with Trina included, began to take a beating. Company stock traded around $28 per share on July 3, and by August had lost 40 percent of its value since the start of 2008.

STORMY WEATHER AHEAD

In July 2008, Trina landed a contract to sell a total of 17 megawatts of solar modules to the Italian company, Enel SpA, and entered into a multiyear, multisystem contract to buy key module line equipment from Spire Corporation, located in Massachusetts. The firm landed another deal in September with a sale of 50 megawatts of solar modules starting in 2009 to Belgium-based Invictus NV.

November 2008 brought the announcement that Trina had chosen San Francisco as the base for its North American operations, and Rotterdam, a key port city in the Netherlands, for the establishment of European warehouse operations. By mid-November, worldwide tightening of credit access, the continued collapse of the crude oil market, and a pullback in government subsidies in key markets such as Spain and Germany caused Trina's stock to lose about 70 percent of its value since October 1. Not even the extension of solar tax credits through 2016 by the U.S. Congress in early October helped stem the tide.

In late January 2009, the company announced an agreement to sell between 20 to 36 megawatts of solar modules to Spanish customer, Gestamp Asetym Solar, S.L. Financial results for 2008, released by the company in early March 2009, showed total revenues at $831.9 million, an increase of 175 percent from 2007. Net income came in at $61.4 million, about 72 percent higher than 2007. Gross margin fell, however, to 19.8 percent compared to 22.4 percent in 2007. The company also reported that it had reached its 2008 capacity expansion goal of 350 megawatts for its ingot, wafer, cell, and module manufacturing lines.

As the entire solar industry hunkered down to ride out the worldwide financial storms in the first quarter of

2009, Trina appeared to be well positioned in the middle of the solar value chain as a maker of ingots, wafers, cells, and modules. With polysilicon prices expected to fall 20 percent in the year ahead, the company's April 2008 decision to kill a $1 billion polysilicon project was looking very prudent in March 2009. Despite the challenging global economic and financial climate, company officials predicted an increase in 2009 solar module shipments ranging from 74 to 99 percent. Investors could only hope that Trina's sunny forecast came true.

Ted Sylvester

PRINCIPAL COMPETITORS

Yingli Green Energy Holding Co. Limited; Suntech Power Holdings Co., Ltd.; Sunways Ag (Germany); Canadian Solar Inc.; JA Solar Holdings Co., Ltd.; Solar-World AG (Germany); ReneSola Ltd; Solarfun Power Holdings Co., Ltd.; erSol Solar Energy AG (Germany); SunPower Corporation (USA); First Solar, Inc. (USA).

FURTHER READING

Alpert, Bill, "China's Solar Boom Loses Its Luster," *Barron's*, October 8, 2007, p. 22.

Bogoslaw, David, "Solar Stocks Get Their Day in the Sun," *BusinessWeek Online*, January 3, 2008.

Chernova, Yuliya, "Trina Solar Close to Signing Its First U.S. Integrator Deals," *Dow Jones News Service*, September 10, 2008.

"Chinese PV Product Makers Face Gloomy Fourth Quarter," *Interfax: China Business Newswire*, December 4, 2008.

Cowan, Lynn, "Deals & Deal Makers: Chinese Firms Rack Up IPO Gains," *Wall Street Journal*, December 20, 2006, p. C4.

Gold, Donald H., "Once-Powerful Solar Stocks Take a Beating," *Investor's Business Daily*, July 3, 2008.

Hua, Judy, "Interview: Trina Solar to Boost Capacity, Eyes U.S. Market," *Reuters News*, January 16, 2008.

Li, Liang, "In the Shadow of the Sun," *China Business Feature*, May 9, 2007.

"Polysilicon Price May Drop in 2010," *China Chemical Reporter*, November 16, 2008.

Reeves, Amy, "Trina Solar Ltd. Changzhou, China; Chinese Manufacturer Works to Lower the Price of Solar Energy," *Investor's Business Daily*, March 9, 2007, p. A09.

———, "Will Investors Warm Up to More Solar Power IPOs?" *Investor's Business Daily*, December 19, 2006, p. A06.

Rocha, Euan, "Trina Profit Soars, but '09 Demand Weighs on Stock," *Reuters News*, August 18, 2008.

Savitz, Eric J., "Prospects of Rain in Spain Make for Gloomy Solar Week," *Barron's*, July 28, 2008, p. 27.

Somodevilla, Chip, "Tax-Credit Vote Boosts Solar Power Firms," *Boston Globe*, September 25, 2008, p. E6.

Spencer, Jane, "China Solar Stocks Shine in U.S., but Some Could Be Overheated," *Wall Street Journal Asia*, May 23, 2007, p. 21.

"SunPower Warning Sends Solar Stocks Tumbling," *AFX Asia*, November 5, 2008.

"Trina Solar to Power North America's Largest Single Rooftop Installation," *PR Newswire* (U.S.), September 24, 2008.

U.S. Bancorp

———————— ■ ————————

U.S. Bank Place
800 Nicollet Mall
Minneapolis, Minnesota 55402
U.S.A.
Telephone: (651) 466-3000
Toll Free: (800) 872-2657
Fax: (612) 303-0782
Web site: http://www.usbank.com

Public Company
Incorporated: 1929 as First Bank Stock Investment
  Company
Employees: 57,904
Total Assets: $265.91 billion (2008)
Stock Exchanges: New York
Ticker Symbol: USB
NAICS: 551111 Offices of Bank Holding Companies;
  522110 Commercial Banking; 522210 Credit Card
  Issuing; 522320 Financial Transactions Processing;
  522390 Other Activities Related to Credit
  Intermediation

■ ■ ■

U.S. Bancorp, a diversified financial holding company headquartered in Minneapolis, is the parent company of the nation's sixth largest commercial bank. U.S. Bank serves 24 states spanning the West and Midwest through 2,791 bank offices and 5,164 ATM locations. In addition to banking services, U.S. Bancorp provides brokerage, insurance, investment, mortgage, trust, and payment service products to consumers, businesses, and

institutions. Formed from the merger of two regional banks headed by brothers, U.S. Bancorp appeared to be weathering the financial industry crisis that erupted in 2008 better than many.

HISTORY OF FIRST BANK SYSTEM INC.

In April 1929, just one-half year before the great stock market crash, 85 banks located in the Ninth Federal Reserve district joined together in a loose confederation called First Bank Stock Investment Corporation. Since the Federal Deposit Insurance Company (FDIC) had not yet been created, the purpose of the confederation was to provide mutual financial support during difficult economic times. Although there was a great deal of speculation going on during this time in Wall Street brokerage houses, most banks throughout the country remained financially conservative and extremely cautious about using their assets for anything except the most stable investments.

Despite their fiscal conservatism, a number of banks were forced to close their doors during the 1920s. With the stock market crash of October 1929 and the onset of the Great Depression, conditions for the banking industry grew harsher and harsher. Many banks were forced to close during the years between 1929 and 1932. As the Depression grew worse during the first few months of Franklin Roosevelt's presidency, he decided in early 1933 to close all the nation's banks for ten days. The purpose of this dramatic decision was to make certain that only those banks with stable financial ledgers would be permitted to reopen their doors to the

COMPANY PERSPECTIVES

At U.S. Bank, our Five Star Service Guarantee means that every teller, every loan officer, every manager and every employee is committed to responsive, respectful, prompt and helpful service. The Five Star Guarantee means putting your needs first and foremost. It means focusing on what you need to maximize your business or personal financial management. It's our promise—to change forever what you expect from a financial institution. And it's a promise WE GUARANTEE!

public. When the ten-day period was over, all First Bank Stock Investment Corporation subsidiaries were allowed by the federal government to reopen without any mandated reorganization. The conservative policies adhered to by First Bank management were so sound, in fact, that the holding company was able to start an acquisitions campaign that lasted through much of the 1930s.

During the 1940s, banks that belonged to the First Bank confederation largely operated independently of one another. Managers at the individual banks were fiercely loyal to their own self-interests, and never hesitated to engage in extensive price cuts if they thought it might take a profitable customer away from another bank within the confederation. In fact, the competition among confederation banks was most intense in the Twin Cities of Minneapolis and St. Paul, Minnesota, where the largest individual banks in the First Bank system fought one another for customers. One cause of this counterproductive competition among the banks was the restrictive and antiquated branching legislation in Minnesota and other states in the region.

In 1954, the Bank Holding Company Act was passed by the U.S. Congress. This legislation gave the First Bank confederation and other bank holding companies throughout the nation the approval for existing multistate banking operations. Banks within the First Bank confederation were spread across a four-state area during this time, including Montana, South Dakota, North Dakota, and Minnesota. For the remainder of the 1950s, and throughout the decade of the 1960s, the banks of the confederation expanded their presence in these states by engaging in an aggressive acquisitions policy. By the 1970s, however, member banks of the confederation were operating so independently of one another that there was not only a

lack of uniformity in services, but an overall lack of direction and centralized decision making.

During the late 1970s and early 1980s, the economy in the United States went into a tailspin, and the First Bank confederation was faced with the challenges of high inflation, uncertain interest rates, and growing competition from nonbank financial service companies. Confederation management recognized the need for more centralized control and in 1982 began to prepare a comprehensive strategy for this purpose. In 1985, First Bank management made its first significant decision by selling 28 smaller, rural banks with little prospect for future growth. This decision resulted in the sale of 45 offices over a four-state region. Another major decision involved the 1988 merger of the large Minneapolis and St. Paul banks, and additional suburban banks in the Twin Cities area, into First Bank National Association. The increase in operational efficiency and reduction in service costs provided the bank with a greater opportunity to compete effectively in the entire Twin Cities metropolitan area. Management at First Bank also purchased banks in the states of Washington and Colorado during this time, taking advantage of federal legislation that weakened many barriers to national banking.

More than the recession of the early 1980s led First Bank to reassess the adequacy and effectiveness of a loose confederation and hands-off management style. The farm crisis of the early to mid-1980s created credit quality problems for the regional banks affiliated with First Bank which were outside of the greater Twin Cities metropolitan area. Under the bank's own credit examination, its credit losses amounted to $424 million by 1986. This loss was compensated for by the $397 million in realized gains when the investment securities were sold. Yet when rising interest rates led to a substantial unrealized loss estimated at $640 million in the long-term bonds which had been bought to replace the securities sold, the company decided upon a hedging strategy to minimize the loss. Unfortunately, the hedging strategy failed, and the bonds were finally sold at a pretax loss of $506 million in 1988.

First Bank's emphasis on merchant banking, capital markets, and lending specializations proved disastrous during the mid-1980s. With decreasing capital levels resulting from the securities and bond losses, rising non-interest costs, an increasing amount of nonperforming assets, and weakening profitability, the company announced a comprehensive reorganization strategy in late 1989. The strategy included a withdrawal from merchant banking and lending specializations and a concentration on more basic banking services, such as merchant processing, credit cards, automated teller

KEY DATES

1891: United States National Bank of Portland is founded.

1902: United States National and Ainsworth National merge.

1925: United States National merges with Ladd and Tilton, Oregon's oldest bank.

1929: First Bank Stock Investment Corporation is formed.

1964: United States National Bank of Portland is renamed United States National Bank of Oregon.

1968: First Bank Stock Investment Corporation is renamed First Bank System, Inc.; United States National Bank reorganizes as a holding company called U.S. Bancorp.

1988: First Bank National Association is formed through the merger of large banks in Minneapolis, St. Paul, and the greater Twin Cities region.

1990: First Bank hires John (Jack) Grundhofer as CEO, chairman, and president.

1993: First Bank acquires U.S. Bancorp's corporate trust operations in Oregon and Washington.

1995: U.S. Bancorp acquires West One Bancorp of Idaho.

1997: In its largest acquisition, First Bank purchases U.S. Bancorp and adopts the U.S. Bancorp name; company also acquires Piper Jaffray Companies Inc.

2001: Firstar Corporation acquires U.S. Bancorp.

2003: Integration problems result in Piper Jaffray spinoff.

2007: New CEO refocuses on retail banking growth.

2009: U.S. Bancorp rethinks participation in bank bailout program.

machines, and cash management. The company also began to capitalize upon and extend its geographic franchise. In 1989, First Bank recorded a restructuring expense of $37.5 million, while also reporting a $175 million provision for credit losses.

After a four-month search, in January 1990 the First Bank board of directors hired John F. (Jack) Grundhofer to act as chairman, president, and chief

executive officer. Grundhofer, a former vice-chairman and senior executive officer at Wells Fargo, immediately initiated a massive cost-cutting strategy designed to bring the bank back to profitability. Grundhofer and his hand-chosen management team examined each line of the bank's business to determine whether or not it could remain competitive in the market. Grundhofer's first move was to stop lending to large corporations and concentrate more on retail banking, trusts and investments, and small and middle-range businesses. As a result, First Bank's portfolio of loans was drastically reduced. All the bank's national lending programs and its indirect auto loan programs were entirely eliminated, thus allowing the company to concentrate on expanding its regional commercial lending program and its direct consumer loan program. In general, First Bank's loan portfolio was gradually restructured to emphasize a larger number and more diverse mix of consumer loans.

The most important move that Grundhofer made, however, was to commit $150 million in First Bank funds to a cost-cutting technology program. When he arrived on the scene in the beginning of 1990, Grundhofer discovered that First Bank was mired in 1950s and 1960s technology. Over 45 banks under First Bank's umbrella had 47 different data processing centers, 715 different kinds of basic consumer deposit accounts, 16 loan processing centers, eight consumer loan centers, and 20 item processing centers. The bank also was without any centralized pricing structure for its products or services, and each bank within the system offered various kinds of products and services. The company's installment loan system was initially brought in during 1959 and was still in use. First Bank's customer information system dated back to 1964, without the benefit of any update since that time. In addition, its online savings system was more than 20 years old.

Within two years Grundhofer consolidated the bank's 47 data processing centers into one, and drastically reduced or eliminated all the other loan and processing centers. He implemented a fixed price structure for the bank's products and services, and standardized the products and services each of the banks offered within the First Bank system. As First Bank's efficiency ratio improved, more customers were attracted to the services provided by the bank. By 1992, a customer could walk into any of First Bank's affiliates in the Twin Cities area and get a cashier's check or automobile loan within ten minutes. The bank also developed an extremely useful and very popular 48-hour turnaround on small business loans; for a $250,000 loan, the customer was asked to fill out a brief two-page application. Other processing capabilities that were improved by the bank's emphasis on technological development included a customer's ability to access account information from a remote site. Finally, all of the bank's numerous customer service phone centers were consolidated into two locations.

When the cost-cutting technology program began to show financial rewards, Grundhofer decided to increase First Bank's asset base through an aggressive acquisitions program. First Bank purchased U.S. Bancorp's Oregon and Washington corporate trust operations in early 1993. Prior to this, it had purchased the California corporate trust subsidiary of Bankers Trust New York Corporation in 1992. The company acquired Colorado National Bank with over $3 billion in assets, and Boulevard Bancorp in Chicago with over $1.5 billion in assets. Perhaps the most important acquisition involved the purchase of the domestic corporate trust of J.P. Morgan & Company, one of the largest and most prestigious banks in the United States. In May 1994, the company confirmed its acquisition of Metropolitan Financial Corporation for approximately $800 million. Metropolitan Financial, a Minneapolis-based bank with $5.7 billion in assets, operated a multistate banking office network located in Minnesota, North Dakota, Iowa, Nebraska, Kansas, and Wyoming. The purchase of Metropolitan helped push First Bank's assets to $34.5 billion, ahead of the assets at First Fidelity Bancorp, the nation's 25th largest bank holding company.

In 1990 and 1991, the bank's capital restoration program involved a private placement of new common stock, which raised some $145 million from an investment partnership headed by Lazard Frères, and $30 million from the State Board of Administration of Florida. The bank also initiated a public offering of $114.5 million of preferred stock. These moves placed First Bank's capital ratio in the top percentile of regional banks in the United States.

Under Grundhofer's leadership, by the beginning of 1995 First Bank had grown into one of the largest and most successful of the regional banks. With its financial condition clearly improved, First Bank began to develop a community initiatives program that became a model for regional banks. First Bank's extensive community outreach program involved volunteerism, youth-employment projects, event sponsorships, and grants to nonprofit organizations. The company offered a comprehensive line of mortgage products and services to help low and moderate income families purchase their own homes. The bank also tailored loans for people with disabilities, provided customer assistance for non-English-speaking people, and offered free accounts and services to individuals with low-income jobs. First Bank also extended credit to small businesses that fostered community development and rehabilitation by working closely with the Small Business Administration.

First Bank continued to focus its efforts on growth through acquisitions, and in March 1995 the company completed its acquisition of holding company First Western Corporation, which owned Western Bank in Sioux Falls, South Dakota. The sale included Western Bank's 12 branches in South Dakota. Also that year First Bank bought Southwest Bank, First Bank of Omaha, and FirsTier Financial Inc., greatly furthering its presence in Nebraska. The acquisitions made First Bank the largest banking firm in Nebraska, with a leading market share in Lincoln and the number two spot in Omaha. The FirsTier purchase was the largest bank acquisition in Nebraska history. Continuing with its flurry of acquisitions in 1995, First Bank bought the corporate trust operations of BankAmerica Corporation, making First Bank the nation's largest corporate trust company in terms of revenues. The following year First Bank added to its corporate trust operations by purchasing the municipal and corporate bond trustee division of Comerica Inc., a banking company based in Detroit.

Although acquisitions were a primary concern of First Bank, the company also focused on streamlining operations. The company's trust and investment division implemented a cost-cutting plan, which included personnel cuts and technology enhancements, to decrease expenses and boost revenues. First Bank also made the decision to depart the mortgage banking industry by selling its FBS Mortgage and Colorado National Mortgage operations. The bank planned to continue offering mortgage loans through its bank branches.

In the mid-1990s First Bank also spent a great deal of time, money, and energy in its attempt to acquire First Interstate Bancorp. First Bank lost out to Wells Fargo & Co., which had made several hostile takeover bids for First Interstate before succeeding. The battle was the largest hostile takeover attempt in the history of U.S. banking and, while it left First Bank without the First Interstate empire, the company gained a $200 million termination fee. First Bank hoped to use these funds to finance a significant acquisition, one that would enhance its operations and make it a strong contender in the rapidly consolidating and highly competitive U.S. banking industry.

HISTORY OF U.S. BANCORP

U.S. Bancorp was organized as a holding company by the United States Bank of Oregon in the late 1960s, a time when many large banks across the country acknowledged and fostered their transformation into diversified financial services organizations by forming bank holding companies. The company's historical roots, however, stretch back nearly a century before the descriptive phrase "diversified financial services organizations" became part of banking nomenclature, reaching back into the late 19th century to a simpler age when the business of banking comprised the rudimentary tasks of receiving deposits, cashing checks, and extending and collecting loans. Banking would develop into a much more sophisticated business by the time U.S. Bancorp first emerged in the late 1960s, but the company's true origins stemmed from the efforts of a handful of wealthy and influential businessmen during the early 1890s and their organization of The United States National Bank of Portland.

From out of the uncharted Portland wilderness, Oregon developed into a bustling commercial and industrial hub during the 19th century, its growth propelled by successive waves of settlers into the Pacific Northwest and the subsequent establishment of a spectrum of businesses and industries. As the community evolved from a secluded settlement into a burgeoning town and finally into one of the principal cities underpinning the Pacific Northwest's economy, banks were there to promote and support its growth, serving as a crucial source of capital in a region far removed from the established financial centers in the eastern United States. Starting in 1859, when the first national bank in Portland, the Ladd and Tilton, was organized, Portland's business operators began to utilize bank loans to develop their enterprises. As the town grew, requiring increasing amounts of capital to fund its development, the number of banks increased, totaling five in the state of Oregon by 1872, then jumping to 16 by 1880. Roughly a decade later, when more than 40 national banks were operating in Oregon, United States National Bank of Portland (U.S. National) was organized by nine businessmen.

Led by Donald MacLeay, an immigrant from Scotland who made his fortune in the grocery and shipping business, and George Washington Ewing Griffith, a wealthy Kansas businessman, the founding directors, all of whom were born outside of Oregon, organized U.S. National on February 5, 1891, then opened the bank four days later in rented offices in downtown Portland. Although U.S. National operated without a vault during its inaugural year, the apparent lack of security did not dissuade customers from bringing their banking business to the city's newest bank. During the bank's first day 15 customers opened new accounts, depositing a total of $21,886.30. By the end of its first year, fledgling U.S. National had become a thriving enterprise, holding $450,000 in deposits and capital stock and administering more than $350,000 in loans. It was an encouraging start for U.S. National, but before there was much chance for celebration, economic conditions in Oregon and throughout the nation soured, providing the bank

with its first great test of resiliency while still in its infancy.

In 1893, two years after U.S. National began operating, a severe economic depression gripped the country, devastating more than 500 of the nation's banks and more than 16,000 businesses by the end of the year. Among the victims of the harsh economic conditions were a number of stable and respected Portland banks, but despite its status as a neophyte in the area's banking community U.S. National beat back the debilitating effects of the economic downturn. The bank's deposits slipped from a high of more than $400,000 in 1892 to less than $340,000 in 1896, but when the discovery of gold in the late 1890s swept away any lingering effects of the economic depression in the Pacific Northwest, U.S. National emerged stronger than ever before. For this strength the bank was indebted to the financial malaise of the early and mid-1890s, a deleterious period for many banks that left U.S. National occupying a more powerful position. Of Oregon's 41 national banks operating in 1892, only 27 remained after the depression, creating a more consolidated banking industry that buoyed U.S. National's position considerably. Of these 27 national banks, only four would survive to compete during the 20th century: Ainsworth National, Merchants National, First National, and the upstart U.S. National.

Less than a decade old in 1900, U.S. National had passed Ainsworth National in volume of business to rank as the third largest bank and was gaining ground on Merchants National to secure the industry's second position. Growth would come quickly during the first decades of the new century as bankers recouped their losses from the 1890s and shared in the prosperity of the times. During the first decade of the century, the number of national banks in Oregon increased from 27 to 75, and deposits quadrupled as the city of Portland, with 200,000 residents by 1910, flourished economically. As one of the city's stalwart banks, U.S. National benefited greatly from the more robust economic conditions and was able to conclude several pivotal transactions that secured its inclusion among the region's leading banks. In 1902 U.S. National and Ainsworth National, the fourth largest bank, agreed to merge, creating a banking entity that kept the U.S. National corporate title and controlled resources valued at more than $2 million. Three years later U.S. National merged with Wells Fargo Company's Portland bank as growth and prosperity reigned, then in 1917 the bank merged with another large Portland bank, Lumbermens National. The merger with Lumbermens National increased U.S. National's deposits by $6.5 million and made it the second largest bank in the Pacific Northwest.

By the beginning of the 1920s U.S. National had deposits of more than $36 million, having grown considerably during its first 30 years of operation. In 1925 the bank set the tone for the magnitude of growth ahead when it merged with the venerable Ladd and Tilton. Aside from being the region's oldest bank, Ladd and Tilton represented a potent banking competitor with more than $20 million in deposits and 30,000 depositors. Once Ladd and Tilton was merged into U.S. National, U.S. National received a substantial boost to its stature, becoming the largest bank north of San Francisco and west of Minneapolis, with resources totaling $64.6 million, deposits reaching $60 million, and a large base of 75,000 depositors.

The 1920s were heady years for U.S. National, but as the events of the next decade unfolded, the bank faced economic conditions far more menacing than those surmounted during the 1890s. During the Great Depression more than half of the country's banks were financially ruined, thousands of businesses were devastated, and the ranks of the unemployed swelled beyond precedent. Like the economic depression touched off in 1893, however, U.S. National withstood the pernicious effects of financial collapse all around it, although deposits once again shrank during the period. Deposits reached a high of $71 million in September 1931, then over the next eight months fell by $10 million; however, by the late 1930s business began to recover and the bank's deposits eclipsed $100 million. Perhaps the most important occurrence during the otherwise crippling 1930s was the enactment of legislation enabling banks to establish branches, which U.S. National began doing in 1933 and would continue to do thereafter.

During the 1940s U.S. National expanded its presence geographically by acquiring existing banks and converting them to U.S. National branches, such as the bank's 1940 purchase of the Medford National Bank, First National of Corvallis, and the Ladd and Bush Bank of Salem. Although the number of banking units comprising U.S. National's growing branch network rose only modestly during World War II, climbing from 26 to 29, deposits nearly tripled during the war years, leaping to $581 million by the end of 1945. Following the war, when an era of widespread prosperity gave large segments of the American population substantially more disposable income than ever before, the national banking industry underwent a dramatic shift as banks across the country began focusing on the consumer with concerted intensity. Loans for consumer purchases proliferated, and U.S. National responded by augmenting its consumer credit department with a branch consumer credit department in 1949. Bank advertising during the era reflected the significant shift in focus, as advertisements began to emphasize the availability of loans for individuals and the use of bank credit, rather than encouraging thrift as they had done since U.S. National's inception.

Between 1945 and 1955, 35 banking units were added to U.S. National's branch system, the bulk of which, 29, were acquired through mergers and acquisitions as the bank swallowed smaller competitors and outpaced larger competitors with its aggressive expansion across the state of Oregon. Aside from ranking as one of the larger state banks in the nation, U.S. National also began to distinguish itself as an industry pioneer during the 1950s by offering such innovative services as drive-up banking, erecting the first motor banking facility in Oregon in 1956, and leading the way with a computerized system to post checks in 1957.

In contrast to the 1950s, U.S. National expanded its branch network through internal means during the 1960s, creating new banking facilities rather than absorbing existing banking units through mergers or acquisitions. By 1965 the bank operated 100 branches across the state, a considerable presence that the bank's directors had acknowledged the previous year by changing the bank's name from United States National Bank of Portland to United States National Bank of Oregon. Other, more significant changes were in the offing as the bank entered the late 1960s and began to formulate a plan for the future, in search of a way to contend with the mounting pressures affecting banks during the period.

The business of banking had become a complex and highly competitive endeavor by the 1960s, substantially more sophisticated than when U.S. National first opened its doors in 1891. In addition to a much broader range of financial services offered by commercial banks, the market for these services had become more competitive since World War II. Between 1945 and 1960, savings in commercial banks such as U.S. National had doubled, whereas the amount in savings and loan associations had sextupled and the amount in credit unions had increased an enormous tenfold, absorbing business that would traditionally have gone to commercial banks.

In response, commercial banks began to form one-bank holding companies during the late 1960s, enabling them to acquire and organize other subsidiaries that could legally offer a broader range of services. In so doing, banks hoped to beat back the competition and keep noncommercial banks from entering into financial activities that historically had been under the exclusive purview of commercial banks. On September 9, 1968, U.S. National followed the nationwide trend by forming U.S. Bancorp as a one-bank holding company, heralding the development of a vast financial services network and the extension of U.S. Bancorp beyond Oregon's borders.

Once able to delve into new businesses, U.S. Bancorp did so with fervor, organizing a host of financial services subsidiaries during the 1970s: Bancorp Leasing, Inc., which was organized to enhance service to business customers through lease financing; U.S. Bancorp Financial, Inc., a subsidiary formed to specialize in asset-based commercial financing; and Mount Hood Credit Life Insurance Agency, which was created to centralize and streamline credit-related insurance activities throughout the U.S. National system. Numerous other subsidiaries were formed in the wake of U.S. Bancorp's founding, transforming the U.S. National-U.S. Bancorp network into a genuine regional financial services organization.

By the beginning of the 1980s, U.S. Bancorp was well on its way to becoming one of the preeminent regional financial services organizations in the country. Decidedly acquisitive throughout the 1980s, the holding company started the decade by establishing The Bank of Milwaukee, a state-chartered bank, in 1980, making U.S. Bancorp a multibank holding company. During the year, the company also acquired State Finance and Thrift Company of Logan, Utah, and established Citizen's Industrial Bank in Littleton, Colorado, further bolstering its out-of-state presence in regions where U.S. National was not allowed to operate. By the end of the year U.S. Bancorp's territory included California, Texas, Washington, Utah, Idaho, Colorado, Montana, and its home state of Oregon, giving the company ample room to grow as the decade progressed.

With the acquisition of Spokane-based Old National Bancorp and Seattle-based Peoples Bancorp in 1987, U.S. Bancorp became the largest bank holding company based in the Northwest. During the late 1980s, the company continued to aggressively pursue smaller rival banks, hoping to achieve a dominant position in markets opened up earlier in the decade. Other large banking organizations followed a similar strategy, creating a nationwide trend toward consolidation that left U.S. Bancorp as the last major independent bank in the Pacific Northwest by the early 1990s. With $19 billion in assets in 1992, the company ranked as the 32nd largest bank in the United States.

During the next two years, U.S. Bancorp's management began to focus its efforts on achieving greater efficiency by streamlining the company's operations and eliminating nearly a quarter of its workforce through layoffs and the divestiture of noncore subsidiaries. After two years of implementing severe downsizing measures, the company announced a momentous acquisition in 1995 that added substantially to U.S. Bancorp's sizable

holdings. Intent on strengthening its position in Idaho, where the company maintained only a token presence, U.S. Bancorp officials announced the $1.6 billion acquisition of West One Bancorp of Idaho in May, which the shareholders of both banking organizations agreed to in October. Completed at the end of 1995, the deal made U.S. Bancorp one of the 30 largest banking organizations in the country, with $30 billion in assets and $21 billion in deposits.

Buoyed by its purchase of West One, U.S. Bancorp continued its quest for growth in 1996. In an age of industry consolidation, U.S. Bancorp hoped to expand and grow to stave off takeover attempts, and acquisitions proved an optimal way to grow quickly. The company bought Northern California-based California Bancshares Inc. for about $327 million, boosting its presence there from 57 branches to 93 and expanding its area of operations from 22 counties to 27. In December 1996 U.S. Bancorp grew its presence in northern California further with the acquisition of Sacramento-based Business & Professional Bank. The small bank had four offices in the Sacramento region. U.S. Bancorp picked up another small bank with the purchase of Sun Capital Bancorp of Utah. The fast-growing Sun Capital had three branches in St. George, in the southern portion of Utah. U.S. Bancorp also hoped to capitalize on the growth of in-store banking and made plans to open about 200 supermarket branches from 1996 to 2000. The company inked a deal with Albertsons Inc. to provide exclusive banking services to about 170 Albertsons stores in Oregon, Washington, Idaho, and Nevada.

Although U.S. Bancorp continued to strengthen operations and grow, industry analysts believed the bank was not immune to takeover attempts. U.S. Bancorp's strategy of acquiring small companies, some analysts felt, was insufficient and would not protect the bank from larger adversaries. In addition, small to midsized banks were growing ever more scarce, leaving U.S. Bancorp with few potential acquisitions, and competition was growing. The bank ran into a small obstacle when its attempt to buy 61 branches in California from Wells Fargo & Co. in 1996 failed. Still, U.S. Bancorp remained confident and hopeful that it would be able to continue functioning independently.

FIRST BANK SYSTEM ACQUIRES U.S. BANCORP: 1997–2000

In early 1997 First Bank System announced it would acquire U.S. Bancorp for about $8.8 billion, extending First Bank's reach to the Pacific Ocean. The deal, which was one of the largest in U.S. banking history, nearly doubled First Bank's asset size and created a mega-bank serving about 17 states in the Midwest and West. The merged entity took the name U.S. Bancorp, with headquarters remaining in Minneapolis. First Bank's Grundhofer served as president and CEO, while U.S. Bancorp's Gerry Cameron continued as chairman until his retirement in 1998. According to the *Star-Tribune*, Grundhofer commented on the merger at a press conference and said, "Our regions are contiguous, compatible and are in attractive growth markets. Our banks both have strong market presence. Our business strategies are virtually identical."

As part of the consolidation efforts, nearly 4,000 staff members were laid off, the bulk of them from among U.S. Bancorp's 14,000 workers, including about 2,000 positions in the Portland region. Loan servicing operations in Portland were moved to Minneapolis, and credit card processing operations were moved to Fargo, North Dakota, where First Bank's credit card division was based.

In late 1997 the new U.S. Bancorp announced it would buy Minneapolis-based Piper Jaffray Companies Inc. for about $730 million. The acquisition greatly enhanced U.S. Bancorp's ability to provide investment banking and securities brokerage services to customers and created the 11th largest brokerage in the nation. U.S. Bancorp continued to grow in 1998 and bought Northwest National Bank, a small, family-owned bank in Vancouver, Washington, near Portland, Oregon. In the summer of 1998 U.S. Bancorp gained an exclusive contract to provide the Department of Defense with purchasing cards and electronic commerce systems. The bank beat out several competitors to gain the lucrative contract.

In 1999 U.S. Bancorp exited the retail banking scene in Kansas when it sold its 20 branches to INTRUST Bank of Wichita, Kansas's largest bank. The company also sold eight branches in Iowa. Although U.S. Bancorp left Kansas, it strove to increase its presence in Southern California in 1999 by acquiring several banks. The bank purchased Bank of Commerce, based in San Diego, for $314 million in stock. Bank of Commerce operated ten branches. U.S. Bancorp also bought Western Bancorp of Newport Beach for about $958 million in stock. Western Bancorp operated Santa Monica Bank and Southern California Bank and had 31 branches. The bank was known for its commercial lending operations. In the fall of 1999 U.S. Bancorp announced it would buy Peninsula Bank of San Diego for about $104 million in stock. Prior to the three acquisitions, U.S. Bancorp had 88 branches in Southern California.

U.S. Bancorp grew its U.S. Bancorp Piper Jaffray division with the acquisition of Libra Investments, Inc., in early 1999 and the investment banking operations of

John Nuveen Co. in September. The following year the company bought specialty leasing company Oliver-Allen Corporation. Also in 2000 the bank continued its acquisition streak in Southern California when it purchased Scripps Financial Corp. of San Diego. The buy included nine branches of Scripps Bank, primarily a commercial bank.

Although U.S. Bancorp appeared to be on the fast track of growth in the late 1990s, its consumer banking operations, which accounted for about one-third of U.S. Bancorp's earnings, struggled, and retail revenue grew a mere 4 percent in 1999. U.S. Bancorp's 1999 net income was $1.51 billion, up from 1998 net income of $1.33 billion, but the company failed to meet its growth goals. To stoke up its consumer banking division, U.S. Bancorp hired hundreds of new branch tellers, customer service representatives for its telephone operations, and small business bankers. The bank also added new electronic banking services and began to overhaul more than 1,000 branches. Still, the company's stock continued to sag, and during the first half of 2000 its stock price fell 11 percent. U.S. Bancorp's Grundhofer remained optimistic and confident about the bank's future, stating in his letter to shareholders in the company's 1999 annual report that U.S. Bancorp hoped to meet its growth goal of 12 to 15 percent by the end of 2001.

BROTHERS UNITED: A NEW CENTURY

U.S. Bancorp agreed, in 2000, to be purchased by Firstar Corporation of Milwaukee. The deal, valued at roughly $20 billion, was struck between brothers Jerry A. Grundhofer, Firstar CEO, and John F. Grundhofer, head of U.S. Bancorp.

The all-stock transaction consisted of 1.265 shares of Firstar for each share of U.S. Bancorp. Following completion of the merger, Jerry Grundhofer would serve as president and CEO, with John Grundhofer acting as chairman until retirement in 2002. While Firstar would hold 50.5 percent of the stock and seat 14 of 25 members on the board, its name would be relinquished.

The combination linked Firstar's significantly stronger retail operation with U.S. Bancorp's fee generation capabilities. According to an October 5, 2000, article in the *New York Times,* the Firstar retail franchise had been growing at 21 percent a year versus 6 percent for U.S. Bancorp.

The Minnesota-based bank's more robust fee-generating activities, on the other hand, provided an antidote to income slumps tied to credit cycles and interest rate shifts. U.S. Bancorp also brought a retail banking presence in the growing metropolitan areas of California and the Pacific Northwest to the new alliance, which would span 24 states.

Firstar's merger strategy had taken it from $20 billion in assets to $74 billion in assets, during the late 1990s. The integration of the $86 billion asset U.S. Bancorp, though, would be its most challenging to date. Cincinnati-based Star Banc Corp bought Firstar for $7.2 billion in 1998, retaining the Firstar name. The new Firstar then bought Mercantile Bancorp of St. Louis for $10 billion, the following year. When Banking veteran Jerry Grundhofer took charge of Star Banc in 1993, it had $7.6 billion in assets and operated in three states.

Initially the stock market reacted negatively to the pending Firstar-U.S. Bancorp deal, but share price rebounded as the year wound down. Bank stocks in general had climbed with the expectation of interest rate cuts by the Federal Reserve Board, according to the *Business Journal-Milwaukee*.

The period was marked by both a slowing U.S. economy and some troubled large commercial loans. Although Firstar and U.S. Bancorp had some problem loans on their books, an analyst with Dain Rauscher Wessels in Minneapolis told the *Business Journal*, "their assets are pretty clean," with both appearing to have "nonperformers and net charge-offs under control." The analyst, Jon Arfstrom, held a "long investment position in U.S. Bancorp," according to the December 29, 2000, article.

NOT SO EASY: 2001–06

The $22.1 billion deal closed in February 2001. In August, the bank reported it had incurred greater than expected merger and restructuring charges, upping the total to $1.4 billion from $800 million. The shutdown of one unit and the restructuring of another, led to the additional charges. According to *American Banker,* the new U.S. Bancorp, consisting of $160 billion in assets, ten million customers, and 2,200 branches, planned to focus "on sustaining the consumer-banking unit's growth." The company, which employed 50,000 nationwide, expected to cut about 2,500 jobs due to the merger.

Significant segments of U.S. Bancorp's card business were touched by the September 11, 2001, terrorist attacks on the United States. Declining corporate travel suddenly halted with the shutdown of the airports. Then in the wake of the tragedy, as the country grappled with fear and uncertainty, businesses canceled trips, hurting card-related revenues. On the other hand, Department of Defense spending on cards for procurements ramped up with the advent of the "war on terrorism," *Cardline* reported.

During the third quarter of 2001, U.S. Bancorp recorded an unanticipated $1 billion charge related loan loss reserves and loan charge-offs. In 2002 U.S. Bancorp moved Piper Jaffray from its position as a unit in the company to one of a subsidiary, while retaining 100 percent ownership. Not only had Piper Jaffray's profits fallen, its culture clashed with the workings of the bank. "We find growth companies in the very early stages and invest capital, which is very different than a large commercial bank with *Fortune* 500 clients and huge balance sheets," Piper Jaffray CEO Andrew Duff told *American Banker*. He added that unlike U.S. Bancorp, the high-net-worth investment bank did "not use pricing as [its] core strategy." Piper Jaffray was spun off as an independent, public company in late 2003.

Jerry Grundhofer, meanwhile, focused on the core banking business of collecting deposits and making loans. The bank improved customer service at the branch level, tied branch manager bonuses to performance, promoted products to customers shopping in its grocery store locations, eliminated a monthly fee for Internet bill payment, and introduced a check cash reward program, Chris Serres outlined in a April 2004 *Minneapolis Star Tribune* article. The cumulative result was a positive influx of deposits. Also on the plus side, U.S. Bancorp had been able to reduce the level of funds set aside for possible loan losses.

U.S. Bancorp's performance remained solid, going into the middle of the decade but its share price stagnated. "While rising interest rates have hurt all bank stocks, U.S. Bancorp consistently lags behind its peers," Thomas Lee wrote for the *Star Tribune*. "Banks make money by offering consumers interest on their deposits, then loaning that money at a higher rate, thus pocketing the difference, or 'spread.' Unfortunately for banks, the spread between deposits and loans has virtually disappeared since the Fed began raising rates in June 2004, which means tighter profit margins."

Analysts floated a variety of explanations for investors' attitude toward U.S. Bancorp. Peers who raised interest rates to attract customers or practiced aggressive cross selling fared better in the market. U.S. Bancorp, instead, relied on less revered fee-based sales to stabilize income, according to the April 2006 *Star Tribune* article. Additionally, some investors expressed concern Grundhofer might launch another large merger, one that could set the company back. Prior to the U.S. Bancorp acquisition Firstar ranked among the nation's most profitable banks.

In July 2006, U.S. Bancorp announced Grundhofer's pending retirement. President and COO Richard Davis would succeed his longtime boss as CEO in

December, with Grundhofer continuing to serve as chairman until the end of 2007.

BROADER PROBLEMS: 2007–09

Richard Davis, faced with declining retail market share, implemented a plan to reverse the trend and lessen the company's dependency on fee-generating services, such as credit card transactions, to bolster income. Among the tactics were expanded hours and staffing at key retail branches, added high-traffic locations in retail stores and supermarkets, and improved product cross selling.

The sixth largest U.S. bank returned about 80 percent of its profits to its shareholders through buying back shares and paying out dividends. To continue this practice, along with building or buying new branches, U.S. Bancorp had to grow deposits and loans, analyst Richard Bove surmised in a June 2007 *Star Tribune* article.

While U.S. Bancorp increased deposit and loan volume and retained capital strength, it still suffered the effects of the mortgage-market triggered economic meltdown, which began toward the end of 2007. An increase in the credit loss provision, and in net charge-offs, mitigated improvements in net interest income during 2008. The company continued to be profitable, but overall earnings declined. Rattled banking customers, meanwhile, turned to institutions perceived as solid, seeking a safe haven.

In November 2008, U.S. Bancorp had announced its intention to participate in the U.S. Treasury's Capital Purchase Program, later issuing $6.6 billion of preferred stock and related warrants. By early 2009, Davis was expressing his disenchantment with the program.

Katie Kuehner-Hebert wrote in *American Banker:* Davis "complained that the program's goals and rules have been a moving target since it was created. He also said the [Troubled Asset Relief Program (TARP)] was hurting healthy banking companies like his, which were 'told, not asked' by the government to take the money last fall."

The plan had morphed from capital infusion into an otherwise frozen market to the shoring up of troubled institutions, under TARP. U.S. Bancorp cut its dividend, partly due to the deepening economic turndown, but also to expedite the payback of government funds.

In April 2009, the Financial Accounting Standards Board eased rules related to how companies valued their assets, untying them from current market conditions. "Bankers have argued that the rules are unfair at a time when the market for assets is basically shut down. The

rules have forced financial institutions to raise new capital to offset the losses. Opponents have said the revisions, which some analysts have estimated could boost earnings by as much as 20 percent, could obscure the true picture of some institutions' true financial health," Susan Feyder explained for the *Star Tribune.* U.S. Bancorp, holder of some deteriorating assets, received a bump in stock price upon the news.

The government, meanwhile, was administering stress tests of the nation's 19 largest banks to determine their capacity to survive even more dire economic conditions, complete with higher unemployment and greater losses in mortgage, home equity, commercial and industrial, real estate, and credit card portfolios. U.S. Bancorp's outlook, for the time being, appeared positive.

Jeffrey L. Covell; Thomas Derdak
Updated, Mariko Fujinaka; Kathleen Peippo

PRINCIPAL SUBSIDIARIES

U.S. Bank; U.S. Bancorp Investments, Inc.; FAF Advisors Inc.; U.S. Bancorp Fund Services, LLC; U.S. Bancorp Insurance Services, LLC; Elavon, Inc., Elan Financial Services.

PRINCIPAL OPERATING UNITS

Payment Services; Wholesale Banking; Consumer Banking; Wealth Management and Securities Services.

PRINCIPAL COMPETITORS

Bank of America Corporation; JPMorgan Chase & Co.; Wells Fargo & Company.

FURTHER READING

Anderson, Michael A., "U.S. Bancorp's Interstate Bid Begins Anew," *Business Journal-Portland,* May 19, 1986, p. 1.

Atlas, Riva, "U.S. Bancorp to Be Acquired by Firstar for $21 Billion," *New York Times,* October 2, 2000, p. C4.

Bennett, Robert A., "Roger Faces Goliath," *United States Banker,* June 1992, p. 20.

Condon, Bernard, "Brother, Can You Spare a Bank?" *Forbes,* April 3, 2000.

Crockett, Barton, "U.S. Bancorp to Ax 52 Branches After Merger," *American Banker,* October 27, 1995, p. 4.

DePass, Dee, "FBS Reaches West," *Minneapolis Star Tribune,* March 21, 1997, p. D1.

Dobbs, Kevin, "Lifetime Achievement: Jerry Grundhofer," *American Banker,* December 5, 2008, p. A26.

Feyder, Susan, "Regulatory Change May Boost Banks' Bottom Lines," *Minneapolis Star Tribune,* April 3, 2009, p. 1D.

Fitch, Mike, "Mother Lode's Buyer Got Good Deal, Say Observers," *Puget Sound Business Journal,* November 6, 1989, p. 22.

Gewirtz, Lisa, "U.S. Bank Corp Pushes Piper Jaffray Off to Arm's Length," *Wall Street Letter,* April 15, 2002, pp. 1+.

Gores, Paul, "A Year After Merger," *Milwaukee Journal Sentinel,* October 1, 2001, p. 1D.

Heind, John, "Buy or Be Bought," *Forbes,* May 18, 1987, p. 48.

Jaffe, Thomas, "Cheap Bank," *Forbes,* June 29, 1987, p. 122.

Jordon, Steve, "First Bank Is Poised to Grow in Nebraska," *Omaha World-Herald,* June 9, 1995, p. 14.

———, "U.S. Bancorp Chairman Is Building for Long Haul," *Omaha World-Herald,* June 21, 2000, p. 18.

Kapiloff, Howard, "Fourth-of-July Merger Fireworks," *American Banker,* July 5, 1994, p. 1.

Klinkerman, Steve, and Karen Gullo, "First Bank System to Purchase Morgan's Corporate Trust Unit," *American Banker,* January 5, 1993, p. 5.

Kuehner-Hebert, Katie, "Eye on Exit, USB Slashes Dividend," *American Banker,* March 5, 2009, p. 1.

Lee, Thomas, "Continuity Likely in U.S. Bank Transition," *Minneapolis Star Tribune,* July 19, 2006, p. 1D.

———, "A Stock That's Stuck in Neutral," *Minneapolis Star Tribune,* April 7, 2006, p. 1D.

———, "U.S. Bank Looks for a Bounce," *Minneapolis Star Tribune,* June 3, 2007, p. 1D.

Leibowitz, Alissa, "Grundhofer Brothers Ready to Close Merger," *American Banker,* January 3, 2001, p. 1.

Manning, Jeff, "Bankruptcies May Be Lever for U.S. Bank," *Business Journal-Portland,* December 9, 1991, p. 1.

Milligan, John W., "Making First Bank Work," *US Banker,* March 1, 1997, p. 32.

Ota, Alan K., "First Bank Begins to Issue Pink Slips at U.S. Bancorp," *Portland Oregonian,* June 4, 1997, p. C1.

———, "U.S. Bancorp: Hunter or Prey?" *Portland Oregonian,* September 12, 1996, p. B1.

———, "U.S. Bancorp on Guard Duty," *Portland Oregonian,* May 8, 1996, p. B1.

Ota, Alan K., and Steve Woodward, "First Bank Wooed U.S. Bank in Polite but Insistent Romance," *Portland Oregonian,* March 26, 1997.

"Purchase by U.S. Bancorp to Create Northwest Giant," *New York Times,* May 9, 1995, p. D2.

Reilly, Patrick, "U.S. Bancorp Revises Merger Charges," *American Banker,* August 16, 2001, p. 20.

Rhoads, Christopher, "First Bank System Buying U.S. Bancorp; Pricey $8.4B Deal Is Banking Industry's Fourth Largest Ever," *American Banker,* March 21, 1997, p. 1.

Schwab, Paul, "Wall Street Renews Its Love Affair with Firstar," *Business Journal-Milwaukee,* December 29, 2000, p. 1.

Serres, Chris, "No More Merger Mania at Piper," *Minneapolis Star Tribune,* July 7, 2004, p. 1D.

———, "U.S. Bancorp Profit Beats Analysts' Estimates: Shareholders at Tuesday's Annual Meeting Vented Some Frustration," *McClatchy-Tribune Business News,* April 22, 2209.

———, "U.S. Bancorp Regains Strength," *Minneapolis Star Tribune,* April 21, 2004, p. 1D.

"Shareholders Approve Merger of U.S. Bancorp & West One, Bancorp," *PR Newswire,* October 3, 1995, p. 1.

Silvestri, Scott, and Laura Mandaro, "U.S. Bancorp CEO Talks Like a Buyer," *American Banker,* June 19, 2000, p. 1.

Solomon, Debra, "Friday Is Banks' Stress-Test Moment of Truth," *Wall Street Journal Asia,* April 23, 2009, p. M4.

Talley, Karen, "U.S. Bancorp's Piper Deal an Integration Success," *American Banker,* November 10, 1999, p. 1.

Taylor, John H., "No Chest-Beater," *Forbes,* May 11, 1992, p. 172.

"U.S. Bancorp Loses and Wins As Result of Terrorist Attacks," *Cardline,* September 21, 2001, p. 1.

"U.S. Bancorp Will Acquire Piper Jaffray," *Portland Oregonian,* December 16, 1997, p. B1.

Wagner, Daniel, "Fed Harder on Regional Banks?" *Deseret News,* April 22, 2009, p. A 11.

Zack, Jeffrey, "Technology Gives First Bank's Grundhofer a Cost-Cutting Edge," *American Banker,* May 9, 1994, p. 1.

Zimmerman, Rachel, "Branch Closures Likely in U.S. Bank-West One Deal," *Puget Sound Business Journal,* August 25, 1995, p. 7.

UnitedHealth Group Incorporated

———— ∎ ————

UnitedHealth Group Center
9900 Bren Road East
Minnetonka, Minnesota 55343
U.S.A.
Telephone: (952) 936-1300
Toll Free: (800) 328-5979
Fax: (952) 936-1819
Web site: http://www.unitedhealthgroup.com

Public Company
Incorporated: 1977 as United HealthCare Corporation
Employees: 75,000
Sales: $81.19 billion (2008)
Stock Exchanges: New York
Ticker Symbol: UNH
NAICS: 524114 Direct Health and Medical Insurance Carriers; 424210 Drugs and Druggists' Sundries Merchant Wholesalers; 524113 Direct Life Insurance Carriers; 551112 Offices of Other Holding Companies

∎ ∎ ∎

UnitedHealth Group Incorporated is one of the largest and most diversified healthcare companies in the United States. Its core healthcare insurance services business offers a variety of network-based managed-care plans for several sectors of the market, including small to large companies, individuals, students, Medicaid enrollees, and seniors. In addition to its health maintenance organizations (HMOs), preferred provider organizations (PPOs), and point-of-service plans, UnitedHealth in

partnership with AARP offers a variety of Medicare plans to the nation's seniors through its Ovations unit. In addition, the company's AmeriChoice unit offers plans for beneficiaries of government-sponsored healthcare programs, such as State Medicaid Children's Health Insurance Programs (SCHIP). Through these operations, UnitedHealth provides health coverage to about 36 million members. Among the company's other operations are OptumHealth, which offers a range of health, financial, and specialty benefit services, such as personalized health management programs, employee assistance programs, dental and vision plans, and health savings accounts; Ingenix, a provider of healthcare information services; and the firm's pharmacy benefit management services unit, Prescription Solutions.

HMO PIONEER

UnitedHealth Group Incorporated, originally known as United HealthCare Corporation, informally traces its roots to the development of the HMO as a model for organized healthcare. The HMO's leading spokesperson, Dr. Paul Ellwood, helped develop several HMO companies in Minnesota and nearly singlehandedly thrust managed healthcare onto the national stage during the early 1970s. In 1970 Ellwood, who later became known as the "Father of the HMO," founded the Minnesota-based healthcare think tank, Interstudy, and later succeeded in getting congressional approval for his HMO model. In 1971 Ellwood hired Richard Burke to help put the HMO model to practice. Three years later Burke founded Charter Med Incorporated as a Minnetonka, Minnesota-based for-profit company organized to manage the newly created Physicians Health Plan of

Minnesota, which under Minnesota's HMO law at the time was required to be a nonprofit company.

In January 1977 United HealthCare Corporation was incorporated and acquired Charter Med. Through acquisitions and expansion of its management services United grew steadily as an owner and manager of HMOs, and by 1984 the company was running 11 HMOs in ten states.

With plans to step up expansion and acquisition efforts, United HealthCare went public in 1984 and began trading as an over-the-counter stock. Soon thereafter the company launched an ambitious national expansion program, which included starting new HMOs and acquiring multistate HMO companies.

In June 1985 United HealthCare made its first major acquisition since going public, acquiring Share Development Corporation, an Indiana-based multistate HMO, through a stock swap valued at nearly $60 million. Share Development increased United Health-Care's health plan membership by 167,000 enrollees, and by the end of the year United HealthCare and its subsidiaries were active in 22 states, covering 822,400 members through company-owned or company-managed health plans.

In November 1986 United HealthCare paid $83 million to acquire the Colorado-based Peak Health Care Inc., a four-state HMO network with 104,000 enrollees.

By the end of the year United HealthCare owned or managed healthcare plans serving about 1.6 million people. The expansion efforts paid short-term dividends, and for the year the company earned $7.2 million on revenues of more than $216 million, which was more than double the company's 1985 revenues and more than six times United HealthCare's 1984 revenues.

GROWING PAINS

In April 1987 Kenneth Simmons, the former president of Peak Health Care, was named chief operating officer of United HealthCare, succeeding Robert Ditmore, who remained president. Seven months later Simmons was named to replace Richard Burke as chief executive in order to pacify Physician Health Plan (PHP) doctors who were balking at Burke's management style. Burke, who remained chairperson, also gave up his post as chief executive of PHP in November 1987 and lost his status as the company's largest shareholder that month when United HealthCare, with finances strained by rapid expansion, turned to the New York investment group Warburg, Pincus Capital Company L.P. for an infusion of cash. With an annual loss looming as a result of unprofitable and marginally profitable HMO start-ups, Warburg agreed to purchase $9.8 million worth of newly issued preferred voting stock and acquire a 39.5 percent stake in the company.

Although United HealthCare doubled its revenues in 1987 to more than $440 million, its operating expenses had grown at a faster rate, and the company lost $15.8 million for the year while its stock value fell from a 1986 high of $15.88 to $4.25 by the end of 1987. Unsteady market conditions, excessive administrative costs and price competition battles with traditional insurance companies led United HealthCare to abandon several health plans, including HMO start-ups in six large cities and another well-established HMO operation in Phoenix.

In 1988 United HealthCare completed its restructuring program, selling several unpromising businesses in areas in which it had entered highly competitive markets too late. In another restructuring move designed to shore up its relationship with PHP, United agreed to a new five-year contract in April 1988, which gave the PHP board of directors the power to appoint its own chief executive and other key officers.

In September 1988 United sold its interest in Peak Health Care Corporation for $41.5 million and raised an additional $31.6 million through a secondary public stock offering. Despite revenues that reached nearly $440 million that year, the company lost $36.7 million, bringing the cost of its extensive two-year restructuring to $53 million.

KEY DATES

1977: United HealthCare Corporation is incorporated as a pioneering HMO company based in Minnetonka, Minnesota.

1984: Company goes public to fund ambitious national expansion program.

1991: William McGuire is named chairman and CEO.

1994: United sells Diversified Pharmaceutical Services, Inc., for $2.3 billion.

1995: MetraHealth Companies, Inc., is acquired for about $1.69 billion.

1998: Company begins providing supplemental Medicare insurance through a partnership with the American Association of Retired Persons (AARP); company reorganizes around five core operating units and begins calling itself UnitedHealth Group.

2000: Company name is officially changed to UnitedHealth Group Incorporated.

2004: In deals totaling $7.7 billion, UnitedHealth acquires Rockville, Maryland-based Mid Atlantic Medical Services, Inc., and Oxford Health Plans, Inc., based in Trumbull, Connecticut.

2005: PacifiCare Health Systems, Inc., of Cypress, California, is acquired for $8.8 billion.

2006: McGuire is forced to resign over a scandal involving the backdating of stock options; Stephen J. Hemsley is named CEO.

Nevertheless, the restructuring program eventually returned United to profitability, and by the end of 1989 it was one of the largest publicly traded HMOs in the United States, serving about one million people in 15 states. The company was managing not only PHP, the largest HMO in Minnesota, but also Share Health Plan, the state's fourth largest HMO. For the year, United HealthCare earned $13.6 million on revenues of $412 million.

A RETURN TO EXPANSION

With its restructuring completed, the company began buying specialty companies designed to control some of the most exorbitant medical costs, including companies that managed programs for the aged, prescription drugs, mental health treatments, and organ transplants. At the same time, the company launched a new expansion and acquisition plan under the direction of Dr. William McGuire, a former Peak Health Care president who was promoted to United HealthCare president in 1989. The new program focused on geographic markets where the company was already operating.

In March 1990 United HealthCare held a secondary public offering of three million shares, adding about $100 million to the $60 million the company had at its disposal for acquisitions and operations. That month United HealthCare acquired PrimeCare Health Plan Inc., a Milwaukee-based HMO and the second largest HMO in Wisconsin with 103,000 members. The acquisition was designed to complement the services of a growing United HealthCare subsidiary, Diversified Pharmaceutical Services, Inc. (DPS), a provider of managed-care drug services to about 200,000 members of several Wisconsin HMOs. The acquisition also sent a signal to the business world that United HealthCare was ready to spend more of its resources to continue expanding its core business.

In July 1990 United became the first managed healthcare company to go after clients already associated with other HMOs, offering three types of healthcare services separately rather than in a package. The new services were designed to attract customers who already belonged to an HMO but wanted programs to further contain exorbitant medical costs. The services included: United Resource Network, a program designed to manage the delivery of high-cost, low-volume procedures such as organ transplants; Healthmarc, a program offering healthcare utilization review and case management services for workers' compensation claims; and Employee Performance Design, a group of employee assistance programs offering financial, personal, legal, and other advice to workers.

By the close of 1990 United HealthCare, with about 1.5 million members enrolled in its health plans, was serving more patients than any other independent HMO company. The company's members included those belonging to United HealthCare–owned HMOs in Chicago, Atlanta, Salt Lake City, Des Moines, and Milwaukee, as well as members belonging to HMOs United HealthCare was contracted to manage in other areas.

In capitalizing on the growing trend toward managed healthcare and the monitoring of medical expenses and claims procedures, United HealthCare's net income surged from $13.7 million in 1989 to $33.9 million in 1990, as revenues rose from $412 million to $605.5 million. Pacing the revenue growth were the increasing numbers of customers served by HMOs that United HealthCare owned or managed, as well as the company's growing list of specialty programs, particularly DPS.

ACQUISITIONS PUSH UNDER MCGUIRE

In February 1991 McGuire was named to the additional positions of chair and chief executive, succeeding Burke and Simmons. In April 1991 United acquired the Institute of Human Resources (IHR), a Rockville, Maryland-based employee assistance company operating one of the largest networks of employee counselors in the United States and providing phone counseling services to workers with mental health, drug abuse, or alcohol problems. United HealthCare's own employee assistance operation, Employee Performance Design, was merged into IHR with the combined operation comprising 2,650 mental health and employee assistance professionals working in 15 separate specialist networks in various regions of the United States.

In July 1991 two of the largest HMOs United HealthCare was managing, PHP and Share Health Plan, were merged into a single company, bringing more than 480,000 Minnesota medical plan enrollees together under one HMO. The merger allowed the new company, Medica, to provide for a wider range of healthcare benefit packages offered by a single company and also served to shore up the Share Health Plan organization, which had been experiencing financial difficulties and was losing members. As a result of the merger, PHP was renamed Medica Choice, and Share Health became Medica Primary.

That same month United purchased the Wauwatosa, Wisconsin-based Samaritan Health Plan Insurance Corporation, one of the first hospital-sponsored HMOs in the country. Four months later Samaritan was merged into PrimeCare, creating the second largest HMO in the Milwaukee area with a total of 157,000 members. The following month United expanded its presence in New England when it acquired Ocean State Physicians Health Plan, a Rhode Island-based HMO previously managed by United HealthCare. By the time United HealthCare closed its books on 1991 it was trading on the New York Stock Exchange and had more than doubled its previous year's income to $74.8 million on revenues of $847.1 million.

In January 1992 United HealthCare paid $84 million to acquire Physicians Health Plan of Ohio, a Columbus-based HMO with 154,000 members. In March United HealthCare staged another secondary public offering, generating $200 million. Then, in July, United HealthCare acquired the assets of HealthPro, Inc., a Massachusetts-based benefits management

company providing utilization management and medical review services to government agencies, labor union health and welfare funds, and corporations. One month later United HealthCare agreed to acquire a 50 percent stake in Physicians Health Plan of North Carolina, a 50,000-member health plan.

By the end of 1992 United HealthCare was considered an industry leader in product diversification among managed healthcare companies, as well as an HMO force in Minneapolis and a growing HMO factor in Milwaukee, Ohio, and Rhode Island. Acquisitions, enrollment growth, and increased sales in specialty operations all contributed to significant financial gains, and for 1992 United HealthCare's revenues leaped 70 percent to $1.4 billion, while income rose 54 percent to $111.5 million.

In early 1993 United HealthCare became Ohio's preeminent HMO when it paid $100 million to acquire Western Ohio Health Care Corporation, a 185,000-member health plan and the largest HMO in Dayton, Ohio. The deal was the fifth and largest acquisition of an HMO by United HealthCare since 1991 and gave United HealthCare 338,000 HMO members in Ohio, or 20 percent of the state's HMO enrollment.

In March 1993 DPS reconfigured its product lines in order to become more competitive and began targeting the public sector market, including state and federal government health insurance programs. In July, United HealthCare completed its first divestiture since 1987, selling its Des Moines-based health plan with about 26,000 members. A month later, United acquired HMO America, Inc., in an exchange of stock valued at around $370 million. HMO America was the second largest HMO in Chicago, owning and operating a 300,000-member plan, Chicago HMO Ltd. This operation was combined with United HealthCare's Share Illinois company, a 97,300-member plan, to form United HealthCare of Illinois, which ranked as the largest managed-care health system in the Chicago area.

United HealthCare's deal making accelerated in 1994. Two significant acquisitions were completed in May of that year, the stock-swap takeovers of Complete Health Services, Inc., and Ramsay-HMO, Inc. Birmingham, Alabama-based Complete Health, acquired for about $241 million in stock, owned or managed HMOs in Alabama, Louisiana, Tennessee, Arkansas, Georgia, Mississippi, and Florida with an aggregate total of 272,000 members. Ramsay-HMO, based in Coral Gables, Florida, owned and operated a 177,000-member HMO in southern and central Florida. Valued at roughly $560 million, it was United's largest acquisition to that time. United was particularly interested in Complete Health and Ramsay because they operated in markets that had been relatively underpenetrated in managed care and therefore held solid potential for further growth. Also in 1994, United HealthCare completed a major divestment, selling DPS to a U.S. subsidiary of London-based SmithKline Beecham plc for $2.3 billion in cash. As part of the deal, United and SmithKline entered into an alliance through which United continued to provide management and administrative services to DPS and continued to use DPS's services for its health plans. United HealthCare recorded a net gain of $1.38 billion from this sale.

BLOCKBUSTER METRAHEALTH DEAL

United used some of its hoard of cash on its January 1995 purchase of GenCare Health Systems, Inc., which owned and operated the largest health plan in St. Louis, with 230,000 members. The purchase price was $515.4 million in cash. Then, in its biggest acquisition thus far, United acquired MetraHealth Companies, Inc., in October 1995 for about $1.69 billion. MetraHealth, which had been formed earlier in 1995 from the combination of the group healthcare operations of Metropolitan Life Insurance Company and the Travelers Insurance Group, provided healthcare coverage to more than ten million individuals. Only about 5.9 million of these individuals were enrolled in managed-care plans, with the remainder in traditional indemnity insurance plans making this deal something of a departure for United, which had made its mark running HMOs. The purchase of MetraHealth was nevertheless strategically important because it moved United HealthCare into several major new markets, including New York City, Los Angeles, San Francisco, Houston, and Dallas. It also beefed up the company's client list to include nearly half of the largest publicly held firms in the United States, which provided United with a lucrative platform for selling its specialty healthcare services, including its mental health, employee assistance, and organ transplant management programs.

Two much smaller deals were completed in 1996, the purchases of PHP, Inc., a North Carolina HMO with 132,000 members, and Nashville-based Health-Wise of America, Inc., the owner or operator of HMOs serving 154,000 members in Maryland, Kentucky, Tennessee, and Arkansas. At the end of 1996, United HealthCare had nearly 13.8 million members enrolled in its core health plans. The firm's operations encompassed all 50 states. Its revenues that year, swelled by the string of acquisitions, nearly doubled to $10.07 billion, while its net earnings had reached $355.6 million. Also in 1996, United broke ranks with its managed-care brethren by rolling out an "open-access"

HMO plan allowing members to visit specialists without first gaining approval from their primary-care physician.

During 1997 United HealthCare concentrated mainly on consolidating its acquisitions, although it did strengthen its healthcare information operations by purchasing Medicode, Inc., a Salt Lake City-based developer and marketer of financial and clinical management tools for healthcare payers, purchasers, and providers. United that year also entered into a long-term alliance with the American Association of Retired Persons (AARP) to provide supplemental Medicare insurance, so-called Medigap coverage, marketed through the AARP. In early 1998 the company took over the servicing of AARP's existing Medigap policies, which had been administered by the Prudential Insurance Company of America. That first year, United HealthCare's portion of the premium revenue generated from the approximately four million Medigap policies that had been purchased through AARP amounted to about $3.5 billion.

In May 1998 United HealthCare agreed to acquire Louisville-based Humana Inc. in a stock swap initially valued at $5.5 billion. The deal promised to create the largest managed healthcare company in the United States, with annual revenues of $28 billion and 10.4 million full-paying HMO and PPO members (and overall membership of more than 19 million), exceeding the nine million of Kaiser Permanente. In August 1998, however, United HealthCare's stock plummeted after the company disclosed it was taking a $900 million charge for a restructuring involving about 4,000 layoffs and the divestment of several peripheral operations. This cost-cutting effort was taken in particular to offset unexpectedly high costs in HMO plans for Medicare enrollees. The stock dive sharply lessened the value of the deal to Humana shareholders, and Humana walked away from the merger.

REORGANIZATION AS UNITEDHEALTH GROUP

In an additional restructuring undertaken in 1998, United reorganized itself into a healthcare holding company with a handful of key operating units: United-Healthcare, concentrating on locally based health plans; Uniprise, specializing in healthcare insurance and related services for large, multistate employers; Ovations, handling the firm's healthcare programs for older Americans, including those offered in partnership with AARP as well as EverCare, a provider of medical services to nursing home residents; Specialized Care Services, which included United's mental health, employee assistance, and organ transplant businesses; and Ingenix, centering on healthcare information operations. In connection with this overhaul, the company began calling itself UnitedHealth Group, although the official name of the parent company was not changed to UnitedHealth Group Incorporated until early 2000.

Back on the acquisition front, UnitedHealth in October 1998 became the largest health insurer in Arizona by paying $235 million in cash for HealthPartners of Arizona, Inc., which ran a statewide health plan with 509,000 members. The company's Specialized Care Services unit expanded in June of the following year by purchasing Dental Benefit Providers, Inc., (DBP) for $105 million. DBP ranked as one of the largest managed dental plan companies in the United States, serving nearly two million people in 29 states and the District of Columbia. In a $214 million, September 1999 deal, the Ingenix unit acquired Worldwide Clinical Trials, Inc. (WCT), a leading contract research organization. WCT and the 1998-acquired Kern-McNeill International formed the basis for the creation in 2000 of Ingenix Pharmaceutical Services, which conducted clinical trials for pharmaceutical and biotechnology companies around the world on a contract basis.

Late in 1999 UnitedHealth Group made a considerable splash when it announced it would eliminate the precertification procedures that had long been employed by managed-care health plans to control costs, and had long been the bane of patients frustrated by insurers overruling the decisions of their doctors. UnitedHealth had determined that it was actually spending more than it saved scrutinizing doctors' decisions. Although the company eliminated precertification, it retained the right to refuse to pay for treatments it deemed unwarranted, which to a degree undercut the move. Nevertheless, as a replacement for precertification, UnitedHealth put into place an effort to push doctors to practice better medicine based on nationally accepted benchmarks for medical care, such as recommending mammograms and regularly screening patients' cholesterol levels.

By 2001, UnitedHealth's revenues had ballooned to $25.45 billion, which translated into a remarkable compound annual growth rate of 25 percent over the decade since McGuire took over as chairman and CEO. Profits for 2001 reached $913 million. In October of that year, the firm's Specialized Care Services unit expanded once again, moving into vision-care benefits via the $143 million purchase of Spectera, Inc. Baltimore-based Spectera administered group vision-care benefits for 4.7 million individuals across the country based on a network of 8,200 doctors, more than 80 retail vision-care facilities, and a laboratory churning out more than 6,000 pairs of glasses each week. In September 2002 UnitedHealth Group acquired Ameri-

Choice Corporation for about $500 million in stock. AmeriChoice provided healthcare benefits and services for Medicaid recipients in New York, New Jersey, and Pennsylvania. The deal boosted UnitedHealth's Medicaid business membership to one million in 17 states. This business subsequently adopted the AmeriChoice name.

ANOTHER ACQUISITION SPREE

A new string of acquisitions, including three billion-dollar-plus blockbusters, was the driving force behind UnitedHealth Group's skyrocketing revenues, which reached $71.54 billion in 2006. In two of the smaller deals, UnitedHealth moved headlong into the nascent field for medical savings accounts. In November 2003 the company acquired Indianapolis-based Golden Rule Financial Corporation, a market leader in medical savings accounts set up by individuals, for $495 million. Golden Rule also ran a life insurance and annuity business, but UnitedHealth subsequently sold it to OneAmerica Financial Partners, Inc. In December 2004 UnitedHealth spent $305 million for Minneapolis-based Definity Health Corporation, which offered so-called consumer-directed health plans centering on high deductibles and health savings accounts. Because it specialized in administering such plans for large self-insured U.S. employers, Definity became part of UnitedHealth's Uniprise unit.

The three blockbuster deals completed during this period greatly enhanced UnitedHealth's national reach. In February 2004 the company more than doubled its presence in the mid-Atlantic region by acquiring Rockville, Maryland-based Mid Atlantic Medical Services, Inc., for $2.7 billion in stock and cash. Mid Atlantic Medical operated HMOs and related services for about two million people in that region. UnitedHealth next bolstered its position in the highly competitive northeastern market by purchasing Oxford Health Plans, Inc., in a deal valued at approximately $5 billion. Headquartered in Trumbull, Connecticut, and operating within New York City, northern New Jersey, and southern Connecticut, Oxford had about 1.5 million members in its HMOs, PPOs, point-of-service plans, and consumer-directed health plans.

Then, in its largest acquisition to that time, UnitedHealth greatly enhanced its operations in the western United States and particularly in California when it acquired PacifiCare Health Systems, Inc., for $8.8 billion in December 2005. PacifiCare, based in Cypress, California, offered individuals, employers, and Medicare recipients a variety of health plans, and its more than three million members pushed UnitedHealth's total membership to around 23 million, second only to Well-

Point, Inc.'s 32 million. In addition to California, PacifiCare's main markets included Arizona, Colorado, Nevada, Oklahoma, Oregon, Texas, and Washington. PacifiCare also operated several specialty healthcare businesses, including behavioral health, dental, and vision services operations, and these were integrated into UnitedHealth's established businesses. This acquisition also marked UnitedHealth Group's return to the pharmacy benefit management business via its inheritance of PacifiCare's Prescription Solutions unit.

In the meantime, the Medicare Modernization Act of 2003 had brought sweeping changes to the government-administered healthcare program. In addition to an expansion of the privately administered Medicare Advantage program, the legislation also mandated the January 2006 launch of a new voluntary Medicare prescription drug plan known as Part D. Under a contract with the Centers for Medicare & Medicaid Services, UnitedHealth became one of a small number of insurers offering these plans on a nationwide basis. By the end of 2006, the company's Ovations unit had enrolled around 5.7 million members in the Part D program, including 4.5 million in standalone drug plans and 1.2 million in Medicare Advantage plans incorporating Part D coverage. In 2007 UnitedHealth extended and broadened its partnership with AARP in a new seven-year agreement that encompassed Medicare Advantage, Medicare Part D, and Medicare supplemental and indemnity insurance.

STOCK OPTIONS AND BILLING CONTROVERSIES

During the astounding stretch of growth McGuire had engineered, the chairman and CEO was the subject of occasional criticism for his huge compensation packages, which often made him the highest-paid CEO in Minnesota, as calculated by the *Minneapolis Star Tribune*. By the end of 2005, McGuire had amassed unexercised stock options valued at $1.78 billion, more than any other U.S. corporate chieftain. These stock options eventually proved his downfall after an internal investigation revealed that at least some of them were "likely" backdated, a practice that served to further increase their value. After months of controversy surrounding his stock options, McGuire resigned in late 2006. Stephen J. Hemsley was named the new CEO, while longtime board member and former CEO and Chairman Richard Burke assumed the chairmanship once again.

In further fallout from the scandal, McGuire and Hemsley in November 2006 agreed to forfeit stock options worth about $390 million, and in March 2007 UnitedHealth reduced its earnings over the previous 12 years by $1.53 billion. To settle two civil actions that had been filed against him, McGuire in late 2007 agreed to forfeit an additional $420 million in stock options. About a year later, the Securities and Exchange Commission fined him $7 million, which was the largest stock-option-backdating civil penalty levied against an individual. McGuire was also barred from serving as an officer or director of a public company for ten years. In July 2008 UnitedHealth agreed to pay $912 million to resolve shareholder class-action lawsuits that had been brought against it because of the backdated stock options.

Late in 2007 UnitedHealth reorganized itself into four units: Health Care Services, which included UnitedHealthcare, Uniprise, Ovations, and AmeriChoice; OptumHealth, the rebranded Specialized Care Services unit; Ingenix; and Prescription Solutions, which had previously been included in the Ovations business. That year, the company also agreed to acquire Las Vegas-based Sierra Health Services, Inc., but the deal was the subject of a lengthy antitrust review and did not close until February 2008. Purchased for about $2.6 billion in cash, Sierra further strengthened UnitedHealth's position in the West with its more than 800,000 HMO members in Nevada, Arizona, and Texas. To gain antitrust approval, UnitedHealth was forced to divest its Medicare Advantage business in the Las Vegas area, which encompassed about 30,000 members. Other 2008 acquisitions included the $730 million purchase of Fiserv, Inc.'s health businesses, which provided medical benefits administration, care-facilitation, pharmacy benefit management, and other healthcare services; and the $930 million buyout of Unison Health Plans, a provider of government-sponsored health plan coverage to individuals in Pennsylvania, Ohio, Tennessee, Delaware, South Carolina, and Washington, D.C. Unison was merged into AmeriChoice, the operations of which consequently stretched across 21 states and the District of Columbia.

The stock options controversy had barely died down when UnitedHealth Group was embroiled in another controversy surrounding its billing practices. In one of a string of state actions, California in early 2008 fined the company $3.5 million for improper handling of insurance claims, including wrongful denials of claims, incorrect payments, and repeated requests for documentation. The state further found more than 130,000 violations of state rules concerning health claims, an amount that could lead to fines approaching $1.3 billion. In January 2009 UnitedHealth reached an agreement with the attorney general of New York to pay $50 million to help create a new, independent database for determining the amount managed-care insurers pay for out-of-network claims. This database was slated to replace one run by UnitedHealth's Ingenix that had been at the center of some of the billing controversies. The company also agreed to pay $350 million to settle a class-action lawsuit, spearheaded by the American Medical Association, over the way Ingenix had determined the out-of-network payments.

At this time, UnitedHealth was also contending with the deep economic downturn, and the loss of a considerable number of health plan enrollees as companies across the country slashed their workforces and the unemployment rate shot up. Although revenues grew an additional 7.6 percent in 2008 to $81.19 billion, profits fell 36 percent to $2.98 billion. Concurrently, pressure for significant reform of the U.S. healthcare system was building, particularly following the election of Barack Obama to the U.S. presidency. The Obama administration was expected to increase regulation of the insurance industry and also push cost-cutting initiatives that were likely to dent insurers' profits. An early example arose in April 2009 when the federal government announced that it would cut payments for Medicare Advantage plans starting in 2010. This action was sure to have a fairly significant impact on UnitedHealth given its position as the largest provider of these plans with about 1.5 million members.

Roger W. Rouland
Updated, David E. Salamie

PRINCIPAL SUBSIDIARIES

AmeriChoice Corporation; Ingenix, Inc.; OptumHealth, Inc.; Oxford Health Plans LLC; Ovations, Inc.; PacifiCare Health Systems, LLC; RxSolutions, Inc.; UnitedHealthcare, Inc.; United HealthCare Services, Inc.

PRINCIPAL COMPETITORS

WellPoint, Inc.; Aetna Inc.; CIGNA Corporation; Humana Inc.; Kaiser Foundation Health Plan, Inc.; Health Net, Inc.; Coventry Health Care, Inc.; Medco Health Solutions, Inc.; CVS Caremark Corporation; Express Scripts, Inc.

FURTHER READING

Bandler, James, and Charles Forelle, "Bad Options: How a Giant Insurer Decided to Oust Hugely Successful CEO," *Wall Street Journal,* December 7, 2006, p. A1.

———, "Embattled CEO to Step Down at UnitedHealth," *Wall Street Journal,* October 16, 2006, p. A1.

Berman, Dennis K., and Vanessa Fuhrmans, "UnitedHealth Agrees to Buy Oxford," *Wall Street Journal,* April 27, 2004, p. A3.

Booth, Michael, "The Latest from the Father of the HMO," *Corporate Report–Minnesota,* October 1991, p. 28.

Brin, Dinah Wisenberg, "UnitedHealth's Net Falls 40%," *Wall Street Journal,* January 23, 2009, p. B6.

Burton, Thomas M., "United HealthCare Takes a Big Charge," *Wall Street Journal,* August 7, 1998, p. A3.

———, "United Health, Humana Deal Is Terminated," *Wall Street Journal,* August 10, 1998, p. A3.

———, "UnitedHealth to End Ruling on Treatments," *Wall Street Journal,* November 9, 1999, p. A3.

Burton, Thomas M., and Steven Lipin, "United HealthCare to Acquire Humana," *Wall Street Journal,* May 29, 1998, p. A3.

Fiedler, Terry, "The Quiet Giant," *Minneapolis Star Tribune,* September 29, 2002, p. 1D.

Fuhrmans, Vanessa, "Incentive Plan; A Big Insurer Bets on Hot Trend: Shopping Around for Health Care," *Wall Street Journal,* October 24, 2005, p. A1.

———, "UnitedHealth Agrees to Pay $912 Million to Settle Suits," *Wall Street Journal,* July 3, 2008, p. B1.

———, "UnitedHealth Settles Class Actions," *Wall Street Journal,* January 16, 2009, p. B3.

———, "UnitedHealth's Quest: Firm to Buy Sierra for $2.6 Billion," *Wall Street Journal,* March 13, 2007, p. A12.

Fuhrmans, Vanessa, and James Bandler, "Ex-CEO Forfeits $620 Million in Options Case," *Wall Street Journal,* December 7, 2007, p. A1.

Fuhrmans, Vanessa, Dennis K. Berman, and Rhonda Rundle, "Two Health Plans Agree on a Deal for $8.1 Billion: UnitedHealth Adds Heft in California and Medicare with Move on PacifiCare," *Wall Street Journal,* July 7, 2005, p. A1.

Gibson, Richard, "United HealthCare to Buy GenCare, St. Louis HMO, in $520 Million Pact," *Wall Street Journal,* September 13, 1994, p. A5.

Gold, Jacqueline S., "Future Doc?: Meet the Current Health-Care Darling," *Financial World,* November 10, 1992, pp. 25–26.

Hamburger, Tom, and Glenn Howatt, "United HealthCare to Handle AARP's Medigap Business," *Minneapolis Star Tribune,* February 28, 1997, p. 1A.

Hirschman, Carolyn, "United HealthCare to Be Ohio's Largest HMO," *Business First–Columbus,* January 25, 1993, p. 3.

Howatt, Glenn, "Restructuring United HealthCare Corp. Changes Name to UnitedHealth Group," *Minneapolis Star Tribune,* December 11, 1998, p. 3D.

———, "United HealthCare Corp. Is Buying Largest St. Louis HMO for $520 Million," *Minneapolis Star Tribune,* September 13, 1994, p. 1D.

———, "United HealthCare Corp. to Buy Chicago-Based HMO America," *Minneapolis Star Tribune,* May 14, 1993, p. 1D.

———, "United HealthCare Plans to Acquire MetraHealth," *Minneapolis Star Tribune,* June 27, 1995, p. 1D.

————, "United HealthCare Resuscitates Itself," *Minneapolis Star Tribune*, February 28, 1994, p. 1D.

————, "United HealthCare Selling DPS Unit to SmithKline," *Minneapolis Star Tribune*, May 4, 1994, p. 1D.

————, "United HealthCare to Buy Arizona HMO," *Minneapolis Star Tribune*, June 13, 1998, p. 1D.

————, "United HealthCare to Buy N. Carolina HMO," *Minneapolis Star Tribune*, November 29, 1995, p. 1D.

Kertesz, Louise, "United Blazes a Trail in Managed Care," *Modern Healthcare*, April 8, 1996, p. 46.

Miller, James P., "United HealthCare to Buy Healthwise for $290 Million," *Wall Street Journal*, February 2, 1996, p. B2.

————, "United HealthCare Vows Sale Cash Won't Turn Its Head," *Wall Street Journal*, May 5, 1994, p. B4.

————, "United Health Plans to Acquire Ramsay-HMO," *Wall Street Journal*, February 16, 1994, p. B5.

Nissen, Todd, "United HealthCare Adds Three Divisions," *Minneapolis–St. Paul CityBusiness*, July 30, 1990, p. 8.

————, "United HealthCare Again Looking to Buy," *Minneapolis–St. Paul CityBusiness*, December 11, 1989, p. 6.

————, "With an M.D. As CEO, Firm Hopes for Health Growth," *Minneapolis–St. Paul CityBusiness*, March 18, 1991, p. 1.

"Pact Is Signed to Sell Stake to Warburg Pincus Capital," *Wall Street Journal*, November 17, 1987, p. 5.

Phelps, David, "McGuire Leaving over Stock Options," *Minneapolis Star Tribune*, October 16, 2006, p. 1A.

————, "A Medical Miracle's Second Act," *Minneapolis Star Tribune*, December 29, 2003, p. 1D.

————, "United CEO Says He'll Take No More Stock Options," *Minneapolis Star Tribune*, April 19, 2006, p. 1A.

————, "United Goes West with Its Latest Deal," *Minneapolis Star Tribune*, March 13, 2007, p. 1D.

————, "UnitedHealth to Buy Rival Company for $2.8 Billion," *Minneapolis Star Tribune*, October 28, 2003, p. 1D.

————, "United's Stock-Option Tab: $1.53 Billion," *Minneapolis Star Tribune*, March 7, 2007, p. 1D.

Phelps, David, and David Shaffer, "McGuire's Rise Ends with His Fall," *Minneapolis Star Tribune*, November 26, 2006, p. 1A.

Shaffer, David, "Billing Flaws Persisted As UnitedHealth Grew," *Minneapolis Star Tribune*, December 9, 2007, p. 1A.

Shapiro, Joseph P., "Giving Doctors the Final Word," *U.S. News and World Report*, November 22, 1999, p. 20.

Smith, Scott D., "UnitedHealth Poised for No. 1," *Minneapolis–St. Paul CityBusiness*, July 20, 2001, p. 1.

Solberg, Carla, "Shock Treatment: New CEO Tries to Cure What Ails United HealthCare," *Corporate Report–Minnesota*, December 1998, pp. 38+.

Stecklow, Steve, and Vanessa Fuhrmans, "UnitedHealth Executives Forfeit $390 Million in Options," *Wall Street Journal*, November 9, 2006, p. B1.

Stires, David, "The HMO (Almost) Nobody Hates," *Fortune*, September 15, 2003, p. 189.

Straumanis, Andris, "United HealthCare: Not Just an HMO Manager," *Corporate Report–Minnesota*, February 1991, p. 60.

Tooher, Nora Lockwood, "Local HMO Parent Has Big Plans to Extend Reach," *Providence Journal-Bulletin*, September 29, 1991, p. F1.

Weber, Joseph, "He Collects Butterflies—and Companies," *Business Week*, November 4, 2002, p. 120.

Winslow, Ron, "United HealthCare's McGuire: From a Doctor to a Deal Maker," *Wall Street Journal*, June 27, 1995, p. B1.

Yee, Chen May, "An Angry California Fines UnitedHealth $3.5 Million," *Minneapolis Star Tribune*, January 30, 2008, p. 1A.

————, "Mystery Player in the Spotlight; Ingenix Who?" *Minneapolis Star Tribune*, March 16, 2008, p. 1D.

————, "UNH Faces Big Job Cuts, Big Payout over Lawsuit," *Minneapolis Star Tribune*, July 3, 2008, p. 1A.

————, "UnitedHealth Settles Ingenix Suit," *Minneapolis Star Tribune*, January 16, 2009, p. 1D.

————, "UnitedHealth Working to Get Back on Course," *Minneapolis Star Tribune*, December 7, 2007, p. 1D.

VNUS Medical Technologies, Inc.

———■———

5799 Fontanoso Way
San Jose, California 95138-1015
U.S.A.
Telephone: (408) 360-7200
Toll Free: (888) 797-8346
Fax: (408) 365-8480
Web site: http://www.vnus.com

Public Company
Incorporated: 1995
Employees: 218
Sales: $101.15 million (2008)
Stock Exchanges: NASDAQ
Ticker Symbol: VNUS
NAICS: 339113 Surgical Appliances and Supplies

■ ■ ■

VNUS Medical Technologies, Inc., is one of the leading developers and manufacturers of medical devices for the treatment of venous reflux disease. The company's proprietary vein ablation systems offer physicians and their patients a minimally invasive technique with few side effects and a rapid rate of recovery. VNUS products include radio frequency generators, sterile, disposable catheters, and accessories for efficiently implementing the procedure. Complementary products offered by VNUS include the ClosureRFS Stylet, for treatment of incompetent perforating veins, an advanced condition of venous reflux disease. The VeinLite Transilluminator is an under skin light source for vein mapping, and the Logiq e System provides endovenous ultrasound-image guidance. The VNUS Tumescent Infiltration Pump administers local anesthesia.

The VNUS Closure System is available as an outpatient procedure, and it is covered by more than 100 healthcare insurance providers in the United States and by national healthcare systems in several European countries. VNUS sales offices are located in the United States, France, Germany, and England, and distributors sell VNUS products in more than 40 countries across Europe, South America, and Asia, as well as in Canada.

STATE OF THE ART
TECHNOLOGY ADVANCES
TREATMENT OF VENOUS REFLUX

VNUS Medical Technologies formed in 1995 for the purpose of developing a state-of-the-art radio frequency technology that would greatly improve treatment of venous reflux disease. The disease affects the saphenous vein, the major blood vessel of the leg, which is responsible for returning oxygen-depleted blood to the heart for replenishment. Deterioration of the valve that regulates the forward movement of blood flow causes venous reflux, the backward flow of deficient blood into the veins. The varicose condition occurs when the veins become inflamed, then bulge and twist, looking like a blue cord under the skin. Without some treatment for reducing venous reflux and varicose veins, patients may suffer painful swelling, ulcers, open wounds, and leg fatigue.

VNUS's method of treatment involved administering a radio frequency to the saphenous vein through a small catheter in order to shrink the collagen and close

COMPANY PERSPECTIVES

Our mission is to create innovative products and procedures for the treatment of venous reflux disease in order to significantly improve patients' lives.

the vein. The VNUS Closure System consisted of two components, the radio frequency (RF) generator and the endovenous catheter, collapsible electrodes inserted into the vein to deliver the RF to the vein wall. An ultrasound image guides the physician in moving the catheter through the saphenous vein. Heat from the RF generator causes a swollen blood vessel to shrink. When the catheter is removed, the vein collapses and seals completely, forcing healthy veins to take control of blood flow.

After obtaining patents and government approval for the technology, VNUS began marketing the VNUS Closure System in Europe in 1998. The Food and Drug Administration (FDA) approved use of the product in March 1999, and VNUS immediately began marketing the product in the United States. VNUS offered two models, one with a 5F catheter with electrodes that expand to seven millimeters for use in smaller veins, and an 8F catheter that expands to 12 millimeters.

The VNUS Closure System had several advantages over other methods of vascular surgery. The system required a local anesthetic, rather than general anesthesia, and the procedure could be performed as outpatient care. Vein-stripping, the most common method of treatment for varicose veins since the early 1900s, involved open surgery. The treatment called for removal of blood vessels by turning them inside out with a threading rod, then stripping them from the body. Patients required one to two weeks of bed rest after surgery, compared to VNUS Closure, which required only a day or two of rest. An updated version of sclerotherapy worked in a manner similar to the VNUS system, in that ultrasound guides passage for application of medicine to reduce blood vessel membranes. Laser techniques applied heat to reduce vein size, enabling the valves to function normally. While laser medical devices were most competitive with the VNUS system, they were considered experimental at this time.

Complications of the VNUS Closure procedure included pulmonary embolism, a blood clot that quickly moves into the lungs; however, VNUS reported very low incidence of the problem. Overall, VNUS Closure proved to be safer, more effective, and with fewer side

effects than other forms of venous reflux treatment. The treatment was fairly painless and patients experienced less pain after the procedure.

ACCEPTANCE OF VNUS CLOSURE SYSTEM CULTIVATES GROWTH AND EXPANSION

With physicians advocating the Closure System, health insurance providers began allowing coverage of the procedure. Aetna/US Healthcare established coverage in 2002. The Blue Cross and Blue Shield Association, which established coverage policy for member organizations, gave a favorable review of the Closure System. The association's Medical Policy Panel determined that, in certain cases, the procedure could be the preferred, medically necessary substitute to vein stripping. Beginning July 1, 2002, Medicare established VNUS Closure as a new medical device category, and allowed supplemental pass-through payment for the procedure as hospital outpatient care.

As VNUS Closure became an accepted method of treating venous reflux, the company experienced rapid growth. Sales doubled from $5.56 million in 2001 to $10.04 million in 2002, then doubled again to $21.84 million in 2003. By late 2003, VNUS equipment users had performed 30,000 procedures successfully. More healthcare insurance providers recognized the value of the technology and began to cover treatment.

VNUS fostered growth by developing its existing technology. In September 2003, VNUS launched the Closure Plus unit, improved with ergonomic design. The introduction of disposable catheters meant that sterilization of instrument cables was no longer necessary. VNUS launched a new RF device, the RFG2, in the fall of 2004. In addition to improving the user interface and providing a large color screen for easier use, the new device improved vein wall monitoring. Improved observation of temperature and vein obstructions allowed the physician to perform the closure procedure more effectively.

The company's growth strategy included offering complementary products to its customers. In March 2004 VNUS began offering a line of surgical instruments used to remove varicose veins. The VarEx instrument line for ambulatory phlebectomy involved a less invasive form of the stripping surgical procedure. The tools complemented the Closure System. Through an agreement with VENOSAN, VNUS began selling medical compression stockings, a high-quality form of support stockings. Made with Tactel, a Lycra microfiber, the compression stockings stimulated blood circulation in the legs.

In December 2004, VNUS signed a distribution agreement with SonoPrep, maker of an ultrasound local anesthetic device. The skin permeation of the ultrasonic technique created an immediate anesthetic effect, compared to up to one hour for a topical anesthesia. Hence, SonoPrep was a natural companion device to the Closure system, providing physicians and patients with significant time savings.

As the use of its medical devices increased, VNUS became a profitable company. The number of procedures performed more than doubled from 30,000 completed between 1998 and 2003, to 70,000 in 2004 alone. After eight years of operating at a loss, VNUS began to earn an operating profit by the end of 2004. That year, revenues of $38.16 million garnered $2.65 million in net income, compared to $21.84 million in revenues and a $2.58 million net loss in 2003.

Assured of its viability as a profitable company, VNUS prepared for continued growth with an initial public offering (IPO) of stock. In October 2004, the company launched its IPO on the NASDAQ. VNUS offered 5.375 million shares of common stock at $15 per share.

AWARENESS OF VNUS CLOSURE PROCEDURE SPREADS

A growing body of evidence affirmed the efficacy of the VNUS products, especially compared to other procedures. One clinical study showed that patients experienced an improved quality of life, free of pain, for two years after treatment. Moreover, 84 percent of limbs treated remained disease free after five years. Another study showed that VNUS Closure maintained a higher rate of vein occlusion one year after treatment, when compared to endovenous laser ablation.

VNUS sought to increase exposure of the RF method to both physicians and the general public. VNUS targeted people suffering from venous reflux disease directly by advertising on television. In June 2005, Rush University Medical University in Chicago conducted the procedure via live webcast. Also, that year, the company began a public education and outreach campaign, promoting its procedure on select cable television stations with national audiences.

Opportunities for public investment improved in 2005, when the NASDAQ added VNUS to its Health Care Index, a value composite of health maintenance organizations, medical device manufacturers and suppliers, healthcare facilities, and pharmaceutical and biotechnology companies. The company was named to the broad-market Russell 3000 Index, the small-cap Russell 2000 Index, and the Russell Microcap Index.

TECHNIQUE PUTS VNUS AHEAD OF THE COMPETITION

In 2006, VNUS introduced the ClosureFast Catheter, which doubled the speed of vein ablation. Sensitive heat modulation allowed the physician to stop the catheter, heating veins in seven centimeter segments, thus reducing potential side effects from continuous movement of the catheter upon removal. Hence, the ClosureFast Catheter quickly sealed veins with less discomfort during and after treatment. The catheter could be removed in three to five minutes, compared to 20 minutes with the previous technology. Overall treatment was reduced from 40 minutes to fewer than 20 minutes from the time of insertions to removal. Initially instituted at medical and cosmetic centers in Europe in 2006, a clinical trial showed 100 percent occlusion after three months for 164 limbs and six months for 62 limbs (a total of 194 patients). The study did not find any serious complications, such as deep venous thrombosis or thermal skin injury. Moreover, the ClosureFast Catheter addressed problems associated with competing laser technology, whose side effects included vein perforations and post-procedure pain.

The FDA approved the technology for distribution in the United States in the spring of 2007. VNUS supported the launch of ClosureFast with a number of public relations events, such as patient screening events, and national television advertising. Advertisements direct to potential patients included 1,100 television spots nationwide. A 30-second commercial for local use by VNUS customers was derived from the longer spots.

Introduction of VNUS ClosureFast increased sales significantly. Catheter unit sales increased 35 percent in 2007, with the ClosureFast representing 70 percent of units sold. Also, the introduction of the VNUS ClosureRFS Stylet, for treatment of incompetent perforating veins, an advanced condition of venous reflux disease, contributed to an overall 29 percent increase in revenues. Revenues rose from $51.68 million in 2006 to $70.9 million in 2007. The company's market share for vein ablation devices increased from 50 percent in 2006 to 56 percent in 2007. Growth continued apace in 2008, with revenues increasing 43 percent and net income reaching $13.5 million.

VNUS Closure Systems continued to gain credibility with health insurers. Medicare reimbursement for the VNUS closure procedure improved compared to laser techniques. Medicare provided $1,900 in reimbursement for ClosureFast compared to $1,645 for laser procedures. By this time more than 100 healthcare insurers covered VNUS treatments. In the United Kingdom, the National Health Service's National Innovation Center selected the ClosureFast system as the procedure of choice for treating venous reflux. The procedure freed space for other operations, required no overnight stay, and required less staff time, resulting in significant cost savings for the National Health Service.

Mary Tradii

PRINCIPAL COMPETITORS

AngioDynamics, Inc.; biolitect AG; BTG plc; Dornier MedTech GmbH; New Star Lasers, Inc. (dba Cool Touch, Inc.); Sciton, Inc.; Total Vein Systems and Vascular Solutions, Inc.

FURTHER READING

Johnson, Steve, "Mining Waves to Treat Varicose Veins—Vnus' Radio-Frequency System Gaining Acceptance—And Profit," *San Jose Mercury News,* September 7, 2005, p. 1C.

"Randomized Trial Shows VNUS Closure System Produces Advantages over Traditional Vein Stripping for Patients with Symptomatic Varicose Veins and Saphenous Vein Reflux," *PR Newswire,* May 29, 2002.

"VNUS ClosureFast Catheter Clinical Trial Has Favorable Results," *Biotech Equipment Update,* April 1, 2007.

"VNUS Medical Technologies Achieves Two Major Milestones: Blue Cross and Blue Shield Association Recognition of Closure Procedure and New Medicare Pass-Through Device Code for the Closure Catheter," *PR Newswire,* June 6, 2002.

"VNUS Medical Technologies, Inc. Announces Management and Organizational Changes," *PR Newswire,* April 21, 2005.

"VNUS Medical Technologies Launches Television Ad Campaign Directed at Patients with Painful Varicose Veins," *PR Newswire,* June 28, 2005.

"VNUS Medical Technologies Receives FDA Clearance for Its Closure System for Endovascular Coagulation of Blood Vessels in Patients with Superficial Vein Reflux," *PR Newswire,* March 29, 1999, p. 9732.

The Vons Companies, Inc.

618 Michillinda Avenue
Arcadia, California 91007-6300
U.S.A.
Telephone: (626) 821-7000
Toll Free: (877) 723-3929
Fax: (626) 821-7933
Web site: http://www.vons.com

Wholly Owned Subsidiary of Safeway Inc.
Incorporated: 1906 as Vons Grocery Company
Employees: 29,700
Sales: $2.14 billion (2007)
NAICS: 445110 Supermarkets and Other Grocery (Except Convenience) Stores

∎ ∎ ∎

The Vons Companies, Inc., operates approximately 300 stores primarily in central and Southern California. The company operates 20 stores in Nevada. Vons competes under two main brands: Vons supermarkets and Pavilions stores, the latter of which are larger-format stores featuring wider selections of items and enhanced services. Vons is vertically integrated, operating facilities that produce baked goods and dairy products for sale in its stores. The company is owned by Pleasanton, California-based Safeway Inc., a supermarket chain comprising more than 1,700 stores.

ENTREPRENEURIAL ORIGINS

Vons was created by Charles Von der Ahe, an entrepreneur instrumental in the development of the

modern supermarket. Von der Ahe's first experience in the grocery business was as a delivery boy in Illinois. On the way to California, where he would eventually settle, Von der Ahe worked in several markets, observing merchandising techniques and customer buying patterns firsthand. In 1906, with a total capital investment of $1,200, Von der Ahe opened a small grocery store named Von's Groceteria on the corner of Seventh and Figueroa in Los Angeles. Over the next few years, he opened additional stores, implementing a number of innovative strategies which fueled dynamic growth in his business. Von der Ahe was the first grocer to introduce cash-and-carry and self-service. In leasing his open storefronts to produce vendors and butchers, Vons also pioneered the combination store concept which would later lead to his first supermarket. By 1929 the Vons Grocery Company numbered 87 stores.

Von der Ahe had the foresight to sell his stores to McMarr Stores in 1929, before the stock market crash decimated the value of commercial properties. McMarr would in turn eventually be purchased by Safeway. In the meantime, Von der Ahe enjoyed three years of retirement before being lured back into the grocery business by his sons Ted and Will, who decided to open a new chain of Vons stores in the Los Angeles area. Von der Ahe helped his sons out with investment capital and industry expertise, and Vons stores began to multiply. The partnership culminated in the opening of a 50,300-square-foot food market in downtown Los Angeles in 1948. The prototype of the supermarket, this location boasted a number of innovative features which today are taken for granted, notably self-service produce, meat, and delicatessen departments. The store confirmed the

COMPANY PERSPECTIVES

The marketing area which Vons covers comprises some of the most affluent, forward thinking, culturally mixed communities in the U.S. The Vons business strategy has always been to provide for the needs of these communities with the highest quality meat and produce at competitive prices. Equally important, Vons has been changing as Southern California changes. Capital spending insures a continuing pace of replacement stores and remodels.

Von der Ahe family's role as innovators in the retail food industry.

In 1960, Vons merged with Shopping Bag Food Stores, bringing the total number of stores under family management to 66. Particular emphasis was placed on understanding local markets and arranging shelf space accordingly, a practice that has continued to the present day. In 1967 the merger was challenged by the Federal Trade Commission. The case went all the way to the U.S. Supreme Court, which ordered Vons to divest itself of the Shopping Bag locations immediately. In 1969 Vons was bought out by the Household Finance Corporation, later Household International, which added the chain to its Household Merchandising division.

DYNAMIC GROWTH: SEVENTIES AND EARLY EIGHTIES

The expansion of Vons Stores into the San Diego area during the 1970s corresponded with a period of dynamic growth when the chain widened operations to include wholesale marketing to other retailers and fast-food chains. In the mid-1970s, Vons opened a series of midsized units called Value Centers, which sold food and drugs in one location. This "combo" concept would develop into Pavilions Stores in 1987. In the early 1980s, Vons expanded north into the Fresno area. In the same period, the company began to stress the importance of combining coupon promotions with in-store product demonstrations as a means of persuading more conservative customers to try new foods. Vons was among the first stores to operate its product promotion department as a profit center funded by fees from participating companies.

Vons scored a tremendous coup in 1984 when the company was designated the official supermarket of the Los Angeles Olympics. Under a deal worked out with the Olympic Committee, the chain agreed to provide food for more than 12,000 athletes, coaches, and trainers in the Olympic Village. Food worth $8 million was provided to the committee at cost for preparation by an independent foodservice organization. The balance, worth $2 million, was donated by the company. In return, Vons was guaranteed a number of exclusive merchandising and advertising opportunities. Store décor was changed to highlight the Olympic theme, and the Olympic logo was placed on a number of perishable items that were considered to have particular nutritional value.

VONS REGAINS INDEPENDENCE IN 1986

In January 1986 top management in the Household Merchandising branch of Household International negotiated a $757 million leveraged buyout of their division. The deal, which was the largest retail buyout in the United States at the time, was masterminded by Roger E. Stangeland, who went on to become chairperson of the newly independent Vons Companies. Stangeland had been an executive at Household International since 1961, and had been responsible for Vons Stores since 1982. While the buyout successfully separated Vons from Household International, it also burdened the company with an unacceptable level of debt. Stangeland announced that reducing the debt-to-equity ratio would be a priority over the next few years. In the meantime, he added the ten-store Pantry chain to the Vons portfolio. He also charged William S. Davila, the company's president, with developing an expanded "combination store" concept. Started in 1986, the year of the leveraged buyout, the Pavilions subchain would number 28 stores by 1991.

At 75,000 square feet, the first Pavilions store was the company's largest to date. A combination store, Pavilions offered huge food and nonfood sections. Different departments were identified with banners and decked with white awnings which created the effect of tented "pavilions." Joe Raymond, a merchandising executive with Pavilions, described the concept as "breaking away from the pack." Important features included the plain white décor, designed to focus customer attention on the items on display. The store carried a greater selection of produce than comparable stores, and shoppers were invited to sample new products at a permanently staffed demonstration booth. In order to emphasize the freshness of the perishable goods, all food preparation was done in full view of the shopping public. At the same time, the nonfood area stressed value for money, with a large variety of health

KEY DATES

1906: Using $1,200, Charles Von der Ahe opens his first grocery store, Von's Groceteria, in Los Angeles.

1929: Vons Grocery Company operates 87 stores when Von der Ahe sells the chain to McMarr Stores.

1932: With the help of his sons, Ted and Will, Von der Ahe begins building a new chain of grocery stores.

1948: The opening of a 50,300-square-foot store in downtown Los Angeles ushers in the age of the supermarkets.

1969: Vons is acquired by Household Finance Corporation.

1970s: Expansion into the San Diego area coincides with the development of a second brand, Value Centers, which is the precursor to the company's Pavilions Stores chain.

1986: The Vons chain gains independence through a management-led leveraged buyout, creating The Vons Companies, Inc.

1987: Vons becomes a publicly traded company, debuting on the New York Stock Exchange.

1988: As part of a transaction that gives Vons ownership of 172 stores operated by Safeway Inc., Safeway takes a more than one-third equity interest in Vons.

1992: Vons acquires the 18-store Williams Brothers Markets chain.

1997: Safeway acquires Vons for $2.5 billion, purchasing the 65 percent of the chain it did not already own.

2002: Vons launches vons.com, a web site offering home delivery of groceries.

2004: A four-and-half-month strike begins by members of the United Food and Commercial Workers International Union.

2007: A decade after being acquired by Safeway, Vons operates 304 stores, 16 fewer stores than when Safeway acquired the chain.

and beauty aids offered at discounts of up to 30 percent on average retail prices, and a professionally staffed pharmacy selling prescription drugs at discounts of up to 50 percent. In some areas, Pavilions competed directly with adjacent Vons stores, a situation that traditional marketing strategists would tend to avoid. Vons executives remained unruffled, however, articulating their belief that if Pavilions did not go head-to-head with the older stores, a competitor certainly would.

A PUBLIC COMPANY IN 1987

In December 1986, Vons announced that a $700 million deal had been struck with Allied Supermarkets, Inc., a publicly listed Detroit retail and wholesale food marketer. The goal of the merger was to take Vons public while controlling the company's debt load. Roger Stangeland became chair and CEO of Vons, and William S. Davila was named president and COO. Since Vons had no ambitions to expand to the Midwest, Allied's Detroit assets were sold to members of the existing management. The merger achieved its goal; Vons went public on the New York Stock Exchange in early 1987.

Constantly in search of new merchandising techniques, Vons executives turned their attention to the ethnic composition of their customers in 1987. They observed that by 1990 an estimated 40 percent of Southern California's population would be of Hispanic origin. In January 1987 the company opened its first Tianguis superstore in Montebello, California, designed to cater to the specific needs of Hispanic customers, especially first-generation immigrants. Tianguis, meaning "marketplace" in Aztec, denotes the place where the community meets to shop and to socialize; commenting on the choice of name, CEO Stangeland said in August 1986 that Vons hoped to "position our stores as an important center in the community" and to "differentiate ourselves strongly from the competition." By 1991 the company was operating nine Tianguis stores throughout Southern California and had plans to open two to three stores per year.

Tianguis differed from its predecessors in many ways. All advertising and store signs were bilingual, as were the stores' employees, hired from the local community. The produce section was greatly expanded to include a wide variety of Mexican herbs, fruits, and vegetables, while some product categories were eliminated completely. As in the Pavilions stores, meat preparation was done in front of customers. The grocery section included an extensive selection of Mexican imports, sharing shelf space with their U.S. counterparts. Distribution of imports was guaranteed through the early establishment of a subsidiary called Central de Abastos Internacional in 1986. To enhance the social aspect of the stores, aisles were widened to allow patrons to stop and chat. Diaper-changing rooms were installed at the back of each store since, in Vons President Davila's words, "shopping tends to be a family event for Hispanics." The introduction of the Tianguis stores was widely discussed in the industry. Vons had demonstrated once again its strength in adapting to the changing needs of the market before its competitors.

PURCHASING SAFEWAY'S SOUTHERN CALIFORNIA STORES IN 1988

On August 29, 1988, Vons took over 172 of Safeway's Southern California operations, paying $297 million in cash and giving up 11.67 million shares of Vons common stock, leading to Safeway holding a more than one-third stake in Vons. As a result of this transaction, the number of stores under Vons control doubled, but the company's debt load also soared. In spite of its highly leveraged position, the company immediately embarked on an ambitious remodeling of the former Safeway stores, spending an average of $1.3 million on each location. Together with more efficient inventory control and labor scheduling, the remodeling was intended to increase per-store profitability, money that in turn would be used to pay off debt. A number of in-store innovations were also implemented, including an electronic coupon program and other cost-saving technology. The strategy worked. By November 1990, sales per square foot at the former Safeway stores had risen to $615 from an average of $447 at the time of the buyout. The industry average at the time was $550. Meanwhile, corporate finances also improved. Vons went from a $25 million loss in 1989 to a $50 million profit in 1990 and a $65 million profit in 1991. By 1991, the company's debt-to-total capitalization ratio had dropped to 60 percent. The company's financial position was also strengthened by a successful equity issue in 1991.

In January 1992 Vons acquired family-owned Williams Brothers Markets for $48 million in cash and a liability of $10 million on Williams Brothers' outstanding mortgages. The transaction was financed using Vons' existing revolving loan. Located in central California, the 18 Williams Brothers stores were well-known for their customer service and successful niche in marketing to local communities. As such, they integrated well with other stores in the Vons portfolio, while allowing Vons to expand farther north.

During the course of the riots in Los Angeles in May 1992, several Vons stores were looted and burned. The cost of restoring the damaged properties, however, was largely covered by insurance. In the aftermath of the riots, attention was focused on the dearth of quality supermarkets in south central Los Angeles. Vons Companies announced that the chain would commit $100 million to developing markets in neglected areas over the next few years. Then in January 1993, an outbreak of food poisoning in Washington State that claimed the lives of three children was traced to hamburgers purchased at the Jack in the Box fast-food chain, which had purchased the meat tainted with the deadly *E. coli* bacteria from Foodmaker, parent company of Jack in the Box. Vons, as the meat processor for Foodmaker, was involved in the early stages of the investigation. After being commended by health authorities for its clean processing facility, Vons aided health authorities by tracing the source of the contaminated beef to one Foodmaker beef supplier. The incident had wide-ranging implications for U.S. Department of Agriculture inspection procedures, which were deemed inadequate.

In the early 1990s, Vons renewed a commitment to technological progress by announcing a dramatic increase in its Information Systems (IS) budget. IS initiatives were piloted in a number of metropolitan locations and included electronic shelf tags, which would be updated automatically when the checkout scanner price was changed. This system was intended to enhance customer service and decrease labor costs. The early 1990s also brought two new store formats: the warehouse-club-style Expo, a format abandoned in 1995; and Super Combo stores, which included banking services, catering facilities, a dry cleaner, photo processing, a pharmacy, as well as an expanded grocery section. Later in the decade the Super Combo format essentially was melded into the Vons and Pavilions formats, many of which included the added services and sections that were becoming increasingly common in grocery stores.

RESTRUCTURING IN THE EARLY NINETIES

Overall, the early 1990s were difficult years for Vons not only because of the severe Southern California recession but also as a result of a number of other factors: the heavy debt-load that was taken on to acquire the Safeway stores; the cost of acquiring William Brothers, remodeling 59 stores in 1993 alone, opening 12 new stores in 1993, and opening a new headquarters; the temporary closing of 45 stores due to damage from the 1994 Northridge earthquake; and the loss of some customers as a result of the Jack-in-the-Box food poisoning outbreak. Same-store sales fell 2 percent in 1992 and another 9 percent in 1993. In response, Vons instituted a restructuring program in the third quarter of 1993, taking a $57 million charge for a cost-cutting program that involved a workforce reduction of about 15 percent, salary freezes, and other initiatives. Simultaneously, the company launched the Vons Value program, which began in January 1994 and featured 18,000 price reductions.

Continuing its recovery efforts, Vons spent $175 million in 1995 to open ten new stores and remodel 65 existing stores. The company also closed down a number of unprofitable stores and consolidated three distribution centers into two, while laying plans for a three-year, 15-unit expansion of the Pavilions subchain. Same-store sales fell 2.4 percent in 1994 and increased 3.5 percent in 1995, signaling a company on the rebound, having also been aided by the strengthening of the Southern California economy.

UNDER THE SAFEWAY UMBRELLA: APRIL 1997

In 1996 Vons added 12 new stores to its chain, eight of them replacements for older units that were closed down and four of them bought from Smith's Food & Drug. Late in the year as the company was laying plans to open 12 to 15 stores in 1997 (6 of them Pavilions, including the first San Diego stores for that format) Safeway offered to purchase the 65 percent of Vons it did not already own. The deal was completed in April 1997, with Safeway paying about $2.5 billion to complete the purchase, including $565 million in debt. Vons thereby became a wholly owned subsidiary of Safeway, but its 320 stores continued to operate under the Vons and Pavilions names. Shortly after completion of the deal, Safeway eliminated 240 administrative positions at Vons, representing 37 percent of the 650 Vons headquarters staff.

In February 1998 Vons contributed, along with several meatpackers and other companies, to a $58.5 million payment to Foodmaker to settle a lawsuit Foodmaker had filed in 1993 in connection with the Jack-in-the-Box food poisoning outbreak. In December 1998 Vons bought eight stores from the Ralphs chain and subsequently remodeled them and reopened them under the Vons banner. By January 1999 there were a total of 324 Vons and Pavilions stores. This number was likely to increase at a more rapid rate than in the past as Vons could take advantage of the deeper pockets of its parent, which was the second largest grocery chain in North America, trailing only The Kroger Company.

VONS IN THE 21ST CENTURY

During Safeway's first decade of ownership, expansion occurred, but the addition of stores did not factor as the period's most noteworthy development. Vons, in fact, became a smaller chain under Safeway's control, with the closing of underperforming stores outpacing the

establishment of new stores. By 2007, a decade after Safeway acquired the chain, Vons operated 304 stores, 16 fewer units than when Safeway purchased the chain. "We open and close stores all the time," a Safeway spokesperson remarked in the December 21, 2007 edition of the *Las Vegas Review-Journal*, explaining how Vons' expansion program resulted in negative growth.

Instead of expansion, other events took center stage as Vons entered the 21st century. In 2002, the company launched vons.com, marking its entry into the online grocery business. The launch of the web site, coordinated with the debut of safeway.com, gave consumers the option of having their groceries delivered to their home. The service, offered through Grocery Works, an Internet-based home-shopping and delivery service 50 percent owned by Safeway, offered products sold at the same prices seen at stores. For a delivery fee of $4.95 for orders totaling $150 or more and $9.95 for orders under $150, customers could specify a two-hour period between 10 A.M. and 8 P.M. seven days a week to have their groceries delivered at home. Select stores, referred to as "pick stores," received the online orders, which were transmitted to computer-equipped shopping carts navigated by personal shoppers.

NEW STORE FORMAT AND WORKER UNREST

The foray into the online grocery business proved to be a success, as did a new store format that debuted in 2004. Referred to as the "lifestyle" format by Vons officials, the new version of supermarkets featured hardwood floors, an expanded deli section, and an increased emphasis on prepared foods. The new format, developed to compete against smaller chains such as Trader Joe's and Fresh & Easy, became the focal point of the chain's expansion efforts, resulting in the opening of more than 50 lifestyle stores by 2007.

The launch of an online business and the development of a new format represented two highlights during Safeway's first decade of ownership, but their significance was overshadowed by the predominant event of the period: labor troubles. The specter of a strike loomed in mid-2003, when industry observers revealed troubled negotiations among Vons, Kroger-owned Ralphs Grocery, Albertsons, and seven local chapters of the United Food and Commercial Workers International Union (UFCW). The supermarket chains offered proposals "designed to address the employers' competitive disadvantage ... with respect to union and non-union companies operating without such restrictions," as reported in the September 22, 2003 issue of

Supermarket News. The proposals, *Supermarket News* theorized, were developed with the impending arrival of a giant, non-union competitor in mind. Wal-Mart Stores was planning to open supercenters in Southern California in early 2004, part of an expansion program that called for the opening of 40 stores in the region by 2008. The proposals included a lower wage system for new employees, reductions in the amount of pay on Sundays and holidays, reductions in pension plans, and increased healthcare premiums. The union objected to the terms of the new contract, which lent an air of uncertainty to negotiations in the weeks leading up to the expiration of the existing contract on October 5, 2003.

Vons, Ralphs Grocery, and Albertsons joined forces in preparation for what was expected to be an ordeal. The three chains negotiated as a single bargaining entity with UFCW Local 770, the largest of the seven chapters. With the other six locals, the companies negotiated independently. October 5 passed without a new contract being signed, and six days later, 70,000 members of the UFCW went on strike against stores operated by Vons. In response, Ralphs Grocery and Albertsons locked out UFCW members the following day. The strike dragged on for four-and-a-half months, becoming one of the longest grocery strikes in the history of the nation. The parties settled their differences by implementing a two-tier system that allowed existing workers to keep their higher pay and benefits and allowed the supermarket chains to replace departing employees with lower-compensated workers.

The two-tier system resolved a protracted battle between employers and employees in 2004, but it did not serve as a permanent solution. When the 2004 contract expired in March 2007, the two-tier system was a major point of contention by UFCW members. Again, a strike threatened to disrupt Vons' business, but the expiration of the contract was extended, averting labor troubles. After months of negotiations, the three grocery chains agreed to eliminate the two-tier system, a decision ratified by the union in July 2007.

As Vons prepared for the future, the company faced the likely prospect of further labor troubles. In his July 30, 2007 article, the *Los Angeles Business Journal's* Charles Crumpley noted, "The march of history is against grocery chains that employ many full-time workers with benefits, just as it was against shoe stores, department stores, and gasoline stations. As long as customers keep demanding low-priced food, grocery owners will be compelled to cut costs. That means more workers without benefits some time in the future." If Crumpley's word proved true, Vons, at some point, faced an epic battle with the UFCW, one that promised

to have a lasting effect on the way the company operated.

Moya Verzhbinsky
Updated, David E. Salamie; Jeffrey L. Covell

PRINCIPAL SUBSIDIARIES

Vons REIT, Inc.; Vons Sherman Oaks, LLC.

PRINCIPAL COMPETITORS

Ralphs Grocery Company; SuperValu Inc.; Stater Bros. Holdings Inc.

FURTHER READING

Allen, Mike, "Grocers' Union Stands Firm on Health Benefits Issue," *San Diego Business Journal,* October 20, 2003, p. 3.

Armstrong, Larry, "Coupon Clippers, Save Your Scissors," *Business Week,* June 20, 1994, pp. 164, 166.

Crumpley, Charles, "The Decision by Vons, Ralphs and Albertsons to Scrap the Two-Tier Employee System, a Decision Ratified by the Union Last Week, Was Probably As Much a Victory for the Companies As the Workers," Los Angeles Business Journal, July 30, 2007, p. 54.

Deutschman, Alan, "America's Fastest Risers," *Fortune,* October 7, 1991.

Duff, Mike, "Superstores," *Supermarket Business,* January 1991.

Gutner, Todd, "'Focus on the Customer,'" *Forbes,* August 2, 1993, pp. 45+.

Jereski, Laura, "Vons, Mired in California's Downturn, Draws Far More Negative Reviews Than Positive Ones," *Wall Street Journal,* December 30, 1993, p. C2.

McClintock, Jamie, "Vons' Online Grocery Shopping Option Well Received in Southern California," *San Gabriel Valley Tribune,* September 25, 2003.

McDermott, Terry, "*E. Coli* Investigation Finds Vons Supplier," *Seattle Times,* February 23, 1993.

"So. Calif. Grocery Strike Intensifies," *Drug Store News,* December 15, 2003, p. 6.

Spillman, Benjamin, "Safeway to Close Vons Grocery by Year's End," *Las Vegas Review-Journal,* December 21, 2007.

Tosh, Mark, "Vons Is Fighting Sales Declines with Price Cuts, Staff Upgrades," *Supermarket News,* January 17, 1994, pp. 4+.

Weidemann, Liz, "Vons Opens Upscale 'Lifestyle' Store at Liberty Station Marketplace," *San Diego Business Journal,* November 12, 2007, p. 9.

Weinstein, Steve, "'This Company Is Not Broken,'" *Progressive Grocer,* July 1994, p. 30.

Zwiebach, Elliott, "Del Santo to Take Vons Helm," Supermarket News, May 1, 1995, pp. 4+.

———, "Ready for Launch," Supermarket News, September 30, 1996, pp. 1+.

———, "Safeway, Vons Are Poised to Benefit from Tie's Synergy," *Supermarket News,* December 23, 1996, pp. 1+.

———, "Supermarkets, Labor Square Off in Southern California," *Supermarket News,* September 22, 2003, p. 1.

———, "Vons: Diversifying Formats for Diversified Needs," *Supermarket News,* April 7, 1986.

———, "Vons' New Accent," *Supermarket News,* February 9, 1987.

———, "Vons, Safeway Set to Tie Knot Tomorrow," *Supermarket News,* April 7, 1997, pp. 1+.

Voortman Cookies Limited

———— ■ ————

4455 North Service Road
Burlington, Ontario L7L 4X7
Canada
Telephone: (905) 335-9500
Fax: (905) 332-5499
Web site: http://www.voortman.com

Private Company
Incorporated: 1951
Employees: 450
Sales: $46.3 million (2007)
NAICS: 311821 Cookie and Cracker Manufacturing

■ ■ ■

Voortman Cookies Limited makes cookies and sugar wafers, selling its products throughout North America and in Puerto Rico. All of the company's products are made at its 250,000-square-foot production facility in Burlington, Ontario. The plant is capable of making 20 million cookies per day, using seven cookie lines, three wafer lines, and ten ovens to produce more than 60 varieties of cookies and sugar wafers. Voortman Cookies, a family-owned and -managed company, relies on a network of more than 500 distributors who have accounts with more than 50,000 grocery stores in Canada and the United States. A separate company, Appleby Transportation Limited, serves as Voortman Cookies' exclusive transportation carrier, supplying the company with the ingredients used to make its cookies and supplying the finished products to distributors. A second manufacturing plant in Bloomington, California, is owned and operated by the second generation of the Voortman family, conducting its business as a separate company under the name Traditional Baking.

FROM HELLENDOORN TO HAMILTON

As a baker in the Dutch town of Hellendoorn, John Voortman contended with less than ideal conditions. The frustration he felt had nothing to do with his ability as a baker. If the consumption of flour was the measure of a successful baker, then there was no baker more successful in Hellendoorn than Voortman; he went through 20 bags of flour per week, more than any of his rivals used. Voortman's problem was that there were too many rivals. He was one of 16 bakers serving a population of 4,000, stuck in a situation he found untenable. Rather than battle it out in Hellendoorn, Voortman, a widowed father of four sons, decided to try his luck elsewhere. In 1948, he booked passage for his family on the *Tabinta* and left his native country behind.

The Voortmans immigrated to Canada, settling in Picton, a small town in southern Ontario. Once John Voortman made Picton his new home, he left his baking days behind him, preferring to make his living working on a farm. The association of the Voortman name with baking did not end with John Voortman's decision to become a farmer, however. Two of his sons, Bill and Harry, were eager to follow in their father's footsteps. They wanted to start their own bakery, but they realized they could not instantly become entrepreneurs. "Our goal was to start our own business someday, but first we had to get our foot in the door," Harry Voortman noted on the Voortman Cookies web site.

Our purpose: To delight consumers across North America with a unique selection of delicious cookies at an affordable price. Our commitment: To deliver products of consistently high quality with a fresh, home-baked taste.

The two brothers, both teenagers, were hired by National System Baking Co. in Hamilton, Ontario, securing jobs that paid them CAD 28 per week. Saving what they could, the brothers were able to purchase a used oven, some basic baking equipment, and rent a back room of a house in Hamilton for CAD 50 per month. They rented the room in October 1951, put their baking equipment in the 100-square-foot room, and embarked on their careers as bakers, but only on a part-time basis. Their days were spent at National System Baking; their nights, in the rented room baking *snijkoek* and *roggebrood*. They baked the goods, honey cake and pumpernickel bread, for their fellow expatriates, the Dutch immigrants who were entirely responsible for supporting the Voortmans' business during its fledgling years.

At the end of the Voortmans' first year in business, the financial figures were less than inspiring. They baked CAD 6,000 worth of baked goods, earning CAD 50 in profit. The income was just one-third of the amount the brothers earned at National System Baking, but they looked at the figures and decided to devote all their time to running the bakery. Credit was hard to come by, 16-hour days became too frequent, but the brothers could celebrate one bright moment as they set out as entrepreneurs. They were able to rent a two-story building for the same rent as the back room they had used, albeit without heat. In that building, Bill and Harry Voortman began trying to expand their product line beyond *snijkoek* and *roggebrood*.

PRODUCT EXPERIMENTATION

"We began wholesaling pies to restaurants, but this didn't succeed," Harry Voortman recalled on the Voortman Cookies web site. "Then we went into doughnuts. What a time we had. There was no heat in the building, so we stood there at four o'clock in the morning frying doughnuts with our overcoats on." Next, the Voortmans experimented with the product that would drive their business' growth for the following half-century. They began making cookies.

Bill and Harry Voortman began making cookies by hand at first. When someone they knew brought a cookie machine from the Netherlands to Ontario, the brothers bought the machine and began making cookies in volume for the same Dutch immigrants who had purchased their honey cake and pumpernickel bread.

PRODUCTION PLANT EXPANSIONS

Cookies proved to be more profitable than *snijkoek* and *roggebread*. The Voortmans' business grew, requiring the brothers to find a larger manufacturing facility. In 1956, five years after they started out, Bill and Harry hired a builder to construct a 4,600-square-foot building in Burlington, Ontario, to house their growing operations. Bill Voortman took on the responsibilities of president for the business, and celebrated the company's first major success the year it moved into its substantially larger quarters. In 1956, a grocery store chain agreed to give the Voortmans space on its shelves, touching off a period of robust growth for Voortman Cookies.

Once their cookies began to appear in the grocery stores, the Voortmans' business began to evolve toward its eventual stature as a mass producer of cookies. A dozen employees occupied the new manufacturing facility built in 1956, but Voortman Cookies' payroll did not remain at that level for long. Within five years, the company needed a larger production plant, which led to another move in 1961 to an 18,000-square-foot building on King Road in Burlington. As the company's distribution network expanded and increasing numbers of grocery stores in Canada began to stock Voortman cookies, more production space was needed. After several additions to the King Road facility, square footage was increased to 38,000, which sustained the company's operations until it moved to a ten-acre site in eastern Burlington in 1975.

During the 1980s, Voortman Cookies cemented its reputation as a mass producer of cookies. The company was able to make the transition to volume production because of the popularity of its cookies, its success in cultivating relationships with distributors, and the development of packaging that facilitated the shipment of baked goods in large quantities. The Voortmans developed what they called "Cookie Huts," which originally were made out of cardboard. Once they began using Cookie Huts to ship their products to grocery stores, Voortman Cookies' sales began to increase substantially. "We tried them in the early 1980s when bulk food came into vogue," Harry Voortman recalled on the company's web site. "They were accepted extremely well and made a great contribution to the success of Voortman Cookies." Later versions of the Cookie

KEY DATES

1951: Bill and Harry Voortman begin baking honey cake and pumpernickel in a rented room in Hamilton, Ontario.

1956: The Voortmans move to larger quarters in Burlington, Ontario.

1975: The company moves to a ten-acre site in eastern Burlington.

1988: Bill Voortman retires as president and Harry Voortman takes on his responsibilities.

2004: Voortman Cookies eliminates all trans fatty acids from its cookies.

2009: Harry Voortman celebrates his 58th year with the company.

Huts featured plastic lids, playing an instrumental role in the company's ability to enter the U.S. market, which eventually accounted for 70 percent of its business.

The decade also included the first transfer of power in the company's history. Bill Voortman retired in 1988 and handed the reins of command to Harry Voortman. The following year, the company's presence in the U.S. market was increased indirectly by the formation of a sister company. Bill Voortman's children, Kathy and John Voortman, acquired the exclusive license to make and to sell Voortman Cookies in the southwestern United States. At the time, their father and uncle had limited their U.S. sales efforts primarily to regions in the north and the northeast, but after three years of assessing the market in several southwestern states, John Voortman was convinced he could sell the family's cookies in the four-state region he had studied. He and his sister purchased the rights to operate in California, Nevada, Arizona, and Utah, established a network of 35 independent distributors, and, with the help of their recently retired father, opened a 42,000-square-feet manufacturing facility in Bloomington, California. Their company, a separate entity from Voortman Cookies, operated under the name Traditional Baking.

A VOLUME PRODUCER

As Voortman Cookies approached its 50th anniversary, the company possessed impressive capabilities as a cookie producer. At the site where it moved in 1975, the company operated a 250,000-square-foot production plant outfitted with robotic arms. More than 400 employees worked on seven cookie lines, three wafer lines, and used ten ovens to produce vast quantities of cookies and sugar wafers. The plant had the capability to produce 20 million cookies each day, a capacity that enabled Voortman Cookies to ship 30,000 tons of cookies in 2000. The company relied on the efforts of more than 500 distributors to deliver its products to the marketplace, using a distributor network that serviced more than 50,000 stores. Every other week, the distributors received their cookie orders and took responsibility for store deliveries, inventory control, and product code freshness.

Another aspect of Voortman Cookies' production and delivery operations involved Appleby Transportation Ltd., a trucking company. Although housed within the company's main offices in Burlington, Appleby Transportation operated as a separate company. It owned a fleet of 32 tractors, 60 dry van trailers, and several refrigerated trailers, serving as the link between Voortman Cookies and its distributors.

VOORTMAN COOKIES OPTS FOR A HEALTHIER ALTERNATIVE

As Voortman Cookies concluded its first half-century of business, the company was preparing for a major change in the way it made its cookies. The impetus for the change was Lynn Voortman, the daughter of Harry Voortman. Lynn Voortman, a naturopathic doctor residing in Oakville, Ontario, began persuading her father in 1999 to eliminate trans fatty acids from the family's cookies. Trans fatty acids were caused by bubbling hydrogen gas through vegetable oil at high temperatures, a process known as partial hydrogenation that altered the molecular structure of unsaturated liquid fats and turned them into semi-solid trans fatty acids. Partial hydrogenation made foods more pliable and extended their shelf life, but the process was believed to increase the risk of heart disease, diabetes, and Alzheimer's.

Harry Voortman listened to his daughter, but eliminating trans fatty acids from Voortman Cookies was not a task that could be completed overnight. It took four years of experimentation to develop a formulation that eliminated trans fatty acids yet retained the taste and look of the family's cookies. In November 2003, Voortman Cookies announced all of its cookies would be made from non-hydrogenated oils by March 2004, which made it the first major company to eliminate all trans fatty acids from its food products. "We're number one at making this switch and it's only a matter of time before everyone else follows our example," Harry Voortman said in the November 25, 2003 edition of the *Globe & Mail*.

With a healthier product line and nearly 60 years of steady expansion, Voortman Cookies could look toward the future with confidence. The company stood as a formidable competitor in the cookie industry, representing one of Canada's most successful and enduring family-owned businesses. The one uncertainty about the years ahead was the inevitable change in leadership that would occur when Harry Voortman retired. He helped establish the company during his teenage years, which made for an exceptionally long career as a senior executive. Harry Voortman continued to serve as the company's president in 2009, 58 years after he and his brother rented a room in Hamilton and began baking honey cake and pumpernickel bread. The process of handing the reins of command to his successor promised to be a significant event in the years ahead.

Jeffrey L. Covell

PRINCIPAL COMPETITORS

Kellogg Company; Kraft North America; Parmalat Canada Limited.

FURTHER READING

Colman, Robert, "A Social Statement, a Streamlined Brand," *CMA Management,* February 2005, p. 40.

Malovany, Dan, "Traditional Values," *Snack Food & Wholesale Bakery,* January 2001, p. 26.

Picard, Andre, "Companies Struggle to End Growing Threat of Trans Fat," *Globe & Mail,* November 26, 2003, p. A1.

———, "Cookie Maker Crumbles on Fat," *Globe & Mail,* November 25, 2003, p. A1.

Vulcabras|azaleia

Vulcabras S.A.

───────── ■ ─────────

Av Antonio Frederico Ozanam 1440
Jundiaí, São Paulo 13219-001
Brazil
Telephone: (55 11) 4532-1000
Fax: (55 11) 4532-1082
Web site: http://www.vulcabras.com.br

Public Company
Incorporated: 1977
Employees: 28,984
Sales: BRL 1.31 billion ($689.47 million) (2007)
Stock Exchanges: Bolsa de Valores de São Paulo
Ticker Symbol: VULC
NAICS: 316213 Men's Footwear (Except Athletic) Manufacturing; 316214 Women's Footwear (Except Athletic) Manufacturing; 316219 Other Footwear Manufacturing; 339920 Sporting and Athletic Good Manufacturing

■ ■ ■

With its purchase of rival Calçados Azaléia S.A., Vulcabras S.A. has become the largest manufacturer of footwear not only in Brazil but in all Latin America. Vulcabras turns out athletic and industrial safety shoes, rubber working boots, and dress shoes under its own name but is best known for licensed sports footwear under the Reebok name. The Azaleia brand is Latin America's leader for women's shoes, and the Olympikus sneaker is a popular brand, too.

AZALÉIA, A SUCCESSFUL START-UP: 1958–93

The larger of the two companies and the most prominent prior to their merger was Calçados Azaléia, which was founded by Nestor Herculano de Paula in Parobé, Rio Grande do Sul. De Paula's mother died when he was seven and his father, when he was nine. He was raised by a sister and learned about making shoes from her husband, whose job was to stitch on the soles. His first formal job was as a fare collector on buses. In 1958 de Paula sold the house he had inherited and joined three friends and a brother in opening a small shoe factory in Parobé under the name Berlitz, Lauck e Cia. Ltda. In the beginning they, their wives, and four employees turned out 100 pairs of women's shoes per day. Their first brands, prior to Azaléia (named for the flower), were Laika and Nectar.

Azaléia's Olympikus sneaker, introduced in 1975, was made of leather and thus was better suited for durability than the traditional canvas one of the era. At the start of the 1980s, international sports footwear brands were introduced to Brazil with new technology, innovative marketing, and endorsements by popular athletes, but Olympikus continued to prosper. By this time Azaléia had taken the lead in footwear sales in Brazil, with a 12 to 15 percent share of the market. It was specializing in sandals, especially suitable in a mostly tropical country (although, ironically, the company probably experienced Brazil's coolest weather, since it was located in the nation's southernmost state).

By 1992 Azaléia, one of the most popular women's shoe brand names in Brazil, was turning out 75,000 pairs of footwear per day. Its annual sales passed $100 million. The following year, when it was named the nation's best clothing company, a distinction it earned again in 1994, by the business magazine *Exame,* revenues more than doubled, and the company reached second place among footwear manufacturers. It was first in women's shoes.

Azaléia was vertically organized, with five factories, two of them in northeastern Brazil, and additional production from other firms in Rio Grande do Sul, which had many shoemakers. It spent freely on advertising and employed 185 salespeople, who were the first in their sector to communicate by means of laptops. The company reinvested its profits in new technology instead of seeking bank loans for this purpose. One publication compared 25 different lines of women's shoes and concluded that none of the others could match Azaléia in its capacity to introduce new models quickly.

PROSPEROUS AND SOCIALLY CONSCIOUS: 1990–2000

President and chief shareholder of the firm, de Paula was quick to share its success with the workers. Azaléia paid higher wages than any other company in the region and had established a profit sharing plan in 1984. More than 300 were shareholders, inspiring de Paula to call the firm a rich company of poor partners. When he found that 80 percent of the employees had no education beyond fourth grade, he initiated classes in the company's facilities. They also housed a nursery for hundreds of children, since production was around the clock in eight-hour shifts.

Older children received free education with access to laboratories and libraries. Azaléia built an infirmary for the workers, who were also provided with a cafeteria and transport. A comprehensive health plan, for pensioners as well as employers, included prenatal care, dental work, contact lenses, psychotherapy, and treat-

ment for substance dependence. The company offered many of these benefits to the community and invested millions in the construction of a municipal hospital for Parobé.

Azaléia had grown by selling to the domestic market while other shoemakers were concentrating on exports. This began to change in 1991 because plans were underway to establish Mercosur, a free trade zone encompassing Argentina, Paraguay, and Uruguay as well as Brazil. That year, Azaléia shipped 6 percent of its merchandise abroad, mostly to other South American nations. By the following year, on its third try, it had established Azaléia U.S.A. to sell its wares in the United States. The sales office opened in a Chicago suburb, moved to a St. Louis suburb, where it also opened a warehouse, and later moved to Doral, Florida. By 1996 Azaléia was selling specially designed U.S. lines to 1,250 retail clients, including Sears, Nordstrom, and Carson Pirie Scott.

Among Azaléia's popular models at this time were its leather sandals featuring what was called an "air support system" with an injected insole and a flexible outsole. Its loafers and lace-up footwear in the United States had this system in full or part, as did the "Rock'n Sole," featuring moccasins, loafers, and booties in four different leathers. The company was also marketing the popular transparent sandals called jellies. Wholesale export prices averaged $11 to $12 a pair, and nothing sold at retail for over $50. For the home market, Azaléia began making a popular low priced canvas shoe called the "Shanghai."

AZALÉIA IN THE 21ST CENTURY: DECLINE AND FALL

By 2000 Azaléia seemed to be unstoppable. There were 16 company-owned plants, 11 contracted ones, and eight workers' cooperatives turning out 140,000 pairs of footwear per day, or more than 30 million a year. Twenty-five million were being sold in Brazil, with the rest exported to 30 countries. By 2003 the company was producing 45 million pairs a year. That year ended badly, however, with sales down about 8 percent, layoffs, and a deficit in the second half of the year. Chinese imports, no longer subject in Brazil to high tariffs, were taking a heavy toll on the company.

Worse yet, de Paula was found to have contracted lung cancer and died six months later, in early 2004. None of his three children was interested in assuming the management of the company. In the time left to him, de Paula appointed as his successor Antonio Britto, former governor of Rio Grande do Sul. Although he had no business experience or expertise in shoes, Britto successfully managed Azaléia for three years. Revenues

KEY DATES

1958: Shoe factory that later becomes Calçados Azaléia is founded.

1971: Vulcabras is formed as a rubber company by the Grendene brothers.

1973: Vulcabras secures a license to make athletic footwear under the adidas name.

1975: Azaléia introduces its popular Olympikus sneaker.

1989: Vulcabras is Brazil's second largest manufacturer of athletic footwear.

1994: Azaléia is second among Brazil footwear producers and first in women's shoes.

1998: Vulcabras signs production and exclusive distribution contracts with Reebok.

2007: Vulcabras purchases Azaléia and an Argentine footwear manufacturer.

2008: Vulcabras and adidas Group AG form a joint venture company.

passed BRL $1 billion ($417 million) in 2005, and earnings rose in 2004 and 2005, although the profit margin remained low.

Britto kept Azaléia competitive chiefly by controlling costs. He wanted to steer the company toward marketing its brands rather than by emphasizing production. The number of plants was reduced, and more closings were planned in an effort to fend off Chinese competition by outsourcing production to China. Here, however, Britto ran into resistance from shareholders, especially Lauro Volkart, a cofounder of Azaléia and vice-president of the board. Britto submitted his resignation in late 2006 and left the firm at the end of the year.

Azaléia never appointed a new president. The company was sold in July 2007 to Vulcabras by Pilar Empreendimentos Imobiliários S.A. for BRL 387 million ($204 million), which came partly from Vulcabras's own resources and partly from financing by the Brazilian development bank BNDES. Pilar, the holding company that owned Azaléia, was 52 percent owned by the de Paula family and 48 percent by the Volkart family.

VULCABRAS, GRENDENE'S LITTLE BROTHER: 1971–2007

Vulcabras started out as a rubber company tied to Grendene S.A., the shoe manufacturer founded by the twin brothers Alexandre and Pedro Grendene Bartelle in 1971. Vulcabras licensed the adidas name in 1973, but produced the German company's athletic shoes in its own way, tailoring them to the Brazilian market. This meant that, although bearing the Adidas logo, many models of the Vulcabras-made footwear were made of canvas rather than leather and nylon. Despite the company name, the soles of these shoes were generally not of vulcanized rubber but injected with polyvinyl chloride. This allowed Vulcabras to sell its high-top basketball shoes or low-top leisure ones for about $20. Vulcabras also licensed and manufactured athletic shoes in Brazil under the Pony, Panda, Rider, and Le Coq Sportif lines.

The business interests of the Grendene twins diverged in the 1980s, when Grendene branched out, buying farms, hotels, and alcohol distilleries. These diversions from the footwear business and Alexandre's flashy lifestyle apparently were not to the taste of the more restrained Pedro, who settled for a 20 percent stake in Grendene while assuming full ownership of the smaller Vulcabras.

Vulcabras was the nation's second largest athletic footwear manufacturer in 1989, when it was introducing a Puma AG model in the form of an expensive sneaker that had leather and nylon uppers and polyurethane midsoles. Between 1992 and 1993, Vulcabras added Brooks, Lotto, and Reebok models to its lines.

In 1995 Vulcabras moved half of its production from Franca, São Paulo, to Horizonte, Ceará, in northern Brazil, where labor costs were lower than in the south. It signed licensing contracts in 1998 with Reebok International Ltd. allowing it to produce and have exclusive distribution of Reebok's products in Brazil and Argentina.

Vulcabras's rate of growth picked up at the start of the 21st century. In the eight years between 1999 and 2007, its annual revenue increased from BRL 91 million ($50 million) to BRL 563 million ($311 million), a rate of about 30 percent a year. Yet this growth was almost entirely due to the boom in sales of athletic footwear, and of Reebok's sales in particular. By 2007 Reebok was accounting for 40 percent of the Brazilian market, which had grown from BRL 4 billion ($1.67 billion) in 2005 to BRL 7 billion in 2006 ($3.18 billion), and it represented about 90 percent of Vulcabras's revenues.

Then, in July 2007, within little more than a week, Vulcabras made two major acquisitions. The first was of Indular Manufacturas S.A. of Argentina, followed by 51 percent of Azaléia. By the end of the year Vulcabras owned all of Azaléia's common stock. Indular Manufacturas had been the exclusive distributor of Reebok footwear and apparel in Argentina since 2004 and was manufacturing 2.5 million pairs of shoes a year.

VULCABRAS/AZALÉIA IN 2008

With these acquisitions, Vulcabras became an enterprise with 19 factories, almost 30,000 employees, and projected consolidated annual revenues in the neighborhood of BRL 2 billion (about $1.1 billion). The Azaléia acquisition, which included its Olympikus brand (and accounted for about 65 percent of its revenues), raised its share of the Brazilian athletic footwear market to about half. It also meant that women's shoes, a major part of Azaléia's business, would assume less importance, although Vulcabras claimed the Azaléia brand was still the leader in women's shoes in Latin America.

A minor consequence of the union of the two companies was the elimination of the accent mark for what was now the Azaleia brand. Vulcabras had dropped the accent over its own second *a* at some prior time.

In 2008 adidas Group AG, which had acquired Reebok International in 2005, and Vulcabras agreed to form a joint venture company to distribute Reebok footwear, apparel, and accessories in Brazil and Paraguay, with Pedro Grendene as president and chairman of the board. The pact, to expire at the end of 2015, provided that Vulcabras would continue to supply Reebok products to the joint venture and meant that Vulcabras's revenues would come in the form of a share in the profits rather than in royalties.

The agreement also gave Vulcabras the right to buy Reebok products directly from Asian manufacturers, which promised to reduce costs by 15 percent and might constitute 30 percent of its inventory by the end of the contract. The new contract also freed Vulcabras from the restriction barring it from distributing athletic footwear belonging to any foreign company other than adidas.

Adidas and Vulcabras were also planning to sign a similar agreement for Argentina. In addition, Vulcabras was planning to have the Argentine operation market the Olympikus brand there as well as Reebok products. Vulcabras had distribution subsidiaries, inherited from Azaleia, in Chile, Colombia, Peru, and the United States, as well as its own in Argentina.

In addition to its Reebok products, Vulcabras was making a tough, polyurethane chloride-injected boot with a polyester interior and an antiskid sole sometimes made of vulcanized rubber. Besides the women's shoes under its own name, Azaleia in 2006 had introduced AZ, a fashion brand with "attitude" and "personality." Dijean, introduced in 2005, was for adolescent girls,

and Fanny, introduced in 2005, for preteen girls. Openka was the flip-flop brand for both men and women. OLK, created by Olympikus, was a casual sneaker. Signia, established in 1999, was an Argentine sports shoe used for soccer.

The ownership structure in Vulcabras in 2008 was complex. Pedro Grendene owned just over half the shares, directly or through Gianpega S/A, in a company named Gold S/A. Two women, one a relative, owned the rest of the shares in Gold, which owned nearly 55 percent of Vulcabras, while Gianpega owned nearly 35 percent. Grendene owned another 1.5 percent directly, and public shareholders held nearly 9 percent. Pedro Grendene was also vice-president and vice-chairman of Grendene, in which, as of 2007, he owned 20 percent of the stock. Alexandre Grendene, president and chairman of Grendene, was vice-president and chairman of Vulcabras.

Robert Halasz

PRINCIPAL SUBSIDIARIES

Vulcabras do Nordeste S.A.

PRINCIPAL COMPETITORS

Grendene S.A.; São Paulo Alpargatas S.A.

FURTHER READING

Carvalho, Denise, "Dois irmãos contra a China," *Exame,* August 1, 2007, pp. 60–61.

"Ela tem a força," *Exame Melhores e Maiores,* August 1993, p. 153.

"Fundador da *Azaléa* more no RS," *O Estado de São Paulo,* January 24, 2004, p. B8.

Gomes, Maria Tereza, "Azaléia," *Exame,* November 5, 1997, supplement, pp. 18–20.

Gotardello Filho, Wilson, "Vulcabras importará mais de asiáticos," *Gazeta Mercantil,* March 26, 2008.

"O jogo de equipe é o que dá resultado," *Exame Melhores e Maiores,* August 1994, pp. 154, 156.

Kepp, Michael, "Amazing Azaléia," *Footwear News,* February 5, 1996, pp. 64, 66.

———, "Brazilians Take 'License' with Branded Athletics," *Footwear News,* April 11, 1988, p. 19.

———, "Vulcabras Is Launching Puma Brand in Brazil," *Footwear News,* November 20, 1989, p. 24.

Koike, Beth, et al., "Vulcabras pretende se-tornar lider no mercado nacional de calçados," *NoticiasFinancieras,* July 11, 2007, p. 1.

Leand, Judy, "Latin Class," September 13, 1999, p. 22.

Naiditch, Suzana, "Depoi que o dono se vai," *Exame,* May 26, 2004, pp. 48–50.

———, "Primeiro, a liçao de casa," *Exame,* November 29, 2000, supplement, pp. 38–39.

———, "Um problema a mais," *Exame,* December 20, 2006, pp. 68–69.

———, "Três presidentes em um," *Exame,* November 7, 2007, pp. 68–69.

Rieger, Nancy, "Brazil's Azaléia Will Market Branded Footwear in the U.S.," *Footwear News,* July 6, 1992, p. 23.

WellPoint, Inc.

120 Monument Circle
Indianapolis, Indiana 46204-4906
U.S.A.
Telephone: (317) 488-6000
Fax: (317) 488-6028
Web site: http://www.wellpoint.com

Public Company
Founded: 1944 as Mutual Hospital Insurance, Inc.
Incorporated: 2001 as Anthem, Inc.
Employees: 41,700
Sales: $61.25 billion (2008)
Stock Exchanges: New York
Ticker Symbol: WLP
NAICS: 524114 Direct Health and Medical Insurance
Carriers; 424210 Drugs and Druggists' Sundries
Merchant Wholesalers; 524113 Direct Life Insur-
ance Carriers; 524292 Third Party Administration
of Insurance and Pension Funds; 551112 Offices of
Other Holding Companies

■ ■ ■

The largest health insurer in the United States, Well-
Point, Inc., provides health coverage to about 35 million
members. The firm offers health plans as the Blue Cross
licensee for California and as the Blue Cross and Blue
Shield licensee for Colorado, Connecticut, Georgia,
Indiana, Kentucky, Maine, Nevada, New Hampshire,
Ohio, and Wisconsin as well as portions of Missouri,
New York, and Virginia. WellPoint also offers certain
plans throughout the country under the UniCare name.

The company offers a broad array of network-based
managed-care plans for several sectors of the market,
including small to large companies, individuals,
Medicaid enrollees, and seniors. Its core plans include
health maintenance organizations (HMOs), preferred
provider organizations (PPOs), point-of-service plans,
traditional indemnity plans, and hybrid plans, while its
specialty offerings include life and disability insurance,
pharmacy benefit management services, and dental, vision, and specialty pharmacy coverage. WellPoint, Inc.,
was formed in November 2004 via the merger of
Indianapolis-based Anthem, Inc., and Thousand Oaks,
California-based WellPoint Health Networks Inc.

ANTHEM'S INDIANA BEGINNINGS

The Anthem side of WellPoint's history dates back to
1944, when a mutual insurance company called Mutual
Hospital Insurance, Inc., was formed in Indianapolis to
provide a hospital prepayment insurance plan to Indiana
residents under the name Blue Cross of Indiana. Around
the time of its founding, Blue Cross of Indiana was one
of some 80 Blue Cross plans around the country with a
collective enrollment of 19 million. Unlike with other
Blue Cross plans, the state legislation that established
Blue Cross of Indiana did not exempt the company
from state taxes and did not require hospitals to provide
the company with discounts on their normal charges. In
other respects, the Indiana company operated like other
Blue Cross plans, taking in premiums that were essentially considered prepayment for necessary hospital
stays.

At this same time, Blue Shield plans were being set
up across the country at the behest of state medical as-

COMPANY PERSPECTIVES

At WellPoint, our mission is to improve the lives of the people we serve and the health of our communities. We achieve our mission every day by linking nearly 35 million members to the resources they need—doctors, health care facilities, and community resources. Our portfolio of products and services is designed to meet the unique needs of each of our members, by giving them the ability to choose what works best for them and their families at every stage throughout the continuum of their lives.

sociations to provide prepaid physicians' services. In 1946 the Indiana State Medical Association raised $100,000 to set up Mutual Medical Insurance, Inc., a mutual insurance company based in Indianapolis serving Indiana residents as Blue Shield of Indiana. In another departure from the typical practice at this time, the physicians group that set up Blue Shield of Indiana decided they did not want to be involved in the marketing and administration of the plan. They entered into a unique arrangement with Blue Cross of Indiana whereby the latter assumed responsibility for acquiring new business and managing the operations of the Blue Shield plan. Blue Shield of Indiana was thus responsible solely for setting the amounts paid for medical services.

From the 1950s into the 1970s, the Indiana Blue Cross and Blue Shield companies enjoyed tremendous growth, eventually grabbing more than 80 percent of the state's insurance market. During the 1970s, however, contraction and consolidation in the state's core automotive and steel industries undermined the companies' business base. At the same time, rapid and sustained increases in healthcare expenses made cost containment a prime issue and thereby provided the impetus for the evolution of HMOs and PPOs. As a result, the Indiana Blue Cross and Blue Shield companies during the 1970s and the early 1980s suffered from falling market share, increased competition, and exposure to the viciously cyclical ups and downs that marked the health insurance industry during this period.

MERGER AND DIVERSIFICATION

In 1985 Mutual Hospital Insurance, Inc., and Mutual Medical Insurance, Inc., merged under a newly formed holding company called Associated Insurance Companies, Inc., also known as the Associated Group.

Associated Insurance initially was focused solely on its single operating entity, the combined Blue Cross and Blue Shield of Indiana. Yet under the leadership of Lloyd J. Banks, the firm's CEO, and L. Ben Lytle, the executive vice-president in charge of operations, Associated Insurance embarked on a strategy of business-line and geographic diversification to escape from the vulnerabilities inherent in a one-state, one-product operation.

Associated Insurance over the course of several years acquired or established numerous subsidiaries operating outside its original business. By 1992 its operations included Acordia, Inc., which ran brokerages selling and servicing insurance and employee benefit programs for certain niche markets; Anthem Health, Inc., a nationwide operation offering group life and health insurance, including HMOs and PPOs; Raffensperger, Hughes & Co., Inc., Indiana's largest investment banking concern; and the Shelby Insurance Co., a property and casualty insurance business whose annual premiums were approaching $200 million. By that time, too, Lytle had succeeded Banks as CEO.

In 1992 Associated Insurance took Acordia public through an initial public offering (IPO) of a minority portion of the subsidiary's stock. A year later Acordia substantially bolstered its property and casualty insurance brokerage business by acquiring American Business Insurance, Inc., for about $130 million. Two other significant acquisitions were completed in 1993, including the $100 million purchase of property and casualty insurance specialist Federal Kemper Insurance Company. Most significantly, however, Associated Insurance purchased Southeastern Mutual Insurance Company, operator of Blue Cross and Blue Shield of Kentucky. This was the first cross-state merger of two major Blues plans. Under pressure to lower its costs to compete with its hyper-cost-conscious managed-care competitors, Associated aimed to expand its core health insurance business beyond its home state and thereby gain economies of scale by spreading fixed costs over a greater number of customers. Aided by its latest acquisitions, Associated Insurance enjoyed its best year ever in 1993, with profits of $65.4 million on $3.4 billion in revenue.

RETURN TO THE CORE

A key turning point occurred in 1995, when Associated Insurance acquired Community Mutual Insurance Company, a Cincinnati firm that was one of three Blue Cross/Blue Shield licensees in Ohio. Community Mutual provided healthcare coverage to 1.9 million people in Ohio, and its annual revenues were around $2.2 billion. Following the takeover of Community Mutual, Associated set up Anthem Blue Cross and Blue Shield to manage its three-state Blue Cross/Blue Shield

KEY DATES

1936: Blue Cross of Northern California is founded.

1937: Blue Cross of Southern California is founded.

1944: Mutual Hospital Insurance, Inc., is formed in Indianapolis to offer prepaid hospital insurance to Indiana residents under the name Blue Cross of Indiana.

1946: Another Indianapolis-based firm, Mutual Medical Insurance, Inc., is set up to offer prepaid medical insurance to Indiana residents under the name Blue Shield of Indiana.

1982: The two California Blue Cross companies merge to form Blue Cross of California (BCC).

1985: Mutual Hospital Insurance and Mutual Medical Insurance merge under the newly formed holding company Associated Insurance Companies, Inc., which oversees Blue Cross and Blue Shield of Indiana.

1992: WellPoint Health Networks Inc. is established to run BCC's managed healthcare operations.

1993: Associated Insurance acquires Southeastern Mutual Insurance Company, operator of Blue Cross and Blue Shield of Kentucky; WellPoint Health is taken public.

1995: Associated acquires Community Mutual Insurance Company, a Cincinnati-based Blue Cross/Blue Shield licensee.

1996: Associated Insurance is renamed Anthem Insurance Companies, Inc.; BCC is merged into WellPoint Health.

2001: Anthem Insurance demutualizes and goes public as Anthem, Inc.; WellPoint Health acquires Cerulean Companies, Inc., parent of Blue Cross and Blue Shield of Georgia.

2002: Anthem acquires Trigon Healthcare, Inc., a Blue Cross/Blue Shield licensee in Virginia; WellPoint Health purchases RightChoice Managed Care, Inc., owner of Blue Cross and Blue Shield of Missouri.

2004: In a $15.8 billion deal, Anthem and WellPoint Health merge to form WellPoint, Inc.

2005: Company acquires WellChoice, Inc., operator of New York-based Empire Blue Cross Blue Shield.

health plans. At the same time, Lytle shifted the company's focus back to this core area and recentered the diversification efforts on geographic expansion through the acquisition of additional Blue Cross/Blue Shield companies. The prospects for this business had turned brighter with the scuttling of the healthcare reform initiatives of President Bill Clinton's administration.

The divestment of those operations that had been deemed noncore began in 1995 with the sale of Raffensperger, Hughes to National City Corporation. Gradually, through 1998, the other noncore operations were jettisoned, including Acordia and the various property and casualty insurance businesses. In the meantime, Associated Insurance changed its name to Anthem Insurance Companies, Inc., in 1996.

Over the remainder of the 1990s, Anthem aggressively sought to broaden its geographic footprint. In May 1996 the company announced plans to acquire New Jersey Blue Cross and Blue Shield, the largest health insurer in New Jersey with 1.9 million enrollees. The deal hit a snag, however, because of the New Jersey outfit's nonprofit status. In order for New Jersey Blue Cross to merge with Anthem it needed to first convert into a mutual insurance company. State regulators, however, would not permit this to occur unless New Jersey Blue Cross transferred hundreds of millions of dollars to a healthcare foundation as repayment for the concessions the state had granted it over the years in return for serving as the insurer of last resort for people with expensive illnesses. Anthem did manage to complete the purchase of Blue Cross & Blue Shield of Connecticut, Inc., which had 916,000 subscribers, in 1997, boosting its total enrollment to 5.3 million. Then in 1999 Anthem purchased Blue Cross and Blue Shield companies in New Hampshire (366,000 enrollees), Colorado (395,000), and Nevada (91,000).

By 1999 Anthem's revenues had grown to nearly $6.3 billion. Net income that year, which totaled $44.9 million, was substantially reduced by the company's contribution of $114.1 million to nonprofit foundations in Kentucky, Ohio, and Connecticut to settle asset claims similar to the one that had unraveled the New Jersey Blue Cross deal. At this time, Anthem's membership base across its seven-state operating area included 2.4 million PPO enrollees, a little more than a million in traditional indemnity plans, 964,000 in HMOs, and 723,000 in point-of-service plans. In October 1999 Lytle retired and was succeeded by Larry C. Glasscock, who had joined the company the previous year and had led the company overseeing the Blue Cross/Blue Shield plan for the District of Columbia.

DEMUTUALIZATION AND IPO

Under Glasscock, Anthem at least initially continued down the same path, with the new leader seeing through to completion the 2000 purchase of Associated Hospital Service of Maine, which operated as Blue Cross and Blue Shield of Maine and had nearly 500,000 enrollees. Early the following year, however, Anthem embarked on a new phase in its history when it announced plans to convert from a mutual insurance company, owned by its policyholders, into a publicly traded company, owned by shareholders. The changeover was designed to make it easier for Anthem to raise money for capital investments and acquisitions, while also enabling executives to receive part of their compensation in the form of stock and stock options. On October 30, 2001, Anthem completed its demutualization and an IPO of stock in Anthem, Inc., on the New York Stock Exchange. More than 55 million shares of stock were sold at $36 a share, with nearly all of the more than $1.9 billion raised going to the company's policyholders/owners. Anthem immediately ranked as the fourth largest publicly traded health insurance company in the nation.

Over the next two years, Anthem increased its enrollment by more than 50 percent to 11.9 million members. In addition to significant organic growth within its existing geographic footprint, the company in July 2002 completed the major acquisition of Trigon Healthcare, Inc., for $4.04 billion in cash and stock. Trigon was the largest health insurer in Virginia with 2.2 million members and was the Blue Cross/Blue Shield licensee for the entire state except for the immediate suburbs of the District of Columbia. Anthem suffered a setback in 2003 when the Kansas Supreme Court blocked its proposed $190 million purchase of Topeka-based Blue Cross Blue Shield of Kansas, upholding the Kansas Insurance Department's contention that the deal would "weaken the financial standing of the state's dominant health insurer." In spite of this disappointing development on the acquisition front, Anthem enjoyed stellar growth between 2001 and 2003 as revenues jumped from $10.12 billion to $16.48 billion and net income more than doubled to $774.3 million. In October 2003 Anthem announced a blockbuster takeover of rival WellPoint Health Networks Inc. in a deal valued at more than $12 billion.

WELLPOINT HEALTH'S EVOLUTION OUT OF BLUE CROSS OF CALIFORNIA

The ultimate origins of WellPoint Health Networks date back to the 1936 founding of Blue Cross of Northern California and the establishment of Blue Cross of Southern California a year later. These two nonprofit entities merged in 1982 to form Blue Cross of California (BCC). In the mid-1980s, after a tumultuous period when the cost of medical care increased rapidly, the group found itself in precarious financial straits. As company CEO Leonard Schaeffer described the situation in *Health Affairs,* "BCC's very existence was threatened." Blue Cross ran a $55 million deficit in 1986. The sale of its Woodland Hills, California, headquarters building provided temporary help, balancing out BCC's 1987 stock market and underwriting losses. In April 1988 Schaeffer announced the worst was past. The following August, however, the group reported second-quarter losses of $20.5 million and was able to stave off insolvency at the end of the year only when it found a buyer for its TakeCare HMO.

In early 1989 BCC completed an initial restructuring implemented by Schaeffer. Within a few months, the group's staff had been cut from 6,500 to 3,825 and BCC could report a fourth quarter profit of $41.9 million. A new California law enacted in the fall of 1990 enabled BCC to be licensed as a healthcare services plan. By 1991 BCC could report a dramatic turnaround: full-year profits of $159.7 million. It boasted the largest growth in enrollment and earnings of any healthcare plan in California, and of any Blue Cross or Blue Shield plan in the entire country. Nonetheless, as Schaeffer wrote in 1996, "BCC faced significant challenges: uncertainty over future government policy and regulations, limited access to capital markets, and increasing competition in a rapidly growing marketplace. BCC thus began to look for a way to compete on the same regulatory and marketing playing field with its competitors."

Against this background, WellPoint Health Networks Inc. was organized in 1992 as the division responsible for BCC's managed healthcare operations. BCC's most profitable operations were concentrated in the new company—the health maintenance organization, the preferred provider organization, and the various specialty plans. Blue Cross of California retained the traditional health insurance plans. In August 1992 BCC management presented a restructuring plan to the California Department of Corporations (DOC) calling for the creation of a wholly owned, for-profit subsidiary, WellPoint Health Networks, whose stock would be sold in a public offering. The plan was designed to further improve Blue Cross's financial position by giving it access to the country's capital markets.

Under the plan, Blue Cross of California would retain 80 percent of WellPoint Health and the BCC board would hold 97.5 percent of the voting shares in the new company. BCC would also restructure but would not convert to for-profit status. An important consideration in that decision was a Blue Cross and Blue Shield Association rule that prevented a for-profit entity from being the primary licensee of the Blue Cross name and trademark.

In January 1993 the DOC approved BCC's proposal. The first public offering of WellPoint Health stock took place in late January 1993. At first BCC planned to sell 15 million shares at a cost of $22 to $24 a share, but stronger than expected investor demand led to the sale of some 18 million shares at $28 a share. The strong showing could be traced to WellPoint Health's large membership base—423,000 HMO members and 1.5 million PPO members—and its healthy 1992 earnings of $142.8 million, an exceptionally good year for a Blue Cross division. Also contributing to investor interest were WellPoint Health's high-profit services, which indicated the company would probably experience quick growth.

CONTROVERSY STEMMING FROM PUBLIC OFFERING

The deal created one of the largest public managed healthcare companies in the United States and brought $517 million to Blue Cross of California. Afterward, though, the restructuring proved to be extremely controversial. Under California law, when a nonprofit converted to for-profit status it was required to compensate the public for the years it was allowed to operate on a tax-free basis. That normally entailed contributing the full value of the assets of the converted organization to a charitable foundation. In this case, however, the nonprofit BCC had not *itself* converted to for-profit status; its subsidiary had, though, and BCC controlled it completely.

There was no provision in California law requiring a contribution in such a case. The DOC's initial ruling absolved BCC from owing any compensation. The decision drew criticism from the California Office of Consumers Union and the California Medical Association. In transferring most of its assets to Well-Point Health while remaining nonprofit, critics maintained Blue Cross had taken advantage of a loophole in the law and that Blue Cross executives, who also sat on the board of WellPoint Health, stood to profit personally from the change through stock option plans and other considerations.

In April members of the California legislature became involved in the dispute. Accusing Blue Cross of ducking its public responsibility, a bill was introduced to penalize Blue Cross retroactively for hundreds of millions of dollars. After weeks of negotiations between Blue Cross and legislators, an agreement was reached in

the summer of 1993: BCC would pay a $100 million lump sum to charity as well as increasing its annual charitable contributions by $5 million.

In August 1993, however, Gary S. Mendoza was appointed to head the DOC. In December 1993 the new, more aggressive commissioner informed Blue Cross that he did not consider the agreement with the legislature to be sufficient. Eventually, in April 1994, he informed Blue Cross it should commit not less than $100 million to charitable purposes in 1994, and at least 40 percent of Blue Cross of California's WellPoint Health holdings to a new charitable foundation. By comparison, when Health Net, another California health insurance provider, went for-profit in 1992, it had to endow the California Wellness Foundation with $300 million and 80 percent of its stock; BCC was nearly ten times larger than Health Net.

The DOC's demand took BCC by surprise, and the firm responded by telling Mendoza that it did not believe there was any statutory basis to justify the stock turnover or the loss of control of WellPoint Health that it would entail for BCC. With Mendoza threatening enforcement action, an event occurred in May 1994 that seemed to offer a way out of the impasse. The Blue Cross and Blue Shield Association amended its bylaws to allow a for-profit organization to hold a primary Blue Cross license. Blue Cross of California drew up a new plan that it presented to DOC in September 1994. Blue Cross would separate its nonprofit and for-profit activities completely by donating all of its remaining assets to two brand new charitable foundations that it would found and then convert itself to for-profit status. All of BCC's insurance activities would be merged into Well-Point Health, which would also take over the rights to the Blue Cross license and logo. Some analysts observed that Blue Cross was exactly where it would have been if it had acceded to critics' demands in 1992. Yet to go completely for-profit at that time would have entailed surrendering the rights to the company's respected, and valuable, Blue Cross affiliation.

All that remained to be established was WellPoint Health's actual value as an asset. BCC proposed using the company's publicly traded price as a yardstick, despite a year and a half of wrangling, it had remained remarkably stable at just over $27. "The DOC," according to Schaeffer, "said that the company could be better valued by putting it up for auction through a 'market assessment' process." WellPoint Health disagreed fundamentally with this approach but proceeded nonetheless. In March 1995 Blue Shield of California, attempting to develop its HMO business, offered first $4.5 billion, then $4.8 billion, for WellPoint Health. If its bid were successful, Blue Shield said, it would follow

WellPoint Health's example and convert to for-profit status.

WellPoint Health rejected both Blue Shield offers. It had been pursuing negotiations to acquire Health Systems International, a company headquartered near WellPoint Health in Woodland Hills, California. On April 4, 1995, the two companies formally announced that they were merging. Terms of the deal entailed the exchange of $1.9 billion in stock. This deal, which provoked new controversies, was eventually approved by the DOC only to then fall apart later in 1995 when the two sides were unable to iron out the final terms.

MERGER OF BCC INTO WELLPOINT HEALTH

In the wake of the failed merger, WellPoint Health filed a third recapitalization plan with the DOC in February 1996. It called for the creation of two foundations that would receive about 80 percent of Blue Cross's WellPoint Health stock. WellPoint Health would pay out additional monies to acquire remaining Blue Cross commercial assets. The total endowment would amount to approximately $3 billion. Over a five-year period, the foundations would be required to reduce their voting share to less than 5 percent in WellPoint Health through sales or transfers. On May 20, 1996, Blue Cross of California and its remaining assets were merged into WellPoint Health, which assumed the rights to the Blue Cross name and logo.

WellPoint Health's service plans and networks had been expanding under Schaeffer's leadership during 1995. In May 1995 that company acquired nine San Francisco Bay Area dental practices with 800,000 patients to form what it called a "dental service organization" (DSO), similar in organization to the management-services organization in the medical world. Participating dentists would be part owners of the organization, and in effect pool their resources with WellPoint Health's to create advantageous economies of scale. WellPoint Health's DSO was said to be the first of its kind in the country, and the company hoped within 18 months to have a network in place that would reach a quarter of all Californians.

Schaeffer's sights were set much higher though as he aimed to make the firm a national company. A key step in this direction took place in March 1996 when WellPoint Health acquired the Group Life and Health subsidiary of Massachusetts Mutual Life Insurance Company for $402.2 million. The acquired unit's one million members, combined with WellPoint Health's 2.8 million, created the second largest publicly held managed health company in the United States. This first major acquisition outside California enabled WellPoint Health to expand its coverage into ten states, including Massachusetts, New York, and New Jersey, and to add Mass Mutual's sizable dental insurance and group life and disability insurance business to its own rosters.

In March 1997 WellPoint Health bought the group benefit operations of the John Hancock Mutual Life Insurance Company for $86.7 million, gaining a unit that concentrated on serving the needs of large employers. The purchase extended WellPoint Health's presence to a number of new states, including Michigan, Texas, and the mid-Atlantic area. The purchase of the Hancock and Mass Mutual units, with their more traditional types of policies, reflected WellPoint Health's unconventional conviction at the time: The popularity of HMOs had peaked, and both employers and workers were looking for healthcare plans that offered them greater latitude. WellPoint Health made its UNICARE subsidiary responsible for the Mass Mutual and Hancock operations.

Despite healthy profits (even in 1994 during the uncertainty with the DOC its profit margin was 13 percent), WellPoint Health had a bad reputation among California doctors, who complained of the firm's tight-fisted payment practices and strong-arm tactics. Studies released by the California Medical Association (CMA) between 1994 and 1996 claimed that WellPoint Health's CaliforniaCare HMO spent less of its total revenues on patient care and more on profits and overhead than any other plan in California. WellPoint Health maintained the CMA's survey was flawed pointing out that it ignored differences in accounting practice in nonprofit and for-profit entities, and the higher overhead required to support independent sales agents. Hospitals in California also voiced objection to the company's 1995 organization of a two-tier co-payment scheme for the state's hospitals. Among other groups giving WellPoint Health poor ratings, the National Committee for Quality Assurance, which evaluates managed healthcare, refused to give its accreditation to a company HMO.

Throughout the remainder of the 1990s and into the 21st century, WellPoint Health Networks was the subject of a barrage of similar criticism along with periodic lawsuits. Some critics blamed the rising costs of healthcare on the thirst for profits of WellPoint and its for-profit rivals. WellPoint Health certainly posted consistently profitable results, placing it in position to pursue growth through acquisition. By 2000 net income had grown to $342.3 million on revenues of $9.23 billion. That year, WellPoint Health spent $204 million for Rush Prudential Health Plans, which served about 300,000 members, mainly in the Chicago area. The company in 2000 also joined with ING Groep N.V. to approach Aetna Inc. about a possible takeover, but the overture was rebuffed.

EARLY 21ST-CENTURY ACQUISITION SPREE

WellPoint Health continued its efforts to grow outside of its California base, completing a $700 million acquisition of Cerulean Companies, Inc., in March 2001. Cerulean was the parent company of Blue Cross and Blue Shield of Georgia, which had around 1.8 million members. In January 2002 WellPoint Health acquired RightChoice Managed Care, Inc., for approximately $1.5 billion in cash and stock. Based in St. Louis, RightChoice was the largest managed-care company in Missouri, with 2.8 million members, and owned Blue Cross and Blue Shield of Missouri. Its other operations included HealthLink, a provider of medical networks and administrative services to employers and insurers in seven states in the Midwest. WellPoint Health also bolstered its UNICARE unit via the April 2002 acquisition of MethodistCare, which operated an HMO in the Greater Houston area serving more than 70,000 members.

The company completed two more deals in 2003, adding Golden West Dental and Vision of Camarillo, California, which provided dental and vision insurance coverage to more than 275,000 members in California, and Cobalt Corporation, parent of Blue Cross and Blue Shield United of Wisconsin. The latter deal, completed for $884.9 million in cash and stock, added an additional 675,000 members into the company fold, bringing its nationwide total at the end of 2003 to 15 million. In a setback for WellPoint Health, its proposed $1.37 billion acquisition of CareFirst, Inc., a Blue Cross/Blue Shield licensee in Maryland, Delaware, northern Virginia, and the District of Columbia with 3.1 million members, was terminated when Maryland's insurance commissioner blocked CareFirst's conversion to for-profit status, a prerequisite for the takeover. WellPoint Health nevertheless enjoyed record results for 2003, net income of $935.2 million on revenues of $19.16 billion.

MERGER OF ANTHEM AND WELLPOINT HEALTH

Over the course of the 1990s and into the 21st century, Anthem and WellPoint Health Networks had been two of the most acquisitive managed-care companies in the country and had mainly concentrated on snapping up Blue Cross/Blue Shield plans around the country. With cost savings at the heart of these takeovers, it was certainly not surprising when the two firms pursued an even larger cost-cutting opportunity: their own merger. The deal, which was announced in October 2003 and completed on November 30, 2004, was structured as an Anthem takeover of WellPoint Health and was valued at $15.8 billion. Along the way, the companies ran into some regulatory roadblocks, and the parties had to pledge $265 million to boost healthcare in California and $126.5 million to boost healthcare in Georgia. Upon completion of the deal, Anthem changed its name to WellPoint, Inc. The company remained based in Indianapolis, and Glasscock, Anthem's CEO, continued in the same position at the new WellPoint.

WellPoint, Inc., immediately ranked as the largest health insurer in the United States, serving more than 27 million members around the country. The core of its operations were its Blue Cross and Blue Shield plans in 13 states, with its other operations headed by the nationwide UniCare unit. Among its actions during the first year following the megamerger, WellPoint launched a $250 million program to overhaul its bill-payment and other operations as part of an effort to improve its relations with physicians. The company also agreed to make payments totaling about $200 million to settle class-action lawsuits that had been filed by more than 700,000 physicians around the country accusing WellPoint and other managed-care companies of unfairly cutting reimbursements to them.

WellPoint continued to make news on the acquisition front as well. In June 2005 the company spent $185 million for Lumenos, Inc. This Alexandria, Virginia, firm was a pioneer in the field of so-called consumer-driven health plans, which were marketed as a way for individuals to take a more active role in their healthcare and were centered around health savings accounts and health reimbursement accounts. In a deal with a far larger immediate impact, WellPoint acquired WellChoice, Inc., for $6.5 billion in cash and stock. WellChoice, operating as Empire Blue Cross Blue Shield, had about five million members in New York City, ten downstate counties of New York, and New Jersey. WellPoint thus gained a significant foothold in New York City, the headquarters of more *Fortune* 500 companies than any other single market.

During 2006 WellPoint was essentially forced to shift away from acquisition-led growth because of a dearth of targets. The companies that had been rolled up into WellPoint over the years were primarily for-profit Blue Cross/Blue Shield operators; there were none of these left to acquire, and state governments had been blocking further attempts by nonprofit plans to convert to for-profit status. In addition, WellPoint faced a specific limit in the growth of its non-Blues business because to keep its licenses from the Blue Cross Blue Shield Association, it was required to generate two-thirds of its national insurance revenues from Blues operations. Organic growth thus became a renewed point of emphasis, and WellPoint added 245,000 customers during 2006 without the benefit of an acquisition. New product launches helped in this effort. Leveraging the Lumenos acquisition, WellPoint became the first health insurance company to introduce on a national basis an array of consumer-driven health plans in all market segments, from individuals to large employers. The company's 2006 results showed net income of more than $3 billion on revenues of $56.95 billion.

In June 2007 Glasscock retired as CEO while remaining chairman. His successor, Angela F. Braly, had been the firm's general counsel and an executive vice-president and had previously headed Blue Cross and Blue Shield of Missouri. Braly's background in corporate law and public affairs was seen by analysts as ideal at a time when pressure for reform of the U.S. healthcare industry was building. Even before the election of Barack Obama to the U.S. presidency, which increased the chances that significant reform might actually be enacted, WellPoint was struggling to deal with another challenge: the severe economic downturn. The company began losing thousands and thousands of enrollees as companies across the country slashed their workforces and the unemployment rate shot up. At the same time, the doldrums on Wall Street had a major impact on WellPoint's investment portfolio. Over the course of 2008, the company incurred after-tax investment losses of $759.6 million, which helped push net income down 25.5 percent to $2.49 billion. Among its initial reactions to the downturn were announcements in early 2009 to eliminate about 1,500 jobs, or about 3.6 percent of its workforce, and to sell its in-house pharmacy benefit management business, NextRx, which was the fourth largest such business in the country.

Gerald Brennan
Updated, David E. Salamie

PRINCIPAL SUBSIDIARIES

American Imaging Management, Inc.; Anthem Blue Cross Blue Shield Partnership Plan, Inc.; Anthem Blue Cross Life and Health Insurance Company; Anthem Health Insurance Company of Nevada; Anthem Health Plans of Kentucky, Inc.; Anthem Health Plans of Maine, Inc.; Anthem Health Plans of New Hampshire, Inc.; Anthem Health Plans of Virginia, Inc.; Anthem Health Plans, Inc.; Anthem HMO of Nevada; Anthem Holding Corp.; Anthem Life Insurance Company; Anthem Southeast, Inc.; Blue Cross and Blue Shield of Georgia, Inc.; Blue Cross Blue Shield of Wisconsin; Blue Cross of California; Empire HealthChoice Assurance, Inc.; Empire HealthChoice HMO, Inc.; Golden West Health Plan, Inc.; Health Core, Inc.; HealthLink, Inc.; Health Management Corporation; HMO Colorado, Inc.; HMO Missouri, Inc.; Meridian Resource Company, LLC; National Capital Preferred Provider Organization, Inc.; National Government Services, Inc.; Resolution Health, Inc.; UNICARE Health Benefit Services of Texas, Inc.; UNICARE Health Insurance Company of Texas; UNICARE Health Insurance Company of the Midwest; UNICARE Health Plan of Kansas, Inc.; UNICARE Health Plan of South Carolina, Inc.; UNICARE Health Plan of West Virginia, Inc.; UNICARE Health Plans of Texas, Inc.; UNICARE Health Plans of the Midwest, Inc.; UNICARE Illinois Services, Inc.; UniCare Life & Health Insurance Company; UNICARE National Services, Inc.; UNICARE of Texas Health Plans, Inc.; UNICARE Specialty Services, Inc.; WellPoint Behavioral Health, Inc.; WellPoint Dental Services, Inc.

PRINCIPAL DIVISIONS

PrecisionRx Specialty Solutions; WellPoint NextRx; WellPoint Workers' Compensation Managed Care Services.

PRINCIPAL COMPETITORS

UnitedHealth Group Incorporated; Aetna Inc.; CIGNA Corporation; Humana Inc.; Kaiser Foundation Health Plan, Inc.; Health Care Service Corporation.

FURTHER READING

"After Two-Year Buildup, Lytle Prepares to Step Down," *Indianapolis Business Journal*, September 6, 1999, p. 5A.

Anders, George, "Blue Cross of California Sells Stake in Well-Point Health for $476 Million," *Wall Street Journal*, January 28, 1993.

Andrews, Greg, "Restructuring Leaves Associated Stronger, Streamlined," *Indianapolis Business Journal*, January 27, 1992, pp. 14A+.

"Anthem Blue Cross and Blue Shield," *Indianapolis Business Journal*, December 1999, p. 82B.

Barnum, Alex, "Blue Cross IPO Tantalizes Wall Street," *San Francisco Chronicle*, January 28, 1993.

Brin, Dinah Wisenberg, "Blue Cross Plans Feeling Pressure to Consolidate," *Wall Street Journal*, August 25, 2008, p. B7.

Burton, Thomas M., and Ann Carrns, "Anthem to Buy Trigon Healthcare," *Wall Street Journal*, April 30, 2002, p. A3.

Colliver, Victoria, "Anthem-WellPoint Deal OK'd," *San Francisco Chronicle*, November 10, 2004, p. C1.

Connolly, Jim, "California Blue Cross Plans to Start For-Profit Sub," *National Underwriter—Life and Health/Financial Services,* September 14, 1992.

Deveny, Kathleen, "What's Ailing Blue Cross: Just About Everything," *Business Week,* February 15, 1988, pp. 32+.

Dorman, Shirleen, "WellPoint to Cut About 1,500 Jobs," *Wall Street Journal,* January 20, 2009, p. B5.

Ellison, Evelyn, "String of Deals Pays Off Big for Anthem," *Indianapolis Business Journal,* August 11, 1997, p. 17.

Feder, Barnaby J., "Anthem's Strategy: Bigger the Better," *New York Times,* May 30, 1996, p. D6.

Freudenheim, Milt, "Acquisition Would Create Nation's Largest Health Insurer," *New York Times,* October 28, 2003, p. C1.

———, "Battling, Politely, for Health Care's Biggest Prize," *New York Times,* May 26, 2002, sec. 3, p. 1.

Fuhrmans, Vanessa, "Anthem Acquires WellPoint, Creating No. 1 Health Insurer," *Wall Street Journal,* December 1, 2004, p. C4.

———, "Pricing Strategy Puts WellPoint in Bind," *Wall Street Journal,* September 3, 2008, p. B1.

———, "WellPoint Profit Slides 61% As Plan Numbers Fall," *Wall Street Journal,* January 29, 2009, p. B6.

———, "WellPoint Settles Doctors' Lawsuit," *Wall Street Journal,* July 12, 2005, p. A3.

Fuhrmans, Vanessa, and Carol Hymowitz, "WellPoint's CEO Takes the Reins, Facing Challenges," *Wall Street Journal,* June 6, 2007, p. B1.

Fuhrmans, Vanessa, and Matthew Karnitschnig, "WellPoint Puts NextRx on the Auction Block," *Wall Street Journal,* March 6, 2009, p. B3.

Gallagher, Leigh, "WellPoint: Zag When Everyone Else Is Zigging," *Forbes,* January 10, 2000, p. 142.

Hagerty, Alfred G., "California Wants More Funds from Blue Cross for Non-Profit Unit," *National Underwriter—Life and Health/Financial Services,* May 30, 1994.

Hall, Carl T., "Deal to Create Huge HMO Dies," *San Francisco Chronicle,* December 15, 1995.

———, "WellPoint Confirms Health Care Merger," *San Francisco Chronicle,* April 4, 1995.

Johnson, J. Douglas, "The Best of the Blues ... and a Whole Lot More," *Indiana Business Magazine,* September 1992, pp. 10+.

Ketzenberger, John, "New Tune: Associated No Longer Just Playing the Blues," *Indianapolis Business Journal,* May 21, 1990, pp. 1+.

Lagnado, Lucette, "Anthem Inc. Seeks 'Blues' of Connecticut," *Wall Street Journal,* October 1, 1996, p. B5.

Laing, Jonathan R., "A Clean Bill of Health," *Barron's,* May 7, 2007, pp. 31–33.

Louis, Arthur M., "HMO Merger Takes a Turn," *San Francisco Chronicle,* March 28, 1995.

Lytle, L. Ben, *The Associated Group: "A Tradition Transformed,"* New York: Newcomen Society of the United States, 1990, 24 p.

Martinez, Barbara, "WellPoint Gets New York Foothold in $6.5 Billion WellChoice Deal," *Wall Street Journal,* September 28, 2005, p. A3.

McKimmie, Kathy, "National Anthem: Once Just the Indiana Blue Cross and Blue Shield Plan, Anthem Inc. Is Now the Fifth-Largest Publicly Held Health-Benefits Company, with 7.9 Million Members," *Indiana Business Magazine,* March 2002, pp. 10–14, 16.

Morrison, Patrick, "Markets Embrace Anthem Offering," *Indianapolis Business Journal,* November 5, 2001, pp. 1A, 2A.

———, "Trigon Deal Cements Anthem Position," *Indianapolis Business Journal,* May 6, 2002, pp. 3, 56.

Murphy, Tom, "Anthem Trumpets Steady Growth," *Indianapolis Business Journal,* October 6, 2003, pp. 3A, 71A.

———, "Savings at Core of Merger," *Indianapolis Business Journal,* November 3, 2003, pp. 1, 50–51.

Niedzielski, Joe, "Plan Set to Recapitalize WellPoint," *National Underwriter—Life and Health/Financial Services,* March 4, 1996.

Olson, Scott, "WellPoint's Restructuring Nearing Completion," *Indianapolis Business Journal,* October 16, 2006, pp. 21, 27.

Pondel, Evan, "WellPoint Grows in Texas: Firm Diversifies by Acquiring Methodist Care," *Los Angeles Daily News,* January 26, 2002, p. B1.

Rauber, Chris, "WellPoint Picks up String of Bay Area Dental Practices," *Business Journal,* May 22, 1995, p. 20.

Rundle, Rhonda L., "Blue Cross of California to Turn Over Most Assets to New Charity Foundation," *Wall Street Journal,* September 16, 1994.

———, "California in Talks with Blue Cross over Public Sale, " *Wall Street Journal,* August 23, 1993.

———, "California Pressing Blue Cross to Give $1 Billion to Charity," *Wall Street Journal,* May 13, 1994.

———, "Calling the Shots: California Health Plan Thrives, but Doctors Claim Care Suffers," *Wall Street Journal,* May 31, 2000, p. A1.

———, "Cerulean Accepts $700 Million WellPoint Offer," *Wall Street Journal,* November 30, 2000, p. B13.

———, "Observers Detect a Health-Care Giant Looming in WellPoint-Health Systems," *Wall Street Journal,* April 4, 1995.

———, "WellPoint Agrees to Buy RightChoice for Cash, Stock Totaling $1.3 Billion," *Wall Street Journal,* October 19, 2001, p. B8.

———, "WellPoint Set to Buy Georgia Medical Firm," *Wall Street Journal,* July 10, 1998, p. A6.

Rundle, Rhonda L., and Leslie Scism, "WellPoint Faces Fight As Doctors, Hospitals Challenge Its Tightfisted Payment Practices," *Wall Street Journal,* June 1, 1998, p. C4.

Russell, Sabin, "Blue Cross Spin-Off Under Attack," *San Francisco Chronicle,* April 29, 1993.

Schaeffer, Leonard D., "Health Plan Conversions: The View from Blue Cross of California," *Health Affairs,* Winter 1996, pp. 183–87.

Schneider, A. J., "Associated Group on the Grow Again," *Indianapolis Business Journal,* December 5, 1994, pp. 1A, 42A.

Scism, Leslie, and Rhonda L. Rundle, "WellPoint Is Close to Deal with Hancock," *Wall Street Journal,* October 3, 1996, p. A3.

Shinkman, Ronald, "Blue Cross, State Bump Heads," *Los Angeles Business Journal,* September 4, 1995, pp. 1+.

———, "Blue Cross Submits Plan for Charitable Units," *Los Angeles Business Journal,* March 4, 1996, p. 6.

Sidel, Robin, and Rhonda L. Rundle, "Anthem to Acquire WellPoint Health," *Wall Street Journal,* October 27, 2003, p. A3.

———, "WellPoint Agrees to Acquire Cobalt for $960 Million," *Wall Street Journal,* June 5, 2003, p. B2.

Tokarski, Cathy, "Forget Everything You Thought You Knew About the Blues," *Medical Economics,* March 25, 1996, pp. 107+.

Treaster, Joseph B., "Anthem Is Expected to Be Publicly Held," *New York Times,* February 1, 2001, p. C7.

Wall, J. K., "Rough Road Ahead? WellPoint's New CEO Likely to Encounter More Obstacles Than Her Predecessor," *Indianapolis Business Journal,* March 5, 2007, pp. 1, 40.

———, "WellPoint Expected to Go Global," *Indianapolis Business Journal,* July 28, 2008, pp. 3, 44.

Ward, Sandra, "WellPoint's Advantage," *Barron's,* July 25, 2005, pp. 37–38.

Weber, Joseph, "In the Pink of Health: How CEO Larry Glasscock Keeps WellPoint So Fit," *Business Week,* May 23, 2005, pp. 72, 75.

———, "Making Health Insurance Hip: WellPoint Sees Growth Selling No-Frills Coverage to Twentysomethings," *Business Week,* March 19, 2007, p. 84.

Weintraub, Arlene, "Leonard the Giant Killer?" *Business Week,* May 14, 2001, pp. 78, 81.

Whelan, David, "This Won't Hurt a Bit," *Forbes,* September 17, 2007, pp. 116–18+.

Williams-Sonoma, Inc.

_____ ■ _____

3250 Van Ness Avenue
San Francisco, California 94109
U.S.A.
Telephone: (415) 421-7900
Fax: (415) 616-8359
Web site: http://www.williams-sonomainc.com

Public Company
Incorporated: 1956
Employees: 30,000
Sales: $3.4 billion (2009)
Stock Exchanges: New York
Ticker Symbol: WSM
NAICS: 454110 Electronic Shopping and Mail-Order
Houses; 442299 All Other Home Furnishings
Stores

■ ■ ■

Williams-Sonoma, Inc., is a specialty retailer with a wide range of products for the home. Beginning with gourmet kitchen utensils and appliances, the company has steadily expanded its wares to include home furnishings for virtually every room in the house including items for adults, teens, and children. The company also runs online bridal and gift registries and has long harnessed the power of catalog and web sales in addition to brick-and-mortar stores. With nearly 630 stores in 46 states, Washington, D.C., Canada, and Puerto Rico, Williams-Sonoma remains one of the most popular home furnishing and accessories retailers in the United States.

A PASSION FOR COOKING: FIFTIES TO SEVENTIES

After serving as an Air Force mechanic in North Africa and India during World War II, Charles Williams moved to Sonoma, California, where he worked as a self-taught carpenter. A passionate cook, Williams made a trip to Paris in the early 1950s aboard the famed _Ile de France_ cruise ship. While in Paris, he discovered a range of cookware and accessories unknown to the rather bland American kitchen of the period. In 1956, tired of his carpentry career, Williams bought and began to renovate a building in Sonoma that included a failed hardware store. Williams proceeded to dispose of the store's traditional hardware supplies and stock it with the professional quality cooking equipment he had discovered overseas.

The store caught on quickly, becoming popular with many professional and serious cooks. Encouraged by friends such as Julia Child and James Beard, who would be instrumental in sparking an interest in fine cooking in the United States, Williams moved his store to San Francisco, renaming it Williams-Sonoma in honor of its original location. Throughout the next decade the store prospered, attracting customers from around the country. Williams continued making trips to Europe, discovering new products to bring back to his store.

By the late 1960s the nature of houseware sales in the United States had changed. The popularity of international cuisine was on the rise, generating interest in professional quality cooking equipment. Department stores such as Macy's began expanding their kitchenware departments, but none could compete with Williams-Sonoma. In the early 1970s, Williams, exhausted from shouldering the burden of stocking and operating his store, and running every aspect of the business, began to look for help.

One frequent customer and close friend was Edward Marcus of Neiman Marcus retail fame. Marcus suggested Williams either sell his company or expand it into a chain. Williams decided to expand, and in 1972, Marcus and Williams formed a corporation, Williams-Sonoma, Inc. Williams continued to handle purchasing and merchandising, while Marcus brought in a team of executives to guide the company's business end. A second store was opened in Beverly Hills by 1973, the same year the company issued its first mail-order catalog. Williams soon found products that did not sell well in the store often sold very well in the catalog, due to descriptions and stories about unusual products. One such example was a cooks catalog featuring photographs of each product in use. The first mailing of the catalog went to 5,000 people. Sales took off, and the cooks catalog mailing list quickly went nationwide as more stores were opened as well.

By 1977 the Williams-Sonoma chain had grown to five stores. The following year Marcus, who held one-third of the company, died, and a change in management led the company into trouble. With $4.9 million in sales, the company carried a debt of $700,000 and posted a net loss of $173,000. Williams made the difficult decision to sell.

NEW OWNERSHIP: 1978–86

In 1978 Williams sold the company for $100,000 to W. Howard Lester, a former IBM salesman and founder of several computer services firms, and his partner, James McMahan. With the sale came the requirement that Williams remain in charge of selecting merchandise and running the catalog.

Williams-Sonoma turned around quickly under Lester. Within five years, the retail chain grew to 19 stores. In 1982 the company's catalog sales expanded with the acquisition of the Gardeners Eden catalog, then posting about $100,000 in annual sales. By the following year, 1983, catalog mailings reached 30 million customers, with sales accounting for more than 75 percent of the company's overall $35 million annual revenues. To finance further expansion, Lester took the company public in 1983, with an initial public offering (IPO) of one million shares at $23 per share. Lester retained about 22 percent of the company; Williams, who continued to lead the company's catalog division, held about 1.9 percent of the company's stock.

With the money raised in its IPO, the company established a new distribution and warehouse facility in Memphis, Tennessee. Over the next three years, the retail chain grew to 31 stores in 14 states, and the company opened a second retail chain, Hold Everything, which would grow to five stores. The company also sought to expand its catalog business, introducing one featuring table settings and another with more exotic cookware, both of which did poorly. Coupled with the catalog losses and the Memphis warehouse, profits fell to $445,000 in 1983 from a net of $1.5 million in 1982. By 1984, with sales reaching nearly $52 million, earnings had sunk to a mere $38,000.

Williams-Sonoma's setbacks proved short-lived. By 1985 sales climbed to $68 million, earning the company a net of $2.4 million in profit. The company continued to expand, adding 14 Williams-Sonoma stores by the end of the following year. Expansion also included the acquisition of the struggling Pottery Barn chain of 27 retail home furnishings stores, bought for $6 million from The Gap. Pottery Barn also was added to the company's growing line of catalogs, along with Hold Everything and Gardeners Eden. Meanwhile, the retail end was contributing a growing percentage of the company's sales, up to 36 percent of fiscal 1986 sales of just over $100 million.

EXPANSION, RECESSION, AND RECOVERY: 1987–92

The company continued to grow aggressively, raising the number of Williams-Sonoma stores to 64 in 1988. A joint venture with Tokyo Department Store brought the first Williams-Sonoma store, and the Catalog for Cooks, to Japan. The company's sales surged to $136.8 million and net earnings reached $3.4 million by year-end

KEY DATES

■

1956: Charles Williams opens a store in Sonoma, California.

1972: Williams-Sonoma, Inc., is formed as a corporation.

1973: Second store opens in Beverly Hills; the company launches its first mail-order catalog.

1978: Company is sold to W. Howard Lester and James McMahan.

1982: Gardeners Eden catalog is acquired.

1983: Williams-Sonoma goes public with an initial public offering.

1985: Firm establishes a second retail chain, Hold Everything.

1986: Pottery Barn chain of stores is purchased from The Gap.

1989: Chambers, a new catalog, is mailed to customers.

1992: Company partners with Time-Life Books to create Williams-Sonoma Kitchen Library cookbooks.

1994: Williams-Sonoma and Pottery Barn stores undergo changes, including new store formats.

1998: Company gains a listing on the New York Stock Exchange and launches an e-commerce web site.

2000: Pottery Barn begins selling merchandise on-line and the first Pottery Barn Kids store opens.

2001: Company crosses the border into Canada with five stores in the Toronto area.

2002: West Elm, a competitively priced home décor brand for younger shoppers, is introduced.

2004: Williams-Sonoma Home replaces the Chambers home décor brand.

2006: Company celebrates its 50th anniversary by stocking products from its original store.

2008: Two stores open in Puerto Rico; Williams-Sonoma Home debuts in midtown New York City.

1987. To guide the burgeoning empire, Lester brought in former Pillsbury Company President Kent Larson as president of Williams-Sonoma.

Under Larson, the company formed a joint venture with Ralph Lauren to open a chain of Polo/Ralph Lau-

ren Home Collection stores. A fifth catalog was added to the Williams-Sonoma ranks in early 1989, called Chambers, and featured bed and bath products. By this time, retail sales had grown to 53 percent of Williams-Sonoma's overall sales.

In the late 1980s the company added an average of 12 stores per year, bringing the total number of Williams-Sonoma, Pottery Barn, and Hold Everything retail units to 102 U.S. stores and one unit in Japan. Not all of Williams-Sonoma's ventures were successful, however. After one year, the company and Ralph Lauren agreed to dissolve their joint-venture partnership. An attempt to establish a Gardeners Eden retail chain also failed, in part because of the inherently seasonal nature of that market. Nevertheless, the company's revenues, led by its growing retail chain, continued to make steady gains, rising from $174 million in 1988 to $287 million in 1990.

The onset of a recession and William-Sonoma's rapid expansion left the company vulnerable in the early 1990s. While revenues were relatively solid, earnings were significantly affected: The company's $11.2 million net profit in 1990 fell to $1.6 million and $1.8 million in the next two years, while revenues increased slowly, to $312 million in 1991 and $344 million in 1992, the latter helped by a partnership with Time-Life Books to create a series of Williams-Sonoma Kitchen Library cookbooks.

To prevent further earnings slippage, Williams-Sonoma's management was restructured, new merchandising strategies and catalog designs were introduced, and catalog production was brought in-house. Retail expansion was slowed, focusing instead on improving store design and increasing store square footage. By year-end 1993 the company had experienced a strong turnaround with revenues of $410 million, and earnings topping $11 million. Chief architect of the transformation was executive vice-president Gary Friedman who revamped the company's Catalog for Cooks from digest to full size, spurring an increase of 40 percent in sales. Friedman also initiated monthly themed promotions for Williams-Sonoma stores, added professional demonstration kitchens, larger cookbook libraries, tasting bars, and a line of high-quality private-label foods.

For the Pottery Barn division, which had lost more than $5 million in 1992, Friedman introduced even more dramatic changes including replacing more than 80 percent of the retail stores' merchandise, while increasing square footage in new and future stores. The new format included an average of more than 10,000 square feet, about triple the size of older Pottery Barn stores, featuring a design studio, lighting gallery, and interior finishings products. The newly designed Pottery Barn reflected Friedman's own frustration when trying to furnish his home, as he told the *Dallas Morning News,* "I wanted a store that would sell me window treatments, lamps, sofas and chairs." The Pottery Barn redesign proved immediately successful and helped spark the division's growth from combined store and catalog sales of $103 million in 1992 to $165 million in 1993.

Additionally, Williams-Sonoma started construction on a 300,000-square-foot addition to its 750,000-square-foot Memphis distribution and warehouse facility and signed with Time Warner and Spiegel to introduce a 24-hour television shopping network. By 1994 Williams-Sonoma was once again on the fast track with sales reaching $528.5 million and net earnings of $19.6 million. The following year, 1995, Williams-Sonoma was honored with a Lifetime Achievement Award from the James Beard Foundation. Revenues for the year jumped to $644.7 million as the total number of Williams-Sonoma, Hold Everything, and Pottery Barn stores topped 200.

THE INTERNET AND BRAND STRENGTHENING: 1998–2003

In 1998 Williams-Sonoma was listed on the New York Stock Exchange as annual sales reached $1.1 billion. Management began to focus on a multichannel marketing strategy that included its stores and catalogs, as well as the burgeoning power of the Internet. The company began an extensive program to capture additional sales via a company web site, followed by an online bridal registry in June 1999. The Gardeners Eden catalog was sold in 1999, as part of the firm's new strategy to focus on its core brands and Internet business. The Williams-Sonoma catalog also was overhauled to include more product information, special features, and quick tips. By the end of the decade there were more than 300 stores in operation across the United States.

Williams-Sonoma entered the new millennium determined to remain a leader in the specialty retail and home furnishings market. A new catalog, Pottery Barn Bed + Bath, with moderately priced bed and bath items, was launched in 2000, while eight Pottery Barn Kids stores were slated to open after the success of the brand's catalog the previous year.

A new magazine also debuted in 2000, *Williams-Sonoma TASTE,* adding another publication to the company's arsenal. The new lifestyle magazine focused on food, drink, travel, and entertaining. Plans were also set in motion to develop a concept called Elm Street, a new brand selling lower-end kitchen and housewares to complement the Williams-Sonoma and Pottery Barn brands.

In 2001 Lester, who had run daily operations of the company since 1979, turned over his CEO duties to Dale Hilpert, while retaining his title as chairman of the board. Fiscal (January) 2001 was a year with record revenues ($1.8 billion) yet plummeting net income during the third quarter. The decline was attributed to a number of factors including aggressive growth strategies, higher catalog and web costs, higher advertising costs, and economic woes after the September 11 terrorist attacks on the United States.

In 2002 Williams-Sonoma seemed to rally somewhat under Hilpert's direction, moving forward with the new Elm Street catalog, targeting younger, hipper homeowners bent on outdoing the Joneses at affordable prices. An Elm Street web site debuted a year later, along with bricks-and-mortar stores, the first in Brooklyn, New York. The company followed the same pattern with another Pottery Barn brand, PBteen, featuring home décor for teenagers, introducing a catalog and fully functional web site. Revenues for 2002 reached just under $2.1 billion with weak net earnings of $75.1 million.

In January 2003 Hilpert stepped down and was replaced by Edward A. Mueller, one of the board directors. Citing the need for a different type of leadership in the *New York Times* (January 10, 2003), Mueller's take-charge attitude led the company to a slight rise in revenues to $2.36 billion for 2003, but with a significant leap in net income to $124.4 million as the company workforce had grown to 32,000 employees worldwide.

SETBACKS AND STRATEGIES: 2004 AND BEYOND

In 2004 the company expanded its home décor reach by replacing the older Chambers brand with a new name and snazzy launch: Williams-Sonoma Home, featuring high-end, classic home furnishings and lifestyle accessories was introduced via an 80-page catalog and web site. Another new venue, Hold Everything, featuring organizational products for the home and office, was also launched in 2004 following the same pattern.

As the first Williams-Sonoma Home stores opened in 2005 in California, Indiana, and Ohio, management had decided to integrate Hold Everything merchandise into its existing stores. The brand had not attracted the customers nor sufficient revenue, so its handful of stores were closed in 2005 and early 2006. Catalog and web site operations were ceased in mid-2006 as Williams-Sonoma Home's new web site was launched. The Pottery Barn brands continued to grow, while the original Williams-Sonoma kitchen and cookware brand, with more than 250 stores in North America, remained a strong performer. Revenues for 2005 and 2006 were an impressive $3.1 and $3.5 billion, with net income climbing to $191.2 and $214.9 million, respectively.

Fiscal 2007 brought the first Pottery Barn Bed & Bath store, followed by plans for the company's 50th anniversary. To honor founder Chuck Williams and the first Williams-Sonoma store's famous green awning, two popular products of the day were brought back: the KitchenAid Artisan Mixer and Le Creuset Round Dutch Oven in the company's signature green. Additionally, Williams was honored as a Visionary of Design at *House Beautiful*'s seventh annual Giants of Design awards presentation in New York City.

The following year came another accolade for Williams and CEO/Chairman Lester when *Inc.* magazine honored them with Bernard A. Goldhirsh Lifetime Achievement Awards, for their roles in furthering the values and virtues of American entrepreneurship. The company, meanwhile, ventured outside its borders again with the opening of two new stores (one Pottery barn, one West Elm) in Puerto Rico and a flagship Williams-Sonoma Home store in midtown New York City. Revenues for fiscal 2008 were a robust $3.9 billion with net income of $195.8 million. Unfortunately, as the U.S. economy faltered in late 2008 and early 2009, the company figures for fiscal 2009 fell slightly to $3.4 billion in sales with a sharp downturn in net income to only $30 million, primarily due to restructuring charges, store closures, and reducing inventory by slashing prices for some of its brands.

Despite the economic woes of 2009 and a soft retail sector, Williams-Sonoma continued to be synonymous with quality home furnishings, whether classic or up-to-the-minute trendy. The company had become more about *lifestyle* than product, offering its growing clientele items for every day or special occasions, for every room in the house, for kids, teens, and adults, and with the added convenience of shopping in retail stores, by catalog, or online.

M. L. Cohen
Updated, Christina M. Stansell; Nelson Rhodes

PRINCIPAL DIVISIONS

Williams-Sonoma (Williams-Sonoma, Williams-Sonoma Home); Pottery Barn (Pottery Barn, PBteen; Pottery Barn Kids); West Elm.

PRINCIPAL COMPETITORS

Bed Bath & Beyond Inc.; Euromarket Designs Inc.; Pier 1 Imports Inc.

FURTHER READING

Barnett, Frank, and Sharon Barnett, "Williams-Sonoma's Multi-Channel Marketing Leads to Niche Dominance," *Direct Marketing,* March 1999, p. 41.

Breyer, R. Michelle, "Pottery Barn Bringing New Format to City," *Austin American-Statesman,* August 19, 1995, p. D1.

Feldman, Amy, "Irrational Pessimism," *Business Week,* April 6, 2009, p. 79.

Fisher, Lawrence M., "Store for the Gourmet Cook," *New York Times,* July 30, 1986, p. D1.

Garry, Michael, "Upscale Image Reaps $35 Mil for Williams-Sonoma," *Merchandising,* September 1984, p. 17.

Halkias, Maria, "Mending Cracks at Pottery Barn," *Dallas Morning News,* July 6, 1995, p. 1D.

Jenkins, Caroline, and Susan Posnock, "Magazine Taste Test," *Folio: The Magazine for Magazine Management,* January 2001, p. 61.

Joss, John, "The Kitchen God's Life," *Gentry,* January/February 1994, p. 61.

Jung, Carolyn, "The Man Who Put Gourmet into Everyday Kitchens," *San Jose Mercury News,* October 3, 2005.

Kehoe, Ann-Margaret, "Team Spirit: Unity of Vision Gives Power Retailer Its Edge," *HFN: The Weekly Newspaper for the Home Furnishing Network,* April 28, 1997, pp. 1+.

Lee, Louise, "Williams-Sonoma Tries a New Recipe," *Business Week,* May 6, 2002, p. 36.

Marler, Serena, "Williams-Sonoma Eyes Web for Growth," *HFN,* June 7, 1999, p. 5.

Meeks, Fleming, "Williams-Sonoma," *Forbes,* February 18, 1991, p. 60.

Nicksin, Carole, "Lester Taps Hilpert As CEO of Williams-Sonoma," *HFN,* February 19, 2001, p. 1.

Pascale, Moira, "W-S Cooks Up New Look," *Catalog Age,* October 1999, p. 7.

"Profits at Williams-Sonoma Plunge 73% in Quarter," *New York Times,* August 25, 2001, p. B4.

Rohrlich, Marianne, "Custom Made Comes in a Catalog," *New York Times,* August 12, 2004, p. F1.

———, "Out of the Catalog, into the Store," *New York Times,* September 18, 2008, p. F3.

Saeks, Diane Dorrans, "Williams-Sonoma Net Off Despite Launches in 2000," *HFN,* May 28, 2001, p. 41.

Scheraga, Dan, "Homestyle Success: Williams-Sonoma Is a Consistently High Performer," *Chain Store Age,* November 2005, p. 46.

Shaw, Jan, "Williams Learned to Delegate, but He Hasn't Given Up Working," *San Francisco Business Times,* December 19, 1988, p. 12.

———, "Williams-Sonoma Cooks Up Growth," *San Francisco Business Times,* November 28, 1988, p. 1.

Springer, Bobbi, "Cooking on Four Burners," *San Francisco Business Magazine,* July 1989, p. 44.

Vincenti, Lisa, "Williams-Sonoma to Broaden Reach of Home Furnishings," *HFN,* October 25, 1999, p. 4.

"Williams-Sonoma Chief Retires Suddenly," *New York Times,* July 12, 2006, p. C7.

"Williams-Sonoma Cuts Full-Year Forecast Again," *New York Times,* August 25, 2006, p. C7.

"Williams-Sonoma Expects to Meet Profit Estimates," *New York Times,* October 4, 2001, p. C4.

"Williams-Sonoma Says Director Is Taking Over As Chief," *New York Times,* January 10, 2003, p. C3.

"Williams-Sonoma Sets Catalog Redeployment," *HFN,* January 19, 1998, p. 4.

"Williams-Sonoma Tops Expectations," *New York Times,* August 30, 2007, p. C9.

Yawn, David, "Williams Sonoma Expanding Distribution," *Memphis Business Journal,* April 29, 1996, p. 1.

Zimbalist, Kristina, "The Guru of Home Decor: Dave DeMattei," *Time,* April 26, 2005, p. 22.

WonderWorks, Inc.

7231 Remmet Avenue
Canoga Park, California 91303
U.S.A.
Telephone: (818) 992-8811
Fax: (818) 347-4330
Web site: http://www.wonderworksweb.com

Private Company
Founded: 1977
Sales: $6 million (2001 est.)
NAICS: 512199 Other Motion Picture and Video
Industries

■ ■ ■

WonderWorks, Inc., designs, fabricates, and installs special effects for motion picture and television productions, theme parks, museums, trade shows, and live music performances. In particular, WonderWorks excels at making scale or full-size models of space vehicles, including space shuttles, space ships, and their technical interiors. These models are used for motion picture production, museum displays, theme park attractions, aerospace prototypes, and NASA promotional videos. In addition to producing custom models, WonderWorks has a standing inventory of rental products, including planes, trains, boats, buildings, cars, as well as space vehicles and props. WonderWorks also offers conceptual design services to theme parks and museums, including ride and show engineering, story and character development, interactive displays, and effects design and development.

A CHILD'S TALENT FOR SPACE DESIGN

Brick Price's interest in futuristic designs began during his childhood in the 1950s, when jet propulsion and space travel were still novel ideas. Price's fascination with complex, futuristic technology was kindled by his father's professional life as a physicist. His father worked as a professor at the California Institute of Technology and on confidential projects at the Jet Propulsion Laboratory and the Hughes think tank. In school, history bored Price, but comic books and Disney movies stimulated ideas about the world of the future. His mother worked as a cartoonist for Walt Disney Studios, so Price readily found the self-assurance to put his imagination to paper in drawings and designs. Price followed his interest in space and the future via a position in the aerospace industry, but he found that working in a cubicle restrained his creativity.

Oddly, Price's talent for visual arts came to fruition while he was in the U.S. Army during the Vietnam War. Price drew political cartoons that lampooned the officers and the military, but when the commanding officer discovered the offense, he did not punish Price. Instead, the colonel directed Price's talent toward Army uses.

Price's transition into special effects design originated from his involvement in model-making for publication. While publisher of *International Model Magazine,* for which he won a Maggie Award, Price discovered that he could make miniature scenes that created the illusion of sweeping perspective in motion pictures. Hence, Brick and his wife, Laura, founded Brick Price Movie Miniatures in 1977. During its first year, Movie Miniatures garnered $150,000 in revenues. The company almost went bankrupt, however, due to cost overruns on workers' compensation, health insurance, and other unexpected expenses. John Palmer joined the company in 1980 to handle finance and marketing.

Price's publication of a model magazine provided him with the professional breakthrough he needed in special effects design. Gene Roddenberry knew of Price from reading an article Price wrote about the *Starship Enterprise,* from the *Star Trek* television series. Price's work impressed Roddenberry, who was involved with making the first *Star Trek* movie. Roddenberry contacted Price to design and fabricate the props, familiar from the science-fiction space travel show. The work included phaser guns, tricorders, belt buckles, Spock's space suit, and a model of the *Starship Enterprise.* The success of *Star Trek: The Motion Picture,* released in 1980, brought Brick and Laura Price a Saturn Award from The Academy of Science Fiction, Fantasy & Horror Films, as well as additional work in sequels to the first movie. WonderWorks' realistic designs appeared in *Star Trek II: The Wrath of Khan,* released in 1982, and *Star Trek III: The Search for Spock,* released in 1983.

PRICE DEVELOPS A PHILOSOPHY OF SUCCESSFUL EFFECTS

Price believed that his job involved convincing people that a scene was real, and he gained a reputation in the movie industry for creating realistic visual effects. Moreover, his team completed the work on schedule, with superior props, sets, and miniature models. Rather than employ newer techniques, Price used techniques from an earlier era. Other special effects companies filmed against a green or blue screen and filled in the background later. However, the technique often required adjustments months after the filming, compared to the immediate feedback of video playback used by WonderWorks. Price filmed models, miniatures, and sets in the actual location background, and he used modern equipment for depth perception camera techniques to produce a realistic image.

Price took a collaborative approach to design. His cinematic philosophy focused on the drama of the action rather than the technology. Moreover, Price felt his creative imagination in movies contributed more to the space program than direct participation at the National Aeronautics and Space Administration (NASA). Price sensed that the company's futuristic props and sets sparked the imagination of space movie fans and motivated some to become involved in space travel. Indeed, WonderWorks produced models for NASA, such as the Space Station Freedom USA, used for promotional films. Also, the company built mockups of the Crew Exploration Vehicle (CEV) for Rocketdyne.

SPECIAL EFFECTS FOR SCIENCE-FICTION FILMS

Science-fiction motion pictures quickly became a specialty at the newly renamed company, WonderWorks, Inc. WonderWorks designed sets and props for the 1985 television miniseries *Space,* based on James Michener's historical novel about the NASA space program. The company contributed futuristic elements to the full-season series *Amazing Stories,* produced from 1985 to 1987. Movies about space travel included *The Right Stuff* (1983) and *SpaceCamp* (1986). Some projects involved a futuristic sensibility, but were not necessarily related to space travel. These included *Back to the Future* (1985) and *Back to the Future III* (1990). Work on *The Abyss,* an underwater science-fiction movie directed by James Cameron and released in 1989, involved developing visual effects for wet scenes and "dry-for-wet" scenes, as well as fabricating undersea vehicles. Price was among the team of special effects designers to be nominated for an Academy Award for Best Visual Effects for *The Abyss.*

EXPANDING DESIGN VENUES

During the late 1980s, WonderWorks diversified into design mediums compatible with model-making, such as museum interiors, theme parks, and scale model automotive prototypes. For Chevrolet, Wonderworks produced miniature models of the C4 Corvette, which allowed the company to circulate samples of prototypes among executives for feedback.

The design, fabrication, and installation of miniature models fit the needs of museums and theme parks. The company's illusionists, designers, and engineers easily applied their expertise to these venues. WonderWorks' first experience with theme park attractions involved designing and building the "Captain EO" attraction for Disneyland, based on Michael Jackson's space opera. Another project involved designing an interactive laser game in Japan. In 1990 WonderWorks designed the world's first interactive space museum,

KEY DATES

1978: Special effects for the first *Star Trek* movie launches company into space movie special effects as Brick Price Movie Miniatures.
1985: Company takes the WonderWorks name.
1989: WonderWorks enters theme park and museum interiors business.
1995: Company wins Emmy Award for special visual effects for *Star Trek: Voyager* episode.
2002: WonderWorks begins redevelopment of home studio in Canoga Park.
2009: Price begins writing screenplay for a sequel to *SpaceCamp* movie.

located in Caracas, Venezuela. Life-size replicas in the museum included space suits and an *Apollo 11* orbiter and lander. The space museum provided visitors with an interactive learning experience through authentic motion simulation rides and computer simulations.

New design contracts included sets, props, and special effects for concerts. WonderWorks handled aspects of Michael Jackson's concert and music video compilation *Moonwalker*, in 1988, and special effects for Janet Jackson's Rhythm Nation tour in 1990. In 1991 WonderWorks formed a partnership with Vertex Productions for the purpose of designing attractions for theme parks and other entertainment venues.

INVOLVEMENT IN SCIENCE-FICTION FILMS CONTINUES

WonderWorks continued to be the company-to-hire for motion picture spacecraft set and prop design. The company designed and built space vehicles for the 1995 movie *Apollo 13*. The film was released in IMAX format in 2000. For the 1995 television movie *Star Trek: Voyager*, WonderWorks designed and constructed miniatures for which Price won an Emmy Award for Outstanding Achievement in Special Visual Effects. The company provided spacecraft interiors for *Apollo 11*, a made-for-television movie released in 1996. For the 1998 movie *Armageddon*, WonderWorks provided space shuttle models and life-size shuttle and space station interiors. Special effects for this movie included a space shuttle destroyed by meteors and an exploding space station cockpit. For *Deep Impact* WonderWorks designed props and special effects including an exploding cockpit and a space shuttle set. Film credits for 2000 included

Space Cowboys and *Race to Space*. WonderWorks provided a space station set for *The Day After Tomorrow* in 2004. That year, WonderWorks provided technical sets for the television movie *Space Odyssey: Voyage to the Planets*.

THEME PARK DEVELOPMENT COMPENSATES FOR DECLINE IN MINIATURES BUSINESS

Computer-generated graphics led to a decline in the use of miniature models in Hollywood films, prompting WonderWorks to increase its involvement in diverse entertainment venues, particularly in theme park development. WonderWorks developed five major attractions for Future Extravaganza, a Shanghai, China, theme park. For instance, a "Frobeland" attraction featured a jousting event, for which WonderWorks designed and constructed the arena and trained the performers.

Once it became known that WonderWorks handled such projects, other contracts followed. Disney MGM Studios in Florida and Universal Studios Hollywood hired WonderWorks for projects at their theme parks. By 1997, 20 percent of revenues originated from theme park business. By 2001, 75 percent of $6 million in revenues came from theme park business.

In 1999, the Damo Company in Seoul, Korea, hired WonderWorks to build the World Village theme park. The $10 million contract covered the creation of miniature models, in 1/24th scale, of the world's architectural wonders. The 20-acre park carried 90 notable structures, including the Eiffel Tower, the Leaning Tower of Pisa, Aztec and Egyptian pyramids, the Great Wall of China, the Hong Kong skyline, Buckingham Palace, and the Statue of Liberty. The Manhattan skyline, planned before the World Trade Center was destroyed in 2001, retained the twin towers as a memorial. The Empire State Building held a King Kong replica and featured remotely controlled planes attacking the ape, imitating the famous movie. Other active structures included the Space Shuttle, featuring the re-creation of a countdown to launch, including sound, vibration, and smoke. More than 100 rides at the park included a roller coaster, a Ferris wheel, and Space and Future World.

Theme park development required the Wonder-Works team to resolve several challenging problems. These included making structures in appropriate scale to each other and arranging the diverse aesthetics of many countries in a visually pleasing order. Also, the models had to be capable of withstanding 90-mile-per-hour typhoons common in Korea. The World Village theme park opened in Yul-dong, in the summer of 2004.

A departure from the company's common space repertoire involved warship models for the National Civil War Naval Museum in Port Columbus, Georgia. WonderWorks fabricated a full-size model of the CSS *Hunley,* a Confederate submarine, and a replica of a gun deck. A lifelike action theme simulated the interior of a naval ship under attack, with sound effects and hydraulics that rocked the floor. Film showing outside the mock windows contributed to the realism of the battle. The upgraded museum opened in March 2001.

WonderWorks' expertise in NASA re-creations attracted significant museum business. These projects included reproductions for the Smithsonian Institution's Air and Space Museum in Washington, D.C. Wonder-Works built a replica of the *Mercury* capsule for the Ronald Reagan Presidential Library in Simi Valley, California, and spaceships and interior displays for the Challenger Center, commemorating the space shuttle *Challenger* that exploded before leaving the atmosphere in 1987.

Other projects included the development of a hotel waterpark for SouthSeas Island Resorts in Milwaukee, through its joint venture with Vertex Productions, Inc. WonderWorks entertainment show special effects included designing the transformation of a Ford F150 prototype truck into a stage for country music star Toby Keith's 2003 summer tour. The project required the WonderWorks team to replace the 40-gallon fuel tank with a four-gallon fuel cell. The change created space for hydraulic equipment used to propel moving parts, including hidden arms that folded down the sides of the truck to form the stage. Another set of arms moved lights, speakers, and guitar amplifiers into place.

STAYING BUSY DESPITE EXPANSION SETBACKS

During the early 2000s, WonderWorks became involved in studio projects that did not come to fruition. The company created designs for the Haikou-Hollywood International Motion Picture Studio and Theme Park in China, but the facilities stalled in development. In 2003 WonderWorks initiated redevelopment of its existing facilities in Canoga Park. The company planned to add a 130,000-square-foot entertainment studio and a 500,000-square-foot motion picture studio and film lot consisting of four sound stages and 200,000 square feet in office space for postproduction, special effects design, and other operations. Unfortunately, redevelopment plans by the Metropolitan Transit Authority took precedence, so WonderWorks managed with existing facilities while looking for other location expansion opportunities.

Taking his interest in space in a new direction, Price began cohosting the show *UFO Hunters,* and Wonder-Works provided replicas and miniatures that realistically re-created UFO sightings. On one episode, Wonder-Works constructed a replica of a pre-Columbian artifact that resembled a spacecraft or jet. The 15-foot model flew on the first attempt, confirming that the artifact represented accurate knowledge of space travel in ancient times.

WonderWorks continued to work on diverse projects related to space travel in 2008 and 2009. The company began conceptual design for the Yanks Air Museum in Chino, California. The contract for the facility upgrade included fabrication and installation of the designs. In 2008 Price received authorization to write the screenplay for a sequel to the *SpaceCamp* movie. For Rocketdyne, WonderWorks fabricated a prototype for the new Orion space shuttle. Another four full-size replicas would be used by the aerospace company to finalize its plans for the space shuttle.

Mary Tradii

PRINCIPAL OPERATING UNITS

Motion Picture Special Effects; Theme Park and Museum Design.

PRINCIPAL COMPETITORS

Gardly, Inc.

FURTHER READING

Emmons, Natasha, "A Brand New 'World': California Company Works with Korean Park," *Amusement Business,* April 29, 2002, p. 5.

Hernandez, Greg, "World of Wonders Miniatures, Special Effects Company Getting Bigger with Each Passing Year," *Daily News,* June 30, 2002, p. B1.

Lee, Don, "WonderWorks: Model Masters of Illusion Miniatures: Canoga Park Firm Makes Replicas for Movies, Museums and NASA," *Los Angeles Times,* October 26, 1993, p. 9.

Martinez, Carlos, "Effects House Concentrates on Theme Parks," *San Fernando Valley Business Journal,* July 8, 2002, p. 5.

———, "Plan for Studio Complex in Canoga Park Trips on MTA," *San Fernando Valley Business Journal,* March 3, 2003, p. 4.

———, "Valley Special Effects Studio Going on Stage for Concert," *San Fernando Valley Business Journal,* August 18, 2003.

Satzman, Darrell, et al., "Small World," *Los Angeles Business Journal,* September 9, 2002, p. 4.

Walker, Sally J. "Brick Price: A Man of SFX Vision," *Movi-eScope,* Spring 2007.

WuXi AppTec Company Ltd.

288 Fute Zhong Road
Waigaoqiao Free Trade Zone
Shanghai, 200131
China
Telephone: (+86 21) 5046-1111
Fax: (+86 21) 5046-1000
Web site: http://www.pharmatechs.com

Public Company
Incorporated: 2000
Employees: 3,172
Sales: $235.5 million (2008)
Stock Exchanges: New York
Ticker Symbol: WX
NAICS: 541710 Research and Development in the
    Physical Sciences and Engineering Sciences

■ ■ ■

WuXi AppTec Company Ltd. is one of the world's fastest-growing contract research organizations (CROs). The Shanghai, China-based company provides a full range of drug discovery and development services, as well as biological and clinical trial testing services, toxicology services, and other services from the discovery phase through to product commercialization. The company also provides similar services to the medical equipment industry. WuXi's client list includes nearly all of the world's largest pharmaceutical companies. Such companies have turned to the CRO sector in order to reduce the heavy cost of new pharmaceutical development. WuXi, which employs more than 2,500

scientists at several facilities in Shanghai, expects to complete new facilities in Tianjin and Suzhou in 2009. Since 2008 WuXi has also been present in the United States, following its acquisition of Minnesota-based AppTec Inc. That purchase added research and development facilities in St. Paul, Minnesota; Atlanta, Georgia; and Philadelphia, Pennsylvania. WuXi was founded in December 2000 by Dr. Ge Li, who earlier had cofounded the Princeton, New Jersey-based Pharmacopeia. WuXi is listed on the New York Stock Exchange. In 2008 the group's revenues jumped nearly 90 percent, to $235.5 million.

OUTSOURCING FOR SURVIVAL IN THE NEW CENTURY

WuXi PharmaTech, the company that later became WuXi AppTec, was the brainchild of Ge Li. The Chinese native earned a bachelor's degree in chemistry at Peking University in 1989. Like many of China's most brilliant students at the time, Li then traveled to the United States to continue his education. He enrolled in Columbia University, where he soon earned a master's degree and then a Ph.D. in organic chemistry.

While at Columbia, Li was part of the team that pioneered the use of combinatorial chemistry for new drug discovery. This method provided a faster and more efficient means of identifying potentially viable pharmaceutical compounds. The new drug discovery technology served as the basis for the launch in 1993 of a new company, Pharmacopeia, of which Li was one of the cofounders.

From the start, Li's interests reached beyond science and into the commercial sector. As Pharmacopeia's chairman told *Forbes Global* in 2008: "[Li] was always in my office, coming up with better ways to push our products. He was clearly thinking about ways to make this a more efficient process for everyone."

Like many Chinese who left to study and work abroad, Li had prepared to stay in the United States, becoming a U.S. citizen. In 1999, however, Li returned to China on a business trip to assist in setting up a joint venture between Pharmacopeia and a local Chinese company. That joint venture eventually fell through, however. Nonetheless, the trip had a significant impact on Li.

GROWTH OF THE CRO MARKET IN THE NINETIES

China had undergone a dramatic transformation in the decade since Li's departure. By the late 1990s the country had emerged as a major manufacturing center for the increasingly global world economy. China profited especially from the outsourcing trend, which saw companies across nearly every industry shutting down their own factories and turning instead to contract manufacturers based in China and other developing markets. China's vast labor force and low wages made the country a particularly attractive target for the outsourcing movement.

The pharmaceuticals industry was in the meantime in the process of developing its own outsourcing model. In the past, drug companies had for the most part carried out their drug discovery and development operations in-house. The rising costs and increasing complexity of the drug development process, however, encouraged the pharmaceutical majors to turn over parts of the process to third parties. The 1990s witnessed the growth of the new industry of CROs, which were capable of taking over large parts of the drug development cycle, starting from the drug discovery phase and continuing through the final clinical trials before a product's launch.

For the most part, the CRO industry remained based in the United States and Europe, close to the major pharmaceutical companies. On his trip to China, however, Li recognized the potential of building a drug discovery business there. Although many of the country's most brilliant scientists had left China permanently, the country's universities continued to produce large numbers of highly trained chemists, biologists, physicists, and other researchers. At the start of the 21st century, however, increasing numbers of the expatriate Chinese had begun to return to take advantage of the new economic opportunities in China. The trend earned them the nickname "sea turtles," given that animal's instinct to return to its birthplace in order to reproduce.

RETURNING SEA TURTLE IN 2001

China held a number of benefits over the West as a potential research center. The lower wages (top researchers' salaries were only one-tenth of researchers' pay in the United States, for example) and less rigorous ethical imperatives (especially in regard to animal research), as well as a large pool of low-paid human test subjects, represented some of the advantages.

Li initially approached Pharmacopeia with the idea of setting up a research facility for the company in Beijing. Pharmacopeia declined the idea, however, stating that the move did not fit in with its own product focus. However, as one WuXi executive told *Forbes Global* in 2008: "[Li] felt that the idea was so compelling that he had to do this on his own."

Li returned to China in 2000, and joined by three other partners, founded WuXi PharmaTech in the city of Wuxi (pronounced Woo-she) in Jiangsu Province, about an hour by train from Shanghai. The major economic capital of Shanghai became the site of WuXi PharmaTech's initial operations, as the company set up a laboratory in a leased facility in the city's Waigaoqiao Free Trade Zone (FTZ). This location was chosen because it allowed the company to import both equipment and spare parts tax-free, which represented significant savings for the young company. The Waigaoqiao FTZ also provided the company with quick access to imported chemicals.

Li did not need to look far for WuXi PharmaTech's first customer as the company signed a contract to provide drug discovery services for Pharmacopeia. The two companies later broadened their relationship, creating a strategic partnership to provide contract chemistry and research services to the global pharmaceutical market in April 2003. Under the agreement, Pharmacopeia provided technology and scientific oversight, while WuXi PharmaTech provided the manpower.

KEY DATES

2000: WuXi PharmaTech is established as a contract research organization in Wuxi, China.

2001: WuXi PharmaTech begins operations at a leased facility in the Waigaoqiao Free Trade Zone (FTZ) in Shanghai.

2004: The company builds its own 630,000-square-foot headquarters and research facility in the Waigaoqiao FTZ, and launches contract manufacturing at a second plant in Jinshan, Shanghai.

2007: WuXi goes public with a listing on the New York Stock Exchange.

2008: WuXi acquires U.S.-based AppTec Inc. and becomes WuXi AppTec.

In the meantime, WuXi PharmaTech had begun to build up an impressive list of clients, including such giants as Merck, Eli Lilly, and Sumitomo. The dawn of the 21st century marked a surge in the CRO industry, in part as drug companies sought relief from the skyrocketing costs of the drug development cycle. Indeed, into the later years of the first decade of the 2000s, developing a successful new drug through to its commercialization often cost companies more than $1 billion, and even up to $2 billion.

With its far lower operating costs, WuXi PharmaTech offered significant savings to the pharmaceuticals industry. As a result, the company picked up a growing number of contracts. By the middle of the decade, WuXi PharmaTech boasted a client base of some 70 companies, including nine of the world's top ten drug companies.

PUBLIC OFFERING IN 2007

WuXi PharmaTech grew strongly in the first half of the decade. By the end of 2002, company sales had topped $3 million. Just one year later, revenues had tripled, then doubled again through 2004. The company's workforce kept pace, growing from 45 employees in 2002 to more than 200 by the beginning of 2004.

This success encouraged the company to set up shop permanently in the Waigaoqiao FTZ. The company launched construction of a new 630,000-square-foot headquarters and laboratory facility in 2004. Around this same time, WuXi, which had initially focused on drug discovery, began to broaden its range of

services. In 2003 the group had entered the pharmaceutical manufacturing sector as well. For this, the company launched construction of a second facility, based in Jinshan, on the other side of Shanghai. The Jinshan facility allowed WuXi to begin producing advanced intermediates and active pharmaceutical ingredients, in both large and small quantities.

WuXi's pharmaceutical services business more than tripled between 2004 and 2006, while the addition of manufacturing operations brought its total revenues to nearly $70 million that year. This growth led the company to a position on the Deloitte Technology Fast 500 Asia Pacific list in 2007, as well as a spot among the Chinese Ministry of Science and Technology's Top 103 National Innovative Companies rankings in 2006. WuXi's payroll kept pace with its turnover, growing to more than 530 by the end of 2004, then nearing 1,000 in 2005. By the middle of 2007, WuXi employed nearly 2,000.

The company marked a number of new milestones in 2007. At the beginning of the year, WuXi inaugurated a new 120,000-square-foot drug discovery laboratory in Tianjin. The company also signed a major drug manufacturing contract with Vertex Pharmaceuticals. The deal raised the company's manufacturing operations to 30 percent of its total revenues. By then, too, WuXi had expanded its range of services to service biology, including assay development and high-throughput screening.

WuXi's rapid growth also led to the company's decision to go public with a listing on the New York Stock Exchange in August 2007. The initial public offering (IPO) was highly successful, raising approximately $150 million for the company. Within a month of the company's IPO, WuXi's share price had nearly doubled. By the end of the year, the company's market capitalization had soared past $1.4 billion.

U.S. RETURN IN 2008

The successful IPO helped support a new services extension by the company, as it launched toxicology services, including preclinical drug-safety evaluation testing and other services, in September 2007. WuXi then launched construction of a dedicated toxicology facility in Suzhou. The 215,000-square-foot facility was expected to be fully operational by 2009.

In addition, WuXi also saw an opportunity to expand its operations elsewhere. Although the company envisaged working with Chinese companies in the future, especially as a number of Chinese pharmaceuticals companies initiated their first drug development projects, the United States remained the company's primary source of clients. This led WuXi to decide to establish its own U.S. base.

For this, the company looked to acquire an existing company. Its focus fell on AppTec Inc., a CRO based in St. Paul, Minnesota. That company, founded in 2001, had expanded strongly through the decade, establishing additional drug discovery facilities in Atlanta as well as its own biological manufacturing unit in Philadelphia. WuXi paid $163 million for AppTec. Following the acquisition, the company adopted a new name, WuXi AppTec.

The AppTec acquisition helped WuXi maintain its strong revenue growth, despite the increasingly gloomy economic climate. By the end of 2008, WuXi's revenues had jumped ahead by another 74 percent, to nearly $262 million. Much of that growth, however, was attributed to AppTec, which contributed over $60 million during the year. Part of that contribution came from AppTec's biological manufacturing unit. In December 2008, however, the company announced its decision to phase out that division from its U.S. operations.

Despite the company's move into the United States, China remained the company's core area of operations. Although observers had begun to question just how long China would be able to sustain a growth model based on low wages, the country nonetheless had begun to play a central role in the global effort to discover and develop new drugs. As the largest CRO in China, and one of the fastest-growing CROs in the world, WuXi AppTec appeared to have discovered its own medicine for growth in the new century.

M. L. Cohen

PRINCIPAL SUBSIDIARIES

Shanghai PharmaTech Chemical Technology Co. Ltd.; Shanghai SynTheAll Pharmaceutical Co. Ltd.; Suzhou PharmaTech Co. Ltd.; Tianjin PharmaTech Co. Ltd.; WuXi AppTec Co., Ltd. (China); WuXi AppTec, Inc. (USA).

PRINCIPAL OPERATING UNITS

Laboratory Services; Manufacturing.

PRINCIPAL COMPETITORS

PAREXEL International Corp.; Quintiles Transnational Corporation; Covance Inc.; Pharmaceutical Product Development, Inc.

FURTHER READING

"Bringing It Back to the States," *Contract Pharma,* January 22, 2008.

Kitchens, Susan, "Farmed Out Pharma," *Forbes Global,* February 11, 2008, p. 35.

Lee, Thomas, "AppTec CEO Baskin Will Depart Soon, WuXi Says," *Minneapolis Star Tribune,* January 5, 2008, p. 1D.

Orelli, Brian, "No Slowdown for China's WuXi," *China Daily,* March 14, 2008.

Pettypiece, Shannon, "WuXi Has More Chemists Than Pfizer As Shanghai Research Surges," *International Herald Tribune,* December 26, 2007.

———, "WuXi Reaps Outsourcing Rewards," *International Herald Tribune,* December 27, 2007.

"Pharmacopeia Forms Strategic Alliance with Shanghai-Based Company," *Biotech Week,* April 9, 2003, p. 112.

"Putting China on Clinical Trial," *Investor's Business Daily,* October 22, 2007, p. B02.

Qian Yanfeng, "Right Mix," *China Daily,* March 24, 2008.

Reeves, Amy, "WuXi PharmaTech Cuts Expenses for New Drugs Coming to Market," *Investor's Business Daily,* August 7, 2007, p. A06.

Scheidt, Zachary, "Drug Services Enhancing Performance," *Seeking Alpha,* December 27, 2007.

"Talent Arbitrage," *Economist,* September 22, 2007, p. 82US.

"WuXi Pharma's US Operations to Shift Focus away from Biological Manufacturing," *China Business News,* December 3, 2008.

"WuXi PharmaTech Disappointed by AppTec Acquisition," *China Bio Today,* March 27, 2009.

"WuXi PharmaTech's New Drug Safety Center Underway," *China Business News,* October 9, 2007.

"WuXi Revenues up 87% in 2008," *Clinical Trials Today,* March 26, 2009.

Zamiska, Nicholas, "WuXi's AppTec Deal Is Move for Bigger Market Share," *Wall Street Journal,* January 5, 2008.

Yingli Green Energy Holding Company Limited

———————————— ■ ————————————

3055 Fuxing Middle Road
Baoding, Hebei 071051
China
Telephone: (86 312) 8929700
Fax: (86 312) 3151881
Web site: http://www.yinglisolar.com

Public Company
Incorporated: 1998 as Baoding Tianwei Yingli New
Energy Resources Co., Ltd.
Employees: 3,000
Sales: $1.11 billion (2008)
Stock Exchanges: New York
Ticker Symbol: YGE
NAICS: 334413 Semiconductor and Related Device
Manufacturing

■ ■ ■

Yingli Green Energy Holding Company Limited, or Yingli, through its principal subsidiary, Baoding Tianwei Yingli New Energy Resources Co., Ltd., or Tianwei Yingli, is one of the world's leading manufacturers of solar photovoltaic (PV) modules. Yingli produces polysilicon ingots and wafers, solar cells, and finished solar modules from its main facility in Baoding, in the northern province of Hebei, in the People's Republic of China (PRC). With help from affiliates, the company designs, manufactures, and markets PV modules and systems under the brand name Yingli Solar to PV system integrators and distributors located in China and in various markets around the world, including Europe and the United States.

LAYING THE FOUNDATION

Liansheng Miao, as the founder and sole owner of Baoding Yingli Group Co., Ltd., established Tianwei Yingli as a PRC limited liability company in August 1998 to manufacture solar PV products and components. In 1999, Yingli Group began a cooperative and long-term relationship with Hebei-based Tianwei Baobian Electric Co., a firm controlled by Baoding Tianwei Group Co., Ltd., a wholly state-owned limited liability company established in the PRC in January 1991. The principal business of Tianwei Baobian, since its founding in 1999, was the manufacture of large electricity transformers.

Tianwei Yingli acquired its first turnkey production line for PV modules in 2001. In April 2002, Tianwei Baobian officially became a shareholder of Tianwei Yingli. That same year, Tianwei Yingli completed construction of its first manufacturing facilities for PV modules. Production capacity for 2002 amounted to three megawatts (MW).

Also in 2002, the company established its first subsidiary, Chengdu Yingli New Energy Resources Co., Ltd., or Chengdu Yingli, in the city of Chengdu, located in Sichuan Province. Tianwei Yingli initially held a 55 percent equity interest in the operation, which was set up to sell and install PV systems in the central Chinese province.

COMPANY PERSPECTIVES

As one of the world's leading vertically integrated PV product manufacturers, Yingli Green Energy controls the entire production process and optimizes each individual component that goes into making PV modules. From the latest generation technology used in our wafer and cell manufacturing process, to the superior quality components used in module assembly, Yingli Green Energy is committed to delivering top quality modules. We produce a wide variety of module types that are used in on-grid systems, off-grid systems and other configurations.

ESTABLISHING A PRIMARY MARKET

Until October 2003, when Tianwei Yingli began manufacturing its own polysilicon ingots and wafers at an annual production capacity of 6 MW, the company purchased all of its solar module components from third parties. In March 2004, Tianwei Yingli began producing another solar module component, PV cells, with an initial manufacturing capacity of three MW.

In May 2004, Tianwei Yingli increased its equity interest in Chengdu Yingli to 64 percent, and before the end of the year, the company acquired a 10 percent equity interest in Tibet Tianwei Yingli New Resources Co., Ltd., or Tibetan Yingli, a firm that sold and installed PV systems in Tibet.

While Tianwei Yingli sold most of its products in China in 2003, sales to foreign markets increased significantly in 2004. That year, Germany became the company's largest market and accounted for about two-thirds of total annual revenues.

In September 2005, Tianwei Yingli increased its stake in Tibetan Yingli to 50 percent. Germany continued to be Yingli's number one market in 2005, accounting for 65 percent of the company's total revenues for the year.

REFINING CORPORATE STRUCTURE

Tianwei Yingli began a complicated and significant corporate restructuring in 2006. In June, Liansheng Miao established Yingli Power Holding Company, Ltd., in the British Virgin Islands. On August 7, Yingli Power then established Yingli Green Energy Holding Company

Limited, or Yingli Green Energy, in the Cayman Islands. In connection with that transaction, Yingli Power became Yingli Green Energy's controlling shareholder, with 59.58 percent of its share capital.

On August 25, 2006, Tianwei Yingli, entered into a joint-venture contract with Tianwei Baobian. The agreement entitled Tianwei Baobian to appoint three of seven seats on the company's board of directors. On September 5, 2006, Yingli Group transferred its 51 percent majority equity interest in Tianwei Yingli to Yingli Green Energy. As a result of the transaction, Tianwei Yingli became a subsidiary of its holding company, Yingli Green Energy.

On December 18, 2006, Yingli Green Energy increased its equity interest in Tianwei Yingli from 51 percent to 62.13 percent, which left its joint-venture partner, the state-controlled Tianwei Baobian, holding a 37.97 percent stake. As founder, the 49-year-old Miao assumed the roles of chairman and chief executive of the company.

Germany still accounted for the majority of the company's total revenues for 2006, but with 14.3 percent of total sales, Spain overtook China as the firm's second largest market. At the end of 2006, Yingli signed a 42 MW contract with Spain-based Acciona Energy to help build the world's largest solar plant in Moah, Portugal. As of December 31, 2006, Tianwei Yingli had 1,552 employees, and according to company reports, netted $47 million on total revenues of $210 million for the year.

GOING PUBLIC IN THE BIG APPLE

In May 2007, Yingli Green Energy announced that it would list American Depositary Shares (ADS) in an initial public offering (IPO) on the New York Stock Exchange (NYSE). The company hoped to raise $350 million to fund a manufacturing capacity expansion of its principal operating subsidiary, Tianwei Yingli. At the time, the firm had an annual production capacity of 95 MW of polysilicon ingots and wafers, 90 MW of PV cells, and 100 MW of PV modules.

On June 8, 2007, trading under the trading symbol "YGE," Yingli Power and Yingli Green Energy offered 29 million shares on the NYSE. The IPO raised $319 million and gave the company an initial market capitalization of $1.39 billion. On June 25, Yingli Green Energy, or Yingli, increased its equity interest in Tianwei Yingli to 70.11 percent.

In 2007, Spain emerged for a period as the company's largest market. In the first six months of

KEY DATES

1998: Liansheng Miao establishes Tianwei Yingli in China's northern Hebei Province.

2001: Tianwei Yingli begins solar photovoltaic (PV) module production.

2002: First subsidiary, Chengdu Yingli, begins operations in central Sichuan Province.

2003: Company starts manufacturing its own polysilicon ingots and wafers.

2004: PV cell production begins; Tianwei Yingli acquires a stake in Tibetan Yingli.

2006: Yingli Green Energy is incorporated as a holding company for Tianwei Yingli and affiliates.

2007: Firm makes its market debut on the New York Stock Exchange.

2008: Yingli reaches milestone annual production capacity of 400 megawatts.

2009: Polysilicon producer, Cyber Power, is acquired.

2007, Yingli entered into sales contracts with Spain-based Unitec Europa, S.A., and Laxtron Energías Renovables, as well as Sinolink Development Limited, of China, for delivery of over 40 MW of PV modules. July brought the firm a contract with Control y Montages Industriales CYMI S.A., of Spain, to supply 9.55 MW of PV modules in 2007.

DOUBLING PRODUCTION CAPACITY

In July 2007, Yingli secured a long-term supply contract for the period from 2010 through 2018 for its most important raw material, polysilicon, with Wacker Chemie AG of Germany, a supplier for the company since 2003. The deal was in addition to two existing long-term supply agreements with Wacker scheduled from 2009 through 2013 and 2017. Also in July, Yingli announced the completion of the first phase of its expansion, doubling its total annual production capacity with the addition of 100 MW production lines of polysilicon ingots and wafers, PV cells, and PV modules.

On September 28, 2007, Yingli Green Energy added $236.6 million to its joint venture with Tianwei Baobian, which increased the firm's stake in Tianwei Yingli to 74 percent. With the transaction, Yingli Green Energy's total investment in Tianwei Yingli rose to about $456.1 million. By October 11, 2007, company

stock had soared more than 150 percent since its June debut. On October 29, after amending an existing supply deal with Sichuan Xinguang Silicon Science and Technology Co. Ltd. that adjusted polysilicon prices, company stock jumped 10 percent to close near its 52-week high of $38.

According to the company, in October 2007, Yingli Energy (China) Company Ltd., or Yingli China, was incorporated, "to strengthen the Company's ability to effectively execute its strategies." The following month, Yingli Energy (Beijing) Co., Ltd., was established "to advance the Company's strategic execution and development by taking advantage of Beijing's location and diversified professional talent." Also, Yingli Green Energy Europe GmbH was set up in Munich, Germany, to facilitate further expansion into the European PV market.

Yingli continued to build its market presence in Spain with a November 2007 agreement to sell 16.5 MW of PV modules to Aplicaciones Tecnicas de la Energia, S.L. In late November, the company again moved forward on expansion plans when it signed a $56 million contract to buy silicon ingot furnaces from New Hampshire-based GT Solar Incorporated.

EXPANDING GLOBAL SALES

January 2008 started out with a sales agreement for seven MW of PV modules with EDF Energies Nouvelles, of France, and an 11.56 MW deal from Iberdrola Ingeniería Y Construcción S.A.U., of Spain. In February, Yingli reported its 2007 financial and operating highlights, which included a $53.3 million profit on total revenues of $556 million. PV module shipments for the year more than tripled from 2006 to 142.5 MW. However, falling oil prices, an expectation of high polysilicon costs, and rising concerns about the U.S. economy began to take its toll on company stock value, which fell to around $14 a share on March 19, 2008.

Yingli broke into the Korean market in April 2008 with sales contracts with two South Korean energy companies, Korea Electric Power Industrial Development Corp., and Kaycom Corp. May brought deals for the company to sell 17.35 MW of PV modules to Eiko Trading Corporation JP, of Japan, and a minimum of 35 MW of PV modules to IBC Solar AG, of Germany.

Revenue for the first quarter of 2008, as reported by the firm in May, jumped 272 percent from the same quarter of 2007, to $227.5 million. At the end of May, Yingli inked a critical polysilicon supply agreement with Sailing New Energy Resources Co., Ltd., of China. It also finalized a sales contract with Germany's S.A.G. Solarstrom AG to supply 5.75 MW of PV modules. In

June, the company scored four new sales contracts totaling 64 MW of PV modules with two leading German PV firms at the Intersolar 2008 Technology Trade Fair held in Munich, Germany.

July 2008 brought the announcement that Yingli, together with the Brazilian company MPX Energia S.A., had plans to construct a 50-MW solar power plant in Taua, Brazil. Also in July, the company expanded its presence in South Korea with five new sales contracts with an aggregate total of seven MW.

RAMPING UP IN A GLOBAL DOWNTURN

In the summer of 2008, as Yingli was just firing up small-scale production of its planned 200 MW expansion project, the governments of both Spain and Germany announced pullbacks on their solar subsidy programs. That did not stop Germany-based Payom Solar from ordering 8.5 MW of PV modules from Yingli in early August 2008.

Year over year, second-quarter 2008 profit more than tripled to $30.2 million, and revenue more than doubled to $298.7 million, as reported by the company on August 6, 2008. The company also upped its full-year guidance on net revenue to over $1 billion. Also in August, the firm announced an agreement with the local government of a county in Beijing to build a ten MW solar power plant.

Yingli's subsidiary, Tianwei Yingli, in September 2008 signed a $50 million credit facility with two European banks in order to fund further expansion plans. In September, the company also signed a sales contract to supply 16 MW of PV modules to Fire Energy, S.L., of Spain. Solar stocks that were tumbling in the wake of a global financial crisis, including Yingli's, jumped briefly in late September after the U.S. Senate voted to extend solar tax credits worth $18 billion for renewable energy.

October 2008 brought a sales contract for 28 MW of PV modules with Germany-based GeckoLogic GmbH, and two smaller deals with Sinosol AG and En-Neo Neue Energien GmbH. The month also marked a milestone for Yingli when it completed the installation of an additional 200 MW of annual manufacturing capacity for ingots, wafers, cells, and modules, bringing its total to 400 MW.

EXPLORING THE DEPTHS

In early November 2008, Yingli secured a new credit line of $73 million with the central government-owned Export-Import Bank of China. By mid-November, worldwide tightening of credit access, the continued collapse of the crude oil market, and a general worldwide economic meltdown had taken its toll on the solar industry in general, and Yingli was no exception. Company stock on November 20, after starting the year trading above $38 a share, closed the day at $2.56.

In late November, Yingli attracted $75 million in venture-capital funding from France's Promotion et Participation pour la Coopération économique, Dutch Development Bank, and German Investment and Development Company. On November 26, Yingli signed a letter of intent to purchase China-based polysilicon maker Fine Silicon Co., Ltd., a wholly owned subsidiary of Cyber Power Group Limited, a development stage enterprise, for between $70 million and $80 million.

In December, Yingli signed another multiyear polysilicon supply agreement with Wacker that was set to start in 2010. At the same time, the company inked a contract to sell 91 MW of PV modules to IBC Solar AG, of Germany. The company closed out 2008 by securing an eight-year $70 million expansion loan agreement with China Development Bank, a government policy bank.

FORECASTING A GREENER FUTURE

The company began 2009 by closing a deal with Goldbeck Solar GmbH, of Germany, for at least 15 MW of PV modules. On January 7, Yingli announced that it had completed the acquisition of Cyber Power, and planned to begin production of solar-grade polysilicon in the second half of 2009. Cyber Power was purchased for $77.6 million from Baoding Yingli Group Company Limited, a company wholly owned by Yingli Chairman and CEO Liansheng Miao.

On February 10, 2009, Yingli announced its year-end financial results. Revenues for 2008 totaled $1.11 billion, an 86 percent increase from 2007. At a time when many of its rivals were posting losses, the company reported a net income of $99.9 million, or $0.77 a share. Total PV module shipments for the year almost doubled to 281.5 MW.

The *China Daily* reported in late February 2009 that Yingli teamed up with real estate developer Longjitaihe Industry Group to set up a new business in China, Lightway Green Energy Corporation, to manufacture PV solar systems. The Baoding realtor committed $4.2 billion to the project, which has a planned production capacity of 600 MW by 2010. In early March 2009, three Yingli subsidiaries, Tianwei Yingli, Yingli Energy (China) Co., and Fine Silicon Co., Ltd., received short-term loans from domestic banks and an affiliate of the company totaling RMB 420 million.

As the second quarter of 2009 began, Yingli's growth projections of 90 to 100 percent for the year seemed optimistic given the very difficult global economic and market conditions that prevailed. Signed contracts for delivery of about 317 MW of PV modules in 2009 signaled a good start but hitting that target depended on the company's ability to install and ramp up an additional 200 MW of ingot, wafer, cell, and module production capacity scheduled for the third quarter. On the positive side, the January acquisition of the last piece of the firm's vertical integration model, a polysilicon manufacturing facility, was expected to help stabilize sourcing of the company's most important raw material and boost margins. In addition, Yingli's cash on hand, expected cash flow from operations, and available lines of credit were expected to give the company at least a fighting chance of meeting its ambitious goals.

Ted Sylvester

PRINCIPAL SUBSIDIARIES

Baoding Tianwei Yingli New Energy Resources Co., Ltd. (74%); Chengdu Yingli New Energy Resources Co., Ltd. (50%); Tibet Tianwei Yingli New Resources Co., Ltd. (50%); Yingli Energy (China) Co., Ltd.; Yingli Energy (Beijing) Co., Ltd. (90%).

PRINCIPAL COMPETITORS

BP Solar; Suntech Power Holdings Co., Ltd.; Renewable Energy Corporation ASA; Sharp Corporation; SunPower Corporation; Ersol Solar Energy AG; LDK Solar Co., Ltd.; Trina Solar Limited; SolarWorld AG; Solarfun Power Holdings Co., Ltd.; First Solar, Inc.; Canadian Solar Inc.

FURTHER READING

Alpert, Bill, "China's Solar Boom Loses Its Luster," *Barron's,* October 8, 2007, p. 22.

Ball, Yvonne, "IPO Outlook: Deals & Deal Makers: Ten IPOs from China Set Record," *Wall Street Journal,* June 11, 2007, p. C5.

————, "Limelight IPO Grabs the Spotlight with 48% Gain, Latest Tech Rally," *Wall Street Journal,* June 9, 2007, p. B3.

Bogoslaw, David, "Solar Stocks Get Their Day in the Sun," *BusinessWeek Online,* January 3, 2008.

Burnham, Michael, "Solar Power; Flush with Silicon, China Company Enters Korean Market," *Greenwire,* April 3, 2008.

Chen Jialu, "More Solar Companies to List on New York Exchange," *China Daily,* May 30, 2007.

"China's Offshore-Listed Solar Firms See 77% Market Cap Drop," *China Perspective,* November 23, 2008.

"Event Brief of Q3 2008 Yingli Green Energy Holding Co. Ltd. Earnings Conference Call," *Voxant FD Wire,* November 26, 2008.

Gage, Jack, "High Energy Stocks; Demand for Energy Has Made It the Hottest Industry on Wall Street," *Forbes,* June 16, 2008.

Gold, Donald H., "Once-Powerful Solar Stocks Take a Beating," *Investor's Business Daily,* July 3, 2008.

Groom, Nichola, "Solar Stocks Soar on Outlook for U.S. Subsidies," *Reuters News,* April 4, 2008.

————, "Yingli Profit Soars, Shares Drop on '09 Outlook," *Reuters News,* 6 August 6, 2008.

"Polysilicon Price May Drop in 2010," *China Chemical Reporter,* November 16, 2008.

Savitz, Eric J., "Prospects of Rain in Spain Make for Gloomy Solar Week," *Barron's,* July 28, 2008, p. 27.

"Solar Module Manufacturers—Daniel Ries—Collins Stewart LLC: Analyst Interview," *Wall Street Transcript,* March 3, 2008.

Spencer, Jane, "China Solar Stocks Shine in U.S., but Some Could Be Overheated," *Wall Street Journal Asia,* May 23, 2007, p. 21.

Womack, Brian, "Yingli Shines Among Solar Energy Stars," *Investor's Business Daily,* October 11, 2007.

"Yingli Green Energy Will Supply PV Modules to Largest University Campus Solar Energy Facility in the United States," *Science Letter,* October 7, 2008.

Zhang Qi, "Yingli Fostering Lightway's Green Dreams," *China Daily,* February 28, 2009.

Cumulative Index to Companies

Listings in this index are arranged in alphabetical order under the company name. Company names beginning with a letter or proper name such as Eli Lilly & Co. will be found under the first letter of the company name. Definite articles (The, Le, La) are ignored for alphabetical purposes as are forms of incorporation that precede the company name (AB, NV). Company names printed in **bold** *type have full, historical essays on the page numbers appearing in bold. Updates to entries that appeared in earlier volumes are signified by the notation* **(upd.)**. *This index is cumulative with volume numbers printed in bold type.*

A

A&E Television Networks, 32 3–7

A&P *see* The Great Atlantic & Pacific Tea Company, Inc.

A & W Brands, Inc., 25 3–5 *see also* Cadbury Schweppes PLC.

A-dec, Inc., 53 3–5

A-Mark Financial Corporation, 71 3–6

A.B. Chance Industries Co., Inc. *see* Hubbell Inc.

A.B.Dick Company, 28 6–8

A.B. Watley Group Inc., 45 3–5

A.C. Moore Arts & Crafts, Inc., 30 3–5

A.C. Nielsen Company, 13 3–5 *see also* ACNielsen Corp.

A. Duda & Sons, Inc., 88 1–4

A. F. Blakemore & Son Ltd., 90 1–4

A.G. Edwards, Inc., 8 3–5; **32** 17–21 **(upd.)**

A.H. Belo Corporation, 10 3–5; **30** 13–17 **(upd.)** *see also* Belo Corp.

A.L. Pharma Inc., 12 3–5 *see also* Alpharma Inc.

A.M. Castle & Co., 25 6–8

A. Moksel AG, 59 3–6

A. Nelson & Co. Ltd., 75 3–6

A. O. Smith Corporation, 11 3–6; **40** 3–8 **(upd.)**; **93** 1–9 **(upd.)**

A.P. Møller - Maersk A/S, 57 3–6

A.S. Watson & Company Ltd., 84 1–4

A.S. Yakovlev Design Bureau, 15 3–6

A. Schulman, Inc., 8 6–8; **49** 3–7 **(upd.)**

A.T. Cross Company, 17 3–5; **49** 8–12 **(upd.)**

A.W. Faber-Castell Unternehmensverwaltung GmbH & Co., 51 3–6

A/S Air Baltic Corporation, 71 35–37

AAF-McQuay Incorporated, 26 3–5

Aalborg Industries A/S, 90 5–8

AAON, Inc., 22 3–6

AAR Corp., 28 3–5

Aardman Animations Ltd., 61 3–5

Aarhus United A/S, 68 3–5

Aaron Brothers Holdings, Inc. *see* Michaels Stores, Inc.

Aaron Rents, Inc., 14 3–5; **35** 3–6 **(upd.)**

AARP, 27 3–5

Aavid Thermal Technologies, Inc., 29 3–6

AB Volvo, I 209–11; **7** 565–68 **(upd.)**; **26** 9–12 **(upd.)**; **67** 378–83 **(upd.)**

Abar Corporation *see* Ipsen International Inc.

ABARTA, Inc., 100 1–4

Abatix Corp., 57 7–9

Abaxis, Inc., 83 1–4

ABB Ltd., II 1–4; **22** 7–12 **(upd.)**; **65** 3–10 **(upd.)**

Abbey National plc, 10 6–8; **39** 3–6 **(upd.)**

Abbott Laboratories, I 619–21; **11** 7–9 **(upd.)**; **40** 9–13 **(upd.)**; **93** 10–18 **(upd.)**

ABC Appliance, Inc., 10 9–11

ABC Carpet & Home Co. Inc., 26 6–8

ABC Family Worldwide, Inc., 52 3–6

ABC, Inc. *see* Capital Cities/ABC Inc.

ABC Learning Centres Ltd., 93 19–22

ABC Rail Products Corporation, 18 3–5

ABC Stores *see* MNS, Ltd.

ABC Supply Co., Inc., 22 13–16

Abengoa S.A., 73 3–5

Abercrombie & Fitch Company, 15 7–9; **35** 7–10 **(upd.)**; **75** 7–11 **(upd.)**

Abertis Infraestructuras, S.A., 65 11–13

ABF *see* Associated British Foods plc.

Abigail Adams National Bancorp, Inc., 23 3–5

Abiomed, Inc., 47 3–6

AbitibiBowater Inc., IV 245–47; **25** 9–13 **(upd.)**; **99** 1–11 **(upd.)**

ABM Industries Incorporated, 25 14–16 **(upd.)**

ABN *see* Algemene Bank Nederland N.V.

ABN AMRO Holding, N.V., 50 3–7

Abrams Industries Inc., 23 6–8 *see also* Servidyne Inc.

Abraxas Petroleum Corporation, 89 1–5

Abril S.A., 95 1–4

Abt Associates Inc., 95 5–9

Abu Dhabi National Oil Company, IV 363–64; **45** 6–9 **(upd.)**

Academic Press *see* Reed Elsevier plc.

Academy of Television Arts & Sciences, Inc., 55 3–5

Aveda Corporation, 24 55–57

Avedis Zildjian Co., 38 66–68

Avendt Group, Inc. *see* Marmon Group, Inc.

Aventine Renewable Energy Holdings, Inc., 89 83–86

Avery Dennison Corporation, IV 251–54; 17 27–31 (upd.); 49 34–40 (upd.)

Aviacionny Nauchno-Tehnicheskii Komplex im. A.N. Tupoleva, 24 58–60

Aviacsa *see* Consorcio Aviacsa, S.A. de C.V.

Aviall, Inc., 73 42–45

Avianca Aerovías Nacionales de Colombia SA, 36 52–55

Aviation Sales Company, 41 37–39

Avid Technology Inc., 38 69–73

Avionics Specialties Inc. *see* Aerosonic Corp.

Avions Marcel Dassault-Breguet Aviation, I 44–46 *see also* Groupe Dassault Aviation SA.

Avis Group Holdings, Inc., 6 356–58; 22 54–57 (upd.); 75 44–49 (upd.)

Avista Corporation, 69 48–50 (upd.)

Aviva PLC, 50 65–68 (upd.)

Avnet Inc., 9 55–57

Avocent Corporation, 65 56–58

Avon Products, Inc., III 15–16; 19 26–29 (upd.); 46 43–46 (upd.)

Avondale Industries, Inc., 7 39–41; 41 40–43 (upd.)

AVTOVAZ Joint Stock Company, 65 59–62

AVX Corporation, 67 41–43

AWA *see* America West Holdings Corp.

AWB Ltd., 56 25–27

Awrey Bakeries, Inc., 56 28–30

AXA Colonia Konzern AG, III 210–12; 49 41–45 (upd.)

Axcan Pharma Inc., 85 25–28

Axcelis Technologies, Inc., 95 36–39

Axel Johnson Group, I 553–55

Axel Springer Verlag AG, IV 589–91; 20 50–53 (upd.)

Axsys Technologies, Inc., 93 65–68

Aydin Corp., 19 30–32

Aynsley China Ltd. *see* Belleek Pottery Ltd.

Azcon Corporation, 23 34–36

Azelis Group, 100 44–47

Azerbaijan Airlines, 77 46–49

Azienda Generale Italiana Petroli *see* ENI S.p.A.

Aztar Corporation, 13 66–68; 71 41–45 (upd.)

AZZ Incorporated, 93 69–72

B

B&D *see* Barker & Dobson.

B&G Foods, Inc., 40 51–54

B&J Music Ltd. *see* Kaman Music Corp.

B&Q plc *see* Kingfisher plc.

B.A.T. Industries PLC, 22 70–73 (upd.) *see also* Brown and Williamson Tobacco Corporation

B. Dalton Bookseller Inc., 25 29–31 *see also* Barnes & Noble, Inc.

B.F. Goodrich Co. *see* The BFGoodrich Co.

B.J. Alan Co., Inc., 67 44–46

The B. Manischewitz Company, LLC, 31 43–46

B.R. Guest Inc., 87 43–46

B.W. Rogers Company, 94 49–52

B/E Aerospace, Inc., 30 72–74

BA *see* British Airways plc.

BAA plc, 10 121–23; 33 57–61 (upd.)

Baan Company, 25 32–34

Babbage's, Inc., 10 124–25 *see also* GameStop Corp.

The Babcock & Wilcox Company, 82 26–30

Babcock International Group PLC, 69 51–54

Babolat VS, S.A., 97 63–66

Baby Lock USA *see* Tacony Corp.

Baby Superstore, Inc., 15 32–34 *see also* Toys 'R Us, Inc.

Bacardi & Company Ltd., 18 39–42; 82 31–36 (upd.)

Baccarat, 24 61–63

Bachman's Inc., 22 58–60

Bachoco *see* Industrias Bachoco, S.A. de C.V.

Back Bay Restaurant Group, Inc., 20 54–56; 102 34–38 (upd.)

Back Yard Burgers, Inc., 45 33–36

Backus y Johnston *see* Unión de Cervecerías Peruanas Backus y Johnston S.A.A.

Bad Boy Worldwide Entertainment Group, 58 14–17

Badger Meter, Inc., 22 61–65

Badger Paper Mills, Inc., 15 35–37

Badger State Ethanol, LLC, 83 33–37

BAE Systems Ship Repair, 73 46–48

Bahamas Air Holdings Ltd., 66 24–26

Bahlsen GmbH & Co. KG, 44 38–41

Baidu.com Inc., 95 40–43

Bailey Nurseries, Inc., 57 59–61

Bain & Company, 55 41–43

Baird & Warner Holding Company, 87 47–50

Bairnco Corporation, 28 42–45

Bajaj Auto Limited, 39 36–38

Baker *see* Michael Baker Corp.

Baker & Daniels LLP, 88 17–20

Baker & Hostetler LLP, 40 55–58

Baker & McKenzie, 10 126–28; 42 17–20 (upd.)

Baker & Taylor Corporation, 16 45–47; 43 59–62 (upd.)

Baker and Botts, L.L.P., 28 46–49

Baker Hughes Incorporated, III 428–29; 22 66–69 (upd.); 57 62–66 (upd.)

Bakkavör Group hf., 91 35–39

Balance Bar Company, 32 70–72

Balchem Corporation, 42 21–23

Baldor Electric Company, 21 42–44; 97 63–67 (upd.)

Baldwin & Lyons, Inc., 51 37–39

Baldwin Piano & Organ Company, 18 43–46 *see also* Gibson Guitar Corp.

Baldwin Richardson Foods Company, 100 48–52

Baldwin Technology Company, Inc., 25 35–39

Balfour Beatty Construction Ltd., 36 56–60 (upd.)

Ball Corporation, I 597–98; 10 129–31 (upd.); 78 25–29 (upd.)

Ball Horticultural Company, 78 30–33

Ballantine Books *see* Random House, Inc.

Ballantyne of Omaha, Inc., 27 56–58

Ballard Medical Products, 21 45–48 *see also* Kimberly-Clark Corp.

Ballard Power Systems Inc., 73 49–52

Ballistic Recovery Systems, Inc., 87 51–54

Bally Manufacturing Corporation, III 430–32

Bally Total Fitness Corporation, 25 40–42; 94 53–57 (upd.)

Balmac International, Inc., 94 58–61

Bâloise-Holding, 40 59–62

Baltek Corporation, 34 59–61

Baltika Brewery Joint Stock Company, 65 63–66

Baltimore & Ohio Railroad *see* CSX Corp.

Baltimore Aircoil Company, Inc., 66 27–29

Baltimore Gas and Electric Company, V 552–54; 25 43–46 (upd.)

Baltimore Orioles L.P., 66 30–33

Baltimore Technologies Plc, 42 24–26

The Bama Companies, Inc., 80 13–16

Banamex *see* Grupo Financiero Banamex S.A.

Banana Republic Inc., 25 47–49 *see also* Gap, Inc.

Banc One Corporation, 10 132–34 *see also* JPMorgan Chase & Co.

Banca Commerciale Italiana SpA, II 191–93

Banca Fideuram SpA, 63 52–54

Banca Intesa SpA, 65 67–70

Banca Monte dei Paschi di Siena SpA, 65 71–73

Banca Nazionale del Lavoro SpA, 72 19–21

Banca Serfin *see* Grupo Financiero Serfin, S.A.

Banco Bilbao Vizcaya Argentaria S.A., II 194–96; 48 47–51 (upd.)

Banco Bradesco S.A., 13 69–71

Banco Central, II 197–98; 56 65 *see also* Banco Santander Central Hispano S.A.

Banco Central del Paraguay, 100 53–56

Banco Comercial Português, SA, 50 69–72

Banco de Chile, 69 55–57

Banco de Comercio, S.A. *see* Grupo Financiero BBVA Bancomer S.A.

Banco de Crédito del Perú, 92 73–76

Banco de Comercio e Inversiones *see* Bci.

Banco do Brasil S.A., II 199–200

Banco Espírito Santo e Comercial de Lisboa S.A., 15 38–40 *see also* Espírito Santo Financial Group S.A.

Banco Itaú S.A., 19 33–35

bebe stores, inc., 31 50–52; 103 47–51
(upd.)
Bechtel Corporation, I 558–59; 24
64–67 (upd.); 99 55–60 (upd.)
Beckett Papers, 23 48–50
Beckman Coulter, Inc., 22 74–77
Beckman Instruments, Inc., 14 52–54
Becton, Dickinson and Company, I
630–31; 11 34–36 (upd.); 36 84–89
(upd.); 101 69–77 (upd.)
Bed Bath & Beyond Inc., 13 81–83; 41
49–52 (upd.)
Beech Aircraft Corporation, 8 49–52 see
also Raytheon Aircraft Holdings Inc.
Beech-Nut Nutrition Corporation, 21
53–56; 51 47–51 (upd.)
Beef O'Brady's see Family Sports
Concepts, Inc.
Beer Nuts, Inc., 86 30–33
Beggars Group Ltd., 99 61–65
Behr GmbH & Co. KG, 72 22–25
Behring Diagnostics see Dade Behring
Holdings Inc.
BEI Technologies, Inc., 65 74–76
Beiersdorf AG, 29 49–53
Bekaert S.A./N.V., 90 53–57
Bekins Company, 15 48–50
Bel see Fromageries Bel.
Bel Fuse, Inc., 53 59–62
Bel/Kaukauna USA, 76 46–48
Belco Oil & Gas Corp., 40 63–65
Belden CDT Inc., 19 43–45; 76 49–52
(upd.)
Belgacom, 6 302–04
Belk, Inc., V 12–13; 19 46–48 (upd.);
72 26–29 (upd.)
Bell and Howell Company, 9 61–64; 29
54–58 (upd.)
Bell Atlantic Corporation, V 272–74; 25
58–62 (upd.) see also Verizon
Communications.
Bell Canada Enterprises Inc. see BCE, Inc.
Bell Canada International, Inc., 6
305–08
Bell Helicopter Textron Inc., 46 64–67
Bell Industries, Inc., 47 40–43
Bell Resources see TPG NV.
Bell Sports Corporation, 16 51–53; 44
51–54 (upd.)
Bellcore see Telcordia Technologies, Inc.
Belleek Pottery Ltd., 71 50–53
Belleville Shoe Manufacturing
Company, 92 17–20
Bellisio Foods, Inc., 95 51–54
BellSouth Corporation, V 276–78; 29
59–62 (upd.) see also AT&T Corp.
Bellway Plc, 45 37–39
Belo Corporation, 98 19–25 (upd.)
Beloit Corporation, 14 55–57 see also
Metso Corp.
Belron International Ltd., 76 53–56
Belvedere S.A., 93 77–81
Bemis Company, Inc., 8 53–55; 91
53–60 (upd.)
Ben & Jerry's Homemade, Inc., 10
146–48; 35 58–62 (upd.); 80 22–28
(upd.)
Ben Bridge Jeweler, Inc., 60 52–54

Ben E. Keith Company, 76 57–59
Benchmark Capital, 49 50–52
Benchmark Electronics, Inc., 40 66–69
Benckiser N.V. see Reckitt Benckiser plc.
Bendix Corporation, I 141–43
Beneficial Corporation, 8 56–58
Benesse Corporation, 76 60–62
Bénéteau SA, 55 54–56
Benetton Group S.p.A., 10 149–52; 67
47–51 (upd.)
Benfield Greig Group plc, 53 63–65
Benguet Corporation, 58 21–24
Benihana, Inc., 18 56–59; 76 63–66
(upd.)
Benjamin Moore and Co., 13 84–87; 38
95–99 (upd.)
BenQ Corporation, 67 52–54
Benton Oil and Gas Company, 47
44–46
Berean Christian Stores, 96 40–43
Beretta see Fabbrica D' Armi Pietro
Beretta S.p.A.
Bergdorf Goodman Inc., 52 45–48
Bergen Brunswig Corporation, V
14–16; 13 88–90 (upd.) see also
AmerisourceBergen Corp.
Berger Bros Company, 62 31–33
Beringer Blass Wine Estates Ltd., 22
78–81; 66 34–37 (upd.)
Berjaya Group Bhd., 67 55–57
Berkeley Farms, Inc., 46 68–70
Berkshire Hathaway Inc., III 213–15;
18 60–63 (upd.); 42 31–36 (upd.);
89 92–99 (upd.)
Berkshire Realty Holdings, L.P., 49
53–55
Berlex Laboratories, Inc., 66 38–40
Berliner Stadtreinigungsbetriebe, 58
25–28
Berliner Verkehrsbetriebe (BVG), 58
29–31
Berlinwasser Holding AG, 90 58–62
Berlitz International, Inc., 13 91–93; 39
47–50 (upd.)
Bernard C. Harris Publishing Company,
Inc., 39 51–53
Bernard Chaus, Inc., 27 59–61
Bernard Hodes Group Inc., 86 34–37
Bernard Matthews Ltd., 89 100–04
The Bernick Companies, 75 62–65
Bernina Holding AG, 47 47–50
Bernstein-Rein, 92 21–24
The Berry Company see L. M. Berry and
Company
Berry Petroleum Company, 47 51–53
Berry Plastics Group Inc., 21 57–59; 98
26–30 (upd.)
Bertelsmann A.G., IV 592–94; 43 63–67
(upd.); 91 61–68 (upd.)
Bertucci's Corporation, 16 54–56; 64
51–54 (upd.)
Berwick Offray, LLC, 70 17–19
Berwind Corporation, 100 61–64
Besix Group S.A./NV, 94 66–69
Besnier SA, 19 49–51 see also Groupe
Lactalis
Best Buy Co., Inc., 9 65–66; 23 51–53
(upd.); 63 61–66 (upd.)

Best Kosher Foods Corporation, 82
41–44
Bestfoods, 22 82–86 (upd.)
Bestseller A/S, 90 63–66
Bestway Transportation see TNT
Freightways Corp.
BET Holdings, Inc., 18 64–66
Beth Abraham Family of Health
Services, 94 70–74
Beth Israel Medical Center see Continuum
Health Partners, Inc.
Bethlehem Steel Corporation, IV 35–37;
7 48–51 (upd.); 27 62–66 (upd.)
Betsey Johnson Inc., 100 65–69
Better Made Snack Foods, Inc., 90
67–69
Bettys & Taylors of Harrogate Ltd., 72
30–32
Betz Laboratories, Inc., I 312–13; 10
153–55 (upd.)
Beverly Enterprises, Inc., III 76–77; 16
57–59 (upd.)
Bewag AG, 39 54–57
BFC Construction Corporation, 25
63–65
The BFGoodrich Company, V 231–33;
19 52–55 (upd.) see also Goodrich
Corp.
BFI see The British Film Institute;
Browning-Ferris Industries, Inc.
BFP Holdings Corp. see Big Flower Press
Holdings, Inc.
BG&E see Baltimore Gas and Electric Co.
BG Products Inc., 96 44–47
Bharti Tele-Ventures Limited, 75 66–68
BHC Communications, Inc., 26 32–34
BHP Billiton, 67 58–64 (upd.)
Bhs plc, 17 42–44
Bianchi International (d/b/a Gregory
Mountain Products), 76 67–69
Bibliographisches Institut & F.A.
Brockhaus AG, 74 30–34
BIC Corporation, 8 59–61; 23 54–57
(upd.)
BICC PLC, III 433–34 see also Balfour
Beatty plc.
Bicoastal Corporation, II 9–11
Biffa plc, 92 25–28
Big 5 Sporting Goods Corporation, 55
57–59
Big A Drug Stores Inc., 79 62–65
Big B, Inc., 17 45–47
Big Bear Stores Co., 13 94–96
Big Brothers Big Sisters of America, 85
29–33
Big Dog Holdings, Inc., 45 40–42
Big Flower Press Holdings, Inc., 21
60–62 see also Vertis Communications.
The Big Food Group plc, 68 50–53
(upd.)
Big Idea Productions, Inc., 49 56–59
Big Lots, Inc., 50 98–101
Big O Tires, Inc., 20 61–63
Big Rivers Electric Corporation, 11
37–39
Big V Supermarkets, Inc., 25 66–68
Big Y Foods, Inc., 53 66–68
Bigard see Groupe Bigard S.A.

Books-A-Million, Inc., 14 61–62; 41 59–62 (upd.); 96 57–61 (upd.)

Books Are Fun, Ltd. *see* The Reader's Digest Association, Inc.

Bookspan, 86 42–46

Boole & Babbage, Inc., 25 86–88 *see also* BMC Software, Inc.

Booth Creek Ski Holdings, Inc., 31 65–67

Boots & Coots International Well Control, Inc., 79 70–73

The Boots Company PLC, V 17–19; 24 72–76 (upd.) *see also* Alliance Boots plc.

Booz Allen Hamilton Inc., 10 172–75; 101 78–84 (upd.)

Boral Limited, III 672–74; 43 72–76 (upd.); 103 52–59 (upd.)

Borden, Inc., II 470–73; 22 91–96 (upd.)

Borders Group, Inc., 15 61–62; 43 77–79 (upd.)

Borealis AG, 94 83–86

Borg-Warner Automotive, Inc., 14 63–66; 32 93–97 (upd.)

Borg-Warner Corporation, III 438–41 *see also* Burns International.

BorgWarner Inc., 85 38–44 (upd.)

Borland International, Inc., 9 80–82

Boron, LePore & Associates, Inc., 45 43–45

Bosch *see* Robert Bosch GmbH.

Boscov's Department Store, Inc., 31 68–70

Bose Corporation, 13 108–10; 36 98–101 (upd.)

Boss Holdings, Inc., 97 78–81

Boston Acoustics, Inc., 22 97–99

The Boston Beer Company, Inc., 18 70–73; 50 111–15 (upd.)

Boston Celtics Limited Partnership, 14 67–69

Boston Chicken, Inc., 12 42–44 *see also* Boston Market Corp.

The Boston Consulting Group, 58 32–35

Boston Edison Company, 12 45–47

Boston Market Corporation, 48 64–67 (upd.)

Boston Pizza International Inc., 88 33–38

Boston Professional Hockey Association Inc., 39 61–63

Boston Properties, Inc., 22 100–02

Boston Scientific Corporation, 37 37–40; 77 58–63 (upd.)

The Boston Symphony Orchestra Inc., 93 95–99

Bou-Matic, 62 42–44

Boulanger S.A., 102 57–60

Bourbon *see* Groupe Bourbon S.A.

Bourbon Corporation, 82 49–52

Bouygues S.A., I 562–64; 24 77–80 (upd.); 97 82–87 (upd.)

Bovis *see* Peninsular and Oriental Steam Navigation Company (Bovis Division)

Bowater PLC, IV 257–59

Bowlin Travel Centers, Inc., 99 71–75

Bowne & Co., Inc., 23 61–64; 79 74–80 (upd.)

Bowthorpe plc, 33 70–72

The Boy Scouts of America, 34 66–69

Boyd Bros. Transportation Inc., 39 64–66

Boyd Coffee Company, 53 73–75

Boyd Gaming Corporation, 43 80–82

The Boyds Collection, Ltd., 29 71–73

Boyne USA Resorts, 71 65–68

Boys & Girls Clubs of America, 69 73–75

Bozell Worldwide Inc., 25 89–91

Bozzuto's, Inc., 13 111–12

BP p.l.c., 45 46–56 (upd.); 103 60–74 (upd.)

BPB plc, 83 46–49

Braathens ASA, 47 60–62

Brach's Confections, Inc., 15 63–65; 74 43–46 (upd.)

Bradford & Bingley PLC, 65 77–80

Bradlees Discount Department Store Company, 12 48–50

Bradley Air Services Ltd., 56 38–40

Brady Corporation, 78 50–55 (upd.)

Brake Bros plc, 45 57–59

Bramalea Ltd., 9 83–85

Brambles Industries Limited, 42 47–50

Brammer PLC, 77 64–67

The Branch Group, Inc., 72 43–45

BrandPartners Group, Inc., 58 36–38

Brannock Device Company, 48 68–70

Brascan Corporation, 67 71–73

Brasfield & Gorrie LLC, 87 72–75

Brasil Telecom Participaçoes S.A., 57 67–70

Brass Eagle Inc., 34 70–72

Brauerei Beck & Co., 9 86–87; 33 73–76 (upd.)

Braun GmbH, 51 55–58

Brazil Fast Food Corporation, 74 47–49

Brazos Sportswear, Inc., 23 65–67

Breeze-Eastern Corporation, 95 67–70

Bremer Financial Corp., 45 60–63

Brenntag Holding GmbH & Co. KG, 8 68–69; 23 68–70 (upd.); 101 85–90 (upd.)

Brescia Group *see* Grupo Brescia.

Briazz, Inc., 53 76–79

The Brickman Group, Ltd., 87 76–79

Bricorama S.A., 68 62–64

Bridgeport Machines, Inc., 17 52–54

Bridgestone Corporation, V 234–35; 21 72–75 (upd.); 59 87–92 (upd.)

Bridgford Foods Corporation, 27 71–73

Briggs & Stratton Corporation, 8 70–73; 27 74–78 (upd.)

Brigham Exploration Company, 75 72–74

Brigham's Inc., 72 46–48

Bright Horizons Family Solutions, Inc., 31 71–73

Brightpoint, Inc., 18 74–77

Brillstein-Grey Entertainment, 80 41–45

Brinker International, Inc., 10 176–78; 38 100–03 (upd.); 75 75–79 (upd.)

The Brink's Company, 58 39–43 (upd.)

BRIO AB, 24 81–83; 103 75–79 (upd.)

Brioche Pasquier S.A., 58 44–46

Brioni Roman Style S.p.A., 67 74–76

BRISA Auto-estradas de Portugal S.A., 64 55–58

Bristol Farms, 101 91–95

Bristol Hotel Company, 23 71–73

Bristol-Myers Squibb Company, III 17–19; 9 88–91 (upd.); 37 41–45 (upd.)

Bristow Helicopters Ltd., 70 26–28

Britannia Soft Drinks Ltd. (Britvic), 71 69–71

Britannica.com *see* Encyclopaedia Britannica, Inc.

Brite Voice Systems, Inc., 20 75–78

British Aerospace plc, I 50–53; 24 84–90 (upd.)

British Airways plc, I 92–95; 14 70–74 (upd.); 43 83–88 (upd.)

British American Tobacco PLC, 50 116–19 (upd.)

British-Borneo Oil & Gas PLC, 34 73–75

British Broadcasting Corporation Ltd., 7 52–55; 21 76–79 (upd.); 89 111–17 (upd.)

British Coal Corporation, IV 38–40

British Columbia Telephone Company, 6 309–11

British Energy Plc, 49 65–68 *see also* British Nuclear Fuels PLC.

The British Film Institute, 80 46–50

British Gas plc, V 559–63 *see also* Centrica plc.

British Land Plc, 54 38–41

British Midland plc, 38 104–06

The British Museum, 71 72–74

British Nuclear Fuels PLC, 6 451–54

British Oxygen Co *see* BOC Group.

The British Petroleum Company plc, IV 378–80; 7 56–59 (upd.); 21 80–84 (upd.) *see also* BP p.l.c.

British Railways Board, V 421–24

British Sky Broadcasting Group plc, 20 79–81; 60 66–69 (upd.)

British Steel plc, IV 41–43; 19 62–65 (upd.)

British Sugar plc, 84 25–29

British Telecommunications plc, V 279–82; 15 66–70 (upd.) *see also* BT Group plc.

The British United Provident Association Limited, 79 81–84

British Vita plc, 9 92–93; 33 77–79 (upd.)

British World Airlines Ltd., 18 78–80

Britvic Soft Drinks Limited *see* Britannia Soft Drinks Ltd. (Britvic)

Broadcast Music Inc., 23 74–77; 90 74–79 (upd.)

Broadcom Corporation, 34 76–79; 90 80–85 (upd.)

The Broadmoor Hotel, 30 82–85

Broadwing Corporation, 70 29–32

Brobeck, Phleger & Harrison, LLP, 31 74–76

Brockhaus *see* Bibliographisches Institut & F.A. Brockhaus AG.

Food Lion LLC, II 626–27; 15 176–78 (upd.); 66 112–15 (upd.)

Foodarama Supermarkets, Inc., 28 143–45 *see also* Wakefern Food Corp.

FoodBrands America, Inc., 23 201–04 *see also* Doskocil Companies, Inc.; Tyson Foods, Inc.

Foodmaker, Inc., 14 194–96 *see also* Jack in the Box Inc.

Foot Locker, Inc., 68 157–62 (upd.)

Foot Petals L.L.C., 95 151–54

Foote, Cone & Belding Worldwide, I 12–15; 66 116–20 (upd.)

Footstar, Incorporated, 24 167–69 *see also* Foot Locker, Inc.

Forbes Inc., 30 199–201; 82 115–20 (upd.)

Force Protection Inc., 95 155–58

The Ford Foundation, 34 170–72

Ford Gum & Machine Company, Inc., 102 128–31

Ford Motor Company, I 164–68; 11 136–40 (upd.); 36 215–21 (upd.); 64 128–34 (upd.)

Ford Motor Company, S.A. de C.V., 20 219–21

FORE Systems, Inc., 25 161–63 *see also* Telefonaktiebolaget LM Ericsson.

Foremost Farms USA Cooperative, 98 116–20

FöreningsSparbanken AB, 69 177–80

Forest City Enterprises, Inc., 16 209–11; 52 128–31 (upd.)

Forest Laboratories, Inc., 11 141–43; 52 132–36 (upd.)

Forest Oil Corporation, 19 161–63; 91 182–87 (upd.)

Forever 21, Inc., 84 127–129

Forever Living Products International Inc., 17 186–88

FormFactor, Inc., 85 128–31

Formica Corporation, 13 230–32

Formosa Plastics Corporation, 14 197–99; 58 128–31 (upd.)

Forrester Research, Inc., 54 113–15

Forstmann Little & Co., 38 190–92

Fort Howard Corporation, 8 197–99 *see also* Fort James Corp.

Fort James Corporation, 22 209–12 (upd.) *see also* Georgia-Pacific Corp.

Fortis, Inc., 15 179–82; 47 134–37 (upd.); 50 4–6

Fortum Corporation, 30 202–07 (upd.) *see also* Neste Oil Corp.

Fortune Brands, Inc., 29 193–97 (upd.); 68 163–67 (upd.)

Fortunoff Fine Jewelry and Silverware Inc., 26 144–46

Forward Air Corporation, 75 147–49

Forward Industries, Inc., 86 152–55

The Forzani Group Ltd., 79 172–76

Fossil, Inc., 17 189–91

Foster Poultry Farms, 32 201–04

Foster Wheeler Corporation, 6 145–47; 23 205–08 (upd.); 76 152–56 (upd.)

FosterGrant, Inc., 60 131–34

Foster's Group Limited, 7 182–84; 21 227–30 (upd.); 50 199–203 (upd.)

Foundation Health Corporation, 12 175–77

Fountain Powerboats Industries, Inc., 28 146–48

Four Seasons Hotels Inc., 9 237–38; 29 198–200 (upd.)

Four Winns Boats LLC, 96 124–27

4Kids Entertainment Inc., 59 187–89

Fourth Financial Corporation, 11 144–46

Fox Entertainment Group, Inc., 43 173–76

Fox Family Worldwide, Inc., 24 170–72 *see also* ABC Family Worldwide, Inc.

Fox, Inc. *see* Twentieth Century Fox Film Corp.

Foxboro Company, 13 233–35

FoxHollow Technologies, Inc., 85 132–35

FoxMeyer Health Corporation, 16 212–14 *see also* McKesson Corp.

Fox's Pizza Den, Inc., 98 121–24

Foxworth-Galbraith Lumber Company, 91 188–91

FPL Group, Inc., V 623–25; 49 143–46 (upd.)

Framatome SA, 19 164–67 aee also Alcatel S.A.; AREVA.

France Telecom S.A., V 291–93; 21 231–34 (upd.); 99 173–179 (upd.)

Francotyp-Postalia Holding AG, 92 123–27

Frank J. Zamboni & Co., Inc., 34 173–76

Frank Russell Company, 46 198–200

Franke Holding AG, 76 157–59

Frankel & Co., 39 166–69

Frankfurter Allgemeine Zeitung GmbH, 66 121–24

Franklin Covey Company, 11 147–49; 37 149–52 (upd.)

Franklin Electric Company, Inc., 43 177–80

Franklin Electronic Publishers, Inc., 23 209–13

The Franklin Mint, 69 181–84

Franklin Resources, Inc., 9 239–40

Frank's Nursery & Crafts, Inc., 12 178–79

Franz Inc., 80 122–25

Fraport AG Frankfurt Airport Services Worldwide, 90 197–202

Fraser & Neave Ltd., 54 116–18

Fred Alger Management, Inc., 97 168–72

Fred Meyer Stores, Inc., V 54–56; 20 222–25 (upd.); 64 135–39 (upd.)

Fred Usinger Inc., 54 119–21

The Fred W. Albrecht Grocery Co., 13 236–38

Fred Weber, Inc., 61 100–02

Freddie Mac, 54 122–25

Frederick Atkins Inc., 16 215–17

Frederick's of Hollywood Inc., 16 218–20; 59 190–93 (upd.)

Fred's, Inc., 23 214–16; 62 144–47 (upd.)

Freedom Communications, Inc., 36 222–25

Freeport-McMoRan Copper & Gold, Inc., IV 81–84; 7 185–89 (upd.); 57 145–50 (upd.)

Freescale Semiconductor, Inc., 83 151–154

Freeze.com LLC, 77 156–59

FreightCar America, Inc., 101 192–95

Freixenet S.A., 71 162–64

French Connection Group plc, 41 167–69

French Fragrances, Inc., 22 213–15 *see also* Elizabeth Arden, Inc.

Frequency Electronics, Inc., 61 103–05

Fresenius AG, 56 138–42

Fresh America Corporation, 20 226–28

Fresh Choice, Inc., 20 229–32

Fresh Enterprises, Inc., 66 125–27

Fresh Express Inc., 88 97–100

Fresh Foods, Inc., 29 201–03

FreshDirect, LLC, 84 130–133

Fretter, Inc., 10 304–06

Freudenberg & Co., 41 170–73

Fried, Frank, Harris, Shriver & Jacobson, 35 183–86

Fried. Krupp GmbH, IV 85–89 *see also* ThyssenKrupp AG.

Friedman, Billings, Ramsey Group, Inc., 53 134–37

Friedman's Inc., 29 204–06

Friedrich Grohe AG & Co. KG, 53 138–41

Friendly Ice Cream Corporation, 30 208–10; 72 141–44 (upd.)

Friesland Coberco Dairy Foods Holding N.V., 59 194–96

Frigidaire Home Products, 22 216–18

Frisch's Restaurants, Inc., 35 187–89; 92 121–32 (upd.)

Frito-Lay North America, 32 205–10; 73 151–58 (upd.)

Fritz Companies, Inc., 12 180–82

Fromageries Bel, 23 217–19; 25 83–84

Frontera Foods, Inc., 100 170–73

Frontier Airlines Holdings Inc., 22 219–21; 84 134–138 (upd.)

Frontier Corp., 16 221–23

Frontier Natural Products Co-Op, 82 121–24

Frontline Ltd., 45 163–65

Frost & Sullivan, Inc., 53 142–44

Frozen Food Express Industries, Inc., 20 233–35; 98 125–30 (upd.)

Frucor Beverages Group Ltd., 96 128–31

Fruehauf Corp., I 169–70

Fruit of the Loom, Inc., 8 200–02; 25 164–67 (upd.)

Fruth Pharmacy, Inc., 66 128–30

Frymaster Corporation, 27 159–62

Fry's Electronics, Inc., 68 168–70

FSI International, Inc., 17 192–94 *see also* FlightSafety International, Inc.

FTD Group, Inc., 99 180–185 (upd.)

FTI Consulting, Inc., 77 160–63

FTP Software, Inc., 20 236–38

Fubu, 29 207–09

Kumon Institute of Education Co., Ltd., 72 211–14

Kuoni Travel Holding Ltd., 40 284–86

Kurzweil Technologies, Inc., 51 200–04

The Kushner-Locke Company, 25 269–71

Kuwait Airways Corporation, 68 226–28

Kuwait Flour Mills & Bakeries Company, 84 232–234

Kuwait Petroleum Corporation, IV 450–52; 55 240–43 (upd.)

Kvaerner ASA, 36 321–23

Kwang Yang Motor Company Ltd., 80 193–96

Kwik-Fit Holdings plc, 54 205–07

Kwik Save Group plc, 11 239–41

Kwizda Holding GmbH, 102 209–12

Kymmene Corporation, IV 299–303 see also UPM-Kymmene Corp.

Kyocera Corporation, II 50–52; 21 329–32 (upd.); 79 231–36 (upd.)

Kyokuyo Company Ltd., 75 228–30

Kyowa Hakko Kogyo Co., Ltd., III 42–43; 48 248–50 (upd.)

Kyphon Inc., 87 292–295

Kyushu Electric Power Company Inc., V 649–51

L

L-3 Communications Holdings, Inc., 48 251–53

L. and J.G. Stickley, Inc., 50 303–05

L.A. Darling Company, 92 203–06

L.A. Gear, Inc., 8 303–06; 32 313–17 (upd.)

L.A. T Sportswear, Inc., 26 257–59

L.B. Foster Company, 33 255–58

L.D.C. SA, 61 155–57

L. Foppiano Wine Co., 101 290–93

L.L. Bean, Inc., 10 388–90; 38 280–83 (upd.); 91 307–13 (upd.)

The L.L. Knickerbocker Co., Inc., 25 272–75

L. Luria & Son, Inc., 19 242–44

L. M. Berry and Company, 80 197–200

L.S. Starrett Company, 13 301–03; 64 227–30 (upd.)

La Choy Food Products Inc., 25 276–78

La Doria SpA, 101 294–97

La Madeleine French Bakery & Café, 33 249–51

La Poste, V 270–72; 47 213–16 (upd.)

The La Quinta Companies, 11 242–44; 42 213–16 (upd.)

La Reina Inc., 96 252–55

La Seda de Barcelona S.A., 100 260–63

La Senza Corporation, 66 205–07

La Serenísima see Mastellone Hermanos S.A.

La-Z-Boy Incorporated, 14 302–04; 50 309–13 (upd.)

LAB see Lloyd Aéreo Boliviano S.A

Lab Safety Supply, Inc., 102 213–16

LaBarge Inc., 41 224–26

Labatt Brewing Company Limited, I 267–68; 25 279–82 (upd.)

Labeyrie SAS, 80 201–04

LabOne, Inc., 48 254–57

Labor Ready, Inc., 29 273–75; 88 231–36 (upd.)

Laboratoires Arkopharma S.A., 75 231–34

Laboratoires de Biologie Végétale Yves Rocher, 35 262–65

Laboratoires Pierre Fabre S.A., 100 353–57

Laboratory Corporation of America Holdings, 42 217–20 (upd.)

LaBranche & Co. Inc., 37 223–25

LaCie Group S.A., 76 232–34

Lacks Enterprises Inc., 61 158–60

Laclede Steel Company, 15 271–73

LaCrosse Footwear, Inc., 18 298–301; 61 161–65 (upd.)

Ladbroke Group PLC, II 141–42; 21 333–36 (upd.) see also Hilton Group plc

LADD Furniture, Inc., 12 299–301 see also La-Z-Boy Inc.

Ladish Co., Inc., 30 282–84

Lafarge Cement UK, 54 208–11 (upd.)

Lafarge Coppée S.A., III 703–05

Lafarge Corporation, 28 228–31

Lafuma S.A., 39 248–50

Laidlaw International, Inc., 80 205–08

Laing O'Rourke PLC, 93 282–85 (upd.)

L'Air Liquide SA, I 357–59; 47 217–20 (upd.)

Lakeland Industries, Inc., 45 245–48

Lakes Entertainment, Inc., 51 205–07

Lakeside Foods, Inc., 89 297–301

Lala see Grupo Industrial Lala, S.A. de C.V.

Lam Research Corporation, 11 245–47; 31 299–302 (upd.)

Lam Son Sugar Joint Stock Corporation (Lasuco), 60 195–97

Lamar Advertising Company, 27 278–80; 70 150–53 (upd.)

The Lamaur Corporation, 41 227–29

Lamb Weston, Inc., 23 319–21

Lamborghini see Automobili Lamborghini S.p.A.

Lamonts Apparel, Inc., 15 274–76

The Lamson & Sessions Co., 13 304–06; 61 166–70 (upd.)

Lan Chile S.A., 31 303–06

Lancair International, Inc., 67 224–26

Lancaster Colony Corporation, 8 307–09; 61 171–74 (upd.)

Lance, Inc., 14 305–07; 41 230–33 (upd.)

Lancer Corporation, 21 337–39

Land O'Lakes, Inc., II 535–37; 21 340–43 (upd.); 81 222–27 (upd.)

Land Securities PLC, IV 704–06; 49 246–50 (upd.)

LandAmerica Financial Group, Inc., 85 213–16

Landauer, Inc., 51 208–10

Landec Corporation, 95 235–38

Landmark Communications, Inc., 12 302–05; 55 244–49 (upd.)

Landmark Theatre Corporation, 70 154–56

Landor Associates, 81 228–31

Landry's Restaurants, Inc., 15 277–79; 65 203–07 (upd.)

Lands' End, Inc., 9 314–16; 29 276–79 (upd.); 82 195–200 (upd.)

Landsbanki Islands hf, 81 232–35

Landstar System, Inc., 63 236–38

Lane Bryant, Inc., 64 231–33

The Lane Co., Inc., 12 306–08

Lanier Worldwide, Inc., 75 235–38

Lanoga Corporation, 62 222–24 see also Pro-Build Holdings Inc.

Lapeyre S.A. see Groupe Lapeyre S.A.

Larry Flynt Publishing Inc., 31 307–10

Larry H. Miller Group, 29 280–83

Las Vegas Sands, Inc., 50 306–08

Laserscope, 67 227–29

LaSiDo Inc., 58 209–11

Lason, Inc., 31 311–13

Lassonde Industries Inc., 68 229–31

Lasuco see Lam Son Sugar Joint Stock Corp.

Latécoère S.A., 100 264–68

Latham & Watkins, 33 252–54

Latrobe Brewing Company, 54 212–14

Lattice Semiconductor Corp., 16 315–17

Lauda Air Luftfahrt AG, 48 258–60

Laura Ashley Holdings plc, 13 307–09; 37 226–29 (upd.)

The Laurel Pub Company Limited, 59 255–57

Laurent-Perrier SA, 42 221–23

Laurus N.V., 65 208–11

Lavoro Bank AG see Banca Nazionale del Lavoro SpA.

Lawson Software, 38 284–88

Lawter International Inc., 14 308–10 see also Eastman Chemical Co.

Layne Christensen Company, 19 245–47

Lazard LLC, 38 289–92

Lazare Kaplan International Inc., 21 344–47

Lazio see Società Sportiva Lazio SpA.

Lazy Days RV Center, Inc., 69 228–30

LCA-Vision, Inc, 85 217–20

LCC International, Inc., 84 235–238

LCI International, Inc., 16 318–20 see also Qwest Communications International, Inc.

LDB Corporation, 53 204–06

LDC, 68 232–34

LDC S.A. see L.D.C. S.A.

LDDS-Metro Communications, Inc., 8 310–12 see also MCI WorldCom, Inc.

LDI Ltd., LLC, 76 235–37

LDK Solar Co., Ltd., 101 298–302

Le Bon Marché see The Bon Marché.

Le Chateau Inc., 63 239–41

Le Cordon Bleu S.A., 67 230–32

Le Duff see Groupe Le Duff S.A.

Le Monde S.A., 33 308–10

Léa Nature see Groupe Léa Nature.

Leap Wireless International, Inc., 69 231–33

LeapFrog Enterprises, Inc., 54 215–18

Lear Corporation, 16 321–23; 71 191–95 (upd.)
Lear Siegler Inc., I 481–83
Learjet Inc., 8 313–16; 27 281–85 (upd.)
Learning Care Group, Inc., 76 238–41 (upd.)
The Learning Company Inc., 24 275–78
Learning Tree International Inc., 24 279–82
LeaRonal, Inc., 23 322–24 *see also* Rohm and Haas Co.
Leaseway Transportation Corp., 12 309–11
Leatherman Tool Group, Inc., 51 211–13
Lebhar-Friedman, Inc., 55 250–52
Leblanc Corporation *see* G. Leblanc Corp.
LeBoeuf, Lamb, Greene & MacRae, L.L.P., 29 284–86
LECG Corporation, 93 286–89
Leche Pascual *see* Grupo Leche Pascual S.A.
Lechmere Inc., 10 391–93
Lechters, Inc., 11 248–50; 39 251–54 (upd.)
Leclerc *see* Association des Centres Distributeurs E. Leclerc.
LeCroy Corporation, 41 234–37
Ledcor Industries Limited, 46 266–69
Ledesma Sociedad Anónima Agrícola Industrial, 62 225–27
Lee Apparel Company, Inc., 8 317–19
Lee Enterprises, Incorporated, 11 251–53; 64 234–37 (upd.)
Leeann Chin, Inc., 30 285–88
Lefrak Organization Inc., 26 260–62
Legal & General Group Plc, III 272–73; 24 283–85 (upd.); 101 303–08 (upd.)
The Legal Aid Society, 48 261–64
Legal Sea Foods Inc., 96 256–60
Legent Corporation, 10 394–96 *see also* Computer Associates International, Inc.
Legg Mason, Inc., 33 259–62
Leggett & Platt, Inc., 11 254–56; 48 265–68 (upd.)
Lego A/S, 13 310–13; 40 287–91 (upd.)
Legrand SA, 21 348–50
Lehigh Portland Cement Company, 23 325–27
Lehman Brothers Holdings Inc., 99 249–253 (upd.)
Leica Camera AG, 35 266–69
Leica Microsystems Holdings GmbH, 35 270–73
Leidy's, Inc., 93 290–92
Leinenkugel Brewing Company *see* Jacob Leinenkugel Brewing Co.
Leiner Health Products Inc., 34 250–52
Lend Lease Corporation Limited, IV 707–09; 17 283–86 (upd.); 52 218–23 (upd.)
LendingTree, LLC, 93 293–96
Lennar Corporation, 11 257–59
Lennox International Inc., 8 320–22; 28 232–36 (upd.)
Lenovo Group Ltd., 80 209–12
Lenox, Inc., 12 312–13

LensCrafters Inc., 23 328–30; 76 242–45 (upd.)
L'Entreprise Jean Lefebvre, 23 331–33 *see also* Vinci.
Leo Burnett Company, Inc., I 22–24; 20 336–39 (upd.)
The Leona Group LLC, 84 239–242
Leoni AG, 98 231–36
Leprino Foods Company, 28 237–39
Leroux S.A.S., 65 212–14
Leroy Merlin SA, 54 219–21
Les Boutiques San Francisco, Inc., 62 228–30
Les Echos *see* Groupe Les Echos.
Les Schwab Tire Centers, 50 314–16
Lesaffre *see* Societe Industrielle Lesaffre.
Lesco Inc., 19 248–50
The Leslie Fay Company, Inc., 8 323–25; 39 255–58 (upd.)
Leslie's Poolmart, Inc., 18 302–04
Leucadia National Corporation, 11 260–62; 71 196–200 (upd.)
Leupold & Stevens, Inc., 52 224–26
Level 3 Communications, Inc., 67 233–35
Levenger Company, 63 242–45
Lever Brothers Company, 9 317–19 *see also* Unilever.
Levi, Ray & Shoup, Inc., 96 261–64
Levi Strauss & Co., V 362–65; 16 324–28 (upd.); 102 217–23 (upd.)
Levitz Furniture Inc., 15 280–82
Levy Restaurants L.P., 26 263–65
Lewis Drug Inc., 94 272–76
Lewis Galoob Toys Inc., 16 329–31
Lewis-Goetz and Company, Inc., 102 224–27
LEXIS-NEXIS Group, 33 263–67
Lexmark International, Inc., 18 305–07; 79 237–42 (upd.)
LG&E Energy Corporation, 6 516–18; 51 214–17 (upd.)
LG Corporation, 94 277–83 (upd.)
Li & Fung Limited, 59 258–61
Libbey Inc., 49 251–54
The Liberty Corporation, 22 312–14
Liberty Livewire Corporation, 42 224–27
Liberty Media Corporation, 50 317–19
Liberty Mutual Holding Company, 59 262–64
Liberty Orchards Co., Inc., 89 302–05
Liberty Property Trust, 57 221–23
Liberty Travel, Inc., 56 203–06
Libyan National Oil Corporation, IV 453–55 *see also* National Oil Corp.
Liebherr-International AG, 64 238–42
Life Care Centers of America Inc., 76 246–48
Life is good, Inc., 80 213–16
Life Technologies, Inc., 17 287–89
LifeCell Corporation, 77 236–39
Lifeline Systems, Inc., 32 374; 53 207–09
LifeLock, Inc., 91 314–17
LifePoint Hospitals, Inc., 69 234–36

Lifetime Brands, Inc., 27 286–89; 73 207–11 (upd.)
Lifetime Entertainment Services, 51 218–22
Lifetouch Inc., 86 243–47
Lifeway Foods, Inc., 65 215–17
LifeWise Health Plan of Oregon, Inc., 90 276–79
Ligand Pharmaceuticals Incorporated, 10 48; 47 221–23
LILCO *see* Long Island Lighting Co.
Lillian Vernon Corporation, 12 314–15; 35 274–77 (upd.); 92 207–12 (upd.)
Lilly & Co *see* Eli Lilly & Co.
Lilly Endowment Inc., 70 157–59
Limagrain *see* Groupe Limagrain.
The Limited, Inc., V 115–16; 20 340–43 (upd.)
LIN Broadcasting Corp., 9 320–22
Linamar Corporation, 18 308–10
Lincare Holdings Inc., 43 265–67
Lincoln Center for the Performing Arts, Inc., 69 237–41
Lincoln Electric Co., 13 314–16
Lincoln National Corporation, III 274–77; 25 286–90 (upd.)
Lincoln Property Company, 8 326–28; 54 222–26 (upd.)
Lincoln Snacks Company, 24 286–88
Lincoln Telephone & Telegraph Company, 14 311–13
Lindal Cedar Homes, Inc., 29 287–89
Linde AG, I 581–83; 67 236–39 (upd.)
Lindley *see* Corporación José R. Lindley S.A.
Lindsay Manufacturing Co., 20 344–46
Lindt & Sprüngli *see* Chocoladefabriken Lindt & Sprüngli AG.
Linear Technology Corporation, 16 332–34; 99 254–258 (upd.)
Linens 'n Things, Inc., 24 289–92; 75 239–43 (upd.)
LinkedIn Corporation, 103 246–49
Lintas: Worldwide, 14 314–16
The Lion Brewery, Inc., 86 248–52
Lion Corporation, III 44–45; 51 223–26 (upd.)
Lion Nathan Limited, 54 227–30
Lionel L.L.C., 16 335–38; 99 259–265 (upd.)
Lions Gate Entertainment Corporation, 35 278–81
Lipman Electronic Engineering Ltd., 81 236–39
Lipton *see* Thomas J. Lipton Co.
Liqui-Box Corporation, 16 339–41
Liquidity Services, Inc., 101 309–13
Liquidnet, Inc., 79 243–46
LIRR *see* The Long Island Rail Road Co.
Litehouse Inc., 60 198–201
Lithia Motors, Inc., 41 238–40
Littelfuse, Inc., 26 266–69
Little Caesar Enterprises, Inc., 7 278–79; 24 293–96 (upd.) *see also* Ilitch Holdings Inc.
Little Switzerland, Inc., 60 202–04
Little Tikes Company, 13 317–19; 62 231–34 (upd.)

McKinsey & Company, Inc., 9 343–45

McLane Company, Inc., 13 332–34

McLeodUSA Incorporated, 32 327–30

McMenamins Pubs and Breweries, 65 224–26

McMoRan *see* Freeport-McMoRan Copper & Gold, Inc.

MCN Corporation, 6 519–22

McNaughton Apparel Group, Inc., 92 236–41 (upd.)

McPherson's Ltd., 66 220–22

McQuay International *see* AAF-McQuay Inc.

MCSi, Inc., 41 258–60

McWane Corporation, 55 264–66

MDC Partners Inc., 63 290–92

MDU Resources Group, Inc., 7 322–25; 42 249–53 (upd.)

The Mead Corporation, IV 310–13; 19 265–69 (upd.) *see also* MeadWestvaco Corp.

Mead Data Central, Inc., 10 406–08 *see also* LEXIS-NEXIS Group.

Mead Johnson & Company, 84 257–262

Meade Instruments Corporation, 41 261–64

Meadowcraft, Inc., 29 313–15; 100 283–87 (upd.)

MeadWestvaco Corporation, 76 262–71 (upd.)

Measurement Specialties, Inc., 71 222–25

MEC *see* Mitsubishi Estate Company, Ltd.

Mecalux S.A., 74 183–85

Mechel OAO, 99 278–281

Mecklermedia Corporation, 24 328–30 *see also* Jupitermedia Corp.

Medarex, Inc., 85 256–59

Medco Containment Services Inc., 9 346–48 *see also* Merck & Co., Inc.

Médecins sans Frontières, 85 260–63

MEDecision, Inc., 95 263–67

Media Arts Group, Inc., 42 254–57

Media General, Inc., 7 326–28; 38 306–09 (upd.)

Mediacom Communications Corporation, 69 250–52

MediaNews Group, Inc., 70 177–80

Mediaset SpA, 50 332–34

Medical Action Industries Inc., 101 338–41

Medical Information Technology Inc., 64 266–69

Medical Management International, Inc., 65 227–29

Medical Staffing Network Holdings, Inc., 89 320–23

Medicine Shoppe International, Inc., 102 253–57

Medicis Pharmaceutical Corporation, 59 284–86

Medifast, Inc., 97 281–85

MedImmune, Inc., 35 286–89

Mediolanum S.p.A., 65 230–32

Medis Technologies Ltd., 77 257–60

Meditrust, 11 281–83

Medline Industries, Inc., 61 204–06

Medtronic, Inc., 8 351–54; 30 313–17 (upd.); 67 250–55 (upd.)

Medusa Corporation, 24 331–33

Mega Bloks, Inc., 61 207–09

Megafoods Stores Inc., 13 335–37

Meggitt PLC, 34 273–76

Meguiar's, Inc., 99 282–285

Meidensha Corporation, 92 242–46

Meier & Frank Co., 23 345–47 *see also* Macy's, Inc.

Meijer, Inc., 7 329–31; 27 312–15 (upd.); 101 342–46 (upd.)

Meiji Dairies Corporation, II 538–39; 82 231–34 (upd.)

Meiji Mutual Life Insurance Company, III 288–89

Meiji Seika Kaisha Ltd., II 540–41; 64 270–72 (upd.)

Mel Farr Automotive Group, 20 368–70

Melaleuca Inc., 31 326–28

Melamine Chemicals, Inc., 27 316–18 *see also* Mississippi Chemical Corp.

Melco Crown Entertainment Limited, 103 262–65

Melitta Unternehmensgruppe Bentz KG, 53 218–21

Mello Smello *see* The Miner Group International.

Mellon Financial Corporation, II 315–17; 44 278–82 (upd.)

Mellon-Stuart Co., I 584–85 *see also* Michael Baker Corp.

The Melting Pot Restaurants, Inc., 74 186–88

Melville Corporation, V 136–38 *see also* CVS Corp.

Melvin Simon and Associates, Inc., 8 355–57 *see also* Simon Property Group, Inc.

MEMC Electronic Materials, Inc., 81 249–52

Memorial Sloan-Kettering Cancer Center, 57 239–41

Memry Corporation, 72 225–27

The Men's Wearhouse, Inc., 17 312–15; 48 283–87 (upd.)

Menasha Corporation, 8 358–61; 59 287–92 (upd.)

Mendocino Brewing Company, Inc., 60 205–07

The Mentholatum Company Inc., 32 331–33

Mentor Corporation, 26 286–88

Mentor Graphics Corporation, 11 284–86

MEPC plc, IV 710–12

Mercantile Bankshares Corp., 11 287–88

Mercantile Stores Company, Inc., V 139; 19 270–73 (upd.) *see also* Dillard's Inc.

Mercer International Inc., 64 273–75

The Merchants Company, 102 258–61

Mercian Corporation, 77 261–64

Merck & Co., Inc., I 650–52; 11 289–91 (upd.); 34 280–85 (upd.); 95 268–78 (upd.)

Mercury Air Group, Inc., 20 371–73

Mercury Communications, Ltd., 7 332–34 *see also* Cable and Wireless plc.

Mercury Drug Corporation, 70 181–83

Mercury General Corporation, 25 323–25

Mercury Interactive Corporation, 59 293–95

Mercury Marine Group, 68 247–51

Meredith Corporation, 11 292–94; 29 316–19 (upd.); 74 189–93 (upd.)

Merge Healthcare, 85 264–68

Merial Ltd., 102 262–66

Meridian Bancorp, Inc., 11 295–97

Meridian Gold, Incorporated, 47 238–40

Merillat Industries, LLC, 13 338–39; 69 253–55 (upd.)

Merisant Worldwide, Inc., 70 184–86

Merisel, Inc., 12 334–36

Merit Medical Systems, Inc., 29 320–22

Meritage Corporation, 26 289–92

MeritCare Health System, 88 257–61

Merix Corporation, 36 329–31; 75 257–60 (upd.)

Merriam-Webster Inc., 70 187–91

Merrill Corporation, 18 331–34; 47 241–44 (upd.)

Merrill Lynch & Co., Inc., II 424–26; 13 340–43 (upd.); 40 310–15 (upd.)

Merry-Go-Round Enterprises, Inc., 8 362–64

The Mersey Docks and Harbour Company, 30 318–20

Mervyn's California, 10 409–10; 39 269–71 (upd.) *see also* Target Corp.

Merz Group, 81 253–56

Mesa Air Group, Inc., 11 298–300; 32 334–37 (upd.); 77 265–70 (upd.)

Mesaba Holdings, Inc., 28 265–67

Messerschmitt-Bölkow-Blohm GmbH., I 73–75 *see also* European Aeronautic Defence and Space Company EADS N.V.

Mestek, Inc., 10 411–13

Metal Box plc, I 604–06 *see also* Novar plc.

Metal Management, Inc., 92 247–50

Metaleurop S.A., 21 368–71

Metalico Inc., 97 286–89

Metallgesellschaft AG, IV 139–42; 16 361–66 (upd.)

Metalurgica Mexicana Penoles, S.A. *see* Industrias Penoles, S.A. de C.V.

Metatec International, Inc., 47 245–48

Metavante Corporation, 100 288–92

Metcash Trading Ltd., 58 226–28

Meteor Industries Inc., 33 295–97

Methanex Corporation, 40 316–19

Methode Electronics, Inc., 13 344–46

MetLife *see* Metropolitan Life Insurance Co.

Metris Companies Inc., 56 224–27

Metro AG, 50 335–39

Metro-Goldwyn-Mayer Inc., 25 326–30 (upd.); 84 263–270 (upd.)

Métro Inc., 77 271–75

Metro Information Services, Inc., 36 332–34

Mitsui & Co., Ltd., I 505–08; 28 280–85 (upd.)

Mitsui Bank, Ltd., II 325–27 *see also* Sumitomo Mitsui Banking Corp.

Mitsui Marine and Fire Insurance Company, Limited, III 295–96

Mitsui Mining & Smelting Co., Ltd., IV 145–46; 102 274–78 (upd.)

Mitsui Mining Company, Limited, IV 147–49

Mitsui Mutual Life Insurance Company, III 297–98; 39 284–86 (upd.)

Mitsui O.S.K. Lines Ltd., V 473–76; 96 282–87 (upd.)

Mitsui Petrochemical Industries, Ltd., 9 352–54

Mitsui Real Estate Development Co., Ltd., IV 715–16

Mitsui Trust & Banking Company, Ltd., II 328

Mitsukoshi Ltd., V 142–44; 56 239–42 (upd.)

Mity Enterprises, Inc., 38 310–12

MIVA, Inc., 83 271–275

Mizuho Financial Group Inc., 25 344–46; 58 229–36 (upd.)

MNS, Ltd., 65 236–38

Mo och Domsjö AB, IV 317–19 *see also* Holmen AB

Mobil Corporation, IV 463–65; 7 351–54 (upd.); 21 376–80 (upd.) *see also* Exxon Mobil Corp.

Mobile Mini, Inc., 58 237–39

Mobile Telecommunications Technologies Corp., 18 347–49

Mobile TeleSystems OJSC, 59 300–03

Mocon, Inc., 76 275–77

Modell's Sporting Goods *see* Henry Modell & Company Inc.

Modern Times Group AB, 36 335–38

Modern Woodmen of America, 66 227–29

Modine Manufacturing Company, 8 372–75; 56 243–47 (upd.)

MoDo *see* Mo och Domsjö AB.

Modtech Holdings, Inc., 77 284–87

Moen Incorporated, 12 344–45

Moët-Hennessy, I 271–72 *see also* LVMH Moët Hennessy Louis Vuitton SA.

Mohawk Industries, Inc., 19 274–76; 63 298–301 (upd.)

Mohegan Tribal Gaming Authority, 37 254–57

Moksel *see* A. Moksel AG.

MOL *see* Mitsui O.S.K. Lines, Ltd.

MOL Rt, 70 192–95

Moldflow Corporation, 73 227–30

Molex Incorporated, 11 317–19; 14 27; 54 236–41 (upd.)

Moliflor Loisirs, 80 252–55

Molinos Río de la Plata S.A., 61 219–21

Molins plc, 51 249–51

The Molson Companies Limited, I 273–75; 26 303–07 (upd.)

Molson Coors Brewing Company, 77 288–300 (upd.)

Monaco Coach Corporation, 31 336–38

Monadnock Paper Mills, Inc., 21 381–84

Monarch Casino & Resort, Inc., 65 239–41

The Monarch Cement Company, 72 231–33

Mondadori *see* Arnoldo Mondadori Editore S.p.A.

Mondragón Corporación Cooperativa, 101 347–51

MoneyGram International, Inc., 94 315–18

Monfort, Inc., 13 350–52

Monnaie de Paris, 62 246–48

Monnoyeur Group *see* Groupe Monnoyeur.

Monoprix S.A., 86 282–85

Monro Muffler Brake, Inc., 24 337–40

Monrovia Nursery Company, 70 196–98

Monsanto Company, I 365–67; 9 355–57 (upd.); 29 327–31 (upd.); 77 301–07 (upd.)

Monsoon plc, 39 287–89

Monster Cable Products, Inc., 69 256–58

Monster Worldwide Inc., 74 194–97 (upd.)

Montana Coffee Traders, Inc., 60 208–10

The Montana Power Company, 11 320–22; 44 288–92 (upd.)

Montblanc International GmbH, 82 240–44

Montedison S.p.A., I 368–69; 24 341–44 (upd.)

Monterey Pasta Company, 58 240–43

Montgomery Ward & Co., Incorporated, V 145–48; 20 374–79 (upd.)

Montres Rolex S.A., 13 353–55; 34 292–95 (upd.)

Montupet S.A., 63 302–04

Moody's Corporation, 65 242–44

Moog Inc., 13 356–58

Moog Music, Inc., 75 261–64

Mooney Aerospace Group Ltd., 52 252–55

Moore Corporation Limited, IV 644–46 *see also* R.R. Donnelley & Sons Co.

Moore-Handley, Inc., 39 290–92

Moore Medical Corp., 17 331–33

Moran Towing Corporation, Inc., 15 301–03

The Morgan Crucible Company plc, 82 245–50

Morgan Grenfell Group PLC, II 427–29 *see also* Deutsche Bank AG.

The Morgan Group, Inc., 46 300–02

Morgan, Lewis & Bockius LLP, 29 332–34

Morgan's Foods, Inc., 101 352 |B5–55

Morgan Stanley Dean Witter & Company, II 430–32; 16 374–78 (upd.); 33 311–14 (upd.)

Morgans Hotel Group Company, 80 256–59

Morguard Corporation, 85 287–90

Morinaga & Co. Ltd., 61 222–25

Morinda Holdings, Inc., 82 251–54

Morningstar Inc., 68 259–62

Morris Communications Corporation, 36 339–42

Morris Travel Services L.L.C., 26 308–11

Morrison & Foerster LLP, 78 220–23

Morrison Knudsen Corporation, 7 355–58; 28 286–90 (upd.) *see also* The Washington Companies.

Morrison Restaurants Inc., 11 323–25

Morrow Equipment Co. L.L.C., 87 325–327

Morse Shoe Inc., 13 359–61

Morton International, Inc., 9 358–59 (upd.); 80 260–64 (upd.)

Morton Thiokol Inc., I 370–72 *see also* Thiokol Corp.

Morton's Restaurant Group, Inc., 30 329–31; 88 262–66 (upd.)

The Mosaic Company, 91 330–33

Mosinee Paper Corporation, 15 304–06 *see also* Wausau-Mosinee Paper Corp.

Moss Bros Group plc, 51 252–54

Mossimo, 27 328–30; 96 288–92 (upd.)

Mota-Engil, SGPS, S.A., 97 290–93

Motel 6, 13 362–64; 56 248–51 (upd.) *see also* Accor SA

Mothercare plc, 17 334–36; 78 224–27 (upd.)

Mothers Against Drunk Driving (MADD), 51 255–58

Mothers Work, Inc., 18 350–52

The Motley Fool, Inc., 40 329–31

Moto Photo, Inc., 45 282–84

Motor Cargo Industries, Inc., 35 296–99

Motorcar Parts & Accessories, Inc., 47 253–55

Motorola, Inc., II 60–62; 11 326–29 (upd.); 34 296–302 (upd.); 93 313–23 (upd.)

Motown Records Company L.P., 26 312–14

Mott's Inc., 57 250–53

Moulinex S.A., 22 362–65 *see also* Groupe SEB.

Mount *see also* Mt.

Mount Washington Hotel *see* MWH Preservation Limited Partnership.

Mountain States Mortgage Centers, Inc., 29 335–37

Mouvement des Caisses Desjardins, 48 288–91

Movado Group, Inc., 28 291–94

Movie Gallery, Inc., 31 339–41

Movie Star Inc., 17 337–39

Moy Park Ltd., 78 228–31

MPI *see* Michael Page International plc.

MPRG *see* Matt Prentice Restaurant Group.

MPS Group, Inc., 49 264–67

MPW Industrial Services Group, Inc., 53 231–33

Mr. Bricolage S.A., 37 258–60

Mr. Coffee, Inc., 15 307–09

Mr. Gasket Inc., 15 310–12

Red Hat, Inc., 45 361–64
Red McCombs Automotive Group, 91 400–03
Red Robin Gourmet Burgers, Inc., 56 294–96
Red Roof Inns, Inc., 18 448–49 *see also* Accor S.A.
Red Spot Paint & Varnish Company, 55 319–22
Red Wing Pottery Sales, Inc., 52 294–96
Red Wing Shoe Company, Inc., 9 433–35; 30 372–75 (upd.); 83 315–321 (upd.)
Redback Networks, Inc., 92 319–22
Redcats S.A., 102 348–52
Reddy Ice Holdings, Inc., 80 304–07
Redhook Ale Brewery, Inc., 31 381–84; 88 317–21 (upd.)
Redken Laboratories Inc., 84 327–330
Redland plc, III 734–36 *see also* Lafarge Cement UK.
Redlon & Johnson, Inc., 97 331–34
RedPeg Marketing, 73 277–79
RedPrairie Corporation, 74 257–60
Redrow Group plc, 31 385–87
Reebok International Ltd., V 375–77; 9 436–38 (upd.); 26 396–400 (upd.)
Reed & Barton Corporation, 67 322–24
Reed Elsevier plc, 31 388–94 (upd.)
Reed International PLC, IV 665–67; 17 396–99 (upd.)
Reed's, Inc., 103 351–54
Reeds Jewelers, Inc., 22 447–49
Regal-Beloit Corporation, 18 450–53; 97 335–42 (upd.)
Regal Entertainment Group, 59 340–43
The Regence Group, 74 261–63
Regency Centers Corporation, 71 304–07
Regent Communications, Inc., 87 416–420
Regent Inns plc, 95 354–57
Régie Nationale des Usines Renault, I 189–91 *see also* Renault S.A.
Regis Corporation, 18 454–56; 70 261–65 (upd.)
REI *see* Recreational Equipment, Inc.
Reichhold Chemicals, Inc., 10 465–67
Reiter Dairy, LLC, 94 361–64
Rejuvenation, Inc., 91 404–07
Reliance Electric Company, 9 439–42
Reliance Group Holdings, Inc., III 342–44
Reliance Industries Ltd., 81 332–36
Reliance Steel & Aluminum Company, 19 343–45; 70 266–70 (upd.)
Reliant Energy Inc., 44 368–73 (upd.)
Reliv International, Inc., 58 292–95
Remedy Corporation, 58 296–99
RemedyTemp, Inc., 20 448–50
Remington Arms Company, Inc., 12 415–17; 40 368–71 (upd.)
Remington Products Company, L.L.C., 42 307–10
Remington Rand *see* Unisys Corp.
Rémy Cointreau Group, 20 451–53; 80 308–12 (upd.)

Renaissance Learning, Inc., 39 341–43; 100 367–72 (upd.)
Renal Care Group, Inc., 72 297–99
Renault Argentina S.A., 67 325–27
Renault S.A., 26 401–04 (upd.); 74 264–68 (upd.)
Renfro Corporation, 99 362–365
Rengo Co., Ltd., IV 326
Renishaw plc, 46 358–60
RENK AG, 37 325–28
Renner Herrmann S.A., 79 353–56
Reno Air Inc., 23 409–11
Reno de Medici S.p.A., 41 325–27
Rent-A-Center, Inc., 45 365–67
Rent-Way, Inc., 33 366–68; 75 336–39 (upd.)
Rental Service Corporation, 28 386–88
Rentokil Initial Plc, 47 332–35
Rentrak Corporation, 35 371–74
Repco Corporation Ltd., 74 269–72
REpower Systems AG, 101 424–27
Repsol-YPF S.A., IV 527–29; 16 423–26 (upd.); 40 372–76 (upd.)
Republic Engineered Steels, Inc., 7 446–47; 26 405–08 (upd.)
Republic Industries, Inc., 26 409–11 *see also* AutoNation, Inc.
Republic New York Corporation, 11 415–19 *see also* HSBC Holdings plc.
Republic Services, Inc., 92 323–26
Res-Care, Inc., 29 399–402
Research in Motion Ltd., 54 310–14
Research Triangle Institute, 83 322–325
Réseau Ferré de France, 66 266–68
Reser's Fine Foods, Inc., 81 337–40
Resorts International, Inc., 12 418–20
Resource America, Inc., 42 311–14
Resources Connection, Inc., 81 341–44
Response Oncology, Inc., 27 385–87
Restaurant Associates Corporation, 66 269–72
Restaurants Unlimited, Inc., 13 435–37
Restoration Hardware, Inc., 30 376–78; 96 347–51 (upd.)
Retail Ventures, Inc., 82 299–03 (upd.)
Retractable Technologies, Inc., 99 366–369
Reuters Group PLC, IV 668–70; 22 450–53 (upd.); 63 323–27 (upd.)
Revco D.S., Inc., V 171–73 *see also* CVS Corp.
Revell-Monogram Inc., 16 427–29
Revere Electric Supply Company, 96 352–55
Revere Ware Corporation, 22 454–56
Revlon Inc., III 54–57; 17 400–04 (upd.); 64 330–35 (upd.)
Rewards Network Inc., 70 271–75 (upd.)
REWE-Zentral AG, 103 355–59
REX Stores Corp., 10 468–69
Rexam PLC, 32 380–85 (upd.); 85 353–61 (upd.)
Rexel, Inc., 15 384–87
Rexnord Corporation, 21 429–32; 76 315–19 (upd.)
The Reynolds and Reynolds Company, 50 376–79

Reynolds Metals Company, IV 186–88; 19 346–48 (upd.) *see also* Alcoa Inc.
RF Micro Devices, Inc., 43 311–13
RFC Franchising LLC, 68 317–19
RFF *see* Réseau Ferré de France.
RGI *see* Rockefeller Group International.
Rheinmetall AG, 9 443–46; 97 343–49 (upd.)
RHI AG, 53 283–86
Rhino Entertainment Company, 18 457–60; 70 276–80 (upd.)
RHM *see* Ranks Hovis McDougall.
Rhodes Inc., 23 412–14
Rhodia SA, 38 378–80
Rhône-Poulenc S.A., I 388–90; 10 470–72 (upd.)
Rhythm & Hues Studios, Inc., 103 360–63
Rica Foods, Inc., 41 328–30
Ricardo plc, 90 352–56
Rich Products Corporation, 7 448–49; 38 381–84 (upd.); 93 368–74 (upd.)
The Richards Group, Inc., 58 300–02
Richardson Electronics, Ltd., 17 405–07
Richardson Industries, Inc., 62 298–301
Richfood Holdings, Inc., 7 450–51; *see also* Supervalu Inc.
Richton International Corporation, 39 344–46
Richtree Inc., 63 328–30
Richwood Building Products, Inc. *see* Ply Gem Industries Inc.
Rickenbacker International Corp., 91 408–12
Ricoh Company, Ltd., III 159–61; 36 389–93 (upd.)
Ricola Ltd., 62 302–04
Riddell Sports Inc., 22 457–59; 23 449
Ride, Inc., 22 460–63
Ridley Corporation Ltd., 62 305–07
Riedel Tiroler Glashuette GmbH, 99 370–373
The Riese Organization, 38 385–88
Rieter Holding AG, 42 315–17
Riggs National Corporation, 13 438–40
Right Management Consultants, Inc., 42 318–21
Riklis Family Corp., 9 447–50
Rimage Corp., 89 369–72
Rinascente S.p.A., 71 308–10
Rinker Group Ltd., 65 298–301
Rio Tinto plc, 19 349–53 (upd.) 50 380–85 (upd.)
Ripley Corp S.A., 102 353–56
Ripley Entertainment, Inc., 74 273–76
Riser Foods, Inc., 9 451–54 *see also* Giant Eagle, Inc.
Ritchie Bros. Auctioneers Inc., 41 331–34
Rite Aid Corporation, V 174–76; 19 354–57 (upd.); 63 331–37 (upd.)
Ritter Sport *see* Alfred Ritter GmbH & Co. KG.
Ritter's Frozen Custard *see* RFC Franchising LLC.
Ritz Camera Centers, 34 375–77

Smithfield Foods, Inc., 7 477–78; 43 381–84 (upd.)

SmithKline Beckman Corporation, I 692–94 *see also* GlaxoSmithKline plc.

SmithKline Beecham plc, III 65–67; 32 429–34 (upd.) *see also* GlaxoSmithKline plc.

Smith's Food & Drug Centers, Inc., 8 472–74; 57 324–27 (upd.)

Smiths Industries PLC, 25 429–31

Smithsonian Institution, 27 410–13

Smithway Motor Xpress Corporation, 39 376–79

Smoby International SA, 56 333–35

Smorgon Steel Group Ltd., 62 329–32

Smucker's *see* The J.M. Smucker Co.

Smurfit-Stone Container Corporation, 26 442–46 (upd.) ; 83 360–368 (upd.)

Snap-On, Incorporated, 7 479–80; 27 414–16 (upd.)

Snapfish, 83 369–372

Snapple Beverage Corporation, 11 449–51

SNC-Lavalin Group Inc., 72 330–33

SNCF *see* Société Nationale des Chemins de Fer Français.

SNEA *see* Société Nationale Elf Aquitaine.

Snecma Group, 46 369–72 *see also* SAFRAN.

Snell & Wilmer L.L.P., 28 425–28

SNET *see* Southern New England Telecommunications Corp.

Snow Brand Milk Products Company, Ltd., II 574–75; 48 362–65 (upd.)

Soap Opera Magazine see American Media, Inc.

Sobeys Inc., 80 348–51

Socata *see* EADS SOCATA.

Sociedad Química y Minera de Chile S.A.,103 382–85

Società Finanziaria Telefonica per Azioni, V 325–27

Società Sportiva Lazio SpA, 44 386–88

Société Air France, 27 417–20 (upd.).

Société BIC S.A., 73 312–15

Societe des Produits Marnier-Lapostolle S.A., 88 373–76

Société d'Exploitation AOM Air Liberté SA (AirLib), 53 305–07

Société du Figaro S.A., 60 281–84

Société du Louvre, 27 421–23

Société Générale, II 354–56; 42 347–51 (upd.)

Société Industrielle Lesaffre, 84 356–359

Société Luxembourgeoise de Navigation Aérienne S.A., 64 357–59

Société Nationale des Chemins de Fer Français, V 512–15; 57 328–32 (upd.)

Société Nationale Elf Aquitaine, IV 544–47; 7 481–85 (upd.)

Société Norbert Dentressangle S.A., 67 352–54

Société Tunisienne de l'Air-Tunisair, 49 371–73

Society Corporation, 9 474–77

Sodexho SA, 29 442–44; 91 433–36 (upd.)

Sodiaal S.A., 19 50; 36 437–39 (upd.)

SODIMA, II 576–77 *see also* Sodiaal S.A.

Soft Sheen Products, Inc., 31 416–18

Softbank Corporation, 13 481–83; 38 439–44 (upd.); 77 387–95 (upd.)

Sojitz Corporation, 96 395–403 (upd.)

Sol Meliá S.A., 71 337–39

Sola International Inc., 71 340–42

Solar Turbines Inc., 100 402–06

Sole Technology Inc., 93 405–09

Solectron Corporation, 12 450–52; 48 366–70 (upd.)

Solo Serve Corporation, 28 429–31

Solutia Inc., 52 312–15

Solvay & Cie S.A., I 394–96; 21 464–67 (upd.)

Solvay S.A., 61 329–34 (upd.)

Somerfield plc, 47 365–69 (upd.)

Sommer-Allibert S.A., 19 406–09 *see also* Tarkett Sommer AG.

Sompo Japan Insurance, Inc., 98 359–63 (upd.)

Sonae SGPS, S.A., 97 378–81

Sonat, Inc., 6 577–78 *see also* El Paso Corp.

Sonatrach, 65 313–17 (upd.)

Sonera Corporation, 50 441–44 *see also* TeliaSonera AB.

Sonesta International Hotels Corporation, 44 389–91

Sonic Automotive, Inc., 77 396–99

Sonic Corp., 14 451–53; 37 360–63 (upd.); 103 386–91 (upd.)

Sonic Innovations Inc., 56 336–38

Sonic Solutions, Inc., 81 375–79

SonicWALL, Inc., 87 421–424

Sonnenschein Nath and Rosenthal LLP, 102 384–87

Sonoco Products Company, 8 475–77; 89 415–22 (upd.)

SonoSite, Inc., 56 339–41

Sony Corporation, II 101–03; 12 453–56 (upd.); 40 404–10 (upd.)

Sophus Berendsen A/S, 49 374–77

Sorbee International Ltd., 74 309–11

Soriana *see* Organización Soriana, S.A. de C.V.

Soros Fund Management LLC, 28 432–34

Sorrento, Inc., 19 51; 24 444–46

SOS Staffing Services, 25 432–35

Sotheby's Holdings, Inc., 11 452–54; 29 445–48 (upd.); 84 360–365 (upd.)

Soufflet SA *see* Groupe Soufflet SA.

Sound Advice, Inc., 41 379–82

Souper Salad, Inc., 98 364–67

The Source Enterprises, Inc., 65 318–21

Source Interlink Companies, Inc., 75 350–53

The South African Breweries Limited, I 287–89; 24 447–51 (upd.) *see also* SABMiller plc.

South Beach Beverage Company, Inc., 73 316–19

South Dakota Wheat Growers Association, 94 397–401

South Jersey Industries, Inc., 42 352–55

Southam Inc., 7 486–89 *see also* CanWest Global Communications Corp.

Southcorp Limited, 54 341–44

Southdown, Inc., 14 454–56 *see also* CEMEX S.A. de C.V.

Southeast Frozen Foods Company, L.P., 99 423–426

The Southern Company, V 721–23; 38 445–49 (upd.)

Southern Connecticut Gas Company, 84 366–370

Southern Electric PLC, 13 484–86 *see also* Scottish and Southern Energy plc.

Southern Financial Bancorp, Inc., 56 342–44

Southern Indiana Gas and Electric Company, 13 487–89 *see also* Vectren Corp.

Southern New England Telecommunications Corporation, 6 338–40

Southern Pacific Transportation Company, V 516–18 *see also* Union Pacific Corp.

Southern Peru Copper Corporation, 40 411–13

Southern Poverty Law Center, Inc., 74 312–15

Southern Progress Corporation, 102 388–92

Southern States Cooperative Incorporated, 36 440–42

Southern Union Company, 27 424–26

Southern Wine and Spirits of America, Inc., 84 371–375

The Southland Corporation, II 660–61; 7 490–92 (upd.) *see also* 7–Eleven, Inc.

Southtrust Corporation, 11 455–57 *see also* Wachovia Corp.

Southwest Airlines Co., 6 119–21; 24 452–55 (upd.); 71 343–47 (upd.)

Southwest Gas Corporation, 19 410–12

Southwest Water Company, 47 370–73

Southwestern Bell Corporation, V 328–30 *see also* SBC Communications Inc.

Southwestern Electric Power Co., 21 468–70

Southwestern Public Service Company, 6 579–81

Southwire Company, Inc., 8 478–80; 23 444–47 (upd.)

Souza Cruz S.A., 65 322–24

Sovereign Bancorp, Inc., 103 392–95

Sovran Self Storage, Inc., 66 299–301

SP Alpargatas *see* Sao Paulo Alpargatas S.A.

Spacehab, Inc., 37 364–66

Spacelabs Medical, Inc., 71 348–50

Spaghetti Warehouse, Inc., 25 436–38

Spago *see* The Wolfgang Puck Food Company, Inc.

Spangler Candy Company, 44 392–95

Spanish Broadcasting System, Inc., 41 383–86

Spansion Inc., 80 352–55

Taittinger S.A., 43 401–05

Taiwan Semiconductor Manufacturing Company Ltd., 47 383–87

Taiwan Tobacco & Liquor Corporation, 75 361–63

Taiyo Fishery Company, Limited, II 578–79 *see also* Maruha Group Inc.

Taiyo Kobe Bank, Ltd., II 371–72

Takara Holdings Inc., 62 345–47

Takashimaya Company, Limited, V 193–96; 47 388–92 (upd.)

Take-Two Interactive Software, Inc., 46 389–91

Takeda Chemical Industries, Ltd., I 704–06; 46 392–95 (upd.)

The Talbots, Inc., 11 497–99; 31 429–32 (upd.); 88 393–98 (upd.)

Talisman Energy Inc., 9 490–93; 47 393–98 (upd.); 103 425–34 (upd.)

Talk America Holdings, Inc., 70 316–19

Talley Industries, Inc., 16 482–85

TALX Corporation, 92 361–64

TAM Linhas Aéreas S.A., 68 363–65

Tambrands Inc., 8 511–13 *see also* Procter & Gamble Co.

TAME (Transportes Aéreos Militares Ecuatorianos), 100 407–10

Tamedia AG, 53 323–26

Tamfelt Oyj Abp, 62 348–50

Tamron Company Ltd., 82 378–81

TAMSA *see* Tubos de Acero de Mexico, S.A.

Tandem Computers, Inc., 6 278–80 *see also* Hewlett-Packard Co.

Tandy Corporation, II 106–08; 12 468–70 (upd.) *see also* RadioShack Corp.

Tandycrafts, Inc., 31 433–37

Tanger Factory Outlet Centers, Inc., 49 386–89

Tanimura & Antle Fresh Foods, Inc., 98 379–83

Tanox, Inc., 77 429–32

TAP—Air Portugal Transportes Aéreos Portugueses S.A., 46 396–99 (upd.)

Tapemark Company Inc., 64 373–75

TAQA North Ltd., 95 403–06

Target Corporation, 10 515–17; 27 451–54 (upd.); 61 352–56 (upd.)

Targetti Sankey SpA, 86 385–88

Tarkett Sommer AG, 25 462–64

Tarmac Limited, III 751–54; 28 447–51 (upd.); 95 407–14 (upd.)

Taro Pharmaceutical Industries Ltd., 65 335–37

TAROM S.A., 64 376–78

Tarragon Realty Investors, Inc., 45 399–402

Tarrant Apparel Group, 62 351–53

Taschen GmbH, 101 –465–68

Taser International, Inc., 62 354–57

Tastefully Simple Inc., 100 411–14

Tasty Baking Company, 14 485–87; 35 412–16 (upd.)

Tata Iron & Steel Co. Ltd., IV 217–19; 44 411–15 (upd.)

Tata Tea Ltd., 76 339–41

Tate & Lyle PLC, II 580–83; 42 367–72 (upd.); 101 469–77 (upd.)

Tati SA, 25 465–67

Tatneft *see* OAO Tatneft.

Tattered Cover Book Store, 43 406–09

Tatung Co., 23 469–71

Taubman Centers, Inc., 75 364–66

TaurusHolding GmbH & Co. KG, 46 400–03

Taylor & Francis Group plc, 44 416–19

Taylor Corporation, 36 465–67

Taylor Devices, Inc., 97 403–06

Taylor Guitars, 48 386–89

Taylor Made Group Inc., 98 384–87

Taylor Nelson Sofres plc, 34 428–30

Taylor Publishing Company, 12 471–73; 36 468–71 (upd.)

Taylor Woodrow plc, I 590–91; 38 450–53 (upd.)

TaylorMade-adidas Golf, 23 472–74; 96 423–28 (upd.)

TB Wood's Corporation, 56 355–58

TBA Global, LLC, 99 435–438

TBS *see* Turner Broadcasting System, Inc.

TBWA/Chiat/Day, 6 47–49; 43 410–14 (upd.) *see also* Omnicom Group Inc.

TC Advertising *see* Treasure Chest Advertising, Inc.

TCBY Systems LLC, 17 474–76; 98 388–92 (upd.)

TCF Financial Corporation, 47 399–402; 103 435–41 (upd.)

Tchibo GmbH, 82 382–85

TCI *see* Tele-Communications, Inc.

TCO *see* Taubman Centers, Inc.

TD Bank *see* The Toronto-Dominion Bank.

TDC A/S, 63 371–74

TDK Corporation, II 109–11; 17 477–79 (upd.); 49 390–94 (upd.)

TDL Group Ltd., 46 404–06

TDS *see* Telephone and Data Systems, Inc.

TEAC Corporation, 78 377–80

Teachers Insurance and Annuity Association-College Retirement Equities Fund, III 379–82; 45 403–07 (upd.)

Teamsters Union *see* International Brotherhood of Teamsters.

TearDrop Golf Company, 32 445–48

Tech Data Corporation, 10 518–19; 74 335–38 (upd.)

Tech-Sym Corporation, 18 513–15; 44 420–23 (upd.)

TechBooks Inc., 84 390–393

TECHNE Corporation, 52 345–48

Technical Olympic USA, Inc., 75 367–69

Technip, 78 381–84

Technitrol, Inc., 29 459–62

Technology Research Corporation, 94 411–14

Technology Solutions Company, 94 415–19

TechTarget, Inc., 99 439–443

Techtronic Industries Company Ltd., 73 331–34

Teck Corporation, 27 455–58

TECO Energy, Inc., 6 582–84

Tecumseh Products Company, 8 514–16; 71 351–55 (upd.)

Ted Baker plc, 86 389–92

Tee Vee Toons, Inc., 57 357–60

Teekay Shipping Corporation, 25 468–71; 82 386–91 (upd.)

Teijin Limited, V 380–82; 61 357–61 (upd.)

Tejon Ranch Company, 35 417–20

Tekelec, 83 395–399

Teknor Apex Company, 97 407–10

Tektronix, Inc., 8 517–21; 78 385–91 (upd.)

Telcordia Technologies, Inc., 59 399–401

Tele-Communications, Inc., II 160–62

Tele Norte Leste Participações S.A., 80 369–72

Telecom Argentina S.A., 63 375–77

Telecom Australia, 6 341–42 *see also* Telstra Corp. Ltd.

Telecom Corporation of New Zealand Limited, 54 355–58

Telecom Eireann, 7 508–10 *see also* eircom plc.

Telecom Italia Mobile S.p.A., 63 378–80

Telecom Italia S.p.A., 43 415–19

Teledyne Technologies Inc., I 523–25; 10 520–22 (upd.); 62 358–62 (upd.)

Telefonaktiebolaget LM Ericsson, V 334–36; 46 407–11 (upd.)

Telefónica de Argentina S.A., 61 362–64

Telefónica de España, S.A., V 337–40

Telefónica S.A., 46 412–17 (upd.)

Telefonos de Mexico S.A. de C.V., 14 488–90; 63 381–84 (upd.)

Telegraaf Media Groep N.V., 98 393–97 (upd.)

Telekom Malaysia Bhd, 76 342–44

Telekomunikacja Polska SA, 50 464–68

Telenor ASA, 69 344–46

Telephone and Data Systems, Inc., 9 494–96

TelePizza S.A., 33 387–89

Television de Mexico, S.A. *see* Grupo Televisa, S.A.

Television Española, S.A., 7 511–12

Télévision Française 1, 23 475–77

TeliaSonera AB, 57 361–65 (upd.)

Tellabs, Inc., 11 500–01; 40 426–29 (upd.)

Telsmith Inc., 96 429–33

Telstra Corporation Limited, 50 469–72

Telxon Corporation, 10 523–25

Tembec, Inc., 66 322–24

Temple-Inland Inc., IV 341–43; 31 438–42 (upd.); 102 410–16 (upd.)

Tempur-Pedic Inc., 54 359–61

Ten Cate *see* Royal Ten Cate N.V.

Tenaris SA, 63 385–88

Tenedora Nemak, S.A. de C.V., 102 417–20

Tenet Healthcare Corporation, 55 368–71 (upd.)

TenFold Corporation, 35 421–23

Tengasco, Inc., 99 444–447

UAL Corporation, 34 462–65 (upd.)

UAP *see* Union des Assurances de Paris.

UAW (International Union, United Automobile, Aerospace and Agricultural Implement Workers of America), 72 354–57

Ube Industries, Ltd., III 759–61; 38 463–67 (upd.)

Ubi Soft Entertainment S.A., 41 407–09

UBS AG, 52 352–59 (upd.)

UCB Pharma SA, 98 409–12

UFA TV & Film Produktion GmbH, 80 382–87

UGI Corporation, 12 498–500

Ugine S.A., 20 498–500

Ugly Duckling Corporation, 22 524–27 *see also* DriveTime Automotive Group Inc.

UICI, 33 418–21 *see also* HealthMarkets, Inc.

Ukrop's Super Markets Inc., 39 402–04; 101 478–82 (upd.)

UL *see* Underwriters Laboratories, Inc.

Ulster Television PLC, 71 366–68

Ulta Salon, Cosmetics & Fragrance, Inc., 92 471–73

Ultimate Electronics, Inc., 18 532–34; 69 356–59 (upd.)

Ultimate Leisure Group PLC, 75 383–85

Ultra Pac, Inc., 24 512–14

Ultra Petroleum Corporation, 71 369–71

Ultrak Inc., 24 508–11

Ultralife Batteries, Inc., 58 345–48

Ultramar Diamond Shamrock Corporation, IV 565–68; 31 453–57 (upd.)

ULVAC, Inc., 80 388–91

Umbro plc, 88 414–17

Umpqua Holdings Corporation, 87 443–446

Uncle Ben's Inc., 22 528–30

Uncle Ray's LLC, 90 417–19

Under Armour Performance Apparel, 61 381–83

Underberg AG, 92 388–393

Underwriters Laboratories, Inc., 30 467–70

UNG *see* United National Group, Ltd.

Uni-Marts, Inc., 17 499–502

Unibail SA, 40 444–46

Unibanco Holdings S.A., 73 350–53

Unica Corporation, 77 450–54

UNICEF *see* United Nations International Children's Emergency Fund (UNICEF).

Unicharm Corporation, 84 414–417

Unicom Corporation, 29 486–90 (upd.) *see also* Exelon Corp.

Uniden Corporation, 98 413–16

Unifi, Inc., 12 501–03; 62 372–76 (upd.)

Unified Grocers, Inc., 93 474–77

UniFirst Corporation, 21 505–07

Unigate PLC, II 586–87; 28 488–91 (upd.) *see also* Uniq Plc.

Unilever, II 588–91; 7 542–45 (upd.); 32 472–78 (upd.); 89 464–74 (upd.)

Unilog SA, 42 401–03

Union Bank of California, 16 496–98 *see also* UnionBanCal Corp.

Union Bank of Switzerland, II 378–79 *see also* UBS AG.

Union Camp Corporation, IV 344–46

Union Carbide Corporation, I 399–401; 9 516–20 (upd.); 74 358–63 (upd.)

Unión de Cervecerias Peruanas Backus y Johnston S.A.A., 92 394–397

Union des Assurances de Paris, III 391–94

Union Electric Company, V 741–43 *see also* Ameren Corp.

Unión Fenosa, S.A., 51 387–90

Union Financière de France Banque SA, 52 360–62

Union Pacific Corporation, V 529–32; 28 492–500 (upd.); 79 435–46 (upd.)

Union Planters Corporation, 54 387–90

Union Texas Petroleum Holdings, Inc., 9 521–23

UnionBanCal Corporation, 50 496–99 (upd.)

Uniq plc, 83 428–433 (upd.)

Unique Casual Restaurants, Inc., 27 480–82

Unison HealthCare Corporation, 25 503–05

Unisys Corporation, III 165–67; 6 281–83 (upd.); 36 479–84 (upd.)

Unit Corporation, 63 407–09

United Airlines, I 128–30; 6 128–30 (upd.) *see also* UAL Corp.

United Auto Group, Inc., 26 500–02; 68 381–84 (upd.)

United Biscuits (Holdings) plc, II 592–94; 42 404–09 (upd.)

United Brands Company, II 595–97

United Business Media plc, 52 363–68 (upd.)

United Community Banks, Inc., 98 417–20

United Dairy Farmers, Inc., 74 364–66

United Defense Industries, Inc., 30 471–73; 66 346–49 (upd.)

United Dominion Industries Limited, 8 544–46; 16 499–502 (upd.)

United Dominion Realty Trust, Inc., 52 369–71

United Farm Workers of America, 88 418–22

United Foods, Inc., 21 508–11

United HealthCare Corporation, 9 524–26 *see also* Humana Inc.

The United Illuminating Company, 21 512–14

United Industrial Corporation, 37 399–402

United Industries Corporation, 68 385–87

United Internet AG, 99 466–469

United Jewish Communities, 33 422–25

United Merchants & Manufacturers, Inc., 13 534–37

United Microelectronics Corporation, 98 421–24

United National Group, Ltd., 63 410–13

United Nations International Children's Emergency Fund (UNICEF), 58 349–52

United Natural Foods, Inc., 32 479–82; 76 360–63 (upd.)

United Negro College Fund, Inc., 79 447–50

United News & Media plc, 28 501–05 (upd.) *see also* United Business Media plc.

United Newspapers plc, IV 685–87 *see also* United Business Media plc.

United Online, Inc., 71 372–77 (upd.)

United Overseas Bank Ltd., 56 362–64

United Pan-Europe Communications NV, 47 414–17

United Paper Mills Ltd., IV 347–50 *see also* UPM-Kymmene Corp.

United Parcel Service, Inc., V 533–35; 17 503–06 (upd.); 63 414–19; 94 425–30 (upd.)

United Press International, Inc., 25 506–09; 73 354–57 (upd.)

United Rentals, Inc., 34 466–69

United Retail Group Inc., 33 426–28

United Road Services, Inc., 69 360–62

United Service Organizations, 60 308–11

United States Cellular Corporation, 9 527–29 *see also* U.S. Cellular Corp.

United States Filter Corporation, 20 501–04 *see also* Siemens AG.

United States Health Care Systems, Inc. *see* U.S. Healthcare, Inc.

United States Pipe and Foundry Company, 62 377–80

United States Playing Card Company, 62 381–84

United States Postal Service, 14 517–20; 34 470–75 (upd.)

United States Shoe Corporation, V 207–08

United States Steel Corporation, 50 500–04 (upd.)

United States Surgical Corporation, 10 533–35; 34 476–80 (upd.)

United Stationers Inc., 14 521–23

United Talent Agency, Inc., 80 392–96

United Technologies Automotive Inc., 15 513–15

United Technologies Corporation, I 84–86; 10 536–38 (upd.); 34 481–85 (upd.)

United Telecommunications, Inc., V 344–47 *see also* Sprint Corp.

United Utilities PLC, 52 372–75 (upd.)

United Video Satellite Group, 18 535–37 *see also* TV Guide, Inc.

United Water Resources, Inc., 40 447–50; 45 277

United Way of America, 36 485–88

UnitedHealth Group Incorporated, 103 476–84 (upd.)

Index to Industries

Norrell Corporation, 25
Norwood Promotional Products, Inc., 26
The NPD Group, Inc., 68
O.C. Tanner Co., 69
Oakleaf Waste Management, LLC, 97
Obie Media Corporation, 56
Observer AB, 55
OfficeTiger, LLC, 75
The Ogilvy Group, Inc., I
Olsten Corporation, 6; 29 (upd.)
Omnicom Group, I; 22 (upd.); 77 (upd.)
On Assignment, Inc., 20
1-800-FLOWERS.COM, Inc., 26; 102
  (upd.)
Opinion Research Corporation, 46
Oracle Corporation, 67 (upd.)
Orbitz, Inc., 61
The Orchard Enterprises, Inc., 103
Outdoor Systems, Inc., 25
Paris Corporation, 22
Paychex, Inc., 15; 46 (upd.)
PDI, Inc., 52
Pegasus Solutions, Inc., 75
Pei Cobb Freed & Partners Architects
  LLP, 57
Penauille Polyservices SA, 49
PFSweb, Inc., 73
Philip Services Corp., 73
Phillips, de Pury & Luxembourg, 49
Pierce Leahy Corporation, 24
Pinkerton's Inc., 9
Plante & Moran, LLP, 71
PMT Services, Inc., 24
Posterscope Worldwide, 70
Priceline.com Incorporated, 57
Publicis Groupe, 19; 77 (upd.)
Publishers Clearing House, 23; 64 (upd.)
Quintiles Transnational Corporation, 68
  (upd.)
Quovadx Inc., 70
@radical.media, 103
Randstad Holding n.v., 16; 43 (upd.)
RedPeg Marketing, 73
RedPrairie Corporation, 74
RemedyTemp, Inc., 20
Rental Service Corporation, 28
Rentokil Initial Plc, 47
Research Triangle Institute, 83
Resources Connection, Inc., 81
Rewards Network Inc., 70 (upd.)
The Richards Group, Inc., 58
Right Management Consultants, Inc., 42
Ritchie Bros. Auctioneers Inc., 41
Robert Half International Inc., 18
Roland Berger & Partner GmbH, 37
Ronco Corporation, 15; 80 (upd.)
Russell Reynolds Associates Inc., 38
Saatchi & Saatchi, I; 42 (upd.)
Sanders\Wingo, 99
Schenck Business Solutions, 88
Securitas AB, 42
ServiceMaster Limited Partnership, 6
Servpro Industries, Inc., 85
Shared Medical Systems Corporation, 14
Sir Speedy, Inc., 16
Skidmore, Owings & Merrill LLP, 13; 69
  (upd.)
SmartForce PLC, 43

SOS Staffing Services, 25
Sotheby's Holdings, Inc., 11; 29 (upd.);
  84 (upd.)
Source Interlink Companies, Inc., 75
Spencer Stuart and Associates, Inc., 14
Spherion Corporation, 52
SSI (U.S.) Inc., 103 (upd.)
Steiner Corporation (Alsco), 53
Strayer Education, Inc., 53
Superior Uniform Group, Inc., 30
Sykes Enterprises, Inc., 45
Sylvan Learning Systems, Inc., 35
Synchronoss Technologies, Inc., 95
TA Triumph-Adler AG, 48
Taylor Nelson Sofres plc, 34
TBA Global, LLC, 99
TBWA/Chiat/Day, 6; 43 (upd.)
Thomas Cook Travel Inc., 33 (upd.)
Ticketmaster, 76 (upd.)
Ticketmaster Group, Inc., 13; 37 (upd.)
TMP Worldwide Inc., 30
TNT Post Group N.V., 30
Towers Perrin, 32
Trader Classified Media N.V., 57
Traffix, Inc., 61
Transmedia Network Inc., 20
Treasure Chest Advertising Company, Inc.,
  32
TRM Copy Centers Corporation, 18
True North Communications Inc., 23
24/7 Real Media, Inc., 49
Tyler Corporation, 23
U.S. Office Products Company, 25
Unica Corporation, 77
UniFirst Corporation, 21
United Business Media plc, 52 (upd.)
United News & Media plc, 28 (upd.)
Unitog Co., 19
Valassis Communications, Inc., 37 (upd.);
  76 (upd.)
ValleyCrest Companies, 81 (upd.)
ValueClick, Inc., 49
Vebego International BV, 49
Vedior NV, 35
Vertis Communications, 84
Vertrue Inc., 77
Viad Corp., 73
W.B Doner & Co., 56
The Wackenhut Corporation, 14; 63
  (upd.)
Waggener Edstrom, 42
Warrantech Corporation, 53
WebEx Communications, Inc., 81
Welcome Wagon International Inc., 82
Wells Rich Greene BDDP, 6
Westaff Inc., 33
Whitman Education Group, Inc., 41
Wieden + Kennedy, 75
William Morris Agency, Inc., 23; 102
  (upd.)
Williams Scotsman, Inc., 65
Workflow Management, Inc., 65
WPP Group plc, 6; 48 (upd.)
Wunderman, 86
Xerox Corporation, III; 6 (upd.); 26
  (upd.); 69 (upd.)
Young & Rubicam, Inc., I; 22 (upd.); 66
  (upd.)

Ziment Group Inc., 102
Zogby International, Inc., 99

Aerospace

A.S. Yakovlev Design Bureau, 15
Aerojet-General Corp., 63
Aeronca Inc., 46
Aerosonic Corporation, 69
The Aerospatiale Group, 7; 21 (upd.)
AeroVironment, Inc., 97
AgustaWestland N.V., 75
Airborne Systems Group, 89
Alliant Techsystems Inc., 30 (upd.)
Antonov Design Bureau, 53
Arianespace S.A., 89
Aviacionny Nauchno-Tehnicheskii
  Komplex im. A.N. Tupoleva, 24
Aviall, Inc., 73
Avions Marcel Dassault-Breguet Aviation,
  I
B/E Aerospace, Inc., 30
Ballistic Recovery Systems, Inc., 87
Banner Aerospace, Inc., 14
BBA Aviation plc, 90
Beech Aircraft Corporation, 8
Bell Helicopter Textron Inc., 46
The Boeing Company, I; 10 (upd.); 32
  (upd.)
Bombardier Inc., 42 (upd.); 87 (upd.)
British Aerospace plc, I; 24 (upd.)
CAE USA Inc., 48
Canadair, Inc., 16
Cessna Aircraft Company, 8
Cirrus Design Corporation, 44
Cobham plc, 30
CPI Aerostructures, Inc., 75
Daimler-Benz Aerospace AG, 16
DeCrane Aircraft Holdings Inc., 36
Derco Holding Ltd., 98
Diehl Stiftung & Co. KG, 79
Ducommun Incorporated, 30
Duncan Aviation, Inc., 94
EADS SOCATA, 54
Eclipse Aviation Corporation, 87
EGL, Inc., 59
Empresa Brasileira de Aeronáutica S.A.
  (Embraer), 36
European Aeronautic Defence and Space
  Company EADS N.V., 52 (upd.)
Fairchild Aircraft, Inc., 9
Fairchild Dornier GmbH, 48 (upd.)
Finmeccanica S.p.A., 84
First Aviation Services Inc., 49
G.I.E. Airbus Industrie, I; 12 (upd.)
General Dynamics Corporation, I; 10
  (upd.); 40 (upd.); 88 (upd.
GKN plc, III; 38 (upd.); 89 (upd.)
Goodrich Corporation, 46 (upd.)
Groupe Dassault Aviation SA, 26 (upd.)
Grumman Corporation, I; 11 (upd.)
Grupo Aeropuerto del Sureste, S.A. de
  C.V., 48
Gulfstream Aerospace Corporation, 7; 28
  (upd.)
HEICO Corporation, 30
International Lease Finance Corporation,
  48
Irkut Corporation, 68

Conglomerates

Sojitz Corporation, 96 (upd.)
Sonae SGPS, S.A., 97
Standex International Corporation, 17; 44 (upd.)
Steamships Trading Company Ltd., 82
Stinnes AG, 23 (upd.)
Sudbury Inc., 16
Sumitomo Corporation, I; 11 (upd.); 102 (upd.)
Swire Pacific Limited, I; 16 (upd.); 57 (upd.)
Talley Industries, Inc., 16
Tandycrafts, Inc., 31
TaurusHolding GmbH & Co. KG, 46
Teijin Limited, 61 (upd.)
Teledyne, Inc., I; 10 (upd.)
Tenneco Inc., I; 10 (upd.)
Textron Inc., I; 34 (upd.); 88 (upd.)
Thomas H. Lee Co., 24
Thorn Emi PLC, I
Thorn plc, 24
TI Group plc, 17
Time Warner Inc., IV; 7 (upd.)
Tokyu Corporation, 47 (upd.)
Tomen Corporation, 24 (upd.)
Tomkins plc, 11; 44 (upd.)
Toshiba Corporation, I; 12 (upd.); 40 (upd.); 99 (upd.)
Tractebel S.A., 20
Transamerica–An AEGON Company, I; 13 (upd.); 41 (upd.)
The Tranzonic Cos., 15
Triarc Companies, Inc., 8
Triple Five Group Ltd., 49
TRW Inc., I; 11 (upd.)
Tyco International Ltd., 63 (upd.)
Unilever, II; 7 (upd.); 32 (upd.); 89 (upd.)
Unión Fenosa, S.A., 51
United Technologies Corporation, 34 (upd.)
Universal Studios, Inc., 33; 100 (upd.)
Valhi, Inc., 19
Valorem S.A., 88
Valores Industriales S.A., 19
Veba A.G., I; 15 (upd.)
Vendôme Luxury Group plc, 27
Viacom Inc., 23 (upd.); 67 (upd.)
Virgin Group Ltd., 12; 32 (upd.); 89 (upd.)
Vivartia S.A., 82
Votorantim Participaçoes S.A., 76
W.R. Grace & Company, I; 50
Walter Industries, Inc., 72 (upd.)
The Washington Companies, 33
Watsco Inc., 52
Wheaton Industries, 8
Whitbread PLC, I; 20 (upd.); 52 (upd.); 97 (upd.)
Whitman Corporation, 10 (upd.)
Whittaker Corporation, I
Wilh. Werhahn KG, 101
Wirtz Corporation, 72
WorldCorp, Inc., 10
Worms et Cie, 27
Yamaha Corporation, III; 16 (upd.); 40 (upd.); 99 (upd.)

Construction

A. Johnson & Company H.B., I
ABC Supply Co., Inc., 22
Abertis Infraestructuras, S.A., 65
Abrams Industries Inc., 23
Acergy SA, 97
Aegek S.A., 64
Alberici Corporation, 76
Amec Spie S.A., 57
AMREP Corporation, 21
Anthony & Sylvan Pools Corporation, 56
Asplundh Tree Expert Co., 59 (upd.)
Astec Industries, Inc., 79
ASV, Inc., 34; 66 (upd.)
The Auchter Company, 78
The Austin Company, 8
Autoroutes du Sud de la France SA, 55
Autostrada Torino-Milano S.p.A., 101
Balfour Beatty plc, 36 (upd.)
Baratt Developments PLC, I
Barton Malow Company, 51
Bauerly Companies, 61
BE&K, Inc., 73
Beazer Homes USA, Inc., 17
Bechtel Corporation, I; 24 (upd.); 99 (upd.)
Bellway Plc, 45
BFC Construction Corporation, 25
Bilfinger & Berger AG, I; 55 (upd.)
Bird Corporation, 19
Birse Group PLC, 77
Black & Veatch LLP, 22
Boral Limited, III; 43 (upd.); 103 (upd.)
Bouygues S.A., I; 24 (upd.); 97 (upd.)
The Branch Group, Inc., 72
Brasfield & Gorrie LLC, 87
BRISA Auto-estradas de Portugal S.A., 64
Brown & Root, Inc., 13
Bufete Industrial, S.A. de C.V., 34
Building Materials Holding Corporation, 52
Bulley & Andrews, LLC, 55
C.R. Meyer and Sons Company, 74
CalMat Co., 19
Cavco Industries, Inc., 65
Centex Corporation, 8; 29 (upd.)
Chugach Alaska Corporation, 60
Cianbro Corporation, 14
The Clark Construction Group, Inc., 8
Colas S.A., 31
Comfort Systems USA, Inc., 101
Consorcio ARA, S.A. de C.V., 79
Corporación Geo, S.A. de C.V., 81
D.R. Horton, Inc., 58
Day & Zimmermann, Inc., 31 (upd.)
Desarrolladora Homex, S.A. de C.V., 87
Dick Corporation, 64
Dillingham Construction Corporation, I; 44 (upd.)
Dominion Homes, Inc., 19
The Drees Company, Inc., 41
Dycom Industries, Inc., 57
E.W. Howell Co., Inc., 72
Edw. C. Levy Co., 42
Eiffage, 27
Ellerbe Becket, 41
EMCOR Group Inc., 60

Empresas ICA Sociedad Controladora, S.A. de C.V., 41
Encompass Services Corporation, 33
Engle Homes, Inc., 46
Environmental Industries, Inc., 31
Eurotunnel PLC, 13
Fairclough Construction Group PLC, I
Flatiron Construction Corporation, 92
Fleetwood Enterprises, Inc., III: 22 (upd.); 81 (upd.)
Fluor Corporation, I; 8 (upd.); 34 (upd.)
Forest City Enterprises, Inc., 52 (upd.)
Fred Weber, Inc., 61
Furmanite Corporation, 92
George Wimpey plc, 12; 51 (upd.)
Gilbane, Inc., 34
Granite Construction Incorporated, 61
Granite Rock Company, 26
Great Lakes Dredge & Dock Company, 69
Grupo Dragados SA, 55
Grupo Ferrovial, S.A., 40
H.J. Russell & Company, 66
Habitat for Humanity International, 36
Heery International, Inc., 58
Heijmans N.V., 66
Henry Boot plc, 76
Hensel Phelps Construction Company, 72
Hillsdown Holdings plc, 24 (upd.)
Hochtief AG, 33; 88 (upd.)
Hoffman Corporation 78
Horton Homes, Inc., 25
Hospitality Worldwide Services, Inc., 26
Hovnanian Enterprises, Inc., 29; 89 (upd.)
IHC Caland N.V., 71
Irex Contracting Group, 90
J.A. Jones, Inc., 16
J C Bamford Excavators Ltd., 83
J.F. Shea Co., Inc., 55
J.H. Findorff and Son, Inc., 60
Jaiprakash Associates Limited, 101
Jarvis plc, 39
JE Dunn Construction Group, Inc., 85
JLG Industries, Inc., 52
John Brown PLC, I
John Laing plc, I; 51 (upd.)
John W. Danforth Company, 48
Kajima Corporation, I; 51 (upd.)
Kaufman and Broad Home Corporation, 8
KB Home, 45 (upd.)
Kellogg Brown & Root, Inc., 62 (upd.)
Kitchell Corporation, 14
The Koll Company, 8
Komatsu Ltd., 16 (upd.)
Kraus-Anderson Companies, Inc., 36; 83 (upd.)
Kumagai Gumi Company, Ltd., I
L'Entreprise Jean Lefebvre, 23
Laing O'Rourke PLC, 93 (upd.)
Ledcor Industries Limited, 46
Lennar Corporation, 11
Lincoln Property Company, 8
Lindal Cedar Homes, Inc., 29
Linde A.G., I
MasTec, Inc., 55
Matrix Service Company, 65
May Gurney Integrated Services PLC, 95

Containers

Drugs & Pharmaceuticals

Fisons plc, 9; 23 (upd.)
Forest Laboratories, Inc., 52 (upd.)
FoxMeyer Health Corporation, 16
Fujisawa Pharmaceutical Company Ltd., I
G.D. Searle & Co., I; 12 (upd.); 34
   (upd.)
Galenica AG, 84
GEHE AG, 27
Genentech, Inc., I; 8 (upd.); 75 (upd.)
Genetics Institute, Inc., 8
Genzyme Corporation, 13, 77 (upd.)
Glaxo Holdings PLC, I; 9 (upd.)
GlaxoSmithKline plc, 46 (upd.)
Groupe Fournier SA, 44
Groupe Léa Nature, 88
H. Lundbeck A/S, 44
Hauser, Inc., 46
Heska Corporation, 39
Hexal AG, 69
Hikma Pharmaceuticals Ltd., 102
Hospira, Inc., 71
Huntingdon Life Sciences Group plc, 42
ICN Pharmaceuticals, Inc., 52
Immucor, Inc., 81
Integrated BioPharma, Inc., 83
IVAX Corporation, 55 (upd.)
Janssen Pharmaceutica N.V., 80
Johnson & Johnson, III; 8 (upd.)
Jones Medical Industries, Inc., 24
The Judge Group, Inc., 51
King Pharmaceuticals, Inc., 54
Kinray Inc., 85
Kos Pharmaceuticals, Inc., 63
Kyowa Hakko Kogyo Co., Ltd., 48 (upd.)
Laboratoires Arkopharma S.A., 75
Laboratoires Pierre Fabre S.A., 100
Leiner Health Products Inc., 34
Ligand Pharmaceuticals Incorporated, 47
MannKind Corporation, 87
Marion Merrell Dow, Inc., I; 9 (upd.)
Matrixx Initiatives, Inc., 74
McKesson Corporation, 12; 47 (upd.)
Medicis Pharmaceutical Corporation, 59
MedImmune, Inc., 35
Merck & Co., Inc., I; 11 (upd.); 34
   (upd.); 95 (upd.)
Merial Ltd., 102
Merz Group, 81
Miles Laboratories, I
Millennium Pharmaceuticals, Inc., 47
Monsanto Company, 29 (upd.), 77 (upd.)
Moore Medical Corp., 17
Murdock Madaus Schwabe, 26
Mylan Laboratories Inc., I; 20 (upd.); 59
   (upd.)
Myriad Genetics, Inc., 95
Nadro S.A. de C.V., 86
Nastech Pharmaceutical Company Inc., 79
National Patent Development
   Corporation, 13
Natrol, Inc., 49
Natural Alternatives International, Inc., 49
Nektar Therapeutics, 91
Novartis AG, 39 (upd.)
Noven Pharmaceuticals, Inc., 55
Novo Nordisk A/S, I; 61 (upd.)
Obagi Medical Products, Inc., 95
Omnicare, Inc., 49

Omrix Biopharmaceuticals, Inc., 95
Par Pharmaceutical Companies, Inc., 65
PDL BioPharma, Inc., 90
Perrigo Company, 59 (upd.)
Pfizer Inc., I; 9 (upd.); 38 (upd.); 79
   (upd.)
Pharmacia & Upjohn Inc., I; 25 (upd.)
Pharmion Corporation, 91
PLIVA d.d., 70
PolyMedica Corporation, 77
POZEN Inc., 81
QLT Inc., 71
The Quigley Corporation, 62
Quintiles Transnational Corporation, 21
R.P. Scherer, I
Ranbaxy Laboratories Ltd., 70
ratiopharm Group, 84
Reckitt Benckiser plc, II; 42 (upd.); 91
   (upd.)
Roberts Pharmaceutical Corporation, 16
Roche Bioscience, 14 (upd.)
Rorer Group, I
Roussel Uclaf, I; 8 (upd.)
Salix Pharmaceuticals, Ltd., 93
Sandoz Ltd., I
Sankyo Company, Ltd., I; 56 (upd.)
The Sanofi-Synthélabo Group, I; 49
   (upd.)
Schering AG, I; 50 (upd.)
Schering-Plough Corporation, I; 14
   (upd.); 49 (upd.); 99 (upd.)
Sepracor Inc., 45
Serono S.A., 47
Shionogi & Co., Ltd., III; 17 (upd.); 98
   (upd.)
Sigma-Aldrich Corporation, I; 36 (upd.);
   93 (upd.)
SmithKline Beecham plc, I; 32 (upd.)
Solvay S.A., 61 (upd.)
Squibb Corporation, I
Sterling Drug, Inc., I
Stiefel Laboratories, Inc., 90
Sun Pharmaceutical Industries Ltd., 57
The Sunrider Corporation, 26
Syntex Corporation, I
Takeda Chemical Industries, Ltd., I
Taro Pharmaceutical Industries Ltd., 65
Teva Pharmaceutical Industries Ltd., 22;
   54 (upd.)
UCB Pharma SA, 98
The Upjohn Company, I; 8 (upd.)
Vertex Pharmaceuticals Incorporated, 83
Virbac Corporation, 74
Vitalink Pharmacy Services, Inc., 15
Warner Chilcott Limited, 85
Warner-Lambert Co., I; 10 (upd.)
Watson Pharmaceuticals Inc., 16; 56
   (upd.)
The Wellcome Foundation Ltd., I
WonderWorks, Inc., 103
Zentiva N.V./Zentiva, a.s., 99
Zila, Inc., 46

Electrical & Electronics

ABB ASEA Brown Boveri Ltd., II; 22
   (upd.)
ABB Ltd., 65 (upd.)
Acer Incorporated, 16; 73 (upd.)

Acuson Corporation, 10; 36 (upd.)
ADC Telecommunications, Inc., 30 (upd.)
Adtran Inc., 22
Advanced Micro Devices, Inc., 6; 30
   (upd.); 99 (upd.)
Advanced Technology Laboratories, Inc., 9
Agere Systems Inc., 61
Agilent Technologies Inc., 38; 93 (upd.)
Agilysys Inc., 76 (upd.)
Aiwa Co., Ltd., 30
AKG Acoustics GmbH, 62
Akzo Nobel N.V., 13; 41 (upd.)
Alienware Corporation, 81
Alliant Techsystems Inc., 30 (upd.); 77
   (upd.)
AlliedSignal Inc., 22 (upd.)
Alpine Electronics, Inc., 13
Alps Electric Co., Ltd., II
Altera Corporation, 18; 43 (upd.)
Altron Incorporated, 20
Amdahl Corporation, 40 (upd.)
American Power Conversion Corporation,
   24; 67 (upd.)
American Superconductor Corporation,
   97
American Technical Ceramics Corp., 67
American Technology Corporation, 103
Amerigon Incorporated, 97
Amkor Technology, Inc., 69
AMP Incorporated, II; 14 (upd.)
Amphenol Corporation, 40
Amstrad plc, 48 (upd.)
Analog Devices, Inc., 10
Analogic Corporation, 23
Anam Group, 23
Anaren Microwave, Inc., 33
Andrew Corporation, 10; 32 (upd.)
Anixter International Inc., 88
Anritsu Corporation, 68
Apex Digital, Inc., 63
Apple Computer, Inc., 36 (upd.); 77
   (upd.)
Applied Power Inc., 32 (upd.)
Applied Signal Technology, Inc., 87
Argon ST, Inc., 81
Arotech Corporation, 93
ARRIS Group, Inc., 89
Arrow Electronics, Inc., 10; 50 (upd.)
Ascend Communications, Inc., 24
Astronics Corporation, 35
Atari Corporation, 9; 23 (upd.); 66 (upd.)
ATI Technologies Inc., 79
Atmel Corporation, 17
ATMI, Inc., 93
AU Optronics Corporation, 67
Audiovox Corporation, 34; 90 (upd.)
Ault Incorporated, 34
Autodesk, Inc., 10; 89 (upd.)
Avnet Inc., 9
AVX Corporation, 67
Axcelis Technologies, Inc., 95
Axsys Technologies, Inc., 93
Ballard Power Systems Inc., 73
Bang & Olufsen Holding A/S, 37; 86
   (upd.)
Barco NV, 44
Bell Microproducts Inc., 69
Benchmark Electronics, Inc., 40

Engineering & Management Services

Entertainment & Leisure

Financial Services: Banks

Financial Services: Excluding Banks

Stephens Inc., 92
Student Loan Marketing Association, II
Sun Life Financial Inc., 85
T. Rowe Price Associates, Inc., 11; 34
   (upd.)
Teachers Insurance and Annuity
   Association-College Retirement Equities
   Fund, 45 (upd.)
Texas Pacific Group Inc., 36
3i Group PLC, 73
Total System Services, Inc., 18
TradeStation Group, Inc., 83
Trilon Financial Corporation, II
United Jewish Communities, 33
The Vanguard Group, Inc., 14; 34 (upd.)
VeriFone Holdings, Inc., 18; 76 (upd.)
Viel & Cie, 76
Visa International, 9; 26 (upd.)
Wachovia Corporation, 12; 46 (upd.)
Waddell & Reed, Inc., 22
Washington Federal, Inc., 17
Waterhouse Investor Services, Inc., 18
Watson Wyatt Worldwide, 42
Western Union Financial Services, Inc., 54
WFS Financial Inc., 70
Working Assets Funding Service, 43
World Acceptance Corporation, 57
Yamaichi Securities Company, Limited, II
The Ziegler Companies, Inc., 24; 63
   (upd.)
Zurich Financial Services, 42 (upd.); 93
   (upd.)

Food Products

A. Duda & Sons, Inc., 88
A. Moksel AG, 59
Adecoagro LLC, 101
Agri Beef Company, 81
Agway, Inc., 7
Ajinomoto Co., Inc., II; 28 (upd.)
Alabama Farmers Cooperative, Inc., 63
The Albert Fisher Group plc, 41
Alberto-Culver Company, 8; 36 (upd.); 91
   (upd.)
Alfred Ritter GmbH & Co. KG, 58
Alfesca hf, 82
Allen Brothers, Inc., 101
Allen Canning Company, 76
Alpine Confections, Inc., 71
Alpine Lace Brands, Inc., 18
American Crystal Sugar Company, 11; 32
   (upd.)
American Foods Group, 43
American Italian Pasta Company, 27; 76
   (upd.)
American Licorice Company, 86
American Maize-Products Co., 14
American Pop Corn Company, 59
American Rice, Inc., 33
Amfac/JMB Hawaii L.L.C., 24 (upd.)
Amy's Kitchen Inc., 76
Annie's Homegrown, Inc., 59
Archer-Daniels-Midland Company, 32
   (upd.)
Archway Cookies, Inc., 29
Arcor S.A.I.C., 66
Arla Foods amba, 48
Arnott's Ltd., 66

Artisan Confections Company, 103
Asher's Chocolates, Inc., 103
Associated British Foods plc, II; 13 (upd.);
   41 (upd.)
Associated Milk Producers, Inc., 11; 48
   (upd.)
Atkinson Candy Company, 87
Atlantic Premium Brands, Ltd., 57
August Storck KG, 66
Aurora Foods Inc., 32
Auvil Fruit Company, Inc., 95
Awrey Bakeries, Inc., 56
B&G Foods, Inc., 40
The B. Manischewitz Company, LLC, 31
Bahlsen GmbH & Co. KG, 44
Bakkavör Group hf., 91
Balance Bar Company, 32
Baldwin Richardson Foods Company, 100
Baltek Corporation, 34
The Bama Companies, Inc., 80
Bar-S Foods Company, 76
Barbara's Bakery Inc., 88
Barilla G. e R. Fratelli S.p.A., 17; 50
   (upd.)
Barry Callebaut AG, 71 (upd.)
Baxters Food Group Ltd., 99
Bear Creek Corporation, 38
Beatrice Company, II
Beech-Nut Nutrition Corporation, 21; 51
   (upd.)
Beer Nuts, Inc., 86
Bel/Kaukauna USA, 76
Bellisio Foods, Inc., 95
Ben & Jerry's Homemade, Inc., 10; 35
   (upd.); 80 (upd.)
Berkeley Farms, Inc., 46
Bernard Matthews Ltd., 89
Besnier SA, 19
Best Kosher Foods Corporation, 82
Bestfoods, 22 (upd.)
Better Made Snack Foods, Inc., 90
Bettys & Taylors of Harrogate Ltd., 72
Birds Eye Foods, Inc., 69 (upd.)
Blue Bell Creameries L.P., 30
Blue Diamond Growers, 28
Bob's Red Mill Natural Foods, Inc., 63
Bobs Candies, Inc., 70
Bolton Group B.V., 86
Bonduelle SA, 51
Bongrain S.A., 25; 102 (upd.)
Booker PLC, 13; 31 (upd.)
Borden, Inc., II; 22 (upd.)
Boyd Coffee Company, 53
Brach and Brock Confections, Inc., 15
Brake Bros plc, 45
Bridgford Foods Corporation, 27
Brigham's Inc., 72
Brioche Pasquier S.A., 58
British Sugar plc, 84
Brossard S.A., 102
Brothers Gourmet Coffees, Inc., 20
Broughton Foods Co., 17
Brown & Haley, 23
Bruce Foods Corporation, 39
Bruegger's Corporation, 63
Bruster's Real Ice Cream, Inc., 80
BSN Groupe S.A., II
Bumble Bee Seafoods L.L.C., 64

Bunge Brasil S.A. 78
Bunge Ltd., 62
Bourbon Corporation, 82
Burns, Philp & Company Ltd., 63
Bush Boake Allen Inc., 30
Bush Brothers & Company, 45
The C.F. Sauer Company, 90
C.H. Robinson Worldwide, Inc., 40
   (upd.)
C.H. Guenther & Son, Inc., 84
Cabot Creamery Cooperative, Inc., 102
Cactus Feeders, Inc., 91
Cadbury Schweppes PLC, II; 49 (upd.)
Cagle's, Inc., 20
Cal-Maine Foods, Inc., 69
Calavo Growers, Inc., 47
Calcot Ltd., 33
Callard and Bowser-Suchard Inc., 84
Campagna-Turano Bakery, Inc., 99
Campbell Soup Company, II; 7 (upd.); 26
   (upd.); 71 (upd.)
The Campina Group, 78
Campofrío Alimentación S.A, 59
Canada Bread Company, Limited, 99
Canada Packers Inc., II
Cape Cod Potato Chip Company, 90
Cargill, Incorporated, II; 13 (upd.); 40
   (upd.); 89 (upd.)
Carnation Company, II
The Carriage House Companies, Inc., 55
Carroll's Foods, Inc., 46
Carvel Corporation, 35
Castle & Cooke, Inc., II; 20 (upd.)
Cattleman's, Inc., 20
Ce De Candy Inc., 100
Celestial Seasonings, Inc., 16
Cemoi S.A., 86
Central Soya Company, Inc., 7
Cerebos Gregg's Ltd., 100
Chaoda Modern Agriculture (Holdings)
   Ltd., 87
Charal S.A., 90
Chase General Corporation, 91
Chattanooga Bakery, Inc., 86
Chef Solutions, Inc., 89
Chelsea Milling Company, 29
Chicken of the Sea International, 24
   (upd.)
China National Cereals, Oils and
   Foodstuffs Import and Export
   Corporation (COFCO), 76
Chiquita Brands International, Inc., 7; 21
   (upd.); 83 (upd.)
Chock Full o'Nuts Corp., 17
Chocoladefabriken Lindt & Sprüngli AG,
   27
Chocolat Frey AG, 102
Chr. Hansen Group A/S, 70
CHS Inc., 60
Chupa Chups S.A., 38
The Clemens Family Corporation, 93
Clif Bar Inc., 50
Cloetta Fazer AB, 70
The Clorox Company, III; 22 (upd.); 81
   (upd.)
Clougherty Packing Company, 72
Coca-Cola Enterprises, Inc., 13
Coffee Holding Co., Inc., 95

Food Services & Retailers

Health & Personal Care Products

Anteon Corporation, 57
AOL Time Warner Inc., 57 (upd.)
Apollo Group, Inc., 24
Apple Computer, Inc., III; 6 (upd.); 77
  (upd.)
aQuantive, Inc., 81
The Arbitron Company, 38
Ariba, Inc., 57
Asanté Technologies, Inc., 20
Ascential Software Corporation, 59
AsiaInfo Holdings, Inc., 43
ASK Group, Inc., 9
Ask Jeeves, Inc., 65
ASML Holding N.V., 50
The Associated Press, 73 (upd.)
AST Research Inc., 9
At Home Corporation, 43
AT&T Bell Laboratories, Inc., 13
AT&T Corporation, 29 (upd.)
AT&T Istel Ltd., 14
Atos Origin S.A., 69
Attachmate Corporation, 56
Autodesk, Inc., 10; 89 (upd.)
Autologic Information International, Inc.,
  20
Automatic Data Processing, Inc., III; 9
  (upd.); 47 (upd.)
Autotote Corporation, 20
Avantium Technologies BV, 79
Avid Technology Inc., 38
Avocent Corporation, 65
Aydin Corp., 19
Baan Company, 25
Baidu.com Inc., 95
Baltimore Technologies Plc, 42
Bankrate, Inc., 83
Banyan Systems Inc., 25
Battelle Memorial Institute, Inc., 10
BBN Corp., 19
BEA Systems, Inc., 36
Bell and Howell Company, 9; 29 (upd.)
Bell Industries, Inc., 47
Billing Concepts, Inc., 26; 72 (upd.)
Blackbaud, Inc., 85
Blackboard Inc., 89
Blizzard Entertainment 78
Bloomberg L.P., 21
Blue Martini Software, Inc., 59
BMC Software, Inc., 55
Boole & Babbage, Inc., 25
Booz Allen Hamilton Inc., 10; 101 (upd.)
Borland International, Inc., 9
Bowne & Co., Inc., 23
Brite Voice Systems, Inc., 20
Broderbund Software, 13; 29 (upd.)
BTG, Inc., 45
Bull S.A., 43 (upd.)
Business Objects S.A., 25
C-Cube Microsystems, Inc., 37
CACI International Inc., 21; 72 (upd.)
Cadence Design Systems, Inc., 11
Caere Corporation, 20
Cahners Business Information, 43
CalComp Inc., 13
Cambridge Technology Partners, Inc., 36
Candle Corporation, 64
Canon Inc., III
Cap Gemini Ernst & Young, 37

Captaris, Inc., 89
CareerBuilder, Inc., 93
Caribiner International, Inc., 24
Cass Information Systems Inc., 100
Catalina Marketing Corporation, 18
CDC Corporation, 71
CDW Computer Centers, Inc., 16
Cerner Corporation, 16
CheckFree Corporation, 81
Cheyenne Software, Inc., 12
CHIPS and Technologies, Inc., 9
Ciber, Inc., 18
Cincom Systems Inc., 15
Cirrus Logic, Incorporated, 11
Cisco-Linksys LLC, 86
Cisco Systems, Inc., 11; 77 (upd.)
Citizen Watch Co., Ltd., III; 21 (upd.);
  81 (upd.)
Citrix Systems, Inc., 44
CMGI, Inc., 76
CNET Networks, Inc., 47
Cogent Communications Group, Inc., 55
Cognizant Technology Solutions
  Corporation, 59
Cognos Inc., 44
Commodore International Ltd., 7
Compagnie des Machines Bull S.A., III
Compaq Computer Corporation, III; 6
  (upd.); 26 (upd.)
Complete Business Solutions, Inc., 31
CompuAdd Computer Corporation, 11
CompuCom Systems, Inc., 10
CompUSA, Inc., 35 (upd.)
CompuServe Interactive Services, Inc., 10;
  27 (upd.)
Computer Associates International, Inc.,
  6; 49 (upd.)
Computer Data Systems, Inc., 14
Computer Sciences Corporation, 6
Computervision Corporation, 10
Compuware Corporation, 10; 30 (upd.);
  66 (upd.)
Comshare Inc., 23
Conner Peripherals, Inc., 6
Control Data Corporation, III
Control Data Systems, Inc., 10
Corbis Corporation, 31
Corel Corporation, 15; 33 (upd.); 76
  (upd.)
Corporate Software Inc., 9
CoStar Group, Inc., 73
craigslist, inc., 89
Cray Research, Inc., III
Credence Systems Corporation, 90
CSX Corporation, 79 (upd.)
CTG, Inc., 11
Ctrip.com International Ltd., 97
Cybermedia, Inc., 25
Dairyland Healthcare Solutions, 73
Dassault Systèmes S.A., 25
Data Broadcasting Corporation, 31
Data General Corporation, 8
Datapoint Corporation, 11
Dell Computer Corp., 9
Dendrite International, Inc., 70
Deutsche Börse AG, 59
Dialogic Corporation, 18
DiamondCluster International, Inc., 51

Digex, Inc., 46
Digital Equipment Corporation, III; 6
  (upd.)
Digital River, Inc., 50
Digitas Inc., 81
Dimension Data Holdings PLC, 69
ditech.com, 93
Documentum, Inc., 46
The Dun & Bradstreet Corporation, IV;
  19 (upd.)
Dun & Bradstreet Software Services Inc.,
  11
DynCorp, 45
E.piphany, Inc., 49
EarthLink, Inc., 36
eCollege.com, 85
ECS S.A, 12
EDGAR Online, Inc., 91
Edmark Corporation, 14; 41 (upd.)
Egghead Inc., 9
El Camino Resources International, Inc.,
  11
Electronic Arts Inc., 10; 85 (upd.)
Electronic Data Systems Corporation, III;
  28 (upd.)
Electronics for Imaging, Inc., 43 (upd.)
EMC Corporation, 12; 46 (upd.)
Encore Computer Corporation, 13; 74
  (upd.)
Environmental Systems Research Institute
  Inc. (ESRI), 62
EPAM Systems Inc., 96
Epic Systems Corporation, 62
EPIQ Systems, Inc., 56
Evans and Sutherland Computer
  Company 19, 78 (upd.)
Exabyte Corporation, 12
Experian Information Solutions Inc., 45
Facebook, Inc., 90
FactSet Research Systems Inc., 73
FASTWEB S.p.A., 83
F5 Networks, Inc., 72
First Financial Management Corporation,
  11
Fiserv Inc., 11
FlightSafety International, Inc., 9
FORE Systems, Inc., 25
Franklin Electronic Publishers, Inc., 23
Franz Inc., 80
FTP Software, Inc., 20
Fujitsu Limited, III; 16 (upd.); 42 (upd.);
  103 (upd.)
Fujitsu-ICL Systems Inc., 11
Future Now, Inc., 12
Gartner, Inc., 21; 94 (upd.)
Gateway, Inc., 10; 27 (upd.)
GEAC Computer Corporation Ltd., 43
Geek Squad Inc., 102
Genesys Telecommunications Laboratories
  Inc., 103
Gericom AG, 47
Getronics NV, 39
GFI Informatique SA, 49
Global Imaging Systems, Inc., 73
The Go Daddy Group Inc., 102
Google, Inc., 50; 101 (upd.)
Groupe Ares S.A., 102
Groupe Open, 74

Insurance

Legal Services

Andrews Kurth, LLP, 71
Arnold & Porter, 35
Baker & Daniels LLP, 88
Baker & Hostetler LLP, 40
Baker & McKenzie, 10; 42 (upd.)
Baker and Botts, L.L.P., 28
Bingham Dana LLP, 43
Brobeck, Phleger & Harrison, LLP, 31
Cadwalader, Wickersham & Taft, 32
Chadbourne & Parke, 36
Cleary, Gottlieb, Steen & Hamilton, 35
Clifford Chance LLP, 38
Coudert Brothers, 30
Covington & Burling, 40
CRA International, Inc., 93
Cravath, Swaine & Moore, 43
Davis Polk & Wardwell, 36
Debevoise & Plimpton, 39
Dechert, 43
Dewey Ballantine LLP, 48
Dorsey & Whitney LLP, 47
Drinker, Biddle and Reath L.L.P., 92
Faegre & Benson LLP, 97
Fenwick & West LLP, 34
Fish & Neave, 54
Foley & Lardner, 28
Fried, Frank, Harris, Shriver & Jacobson, 35
Fulbright & Jaworski L.L.P., 47
Gibson, Dunn & Crutcher LLP, 36
Greenberg Traurig, LLP, 65
Heller, Ehrman, White & McAuliffe, 41
Hildebrandt International, 29
Hogan & Hartson L.L.P., 44
Holland & Knight LLP, 60
Holme Roberts & Owen LLP, 28
Hughes Hubbard & Reed LLP, 44
Hunton & Williams, 35
Jenkens & Gilchrist, P.C., 65
Jones, Day, Reavis & Pogue, 33
Kelley Drye & Warren LLP, 40
King & Spalding, 23
Kirkland & Ellis LLP, 65
Latham & Watkins, 33
LeBoeuf, Lamb, Greene & MacRae, L.L.P., 29
LECG Corporation, 93
The Legal Aid Society, 48
Mayer, Brown, Rowe & Maw, 47
Milbank, Tweed, Hadley & McCloy, 27
Morgan, Lewis & Bockius LLP, 29
Morrison & Foerster LLP 78
O'Melveny & Myers, 37
Oppenheimer Wolff & Donnelly LLP, 71
Orrick, Herrington and Sutcliffe LLP, 76
Patton Boggs LLP, 71
Paul, Hastings, Janofsky & Walker LLP, 27
Paul, Weiss, Rifkind, Wharton & Garrison, 47
Pepper Hamilton LLP, 43
Perkins Coie LLP, 56
Phillips Lytle LLP, 102
Pillsbury Madison & Sutro LLP, 29
Pre-Paid Legal Services, Inc., 20
Proskauer Rose LLP, 47
Quinn Emanuel Urquhart Oliver & Hedges, LLP, 99

Robins, Kaplan, Miller & Ciresi L.L.P., 89
Ropes & Gray, 40
Saul Ewing LLP, 74
Seyfarth Shaw LLP, 93
Shearman & Sterling, 32
Sidley Austin Brown & Wood, 40
Simpson Thacher & Bartlett, 39
Skadden, Arps, Slate, Meagher & Flom, 18
Snell & Wilmer L.L.P., 28
Sonnenschein Nath and Rosenthal LLP, 102
Southern Poverty Law Center, Inc., 74
Strook & Strook & Lavan LLP, 40
Sullivan & Cromwell, 26
Troutman Sanders L.L.P., 79
Vinson & Elkins L.L.P., 30
Wachtell, Lipton, Rosen & Katz, 47
Weil, Gotshal & Manges LLP, 55
White & Case LLP, 35
Williams & Connolly LLP, 47
Willkie Farr & Gallagher LLP, 95
Wilson Sonsini Goodrich & Rosati, 34
Winston & Strawn, 35
Womble Carlyle Sandridge & Rice, PLLC, 52

Manufacturing

A-dec, Inc., 53
A. Schulman, Inc., 49 (upd.)
A.B.Dick Company, 28
A.O. Smith Corporation, 11; 40 (upd.); 93 (upd.)
A.T. Cross Company, 17; 49 (upd.)
A.W. Faber-Castell Unternehmensverwaltung GmbH & Co., 51
AAF-McQuay Incorporated, 26
Aalborg Industries A/S, 90
AAON, Inc., 22
AAR Corp., 28
Aarhus United A/S, 68
ABB Ltd., 65 (upd.)
ABC Rail Products Corporation, 18
Abiomed, Inc., 47
ACCO World Corporation, 7; 51 (upd.)
Accubuilt, Inc., 74
Acindar Industria Argentina de Aceros S.A., 87
Acme United Corporation, 70
Acme-Cleveland Corp., 13
Acorn Products, Inc., 55
Acuity Brands, Inc., 90
Acushnet Company, 64
Acuson Corporation, 36 (upd.)
Adams Golf, Inc., 37
Adolf Würth GmbH & Co. KG, 49
Advanced Circuits Inc., 67
Advanced Neuromodulation Systems, Inc., 73
AEP Industries, Inc., 36
AeroGrow International, Inc., 95
Aftermarket Technology Corp., 83
Ag-Chem Equipment Company, Inc., 17
Aga Foodservice Group PLC, 73
AGCO Corporation, 13; 67 (upd.)
Agfa Gevaert Group N.V., 59
Agrium Inc., 73

Ahlstrom Corporation, 53
Ainsworth Lumber Co. Ltd., 99
Airgas, Inc., 54
Aisin Seiki Co., Ltd., III
AK Steel Holding Corporation, 41 (upd.)
Akeena Solar, Inc., 103
AKG Acoustics GmbH, 62
Aktiebolaget Electrolux, 22 (upd.)
Aktiebolaget SKF, III; 38 (upd.); 89 (upd.)
Alamo Group Inc., 32
ALARIS Medical Systems, Inc., 65
Alberto-Culver Company, 8; 36 (upd.); 91 (upd.)
Aldila Inc., 46
Alfa Laval AB, III; 64 (upd.)
Allen Organ Company, 33
Allen-Edmonds Shoe Corporation, 61
Alliance Laundry Holdings LLC, 102
Alliant Techsystems Inc., 8; 30 (upd.); 77 (upd.)
The Allied Defense Group, Inc., 65
Allied Healthcare Products, Inc., 24
Allied Products Corporation, 21
Allied Signal Engines, 9
AlliedSignal Inc., 22 (upd.)
Allison Gas Turbine Division, 9
Alltrista Corporation, 30
Alps Electric Co., Ltd., 44 (upd.)
Alticor Inc., 71 (upd.)
Aluar Aluminio Argentino S.A.I.C., 74
Alvis Plc, 47
Amer Group plc, 41
American Axle & Manufacturing Holdings, Inc., 67
American Biltrite Inc., 43 (upd.)
American Business Products, Inc., 20
American Cast Iron Pipe Company, 50
American Greetings Corporation, 59 (upd.)
American Homestar Corporation, 18; 41 (upd.)
American Locker Group Incorporated, 34
American Power Conversion Corporation, 67 (upd.)
American Seating Company 78
American Standard Companies Inc., 30 (upd.)
American Technical Ceramics Corp., 67
American Technology Corporation, 103
American Tourister, Inc., 16
American Woodmark Corporation, 31
Ameriwood Industries International Corp., 17
Amerock Corporation, 53
Ameron International Corporation, 67
AMETEK, Inc., 9
AMF Bowling, Inc., 40
Ampacet Corporation, 67
Ampco-Pittsburgh Corporation, 79
Ampex Corporation, 17
Amway Corporation, 30 (upd.)
Analogic Corporation, 23
Anchor Hocking Glassware, 13
Andersen Corporation, 10
The Andersons, Inc., 31
Andis Company, Inc., 85

Simplex Technologies Inc., 21
Siskin Steel & Supply Company, 70
Solutia Inc., 52
Sommer-Allibert S.A., 19
Southdown, Inc., 14
Spartech Corporation, 19; 76 (upd.)
Ssangyong Cement Industrial Co., Ltd., III; 61 (upd.)
Steel Technologies Inc., 63
Sun Distributors L.P., 12
Symyx Technologies, Inc., 77
Tarmac Limited, III; 28 (upd.); 95 (upd.)
Tergal Industries S.A.S., 102
Tilcon-Connecticut Inc., 80
TOTO LTD., III; 28 (upd.)
Toyo Sash Co., Ltd., III
Tuscarora Inc., 29
U.S. Aggregates, Inc., 42
Ube Industries, Ltd., III
United States Steel Corporation, 50 (upd.)
USG Corporation, III; 26 (upd.); 81 (upd.)
Usinas Siderúrgicas de Minas Gerais S.A., 77
Vicat S.A., 70
voestalpine AG, 57 (upd.)
Vulcan Materials Company, 7; 52 (upd.)
Wacker-Chemie GmbH, 35
Walter Industries, Inc., III
Waxman Industries, Inc., 9
Weber et Broutin France, 66
Wienerberger AG, 70
Wolseley plc, 64
ZERO Corporation, 17; 88 (upd.)
Zoltek Companies, Inc., 37

Mining & Metals

A.M. Castle & Co., 25
Acindar Industria Argentina de Aceros S.A., 87
African Rainbow Minerals Ltd., 97
Aggregate Industries plc, 36
Agnico-Eagle Mines Limited, 71
Aktiebolaget SKF, III; 38 (upd.); 89 (upd.)
Alcan Aluminium Limited, IV; 31 (upd.)
Alcoa Inc., 56 (upd.)
Alleghany Corporation, 10
Allegheny Ludlum Corporation, 8
Alliance Resource Partners, L.P., 81
Alrosa Company Ltd., 62
Altos Hornos de México, S.A. de C.V., 42
Aluminum Company of America, IV; 20 (upd.)
AMAX Inc., IV
AMCOL International Corporation, 59 (upd.)
Amsted Industries Incorporated, 7
Anglo American Corporation of South Africa Limited, IV; 16 (upd.)
Anglo American PLC, 50 (upd.)
Aquarius Platinum Ltd., 63
ARBED S.A., IV; 22 (upd.)
Arcelor Gent, 80
Arch Coal Inc., 98
Arch Mineral Corporation, 7
Armco Inc., IV
ASARCO Incorporated, IV

Ashanti Goldfields Company Limited, 43
Atchison Casting Corporation, 39
Barrick Gold Corporation, 34
Battle Mountain Gold Company, 23
Benguet Corporation, 58
Bethlehem Steel Corporation, IV; 7 (upd.); 27 (upd.)
BHP Billiton, 67 (upd.)
Birmingham Steel Corporation, 13; 40 (upd.)
Boart Longyear Company, 26
Bodycote International PLC, 63
Boliden AB, 80
Boral Limited, III; 43 (upd.); 103 (upd.)
British Coal Corporation, IV
British Steel plc, IV; 19 (upd.)
Broken Hill Proprietary Company Ltd., IV; 22 (upd.)
Brush Engineered Materials Inc., 67
Brush Wellman Inc., 14
Bucyrus International, Inc., 17; 103 (upd.)
Buderus AG, 37
Cameco Corporation, 77
Caparo Group Ltd., 90
Carpenter Technology Corporation, 13; 95 (upd.)
Chaparral Steel Co., 13
Charter Manufacturing Company, Inc., 103
China Shenhua Energy Company Limited, 83
Christensen Boyles Corporation, 26
Cleveland-Cliffs Inc., 13; 62 (upd.)
Coal India Ltd., IV; 44 (upd.)
Cockerill Sambre Group, IV; 26 (upd.)
Coeur d'Alene Mines Corporation, 20
Cold Spring Granite Company Inc., 16; 67 (upd.)
Cominco Ltd., 37
Commercial Metals Company, 15; 42 (upd.)
Companhia Siderúrgica Nacional, 76
Companhia Vale do Rio Doce, IV; 43 (upd.)
Compañia de Minas Buenaventura S.A.A., 93
CONSOL Energy Inc., 59
Corporacion Nacional del Cobre de Chile, 40
Corus Group plc, 49 (upd.)
CRA Limited, IV
Cyprus Amax Minerals Company, 21
Cyprus Minerals Company, 7
Daido Steel Co., Ltd., IV
De Beers Consolidated Mines Limited/De Beers Centenary AG, IV; 7 (upd.); 28 (upd.)
Degussa Group, IV
Diavik Diamond Mines Inc., 85
Dofasco Inc., IV; 24 (upd.)
Dynatec Corporation, 87
Earle M. Jorgensen Company, 82
Echo Bay Mines Ltd., IV; 38 (upd.)
Engelhard Corporation, IV
Eramet, 73
Evergreen Energy, Inc., 97
Evraz Group S.A., 97

Falconbridge Limited, 49
Fansteel Inc., 19
Fluor Corporation, 34 (upd.)
Freeport-McMoRan Copper & Gold, Inc., IV; 7 (upd.); 57 (upd.)
Fried. Krupp GmbH, IV
Gencor Ltd., IV; 22 (upd.)
Geneva Steel, 7
Gerdau S.A., 59
Glamis Gold, Ltd., 54
Gold Fields Ltd., IV; 62 (upd.)
Goldcorp Inc., 87
Grupo Mexico, S.A. de C.V., 40
Gruppo Riva Fire SpA, 88
Handy & Harman, 23
Hanson Building Materials America Inc., 60
Hanson PLC, 30 (upd.)
Harmony Gold Mining Company Limited, 63
Haynes International, Inc., 88
Hecla Mining Company, 20
Hemlo Gold Mines Inc., 9
Heraeus Holding GmbH, IV
Highland Gold Mining Limited, 95
Highveld Steel and Vanadium Corporation Limited, 59
Hitachi Metals, Ltd., IV
Hoesch AG, IV
Homestake Mining Company, 12; 38 (upd.)
Horsehead Industries, Inc., 51
The Hudson Bay Mining and Smelting Company, Limited, 12
Hylsamex, S.A. de C.V., 39
IMCO Recycling, Incorporated, 32
Imerys S.A., 40 (upd.)
Imetal S.A., IV
Inco Limited, IV; 45 (upd.)
Industrias Penoles, S.A. de C.V., 22
Inland Steel Industries, Inc., IV; 19 (upd.)
Intermet Corporation, 32
Iscor Limited, 57
Ispat Inland Inc., 30; 40 (upd.)
JFE Shoji Holdings Inc., 88
Johnson Matthey PLC, IV; 16 (upd.)
JSC MMC Norilsk Nickel, 48
K.A. Rasmussen AS, 99
Kaiser Aluminum Corporation, IV; 84 (upd.)
Kawasaki Heavy Industries, Ltd., 63 (upd.)
Kawasaki Steel Corporation, IV
Kennecott Corporation, 7; 27 (upd.)
Kentucky Electric Steel, Inc., 31
Kerr-McGee Corporation, 22 (upd.)
Kinross Gold Corporation, 36
Klockner-Werke AG, IV
Kobe Steel, Ltd., IV; 19 (upd.)
Koninklijke Nederlandsche Hoogovens en Staalfabrieken NV, IV
Laclede Steel Company, 15
Layne Christensen Company, 19
Lonmin plc, 66 (upd.)
Lonrho Plc, 21
The LTV Corporation, I; 24 (upd.)
Lukens Inc., 14
Magma Copper Company, 7

Paper & Forestry

Personal Services

Petroleum

Publishing & Printing

Retail & Wholesale

Rubber & Tires

Telecommunications

Textiles & Apparel

Tobacco

Transport Services

Utilities

Geographic Index

Fanuc Ltd., III; 17 (upd.); 75 (upd.)
The Fuji Bank, Ltd., II
Fuji Electric Co., Ltd., II; 48 (upd.)
Fuji Photo Film Co., Ltd., III; 18 (upd.); 79 (upd.)
Fuji Television Network Inc., 91
Fujisawa Pharmaceutical Company, Ltd., I; 58 (upd.)
Fujitsu Limited, III; 16 (upd.); 42 (upd.); 103 (upd.)
Funai Electric Company Ltd., 62
The Furukawa Electric Co., Ltd., III
General Sekiyu K.K., IV
Hakuhodo, Inc., 6; 42 (upd.)
Hankyu Department Stores, Inc., V; 23 (upd.); 62 (upd.)
Hagoromo Foods Corporation, 84
Hino Motors, Ltd., 7; 21 (upd.)
Hitachi, Ltd., I; 12 (upd.); 40 (upd.)
Hitachi Metals, Ltd., IV
Hitachi Zosen Corporation, III; 53 (upd.)
Hokkaido Electric Power Company Inc. (HEPCO), V; 58 (upd.)
Hokuriku Electric Power Company, V
Honda Motor Company Ltd., I; 10 (upd.); 29 (upd.); 96 (upd.)
Honshu Paper Co., Ltd., IV
Hoshino Gakki Co. Ltd., 55
Idemitsu Kosan Co., Ltd., IV; 49 (upd.)
The Industrial Bank of Japan, Ltd., II
INPEX Holdings Inc., 97
Isetan Company Limited, V; 36 (upd.)
Ishikawajima-Harima Heavy Industries Company, Ltd., III; 86 (upd.)
Isuzu Motors, Ltd., 9; 23 (upd.); 57 (upd.)
Ito En Ltd., 101
Ito-Yokado Co., Ltd., V; 42 (upd.)
ITOCHU Corporation, 32 (upd.)
Itoham Foods Inc., II; 61 (upd.)
Japan Airlines Company, Ltd., I; 32 (upd.)
JAFCO Co. Ltd. 79
Japan Broadcasting Corporation, 7
Japan Leasing Corporation, 8
Japan Pulp and Paper Company Limited, IV
Japan Tobacco Inc., V; 46 (upd.)
JFE Shoji Holdings Inc., 88
JSP Corporation, 74
Jujo Paper Co., Ltd., IV
JUSCO Co., Ltd., V
Kajima Corporation, I; 51 (upd.)
Kanebo, Ltd., 53
Kanematsu Corporation, IV; 24 (upd.); 102 (upd.)
The Kansai Electric Power Company, Inc., V; 62 (upd.)
Kansai Paint Company Ltd., 80
Kao Corporation, III; 20 (upd.); 79 (upd.)
Katokichi Company Ltd., 82
Kawai Musical Instruments Mfg Co. Ltd. 78
Kawasaki Heavy Industries, Ltd., III; 63 (upd.)
Kawasaki Kisen Kaisha, Ltd., V; 56 (upd.)
Kawasaki Steel Corporation, IV

Keio Corporation, V; 96 (upd.)
Kenwood Corporation, 31
Kewpie Kabushiki Kaisha, 57
Kikkoman Corporation, 14; 47 (upd.)
Kinki Nippon Railway Company Ltd., V
Kirin Brewery Company, Limited, I; 21 (upd.); 63 (upd.)
Kobe Steel, Ltd., IV; 19 (upd.)
Kodansha Ltd., IV; 38 (upd.)
Komatsu Ltd., III; 16 (upd.); 52 (upd.)
Konami Corporation, 96
Konica Corporation, III; 30 (upd.)
Kotobukiya Co., Ltd., V; 56 (upd.)
Kubota Corporation, III; 26 (upd.)
Kumagai Gumi Company, Ltd., I
Kumon Institute of Education Co., Ltd., 72
Kyocera Corporation, II; 21 (upd.); 79 (upd.)
Kyokuyo Company Ltd., 75
Kyowa Hakko Kogyo Co., Ltd., III; 48 (upd.)
Kyushu Electric Power Company Inc., V
Lion Corporation, III; 51 (upd.)
Long-Term Credit Bank of Japan, Ltd., II
Mabuchi Motor Co. Ltd., 68
Makita Corporation, 22; 59 (upd.)
Mandom Corporation, 82
Marubeni Corporation, I; 24 (upd.)
Maruha Group Inc., 75 (upd.)
Marui Company Ltd., V; 62 (upd.)
Maruzen Co., Limited, 18
Matsushita Electric Industrial Co., Ltd., II; 64 (upd.)
Matsushita Electric Works, Ltd., III; 7 (upd.)
Matsuzakaya Company Ltd., V; 64 (upd.)
Mazda Motor Corporation, 9; 23 (upd.); 63 (upd.)
Meidensha Corporation, 92
Meiji Dairies Corporation, II; 82 (upd.)
The Meiji Mutual Life Insurance Company, III
Meiji Seika Kaisha Ltd., II; 64 (upd.)
Mercian Corporation, 77
Millea Holdings Inc., 64 (upd.)
Minebea Co., Ltd., 90
Minolta Co., Ltd., III; 18 (upd.); 43 (upd.)
The Mitsubishi Bank, Ltd., II
Mitsubishi Chemical Corporation, I; 56 (upd.)
Mitsubishi Corporation, I; 12 (upd.)
Mitsubishi Electric Corporation, II; 44 (upd.)
Mitsubishi Estate Company, Limited, IV; 61 (upd.)
Mitsubishi Heavy Industries, Ltd., III; 7 (upd.); 40 (upd.)
Mitsubishi Materials Corporation, III
Mitsubishi Motors Corporation, 9; 23 (upd.); 57 (upd.)
Mitsubishi Oil Co., Ltd., IV
Mitsubishi Rayon Co., Ltd., V
The Mitsubishi Trust & Banking Corporation, II
Mitsubishi UFJ Financial Group, Inc., 99 (upd.)

Mitsui & Co., Ltd., 28 (upd.)
The Mitsui Bank, Ltd., II
Mitsui Bussan K.K., I
Mitsui Marine and Fire Insurance Company, Limited, III
Mitsui Mining & Smelting Company, Ltd., IV; 102 (upd.)
Mitsui Mining Company, Limited, IV
Mitsui Mutual Life Insurance Company, III; 39 (upd.)
Mitsui O.S.K. Lines, Ltd., V; 96 (upd.)
Mitsui Petrochemical Industries, Ltd., 9
Mitsui Real Estate Development Co., Ltd., IV
The Mitsui Trust & Banking Company, Ltd., II
Mitsukoshi Ltd., V; 56 (upd.)
Mizuho Financial Group Inc., 58 (upd.)
Mizuno Corporation, 25
Morinaga & Co. Ltd., 61
Nagasakiya Co., Ltd., V; 69 (upd.)
Nagase & Co., Ltd., 8; 61 (upd.)
NEC Corporation, II; 21 (upd.); 57 (upd.)
NGK Insulators Ltd., 67
NHK Spring Co., Ltd., III
Nichii Co., Ltd., V
Nichimen Corporation, IV; 24 (upd.)
Nichirei Corporation, 70
Nichiro Corporation, 86
Nidec Corporation, 59
Nihon Keizai Shimbun, Inc., IV
The Nikko Securities Company Limited, II; 9 (upd.)
Nikon Corporation, III; 48 (upd.)
Nintendo Co., Ltd., III; 7 (upd.); 28 (upd.); 67 (upd.)
Nippon Credit Bank, II
Nippon Electric Glass Co. Ltd., 95
Nippon Express Company, Ltd., V; 64 (upd.)
Nippon Life Insurance Company, III; 60 (upd.)
Nippon Light Metal Company, Ltd., IV
Nippon Meat Packers Inc., II, 78 (upd.)
Nippon Mining Holdings Inc., 102 (upd.)
Nippon Oil Corporation, IV; 63 (upd.)
Nippon Seiko K.K., III
Nippon Sheet Glass Company, Limited, III
Nippon Shinpan Co., Ltd., II; 61 (upd.)
Nippon Soda Co., Ltd., 85
Nippon Steel Corporation, IV; 17 (upd.); 96 (upd.)
Nippon Suisan Kaisha, Ltd., II; 92 (upd.)
Nippon Telegraph and Telephone Corporation, V; 51 (upd.)
Nippon Yusen Kabushiki Kaisha (NYK), V; 72 (upd.)
Nippondenso Co., Ltd., III
Nissan Motor Company Ltd., I; 11 (upd.); 34 (upd.); 92 (upd.)
Nisshin Seifun Group Inc., II; 66 (upd.)
Nisshin Steel Co., Ltd., IV
Nissho Iwai K.K., I
Nissin Food Products Company Ltd., 75
NKK Corporation, IV; 28 (upd.)
NOF Corporation, 72

United States

Colt Industries Inc., I
Colt's Manufacturing Company, Inc., 12
Columbia Forest Products Inc., 78
The Columbia Gas System, Inc., V; 16 (upd.)
Columbia House Company, 69
Columbia Sportswear Company, 19; 41 (upd.)
Columbia TriStar Motion Pictures Companies, II; 12 (upd.)
Columbia/HCA Healthcare Corporation, 15
Columbus McKinnon Corporation, 37
Comair Holdings Inc., 13; 34 (upd.)
Combe Inc., 72
Comcast Corporation, 7; 24 (upd.)
Comdial Corporation, 21
Comdisco, Inc., 9
Comerica Incorporated, 40; 101 (upd.)
COMFORCE Corporation, 40
Comfort Systems USA, Inc., 101
Command Security Corporation, 57
Commerce Clearing House, Inc., 7
Commercial Credit Company, 8
Commercial Federal Corporation, 12; 62 (upd.)
Commercial Financial Services, Inc., 26
Commercial Metals Company, 15; 42 (upd.)
Commercial Vehicle Group, Inc., 81
Commodore International Ltd., 7
Commonwealth Edison Company, V
Commonwealth Energy System, 14
Commonwealth Telephone Enterprises, Inc., 25
CommScope, Inc., 77
Community Coffee Co. L.L.C., 53
Community Health Systems, Inc., 71
Community Newspaper Holdings, Inc., 91
Community Psychiatric Centers, 15
Compaq Computer Corporation, III; 6 (upd.); 26 (upd.)
Compass Bancshares, Inc., 73
Compass Minerals International, Inc. 79
CompDent Corporation, 22
CompHealth Inc., 25
Complete Business Solutions, Inc., 31
Comprehensive Care Corporation, 15
CompuAdd Computer Corporation, 11
CompuCom Systems, Inc., 10
CompuDyne Corporation, 51
CompUSA, Inc., 10; 35 (upd.)
CompuServe Interactive Services, Inc., 10; 27 (upd.)
Computer Associates International, Inc., 6; 49 (upd.)
Computer Data Systems, Inc., 14
Computer Learning Centers, Inc., 26
Computer Sciences Corporation, 6
Computerland Corp., 13
Computervision Corporation, 10
Compuware Corporation, 10; 30 (upd.); 66 (upd.)
Comsat Corporation, 23
Comshare Inc., 23
Comstock Resources, Inc., 47
Comtech Telecommunications Corp., 75

Comverse Technology, Inc., 15; 43 (upd.)
Con-way Inc., 101
ConAgra Foods, Inc., II; 12 (upd.); 42 (upd.); 85 (upd.)
Conair Corporation, 17; 69 (upd.)
Concentra Inc., 71
Concepts Direct, Inc., 39
Concord Camera Corporation, 41
Concord EFS, Inc., 52
Concord Fabrics, Inc., 16
Concurrent Computer Corporation, 75
Condé Nast Publications, Inc., 13; 59 (upd.)
Cone Mills LLC, 8; 67 (upd.)
Conexant Systems, Inc., 36
Confluence Holdings Corporation, 76
Congoleum Corporation, 18; 98 (upd.)
CONMED Corporation, 87
Conn's, Inc., 67
Conn-Selmer, Inc., 55
Connecticut Light and Power Co., 13
Connecticut Mutual Life Insurance Company, III
The Connell Company, 29
Conner Peripherals, Inc., 6
Connetics Corporation, 70
ConocoPhillips, IV; 16 (upd.); 63 (upd.)
Conrad Industries, Inc., 58
Conseco, Inc., 10; 33 (upd.)
Conso International Corporation, 29
CONSOL Energy Inc., 59
Consolidated Delivery & Logistics, Inc., 24
Consolidated Edison, Inc., V; 45 (upd.)
Consolidated Freightways Corporation, V; 21 (upd.); 48 (upd.)
Consolidated Graphics, Inc., 70
Consolidated Natural Gas Company, V; 19 (upd.)
Consolidated Papers, Inc., 8; 36 (upd.)
Consolidated Products Inc., 14
Consolidated Rail Corporation, V
Constar International Inc., 64
Constellation Brands, Inc., 68 (upd.)
Consumers Power Co., 14
Consumers Union, 26
Consumers Water Company, 14
The Container Store, 36
ContiGroup Companies, Inc., 43 (upd.)
Continental Airlines, Inc., I; 21 (upd.); 52 (upd.)
Continental Bank Corporation, II
Continental Cablevision, Inc., 7
Continental Can Co., Inc., 15
The Continental Corporation, III
Continental General Tire Corp., 23
Continental Grain Company, 10; 13 (upd.)
Continental Group Company, I
Continental Medical Systems, Inc., 10
Continental Resources, Inc., 89
Continucare Corporation, 101
Continuum Health Partners, Inc., 60
Control Data Corporation, III
Control Data Systems, Inc., 10
Converse Inc., 9; 31 (upd.)
Cook Group Inc., 102

Cooker Restaurant Corporation, 20; 51 (upd.)
CoolSavings, Inc., 77
Cooper Cameron Corporation, 20 (upd.); 58 (upd.)
The Cooper Companies, Inc., 39
Cooper Industries, Inc., II; 44 (upd.)
Cooper Tire & Rubber Company, 8; 23 (upd.)
Coopers & Lybrand, 9
Copart Inc., 23
The Copley Press, Inc., 23
The Copps Corporation, 32
Corbis Corporation, 31
The Corcoran Group, Inc., 58
Cordis Corporation, 19; 46 (upd.)
CoreStates Financial Corp, 17
Corinthian Colleges, Inc., 39; 92 (upd.)
The Corky McMillin Companies, 98
Corning Inc., III; 44 (upd.); 90 (upd.)
The Corporate Executive Board Company, 89
Corporate Express, Inc., 22; 47 (upd.)
Corporate Software Inc., 9
Corporation for Public Broadcasting, 14; 89 (upd.)
Correctional Services Corporation, 30
Corrections Corporation of America, 23
Corrpro Companies, Inc., 20
CORT Business Services Corporation, 26
Corus Bankshares, Inc., 75
Cosi, Inc., 53
Cosmair, Inc., 8
The Cosmetic Center, Inc., 22
Cosmolab Inc., 96
Cost Plus, Inc., 27
Cost-U-Less, Inc., 51
CoStar Group, Inc., 73
Costco Wholesale Corporation, V; 43 (upd.)
Cotter & Company, V
Cotton Incorporated, 46
Coty, Inc., 36
Coudert Brothers, 30
Council on International Educational Exchange Inc., 81
Country Kitchen International, Inc., 76
Countrywide Financial, 16; 100 (upd.)
County Seat Stores Inc., 9
Courier Corporation, 41
Cousins Properties Incorporated, 65
Covance Inc., 30; 98 (upd.)
Covanta Energy Corporation, 64 (upd.)
Coventry Health Care, Inc., 59
Covington & Burling, 40
Cowen Group, Inc., 92
Cowles Media Company, 23
Cox Enterprises, Inc., IV; 22 (upd.); 67 (upd.)
Cox Radio, Inc., 89
CPAC, Inc., 86
CPC International Inc., II
CPI Aerostructures, Inc., 75
CPI Corp., 38
CPP International, LLC, 103
CR England, Inc., 63
CRA International, Inc., 93